LAW AND MORALITY:
READINGS IN LEGAL PHILOSOPHY

Third Edition

Edited by David Dyzenhaus, Sophia Reibetanz Moreau,
and Arthur Ripstein

Since its first publication in 1996, *Law and Morality* has filled a long-standing need for a contemporary Canadian textbook in the philosophy of law. Now in its third edition, this anthology has been thoroughly revised and updated, and includes new chapters on equality, judicial review, and terrorism and the rule of law.

The volume begins with essays that explore general questions about morality and law, surveying the traditional literature on legal positivism and contemporary debates about the connection between law and morality. These essays explore the tensions between law as a protector of individual liberty and as a tool of democratic self-rule, and introduce debates about adjudication and the contribution of feminist approaches to the philosophy of law. New material on the Chinese Canadian head tax case is also featured. The second part of *Law and Morality* deals with philosophical questions as they apply to contemporary issues. Excerpts from judicial decisions as well as essays by practising lawyers are included to provide theoretically informed legal analyses of the issues.

Striking a balance between practical and more analytic, philosophical approaches, the volume's treatment of the philosophy of law as a branch of political philosophy enables students to understand law in its function as a social institution. *Law and Morality* has proved to be an essential text in both departments of philosophy and faculties of law and this latest edition brings the debates fully up to date, filling gaps in the earlier editions and adding to the array of contemporary issues previously covered.

(Toronto Studies in Philosophy)

DAVID DYZENHAUS is a professor in the Faculty of Law and the Department of Philosophy at the University of Toronto.
SOPHIA REIBETANZ MOREAU is an assistant professor in the Faculty of Law and the Department of Philosophy at the University of Toronto.
ARTHUR RIPSTEIN is a professor in the Faculty of Law and the Department of Philosophy at the University of Toronto.

EDITED BY DAVID DYZENHAUS,
SOPHIA REIBETANZ MOREAU,
AND ARTHUR RIPSTEIN

Law and Morality:
Readings in Legal Philosophy

Third Edition

UNIVERSITY OF TORONTO PRESS
Toronto Buffalo London

©University of Toronto Press 2007
Toronto Buffalo London
Printed in the U.S.A.

Reprinted 2008, 2014

First edition published 1996; reprinted 1998
Second edition published 2001; reprinted 2003

ISBN 978-0-8020-9489-6

Printed on acid-free paper

Toronto Studies in Philosophy
Editors: Donald Ainslie and Amy Mullin

Library and Archives Canada Cataloguing in Publication

Law and morality: readings in legal philosophy / edited by
David Dyzenhaus, Arthur Ripstein and Sophia Reibetanz
Moreau. – 3rd ed.

(Toronto studies in philosophy)
Includes bibliographical references.
ISBN 978-0-8020-9489-6

1. Law and ethics. 2. Law – Philosophy. I. Dyzenhaus, David.
II. Ripstein, Arthur. III. Reibetanz Moreau, Sophia. IV. Series.

K235.L39 2007   340'.112   C2007-900048-7

University of Toronto Press acknowledges the financial assistance to its
publishing program of the Canada Council and the Ontario Arts Council.

University of Toronto Press acknowledges the financial support for its
publishing activities of the Government of Canada through the Book
Publishing Industry Development Program (BPIDP).

Contents

Chapter 2: Adjudication 167

Chapter 3: Feminist Approaches to the Rule of Law 257

viii Contents

Preface to the Third Edition

In the years since the publication of the second edition of *Law and Morality*, it has become clear that some of the topics covered in that edition have a waning attraction as focal points for debate in philosophy of law. At the same time, other topics have arisen that were not covered but yet seem fruitful sites for such debate. Thus, we have included in the third edition new chapters on "Judicial Review" and "Terrorism, States of Emergency, and the Rule of Law," while we have dropped chapters on "Civil Disobedience," "The Limits of Legal Order," and "Abortion." We have changed the focus of the chapter on "Defining Family," a change reflected in its new title, "Equality." All the other chapters have been revised with perhaps the most significant addition – one made to reflect a growing interest in the topic of reparations for historic injustice – the material in chapter 2, "Adjudication," on the Chinese Head Tax Case.

THE EDITORS

David Dyzenhaus is Professor of Law and Philosophy at the University of Toronto, Associate Dean, Graduate Studies, of the Faculty of Law, and a Fellow of the Royal Society of Canada. In 2002, he was the Law Foundation Visiting Fellow in the Faculty of Law, University of Auckland. In 2005–6 he was Herbert Smith Visiting Professor in the Cambridge Law Faculty and a Senior Scholar of Pembroke College, Cambridge. He is the author of *Hard Cases in Wicked Legal Systems: South African Law in the Perspective of Legal Philosophy*; *Legality and Legitimacy: Carl Schmitt, Hans Kelsen, and Hermann Heller in Weimar*; and *Judging the Judges, Judging Ourselves: Truth, Reconciliation and the Apartheid Legal*

Order. He has published two edited collections of essays, *Law as Politics: Carl Schmitt's Critique of Liberalism* and *Recrafting the Rule of Law: The Limits of Legal Order.* In 2004 he gave the JC Smuts Memorial Lectures to the Faculty of Law, Cambridge University, which were published by Cambridge University Press in 2006 under the title *The Constitution of Law.*

Sophia Reibetanz Moreau is Assistant Professor of Law and Philosophy at the University of Toronto. In 2002–3, Professor Moreau served as law clerk to Chief Justice Beverley McLachlin of the Supreme Court of Canada. She has also been a Frank Knox Memorial Fellow at Harvard University, where she wrote a doctoral dissertation in the Department of Philosophy on practical deliberation, the nature of autonomy, and the significance of character; and a Commonwealth Scholar at the University of Oxford, where she completed a B.Phil. in legal and political philosophy. Her published work has appeared in *Ethics,* the *Proceedings of the Aristotelian Society,* the *University of Toronto Faculty of Law Journal,* the *Journal of Law and Equality,* and in several edited volumes. She has also written a report on discrimination for the Government of Canada, entitled "What Is a Ground of Discrimination?" Professor Moreau is currently working on a book on equality rights and anti-discrimination law in the public and private sectors.

Arthur Ripstein is Professor of Law and Philosophy at the University of Toronto. He was Laurance S. Rockefeller Visiting Fellow at Princeton in 1995–6, and held a Connaught Fellowship in the spring term of 2000. His research and teaching interests include torts, criminal law, legal theory, and political philosophy. In addition to numerous articles in legal theory and political philosophy, he is the author of *Equality, Responsibility and the Law* (1999), editor of *Ronald Dworkin* (2007), and co-editor of *Practical Rationality and Preference* (2001). He is currently writing a book on Kant's legal and political philosophy. An associate editor of *Philosophy and Public Affairs* and a former editor of *Ethics* and the *Canadian Journal of Philosophy,* he serves on the editorial board of *Legal Theory* and is advisory editor of the *Canadian Journal of Law and Jurisprudence.* His popular work has appeared on *Ideas* on CBC Radio.

Preface to the Second Edition

The five years since the first edition of *Law and Morality* have been momentous for Canadian law and legal culture. The Supreme Court has broken new ground on many of the issues explored in the first edition. The most prominent decision was the *Quebec Secession Reference*, in which the Court both decided that Quebec has no constitutional right to unilateral secession, and considered between the legal and political obligations of the Canadian state in the event that Quebec declares independence unilaterally. We have included the *Secession Reference*, and to complement it a series of further readings on challenges to the legitimacy of the legal order. These include two essays concerning the particular challenges posed by Canada's Aboriginal peoples.

In addition, a case about foetal rights, which was discussed in one of the reading questions in the first edition, has now been decided by the Court. A new case on sexual orientation discrimination has also been decided. Excerpts from both cases have been included.

Other debates have risen to new prominence. Although the *Butler* pornography decision purported to incorporate Catharine MacKinnon's feminist analysis of pornography, another group of feminists has objected to it, in part in response to issues of enforcement to which it gave rise. We include an article on that topic.

We have also modified our selection of more theoretical material, including a discussion of legal authority, and a further piece from the critical legal studies movement. And we have made numerous other small additions and as many deletions, all prompted by our and others' experience in teaching from this book.

We are grateful to our editor, Ron Schoeffel, for his help and support at every stage of this project.

Preface to the First Edition

For most students, a course in legal philosophy marks their first encounter with a rigorous examination of the conceptual apparatus of the law. Yet it is hardly their first encounter with many of the law's central questions. Law has long shaped ordinary life. From regulations concerning auto emissions to common-law rules governing warranties and product liability, the law affects our everyday existence. Indeed, these rules and regulations are so pervasive that most people seldom notice them, let alone reflect on them. By providing conceptual tools with which to consider the general problems of jurisprudence, this book aims to be an aid to students both in their intellectual pursuits and in their role as informed citizens.

Courses in the philosophy of law often break up into two sharply divided sections, one exploring conceptual questions about the nature of law, the other looking at a series of questions concerning the proper limits of the criminal law. These two sections sometimes sit together uneasily. In our view, the philosophy of law is far too important a subject to be treated in such a disjointed way. Part of the difficulty is that most discussion of the nature of law focuses on administrative rules or grand questions of constitutional theory. As a result, questions about the reach of the criminal law too often seem unrelated to those about its nature. A deeper reason for avoiding the usual approach is that it probably rests on a particular resolution to one of the problems considered in the first part of such courses in the philosophy of law. Standard versions of legal positivism suppose that the law can take on any content whatsoever. One consequence of such a view is that questions about the appropriate reach of the criminal law are in principle open to any sort of argumentation, because the concept of law by itself provides no constraints on its content. Yet legal reasoning often employs reasoning from other areas of the law, and these often seem to constrain the law's content. An adequate understanding of these challenges to positivism, or a version of positivism adequate to meet them, allows for a more sophisticated approach to contemporary issues. While we do not offer this anthology for use only by anti-positivists, we regard it as a virtue of our approach that it is neutral on those questions. Our central organizing assumption in compiling this anthology is that questions about morality and the law are at root questions of political theory.

The traditional questions of jurisprudence concern the distinguishing features of a legal order. What makes a legal order different from other types of social order? Answers to those questions, in turn, make a difference to the ways in which law can be used. For example, different views of legal order have profound implications for any account of the relation between democracy and the rule of law, and so for questions about the limits to criminalization. Again, views about the nature of law have implications for the ways in which the law might appropriately address those who object to it on moral grounds. Of course, there is no direct relationship – one might be a positivist or anti-positivist and still suppose the criminal law should be limited. But views about the general relation between law, morality, and democracy give shape to the types of arguments that are available, and assumptions about the nature of law will sometimes dictate which of those arguments seem most compelling. At the same time, views about the appropriate limits of state action may well lend credence to views about what is or is not an acceptable account of the nature of law. Again, questions about the nature of adjudication seem to straddle both sets of issues. In the end, all of the issues revolve around whether, or under what conditions, law is an appropriate place to pin our hopes for justice.

Since the introduction of the *Charter of Rights and Freedoms* in 1982, Canada's legal and political culture has changed dramatically. The political vocabulary of Canadians has become increasingly legalized. Perhaps the most noticeable feature is the way in which claims about fundamental justice and individual rights are traded in debates about most issues of public concern. But there have been subtler and deeper changes also. Although this collection contains brief excerpts from and discussions of American cases, its main focus will be Canadian. While some critics have described the introduction of the *Charter* as the "Americanization" of Canadian law, such a characterization is at best misleading. Judicial review has assumed an increased importance since the *Charter* was introduced, but the content of Canadian and American legal thought is very different. The differences are perhaps most obvious on issues of freedom of expression, where Canadian and American courts have come to such different conclusions. Those conclusions reveal yet deeper differences in their views of equality and the rule of law more generally. The central debates of legal theory and public policy that face Canadians in the 1990s are not the same as those that divided the United States in the 1960s. While those American struggles, especially the struggle for racial equality, are worthy of serious study, America's specific political and constitutional history has given these issues a shape that does not transfer readily to the rest of the world. Canada's legal culture is distinctive and important, and must be taken seriously in its own right. For similar reasons, we include a sample of the feminist writings which have been so influential in both legal theory and Canadian law.

The collection is divided into two sections. The first deals with general questions about morality and law, drawing both on the traditional literature discussing legal positivism and on contemporary debates about the role of law as a tool in pursuit of equality. Then it looks at a series of questions revolving around the tensions between the role of law as a protector of individual liberty and as a tool of democratic self-rule. Law has been defended as each of these, yet they are in apparent tension. The second section considers a series of contemporary issues in which the questions considered in the first section present themselves especially forcefully. The collection contains somewhat more material than would ordinarily be included in a one-semester course, so as to allow instructors some flexibility in designing a course using it, and in varying the course from year to year. For example, different contemporary problems might be covered, and the conceptual and practical materials integrated in a number of ways. At the same time, it does not contain so much material as to make prohibitive the cost of using additional material, either because this is better suited to the particular instructor's aims or because the instructor wishes to use the collection as the basis for a full-year course.

We have included reading questions for each of the selections. We have not suggested additional readings, leaving that instead to the discretion of instructors using the book.

PART ONE

MORALITY AND THE RULE OF LAW

1

Positivism, Legal Order, and Morality

Careful reflection about the law's relationship to morality requires inquiry into a variety of questions about its other features. Lawyers regularly make claims about what the law requires in a particular case. What other facts fix the truth of such claims? Does moral argument enter into them? If so, what sorts of moral argument? What determines whether a moral argument is admissible? Must every legal system incorporate moral arguments?

Philosophical thought about the nature of law has fallen into two broad camps. Legal positivism is the view that law is best understood as a sociological phenomenon, a particular way of structuring social life. For the positivist, it is essential to the nature of law that it can be identified without appeal to controversial moral arguments. Law is thus identified with positive law, that is law that has been promulgated or enacted in appropriate ways. Different positivists have different views of the necessary and sufficient conditions for appropriate enactment. Some make the command of a sovereign essential; others the existence of structures for changing laws, and others the availability of non-controversial ways of applying the law to particular cases. Whatever their other differences, positivists share the view that it is essential to a legal system that what the law *is* can be established without considering what the law morally *ought to be*.

Opposed to positivists are defenders of natural law, according to whom a system of official power only qualifies as a legal system if it meets certain moral demands. Natural lawyers differ on what those demands might be, but share an insistence that the difference between the rule of law and other ways of organizing power can only be drawn in terms of the fundamental moral conceptions at the heart of a legal system.

So described, the traditional questions of jurisprudence sometimes seem narrowly conceptual and lacking in political implications. At one level, this is plainly true: answers to them do not, by themselves, dictate answers to pressing political disputes. Yet jurisprudence was born of political ferment, and many people continue to see it as profoundly related to questions of justice and legitimacy. The connection can be found in the issue of adjudication. Any account of the nature of law is thereby also an account of the distinction between a judge or other official *applying* established law and *making* new law. One of the core ideals of the rule of law is that the task of judges is to apply the law rather than to make it. Depending on how this distinction is drawn, the role of courts can be seen as anything from a usurpation of majority rule (or a bulwark against tyranny), to a direct instrument of state control. Positivists will regard most intrusions of morality into official decisions as making law rather than applying it; natural lawyers will suppose that correctly applying the law requires moral argument. The distinction between making and applying law also has important implications for understanding the demands placed on judges as legal actors. Does the law allow a judge to reach morally desirable results contrary to the wishes of the state? Does it ever require such results?

Both positivists and their opponents sometimes accuse each other of authoritarianism. Positivists claim that seeing law as essentially moral is likely to lead to either of two pathologies. It may lead to authoritarianism, because people will suppose that whatever law is on the books is therefore just, and thus blindly obey it. Alternatively, it may lead to anarchy, as people suppose themselves to be the appropriate judges of whether or not to obey. For their part, anti-positivists sometimes charge that positivism leads to a sort of rule-worship, and an implicit moral admiration for order, regardless of its injustices.

In the seventeenth century, Thomas Hobbes first articulated legal positivism in support of the consolidation of state power. Virtually all human societies have resolved disputes by granting authority to people not involved in the disputes. Such courts are not necessarily directly connected with either state power or the more general directions of public policy. Our own legal system is a descendent of a system in which nobles held courts of their own in addition to the royal courts. In the English-speaking world, religious courts remained a separate center of legal power well into the nineteenth century. Similar systems of adjudication can be found today in the form of disciplinary procedures in workplaces and universities. The idea that the state should be the only lawmaking institution is thus comparatively new.

On Hobbes's view, law cannot be understood as anything but the command of a sovereign. If courts lie outside the direct control of the state, judges are making law rather than applying it. The result is divided sovereignty and conflict. A century and a half later, Jeremy Bentham offered a different version of positivism in support of a forward-looking version of public policy. The role of law is to provide incentives to behavior, and laws must have coercive sanctions attached to them in order to qualify as laws. For both Hobbes and Bentham, courts can only properly apply the law if judges follow clear instructions from the state.

Recent versions of positivism have had less of a tone of political urgency about them. H.L.A. Hart's influential development of positivism emphasizes the role of rules in a legal system. According to Hart, a legal system must contain both "primary" rules regulating behavior and "secondary" rules regulating the changing of the primary rules. In order to govern behavior effectively, these rules must be largely accepted by both the population they govern and the officials applying them. For Hart, any such system of rules will face cases to which they do not straightforwardly apply. In such circumstances, the judge will have no choice but to exercise discretion, making law rather than simply applying it. Hart maintains that these distinctions are descriptive and conceptual, but politically important, because keeping them in mind enables us to evaluate existing law with an open mind, rather than seeing it as either a nightmare of power politics or a noble dream of perfect justice.

The readings explore the political charges made by both positivists and their critics. Those issues come to a head in the issue of wicked legal systems. Whether the example is Nazi law, South African law under Apartheid, or slavery in the United States, positivists insist that wicked legal systems must nonetheless be seen as involving law. Opponents of positivism have two options: some insist that such systems are not legal systems at all; others insist that precisely because they are legal systems, they cannot consistently enforce their unjust dictates. According to the anti-positivist, positivist judges serve unjust regimes when they suppose that their choices are to either enforce the wishes of their political masters or give up on being judges.

The debate about whether the law is an instrument of justice carries over into recent feminist scholarship about the law. The readings approach the same set of issues in light of recent feminist scholarship. Historically, the law has treated women badly. At common law, women were not allowed to own property, husbands were allowed to beat their wives, and victims of sexual assault were presumed to have consented. Feminist scholarship has criticized these implicit (sometimes explicit) biases. Some feminist scholarship has supposed that the law can nonetheless be reclaimed for feminist purposes; other feminists take a less optimistic view.

The selections in this opening chapter look at the traditional jurisprudential question, "What is law?" Both positivists and anti-positivists agree that law is a distinctive type of social ordering, but disagree about what makes it distinctive. Positivists suppose that law can be identified solely by its sources, while their critics suppose it must be identified by its particular moral content.

Thomas Hobbes
Leviathan (1651)

Hobbes is widely regarded as the greatest of the English political philosophers. He is also plausibly credited with being the founder of modern legal philosophy. Various forms of dispute resolution, legislation, and punishment have been found in all human societies. In early modern England, the church had its own laws and courts, as did various nobles, just as universities and workplaces have analogous disciplinary practices to this day. Hobbes, writing at the dawn of the modern age, was the first philosopher to identify law as a type of order exercised above all by the state. Thus, Hobbes understands legal order in terms of its sources, rather than its particular content. The selections included here set the context for Hobbes's view of law with his description of what he calls "the natural condition of mankind." Hobbes views the state as the solution to a practical problem of order. Laws provide predictability, and are backed with threats. As a result, they change the structure of social life from one of opposition and distrust to one of coordination. For Hobbes, such coordination is only possible if there is a single sovereign charged with making, applying, and enforcing law. Anything else, including any kind of moral limitation on the sovereign, risks controversy and eventual war. As a result, law must be identified with whatever the sovereign commands.

CHAPTER 5

And as in Arithmetique, unpractised men must, and Professors them-selves may often erre, and cast up false; so also in any other subject of Reasoning, the ablest, most attentive, and most practised men, may deceive themselves, and inferre false Conclusions; Not but that Reason it selfe is always Right Reason, as well as Arithmetique is a certain and infallible Art: But no one mans Reason, nor the Reason of any one number of men, makes the certaintie; no more than an account is there-fore well cast up, because a great many men have unanimously ap-proved it. And therefore, as when there is a controversy in [19] an account, the parties must by their own accord, set up for right Reason, the Reason of some Arbitrator, or Judge, to whose sentence they will both stand, or their controversie must either come to blowes, or be un-decided, for want of a right Reason constituted by Nature; so is it also in all debates of what kind soever: And when men that think them-selves wiser than all others, clamour and demand right Reason for judge; yet seek no more, but that things should be determined, by no other mens reason but their own, it is as intolerable in the society of men, as it is in play after trump is turned, to use for trump on every occasion, that suite whereof they have most in their hand. For they do nothing els, that will have every of their passions, as it comes to bear sway in them, to be taken for right Reason, and that in their own con-troversies: bewraying their want of right Reason, by the claym they lay to it.

CHAPTER 6

But whatsoever is the object of any mans Appetite or Desire; that is it, which he for his part calleth *Good:* And the object of his Hate, and Aversion, *Evill*; And of his Contempt, *Vile, and Inconsiderable.* For these words of Good, Evill, and Contemptible, are ever used with relation to the person that useth them: There being nothing simply and absolutely so; nor any common Rule of Good and Evill, to be taken from the nature of the objects themselves; but from the Person of the man (where there is no Common-wealth;) or, (in a Common-wealth,) from the Person that representeth it; or from an Arbitrator or Judge, whom men disagreeing shall by consent set up, and make his sentence the Rule thereof.

CHAPTER 13: OF THE NATURALL CONDITION OF MANKIND, AS CONCERNING
THEIR FELICITY, AND MISERY

Nature hath made men so equall, in the faculties of body, and mind; as
that though there bee found one man sometimes manifestly stronger in
body, or of quicker mind than another; yet when all is reckoned together, the difference between man, and man, is not so considerable, as
that one man can thereupon claim to himselfe any benefit, to which
another may not pretend, as well as he. For as to the strength of body,
the weakest has strength enough to kill the strongest, either by secret
machination, or by confederacy with others, that are in the same danger
with himselfe.

And as to the faculties of the mind, (setting aside the arts grounded
upon words, and especially that skill of proceeding upon generall, and
infallible rules, called Science; which very few have, and but in few
things; as being not a native faculty, born with us; nor attained, (as
Prudence,) while we look after somewhat els,) I find yet a greater equality amongst men, than that of strength. For Prudence, is but Experience;
which equall time, equally bestows on all men, in [61] those things they
equally apply themselves unto. That which may perhaps make such
equality incredible, is but a vain conceipt of ones own wisdom, which
almost all men think they have in a greater degree, than the Vulgar; that
is, than all men but themselves, and a few others, whom by Fame, or for
concurring with themselves, they approve. For such is the nature of
men, that howsoever they may acknowledge many others to be more
witty, or more eloquent, or more learned; Yet they will hardly believe
there be many so wise as themselves: For they see their own wit at
hand, and other mens at a distance. But this proveth rather that men are
in that point equall, than unequall. For there is not ordinarily a greater
signe of the equall distribution of any thing, than that every man is
contented with his share.

From this equality of ability, ariseth equality of hope in the attaining
of our Ends. And therefore if any two men desire the same thing, which
neverthelesse they cannot both enjoy, they become enemies; and in the
way to their End, (which is principally their owne conservation, and
sometimes their delectation only,) endeavour to destroy, or subdue one
an other. And from hence it comes to passe, that where an Invader hath
no more to feare, than an other mans single power; if one plant, sow,
build, or possesse a convenient Seat, others may probably be expected
to come prepared with forces united, to dispossesse, and deprive him,

not only of the fruit of his labour, but also of his life, or liberty. And the Invader again is in the like danger of another.

And from this diffidence of one another, there is no way for any man to secure himselfe, so reasonable, as Anticipation; that is, by force, or wiles, to master the persons of all men he can, so long, till he see no other power great enough to endanger him: And this is no more than his own conservation requireth, and is generally allowed. Also because there be some, that taking pleasure in contemplating their own power in the acts of conquest, which they pursue farther than their security requires; if others, that otherwise would be glad to be at ease within modest bounds, should not by invasion increase their power, they would not be able, long time, by standing only on their defence, to sub-sist. And by consequence, such augmentation of dominion over men, being necessary to a mans conservation, it ought to be allowed him.

Againe, men have no pleasure, (but on the contrary a great deale of griefe) in keeping company, where there is no power able to over-awe them all. For every man looketh that his companion should value him, at the same rate he sets upon himselfe: And upon all signes of contempt, or undervaluing, naturally endeavours, as far as he dares (which amongst them that have no common power, to keep them in quiet, is far enough to make them destroy each other,) to extort a greater value from his contemners, by dommage; and from others, by the example.

So that in the nature of man, we find three principall causes of quarrell. First, Competition; Secondly, Diffidence; Thirdly, Glory.

[62] The first, maketh men invade for Gain; the second, for Safety; and the third, for Reputation. The first use Violence, to make them-selves Masters of other mens persons, wives, children, and cattell; the second, to defend them; the third, for trifles, as a word, a smile, a different opinion, and any other signe of undervalue, either direct in their Persons, or by reflexion in their Kindred, their Friends, their Na-tion, their Profession, or their Name.

Hereby it is manifest, that during the time men live without a com-mon Power to keep them all in awe, they are in that condition which is called Warre; and such a warre, as is of every man, against every man. For Warre, consisteth not in Battell onely, or the act of fighting; but in a tract of time, wherein the Will to contend by Battell is sufficiently known: and therefore the notion of *Time*, is to be considered in the nature of Warre; as it is in the nature of Weather. For as the nature of Foule weather, lyeth not in a showre or two of rain; but in an inclination thereto of many days together: So the nature of War, consisteth not in actuall fighting; but in the known disposition thereto, during all the time there is no assurance to the contrary. All other time is Peace.

Whatsoever therefore is consequent to a time of Warre, where every man is Enemy to every man; the same is consequent to the time, wherein men live without other security, than what their own strength, and their own invention shall furnish them withall. In such condition, there is no place for Industry; because the fruit thereof is uncertain: and consequently no Culture of the Earth; no Navigation, nor use of the commodities that may be imported by Sea; no commodious Building; no Instruments of moving, and removing such things as require much force; no Knowledge of the face of the Earth; no account of Time; no Arts; no Letters; no Society; and which is worst of all, continuall feare, and danger of violent death; And the life of man, solitary, poore, nasty, brutish, and short.

It may seem strange to some man, that has not well weighed these things; that Nature should thus dissociate, and render men apt to invade, and destroy one another: and he may therefore, not trusting to this Inference, made from the Passions, desire perhaps to have the same confirmed by Experience. Let him therefore consider with himselfe, when taking a journey, he armes himselfe, and seeks to go well accompanied; when going to sleep, he locks his dores; when even in his house he locks his chests; and this when he knows there bee Lawes, and publike Officers, armed, to revenge all injuries shall bee done him; what opinion he has of his fellow subjects, when he rides armed; of his fellow Citizens, when he locks his dores; and of his children, and servants, when he locks his chests. Does he not there as much accuse mankind by his actions, as I do by my words? But neither of us accuse mans nature in it. The Desires, and other Passions of man, are in themselves no Sin. No more are the Actions, that proceed from those Passions, till they know a Law that forbids them: which till Lawes be made they cannot know: nor can any Law be made, till they have agreed upon the Person that shall make it.

[63] It may peradventure be thought, there was never such a time, nor condition of warre as this; and I believe it was never generally so, over all the world: but there are many places, where they live so now. For the savage people in many places of *America*, except the government of small Families, the concord whereof dependeth on naturall lust, have no government at all; and live at this day in that brutish manner, as I said before. Howsoever, it may be perceived what manner of life there

would be, where there were no common Power to feare; by the manner of life, which men that have formerly lived under a peacefull government, use to degenerate into, in a civill Warre.

But though there had never been any time, wherein particular men were in a condition of warre one against another; yet in all times, Kings, and Persons of Soveraigne authority, because of their Independency, are in continuall jealousies, and in the state and posture of Gladiators; having their weapons pointing, and their eyes fixed on one another; that is, their Forts, Garrisons, and Guns upon the Frontiers of their Kingdomes; and continuall Spyes upon their neighbours; which is a posture of War. But because they uphold thereby, the Industry of their Subjects; there does not follow from it, that misery, which accompanies the Liberty of particular men.

To this warre of every man against every man, this also is consequent; that nothing can be Unjust. The notions of Right and Wrong, Justice and Injustice have there no place. Where there is no common Power, there is no Law: where no Law, no Injustice. Force, and Fraud, are in warre the two Cardinall vertues. Justice, and Injustice are none of the Faculties neither of the Body, nor Mind. If they were, they might be in a man that were alone in the world, as well as his Senses, and Passions. They are Qualities, that relate to men in Society, not in Solitude. It is consequent also to the same condition, that there be no Propriety, no Dominion, no *Mine* and *Thine* distinct; but onely that to be every mans that he can get; and for so long, as he can keep it. And thus much for the ill condition, which man by meer Nature is actually placed in; though with a possibility to come out of it, consisting partly in the Passions, partly in his Reason.

The Passions that encline men to Peace, are Feare of Death; Desire of such things as are necessary to commodious living; and a Hope by their Industry to obtain them. And Reason suggesteth convenient Articles of Peace, upon which men may be drawn to agreement. These Articles, are they, which otherwise are called the Lawes of Nature: whereof I shall speak more particularly, in the two following Chapters. [64]

CHAPTER 14: OF THE FIRST AND SECOND NATURALL LAWES, AND OF CONTRACTS

The Right of Nature, which Writers commonly call *Jus Naturale,* is the Liberty each man hath, to use his own power, as he will himselfe, for the preservation of his own Nature; that is to say, of his own Life; and consequently, of doing any thing, which in his own Judgement, and Reason, hee shall conceive to be the aptest means thereunto.

By Liberty, is understood, according to the proper signification of the word, the absence of externall Impediments: which Impediments, may oft take away part of a mans power to do what hee would; but cannot hinder him from using the power left him, according as his judgement, and reason shall dictate to him.

A Law of Nature, *(Lex Naturalis,)* is a precept, or generall Rule, found out by Reason, by which a man is forbidden to do, that, which is destructive of his life, or taketh away the means of preserving the same; and to omit, that, by which he thinketh it may be best preserved. For though they that speak of this subject, use to confound *Jus*, and *Lex*, *Right* and *Law;* yet they ought to be distinguished; because RIGHT, consisteth in liberty to do, or to forbeare; Whereas LAW, determineth, and bindeth to one of them: so that Law, and Right, differ as much, as Obligation, and Liberty; which in one and the same matter are inconsistent.

And because the condition of Man, (as hath been declared in the precedent Chapter) is a condition of Warre of every one against every one; in which case every one is governed by his own Reason; and there is nothing he can make use of, that may not be a help unto him, in preserving his life against his enemyes; It followeth, that in such a condition, every man has a Right to every thing; even to one anothers body. And therefore, as long as this naturall Right of every man to every thing endureth, there can be no security to any man, (how strong or wise soever he be,) of living out the time, which Nature ordinarily alloweth men to live. And consequently it is a precept, or generall rule of Reason, *That every man, ought to endeavour Peace, as farre as he has hope of obtaining it; and when he cannot obtain it, that he may seek, and use, all helps, and advantages of Warre.* The first branch of which Rule, containeth the first, and Fundamentall Law of Nature; which is, *to seek Peace, and follow it.* The Second, the summe of the Right of Nature; which is, By *all means we can, to defend our selves.*

From this Fundamentall Law of Nature, by which men are commanded to endeavour Peace, is derived this second Law; *That a man be willing, when others are so too, as farre-forth, as for Peace, and* [65] *defence of himselfe he shall think it necessary, to lay down this right to all things; and be contented with so much liberty against other men, as he would allow other men against himselfe.* For as long as every man holdeth this Right, of doing any thing he liketh; so long are all men in the condition of Warre. But if other men will not lay down their Right, as well as he; then there is no Reason for any one, to devest himselfe of his: For that were to expose himselfe to Prey, (which no man is bound to) rather than to dispose himselfe to Peace. This is that Law of the Gospell; *Whatsoever you require that others should do to you, that do ye to them.* And that Law of all men, *Quod tibi fieri non vis, alteri ne feceris ...*

A Covenant not to defend my selfe from force, by force, is alwayes voyd. For (as I have shewed before) no man can transferre or lay down his Right to save himselfe from Death, Wounds, and Imprisonment, (the avoyding whereof is the onely End of laying [70] down any Right, and therefore the promise of not resisting force, in no Covenant transferreth any right; nor is obliging. For though a man may Covenant thus, *Unlesse I do so, or so, kill* me; he cannot Covenant thus, *Unlesse I do so, or so, I will not resist you, when you come to kill me.* For man by nature chooseth the lesser evill, which is danger of death in resisting; rather than the greater, which is certain and present death in not resisting. And this is granted to be true by all men, in that they lead Criminals to Execution, and Prison, with armed men, notwithstanding that such Criminals have consented to the Law, by which they are condemned.

CHAPTER 15: OF OTHER LAWES OF NATURE

From that law of Nature, by which we are obliged to transferre to another, such Rights, as being retained, hinder the peace of Mankind, there followeth a Third; which is this, *That men performe their Covenants made*: without which, Covenants are in vain, and but Empty words; and the Right of all men to all things remaining, wee are still in the condition of Warre.

And in this law of Nature, consisteth the Fountain and Originall of JUSTICE. For where no Covenant hath preceded, there hath no Right been transferred, and every man has right to every thing; and consequently, no action can be Unjust. But when a Covenant is made, then to break it is *Unjust*: And the definition of INJUSTICE, is no other than *the not Performance of Covenant*. And whatsoever is not Unjust, is *Just*.

But because Covenants of mutuall trust, where there is a feare of not performance on either part, (as hath been said in the former Chapter,) are invalid; though the Originall of Justice be the making of Covenants; yet Injustice actually there can be none, till the cause of such feare be taken away; which while men are in the naturall condition of Warre, cannot be done. Therefore before the names of Just, and Unjust can have place, there must be some coercive Power, to compell men equally to the performance of their Covenants, by the terrour of some punishment, greater than the benefit they expect [72] by the breach of their Covenant; and to make good that Propriety, which by mutuall Contract men acquire, in recompence of the universall Right they abandon: and such power there is none before the erection of a Commonwealth. And this is also to be gathered out of the ordinary definition of Justice in the Schooles; For they say, that *Justice is the constant Will of giving to every man his own*. And therefore where there is no *Own*, that is, no Propriety, there is no Injustice; and where there is no coercive Power erected, that is, where there is no Common-wealth, there is no Propriety; all men having Right to all things: Therefore where there is no Common-wealth, there nothing is Unjust. So that the nature of Justice, consisteth in keeping of valid Covenants; but the Validity of Covenants begins not but with the Constitution of a Civill Power, sufficient to compell men to keep them: And then it is also that Propriety begins.

The Foole hath sayd in his heart, there is no such thing as Justice; and sometimes also with his tongue; seriously alleaging, that every mans conservation, and contentment, being committed to his own care, there could be no reason, why every man might not do what he thought conduced thereunto: and therefore also to make, or not make; keep, or not keep Covenants, was not against Reason, when it conduced to ones benefit. He does not therein deny, that there be Covenants; and that they are sometimes broken, sometimes kept; and that such breach of them may be called Injustice, and the observance of them Justice: but he questioneth, whether Injustice, taking away the feare of God, (for the same Foole hath said in his heart there is no God,) may not sometimes stand with that Reason, which dictateth to every man his own good; and particularly then, when it conduceth to such a benefit, as shall put a man in a condition, to neglect not onely the dispraise, and revilings, but also the power of other men. The Kingdome of God is gotten by violence: but what if it could be gotten by unjust violence? were it against Reason so to get it, when it is impossible to receive hurt by it? And if it be not against Reason, it is not against Justice: or else Justice is not to be approved for good. From such reasoning as this, Successful wickednesse hath obtained the name of Vertue: and some that in all other things have disallowed the violation of Faith; yet have allowed it, when it is for the getting of a Kingdome. And the Heathen that believed, that *Saturn* was deposed by his son *Jupiter*, believed neverthelesse the same *Jupiter* to be the avenger of Injustice: Somewhat like to a piece of Law in *Cokes* Commentaries on *Litleton*; where he sayes, If the right Heire of the Crown be attainted of Treason; yet the Crown shall descend to him, and *eo instante* the Atteynder be voyd: From which instances a man will be very prone to inferre; that when the Heire apparent of a Kingdome, shall kill him that is in possession, though his father; you may call it Injustice, or by what other name you will; yet it can never be against reason, seeing all the voluntary actions of men tend to the benefit of themselves; and those actions are most reasonable, that conduce most to their [73] ends. This specious reasoning is neverthelesse false.

For the question is not of promises mutuall, where there is no security of performance on either side; as when there is no Civill Power erected over the parties promising; for such promises are no Covenants: But either where one of the parties has performed already; or where there is a Power to make him performe; there is the question whether it be against reason, that is, against the benefit of the other to performe, or not. And I say it is not against reason. For the manifestation whereof, we are to consider; First, that when a man doth a thing, which notwithstanding any thing can be foreseen, and reckoned on, tendeth to his own destruction, howsoever some accident which he could not expect, arriving may turne it to his benefit; yet such events do not make it reasonably or wisely done. Secondly, that in a condition of Warre, wherein every man to every man, for want of a common Power to keep them all in awe, is an Enemy, there is no man can hope by his own strength, or wit, to defend himselfe from destruction, without the help of Confederates; where every one expects the same defence by the Confederation, that any one else does: and therefore he which declares he thinks it reason to deceive those that help him, can in reason expect no other means of safety, than what can be had from his own single Power. He therefore that breaketh his Covenant, and consequently declareth that he thinks he may with reason do so, cannot be received into any Society, that unite themselves for Peace and Defence, but by the errour of them that receive him; nor when he is received, be retayned in it, without seeing the danger of their errour; which errours a man cannot reasonably reckon upon as the means of his security: and therefore if he be left, or cast out of Society, he perisheth; and if he live in Society, it is by the errours of other men, which he could not foresee, nor reckon upon; and consequently against the reason of his preservation; and so, as all men that contribute not to his destruction, forbear him onely out of ignorance of what is good for themselves.

As for the Instance of gaining the secure and perpetuall felicity of Heaven, by any way; it is frivolous: there being but one way imaginable; and that is not breaking, but keeping of Covenant.

And for the other Instance of attaining Soveraignty by Rebellion; it is manifest, that though the event follow, yet because it cannot reasonably be expected, but rather the contrary; and because by gaining it so, others are taught to gain the same in like manner, the attempt thereof is against reason. Justice therefore, that is to say, Keeping of Covenant, is a Rule of Reason, by which we are forbidden to do any thing destructive to our life; and consequently a law of Nature.

CHAPTER 25

Command is, where a man saith, *Doe this, or Doe not this,* without expecting other reason than the Will of him that sayes it. From this it followeth manifestly, that he that Commandeth, pretendeth thereby his own Benefit: For the reason of his Command is his own [132] Will onely, and the proper object of every mans Will, is some Good to himselfe.

Counsell, is where a man saith, *Doe, or Doe not this,* and deduceth his reasons from the benefit that arriveth by it to him to whom he saith it. And from this it is evident, that he that giveth Counsell, pretendeth onely (whatsoever he intendeth) the good of him, to whom he giveth it ...

CHAPTER 26: OF CIVILL LAWES

By Civill Lawes, I understand the Lawes, that men are therefore bound to observe, because they are Members, not of this, or that Commonwealth in particular, but of a Common-wealth. For the knowledge of particular Lawes [137] belongeth to them, that professe the study of the Lawes of their severall Countries; but the knowledge of Civill Law in generall, to any man. The antient Law of *Rome* was called their *Civil Law,* from the word *Civitas,* which signifies a Common-wealth: And those Countries, which having been under the Roman Empire, and governed by that Law, retaine still such part thereof as they think fit, call that part the Civill Law, to distinguish it from the rest of their own Civill Lawes. But that is not it I intend to speak of here; my designe being not to shew what is Law here, and there; but what is Law; as *Plato, Aristotle, Cicero,* and divers others have done, without taking upon them the profession of the study of the Law.

And first it is manifest, that Law in generall, is not Counsell, but Command; nor a Command of any man to any man; but only of him, whose Command is addressed to one formerly obliged to obey him. And as for Civill Law, it addeth only the name of the person Commanding, which is *Persona Civitatis*, the Person of the Common-wealth.

Which considered, I define Civill Law in this manner. Civill Law, *Is to every Subject, those Rules, which the Common-wealth hath Commanded him, by Word, Writing, or other sufficient Sign of the Will, to make use of, for the Distinction of Right, and Wrong; that is to say, of what is contrary, and what is not contrary to the Rule.*

In which definition, there is nothing that is not at first sight evident. For every man seeth, that some Lawes are addressed to all the Subjects in generall; some to particular Provinces; some to particular Vocations; and some to particular Men; and are therefore Lawes, to every of those to whom the Command is directed; and to none else. As also, that Lawes are the Rules of Just, and Unjust; nothing being reputed Unjust, that is not contrary to some Law. Likewise, that none can make Lawes but the Common-wealth; because our Subjection is to the Common-wealth only: and that Commands, are to be signified by sufficient Signs; because a man knows not otherwise how to obey them. And therefore, whatsoever can from this definition by necessary consequence be deduced, ought to be acknowledged for truth. Now I deduce from it this that followeth.

1. The Legislator in all Common-wealths, is only the Soveraign, be he one Man, as in a Monarchy, or one Assembly of men, as in a Democracy, or Aristocracy. For the Legislator, is he that maketh the Law. And the Common-wealth only, præscribes, and commandeth the observation of those rules, which we call Law: Therefore the Common-wealth is the Legislator. But the Common-wealth is no Person, nor has capacity to doe any thing, but by the Representative, (that is, the Soveraign;) and therefore the Soveraign is the sole Legislator. For the same reason, none can abrogate a Law made, but the Soveraign; because a Law is not abrogated, but by another Law, that forbiddeth it to be put in execution.

2. The Soveraign of a Common-wealth, be it an Assembly, or one Man, is not Subject to the Civill Lawes. For having power to [138] make, and repeale Lawes, he may when he pleaseth, free himselfe from that subjection, by repealing those Lawes that trouble him, and making of new; and consequently he was free before. For he is free, that can be free when he will: Nor is it possible for any person to be bound to himselfe; because he that can bind, can release; and therefore he that is bound to himselfe only, is not bound.

3. When long Use obtaineth the authority of a Law, it is not the Length of Time that maketh the Authority, but the Will of the Soveraign signified by his silence, (for Silence is sometimes an argument of Consent;) and it is no longer Law, then the Soveraign shall be silent therein. And therefore if the Soveraign shall have a question of Right grounded, not upon his present Will, but upon the Lawes formerly made; the Length of Time shal bring no prejudice to his Right; but the question shal be judged by Equity. For many unjust Actions, and unjust Sentences, go uncontrolled a longer time, than any man can remember. And our Lawyers account no Customes Law, but such as are reasonable, and that eville Customes are to be abolished: But the Judgement of what is reasonable, and of what is to be abolished, belongeth to him that maketh the Law, which is the Soveraign Assembly, or Monarch.

4. The Law of Nature, and the Civill Law, contain each other, and are of equall extent. For the Lawes of Nature, which consist in Equity, Justice, Gratitude, and other morall Vertues on these depending, in the condition of meer Nature (as I have said before in the end of the 15th Chapter,) are not properly Lawes, but qualities that dispose men to peace, and to obedience. When a Common-wealth is once settled, then are they actually Lawes, and not before; as being then the commands of the Common-wealth; and therefore also Civill Lawes: For it is the Soveraign Power that obliges men to obey them. For in the differences of private men, to declare, what is Equity, what is Justice, and what is morall Vertue, and to make them binding, there is need of the Ordinances of Soveraign Power, and Punishments to be ordained for such as shall break them; which Ordinances are therefore part of the Civill Law. The Law of Nature therefore is a part of the Civill Law in all Common-wealths of the world. Reciprocally also, the Civill Law is a part of the Dictates of Nature. For Justice, that is to say, Performance of Covenant, and giving to every man his own, is a Dictate of the Law of Nature. But every subject in a Common-wealth, hath covenanted to obey the Civill Law, (either one with another, as when they assemble to make a common Representative, or with the Representative it selfe one by one, when subdued by the Sword they promise obedience, that they may receive life;) And therefore Obedience to the Civill Law is part also of the Law of Nature. Civill, and Naturall Law are not different kinds, but different parts of Law; whereof one part being written, is called Civill, the other unwritten, Naturall. But the Right of Nature, that is, the naturall Liberty of man, may by the Civill Law be abridged, and restrained: nay, the end of making Lawes, is no other, but such Restraint;

without the which there cannot possibly be any Peace. And Law was brought into the world for nothing else, [139] but to limit the naturall liberty of particular men, in such manner, as they might not hurt, but assist one another, and joyn together against a common Enemy.

5. If the Soveraign of one Common-wealth, subdue a People that have lived under other written Lawes, and afterwards govern them by the same Lawes, by which they were governed before; yet those Lawes are the Civill Lawes of the Victor, and not of the Vanquished Common-wealth. For the Legislator is he, not by whose authority the Lawes were first made, but by whose authority they now continue to be Lawes. And therefore where there be divers Provinces, within the Dominion of a Common-wealth, and in those Provinces diversity of Lawes, which commonly are called the Customes of each severall Province, we are not to understand that such Customes have their force, onely from Length of Time; but that they were antiently Lawes written, or otherwise made known, for the Constitutions, and Statutes of their Soveraigns; and are now Lawes, not by vertue of the Præscription of time, but by the Constitutions of their present Soveraigns. But if an unwritten Law, in all the Provinces of a Dominion, shall be generally observed, and no iniquity appear in the use thereof; that Law can be no other but a Law of Nature, equally obliging all man-kind.

6. Seeing then all Lawes, written, and unwritten, have their Authority, and force, from the Will of the Common-wealth; that is to say, from the Will of the Representative; which in a Monarchy is the Monarch, and in other Common-wealths the Soveraign Assembly; a man may wonder from whence proceed such opinions, as are found in the Books of Lawyers of eminence in several Commonwealths, directly, or by consequence making the Legislative Power depend on private men, or subordinate Judges. As for example, *That the Common Law, hath no Controuler but the Parlament;* which is true onely where a Parlament has the Soveraign Power, and cannot be assembled, not dissolved, but by their own discretion. For if there be a right in any else to dissolve them, there is a right also to controule them, and consequently to controule their controulings. And if there be no such right, then the Controuler of Lawes is not *Parlamentum,* but *Rex in Parlamento.* And where a Parlament is Soveraign, if it should assemble never so many, or so wise men, from the Countries subject to them, for whatsoever cause; yet there is no man will believe, that such an Assembly hath thereby acquired to themselves a Legislative Power. *Item,* that the two arms of a Common-wealth, are *Force, and Justice; the first whereof is in the King; the other*

deposited in the hands of the Parlament. As if a Common-wealth could consist, where the Force were in any hand, which justice had not the Authority to command and govern.

7. That Law can never be against Reason, our Lawyers are agreed; and that not the Letter, (that is every construction of it,) but that which is according to the Intention of the Legislator, is the Law. And it is true: but the doubt is, of whose Reason it is, that shall be received for Law. It is not meant of any private Reason; for [140] then there would be as much contradiction in the Lawes, as there is in the Schooles; nor yet, (as Sr. *Ed. Coke* makes it,) an *Artificiall perfection of Reason, gotten by long study, observation, and experience,* (as his was.) For it is possible long study may encrease, and confirm erroneous Sentences: and where men build on false grounds, the more they build, the greater is the ruine: and of those that study, and observe with equall time, and diligence, the reasons and resolutions are, and must remain discordant: and therefore it is not that *Juris prudentia,* or wisedome of subordinate Judges; but the Reason of this our Artificiall Man the Common-wealth, and his Command, that maketh Law: And the Common-wealth being in their Representative but one Person, there cannot easily arise any contradiction in the Lawes; and when there doth, the same Reason is able, by interpretation, or alteration, to take it away. In all Courts of Justice, the Soveraign (which is the Person of the Common-wealth,) is he that Judgeth: The subordinate Judge, ought to have regard to the reason, which moved his Soveraign to make such Law, that his Sentence may be according thereunto; which then is his Soveraigns Sentence; otherwise it is his own, and an unjust one.

8. From this, that the Law is a Command, and a Command consisteth in declaration, or manifestation of the will of him that commandeth, by voyce, writing, or some other sufficient argument of the same, we may understand, that the Command of the Common-wealth, is Law onely to those, that have means to take notice of it. Over naturall fooles, children, or mad-men there is no Law, no more than over brute beasts; nor are they capable of the title of just, or unjust; because they had never power to make any covenant, or to understand the consequences thereof; and consequently never took upon them to authorise the actions of any Soveraign, as they must do that make to themselves a Common-wealth. And as those from whom Nature, or Accident hath taken away the notice of all Lawes in generall; so also every man, from whom any accident, not proceeding from his own default, hath taken away the means to take notice of any particular Law, is excused, if he

observe it not; And to speak properly, that Law is no Law to him. It is therefore necessary, to consider in this place, what arguments, and signes be sufficient for the knowledge of what is the Law; that is to say, what is the will of the Soveraign, as well in Monarchies, as in other formes of government.

And first, if it be a Law that obliges all the Subjects without exception, and is not written, nor otherwise published in such places as they may take notice thereof, it is a Law of Nature. For whatsoever men are to take knowledge of for Law, not upon other mens words, but every one from his own reason, must be such as is agreeable to the reason of all men; which no Law can be, but the Law of Nature. The Lawes of Nature therefore need not any publishing, nor Proclamation; as being contained in this one Sentence, approved by all the world, *Do not that to another, which thou thinkest unreasonable to be done by another to thy selfe.*

[141] Secondly, if it be a Law that obliges only some condition of men, or one particular man, and be not written, nor published by word, then also it is a Law of Nature; and known by the same arguments, and signs, that distinguish those in such a condition, from other Subjects. For whatsoever Law is not written, or some way published by him that makes it Law, can be known no way, but by the reason of him that is to obey it; and is therefore also a Law not only Civill, but Naturall. For Example, if the Soveraign employ a Publique Minister, without written Instructions what to doe; he is obliged to take for Instructions the Dictates of Reason; As if he make a Judge, The Judge is to take notice, that his Sentence ought to be according to the reason of his Soveraign, which being alwaies understood to be Equity, he is bound to it by the Law of Nature: Or if an Ambassador, he is (in all things not conteined in his written Instructions) to take for Instruction that which Reason dictates to be most conducing to his Soveraigns interest; and so of all other Ministers of the Soveraignty, publique and private. All which Instructions of naturall Reason may be comprehended under one name of *Fidelity*; which is a branch of naturall Justice ...

Nor is it enough the Law be written, and published; but also that there be manifest signs, that it proceedeth from the will of the Soveraign. For private men, when they have, or think they have force enough to secure their unjust designes, and convoy them safely to their ambitious ends, may publish for Lawes what they please, without, or against the Legislative Authority. There is therefore requisite, not only a Declaration of the Law, but also sufficient signes of the Author, and Authority. The Author, or Legislator is supposed in every Common-wealth to be evident, because he is the Soveraign, who having been Constituted by the consent of every one, is supposed by every one to be sufficiently known. And though the ignorance, and security of men be such, for the most part, as that when [142] the memory of the first Constitution of their Common-wealth is worn out, they doe not consider, by whose power they use to be defended against their enemies, and to have their industry protected, and to be righted when injury is done them; yet because no man that considers, can make question of it, no excuse can be derived from the ignorance of where the Soveraignty is placed. And it is a Dictate of Naturall Reason, and consequently an evident Law of Nature, that no man ought to weaken that power, the protection whereof he hath himself demanded, or wittingly received against others. Therefore of who is Soveraign, no man, but by his own fault, (whatsoever evill men suggest,) can make any doubt. The difficulty consisteth in the evidence of the Authority derived from him; The removing whereof, dependeth on the knowledge of the publique Registers, publique Counsels, publique Ministers, and publique Seales; by which all Lawes are sufficiently verified; Verifyed, I say, not Authorised: for the Verification, is but the Testimony and Record; not the Authority of the Law; which consisteth in the Command of the Soveraign only.

If therefore a man have a question of Injury, depending on the Law of Nature; that is to say, on common Equity; the Sentence of the Judge, that by Commission hath Authority to take cognisance of such causes, is a sufficient Verification of the Law of Nature in that individuall case. For though the advice of one that professeth the study of the Law, be usefull for the avoyding of contention; yet it is but advice: tis the Judge must tell men what is Law, upon the hearing of the Controversy.

But when the question is of injury, or crime, upon a written Law; every man by recourse to the Registers, by himself, or others, may (if he will) be sufficiently enformed, before he doe such injury, or commit the crime, whither it be an injury, or not: Nay he ought to doe so: For when a man doubts whether the act he goeth about, be just, or injust; and may informe himself, if he will; the doing is unlawfull. In like manner, he that supposeth himself injured, in a case determined by the written Law, which he may by himself, or others see and consider; if he complaines before he consults with the Law, he does unjustly, and bewrayeth a disposition rather to vex other men, than to demand his own right.

If the question be of Obedience to a publique Officer; To have seen his Commission, with the Publique Seale, and heard it read; or to have had the means to be informed of it, if a man would, is a sufficient Verification of his Authority. For every man is obliged to doe his best endeavour, to informe himself of all written Lawes, that may concerne his own future actions.

The Legislator known; and the Lawes, either by writing, or by the light of Nature, sufficiently published; there wanteth yet another very materiall circumstance to make them obligatory. For it is not the Letter, but the Intendment, or Meaning; that is to say, the authentique Interpretation of the Law (which is the sense of the Legislator,) in which the nature of the Law consisteth; And therefore [143] the Interpretation of all Lawes dependeth on the Authority Soveraign; and the Interpreters can be none but those, which the Soveraign, (to whom only the Subject oweth obedience) shall appoint. For else, by the craft of an Interpreter, the Law may be made to beare a sense, contrary to that of the Soveraign; by which means the Interpreter becomes the Legislator.

All Laws, written, and unwritten, have need of Interpretation. The unwritten Law of Nature, though it be easy to such, as without partiality, and passion, make use of their naturall reason, and therefore leaves the violaters thereof without excuse; yet considering there be very few, perhaps none, that in some cases are not blinded by self love, or some other passion, it is now become of all Laws the most obscure; and has consequently the greatest need of able Interpreters. The written Laws, if they be short, are easily mis-interpreted, from the divers significations of a word, or two: if long, they be more obscure by the diverse significations of many words: in so much as no written Law, delivered in few, or many words, can be well understood, without a perfect understanding of the finall causes, for which the Law was made; the knowledge of which finall causes is in the Legislator. To him therefore there can not be any knot in the Law, insoluble; either by finding out the ends, to undoe it by; or else by making what ends he will, (as *Alexander* did with his sword in the Gordian Knot,) by the Legislative power; which no other Interpreter can doe.

The Interpretation of the Lawes of Nature, in a Common-wealth, dependeth not on the books of Morall Philosophy. The Authority of writers, without the Authority of the Common-wealth, maketh not their opinions Law, be they never so true. That which I have written in this Treatise, concerning the Morall Vertues, and of their necessity, for the procuring, and maintaining peace, though it bee evident Truth, is not therefore presently Law; but because in all Common-wealths in the world, it is part of the Civill Law: For though it be naturally reasonable;

yet it is by the Soveraigne Power that it is Law: Otherwise, it were a great errour, to call the Lawes of Nature unwritten Law; whereof wee see so many volumes published, and in them so many contradictions of one another, and of themselves.

The Interpretation of the Law of Nature, is the Sentence of the Judge constituted by the Soveraign Authority, to heare and determine such controversies, as depend thereon; and consisteth in the application of the Law to the present case. For in the act of Judicature, the Judge doth no more but consider, whither the demand of the party, be consonant to naturall reason, and Equity; and the Sentence he giveth, is therefore the Interpretation of the Law of Nature; which Interpretation is Authentique; not because it is his private Sentence; but because he giveth it by Authority of the Soveraign, whereby it becomes the Soveraigns Sentence; which is Law for that time, to the parties pleading.

[144] But because there is no Judge Subordinate, nor Soveraign, but may erre in a Judgement of Equity; if afterward in another like case he find it more consonant to Equity to give a contrary Sentence, he is obliged to doe it. No mans error becomes his own Law; nor obliges him to persist in it. Neither (for the same reason) becomes it a Law to other Judges, though sworn to follow it. For though a wrong Sentence given by authority of the Soveraign, if he know and allow it, in such Lawes as are mutable, be a constitution of a new Law, in cases, in which every little circumstance is the same; yet in Lawes immutable, such as are the Lawes of Nature, they are no Lawes to the same, or other Judges, in the like cases for ever after. Princes succeed one another; and one Judge passeth, another commeth; nay, Heaven and Earth shall passe; but not one title of the Law of Nature shall passe; for it is the Eternall Law of God. Therefore all the Sentences of precedent Judges that have ever been, cannot all altogether make a Law contrary to naturall Equity: Nor any Examples of former Judges, can warrant an unreasonable Sentence, or discharge the present Judge of the trouble of studying what is Equity (in the case he is to Judge,) from the principles of his own naturall reason. For example sake, 'Tis against the Law of Nature, *To punish the Innocent*; and Innocent is he that acquitteth himselfe Judicially, and is acknowledged for Innocent by the Judge. Put the case now, that a man is accused of a capitall crime, and seeing the power and malice of some enemy, and the frequent corruption and partiality of Judges, runneth away for feare of the event, and afterwards is taken, and brought to a legall triall, and maketh it sufficiently appear, he was not guilty of the

crime, and being thereof acquitted, is neverthelesse condemned to lose his goods; this is a manifest condemnation of the Innocent. I say therefore, that there is no place in the world, where this can be an interpretation of a Law of Nature, or be made a Law by the Sentences of precedent Judges, that had done the same. For he that judged it first, judged unjustly; and no Injustice can be a pattern of Judgement to succeeding Judges. A written Law may forbid innocent men to fly, and they may be punished for flying: But that flying for feare of injury, should be taken for presumption of guilt, after a man is already absolved of the crime Judicially, is contrary to the nature of a Presumption, which hath no place after Judgement given. Yet this is set down by a great Lawyer for the common Law of *England*. *If a man* (saith he) *that is Innocent, be accused of Felony, and for feare flyeth for the same; albeit he judicially acquitteth himselfe of the Felony; yet if it be found that he fled for the Felony, he shall notwithstanding his Innocency, Forfeit all his goods, chattells, debts, and duties. For as to the Forfeiture of them, the Law will admit no proofe against the Presumption in Law, grounded upon his flight.* Here you see, *An Innocent man, Judicially acquitted, notwithstanding his Innocency,* (when no written Law forbad him to fly) after his acquittall, *upon a Presumption in Law,* condemned to lose all the goods he hath. If the Law ground upon his flight a Presumption of the fact, (what was Capitall,) the Sen[145]tence ought to have been Capitall: if the Presumption were not of the Fact, for what then ought he to lose his goods? This therefore is no Law of *England*; nor is the condemnation grounded upon a Presumption of Law, but upon the Presumption of the Judges. It is also against Law, to say that no Proofe shall be admitted against a Presumption of Law. For all Judges, Soveraign and subordinate, if they refuse to heare Proofe, refuse to do Justice: for though the Sentence be Just, yet the Judges that condemn without hearing the Proofes offered, are Unjust Judges; and their Presumption is but Prejudice; which no man ought to bring with him to the Seat of Justice, whatsoever precedent judgements, or examples he shall pretend to follow. There be other things of this nature, wherein mens Judgements have been perverted, by trusting to Precedents: but this is enough to shew, that though the Sentence of the Judge, be a Law to the party pleading, yet it is no Law to any Judge, that shall succeed him in that Office.

In like manner, when question is of the Meaning of written Lawes, he is not the Interpreter of them, that writeth a Commentary upon them. For Commentaries are commonly more subject to cavill, than the

Text; and therefore need other Commentaries; and so there will be no end of such Interpretation. And therefore unlesse there be an Interpreter authorised by the Soveraign, from which the subordinate Judges are not to recede, the Interpreter can be no other than the ordinary Judges, in the same manner, as they are in cases of the unwritten Law; and their Sentences are to be taken by them that plead, for Lawes in that particular case; but not to bind other Judges, in like cases to give like judgements. For a Judge may erre in the Interpretation even of written Lawes; but no errour of a subordinate Judge, can change the Law, which is the generall Sentence of the Soveraigne.

In written Lawes, men use to make a difference between the Letter, and the Sentence of the Law: And when by the Letter, is meant whatsoever can be gathered from the bare words, 'tis well distinguished. For the significations of almost all words, are either in themselves, or in the metaphoricall use of them, ambiguous; and may be drawn in argument, to make many senses; but there is onely one sense of the Law. But if by the Letter, be meant the literall sense, then the Letter, and the Sentence or intention of the Law, is all one. For the literall sense is that, which the Legislator intended, should by the letter of the Law be signified. Now the Intention of the Legislator is always supposed to be Equity: For it were a great contumely for a Judge to think otherwise of the Soveraigne. He ought therefore, if the Word of the Law doe not fully authorise a reasonable Sentence, to supply it with the Law of Nature; or if the case be difficult, to respit Judgement till he have received more ample authority. For Example, a written Law ordaineth, that he which is thrust out of his house by force, shall be restored by force: It happens that a man by negligence leaves his house empty, and returning is kept out by force, in which case there is no speciall Law ordained. It is evi[146]dent, that this case is contained in the same Law: for else there is no remedy for him at all; which is to be supposed against the Intention of the Legislator. Again, the word of the Law, commandeth to Judge according to the Evidence: A man is accused falsly of a fact, which the Judge saw himself done by another; and not by him that is accused. In this case neither shall the Letter of the Law be followed to the condemnation of the Innocent, nor shall the Judge give Sentence against the evidence of the Witnesses; because the Letter of the Law is to the contrary: but procure of the Soveraign that another be made Judge, and himselfe Witnesse. So that the incommodity that follows the bare words of a written Law, may lead him to the Intention of the Law, whereby to interpret the same the better; though no Incommodity can warrant a Sentence against the Law. For every Judge of Right, and Wrong, is not Judge of what is Commodious, or Incommodious to the Common-wealth.

The abilities required in a good Interpreter of the Law, that is to say, in a good Judge, are not the same with those of an Advocate; namely the study of the Lawes. For a Judge, as he ought to take notice of the Fact, from none but the Witnesses; so also he ought to take notice of the Law, from nothing but the Statutes, and Constitutions of the Soveraign, alledged in the pleading, or declared to him by some that have authority from the Soveraign Power to declare them; and need not take care before-hand, what hee shall Judge; for it shall bee given him what hee shall say concerning the Fact, by Witnesses; and what hee shall say in point of Law, from those that shall in their pleadings shew it, and by authority interpret it upon the place. The Lords of Parlament in *England* were Judges, and most difficult causes have been heard and determined by them; yet few of them were much versed in the study of the Lawes, and fewer had made profession of them: and though they consulted with Lawyers, that were appointed to be present there for that purpose; yet they alone had the authority of giving Sentence. In like manner, in the ordinary trialls of Right, Twelve men of the common People, are the Judges, and give Sentence, not onely of the Fact, but of the Right; and pronounce simply for the Complaynant, or for the Defendant; that is to say, are Judges not onely of the Fact, but also of the Right: and in a question of crime, not onely determine whether done, or not done; but also whether it be *Murder, Homicide, Felony, Assault*, and the like, which are determinations of Law: but because they are not supposed to know the Law of themselves, there is one that hath Authority to enforme them of it, in the particular case they are to Judge of. But yet if they judge not according to that he tells them, they are not subject thereby to any penalty; unlesse it be made appear, they did it against their consciences, or had been corrupted by reward.

The things that make a good Judge, or good Interpreter of the Lawes, are, first, *A right understanding* of that principall Law of Nature called *Equity*; which depending not on the reading of other mens Writings, but on the goodnesse of a mans own naturall [147] Reason, and Meditation, is presumed to be in those most, that have had most leisure, and had the most inclination to meditate thereon. Secondly, *Contempt of unnecessary Riches*, and Preferments. Thirdly, *To be able in judgement to devest himselfe of all feare, anger, hatred, love,* and *compassion.* Fourthly, and lastly, *Patience to heare; diligent attention in hearing, and memory to retain, digest and apply what he hath heard ...*

READING QUESTIONS ON HOBBES

1 How realistic is Hobbes's view of the "Natural Condition of Mankind"? (Don't ask yourself if Hobbes accurately describes your motives; ask instead if he describes other people you know.)
2 Can the Hobbesian sovereign appeal to moral considerations?
3 What is the role of judges in Hobbes's theory? Could someone actually carry out the task of judging as Hobbes describes it?
4 Hobbes appeals to ideas of equity in deciding cases. How is this related to his more general positivism? Is there a tension in his view? Can you think of any way it might be resolved?

H.L.A. Hart
"Positivism and the Separation of Law and Morals" (1958)

Jurisprudence had lain moribund for close to half a century before Hart's classic essay. Hart's aim is to offer a rigorous statement of legal positivism, the view that law and morality are distinct modes of social ordering. Hart's essay is important both for its historical place and because of its emphasis on the importance, both moral and conceptual, of keeping law and morality apart. In *The Concept of Law,* Hart elaborates his idea of a fundamental rule which has to be accepted by legal officials.

Positivism and the Separation of Law and Morals

... I shall present the subject as part of the history of an idea ...

Bentham's general recipe for life under the government of laws was simple: it was *"to obey punctually; to censure freely."* But Bentham was especially aware, as an anxious spectator of the French revolution, that this was not enough: the time might come in any society when the law's commands were so evil that the question of resistance had to be faced, and it was then essential that the issues at stake at this point should neither be oversimplified nor obscured. Yet this was precisely what the confusion between law and morals had done, and Bentham found that the confusion had spread symmetrically in two different directions. On the one hand Bentham had in mind the anarchist who argues thus: "This ought not to be the law, therefore it is not and I am free not merely to censure but to disregard it." On the other hand he thought of the reactionary who argues: "This is the law, therefore it is what it ought to be," and thus stifles criticism at its birth. Both errors, Bentham thought, were to be found in Blackstone: there was his incautious statement that human laws were invalid if contrary to the law of God, and "that spirit of obsequious *quietism* that seems constitutional in our Author" which "will scarce ever let him recognise a difference" between what is and what ought to be. This indeed was for Bentham the occupational disease of lawyers: "[I]n the eyes of lawyers – not to speak their dupes – that is to say, as yet, the generality of non-lawyers – the *is* and the *ought to be* ... were one and indivisible." There are therefore two dangers between which insistence on this distinction will help us to steer: the danger that law and its authority may be dissolved in man's conceptions of what law ought to be and the danger that the existing law may supplant morality as a final test of conduct and so escape criticism.

In view of later criticisms it is also important to distinguish several things that the Utilitarians did not mean by insisting on their separation of law and morals. They certainly accepted many of the things that might be called "the intersection of law and morals." First, they never denied that, as a matter of historical fact, the development of legal systems had been powerfully influenced by moral opinion, and, conversely, that moral standards had been profoundly influenced by law, so that the content of many legal rules mirrored moral rules or principles. It is not in fact always easy to trace this historical causal connection, but Bentham was certainly ready to admit its existence; so too Austin spoke of the "frequent coincidence" of positive law and morality and attributed the confusion of what law is with what law ought to be to this very fact.

Second, neither Bentham nor his followers denied that by explicit legal provisions moral principles might at different points be brought into a legal system and form part of its rules, or that courts might be legally bound to decide in accordance with what they thought just or best. Bentham indeed recognized, as Austin did not, that even the supreme legislative power might be subjected to legal restraints by a constitution and would not have denied that moral principles, like those of the Fifth Amendment, might form the content of such legal constitutional restraints. Austin differed in thinking that restraints on the supreme legislative power could not have the force of law, but would remain merely political or moral checks; but of course he would have recognized that a statute, for example, might confer a delegated legislative power and restrict the area of its exercise by reference to moral principles.

What both Bentham and Austin were anxious to assert were the following two simple things: first, in the absence of an expressed constitutional or legal provision, it could not follow from the mere fact that a rule violated standards of morality that it was not a rule of law; and, conversely, it could not follow from the mere fact that a rule was morally desirable that it was a rule of law ...

So much for the doctrine in the heyday of its success. Let us turn now to some of the criticisms. Undoubtedly, when Bentham and Austin insisted on the distinction between law as it is and as it ought to be, they had in mind *particular* laws, the meanings of which were clear and so not in dispute, and they were concerned to argue that such laws, even if morally outrageous, were still laws. It is, however, necessary, in considering the criticisms which later developed, to consider more than those criticisms which were directed to this particular point if we are to get at the root of the dissatisfaction felt; we must also take account of the objection that, even if what the Utilitarians said on this particular point were true, their insistence on it, in a terminology suggesting a general cleavage between what is and ought to be law, obscured the fact that at other points there is an essential point of contact between the two. So in what follows I consider not only criticisms of the particular point which the Utilitarians had in mind, but also the claim that an essential connection between law and morals emerges if we examine how laws, the meanings of which are in dispute, are interpreted and applied in concrete cases; and that this connection emerges again if we widen our point of view and ask, not whether every particular rule of law must satisfy a moral minimum in order to be a law, but whether a system of rules which altogether failed to do this could be a legal system.

There is, however, one major initial complexity by which criticism has been much confused. We must remember that the Utilitarians combined with their insistence on the separation of law and morals two other equally famous but distinct doctrines. One was the important truth that a purely analytical study of legal concepts, a study of the meaning of the distinctive vocabulary of the law, was as vital to our understanding of the nature of law as historical or sociological studies, though of course it could not supplant them. The other doctrine was the famous imperative theory of law – that law is essentially a command.

These three doctrines constitute the utilitarian tradition in jurisprudence; yet they are distinct doctrines. It is possible to endorse the separation between law and morals and to value analytical inquiries into the meaning of legal concepts and yet think it wrong to conceive of law as essentially a command. One source of great confusion in the criticism of the separation of law and morals was the belief that the falsity of any one of these three doctrines in the utilitarian tradition showed the other two to be false; what was worse was the failure to see that there were three quite separate doctrines in this tradition. The indiscriminate use of the label "positivism" to designate ambiguously each one of these three separate doctrines (together with some others which the Utilitarians never professed) has perhaps confused the issue more than any other single factor ...[1]

The famous theory that law is a command was a part of a wider and more ambitious claim. Austin said that the notion of a command was "the *key* to the sciences of jurisprudence and morals," and contemporary attempts to elucidate moral judgments in terms of "imperative" or "prescriptive" utterances echo this ambitious claim. But the command theory, viewed as an effort to identify even the quintessence of law, let alone the quintessence of morals, seems breathtaking in its simplicity and quite inadequate. There is much, even in the simplest legal system, that is distorted if presented as a command. Yet the Utilitarians thought that the essence of a legal system could be conveyed if the notion of a command were supplemented by that of a habit of obedience. The simple scheme was this: What is a command? It is simply an expression by one person of the desire that another person should do or abstain from some action, accompanied by a threat of punishment which is likely to follow disobedience. Commands are laws if two conditions are satisfied: first, they must be general; second they must be commanded by what (as both Bentham and Austin claimed) exists in every political society whatever its constitutional form, namely, a person or a group of persons who are in receipt of habitual obedience from most of the society but pay no such obedience to others. These persons are its sovereign. Thus law is the command of the uncommanded commanders of society – the creation of the legally untrammelled will of the sovereign who is by definition outside the law.

It is easy to see that this account of a legal system is threadbare. One can also see why it might seem that its inadequacy is due to the omission of some essential connection with morality. The situation which the simple trilogy of command, sanction, and sovereign avails to describe, if you take these notions at all precisely, is like that of a gunman saying to his victim, "Give me your money or your life." The only difference is that in the case of a legal system the gunman says it to a large number of people who are accustomed to the racket and habitually surrender to it. Law surely is not the gunman situation writ large, and legal order is surely not to be thus simply identified with compulsion.

This scheme, despite the points of obvious analogy between a statute and a command, omits some of the most characteristic elements of law. Let me cite a few. It is wrong to think of a legislature (and *a fortiori* an electorate) with a changing membership as a group of persons habitually obeyed: this simple idea is suited only to a monarch sufficiently long-lived for a "habit" to grow up. Even if we waive this point, nothing which legislators do makes law unless they comply with fundamental accepted rules specifying the essential law-making procedures. This is true even in a system having a simple unitary constitution like the British. These fundamental accepted rules specifying what the legislature must do to legislate are not commands habitually obeyed, nor can they be expressed as habits of obedience to persons. They lie at the root of a legal system, and what is most missing in the utilitarian scheme is an analysis of what it is for a social group and its officials to accept such rules. This notion, not that of a command as Austin claimed, is the "key to the science of jurisprudence," or at least one of the keys.

Again, Austin, in the case of a democracy, looked past the legislators to the electorate as "the sovereign" (or in England as part of it). He thought that in the United States the mass of the electors to the state and federal legislatures were the sovereign whose commands, given by their "agents" in the legislatures, were law. But on this footing the whole notion of the sovereign outside the law being "habitually obeyed" by the "bulk" of the population must go: for in this case the "bulk" obeys the bulk, that is, it obeys itself. Plainly the general acceptance of the authority of a law-making procedure, irrespective of the changing individuals who operate it from time to time, can be only distorted by an analysis in terms of mass habitual obedience to certain persons who are by definition outside the law, just as the cognate but much simpler phenomenon of the general social acceptance of a rule, say of taking off the hat when entering a church, would be distorted if represented as habitual obedience by the mass to specific persons.

Other critics dimly sensed a further and more important defect in the command theory, yet blurred the edge of an important criticism by assuming that the defect was due to the failure to insist upon some important connection between law and morals. This more radical defect is as follows. The picture that the command theory draws of life under law is essentially a simple relationship of the commander to the commanded, of superior to inferior, of top to bottom; the relationship is vertical between the commanders or authors of the law conceived of as essentially outside the law and those who are commanded and subject to the law. In this picture no place, or only an accidental or subordinate place, is afforded for a distinction between types of legal rules which are in fact radically different. Some laws require men to act in certain ways or to abstain from acting whether they wish to or not. The criminal law consists largely of rules of this sort: like commands they are simply "obeyed" or "disobeyed." But other legal rules are presented to society in quite different ways and have quite different functions. They provide facilities more or less elaborate for individuals to create structures of rights and duties for the conduct of life within the coercive framework of the law. Such are the rules enabling individuals to make contracts, wills, and trusts, and generally to mould their legal relations with others. Such rules, unlike the criminal law, are not factors designed to obstruct wishes and choices of an antisocial sort. On the contrary, these rules provide facilities for the realization of wishes and choices. They do not say (like commands) "do this whether you wish it or not," but rather "if you wish to do this, here is the way to do it." Under these rules we exercise powers, make claims, and assert rights. These phrases mark off characteristic features of laws that confer rights and powers; they are laws which are, so to speak, put at the disposition of individuals in a way in which the criminal law is not. Much ingenuity has gone into the task of "reducing" laws of this second sort to some complex variant of laws of the first sort. The effort to show that laws conferring rights are "really" only conditional stipulations of sanctions to be exacted from the person ultimately under a legal duty characterizes much of Kelsen's work. Yet to urge this is really just to exhibit dogmatic determination to suppress one aspect of the legal system in order to maintain the theory that the stipulation of a sanction, like Austin's command, represents the quintessence of law. One might as well urge that the rules of baseball were "really" only complex conditional directions to the scorer and that this showed their real or "essential" nature.

One of the first jurists in England to break with the Austinian tradition, Salmond, complained that the analysis in terms of commands left the notion of a right unprovided with a place. But he confused the point. He argued first, and correctly, that if laws are merely commands it is inexplicable that we should have come to speak of legal rights and powers as conferred or arising under them, but then wrongly concluded that the rules of a legal system must necessarily be connected with moral rules or principles of justice and that only on this footing could the phenomenon of legal rights be explained. Otherwise, Salmond thought, we would have to say that a mere "verbal coincidence" connects the concepts of legal and moral right. Similarly, continental critics of the Utilitarians, always alive to the complexity of the notion of a subjective right, insisted that the command theory gave it no place. Hägerström insisted that if laws were merely commands the notion of an individual's right was really inexplicable, for commands are, as he said, something which we either obey or we do not obey; they do not confer rights. But he, too, concluded that moral, or, as he put it, common-sense, notions of justice must therefore be necessarily involved in the analysis of any legal structure elaborate enough to confer rights.

Yet, surely these arguments are confused. Rules that confer rights, though distinct from commands, need not be moral rules or coincide with them. Rights, after all, exist under the rules of ceremonies, games, and in many other spheres regulated by rules which are irrelevant to the question of justice or what the law ought to be. Nor need rules which confer rights be just or morally good rules. The rights of a master over his slaves show us that. "Their merit or demerit," as Austin termed it, depends on how rights are distributed in society and over whom or what they are exercised. These critics indeed revealed the inadequacy of the simple notions of command and habit for the analysis of law; at many points it is apparent that the social acceptance of a rule or standard of authority (even if it is motivated only by fear or superstition or rests on inertia) must be brought into the analysis and cannot itself be reduced to the two simple terms. Yet nothing in this showed the utilitarian insistence on the distinction between the existence of law and its "merits" to be wrong.

III

I now turn to a distinctively American criticism of the separation of the law that is from the law that ought to be. It emerged from the critical study of the judicial process with which American jurisprudence has been on the whole so beneficially occupied. The most sceptical of these critics – the loosely named "Realists" of the 1930s – perhaps too naively accepted the conceptual framework of the natural sciences as adequate for the characterization of law and for the analysis of rule-guided action of which a living system of law at least partly consists. But they opened men's eyes to what actually goes on when courts decide cases, and the contrast they drew between the actual facts of judicial decision and the traditional terminology for describing it as if it were a wholly logical operation was usually illuminating; for in spite of some exaggeration the Realists made us acutely conscious of one cardinal feature of human language and human thought, emphasis on which is vital not only for the understanding of law but in areas of philosophy far beyond the confines of jurisprudence. The insight of this school may be presented in the following example. A legal rule forbids you to take a vehicle into the public park. Plainly this forbids an automobile, but what about bicycles, roller skates, toy automobiles? What about aeroplanes? Are these, as we say, to be called "vehicles" for the purpose of the rule or not? If we are to communicate with each other at all, and if, as in the most elementary form of law, we are to express our intentions that a certain type of behaviour be regulated by rules, then the general words we use – like "vehicle" in the case I consider – must have some standard instance in which no doubts are felt about its application. There must be a core of settled meaning, but there will be, as well, a penumbra of debatable cases in which words are neither obviously applicable nor obviously ruled out. These cases will each have some features in common with the standard case; they will lack others or be accompanied by features not present in the standard case. Human invention and natural processes continually throw up such variants on the familiar, and if we are to say that these ranges of facts do or do not fall under existing rules, then the classifier must make a decision which is not dictated to him, for the facts and phenomena to which we fit our words and apply our rules are as it were *dumb*. The toy automobile cannot speak up and say, "I am a vehicle for the purpose of this legal rule," nor can the roller skates chorus, "We are not a vehicle." Fact situations do not await us neatly labelled, creased, and folded; nor is their legal classification written on them to be simply read off by the judge. Instead, in applying legal rules, someone must take the responsibility of deciding that words do or do not cover some case in hand, with all the practical consequences involved in this decision.

We may call the problems which arise outside the hard core of standard instances or settled meaning "problems of the penumbra"; they are always with us whether in relation to such trivial things as the regulation of the use of the public park or in relation to the multidimensional generalities of a constitution. If a penumbra of uncertainty must surround all legal rules, then their application to specific cases in the penumbral area cannot be a matter of logical deduction, and so deductive reasoning, which for generations has been cherished as the very perfection of human reasoning, cannot serve as a model for what judges, or indeed anyone, should do in bringing particular cases under general rules. In this area men cannot live by deduction alone. And it follows that if legal arguments and legal decisions of penumbral questions are to be rational, their rationality must lie in something other than a logical relation to premises. So if it is rational or "sound" to argue and to decide that for the purposes of this rule an aeroplane is not a vehicle, this argument must be sound or rational without being logically conclusive. What is it then that makes such decisions correct or at least better than alternative decisions? Again, it seems true to say that the criterion which makes a decision sound in such cases is some concept of what the law ought to be; it is easy to slide from that into saying that it must be a moral judgment about what law ought to be. So here we touch upon a point of necessary "intersection between law and morals" which demonstrates the falsity or, at any rate, the misleading character of the Utilitarians' emphatic insistence on the separation of law as it is and ought to be. Surely, Bentham and Austin could only have written as they did because they misunderstood or neglected this aspect of the judicial process, because they ignored the problems of the penumbra.

The misconception of the judicial process which ignores the problems of the penumbra and which views the process as consisting preeminently in deductive reasoning is often stigmatized as the error of "formalism" or "literalism." My question now is, how and to what extent does the demonstration of this error show the utilitarian distinction to be wrong or misleading? Here there are many issues which have been confused, but I can only disentangle some. The charge of formalism has been levelled both at the "positivist" legal theorist and at the courts, but of course it must be a very different charge in each case. Levelled at the legal theorist, the charge means that he has made a theoretical mistake about the character of legal decision; he has thought of the reasoning involved as consisting in deduction from premises in which the judges' practical choices or decisions play no part. It would be easy to show that Austin was guiltless of this error; only an entire misconception of what analytical jurisprudence is and why he thought it important has led to the view that he, or any other analyst, believed that the law was a closed logical system in which judges deduced their decisions from premises. On the contrary, he was very much alive to the character of language, to its vagueness or open character; he thought that in the penumbral situation judges must necessarily legislate, and, in accents that sometimes recall those of the late Judge Jerome Frank, he berated the common-law judges for legislating feebly and timidly and for blindly relying on real or fancied analogies with past cases instead of adapting their decisions to the growing needs of society as revealed by the moral standard of utility. The villains of this piece, responsible for the conception of the judge as an automaton, are not the utilitarian thinkers. The responsibility, if it is to be laid at the door of any theorist, is with thinkers like Blackstone and, at an earlier stage, Montesquieu. The root of this evil is preoccupation with the separation of powers and Blackstone's "childish fiction" (as Austin termed it) that judges only "find," never "make," law.

But we are concerned with "formalism" as a vice not of jurists but of judges. What precisely is it for a judge to commit this error, to be a "formalist," "automatic," a "slot machine"? Curiously enough the literature, which is full of the denunciation of these vices, never makes this clear in concrete terms; instead we have only descriptions which cannot mean what they appear to say; it is said that in the formalist error courts make an excessive use of logic, take a thing to "a dryly logical extreme," or make an excessive use of analytical methods. But just how in being a formalist does a judge make an excessive use of logic? It is clear that the essence of his error is to give some general term an interpretation which is blind to social values and consequences (or which is in some other way stupid or perhaps merely disliked by critics). But logic does not prescribe interpretation of terms; it dictates neither the stupid nor intelligent interpretation of any expression. Logic only tells you hypothetically that *if* you give a certain term a certain interpretation then a certain conclusion follows. Logic is silent on how to classify particulars – and this is the heart of a judicial decision. So this reference to logic and to logical extremes is a misnomer for something else, which must be this. A judge has to apply a rule to a concrete case – perhaps the rule that one may not take a stolen "vehicle" across State lines, and in this case an aeroplane has been taken. He either does not see or pretends not to see that the general terms of this rule are susceptible of different interpretations and that he has a choice left open uncontrolled by linguistic conventions. He ignores, or is blind to, the fact that he is in the area of the penumbra and is not dealing with a standard case. Instead of choosing in the light of social aims the judge fixes the meaning in a different way. He either takes the meaning that the word most obviously suggests in its ordinary non-legal context to ordinary men, or one which the word has been given in some other legal context, or, still worse, he thinks of a standard case and then arbitrarily identifies certain features in it – for example, in the case of a vehicle, (1) normally used on land, (2) capable of carrying a human person, (3) capable of being self-propelled – and treats these three as always necessary and always sufficient conditions for the use in all contexts of the word "vehicle," irrespective of the social consequences of giving it this interpretation. This choice, not "logic," would force the judge to include a toy motor car (if electrically propelled) and to exclude bicycles and the aeroplane. In all this there is possibly great stupidity, but no more "logic," and no less, than in cases in which the interpretation given to a general term and the consequent application of some general rule to a particular case is consciously controlled by some identified social aim.

Decisions made in a fashion as blind as this would scarcely deserve the name of decisions; we might as well toss a penny in applying a rule of law. But it is at least doubtful whether any judicial decisions (even in England) have been quite as automatic as this. Rather, either the interpretations stigmatized as automatic have resulted from the conviction that it is fairer in a criminal statute to take a meaning which would jump to the mind of the ordinary man at the cost even of defeating other values, and this itself is a social policy (though possibly a bad one); or much more frequently, what is stigmatized as "mechanical" and "automatic" is a determined choice made indeed in the light of a social aim but of a conservative social aim. Certainly many of the Supreme Court decisions at the turn of the century which have been so stigmatized represent clear choices in the penumbral area to give effect to a policy of a conservative type. This is peculiarly true of Mr Justice Peckham's opinions defining the spheres of police power and due process.

But how does the wrongness of deciding cases in an automatic and mechanical way and the rightness of deciding cases by reference to social purposes show that the utilitarian insistence on the distinction between what the law is and what it ought to be is wrong? I take it that no one who wished to use these vices of formalism as proof that the distinction between what is and what ought to be is mistaken would deny that the decisions stigmatized as automatic are law; nor would he deny that the system in which such automatic decisions are made is a legal system. Surely he would say that they are law, but they are bad law; they ought not to be law. But this would be to use the distinction, not to refute it; and of course both Bentham and Austin used it to attack judges for failing to decide penumbral cases in accordance with the growing needs of society.

Clearly, if the demonstration of the errors of formalism is to show the utilitarian distinction to be wrong, the point must be drastically re-stated. The point must be not merely that a judicial decision to be rational must be made in the light of some conception of what ought to be, but that the aims, the social policies and purposes to which judges should appeal if their decisions are to be rational, are themselves to be considered as part of the law in some suitably wide sense of "law" which is held to be more illuminating than that used by the Utilitarians. This restatement of the point would have the following consequence: instead of saying that the recurrence of penumbral questions shows us that legal rules are essentially incomplete, and that, when they fail to determine decisions, judges must legislate and so exercise a creative choice between alternatives, we shall say that the social policies which guide the judges' choice are in a sense there for them to discover; the judges are only "drawing out" of the rule what, if it is properly under-stood, is "latent" within it. To call this judicial legislation is to obscure some essential continuity between the clear cases of the rule's applica-tion and the penumbral decisions. I shall question later whether this way of talking is salutary, but I wish at this time to point out something obvious, but likely, if not stated, to tangle the issues. It does not follow that, because the opposite of a decision reached blindly in the formalist or literalist manner is a decision intelligently reached by reference to some conception of what ought to be, we have a junction of law and morals. We must, I think, beware of thinking in a too simple-minded fashion about the word "ought." This is not because there is no distinc-tion to be made between law as it is and ought to be. Far from it. It is because the distinction should be between what is and what from many different points of view ought to be. The word "ought" merely reflects the presence of some standard of criticism; one of these standards is a moral standard, but not all standards are moral. We say to our neigh-bour, "You ought not to lie," and that may certainly be a moral judgment, but we should remember that the baffled poisoner may say, "I ought to have given her a second dose." The point here is that intelligent decisions which we oppose to mechanical or formal decisions are not necessarily identical with decisions defensible on moral grounds. We may say of many a decision: "Yes, that is right; that is as it ought to be," and we may mean only that some accepted purpose or policy has been thereby advanced; we may not mean to endorse the moral propriety of the policy or the decision. So the contrast between the mechanical decision and the intelligent one can be reproduced inside a system dedicated to the pursuit of the most evil aims. It does not exist as a contrast to be found only in legal systems which, like our own, widely recognize principles of justice and moral claims of individuals.

An example may make this point plainer. With us the task of sentencing in criminal cases is the one that seems most obviously to demand from the judge the exercise of moral judgment. Here the factors to be weighed seem clearly to be moral factors: society must not be exposed to wanton attack; too much misery must not be inflicted on either the victim or his dependants; efforts must be made to enable him to lead a better life and regain a position in the society whose laws he has violated. To a judge striking the balance among these claims, with all the discretion and perplexities involved, his task seems as plain an example of the exercise of moral judgment as could be; and it seems to be the polar opposite of some mechanical application of a tariff of penalties fixing a sentence careless of the moral claims which in our system have to be weighed. So here intelligent and rational decision is guided however uncertainly by moral aims. But we have only to vary the example to see that this need not necessarily be so and surely, if it need not necessarily be so, the utilitarian point remains unshaken. Under the Nazi regime men were sentenced by courts for criticism of the regime. Here the choice of sentence might be guided exclusively by consideration of what was needed to maintain the state's tyranny effectively. What sentence would both terrorize the public at large and keep the friends and family of the prisoner in suspense so that both hope and fear would cooperate as factors making for subservience? The prisoner of such a system would be regarded simply as an object to be used in pursuit of these aims. Yet, in contrast with a mechanical decision, decision on these grounds would be intelligent and purposive, and from one point of view the decision would be as it ought to be. Of course, I am not unaware that a whole philosophical tradition has sought to demonstrate the fact that we cannot correctly call decisions or behaviour truly rational unless they are in conformity with moral aims and principles. But the example I have used seems to me to serve at least as a warning that we cannot use the errors of formalism as something which *per se* demonstrates the falsity of the utilitarian insistence on the distinction between law as it is and law as *morally* it ought to be.

We can now return to the main point. If it is true that the intelligent decision of penumbral questions is one made not mechanically but in the light of aims, purposes, and policies, though not necessarily in the light of anything we would call moral principles, is it wise to express this important fact by saying that the firm utilitarian distinction between what the law is and what it ought to be should be dropped? Perhaps the claim that it is wise cannot be theoretically refuted, for it is, in effect, an *invitation* to revise *our conception* of what a legal rule is. We are invited to include in the "rule" the various aims and policies in the light of which its penumbral cases are decided on the ground that these aims have, because of their importance, as much right to be called law as the core of legal rules whose meaning is settled. But though an invitation cannot be refuted, it may be refused, and I would proffer two reasons for refusing this invitation. First, everything we have learned about the judicial process can be expressed in other less mysterious ways. We can say laws are incurably incomplete and we must decide the penumbral cases rationally by reference to social aims. I think Holmes, who had such a vivid appreciation of the fact that "general propositions do not decide concrete cases," would have put it that way. Secondly, to insist on the utilitarian distinction is to emphasize that the hard core of settled meaning is law in some centrally important sense and that even if there are borderlines, there must first be lines. If this were not so the notion of rules controlling courts' decisions would be senseless, as some of the "Realists" – in their most extreme moods, and, I think, on bad grounds – claimed.

By contrast, to soften the distinction, to assert mysteriously that there is some fused identity between law as it is and as it ought to be, is to suggest that all legal questions are fundamentally like those of the penumbra. It is to assert that there is no central element of actual law to be seen in the core of central meaning which rules have, that there is nothing in the nature of a legal rule inconsistent with *all* questions being open to reconsideration in the light of social policy. Of course, it is good to be occupied with the penumbra. Its problems are rightly the daily diet of the law schools. But to be occupied with the penumbra is one thing, to be preoccupied with it another. And preoccupation with the penumbra is, if I may say so, as rich a source of confusion in the American legal tradition as formalism in the English. Of course we might abandon the notion that rules have authority; we might cease to attach force or even meaning to an argument that a case falls clearly within a rule and the scope of a precedent. We might call all such reasoning "automatic" or "mechanical," which is already the routine invective of the courts. But until we decide that this *is* what we want, we should not encourage it by obliterating the utilitarian distinction ...

IV

The third criticism of the separation of law and morals is of a very different character; it certainly is less an intellectual argument against the utilitarian distinction than a passionate appeal supported not by detailed reasoning but by reminders of a terrible experience. For it consists of the testimony of those who have descended into Hell, and, like Ulysses or Dante, brought back a message for human beings. Only in this case the Hell was not beneath or beyond earth, but on it; it was a Hell created on earth by men for other men.

This appeal comes from those German thinkers who lived through the Nazi regime and reflected upon its evil manifestations in the legal system. One of these thinkers, Gustav Radbruch, had himself shared the "positivist" doctrine until the Nazi tyranny, but he was converted by this experience and so his appeal to other men to discard the doctrine of the separation of law and morals has the special poignancy of a recantation. What is important about this criticism is that it really does confront the particular point which Bentham and Austin had in mind in urging the separation of law as it is and as it ought to be. These German thinkers put their insistence on the need to join together what the Utilitarians separated just where this separation was of most importance in the eyes of the Utilitarians; for they were concerned with the problem posed by the existence of morally evil laws.

Before his conversion Radbruch held that resistance to law was a matter for the personal conscience, to be thought out by the individual as a moral problem, and the validity of a law could not be disproved by showing that its requirements were morally evil or even by showing that the effect of compliance with the law would be more evil than the effect of disobedience. Austin, it may be recalled, was emphatic in condemning those who said that if human laws conflicted with the fundamental principles of morality then they cease to be laws, as talking "stark nonsense."

The most pernicious laws, and therefore those which are most opposed to the will of God, have been and are continually enforced as laws by judicial tribunals. Suppose an act innocuous, or positively beneficial, be prohibited by the sovereign under the penalty of death; if I commit this act, I shall be tried and condemned, and if I object to the sentence, that it is contrary to the law of God ... the court of justice will demonstrate the inconclusiveness of my reasoning by hanging me up, in pursuance of the law of which I have impugned the validity. An exception, demurrer, or plea, founded on the law of God was never heard in a Court of Justice, from the creation of the world down to the present moment.

These are strong, indeed brutal words, but we must remember that they went along – in the case of Austin and, of course, Bentham – with the conviction that if laws reached a certain degree of iniquity then there would be a plain moral obligation to resist them and to withhold obedience. We shall see, when we consider the alternatives, that this simple presentation of the human dilemma which may arise has much to be said for it.

Radbruch, however, had concluded from the ease with which the Nazi regime had exploited subservience to mere law – expressed, as he thought, in the "positivist" slogan "law as law" (*Gesetz als Gesetz*) – and from the failure of the German legal profession to protest against the enormities which they were required to perpetrate in the name of law, that "positivism" (meaning here the insistence on the separation of law as it is from law as it ought to be) had powerfully contributed to the horrors. His considered reflections led him to the doctrine that the fundamental principles of humanitarian morality were part of the very concept of *Recht* or Legality and that no positive enactment or statute, however clearly it was expressed and however clearly it conformed with the formal criteria of validity of a given legal system, could be valid if it contravened basic principles of morality. This doctrine can be appreciated fully only if the nuances imported by the German word *Recht* are grasped. But it is clear that the doctrine meant that every lawyer and judge should denounce statutes that transgressed the fundamental principles not as merely immoral or wrong but as having no legal character, and enactments which on this ground lack the quality of law should not be taken into account in working out the legal position of any given individual in particular circumstances. The striking recantation of his previous doctrine is unfortunately omitted from the translation of his works, but it should be read by all who wish to think afresh on the question of the interconnection of law and morals.

It is impossible to read without sympathy Radbruch's passionate demand that the German legal conscience should be open to the demands of morality and his complaint that this has been too little the case in the German tradition. On the other hand there is an extraordinary naïvety in the view that insensitiveness to the demands of morality and subservience to state power in a people like the Germans should have arisen from the belief that law might be law though it failed to conform with the minimum requirements of morality. Rather this terrible history prompts inquiry into why emphasis on the slogan "law is law," and the distinction between law and morals, acquired a sinister character in Germany, but elsewhere, as with the Utilitarians themselves, went along with the most enlightened liberal attitudes. But something more disturbing than naïvety is latent in Radbruch's whole presentation of the issues to which the existence of morally iniquitous laws give rise. It is not, I think, uncharitable to say that we can see in his argument that he has only half digested the spiritual message of liberalism which he is seeking to convey to the legal profession. For everything that he says is really dependent upon an enormous overvaluation of the importance of the bare fact that a rule may be said to be a valid rule of law, as if this, once declared, was conclusive of the final moral question: "Ought this rule of law to be obeyed?" Surely the truly liberal answer to any sinister use of the slogan "law is law" or of the distinction between law and morals is, "Very well, but that does not conclude the question. Law is not morality; do not let it supplant morality."

However, we are not left to a mere academic discussion in order to evaluate the plea which Radbruch made for the revision of the distinction between law and morals. After the war Radbruch's conception of law as containing in itself the essential moral principle of humanitarianism was applied in practice by German courts in certain cases in which local war criminals, spies, and informers under the Nazi regime were punished. The special importance of these cases is that the persons accused of these crimes claimed that what they had done was not illegal under the laws of the regime in force at the time these actions were performed. This plea was met with the reply that the laws upon which they relied were invalid as contravening the fundamental principles of morality. Let me cite briefly one of these cases.

In 1944 a woman, wishing to be rid of her husband, denounced him to the authorities for insulting remarks he had made about Hitler while home on leave from the German army. The wife was under no legal duty to report his acts, though what he had said was apparently in violation of statutes making it illegal to make statements detrimental to the government of the Third Reich or to impair by any means the military defence of the German people. The husband was arrested and sentenced to death, apparently pursuant to these statutes, though he was not executed but was sent to the front. In 1949 the wife was prosecuted in a West German court for an offence which we would describe as illegally depriving a person of his freedom (*rechtswidrige Freiheitsberaubung*). This was punishable as a crime under the German Criminal Code of 1871 which had remained in force continuously since its enactment. The wife pleaded that her husband's imprisonment was pursuant to the Nazi statutes and hence that she had committed no crime. The court of appeal to which the case ultimately came held that the wife was guilty of procuring the deprivation of her husband's liberty by denouncing him to the German courts, even though he had been sentenced by a court for having violated a statute, since, to quote the words of the court, the statute "was contrary to the sound con-science and sense of justice of all decent human beings." This reasoning was followed in many cases which have been hailed as a triumph of the doctrines of natural law and as signalling the overthrow of positivism. The unqualified satisfaction with this result seems to me to be hysteria. Many of us might applaud the objective – that of punishing a woman for an outrageously immoral act – but this was secured only by declaring a statute established since 1934 not to have the force of law, and at least the wisdom of this course must be doubted. There were, of course, two other choices. One was to let the woman go unpunished; one can sympathize with and endorse the view that this might have been a bad thing to do. The other was to face the fact that if the woman were to be punished it must be pursuant to the introduction of a frankly retrospective law and with a full consciousness of what was sacrificed in securing her punishment in this way. Odious as retrospective criminal legislation and punishment may be, to have pursued it openly in this case would at least have had the merits of candour. It would have made plain that in punishing the woman a choice had to be made between two evils, that of leaving her unpunished and that of sacrific-ing a very precious principle of morality endorsed by most legal systems. Surely if we have learned anything from the history of morals it is that the thing to do with a moral quandary is not to hide it. Like nettles, the occasions when life forces us to choose the lesser of two evils must be grasped with the consciousness that they are what they are. The vice of this use of the principle that, at certain limiting points, what is utterly immoral cannot be law or lawful is that it will serve to cloak the true nature of the problems with which we are faced and will encourage the romantic optimism that all the values we cherish ultimately will fit into a single system, that no one of them has to be sacrificed or compromised to accommodate another.

> All Discord Harmony not understood
> All Partial Evil Universal Good

This is surely untrue, and there is an insincerity in any formulation of our problem which allows us to describe the treatment of the dilemma as if it were the disposition of the ordinary case.

It may seem perhaps to make too much of forms, even perhaps of words, to emphasize one way of disposing of this difficult case as compared with another which might have led, so far as the woman was concerned, to exactly the same result. Why should we dramatize the difference between them? We might punish the woman under a new retrospective law and declare overtly that we were doing something inconsistent with our principles as the lesser of two evils; or we might allow the case to pass as one in which we do not point out precisely where we sacrifice such a principle. But candour is not just one among many minor virtues of the administration of law, just as it is not merely a minor virtue of morality. For if we adopt Radbruch's view, and with him and the German courts make our protest against evil law in the form of an assertion that certain rules cannot be law because of their moral iniquity, we confuse one of the most powerful, because it is the simplest, forms of moral criticism. If with the Utilitarians we speak plainly, we say that laws may be law but too evil to be obeyed. This is a moral condemnation which everyone can understand and it makes an immediate and obvious claim to moral attention. If, on the other hand, we formulate our objection as an assertion that these evil things are not law, here is an assertion which many people do not believe, and if they are disposed to consider it at all, it would seem to raise a whole host of philosophical issues before it can be accepted. So perhaps the most important single lesson to be learned from this form of the denial of the utilitarian distinction is the one that the Utilitarians were most concerned to teach; when we have the ample resources of plain speech we must not present the moral criticism of institutions as propositions of a disputable philosophy.

V

I have endeavoured to show that, in spite of all that has been learned and experienced since the Utilitarians wrote, and in spite of the defects of other parts of their doctrine, their protest against the confusion of what is and what ought to be law has a moral as well as an intellectual value. Yet it may well be said that, though this distinction is valid and important if applied to any particular law of a system, it is at least misleading if we attempt to apply it to "law," that is, to the notion of a legal system, and that if we insist, as I have, on the narrower truth (or truism), we obscure a wider (or deeper) truth. After all, it may be urged, we have learned that there are many things which are untrue of laws taken separately, but which are true and important in a legal system considered as a whole. For example, the connection between law and sanctions and between the existence of law and its "efficacy" must be understood in this more general way. It is surely not arguable (without some desperate extension of the word "sanction" or artificial narrowing of the word "law") that every law in a municipal legal system must have a sanction, yet it is at least plausible to argue that a legal system must, to be a legal system, provide sanctions for certain of its rules. So too, a rule of law may be said to exist though enforced or obeyed in only a minority of cases, but this could not be said of a legal system as a whole. Perhaps the differences with respect to laws taken separately and a legal system as a whole are also true of the connection between moral (or some other) conceptions of what law ought to be and law in this wider sense.

This line of argument, found (at least in embryo form) in Austin, where he draws attention to the fact that every developed legal system contains certain fundamental notions which are "necessary" and "bottomed in the common nature of man," is worth pursuing – up to a point – and I shall say briefly why and how far this is so.

We must avoid, if we can, the arid wastes of inappropriate definition, for, in relation to a concept as many-sided and vague as that of a legal system, disputes about the "essential" character, or necessity to the whole, of any single element soon begin to look like disputes about whether chess could be "chess" if played without pawns. There is a wish, which may be understandable, to cut straight through the question whether a legal system, to be a legal system, must measure up to some moral or other standard with simple statements of fact: for example, that no system which utterly failed in this respect has ever existed or could endure; that the normally fulfilled assumption that a legal system aims at some form of justice colours the whole way in which we interpret specific rules in particular cases, and if this normally fulfilled assumption were not fulfilled no one would have any reason to obey except fear (and probably not that), and still less, of course, any moral obligation to obey. The connection between law and moral standards and principles of justice is therefore as little arbitrary and as "necessary" as the connection between law and sanctions, and the pursuit of the question whether this necessity is logical (part of the "meaning" of law) or merely factual or causal can safely be left as an innocent pastime for philosophers.

Yet in two respects I should wish to go further (even though this involves the use of a philosophical fantasy) and show what could intelligibly be meant by the claim that certain provisions in a legal system are "necessary." The world in which we live, and we who live in it, may one day change in many different ways; and if this change were radical enough not only would certain statements of fact now true be false and vice versa, but whole ways of thinking and talking which constitute our present conceptual apparatus, through which we see the world and each other, would lapse. We have only to consider how the whole of our social, moral, and legal life, as we understand it now, depends on the contingent fact that though our bodies do change in shape, size, and other physical properties they do not do this so drastically nor with such quicksilver rapidity and irregularity that we cannot identify each other as the same persistent individual over considerable spans of time. Though this is but a contingent fact which may one day be different, on it at present rest huge structures of our thought and principles of action and social life. Similarly, consider the following possibility (not because it is more than a possibility but because it reveals why we think certain things necessary in a legal system and what we mean by this): suppose that men were to become invulnerable to attack by each other, were clad perhaps like giant land crabs with an impenetrable carapace, and could extract the food they needed from the air by some internal chemical process. In such circumstances (the details of which can be left to science fiction) rules forbidding the free use of violence and rules constituting the minimum form of property – with its rights and duties sufficient to enable food to grow and be retained until eaten – would not have the necessary non-arbitrary status which they have for us, constituted as we are in a world like ours. At present, and until such radical changes supervene, such rules are so fundamental that if a legal system did not have them there would be no point in having any other rules at all. Such rules overlap with basic moral principles vetoing murder, violence, and theft; and so we can add to the factual statement that all legal systems in fact coincide with morality at such vital points, the statement that this is, in this sense, necessarily so. And why not call it a "natural" necessity?

Of course even this much depends on the fact that in asking what content a legal system must have we take this question to be worth asking only if we who consider it cherish the humble aim of survival in close proximity to our fellows. Natural-law theory, however, in all its protean guises, attempts to push the argument much further and to assert that human beings are equally devoted to and united in their conception of aims (the pursuit of knowledge, justice to their fellow men) other than that of survival and these dictate a further necessary content to a legal system (over and above my humble minimum) without which it would be pointless. Of course we must be careful not to exaggerate the differences among human beings, but it seems to me that above this minimum the purposes men have for living in society are too conflicting and varying to make possible much extension of the argument that some fuller overlap of legal rules and moral standards is "necessary" in this sense.

Another aspect of the matter deserves attention. If we attach to a legal system the minimum meaning that it must consist of general rules – general both in the sense that they refer to courses of action, not single actions and to multiplicities of men, not single individuals – this meaning connotes the principle of treating like cases alike, though the criteria of when cases are alike will be, so far, only the general elements specified in the rules. It is, however, true that *one* essential element of the concept of justice is the principle of treating like cases alike. This is justice in the administration of the law, not justice of the law. So there is, in the very notion of law consisting of general rules, something which prevents us from treating it as if morally it is utterly neutral, without any necessary contact with moral principles. Natural procedural justice consists therefore of those principles of objectivity and impartiality in the administration of the law which implement just this aspect of law and which are designed to ensure that rules are applied only to what are genuinely cases of the rule or at least to minimize the risks of inequalities in this sense.

These two reasons (or excuses) for talking of a certain overlap between legal and moral standards as necessary and natural, of course, should not satisfy anyone who is really disturbed by the utilitarian or "positivist" insistence that law and morality are distinct. This is so because a legal system that satisfied these minimum requirements might apply, with the most pedantic impartiality as between the persons affected, laws which were hideously oppressive, and might deny to a vast rightless slave population the minimum benefits of protection from violence and theft. The stink of such society is, after all, still in our nostrils, and to argue that they have (or had) no legal system would only involve the repetition of the argument. Only if the rules failed to provide these essential benefits and protection for anyone – even for a slave-owning group – would the minimum be unsatisfied and the system sink to the status of a set of meaningless taboos. Of course no one denied those benefits would have any reason to obey except fear and would have every moral reason to revolt.

VI

... When rules are recognized as applying to instances beyond any that legislators did or could have considered, their extension to such new cases often presents itself not as a deliberate choice or fiat on the part of those who so interpret the rule. It appears neither as a decision to give the rule a new or extended meaning nor as a guess as to what legislators, dead perhaps in the eighteenth century, would have said had they been alive in the twentieth century. Rather, the inclusion of the new case under the rule takes its place as a natural elaboration of the rule, as something implementing a "purpose" which it seems natural to attribute (in some sense) to the rule itself rather than to any particular person dead or alive. The utilitarian description of such interpretative extension of old rules to new cases as judicial legislation fails to do justice to this phenomenon; it gives no hint of the differences between a deliberate fiat or decision to treat the new case in the same way as past cases and a recognition (in which there is little that is deliberate or even voluntary) that inclusion of the new case under the rule will implement or articulate a continuing and identical purpose, hitherto less specifically apprehended.

Perhaps many lawyers and judges will see in this language something that precisely fits their experience; others may think it a romantic gloss on facts better stated in the utilitarian language of judicial "legislation" or in the modern American terminology of "creative choice."

To make the point clear Professor Fuller uses a non-legal example from the philosopher Wittgenstein which is, I think, illuminating.

Someone says to me: "Show the children a game." I teach them gaming with dice and the other says "I did not mean that sort of game." Must the exclusion of the game with dice have come before his mind when he gave me the order?

Something important does seem to me to be touched on in this example. Perhaps there are the following (distinguishable) points. First, we normally do interpret not only what people are trying to do but what they say in the light of assumed common human objectives, so that unless the contrary were expressly indicated we would not interpret an instruction to show a young child a game as a mandate to introduce him to gambling even though in other contexts the word "game" would be naturally so interpreted. Secondly, very often, the speaker whose words are thus interpreted might say: "Yes, that's what I mean [or "that's what I meant all along"] though I never thought of it until you put this particular case to me." Third, when we thus recognize, perhaps after argument or consultation with others, a particular case not specifically envisaged beforehand as falling within the ambit of some vaguely expressed instruction, we may find this experience falsified by description of it as a mere decision on our part so to treat the particular case, and that we can only describe this faithfully as coming to realize and to articulate what we "really" want or our "true purpose" – phrases which Professor Fuller uses later in the same article.

I am sure that many philosophical discussions of the character of moral argument would benefit from attention to cases of the sort instanced by Professor Fuller. Such attention would help to provide a corrective to the view that there is a sharp separation between "ends" and "means" and that in debating "ends" we can only work on each other non-rationally, and that rational argument is reserved for discussion of "means." But I think the relevance of his point to the issue whether it is correct or wise to insist on the distinction between law as it is and law as it ought to be is very small indeed. Its net effect is that in interpreting legal rules there are some cases which we find after reflection to be so natural an elaboration or articulation of the rule that to think of and refer to this as "legislation," "making law," or a "fiat" on our part would be misleading. So, the argument must be, it would be misleading to distinguish in such cases between what the rule is and what it ought to be – at least in some sense of ought. We think it ought to include the new case and come to see after reflection that it really does. But even if this way of presenting a recognizable experience as an example of a fusion between is and ought to be is admitted, two caveats must be borne in mind. The first is that "ought" in this case need have nothing to do with morals for the reasons explained already in section III: there may be just the same sense that a new case will implement and articulate the purpose of a rule in interpreting the rules of a game or some hideously immoral code of oppression whose immorality is appreciated by those called in to interpret it. They too can see what the "spirit" of the game they are playing requires in previously unenvisaged cases. More important is this: after all is said and done we must remember how rare in the law is the phenomenon held to justify this way of talking, how exceptional is this feeling that one way of deciding a case is imposed upon us as the only natural or rational elaboration of some rule. Surely it cannot be doubted that, for most cases of interpretation, the language of choice between alternatives, "judicial legislation" or even "fiat" (though not arbitrary fiat), better conveys the realities of the situation.

Within the framework of relatively well-settled law there jostle too many alternatives too nearly equal in attraction between which judge and lawyer must uncertainly pick their way to make appropriate here language which may well describe those experiences which we have in interpreting our own or others' principles of conduct, intention, or wishes, when we are not conscious of exercising a deliberate choice, but rather of recognizing something awaiting recognition. To use in the description of the interpretation of laws the suggested terminology of a fusion or inability to separate what is law and ought to be will serve (like earlier stories that judges only find, never make, law) only to conceal the facts, that here if anywhere we live among uncertainties between which we have to choose, and that the existing law imposes only limits on our choice and not the choice itself.

NOTE

1   It may help to identify five (there may be more) meanings of "positivism" bandied about in contemporary jurisprudence:
    (1) the contention that laws are commands of human beings; see 31–4 *infra*;
    (2) the contention that there is no necessary connection between law and morals or law as it is and ought to be; see 28–30 *supra*;
    (3) the contention that the analysis (or study of the meaning) of legal concepts is (a) worth pursuing and (b) to be distinguished from historical inquiries into the causes or origins of laws, from sociological inquiries into the relation of law and other social phenomena, and from the criti-

cism or appraisal of law whether in terms of morals, social aims, "functions," or otherwise; see 34–9 *infra;*

(4) the contention that a legal system is a "closed logical system" in which correct legal decisions can be deduced by logical means from predetermined legal rules without reference to social aims, policies, moral standards; see 34–9 *infra,* and

(5) the contention that moral judgments cannot be established or defended, as statements of facts can, by rational argument, evidence, or proof ('noncognitivism" in ethics).

Bentham and Austin held the views described in (1), (2), and (3), but not those in (4) and (5). Opinion (4) is often ascribed to analytical jurists; see 34–9 *infra,* but I know of no "analyst" who held this view.

H.L.A. Hart
The Concept of Law (1961)

PRIMARY AND SECONDARY RULES

The Elements of Law

It is, of course, possible to imagine a society without a legislature, courts or officials of any kind. Indeed, there are many studies of primitive communities which not only claim that this possibility is realized but depict in detail the life of a society where the only means of social control is that general attitude of the group towards its own standard modes of behaviour in terms of which we have characterized rules of obligation. A social structure of this kind is often referred to as one of "custom"; but we shall not use this term, because it often implies that the customary rules are very old and supported with less social pressure than other rules. To avoid these implications we shall refer to such a social structure as one of primary rules of obligation. If a society is to live by such primary rules alone, there are certain conditions which, granted a few of the most obvious truisms about human nature and the world we live in, must clearly be satisfied. The first of these conditions is that the rules must contain in some form restrictions on the free use of violence, theft, and deception to which human beings are tempted but which they must, in general, repress, if they are to coexist in close proximity to each other. Such rules are in fact always found in the primitive societies of which we have knowledge, together with a variety of others imposing on individuals various positive duties to perform services or make contributions to the common life. Secondly, though such a society may exhibit the tension, already described, between those who accept the rules and those who reject the rules except where fear of social pressure induces them to conform, it is plain that the latter cannot be more than a minority, if so loosely organized a society of persons, approximately equal in physical strength, is to endure: for otherwise those who reject the rules would have too little social pressure to fear. This too is confirmed by what we know of primitive communities where, though there are dissidents and malefactors, the majority live by the rules seen from the internal point of view.

More important for our present purpose is the following consideration. It is plain that only a small community closely knit by ties of kinship, common sentiment, and belief, and placed in a stable environment, could live successfully by such a régime of unofficial rules. In any other conditions such a simple form of social control must prove defective and will require supplementation in different ways. In the first place, the rules by which the group lives will not form a system, but will simply be a set of separate standards, without any identifying or common mark, except of course that they are the rules which a particular group of human beings accepts. They will in this respect resemble our own rules of etiquette. Hence if doubts arise as to what the rules are or as to the precise scope of some given rule, there will be no procedure for settling this doubt, either by reference to an authoritative text or to an official whose declarations on this point are authoritative. For, plainly, such a procedure and the acknowledgement of either authoritative text or persons involve the existence of rules of a type different from the rules of obligation or duty which *ex hypothesi* are all that the group has. This defect in the simple social structure of primary rules we may call its *uncertainty*.

A second defect is the *static* character of the rules. The only mode of change in the rules known to such a society will be the slow process of growth, whereby courses of conduct once thought optional become first habitual or usual, and then obligatory, and the converse process of decay, when deviations, once severely dealt with, are first tolerated and then pass unnoticed. There will be no means, in such a society, of deliberately adapting the rules to changing circumstances, either by eliminating old rules or introducing new ones: for, again, the possibility of doing this presupposes the existence of rules of a different type from the primary rules of obligation by which alone the society lives. In an extreme case the rules may be static in a more drastic sense. This, though never perhaps fully realized in any actual community, is worth considering because the remedy for it is something very characteristic of law. In this extreme case, not only would there be no way of deliberately changing the general rules, but the obligations which arise under the rules in particular cases could not be varied or modified by the deliberate choice of any individual. Each individual would simply have fixed obligations or duties to do or abstain from doing certain things. It might indeed very often be the case that others would benefit from the performance of these obligations; yet if there are only primary rules of obligation they would have no power to release those bound from performance or to transfer to others the benefits which would accrue from performance. For such operations of release or transfer create changes in the initial positions of individuals under the primary rules of obligation, and for these operations to be possible there must be rules of a sort different from the primary rules.

The third defect of this simple form of social life is the *inefficiency* of the diffuse social pressure by which the rules are maintained. Disputes as to whether an admitted rule has or has not been violated will always occur and will, in any but the smallest societies, continue interminably, if there is no agency specially empowered to ascertain finally, and authoritatively, the fact of violation. Lack of such final and authoritative determinations is to be distinguished from another weakness associated with it. This is the fact that punishments for violations of the rules, and other forms of social pressure involving physical effort or the use of force, are not administered by a special agency but are left to the individuals affected or to the group at large. It is obvious that the waste of time involved in the group's unorganized efforts to catch and punish offenders, and the smouldering vendettas which may result from self-help in the absence of an official monopoly of "sanctions," may be serious. This history of law does, however, strongly suggest that the lack of official agencies to determine authoritatively the fact of violation of the rules is a much more serious defect; for many societies have remedies for this defect long before the other.

The remedy for each of these three main defects in this simplest form of social structure consists in supplementing the *primary* rules of obligation with *secondary* rules which are rules of a different kind. The introduction of the remedy for each defect might, in itself, be considered a step from the pre-legal into the legal world; since each remedy brings with it many elements that permeate law: certainly all three remedies together are enough to convert the régime of primary rules into what is indisputably a legal system. We shall consider in turn each of these remedies and show why law may most illuminatingly be characterized as a union of primary rules of obligation with such secondary rules. Before we do this, however, the following general points should be noted. Though the remedies consist in the introduction of rules which are certainly different from each other, as well as from the primary rules of obligation which they supplement, they have important features in common and are connected in various ways. Thus they may all be said to be on a different level from the primary rules, for they are all *about* such rules; in the sense that while primary rules are concerned with the actions that individuals must or must not do, these secondary rules are all concerned with the primary rules themselves. They specify the ways in which the primary rules may be conclusively ascertained, introduced, eliminated, varied, and the fact of their violation conclusively determined.

The simplest form of remedy for the *uncertainty* of the régime of primary rules is the introduction of what we shall call a "rule of recognition." This will specify some feature or features possession of which by a suggested rule is taken as a conclusive affirmative indication that it is a rule of the group to be supported by the social pressure it exerts. The existence of such a rule of recognition may take any of a huge variety of forms, simple or complex. It may, as in the early law of many societies, be no more than that an authoritative list or text of the rules is to be found in a written document or carved on some public monument. No doubt as a matter of history this step from the pre-legal to the legal may be accomplished in distinguishable stages, of which the first is the mere reduction to writing of hitherto unwritten rules. This is not itself the crucial step, though it is a very important one: what is crucial is the acknowledgement of reference to the writing or inscription as *authoritative*, i.e., as the *proper* way of disposing of doubts as to the existence of the rule. Where there is such an acknowledgement there is a very simple form of secondary rule: a rule for conclusive identification of the primary rules of obligation.

In a developed legal system the rules of recognition are of course more complex; instead of identifying rules exclusively by reference to a text or list they do so by reference to some general characteristic possessed by the primary rules. This may be the fact of their having been enacted by a specific body, or their long customary practice, or their relation to judicial decisions. Moreover, where more than one of such general characteristics are treated as identifying criteria, provision may be made for their possible conflict by their arrangement in an order of superiority, as by the common subordination of custom or precedent to statute, the latter being a "superior source" of law. Such complexity may make the rules of recognition in a modern legal system seem very different from the simple acceptance of an authoritative text: yet even in this simplest form, such a rule brings with it many elements distinctive of law. By providing an authoritative mark it introduces, although in embryonic form, the idea of a legal system: for the rules are now not just a discrete unconnected set but are, in a simple way, unified. Further, in the simple operation of identifying a given rule as possessing the required feature of being an item on an authoritative list of rules we have the germ of the idea of legal validity.

The remedy for the *static* quality of the régime of primary rules consists in the introduction of what we shall call "rules of change." The simplest form of such a rule is that which empowers an individual or body of persons to introduce new primary rules for the conduct of the life of the group, or of some class within it, and to eliminate old rules. As we have already argued in Chapter IV it is in terms of such a rule, and not in terms of orders backed by threats, that the ideas of legislative enactment and repeal are to be understood. Such rules of change may be very simple or very complex: the powers conferred may be unrestricted or limited in various ways: and the rules may, besides specifying the persons who are to legislate, define in more or less rigid terms the procedure to be followed in legislation. Plainly, there will be a very close connexion between the rules of change and the rules of recognition: for where the former exists the latter will necessarily incorporate a reference to legislation as an identifying feature of the rules, though it need not refer to all the details of procedure involved in legislation. Usually some official certificate or official copy will, under the rules of recognition, be taken as a sufficient proof of due enactment. Of course if there is a social structure so simple that the only "source of law" is legislation, the rule of recognition will simply specify enactment as the unique identifying mark or criterion of validity of the rules. This will be the case for example in the imaginary kingdom of Rex I depicted in Chapter IV: there the rule of recognition would simply be that whatever Rex I enacts is law.

We have already described in some detail the rules which confer on individuals power to vary their initial positions under the primary rules. Without such private power-conferring rules society would lack some of the chief amenities which law confers upon it. For the operations which these rules make possible are the making of wills, contracts, transfers of property, and many other voluntarily created structures of rights and duties which typify life under law, though of course an elementary form of power-conferring rule also underlies the moral institution of a promise. The kinship of these rules with the rules of change involved in the notion of legislation is clear, and as recent theory such as Kelsen's has shown, many of the features which puzzle us in the institutions of contract or property are clarified by thinking of the operations of making a contract or transferring property as the exercise of limited legislative powers by individuals.

The third supplement to the simple régime of primary rules, intended to remedy the *inefficiency* of its diffused social pressure, consists of secondary rules empowering individuals to make authoritative determinations of the question whether, on a particular occasion, a primary rule has been broken. The minimal form of adjudication consists in such determinations, and we shall call the secondary rules which confer the power to make them "rules of adjudication." Besides identifying the individuals who are to adjudicate, such rules will also define the procedure to be followed. Like the other secondary rules these are on a different level from the primary rules: though they may be reinforced by further rules imposing duties on judges to adjudicate, they do not impose duties but confer judicial powers and a special status on judicial declarations about the breach of obligations. Again these rules, like the other secondary rules, define a group of important legal concepts: in this case the concepts of judge or court, jurisdiction and judgment. Besides these resemblances to the other secondary rules, rules of adjudication have intimate connexions with them. Indeed, a system which has rules of adjudication is necessarily also committed to a rule of recognition of an elementary and imperfect sort. This is so because, if courts are empowered to make authoritative determinations of the fact that a rule has been broken, these cannot avoid being taken as authoritative determinations of what the rules are. So the rule which confers jurisdiction will also be a rule of recognition, identifying the primary rules through the judgments of the courts and these judgments will become a "source" of law. It is true that this form of rule of recognition, inseparable from the minimum form of jurisdiction, will be very imperfect. Unlike an authoritative text or a statute book, judgments may not be couched in general terms and their use as authoritative guides to the rules depends on a somewhat shaky inference from particular decisions, and the reliability of this must fluctuate both with the skill of the interpreter and the consistency of the judges.

It need hardly be said that in few legal systems are judicial powers confined to authoritative determinations of the fact of violation of the primary rules. Most systems have, after some delay, seen the advantages of further centralization of social pressure; and have partially prohibited the use of physical punishments or violent self help by private individuals. Instead they have supplemented the primary rules of obligation by further secondary rules, specifying or at least limiting the penalties for violation, and have conferred upon judges, where they have ascertained the fact of violation, the exclusive power to direct the application of penalties by other officials. These secondary rules provide the centralized official "sanctions" of the system ...

New Questions

Once we abandon the view that the foundations of a legal system consist in a habit of obedience to a legally unlimited sovereign and substitute for this the conception of an ultimate rule of recognition which provides a system of rules with its criteria of validity, a range of fascinating and important questions confronts us. They are relatively new questions; for they were veiled so long as jurisprudence and political theory were committed to the older ways of thought. They are also difficult questions, requiring for a full answer, on the one hand a grasp of some fundamental issues of constitutional law and on the other an appreciation of the characteristic manner in which legal forms may silently shift and change. We shall therefore investigate these questions only so far as they bear upon the wisdom or unwisdom of insisting, as we have done, that a central place should be assigned to the union of primary and secondary rules in the elucidation of the concept of law.

The first difficulty is that of classification; for the rule which, in the last resort, is used to identify the law escapes the conventional categories used for describing a legal system, though these are often taken to be exhaustive. Thus, English constitutional writers since Dicey have usually repeated the statement that the constitutional arrangements of the United Kingdom consist partly of laws strictly so called (statutes, orders in council, and rules embodied in precedents) and partly of conventions which are mere usages, understandings, or customs. The latter include important rules such as that the Queen may not refuse her consent to a bill duly passed by Peers and Commons; there is, however, no legal duty on the Queen to give her consent and such rules are called conventions because the courts do not recognize them as imposing a legal duty. Plainly the rule that what the Queen in Parliament enacts is law does not fall into either of these categories. It is not a convention, since the courts are most intimately concerned with it and they use it in identifying the law; and it is not a rule on the same level as the "laws strictly so called" which it is used to identify. Even if it were enacted by statute, this would not reduce it to the level of a statute; for the legal status of such an enactment necessarily would depend on the fact that the rule existed antecedently to and independently of the enactment. Moreover, as we have shown in the last section, its existence, unlike that of a statute, must consist in an actual practice.

This aspect of things extracts from some a cry of despair: how can we show that the fundamental provisions of a constitution which are surely law are really law? Others reply with the insistence that at the base of legal systems there is something which is "not law," which is "pre-legal," "meta-legal," or is just "political fact." This uneasiness is a sure sign that the categories used for the description of this most important feature in any system of law are too crude. The case for calling the rule of recognition "law" is that the rule providing criteria for the identification of other rules of the system may well be thought a defining feature of a legal system, and so itself worth calling "law"; the case for calling it "fact" is that to assert that such a rule exists is indeed to make an external statement of an actual fact concerning the manner in which the rules of an "efficacious" system are identified. Both these aspects claim attention but we cannot do justice to them both by choosing one of the labels "law" or "fact." Instead, we need to remember that the ultimate rule of recognition may be regarded from two points of view: one is expressed in the external statement of fact that the rule exists in the actual practice of the system; the other is expressed in the internal statements of validity made by those who use it in identifying the law.

A second set of questions arises out of the hidden complexity and vagueness of the assertion that a legal system *exists* in a given country or among a given social group. When we make this assertion we in fact refer in compressed, portmanteau form to a number of heterogeneous social facts, usually concomitant. The standard terminology of legal and political thought, developed in the shadow of a misleading theory, is apt to over-simplify and obscure the facts. Yet when we take off the spectacles constituted by this terminology and look at the facts, it becomes apparent that a legal system, like a human being, may at one stage be unborn, at a second not yet wholly independent of its mother, then enjoy a healthy independent existence, later decay and finally die. These half-way stages between birth and normal, independent existence and, again, between that and death, put out of joint our familiar ways of describing legal phenomena. They are worth our study because, baffling as they are, they throw into relief the full complexity of what we take for granted when, in the normal case, we make the confident and true assertion that in a given country a legal system exists.

One way of realizing this complexity is to see just where the simple, Austinian formula of a general habit of obedience to orders fails to reproduce or distorts the complex facts which constitute the minimum conditions which a society must satisfy if it is to have a legal system. We may allow that this formula does designate one necessary condition: namely, that where the laws impose obligations or duties these should be generally obeyed or at any rate not generally disobeyed. But, though essential, this only caters for what we may term the "end product" of the legal system, where it makes its impact on the private citizen; whereas its day-to-day existence consists also in the official creation, the official identification, and the official use and application of law. The relationship with law involved here can be called "obedience" only if that word is extended so far beyond its normal use as to cease to characterize informatively these operations. In no ordinary sense of "obey" are legislators obeying rules when, in enacting laws, they conform to the rules conferring their legislative powers, except of course when the rules conferring such powers are reinforced by rules imposing a duty to follow them. Nor, in failing to conform with these rules do they "disobey" a law, though they may fail to make one. Nor does the word "obey" describe well what judges do when they apply the system's rule of recognition and recognize a statute as valid law and use it in the determination of disputes. We can of course, if we wish, preserve the simple terminology of "obedience" in face of the facts by many devices. One is to express, e.g. the use made by judges of general criteria of validity in recognizing a statute, as a case of obedience to orders given by the "Founders of the Constitution," or (where there are no "Founders") as obedience to a "depsychologized command," i.e., a command without a commander. But this last should perhaps have no more serious claims on our attention than the notion of a nephew without an uncle. Alternatively we can push out of sight the whole official side to law and forgo the description of the use of rules made in legislation and adjudication, and instead, think of the whole official world as one person (the "sovereign") issuing orders, through various agents or mouthpieces, which are habitually obeyed by the citizen. But this is either no more than a convenient shorthand for complex facts which still await description, or a disastrously confusing piece of mythology.

It is natural to react from the failure of attempts to give an account of what it is for a legal system to exist, in the agreeably simple terms of the habitual obedience which is indeed characteristic of (though it does not always exhaustively describe) the relationship of the ordinary citizen to law, by making the opposite error. This consists in taking what is characteristic (though again not exhaustive) of the official activities, especially the judicial attitude or relationship to law, and treating this as an adequate account of what must exist in a social group which has a legal system. This amounts to replacing the simple conception that the bulk of society habitually obey the law with the conception that they must generally share, accept, or regard as binding the ultimate rule of recognition specifying the criteria in terms of which the validity of laws are ultimately assessed. Of course we can imagine, as we have done in Chapter III, a simple society where knowledge and understanding of the sources of law are widely diffused. There the "constitution" was so simple that no fiction would be involved in attributing knowledge and acceptance of it to the ordinary citizen as well as to the officials and lawyers. In the simple world of Rex I we might well say that there was more than mere habitual obedience by the bulk of the population to his word. There it might well be the case that both they and the officials of the system "accepted," in the same explicit, conscious way, a rule of recognition specifying Rex's word as the criterion of valid law for the whole society, though subjects and officials would have different roles to play and different relationships to the rules of law identified by this criterion. To insist that this state of affairs, imaginable in a simple society, always or usually exists in a complex modern state would be to insist on a fiction. Here surely the reality of the situation is that a great proportion of ordinary citizens – perhaps a majority – have no general conception of the legal structure or of its criteria of validity. The law which he obeys is something which he knows of only as "the law." He may obey it for a variety of different reasons and among them may often, though not always, be the knowledge that it will be best for him to do so. He will be aware of the general likely consequences of disobedience: that there are officials who may arrest him and others who will try him and send him to prison for breaking the law. So long as the laws which are valid by the system's tests of validity are obeyed by the bulk of the population this surely is all the evidence we need in order to establish that a given legal system exists.

But just because a legal system is a complex union of primary and secondary rules, this evidence is not all that is needed to describe the relationships to law involved in the existence of a legal system. It must be supplemented by a description of the relevant relationship of the officials of the system to the secondary rules which concern them as officials. Here what is crucial is that there should be a unified or shared official acceptance of the rule of recognition containing the system's criteria of validity. But it is just here that the simple notion of general obedience, which was adequate to characterize the indispensable minimum in the case of ordinary citizens, is inadequate. The point is not, or not merely, the "linguistic" one that "obedience" is not naturally used to refer to the way in which these secondary rules are respected as rules by courts and other officials. We could find, if necessary, some wider expression like "follow," "comply," or "conform to" which would characterize both what ordinary citizens do in relation to law when they report for military service and what judges do when they identify a particular statute as law in their courts, on the footing that what the Queen in Parliament enacts is law. But these blanket terms would merely mask vital differences which must be grasped if the minimum conditions involved in the existence of the complex social phenomenon which we call a legal system is to be understood.

What makes "obedience" misleading as a description of what legislators do in conforming to the rules conferring their powers, and of what courts do in applying an accepted ultimate rule of recognition, is that obeying a rule (or an order) *need* involve no thought on the part of the person obeying that what he does is the right thing both for himself and for others to do: he need have no view of what he does as a fulfilment of a standard of behaviour for others of the social group. He need not think of his conforming behaviour as "right," "correct," or "obligatory." His attitude, in other words, need not have any of that critical character which is involved whenever social rules are accepted and types of conduct are treated as general standards. He need not, though he may, share the internal point of view accepting the rules as standards for all to whom they apply. Instead, he may think of the rule only as something demanding action from *him* under threat of penalty; he may obey it out of fear of the consequences, or from inertia, without thinking of himself or others as having an obligation to do so and without being disposed to criticize either himself or others for deviations. But this merely personal concern with the rules, which is all the ordinary citizen *may* have in obeying them, cannot characterize the attitude of the courts to the rules with which they operate as courts. This is most patently the case with the ultimate rule of recognition in terms of which the validity of other rules is assessed. This, if it is to exist at all, must be regarded from the internal point of view as a public, common standard of correct judicial decision, and not as something which each judge merely obeys for his part only. Individual courts of the system though they may, on occasion, deviate from these rules must, in general, be critically concerned with such deviations as lapses from standards, which are essentially common or public. This is not merely a matter of the efficiency or health of the legal system, but is logically a necessary condition of our ability to speak of the existence of a single legal system. If only some judges acted "for their part only" on the footing that what the Queen in Parliament enacts is law, and made no criticisms of those who did not respect this rule of recognition, the characteristic unity and continuity of a legal system would have disappeared. For this depends on the acceptance, at this crucial point, of common standards of legal validity. In the interval between these vagaries of judicial behaviour and the chaos which would ultimately ensue when the ordinary man was faced with contrary judicial orders, we would be at a loss to describe the situation. We would be in the presence of a *lusus naturae* worth thinking about only because it sharpens our awareness of what is often too obvious to be noticed.

There are therefore two minimum conditions necessary and sufficient for the existence of a legal system. On the one hand those rules of behaviour which are valid according to the system's ultimate criteria of validity must be generally obeyed, and, on the other hand, its rules of recognition specifying the criteria of legal validity and its rules of change and adjudication must be effectively accepted as common public standards of official behaviour by its officials. The first condition is the only one which private citizens *need* satisfy: they may obey each "for his part only" and from any motive whatever; though in a healthy society they will in fact often accept these rules as common standards of behaviour and acknowledge an obligation to obey them, or even trace this obligation to a more general obligation to respect the constitution. The second condition must also be satisfied by the officials of the system. They must regard these as common standards of official behaviour and appraise critically their own and each other's deviations as lapses. Of course it is also true that besides these there will be many primary rules which apply to officials in their merely personal capacity which they need only obey.

The assertion that a legal system exists is therefore a Janus-faced statement looking both towards obedience by ordinary citizens and to the acceptance by officials of secondary rules as critical common standards of official behaviour. We need not be surprised at this duality. It is merely the reflection of the composite character of a legal system as compared with a simpler decentralized pre-legal form of social structure which consists only of primary rules. In the simpler structure, since there are no officials, the rules must be widely accepted as setting critical standards for the behaviour of the group. If, there, the internal point of view is not widely disseminated there could not logically be any rules. But where there is a union of primary and secondary rules, which is, as we have argued, the most fruitful way of regarding a legal system, the acceptance of the rules as common standards for the group may be split off from the relatively passive matter of the ordinary individual acquiescing in the rules by obeying them for his part alone. In an extreme case the internal point of view with its characteristic normative use of legal language ("This is a valid rule") might be confined to the official world. In this more complex system, only officials might accept and use the system's criteria of legal validity. The society in which this was so might be deplorably sheeplike; the sheep might end in the slaughter-house. But there is little reason for thinking that it could not exist or for denying it the title of a legal system ...

READING QUESTIONS ON HART

1 What are Hart's criticisms of the command theory?
2 What is the "internal point of view"? Is there a difference between it and a moral point of view?
3 Why are secondary rules important to a legal system?

Whitely v. Chapel (1868) LR 4 QB 147

In this nineteenth-century English case, the accused had used the names of people recently deceased whose names appeared on the voting list; the issue was whether that constituted personating another for purposes of the statute. (Footnotes omitted.)

By 14 & 15 Vict. c. 105, s. 3, if any person, pending or after the election of any guardian [of the poor], shall wilfully, fraudulently, and with intent to affect the result of such election ... "personate any person entitled to vote at such election," he is made liable on conviction to imprisonment for not exceeding three months.

The appellant was charged with having personated one J. Marston, a person entitled to vote at an election of guardians for the township of Bradford; and it was proved that Marston was duly qualified as a rate-payer on the rate book to have voted at the election, but that he had died before the election. The appellant delivered to the person appointed to collect the voting papers a voting paper apparently duly signed by Marston.

The magistrate convicted the appellant.

The question for the Court was, whether the appellant was rightly convicted.

Mellish, QC (with him *McIntyre)*, for the appellant. A dead person cannot be said to be "a person entitled to vote;" and the appellant therefore could not be guilty of personation under 14 & 15 Vict. c. 105, s. 3. Very possibly he was within the spirit, but he was not within the letter, of the enactment, and in order to bring a person within a penal enactment, both must concur. In Russell on Crimes (vol. ii. p. 1013, 4th ed., p. 541, 3rd ed.), under a former statute, in which the words were similar to those of 2 Wm. 4, c. 53, s. 49, which makes it a misdemeanor to personate "a person entitled or supposed to be entitled to any prize money," &c., *Brown's Case* is cited, in which it was held that the personation must be of some person prima facie entitled to prize money. In the Parliamentary Registration Act (6 Vict. c. 18), s. 83, the words are "any person who shall knowingly personate ... any person whose name appears on the register of voters, whether such person be alive or dead;" but under the present enactment the person must be entitled, that is, could have voted himself.

Crompton, for the respondent. *Brown's Case* is, in effect, overruled by the later cases of *Rex v. Martin, and Rex v. Cramp,* in which the judges decided that the offence of personating a person "supposed to be entitled" could be committed, although the person, to the knowledge or belief of the authorities, was dead. Those cases are directly in point. The gist of the offence is the fraudulently voting under another's name; the mischief is the same, whether the supposed voter be alive or dead; and the Court will put a liberal construction on such an enactment: *Reg. v. Hague.*

Mellish, QC, in reply. "Supposed to be entitled" must have been held by the judges in the cases cited to mean supposed by the person personating.

Lush, J.: – I do not think we can, without straining them, bring the case within the words of the enactment. The legislature has not used words wide enough to make the personation of a dead person an offence. The words "a person entitled to vote" can only mean, without a forced construction, a person who is entitled to vote at the time at which the personation takes place; in the present case, therefore, I feel bound to say the offence has not been committed. In the cases of *Rex v. Martin,* and *Rex v. Cramp,* the judges gave no reasons for their decision; they probably held that "supposed to be entitled" meant supposed by the person personating.

Hannen, J.: – l regret that we are obliged to come to the conclusion that the offence charged was not proved; but it would be wrong to strain words to meet the justice of the present case, because it might make a precedent, and lead to dangerous consequences in other cases.

Hayes, J., concurred.

Lon L. Fuller
"Positivism and Fidelity to Law – A Reply to Professor Hart" (1958)

Fuller takes Hart to be advancing what he describes as an "ideal of fidelity to law," that is, a positivist position that seeks to make sense of law as an inherently moral project. Fuller argues that because Hart takes this step, meaningful debate between positivists and anti-positivists is for the first time possible. However, Fuller takes Hart's position to be deeply flawed and he thus sketches an alternative, based on what he describes as an "internal morality of law." In later work, Fuller accused legal positivism of having a "managerial" view of law: law is conceived as a "one-way projection of authority, originating with government and imposing itself on the citizen." He also said that the internal morality of law consisted of eight principles: generality, publicity, non-retroactivity, clarity or intelligibility, non-contradiction, possibility of compliance, constancy through time, and congruence between declared rule and official action. If these basically procedural principles of legality or the rule of law were observed, he argued, the citizenry would have a "sound and stable framework for their interactions with one another, the role of government being that of standing as a guardian of the integrity of this system." (Fuller, *The Morality of Law* [New Haven: Yale University Press, 1969, revised edition] 204–10.)

Professor Hart has made an enduring contribution to the literature of legal philosophy. I doubt if the issues he discusses will ever again assume quite the form they had before being touched by his analytical powers. His argument is no mere restatement of Bentham, Austin, Gray, and Holmes. Their views receive in his exposition a new clarity and a new depth that are uniquely his own.

I must confess that when I first encountered the thoughts of Professor Hart's essay, his argument seemed to me to suffer from a deep inner contradiction. On the one hand, he rejects emphatically any confusion of "what is" with "what ought to be." He will tolerate no "merger" of law and conceptions of what law ought to be, but at the most an antiseptic "intersection." Intelligible communication on any subject, he seems to imply, becomes impossible if we leave it uncertain whether we are talking about "what is" or "what ought to be." Yet it was precisely this uncertainty about Professor Hart's own argument which made it difficult for me at first to follow the thread of his thought. At times he seemed to be saying that the distinction between law and morality is something that exists, and will continue to exist, however we may talk about it. It expresses a reality which, whether we like it or not, we must accept if we are to avoid talking nonsense. At other times, he seemed to be warning us that the reality of the distinction is itself in danger and that if we do not mend our ways of thinking and talking we may lose a "precious moral ideal," that of fidelity to law. It is not clear, in other words, whether in Professor Hart's own thinking the distinction between law and morality simply "is," or is something that "ought to be" and that we should join with him in helping to create and maintain.

These were the perplexities I had about Professor Hart's argument when I first encountered it. But on reflection I am sure any criticism of his essay as being self-contradictory would be both unfair and unprofitable. There is no reason why the argument for a strict separation of law and morality cannot be rested on the double ground that this separation serves both intellectual clarity and moral integrity. If there are certain difficulties in bringing these two lines of reasoning into proper relation to one another, these difficulties affect also the position of those who reject the views of Austin, Gray, and Holmes. For those of us who find the "positivist" position unacceptable do ourselves rest our argument on the double ground that its intellectual clarity is specious and that its effects are, or may be, harmful. On the one hand, we assert that Austin's definition of law, for example, violates the reality it purports to describe. Being false in fact, it cannot serve effectively what Kelsen calls "an interest of cognition." On the other hand, we assert that under some conditions the same conception of law may become dangerous, since in human affairs what men mistakenly accept as real tends, by the very act of their acceptance, to become real.

It is a cardinal virtue of Professor Hart's argument that for the first time it opens the way for a truly profitable exchange of views between those whose differences center on the distinction between law and morality. Hitherto there has been no real joinder of issue between the opposing camps. On the one side, we encounter a series of definitional fiats. A rule of law is – that is to say, it really and simply and always is – the command of a sovereign, a rule laid down by a judge, a prediction of the future incidence of state force, a pattern of official behavior, etc. When we ask what purpose these definitions serve, we receive the answer, "Why, no purpose, except to describe accurately the social reality that corresponds to the word 'law.'" When we reply, "But it doesn't look like that to me," the answer comes back, "Well, it does to me." There the matter has to rest.

This state of affairs has been most unsatisfactory for those of us who are convinced that "positivistic" theories have had a distorting effect on the aims of legal philosophy. Our dissatisfaction arose not merely from the impasse we confronted, but because this impasse seemed to us so unnecessary. All that was needed to surmount it was an acknowledgment on the other side that its definitions of "what law really is" are not mere images of some datum of experience, but direction posts for the application of human energies. Since this acknowledgment was not forthcoming, the impasse and its frustrations continued. There is indeed no frustration greater than to be confronted by a theory which purports merely to describe, when it not only plainly prescribes, but owes its special prescriptive powers precisely to the fact that it disclaims prescriptive intentions. Into this murky debate, some shafts of light did occasionally break through, as in Kelsen's casual admission, apparently never repeated, that his whole system might well rest on an emotional preference for the ideal of order over that of justice.[1] But I have to confess that in general the dispute that has been conducted during the last twenty years has not been very profitable.

Now, with Professor Hart's paper, the discussion takes a new and promising turn. It is now explicitly acknowledged on both sides that one of the chief issues is how we can best define and serve the ideal of fidelity to law. Law, as something deserving loyalty, must represent a human achievement; it cannot be a simple fiat of power or a repetitive pattern discernible in the behavior of state officials. The respect we owe to human laws must surely be something different from the respect we accord to the law of gravitation. If laws, even bad laws, have a claim to our respect, then law must represent some general direction of human effort that we can understand and describe, and that we can approve in principle even at the moment when it seems to us to miss its mark.

If, as I believe, it is a cardinal virtue of Professor Hart's argument that it brings into the dispute the issue of fidelity to law, its chief defect, if I may say so, lies in a failure to perceive and accept the implications that this enlargement of the frame of argument necessarily entails. This defect seems to me more or less to permeate the whole essay, but it comes most prominently to the fore in his discussion of Gustav Radbruch and the Nazi regime.[2] Without any inquiry into the actual workings of whatever remained of a legal system under the Nazis, Professor Hart assumes that something must have persisted that still deserved the name of law in a sense that would make meaningful the ideal of fidelity to law. Not that Professor Hart believes the Nazis' laws should have been obeyed. Rather he considers that a decision to disobey them presented not a mere question of prudence or courage, but a genuine moral dilemma in which the ideal of fidelity to law had to be sacrificed in favor of more fundamental goals. I should have thought it unwise to pass such a judgment without first inquiring with more particularity what "law" itself meant under the Nazi regime.

I shall present later my reasons for thinking that Professor Hart is profoundly mistaken in his estimate of the Nazi situation and that he gravely misinterprets the thought of Professor Radbruch. But first I shall turn to some preliminary definitional problems in which what I regard as the central defect in Professor Hart's thesis seems immediately apparent.

I THE DEFINITION OF LAW

Throughout his essay Professor Hart aligns himself with a general position which he associates with the names of Bentham, Austin, Gray, and Holmes. He recognizes, of course, that the conceptions of these men as to "what law is" vary considerably, but this diversity he apparently considers irrelevant in his defense of their general school of thought.

If the only issue were that of stipulating a meaning for the word "law" that would be conducive to intellectual clarity, there might be much justification for treating all of these men as working in the same direction. Austin, for example, defines law as the command of the highest legislative power, called the sovereign. For Gray, on the other hand, law consists in the rules laid down by judges. A statute is, for Gray, not a law, but only a source of law, which becomes law only after it has been interpreted and applied by a court. Now if our only object were to obtain that clarity which comes from making our definitions explicit and then adhering strictly to those definitions, one could argue plausibly that either conception of the meaning of "law" will do. Both conceptions appear to avoid a confusion of morals and law, and both writers let the reader know what meaning they propose to attribute to the word "law."

The matter assumes a very different aspect, however, if our interest lies in the ideal of fidelity to law, for then it may become a matter of capital importance what position is assigned to the judiciary in the general frame of government. Confirmation for this observation may be found in the slight rumbling of constitutional crisis to be heard in this country today. During the past year readers of newspapers have been writing to their editors urging solemnly, and even apparently with sincerity, that we should abolish the Supreme Court as a first step toward a restoration of the rule of law. It is unlikely that this remedy for our governmental ills derives from any deep study of Austin or Gray, but surely those who propose it could hardly be expected to view with indifference the divergent definitions of law offered by those two jurists. If it be said that it is a perversion of Gray's meaning to extract from his writings any moral for present controversies about the role of the Supreme Court, then it seems to me there is equal reason for treating what he wrote as irrelevant to the issue of fidelity to law generally.

Another difference of opinion among the writers defended by Professor Hart concerns Bentham and Austin and their views on constitutional limitations on the power of the sovereign. Bentham considered that a constitution might preclude the highest legislative power from issuing certain kinds of laws. For Austin, on the other hand, any legal limit on the highest lawmaking power was an absurdity and an impossibility. What guide to conscience would be offered by these two writers in a crisis that might some day arise out of the provision of our constitution to the effect that the amending power can never be used to deprive any state without its consent of its equal representation in the Senate?[3] Surely it is not only in the affairs of everyday life that we need clarity about the obligation of fidelity to law, but most particularly and urgently in times of trouble. If all the positivist school has to offer in such times is the observation that, however you may choose to define law, it is always something different from morals, its teachings are not of much use to us.

I suggest, then, that Professor Hart's thesis as it now stands is essentially incomplete and that before he can attain the goals he seeks he will have to concern himself more closely with a definition of law that will make meaningful the obligation of fidelity to law.

II THE DEFINITION OF MORALITY

It is characteristic of those sharing the point of view of Professor Hart that their primary concern is to preserve the integrity of the concept of law. Accordingly, they have generally sought a precise definition of law, but have not been at pains to state just what it is they mean to exclude by their definitions. They are like men building a wall for the defense of a village, who must know what it is they wish to protect, but who need not, and indeed cannot, know what invading forces those walls may have to turn back.

When Austin and Gray distinguish law from morality, the word "morality" stands indiscriminately for almost every conceivable standard by which human conduct may be judged that is not itself law. The inner voice of conscience, notions of right and wrong based on religious belief, common conceptions of decency and fair play, culturally conditioned prejudices – all of these are grouped together under the heading of "morality" and are excluded from the domain of law. For the most part Professor Hart follows in the tradition of his predecessors. When he speaks of morality he seems generally to have in mind all sorts of extralegal notions about "what ought to be," regardless of their sources, pretensions, or intrinsic worth. This is particularly apparent in his treatment of the problem of interpretation, where uncodified notions of what ought to be are viewed as affecting only the penumbra of law, leaving its hard core untouched.

Toward the end of the essay, however, Professor Hart's argument takes a turn that seems to depart from the prevailing tenor of his thought. This consists in reminding us that there is such a thing as an immoral morality and that there are many standards of "what ought to be" that can hardly be called moral.[4] Let us grant, he says, that the judge may properly and inevitably legislate in the penumbra of a legal enactment, and that this legislation (in default of any other standard) must be guided by the judge's notions of what ought to be. Still, this would be true even in a society devoted to the most evil ends, where the judge would supply the insufficiencies of the statute with the iniquity that seemed to him most apt for the occasion. Let us also grant, says Professor Hart toward the end of his essay, that there is at times even something that looks like discovery in the judicial process, when a judge by restating a principle seems to bring more clearly to light what was really sought from the beginning. Again, he reminds us, this could happen in a society devoted to the highest refinements of sin, where the implicit demands of an evil rule might be a matter for discovery when the rule was applied to a situation not consciously considered when it was formulated.

I take it that this is to be a warning addressed to those who wish "to infuse more morality into the law." Professor Hart is reminding them that if their program is adopted the morality that actually gets infused may not be to their liking. If this is his point it is certainly a valid one, though one wishes it had been made more explicitly, for it raises much the most fundamental issue of his whole argument. Since the point is made obliquely, and I may have misinterpreted it, in commenting I shall have to content myself with a few summary observations and questions.

First, Professor Hart seems to assume that evil aims may have as much coherence and inner logic as good ones. I, for one, refuse to accept that assumption. I realize that I am here raising, or perhaps dodging, questions that lead into the most difficult problems of the epistemology of ethics. Even if I were competent to undertake an excursus in that direction, this is not the place for it. I shall have to rest on the assertion of a belief that may seem naive, namely, that coherence and goodness have more affinity than coherence and evil. Accepting this belief, I also believe that when men are compelled to explain and justify their decisions, the effect will generally be to pull those decisions toward goodness, by whatever standards of ultimate goodness there are.

Accepting these beliefs, I find a considerable incongruity in any conception that envisages a possible future in which the common law would "work itself pure from case to case" toward a more perfect realization of iniquity.

Second, if there is a serious danger in our society that a weakening of the partition between law and morality would permit an infusion of "immoral morality," the question remains, what is the most effective protection against this danger? I cannot myself believe it is to be found in the positivist position espoused by Austin, Gray, Holmes, and Hart. For those writers seem to me to falsify the problem into a specious simplicity which leaves untouched the difficult issues where real dangers lie.

Third, let us suppose a judge bent on realizing through his decisions an objective that most ordinary citizens would regard as mistaken or evil. Would such a judge be likely to suspend the letter of the statute by openly invoking a "higher law"? Or would he be more likely to take refuge behind the maxim that "law is law" and explain his decision in such a way that it would appear to be demanded by the law itself?

Fourth, neither Professor Hart nor I belong to anything that could be said in a significant sense to be a "minority group" in our respective countries. This has its advantages and disadvantages to one aspiring to a philosophic view of law and government. But suppose we were both transported to a country where our beliefs were anathemas, and where we, in turn, regarded the prevailing morality as thoroughly evil. No doubt in this situation we would have reason to fear that the law might be covertly manipulated to our disadvantage; I doubt if either of us would be apprehensive that its injunctions would be set aside by an appeal to a morality higher than law. If we felt that the law itself was our safest refuge, would it not be because even in the most perverted regimes there is a certain hesitancy about writing cruelties, intolerances, and inhumanities into law? And is it not clear that this hesitancy itself derives, not from a separation of law and morals, but precisely from an identification of law with those demands of morality that are the most urgent and the most obviously justifiable, which no man need be ashamed to profess?

Fifth, over great areas where the judicial process functions, the danger of an infusion of immoral, or at least unwelcome, morality does not, I suggest, present a real issue. Here the danger is precisely the opposite. For example, in the field of commercial law the British courts in recent years have, if I may say so, fallen into a "law-is-law" formalism that constitutes a kind of belated counterrevolution against all that was accomplished by Mansfield.[5] The matter has reached a stage approaching crisis as commercial cases are increasingly being taken to arbitration. The chief reason for this development is that arbitrators are willing to take into account the needs of commerce and ordinary standards of commercial fairness. I realize that Professor Hart repudiates "formalism," but I shall try to show later why I think his theory necessarily leads in that direction.[6]

Sixth, in the thinking of many there is one question that predominates in any discussion of the relation of law and morals, to the point of coloring everything that is said or heard on the subject. I refer to the kind of question raised by the Pope's pronouncement concerning the duty of Catholic judges in divorce actions.[7] This pronouncement does indeed raise grave issues. But it does not present a problem of the relation between law, on the one hand, and, on the other, generally shared views of right conduct that have grown spontaneously through experience and discussion. The issue is rather that of a conflict between two pronouncements, both of which claim to be authoritative; if you will, it is one kind of law against another. When this kind of issue is taken as the key to the whole problem of law and morality, the discussion is so denatured and distorted that profitable exchange becomes impossible. In mentioning this last aspect of the dispute about "positivism," I do not mean to intimate that Professor Hart's own discussion is dominated by any *arrière-pensée*; I know it is not. At the same time I am quite sure that I have indicated accurately the issue that will be uppermost in the minds of many as they read his essay.

In resting content with these scant remarks, I do not want to seem to simplify the problem in a direction opposite to that taken by Professor Hart. The questions raised by "immoral morality" deserve a more careful exploration than either Professor Hart or I have offered in these pages.

III THE MORAL FOUNDATIONS OF A LEGAL ORDER

Professor Hart emphatically rejects "the command theory of law," according to which law is simply a command backed by a force sufficient to make it effective. He observes that such a command can be given by a man with a loaded gun, and "law surely is not the gunman situation writ large."[8] There is no need to dwell here on the inadequacies of the command theory, since Professor Hart has already revealed its defects more clearly and succinctly than I could. His conclusion is that the foundation of a legal system is not coercive power, but certain "fundamental accepted rules specifying the essential lawmaking procedures."[9]

When I reached this point in his essay, I felt certain that Professor Hart was about to acknowledge an important qualification on his thesis. I confidently expected that he would go on to say something like this: I have insisted throughout on the importance of keeping sharp the distinction between law and morality. The question may now be raised, therefore, as to the nature of these fundamental rules that furnish the framework within which the making of law takes place. On the one hand, they seem to be rules, not of law, but of morality. They derive their efficacy from a general acceptance, which in turn rests ultimately on a perception that they are right and necessary. They can hardly be said to be law in the sense of an authoritative pronouncement, since their function is to state when a pronouncement is authoritative. On the other hand, in the daily functioning of the legal system they are often treated and applied much as ordinary rules of law are. Here, then, we must confess there is something that can be called a "merger" of law and morality, and to which the term "intersection" is scarcely appropriate.

Instead of pursuing some such course of thought, to my surprise I found Professor Hart leaving completely untouched the nature of the fundamental rules that make law itself possible, and turning his attention instead to what he considers a confusion of thought on the part of the critics of positivism. Leaving out of account his discussion of analytical jurisprudence, his argument runs something as follows: Two views are associated with the names of Bentham and Austin. One is the command theory of law, the other is an insistence on the separation of law and morality. Critics of these writers came in time to perceive – "dimly" Professor Hart says – that the command theory is untenable. By a loose association of ideas they wrongly supposed that in advancing reasons for rejecting the command theory they had also refuted the view that law and morality must be sharply separated. This was a "natural mistake," but plainly a mistake just the same.

I do not think any mistake is committed in believing that Bentham and Austin's error in formulating improperly and too simply the problem of the relation of law and morals was part of a larger error that led to the command theory of law. I think the connection between these two errors can be made clear if we ask ourselves what would have happened to Austin's system of thought if he had abandoned the command theory.

One who reads Austin's Lectures V and VI[10] cannot help being impressed by the way he hangs doggedly to the command theory, in spite of the fact that every pull of his own keen mind was toward abandoning it. In the case of a sovereign monarch, law is what the monarch commands. But what shall we say of the "laws" of succession which tell who the "lawful" monarch is? It is of the essence of a command that it be addressed by a superior to an inferior, yet in the case of a "sovereign many," say, a parliament, the sovereign seems to command itself since a member of parliament may be convicted under a law he himself drafted and voted for. The sovereign must be unlimited in legal power, for who could adjudicate the legal bounds of a supreme lawmaking power? Yet a "sovereign many" must accept the limitation of rules before it can make law at all. Such a body can gain the power to issue commands only by acting in a "corporate capacity"; this it can do only by proceeding "agreeably to the modes and forms" established and accepted for the making of law. Judges exercise a power delegated to them by the supreme lawmaking power, and are commissioned to carry out its "direct or circuitous commands." Yet in a federal system it is the courts which must resolve conflicts of competence between the federation and its components.

All of these problems Austin sees with varying degrees of explicitness, and he struggles mightily with them. Over and over again he teeters on the edge of an abandonment of the command theory in favor of what Professor Hart has described as a view that discerns the foundations of a legal order in "certain fundamental accepted rules specifying the essential lawmaking procedures." Yet he never takes the plunge. He does not take it because he had a sure insight that it would forfeit the black-and-white distinction between law and morality that was the whole object of his Lectures – indeed, one may say, the enduring object of a dedicated life. For if law is made possible by "fundamental accepted rules" – which for Austin must be rules, not of law, but of positive morality – what are we to say of the rules that the lawmaking power enacts to regulate its own lawmaking? We have election laws, laws allocating legislative representation to specific geographic areas, rules of parliamentary procedure, rules for the qualification of voters, and many other laws and rules of similar nature. These do not remain fixed, and all of them shape in varying degrees the lawmaking process. Yet how are we to distinguish between those basic rules that owe their validity to acceptance, and those which are properly rules of law, valid even when men generally consider them to be evil or ill-advised? In other words, how are we to define the words "fundamental" and "essential" in Professor Hart's own formulation: "certain fundamental accepted rules specifying the essential lawmaking procedure"?

The solution for this problem in Kelsen's theory is instructive. Kelsen does in fact take the plunge over which Austin hesitated too long. Kelsen realizes that before we can distinguish between what is law and what is not, there must be an acceptance of some basic procedure by which law is made. In any legal system there must be some fundamental rule that points unambiguously to the source from which laws must come in order to be laws. This rule Kelsen called "the basic norm." In his own words,

The basic norm is not valid because it has been created in a certain way, but its validity is assumed by virtue of its content. It is valid, then, like a norm of natural law ... The idea of a pure positive law, like that of natural law, has its limitations.[11]

It will be noted that Kelsen speaks, not as Professor Hart does, of "fundamental rules" that regulate the making of law, but of a single rule or norm. Of course, there is no such single rule in any modern society. The notion of the basic norm is admittedly a symbol, not a fact. It is a symbol that embodies the positivist quest for some clear and unambiguous test of law, for some clean, sharp line that will divide the rules which owe their validity to their source and those which owe their validity to acceptance and intrinsic appeal. The difficulties Austin avoided by sticking with the command theory, Kelsen avoids by a fiction which simplifies reality into a form that can be absorbed by positivism.

A full exploration of all the problems that result when we recognize that law becomes possible only by virtue of rules that are not law, would require drawing into consideration the effect of the presence or absence of a written constitution. Such a constitution in some ways simplifies the problems I have been discussing, and in some ways complicates them. In so far as a written constitution defines basic lawmaking procedure, it may remove the perplexities that arise when a parliament in effect defines itself. At the same time, a legislature operating under a written constitution may enact statutes that profoundly affect the lawmaking procedure and its predictable outcome.

If these statutes are drafted with sufficient cunning, they may remain within the frame of the constitution and yet undermine the institutions it was intended to establish. If the "court-packing" proposal of the thirties does not illustrate this danger unequivocally, it at least suggests that the fear of it is not fanciful. No written constitution can be self-executing. To be effective it requires not merely the respectful deference we show for ordinary legal enactments, but that willing convergence of effort we give to moral principles in which we have an active belief. One may properly work to amend a constitution, but so long as it remains unamended one must work with it, not against it or around it. All this amounts to saying that to be effective a written constitution must be accepted, at least provisionally, not just as law, but as good law.

What have these considerations to do with the ideal of fidelity to law? I think they have a great deal to do with it, and that they reveal the essential incapacity of the positivistic view to serve that ideal effectively. For I believe that a realization of this ideal is something for which we must plan, and that is precisely what positivism refuses to do.

Let me illustrate what I mean by planning for a realization of the ideal of fidelity to law. Suppose we are drafting a written constitution for a country just emerging from a period of violence and disorder in which any thread of legal continuity with previous governments has been broken. Obviously such a constitution cannot lift itself unaided into legality; it cannot be law simply because it says it is. We should keep in mind that the efficacy of our work will depend upon general acceptance and that to make this acceptance secure there must be a general belief that the constitution itself is necessary, right, and good. The provisions of the constitution should, therefore, be kept simple and understandable, not only in language, but also in purpose. Preambles and other explanations of what is being sought, which would be objectionable in an ordinary statute, may find an appropriate place in our constitution. We should think of our constitution as establishing a basic procedural framework for future governmental action in the enactment and administration of laws. Substantive limitations on the power of government should be kept to a minimum and should generally be confined to those for which a need can be generally appreciated. In so far as possible, substantive aims should be achieved procedurally, on the principle that if men are compelled to act in the right way, they will generally do the right things.

These considerations seem to have been widely ignored in the constitutions that have come into existence since World War II. Not uncommonly these constitutions incorporate a host of economic and political measures of the type one would ordinarily associate with statutory law. It is hardly likely that these measures have been written into the constitution because they represent aims that are generally shared. One suspects that the reason for their inclusion is precisely the opposite, namely, a fear that they would not be able to survive the vicissitudes of an ordinary exercise of parliamentary power. Thus, the divisions of opinion that are a normal accompaniment of lawmaking are written into the document that makes law itself possible. This is obviously a procedure that contains serious dangers for a future realization of the ideal of fidelity to law.

I have ventured these remarks on the making of constitutions not because I think they can claim any special profundity, but because I wished to illustrate what I mean by planning the conditions that will make it possible to realize the ideal of fidelity to law. Even within the limits of my modest purpose, what I have said may be clearly wrong. If so, it would not be for me to say whether I am also wrong clearly. I will, however, venture to assert that if I am wrong, I am wrong significantly. What disturbs me about the school of legal positivism is that it not only refuses to deal with problems of the sort I have just discussed, but bans them on principle from the province of legal philosophy. In its concern to assign the right labels to the things men do, this school seems to lose all interest in asking whether men are doing the right things.

IV THE MORALITY OF LAW ITSELF

Most of the issues raised by Professor Hart's essay can be restated in terms of the distinction between order and good order. Law may be said to represent order *simpliciter*. Good order is law that corresponds to the demands of justice, or morality, or men's notions of what ought to be. This rephrasing of the issue is useful in bringing to light the ambitious nature of Professor Hart's undertaking, for surely we would all agree that it is no easy thing to distinguish order from good order. When it is said, for example, that law simply represents that public order which obtains under all governments – democratic, Fascist, or Communist[12] – the order intended is certainly not that of a morgue or cemetery. We must mean a functioning order, and such an order has to be at least good enough to be considered as functioning by some standard or other. A reminder that workable order usually requires some play in the joints, and therefore cannot be too orderly, is enough to suggest some of the complexities that would be involved in any attempt to draw a sharp distinction between order and good order.

For the time being, however, let us suppose we can in fact clearly separate the concept of order from that of good order. Even in this unreal and abstract form the notion of order itself contains what may be called a moral element. Let me illustrate this "morality of order" in its crudest and most elementary form. Let us suppose an absolute monarch, whose word is the only law known to his subjects. We may further suppose him to be utterly selfish and to seek in his relations with his subjects solely his own advantage. This monarch from time to time issues commands, promising rewards for compliance and threatening punishment for disobedience. He is, however, a dissolute and forgetful fellow, who never makes the slightest attempt to ascertain who have in fact followed his directions and who have not. As a result he habitually punishes loyalty and rewards disobedience. It is apparent that this monarch will never achieve even his own selfish aims until he is ready to accept that minimum self-restraint that will create a meaningful connection between his words and his actions.

Let us now suppose that our monarch undergoes a change of heart and begins to pay some attention to what he said yesterday when, today, he has occasion to distribute bounty or to order the chopping off of heads. Under the strain of this new responsibility, however, our monarch relaxes his attention in other directions and becomes hopelessly slothful in the phrasing of his commands. His orders become so ambiguous and are uttered in so inaudible a tone that his subjects never have any clear idea what he wants them to do. Here, again, it is apparent that if our monarch for his own selfish advantage wants to create in his realm anything like a system of law he will have to pull himself together and assume still another responsibility.

Law, considered merely as order, contains, then, its own implicit morality. This morality of order must be respected if we are to create anything that can be called law, even bad law. Law by itself is powerless to bring this morality into existence. Until our monarch is really ready to face the responsibilities of his position, it will do no good for him to issue still another futile command, this time self-addressed and threatening himself with punishment if he does not mend his ways.

There is a twofold sense in which it is true that law cannot be built on law. First of all, the authority to make law must be supported by moral attitudes that accord to it the competency it claims. Here we are dealing with a morality external to law, which makes law possible. But this alone is not enough. We may stipulate that in our monarchy the accepted "basic norm" designates the monarch himself as the only possible source of law. We still cannot have law until our monarch is ready to accept the internal morality of law itself.

In the life of a nation these external and internal moralities of law reciprocally influence one another; a deterioration of the one will almost inevitably produce a deterioration in the other. So closely related are they that when the anthropologist Lowie speaks of "the generally accepted ethical postulates underlying our ... legal institutions as their ultimate sanction and guaranteeing their smooth functioning,"[13] he may be presumed to have both of them in mind.

What I have called "the internal morality of law" seems to be almost completely neglected by Professor Hart. He does make brief mention of "justice in the administration of the law," which consists in the like treatment of like cases, by whatever elevated or perverted standards the word "like" may be defined.[14] But he quickly dismisses this aspect of law as having no special relevance to his main enterprise.

In this I believe he is profoundly mistaken. It is his neglect to analyze the demands of a morality of order that leads him throughout his essay to treat law as a datum projecting itself into human experience and not as an object of human striving. When we realize that order itself is something that must be worked for, it becomes apparent that the existence of a legal system, even a bad or evil legal system, is always a matter of degree. When we recognize this simple fact of everyday legal experience, it becomes impossible to dismiss the problems presented by the Nazi regime with a simple assertion: "Under the Nazis there was law, even if it was bad law." We have instead to inquire how much of a legal system survived the general debasement and perversion of all forms of social order that occurred under the Nazi rule, and what moral implications this mutilated system had for the conscientious citizen forced to live under it.

It is not necessary, however, to dwell on such moral upheavals as the Nazi regime to see how completely incapable the positivistic philosophy is of serving the one high moral ideal it professes, that of fidelity to law. Its default in serving this ideal actually becomes most apparent, I believe, in the everyday problems that confront those who are earnestly desirous of meeting the moral demands of a legal order, but who have responsible functions to discharge in the very order toward which loyalty is due.

Let us suppose the case of a trial judge who has had an extensive experience in commercial matters and before whom a great many commercial disputes are tried. As a subordinate in a judicial hierarchy, our judge has of course the duty to follow the law laid down by his supreme court. Our imaginary Scrutton has the misfortune, however, to live under a supreme court which he considers woefully ignorant of the ways and needs of commerce. To his mind, many of this court's decisions in the field of commercial law simply do not make sense. If a conscientious judge caught in this dilemma were to turn to the positivistic philosophy what succor could he expect? It will certainly do no good to remind him that he has an obligation of fidelity to law. He is aware of this already and painfully so, since it is the source of his predicament. Nor will it help to say that if he legislates, it must be "interstitially," or that his contributions must be "confined from molar to molecular motions."[15] This mode of statement may be congenial to those who like to think of law, not as a purposive thing, but as an expression of the dimensions and directions of state power. But I cannot believe that the essentially trite idea behind this advice can be lifted by literary eloquence to the point where it will offer any real help to our judge; for one thing, it may be impossible for him to know whether his supreme court would regard any particular contribution of his as being wide or narrow.

Nor is it likely that a distinction between core and penumbra would be helpful. The predicament of our judge may well derive, not from particular precedents, but from a mistaken conception of the nature of commerce which extends over many decisions and penetrates them in varying degrees. So far as his problem arises from the use of particular words, he may well find that the supreme court often uses the ordinary terms of commerce in senses foreign to actual business dealings. If he interprets those words as a business executive or accountant would, he may well reduce the precedents he is bound to apply to a logical shambles. On the other hand, he may find great difficulty in discerning the exact sense in which the supreme court used those words, since in his mind that sense is itself the product of a confusion.

Is it not clear that it is precisely positivism's insistence on a rigid separation of law as it is from law as it ought to be that renders the positivistic philosophy incapable of aiding our judge? Is it not also clear that our judge can never achieve a satisfactory resolution of his dilemma unless he views his duty of fidelity to law in a context which also embraces his responsibility for making law what it ought to be?

The case I have supposed may seem extreme, but the problem it suggests pervades our whole legal system. If the divergence of views between our judge and his supreme court were less drastic, it would be more difficult to present his predicament graphically, but the perplexity of his position might actually increase. Perplexities of this sort are a normal accompaniment of the discharge of any adjudicative function; they perhaps reach their most poignant intensity in the field of administrative law.

One can imagine a case – surely not likely in Professor Hart's country or mine – where a judge might hold profound moral convictions that were exactly the opposite of those held, with equal attachment, by his supreme court. He might also be convinced that the precedents he was bound to apply were the direct product of a morality he considered abhorrent. If such a judge did not find the solution for his dilemma in surrendering his office, he might well be driven to a wooden and literal application of precedents which he could not otherwise apply because he was incapable of understanding the philosophy that animated them. But I doubt that a judge in this situation would need the help of legal positivism to find these melancholy escapes from his predicament. Nor do I think that such a predicament is likely to arise within a nation where both law and good law are regarded as collaborative human achievements in need of constant renewal, and where lawyers are still at least as interested in asking "What is good law?" as they are in asking "What is law?"

V THE PROBLEM OF RESTORING RESPECT FOR LAW AND JUSTICE AFTER THE COLLAPSE OF A REGIME THAT RESPECTED NEITHER

After the collapse of the Nazi regime the German courts were faced with a truly frightful predicament. It was impossible for them to declare the whole dictatorship illegal or to treat as void every decision and legal enactment that had emanated from Hitler's government. Intolerable dislocations would have resulted from any such wholesale outlawing of all that occurred over a span of twelve years. On the other hand, it was equally impossible to carry forward into the new government the effects of every Nazi perversity that had been committed in the name of law; any such course would have tainted an indefinite future with the poisons of Nazism.

This predicament – which was, indeed, a pervasive one, affecting all branches of law – came to a dramatic head in a series of cases involving informers who had taken advantage of the Nazi terror to get rid of personal enemies or unwanted spouses. If all Nazi statutes and judicial decisions were indiscriminately "law," then these despicable creatures were guiltless, since they had turned their victims over to processes which the Nazis themselves knew by the name of law. Yet it was intolerable, especially for the surviving relatives and friends of the victims, that these people should go about unpunished, while the objects of their spite were dead, or were just being released after years of imprisonment, or, more painful still, simply remained unaccounted for.

The urgency of this situation does not by any means escape Professor Hart. Indeed, he is moved to recommend an expedient that is surely not lacking itself in a certain air of desperation. He suggests that a retroactive criminal statute would have been the least objectionable solution to the problem. This statute would have punished the informer, and branded him as a criminal, for an act which Professor Hart regards as having been perfectly legal when he committed it.[16]

On the other hand, Professor Hart condemns without qualification those judicial decisions in which the courts themselves undertook to declare void certain of the Nazi statutes under which the informer's victims had been convicted. One cannot help raising at this point the question whether the issue as presented by Professor Hart himself is truly that of fidelity to law. Surely it would be a necessary implication of a retroactive criminal statute against informers that, for purposes of that statute at least, the Nazi laws as applied to the informers or their victims were to be regarded as void. With this turn the question seems no longer to be whether what was once law can now be declared not to have been law, but rather who should do the dirty work, the courts or the legislature.

But, as Professor Hart himself suggests, the issues at stake are much too serious to risk losing them in a semantic tangle. Even if the whole question were one of words, we should remind ourselves that we are in an area where words have a powerful effect on human attitudes. I should like, therefore, to undertake a defense of the German courts, and to advance reasons why, in my opinion, their decisions do not represent the abandonment of legal principle that Professor Hart sees in them. In order to understand the background of those decisions we shall have to move a little closer within smelling distance of the witches' caldron than we have been brought so far by Professor Hart. We shall have also to consider an aspect of the problem ignored in his essay, namely, the degree to which the Nazis observed what I have called the inner morality of law itself.

Throughout his discussion Professor Hart seems to assume that the only difference between Nazi law and, say, English law is that the Nazis used their laws to achieve ends that are odious to an Englishman. This assumption is, I think, seriously mistaken, and Professor Hart's acceptance of it seems to me to render his discussion unresponsive to the problem it purports to address.

Throughout their period of control the Nazis took generous advantage of a device not wholly unknown to American legislatures, the retroactive statute curing past legal irregularities. The most dramatic use of the curative powers of such a statute occurred on July 3, 1934, after the "Roehm purge." When this intraparty shooting affair was over and more than seventy Nazis had been – one can hardly avoid saying – "rubbed out," Hitler returned to Berlin and procured from his cabinet a law ratifying and confirming the measures taken between June 30, and July 1, 1934, without mentioning the names of those who were now considered to have been lawfully executed.[17] Some time later Hitler declared that during the Roehm purge "the supreme court of the German people ... consisted of myself,"[18] surely not an overstatement of the capacity in which he acted if one takes seriously the enactment conferring retroactive legality on "the measures taken."

Now in England and America it would never occur to anyone to say that "it is in the nature of law that it cannot be retroactive," although, of course, constitutional inhibitions may prohibit certain kinds of retroactivity. We would say it is normal for a law to operate prospectively, and that it may be arguable that it ought never operate otherwise, but there would be a certain occult unpersuasiveness in any assertion that retroactivity violates the very nature of law itself. Yet we have only to imagine a country in which *all* laws are retroactive in order to see that retroactivity presents a real problem for the internal morality of law. If we suppose an absolute monarch who allows his realm to exist in a constant state of anarchy, we would hardly say that he could create a regime of law simply by enacting a curative statute conferring legality on everything that had happened up to its date and by announcing an intention to enact similar statutes every six months in the future.

A general increase in the resort to statutes curative of past legal irregularities represents a deterioration in that form of legal morality without which law itself cannot exist. The threat of such statutes hangs over the whole legal system, and robs every law on the books of some of its significance. And surely a general threat of this sort is implied when a government is willing to use such a statute to transform into lawful execution what was simple murder when it happened.

During the Nazi regime there were repeated rumors of "secret laws." In the article criticized by Professor Hart, Radbruch mentions a report that the wholesale killings in concentration camps were made "lawful" by a secret enactment.[19] Now surely there can be no greater legal monstrosity than a secret statute. Would anyone seriously recommend that following the war the German courts should have searched for unpublished laws among the files left by Hitler's government so that citizens' rights could be determined by a reference to these laws?

The extent of the legislator's obligation to make his laws known to his subjects is, of course, a problem of legal morality that has been under active discussion at least since the Secession of the Plebs. There is probably no modern state that has not been plagued by this problem in one form or another. It is most likely to arise in modern societies with respect to unpublished administrative directions. Often these are regarded in quite good faith by those who issue them as affecting only matters of internal organization. But since the procedures followed by an administrative agency, even in its "internal" actions, may seriously affect the rights and interests of the citizen, these unpublished, or "secret," regulations are often a subject for complaint.

But as with retroactivity, what in most societies is kept under control by the tacit restraints of legal decency broke out in monstrous form under Hitler. Indeed, so loose was the whole Nazi morality of law that it is not easy to know just what should be regarded as an unpublished or secret law. Since unpublished instructions to those administering the law could destroy the letter of any published law by imposing on it an outrageous interpretation, there was a sense in which the meaning of every law was "secret." Even a verbal order from Hitler that a thousand prisoners in concentration camps be put to death was at once an administrative direction and a validation of everything done under it as being "lawful."

But the most important affronts to the morality of law by Hitler's government took no such subtle forms as those exemplified in the bizarre outcroppings I have just discussed. In the first place, when legal forms became inconvenient, it was always possible for the Nazis to bypass them entirely and "to act through the party in the streets." There was no one who dared bring them to account for whatever outrages might thus be committed. In the second place, the Nazi-dominated courts were always ready to disregard any statute, even those enacted by the Nazis themselves, if this suited their convenience or if they feared that a lawyer-like interpretation might incur displeasure "above."

This complete willingness of the Nazis to disregard even their own enactments was an important factor leading Radbruch to take the position he did in the articles so severely criticized by Professor Hart. I do not believe that any fair appraisal of the action of the postwar

German courts is possible unless we take this factor into account, as Professor Hart fails completely to do.

These remarks may seem inconclusive in their generality and to rest more on assertion than evidentiary fact. Let us turn at once, then, to the actual case discussed by Professor Hart.[20]

In 1944 a German soldier paid a short visit to his wife while under travel orders on a reassignment. During the single day he was home, he conveyed privately to his wife something of his opinion of the Hitler government. He expressed disapproval of (*sich abfällig geäussert über*) Hitler and other leading personalities of the Nazi party. He also said it was too bad Hitler had not met his end in the assassination attempt that had occurred on July 20th of that year. Shortly after his departure, his wife, who during his long absence on military duty "had turned to other men" and who wished to get rid of him, reported his remarks to the local leader of the Nazi party, observing that "a man who would say a thing like that does not deserve to live." The result was a trial of the husband by a military tribunal and a sentence of death. After a short period of imprisonment, instead of being executed, he was sent to the front again. After the collapse of the Nazi regime, the wife was brought to trial for having procured the imprisonment of her husband. Her defense rested on the ground that her husband's statements to her about Hitler and the Nazis constituted a crime under the laws then in force. Accordingly, when she informed on her husband she was simply bringing a criminal to justice.

This defense rested on two statutes, one passed in 1934, the other in 1938. Let us first consider the second of these enactments, which was part of a more comprehensive legislation creating a whole series of special wartime criminal offenses. I reproduce below a translation of the only pertinent section:

The following persons are guilty of destroying the national power of resistance and shall be punished by death: Whoever publicly solicits or incites a refusal to fulfill the obligations of service in the armed forces of Germany, or in armed forces allied with Germany, or who otherwise publicly seeks to injure or destroy the will of the German people or an allied people to assert themselves stalwartly against their enemies.[21]

It is almost inconceivable that a court of present-day Germany would hold the husband's remarks to his wife, who was barred from military duty by her sex, to be a violation of the final catchall provision of this statute, particularly when it is recalled that the text reproduced above was part of a more comprehensive enactment dealing with such things as harboring deserters, escaping military duty by self-inflicted injuries, and the like. The question arises, then, as to the extent to which the interpretive principles applied by the courts of Hitler's government should be accepted in determining whether the husband's remarks were indeed unlawful.

This question becomes acute when we note that the act applies only to *public* acts or utterances, whereas the husband's remarks were in the privacy of his own home. Now it appears that the Nazi courts (and it should be noted we are dealing with a special military court) quite generally disregarded this limitation and extended the act to all utterances, private or public.[22] Is Professor Hart prepared to say that the legal meaning of this statute is to be determined in the light of this apparently uniform principle of judicial interpretation?

Let us turn now to the other statute upon which Professor Hart relies in assuming that the husband's utterance was unlawful. This is the act of 1934, the relevant portions of which are translated below:

(1) Whoever publicly makes spiteful or provocative statements directed against, or statements which disclose a base disposition toward, the leading personalities of the nation or of the National Socialist German Workers' Party, or toward measures taken or institutions established by them, and of such a nature as to undermine the people's confidence in their political leadership, shall be punished by imprisonment.

(2) Malicious utterances not made in public shall be treated in the same manner as public utterances when the person making them realized or should have realized they would reach the public.

(3) Prosecution for such utterances shall be only on the order of the National Minister of Justice; in case the utterance was directed against a leading personality of the National Socialist German Workers' Party, the Minister of Justice shall order prosecution only with the advice and consent of the Representative of the Leader.

(4) The National Minister of Justice shall, with the advice and consent of the Representative of the Leader, determine who shall belong to the class of leading personalities for purposes of Section I above.[23]

Extended comment on this legislative monstrosity is scarcely called for, overlarded and undermined as it is by uncontrolled administrative discretion. We may note only: first, that it offers no justification whatever for the death penalty actually imposed on the husband, though never carried out; second, that if the wife's act in informing on her husband made his remarks "public," there is no such thing as a private utterance under this statute. I should like to ask the reader whether he can actually share Professor Hart's indignation that, in the perplexities of the postwar reconstruction, the German courts saw fit to declare this thing not a law. Can it be argued seriously that it would have been more beseeming to the judicial process if the postwar courts had undertaken a study of "the interpretative principles" in force during Hitler's rule and had then solemnly applied those "principles" to ascertain the meaning of this statute? On the other hand, would the courts really have been showing respect for Nazi law if they had construed the Nazi statutes by their own, quite different, standards of interpretation?

Professor Hart castigates the German courts and Radbruch, not so much for what they believed had to be done, but because they failed to see that they were confronted by a moral dilemma of a sort that would have been immediately apparent to Bentham and Austin. By the simple dodge of saying, "When a statute is sufficiently evil it ceases to be law," they ran away from the problem they should have faced.

This criticism is, I believe, without justification. So far as the courts are concerned, matters certainly would not have been helped if, instead of saying, "This is not law," they had said, "This is law but it is so evil we will refuse to apply it." Surely moral confusion reaches its height when a court refuses to apply something it admits to be law, and Professor Hart does not recommend any such "facing of the true issue" by the courts themselves. He would have preferred a retroactive statute. Curiously, this was also the preference of Radbruch.[24] But unlike Professor Hart, the German courts and Gustav Radbruch were living participants in a situation of drastic emergency. The informer problem was a pressing one, and if legal institutions were to be rehabilitated in Germany it would not do to allow the people to begin taking the law into their own hands, as might have occurred while the courts were waiting for a statute.

As for Gustav Radbruch, it is, I believe, wholly unjust to say that he did not know he was faced with a moral dilemma. His postwar writings repeatedly stress the antinomies confronted in the effort to rebuild decent and orderly government in Germany. As for the ideal of fidelity to law, I shall let Radbruch's own words state his position:

We must not conceal from ourselves – especially not in the light of our experiences during the twelve-year dictatorship – what frightful dangers for the rule of law can be contained in the notion of "statutory lawlessness" and in refusing the quality of law to duly enacted statutes.[25]

The situation is not that legal positivism enables a man to know when he faces a difficult problem of choice, while Radbruch's beliefs deceive him into thinking there is no problem to face. The real issue dividing Professors Hart and Radbruch is: How shall we state the problem? What is the nature of the dilemma in which we are caught?

I hope I am not being unjust to Professor Hart when I say that I can find no way of describing the dilemma as he sees it but to use some such words as the following: On the one hand, we have an amoral datum called law, which has the peculiar quality of creating a moral duty to obey it. On the other hand, we have a moral duty to do what we think is right and decent. When we are confronted by a statute we believe to be thoroughly evil, we have to choose between those two duties.

If this is the positivist position, then I have no hesitancy in rejecting it. The "dilemma" it states has the verbal formulation of a problem, but the problem it states makes no sense. It is like saying I have to choose between giving food to a starving man and being mimsy with the borogoves. I do not think it is unfair to the positivistic philosophy to say that it never gives any coherent meaning to the moral obligation of fidelity to law. This obligation seems to be conceived as sui generis, wholly unrelated to any of the ordinary, extralegal ends of human life. The fundamental postulate of positivism – that law must be strictly severed from morality – seems to deny the possibility of any bridge between the obligation to obey law and other moral obligations. No mediating principle can measure their respective demands on conscience, for they exist in wholly separate worlds.

While I would not subscribe to all of Radbruch's postwar views – especially those relating to "higher law" – I think he saw, much more clearly than does Professor Hart, the true nature of the dilemma confronted by Germany in seeking to rebuild her shattered legal institutions. Germany had to restore both respect for law and respect for justice. Though neither of these could be restored without the other, painful antinomies were encountered in attempting to restore both at once, as Radbruch saw all too clearly. Essentially Radbruch saw the dilemma as that of meeting the demands of order, on the one hand, and those of good order, on the other. Of course no pat formula can be derived from this phrasing of the problem. But, unlike legal positivism, it does not present us with opposing demands that have no living contact with one another, that simply shout their contradictions across a vacuum. As we seek order, we can meaningfully remind ourselves that order itself will do us no good unless it is good for something. As we seek to make our order good, we can remind ourselves that justice itself is impossible without order, and that we must not lose order itself in the attempt to make it good.

VI THE MORAL IMPLICATIONS OF LEGAL POSITIVISM

We now reach the question whether there is any ground for Gustav Radbruch's belief that a general acceptance of the positivistic philosophy in pre-Nazi Germany made smoother the route to dictatorship. Understandably, Professor Hart regards this as the most outrageous of all charges against positivism.

Here indeed we enter upon a hazardous area of controversy, where ugly words and ugly charges have become commonplace. During the last half century in this country no issue of legal philosophy has caused more spilling of ink and adrenalin than the assertion that there are "totalitarian" implications in the views of Oliver Wendell Holmes, Jr. Even the most cautiously phrased criticisms of that grand old figure from the age of Darwin, Huxley, and Haeckel seem to stir the reader's mind with the memory of past acerbities.[26] It does no good to suggest that perhaps Holmes did not perceive all the implications of his own philosophy, for this is merely to substitute one insult for another. Nor does it help much to recall the dictum of one of the closest companions of Holmes' youth – surely no imperceptive observer – that Holmes was "composed of at least two and a half different people rolled into one, and the way he keeps them together in one tight skin, without quarreling any more than they do, is remarkable."[27]

In venturing upon these roughest of all jurisprudential waters, one is not reassured to see even so moderate a man as Professor Hart indulging in some pretty broad strokes of the oar. Radbruch disclosed "an extraordinary naïveté" in assessing the temper of his own profession in Germany and in supposing that its adherence to positivism helped the Nazis to power.[28] His judgment on this and other matters shows that he had "only half digested the spiritual message of liberalism" he mistakenly thought he was conveying to his countrymen.[29] A state of "hysteria"[30] is revealed by those who see a wholesome reorientation of German legal thinking in such judicial decisions as were rendered in the informer cases.

Let us put aside at least the blunter tools of invective and address ourselves as calmly as we can to the question whether legal positivism, as practiced and preached in Germany, had, or could have had, any causal connection with Hitler's ascent to power. It should be recalled that in the seventy-five years before the Nazi regime the positivistic philosophy had achieved in Germany a standing such as it enjoyed in no other country. Austin praised a German scholar for bringing international law within the clarity-producing restraints of positivism.[31] Gray reported with pleasure that the "abler" German jurists of his time were "abjuring all *nicht positivisches Recht,*'" and cited Bergbohm as an example.[32] This is an illuminating example, for Bergbohm was a scholar whose ambition was to make German positivism live up to its own pretensions. He was distressed to encounter vestigial traces of natural-law thinking in writings claiming to be positivistic. In particular, he was disturbed by the frequent recurrence of such notions as that law owes its efficacy to a perceived moral need for order, or that it is in the nature of man that he requires a legal order, etc. Bergbohm announced a program, never realized, to drive from positivistic thinking these last miasmas from the swamp of natural law.[33] German jurists generally tended to regard the Anglo-American common law as a messy and unprincipled conglomerate of law and morals.[34] Positivism was the only theory of law that could claim to be "scientific" in an Age of Science. Dissenters from this view were characterized by positivists with that epithet modern man fears above all others: "naïve." The result was that it could be reported by 1927 that "to be found guilty of adherence to natural law theories is a kind of social disgrace."[35]

To this background we must add the observation that the Germans seem never to have achieved that curious ability possessed by the British, and to some extent by the Americans, of holding their logic on short leash. When a German defines law, he means his definition to be taken seriously. If a German writer had hit upon the slogan of American legal realism, "Law is simply the behavior patterns of judges and other state officials," he would not have regarded this as an interesting little conversation-starter. He would have believed it and acted on it.

German legal positivism not only banned from legal science any consideration of the moral ends of law, but it was also indifferent to what I have called the inner morality of law itself. The German lawyer was therefore peculiarly prepared to accept as "law" anything that called itself by that name, was printed at government expense, and seemed to come "*von oben herab.*"

In the light of these considerations I cannot see either absurdity or perversity in the suggestion that the attitudes prevailing in the German legal profession were helpful to the Nazis. Hitler did not come to power by a violent revolution. He was Chancellor before he became the Leader. The exploitation of legal forms started cautiously and became bolder as power was consolidated. The first attacks on the established order were on ramparts which, if they were manned by anyone, were manned by lawyers and judges. These ramparts fell almost without a struggle.

Professor Hart and others have been understandably distressed by references to a "higher law" in some of the decisions concerning informers and in Radbruch's postwar writings. I suggest that if German jurisprudence had concerned itself more with the inner morality of law, it would not have been necessary to invoke any notion of this sort in declaring void the more outrageous Nazi statutes.

To me there is nothing shocking in saying that a dictatorship which clothes itself with a tinsel of legal form can so far depart from the morality of order, from the inner morality of law itself, that it ceases to be a legal system. When a system calling itself law is predicated upon a general disregard by judges of the terms of the laws they purport to enforce, when this system habitually cures its legal irregularities, even the grossest, by retroactive statutes, when it has only to resort to forays of terror in the streets, which no one dares challenge, in order to escape even those scant restraints imposed by the pretence of legality – when all these things have become true of a dictatorship, it is not hard for me, at least, to deny to it the name of law.

I believe that the invalidity of the statutes involved in the informer cases could have been grounded on considerations such as I have just outlined. But if you were raised with a generation that said "law is law" and meant it, you may feel the only way you can escape one law is to set another off against it, and this perforce must be a "higher law." Hence these notions of "higher law," which are a justifiable cause for alarm, may themselves be a belated fruit of German legal positivism.

It should be remarked at this point that it is chiefly in Roman Catholic writings that the theory of natural law is considered, not simply as a search for those principles that will enable men to live together successfully, but as a quest for something that can be called "a higher law." This identification of natural law with a law that is above human laws seems in fact to be demanded by any doctrine that asserts the possibility of an authoritative pronouncement of the demands of natural law. In those areas affected by such pronouncements as have so far been issued, the conflict between Roman Catholic doctrine and opposing views seems to me to be a conflict between two forms of positivism. Fortunately, over most of the area with which lawyers are concerned, no such pronouncements exist. In these areas I think those of us who are not adherents of its faith can be grateful to the Catholic Church for having kept alive the rationalistic tradition in ethics.

I do not assert that the solution I have suggested for the informer cases would not have entailed its own difficulties, particularly the familiar one of knowing where to stop. But I think it demonstrable that the most serious deterioration in legal morality under Hitler took place in branches of the law like those involved in the informer cases; no comparable deterioration was to be observed in the ordinary branches of private law. It was in those areas where the ends of law were most odious by ordinary standards of decency that the morality of law itself was most flagrantly disregarded. In other words, where one would have been most tempted to say, "This is so evil it cannot be a law," one could usually have said instead, "This thing is the product of a system so oblivious to the morality of law, that it is not entitled to be called a law." I think there is something more than accident here, for the overlapping suggests that legal morality cannot live when it is severed from a striving toward justice and decency.

But as an actual solution for the informer cases, I, like Professors Hart and Radbruch, would have preferred a retroactive statute. My reason for this preference is not that this is the most nearly lawful way of making unlawful what was once law. Rather I would see such a statute as a way of symbolizing a sharp break with the past, as a means of isolating a kind of cleanup operation from the normal functioning of the judicial process. By this isolation it would become possible for the judiciary to return more rapidly to a condition in which the demands of legal morality could be given proper respect. In other words, it would make it possible to plan more effectively to regain for the ideal of fidelity to law its normal meaning.

VII THE PROBLEM OF INTERPRETATION: THE CORE AND THE PENUMBRA

It is essential that we be just as clear as we can be about the meaning of Professor Hart's doctrine of "the core and the penumbra,"[36] because I believe the casual reader is likely to misinterpret what he has to say. Such a reader is apt to suppose that Professor Hart is merely describing something that is a matter of everyday experience for the lawyer, namely, that in the interpretation of legal rules it is typically the case (though not universally so) that there are some situations which will seem to fall rather clearly within the rule, while others will be more doubtful. Professor Hart's thesis takes no such jejune form. His extended discussion of the core and the penumbra is not just a complicated way of recognizing that some cases are hard, while others are easy. Instead, on the basis of a theory about language meaning generally, he is proposing a theory of judicial interpretation which is, I believe, wholly novel. Certainly it has never been put forward in so uncompromising a form before.

As I understand Professor Hart's thesis (if we add some tacit assumptions implied by it, as well as some qualifications he would no doubt wish his readers to supply) a full statement would run something as follows: The task of interpretation is commonly that of determining the meaning of the individual words of a legal rule, like "vehicle" in a rule excluding vehicles from a park. More particularly, the task of interpretation is to determine the range of reference of such a word, or the aggregate of things to which it points. Communication is possible only because words have a "standard instance," or a "core of meaning" that remains relatively constant, whatever the context in which the word may appear. Except in unusual circumstances, it will always be proper to regard a word like "vehicle" as embracing its "standard instance," that is, that aggregate of things it would include in all ordinary contexts, within or without the law. This meaning the word will have in any legal rule, whatever its purpose. In applying the word to its "standard instance," no creative role is assumed by the judge. He is simply applying the law "as it is."

In addition to a constant core, however, words also have a penumbra of meaning which, unlike the core, will vary from context to context. When the object in question (say, a tricycle) falls within this penumbral area, the judge is forced to assume a more creative role. He must now undertake, for the first time, an interpretation of the rule in the light of its purpose or aim. Having in mind what was sought by the regulation concerning parks, ought it to be considered as barring tricycles? When questions of this sort are decided there is at least an "intersection" of "is" and "ought," since the judge, in deciding what the rule "is," does so in the light of his notions of what "it ought to be" in order to carry out its purpose.

If I have properly interpreted Professor Hart's theory as it affects the "hard core," then I think it is quite untenable. The most obvious defect of his theory lies in its assumption that problems of interpretation typically turn on the meaning of individual words. Surely no judge applying a rule of the common law ever followed any such procedure as that described (and, I take it, prescribed) by Professor Hart; indeed, we do not normally even think of his problem as being one of "interpretation." Even in the case of statutes, we commonly have to assign meaning, not to a single word, but to a sentence, a paragraph, or a whole page or more of text. Surely a paragraph does not have a "standard instance" that remains constant whatever the context in which it appears. If a statute seems to have a kind of "core meaning" that we can apply without a too precise inquiry into its exact purpose, this is because we can see that, however one might formulate the precise objective of the statute, *this* case would still come within it.

Even in situations where our interpretive difficulties seem to head up in a single word, Professor Hart's analysis seems to me to give no real account of what does or should happen. In his illustration of the "vehicle," although he tells us this word has a core of meaning that in all contexts defines unequivocally a range of objects embraced by it, he never tells us what these objects might be. If the rule excluding vehicles from parks seems easy to apply in some cases, I submit this is because we can see clearly enough what the rule "is aiming at in general" so that we know there is no need to worry about the difference between Fords and Cadillacs. If in some cases we seem to be able to apply the rule without asking what its purpose is, this is not because we can treat a directive arrangement as if it had no purpose. It is rather because, for example, whether the rule be intended to preserve quiet in the park, or to save carefree strollers from injury, we know, "without thinking," that a noisy automobile must be excluded.

What would Professor Hart say if some local patriots wanted to mount on a pedestal in the park a truck used in World War II, while other citizens, regarding the proposed memorial as an eyesore, support their stand by the "no vehicle" rule? Does this truck, in perfect working order, fall within the core or the penumbra?

Professor Hart seems to assert that unless words have "standard instances" that remain constant regardless of context, effective communication would break down and it would become impossible to construct a system of "rules which have authority."[37] If in every context words took on a unique meaning, peculiar to that context, the whole process of interpretation would become so uncertain and subjective that the ideal of a rule of law would lose its meaning. In other words, Professor Hart seems to be saying that unless we are prepared to accept his analysis of interpretation, we must surrender all hope of giving an effective meaning to the ideal of fidelity to law. This presents a very dark prospect indeed, if one believes, as I do, that we cannot accept his theory of interpretation. I do not take so gloomy a view of the future of the ideal of fidelity to law.

An illustration will help to test, not only Professor Hart's theory of the core and the penumbra, but its relevance to the ideal of fidelity to law as well. Let us suppose that in leafing through the statutes, we come upon the following enactment: "It shall be a misdemeanor, punishable by a fine of five dollars, to sleep in any railway station." We have no trouble in perceiving the general nature of the target toward which this statute is aimed. Indeed, we are likely at once to call to mind the picture of a disheveled tramp, spread out in an ungainly fashion on one of the benches of the station, keeping weary passengers on their feet and filling their ears with raucous and alcoholic snores. This vision may fairly be said to represent the "obvious instance" contemplated by the statute, though certainly it is far from being the "standard instance" of the physiological state called "sleep."

Now let us see how this example bears on the ideal of fidelity to law. Suppose I am a judge, and that two men are brought before me for violating this statute. The first is a passenger who was waiting at 3 A.M. for a delayed train. When he was arrested he was sitting upright in an orderly fashion, but was heard by the arresting officer to be gently snoring. The second is a man who had brought a blanket and pillow to the station and had obviously settled himself down for the night. He was arrested, however, before he had a chance to go to sleep. Which of these cases presents the "standard instance" of the word "sleep"? If I disregard that question, and decide to fine the second man and set free the first, have I violated a duty of fidelity to law? Have I violated that duty if I interpret the word "sleep" as used in this statute to mean something like "to spread oneself out on a bench or floor to spend the night, or as if to spend the night"?

Testing another aspect of Professor Hart's theory, is it really ever possible to interpret a word in a statute without knowing the aim of the statute? Suppose we encounter the following incomplete sentence: "All improvements must be promptly reported to ..." Professor Hart's theory seems to assert that even if we have only this fragment before us we can safely construe the word "improvement" to apply to its "standard instance," though we would have to know the rest of the sentence before we could deal intelligently with "problems of the penumbra." Yet surely in the truncated sentence I have quoted, the word "improvement" is almost as devoid of meaning as the symbol "X."

The word "improvement" will immediately take on meaning if we fill out the sentence with the words, ,"the head nurse," or, "the Town Planning Authority," though the two meanings that come to mind are radically dissimilar. It can hardly be said that these two meanings represent some kind of penumbral accretion to the word's "standard instance." And one wonders, parenthetically, how helpful the theory of the core and the penumbra would be in deciding whether, when the report is to be made to the planning authorities, the word "improvement" includes an unmortgageable monstrosity of a house that lowers the market value of the land on which it is built.

It will be instructive, I think, to consider the effect of other ways of filling out the sentence. Suppose we add to, "All improvements must be promptly reported to ..." the words, "the Dean of the Graduate Division." Here we no longer seem, as we once did, to be groping in the dark; rather, we seem now to be reaching into an empty box. We achieve a little better orientation if the final clause reads, "to the Principal of the School," and we feel completely at ease if it becomes, "to the Chairman of the Committee on Relations with the Parents of Children in the Primary Division."

It should be noted that in deciding what the word "improvement" means in all these cases, we do not proceed simply by placing the word in some general context, such as hospital practice, town planning, or education. If this were so, the "improvement" in the last instance might just as well be that of the teacher as that of the pupil. Rather, we ask ourselves, What can this rule be for? What evil does it seek to avert? What good is it intended to promote? When it is "the head nurse" who receives the report, we are apt to find ourselves asking, "Is there, perhaps, a shortage of hospital space, so that patients who improve sufficiently are sent home or are assigned to a ward where they will receive less attention?" If "Principal" offers more orientation than "Dean of the Graduate Division," this must be because we know something about the differences between primary education and education on the postgraduate university level. We must have some minimum acquaintance with the ways in which these two educational enterprises are conducted, and with the problems encountered in both of them, before any distinction between "Principal" and "Dean of the Graduate Division" would affect our interpretation of "improvement." We must, in other words, be sufficiently capable of putting ourselves in the position of those who drafted the rule to know what they thought "ought to be." It is in the light of this "ought" that we must decide what the rule "is."

Turning now to the phenomenon Professor Hart calls "preoccupation with the penumbra," we have to ask ourselves what is actually contributed to the process of interpretation by the common practice of supposing various "borderline" situations. Professor Hart seems to say, "Why, nothing at all, unless we are working with problems of the penumbra." If this is what he means, I find his view a puzzling one, for it still leaves unexplained why, under his theory, if one is dealing with a penumbral problem, it could be useful to think about other penumbral problems.

Throughout his whole discussion of interpretation, Professor Hart seems to assume that it is a kind of cataloguing procedure. A judge faced with a novel situation is like a library clerk who has to decide where to shelve a new book. There are easy cases: the *Bible* belongs under Religion, *The Wealth of Nations* under Economics, etc. Then there are hard cases, when the librarian has to exercise a kind of creative choice, as in deciding whether *Das Kapital* belongs under Politics or Economics, *Gulliver's Travels* under Fantasy or Philosophy. But whether the decision where to shelve is easy or hard, once it is made all the librarian has to do is to put the book away. And so it is with judges, Professor Hart seems to say, in all essential particulars. Surely the judicial process is something more than a cataloguing procedure. The judge does not discharge his responsibility when he pins an apt diagnostic label on the case. He has to do something about it, to treat it, if you will. It is this larger responsibility which explains why interpretative problems almost never turn on a single word, and also why lawyers for generations have found the putting of imaginary borderline cases useful, not only "on the penumbra," but in order to know where the penumbra begins.

These points can be made clear, I believe, by drawing again on our example of the statutory fragment which reads, "All improvements must be promptly reported to ..." Whatever the concluding phrase may be, the judge has not solved his problems simply by deciding what kind of improvement is meant. Almost all of the words in the sentence may require interpretation, but most obviously this is so of "promptly" and "reported." What kind of "report" is contemplated: a written note, a call at the office, entry in a hospital record? How specific must it be? Will it be enough to say "a lot better," or "a big house with a bay window"?

Now it should be apparent to any lawyer that in interpreting words like "improvement," "prompt," and "report," no real help is obtained by asking how some extralegal "standard instance" would define these words. But, much more important, when these words are all parts of a single structure of thought, they are in interaction with one another during the process of interpretation. "What is an `improvement'? Well, it must be something that can be made the subject of a report. So, for purposes of this statute `improvement' really means `reportable improvement.' What kind of `report' must be made? Well, that depends upon the sort of `improvement' about which information is desired and the reasons for desiring the information."

When we look beyond individual words to the statute as a whole, it becomes apparent how the putting of hypothetical cases assists the interpretative process generally. By pulling our minds first in one direction, then in another, these cases help us to understand the fabric of thought before us. This fabric is something we seek to discern, so that we may know truly what it is, but it is also something that we inevitably help to create as we strive (in accordance with our obligation of fidelity to law) to make the statute a coherent, workable whole.

I should have considered all these remarks much too trite to put down here if they did not seem to be demanded in an answer to the theory of interpretation proposed by Professor Hart, a theory by which he puts such store that he implies we cannot have fidelity to law in any meaningful sense unless we are prepared to accept it. Can it be possible that the positivistic philosophy demands that we abandon a view of interpretation which sees as its central concern, not words, but purpose and structure? If so, then the stakes in this battle of schools are indeed high.

I am puzzled by the novelty Professor Hart attributes to the lessons I once tried to draw from Wittgenstein's example about teaching a game to children.[38] I was simply trying to show the role reflection plays in deciding what ought to be done. I was trying to make such simple points as that decisions about what ought to be done are improved by reflection, by an exchange of views with others sharing the same problems, and by imagining various situations that might be presented. I was assuming that all of these innocent and familiar measures might serve to sharpen our perception of what we were trying to do, and that the product of the whole process might be, not merely a more apt choice of means for the end sought, but a clarification of the end itself. I had thought that a famous judge of the English bench had something like this in mind when he spoke of the common law as working "itself pure."[39] If this view of the judicial process is no longer entertained in the country of its origin, I can only say that, whatever the vicissitudes of

Lord Mansfield's British reputation may be, he will always remain for us in this country a heroic figure of jurisprudence.

I have stressed here the deficiencies of Professor Hart's theory as that theory affects judicial interpretation. I believe, however, that its defects go deeper and result ultimately from a mistaken theory about the meaning of language generally. Professor Hart seems to subscribe to what may be called "the pointer theory of meaning,"[40] a theory which ignores or minimizes the effect on the meaning of words of the speaker's purpose and the structure of language. Characteristically, this school of thought embraces the notion of "common usage." The reason is, of course, that it is only with the aid of this notion that it can seem to attain the inert datum of meaning it seeks, a meaning isolated from the effects of purpose and structure.

It would not do to attempt here an extended excursus into linguistic theory. I shall have to content myself with remarking that the theory of meaning implied in Professor Hart's essay seems to me to have been rejected by three men who stand at the very head of modern developments in logical analysis: Wittgenstein, Russell, and Whitehead. Wittgenstein's posthumous *Philosophical Investigations* constitutes a sort of running commentary on the way words shift and transform their meanings as they move from context to context. Russell repudiates the cult of "common usage," and asks what "instance" of the word "word" itself can be given that does not imply some specific intention in the use of it.[41] Whitehead explains the appeal that "the deceptive identity of the repeated word" has for modern philosophers; only by assuming some linguistic constant (such as the "core of meaning") can validity be claimed for procedures of logic which of necessity move the word from one context to another.[42]

VIII THE MORAL AND EMOTIONAL FOUNDATIONS OF POSITIVISM

If we ignore the specific theories of law associated with the positivistic philosophy, I believe we can say that the dominant tone of positivism is set by a fear of a purposive interpretation of law and legal institutions, or at least by a fear that such an interpretation may be pushed too far. I think one can find confirmatory traces of this fear in all of those classified as "positivists" by Professor Hart, with the outstanding exception of Bentham, who is in all things a case apart and who was worlds removed from anything that could be called *ethical* positivism.

Now the belief that many of us hold, that this fear of purpose takes a morbid turn in positivism, should not mislead us into thinking that the fear is wholly without justification, or that it reflects no significant problem in the organization of society.

Fidelity to law *can* become impossible if we do not accept the broader responsibilities (themselves purposive, as all responsibilities are and must be) that go with a purposive interpretation of law. One can imagine a course of reasoning that might run as follows: This statute says absinthe shall not be sold. What is its purpose? To promote health. Now, as everyone knows, absinthe is a sound, wholesome, and beneficial beverage. Therefore, interpreting the statute in the light of its purpose, I construe it to direct a general sale and consumption of that most healthful of beverages, absinthe.

If the risk of this sort of thing is implicit in a purposive interpretation, what measures can we take to eliminate it, or to reduce it to bearable proportions? One is tempted to say, "Why, just use ordinary common sense." But this would be an evasion, and would amount to saying that although we know the answer, we cannot say what it is. To give a better answer, I fear I shall have to depart from those high standards of clarity Professor Hart so rightly prizes and so generally exemplifies. I shall have to say that the answer lies in the concept of *structure*. A statute or a rule of common law has, either explicitly, or by virtue of its relation with other rules, something that may be called a structural integrity. This is what we have in mind when we speak of "the intent of the statute," though we know it is men who have intentions and not words on paper. Within the limits of that structure, fidelity to law not only permits but demands a creative role from the judge, but beyond that structure it does not permit him to go. Of course, the structure of which I speak presents its own "problems of the penumbra." But the penumbra in this case surrounds something real, something that has a meaning and integrity of its own. It is not a purposeless collocation of words that gets its meaning on loan from lay usage.

It is one of the great virtues of Professor Hart's essay that it makes explicit positivism's concern for the ideal of fidelity to law. Yet I believe, though I cannot prove, that the basic reason why positivism fears a purposive interpretation is not that it may lead to anarchy, but that it may push us too far in the opposite direction. It sees in a purposive interpretation, carried too far, a threat to human freedom and human dignity.

Let me illustrate what I mean by supposing that I am a man without religious beliefs living in a community of ardent Protestant Christian faith. A statute in this community makes it unlawful for me to play golf on Sunday. I find this statute an annoyance and accept its restraints reluctantly. But the annoyance I feel is not greatly different from that I might experience if, though it were lawful to play on Sunday, a power failure prevented me from taking the streetcar I would normally use in reaching the course. In the vernacular, "it is just one of those things."

What a different complexion the whole matter assumes if a statute compels me to attend church, or, worse still, to kneel and recite prayers! Here I may feel a direct affront to my integrity as a human being. Yet the purpose of both statutes may well be to increase church attendance. The difference may even seem to be that the first statute seeks its end slyly and by indirection, the second, honestly and openly. Yet surely this is a case in which indirection has its virtues and honesty its heavy price in human dignity.

Now I believe that positivism fears that a too explicit and uninhibited interpretation in terms of purpose may well push the first kind of statute in the direction of the second. If this is a basic concern underlying the positivistic philosophy, that philosophy is dealing with a real problem, however inept its response to the problem may seem to be. For this problem of the impressed purpose is a crucial one in our society. One thinks of the obligation to bargain "in good faith" imposed by the National Labor Relations Act.[43] One recalls the remark that to punish a criminal is less of an affront to his dignity than to reform and improve him. The statutory preamble comes to mind: the increasing use made of it, its legislative wisdom, the significance that should be accorded to it in judicial interpretation. The flag salute cases[44] will, of course, occur to everyone. I myself recall the splendid analysis by Professor von Hippel of the things that were fundamentally wrong about Nazism, and his conclusion that the grossest of all Nazi perversities was that of coercing acts, like the putting out of flags and saying, "Heil Hitler!" that have meaning only when done voluntarily, or, more accurately, have a meaning when coerced that is wholly parasitic on an association of them with past voluntary expressions.[45]

Questions of this sort are undoubtedly becoming more acute as the state assumes a more active role with respect to economic activity. No significant economic activity can be organized exclusively by "don'ts." By its nature economic production requires a co-operative effort. In the economic field there is special reason, therefore, to fear that "This you may not do" will be transformed into "This you must do – but willingly." As we all know, the most tempting opportunity for effecting this transformation is presented by what is called in administrative practice "the prehearing conference," in which the negative threat of a statute's sanctions may be used by its administrators to induce what they regard, in all good conscience, as "the proper attitude."

I look forward to the day when legal philosophy can address itself earnestly to issues of this sort, and not simply exploit them to score points in favor of a position already taken. Professor Hart's essay seems to me to open the way for such a discussion, for it eliminates from the positivistic philosophy a pretense that has hitherto obscured every issue touched by it. I mean, of course, the pretense of the ethical neutrality of positivism. That is why I can say in all sincerity that, despite my almost paragraph-by-paragraph disagreement with the views expressed in his essay, I believe Professor Hart has made an enduring contribution to legal philosophy.

NOTES

1 Kelsen, "Die Idee des Naturrechtes," 7 Zeitschrift für Öffentliches Recht 221, 248 (Austria 1927).
2 Hart, "Positivism and the Separation of Law and Morals," 71 Harv. L. Rev. 593, 615–21 (1958).
3 U.S. Const. Art. V.
4 Hart, *supra* note 2, at 624.
5 For an outstanding example, see G. *Scammell and Nephew, Ltd. v. Ouston*, [1941] AC 251 (1940). I personally would be inclined to put under the same head *Victoria Laundry, Ltd. v. Newman Industries, Ltd.*, [1949] 2 KB 528 (CA).
6 See Hart, *supra* note 2, at 608–12.
7 See N.Y. Times, Nov. 8, 1949, p. 1, col. 4 (late city ed.) (report of a speech made on November 7, 1949 to the Central Committee of the Union of Catholic Italian Lawyers).
8 Hart, *supra* note 2, at 603.
9 Ibid.
10 Austin, *Lectures on Jurisprudence* 167–341 (5th ed. 1885).
11 Kelsen, *General Theory of Law and State* 401 (3rd ed. 1949).
12 E.g., Friedmann, "The Planned State and the Rule of Law," 22 Austr. L.J. 162, 207 (1948).
13 Lowie, *The Origin of the State* 113 (1927).

14 Hart, *supra* note 2, at 623–24.

15 *Southern Pac. Co. v. Jensen*, 244 U.S. 205, 221 (1917) (Holmes, J., dissenting), paraphrasing *Storti v. Commonwealth*, 178 Mass. 549, 554, 60 NE 210, 211 (1901) (Holmes, C.J.), in which it was held that a statute providing for electrocution as a means of inflicting the punishment of death was not cruel or unusual punishment within the Massachusetts Declaration of Rights, Mass. Const. pt. First, art. XXVI, simply because it accomplished its object by molecular, rather than molar, motions.

16 See Hart, *supra* note 2, at 619–20.

17 N.Y. Times, July 4, 1934, p. 3, col. 3 (late city ed.).

18 See N.Y. Times, July 14, 1934, p. 5, col. 2 (late city ed.).

19 Radbruch, "Die Erneuerung des Rechts," 2 Die Wandlung 8, 9 (Germany 1947). A useful discussion of the Nazi practice with reference to the publicity given laws will be found in Giese, "Verkündung and Gesetzeskraft," 76 Archiv des Öffentlichen Rechts 464, 471–72 (Germany 1951). I rely on this article for the remarks that follow in the text.

20 Judgment of July 27, 1949, Oberlandesgericht, Bamberg, 5 Süddeutsche Juristen-Zeitung, 207 (Germany 1950), 64 Harv. L. Rev. 1005 (1951).

21 The passage translated is § 5 of a statute creating a Kriegssonderstrafrecht. Law of Aug. 17, 1938, [1939]. 2 Reichsgesetzblatt pt. 1, at 1456. The translation is mine.

22 See 5 Süddeutsche Juristen-Zeitung, 207, 210 (Germany 1950).

23 The translated passage is article II of A Law Against Malicious Attacks on the State and the Party and for the Protection of the Party Uniform, Law of Dec. 20, 1934, [1934] 1 Reichsgesetzblatt 1269. The translation is mine.

24 See Radbruch, "Die Erneuerung des Rechts," 2 Die Wandlung 8, 10 (Germany 1947).

25 Radbruch, "Gesetzliches Unrecht und Übergesetzliches Recht," 1 Süddeutsche Juristen-Zeitung 105, 107 (Germany 1946) (reprinted in Radbruch, *Rechtsphilosophie* 347, 354 (4th ed. 1950)). The translation is mine.

26 See, e.g., Howe, "The Positivism of Mr. Justice Holmes," 64 Harv. L. Rev. 529 (1951).

27 See Perry, *The Thought and Character of William James* 297 (1935) (quoting a letter written by William James in 1869).

28 Hart, *supra* note 2, at 617–18.

29 Id. at 618.

30 Id. at 619.

31 Austin, *Lectures on Jurisprudence* 173 (5th ed. 1885) (Lecture V).

32 Gray, *The Nature and Sources of the Law* 96 (2d ed. 1921).

33 Bergbohm, *Jurisprudenz und Rechtsphilosophie* 355–552 (1892).

34 See, e.g., Heller, "Die Krisis der Staatslehre," 55 Archiv für Sozialwissenschaft und Sozialpolitik 289, 309 (Germany 1926).

35 Voegelin, "Kelsen's Pure Theory of Law," 42 Pol. Sci. Q. 268, 269 (1927).

36 Hart, *supra* note 2, at 606–8.

37 See id. at 607.

38 Fuller, "Human Purpose and Natural Law," 53 J. Philos. 697, 700 (1956).

39 *Omychund v. Barker*, Atk. 21, 33, 26 Eng. Rep. 15, 22–23 (Ch. 1744) (argument of Solicitor-General Murray, later Lord Mansfield):

> All occasions do not arise at once; ... a statute very seldom can take in all cases, therefore the common law, *that works itself pure* by rules drawn from the fountain of justice, is for this reason superior to an act of parliament.

40 I am speaking of the linguistic theory that seems to be implied in the essay under discussion here. In Professor Hart's brilliant inaugural address, "Definition and Theory in Jurisprudence," 70 L.Q. Rev. 37 (1954), the most important point made is that terms like "rule," "right," and "legal person" cannot be defined by pointing to correspondent things or actions in the external world, but can only be understood in terms of the function performed by them in the larger system, just as one cannot understand the umpire's ruling, "Y're out!" without having at least a general familiarity with the rules of baseball. Even in the analysis presented in the inaugural address, however, Professor Hart seems to think that the dependence of meaning on function and context is a peculiarity of formal and explicit systems, like those of a game or a legal system. He seems not to recognize that what he has to say about explicit systems is also true of the countless informal and overlapping systems that run through language as a whole. These implicit systematic or structural elements in language often enable us to understand at once the meaning of a word used in a wholly novel sense, as in the statement, "Experts regard the English Channel as the most difficult swim in the world." In the essay now being discussed, Professor Hart seems nowhere to recognize that a rule or statute has a structural or systematic quality that reflects itself in some measure into the meaning of every principal term in it.

41 Russell, "The Cult of 'Common Usage,'" in *Portraits from Memory and Other Essays* 166, 170–71 (1956).

42 Whitehead, "Analysis of Meaning," in *Essays in Science and Philosophy* 122, 127 (1947).

43 § 8(d), added by 61 Stat. 142 (1947), 29 USC § 158(d) (1952) ; see NLRA §§
    8(a) (5), (b) (3), as amended, 61 Stat. 141 (1947), 29 USC §§ 158(a) (5), (b)
    (3) (1952).
44 *Minersville School Dist. v. Gobitis*, 310 U.S. 586 (1940), *overruled, West
    Virginia State Bd. of Educ. v. Barnette*, 319 U.S. 624 (1943).
45 Von Hippel, *Die Nationalsozialistische Herrschaftsordnung als Warnung und
    Lehre* 6–7 (1946).

READING QUESTION ON FULLER

1 Positivists and others responded to Fuller by saying that the
   internal morality of law is not a real morality but at most a set of
   principles of efficacy, principles that if observed make the law into
   a more effective instrument of power. If such principles are what
   the rule of law amounts to, their observance could make a wicked
   legal system morally worse. Contrast, for example, a system where
   slavery is instituted by vague and contradictory laws with one that
   is instituted by very precise and coherent laws. Do you think
   Fuller can be so easily dismissed?

Ronald Dworkin
"Law's Ambitions for Itself" (1985)

Dworkin seeks to expand Fuller's point, arguing that fundamental values of
fairness are implicated in every legal decision. Law's ambition is to work
itself pure and rid itself of all morally arbitrary distinctions. Dworkin argues
that positivist judges make bad decisions when they try to steer clear of
making substantive judgments of fairness.

THE 1984 MCCORKLE LECTURE
LAW'S AMBITIONS FOR ITSELF

I

My title is meant to remind you of a set of metaphors that were once
cherished by lawyers but now seem both old-fashioned and silly. "Law

works itself pure." "There is a higher law, within and yet beyond positive law, toward which positive law grows." "Law has its own ambitions."

Three mysteries live in these metaphors; they all recognize the obvious fact that in some sense law changes through adjudication as well as explicit legislation. Judges often describe the law, that is, as different from what people had taken it to be before, and use their novel description to decide the very case in which it is announced. The first mystery argues that these changes are (or at least can be) guided by the law itself, personified, playing out an internal program or design. The second adds that changes guided in this way by the law itself are also improvements, that law purer is law better. The third is more mysterious yet: that such changes are not really changes at all, but on the contrary discoveries of an underlying identity, so that a judge who announces a novel rule may actually be describing existing law more accurately.

There are political claims in each of these mysteries; but the practical claim of the third is most evident because it figures in the political justification of what judges do in hard cases. It seems unfair for judges to change the law in the course of litigation. If change is really self-realization, however, if apparent change is only the discovery of deeper identity, then this complaint is misplaced. On the contrary judges would be acting unfairly in the way the complaint assumes – acting against the idea of legality – if they did not recognize and enforce the apparent change.

This entire set of ideas will strike many of you as not only mysterious but idiotic. It has played no important role in formal legal theory for the better part of a century. It was ridiculed and, so most academic lawyers think, destroyed by the movement that began with the legal positivists, led by Jeremy Bentham and his energetic disciple John Austin in Britain, and by the legal realists of American jurisprudence. Their attack was direct. They argued that the mysterious claims I described employ an illegitimate personification: there is no such thing as the law that can have its own ambitions, that can guide the course of its own change. There are only judges who change the law, from time to time, in order to make it better, in their own entirely human view, or simply to repair its gaps enough to decide cases at hand. We do much better, these critics said, to junk the obscurantism, and to insist that the law already in the books, with all its faults and gaps, is the only law we have. Judges do legislate when they change that law, they do apply new law retrospectively, and we must criticize and explain what they do with our eyes open to those simple facts.

This jurisprudential battle, which almost everyone thinks the positivists and the realists won, had a political dimension. Positivists and realists saw themselves as reformers. They said that the older theorists, who celebrated the metaphors and the mysteries, were formalists blind to the practical consequences of judicial decisions for the community at large, or worse, that they were conscious or unconscious agents of oppressive capitalism who protected the status quo by pretending that their political decisions were the unfolding of the law's own necessity. I mention this political dimension because the old battle has been rejoined in our time and the political alignments are now strikingly different, indeed reversed.

The battle has been rejoined mainly in a new theater: constitutional adjudication. The famous decisions of the "Warren Court" built a jurisprudence of individual constitutional rights against the state; the justices who wrote the famous opinions said these rights were created not by the bare text of the Constitution, nor by the specific, concrete intentions of its "framers," nor by their own fiat, but instead by the constitutional structure itself working itself pure. They relied, that is, on the mysteries latent in the antique metaphors. They have been attacked with the same arguments, and all the fervor and ridicule, the earlier positivists and realists used against what they called natural law; but now the attack comes from the right, not the left, of the political spectrum. Today's skeptics are conservative, not progressive or even liberal.

The nation's attention is drawn to this argument, at least languidly, every four years, because presidential elections concentrate the public's mind on the Supreme Court. Attention was greater during the recent election, because five members of the Court are now at least seventy-five years old, and also because the lawyers President Reagan is tipped to appoint to fill the coming vacancies include several who have declared their judicial philosophies with unusual candor and academic thoroughness. Some of these are former professors of law Reagan has already appointed to the federal circuit courts of appeal, like Richard Posner and Robert Bork, and it is these I have particularly in mind when I say that the banners of positivism now march with the right.

I shall later illustrate the new political alignment by describing, in some detail, a recent decision by Judge Bork in the circuit court for the District of Columbia. But I should first mention two competing explanations of the political reversal. Some of you will think it shows that jurisprudence is epiphenomenal in the following way. If people like the recent drift of law, if they want judges to continue in the spirit of the last few decades, they will be drawn to the old metaphors about law's internal ambitions. If they do not, if they think law has been moving very much in the wrong direction, they will strike realist postures and condemn the metaphors as empty and mischievous personifications. I am not myself attracted to that cynical view of the connection between jurisprudence and legal practice. (You may think I dislike it because it makes my job pointless.) I prefer an alternative explanation: that the realignment is a natural consequence of the growing attraction, to liberals, of the idea that minorities of different types have political rights against the majority. This development, I believe, itself makes the older attitude to law more attractive to liberals and the positivist attitude correspondingly more attractive to conservatives. (I return to this alternate explanation toward the end of this discussion.)

II

I shall now try to rehabilitate the old idea expressed in the metaphors and developed in the mysteries I described. The nerve of my suggestion is this: we can understand the metaphors and mysteries, and also account for their appeal, if we take them to express an *interpretive* model of adjudication. I cannot describe that model in any detail here, though I have tried to do so elsewhere.[1] I can only summarize it here with the caution that needed detail, as well as response to obvious objections, has been left out. The omissions will not, I hope, defeat my present ambition, which is to show how the mysteries I describe become less mysterious, and less vulnerable to the ridicule of the realist attack, if taken to express a model of adjudication of the general character I describe.

The model distinguishes between the positive law – the law in the books, the law declared in the clear statements of statutes and past court decisions – and the full law, which it takes to be the set of principles of political morality that taken together provide the best interpretation of the positive law. It insists on a certain understanding of the idea of interpretation: a set of principles provides the best interpretation of the positive law if it provides the best justification available for the political decisions the positive law announces. It provides the best interpretation, in other words, if it shows the positive law in the best possible light.

That will seem an odd account of interpretation to those of you who believe that interpretation, in its very nature, is the process of recovering the "intention" of the historical author of the material being interpreted. For the positive law is the product of a great many different officials at different times who were moved by very different ambitions and purposes, and retrieving these often conflicting ambitions and purposes would be a very different enterprise from the one I have just described. But the assumption that interpretation, in its very nature, is a process of recovering intentions confuses two different levels at which the character of interpretation can be studied.

Even in the case of literary interpretation, when the "author's intention" account seems most plausible, it is only one of the several competing accounts of interpretation we find in the literature. Some scholars argue, for example, that interpretation is better understood as an attempt to capture the effect a literary work has on contemporary readers. So we must try to find some description of interpretation more abstract than any of these contending theories, a description we can use to explain the argument among them; to explain, that is, both what they are disagreeing about, and how they can all be seen as theories of the same activity. The account I gave – that interpretation seeks to show the material being interpreted as the best it can be – is meant as a candidate for that more abstract description embracing, in that way, the rival theories rather than contending with them. It explains why the author's intention theory seems appealing to some critics but not others. The former believe or assume that the point of literature is essentially communicative, so that discovering an author's communicative intentions, and showing how these are realized in his or her work, is the best way of showing the value that work can properly be claimed to have. The latter hold different views about the sources of value in literature, and these different views spawn rival ideas about which techniques of interpretation show a work in its best light. This view of the matter – this account of the level at which the author's intention thesis provides a theory of interpretation – is, I believe, suggested by the work of Professor Hirsch of the University of Virginia, who is the most powerful and illuminating exponent of that thesis.

If we keep the more abstract account of interpretation in mind, that an interpretation seeks to make of the material being interpreted the best it can be, then we insist that any interpretation of any material must be tested on two dimensions. First, it must fit that material. No interpretation of the positive law can be successful unless it can justify, broadly, the judicial decisions that have actually been reached; otherwise it cannot claim to show *these* decisions in their best light. We can state that requirement by imagining what we know not to be true, that the various decisions that form the positive law were all taken by a single official. Then the first requirement tests a proposed interpretation by asking whether that single official, guided by the principles set out in the proposed interpretation, could have made those decisions. We cannot insist on an exact fit: that every actual decision be explainable in that way. But we do insist that the fit be at least general, that no fundamental or important part of the positive law run contrary to a proposed interpretation, at least if another interpretation, much more successful in this respect, is available.

The second requirement lies on the dimension of justification. An interpretation of positive law is unsuccessful unless it offers a justification of that law, and if, as will ordinarily be the case, two competing interpretations both satisfy the first requirement of fit to an adequate degree, this second requirement of justification will discriminate between them because it will prefer the interpretation that provides the better justification. In the case of law, of course, the justification in question is one of political morality. Showing positive law in its best light means showing it as the best course of statesmanship possible.

That fact will confirm, for many of you, a suspicion that must have been growing throughout this brief account of interpretation. You will think that it makes interpretation irredeemably subjective, that since two interpreters of the law may very well have different convictions about whether a particular interpretation fits well enough to succeed on the first dimension, and are very likely to have different political convictions about which provides a better justification in political morality on the second, interpretation is just a matter of opinion and no one's interpretation could claim to be "objectively" any better than any one else's. I believe that this is the wrong conclusion to draw, that this use of the troublesome distinction between "subjective" and "objective" is confused and adds nothing useful to any discussion of either interpretation or political morality. I have tried to defend that view elsewhere[2] but I will not expand on it now, because I can continue my argument without it.

Construe, if you like, my description of the interpretive model of adjudication "subjectively." It then becomes an account of the questions a judge should put to himself and answer from his own "subjective" convictions about fit and political morality. Since these are in any case different from the questions the positivist model requires him to put to himself, and draws on a different set of "subjective" convictions, the difference between the two models will be preserved, and so will the question I shall shortly consider, which is whether we have any basis for choosing between the two models.

III

My discussion of interpretation, and of the interpretive model of adjudication, has been exceedingly abstract. I shall try to make it somewhat more concrete by showing how a judge who accepted the interpretive model would attack the problem posed by the recent case I referred to earlier, which is *Dronenburg*.[3] The facts of that case can be stated quickly enough. Dronenburg served with distinction in the Navy for many years, but was discharged when he admitted homosexual acts in a barracks. He sued the Navy claiming that his discharge for that reason violated his constitutional rights.

The interpretive model recommends the following method of studying his claim. We begin by identifying the positive law in the neighborhood of the problem. This consists, first, in the text of the constitutional clauses Dronenburg cited, and then in the past decisions of the Supreme Court under those clauses. For our illustration we may limit the positive law to the text of the Due Process Clause and the set of decisions usually called the "privacy" decisions. *Griswold*[4] decided that states may not prohibit the use of contraceptives by married couples. *Eisenstadt*[5] confirmed that the right to contraception extends to unmarried couples as well, and *Carey*[6] condemned a New York statute requiring contraceptives to be bought only from licensed pharmacists and prohibiting their sale to children under sixteen. The Court has upheld the right to "privacy" in other contexts: for example, in *Loving*,[7] which held a Virginia statute prohibiting interracial marriage unconstitutional. The most dramatic of the "privacy" decisions so far, however, is the abortion decision, *Roe v. Wade*.[8] The Court cited the contraception decisions and *Loving* to justify its ruling that the states could not constitutionally prohibit abortion in the first trimester of pregnancy.

This limited description of the positive law provides our preinterpretive base, and we must now ask which set of principles would provide the best interpretation, that is to say the best justification, of it. Which political principles would satisfy the requirement of the first dimension, the requirement of fit? I can think of two principles that might well be thought to fit, and I shall consider only these, though you might well be able to think of more. First, the decisions just described could have been made by a single statesman acting to enforce a version of Mill's famous principle, which holds that the state must not prohibit acts that harm no one just because these acts are widely considered immoral or sinful. Second, they could have been made by a statesman who accepted the narrower principle that the state may not legislate to restrict liberty touching decisions about procreation.

Suppose, each of these two principles does fit the decisions of the positive law.[9] It matters very much which we accept as the better interpretation of that law. If Mill's principle is a better interpretation, then the full or genuine law protects Dronenburg through the constitutional right he claims. If the second principle, limited to procreation, is superior, then it does not (unless some other principle favoring him can be found elsewhere in constitutional law) because the choice of homosexual sex cannot plausibly be treated as a choice about procreation even though it has consequences for it. So our attention shifts to the second dimension of interpretation; we must ask which of our two putative interpretations provides a better justification of the decisions from the point of view of political morality. Can there be much doubt that the first is superior? It states a recognizable ideal of moral independence that will have considerable appeal even to those who cannot accept it in full. The second principle, which declares only that the state may not intervene in personal decisions about procreation, is not really, on a second look, a principle at all. It sets out an arbitrary line unconnected to any recognizable distinction of moral importance. It offers no reason why intimate personal decisions about procreation should be protected from state regulation though other intimate decisions need not be so protected, and we have no reason at hand in either the literature or common culture of morality that could justify that distinction.

Though, as I emphasized earlier, the interpretive model will often produce different results for different people, because the convictions they bring to bear on the questions the model provides are different, *Dronenburg* strikes me as an easy case within that model.[10] Under that model the full, genuine law holds for Dronenburg. Now please reconsider, in the light of this example, the three "mysteries" I described at the beginning of this lecture.

On the surface a decision for Dronenburg, under the claim that the constitutional right of privacy extends to homosexuals, is a change in the law, because that right is not explicit in the text of the Constitution and had not before been recognized by the Supreme Court. But we can now, I hope, see the sense in the claim that if the interpretive argument justifying this change is a good argument the change was directed by the positive law itself, realizing what can sensibly be called its own ambitions. That is only a way – I agree that it is not the most pellucid way – of saying that the positive law constrains what can count as its best interpretation, and this is patently so. The second claim we found mysterious argues that a change produced through adjudication is not neutral but an improvement, that law purer is law better. This, too, can be restated as a feature of the interpretive model we have developed, for it claims only the converse of the second requirement of interpretation we distinguished. Since an interpretation is better if it provides a better justification in political morality, then a change guided by a better interpretation will for that reason alone be an improvement. Our third "mystery" insisted that change guided by the law itself is not genuine change but only clarification of law as it stands already. That is simply the contrast between positive and full law made to sound more mysterious than it is, and the practical upshot we noticed survives the demystification. For the interpretive model insists that if the best inter-pretation of the positive law, and therefore the most accurate statement of the full law, yields a constitutional right for Dronenburg, then denying him that right is not merely refusing to make a change in the law that would improve it, but is itself a denial of legality, an insult to the rule of law.

IV

So the interpretive model does give point to the old metaphors and does show the illuminating power of the attitudes towards adjudication and the law they expressed. The positivist assault on those attitudes rejected not a patently absurd metaphysics but a perfectly practical style of judging. I said that the positivist critique had become the weapon of conservative lawyers in their opposition to the use of our Constitution to protect individual rights against the state. The judge who actually decided *Dronenburg* is, as it happens, a self-conscious member of the school of conservative positivists, and we may therefore turn to his opinion hoping to sharpen our sense of the contrast between the two styles of adjudication we have now distinguished.

Indeed, the contrast could hardly be more complete. Judge Bork set out the positive law I have described, but only to show that it did not contain, as positive law, any explicit recognition of a constitutional right protecting homosexuals. That, for him, was decisive of whether Dronenburg already had the constitutional right he claimed. He did not.

So the only question left for adjudication was whether lower-court federal judges should create a new right in his favor, and this question, for Bork, answered itself. He allowed himself to say that, in his opinion, even the justices of the Supreme Court should not create new constitutional rights because in so doing they exceed their legitimate powers as judges. But he thought it obvious that, whatever the Supreme Court should or should not do, lower-court justices should not usurp powers not rightfully theirs. He decided, on that ground alone, against Dronenburg's claim. This opinion is remarkable for its crude positivist character. The positive law is all the law there is, and any change would be a piece of legislation merely, in this case, a constitutional amendment in defiance of the amending procedures that document itself provides.

V

So we have two models for adjudication: the interpretive model that, in this instance at least, argues for improved protection of individual rights and the positivist model that argues, at least here, against that development. What grounds could we have for choosing between these two models? It is easier to describe the grounds we do *not* have for that choice.

Positivists often appeal to skepticism as a reason for rejecting the ideas that come together in the interpretive model. This is sometimes metaphysical skepticism, expressed in comments like Holmes' scornful remark that law is not a brooding omnipresence in the sky. But this form of skepticism is available only so long as positivism can treat its opponent as committed to some ghostly form of natural law. It is not appropriate when the older tradition is restated as the interpretive model. That model seems to encourage a different form of skepticism, however, which is moral skepticism in the shape of the following argument. If two lawyers disagree about which set of principles shows positive law in the best light, there can be no right answer to that question, and therefore no single answer dictated by the interpretive model. That argument seems to me a poor one, as I said; but even if it were sound it would provide no argument for positivism against interpretation as general styles of adjudication. For positivism requires judges to make controversial judgments of political morality just as often as the interpretive model does. It is true – and important – that the questions of political morality the interpretive model puts to judges are different, and invoke different convictions, from the questions of morality positivism puts, but if there can be no right answer to the former there can be none to the latter either. So moral skepticism provides as strong – or as weak – an objection to each of the two styles of adjudication, and offers no ground for choosing between them (or, indeed, between either of them and any other theory about how judges should decide hard cases).

Legal philosophers once thought that the choice between theories of adjudication could be made on semantic grounds or (what comes to much the same thing) on grounds of conceptual clarity or convenience. Positivism was supposed to capture how lawyers use the word "law," or at least to provide a superior way to use that word. But these claims foundered for two reasons. First, they are false as claims about how lawyers talk: it is not true that almost all lawyers use "law" to refer only to positive law. (Indeed, positivists have had to invent implausible epicycles of linguistic theory to explain why they do not.) Second, since our two models are substantively different – the difference is illustrated dramatically by the different consequences of the two models in *Dronenburg* – the choice we must make is between the models them-selves, not how we should speak about or within them.

We can dismiss a third suggestion, about how to choose between the two models of adjudication, equally quickly. I mean the argument Bork relied on so heavily in *Dronenburg,* that the interpretive model he re-fused to follow is *illegitimate* in the constitutional context because judges who follow that model usurp powers of constitutional amendment. That argument simply and directly begs the question at issue, for what the constitution actually is, at any moment, depends on which model of adjudication is the proper one to use in constitutional adjudication. If the interpretive model is the right one, for us, then our Constitution already consists of what that model identifies as the full constitutional law, and then it is *Bork's* decision declining to enforce the full law that is illegitimate, that amends the Constitution by fiat.

I anticipated this point in remarking, early in this lecture, this practi-cal consequence of the set of ideas we have now restated in the inter-pretive model: it makes the scope of the rule of law, and therefore the legitimate power of judges, turn on what it identifies as the full law rather than the positive law it takes as the object of interpretation. Of course it would beg the question in the opposite direction if I were to argue, on behalf of the interpretive model, that Bork's positivistic deci-sion was a piece of illegitimate usurpation because it amended the con-stitution. Claims of legitimacy or illegitimacy are part of the conclusion of an argument for a model of adjudication, and so cannot themselves figure in that argument.

It is time I turned from arguments we should reject for choosing one of our two models over the other, however, to consider whether there are any we should accept. We might well be tempted to ask which model itself provides a better interpretation of our constitutional practice. It seems plain that the interpretive model fits that practice much better. It is, indeed, a large complaint of the conservative positivists that the Supreme Court has too often decided cases in the interpretive spirit. We should not rely too heavily on that observation, however, because these conservatives might reply that the positivist model fits enough of constitutional practice – or, if not, that it fits enough of legal practice in the United States more generally – to remain eligible on the dimension of fit. So we should compare the two models on the other dimension of interpretation by asking which provides a better justification, in political morality, for the practices it claims to fit. We have an even stronger reason for turning at once to that directly political question. Positivists may claim that it begs the question, in much the way I just said Bork's argument does, to argue for the interpretive model on interpretive grounds. But if we reject the interpretive test, for that reason, then the test of political morality, where the interpretive test was already leading us, would be the only remaining method of comparing the two models.

We might begin the political test by noticing that the interpretive model supposes and serves a distinct political virtue: political integrity. The model assumes that the state, as policeman, must speak with one voice in the following sense. If it relies on one set of political principles to justify its use of coercive power in one area, it must allow those principles their natural extension. If it must rely on some version of Mill's principle, for example, to justify denying the majority the decision whether people should be permitted to use contraceptives, or to marry interracially, or to have abortions in the first trimester of pregnancy, it must extend the protection of that principle to homosexuals as well.

Can we find a comparable underlying political virtue for the positivist model of constitutional adjudication expressed in Bork's opinion? I believe so: it is the virtue of economic efficiency, conceived as the goal of satisfying the preferences of the community overall, including its political and moral as well as its more narrowly economic preferences. It is no accident that the foremost academic supporters of conservative constitutional policy are also the most obdurate advocates of what is called economic analysis in other areas of the law. Their conviction that the majority's political power should be limited as little as possible – that it should be limited only by the explicit text of the Constitution or the unambiguous intentions of its framers – reflects the same unexpressed political theory as their ambition that the rules of contract, tort, and property be constructed so as to maximize social wealth. Both reflect an unrestricted utilitarianism that allows the preferences of many people to override those of a few, in some overall calculation of a social preference, and denies any constraint on the kind of preferences that must be counted in that calculation. My preferences about how you lead your life, in other words, count as much as yours.

The conflict between the underlying virtues we have now identified for our two models – integrity for the interpretive model and efficiency for the positivist model – is clear enough. Integrity is, from the point of view of efficiency, both arbitrary and irrational: arbitrary because it cannot be drawn from unrestricted utilitarianism, and irrational because it will prove, except in the rarest cases, incompatible with it. A social engineer anxious to achieve the fullest possible satisfaction of everyone's preferences in the long run could not accept integrity as a constraint, because the preferences he seeks to satisfy are unlikely themselves to be disciplined by the principled coherence integrity would impose on them. Our leading example shows this dramatically. Many people prefer that others not have contraceptives, abortions, or homosexual sex. But the phenomenological profiles of these different "external" preferences are very different: they differ in their popularity, emotional charge, and connection to other "moral" views. Perhaps the overall satisfaction of preferences would be improved, in the long run, by some constitutional constraint prohibiting temporary majorities from banning contraception. But it hardly follows that a constraint prohibiting punishing homosexuals would have the same consequence, because the mix and character of preferences, not to mention side effects, is so different in that case.

The conflict between the two virtues seems sharper still when we reflect on the ideals of community associated with each. In a community regulated by efficiency each person sees other people as resources and competitors: resources because his preferences include and are supported by preferences about how they should act, competitors because the satisfaction of their preferences is likely to impinge on the satisfaction of his. There is no sorority or fraternity in this picture of society; it is the picture of politics as commerce by other means. A society dedicated to integrity, on the contrary, aims at the most intense version of community compatible with moral diversity.

We are not a community tied together by a concrete moral settlement, by shared opinions about the details of what justice and fairness and a decent and valuable life require. (We would, I believe, be a worse community if we did achieve consensus about these matters.) We debate about justice and fairness through the institutions we have, seeking, as part of that debate, to reform these institutions as we use them, acknowledging that any institutional structure we achieve is provisional, that no decision of majority or executive or court is right just because it has been taken, or right just because it must be respected so long as it stands. We march in this way toward what we hope is a better community, fairer and more just; we march we hope forward though we can believe some steps are backward. But we nevertheless recognize community in our present diversity, and so accept, in the name of community, a special and further constraint. We march together so that the settlements of principle we reach from time to time, as plateaus for further campaigns, extend to everyone. We leave no wounded behind, no abandoned minorities of race or gender or sexual disposition, even when bringing them along delays the gains of others.

If you find that vision of community more attractive than the community of efficiency, as I do, then you will find in it the only kind of argument we can have for one conception of law over another. It points us toward the interpretive model, toward the set of ideas locked in the old metaphors about law's ambitions for itself. You may find one feature of my argument odd. You may find it odd that the lawyers' contest about styles of adjudication finally turns in the way I claim of ideals of community, that volumes of philosophy speak in the fall of every judge's gavel. It may be odd, but I'm sure it's true, and even a little thrilling.

NOTES

1 See, e.g., R. Dworkin, "Law as Interpretation," in *A Matter of Principle*, Pt. 2 (Harvard Univ. Press, 1985).
2 Ibid., p. 167.
3 *Dronenburg v. Zech*, 741 F.2d 1388 (DC Cir. 1984).
4 *Griswold v. Connecticut*, 381 US 479 (1965).
5 *Eisenstadt v. Baird*, 405 US 438 (1971).
6 *Carey v. Population Servs. Int'l*, 431 US 678 (1977).
7 *Loving v. Virginia*, 388 US 1 (1967).
8 410 US 113 (1973).

9 The assumption that the first interpretation, which appeals to Mill's principle, fits the abortion decision requires the controversial further assumption that a fetus is not a person within the first trimester, and this assumption might therefore be a necessary part of any competent interpretation of the full set of privacy decisions. Or, perhaps, Mill's principle might be used to justify the other decisions in the "privacy" group and some further principle found, if any could be, to justify the abortion decision independently. In either case Mill's principle would then be *part* of an interpretation of the decisions as a whole, though not exhaustive of it.

10 I should repeat, however, that this claim is not necessary to my main purpose, which is to show the model at work and how it differs from the positivist model I shall shortly use Bork's actual decision in *Dronenburg* to illustrate.

Ronald Dworkin
Law's Empire **(1986)**

THE CHAIN OF LAW

The Chain Novel

I argued in Chapter 2 that creative interpretation takes its formal structure from the idea of intention, not (at least not necessarily) because it aims to discover the purposes of any particular historical person or group but because it aims to impose purpose over the text or data or tradition being interpreted. Since all creative interpretation shares this feature, and therefore has a normative aspect or component, we profit from comparing law with other forms or occasions of interpretation. We can usefully compare the judge deciding what the law is on some issue not only with the citizens of courtesy deciding what the tradition requires, but with the literary critic teasing out the various dimensions of value in a complex play or poem.

Judges, however, are authors as well as critics. A judge deciding *McLoughlin* or *Brown* adds to the tradition he interprets; future judges confront a new tradition that includes what he has done. Of course literary criticism contributes to the traditions of art in which authors work; the character and importance of that contribution are themselves issues in critical theory. But the contribution of judges is more direct, and the distinction between author and interpreter more a matter of different aspects of the same process. We can find an even more fruitful comparison between literature and law, therefore, by constructing an artificial genre of literature that we might call the chain novel.

In this enterprise a group of novelists writes a novel *seriatim*; each novelist in the chain interprets the chapters he has been given in order to write a new chapter, which is then added to what the next novelist receives, and so on. Each has the job of writing his chapter so as to make the novel being constructed the best it can be, and the complexity of this task models the complexity of deciding a hard case under law as integrity. The imaginary literary enterprise is fantastic but not unrecognizable. Some novels have actually been written in this way, though mainly for a debunking purpose, and certain parlor games for rainy weekends in English country houses have something of the same structure. Television soap operas span decades with the same characters and some minimal continuity of personality and plot, though they are written by different teams of authors even in different weeks. In our example, however, the novelists are expected to take their responsibilities of continuity more seriously; they aim jointly to create, so far as they can, a single unified novel that is the best it can be.

Each novelist aims to make a single novel of the material he has been given, what he adds to it, and (so far as he can control this) what his successors will want or be able to add. He must try to make this the best novel it can be construed as the work of a single author rather than, as is the fact, the product of many different hands. That calls for an overall judgment on his part, or a series of overall judgments as he writes and rewrites. He must take up some view about the novel in progress, some working theory about its characters, plot, genre, theme, and point, in order to decide what counts as continuing it and not as beginning anew. If he is a good critic, his view of these matters will be complicated and multifaceted, because the value of a decent novel cannot be captured from a single perspective. He will aim to find layers and currents of meaning rather than a single, exhaustive theme. We can, however, in our now familiar way give some structure to any interpretation he adopts, by distinguishing two dimensions on which it must be tested. The first is what we have been calling the dimension of fit. He cannot adopt any interpretation, however complex, if he believes that no single author who set out to write a novel with the various readings of character, plot, theme, and point that interpretation describes could have written substantially the text he has been given. That does not mean his interpretation must fit every bit of the text. It is not disqualified simply because he claims that some lines or tropes are accidental, or even that some events of plot are mistakes because they work against the literary ambitions the interpretation states. But the interpretation he takes up must nevertheless flow throughout the text; it must have general explanatory power, and it is flawed if it leaves unexplained some major structural aspect of the text, a subplot treated as having great dramatic importance or a dominant and repeated metaphor. If no interpretation can be found that is not flawed in that way, then the chain novelist will not be able fully to meet his assignment; he will have to settle for an interpretation that captures most of the text, conceding that it is not wholly successful. Perhaps even that partial success is unavailable; perhaps every interpretation he considers is inconsistent with the bulk of the material supplied to him. In that case he must abandon the enterprise, for the consequence of taking the interpretive attitude toward the text in question is then a piece of internal skepticism: that nothing can count as continuing the novel rather than beginning anew.

He may find, not that no single interpretation fits the bulk of the text, but that more than one does. The second dimension of interpretation then requires him to judge which of these eligible readings makes the work in progress best, all things considered. At this point his more substantive aesthetic judgments, about the importance or insight or realism or beauty of different ideas the novel might be taken to express, come into play. But the formal and structural considerations that dominate on the first dimension figure on the second as well, for even when neither of two interpretations is disqualified out of hand as explaining too little, one may show the text in a better light because it fits more of the text or provides a more interesting integration of style and content. So the distinction between the two dimensions is less crucial or profound than it might seem. It is a useful analytical device that helps us give structure to any interpreter's working theory or style. He will form a sense of when an interpretation fits so poorly that it is unnecessary to consider its substantive appeal, because he knows that this cannot outweigh its embarrassments of fit in deciding whether it makes the novel better, everything taken into account, than its rivals. This sense will define the first dimension for him. But he need not reduce his intuitive sense to any precise formula; he would rarely need to decide whether some interpretation barely survives or barely fails, because a bare survivor, no matter how ambitious or interesting it claimed the text to be, would almost certainly fail in the overall comparison with other interpretations whose fit was evident.

We can now appreciate the range of different kinds of judgments that are blended in this overall comparison. Judgments about textual coherence and integrity, reflecting different formal literary values, are interwoven with more substantive aesthetic judgments that themselves assume different literary aims. Yet these various kinds of judgments, of each general kind, remain distinct enough to check one another in an overall assessment, and it is that possibility of contest, particularly between textual and substantive judgments, that distinguishes a chain novelist's assignment from more independent creative writing. Nor can we draw any flat distinction between the stage at which a chain novelist interprets the text he has been given and the stage at which he adds his own chapter, guided by the interpretation he has settled on. When he begins to write he might discover in what he has written a different, perhaps radically different, interpretation. Or he might find it impossible to write in the tone or theme he first took up, and that will lead him to reconsider other interpretations he first rejected. In either case he returns to the text to reconsider the lines it makes eligible.

Scrooge

We can expand this abstract description of the chain novelist's judgment through an example. Suppose you are a novelist well down the chain. Suppose Dickens never wrote *A Christmas Carol,* and the text you are furnished, though written by several people, happens to be the first part of that short novel. You consider these two interpretations of the central character: Scrooge is inherently and irredeemably evil, an embodiment of the untarnished wickedness of human nature freed from the disguises of convention he rejects; or Scrooge is inherently good but progressively corrupted by the false values and perverse demands of high capitalist society. Obviously it will make an enormous difference to the way you continue the story which of these interpretations you adopt. If you have been given almost all of *A Christmas Carol* with only the very end to be written – Scrooge has already had his dreams, re-

pented, and sent his turkey – it is too late for you to make him irredeemably wicked, assuming you think, as most interpreters would, that
the text will not bear that interpretation without too much strain. I do
not mean that no interpreter could possibly think Scrooge inherently
evil after his supposed redemption. Someone might take that putative
redemption to be a final act of hypocrisy, though only at the cost of
taking much else in the text not at face value. This would be a poor
interpretation, not because no one could think it a good one, but because it is in fact, on all the criteria so far described, a poor one.

READING QUESTIONS ON DWORKIN

1 What is Dworkin's middle ground between history and moral
   recommendation?
2 Can Dworkin really rely on law to work itself pure? There's an old
   saying "garbage in, garbage out." Dworkin seems confident that
   any legal system starts with enough good to generate freedom and
   equality in the end. What features of a legal system make him so
   confident? Is his belief realistic?
3 Positivists have conceded that legal systems often include moral
   values, but insist those values simply reflect the views of those
   with the power to make law. How might Dworkin reply to such a
   challenge?

Gustav Radbruch
"Statutory Lawlessness and Supra-Statutory Law" (1946)[1]

You will recall that one of the points of disagreement between Hart and
Fuller was about the German legal philosopher Gustav Radbruch, who
argued that the merits of legal positivism had to be rethought in the light of
the experience of Nazism. The text that follows is a recent translation of
Radbruch's most famous exposition of this view. It is important to know
that the "Radbruch Formula" – extreme injustice is no law – has been used
by German courts after German reunification in order to facilitate the
prosecution of East German border guards who had shot people trying to
escape to the West. They claimed the protection of the German Border Act,
which authorized guards to use lethal force to prevent escapes. More

recently, as you will see in the next chapter, the Radbruch Formula was relied on in argument to Canadian courts.

I

By means of two maxims, "An order is an order" and "a law is a law," National Socialism contrived to bind its followers to itself, soldiers and jurists respectively. The former tenet was always restricted in its applicability; soldiers had no obligation to obey orders serving criminal purposes.[2] "A law is a law," on the other hand, knew no restriction whatever. It expressed the positivistic legal thinking that, almost unchallenged, held sway over German jurists for many decades. "Statutory lawlessness" was, accordingly, a contradiction in terms, just as "supra-statutory law" was.[3] Today, both problems confront legal practice time and time again. Recently, for example, the *Süddeutsche Juristen-Zeitung* published and commented on a decision of the Wiesbaden Municipal Court [handed down in November of 1945], according to which the "statutes that declared the property of the Jews to be forfeited to the State were in conflict with natural law, and null and void the moment they were enacted."[4]

II

In the criminal law, the same problem has been raised, particularly in debates and decisions within the Russian Zone.[5]

1. A justice department clerk named Puttfarken was tried and sentenced to life imprisonment by the Thuringian Criminal Court in Nordhausen for having brought about the conviction and execution of the merchant Göttig by informing on him. Puttfarken had denounced Göttig for writing on the wall of a WC that "Hitler is a mass murderer and to blame for the war." Göttig had been condemned not only because of this inscription, but also because he had listened to foreign radio broadcasts. The argument made at Puttfarken's trial by the Thuringian Chief Public Prosecutor, Dr. Friedrich Kuschnitzki, was reported in detail in the press.[6] Prosecutor Kuschnitzki first takes up the question: Was Puttfarken's act a violation of law?

The defendant's contention that his belief in National Socialism had led him to inform on Göttig is legally insignificant. Whatever one's own political convictions, there is no legal obligation to denounce anyone. Even during the Hitler years, no such legal obligation existed. The decisive question is whether the defendant acted in the interests of the administration of justice, a question presupposing that the judicial system is in a position to administer justice. *Fidelity to statutes, a striving toward justness, legal certainty – these are the requirements of a judicial system.* And all three are lacking in the politicized criminal justice system of the Hitler regime.

Anyone who informed on another during those years had to know – and did in fact know – that he was delivering up the accused to arbitrary power, not consigning him to a lawful judicial procedure with legal guarantees for determining the truth and arriving at a just decision.

With respect to this question, I subscribe fully to the opinion given by Professor Richard Lange, Dean of the Law Faculty of the University of Jena. So well known was the situation in the Third Reich that one could say with certainty: Any person called to account in the third year of the war for writing "Hitler is a mass murderer and to blame for this war" would never come out alive. Someone like Puttfarken certainly could not have had a clear view of just *how* the judiciary would pervert the law, but he could have been sure *that* it would.

No legal obligation to inform on anyone can be drawn from section 139 of the Criminal Code either. It is true that, according to this provision, a person who obtains reliable information of a plan to commit high treason and fails to give timely notice of this plan to the authorities is subject to punishment. It is also true that Göttig had been condemned to death by the Appeal Court at Kassel for *preparing to commit high treason.* In a legal sense, however, there had certainly been no such preparation to commit high treason. After all, Göttig's brave declaration that "Hitler is a mass murderer and to blame for the war" was simply the naked truth. Anyone declaring and spreading this truth threatened neither the Reich nor its security, but sought only to help rid the Reich of its destroyer and thus to rescue it – in other words, the opposite of high treason. Scruples of legal form must not be allowed to obfuscate this plain fact. Furthermore, it is at least questionable whether the so-called Führer and Chancellor of the Reich should ever have been regarded as the legal head of state at all, and therefore questionable whether he was protected by the provisions on high treason. In any event, the defendant had not reflected at all on the legal implications of informing on Göttig, and, given his limited understanding, he could not have done so. Puttfarken himself has never declared that he informed on Göttig because he saw Göttig's inscription as an act of high treason and felt obliged to report it to the authorities.[7]

The Chief Public Prosecutor then addresses the question: Did Puttfarken's act render him culpable?

Puttfarken essentially admits that he intended to send Göttig to the gallows,
and a series of witnesses have confirmed his intention. *This is premeditated
murder, according to section 211 of the Criminal Code.* That it was a court of the
Third Reich that actually condemned Göttig to death does not argue against
Puttfarken's having committed the crime. *He is an indirect perpetrator.* Granted, the concept of the indirect commission of a crime, as it has been developed in Supreme Court adjudication, usually looks to other cases, chiefly
those in which the indirect perpetrator makes use of instruments lacking in
will or the capacity for accountability. No one ever dreamed that a German
court could be the instrument of a criminal. Yet today we face just such
cases. The Puttfarken case *will not be the only one.* That the Court observed
legal *form* in declaring its pernicious decision cannot argue against
Puttfarken's indirect commission of the crime. Any lingering hesitancy on
this score is cleared away by article 2 of the Thuringian Supplementary Law
of 8 February 1946. Article 2, in order to dispel doubts, offers the following
rendition of section 47, paragraph 1, of the Criminal Code: "Whoever is
guilty of carrying out a criminal act, either by himself or through another
person, even if that other person acted lawfully, shall be punished as
perpetrator." This does not establish new, retroactively effective substantive
law; it is simply an authentic interpretation of criminal law in force since
1871.[8]

After a careful weighing of the pros and cons, I myself am of the opinion
that there can be *no* doubt that this is a case of murder committed indirectly.
But let us suppose – and we must take this contingency into account – that
the Court were to arrive at a different opinion. What would come into
question then? If one rejects the view that this is a case of murder committed
indirectly, then one can hardly escape the conclusion that the *judges who
condemned Göttig to death, contrary to law and statute, are themselves to be
regarded as murderers.* The accused would then be an *accomplice to murder* and
punishable as such. Should this view, too, raise serious misgivings – and I
am not unmindful of them – there remains the Allied Control Council Law
No. 10 [of 20 December 1945]. According to article 2, paragraph 1(c),[9] the
accused would be guilty of a crime against humanity. Within the framework
of this statute, the question is no longer whether the national law of the land
is violated. Inhuman acts and persecution for political, racial, or religious
reasons are, without qualification, subject to punishment. According to art-

icle 2, paragraph 3,[10] the criminal is to be sentenced to such punishment as the court deems just. Even capital punishment.[11]

I might add that as a jurist I am accustomed to confining myself to a purely legal evaluation. But one is always well advised to stand, as it were, *outside* the situation and view it in the light of ordinary common sense. Legal technique is, without exception, merely the instrument the responsible jurist uses in order to arrive at a legally defensible decision.[12]

Puttfarken was condemned by the Thuringian Criminal Court not as an indirect perpetrator of the crime, but as an accomplice to murder. Accordingly, the judges who condemned Göttig to death, contrary to law and statute, had to be guilty of murder.[13]

2. In fact, the Chief Public Prosecutor of Saxony, Dr J.U. Schroeder, announces in the press the intention of enforcing the principle of criminal "responsibility for inhuman judicial decisions," even when such decisions are based on National Socialist statutes:

The legislation of the National Socialist state, on the basis of which death sentences like those cited here were pronounced, *has no legal validity whatsoever*.

National Socialist legislation rests on the so-called *"Enabling Act"* [of 24 March 1933], which was passed without the constitutionally required two-thirds majority. Hitler had forcibly prevented the Communist representatives from participating in the parliamentary session by having them arrested, in spite of their immunity. The remaining representatives, namely from the Centre Party, were threatened by Nazi storm troopers (the SA) and thereby compelled to vote for the emergency powers.[14]

A judge can never administer justice by appealing to a statute that is not merely unjust but *criminal*. We appeal to *human rights* that surpass all written laws, and we appeal to the inalienable, immemorial law that denies validity to the criminal dictates of inhuman tyrants.

In light of these considerations, I believe that judges must be prosecuted who have handed down decisions incompatible with the precepts of humanity and have pronounced the death sentence for trifles.[15]

3. A report comes from Halle that the executioner's assistants, Kleine and Rose, are condemned to death for actively participating in numerous lawless executions. From April 1944 to March 1945, Kleine took part in 931 executions, for which he was paid 26,433 RM. The condemna-

tion of Kleine and Rose seems to be based on the Allied Control Council Law No. 10 (crimes against humanity). "Both of the accused practiced their grisly trade willingly, since every executioner's assistant is free to abstain from his activity at any time, for health reasons or otherwise."[16]

4. In Saxony again, the following case comes to light in an article by Chief Public Prosecutor J.U. Schroeder: A soldier from Saxony, assigned to guard prisoners of war on the eastern front, deserted his post in 1943, "disgusted by the inhuman treatment they received. Perhaps he was also tired of serving in Hitler's army." While on the run, he could not resist stopping by his wife's apartment, where he was discovered and was to be taken into custody by a sergeant. He succeeded, unnoticed, in getting hold of his loaded service revolver and shot the sergeant in the back, killing him. In 1945, the deserter returned to Saxony from Switzerland. He was arrested, and the office of the public prosecutor prepared to charge him with having maliciously killed the official. The Chief Public Prosecutor, however, ordered his release and the abandonment of criminal proceedings, appealing to section 54 of the Criminal Code and arguing that the soldier, having acted out of necessity, was blameless, since

what the judiciary called law then is no longer valid today. In our view of the law, deserting the Hitler-Keitel army is no misdemeanor dishonouring the deserter and justifying his punishment; he is not blameworthy because of it.[17]

With statutory lawlessness and supra-statutory law serving, then, as points of reference, the struggle against positivism is being taken up everywhere.

III

Positivism, with its principle that "a law is a law," has in fact rendered the German legal profession defenceless against statutes that are arbitrary and criminal. Positivism is, moreover, in and of itself wholly incapable of establishing the validity of statutes. It claims to have proved the validity of a statute simply by showing that the statute had sufficient power behind it to prevail. But while power may indeed serve as a basis for the "must" of compulsion, it never serves as a basis for the "ought" of obligation or for legal validity. Obligation and legal validity must be based, rather, on a value inherent in the statute. To be sure, *one* value comes with every positive-law statute without reference to its content: Any statute is always better than no statute at all, since it at least creates legal certainty. But legal certainty is not the only value that law must effectuate, nor is it the decisive value. Alongside legal certainty, there are two other values: purposiveness[18] and justice. In ranking these values, we assign to last place the purposiveness of the law in serving the public benefit. By no means is law anything and everything that "benefits the people." Rather, what benefits the people is, in the long run, only that which law is, namely, that which creates legal certainty and strives toward justice. Legal certainty (which is characteristic of every positive-law statute simply in virtue of the statute's having been enacted) takes a curious middle place between the other two values, purposiveness and justice, because it is required not only for the public benefit but also for justice. That the law be certain and sure, that it not be interpreted and applied one way here and now, another way elsewhere and tomorrow, is also a requirement of justice. Where there arises a conflict between legal certainty and justice, between an objectionable but duly enacted statute and a just law that has not been cast in statutory form, there is in truth a conflict of justice with itself, a conflict between apparent and real justice. This conflict is perfectly expressed in the Gospel, in the command to "obey them that have the rule over you, and submit yourselves," and in the dictate, on the other hand, to "obey God rather than men."[19]

The conflict between justice and legal certainty may well be resolved in this way: The positive law, secured by legislation and power, takes precedence even when its content is unjust and fails to benefit the people, unless the conflict between statute and justice reaches such an intolerable degree that the statute, as "flawed law," must yield to justice. It is impossible to draw a sharper line between cases of statutory lawlessness and statutes that are valid despite their flaws. One line of distinction, however, can be drawn with utmost clarity: Where there is not even an attempt at justice, where equality, the core of justice, is deliberately betrayed in the issuance of positive law, then the statute is not merely "flawed law," it lacks completely the very nature of law. For law, including positive law, cannot be otherwise defined than as a system and an institution whose very meaning is to serve justice. Measured by this standard, whole portions of National Socialist law never attained the dignity of valid law.

The most conspicuous characteristic of Hitler's personality, which became through his influence the pervading spirit of the whole of National Socialist "law" as well, was a complete lack of any sense of truth or any sense of right and wrong. Because he had no sense of truth, he could shamelessly, unscrupulously lend the ring of truth to whatever was rhetorically effective at the moment. And because he had no sense of right and wrong, he could without hesitation elevate to a statute the crudest expression of despotic caprice. There is, at the beginning of his regime, his telegram offering sympathy to the Potempa murderers,[20] at the end, the hideous degradation of the martyrs of 20 July 1944.[21] The supporting theory had been provided by the Nazi ideologue, Alfred Rosenberg, writing in response to the Potempa death sentences: People are not alike, and murders are not alike; the murder of the pacifist Jaurès[22] was properly judged in France in a different light than the attempt to murder the nationalist Clemenceau;[23] for it is impossible to subject the patriotically motivated perpetrator to the same punishment as one whose motives are (in the view of the National Socialists) inimical to the people.[24] The explicit intention from the very beginning, then, was that National Socialist "law" would extricate itself from the essential requirement of justice, namely, the equal treatment of equals. It thereby lacks completely the very nature of law; it is not merely flawed law, but rather no law at all. This applies especially to those enactments by means of which the National Socialist Party claimed for itself the whole of the state, flouting the principle that every political party represents only a part of the state. Legal character is also lacking in all the statutes that treated human beings as subhuman and denied them human rights, and it is lacking, too, in all the caveats that, governed solely by the momentary necessities of intimidation, disregarded the varying gravity of offences and threatened the same punishment, often death, for the slightest as well as the most serious of crimes. All these are examples of statutory lawlessness.

We must not fail to recognize – especially in light of the events of those twelve years – what frightful dangers for legal certainty there can be in the notion of "statutory lawlessness," in duly enacted statutes that are denied the very nature of law. We must hope that such lawlessness will remain an isolated aberration of the German people, a never-to-be-repeated madness. We must prepare, however, for every eventuality. We must arm ourselves against the recurrence of an outlaw state like Hitler's by fundamentally overcoming positivism, which rendered impotent every possible defence against the abuses of National Socialist legislation.[25]

IV

That looks to the future. In the face of the statutory lawlessness of the past twelve years, we must seek now to meet the requirement of justice with the smallest possible sacrifice of legal certainty. Not every judge acting on his own initiative should be allowed to invalidate[26] statutes; rather, this task should be reserved to a higher court or to legislation.[27] Such legislation has already been enacted in the American Zone, based on an agreement in the Council of German States. It is "Act No. 29, on the Redress of National Socialist Wrongs Committed in the Administration of Criminal Justice" [31 May 1946]. A provision according to which "political acts undertaken in resistance to National Socialism or militarism are not punishable" surmounts the difficulties, for example, of the previously mentioned case of the deserter.[28] On the other hand, the companion statute, "Act No. 22, concerning the Punishment of National Socialist Crimes" [31 May 1946], applies to the other three cases discussed here[29] only if the deed in question was criminal according to the law at the time the deed was done. We have to consider the criminality of these other three cases, then, according to the law of the German Criminal Code of 1871, without reference to the later statute.

In the case of the informer Puttfarken, the view that he was guilty of indirectly committing murder is unchallengeable if he intended to cause Göttig's death, an intention he realized by using as his instrument the criminal court and as his means the legal automatism of a criminal proceeding. According to the opinion submitted by Professor Lange,[30] such an intention exists especially in those cases "in which the perpetrator had an interest in getting rid of the person he denounced, whether an interest in marrying his victim's wife, taking over his victim's home or job, or an interest in revenge and the like."[31] Just as a person is the indirect perpetrator where, for criminal purposes, he has abused his power of command over someone bound to obey him, so also is a person the indirect perpetrator where, for criminal purposes, he has set the judicial apparatus into motion by informing on someone. The use of the court as a mere instrument is especially clear in those cases where the indirect perpetrator could and did count on a politically tendentious exercise of the office of the criminal judiciary, whether owing to the political fanaticism of the judge or pressure applied by those in power. Suppose, on the other hand, that the informer had no such criminal intent, but intended instead to provide the court with evidence and leave the rest to the court's decision. Then the informer can be punished for complicity – having brought about the conviction and indirectly the execution of the person he denounced – only if the court itself, in virtue of its decision and the carrying out of its sentence, is guilty of having committed murder. This was in fact the route taken by the court in Nordhausen.

The culpability of judges for homicide presupposes the simultaneous determination that they have perverted the law,[32] since the independent judge's decision can be an object of punishment only if he has violated the very principle that his independence was intended to serve, the principle of submission to the statute, that is, to the law. Objectively speaking, perversion of the law exists where we can determine, in light of the basic principles we have developed, that the statute applied was not law at all, or that the degree of punishment imposed – say, the death sentence pronounced at the discretion of the judge – made a mockery of any intention of doing justice. But what of judges who had been so deformed by the prevailing positivism that they knew no other law than enacted law? Could such judges, in applying positive-law statutes, have had the intention of perverting the law? And even if they did have this intention, there remains one last legal defence for them, albeit a painful one. They could invoke the state of necessity contemplated in section 54 of the Criminal Code[33] by pointing out that they would have risked their own lives had they pronounced National Socialist law to be statutory lawlessness. I call this defence a painful one because the judge's ethos ought to be directed toward justice at any price, even at the price of his own life.

The simplest question to deal with is that of the culpability of the two executioner's assistants for carrying out death sentences. One cannot allow oneself to be influenced either by one's impression of people who make a business out of killing other human beings or by the booming prosperity and profitability of that business at the time. Even when their occupation was still a trade of the sort passed down from generation to generation, executioners repeatedly took care to excuse themselves by pointing out that they were merely carrying out sentences, and that the task of pronouncing sentence belonged to the lord judges. "The lords and masters hold evil in check, and I carry out their final judgment."

This 1698 maxim, or something similar, appears frequently on the blades of executioners' swords. Just as a judge's pronouncement of the death sentence can constitute murder only if it is based on perversion of the law, so the executioner can be punished for his deed only if it fits the circumstance described in section 345 of the Criminal Code: the deliberate carrying out of a punishment that should not be carried out. Karl Binding, with reference to this circumstance, writes that the relation of the executioner to the enforceable sentence is analogous to the relation of the judge to the statute; his single, total duty lies in its precise realization. The executioner's entire activity is determined by the sentence:

His action is just, in so far as it complies with the sentence. It becomes unjust in so far as it deviates from the sentence. This amounts to a disavowal of the single authority that matters for the execution as such, and therein lies the kernel of guilt. The delict [in section 345] ... can therefore be characterized as "perversion of a sentence."[34]

Verification of the legality of the sentence is not incumbent on the executioner. The supposition of its illegality, then, cannot be damaging to him, nor can his failure to resign his post be charged against him as culpable nonfeasance.

V

We do not share the opinion expressed at Nordhausen that "scruples of legal form" tend "to obfuscate" the plain facts. Rather, we are of the opinion that after twelve years of denying legal certainty, we need more than ever to arm ourselves with considerations of "legal form" in order to resist the understandable temptations that can easily arise in every person who has lived through those years of menace and oppression. We must seek justice, but at the same time attend to legal certainty, for it is itself a component of justice. And we must rebuild a *Rechtsstaat*, a government of law that serves as well as possible the ideas of both justice and legal certainty. Democracy is indeed laudable, but a government of law is like our daily bread, like water to drink and air to breathe, and the best thing about democracy is precisely that it alone is capable of securing for us such a government.

NOTES

1 "Gesetzliches Unrecht and übergesetzliches Recht," first published in the Süddeutsche Juristen-Zeitung 1 (1946) 105–8, repr. *inter alia* in Gustav Radbruch, *Gesamtausgabe* (Collected Works), 20 vols, ed. Arthur Kaufmann, vol. 3: *Rechtsphilosophie III*, ed. Winfried Hassemer (Heidelberg: C.F. Müller, 1990) 83–93, 282–91 (editor's notes), and in Radbruch, *Rechtsphilosophie, Studienausgabe*, ed. Ralf Dreier and Stanley L. Paulson (Heidelberg: C.F. Müller, 2nd ed., 2003) 211–19, 234–5 (editors' notes). Translated by Bonnie Litschewski Paulson and Stanley L. Paulson. The translators have drawn on the original printing of 1946; on a reprinting in Gustav Radbruch, *Rechtsphilosophie*, 4th–7th ed., ed. Erik Wolf, and 8th ed., ed. Erik Wolf and Hans-Peter Schneider (Stuttgart: K.F. Koehler, 1950–73); and on a partial, unpublished translation by Lon L. Fuller, which appeared, *inter alia*, in his "Supplemental Readings in Jurisprudence, 1958–9" (Harvard Law School). The translation here is published with the kind permission of Mrs Dorothea Kaufmann (Munich). The translators would like to thank Ralf Dreier (Göttingen), Thomas Mertens (Nijmegen), and Julian Rivers (Bristol) for very helpful comments and suggestions.

2 Military Criminal Code of 1940, § 47.

3 [Translating *"Unrecht"* as "lawlessness" here – not as "injustice," "wrong," or "evil," among other possibilities – and *"Recht"* as "law" – not as "justice" or "right" – underscores the legal context of the sharp distinction Radbruch draws between the two terms. Better reflecting the "positivistic legal thinking" he mentions, the phrases themselves might read "statutory (or positive-law) lawlessness" and "supra-statutory (or supra-positive) law."]

4 Heinz Kleine, in Süddeutsche Juristen-Zeitung 1 (1946) 36.

5 [Post-war Germany was divided by the occupying powers into four zones – Russian, French, British, and American – for purposes of Allied administration of the devastated country.]

6 *Thüringer Volk* (Weimar), 10 May 1946. [In the immediate post-war period, official reports of judicial proceedings were not generally available, and so Radbruch quotes extensively here from newspaper accounts.]

7 Ibid. [Emphasis in original.]

8 In his edition of the Criminal Code in its Thüringian rendition (Weimar: Landesverlag Thüringen, 1946), 13, Prof. Richard Lange states that "in those cases where the perpetrator has misused the judicial system to pursue his own criminal purposes (deception during litigation, political denunciation), much uncertainty has arisen about the concept of the

indirect commission of a crime. Therefore, article 2 of the Supplementary Law of 8 February 1946 makes clear that the indirect commission of a crime is punishable even if the instrument that is employed has itself acted lawfully or in compliance with its official duty."

9 [Control Council Law No. 10, article 2, paragraph 1(c): *"Crimes against Humanity.* Atrocities and offenses, including but not limited to murder, extermination, enslavement, deportation, imprisonment, torture, rape, or other inhumane acts committed against any civilian population, or persecutions on political, racial or religious grounds whether or not in violation of the domestic laws of the country where perpetrated."]

10 [Ibid., article 2, paragraph 3: "Any persons found guilty of any of the crimes above mentioned [in article 2, paragraph 1] may upon conviction be punished as shall be determined by the tribunal to be just. Such punishment may consist of one or more of the following: (a) Death. (b) Imprisonment for life or a term of years, with or without hard labour. (c) Fine, and imprisonment with or without hard labour, in lieu thereof. (d) Forfeiture of property. (e) Restitution of property wrongfully acquired. (f) Deprivation of some or all civil rights. Any property declared to be forfeited or the restitution of which is ordered by the Tribunal shall be delivered to the Control Council for Germany, which shall decide on its disposal."]

11 Criminal liability according to Allied Control Council Law No. 10 is not discussed in what follows, for German courts do not have primary jurisdiction here. See article 3, paragraph 1(d). ["Each occupying authority, within its Zone of Occupation, shall have the right to cause all persons so arrested and charged, and not delivered to another authority as herein provided, or released, to be brought to trial before an appropriate tribunal. Such tribunal may, in the case of crimes committed by persons of German citizenship or nationality against other persons of German citizenship or nationality, or stateless persons, be a German Court, if authorized by the occupying authorities."]

12 *Thüringer Volk,* above n. 6 [emphasis in original].

13 Another proceeding involving denunciation took place before the Munich denazification panel, against those who had informed on the Scholls. [Siblings Hans and Sophie Scholl, leading members of the White Rose, a resistance group at the University of Munich, were distributing anti-Nazi leaflets when they were arrested on 18 February 1943. Condemned to death on 22 February 1943, they were executed the same day. Hans was 24 years old, Sophie 21.] Denazification is levelled against a politically and morally inferior sentiment, and need not enquire into the legality or legitimacy or the culpability of putting that sentiment into practice. It

follows then that a line is drawn between denazification and criminal jurisdiction, but it also follows that the two overlap. Compare article 22 of the *Befreiungsgesetz* [Law for Liberation from National Socialism and Militarism, 5 March 1946].

14 Also requiring discussion here would be the extent to which the "normative force of the factual" [Georg Jellinek] makes valid law out of systems that come to power by way of revolution. And my colleague Walter Jellinek has kindly pointed out that it would be inaccurate to suggest that the two-thirds majority was achieved only by eliminating the Communists.

15 *Tägliche Rundschau* (Berlin), 14 March 1946 [emphasis in original]. On criminal responsibility for unlawful judicial decisions, see also Friedrich Buchwald in his notable work, *Gerechtes Recht* (Weimar: Panses Verlag, 1946) at 3–8.

16 *Liberaldemokratische Zeitung* (Halle), 12 June 1946. [See above, n. 9.]

17 *Tägliche Rundschau*, above n. 15, 9 May 1946.

18 [The German "*Zweckmäßigkeit*" is often translated, respectably, as "utility" or "expediency." In the present context, however, any suggestion of utilitarianism would be misleading, as would the connotation of opportunism that attaches to "expediency." "Purposiveness" has the virtue of stemming directly from "purpose," thereby underscoring Radbruch's point.]

19 [*The Holy Bible*, King James Version, 1611, Hebrews 13:17 and Acts 5:29 respectively.]

20 [In 1932, five Nazi storm troopers were condemned to death by a court in Upper Silesia for the brutal murder of a Communist in the village of Potempa. Under pressure from the Nazis, their sentence was commuted to life imprisonment. After Hitler came to power, they were pardoned.]

21 [Wehrmacht officers and others, arrested following their failed attempt to assassinate Hitler on 20 July 1944, were tortured, viciously humiliated in a sham trial, and executed.]

22 [Jean Jaurès, an eloquent politician known as an intellectual champion of socialism, was assassinated in Paris in 1914 by a fanatical nationalist, Raoul Villain. Villain was taken into custody pending trial, but acquitted in 1919 by jurors who reportedly felt he was a patriot who had done France a favour by getting rid of the antiwar Jaurès.]

23 [Georges Clemenceau, a Radical Nationalist politician, survived an attempt on his life made in 1892 by a rival political group, taking revenge for his repudiation of their leader, General Boulanger, a convicted traitor who had committed suicide in 1891. The Boulangist who failed in his attempt to assassinate Clemenceau was unceremoniously executed.]

24 *Völkischer Beobachter* (Munich) [publication of the National Socialist Party], 26 August 1932.

25 Buchwald, too, argues for supra-statutory law in his book, above n. 15, at 8–16. And compare Walter Roemer, Siiddeutsche Juristen-Zeitung 1 (1946) 9–11.

26 ["Entwerten" (translated "invalidate" here) appears in the Wolf editions of Radbruch's *Rechtsphilosophie*, but *"entwerfen"* ("to draft") is used in the original printing as well as in the Collected Works, above at asterisk note. In the context here, "invalidate" is clearly the better fit.]

27 See also Kleine's article in the Siiddeursche Juristen-Zeitung, above n. 4.

28 See § II, case no. 5, above.

29 [See § II, case nos 1–3, above.]

30 [See § II, case no. 1, above, and see above, n. 7.]

31 It is of course the height of subjectivism in the doctrine of complicity, that criminal intent – in the form of a "subjective element of wrongdoing" – entails in the person of the indirect perpetrator illegality that is lacking in the person of the direct agent or instrument.

32 § 336 and § 344 of the Criminal Code.

33 [See also § II, case no. 4, above.]

34 Karl Binding, *Lehrbuch des Gemeinen Deutschen Strafrechts, Besonderer Ted*, vol. 2 (Leipzig: Engelmann-Verlag, 1st ed., 1905) 569.

READING QUESTION ON RADBRUCH

1 There are two interpretations of Radbruch's position. First, one could think of his position as positivism with a minus sign. Law is the law certified as valid by a legal system's criteria of validity except when it is extremely unjust, as judged by moral values that are not necessarily part of legal order. Second, one could think of it as more like Fuller's position – that is, law fails to be law when it grossly offends principles of legality that are intrinsic to legal order. Which do you think is the better interpretation?

Riggs v. Palmer 22 N.E. 188 (1889)

A nineteenth-century New York case involving the right of an heir to inherit from the grandfather he had murdered. This case raises the question of the relation between moral principles and statutory interpretation.

RIGGS ET AL. V. PALMER ET AL.

(Court of Appeals of New York. Oct. 1889)

Rights of Legatees – Murder of Testator

The Laws of New York relating to the probate of wills and the distributions of estates will not be construed so as to secure the benefit of a will to a legatee who has killed the testator in order to prevent a revocation of the will. Gray and Danforth, JJ., dissenting.

Appeal from supreme court, general term, third department.

Leslie W. Russell, for appellants. *W. M. Hawkins,* for respondents.

Earl, J.: – On the 13th day of August, 1880, Francis B. Palmer made his last will and testament, in which he gave small legacies to his two daughters, Mrs Riggs and Mrs Preston, the plaintiffs in this action, and the remainder of his estate to his grandson, the defendant Elmer E. Palmer, subject to the support of Susan Palmer, his mother, with a gift over to the two daughters, subject to the support of Mrs Palmer in case Elmer should survive him and die under age, unmarried, and without any issue. The testator, at the date of his will, owned a farm, and considerable personal property. He was a widower, and thereafter, in March, 1882 he was married to Mrs Bresee, with whom, before his marriage, he entered into an ante-nuptial contract, in which it was agreed that in lieu of dower and all other claims upon his estate in case she survived him she should have her support upon his farm during her life, and such support was expressly charged upon the farm. At the date of the will, and subsequently to the death of the testator, Elmer lived with him as a member of his family, and at his death was 16 years old. He knew of the provisions made in his favor in the will, and, that he might prevent his grandfather from revoking such provisions, which he had manifested some intention to do, and to obtain the speedy enjoyment and immediate possession of his property, he willfully murdered him by poisoning him. He now claims the property, and the sole question for our determination is, can he have it?

The defendants say that the testator is dead; that his will was made in due form, and has been admitted to probate; and that therefore it must have effect according to the letter of the law. It is quite true that statutes regulating the making, proof, and effect of wills and the devolution of property, if literally construed, and if their force and effect can in no way and under no circumstances be controlled or modified, give this property to the murderer. The purpose of those statutes was to enable testators to dispose of their estates to the objects of their bounty at death, and to carry into effect their final wishes legally expressed; and in considering and giving effect to them this purpose must be kept in view ...

In 1 Bl. Comm. 91, the learned author, speaking of the construction of statutes, says: "If there arise out of them collaterally any absurd consequences manifestly contradictory to common reason, they are with regard to those collateral consequences void ... Where some collateral matter arises out of the general words, and happens to be unreasonable, there the judges are in decency to conclude that this consequence was not foreseen by the parliament, and therefore they are at liberty to expound the statute by equity, and only *quo ad hoc* disregard it"; and he gives as an illustration, if an act of parliament gives a man power to try all causes that arise within his manor of Dale, yet, if a cause should arise in which he himself is party, the act is construed not to extend to that, because it is unreasonable that any man should determine his own quarrel. There was a statute in Bologna that whoever drew blood in the streets should be severely punished, and yet it was held not to apply to the case of a barber who opened a vein in the street. It is commanded in the Decalogue that no work shall be done upon the Sabbath, and yet giving the command a rational interpretation founded upon its design, the Infallible Judge held that it did not prohibit works of necessity, charity, or benevolence on that day.

What could be more unreasonable than to suppose that it was the legislative intention in the general laws passed for the orderly, peaceable, and just devolution of property that they should have operation in favor of one who murdered his ancestor that he might speedily come into the possession of his estate? Such an intention is inconceivable. We need not, therefore, be much troubled by the general language contained in the laws. Besides, all laws, as well as all contracts, may be controlled in their operation and effect by general, fundamental maxims of the common law. No one shall be permitted to profit by his own fraud, or to take advantage of his own wrong, or to found any claim upon his own iniquity, or to acquire property by his own crime. These maxims are dictated by public policy, have their foundation in universal law administered in all civilized countries, and have nowhere been superseded by statutes. They were applied in the decision of the case of the *New York Life Mutual Insurance Co. v. Armstrong*. There it was held that the person who procured a policy upon the life of another, payable at his death, and then murdered the assured to make the policy payable, could not recover thereon ...

Here there was no certainty that this murderer would survive the testator, or that the testator would not change his will, and there was no certainty that he would get this property if nature was allowed to take its course. He therefore murdered the testator expressly to vest himself with an estate. Under such circumstances, what law, human or divine, will allow him to take the estate and enjoy the fruits of his crime? The will spoke and became operative at the death of the testator. He caused that death, and thus by his crime made it speak and have operation. Shall it speak and operate in his favor? If he had met the testator, and taken his property by force, he would have had no title to it. Shall he acquire title by murdering him? If he had gone to the testator's house, and by force compelled him, or by fraud or undue influence had induced him, to will him his property, the law would not allow him to hold it. But can he give effect and operation to a will by murder, and yet take the property? To answer these questions in the affirmative it seems to me would be a reproach to the jurisprudence of our state, and an offense against public policy ...

In the Civil Code of Lower Canada the provisions on the subject in the Code Napoleon have been substantially copied. But, so far as I can find, in no country where the common law prevails has it been deemed important to enact a law to provide for such a case. Our revisers and law-makers were familiar with the civil law, and they did not deem it important to incorporate into our statutes its provisions upon this subject. This is not a *casus omissus*. It was evidently supposed that the maxims of the common law were sufficient to regulate such a case, and that a specific enactment for that purpose was not needed. For the same reasons the defendant Palmer cannot take any of this property as heir. Just before the murder he was not an heir, and it was not certain that he ever would be. He might have died before his grandfather, or might have been disinherited by him. He made himself an heir by the murder, and he seeks to take property as the fruit of his crime. What has before been said as to him as legatee applies to him with equal force as an heir. He cannot vest himself with title by crime. My view of this case does not inflict upon Elmer any greater or other punishment for his crime than the law specifies. It takes from him no property, but simply holds that he shall not acquire property by his crime, and thus be rewarded for its commission.

Gray, J. (*dissenting*): – This appeal presents an extraordinary state of facts, and the case, in respect of them, I believe, is without precedent in this state. The respondent, a lad of 16 years of age, being aware of the provisions in his grandfather's will, which constituted him the residuary legatee of the testator's estate, caused his death by poison, in 1882. For this crime he was tried, and was convicted of murder in the second degree, and at the time of the commencement of this action he was serving out his sentence in the state reformatory. This action was brought by two of the children of the testator for the purpose of having those provisions of the will in the respondent's favor canceled and annulled. The appellants' argument for a reversal of the judgment, which dismissed their complaint, is that the respondent unlawfully prevented a revocation of the existing will, or a new will from being made, by his crime; and that he terminated the enjoyment by the testator of his property, and effected his own succession to it, by the same crime. They say that to permit the respondent to take the property willed to him would be to permit him to take advantage of his own wrong. To sustain their position the appellants' counsel has submitted an able and elaborate brief, and, if I believed that the decision of the question could be effected by considerations of an equitable nature, I should not hesitate to assent to views which commend themselves to the conscience. But the matter does not lie within the domain of conscience. We are bound by the rigid rules of law, which have been established by the legislature, and within the limits of which the determination of this question is confined. The question we are dealing with is whether a testamentary disposition can be altered, or a will revoked, after the testator's death, through an appeal to the courts, when the legislature has by its enactments prescribed exactly when and how wills may be made, altered, and revoked, and apparently, as it seems to me, when they have been fully complied with, has left no room for the exercise of an equitable jurisdiction by courts over such matters. Modern jurisprudence, in recognizing the right of the individual, under more or less restrictions, to dispose of his property after his death, subjects it to legislative control, both as to extent and as to mode of exercise. Complete freedom of testamentary disposition of one's property has not been and is not the universal rule, as we see from the provisions of the Napoleonic Code, from the systems of jurisprudence in countries which are modeled upon the Roman law, and from the statutes of many of our states. To the statutory restraints which are imposed upon the disposition of one's property by will are added strict and systematic statutory rules for the execution, alteration, and revocation of the will, which must be, at least substantially, if not exactly, followed to insure validity and performance. The reason for the establishment of such rules, we may naturally assume, consists in the purpose to create those safeguards about these grave and important acts which experience has demonstrated to be the wisest and surest. That freedom which is permitted to be exercised in the testamentary disposition of one's estate by the laws of the state is subject to its being exercised in conformity with the regulations of the statutes. The capacity and the power of the individual to dispose of his property after death, and the mode by which that power can be exercised, are matters of which the legislature has assumed the entire control, and has undertaken to regulate with comprehensive particularity.

The appellants' argument is not helped by reference to those rules of the civil law, or to those laws of other governments, by which the heir, or legatee, is excluded from benefit under the testament if he has been convicted of killing, or attempting to kill, the testator.

In the absence of such legislation here, the courts are not empowered to institute such a system of remedial justice. The deprivation of the heir of his testamentary succession by the Roman law, when guilty of such a crime, plainly was intended to be in the nature of a punishment imposed upon him. The succession, in such a case of guilt, escheated to the exchequer. See Dom. Civil Law, pt. 2, bk. 1, tit. 1, s. 3. I concede that rules of law which annul testamentary provisions made for the benefit of those who have become unworthy of them may be based on principles of equity and of natural justice. It is quite reasonable to suppose that a testator would revoke or alter his will, where his mind has been so angered and changed as to make him unwilling to have his will executed as it stood. But these principles only suggest sufficient reasons for the enactment of laws to meet such cases.

The statutes of this state have prescribed various ways in which a will may be altered or revoked; but the very provision defining the modes of alteration and revocation implies a prohibition of alteration or revocation in any other way. The words of the section of the statute are: "No will in writing, except in the cases hereinafter mentioned, nor any part thereof, shall be revoked or altered otherwise," etc. Where, therefore, none of the cases mentioned are met by the facts, and the revocation is not in the way described in the section, the will of the testator is unalterable. I think that a valid will must continue as a will always, unless revoked in the manner provided by the statutes. Mere intention to revoke a will does not have the effect of revocation.

READING QUESTIONS ON *RIGGS V. PALMER*

1 Earl, J. says that the law will not allow a man to profit from his own wrongdoing. Where does he find this principle? Can you think of exceptions to it? If so, in what sense is it supposed to be binding?
2 Putting aside the question of Riggs's wrongdoing and the appropriate punishment for it, do you find Grey, J.'s view of the judicial role more appealing?

Tony Honoré
"The Necessary Connection between Law and Morality" (2002)

Honoré, one of the twentieth century's most distinguished jurists, worked closely with H.L.A. Hart. In this short essay, he casts significant doubt on the positivist separation thesis and offers a rich resource for reflection on the materials gathered in this chapter.

On a plausible interpretation of legal positivism, lawyers should reject it as inconsistent with positive law.[1]

Positivism has stood historically for a number of different, though related, ideas. They revolve round two problems. How is law to be identified? How does it relate to morality? On identifying law the positivist thesis is that, as Raz puts it, what is or is not law is a matter of social fact.[2] To this thesis there are two aspects. First, there are in every society criteria (for example accepted rules of recognition) according to which certain items, such as constitutionally enacted legislation, count as law. These criteria mark off what is legally authoritative from what is not. Second, nothing that does not satisfy these socially accepted criteria is law. Nothing is law unless it is recognized as authoritative in the society in which it is claimed to be law.

The positivist thesis about the relation of law to morality follows from the thesis about the identification of law. Nothing that is law according to the accepted criteria for identifying law is disqualified from being law merely because it is morally indefensible. In an extreme form, which Raz dubs the "semantic thesis," terms such as "right," "duty" and "obligation" do not mean the same thing in law and morals. A law-giver who prescribes duties or confers rights does not even purport to prescribe morally binding duties or to confer morally defensible rights.

In its less extreme form, however, this thesis about the relation of law to morality is easy enough to defend. There can be evil laws and corrupt legal systems.[3] The Third Reich had a legal system. Apartheid South Africa had a legal system. It is true that not only these societies but every society has some unjust laws. These laws and legal systems are imperfect because, unless rights and duties mean something different in law and morality, laws and legal systems *claim* to be morally in order. But, though imperfect, the unjust laws and corrupt systems are real laws and legal systems. It is not plausible to say, with some old-fashioned natural lawyers, that the morally objectionable laws and legal systems are not laws and legal systems. Their supporters and opponents alike treat the unjust laws as laws and the corrupt systems as legal systems. Law is a human construct and what is treated by humans as law is law. To deny that objectionable laws and systems are law is to express abhorrence of those laws or legal systems. It is to stress that the laws or systems fail to impose the morally binding duties that they claim to impose. But it is to tell a lie.

On the other hand the more extreme thesis about the relation between law and morality – the thesis that right, duty and obligation mean something different in law and morality – cannot be defended. Hart, it is true, thought that rights, duties and obligations meant something different in law and morals, the moral meaning being in some sense stronger than the legal one. No doubt from the citizen's point of view what the law requires is merely one consideration among others in deciding what to do. But that is not because the law *means* the duties it imposes to be treated as merely providing one consideration among others. Theorists, including Raz, have rightly criticized Hart's opinion,[4] which stems from a mistake about constitutional authority. The authority to make law is futile unless it includes the authority to say what people should do *all things considered*, not merely what they should do if their conduct is to be guided by law. It would be self-defeating for a law-maker (legislator, judge or official), when laying down duties or conferring rights, to say, "This is what you should do if you want to abide by the law" rather than "This is what you should do, full stop." The citizen may view compliance with the requirement as conditional on his or her wishing to abide by the law, but the law-maker must at least purport to pre-empt any reasons the citizen may have for not obeying the law. This is not because the law-maker usually attaches a sanction to disregard of the law, though the threat of sanction, if it exists, will be an additional reason for conforming to law. It is rather that the law-maker must claim the authority to lay down what is morally required of the citizen despite any reasons that appear to conflict with what the law requires. The law-maker may be mistaken – may even know that what is required is not morally defensible. But the claim that it is defensible is an ineluctable feature of law making.

The law-maker's claim that what is prescribed is morally binding may take one of two forms. One is that what the law requires is something morally required even apart from law, like supporting one's family. The other is that what is required is morally defensible apart from law, like paying VAT, and morally binding because prescribed by law. For law will sometimes make morally binding what was not binding apart from its being so required.[5] To understand the meaning of a law requires us, then, to attend to its normative aspect – what Kelsen called its normative meaning, its oughtness.[6]

Apart from this constitutional point, it would be strange in the light of history if terms like as "right," "duty" and "obligation" had different meanings in law and morality. These terms are derived from Roman law (*ius, debitum, obligatio*), the system that first conceived law as a balance of rights and obligations subsisting between individuals and between them and the state. From this legal context the terms were extended by analogy to moral discourse, so that moral philosophers now speak of "moral duties," "moral obligations" and "moral rights." It would be strange if this change of context carried with it a change of meaning, and what is more a change from a weaker legal to a stronger moral meaning.

The difference between the legal and moral duties and rights is not a difference of meaning. It is a difference between formal, institutionally recognized duties and rights and their informal, non-institutional equivalents. The use of these notions outside the law implies that we ought to treat certain actions and interests rather as if they formed part of the institutional apparatus that makes up the law, though they do not. If it is said that a father has a moral obligation to support the mother of his child this means that, though perhaps not legally bound to do so, he should regard himself somewhat as if he were legally bound to support her. It need not be implied that the moral right or obligation should be converted into a legal one. It remains an open question whether it would be good policy to convert the moral obligation to support the child's mother into a legal one. Moral rights and obligations can stand on their own feet; but the meaning of the terms "moral right" and "moral obligation" is parasitic on the legal model from which they are historically derived.

That law-makers claim to impose morally binding requirements has an important consequence. It opens the law, when it comes to be interpreted or applied, to challenge on moral grounds. It makes it part of the notion of law, not something external to law, that it is open to moral criticism. One needs to keep an apparent paradox in mind. A law may be law though morally indefensible. But when the interpretation or application or continued existence of a law is in issue it is always open to a litigant or citizen or legislator to argue that it should be interpreted and applied in a way that is morally defensible or amended in such a way that it becomes morally defensible. For brevity I shall use the term "interpretation" but this needs to be understood in a very wide sense. The moral challenge to law may take, and often has taken, the form of inviting a magistrate such as the Roman praetor or the English Chancellor to intervene in order to render the application of the law morally defensible. If the law claims to be morally in good order the moral argument, whether addressed to the judicial or executive or legislative branch of the state, must always be available.

But what does the law's claim to being morally in good order amount to? Does it mean only that the interpretation of the law should be consistent with the morality current in the society in question ("positive morality")? If so, the positivist thesis that law is a matter of social fact is not affected, since it is a matter of social fact what the morality currently practised or endorsed by a society consists in. Raz, who supports the social fact thesis, accepts that this theory may be consistent with there being a necessary connection between law and current morality.[7] Perhaps. But what if the law-maker's meaning, properly understood, is that what the law prescribes really is a moral duty, not merely that one that fits the morality current in the society in question?

There is a distinction between two arguments concerned with morality that can be raised when the interpretation of a law is in issue. One is that a proposed interpretation would offend current morality and so cause unrest or be difficult to enforce. That argument rests on the likely consequences of adopting a particular interpretation. The other is that a proposed interpretation would be morally indefensible, irrespective of whether it would cause unrest or be difficult to enforce. The first argument appeals to social facts, or apprehended facts. The second does not.

But what does it appeal to? Presumably to "critical" as opposed to current morality. At any rate it is not enough, with Dworkin, to say that the appeal is to the best moral justification of the source-based rules and decisions, because there may be no moral justification for some, perhaps even for many of these. But what is the content of critical morality in this context? It cannot refer to the philosophically correct theory of human behaviour, utilitarian, Kantian, Catholic or whatever it may be, since there neither is nor is likely to be agreement on what this is. But the question admits of a rational answer in the context in which it arises. The critical or rational morality to which law-makers implicitly appeal will comprise certain values inherent in law irrespective of the particular legal system concerned. Law seeks to supplant unregulated violence, both within societies and between them, by fostering the values of co-operation and peaceful co-existence.[8] The critical morality to which the law-maker implicitly appeals relates to these values, and to any more specific values consistent with them that the society in question may embrace. That the society embraces them does not make the appeal to them a social fact about that society. They are relevant to legal argument not because the society embraces them, or some of them (it may reject others) but because they tend to promote co-operation and peaceful co-existence.

If this is correct, the claim of law to be morally in good order puts in question the social thesis, according to which what law is or is not is (wholly) a matter of social fact. Whether something is law is rather partly, indeed largely, a matter of social fact but partly a matter of what is morally defensible.

The argument for the existence of a necessary connection between law and morality does not depend on the society in question possessing a constitution that makes reference to moral criteria, for example in a bill of rights. In some societies the list of authoritative sources includes some that incorporate moral considerations. In that case the moral considerations are positive in the sense of being formally recognized in the society as relevant to whether something is or is not law.[9] The necessary connection here asserted is however independent of whether constitutional provisions of this sort are incorporated in the sources of law recognized in a particular society. It exists by virtue of the fact that whatever is identified as law according to criteria such as rules of recognition requires to be interpreted and applied, not that it has any particular moral content. If moral provisions are written into, say, a bill of rights these provisions themselves require interpretation, which includes interpretation from the point of view of critical morality. A person who under a bill of rights has a right to a fair trial has a right to a trial that is objectively fair, not merely to one that fits the current morality of the society in question. But even if there is no constitutional right to a fair trial, the trial procedure prescribed by law falls to be interpreted in the light of critical morality, of which fairness forms a part.

The connection here proposed is a connection between morality and present, not future law. A person's conduct, if subject to legal challenge, is judged by law as it comes later to be interpreted by a court or executive official. The future moral input into interpretation is therefore, from the citizens' point of view, part of the law at the time he or she acted, though from the point of view of a legal historian it was not yet part of the law. But for the positivist thesis that what is law is a matter of social fact it would be question-begging to confine law to official determinations of the law, since the law by which citizens are judged includes determinations that were not made when they did what they did. Given that citizens are exposed to retrospective interpretations of the law governing their conduct, the moral input into interpretation is some protection to those whose seek to be guided by moral considerations.[10]

It is true that the necessary connection with morality here proposed is a connection with morality as a persuasive, not an authoritative source of law. For the argument that a certain interpretation of the law will be morally untenable, even if correct, cannot be guaranteed to convince a court or official. Or it may convince the court or official without being decisive since other considerations of, say, the wording, systematic fit or purpose of a law stand in the way of giving effect to the morally best interpretation. The interpreter has to take account not only of moral but of linguistic, systematic and teleological arguments. Which interpretations are possible given the wording of the law? Which best fits the rest of the system and the purposes of the provision in question? In the thinking of some theorists these considerations would be arranged in lexical order, so that one of them (let us say the moral considerations) would systematically prevail over the others.[11] In the real world this is not the case, and there are good reasons, outside the scope of the present essay, why it should not be. The necessary connection of law with morality does not therefore guarantee that law will be morally reputable, merely that there will be pressure to make it morally reputable. In what way, then, is the connection a necessary one? Does it enhance the claims of law to our respect?

The connection between law and critical morality is necessary in that it is not contingent. It applies to every law and every legal system. The proposed interpretation of every law in every legal system can *legally* be challenged on the ground that it is not morally defensible, whether the challenge succeeds or fails in a particular instance.

It is also a connection that does, in my view, enhance the claims of law to our respect. The positivist doctrine is something of a prison. How is the law to escape from received ideas, including received ideas about morality? It is because of the necessary connection with morality that judges, officials, writers and teachers whose function it is to interpret the law have been able over the centuries to mould it so as to take account of moral considerations. The same connection, arising from the claim of law to be morally in order, has served to inspire reformers and promote law reform. Hence the values of fairness, equity, justice, honesty, humanity, dignity, prudence, abstention from violence and a host of other values that conduce to co-operation and co-existence play a prominent role in the law even when they are not incorporated in any formal source of law. The interpreter's mandate is to apply the law as an item that purports to be morally in order. The requirement that a judge should do justice according to law expresses this mandate, though obliquely.

I have argued that the view here advocated derives from positive law, since the positive law of societies with legal systems, unlike the theory of positivism, makes arguments addressed to critical morality admissible in the interpretation and application of law. But is this true only of the law of certain societies? It is, in the sense that it applies fully only to those societies in which the interpretation of law is a serious intellectual discipline, so that a legal culture exists which in which there are recognized experts, often professionally organized. It would not apply to a society, if there has even been one, in which law was regarded merely as a system of threats. Nor would it apply to one what was not institutionally advanced enough to possess a legal culture. But it applies to any society in which there exists, in the words of the Roman writer Pomponius, "unwritten law that consists in interpretation."[12] In any such society there is an inbuilt pressure towards improving the law morally and in other ways. It is what in Soviet jargon was called a "permanently operative factor." Lawyers can take some comfort from the perception that they are committed to improving the law not by virtue of their individual merits but by the nature of the institution to which they are committed.

NOTES

1 The argument in this paper against a certain version of positivism is an argument about the nature of law but does not imply a commitment to any particular natural law theory.

2 "Legal Positivism and the Sources of Law" in *The Authority of Law. Essays on Law and Morality* (1979) at 37.

3 E.g. H.L.A. Hart, *The Concept of Law* (2nd ed., 1994) at 268: "morally iniquitous provisions may be valid as legal rules or principles." The reason Hart gives for this conclusion, viz. "that there are no necessary conceptual connections between the content of law and morality" is open to objection unless "conceptual" is given a very narrow meaning.

4 Raz, above n. 2 at 39.

5 T. Honoré, "The Dependence of Morality on Law," OJLS 13 (1993) 1–17.

6 *Introduction to the Problems of Legal Theory* (Reine Rechtslehre, 1934) trans. B.L and S.L. Paulson (1992) 32–5.

7 Above n. 1 at 39. He speaks of "popular" morality but that may suggest too down-market a version of morality. "Positive morality" is meant to include that practised or endorsed by the high-minded.

8 T. Honoré, *Making Law Bind* (1985) 106–14.

9 E.g. W.J. Waluchow, *Inclusive Legal Positivism* (1994).

10 On this point I disagree with the point of view expressed by John Eekelaar in his article in this issue. From the citizens' point of law the moral input is part of the law both because this is the way in which citizens normally think of law, and because they are right to do so in view of the fact that the moral input may turn out to affect their rights and obligations.

11 One could read R. Dworkin, *Law's Empire* (1986) in this sense.

12 Digest 1.2.2.12. 'Unwritten' in the sense of not being embodied in a set text.

The Queen v. Dudley and Stephens 14 QBD 273 (1884)

This is an English case from the nineteenth century, with rather unusual facts. Several sailors, cast away on the sea with nothing to eat, killed and ate the cabin boy. The issue before the court was whether the sailors could use the defence of "necessity" to escape a charge of murder.

INDICTMENT for the murder of Richard Parker on the high seas within the jurisdiction of the Admiralty.

At the trial before Huddleston, B., at the Devon and Cornwall Winter Assizes, November 7, 1884, the jury, at the suggestion of the learned judge, found the facts of the case in a special verdict which stated "that, on July 5, 1884, the prisoners, Thomas Dudley and Edward Stephens, with one Brooks, all able-bodied English seamen, and the deceased also an English boy, between seventeen and eighteen years of age, the crew of an English yacht, a registered English vessel, were cast away in a storm on the high seas 1600 miles from the Cape of Good Hope, and were compelled to put into an open boat belonging to the said yacht. That in this boat they had no supply of water and no supply of food, except two 1 lb. tins of turnips, and for three days they had nothing else to subsist upon. That on the fourth day they caught a small turtle, upon which they subsisted for a few days, and this was the only food they had up to the twentieth day when the act now in question was committed. That on the twelfth day the remains of the turtle were entirely consumed, and for the next eight days they had nothing to eat. That they had no fresh water, except such rain as they from time to time caught in their oilskin capes. That the boat was drifting on the ocean, and was probably more than 1000 miles away from land. That on the eighteenth day, when they had been seven days without food and five without water, the prisoners spoke to Brooks as to what should be done if no succour came, and suggested that some one should be sacrificed to save the rest, but Brooks dissented, and the boy, to whom they were understood to refer, was not consulted. That on the 24th of July, the day before the act now in question, the prisoner Dudley proposed to Stephens and Brooks that lots should be cast who should be put to death to save the rest, but Brooks refused to consent, and it was not put to the boy, and in point of fact there was no drawing of lots. That on that day the prisoners spoke of their having families, and suggested it would be better to kill the boy that their lives should be saved, and Dudley proposed that if there was no vessel in sight by the morrow morning, the boy should be killed. That next day, the 25th of July, no vessel appearing, Dudley told Brooks that he had better go and have a sleep, and made signs to Stephens and Brooks that the boy had better be killed. The prisoner Stephens agreed to the act, but Brooks dissented from it. That the boy was then lying at the bottom of the boat quite helpless, and extremely weakened by famine and by drinking sea water, and unable to make any resistance, nor did he ever assent to his being killed. The prisoner Dudley offered a prayer asking forgiveness for them all if either of them should be tempted to commit a rash act, and that their souls might be saved. That Dudley, with the assent of Stephens, went to the boy, and telling him that his time was come, put a knife into his throat and killed him then and there; that the three men fed upon the body and blood of the boy for four days; that on the fourth day after the act had been committed the boat was picked up by a passing vessel, and the prisoners were rescued, still alive, but in the lowest state of prostration. That they were carried to the port of Falmouth, and committed for trial at Exeter. That if the men had not fed upon the body of the boy they would probably not have survived to be so picked up and rescued, but would within the four days have died of famine. That the boy, being in a much weaker condition, was likely to have died before them. That at the time of the act in question there was no sail in sight, nor any reasonable prospect of relief ..."

The judgment of the Court (Lord Coleridge, C.J., Grove and Denman, JJ., Pollock and Huddleston, BB.) was delivered by LORD COLERIDGE, C.J.:

... [T]he prisoners put to death a weak and unoffending boy upon the chance of preserving their own lives by feeding upon his flesh and blood after he was killed, and with the certainty of depriving him, of any possible chance of survival. The verdict finds in terms that "if the men had not fed upon the body of the boy they would probably not have survived," and that "the boy being in a much weaker condition was likely to have died before them." They might possibly have been picked up next day by a passing ship; they might possibly not have been picked up at all; in either case it is obvious that the killing of the boy would have been an unnecessary and profitless act. It is found by the verdict that the boy was incapable of resistance, and, in fact, made none; and it is not even suggested that his death was due to any violence on his part attempted against, or even so much as feared by, those who killed him. Under these circumstances the jury say that they are ignorant whether those who killed him were guilty of murder, and have referred it to this Court to determine what is the legal consequence which follows from the facts which they have found ...

There remains to be considered the real question in the case – whether killing under the circumstances set forth in the verdict be or be not murder. The contention that it could be anything else was, to the minds of us all, both new and strange, and we stopped the Attorney General in his negative argument in order that we might hear what could be said in support of a proposition which appeared to us to be at once dangerous, immoral, and opposed to all legal principle and analogy. All, no doubt, that can be said has been urged before us, and we are now to consider and determine what it amounts to. First it is said that it follows from various definitions of murder in books of authority, which definitions imply, if they do not state, the doctrine, that in order to save your own life you may lawfully take away the life of another, when that other is neither attempting nor threatening yours, nor is guilty of any illegal act whatever towards you or any one else. But if these definitions be looked at they will not be found to sustain this contention. The earliest in point of date is the passage cited to us from Bracton, who lived in the reign of Henry III ... But in the very passage as to necessity, on which reliance has been placed, it is clear that Bracton is speaking of necessity in the ordinary sense – the repelling by violence, violence justified so far as it was necessary for the object, any illegal violence used towards oneself ... It is, if possible, yet clearer that the doctrine contended for receives no support from the great authority of Lord Hale. It is plain that in his view the necessity which justified homicide is that only which has always been and is now considered a justification. "In all these cases of homicide by necessity," says he, "as in pursuit of a felon, in killing him that assaults to rob, or comes to burn or break a house, or the like, which are in themselves no felony ..."

Now it is admitted that the deliberate killing of this unoffending and unresisting boy was clearly murder, unless the killing can be justified by some well-recognised excuse admitted by the law. It is further admitted that there was in this case no such excuse, unless the killing was justified by what has been called "necessity." But the temptation to the act which existed here was not what the law has ever called necessity. Nor is this to be regretted. Though law and morality are not the same, and many things may be immoral which are not necessarily illegal, yet the absolute divorce of law from morality would be of fatal consequence; and such divorce would follow if the temptation to murder in this case were to be held by law an absolute defence of it. It is not so. To preserve one's life is generally speaking a duty, but it may be the plainest and the highest duty to sacrifice it. War is full of instances in which it is a man's duty not to live, but to die. The duty, in case of shipwreck, of a captain to his crew, of the crew to the passengers, of soldiers to women and children, as in the noble case of the *Birkenhead*; these duties impose on men the moral necessity, not of the preservation, but of the sacrifice of their lives for others from which in no country, least of all, it is to be hoped, in England, will men ever shrink, as indeed, they have not shrunk. It is not correct, therefore, to say that there is any absolute or unqualified necessity to preserve one's life ...

It is not needful to point out the awful danger of admitting the principle which has been contended for. Who is to be the judge of this sort of necessity? By what measure is the comparative value of lives to be measured? Is it to be strength, or intellect, or what? It is plain that the principle leaves to him who is to profit by it to determine the necessity which will justify him in deliberately taking another's life to save his own. In this case the weakest, the youngest, the most unresisting, was chosen. Was it more necessary to kill him than one of the grown men? The answer must be "No" – "So spake the Fiend, and with necessity / The tyrant's plea, excused his devilish deeds." It is not suggested that in this particular case the deeds were "devilish," but it is quite plain that such a principle once admitted might be made the legal cloak for unbridled passion and atrocious crime. There is no safe path for judges to tread but to ascertain the law to the best of their ability and to declare it according to their judgment; and if in any case the law appears to be too severe on individuals, to leave it to the Sovereign to exercise that prerogative of mercy which the Constitution has intrusted to the hands fittest to dispense it. It must not be supposed that in refusing to admit temptation to be an excuse for crime it is forgotten how terrible the temptation was; how awful the suffering; how hard in such trials to keep the judgment straight and the conduct pure. We are often compelled to set up standards we cannot reach ourselves, and to lay down rules which we could not ourselves satisfy. But a man has no right to declare temptation to be an excuse, though he might himself have yielded to it, nor allow compassion for the criminal to change or weaken in any manner the legal definition of the crime. It is therefore our duty to declare that the prisoners' act in this case was wilful murder, that the facts as stated in the verdict are no legal justification of the homicide; and to say that in our unanimous opinion the prisoners are upon this special verdict guilty of murder.

[This sentence was afterwards commuted by the Crown to six months' imprisonment].

READING QUESTIONS ON *DUDLEY V. STEPHENS*

1 In deciding that the defence of necessity did not apply in these circumstances, was Lord Coleridge making new law, or applying existing law? How would Hart answer this question? How would Dworkin answer it?
2 How does Lord Coleridge seem to see the relation between law and morality? Does his view seem closer to Hart's, or to Dworkin's?
3 Could Lord Coleridge have appealed to different moral principles in order to reach the opposite result in this case?

Harvard College v. Canada (Commissioner of Patents), [2002] 4 SCR 45

This case concerned whether Harvard College's "oncomouse" (a mouse genetically altered to render it more susceptible to cancer) could be patented in Canada. One of the requirements for gaining a patent is that the claimant demonstrate that the patented object is an "invention" – that is, a non-obvious and useful composition of matter. The Patent Examiner refused to grant the patent on the grounds that higher life forms were not "compositions of matter" and hence were not "inventions." The Supreme Court of Canada upheld this decision by a narrow 5–4 majority. Excerpts from both the majority and the dissenting judgments are given below.

Binnie, J. (dissenting, for himself and McLachlin, C.J., Major and Arbour, JJ.): The biotechnology revolution in the 50 years since discovery of the structure of DNA has been fuelled by extraordinary human ingenuity and financed in significant part by private investment. Like most revolutions, it has wide ramifications, and presents potential and serious dangers as well as past and future benefits. In this appeal, however, we are only dealing with a small corner of the biotechnology controversy. We are asked to determine whether the oncomouse, a genetically modified rodent with heightened genetic susceptibility to cancer, is an invention. The legal issue is a narrow one and does not provide a proper platform on which to engage in a debate over animal rights, or religion, or the arrogance of the human race.

The oncomouse has been held patentable, and is now patented in jurisdictions that cover Austria, Belgium, Denmark, Finland, France, Germany, Greece, Ireland, Italy, Luxembourg, The Netherlands, Portugal, Spain, Sweden, the United Kingdom and the United States. A similar patent has been issued in Japan. New Zealand has issued a patent for a transgenic mouse that has been genetically modified to be susceptible to HIV infection. Indeed, we were not told of any country with a patent system comparable to Canada's (or otherwise) in which a patent on the oncomouse had been applied for and been refused ...

The issue, in the words of s. 2 of the *Patent Act*, is whether the oncomouse that has been produced by a combination of genetic engineering and natural gestation is a "composition of matter" that is new, unobvious and useful. If it is, then the President and Fellows of Harvard University, who funded the research, are entitled to a patent ...

I accept, as does my colleague, that the proper approach to interpretation of this statute is to read the words "in their entire context and in their grammatical and ordinary sense harmoniously with the scheme of the Act, the object of the Act, and the intention of Parliament": E.A. Driedger, *Construction of Statutes* (2nd ed. 1983), at p. 87. In my opinion, with respect, the context and scheme of the *Patent Act* reinforce the expansive sense of the words "composition of matter" to render the oncomouse patentable. The intent that can properly be attributed to Parliament, based on the language it used and the context of patent legislation generally, is that it considered it to be in the public interest to encourage new and useful inventions without knowing what such inventions would turn out to be and to that end inventors who disclosed their work should be rewarded for their ingenuity. A further indication of Parliament's intent is that the Commissioner of Patents was given no discretion to refuse a patent on the grounds of morality, public interest, public order, or any other ground if the statutory criteria are met: *Patent*

Act, s. 40. In my view, the respondent has fulfilled the statutory criteria and "by law" is entitled to the patent ...

Transgenic mice, including the oncomouse, have a role of potential importance. The evidence is that use of transgenic mice improves the effectiveness of the research that can be done, and shortens the time required to produce results ...

The practical application of biotechnology is in large measure the preoccupation of enterprises that need to profit from their successes to finance continued research on a broader front. These successes are few and far between (Statistics Canada, *supra*, at pp. 13–14). It seems Du Pont spent about US$15 million to fund the oncomouse research: C. Arthur, "The onco-mouse that didn't roar" (1993), 138 *New Scientist* 4. Leder, the afore-mentioned co-inventor of the Harvard mouse, made the point to Congress as follows:

[T]he great and costly engine for invention can only be effectively driven with the support from the private sector, motivated to serve a public need.

The patent system offers the only protection available for the intellectual product of this research, and thus, the only hope of a fair return against the great financial risks that investment in biotechnology entails ...

It is common ground that to meet the subject matter criteria of the *Patent Act* the oncomouse must qualify as a "composition of matter" or a "manufacture."

"Composition of matter" is an open-ended expression. Statutory subject matter must be framed broadly because by definition the *Patent Act* must contemplate the unforeseeable. The definition is not expressly confined to inanimate matter, and the appellant Commissioner agrees that composition of organic and certain living matter can be patented. In the case of the oncomouse, the modified genetic material is a physical substance and therefore "matter." The fertilized mouse egg is a form of biological "matter." The combination of these two forms of matter by the process described in the disclosure is thus, as pointed out by Rothstein, J.A. ([2000] 4 FC 528, at para. 120), a "composition of matter."

What, then, is the justification under the *Patent Act* for drawing a line between certain compositions of living matter (lower life forms) and other compositions of living matter (higher life forms)?

My colleague, Bastarache J, quotes from the *Oxford English Dictionary* (2nd ed. 1989), vol. IX, at p. 480, the entry that "matter" is a "[p]hysical or corporeal substance in general ..., contradistinguished from immaterial or incorporeal substance (spirit, soul, mind), and from qualities, actions, or conditions," but this, of course, depends on context. "Matter" is a most chameleon-like word. The expression "grey matter" refers in everyday use to "intelligence" – which is about as incorporeal as "spirit" or "mind." Indeed, the same Oxford editors define "grey matter" as "intelligence, brains" ...

The *Patent Act* does not distinguish, in its definition of invention, between subject matter that is less complex ("lower life forms") and subject matter that is more complex ("higher life forms"). The degree of complexity is not a criterion found in the Act or in the jurisprudence in determining patentability ...

The various distinctions attempted to be made between "patentable" lower life composition of matter and "unpatentable" higher life composition of matter, shows, I think, the arbitrariness of the Commissioner's approach. My colleague writes at para. 199:

The distinction between lower and higher life forms, though not explicit in the Act, is nonetheless defensible on the basis of common sense differences between the two.

With respect, there seems to be as many versions of "common sense" as there are commentators:

1 Some would say all living organisms are excluded (e.g., Brennan, J. for the dissenters in *Chakrabarty*);
2 Some would allow micro-organisms but only those that can be produced *en masse* with identical features, like bacteria. In *Re Abitibi, supra*, the Patent Appeal Board recommended that patents extend "to all new life forms which are produced *en masse* as chemical compounds are prepared, and are formed in such large numbers that any measurable quantity will possess uniform properties and characteristics" (p. 89). "Mass" live organisms have a long history of patentability, including food products such as beer and yogurt.
3 Then there are the proponents of "higher life" organisms versus "lower life" organisms, the latter being defined by the CBAC as having only a single cell.
4 Others divide the universe between prokaryotic cells (e.g., bacteria and certain forms of algae) and eukaryotic cells (more complex

life forms) and consider "higher" life forms to start only with more "complex" multicellular organisms.

5 The Patent Appeal Board allowed multi-celled organisms such as moulds and fungi in Connaught Laboratories, supra.

6 Some argue that "complex life forms" are unpatentable. Nadon, J. took this position at trial in this case, [1998] 3 FC 510, at para. 35.

7 The Commissioner issues patents for genetically modified complex plants (Monsanto, supra) but refuses to issue a patent for a genetically modified complex mouse.

8 Others draw the line at sentient beings.

9 Still others draw the line at "intelligent" beings.

10 The Commissioner opened his argument in this case by asking whether "a complex, intelligent, living being could be considered an invention."

In my view, none of these proposed dividing lines arise out of the present text of the *Patent Act*. All of them are policy driven and, if they are to be introduced at all, should be introduced by Parliament ...

[Binnie, J. then canvassed various objections to the view that the oncomouse was patentable.]

Some opponents object to scientists "playing God." A hint, perhaps, of their objection is reflected in the reasons of my colleague, Bastarache, J., at para. 163:

Although some in society may hold the view that higher life forms are mere "composition[s] of matter," the phrase does not fit well with common understandings of human and animal life.

I do not think that a court is a forum that can properly debate the mystery of mouse life. What we know, in this case, is that the inventors were able to modify a particular gene in the oncomouse genome, and produce a new, useful and unobvious result. That is all we know about the mysteries of oncomouse life and, in my view, it is all we need to know for the purposes of this appeal ...

Animal rights supporters object to the fact that the oncomouse is deliberately designed to cause sentient beings to grow painful malignant tumours. Of course, whatever position is adopted under patent law, animals have been and will continue to be used in laboratories for scientific research. Pets are property. Mice are already commodified. Parliament may wish to address animal rights as a distinct subject matter. If the claim for the patent on the oncomouse itself is refused, the result will not be that Harvard is denied the opportunity to make, construct, use and sell the oncomouse. On the contrary, the result will be that anyone will be able to make, construct, use and sell the oncomouse. The only difference will be that Harvard will be denied the *quid pro quo* for the disclosure of its invention.

Some critics argue that life and property rights are incompatible. Patents, they say, treat "life" as a commodity that can be bought and sold, and therefore diminish the respect with which life ought to be regarded. Living entities become "objects."

The major concern is that human beings constitute a line that cannot be crossed. The CBAC agrees. But others argue that patenting any form of life puts us on a slippery slope. Today the oncomouse; tomorrow Frankenstein's creature. I do not agree. There is a qualitative divide between rodents and human beings. The broadest claim here specifically excepts humans from the scope of transgenic mammals. Moreover, for the reasons already expressed, I do not believe that the issue of patentability of a human being even arises under the *Patent Act*.

Environmental concerns include the diversity of the gene pool and potential escape of genetically modified organisms into the environment. These are serious concerns which serious people would expect Parliament to address. The concerns, however, have little to do with the patent system. Patents or no patents, genetically engineered organisms have arrived in our midst. The genie is out of the bottle. As Rothstein, J.A. observed, "even if the oncomouse were found not to be patentable, such a decision would not prevent inventors from developing the product or indeed, other genetically engineered living organisms" (para. 197). Patentability addresses only the issue of rewarding the inventors for their disclosure of what they have done. Larger questions are answered elsewhere ...

The judgment of the majority was delivered by Bastarache, J.: ... In my opinion, Parliament did not intend higher life forms to be patentable. Had Parliament intended every conceivable subject matter to be patentable, it would not have chosen to adopt an exhaustive definition that limits invention to any "art, process, machine, manufacture or composition of matter." In addition, the phrases "manufacture" and "composition of matter" do not correspond to common understandings of animal and plant life. Even accepting that the words of the definition can support a broad interpretation, they must be interpreted in light of the scheme of the Act and the relevant context. The Act in its current form fails to address many of the unique concerns that are raised by the patenting of higher life forms, a factor which indicates that Parliament never intended the definition of "invention" to extend to this type of subject matter. Given the unique concerns associated with the grant of a monopoly right over higher life forms, it is my view that Parliament would not likely choose the *Patent Act* as it currently exists as the appropriate vehicle to protect the rights of inventors of this type of subject matter ...

With respect to the meaning of the word "manufacture" (*fabrica tion*), although it may be attributed a very broad meaning, I am of the opinion that the word would commonly be understood to denote a non-living mechanistic product or process. For example, the *Oxford English Dictionary* (2nd ed. 1989), vol. IX, at p. 341, defines the noun "manufacture" as the following:

The action or process of making by hand ... The action or process of making articles or material (in modern use, on a large scale) by the application of physical labour or mechanical power.

The *Grand Robert de la langue française* (2nd ed. 2001), vol. 3, at p. 517, defines thus the word "*fabrication*": [translation] Art or action or manufacturing ... The manufacture of a technical object (by someone). Manufacturing by artisans, by hand, by machine, industrially, by mass production.

In *Chakrabarty, supra,* at p. 308, "manufacture" was defined as

the production of articles for use from raw or prepared materials by giving to these materials new forms, qualities, properties, or combinations, whether by hand-labor or by machinery.

These definitions use the terminology of "article," "material," and "*objet technique.*" Is a mouse an "article," "material," or an "*objet technique*"? In my view, while a mouse may be analogized to a "manufacture" when it is produced in an industrial setting, the word in its vernacular sense does not include a higher life form. The definition in *Hornblower v. Boulton* (1799), 8 TR 95, 101 ER 1285 (KB), cited by the respondent, is equally problematic when applied to higher life forms.

In that case, the English courts defined "manufacture" as "something made by the hands of man" (p. 1288). In my opinion, a complex life form such as a mouse or a chimpanzee cannot easily be characterized as "something made by the hands of man" ...

It also is significant that the word "matter" captures but one aspect of a higher life form. As defined by the *Oxford English Dictionary, supra,* vol. IX, at p. 480, "matter" is a "[p]hysical or corporeal substance in general ..., contradistinguished from immaterial or incorporeal substance (spirit, soul, mind), and from qualities, actions, or conditions." "*Matière*" is defined by the *Grand Robert de la langue française, supra,* vol. 4, p. 1260, as [translation] "corporeal substance 'that is perceptible in space and has mechanical mass.'" Although some in society may hold the view that higher life forms are mere "composition[s] of matter," the phrase does not fit well with common understandings of human and animal life. Higher life forms are generally regarded as possessing qualities and characteristics that transcend the particular genetic material of which they are composed. A person whose genetic make-up is modified by radiation does not cease to be him or herself. Likewise, the same mouse would exist absent the injection of the oncogene into the fertilized egg cell; it simply would not be predisposed to cancer. The fact that it has this predisposition to cancer that makes it valuable to humans does not mean that the mouse, along with other animal life forms, can be defined solely with reference to the genetic matter of which it is composed. The fact that animal life forms have numerous unique qualities that transcend the particular matter of which they are composed makes it difficult to conceptualize higher life forms as mere "composition[s] of matter." It is a phrase that seems inadequate as a description of a higher life form ...

This interpretation of the words of the Act finds support in the fact that the patenting of higher life forms raises unique concerns which do not arise with respect to non-living inventions and which cannot be adequately addressed by the scheme of the Act ...

Perhaps the most significant issue addressed by the CBAC is the patentability of human life. The CBAC recommends that if Canada decides to permit patents over higher life forms, human bodies at all stages of development should be excluded. It observes in this regard that although humans are also animals, no country, including Canada, allows patents on the human body. According to the CBAC, this understanding derives from the universal principle of respect for human dignity, one element of which is that humans are not commodities (see CBAC, *supra*, at p. 8).

The potential for commodification of human life arises out of the fact that the granting of a patent is, in effect, a declaration that an invention based on living matter has the potential to be commercialized. The commodification of human beings is not only intrinsically undesirable; it may also engender a number of troubling consequences. Many of the consequentialist concerns (i.e., the creation of "designer human beings" or features) are directed at genetic engineering in general and not at patenting per se, and are perhaps better dealt with outside the confines of the *Patent Act* (see Schrecker, *supra*, at pp. 64–65). Nonetheless, there remains a concern that allowing patents on the human body will lead to human life being reconceptualized as genetic information. A related concern is the potential for objectification. As noted by Schrecker, *supra*, at p. 62: "[t]o objectify something is implicit in treating it as a market commodity, but what is disturbing about objectifying a person or organism is not so much the exchange of money as it is the notion that a subject, a moral agent with autonomy and dignity, is being treated as if it can be used as an instrument for the needs or desires of others without giving rise to ethical objections" ...

Based on the language and the scheme of the Act, both of which are not well accommodated to higher life forms, it is reasonable to assume that Parliament did not intend the monopoly right inherent in the grant of a patent to extend to inventions of this nature. It simply does not follow from the objective of promoting ingenuity that all inventions must be patentable ...

READING QUESTIONS ON HARVARD MOUSE

1 What are the moral issues raised by the existence of the onco-mouse? Why does Binnie, J. not think that these moral issues are the proper focus of this case? Does he appeal to any types of value himself, in his own reasoning about the case? If so, what does he think is the relation of these values to the law?

2 Bastarache, J. openly appeals to certain moral values. What does he seem to think is the relation of these values to the *Patent Act*?

3 Would Hart say that this is a core case, or a penumbral case? Which of the two judgments do you think he would regard as correctly adjudicated? Why?

2

Adjudication

This chapter explores the relationship between law and morality in adjudication by looking at two cases in which judges found that they were compelled to come to conclusions of which they disapproved. The question here is whether a theory like Dworkin's, which presupposes a link between law and morality, is helpful to judges who find themselves in such a predicament.

Herman Melville
Billy Budd, Sailor (1929)

Melville's novella tells the story of a sailor who strikes a superior officer who has severely provoked him. The officer dies from a blow almost anyone would have survived. The central drama of the story comes when the Captain, who has witnessed the death, decides that Budd must be executed, despite the fact he is morally innocent. Vere feels compelled to enforce the law, though he regards it as profoundly unjust.

The court was held in the same cabin where the unfortunate affair had taken place. This cabin, the commander's, embraced the entire area under the poop deck. Aft, and on either side, was a small stateroom, the one now temporarily a jail and the other a dead-house, and a yet smaller compartment, leaving a space between expanding forward into a goodly oblong of length coinciding with the ship's beam. A skylight of moderate dimension was overhead, and at each end of the oblong space were two sashed porthole windows easily convertible back into embrasures for short carronades.

All being quickly in readiness, Billy Budd was arraigned, Captain Vere necessarily appearing as the sole witness in the case, and as such temporarily sinking his rank, though singularly maintaining it in a matter apparently trivial, namely, that he testified from the ship's weather side, with that object having caused the court to sit on the lee side. Concisely he narrated all that had led up to the catastrophe, omitting nothing in Claggart's accusation and deposing as to the manner in which the prisoner had received it. At this testimony the three officers glanced with no little surprise at Billy Budd, the last man they would have suspected either of the mutinous design alleged by Claggart or the undeniable deed he himself had done. The first lieutenant, taking judicial primacy and turning toward the prisoner, said, "Captain Vere has spoken. Is it or is it not as Captain Vere says?"

In response came syllables not so much impeded in the utterance as might have been anticipated. They were these: "Captain Vere tells the truth. It is just as Captain Vere says, but it is not as the master-at-arms said. I have eaten the King's bread and I am true to the King."

"I believe you, my man," said the witness, his voice indicating a suppressed emotion not otherwise betrayed.

"God will bless you for that, your honor!" not without stammering said Billy, and all but broke down. But immediately he was recalled to self-control by another question, to which with the same emotional difficulty of utterance he said, "No, there was no malice between us. I never bore malice against the master-at-arms. I am sorry that he is dead. I did not mean to kill him. Could I have used my tongue I would not have struck him. But he foully lied to my face and in presence of my captain, and I had to say something, and I could only say it with a blow, God help me!"

In the impulsive aboveboard manner of the frank one the court saw confirmed all that was implied in words that just previously had perplexed them, coming as they did from the testifier to the tragedy and promptly following Billy's impassioned disclaimer of mutinous intent – Captain Vere's words, "I believe you, my man."

Next it was asked of him whether he knew of or suspected aught savoring of incipient trouble (meaning mutiny, though the explicit term was avoided) going on in any section of the ship's company.

The reply lingered. This was naturally imputed by the court to the same vocal embarrassment which had retarded or obstructed previous answers. But in main it was otherwise here, the question immediately recalling to Billy's mind the interview with the afterguardsman in the forechains. But an innate repugnance to playing a part at all approaching that of an informer against one's own shipmates – the same erring sense of uninstructed honor which had stood in the way of his reporting the matter at the time, though as a loyal man-of-war's man it was incumbent on him, and failure so to do, if charged against him and proven, would have subjected him to the heaviest of penalties; this, with the blind feeling now his that nothing really was being hatched, prevailed with him. When the answer came it was a negative.

"One question more," said the officer of marines, now first speaking and with a troubled earnestness. "You tell us that what the master-at-arms said against you was a lie. Now why should he have so lied, so maliciously lied, since you declare there was no malice between you?"

At that question, unintentionally touching on a spiritual sphere wholly obscure to Billy's thoughts, he was nonplussed, evincing a confusion indeed that some observers, such as can readily be imagined, would have construed into involuntary evidence of hidden guilt. Nevertheless, he strove some way to answer, but all at once relinquished the vain endeavor, at the same time turning an appealing glance towards Captain Vere as deeming him his best helper and friend. Captain Vere, who had been seated for a time, rose to his feet, addressing the interrogator. "The question you put to him comes naturally enough. But how can he rightly answer it? – or anybody else, unless indeed it be he who lies within there," designating the compartment where lay the corpse. "But the prone one there will not rise to our summons. In effect, though, as it seems to me, the point you make is hardly material. Quite aside from any conceivable motive actuating the master-at-arms, and irrespective of the provocation to the blow, a martial court must needs in the present case confine its attention to the blow's consequence, which consequence justly is to be deemed not otherwise than as the striker's deed."

This utterance, the full significance of which it was not at all likely that Billy took in, nevertheless caused him to turn a wistful interrogative look toward the speaker, a look in its dumb expressiveness not unlike that which a dog of generous breed might turn upon his master, seeking in his face some elucidation of a previous gesture ambiguous to the canine intelligence. Nor was the same utterance without marked effect upon the three officers, more especially the soldier. Couched in it seemed to them a meaning unanticipated, involving a prejudgment on the speaker's part. It served to augment a mental disturbance previously evident enough.

The soldier once more spoke, in a tone of suggestive dubiety addressing at once his associates and Captain Vere: "Nobody is present – none of the ship's company, I mean – who might shed lateral light, if any is to be had, upon what remains mysterious in this matter."

"That is thoughtfully put," said Captain Vere; "I see your drift. Ay, there is a mystery; but, to use a scriptural phrase, it is a 'mystery of iniquity,' a matter for psychologic theologians to discuss. But what has a military court to do with it? Not to add that for us any possible investigation of it is cut off by the lasting tongue-tie of – him – in yonder," again designating the mortuary stateroom. "The prisoner's deed – with that alone we have to do."

To this, and particularly the closing reiteration, the marine soldier, knowing not how aptly to reply, sadly abstained from saying aught. The first lieutenant, who at the outset had not unnaturally assumed primacy in the court, now overrulingly instructed by a glance from Captain Vere, a glance more effective than words, resumed that primacy. Turning to the prisoner, "Budd," he said, and scarce in equable tones, "Budd, if you have aught further to say for yourself, say it now."

Upon this the young sailor turned another quick glance toward Captain Vere; then, as taking a hint from that aspect, a hint confirming his own instinct that silence was now best, replied to the lieutenant, "I have said all, sir."

The marine – the same who had been the sentinel without the cabin door at the time that the foretopman, followed by the master-at-arms, entered it – he, standing by the sailor throughout these judicial proceedings, was now directed to take him back to the after compartment originally assigned to the prisoner and his custodian. As the twain disappeared from view, the three officers, as partially liberated from some inward constraint associated with Billy's mere presence, simultaneously stirred in their seats. They exchanged looks of troubled indecision, yet feeling that decide they must and without long delay. For Captain Vere, he for the time stood – unconsciously with his back toward them, apparently in one of his absent fits – gazing out from a sashed porthole to windward upon the monotonous blank of the twilight sea. But the court's silence continuing, broken only at moments by brief consultations, in low earnest tones, this served to arouse him and energize him. Turning, he to-and-fro paced the cabin athwart; in the returning ascent to windward climbing the slant deck in the ship's lee roll, without knowing it symbolizing thus in his action a mind resolute to surmount difficulties even if against primitive instincts strong as the wind and the sea. Presently he came to a stand before the three. After scanning their faces he stood less as mustering his thoughts for expression than as one inly deliberating how best to put them to well-meaning men not intellectually mature, men with whom it was necessary to demonstrate certain principles that were axioms to himself. Similar impatience as to talking is perhaps one reason that deters some minds from addressing any popular assemblies.

When speak he did, something, both in the substance of what he said and his manner of saying it, showed the influence of unshared studies modifying and tempering the practical training of an active career. This, along with his phraseology, now and then was suggestive of the grounds whereon rested that imputation of a certain pedantry socially alleged against him by certain naval men of wholly practical cast, captains who nevertheless would frankly concede that His Majesty's navy mustered no more efficient officer of their grade than Starry Vere.

What he said was to this effect: "Hitherto I have been but the witness, little more; and I should hardly think now to take another tone, that of your coadjutor for the time, did I not perceive in you – at the crisis too – a troubled hesitancy, proceeding, I doubt not, from the clash of military duty with moral scruple – scruple vitalized by compassion. For the compassion, how can I otherwise than share it? But, mindful of paramount obligations, I strive against scruples that may tend to enervate decision. Not, gentlemen, that I hide from myself that the case is an exceptional one. Speculatively regarded, it well might be referred to a jury of casuists. But for us here, acting not as casuists or moralists, it is a case practical, and under martial law practically to be dealt with.

"But your scruples: do they move as in a dusk? Challenge them. Make them advance and declare themselves. Come now; do they import something like this: If, mindless of palliating circumstances, we are bound to regard the death of the master-at-arms as the prisoner's deed, then does that deed constitute a capital crime whereof the penalty is a mortal one. But in natural justice is nothing but the prisoner's overt act to be considered? How can we adjudge to summary and shameful death a fellow creature innocent before God, and whom we feel to be so? Does that state it aright? You sign sad assent. Well, I too feel that, the full force of that. It is Nature. But do these buttons that we wear attest that our allegiance is to Nature? No, to the King. Though the ocean, which is inviolate Nature primeval, though this be the element where we move and have our being as sailors, yet as the King's officers lies our duty in a sphere correspondingly natural? So little is that true, that in receiving our commissions we in the most important regards ceased to be natural free agents. When war is declared are we the commissioned fighters previously consulted? We fight at command. If our judgments approve the war, that is but coincidence. So in other particulars. So now. For suppose condemnation to follow these present proceedings. Would it be so much we ourselves that would condemn as it would be martial law operating through us? For that law and the rigor of it, we are not responsible. Our vowed responsibility is in this: That however pitilessly that law may operate in any instances, we nevertheless adhere to it and administer it.

"But the exceptional in the matter moves the hearts within you. Even so too is mine moved. But let not warm hearts betray heads that should be cool. Ashore in a criminal case, will an upright judge allow himself off the bench to be waylaid by some tender kinswoman of the accused seeking to touch him with her tearful plea? Well, the heart here, some-times the feminine in man, is as that piteous woman, and hard though it be, she must here be ruled out."

He paused, earnestly studying them for a moment; then resumed.

"But something in your aspect seems to urge that it is not solely the heart that moves in you, but also the conscience, the private conscience. But tell me whether or not, occupying the position we do, private con-science should not yield to that imperial one formulated in the code under which alone we officially proceed?"

Here the three men moved in their seats, less convinced than agitated by the course of an argument troubling but the more the spontaneous conflict within.

Perceiving which, the speaker paused for a moment; then abruptly changing his tone, went on.

"To steady us a bit, let us recur to the facts. – In wartime at sea a man-of-war's man strikes his superior in grade, and the blow kills. Apart from its effect the blow itself is, according to the Articles of War, a capital crime. Furthermore –"

"Ay, sir," emotionally broke in the officer of marines, "in one sense it was. But surely Budd proposed neither mutiny nor homicide."

"Surely not, my good man. And before a court less arbitrary and more merciful than a martial one, that plea would largely extenuate. At the Last Assizes it shall acquit. But how here? We proceed under the law of the Mutiny Act. In feature no child can resemble his father more than that Act resembles in spirit the thing from which it derives – War. In His Majesty's service – in this ship, indeed – there are Englishmen forced to fight for the King against their will. Against their conscience, for aught we know. Though as their fellow creatures some of us may appreciate their position, yet as navy officers what reck we of it? Still less recks the enemy. Our impressed men he would fain cut down in the same swath with our volunteers. As regards the enemy's naval conscripts, some of whom may even share our own abhorrence of the regicidal French Directory, it is the same on our side. War looks but to the frontage, the appearance. And the Mutiny Act, War's child, takes after the father. Budd's intent or non-intent is nothing to the purpose.

"But while, put to it by those anxieties in you which I cannot but respect, I only repeat myself – while thus strangely we prolong proceedings that should be summary – the enemy may be sighted and an engagement result. We must do; and one of two things must we do – condemn or let go."

"Can we not convict and yet mitigate the penalty?" asked the sailing master, here speaking, and falteringly, for the first.

"Gentlemen, were that clearly lawful for us under the circumstances, consider the consequences of such clemency. The people" (meaning the ship's company) "have native sense; most of them are familiar with our naval usage and tradition; and how would they take it? Even could you explain to them – which our official position forbids – they, long molded by arbitrary discipline, have not that kind of intelligent responsiveness that might qualify them to comprehend and discriminate. No, to the people the foretopman's deed, however it be worded in the announcement, will be plain homicide committed in a flagrant act of mutiny. What penalty for that should follow, they know. But it does not follow. *Why*? they will ruminate. You know what sailors are. Will they not revert to the recent outbreak at the Nore? Ay. They know the well-founded alarm – the panic it struck throughout England. Your clement sentence they would account pusillanimous. They would think that we flinch, that we are afraid of them – afraid of practicing a lawful rigor singularly demanded at this juncture, lest it should provoke new troubles. What shame to use such a conjecture on their part, and how deadly to discipline. You see then, whither, prompted by duty and the law, I steadfastly drive. But I beseech you, my friends, do not take me amiss. I feel as you do for this unfortunate boy. But did he know our hearts, I take him to be of that generous nature that he would feel even for us on whom in this military necessity so heavy a compulsion is laid."

With that, crossing the deck he resumed his place by the sashed porthole, tacitly leaving the three to come to a decision. On the cabin's opposite side the troubled court sat silent. Loyal lieges, plain and practical, though at bottom they dissented from some points Captain Vere had put to them, they were without the faculty, hardly had the inclination, to gainsay one whom they felt to be an earnest man, one too not less their superior in mind than in naval rank. But it is not improbable that even such of his words as were not without influence over them, less came home than his closing appeal to their instinct as sea officers: in the forethought he threw out as to the practical consequences to discipline, considering the unconfirmed tone of the fleet at the time, should a man-of-war's man's violent killing at sea of a superior in grade be allowed to pass for aught else than a capital crime demanding prompt infliction of the penalty.

Not unlikely they were brought to something more or less akin to that harassed frame of mind which in the year 1842 actuated the commander of the U.S. brig-of-war *Somers* to resolve, under the so-called Articles of War, Articles modelled upon the English Mutiny Act, to resolve upon the execution at sea of a midshipman and two sailors as mutineers designing the seizure of the brig. Which resolution was carried out though in a time of peace and within not many days' sail of home. An Act vindicated by a naval court of inquiry subsequently convened ashore. History, and here cited without comment. True, the circumstances on board the *Somers* were different from those on board the *Bellipotent*. But the urgency felt, well-warranted or otherwise, was much the same.

Says a writer whom few know, "Forty years after a battle it is easy for a noncombatant to reason about how it ought to have been fought. It is another thing personally and under fire to have to direct the fighting while involved in the obscuring smoke of it. Much so with respect to other emergencies involving considerations both practical and moral, and when it is imperative promptly to act. The greater the fog the more it imperils the steamer, and speed is put on though at the hazard of running somebody down. Little ween the snug card players in the cabin of the responsibilities of the sleepless man on the bridge."

In brief, Billy Budd was formally convicted and sentenced to be hung at the yardarm in the early morning watch, it being now night. Otherwise, as is customary in such cases, the sentence would forthwith have been carried out. In wartime on the field or in the fleet, a mortal punishment decreed by a drumhead court – on the field sometimes decreed by but a nod from the general – follows without delay on the heel of conviction, without appeal.

...

Of a series of incidents with a brief term rapidly following each other, the adequate narration may take up a term less brief, especially if explanation or comment here and there seem requisite to the better understanding of such incidents. Between the entrance into the cabin of him who never left it alive, and him who when he did leave it left it as one condemned to die; between this and the closeted interview just given, less than an hour and a half had elapsed. It was an interval long enough, however, to awaken speculations among no few of the ship's company.

READING QUESTIONS ON MELVILLE

1 Did Captain Vere really have no other option but to convict Billy? What argument might he have used to acquit him?
2 Captain Vere seems less concerned about whether or not the sailors will mutiny than about the duties of his office. He says that if he condemns Billy and the sailors mutiny, it will not be his responsibility. What view of law does this suggest?

Robert Cover
"Of Creon and Captain Vere" (1976)

Cover explores the similarities between Captain Vere's plight and that of Lemuel Shaw, an abolitionist judge in nineteenth-century Massachusetts, who felt compelled to enforce the *Fugitive Slave Acts*. Shaw's situation raised deep puzzles for theories of law. Like Captain Vere, he sees himself as torn between moral and legal duties. On the one hand, he believes slavery is immoral. On the other, he believes he is bound to uphold the rule of law. The two duties come into conflict because the United States Constitution explicitly allowed each state to decide whether or not to allow slavery.

Shaw's commitment to the rule of law did not stand in the way of him campaigning for the legislative abolition of slavery in states that still allowed it. Nor did it prevent him from preventing slaveowners forcibly returning slaves they had voluntarily brought into states that did not allow slavery. In cases involving the return of escaped slaves, Shaw had a more difficult time. The *Fugitive Slave Acts* required their return to their owners; in so doing it also seemed to require that free states participate in a system of slavery.

PRELUDE: OF CREON AND CAPTAIN VERE

I

Antigone's star has shown brightly through the millennia. The archetype for civil disobedience has claimed a constellation of first-magnitude emulators. The disobedient – whether Antigone, Luther, Gandhi, King, or Bonhoeffer – exerts a powerful force upon us. The singular act, the risk, the dramatic appeal to a juster justice, all contribute to the high drama of the moment and the power of the actor's role. No wonder then, that such men and women are celebrated in literature and history. No wonder that a great psychiatrist like Erikson, upon embarking on a venture in history and biography, chose Luther and Gandhi as his first subjects.

Yet, in a curious way, to focus upon the disobedient and the process of disobedience is to accept the perspective of the established order. It is a concession that it is the man who appeals beyond law that is in need of explanation. With the sole exception of Nazi atrocities, the phenomenon of complicity in oppressive legal systems (oppressive from the actor's own perspective) has seldom been studied. Thus, Creon is present only as a foil for Antigone, not himself the object of the artist's study of human character. In *Antigone* note the curious one-dimensional character of the King. How he comes to make his law and at what cost in psychic terms is not treated at all. Indeed, Creon's first conflict is not between right and law, but between his son and his pride. And even in the midst of that conflict he betrays his singular obtuseness to the complexity of the situation he created by crying filial impiety and anarchy in one breath. He is astounded by the possibility of Haemon's sympathy to an affront to authority. Much of the simplicity of Creon lies in the choice of a tyrant as model for legal system. The making of law and its applications are wholly confined to a single will unconstrained by any but the most personal of considerations such as the feelings and actions of a son.

Melville's Captain Vere in *Billy Budd* is one of the few examples of an attempt to portray the conflict patterns of Creon or Creon's minions in a context more nearly resembling the choice situations of judges in modern legal systems. Billy Budd, radical innocence personified, is overwhelmed by a charge of fomenting mutiny, falsely levied against him by the first mate Claggart. Claggart seems to personify dark and evil forces. Struck dumb by the slanderous charges, Billy strikes out and kills the mate with a single blow. Captain Vere must instruct a drum-head court on the law of the Mutiny Act as it is to be applied to Billy Budd – in some most fundamental sense "innocent," though perpetrator of the act of killing the first mate. In what must be, for the legal scholar, the high point of the novella, Vere articulates the "scruples" of the three officers (and his own) and rejects them.

How can we adjudge to summary and shameful death a fellow creature innocent before God, and whom we feel to be so? – Does that state it aright? You sign sad assent. Well, I too feel that, the full force of that. It is Nature. But do these buttons that we wear attest that our allegiance is to Nature? No, to the King.

And, but a few paragraphs farther on, Vere asks the three whether "occupying the position we do, private conscience should not yield to that imperial one formulated in the code under which alone we officially proceed."

In Vere's words we have a positivist's condensation of a legal system's formal character. Five aspects of that formalism may be discerned and specified: First, there is explicit recognition of the role character of the judges – a consciousness of the formal element. It is a uniform, not nature, that defines obligation. Second, law is distinguished from both the transcendent and the personal sources of obligation. The law is neither nature nor conscience. Third, the law is embodied in a readily identifiable source which governs transactions and occurrences of the sort under consideration: here an imperial code of which the Mutiny Act is a part. Fourth, the will behind the law is vague, uncertain, but *clearly not* that of the judges. It is here "imperial will" which, in (either eighteenth- or) nineteenth-century terms as applied to England, is not very easy to describe except through a constitutional law treatise. But, in any event, it is not the will of Vere and his three officers. Fifth, a corollary of the fourth point, the judge is not responsible for the content of the law but for its straightforward application.

> For that law and the rigor of it, we are not responsible. Our vowed responsibility is in this: That however pitilessly that law may operate in any instances, we nevertheless adhere to it and administer it.

These five elements are part of Vere's arguments. But *Billy Budd* is a literary work and much that is most interesting about Vere is not in what he says but in what he is, in overtones of character. For example, we have intimations from the outset of a personality committed to fearful symmetries. His nickname, derived from Marvell's lines

> Under the discipline severe
> Of Fairfax and the starry Vere

suggests an impersonal and unrelaxed severity. And his intellectual bent, too, reinforces this suggestion of rigidity. He eschewed innovations "disinterestedly" and because they seemed "insusceptible of embodiment in lasting institutions." And he lacked "companionable quality." A man emerges who is disposed to approach life institutionally, to avoid the personal realm even where it perhaps ought to hold sway, to be inflexibly honest, righteous, and duty bound.

It is this man who, seeing and appreciating Budd's violent act, exclaimed, "Struck dead by an angel of God! Yet the angel must hang." And, characteristically, it is Vere who assumes the responsibility of conveying the dread verdict to the accused. Melville's speculations on that "interview" are revealing. He stresses the likelihood that Vere revealed his own full part in the "trial." He goes on to speculate that Vere might well have assumed a paternal stance in the manner of Abraham embracing Isaac "on the brink of resolutely offering him up in obedience to the exacting behest." Such a religious conviction of duty characterizes our man. Neither conventional morality, pity, nor personal agony could bend him from a stern duty. But in Vere's case the master is not God but the King. And the King is but a symbol for a social order.

Righteous men, indeed, suffer the agonies of their righteousness. Captain Vere betrayed just such agony in leaving his meeting with Billy Budd. But there is no indication that Vere suffered the agony of doubt about his course. When Billy died uttering "God Bless Captain Vere," there is no intimation that the Captain sensed any irony (whether intended or not) in the parting benediction. If Captain Vere is Abraham, he is the biblical version, not Kierkegaard's shadow poised achingly at the chasm.

Melville has been astonishingly successful in making his readers ask dreadful questions of Vere and his behavior. What deep urge leads a man to condemn unworldly beauty and innocence? To embrace, personally, the opportunity to do an impersonal, distasteful task? How reconcile the flash of recognition of "the angel must die" and the seizing of the opportunity to act Abraham, with declared protestations, unquestionably sincere, that only plain and clear duty overcomes his sense of the victim's cosmic innocence? We have so many doubts about a man who hears and obeys the voice of the Master so quickly, and our doubts are compounded when it is a harsh social system that becomes the Lord.

I venture to suggest that Melville had a model for Captain Vere that may bring us very close to our main story. Melville's father-in-law was Chief Justice Lemuel Shaw of the Massachusetts Supreme Judicial Court. A firm, unbending man of stern integrity, Shaw dominated the Massachusetts judicial system very much as Captain Vere ran his ship. The Chief Justice was a noted, strong opponent to slavery and expressed his opposition privately, in print, and in appropriate judicial opinions. Yet, in the great causes célèbres involving fugitive slaves, Shaw came down hard for an unflinching application of the harsh and summary law. The effort cost Shaw untold personal agony. He was vilified by abolitionists. I cannot claim that Vere is Lemuel Shaw (though he might be), for there is no direct evidence. I can only say that it would be remarkable that in portraying a man caught in the horrible conflict between duty and conscience, between role and morality, between nature and positive law, Melville would be untouched by the figure of his father-in-law in the *Sims Case,* the Latimer affair, or the Burns controversy. We know Melville's predilection to the ship as microcosm for the social order. He used the device quite plainly with respect to slavery in *Benito Cereno.*

The fugitive slave was very Budd-like, though he was as black as Billy was blonde. The Mutiny Act admitted of none of the usual defenses, extenuations, or mitigations. If the physical act was that of the defendant, he was guilty. The Fugitive Slave Act similarly excluded most customary sorts of defenses. The alleged fugitive could not even plead that he was not legally a slave so long as he was the person *alleged* to be a fugitive. The drumhead court was a special and summary proceeding; so was the fugitive rendition process. In both proceedings the fatal judgment was carried out immediately. There was no appeal.

More important, Billy's fatal flaw was his innocent dumbness. He struck because he could not speak. So, under the Fugitive Slave Acts, the alleged fugitive had no right to speak. And, as a rule, slaves had no capacity to testify against their masters or whites, generally. Billy Budd partakes of the slave, generalized. He was seized, impressed, from the ship *Rights of Man* and taken abroad the *Bellipotent*. Aboard the *Bellipotent* the Mutiny Act and Captain Vere held sway. The Mutiny Act was justified because of its necessity for the order demanded on a ship in time of war. So the laws of slavery, often equally harsh and unbending, were justified as necessary for the social order in antebellum America. Moreover, the institution itself was said to have its origin in war.

But most persuasive is Vere and his dilemma – the subject matter of this book. For, if there was a single sort of case in which judges during Melville's lifetime struggled with the moral-formal dilemma, it was slave cases. In these cases, time and again, the judiciary paraded its helplessness before the law; lamented harsh results; intimated that in a more perfect world, or at the end of days, a better law would emerge, but almost uniformly, marched to the music, steeled themselves, and hung Billy Budd.

Of course, *Billy Budd,* like any great work of literature, exists on many levels. I would not deny the theology in the work, nor the clash of elemental good and elemental evil in Budd and Claggart. But the novella is also about a judgment, within a social system, and about the man, who, dimly perceiving the great and abstract forces at work, bears responsibility for that judgment. It is about starry-eyed Vere and Lemuel Shaw.

II

The rest of this book is not about literature, but about Lemuel Shaw and many judges like him. It is the story of earnest, well-meaning pillars of legal respectability and of their collaboration in a system of oppression – Negro slavery. I have chosen to analyze at length only the dilemma of the antislavery judge – the man who would, in some sense, have agreed with my characterization of slavery as oppression. It was he who confronted Vere's dilemma, the choice between the demands of role and the voice of conscience. And it was he who contributed so much to the force of legitimacy that law may provide, for he plainly acted out of impersonal duty.

In a static and simplistic model of law, the judge caught between law and morality has only four choices. He may apply the law against his conscience. He may apply conscience and be faithless to the law. He may resign. Or he may cheat: He may state that the law is not what he believes it to be and, thus preserve an appearance (to others) of conformity of law and morality. Once we assume a more realistic model of law and of the judicial process, these four positions become only poles setting limits to a complex field of action and motive. For in a dynamic model, law is always becoming. And the judge has a legitimate role in determining what it is that the law will become. The flux in law means also that the law's content is frequently unclear. We must speak of direction and of weight as well as of position. Moreover, this frequent lack of clarity makes possible "ameliorist" solutions. The judge may introduce his own sense of what "ought to be" interstitially, where no "hard" law yet exists. And, he may do so without committing the law to broad doctrinal advances (or retreats).

In a given historical context the way in which judges are likely to respond to the moral-formal dilemma is going to be determined by a wide variety of intellectual and institutional variables. Judges, more than most men, are conscious of the baggage of the past. Thus, the traditions that they inherit will be important. For both slavery and the judicial role in antebellum America the judge had a library of works that influenced the idiom in which he thought. The nature of that intellectual tradition is my first inquiry. I shall examine the natural law tradition on slavery as it stood in the late eighteenth century. I shall then explore the actual uses of principled preferences for liberty in the first thirty or forty years of the nineteenth century. This exploration will delineate the areas of accepted usage of preference for liberty in judicial opinion and the areas where the judge could move the law in the direction of freedom. I shall then explore the sorts of demands that were made upon the judiciary to go beyond those accepted areas and the judicial refusal to do so. That refusal will be traced on the cognitive level to carefully formulated ideas about the judicial function that are themselves the products of a heritage of conflict over the values that ought to govern judging. The dialectical context for the judge's response was not constant, and it is necessary to examine responses to many demands varying, in part, with the ideology of the lawyers and the movements they represented.

Finally, I shall confront directly the question of personality. With Captain Vere we have the sense that it is not logic alone that leads him to his response. So, with Lemuel Shaw, John McLean, Joseph Story, and others, we must inquire into the internal forces that produced an almost uniform response of role fidelity. The theory of cognitive dissonance provides a suggestive framework for integrating the uniform response, the personalities of these men, and the professional and intellectual milieu in which they worked.

Make no mistake. The judges we shall examine really squirmed; were intensely uncomfortable in hanging Billy Budd. But they did the job. Like Vere, they were Creon's faithful minions. We must understand them – as much as Antigone – if we are to understand the processes of injustice.

Commonwealth v. Aves 35 Mass. 193 (1836)

A case decided by Shaw, which holds that a slave brought into a free state by his owner is thereby set free. Shaw argues that the alternative would be to allow slave states to export their slavery to free ones.

... The precise question presented by the claim of the respondent is, whether a citizen of any one of the United States, where negro slavery is established by law, coming into this State, for any temporary purpose of business or pleasure, staying some time, but not acquiring a domicil here, who brings a slave with him as a personal attendant, may restrain such slave of his liberty during his continuance here, and convey him out of this State on his return, against his consent. It is not contended that a master can exercise here any other of the rights of a slave owner, than such as may be necessary to retain the custody of the slave during his residence, and to remove him on his return.

Until this discussion, I had supposed that there had been adjudged cases on this subject in this Commonwealth; and it is believed to have been a prevalent opinion among lawyers, that if a slave is brought voluntarily and unnecessarily within the limits of this State, he becomes free, if he chooses to avail himself of the provisions of our laws; not so much because his coming within our territorial limits, breathing our air, or treading on our soil, works any alteration in his *status,* or his condition, as settled by the law of his domicile as because by the operation of our laws, there is no authority on the part of the master, either to restrain the slave of his liberty, whilst here, or forcibly to take him into custody in order to his removal. There seems, however, to be no decided case on the subject reported ...

Without pursuing this inquiry farther, it is sufficient for the purposes of the case before us, that by the constitution adopted in 1780, slavery was abolished in Massachusetts, upon the ground that it is contrary to natural right and the plain principles of justice. The terms of the first article of the declaration of rights are plain and explicit. "All men are born free and equal, and have certain natural, essential, and unalienable rights, which are, the right of enjoying and defending their lives and liberties, that of acquiring, possessing, and protecting property." It would be difficult to select words more precisely adapted to the abolition of negro slavery. According to the laws prevailing in all the States, where slavery is upheld, the child of a slave is not deemed to be born free, a slave has no right to enjoy and defend his own liberty, or to acquire, possess, or protect property. That the description was broad enough in its terms to embrace negroes, and that it was intended by the framers of the constitution to embrace them, is proved by the earliest contemporaneous construction, by an unbroken series of judicial decisions, and by a uniform practice from the adoption of the constitution to the present time. The whole tenor of our policy, of our legislation and jurisprudence, from that time to the present, has been consistent with this construction, and with no other.

Such being the general rule of law, it becomes necessary to inquire how far it is modified or controlled in its operation; either,

1 By the law of other nations and states, as admitted by the comity of nations to have a limited operation within a particular state; or
2 By the constitution and laws of the United States ...

Upon a general review of the authorities, and upon an application of the well established principles upon this subject, we think they fully maintain the point stated, that though slavery is contrary to natural right, to the principles of justice, humanity and sound policy, as we adopt them and found our own laws upon them, yet not being contrary to the laws of nations, if any other state or community see fit to establish and continue slavery by law, so far as the legislative power of that country extends, we are bound to take notice of the existence of those laws, and we are not at liberty to declare and hold an act done within those limits, unlawful and void, upon our views of morality and policy, which the sovereign and legislative power of the place has pronounced to be lawful. If, therefore, an unwarranted interference and wrong is done by our citizens to a foreigner, acting under the sanction of such laws, and within their proper limits, that is, within the local limits of the power by whom they are thus established, or on the high seas, which each and every nation has a right in common with all others to occupy, our laws would no doubt afford a remedy against the wrong done. So, in pursuance of a well known maxim, that in the construction of contracts, the *lex loci contractus* shall govern, if a person, having in other respects a right to sue in our courts, shall bring an action against another, liable in other respects to be sued in our courts, upon a contract made upon the subject of slavery in a state where slavery is allowed by law, the law here would give it effect. As if a note of hand made in New Orleans were sued on here, and the defence should be, that it was on a bad consideration, or without consideration, because given for the price of a slave sold, it may well be admitted, that such a defence could not prevail, because the contract was a legal one by the law of the place where it was made.

This view of the law applicable to slavery, marks strongly the distinction between the relation of master and slave, as established by the local law of particular states, and in virtue of that sovereign power and independent authority which each independent state concedes to every other, and those natural and social relations, which are everywhere and by all people recognized, and which, though they may be modified and regulated by municipal law, are not founded upon it such as the relation of parent and child, and husband and wife. Such also is the principle upon which the general right of property is founded, being in some form universally recognized as a natural right, independently of municipal law.

This affords an answer to the argument drawn from the maxim, that the right of personal property follows the person, and therefore, where by the law of a place a person there domiciled acquires personal property, by the comity of nations the same must be deemed his property everywhere. It is obvious, that if this were true, in the extent in which the argument employs it, if slavery exists anywhere, and if by the laws of any place a property can be acquired in slaves, the law of slavery must extend to every place where such slaves may be carried. The maxim, therefore, and the argument can apply only to those commodities which are everywhere, and by all nations, treated and deemed subjects of property. But it is not speaking with strict accuracy to say, that a property can be acquired in human beings, by local laws. Each state may, for its own convenience, declare that slaves shall be deemed property, and that the relations and laws of personal chattels shall be deemed to apply to them; as, for instance, that they may be bought and sold, delivered, attached, levied upon, that trespass will lie for an injury done to them, or trover for converting them. But it would be a perversion of terms to say, that such local laws do in fact make them personal property generally; they can only determine that the same rules of law shall apply to them as are applicable to property, and this effect will follow only so far as such laws *proprio vigore* can operate ...

Sims's Case 7 **Cush. 285 (1851)**

Another Shaw case, which holds that a fugitive slave must be returned to his master, just as a fugitive from justice must be. The issue is presented in terms of the powers of the commissioner who is charged with deciding whether an alleged fugitive is to be returned. The commissioner's decision is conclusive. Part of the argument in the case concerned whether the commissioner's appointment was an unconstitutional exercise of judicial power; part turned on the fact that fugitive slaves were not entitled to a jury trial. (By contrast, fugitives from justice could only be returned for trial by a jury.) Shaw makes short work of these arguments, arguing instead that the *Fugitive Slave Act is* prerequisite to the stability of the nation. The report includes an *obiter dictum* on the injustice of slavery.

... Shaw, C.J.: – This is a petition for a writ of *habeas corpus* to bring the petitioner before this court, with a view to his discharge from imprisonment, upon the grounds stated in the petition. We were strongly urged to issue the writ, without inquiry into its cause, and to hear an argument upon the petitioner's right to a discharge, on the return of the writ. This we declined to do, on grounds of principle, and common and well settled practice. Before a writ of *habeas corpus* is granted, sufficient probable cause must be shown; but when it appears upon the party's own showing that there is no sufficient ground *prima facie* for his discharge, the court will not issue the writ ...

The evils existing immediately before the adoption of the constitution, and the greater and more appalling evils in prospect, indicated the absolute necessity of forming a more perfect union, in order to secure the peace and prosperity of all the states. This could only be done by the several states renouncing and relinquishing a portion of their powers of sovereignty; and these were the right of war and peace, the right of making treaties with foreign powers and with each other, and the right of exercising absolute power and dominion over all persons and things within their own territories respectively. In order to form this more perfect union, delegates from the several states met together. It was obvious that the renunciation of some of the powers of sovereignty, at least to the extent above mentioned, was the first step to be taken, and was absolutely essential to the success of any scheme of union. Still, it could not but be perceived that the great difference in the condition of the states in regard to the institution of slavery, and the prospect that many of the states would soon become free, from causes then in operation, constituted a difference in their relative condition, which must first be provided for. So long as the states remained sovereign, they could assert their rights in regard to fugitive slaves by war or treaty; and, therefore, before renouncing and surrendering such sovereignty, some substitute, in the nature of a treaty or compact, must necessarily be devised and agreed to. The clause above cited from the constitution seems to have been, in character, precisely such a treaty. It was a solemn compact, entered into by the delegates of states then sovereign and independent, and free to remain so, on great deliberation, and on the highest considerations of justice and policy, and reciprocal benefit, and in order to secure the peace and prosperity of all the states. It carries with it, therefore, all the sanction which can belong to it, either as an international or a social compact, made by parties invested with full powers to deliberate and act; or as a fundamental law, agreed on as the basis of a government, irrepealable, and to be changed only by the power that made it, in the form prescribed by it.

Such being the circumstances, under which this provision of the constitution was adopted; such the relations of the several states to each other; such the manifest object which the framers of the constitution had in view; we are to look at the clause in question, to ascertain its true meaning and effect. We think it was intended to guaranty to the owner of a slave, living within the territory of a state in which slavery is permitted, the rights conferred upon such owner, by the laws of such state; and that no state should make its own territory an asylum and sanctuary for fugitive slaves, by any law or regulation, by which a slave, who had escaped from a state where he owed labor or service into such state or territory, should avoid being reclaimed; it was designed also to provide a practicable and peaceable mode, by which such fugitive, upon the claim of the person to whom such labor or service should be due, might be delivered up ...

And the theory of the general government is, that these subjects, in their full extent and entire details, being placed under the jurisdiction of the general government, are necessarily withdrawn from the jurisdiction of the state, and the jurisdiction of the general government therefore becomes exclusive. And this is necessary to prevent constant collision and interference; and it is obvious that it must be so, because two distinct governments cannot exercise the same power, at the same time, on the same subject matter. This is not left to mere implication. It is expressly declared, in art. 1, s. 8, that congress shall have power to make all laws which shall be necessary and proper, for carrying into execution all the powers vested by the constitution in the government of the United States, or in any department or officer thereof. And by art. 6, "this constitution, and the laws of the United States which shall be made in pursuance thereof, and all treaties made, or which shall be made, under the authority of the United States, shall be the supreme law of the land; and the judges in every state shall be bound thereby, any thing in the constitution or laws of any state to the contrary notwithstanding." All such laws made by the general government, upon the rights, duties and subjects, specially enumerated and confided to their jurisdiction, are necessarily exclusive and supreme, as well by express provision, as by necessary implication. And the general government is provided with its executive, legislative and judicial departments, not only to make laws regulating the rights, duties and subjects thus confided to them, but to administer right and justice respecting them in a regular course of judicature, and cause them to be carried into full execution, by its own powers, without dependence upon state authority, and without any let or restraint imposed by it.

It was, as we believe, under this view of the right of regaining specifically the custody of one from whom service or labor is due by the laws of one state, and who has escaped into another, and under this view of the powers of the general government, and the duty of congress, that the law of February 12, 1793, was passed ...

The manifest intent of this act of congress was, to regulate and give effect to the right given by the constitution. It secured to the claimant the aid and assistance of certain magistrates and officers, to enable him to exercise his right in a more regular and orderly manner, and without being chargeable with a breach of the peace. It obviously contemplated a prompt and summary proceeding, adapted to the exigency of the occasion, in aid of a power, in terms conferred by the constitution on the claimant. It vested the power of inquiry, (whether regarded as judicial or otherwise,) the same power which is now drawn in question, in magistrates of counties, cities or towns corporate. As to the mode of trial contemplated by this act, it is described by Mr Justice McLean, in his opinion in *Prigg v. Pennsylvania*, 16 Peters, 539, 667, in these terms: "Both the constitution and the act of 1793 require the fugitive from labor to be delivered up on claim being made by the party, or his agent, to whom the service is due. Not that a suit should be regularly instituted. The proceeding authorized by the law is summary and informal. The fugitive is seized and taken before a judge or magistrate within the state, and on proof, parol or written, that he owes labor to the claimant, it is made the duty of the judge or magistrate to give the certificate, which authorizes the removal of the fugitive to the state from whence he absconded"...

We have thought it important thus to inquire into the validity and constitutionality of the act of 1793, because it appears to be decisive of that in question. In the only particular in which the constitutionality of the act of congress of 1850 is now called in question, that of 1793 was obnoxious to the same objection, viz., that of authorizing a summary proceeding before officers and magistrates not qualified under the constitution to exercise the judicial powers of the general government. Congress may have thought it necessary to change the preexisting law, not in principle but in detail, because, as we have seen in the case of *Prigg v. Pennsylvania*, some of the judges were of opinion that state magistrates could not act under the authority conferred on them by the act of 1793, when prohibited from doing so by the laws of their own state, and some states had in fact passed such prohibitory laws. The present fugitive slave law may vary in other respects, and provide other and more rigorous means for carrying its provisions into effect, but these are not made grounds of objection to its constitutionality.

We do not mean to say that this court will in no case issue a writ of *habeas corpus* to bring in a party, held under color of process from the courts of the United States, or whose services, and the custody of whose person, are claimed under authority derived from the laws of the

United States. This is constantly done, in cases of soldiers and sailors, held by military and naval officers, under enlistments complained of as illegal and void. But it is manifest that this ought to be done only in a clear case, and in a case where it is necessary to the security of personal liberty from illegal restraint ...

Since the argument in court, this morning, I am reminded by one of the counsel for the petitioner, that the law in question ought to be regarded as unconstitutional, because it makes no provision for a trial by jury. We think that this cannot vary the result. The law of 1850 stands, in this respect, precisely on the same ground with that of 1793, and the same grounds of argument which tend to show the unconstitutionality of one apply with equal force to the other; and the same answer must be made to them.

The principle of adhering to judicial precedent, especially that of the supreme court of the United States, in a case depending upon the constitution and laws of the United States, and thus placed within their special and final jurisdiction, is absolutely necessary to the peace, union and harmonious action of the state and general governments. The preservation of both, with their full and entire powers, each in its proper sphere, was regarded by the framers of the constitution, and has ever since been regarded, as essential to the peace, order and prosperity of all the United States.

If this were a new question, now for the first time presented, we should desire to pause and take time for consideration. But though this act, the construction of which is now drawn in question, is recent, and this point, in the form in which it is now stated, is new, yet the solution of the question depends upon reasons and judicial decisions, upon legal principles and a long course of practice, which are familiar, and which have often been the subject of discussion and deliberation.

Considering, therefore, the nature of the subject, the urgent necessity for a speedy and prompt decision, we have not thought it expedient to delay the judgment. I have, therefore, to state, in behalf of the court, under the weighty responsibility which rests upon us, and as the unanimous opinion of the court, that the writ of *habeas corpus* prayed for cannot be granted.

Writ refused.

...

By the received laws of nations, it seems to be well established, that however odious we may consider slavery and the slave trade, however abhorrent to the dictates of humanity and the plainest principles of justice and natural right, yet each nation has a right, in this respect, to judge for itself, and to allow or prohibit slavery by its own laws, at its own will; and that whenever slavery is thus established by positive law within the limits of such state, all other nations and people are bound to respect it, and cannot rightfully interfere, either by forcibly seizing, or artfully enticing away slaves, within the limits of the territory of the nation establishing it, or on the high seas, which are the common highway of nations. In the case cited, the language of this court is this: "In considering the law of nations, we may assume that the law of this state is analogous to the law of England in this respect; that while slavery is considered as unlawful and inadmissible in both, because contrary to natural right, and the laws designed for the security of personal liberty, yet, in both, the existence of slavery in other countries is recognized, and the claims of foreigners, growing out of that condition, are, to a certain extent, respected." In *Sommersett's case*, before Lord Mansfield, in 1771, 20 Howells's State Trials, 1, 82, which is the leading case on this subject, and establishes the doctrine of the natural right to personal liberty in its fullest extent, we find a clear intimation of the principle above stated. Slavery, said Lord Mansfield, "is of such a nature that it is incapable of being introduced on any reasons, moral or political, but only by positive law." "It is so odious, that nothing can be suffered to support it, but positive law." But this is a clear admission, and indeed this is manifest throughout his opinion, that although odious and contrary to natural right, it may exist by force of positive law. And this may be mere customary law, as well as the enactment of a statute. The term "positive law," in this sense, may be understood to designate those rules, established by long and tacit acquiescence, or by the legislative act of any state, and which derive their force and effect as law from such acquiescence or legislative enactment, and are acted upon as such, whether conformable to the dictates of natural justice or otherwise.

The principle is, that although slavery and the slave trade are contrary to justice and natural right, yet each nation, in this respect, may establish its own law, within its own territory. And even the slave trade is not regarded as piracy, even by those states who regard it in the abstract as unjust, except when it has been declared so by statute, which can only operate within its own limits; or except when it has been so declared by treaty between two or more powers, in which case it may be so regarded as between such powers, their citizens and subjects. This is confirmed by the English and American authorities, although the governments of both the United States and England have made strong declarations and passed very severe laws against the slave trade ...

If then these states, prior to the adoption of the constitution, would have been sovereign and independent, these views of the established and recognized laws of nations indicate clearly what would have been their relative condition, and their respective rights. Slavery was likely to subsist in some states, and to be abolished in others. Each would have been clothed with certain rights, and bound to the performance of certain duties, which each would have a right to defend and enforce by war, to which there would be a constant temptation; and this could only have been avoided by treaty, regulating and providing for the enjoyment and security of such rights. It would have been in vain to say, that slavery being founded in wrong and injustice, any treaty tending to assent to, uphold and sanction it, would be itself immoral and wrong, and so could not conscientiously be made. Nations cannot elect the subjects on which they will treat; treaties are often made under great exigencies, as the best alternative which can be resorted to in order to avoid greater evils. In the infancy of our commerce and of our political power, we thought it not wrong to make treaties with the Algerines, and other piratical powers of the coast of Barbary, who had committed depredations on our commerce, and carried our citizens into captivity. We made treaties for ransoming our citizens held in slavery, and paid tribute to these acknowledged pirates, to induce them to forbear plundering our commerce, although such payments contributed directly to the upholding and encouragement of robbery and piracy. Having made such treaties, nobody would doubt that it was our duty to fulfil them to the letter, any more than they would doubt our perfect right to refuse renewing them, the moment we were able to defend our own rights by our own strength. No; in making a treaty, we must take our relations with others as we find them; and make the best provision for our rights which is practicable under the circumstances. The question is, in adopting or rejecting a proposed mutual stipulation, not whether it is the most desirable on general grounds of expediency, but whether it is preferable to that which is the inevitable alternative if this is rejected.

But if no binding treaty could be made on the subject of slavery, what would have been the necessary alternative? It would have been a state of things in which acknowledged rights were in constant danger of being drawn into conflict between neighboring states, leading to a war likely to be perpetual, or perhaps to a still more disastrous result – that of some states being subjugated by others of superior physical strength, in a contest in which right and wrong would be disregarded, and violence and brute force would supersede the government of law and the reign of peace. Can this be regarded as an inflamed or exaggerated view of the condition of these states, as independent, but without compact with each other, if the views of the laws of nations above stated are correct? The states were equal in right, but unequal in power. In view of the laws of nations, there was no difference between Rhode Island and Virginia, or Pennsylvania and Delaware. With equal rights, constantly in danger of being brought into conflict, with radical differences of opinion and views, both of justice and policy, on the subject of slavery, the danger of hostile collision was imminent. What alternative was there, but either a general treaty of alliance or a league, or a union under one government, to whom should be confided all these subjects of common and mutual interest. The latter expedient was adopted. The several states agreed to renounce their rights of sovereignty to a limited extent; among other subjects, the regulation of their intercourse with foreign powers, with the Indian tribes and with each other; the right of war and peace, and that of making treaties either with foreign powers or with each other. Certain other subjects of common interest were also surrendered, and placed under the exclusive control and jurisdiction of the common government. Instead of enforcing their rights, as they could have done before, only by war, it was agreed to establish a general government, furnished with full and complete legislative, judicial and executive powers, to take cognizance of these rights, to provide by law for the regulation of them, to declare and apply them in an orderly course of judicature, and to carry them into full effect. On coming to this arrangement, it could not be kept out of view, that some states had large numbers of slaves, and were disposed to uphold and sanction the existence of slavery by their laws; whilst others denounced it and held it in abhorrence, as unjust and criminal, alike opposed to natural right and to good policy. It could not, however, but be known to the framers of the constitution, that in the states where slavery was allowed by law, certain rights attached to its citizens, which were recognized by the laws of nations, and which could not be taken away without their consent. They therefore provided for the limited enjoyment of that right, as it existed before, so as to prevent persons owing service under the laws of one state, and escaping therefrom into another, from being discharged by the laws of the latter;

and authorized the general government to prescribe means for their restoration. This is the *casus fœderis*; to this extent the states are bound by their compact, but no further. Slavery was not created, established or perpetuated by the constitution. It existed before; it would have existed if the constitution had not been made. The framers of the constitution could not abrogate slavery, or the qualified rights claimed under it; they took it as they found it, and regulated it to a limited extent. The constitution, therefore, is not responsible for the origin or continuance of slavery. The provision it contains was the best adjustment which could be made of conflicting rights and claims, and was absolutely necessary to effect what may now be considered as the general pacification, by which harmony and peace should take the place of violence and war. These were the circumstances, and this the spirit, in which the constitution was made; the regulation of slavery so far as to prohibit states by law from harboring fugitive slaves, was an essential element in its formation; and the union intended to be established by it was essentially necessary to the peace, happiness and highest prosperity of all the states. In this spirit, and with these views steadily in prospect, it seems to be the duty of all judges and magistrates to expound and apply these provisions in the constitution and laws of the United States; and in this spirit it behooves all persons, bound to obey the laws of the United States, to consider and regard them.

The duties and relations of the states to each other, by the laws of nations, anterior to the making of the constitution, and the qualified but acknowledged right arising from the establishment of slavery in some states, and its exclusion in others, having been alluded to briefly in the opinion of the court, it was thought advisable, in this note, to expand the argument somewhat, arising from that consideration, but more especially to state the judicial authorities upon which it rests.

READING QUESTIONS ON SHAW

1 How can Shaw reach what seem to be opposite conclusions in the two cases?

2 Charles-Henri Sanson was appointed executioner of Paris by Louis XVI, and served him faithfully. After the French Revolution he served new political masters, and became the king's executioner in a new sense. In the counter-terror, he beheaded another former employer, Robespierre. Sanson insisted on professional

detachment at his task, and is said to have argued that were he to have refused to execute those he thought unworthy, he would have been no better than a murderer for those he did behead. Compare his situation with those of Judge Shaw and Captain Vere.

Anthony Sebok
'Judging the Fugitive Slave Acts" (1991)

Sebok argues that Judge Shaw could have decided Sims's case differently had he reasoned in the way that Dworkin recommends.

Robert Cover argues in *Justice Accused* that the *Fugitive Slave Acts* created a "moral/formal" dilemma for Northern judges. As judges, these men had sworn to uphold the Constitution and the laws of the United States. It seemed apparent to many judges that the federal government's intentions were clear, that the Acts had been passed by valid majorities in Congress, and that they were sanctioned by the Constitution. But, as Northern elites, many of them held strong abolitionist beliefs and considered slavery (and, by extension, the capture of Blacks for return to a life of slavery) evil. These judges lived in a world where, with increasing frequency, many politicians, state judges, and other legal elites were arguing for the rejection of the *Fugitive Slave Acts*. The dilemma, then, lay between the judges' moral beliefs and their formal legal obligations.

Cover's conclusion is that the leading legal theory of the age – legal positivism – so dominated these judges that they could see but not act upon the appeals made from natural law in their courtrooms. Cover concludes that it was the very same technical skill that led these men to be judges that barred them from acting on their beliefs and rejecting the slave laws. The conscientious application of positivism led to "cognitive dissonance" amongst many judges of 1850. Cover suggests that these judges responded in two ways. First, they exaggerated the mechanical operation of the law, so as to deny to themselves any discretion and thereby excuse their failure to act. Second, they "raised the formal stakes" in the cases before them by claiming that if political or moral values were introduced into the process of adjudication, the authority of the state over all citizens would be eroded. Put most starkly, Cover depicts the Northern federal judges of 1850 as saying that in such morally charged cases as those concerning fugitive slaves, adjudication did not require moral judgment, and worse, moral judgment would imperil the state's authority ...

Cover implicitly reaffirms the dichotomy ...: natural law (normative communal vision) on the one side; positivism (bureaucracy and order) on the other. Cover thus finds the moral/formal dilemma a necessary element of American constitutional interpretation ... To rebut Cover's view of adjudication, one would either have to dissolve the moral/formal dichotomy or show why the dichotomy is in fact not a dilemma ...

Dworkin believes that the moral/formal dilemma embraced by Cover is a trap set up by the positivist in order to make positivism attractive. The trap creates two artificial categories which bear little relation to legal practice: legal positivism ("which insists that law and morals are made wholly distinct by ... rules everyone accepts for using 'law'") and natural law ("which insists, on the contrary, that [law and morality] are united"). The false dichotomy poses a choice between positivism and natural law, or between setting out the judge's responsibility as searching for what the law "is" as opposed to what it "ought to be" ...

With the exception of some Constitutional Utopians, few argued that the Constitution, with its implicit references to slavery, did not actually permit slavery in some parts of the country. Further, it would have been hard for someone to argue in 1840 that the Constitution actively forbade slavery. Slavery was a matter of state law, and it is unlikely that Dworkin could generate not only a federal prohibition against slavery, but also some theory of federal common law or federal rights applicable to the states to enforce that prohibition. The Constitution did not approve of slavery, nor did it disapprove of it: its three mentions of the institution regulated a practice which the text could have outlawed but did not (until the Thirteenth Amendment) ...

A combination of these two prongs rebuts the objections to Dworkin's arguments by offering the following claim: the *Fugitive Slave Act* of 1850 was not constitutional because its application, given the conditions of 1850, violated the principle of comity that allowed the free states to tolerate slavery without compromising the demands of their own legal practices ...

Little information exists about the intentions and purposes of the Framers of the fugitive slave clause. As we saw above, however,

Dworkin argues that the goal of constitutional interpretation is not to describe the specific state of affairs the Framers intended, but rather to describe the general principle they hoped to build into the Constitution. Just as Dworkin was able to describe a general principle of the Fourteenth Amendment that was "correctly" instantiated by different theories of racial equality at different times, he can do the same with the principle expressed by the fugitive slave clause. The Clause required – most generally – that each state respect the laws of its neighbor; more specifically, it required the states that forbid slavery to deliver runaway slaves to the states that had slavery. But as with the "principle" of racial equality contained in the Fourteenth Amendment, this "principle" of fugitive comity could have had many different theoretical instantiations. One theory Dworkin could advance is as follows: The Constitution, in order to leave questions of the treatment of Blacks within their borders up to each state, could not replace the laws governing the internal regulation of Blacks with federal laws that, in effect, substituted the laws of another state.

If the Clause is read to refer to this theory, then Dworkin's attack on the 1850 Act can be made on two fronts. First, the Clause, which at root was concerned with the *states'* obligation to return runaways, cannot be read as having granted the federal courts the power to invalidate state processes simply because they were slow or – in the eyes of other states – obstructionist. Thus, the Clause should never have been read to forbid state governments from making fundamental choices about the process necessary for a slave to be "delivered up" to a slave state. Second, the due process clause of the Fifth Amendment limited the sort of processes the federal government could erect to ensure the return of runaway slaves. Unless the process due an accused Black was at least equal to that of the state in which the federal proceeding took place, the "home" state's "pro-Black" processes were being derogated in favor of a Southern state's "anti-Black" processes. These two issues, however, are merely logical extensions of the same central issue, which is: what limits did the fugitive slave clause place on the federal government's power to decide how alleged slaves were to be treated within the Northern states' territory? ...

The theory of interstate comity available to judges in the 1790s and the early nineteenth century may have been something like the following: In order to respect each state's views on slavery, federal law guarantees the slave states their citizens' property rights in slaves in the United States. This theory assumes that the protection of Southern property rights would not conflict with Northern states' domestic law. This assumption may have been credible when Northern states had no body of domestic law designed to address the treatment of accused slaves by domestic or foreign actors. If the laws of Northern states did not conflict with the extraterritorial claims of residents of Southern states, and federal law went no further than to enforce Southern claims, then the principle of comity described above would be consistent with the 1793 Act. A change in conditions – in both the nature of the Northern states' relation to slave-catching and the attitude of Northern governments toward slave-catching – made the Clause's principle of comity incompatible with either Act, however ...

The principle of comity changed between 1793 and 1850 as the world changed. In the early years of the 1793 Act there were few Northern laws about slave-catching to conflict with Southern laws. There was simply much less reason for the Northern states to legislate on the issue of fugitives: the lack of an organized abolition movement meant fewer slaves coming across the border and less popular outrage at the slave-catchers who would enter Northern towns and forcibly remove Blacks to Southern states and inevitably to bondage. The gradual transformation in Northern political morality is illustrated by the rise of "personal liberty" laws, as well as an increase in both the frequency and severity of Northern reaction to the use of the 1793 Act by Southern slave-owners.

In the face of this changing political morality in the North, the Clause forced judges into an inescapable dilemma. On the one hand, the Clause specifically called upon states to cooperate in the return of slaves; one could see this federal instruction as a commitment on the part of the federal government to ensure that conflicts over slaves were regulated by more than the usual "interstate comity" rules that governed choice of law disputes. On the other hand, as Northern states passed more laws regulating how slaves were to be caught within their territory, the federal involvement in slave-catching necessarily had to express a preference in upholding either the North's or the South's conception of how slaves were to be caught. Since the activity always took place in the North, to uphold the Southern conception would increasingly void Northern laws regulating conduct within their own borders.

... [F]or Northern states to curb their personal liberty laws (or to choose not to pass them out of regard for the Clause) would have violated the Clause's commitment to the principle of comity described above. It would be misleading to say that the free states were, in any significant way, adopting a view about the treatment of Blacks simply by omitting to act in a way that opposed a slave state's interests. However, once the free states developed and articulated a view – upon which they based positive state action – about how alleged slaves should be treated, then each time they curbed their sense of what process was due, and acted because of the slave state's interests, they were coerced into choosing the Southern regime over their own. That is why Dworkin can say that the change in the political morality and actions in the North made demands on the Clause that exposed its incompatibility with the Acts. Once that point was reached, to the extent that the Northern states were obliged to act because of the Constitution, the Constitution was not just protecting the slaveholder's interest in his slave, but forcing the North to respect that interest through procedures infected with the assumptions of slavery.

... Northern states had begun to develop a coherent policy as to the treatment of fugitive slaves such that in regulating civil life within their territory, these states were taking positive steps toward preventing slave-catching. The Court's optimism that federal law could coexist with state inactivity became untenable as soon as state regulation with regard to the due process necessary to remove a fugitive slave began to look more and more like Pennsylvania's unconstitutional antikidnapping law.

[B] THE CLAUSE AND DUE PROCESS

... [B]y 1850, the Clause could not have been read to allow uncon-strained federal regulation of slave-catching. A related and important point is that even if the Clause were viewed as giving the federal government the power to enforce the Northern states' obligations as set out in the Clause (to "deliver up" slaves), this still does not mean that the federal process used could violate contemporary state standards of due process. A conflict still remained concerning the extent to which the federal rules should reflect the Northern states' belief that any Black brought before a court in the North should enjoy the presumption that she was free until proven otherwise, and the Southern belief that proceedings in the North were little more than summary extradition hearings, where the presumption was reversed, and that any alleged slave could get a full and fair hearing once they were returned to the state of their alleged master.

... We should recall what we determined to be the Clause's general principle: comity between the states with regard to how Blacks were to be treated within their borders. Until 1850, there was no special federal procedure for slave-catching, since there were no special federal officers like commissioners. Until 1850, federal judges (if they ever heard a runaway case) applied the procedure of the state in which they sat. This reflected the Clause's general commitment to comity. Under the pre-1850 scheme, as conceptions of due process changed in a Northern state, the federal procedure, which relied on state procedure, thus changed accordingly. Until 1850, a Dworkinian interpreter could claim that the Clause did not permit a person domiciled in Pennsylvania to receive federal procedural protections so thin that, in effect, that person's only real hearing was in South Carolina, with South Carolina "procedure." The denial of this interpretation would provide slave-catchers with guaranteed access to Southern slave law in every fugitive slave case: upon seizing a Black in the North, they then would need only to invoke a shred of federal procedure in order legitimately to introduce Southern law. On the other hand, obedience to the principle of comity would, according to our Dworkinian interpretation, require that federal due process treat Blacks with at least that process they would have received in the state in which they were seized ...

Dworkin's specific argument about the 1850 Act suggests that Cover's depiction of adjudication in hard cases is a misdescription with serious political consequences. If adjudication in hard cases requires estrangement from one's political commitments, then Cover simultaneously discourages people with political commitments from choosing to become, or remain, judges, while licensing those who remain judges to discount the role of political commitment in the interpretation of the Constitution. Cover's pessimistic view of adjudication is not necessarily correct. Judges in 1850 were not trapped between the formalism of following evil rules or the moral commands of their consciences.

READING QUESTIONS ON SEBOK

1 Summarize Sebok's argument in your own words. What steps in the argument might a positivist reject?
2 Suppose the *Fugitive Slave Act* had been designed to block the response Sebok suggests. What then?

The Chinese Head Tax Case (2002)

This case arose out of the failed attempt by Chinese Canadians to secure an apology and compensation from the federal government for the Head Tax, a tax imposed on Chinese immigrants to Canada between 1885 and 1923. The lawyers used an imaginative combination of private-law and public-law arguments to make the claim that the government should apologize and make restitution to Head Tax payers and their descendants. These arguments are discussed in the essay by Mayo Moran, which follows the judgment of the Ontario Court of Appeal. It is important to know before you start reading the case that one of the most significant obstacles that the lawyers faced is that they relied heavily on the claim that the government had been unjustly enriched by the Head Tax. However, a claim for unjust enrichment is barred when there is a "valid juristic reason" for the enrichment and the Head Tax had been collected in terms of a valid statute at a time when Canada had no entrenched bill of rights. As part of their attempt to surmount this obstacle, the lawyers relied on Gustav Radbruch's claim that extreme injustice is no law, as you will see in the short extract from their Factum, the written argument which is presented to a court and which forms the basis for a lawyer's oral argument.

FACTUM

International Case Law
96.   Canadian courts are not the first to have considered how a court ought to approach the problem of an "evil law." European courts have had to consider what weight should be given to legislation that was properly enacted positive law, that was not unconstitutional at the time of its enactment, but that was nonetheless profoundly at odds with the core values of the law itself.
97.   German courts have most frequently addressed this problem. They have had to confront the import of National Socialist laws that were validly enacted positive law and which contravened no positive constitutional or international law during their period of operation. In such cases, courts have repeatedly refused to defer absolutely to the existence of positive law. Much of this case law concerns the impact of

Nazi Decree 11 which stripped German Jewish émigrés of their citizenship and hence their proprietary rights, including the right to inherit. In assessing whether the effects of that decree could continue to exert force on the right to inherit property, the Federal Constitutional Court noted that law and justice are not entirely at the discretion of the legislator. In order to avoid reinvigorating Nazi law, it was necessary to:

... affirm the possibility of denying national socialist "legal" rules their validity as law because they contradict fundamental principles of justice in such an evident manner that the judge applying or acknowledging their legal consequences would administer injustice instead of law.
  Order of Second Senate, 14 Feb. 1968, citing BVerfGE 3, 58 [119]; 6, 132 [198].

98. Similarly, the German Federal Court of Justice found invalid the German Government's expropriation of property of a Jewish woman who had lost her German citizenship under the Reich's citizenship law, on the ground that the citizenship law was void from the outset "because of its iniquitous content which contradicts the foundational requirements of every order based on the rule of law."
  BGHZ 16, 350 (354), cited in Robert Alexy, "A Defence of Radbruch's Formula," in *Recrafting the Rule of Law: The Limits of Legal Order*, David Dyzenhaus, ed. (Oxford: Hart Publishing, 1999) at 19.

99. Nor is this approach confined to German courts. In fact, the House of Lords took a similar position in a case involving the validity of the German citizenship law. The law revoked the citizenship of Jews and its operation would have resulted in an unjust enrichment based on double taxation of the plaintiff. In finding that the enrichment was invalid notwithstanding the fact that the law which gave rise to it was constitutional, Lord Cross of Chelsea states:

To my mind a law of this sort constitutes so grave an infringement of human rights that the courts of this country ought to refuse to recognize it as a law at all.
  Oppenheimer v. Cattermole, [1976] AC 249 at p. 278 (H of L) (*per* Lord Cross of Chelsea).

100. This reasoning has also been applied more recently by the Berlin State Court in assessing the culpability of East German border guards

for shootings on the former Berlin Wall and the effect in those circumstances of the Border Law of the German Democratic Republic. In the
leading case, the Court notes that even duly enacted positive law must
give way where it violates the legal convictions of all nations in regard
to people's worth and dignity. The Court affirmed, as had other German
courts before it, that the freedom of a state to legislate is limited and
cannot interfere with the core area of law – the principles of fundamental justice. The reasoning is set out as follows:

It was especially the time of the National Socialist regime in Germany that
taught us that the legislator can also legislate injustice. In other words, if
practical legal usage is not to stand defenseless against such historically
thinkable examples, it must be possible, in extreme cases, to evaluate certain
basic principles of material justice more highly than the principle of legal
certainty, such as it is expressed in the applicability of positive law for
routine cases.

Trial of Border Guards, Berlin State Court, Docket no. (523) 2Js 48/90
(9/91), trans. in *Transitional Justice*, vol. 3: *Laws, Rulings, and Reports* Neil J.
Kritz, ed. (Washington: United States Institute of Peace Press, 1995), 576 at
579, quoting BVerfG 3, 232 (1953 Federal Constitutional Court).

101. In determining whether particular laws amounted to such extreme
injustice, the Court drew on the *International Covenant on Civil and
Political Rights* as a source of "guiding principles." Rudolf Geiger, one
of the leading commentators on the border guard cases, notes how the
courts relied on international human rights principles, not as directly
applicable *per se*, but rather as indications of the fundamental principles
of the law:

The Court emphasized for the first time that the core of international human
rights gives substance and meaning to these basic principles because human
rights expressed the shared opinions of all nations on important elements of
justice and human dignity.

R. Geiger, "The German Border Guard Cases and International Human
Rights" *European Journal of International Law* 9, no. 3 (1998) at 540.

102. This reasoning is equally applicable to customary international
law. Customary international law has the same position as conventional
law. A court can equally rely on customary international law as a source

of guiding principle in assessing whether a law in question amounts to an extreme injustice.

103. It is therefore respectfully submitted that in determining whether contemporary Canadian courts ought to give continuing legal effect to a discriminatory law, guidance ought to be drawn from the experience of German and British courts. The values of certainty and democracy that ordinarily require that courts simply defer to the existence of legislation must at a certain point give way, in the very name of law itself, to the most basic of legal values which courts are dedicated to upholding. Otherwise, contemporary Canadian courts will perpetuate injustice instead of law and that law itself will stand defenseless against the most iniquitous uses of its form.

104. The principle that when positive law enshrines extreme injustice courts acting in furtherance of their judicial duties must refuse to give legal effect to that injustice has been recognized by this Honourable Court.

105. In *Canada Trust Co. v. Ontario Human Rights Commission*, the Ontario Court of Appeal had to consider the contemporary validity of a racist trust established in 1923. The trust itself met all the ordinary conditions of legal validity imposed on charitable trusts, and had been in operation for many years. It was challenged as against public policy under the 1981 *Ontario Human Rights Code*. Although in ordinary conditions a court has no power to override the settlor's intent in a validly executed trust, in this case the Ontario Court of Appeal found that notwithstanding its positive validity the trust was invalid as contrary to public policy:

To perpetuate a trust that imposes restrictive criteria on the basis of discriminatory notions espoused in these recitals according to the terms specified by the settlor would not, in my opinion, be conducive to the public interest. The settlor's freedom to dispose of his property through the creation of a charitable trust fashioned along these lines must give way to current principles of public policy under which all races and religions are to be treated on equal footing of equality and accorded equal regard and equal respect.

Canada Trust Co. v. Ontario Human Rights Commission (1990), 74 OR (2d) 481 at p. 496 (CA) (*per* Robins, J.A.)

106. It is respectfully submitted that this reasoning is equally applicable to the case at bar. Retention of the funds paid pursuant to the *Act* is only possible if courts rely on a juristic reason profoundly at odds with the

basic principles of the legal order. Holding that the *Chinese Immigration Act* constitutes a juristic reason for the continued enrichment of the defendant would not only amount to a contemporary validation of this racist legislation but would implicate the court – the ultimate custodian of rights – in its perpetuation. A judge determining whether the enrichment in this case is unjust is acting today, and must act in accord with the principles of the legal order as we understand them now. Therefore, it is submitted, a contemporary court must apply principles of racial equality in order to prevent validation and perpetuation of the racism embodied in the *Chinese Immigration Act*.

Mack v. Attorney General of Canada:
Judgment of the Ontario Court of Appeal (2002)

Moldver and MacPherson, JJ.A.:

1 In the Quebec Secession Reference,[1] the Supreme Court of Canada observed that although the protection of minority rights has played an essential part in the design of Canada's constitutional structure, our record for upholding such rights has by no means been spotless. In this regard, Canada's treatment of people of Chinese origin who sought to immigrate to this country between 1885 and 1947 represents one of the more notable stains on our minority rights tapestry. For the first 38 of those years, until 1923, Parliament passed a series of laws that required persons of Chinese origin to pay a duty or "head tax" upon entering Canada.[2] The tax, which grew progressively from $50 in 1885 to $500 in 1903, was meant to be prohibitive and it placed Canada beyond the reach of many. But not enough, apparently, for the government of the day, which explains why the tax was abolished in 1923 and replaced by legislation that for the next 24 years, until its repeal in 1947, effectively barred all but a select few Chinese people from immigrating to Canada.[3]
2 The appellants represent a class of people who seek redress from the Government of Canada for the harm occasioned by the impugned legislation – legislation which they quite properly characterize as racist and discriminatory. The class includes some individuals who actually

paid the head tax, but in the main it consists of their spouses and descendants.

3 Among other forms of relief, the appellants seek the return, with compound interest, of monies paid as head tax and damages for pain and suffering, injury to dignity and loss of opportunity stemming from the impugned legislation. For present purposes, it is agreed that the appellants base their claim on the following three causes of action:

(1) The impugned legislation is the source of two distinct violations of the appellants' equality rights under s. 15 of the *Charter*.

(2) The impugned legislation was at all times invalid and of no force or effect because it contravened a customary international law, by which Canada was legally bound, prohibiting racial discrimination.

(3) The equitable principle of unjust enrichment applies and it requires the government to disgorge the revenues raised under the head tax legislation.

4 After being served with the statement of claim (the "claim"), the Attorney General of Canada moved under rule 21.01(1)(b) of the *Rules of Civil Procedure*, R.R.O. 1990, Reg. 194, to have the claim struck out on the ground that it disclosed no reasonable cause of action. The motion was argued before Cumming, J. of the Superior Court of Justice for two full days on April 24 and 25, 2001. On July 9, 2001, Cumming, J. released comprehensive written reasons in which he allowed the motion and struck the claim.

5 The appellants appeal from that order and seek to have the claim reinstated. For reasons that follow, we are satisfied that Cumming, J. came to the correct conclusion. Accordingly, we would dismiss the appeal.

BACKGROUND

6 Cumming, J.'s comprehensive reasons for allowing the motion to strike out the appellants' claim include a thorough review of the background facts and the test to be applied on a rule 21.01(1)(b) motion. Accordingly, we propose to move directly to the issues, commencing with the alleged infractions of the appellants' equality rights under s. 15 of the *Charter*.

7 The appellants allege that the impugned legislation is the source of two separate and distinct violations of their equality rights under s. 15 of the *Charter*.

8 First, they submit that the legislation stigmatized people of Chinese origin because it deemed them to be less worthy than other people. That stigma, they contend, continues unabated to this day because of the government's unwillingness to refund the head tax and provide redress for the harm and suffering occasioned by 62 years of government-sponsored anti-Chinese legislation.

9 Second, the appellants point to the 1988 post-*Charter* agreement between the Government of Canada and Japanese Canadians in which the government provided redress for violating the human rights of Japanese Canadians during the Second World War. In the face of that agreement, they submit that the government's failure to provide the Chinese Canadian community with similar redress is discriminatory because it promotes and perpetuates the idea that Chinese Canadians are less worthy of recognition and less valuable to society than Japanese Canadians.

10 Cumming, J. dealt with both issues in his reasons. With respect to the first, he referred to *Benner v. Canada (Secretary of State)*, [1997] 1 SCR 358, for the proposition that "the *Charter* cannot apply retroactively or retrospectively." He then quoted the relevant passages from *Benner* in which Iacobucci, J. identified the test to be applied in determining whether a proposed application of the *Charter* is or is not retrospective. The passages quoted are found at pp. 383–84 of *Benner* and bear repetition:

Section 15 cannot be used to attack a discrete act which took place before the *Charter* came into effect. It cannot, for example, be invoked to challenge a pre-*Charter* conviction: *R. v. Edwards Books and Art Ltd.*, [1986] 2 SCR 713; *Gamble, supra*. Where the effect of a law is simply to impose an on-going discriminatory status or disability on an individual, however, then it will not be insulated from *Charter* review simply because it happened to be passed before April 17, 1985. It if continues to impose its effects on new applicants today, then it is susceptible to *Charter* scrutiny today: *Andrews v. Law Society of British Columbia*, [1989] 1 SCR 143.

The question, then, is one of characterization: is the situation really one of going back to redress an old event which took place before the *Charter* created the right sought to be vindicated, or is it simply one of assessing the contemporary application of a law which happened to be passed before the *Charter* came into effect?

... Successfully determining whether a particular case involves applying the *Charter* to a past event or simply to a current condition or status will involve determining whether, in all the circumstances, the most significant or relevant feature of the case is the past event or the current condition resulting from it. This is, as I already stated, a question of characterization, and will vary with the circumstances. Making this determination will depend on the facts of the case, on the law in question, and on the *Charter* right which the applicant seeks to apply.

11 Cumming, J. then continued as follows:

The plaintiffs argue that they are not asking the court to apply the *Charter* either retroactively or retrospectively. Rather, they contend that their present *Charter* rights are infringed as a result of the government's refusal to provide redress relating to the Head Tax. They argue that repealing the *Chinese Immigration Act* without remedying any of its resulting discriminatory effects violates the *Charter* section 15 right to equality.

Applying the test articulated in *Benner*, this court must ask how the plaintiffs' claim can best be characterized. Here, the claim is founded on a discrete act, that is, the levying of a fee on Chinese immigrants or the outright exclusion of Chinese immigrants under the *Chinese Immigration Act* in its various forms. It is this discrete act that predominates over any of the Head Tax's continuing effects. It is impossible to say that the plaintiffs' claim is grounded in the "contemporary application" of a historical statute, repealed long before 1985, when s. 15 of the *Charter* came into force. The offending law was repealed in 1947. There can be no contemporary application of a repealed law.

Rather, this claim seeks redress for events that took place over fifty years ago. Accepting all the facts as pleaded by the plaintiffs, the proposed application of the *Charter* is retrospective. Therefore, it cannot succeed.

It is not sufficient for the plaintiffs to plead that they continue to suffer from discriminatory legislation that existed, but was repealed, prior to the enactment of the *Charter*. As the court in *Benner, supra*, recognized at 388, quoting Létourneau, J.A. in the Federal Court of Appeal below:

Otherwise, just about every instance of past discrimination since the turn of the century could be reviewed under section 15, provided the victims still suffer from that past discrimination.

The plaintiffs must find a foundation for their claim in the laws applicable to the time of the impugned actions of government. The direct and indirect consequences of acts of discrimination may well last a lifetime and extend beyond to subsequent generations. But the predominating act of discrimination itself ended with the repeal of the *Chinese Immigration Act* in 1947.

12 We agree with Cumming, J.'s analysis and would only note that, unlike the present situation, *Benner* is a clear case where because of his status at birth (born abroad before February 15, 1977 to a Canadian mother and a non-Canadian father) Benner was prevented in 1988 (3 years after s. 15 of the *Charter* had come into effect) from being accorded the automatic right to citizenship granted to children of Canadian fathers. In other words, in 1988, Benner's status at birth was held against him and disentitled him to a benefit accorded to others because of certain provisions of the *Citizenship Act* that the court found to be discriminatory. With respect, the appellants have not shown any such comparable disadvantage.

13 Cumming, J. then turned to the *Japanese Canadian Redress Agreement* ("*Redress Agreement*") and the alleged breach of the appellants' s. 15 *Charter* rights stemming from the government's failure to extend similar redress to the Chinese Canadian community.[4] Cumming, J. refused to allow the claim to proceed on this ground because, in his view, the pleadings were deficient in two respects.

14 First, the pleadings failed to include "facts as to a discrimination claim framed in the post-*Charter* period." Rather, as pleaded, the alleged discrimination flowed solely "from the impugned historical legislation, not from the *Japanese Canadian Redress Agreement*." The pleading in question reads as follows:

The plaintiffs state that the Government of Canada has provided redress for its violation of the human rights of Japanese Canadians during the Second World War, by means of Order-in-Council P.C. 1988–89/2552 ("the Redress Order"). This Order, and other acts of redress by Canadian national and provincial governments, shows acceptance in this country of the right of redress for human rights violations based on international instruments as outlined above and on Canadian domestic human rights law. Failure to extend redress to the Chinese Canadian community, and to persons in the position of the plaintiffs herein is, moreover, a violation of section 15 of the *Charter of Rights*.

15 Second, the pleadings failed to allege facts capable of showing discrimination in accordance with the principles enunciated in *Law v. Canada (Minister of Employment and Immigration)*, [1999] 1 SCR 497 at 529, namely, facts capable of showing that the *Redress Agreement* functioned by device of stereotype or that the exclusion of the appellants from it had the effect of demeaning their worth and dignity. Cumming, J.'s reasons in this regard are reproduced below:

Moreover, the fact that the government gives redress to one group of Canadians in respect of their claim of discrimination through a voluntary agreement does not in itself provide a legal basis for another, unrelated group in respect of their separate claim of discrimination. The government had a purpose through the *Japanese Canadian Redress Agreement* that was consistent with s. 15 of the *Charter*, and the exclusion of non-Japanese Canadians from the agreement did not undermine this purpose or demean the claimants' human dignity. The Government had a targeted ameliorative program for a specific group, that being Japanese Canadians.

The plaintiffs in the case at hand allege that the *Japanese Canadian Redress Agreement* failed to deal with the disadvantages that Chinese Canadians have experienced, even though those disadvantages are unrelated to the discrimination addressed through the government's agreement with Japanese Canadians. However, exclusion from a specifically targeted group "is less likely to be associated with stereotyping or stigmatization or conveying the message that the excluded group is less worthy of recognition and participation in the larger society." See *Lovelace v. Ontario*, [2000] 1 SCR 950 at 1000. The simple fact is that an "*ex gratia* payment to compensate certain members of the Japanese Canadian population is not discrimination pursuant to s. 15 of the *Charter*" in respect of other Canadians: *R. v. Mayrhofer*, [1993] 2 FC 157 (TD) at 175.

16 We agree with Cumming, J.'s analysis. In particular, we note that in their pleadings, the appellants do not suggest that the alleged differential treatment of Japanese Canadians under the *Redress Agreement* reflects the stereotypical application of presumed group or personal characteristics, or otherwise has the effect of perpetuating or promoting the view that they are less capable, or less worthy of recognition or value as human beings or members of Canadian society (see *Law, supra*, at p. 529).

17 Even if the pleadings, read generously, can be said to incorporate

such an allegation, we agree with the Attorney General of Canada that for the purpose of resolving this appeal, it is irrelevant that discrimination in Canada against immigrants of Asian origin generally encompassed both Chinese and Japanese people. At issue here are the specific acts of alleged discrimination pleaded in the statement of claim, and because those acts are so completely different from the acts of discrimination giving rise to the *Redress Agreement*, it is plain and obvious that the appellants cannot use that agreement as a springboard from which to launch their s. 15 *Charter* claim. See *Lovelace v. Ontario*, [2000] 1 SCR 950 at 994–98.

CAUSE OF ACTION BASED ON CUSTOMARY INTERNATIONAL LAW

18 The appellants submit that their claim supports a cause of action based on customary international law. In particular, they argue that it is not plain and obvious that customary international law did not condemn racial discrimination during the period of the impugned legislation and, to the extent that it did, Canada was legally bound to abide by it and can be held accountable for failing to do so.

19 Cumming, J. devoted a considerable amount of time in his reasons to the international law component of the pleadings. In the end, he concluded that the appellants could not ground their claim in conventional international law because the instruments upon which they were relying did not exist at the time of the impugned legislation and to the extent Canada has since incorporated them into its domestic law, they have not been given retroactive effect. With respect to any international norms against racial discrimination that may have existed during the relevant time frame, Cumming, J. found, in accordance with general principles of international law, that absent adoption, such norms were not binding upon Canada.

20 The appellants do not disagree with Cumming, J.'s analysis so far as it goes. They maintain, however, that he failed to consider their customary international law argument and its impact on the viability of their claim.

21 To the extent that Cumming, J. may have neglected the appellants' customary international law argument, his oversight is understandable as the term "customary international law" is not mentioned in the claim and it is questionable whether the pleadings even raise it as supporting a cause of action. That said, the Attorney General of Canada is not pressing the matter and invites us to address the issue on its merits.

22 The Attorney General of Canada submits, correctly in our view, that there are two required elements of customary international law. A proponent must establish:

(1) a practice among States of sufficient duration, uniformity and generality; and
(2) that States consider themselves legally bound by the practice.
    (I. Brownlie, *Principles of Public International Law*, 5th ed. (Oxford: Clarendon Press, 1998) at 4–7).

23   In the same text, at p. 5, Professor Brownlie explains that the evidence needed to establish custom can come from various sources and includes the following:

... diplomatic correspondence, policy statements, press releases, the opinions of official legal advisers, official manuals on legal questions, e.g. manuals of military law, executive decisions and practices, orders to naval forces etc., comments by governments on drafts produced by the International Law Commission, state legislation, international and national judicial decisions, recitals in treaties and other international instruments, a pattern of treaties in the same form, the practice of international organs, and resolutions relating to legal questions in the United Nations General Assembly. Obviously the value of these sources varies and much depends on the circumstances.

24 The appellants rely on a number of sources to establish the pre-1947 existence of a customary international law prohibiting racial discrimination. These include:

- national and international judicial decisions;
- individual opinions expressed by some members of Parliament;
- Canada's membership in the League of Nations and its participation as a signatory to the Treaty of Versailles;
- Canada's participation as a signatory to various treaties regarding the abolition of slavery;
- the constitution of the International Labour Organization and various declarations emanating from it; and,
- writings of various international law scholars.

In addition, the appellants point to the *Canadian Bill of Rights* and the *Charter*, characterizing each as a codification of pre-existing rights, including the right to be free from racial discrimination.

25 The Attorney General of Canada submits that the source materials referred to by the appellants fall short of establishing a pre-1947 international custom prohibiting racial discrimination. According to the Attorney General, these materials, properly construed, represent pockets of enlightenment in an era when the protection of human rights did not figure prominently on the international scene. Support for this conclusion is found in the writings of leading international law scholars, such as Professor Francesco Capatorti. In his essay entitled "Human Rights, the Hard Road Toward Universality,"[5] Professor Capatorti observes that although the "birth of an international system of regulation of human rights has constituted a form of evolution ... and not one of revolution," the year in which the United Nations was created, 1945, is recognized as:

... the starting point of world-wide international activity for the protection of human rights. Indeed, before that date no system of international rules intended to oblige the states to respect a full catalogue of human rights had ever been introduced. (at p. 979)

26 By way of elaboration, Professor Capatorti references certain "phenomena" in the late nineteenth century and first half of the twentieth century that, in his view, represented the "more significant antecedents of the protection of the human person" (at p. 979). At p. 980 however, he points out that these pockets of enlightenment should not be confused with a world-wide perspective on the protection of human rights:

However, the fragmentary character of the clauses mentioned and their evident connection with situations peculiar to a restricted geographical area show that a world-wide perspective on protection of human rights was still totally absent.

   The same consideration applies to the minorities régime created on the basis of the Peace Treaties of 1919–1920; yet some considerable progress reached by such a régime cannot be denied.

27 As indicated, Professor Capatorti maintains that the breakthrough in the field of individual human rights from a fragmentary perspective to a global aim occurred in 1945, with the birth of the United Nations. At pp. 981–82 he notes:

The birth of the United Nations introduced three great novelties into this evolution. In the first place, the shift from a fragmentary perspective to a global aim: no longer the mere defence of religious freedom, the protection of minorities or a more humane treatment of the workers, each of them considered in a different context, but "the respect for human rights and fundamental freedoms for all without distinction as to race, sex, language or religion" (article 1, paragraph 2 of the Charter). Second, the adoption of this global aim among those of a universal organization, and therefore the ambition of establishing a level of protection common to all states (as the organization gradually achieves a real universality). Third, the creation of an organ intended for that purpose and called upon to work exclusively for it – namely the Commission for Human Rights – as well as the conferring of precise competences in the same field both on the Assembly and on the Economic and Social Council.

28 Other international law scholars, such as Professor John Humphrey, describe the adoption of the U.N. Charter in 1945 as a "revolutionary" foundation for the development of international human rights. In his article entitled "The Implementation of International Human Rights Law," (1978) 24 *New York Law School Review* 31 at 32–33, Professor Humphrey writes:

Customary law has the great advantage over treaty law in that it is binding on all states. Thus the law governing the international responsibility of states for the treatment of aliens is binding on all states by virtue of their membership in the international community. This law, as already indicated, has recently undergone significant changes. For the traditional minimum objective international standard (which was sometimes higher than national standards) has been replaced by a new standard under which foreigners and nationals are entitled to the same treatment. This new standard is set forth in the Universal Declaration of Human Rights which, whatever its drafters may have intended in 1948, is now part of the customary law of nations – not because it was adopted as a resolution of the General Assembly but because of juridical consensus resulting from its invocation as law on countless occasions since 1948 both within and outside the United Nations. The Universal Declaration of Human Rights has now become the authentic interpretation of the human rights provisions of the Charter which neither catalogues nor defines the human rights to which it refers.

This human rights law, whether based on treaty or on custom, is not only new, it is revolutionary in the sense that it is radically different from traditional international law which was only concerned with relations between states.

29 To the extent that national judicial decisions from the pre-1947 era are relevant, the cases relied upon by the appellants, such as *Regina v. Corporation of Victoria*, [1888] 1 BCR Pt. II 331 (SC); *Regina v. Mee Wah*, [1886] 3 BCR 403 (Cty. Ct.); *Tai Sing v. Macguire*, [1878] 1 BCR Pt. I 101 (SC) and *R. v. Gold Commissioner of Victoria District*, [1886], 1 BCR Pt. II 260 (Div. Ct.), are of limited assistance since they do not address the issue at hand but relate instead to the separation of powers under ss. 91 and 92 of the *Constitution Act, 1867*. In any event, they must be read in light of *Cunningham v. Tomey Homma*, [1903] AC 151 (PC), a more recent decision and one of higher authority in which the Privy Council held that a statute which restricted entitlement to vote on the basis of race was both *intra vires* and a valid exercise of provincial power. Notably, speaking for the court, the Lord Chancellor observed at pp. 155–56 that "the policy or impolicy of such an enactment as that which excludes a particular race from the franchise is not a topic which their Lordships are entitled to consider." As the Attorney General of Canada points out, *Cunningham*, a decision of the final appellate court of the day, stands in stark contradiction to the appellants' assertion that a customary international law prohibiting racial discrimination existed in that era.

30 As for the foreign decisions cited by the appellants in support of their customary international law argument, we view them as examples of foreign domestic law, not customary international law and thus not binding on Canada. In any event, the appellants do not suggest that Canada adopted those decisions or the principles enunciated in them during the relevant time frame.

31 In sum, based on the evidence presented, it is plain and obvious that the appellants cannot succeed in establishing the existence of a pre-1947 customary international law prohibiting racial discrimination that would render the impugned legislation invalid. For that reason alone, the customary international law pleading must fail.

32 Even if we had decided that the evidence presented by the appellants was capable of passing the threshold test, we would nonetheless have halted the action because of the well-established principle that customary international law may be ousted for domestic purposes by contrary domestic legislation.[6] Professor Brownlie states the principle succinctly in his article entitled *Principles of Public International Law, supra*, at p. 42:

The dominant principle, normally characterized as the doctrine of incorporation, is that customary rules are to be considered part of the law of the land and enforced as such, with the qualification that they are incorporated only so far as is not inconsistent with Acts of parliament or prior judicial decisions of final authority [citations omitted].

See also *Suresh v. Canada (Minister of Citizenship and Immigration)* (2000), 183 DLR (4th) 629 (FCA) at 659, reversed for other reasons at 2002 SCC 1; *R. v. Gordon*, [1980] BCJ No. 381 (SC) at para. 7; and *Chung Chi Cheung v. The King*, [1939] AC 160 at 167–68.

33 Applying that principle to this case, to the extent any customary international law prohibiting racial discrimination may have existed during the relevant time frame, it was clearly ousted by the impugned legislation. Accordingly, for that reason as well, the customary international law aspect of the claim must fail.

UNJUST ENRICHMENT

34 The appellants contend that the equitable principle of unjust enrichment applies in the circumstances of this case and that it requires the Government of Canada to disgorge the revenues raised under the head tax laws. The recipients would be the surviving payors of the tax (a very small number) or their surviving spouses (also a small number) and direct descendants.

35 The three elements of the principle of unjust enrichment are settled. A claim for unjust enrichment requires the claimant to establish "an enrichment, a corresponding deprivation and absence of any juristic reason for the enrichment": see *Pettkus v. Becker*, [1980] 2 SCR 834 at 848 per Dickson, J.; see also *Rathwell v. Rathwell*, [1978] 2 SCR 436 (*"Rathwell"*); *Peel (Regional Municipality) v. Canada*; *Peel (Regional Municipality) v. Ontario*, [1992] 3 SCR 762 (*"Peel"*); and *Peter v. Beblow*, [1993] 1 SCR 980.

36 In the present case, Cumming, J. held, and the Attorney General of Canada concedes, that the appellants have established the first two branches of the test – the head tax enriched the Government of Canada and constituted a corresponding deprivation to the immigrants who paid it. For purposes of this appeal, we accept Cumming, J.'s decision and the respondent's concession on these matters. We also note that it is not disputed that the principle of unjust enrichment "can operate against a government to ground restitutionary recovery": see *Air Canada v. British Columbia*, [1989] 1 SCR 1161 at 1203 per La Forest, J.

37 The resolution of the unjust enrichment issue in this appeal turns on the third branch of the test – the absence of a juristic reason for permitting the government of Canada to retain the revenues raised during the 38 year history of the head tax laws.

38 The Attorney General of Canada contends that there is an obvious and conclusive juristic reason supporting retention in this case – the head tax laws themselves.

39 There is considerable force in this submission. In one of the leading cases, indeed the case in which the three branch test for unjust enrichment was initially set out, namely *Rathwell, supra*, Dickson, J. gave as examples of juristic reasons "a contract or disposition of law" (at p. 455). It would seem obvious that a statute falls within the category of a disposition of law. In a second leading case, *Peter v. Beblow, supra*, Cory, J. expressly stated that a statute can provide a juristic reason for retention of a benefit (at p. 1018). See also *Attorney General of Canada v. Confederation Life Insurance Company* (1995), 24 OR (3d) 717 at 780 (Gen. Div.), aff'd (1997), 32 OR (3d) 102 (CA).

40 In the leading Canadian text, *The Law of Restitution* (Aurora: Canada Law Book Inc., 1990), the learned authors, Professor John McCamus and Peter Maddaugh, devote a section to the topic *Unjust Retention: No Juristic Reason for Enrichment*. In their discussion of the phrase "disposition of law" from *Rathwell*, they state, at p. 46:

Although the principal example of another "disposition of law" is no doubt the making of a gift, it is perhaps self-evident that an unjust enrichment will not be established in any case where enrichment of the defendant at the plaintiff's expense is required by law. The payment of validly imposed taxes may be considered unjust by some, but their payment gives rise to no restitutionary right of recovery.

41 The appellants attempt to overcome these authorities with the submission that not every statute can constitute a juristic reason for retaining a payment. The head tax laws, the appellants contend, should be regarded as an exception to the general rule.

42 It is true that there are exceptions to the general rule that a statute can provide a juristic reason for retention of a benefit. For example, in *Central Guaranty Trust v. Dixdale* (1994), 24 OR (3d) 506, this court held that a first mortgagee who had mistakenly discharged a mortgage was entitled to priority over a second mortgagee despite the provisions of the *Registry Act* which appeared to require a contrary result. Laskin, J.A. said, at pp. 515–16:

But, in my opinion, the statute alone is not dispositive of this appeal. In an appropriate case a court may give effect to the principle of unjust enrichment despite the terms of a statute.

See also *Deglman v. Brunet Estate*, [1954] SCR 725, where the court allowed the plaintiff to recover in *quantum meruit* even though the *Statute of Frauds* rendered unenforceable the oral agreement on which he had sued.

43 *Central Guaranty Trust* and *Deglman* are private law cases. However, the possibility of some exceptions to the general rule that a statute provides a juristic reason for retention of a benefit has also been raised in public law cases, including cases involving the retention by governments of revenues obtained pursuant to taxation statutes. For example, in *Reference re Goods and Services Tax (GST) (Can.)*, [1992] 2 SCR 445, a minor issue was whether suppliers had a right to be reimbursed by the federal government for the expenses they incurred in collecting the GST. One of the arguments made on their behalf was unjust enrichment. The court rejected this argument. Lamer, C.J.C. stated the general proposition linking a statute and juristic reason in strong language; however, he did so without excluding the possibility of exceptions and, indeed, suggested one possible exception. He said, at p. 477:

Under the GST Act the expenses involved in collecting and remitting the GST are borne by registered suppliers. This certainly constitutes a burden to these suppliers and a benefit to the federal government. However, this is precisely the burden contemplated by the statute. Hence, a juridical reason for the retention of the benefit by the federal government exists unless the statute itself is *ultra vires*.

44 Against the backdrop of these authorities, we do not conclude that it is plain and obvious that the appellants' argument on the third branch of the test of unjust enrichment – namely, that in some cases a statute will not provide a juristic reason for retention by a government of revenues received under a tax – cannot succeed. Accordingly, we proceed to a consideration of the substance of the appellants' argument on this issue.

45 At the start of her oral argument, counsel for the appellants submitted that a "moral balancing" is permitted in the analysis of juristic reason and that both the principles of international law and the provisions of the *Charter* would assist in this exercise. The appellants made

the same link between juristic reason and international law and the *Charter* in their factum:

72. It is respectfully submitted that to the extent the *Chinese Immigration Act* is contrary to customary international law, it cannot provide a juristic reason for the enrichment of the defendant at the expense of the plaintiff.

73. If the appellants meet the "plain and obvious" test with respect to the customary international prohibition on racial discrimination, it is respectfully submitted that they clearly meet the "plain and obvious" test in regard to the *Act* failing to provide a juristic reason for the enrichment of the Canadian government at the expense of the Head Tax payers.

...

78. The principle that the law ought to develop in accordance with the *Charter* is applicable to both equity and the common law. Accordingly, wherever possible, the doctrine of unjust enrichment should be construed to maximize consistency with *Charter* values.

46 The problem with these submissions is that they are not independent of the appellants' submissions relating to their customary international law and *Charter* claims. Indeed, as the above paragraphs make clear, the appellants' juristic reason argument is explicitly and inextricably linked to these two arguments.

47 A similar situation arose in *Reference re Goods and Services Tax, supra*. The Canadian Federation of Independent Business ("CFIB"), an intervener, argued that suppliers had a right to be reimbursed by the federal government for the expenses they incurred in collecting the GST. As noted above, the Supreme Court of Canada rejected the CFIB's unjust enrichment argument in support of this position. In doing so, Lamer, C.J.C. succinctly identified, at p. 477, the duplicative quality, and the concomitant irrelevance, of the CFIB's argument:

The CFIB's argument thus involves it in the following dilemma: If the GST Act is *ultra vires*, then registered suppliers cannot be compelled to collect the tax, and it is not necessary to consider the extent of any restitutionary claim this group might have against the federal government. If, on the other hand, the GST Act is *intra vires*, then the statute itself constitutes a valid juristic reason for the retention of the benefit the federal government receives by being able to rely upon registered suppliers to collect the tax at their own expense. In neither case is the outcome urged upon us by the CFIB supportable.

48 In the present case, Cumming J. identified a similar dilemma in the appellants' submissions relating to juristic reason:

The problem with the plaintiffs' submissions in this regard is much the same as their difficulties with respect to their *Charter* and international law arguments. To find that a statute does not constitute a juristic reason, it would be necessary to demonstrate that the legislation is unconstitutional or *ultra vires*.

He then continued by summarizing, and applying, his reasoning on the *Charter* and international law arguments. The *Charter* cannot be used to attack the head tax laws because it cannot be applied retroactively or retrospectively. Customary international law principles relating to non-discrimination, even if they existed during the life of the head tax laws, are superseded by domestic legislation, which includes the head tax laws.

49 Cumming, J. then reached his conclusion on the unjust enrichment issue:

Since the impugned legislation cannot be challenged on either constitutional or international law grounds, I therefore find that it constitutes a juristic reason for any enrichment and corresponding deprivation. As a result, it is plain and obvious that the plaintiffs' claim with respect to unjust enrichment cannot succeed.

50 We agree with this conclusion. In short, the appellants' submissions relating to juristic reason cover precisely the same ground as their submissions on the *Charter* and customary international law issues. Rejection of the latter necessarily entails rejection of the former.

51 We make one final observation on the unjust enrichment issue in this appeal. Throughout their argument, the appellants make reference to concepts, notions and values, including "moral balancing," "good conscience" and "injustice." We agree with the proposition that these factors are part of the foundation of the equitable doctrine of unjust enrichment. However, it is important to recognize that there are limits to the doctrine. In *Peel, supra*, McLachlin, J. articulated, at pp. 802–803, a caution which we think bears repeating in this appeal:

The Argument on Injustice

The municipality is reduced in the final analysis to the contention that it should recover the payments which it made from the federal and provincial governments because this is what the dictates of justice and fairness require; stated otherwise, it would be unjust for the federal and provincial governments to escape these payments. This argument raises two questions. First, where the legal tests for recovery are clearly not met, can recovery be awarded on the basis of justice or fairness alone? Second, if courts can grant judgment on the basis on justice alone, does justice so require in this case?

On my review of the authorities, the first question must be answered in the negative. The courts' concern to strike an appropriate balance between predictability in the law and justice in the individual case has led them in this area, as in others, to choose a middle course between the extremes of inflexible rules and case by case "palm tree" justice. The middle course consists in adhering to legal principles, but recognizing that those principles must be sufficiently flexible to permit recovery where justice so requires having regard to the reasonable expectations of the parties in all the circumstances of the case as well as to public policy. Such flexibility is found in the three-part test for recovery enunciated by this Court in cases such as *Pettkus v. Becker, supra*. Thus recovery cannot be predicated on the bare assertion that fairness so requires. A general congruence with accepted principle must be demonstrated as well.

This is not to say that the concepts of justice and equity play no role in determining whether recovery lies. It is rather to say that the law defines what is so unjust as to require disgorgement in terms of benefit, corresponding detriment and absence of juristic reason for retention. Such definition is required to preserve a measure of certainty in the law, as well as to ensure due consideration of factors such as the legitimate expectation of the parties, the right of parties to order their affairs by contract, and the right of legislators in a federal system to act in accordance with their best judgment without fear of unforeseen future liabilities.

52 In the first paragraph of these reasons, we said: "Canada's treatment of people of Chinese origin who sought to immigrate to this country between 1885 and 1947 represents one of the more notable stains on our minority rights tapestry." We say that again. However, the head tax laws ceased to operate 79 years ago, in 1923. During their life, they were constitutional in domestic law terms and they did not violate any principles of customary international law.

53 The doctrine of unjust enrichment is an equitable doctrine. However, even the broad purview of equity does not provide courts with the jurisdiction to use current Canadian constitutional law and international law to reach back almost a century and remedy the consequences of laws enacted by a democratic government that were valid at the time.[7]

Disposition

54 We would dismiss the appeal. Like Cumming, J., we do not regard this as a case in which costs should be awarded.

Signed: "M.J. Moldaver J.A."
"J.C. MacPherson J.A."
"I agree. Austin J.A."

Released: September 13, 2002

NOTES

1 *Reference re Secession of Quebec*, [1998] 2 SCR 217 at p. 262.
2 *The Chinese Immigration Act 1885*, SC 1885, c. 71 as amended.
3 *The Chinese Immigration Act 1923*, SC 1923, c. 38, repealed by *The Immigration Act*, SC 1947, c. 19.
4 The *Japanese Canadian Redress Agreement*, PC 1988–9/2552, dated October 31, 1998, stemmed from a policy decision on the part of the government of the day, under the leadership of the Rt. Hon. Brian Mulroney, to provide redress for government actions, including internment or relocation within Canada, expulsion or deportation from Canada and deprivation of property, taken against certain Japanese Canadians during the Second World War under the *War Measures Act*, the *National Emergency Transitional Powers Act 1945* and other transitional legislation.
5 F. Capatorti "Human Rights, the Hard Road Towards Universality," in R. St. J. MacDonald and Douglas M. Johnston, eds., *The Structure and Process of International Law Essays in Legal Philosophy, Doctrine and Theory* (The Hague: Martinus Nijhoff Publishers, 1983) 977 at 978–79.
6 The appellants suggested in oral argument that the prohibition against racial discrimination during the relevant time frame was so well recognized that it qualified as "an established pre-emptory norm of customary international law, or *jus cogens.*" The evidence relied upon by the appellants does not meet the *jus cogens* test.
7 We are not here concerned with facially valid laws enacted by a totalitarian or other despotic regime.

1 Recall the reading question on Radbruch in chapter 1 – Is his position a positivist one but which subtracts from the category of valid laws that are extremely unjust or is it more like Fuller's? Law fails to be law when it grossly offends principles of legality that are intrinsic to legal order. Does the Ontario Court of Appeal respond to the lawyers' argument by constructing it more like the first option than the second and does that make it easier for the court to dismiss the argument?

2 It is worth considering, in regard to question 1, the common law position on bills of attainder. These are statutes which offend the rule of law requirement that all laws be general in nature, particularly when a law is punitive. A law which seeks to punish a particular individual or class of individuals is considered suspect from the point of view of the rule of law, not only because it violates the principle of generality, but also because it attempts to declare guilt and stipulate punishment in the same breath, thus bypassing the courts which are supposed to ensure that no one is punished who had not been fairly determined to be guilty of a preexisting crime. Within the common law tradition, statutes that amount to bills of attainder are considered to be invalid because their defects are so grave that they cannot be counted as successful attempts to make law, even if from a technical perspective they appear to be valid. Is there any analogy between the statute at issue in the Head Tax Case and a bill of attainder?

Mayo Moran
"Time, Place, and Values: *Mack* and the
Influence of the *Charter* on Private Law" (2005)

Contemporary courts are facing a whole new category of cases that seek redress for widespread historic wrongdoing. These "reparations" cases are forcing a number of difficult questions including issues concerning the scope of sovereign and other immunities, the passage of time, and the like. Because such cases almost inevitably involve widespread historic wrongdoing, this litigation tends to press the ordinary limits of legal arguments and resources. The consequence is that courts are increasingly asked to consider the significance of the passage of time, the problem of widespread moral ignorance, and the complicity of law in mass dehumanization. Venerable legal doctrines, particularly in private law, have historically placed such questions beyond the scope of legal inquiry. However, changes in our conceptions of responsibility are reverberating throughout private and criminal law. And one important result of this is an erosion of many of the very barriers that used to place difficult questions of widespread historic injustice beyond the reach of legal responsibility, particularly private law.[1] Nonetheless, the recent experience particularly in the United States suggests that courts often decide reparations cases on procedural grounds, thereby avoiding the difficult broader questions of accountability that such cases raise.[2]

Viewed in this light, the Chinese Canadian head tax case, *Mack v. Attorney General of Canada*,[3] has special importance. *Mack* is in some important sense an *easy* reparations case. This is, of course, not the same as saying that it is an easy case. But unlike some of the more long-standing reparations issues, the claim for the recovery of the onerous head tax selectively imposed on immigrants of Chinese origin is relatively recent in that it involves the claims of those who actually paid the tax and their direct descendants. Thus, it is not beleaguered by the difficult questions of tracing both the wrong and the harm that characterize cases such as the recently filed claims involving slavery in the United States and claims by Aboriginal peoples for the return of land. One consequence of this feature of *Mack* is that the courts are forced to directly confront the substantive questions implicated in redressing historic injustice.

However, if the ease of tracing makes *Mack* look somewhat exceptional, there is another very important respect in which it is characteristic of reparations claims more broadly. The heart of the argument in *Mack* seeks to harness the power of the old principle of unjust enrichment to redress widespread historic injustice. So the *Mack* decisions are important in part because of the judicial response to the restitutionary basis of the claim for redress. This is particularly so since *Mack* faces the characteristic difficulty of virtually all reparations claims that invoke the principle of unjust enrichment.

The principle of unjust enrichment has many virtues for redress-seekers, not the least of which is that its focus on the retention of an unjustly exacted benefit avoids the difficulties inherent in extending more culpability-based notions of responsibility (wrongdoing, for example) across time and, even more problematically, persons. Thus, the proprietary nature of the restitution claim responds to our sense that there may be a justification for responsibility even where it would admittedly be impossible to invoke any robust conception of personal blame. But more importantly, the principle of unjust enrichment seems intuitively apt to capture what strikes us as at the heart of many reparations issues. This sense of aptness springs as much from the principle's explicit invocation of "injustice" as from its focus on retained benefits. Yet, as *Mack* reveals, there are significant difficulties establishing that the enrichment was unjust in the sense required by the law of unjust enrichment. So ironically, the very source of the principle's intuitive appeal is also the source of greatest difficulty. For as both courts in *Mack* point out, the fact that a valid law sanctioned and even required the relevant enrichment ordinarily rules out any finding that that enrichment was unjust.

This difficulty is not simply attributable to the sometimes arcane principles of private law. Indeed, it seems undeniable that the problem with giving content to the unjust inquiry in cases for redress of historic wrongdoing ultimately engages a set of extremely difficult moral, political, and legal questions. The core problem revolves around the fact that much of the conduct that we now unequivocally recognize as "unjust" was not only broadly considered right but also, as in *Mack* itself, often enshrined in law. The "unjust" of the time of the transfer or enrichment and of the adjudicating court are in this sense radically incompatible. There is no unproblematic response to this difficulty. And the impossibility of any simple journey across the moral and legal distance between now and then is a central dilemma of all such cases. The problem of the past thus pervades the claim for redress and undermines at least some of the intuitive appeal of the "unjust" aspect of unjust enrichment.

But the past is not quite yet at the heart of the problematic relationship between the redress case and unjust enrichment. The heart of the problem concerns the troubling complicity of law as a tool of massive discrimination and injustice. How ought law now respond to law then? The relationship of contemporary law and legal values to their disconcerting predecessors engages fundamental questions of law's self-identity. These are questions we have not generally confronted. Our own past feels to us in these moments like foreign, uncomfortable terrain. Thus it is unsurprising that we see institutional anxiety on the part of the courts augmenting more general collective anxiety about the scope and implications of our own historic wrongdoing. We may be tempted, as are the courts in *Mack,* to sidestep the confrontation with our past by insisting on the impossibility of any direct engagement on the wisdom of our legal past.

Yet the law does seem to possess the resources for a more nuanced and defensible response to our own past unjust laws. And in a constitutional order like Canada's, the radiating effect of constitutional values is one particularly important such resource. In fact, our own jurisprudence reveals the influence of constitutional values in cases where courts are faced with demands to "blindly" enforce some other legal act or exercise of sovereignty – be it of the past or elsewhere. Paying attention to the resources that courts bring to bear in such moments may thus provide a way of thinking about how to respond to the unjust laws of our past without undermining our contemporary constitutional order. Of course, the journey back to our legal past may well be one which many of us – citizens as well as courts – would prefer not to take. Yet acknowledging the respects in which our past is indeed another country may provide important inspiration here. It may even assist us in reconciling the need to respect our own fundamental values with an acknowledgment of the complexity of judgment across the difficult moral distance of time. This task holds great significance for the very meaning of law. Indeed, it is precisely because reparations cases remind us of the complicity of the legal system in the enforcement of mass injustice that they so pointedly call for law itself to reassert its own moral self-understanding. And so, we might rightly think of *Mack* as the easiest version of the hardest question posed by the reparations case.

MACK AND THE REPARATIONS CONTEXT

Mack began as a class action involving the infamous head tax that Canada selectively imposed on immigrants of Chinese origin from 1885 until 1923. (From 1923 until 1947, immigration to Canada from China was effectively prohibited.)[4] The plaintiff class was composed of those who paid the head tax and their heirs and descendants. They sought, among other things, restitutionary damages on the ground that the Government of Canada was unjustly enriched at their expense. The Attorney General of Canada brought a motion to strike out the statement of claim on the basis that it disclosed no reasonable cause of action. On 9 July 2001, Cumming, J. ruled in their favour, finding that the statement of claim disclosed no reasonable cause of action. The plaintiffs appealed to the Ontario Court of Appeal, which dismissed the appeal. The Supreme Court of Canada dismissed leave to appeal.[5]

Unsurprisingly, the courts find it straightforward to conclude that the Government of Canada benefited at the expense of the plaintiffs. The fact that the first two elements of unjust enrichment are so easily established illustrates the sense in which *Mack* is an easy reparations case. Because the plaintiffs in *Mack* are the actual payers of the tax or their spouses or direct descendants, the case does not face the difficult "tracing" questions that characterize claims involving older wrongs. Indeed, in the recent debate about reparations for slavery in the United States, the question of who would even be the plaintiffs and defendants is very complex, reflecting how the passage of time complicates the ability to establish "enrichment at the expense of the plaintiff."[6] Similarly difficult problems of tracing harm through several interceding centuries plague questions of how to redress the wrongful appropriation of the land of Aboriginal peoples throughout the world by settler societies.[7] And though there may well be a solution to this, the problem of tracing harm is daunting and it considerably complicates the claim for redress.

There also also other important complications that are absent from *Mack*. Because reparations claims often involve the adjudication of the acts of foreign governments in American courts, foreign sovereign immunity and questions of comity frequently work to defeat the claims.[8] Once again *Mack* is a contrast. In common with the American claims for reparations for slavery, it is distinguished by the fact that the claim for reparations is brought against the plaintiff's – and perhaps as importantly, the court's – own government. Given the reluctance of courts to pass judgment on the acts of another sovereign, this too simplifies cases like *Mack*.

Yet in place of anxiety about offending a foreign sovereign and in the absence (in Canada at least) of a formal doctrine of sovereign immunity,[9] cases like *Mack* are animated by a more complicated kind of worry associated with judging the past. Our legal system possesses considerable resources that could be brought to bear in a principled way upon the problem. Of particular significance here is the fact that courts in Canada are adjudicating these claims in a context in which there are overarching constitutional values "radiating" throughout the legal system. As we see in other cases, these values provide important conceptual resources for enabling traditional private law doctrines to respond to cases with a backdrop of profound discrimination. Yet when poised against issues involving the past discriminatory behaviour of private actors in Canada and "evil regimes" elsewhere, the decisions in *Mack* suggest that courts feel more disabled outside the direct sphere of

Charter operation than they may have before the *Charter* came into operation. Thus, oddly, past legalized discrimination actually looks more immune from judicial scrutiny in the *Charter*-era than it was when courts only had the apparently less powerful tools of "public policy" and "division of powers" at their disposal – at least where the courts of a state that does not consider itself to have an "evil past" are sitting in judgment on their own history.

THE DECISIONS IN *MACK*

The unjust enrichment claim failed in *Mack* because the enrichment of the federal government was accomplished by validly enacted positive law that was not contrary to any norm that straightforwardly applied at the time. It is ordinarily uncontroversial, as Cumming, J. notes, that a statutory provision constitutes a valid "juristic reason" which thereby precludes a finding that the relevant enrichment was "unjust."[10] In his view, the legislation constitutes a juristic reason unless it is unconstitutional or *ultra vires*. However, Cumming, J. holds that s. 15 of the *Charter* does not apply prior to 1985 and that at the time of the head tax legislation there was no clear international norm that was capable of overriding explicit legislation to the contrary. The result is that the head tax legislation must be counted as a juristic reason which thereby "justifies" the enrichment of the federal government and precludes a finding of unjust enrichment.

The Court of Appeal upholds the reasoning of Cumming, J. on this issue. They too conclude that the heart of the unjust enrichment analysis in this case turns on the "unjust" inquiry. So the core question is whether the head tax laws constitute a "juristic reason." The Court notes that the plaintiffs made the argument that the principles of international law and the provisions of the *Charter* were of assistance in the "moral balancing" that is required under the analysis of juristic reason in unjust enrichment. It was clear, the plaintiffs pointed out, that private law ought to develop in accordance with the *Charter*. This in turn dictated that unjust enrichment ought to be construed to maximize consistency with *Charter* values.

However, the Court of Appeal finds these submissions fatally flawed because they are not independent of the customary international and *Charter* arguments. Because the two claims are "inextricably linked," the Court of Appeal assumes they are identical. And if they are identical, then the failure of one automatically entails the failure of the other. So, on the Court of Appeal's reasoning, the "duplicative quality" of these two arguments means that Cumming, J. was correct in holding that since the legislation cannot be challenged on either constitutional or international law grounds, it must constitute a juristic reason. Thus rejection of the argument that the legislation was invalid during the time of its operation "necessarily entails" that neither the *Charter* nor international law plays any role in determining the contemporary meaning of juristic reason.

THE "UNJUST" FACTOR

On the face of it, this seems rather odd. One of the central problems in the law of restitution has always been how to conceive of the unjust inquiry. The extreme possibilities at both ends of the spectrum seem untenable. It is clear that the reference to injustice and the invocations of the test of "good conscience" cannot be taken literally and so the "unjust" inquiry cannot be read as an invitation to engage in freestanding moral reasoning. Nonetheless, the reference to "unjust" undoubtedly points to an important quality of the inquiry, a quality that it shares with other "value terms" such as reasonable, legitimate, and the like.[11] Indeed, it is in the very nature of such terms that they invite attentiveness to larger more explicitly normative considerations.[12] This, along with the fact that the roots of unjust enrichment lie in the common law and in equity and invoke the touchstone of "good conscience," militates strongly against an overly rigid or restrictive interpretation of the unjust factor.

The passage that the Court of Appeal in *Mack* cites from *Peel* illustrates the inherently complex and hybrid nature of the resulting inquiry. As Madam Justice McLachlin (as she then was) puts it, the inquiry into what is "unjust" for the purposes of unjust enrichment cannot be a simple broad determination of what is required by general conceptions of "fairness" or some other form of "palm tree justice." Instead she advocates shaping the relatively indeterminate unjust inquiry by adhering to "legal principles." Nonetheless, the legal principles in play in the unjust inquiry

... must be sufficiently flexible to permit recovery where justice so requires having regard to the reasonable expectations of the parties in all the circumstances of the case as well as to public policy.[13]

The Court of Appeal in *Mack* cites this passage to make the point that the unjust inquiry is not simply a matter of freestanding "moral balancing." Yet the core of McLachlin, J.'s point is that the way to solve the apparent tension between the necessary openness of the inquiry and the concomitant need to render it certain and consistent with "accepted principle" is to draw on background legal principles to determine when restitution is required.[14] What this suggests – and it is partly this that has always accounted for the complexity of the unjust inquiry – is that other legal principles and rules, not themselves directly applicable, necessarily figure in the unjust inquiry including the public policy to which McLachlin, J. refers. Indeed, as discussed below, the most principled approaches to public policy have always drawn on background *legal* principles not themselves directly applicable to give content to the idea of fundamental legal values that provide the best understanding of the elusive idea of public policy.

But this suggests that broader legal values and principles inevitably play an important role in the unjust inquiry. The reduction of that inquiry to a matter of the applicability of binding legal rules thus seems at odds with the conventional understanding of the relation between the unjust factor and the principles of other areas of law as well as over-arching principles of public policy. And it is just this possibility that fundamental principles and values from other areas of law might play an important role in shaping the unjust inquiry that the decisions in *Mack* overlook when they insist that the *Charter* and international law arguments either succeed in a frontal attack on the head tax legislation or fail to have any effect at all.

THE INFLUENCE OF *CHARTER* VALUES

These difficulties with *Mack*'s understanding of the unjust inquiry are exacerbated when we consider the significance of the plaintiffs' claim that the values of the *Charter* play a special role in the unjust enrichment claim. The *Charter*, in common with other constitutionalized human rights norms, occupies a distinct place in the legal landscape. And that in turn entails a distinct set of demands. To see the significance of this, it is important to pay attention to the fact that the plaintiffs in *Mack* made two very different *Charter* arguments.

First, the plaintiffs argued that the head tax legislation actually violated s. 15 of the *Charter* and that this violation gave rise to a continuing wrong that had not been redressed. The remedy for this direct *Charter* claim, which I will call the "right of redress," were it successful, would be found under 24(2) of the *Charter*. However, both courts rejected the argument that s. 15 itself gave rise to a right of redress. They held that the *Charter* could not apply directly and give rise to a right of redress because it was not retroactive or retrospective. I will not take up the wisdom of the decisions regarding the *Charter* right of redress for I want to focus on the second *Charter* argument in *Mack*.

This second *Charter* argument arises in the context of the unjust enrichment claim. And the role of the *Charter* in this claim differs in a number of important respects from its role in the right of redress claim. Most obviously, unjust enrichment is a claim in private law, not public law. So while the legislation is crucial, the basis and structure of the claim are found in private law. The private law argument therefore does not directly engage the independent validity of the legislation under the *Charter*. Rather, it asks a different question – can the legislation (valid or not) constitute a "juristic reason," a legal justification in other words, for the enrichment? Thus, the question here does not concern the *Charter*'s impact on the validity of the legislation but rather what kinds of demands the *Charter* exerts on how the legislation can figure in unjust inquiry. The *Charter* thus enters the private law equation because it is clear that private law, particularly its value terms like "unjust," must be construed in a manner that is consistent with "*Charter* values."[15] So while the structure of the claim is found in the private law cause of action, it is also shaped and constrained by the demands of the *Charter*. In this sense, although the two *Charter* arguments are undoubtedly related, they are by no means "duplicative."

In fact, the failure to distinguish between these two *Charter* arguments reveals a fundamental misunderstanding about the difference between the *force* of the *Charter* and its *effect*. Elsewhere I have argued that the distinctive effect of the *Charter*, which I termed "influential authority," cannot be properly grasped within the "traditional model" of legal reasoning that posits the exclusive salience of "force" or so-called binding authority.[16] Indeed, this model underlies the decisions in *Mack*. For if the argument that the *Charter* exerts a kind of mandatory effect on what a contemporary court can count as a juristic reason is reduced to an argument about the binding force of the *Charter*, one is left with a model which has it that the *Charter* either has binding force or has no effect at all. Yet it is clear that whatever power the exclusive binding sources model may have, it cannot explain the legal significance of the *Charter* in the contemporary Canadian legal regime. In fact, the effect of the *Charter* on the elaboration of private common law provides the clearest and most doctrinally accepted illustration of the phenomenon of influential authority. Accordingly, a brief overview of how influential authority operates is crucial to understanding the significance of *Mack*'s approach to the role of the *Charter* and other values in the unjust enrichment analysis.

It is by now uncontroversial in Canada that although the *Charter* does not apply directly to private common law,[17] it is centrally important to its elaboration. This is because the *Charter* exerts a kind of mandatory influence or "influential authority" over the manner in which private common law rights are articulated and developed. This may seem unremarkable but it is worth noticing the specific nature of influential authority and how it takes hold in legal reasoning. The source of its distinctiveness is found in the way that influential authority conjoins "insistence" on attentiveness to it with the fact that this demand cannot be understood in terms of binding rules. Thus, influential authority, although "insistent" in a manner often associated with "binding" sources or rules of law, is nonetheless distinguished from such rules because of the way it takes hold.

Rights and obligations in private common law operate between parties – private or not – engaged in certain kinds of interactions, and these rights and obligations have their own distinctive structure.[18] And although it has been and continues to be the subject of considerable debate, particularly in the post–Second World War constitutional models, the prevailing and in my view better approach is that constitutional human rights do not generally apply directly to private (common law) interactions between purely private parties.[19] This position has been accepted by courts, including those in Canada, considering the relation between constitutionalized human rights norms and private or common law. So, individuals do not recover *Charter* damages against other individuals for violating their right to freedom of expression or their equality rights. Instead, *Charter* rights matter to private relations because, for instance, they may affect the appropriate scope of the private law of libel and defamation.[20] Similarly, the right to equality may be relevant to determining the kinds of agreements a court might be called upon to enforce or the form of deference extended to the exercise of political choices by public authorities.[21] In cases such as these, the *Charter* does not validate or invalidate the relevant legal acts because it does not directly apply to them. Nor is the structure of justification under s. 1 applicable in any straightforward way. So in this realm, the

Charter has no force. And where force and effect are equated, as they are in the *Mack* decisions, this lack of force disposes of the question of the *Charter*.

Perhaps there are settings where the automatic equation of force and effect is compelling, though I suspect that closer examination will often suggest that this is more unlikely than it might seem. But whatever might hold elsewhere, this equation is not available where the *Charter* applies. Indeed, the absence of force and presence of effect is constitutive of the relationship between the *Charter* and private common law. The effect of the *Charter*, moreover, is of a distinctive kind. This effect is not permissive – that is, it would misstate the relation to suggest that judges elaborating private common law *could* look to the *Charter*. Instead, the effect is mandatory or insistent. Thus it is not simply that it is open to judges to look to the *Charter* if it seems significant or useful. The nature of the *Charter*–common law relation is that judges *must* elaborate the common law in light of the *Charter*. The *Charter* therefore does not grant to judges the *power* to look to its terms when elaborating private common law, it imposes an *obligation* to do so. Thus, the influential source (here, the *Charter*) *demands* attention and consideration in arriving at a decision. And this insistence is in no way diminished by the fact that it does not give rise to discrete rights and obligations.

This brings up two other features of the influential authority of *Charter* that are relevant here. Both arise because of the way that influential authority conjoins insistence along with the fact that it cannot be conceived of in terms of a binding "decision rule." If the obligations that the *Charter* imposes on private common law adjudication do not take the form of a "rule" dictating an outcome,[22] then how do they make themselves felt at all? While the mandatory nature of influential authority distinguishes it from purely persuasive authority, persuasive and influential authority also share a feature in common – both are brought to bear on the process of reasoning or decision-making. What influential authority demands is that the influential source be respected, attended to, and considered in decision-making. To satisfy these demands, the decision-maker needs to state in the course of her reasons how she paid attention to the influential source and why she understands her decision as consistent with it. In this sense then influential authority takes hold primarily at the level of justification – a feature it shares with persuasive authority. Unlike persuasive authority, however, influential authority can demand that it be addressed and respected in a way that purely persuasive authority cannot.[23]

There is one more related feature of influential authority that we should note before considering its significance for *Mack*. Where the authority of the *Charter* is influential there is no argument that its provisions are violated or the rights it guarantees infringed. This accounts for a feature that courts and commentators have noted and sometimes decried as incoherent.[24] It is not *Charter rights* that necessarily influence the shape of private and common law, it is rather its fundamental *values*. Thus, when the *Charter* exerts influential authority on the common law, what it demands is attentiveness to and respect for the core or fundamental values of the *Charter*. This focus on fundamental *values* should not be read as a weakness or limitation but rather as signalling the distinctive nature of influential authority and the fact that it takes hold primarily at the level of justification. So what the *Charter* insists is that the articulation and justification of specific rights and duties in private and common law proceed in accordance with the fundamental values of the *Charter* which are, after all, the supreme law of the land.

The *Charter* in this sense can be conceived of as giving rise both to discrete rights and obligations within the "force field" of its operation and as having a broader systemic effect associated with its authoritative expression of our most fundamental values. In the German system, they speak of this latter effect as "objective" or, more poetically, as the "radiating" quality of fundamental constitutional rights. And though what this entails in any particular situation may be complex, the animating idea is simple enough: in a system of law unified by an express overarching commitment to certain fundamental ideals, those ideals place demands and limits on how the exercise of any public power can be justified and this must include the judicial power to develop ancient common law doctrines including the doctrines of private law.[25]

INFLUENTIAL AUTHORITY IN *MACK*

Attending to the distinctive nature of the *Charter*'s influential authority and its impact on the meaning of traditional private common law doctrines helps to illuminate the Court's misreading of the second *Charter* argument in *Mack*. Indeed, focusing on the influential authority of the *Charter* in *Mack* suggests that a court bound to read private common law in line with the fundamental values of the *Charter* may be obliged to refuse to count as a juristic reason a piece of legislation that is explicitly discriminatory and racist. The possibility of this kind of estoppel-like effect may seem radical but it is worth noting the continuity both with how courts in other jurisdictions have responded to the problem of "evil law" and with what courts, including our own, have done when asked to give their imprimatur to laws or legal arrangements that violate the most basic values of the legal order. The existence of these possibilities directs our attention to a particular constellation of difficulties that may account for why *Mack* seems so hard: it asks us to reexamine the past, to pass on the wisdom of long-defunct *laws*, and laws that are – significantly – our own. The unjust enrichment argument in *Mack* thus presses the outer limits of the effect of *Charter* values on the articulation of private common law.

It seems important to begin to examine the relation between *Charter* values and the unjust enrichment argument in *Mack* by noting that the courts called upon to treat the head tax legislation as a juristic reason *themselves* describe that legislation as contrary to our most cherished legal values. Cumming, J.'s closing remarks are especially instructive. As he points out, the acts that imposed the head tax were

patently discriminatory against persons of Chinese origin. By contemporary Canadian morals and values, these pieces of legislation were both repugnant and reprehensible. The Chinese Immigration Act, 1885, and its successors have come to symbolize a period scarred by racial intolerance and prejudice.[26]

When viewed in light of the demands that the influential authority of the *Charter* places on the articulation of private common law, it is telling that Cumming, J. characterizes the legislation as violative of our most fundamental values. In fact, Cumming, J. explicitly engages the values of the *Charter* when he notes the "discriminatory" character of the legislation – discrimination which not only is now explicitly ruled out by s. 15 of the *Charter* but also undercuts the commitment to equal human dignity that is at the heart of the entire *Charter* order. Similarly the judgment of the Ontario Court of Appeal begins with the statement that "Canada's treatment of people of Chinese origin who sought to immigrate to this country between 1885 and 1947 represents one of the more notable stains on our minority rights tapestry."[27] And the Court returns to this at the end of the judgment, stating "We say that again."[28] So if there is one matter on which there is no ambiguity, it is the recognition by the *very courts* called upon to pronounce on whether the

legislation is a juristic reason that that legislation was not only profoundly wrong but also runs directly contrary to the values of the
Charter.

Bringing the courts' own description of the legislation together with
the fact of their *positive duty* to develop private common law in
accordance with the fundamental values of the *Charter* helps to account
for the difficulty of *Mack*. It also suggests that the judicial insistence that
the two *Charter* arguments are "duplicative" effectively counts out the
most challenging and ultimately most central question in the case. The
core dilemma for the courts is surely found in the *legal* tension at the
heart of the case: while a facially valid positive law will ordinarily be a
relatively uncontroversial justification for an enrichment, a court bound
to construe private common law to render it consistent with the
fundamental values of the *Charter* will of course have difficulty counting
a profoundly discriminatory piece of legislation as a legal justification.

Resolution of the tension between private or common law doctrines
and the influential authority of the *Charter* typically takes the form of a
requirement that courts maximize consistency with fundamental legal
values, especially authoritative *Charter* values.[29] So courts are obliged to
make "*Charter*-positive" choices in whatever room to manoeuvre that
private common law, for instance, gives them. This means that the
openness of private common law, especially but not exclusively in its
explicit invocation of "value terms" like reasonable, legitimate, and
unjust, should always be construed to give maximum effect to the
values of constitutional human rights.[30] Thus in a case like *Mack*, the
influential authority of the *Charter* means that courts are under a
constitutional duty to give effect to the values of the *Charter* in construing such terms if at all possible.

If the courts truly are bound in the way that they suggest to give
effect to the fundamental values of the *Charter* in filling out the meaning
of "value concepts" in private law such as "unjust," then how ought
they to treat a piece of legislation that they themselves describe as racist,
discriminatory, and contrary to our most fundamental legal values?
There is no understanding of the relation of public and private law that
will make this an easy question. However, by equating the direct
application argument of the *Charter* with the argument that the *Charter*
exerted influential authority on the private law of unjust enrichment, the
courts in *Mack* avoided this question almost entirely. Since the *Charter*
lacked the force to render the head tax legislation unconstitutional, on
their view it also lacked any effect over what they could count as a

juristic reason. Let us consider two reasons why the *Mack* courts did not consider the influential authority of the *Charter* more seriously: first, they may have felt that the *Charter* could not exert influential authority because of "the problem of the past," and second, they may have felt that the "problem of the sovereign" precluded reliance on influential authority. Exploring these difficulties will help to illustrate both the inherent challenges and the special importance of attending to the influential authority of the *Charter* in a case like *Mack*.

THE PROBLEM OF THE PAST

The "problem of the past" may seem to account for why the courts in *Mack* did not take the *Charter*'s influential authority more seriously. The issue of how to view the past is undoubtedly among the central legal, political, and moral difficulties of all such reparations cases. However, it seems unlikely that the fact of the past alone can account for the unwillingness to recognize the influential authority of the *Charter* in the decisions in *Mack*. In order to see why, let us contrast *Mack* with another case that involved applying the influential authority of the *Charter* to the past – *Canada Trust Co. v. Ontario Human Rights Commission*.[31]

In that case, post-*Charter* Ontario courts had to consider the contemporary validity of the "Leonard Foundation Trust," an explicitly racist charitable trust established in 1923. The trust, which provided educational scholarships, excluded from its benefit a number of different groups, including "all who are not Christians of the White Race." The trust was valid according to all of the standard requirements of the law of charitable trusts and had been in operation for many decades. However, concern about the terms of the trust became more and more widespread and eventually a complaint was filed under the Ontario Human Rights Code. The trustee then applied to the court for advice and direction. The primary question was whether the terms of the trust violated public policy. It seemed clear that when the trust property vested in the trustee in 1923, the terms "would have been held to be certain, valid and not contrary to any public policy."[32] At trial, McKeown J. noted that there was no positive defect with the trust at the time of its formation. Thus, he held that the settlor was within his rights to dispose of his assets as he wished, however invidious those wishes may have been.

However, the Ontario Court of Appeal unanimously rejected this approach and instead held that at least when a court is called upon to pronounce upon the validity of a trust, a settlor's freedom to dispose of property is limited by "current principles of public policy under which all races and religions are to be treated on a footing of equality."[33] The Court of Appeal is thus explicit that it is not applying the public policy of the time when the trust was created, for according to that public policy the trust would be valid. Instead it applies contemporary norms to an act which gained its legal significance in 1923, ironically, the very year that the head tax was abolished in favour of legislation that effectively precluded Chinese immigration to Canada. And in common with the plaintiff's unjust enrichment argument in *Mack*, the Court of Appeal in *Canada Trust* looks to contemporary rights-protecting documents including the *Charter* to fill out its conception of public policy.

The judgment of Justice Tarnopolsky is particularly illuminating for its attentiveness to the sources of public policy. Public policy, in his view, "is not determined by reference to only one statute or even one province, but is gleaned from a number of sources, including provincial and federal statutes, official declarations of government policy and the Constitution."[34] Thus, he draws not only on the *Human Rights Code* but also on various other pieces of legislation, policies, and the like. Unsurprisingly, in grounding a public policy against discrimination he gives explicit recognition to the provisions of the *Charter* that guarantee equality rights and multiculturalism. He also links these guarantees to a number of international instruments and sources, particularly noting those which Canada ratified.[35]

It is possible to discern the contours of the *Charter*'s influential authority in much of Justice Tarnopolsky's method of giving content to "public policy." This is because it is clear that Justice Tarnopolsky is not simply giving effect to broad policy concerns – what the Supreme Court in *Burns* termed "general public policy."[36] Rather by invoking the background influential and persuasive authority of a variety of *legal* sources, he articulates a specifically juridical conception of public policy that is an expression of basic legal principles and values. A further congruence with influential authority is found in the way that he views the relevance of these sources. That his concern is not with their discrete provisions and regimes is evident when he states, "It would be nonsensical to pursue every one of these domestic and international instruments to see whether the public policy invalidity is restricted to any particular activity or service."[37] Instead, it is the general commitments or values, especially regarding equality, that he draws from these sources. And as in more recent cases that explicitly address the *Charter*–private common law relation, the judgment of Tarnopolsky, J. in *Canada Trust* notes the analogical role of equality analysis under the *Charter* and human rights codes in fleshing out the meaning of that principle in the context of determining what kinds of trusts might violate public policy.

Although it is certainly not on all fours with *Mack*, *Canada Trust* does illustrate that the influential authority of the *Charter* can indeed extend to acts that long pre-date the coming into force of the *Charter*. The resultant duty to respect the fundamental values of the legal system is expressed in terms of public policy. And that policy is that of the contemporary court, not of the settlor's time. So through the vehicle of this juridical policy, the influential authority of the *Charter* comes to exert itself on long-established charitable trusts. The consequence in *Canada Trust* itself is that the values of the contemporary court, most authoritatively expressed in the *Charter*, are the court's justification for refusing to enforce the racially repugnant restrictions of a trust set up in 1923. So even though the trust itself was governed by the private law of charitable trusts and even though that trust was valid at the time that the property vested, decades before the *Charter*, the Ontario Court of Appeal gave effect to the influential authority of the *Charter*.

Canada Trust thus illustrates that the influence of the *Charter* can indeed extend back into the past, to a time long before the *Charter* came into effect. And the fact that this seems odd when viewed from the perspective of the settlor of the trust actually points us towards the underlying implication of influential authority's hold over the past – influential authority operates at the level of the norms of the adjudicating court. Though this is implicit in the fact that such authority operates at the level of justification, and that it is so often expressed in terms of public policy, *Canada Trust* makes us more keenly aware of it. At bottom the Court is not asking whether what the settlor did was invalid at the time that he created the trust. The inquiry is not primarily directed to what would have been possible at the time, or to what a settlor on his own could do then or now. At bottom *Canada Trust* seems to concern what a *court* acting judicially and bound to fundamental legal values can recognize. Perhaps a settlor in 1923 would be within his powers in the creation of a white supremacist trust, but a court bound by a constitutional regime that gives pride of place to equality cannot be called upon to enforce or give legal significance to those elements of the trust that contravene fundamental legal values. Perhaps there was no clear legal norm that could have been called upon to invalidate the trust at the time; yet a court situated in a legal order premised on equality cannot discharge its role in that legal order and enforce terms that violate one of the law's most basic values. The fact that influential authority operates at the level of the norms of the court helps to account for its ability to reach into the past. The court faced with a question like that in *Canada Trust* is forced to ask not just about what was open to the settlor but also about the range of responses open to *the court*. And the answer to this question is inevitably shaped by the obligation that the *Charter* imposes on such a court to act consistently with those basic values of the legal order.

Canada Trust also illuminates another feature of influential authority – what we might think of as its outer limit. And it is this outer limit that arguably makes *Mack* so hard. As noted above, the influential authority of the *Charter* will typically require a court to choose the "Charter-positive" precedent or interpretation of a value term over the available alternatives. However, at times a court may be confronted with a demand to give legal effect to an act that runs contrary to the *Charter*'s most basic values. And in such a case, whatever the range of actions, reasons, and motivations that may be – or have been – open to legal actors and whatever freedom they may possess acting on their own, *Canada Trust* calls our attention to the difference that it makes when the court is engaged. For a court, especially in an egalitarian constitutional regime, is constrained in ways that are uniquely linked to the meaning of law in such a regime. The influential authority of the *Charter* is the authoritative and doctrinal expression of this demand of all law. And whatever else may be done or have been done by others, a court may have to decline to give legal significance to claims that contravene law's most basic values, among which equality is perhaps the most prominent. *Canada Trust* thus directs our attention to the fact that although the influential authority of the *Charter* typically assumes the kind of interpretive significance described above, at its outer limit it possesses this estoppel-like quality.[38] And it is this quality that, in a case like *Canada Trust*, effectively precludes the court from giving effect to acts, arguments, and reasons that contravene fundamental legal values, such as those contained in the *Charter*.

Although this estoppel-like feature of the *Charter*'s influential authority is in some sense novel, it has very important conceptual and genealogical links to a venerable judicial tradition often associated with the invocation of public policy. However, this ancient jurisdiction is

significantly fortified and its apparently tenuous foundation strengthened when a legal regime chooses to entrench fundamental human
rights including the right to equality or non-discrimination. It thus does
not seem accidental that *Canada Trust* uses public policy to give
expression to the influential authority of the *Charter*. And although I
shall not detail the matter here, a like idea of "juridical" policy has long
played a similar estoppel-like role, effectively refusing to countenance
as legal those reasons and justifications that cut against the very
foundation of the legal order. In Canada, this can be seen in cases like
Drummond Wren, which struck down a racially restrictive covenant on
public policy grounds. In fact, the explicit link to constitutional human
rights ideals is evident in *Drummond Wren* where the court argues that
it is the very ability of judges to invoke public policy in such cases that
obviates the need for the kind of constitutional protections of human
rights that prevail elsewhere.[39] Similarly, it does not seem accidental that
the United States Supreme Court approached a similar situation by
invoking the idea that the Constitution precluded judicial enforcement
of agreements that violated fundamental constitutional guarantees.[40]

Understandably, there is and should be considerable debate about
the exact nature and scope of this estoppel-like quality that the values
of fundamental human rights might exert on what a court can countenance. But the essential point here is simply that there is a long tradition
behind the idea that the fundamental values of the constitutional and
legal order impose some limits on what courts can treat as valid legal
reasons and acts. And this venerable idea is effectively given new force
and legitimacy in an order with a written bill of rights that is acknowledged to have a "radiating" effect throughout the legal order. Bringing
this back to the influential authority of the *Charter* reveals how the
Charter itself can exercise a similar estoppel-like effect on the meaning
of private common law, even though it does not explicitly apply. And,
as we have seen in *Canada Trust*, because this effect attaches to what an
adjudicating court can countenance, it is no response that the act may
have taken place at a time when the *Charter* was not in force. Instead,
when a court is faced with a contradiction of its own fundamental
values, particularly the values of constitutionalized human rights, as
Canada Trust illustrates, the fact of the past alone will not be sufficient
to preclude the ordinary operation of the influential authority of the
Charter on private common law. This effect may even go so far as to
"estop" a court, as in *Canada Trust*, from giving contemporary legal
significance to an act that violates that court's most fundamental values.

THE PROBLEM OF ACTS OF THE SOVEREIGN

Influential authority can thus be understood as part of a larger picture of the judicial role and the extent to which constitutional commitments to equality in particular might place certain demands and limits on that role. And as *Canada Trust* illustrates, influential authority also encompasses the possibility of an estoppel-like effect where a court would otherwise have to issue a decision that would run contrary to its own fundamental values. But we do not yet have an account of why the *Mack* courts, especially given their view of the legislation, were so reluctant to recognize the *Charter*'s influential authority. As we have seen, the past alone seems unlikely to explain this reluctance. There is, however, one other obvious explanation for the hesitation of the courts in *Mack*. Perhaps it is because the purported justification in *Mack* is in legislative form. Thus, the fact that cases like *Canada Trust, Shelley v. Kramer*, and *DeKlerk* involved private action may have made it easier to acknowledge the influence of constitutional norms precisely because there could never be a question of actual constitutional validity. So where the act is "doubly" outside of direct *Charter* effect, as in *Canada Trust* where it is both past and private, it may actually be less troubling for the courts to extend the influence of the *Charter*, even out to its estoppel-like boundary.

It is possible to see the logic in this: so long as the action is private in nature and the *Charter* does not apply directly, concerns about the non-retroactivity of the *Charter* are not implicated. So outside of the force field of direct application, the preservation of the non-retroactivity of the *Charter* seems relatively unproblematic and thus the influence of the *Charter* is given full play. However, when official action is at issue and along with it at least the possibility of direct *Charter* application, it may seem that the simplest way to avoid undermining the principle of non-retroactivity is to refuse to allow the *Charter* to exert any influence over our judgments about the pre-*Charter* acts of the state. But even allowing the force of the non-retroactivity concern, this solution seems paradoxical. In part this is because past state acts are "immunized" from the demand for consistency with *Charter* values precisely because the *Charter* applies directly to the state's present-day acts. But it surely grants the non-retroactivity concern too much if it ends up ensuring that public officials and bodies – the very entities for whom the salience of the *Charter* is indubitably greatest – actually turn out to have greater protection from the influence of *Charter* values outside the field of direct application than do private actors. It would also seem paradoxical if enacting the *Charter* effectively gave past state action even greater protection from legal scrutiny than it had before the *Charter* came into effect.[41]

Even beyond these conceptual problems, the implications of such a stance would also be very significant. The problem of legalized historic injustice is central not only to *Mack* but also to many reparations claims and other claims of historic injustice. The very fact that the relevant injustice was often widespread or systemic means that it was extremely common. But more usually it was also legislated and enshrined in law in various ways. Examples are sadly easy to identify: the various decrees of the Nazi era including infamous Decree 11 which stripped Jews of their citizenship, the extensive legal apparatus of slavery and its aftermath in the United States, the residential schools policy in Canada, and the legalization of apartheid in South Africa are but a few examples. If the approach taken by the courts in *Mack* is correct, then the legalization of injustice – often thought by lawyers and philosophers at least to be the ultimate tyranny of systems like those of the American South, the Nazis, and apartheid South Africa – effectively means that law provides the definitive refuge for historic injustice.

In fact sensitivity to this danger is apparent in the fact that the "valid positive law" argument that seemed to so beguile the courts in *Mack* has not always been considered so compelling in cases involving extremely discriminatory laws. Indeed, German cases involving Decree 11 and the like and the closely related House of Lords decisions in *Oppenheimer* suggest that the deference to "valid positive law" of the kind that we see in *Mack* is by no means absolute.[42] The Decree 11 cases confronted judges in the post-Nazi era who had to consider various kinds of claims related to inheritance, taxation, and the like that found their source in the infamous Nazi Decree 11. That Decree, which stripped German Jewish émigrés of their citizenship and hence their proprietary rights including the right to inherit, invidious though it was, was also acknowledged to be validly enacted positive law. It was never found unconstitutional and did not contravene any clear prevailing norm extant at the time of its operation. Nonetheless, when faced with the prospect of giving legal effect to that Decree, both post-Nazi German courts and the English House of Lords refused to do so on the ground that its provisions "contradict the fundamental principles of justice in such an evident manner that the judge applying or acknowledging their legal consequences would administer injustice instead of law."[43] Relying on this reasoning, judges in these and related cases such as those involving the East German border guards suggest the limits of the "valid positive law" argument.[44]

Like *Canada Trust* and the other private discrimination cases discussed above, these Decree 11 cases also seem best understood as implicating some principled limitations – understood in terms of fundamental *legal* values – on what a court can give effect to. They confirm the propriety of an estoppel-like response to a contradiction between the act that is claimed to have legal significance and the fundamental values of the court. And they also illustrate that this effect is not displaced simply because the claimed legal act takes the form of legislation. So this suggests that neither the fact of the past nor the fact that the discrimination is contained in validly enacted positive law will necessarily preclude courts from refusing to give effect to legal acts that profoundly violate the basic values and principles of the legal order.

There is, of course, one more possibility. Perhaps the estoppel-like effect is not open to a court when it is the legislation of the court's own jurisdiction that violates that court's fundamental values. That is, contemporary courts that are estopped from giving legal effect to private discrimination even when it occurred long ago and from giving legal effect to foreign laws that violate the fundamental values of our legal order as enunciated in the *Charter* must nonetheless give effect to our own past laws that similarly violate the court's and our fundamental values. If the discriminatory act is private, a court will not enforce it; if the law of another state is profoundly discriminatory, the court will not enforce it; but if it is a law that we ourselves promulgated at some time in the past, the court must give effect to it no matter how profoundly it contradicts our fundamental values. The sovereignty of our own past thus looks uniquely and somewhat surprisingly inviolable.

It would seem odd, however, if our constitutionalization of non-retrospective norms of equality were to debilitate our courts from exercising the kind of critical scrutiny of our own past political choices that we exercise when the past discrimination is private and even, perhaps, when the laws are those of elsewhere. There is of course a worry in the background here about our unwillingness to examine our own past in the way that we might examine – and encourage examination of – that of others. But let us for the moment focus on a more principled version of why the courts might be worried about this. In the discussion of the difference between public and private discrimination we noted how the fact that past private discrimination is "doubly" outside of direct *Charter* application may have made it easier to recognize the force of the *Charter*'s influence without calling into question the doctrine of non-retroactivity. If we think of courts refusing to give full (or any) legal effect to the laws of another state, we can see an analogous phenomenon. That is, just as the privacy of the activity precludes direct applicability, so too does the fact that the legislation in question is the legislation of another state. In the absence of any direct applicability argument, one finds a nicely streamlined question about whether to give judicial effect to such acts or not. But where there is even a possibility of direct application of the *Charter*, the shrinking distance between direct application and influential effect gives rise to an understandable anxiety about preserving the difference between the full retroactivity of direct application and influential authority. This suggests, however, that paying closer attention to how we approach the acts of other states may enable us to respond in a more principled way to our own official past.

THE PAST IS ANOTHER COUNTRY

This suggests that the most difficult problem of the past revolves around how we ought to resolve profound contradictions between our own fundamental values and our legal past. Ironically, we generally embrace the idea that coming to terms with the past is one of the central moral tasks of regimes with evil pasts. But perhaps to preserve the sense of our historical superiority, we avoid this imperative ourselves. And yet our anxiety not to entirely reopen our own legal past leaves us prey to the charge of hypocrisy. It thus seems important to find a way to avoid the most troubling kind of deference to the past without entirely opening it up to legal scrutiny. Some of our hesitation about judging our own past comes from the sense that the past looks, from here, to be foreign and often incomprehensible terrain. Like foreign terrain, our own past is a world we may strive to understand but can never fully inhabit. There, we will always somehow live as strangers. Our awareness of the way that this distance inevitably limits our comprehension of the past also makes us rightly humble about our capacity for judgment.

The moral distance of the past and its consequent inaccessibility to us in the full sense parallels in this way the more general problem of judging the "other." The limits to our understanding of the past also inspire a kind of respect and restraint, even humility, that may not make itself felt in the same way when we judge the "here and now." And so, although one need not entirely equate the past and the foreign, it is possible to glean some insight from thinking about our own past as "another country." This analogy suggests that we may find some illumination in thinking about how to approach our own legal past by examining how courts approach the problem of when to give effect to the laws of other countries, to "foreign law." Courts in these cases are explicitly concerned, not with the validity of the foreign law (which is generally acknowledged), but rather with the extent to which they can give *effect* to the relevant law. Thus, the mandatory influence of the court's own fundamental values can be felt as courts negotiate the tension between respect for those values and treating foreign laws with the deference they seem to require. Let us examine more closely how courts attempt to recognize both the limitations that moral distance places on the ability to judge across geographical distance and the concomitant moral and legal fact that it is ultimately the task of contemporary judges to decide what can have legal effect in their courts and justify those decisions. As we shall see, the courts that seem so timorous about judgment in the face of the distance of history may have something to learn from the judicial encounter with the distance of place.

The distance of place, the legal significance of another country, figures prominently in adjudication when courts are faced with questions about whether and to what extent they ought to give effect to foreign laws. The salience of "distance" is apparent in the fact that differences between the law of the court and the foreign law, far from justifying non-application by the court, actually give rise to the need for deference. As the House of Lords recently put it, "the existence of differences is the very reason why it may be appropriate for the forum court to have recourse to the foreign law."[45] Thus, in its simplest form, the principle of comity requires a kind of deference to the judgments of the other. It is in the very nature of this deference that it requires courts to give legal effect to foreign law that their own jurisdictions may well view as ill advised, even erroneous. But that deference is inherently reasoned, not automatic, for its exercise must ultimately be consistent with the court's understanding of what it is that *it* will enforce.[46] Thus, it is central to this idea of reasoned deference that "blind adherence to foreign law can never be required of an English court."[47] Instead, "Exceptionally and rarely, a provision of foreign law will be disregarded when it would lead to a result wholly alien to fundamental requirements of justice as administered by an English court."[48]

So in the case of foreign law, while the underlying principle of comity generally requires a judge to "defer" and give effect to foreign law, that deference is inherently limited at least by the fact that a court cannot give effect to laws that profoundly violate its own core legal values. Decades ago, Justice Cardozo pointed out that courts will refuse to recognize a foreign law that violates "some fundamental principle of justice, some prevalent conception of good morals, some deep-rooted tradition of the common weal."[49] Similarly, in *Kuwait Airways* the House of Lords explains its own earlier decision in *Oppenheimer v. Cattermole* on the basis that the courts *must* possess a residual power to "disregard a provision of foreign law when to do otherwise would affront basic principles of justice and fairness which the courts seek to apply in the administration of justice in this country."[50] As with the approach to domestic legal problems discussed above, inconsistency with fundamental values is typically expressed in the language of public policy that we find in cases like *Canada Trust*. And here as there foundational inconsistency has the estoppel-like consequence that the relevant legal act must be denied its claimed effect. The consequence is that here too an estoppel-like effect precludes a court from recognizing or giving legal effect to foreign laws that violate the fundamental values of the court itself.

These limits on the recognition of foreign law parallel in important ways our earlier discussion of *Canada Trust* and other examples of influential authority. The underlying view in all of these situations does not see courts as simple neutral enforcers or appliers of values gleaned elsewhere. Instead, the values of the court itself, including prominently the fundamental values of the legal order as most authoritatively expressed in the *Charter*, are inevitably engaged. This is so even if much of the time it may not be visible because through "*Charter*-positive" interpretive choices courts seamlessly ensure general consistency with their own values. And in the foreign law cases, as in *Canada Trust*, the insistence on the "contemporary" nature of public policy serves as a reminder that it implicates the values of the court asked to give effect to the relevant act.[51] Thus, cases such as *Oppenheimer* and the post-Nazi Decree 11 cases also illustrate this dynamic. Although bound by the principle of comity to respect the other and to acknowledge the limitations of their own capacity for judgment, courts in those cases nonetheless recognize that it would be inconsistent with their role to give automatic deference to the legislation of other regimes. Instead, as the House of Lords suggests, it is implicit in the judicial role that a court must decline to give "effect" to foreign law that violates that court's own fundamental values. "Blind adherence," on this view, is no part of the judicial role. Thus the foreign law cases can be read with cases like *Canada Trust* to suggest both the outer limit of influential authority and the continuity of that limit with the more general judicial imperative to give expression to and act in accordance with the fundamental values of the legal order.

This also suggests that the treatment of "evil law" in the recognition of foreign judgments may provide an analogy for thinking more systematically about our own past. It is crucial to the form of deference extended by the courts in the foreign law cases that it is *their* deference. This is why the relevant norms are those of the time (contemporary) and the place of decision-making. And since this deference is a kind of reasoned or principled respect for some "other," the reasons for respect must ultimately be *ours*, not theirs. So the adjudicating court must give its own reasons to accord respect to the decision of another, even though that decision may be one the court considers unwise – a decision that we would not ourselves have made. Importantly, however, our reason is not theirs. This means, first that our reason need not – indeed probably should not – rest on the wisdom of the relevant law. But it also means that since it must be a reason *for us*, it will not be enough to restate the reason that prevailed for them. This difference may well often be obscured because reasons will often equally hold for us and for them. But where there is a divergence, our courts must give their own reasons to accord respect to the relevant acts. To simply say it was their decision will not be a sufficient reason for us – that would amount to the "blind adherence" that courts in recognition of foreign judgments cases describe as inconsistent with their role. And because the reasons for respect must ultimately be reasons why *we* should accord respect to decisions we may disagree with, those reasons must engage the fundamental values of the legal order asked to accord that respect. We must be able to articulate reasons to respect those decisions that invoke the basic values of our legal order and are, at a minimum, not inconsistent with any such values.

Viewed in this way, we might pose the question of our legal past as presented in *Mack* somewhat differently: why should our contemporary courts respect the decisions of our past legislatures? Ordinarily of course there are reasons of institutional legitimacy grounded in democracy for courts to respect the acts of the legislature. Although the judgments in *Mack* resist the idea that they need to give a reason to respect the head tax legislation and instead prefer the "blind adherence" model, they actually do seem to feel the need to give some kind of a reason. It is thus illuminating to reexamine the response of the Court of Appeal in *Mack* to the analogy between their task and that of the courts that had to determine what contemporary legal effect should be given to the Nazi regime's Decree 11. The Court of Appeal closes with a statement that even the broad doctrine of equity does not allow a contemporary court to remedy the consequences of "laws enacted by a democratic government that were valid at that time," and at the end of this statement they place a footnote. That footnote, effectively the Court's last word in the case, reads as follows: "We are not here concerned with facially valid laws enacted by a totalitarian or other despotic regime."[52] So, unsurprisingly, in response to the pressure – felt though not acknowledged – to give its own reason for deference, the Court gestures towards a contemporary democratic reason for deferring to the legislature of the past.

The Court of Appeal, though, is strikingly timorous about this democratic justification, and rightly so. In fact it is extremely difficult to rely on democracy to justify deference to the legislatures that enacted the head tax legislation. Both federal and provincial legislatures restricted the right to vote on racial grounds, disenfranchising citizens of Chinese origin until decades after the head tax legislation was repealed.[53] Recalling the analogy to another country, we should ask ourselves whether we would accord apartheid era laws in South Africa respect on democratic grounds because the franchise existed for whites. If not, then we ought to question why in *Mack* a similarly limited form of democracy justifies respect for a legislature's treatment of those it explicitly excludes. In fact cases like *Mack*, like the residential schools cases, like the legal treatment of the mentally disabled, in this way raise profound reasons to doubt the adequacy of the democratic justification for the relevant laws. In all of these cases and many others, the legislation we now recognize as profoundly dehumanizing was passed by political bodies that explicitly excluded the "subject" groups from political participation. This "democratic deficit" thus seems to fatally undermine any attempt to argue for respect on democratic grounds. That s.15 specifically advises courts to be on the lookout for discriminatory treatment of the very groups at issue in so many of the laws and political exclusions only adds to the untenability of the democratic justification for deference.

This does not mean of course that every legislative decision from an imperfectly constructed political body will be deemed unworthy of respect on this view. It may well be that in matters of general welfare the legislatures were often sufficiently representative to be worthy of our contemporary respect. Thus, many decisions that would now count as unconstitutional may well have been made on a sufficiently inclusive basis for the purpose of those decisions that we could say there exists a democratic justification for extending our contemporary respect to them despite their inconsistency with contemporary constitutional values. But this justification does not seem plausible in cases where decisions concerning a particular group are made by political bodies that explicitly exclude the political participation of the very group that is specifically disadvantaged by the relevant decision. When such a legislature enacts a law to the profound disadvantage of the very groups it has excluded, a contemporary court bound to respect the fundamental value of equality should have great difficulty giving any legal significance to a law whose main message is the denial of full personhood to those it has excluded.

The analogy to the recognition of foreign laws also highlights a somewhat paradoxical possibility. Do we really mean to invoke the non-retroactivity requirement of the *Charter* to immunize our own past laws from consistency with its fundamental values, even though we demand such consistency from foreign laws, past or present? Indeed, something like this worry may be behind the limit that the South African Constitutional Court places on the non-retroactivity of their constitutional guarantees. Thus, while the Court in *Du Plessis v. De Klerk* holds that the operation of the Constitution is not retroactive or retrospective, it also explicitly provides for just the kind of "exception" that would respond to the concern above:

But we leave open the possibility that there may be cases where the enforcement of previously acquired rights would in the light of our present constitutional values be so grossly unjust and abhorrent that it could not be countenanced, whether as being contrary to public policy or on some other basis ...[54]

It does not seem accidental that the nature of this exception seems to draw on something very like the influential authority of constitutional human rights. The Court thus recognizes that implicit in a system committed to overarching constitutional values is the idea of some principled limits – significantly phrased in terms of basic constitutional values – on what a court can countenance and enforce. Here too the Court allows that this may entail the estoppel-like consequence that previously acquired rights could not be enforced. And public policy is invoked to justify the idea that the court will refuse to enforce claims that violate the basic values of the contemporary constitutional order. *De Klerk* thus suggests that this approach is compatible with the general non-retroactivity of constitutional guarantees. And this seems plausible, for it is simply another expression of the familiar idea that the fundamental values of the adjudicating court inevitably impose some principled limitations on what that court can implicate itself in.

This way of thinking about our own past laws only seems strengthened by recognizing that, if there is anything to the analogy to comity, it surely suggests that the reasons for deference to the laws of another state are more pressing than the reasons for deference to our own past laws. While we may legitimately worry about embarrassing another state, the underlying basis of the claim to deference to our own collective past is not so clear. Indeed, the analogy to another country may lead us to ask ourselves what exactly the reason for such uncritical respect might be. We cannot "embarrass" our past; significantly perhaps, the only embarrassment may well be ours. And if so, then we may well worry that when we uncritically defer to our past, we are resisting the kind of accounting for our own past wrongs that we advocate for regimes that have explicitly acknowledged their racist past.

CONCLUSION

Canada is a constitutional order that places primacy on equality and that expresses that primacy in legal form both domestically and internationally. And this fact cannot be without significance when our courts are charged with evaluating our legal past. Regardless of the status of the head tax legislation during the period of its tenure, it is not open to a contemporary Canadian court to give it current legal significance in a constitutional order committed to the radiating value of equality. Such a court can no more "blindly adhere" to the political choices of our past legislatures than it can so adhere to the choices of foreign legislatures or of individuals. The hardest question in *Mack* and many other reparations cases thus seems to engage our attitude to our own past. Why would we, judging in our own cause so to speak, be so deferential to our own past "sovereigns" even when we acknowledge that the acts they proclaimed in our collective name were profoundly wrong and invidious? Indeed, respect for our collective polity may be better expressed by frankly acknowledging now where we went terribly wrong. Our law – a formidable weapon in our past wrongdoing – should no longer serve as a shield to protect the unassailable sovereignty of the past, but rather as a means of rectifying now what we did so terribly wrong then. Periods in our history like that implicated in the *Mack* case are generally recognized as moments not only of collective political failure but also of the failure of law in particular. But this suggests that part of the task here, as in other cases of "transitional justice," is to ask how law can best reassert the possibility of its moral meaning. Though the temptation to do so may be strong, it seems unlikely that this will be accomplished by ignoring law's contemporary imperatives and deferring to the sovereignty of our racist past. Reasserting the primacy of law's own fundamental values and its substantive, now constitutionalized, commitment to equal human dignity thus seems more promising as a path towards the law's reconciliation with its own ignominious past.

NOTES

1 I discuss this phenomenon and what it reveals about the promise and the limits of private law in responding to the reparations challenge in "The Moral Imagination of Private Law" (draft manuscript on file with the author).

2 See for instance Alfred L. Brophy, "Some Conceptual and Legal Problems in Reparations for Slavery" 58 N.Y.U. Annual Survey of American Law 497 (2003).

3 [2001] OJ No. 2794.

4 The *Chinese Immigration Act*, referred to as the *Chinese Exclusion Act*, which came into effect in 1923, was repealed in 1947: *Immigration Act*, RS 1947, c. 19, s. 4.

5 See [2001] OJ No. 2794, and the Supreme Court decision at [2002] SCCA No. 476.

6 See Brophy, *supra* note 2 at 501–5; Eric A. Posner and Adrian Vermeule, "Reparations for Slavery and Other Historical Injustices" 103 Columbia L. Rev. 689 (2003).

7 These questions are considered in detail in the New Zealand/Maori context by Jeremy Waldron, "Redressing Historic Injustice" (2002) 52 U.T.L.J.
135 at 143ff.

8 See for example the dismissed complaint of the so-called comfort women,
Hwang v. Japan, 172 F. Supp. 2d 52, 55 n.1 (DDC 2001), and a case of an
American citizen seeking damages for injuries sustained and slave labour
performed when held in Nazi concentration camps, *Princz v. Federal
Republic of Germany*, 26 F.3d 1166, 307 U.S. App. DC 102.

9 This is not true of the slavery cases because American courts still extend
significant immunities to the domestic sovereign as well. Sovereign
immunity is a primary procedural obstacle to reparations for slavery that
implicate the government: *Cato v. U.S.* 70 F.3d 1103 (9th Cir. 1995). Thus,
most of the recent claims and the strategies surrounding other possible
reparations claims for the harms of slavery are focused on private defendants who cannot invoke the protection of sovereign immunity: *In re
African-American Slave Descendants Litigation*, 231 F.Supp.2d 1357; *Deadria
Farmer-Paellmann v. FleetBoston Financial Corp., et al.*, CA No. 1:02-1862;
Andre Carrington v. FleetBoston Financial Corp., et al., CA No. 1:02-1863;
Mary Lacey Madison v. FleetBoston Financial Corp., et al., CA No. 1:02-1864;
Richard E. Barber, Sr. v. New York Life Insurance Co., et al., CA No. 2:02-
2084; Willie E. Gary, et al., "Making the Case for Racial Reparations,"
Harper's Magazine, Nov. 2000 at 37–51; Brophy, *supra* note 2 at 514–17.

10 *Mack v. Canada, supra* note 5 at para 46.

11 I borrow the reference to "value term" from President Barak of the
Supreme Court of Israel, who uses it in his discussion of the interaction
of constitutional human rights and private law: A. Barak, "Constitutional
Human Rights and Private Law" (1996) 3 Rev. Constit. Studies 218 at
236–7.

12 Ibid.; M. Moran, *Rethinking the Reasonable Person: An Egalitarian Reconstruction of the Objective Standard* (Oxford: Oxford University Press, 2003)
at 283–6 (discussing the meaning of reasonableness).

13 *Mack v. Canada* (2002), 60 OR (3d) 737 (CA) para. 51 citing *Peel (Regional
Municipality) v. Ontario*, [1992] 3 SCR 762 at 802–3.

14 Ibid.

15 Factum of the Appellants, para. 78.

16 M. Moran, "Authority, Influence, and Persuasion: *Baker, Charter* Values
and the Puzzle of Method," in D. Dyzenhaus, ed. *The Unity of Public Law*
(Oxford: Hart Publishing, 2003).

17 I refer to "private common law," since the cause of action in unjust
enrichment is both private in the sense that it is the source of private

obligation and also finds its source in common law and equity. Although in the text at times I shorten the phrase to "private law" or to "common law," it is worth pointing out that the *Charter* does not apply directly to common law itself or generally to private relations unless there is legislation that governs those relations. As both private and common law, unjust enrichment, like other private law causes of action, is doubly outside the direct application of the *Charter*.

Although I focus on Canada and the *Charter* here, this understanding of the relation of constitutionalized human rights norms to private and common law is more broadly characteristic at least of post–Second World War constitutional regimes: L. Weinrib and E. Weinrib, "Constitutional Values and Private Law in Canada," in Daniel Friedmann and Daphne Barak-Erez, eds, *Human Rights in Private Law* (Oxford: Hart Publishing 2001), 43; Barak, *supra* note 11; Murray Hunt, "The Horizontal Effect of the Human Rights Act" (1998) Public Law 423–43; R. Buxton, "The Human Rights Act and Private Law" (2000) 116 L.Q.R. 48.

18 For some important understandings of that structure see, for instance, E. Weinrib, *The Idea of Private Law* (Cambridge, Mass.: Harvard University Press, 1995) and A. Brudner, *The Unity of the Common Law* (Berkeley: University of California Press, 1995).

19 Indeed, it seems plausible that at least some of the differences between the various possibilities in this debate are not as significant as they seem. This is because even assuming, as I do, that in their nature constitutional bills of rights are not directed exclusively to state actors, nonetheless, the very nature of many of the rights is such that it makes little sense to think of them outside of the state-individual interaction. The many rights directed to the nature of the criminal procedure seem obvious examples. Further, the differences between the various views are also somewhat blunted by the fact that at some point even the most confined understandings of the effect of constitutional guarantees are pressed to admit some limits on what a court can be called upon to enforce, however unremittingly private the relevant acts might be. This argument is elaborated below.

20 See for example *Hill v. Church of Scientology*, [1995] 2 SCR 1130. In other jurisdictions, see *Du Plessis v. De Klerk*, 1996 (3) SA 850 (CC); *Douglas and Zeta-Jones v. Hello! Magazine*, [2001] QB 967 (CA), *A v. B*, [2003] QB 195 (CA).

21 *Canada Trust Co v. Ontario Human Rights Commission* (1990), 69 DLR (4th) 321 (Ont. CA), *Jane Doe v. Toronto (Metropolitan) Commissioners of Police* (1989), 58 DLR (4th) 396.

22 I discuss the more general difficulties with understanding adjudication in terms of binding rules in "Authority, Influence and Persuasion," *supra* note 16, drawing on work by David Dyzenhaus, Murray Hunt, Stephen Perry, and Brian Simpson, among others.

23 Though these are not best conceived as water-tight categories, for even notionally persuasive sources may exert themselves in a fashion that approaches the insistence of influential authority and the like.

24 J. Brunnée and S.J. Toope, "A Hesitant Embrace: The Application of International Law by Canadian Courts," in Dyzenhaus, ed., *The Unity of Public Law*, *supra* note 16; P. Macklem, "Secondary Picketing, Consumer Boycotts, and the *Charter*" (2000) 8 Can. Labour and Employment L.J. 9.

25 Though I do not elaborate the links here, this idea has important affinities with John Rawls's conception of public reason: John Rawls, *Political Liberalism* (New York: Columbia University Press, 1993) especially Part Two, Lecture VI, "The Idea of Public Reason" at 212–54.

26 *Supra* note 5 at 9 (para. 52).

27 *Mack Appeal, supra* note 13 at para. 1.

28 Ibid. at para. 52. However, while they share a denunciatory quality, in one respect Cumming, J.'s statement may be more significant. This is because he puts the wrong in terms of discrimination and prejudice – values which have contemporary legal, especially constitutional, significance. The way that the Court of Appeal describes the legislation seems to focus instead on the negative light it casts on our history, rather than on its incompatibility with contemporary legal values.

29 "Authority, Influence and Persuasion," *supra* note 16 discussing *Hill v. Church of Scientology, supra* note 20 and *Du Plessis v. De Klerk, supra* note 20.

30 Barak, *supra* note 11; David Dyzenhaus stresses a similar point regarding the fundamental values that together constitute what Fuller called the "internal morality of the law": "The Juristic Force of Injustice," in this volume. For the implications of this for views for the meaning of "reasonableness," see M. Moran, *Rethinking the Reasonable Person, supra* note 12.

31 (1990), 74 OR (2d) 481.

32 *Canada Trust Appeal, supra* note 21 at 11 (OJ).

33 Ibid. at 496 (*per* Robins, J.A.) (emphasis added).

34 Ibid. at 21 (OJ).

35 In *"Authority, Influence and Persuasion," supra* note 16, I discuss two instances of influential authority, beginning with ratified but unincorporated treaty obligations of the kind discussed by the majority in *Baker v.*

AG Canada. I note how the act of ratification may impose a mandatory obligation of respect for fundamental values that bears an important similarity to the *Charter's* effect upon private and common law.

36 *United States of America v. Burns*, [2001] 1 SCR 283.

37 *Canada Trust Appeal, supra* note 21 at 22 (OJ).

38 The basic idea of estoppel is that a court is barred, for institutional reasons, from giving legal significance to certain kinds of arguments and acts. Although he does not use the language of estoppel, President Barak notes that constitutional human rights will unavoidably have a similar restrictive effect on the freedom of the judiciary although this will typi-cally only be used when other mechanisms fail: "Constitutional Human Rights and Private Law," *supra* note 11 at 280.

39 [1945] OR 778 (HC).

40 *Shelley v. Kramer*, 334 U.S. 1 (1948).

41 For a pre-*Charter* articulation of rule of law values including equality, see John McLaren, "The Head Tax Case and the Rule of Law: The Historical Thread of Judicial Resistance to 'Legalized' Discrimination," chapter 5 in this volume.

42 Julian Rivers, "Gross Statutory Injustice and the Canadian Head Tax Case," in this volume; Robert Alexy "A Defence of Radbruch's Formula" and Julian Rivers "The Interpretation and Invalidity of Unjust Laws," in D. Dyzenhaus, ed., *Recrafting the Rule of Law: The Limits of the Legal Order* (Oxford: Hart Publishing, 1995), 15–39; *Oppenheimer v. Cattermole*, [1976] AC 249 (HL).

43 Order of the Second Senate, 14 Feb. 1968, citing BVerfGE 3, 58 [119]; 6, 132 [198]. For a discussion of these and related cases see ibid.

44 R. Alexy, "A Defence of Radbruch's Formula," in Dyzenhaus, *supra* note 42 at 15; J. Rivers, "The Interpretation and Invalidity of Unjust Laws," *supra* note 42 at 40; J. Rivers, "Gross Statutory Injustice," *supra* note 42.

45 *Kuwait Airways Corpn v. Iraqi Airways Co (Nos 4 and 5)*, [2002] WLR 1353 at 1360 (per Lord Nicholls).

46 In this sense it is possible to recognize a similar conceptual structure, also expressed in terms of deference, in the issue of judicial review of admin-istrative action in the administrative law context. The structure of both inquiries reflects a delicate mediation between the need to respect the integrity of some "other" and respect for one's own fundamental values – values most authoritatively expressed in the influential authority of the *Charter*. The inherently reasoned idea of deference I draw on here is that of "deference as respect" which has been developed by David Dyzenhaus in the administrative law context and embraced by the Supreme Court of

Canada in Baker. See *Baker v. Canada (Minister of Citizenship and Immigration)*, [1999] 2 SCR 817, and Dyzenhaus, "The Politics of Deference: Judicial Review and Democracy," in Michael Taggart, ed., *The Province of Administrative Law* (Oxford: Hart Publishing, 1997), 279.

47 *Kuwait Airways, supra* note 45 at 1360, discussing Scarman J. in *In the Estate of Fuld, decd (No 3)* [1968] P 675.

48 Ibid.

49 *Loucks v. Standard Oil Co of New York*, 120 NE 198 at 202 (1918).

50 *Oppenheimer v. Cattermole, supra* note 42, as explained in *Kuwait Airways, supra* note 45 at 1360–1 (emphasis added). The Radbruch Formula can be understood as a more theoretical account of this limit. In Canada and other post-war constitutional regimes, the most fundamental values are expressed in the constitutional document, and so in those regimes that formula would at a minimum demand that courts could not enforce as law positive norms that violate those fundamental constitutional values. This of course does not necessarily entail that *only* violations of fundamental constitutional values will engage this limit but simply that such a violation is necessarily problematic under any interpretation of the Radbruch Formula. As the House of Lords indicates in *Kuwait Airways*, violations of international law will also engage the public policy exception and have the estoppel-like consequence discussed in the text: *Kuwait Airways* at 1363 discussing *Oppenheim's International Law*, 9th ed (1992), vol. 1, ed Jennings and Watts, 371–6, para. 113.

51 See, for instance, *Kuwait Airways*, ibid. at 1363 discussing Lord Wilberforce in *Blathwayt v. Baron Cawley*, [1976] AC 397, 426 ("The acceptability of a provision of foreign law must be judged by contemporary standards").

52 *Mack Appeal, supra* note 13 at n. 7.

53 *History of the Vote in Canada* (Ottawa: Minister of Public Works and Government Services, Canada, 1997) at 47, 63–4, 80–9. See also *Cunningham v. Tomey Homma*, [1903] AC 151 (P.C.) (upholding the right to restrict the vote on a racial basis).

54 *Du Plessis v. De Klerk, supra* note 20 at para. 20.

3

Feminist Approaches to the Rule of Law

Feminist scholars and lawyers have made important contributions to legal thought and legal change in the past two decades. There are many different strands in contemporary feminist thought about law. Some feminists are critical of the detachment to which law claims to aspire, others of its implicit bias against women, still others of its emphasis on rights and the separateness of persons rather than their connectedness. These selections are not meant to be representative of all of these trends. Instead, they touch on some of the issues already considered about the general relation between morality and the rule of law. Later sections include feminist engagements with particular issues.

Catharine A. MacKinnon
"The Liberal State" (1989)

MacKinnon sees the law as a potentially powerful medium of progressive change, one that has historically not been in women's hands and has largely sided against women.

The difference between the judges and Sir Isaac [Newton] is that a mistake by Sir Isaac in calculating the orbit of the earth would not send it spinning around the sun with an increased velocity... while if the judges... come to a wrong result, it is none the less law.
– John Chipman Gray (1909)

Political revolutions aim to change political institutions in ways that those institutions themselves prohibit.
– Thomas Kuhn (1962)

Feminism has no theory of the state. Just as feminism has a theory of power but lacks a specific theory of its state form, marxism has a theory of value which (through the organization of work in production) becomes class analysis, but also a problematic theory of the state. Marx himself did not address the state much more explicitly than he addressed women. Women were substratum, the state epiphenomenon. He termed the state "a concentrated expression of economics," a reflection of the real action, which occurred elsewhere; it was "the official résumé of society," a unity of ruptures; it, or its "executive," was "but a committee for managing the common affairs of the whole bourgeoisie." Engels frontally analyzed women and the state, and together. But just as he presumed the subordination of women in every attempt to reveal its roots, he presupposed something like the state, or statelike society, in every attempt to find its origins.

Marx tended to use the term *political* narrowly to refer to the state or its laws, criticizing as exclusively political interpretations of the state's organization or behavior which took them as sui generis, as if they were to be analyzed apart from economic conditions. He termed "political power" as embodied in the modern state "the official expression of antagonism in civil society." Changes on this level could, therefore, emancipate the individual only within the framework of the existing social order, termed "civil society." Revolution on this level was "partial, merely political revolution." Accordingly, until recently, most marxist theory has tended to consider as political that which occurs between classes and the state as the instrument of the economically dominant class. That is, it has interpreted the political in terms of the marxist view of social inequality and the state in terms of the class that controls it. The marxist theory of social inequality has been its theory of politics. The state as such was not seen as furthering particular interests through its form. This theory does not so much collapse the state into society (although it goes far in that direction) as conceive the state as determined by the totality of social relations of which the state is one determined and determining part – without specifying which, or how much, is which.

After 1848, having seen the bourgeoisie win revolutions but then not exercise state power directly, Marx tried to understand how states could plainly serve the bourgeoisie's interest yet not represent it as a class. His attempts form the basis for much contemporary marxist work that has tried to grasp the specificity of the institutional state: how it wields class power or operates within class strictures or supplements or moderates class rule or transforms class society or responds to approach by a left aspiring to rulership or other changes. While much liberal theory has seen the state as emanating power, and traditional marxism has seen the state as expressing power constituted elsewhere, recent marxism, much of it structuralist, has tried to analyze state power as specific to the state as a form, yet integral to a determinate social whole understood in class terms.

Politics becomes "an autonomous phenomenon that is constrained by economics but not reducible to it." This state is found "relatively autonomous"; that is, the state, expressed through its functionaries, has a definite class character, is definitely capitalist or socialist, but also has its own interests, which are to some degree independent of those of the ruling class and even of the class structure. The state as such, in this view, has a specific power and interest, termed "the political," such that class power, class interest expressed by and in the state, and state behavior, though inconceivable in isolation from one another, are nevertheless not linearly linked or strictly coextensive. Thus Jon Elster argues that Marx saw that the bourgeoisie perceived their interests best furthered "if they remain outside politics." Much of this work locates "the specificity of the political" in a mediate "region" between the state and its own ground of power (which alone, as in the liberal conception, would set the state above or apart from class) and the state as possessing no special supremacy or priority in terms of power, as in the more orthodox marxist view. For Nicos Poulantzas, for example, the "specific autonomy which is characteristic of the function of the state ... is the basis of the specificity of the political" – whatever that means.

The idea that the state is relatively autonomous, a kind of first among equals of social institutions, has the genius of appearing to take a stand on the issue of reciprocal constitution of state and society while straddling it. Is the state essentially autonomous of class but partly determined by it, or is it essentially determined by class but not exclusively so? Is it relatively constrained within a context of freedom or relatively free within a context of constraint? As to who or what fundamentally moves and shapes the realities and instrumentalities of domination, and where to go to do something about it, what qualifies what is as ambiguous as it is crucial. When this work has investigated law as a particular form of state expression, it has served to relieve the compulsion to find all law – directly or convolutedly, nakedly or clothed in unconscious or devious rationalia – to be simply "bourgeois," without undercutting the notion that it, with all state emanations, is determinately driven by interest.

Feminism has not confronted, on its own terms, the relation between the state and society within a theory of social determination specific to sex. As a result, it lacks a jurisprudence, that is, a theory of the substance of law, its relation to society, and the relationship between the two. Such a theory would comprehend how law works as a form of state power in a social context in which power is gendered. It would answer the questions: What is state power? Where, socially, does it come from? How do women encounter it? What is the law for women? How does law work to legitimate the state, male power, itself? Can law do anything for women? Can it do anything about women's status? Does how the law is used matter?

In the absence of answers, feminist practice has oscillated between a liberal theory of the state on the one hand and a left theory of the state on the other. Both theories treat law as the mind of society: disembodied reason in liberal theory, reflection of material interest in left theory. In liberal moments, the state is accepted on its own terms as a neutral arbiter among conflicting interests. The law is actually or potentially principled, meaning predisposed to no substantive outcome, or manipulable to any ends, thus available as a tool that is not fatally twisted. Women implicitly become an interest group within pluralism, with specific problems of mobilization and representation, exit and voice, sustaining incremental gains and losses. In left moments, the state becomes a tool of dominance and repression, the law legitimating ideology, use of the legal system a form of utopian idealism or gradualist reform, each apparent gain deceptive or cooptive, and each loss inevitable.

Liberalism applied to women has supported state intervention on behalf of women as abstract persons with abstract rights, without scrutinizing the content and limitations of these notions in terms of gender. Marxism applied to women is always on the edge of counseling abdication of the state as an arena altogether – and with it those women whom the state does not ignore or who are in no position to ignore it. As a result, feminism has been left with these tacit alternatives: either the state is a primary tool of women's betterment and status transformation, without analysis (hence strategy) of it as male; or women are left to civil society, which for women has more closely resembled a state of nature. The state, and with it the law, have been either omnipotent or impotent: everything or nothing. The feminist posture toward the state has therefore been schizoid on issues central to women's status. Rape, abortion, pornography, and sex discrimination are examples. To grasp the inadequacies for women of liberalism on the one hand and marxism on the other is to begin to comprehend the role of the liberal state and liberal legalism within a post-marxist feminism of social transformation.

Gender is a social system that divides power. It is therefore a political system. That is, over time, women have been economically exploited, relegated to domestic slavery, forced into motherhood, sexually objectified, physically abused, used in denigrating entertainment, deprived of a voice and authentic culture, and disenfranchised and excluded from public life. Women, by contrast with comparable men, have systematically been subjected to physical insecurity; targeted for sexual denigration and violation; depersonalized and denigrated; deprived of respect, credibility, and resources; and silenced – and denied public presence, voice, and representation of their interests. Men as men have generally not had these things done to them; that is, men have had to be Black or gay (for instance) to have these things done to them as men. Men have done these things to women. Even conventional theories of power – the more individuated, atomistic, and decisional approaches of the pluralists, as well as the more radical theories, which stress structural, tacit, contextual, and relational aspects of power – recognize such conditions as defining positions of power and powerlessness. If one defines politics with Harold Lasswell, who defines a political act as "one performed in power perspectives," and with Robert Dahl, who defines a political system as "any persistent pattern of human relationships that involves, to a significant extent, power, rule, or authority," and with Kate Millett, who defines political relationships as "power structured relationships," the relation between women and men is political.

Unlike the ways in which men systematically enslave, violate, dehumanize, and exterminate other men, expressing political inequalities among men, men's forms of dominance over women have been accomplished socially as well as economically, prior to the operation of law, without express state acts, often in intimate contexts, as everyday life. So what is the role of the state in sexual politics? Neither liberalism nor marxism grants women, as such, a specific relation to the state. Feminism has described some of the state's treatment of the gender difference but has not analyzed the state's role in gender hierarchy. What, in gender terms, are the state's norms of accountability, sources of power, real constituency? Is the state to some degree autonomous of the interests of men or an integral expression of them? Does the state embody and serve male interests in its form, dynamics, relation to society, and specific policies? Is the state constructed upon the subordination of women? If so, how does male power become state power? Can such a state be made to serve the interests of those upon whose powerlessness its power is erected? Would a different relation between state and society, such as may exist under socialism, make a difference? If not, is masculinity inherent in the state form as such, or is some other form of state, or some other way of governing, distinguishable or imaginable? In the absence of answers to these questions, feminism has been caught between giving more power to that state in each attempt to claim it for women and leaving unchecked power in the society to men. Undisturbed, meanwhile, like the assumption that women generally consent to sex, is the assumption that women consent to this government. The question for feminism is: what is this state, from women's point of view?

The state is male in the feminist sense: the law sees and treats women the way men see and treat women. The liberal state coercively and authoritatively constitutes the social order in the interest of men as a gender – through its legitimating norms, forms, relation to society, and substantive policies. The state's formal norms recapitulate the male point of view on the level of design. In Anglo-American jurisprudence, morals (value judgments) are deemed separable and separated from politics (power contests), and both from adjudication (interpretation). Neutrality, including judicial decision making that is dispassionate, impersonal, disinterested, and precedential, is considered desirable and descriptive. Courts, forums without predisposition among parties and with no interest of their own, reflect society back to itself resolved. Government of laws, not of men, limits partiality with written constraints and tempers force with reasonable rule-following.

At least since Langdell's first casebook in 1871, this law has aspired to be a science of rules and a science with rules, a science of the immanent generalization subsuming the emergent particularity, of prediction and control of social regularities and regulations, preferably codified. The formulaic "tests" of "doctrine" aspire to mechanism, classification to taxonomy, legislators to Linnaeus. Courts intervene only in properly "factualized" disputes, cognizing social conflicts as if collecting empirical data; right conduct becomes rule-following. But these demarcations between morals and politics, science and politics, the personality of the judge and the judicial role, bare coercion and the rule of law, tend to merge in women's experience. Relatively seamlessly they promote the dominance of men as a social group through privileging the form of power – the perspective on social life – which feminist consciousness reveals as socially male. The separation of form from substance, process from policy, adjudication from legislation, judicial role from theory or practice, echoes and reechoes at each level of the regime its basic norm: objectivity.

Formally, the state is male in that objectivity is its norm. Objectivity is liberal legalism's conception of itself. It legitimates itself by reflecting its view of society, a society it helps make by so seeing it, and calling that view, and that relation, rationality. Since rationality is measured by point-of-viewlessness, what counts as reason is that which corresponds to the way things are. Practical rationality, in this approach, means that which can be done without changing anything. In this framework, the task of legal interpretation becomes "to perfect the state as mirror of the society." Objectivist epistemology is the law of law. It ensures that the law will most reinforce existing distributions of power when it most closely adheres to its own ideal of fairness. Like the science it emulates, this epistemological stance cannot see the social specificity of reflexion as method or its choice to embrace that which it reflects. Such law not only reflects a society in which men rule women; it rules in a male way insofar as "the phallus means everything that sets itself up as a mirror." Law, as words in power, writes society in state form and writes the state onto society. The rule form, which unites scientific knowledge with state control in its conception of what law is, institutionalizes the objective stance as jurisprudence.

The state is male jurisprudentially, meaning that it adopts the standpoint of male power on the relation between law and society. This stance is especially vivid in constitutional adjudication, thought legitimate to the degree it is neutral on the policy content of legislation. The foundation for its neutrality is the pervasive assumption that conditions that pertain among men on the basis of gender apply to women as well – that is, the assumption that sex inequality does not really exist in society. The Constitution – the constituting document of this state society – with its interpretations assumes that society, absent government intervention, is free and equal; that its laws, in general, reflect that; and that government need and should right only what government has pre-viously wronged. This posture is structural to a constitution of absti-nence: for example, "Congress shall make no law abridging the freedom of ... speech." Those who have freedoms like equality, liberty, privacy, and speech socially keep them legally, free of governmental intrusion. No one who does not already have them socially is granted them legally.

In this light, once gender is grasped as a means of social stratifica-tion, the status categories basic to medieval law, thought to have been superseded by liberal regimes in aspirational nonhierarchical constructs of abstract personhood, are revealed deeply unchanged. Gender as a status category was simply assumed out of legal existence, suppressed into a presumptively pre-constitutional social order through a constitu-tional structure designed not to reach it. Speaking descriptively rather than functionally or motivationally, the strategy is first to constitute society unequally prior to law; then to design the constitution, including the law of equality, so that all its guarantees apply only to those values that are taken away by law; then to construct legitimating norms so that the state legitimates itself through noninterference with the status quo. Then, so long as male dominance is so effective in society that it is unnecessary to impose sex inequality through law, such that only the most superficial sex inequalities become *de jure,* not even a legal guar-antee of sex equality will produce social equality.

The posture and presumptions of the negative state, the view that government best promotes freedom when it stays out of existing social arrangements, reverberates throughout constitutional law. Doctrinally, it is embodied in rubrics like the "state action" requirement of equal protection law, in the law of freedom of speech, and in the law of privacy. The "state action" requirement restricts the Constitution to securing citizens' equality rights only from violations by governments, not by other citizens. The law of the First Amendment secures freedom of speech only from governmental deprivation. In the law of privacy, governmental intervention itself is unconstitutional.

In terms of judicial role, these notions are defended as the "passive virtues": courts should not (and say they do not) impose their own substantive views on constitutional questions. Judges best vindicate the Constitution when they proceed as if they have no views, when they reflect society back to itself from the angle of vision at which society is refracted to them. In this hall of mirrors, only in extremis shall any man alter what any other man has wrought. The offspring of proper passiv-ity is substancelessness. Law produces its progeny immaculately, with-out messy political intercourse.

Philosophically, this posture is expressed in the repeated constitutional invocation of the superiority of "negative freedom" – staying out, letting be – over positive legal affirmations. Negative liberty gives one the right to be "left to do or be what [he] is able to do or be, without interference from other persons." The state that pursues this value promotes freedom when it does not intervene in the social status quo. Positive freedom, freedom to do rather than to keep from being done to, by distinction, gives one the right to "control or ... determine someone to do, or be, this rather than that." If one group is socially granted the positive freedom to do whatever it wants to another group, to determine that the second group will be and do this rather than that, no amount of negative freedom legally guaranteed to the second group will make it the equal of the first. For women, this has meant that civil society, the domain in which women are distinctively subordinated and deprived of power, has been placed beyond reach of legal guarantees. Women are oppressed socially, prior to law, without express state acts, often in intimate contexts. The negative state cannot address their situation in any but an equal society – the one in which it is needed least.

This posture is enforced through judicial methodology, the formative legal experience for which is *Lochner v. New York,* a case that arose out of the struggle of the working class to extract livable working conditions from a capitalist state through legislated reform. Invalidating legislation that would have restricted the number of hours bakers could work on grounds of freedom of contract, the Supreme Court sided with capitalism over workers. The dissenters' view, ultimately vindicated, was that the majority had superimposed its own views on the Constitution; they, by contrast, would passively reflect the Constitution by upholding the legislation. Soon after, in *Muller v. Oregon,* the Supreme Court upheld restrictive hours legislation for women only. The opinion distinguished *Lochner* on the basis that women's unique frailty, dependency, and breeding capacity placed her "at a disadvantage in the struggle for subsistence." A later ruling, *West Coast Hotel v. Parrish,* generally regarded as ending the *Lochner* era, also used women as a lever against capitalism. Minimum-wage laws were upheld for women because "the exploitation of a class of workers who are in an unequal position with respect to bargaining power and are thus relatively defenseless against the denial of a living wage ... casts a direct burden for their support upon the community."

Concretely, it is unclear whether these special protections, as they came to be called, helped or hurt women. These cases did do something for some workers (female) concretely; they also demeaned all women ideologically. They did assume that women were marginal and second-class members of the workforce; they probably contributed to keeping women marginal and second-class workers by keeping some women from competing with men at the male standard of exploitation. This benefited both male workers and capitalists. These rulings supported one sector of workers against all capitalists by benefiting male workers at the expense of female workers. They did help the working class by setting precedents that eventually supported minimum-wage and maximum-hours laws for all workers. They were a victory against capitalism and for sexism, for some women perhaps at the expense of all women (maybe including those they helped), for the working class perhaps at women's expense, at least so long as they were "women only."

The view of women in *Muller* and *West Coast Hotel* was that of the existing society: demeaning, paternalistic, and largely unrealistic; as with most pedestalization, its concrete benefits were equivocal at best. The view of workers in *Lochner* left capitalism unchecked and would have precluded most New Deal social reforms men wanted. (Protecting all workers was not considered demeaning by anyone.) For these reasons, these cases have come to stand for a critique of substantivity in adjudication as such. But their methodological solution – judicial neutrality – precludes from constitutional relief groups who are socially abject and systematically excluded from the usual political process. Despite universal rejections of "Lochnering," this substantive approach in neutral posture has continued to be incorporated in constitutional method, including in the law of equality. If over half the population has no voice in the Constitution, why is upholding legislation to give them a voice impermissibly substantive and activist, while striking down such legislation is properly substanceless and passive? Is permitting such an interpretation of, for example, the equality principle in a proper case activism, while not permitting it is properly nonsubstantive? Overruling *Lochner* was at least as judicially active as *Lochner* itself was. Further, why are legislation and adjudication regarded as exercises of state power, but passivity in the face of social inequality – even under a constitutional equality principle – is not? The result is, substantivity and activism are hunted down, flailed, and confined, while their twins, neutrality and passivity, roam at large.

To consider the "passive virtues" of judicial restraint as a tool for social change suggests that change for workers was constitutional only because workers were able to get power in legislatures. To achieve such changes by constitutional principle before achieving them socially and politically would be to engage in exactly the kind of substantive judicial activism that those who supported the changes said they opposed. The reasoning was: if courts make substantive decisions, they will express their prejudices, here, exploitive of workers, demeaning and unhelpful of women. The alternatives have been framed, then, as substantive adjudication that demeans and deprives on the one hand, or as substanceless adjudication that, passively virtuous, upholds whatever power can get out of the political process as it is.

The underlying assumption of judicial neutrality is that a status quo exists which is preferable to judicial intervention – a common law status quo, a legislative status quo, an economic status quo, or a gender status quo. For women, it also tends to assume that access to the conventional political realm might be available in the absence of legal rights. At the same time it obscures the possibility that a substantive approach to women's situation could be adequate to women's distinctive social exploitation – ground a claim to civil equality, for example – and do no more to license judicial arbitrariness than current standards do. From women's point of view, adjudications are already substantive; the view from nowhere already has content. *Lochner* saw workers legally the way capitalists see workers socially: as free agents, bargaining at arm's length. *Muller* saw women legally the way men see women socially: as breeders, marginal workers, excludable. If one wants to claim no more for a powerless group than what can be extracted under an established system of power, one can try to abstract them into entitlement by blurring the lines between them and everyone else. Neutrality as pure means makes some sense. If, however, the claim is against the definition and distribution of power itself, one needs a critique not so much of the substantivity of cases like *Lochner* and *Muller,* but of their substance. Such a critique must also include that aspect of the liberal tradition in which one strategy for dominance has been substancelessness.

If the content of positive law is surveyed more broadly from women's point of view, a pattern emerges. The way the male point of view frames an experience is the way it is framed by state policy. Over and over again, the state protects male power through embodying and ensuring existing male control over women at every level – cushioning, qualifying, or *de jure* appearing to prohibit its excesses when necessary to its normalization. *De jure* relations stabilize de facto relations. Laws that touch on sexuality provide illustrations of this argument. As in society, to the extent possession is the point of sex, rape in law is sex with a woman who is not yours, unless the act is so as to make her yours. Social and legal realities are consistent and mutually determinate: since law has never effectively interfered with men's ability to rape women on these terms, it has been unnecessary to make this an express rule of law. Because part of the kick of pornography involves eroticizing the putatively prohibited, obscenity law putatively prohibits pornography enough to maintain its desirability without ever making it unavailable or truly illegitimate. Because the stigma of prostitution is the stigma of sexuality is the stigma of the female gender, prostitution may be legal or illegal, but so long as women are unequal to men and that inequality is sexualized, women will be bought and sold as prostitutes, and law will do nothing about it.

Women as a whole are kept poor, hence socially dependent on men, available for sexual or reproductive use. To the extent that abortion exists to control the reproductive consequences of intercourse, hence to facilitate male sexual access to women, access to abortion will be controlled by "a man or The Man." So long as this is effectively done socially, it is unnecessary to do it by law. Law need merely stand passively by, reflecting the passing scene. The law of sex equality stays as far away as possible from issues of sexuality. Rape, pornography, prostitution, incest, battery, abortion, gay and lesbian rights: none have been sex equality issues under law. In the issues the law of sex discrimination does treat, male is the implicit reference for human, maleness the measure of entitlement to equality. In its mainstream interpretation, this law is neutral: it gives little to women that it cannot also give to men, maintaining sex inequality while appearing to address it. Gender, thus elaborated and sustained by law, is maintained as a division of power. The negative state views gender and sexual relations as neutrally as *Lochner* viewed class relations.

The law on women's situation produced in this way views women's situation from the standpoint of male dominance. It assumes that the conditions that pertain among men on the basis of sex – consent to sex, comparative privacy, voice in moral discourse, and political equality on the basis of gender – apply to women. It assumes on the epistemic level that sex inequality in society is not real. Rape law takes women's usual response to coercion – acquiescence, the despairing response to hopelessness to unequal odds – and calls that consent. Men coerce women; women "consent." The law of privacy treats the private sphere as a sphere of personal freedom. For men, it is. For women, the private is the distinctive sphere of intimate violation and abuse, neither free nor particularly personal. Men's realm of private freedom is women's realm of collective subordination. The law of obscenity treats pornography as "ideas." Whether or not ideas are sex for men, pornography certainly is sex for men. From the standpoint of women, who live the sexual abuse in pornography as everyday life, pornography is reality. The law of obscenity treats regulation of pornography from the standpoint of what is necessary to protect it: as regulation of morals, as some men telling other men what they may not see and do and think and say about sex. From the standpoint of women, whose torture pornography makes entertainment, pornography is the essence of a powerless condition, its effective protection by the state the essence of sexual politics. Obscenity law's "moral ideas" are a political reality of women's subordination. Just as, in male law, public oppression masquerades as private freedom and coercion is guised as consent, in obscenity law real political domination is presented as a discourse in ideas about virtue and vice.

Rape law assumes that consent to sex is as real for women as it is for men. Privacy law assumes that women in private have the same privacy men do. Obscenity law assumes that women have the access to speech men have. Equality law assumes that women are already socially equal to men. Only to the extent women have already achieved social equality does the mainstream law of equality support their inequality claims. The laws of rape, abortion, obscenity, and sex discrimination show how the relation between objectification, understood as the primary process of the subordination of women, and the power of the state is the relation between the personal and the political at the level of government. These laws are not political because the state is presumptively the sphere of politics. They are integral to sexual politics because the state, through law, institutionalizes male power over women through institutionalizing the male point of view in law. Its first state act is to see women from the standpoint of male dominance; its next act is to treat them that way. This power, this state, is not a discrete location, but a web of sanctions throughout society which "control[s] the principal means of coercion" that structures women's everyday lives. The Weberian monopoly on the means of legitimate coercion, thought to distinguish the state as an entity, actually describes the power of men over women in the home, in the bedroom, on the job, in the street, throughout social life. It is difficult, actually, to find a place it does not circumscribe and describe. Men are sovereign in society in the way Austin describes law as sovereign: a person or group whose commands are habitually obeyed and who is not in the habit of obeying anyone else. Men are the group that has had the authority to make law, embodying H.L.A. Hart's "rule of recognition" that, in his conception, makes law authoritative. Distinctively male values (and men) constitute the authoritative interpretive community that makes law distinctively lawlike to the likes of Ronald Dworkin. If one combines "a realistic conception of the state with a revolutionary theory of society," the place of gender in state power is not limited to government, nor is the rule of law limited to police and courts. The rule of law and the rule of men are one thing, indivisible, at once official and unofficial – officially circumscribed, unofficially not. State power, embodied in law, exists throughout society as male power at the same time as the power of men over women throughout society is organized as the power of the state.

Perhaps the failure to consider gender as a determinant of state behavior has made the state's behavior appear indeterminate. Perhaps the objectivity of the liberal state has made it appear autonomous of class. Including, but beyond, the bourgeois in liberal legalism, lies what is male about it. However autonomous of class the liberal state may appear, it is not autonomous of sex. Male power is systemic. Coercive, legitimated, and epistemic, it *is* the regime.

READING QUESTIONS ON MACKINNON

1   What exactly is the tension MacKinnon identifies in the law?
2   Can the tension she identifies form the basis of a progressive legal strategy?

Kathleen A. Kenealy
"Sexual Harassment and the Reasonable Woman Standard" (1992)

The reasonable woman standard is a recent judicial innovation applicable to workplace sexual harassment litigation.[1] The reasonable woman standard assesses the validity of sexual harassment claims from the victim's viewpoint. Under this standard, "a female plaintiff states a prima facie case of hostile environment sexual harassment when she alleges conduct which a reasonable woman would consider sufficiently severe or pervasive to alter the conditions of employment and create an abusive working environment."[2] This new legal standard, if accepted among the federal circuits, could become the prevailing test throughout the country.[3]

While it appears to be a legal victory, the new standard may represent a legal setback for women. The reasonable woman standard, we are told, has been devised to benefit women litigants because "[c]onduct that many men consider unobjectionable may offend many women."[4] The reasonable woman standard appears to represent judicial recognition of the sexism suffered by women in the workplace. But in fact it is an artificial intellectual construct that serves only to obscure and mask the problem of sexual harassment in the workplace, without providing the framework for an effective legal response.

It is interesting to note that courts implementing the reasonable woman standard have provided no gauge for ascertaining the contents of such a standard. They have simply announced that such claims will be analyzed from the viewpoint of a reasonable woman. As such, this "new" standard does not provide a new solution. Although the reasonable person standard can be viewed as a mechanism for enforcing an essentially male viewpoint under the guise of universality, the emerging reasonable woman standard, as it will be defined by a male judiciary, is also likely to constitute a reflection of preexisting norms of womanhood as defined by men. The net result of the reasonable woman standard may end up being merely a shift in perspective, rather than a new framework for analysis. The heralded new solution is really only a Band-Aid when in fact surgery is needed.

At worst the reasonable woman standard could be used in other contexts as a rationale to support the idea that women require special treatment. Women need only look at the debate affirmative action laws have engendered, particularly toward racial minorities, to understand the destructive potential of the reasonable woman standard.[5] Women will have achieved little of value in sexual harassment litigation until courts examine the problem of sexual harassment without focusing on the gender or sensibilities of the victim. In doing so, courts would be recognizing that sexual harassment is a legitimate problem in the workforce, often but not always perpetuated by males. Harassment has nothing whatever to do with a sliding scale of "reasonableness," which is only capable of recognizing a problem when seen through the eyes of a woman. By employing a general reasonableness standard, courts implicitly would recognize that sexual harassment is as visible and recognizable to men as it is to women, and that men whose conduct rises to the level of harassment are neither ignorant nor well-intentioned.

Indeed, sexual harassment has more to do with power than with sex. The respective genders of the actors is simply one aspect of the overall context in which the harassment occurs.[6] The act of sexually harassing a subordinate is a means by which the superior enhances his feelings of power over the victim. By intimidating and manipulating her, the harasser is sending a message to the subordinate that she is in his domain and under his control. Thus, analyzing sexual harassment within a framework of gender-perspective misunderstands the underlying nature of the harassment itself.

Examined in this light, as a power play, the purportedly well-intentioned male to female / supervisor to subordinate "compliment" is not a compliment at all. The true message is not that the object of the comment is a beautiful woman, but that the object is not in control. Typically, courts have recognized this distinction. "A male supervisor might believe, for example, that it is legitimate for him to tell a female subordinate that she has a 'great figure' or 'nice legs.' The female subordinate, however, may find such comments offensive."[7] Any reasonably alert woman would find such comments offensive because such comments are not intended to compliment her and make her feel good, nor are they about her beauty or her body. Rather, in the context of a work environment, superior to subordinate, the comments are intended to notify her that her separate status as a female has not been forgotten and that she is unlike those around her. The boss, presumably busy with other duties, has not taken the time to visit her and praise her good work, her superior skill. Instead he has made it a point to notice her physical attributes and ensure that she understand she has been placed within the confines of her body. She is surplusage, not a member of the team.[8]

Because the reasonable woman standard scrutinizes the perspective of the victim rather than the circumstances existing in the workplace, it dilutes the impact of sexual harassment claims brought by women plaintiffs. Before the new standard, litigants theoretically came before a court on equal footing. The reasonable woman standard abandons the notion that reasonableness is a largely objective criterion and endorses the idea that reasonableness is in the eye of the beholder. In effect, men are objectively reasonable while women possess some other undefined viewpoint, thus requiring special treatment and a special legal standard.[9] The dissenter in *Ellison v. Brady* aptly wrote that "[a]pplication of the 'new standard' presents a puzzlement which is born of the assumption that men's eyes do not see what a woman sees through her eyes."[10]

While it is likely that women often are more victimized by workplace harassment than men, both men and women can be the objects of harassment. As such, a workable legal standard ought to be gender neutral and independent of the characteristics of the plaintiff.[11] Rather than reflecting the differences in perspective and experience between men and women, the reasonable woman standard functions as a disclaimer. The new standard serves to exculpate male conduct that should be recognizable as offensive and disturbing by both men and women. Whether or not sexual harassment occurred ought to be more a question of fact than a matter of perspective.[12] Instead, the law now says that some well-intentioned behavior, when filtered through the perspective of the victim, is transformed into harassment.

The reasonable woman standard threatens to inject needless confusion into the law by attempting to convert a general standard into an ambiguous individualized standard. It is true that men and women face a society that does not view them as equals. Consequently, both men and women often may have differing perspectives and sensitivities, either individually or as a group. Dissimilarities, however, should not be ingrained into a reasonableness standard.

Any reasonableness standard will embody some level of subjectivity when it is made applicable to the facts of a particular case.

[T]he infinite variety of situations which may arise makes it impossible to fix definite rules in advance for all conceivable human conduct. ... The standard of conduct which the community demands must be an external and objective one, rather than the individual judgment, good or bad, of the particular actor ... since the law can have no favorites. At the same time, it must make proper allowance for the risk apparent to the actor, for his capacity to meet it, and for the circumstances under which he must act.[13]

Thus, because a determination of reasonableness can be assessed only within the context of a given factual scenario, the linchpin in the analysis of whether or not sexual harassment has occurred should be overall context and not the nature of the victim.

REASONABLE WOMAN STANDARD SIDESTEPS THE ISSUE

The reasonable woman standard has less to do with judicial concern for women victims of sexual harassment than it does with the reluctance of courts to deal squarely with sexual harassment and to recognize it when it occurs.[14] By suggesting that incidents of harassment merely are misunderstood compliments,[15] this legal standard of plausible deniability allows both harassers and society to evade responsibility for harassment. It institutionalizes and trivializes the perceived severity of sexual harassment. If sexual harassment were truly a serious problem, surely it would be recognizable as such by reasonable men. Through the reasonable woman standard, courts send a different message: Men, intending only to be complimentary, unknowingly sexually harass women. Because women find it so unsettling, the courts will recognize a cause of action which would otherwise go undetected by reasonable men. Buttressing the notion that male harassers are not aware of the nature of their actions, the *Ellison* court suggested that "employers may have to educate and sensitize their workforce" in order to eliminate harassing conduct.[16]

Analyzing the facts from the victim's perspective tends to exculpate the harasser.[17] For example, although the court in *Ellison* held that the male employee, Gray, engaged in sexually harassing conduct, it stressed the "importance of considering the victim's perspective."[18] "Analyzing the facts from the alleged harasser's viewpoint, Gray could be portrayed as a modern-day Cyrano de Bergerac wishing no more than to woo Ellison with his words."[19] The court went on, "[e]xamined in this light, it is not difficult to see why the district court characterized Gray's conduct as isolated and trivial."[20] In noting that the conduct could be characterized as "isolated and trivial," while at the same time finding that the victim stated a cause of action for sexual harassment,[21] the court conveyed a message that while sexual harassment is not a serious issue, a remedy will be provided to women because they find it so upsetting.

In *Ellison*, the court gave its rationale for the new standard. Any "sex-blind reasonable person standard tends to be male biased and tends to systematically ignore the experiences of women."[22] If this is so, then the question arises whether race-blind standards are "white" biased, thereby systematically ignoring the experiences of other races. While a reasonable African-American standard or a reasonable Japanese-American standard would account for differences among groups, further subdivision of the reasonable man standard needlessly will complicate the law. The standard of objectivity already in place can account for some of the subjective qualities of the reasonable person.

[I]t would appear that there is no standardized man; that there is only in part an objective test; that there is no such thing as reasonable or unreasonable conduct except as viewed with reference to certain qualities of the actor – his physical attributes, his intellectual powers, probably, if superior, his knowledge and the knowledge he would have acquired had he exercised standard moral and at least average mental qualities at the time of action or at some connected time.[23]

The reasonable woman standard assumes that members of disparate groups have disparate sensibilities and cannot recognize behavior that is offensive to members of other groups. But this is not necessarily so.[24] Simply because individuals have differing perspectives does not mean that they are incapable of understanding the reasonableness or unreasonableness of conduct in various settings. It does not take a reasonable African-American standard for one to recognize that a noose hung over an employee's work station is a racially hostile act.[25] Neither is a reasonable woman standard necessary for men to recognize sexual harassment.

FOCUS ON THE VICTIM

In *Robinson v. Jacksonville Shipyards, Inc.*, the court noted that "the standards for assessing women's psychological harm due to harassment must begin to reflect women's sensitivity to behavior once condoned as acceptable."[26] Trivializing the nature of sexual harassment, the statement conveys the message that a woman's point of view is needed in order for the law to reflect her *sensitivity* to such behavior. Harassers, it seems, are simply insensitive and mistakenly think that their behavior is flattering or courtly. The idea that men are incapable of recognizing harassment because they have long viewed it as acceptable makes no more sense than the proposition that racist remarks at a Ku Klux Klan rally are spoken innocently and without understanding as to their wrongfulness because this behavior has been condoned as acceptable by Klansmen. However, we are told that sexism, which cuts across humanity in all its racial variations, must be viewed through the eyes of women, for only then can it be seen.

By examining the effect of the conduct at issue on its target, the reasonable woman standard takes the court's focus off of the harasser and focuses instead on the victim.[27] Sexual harassment, we are told, is primarily a woman's problem anyway. Analyzing workplace norms, one writer opined that "[b]ecause of the inequality and coercion with which it is so frequently associated *in the minds of women*, the appearance of sexuality in an unexpected context or a setting of ostensible equality can be an anguishing experience."[28] Sexual harassment, it seems, is more a matter of perception than a fact of reality.[29]

CONCLUSION

While some courts may have created the reasonable woman standard in response to a lack of recognition by other judicial bodies of sexual harassment claims,[30] such good intentions could prove detrimental to women in the long run. A better course may be to examine sexual harassment through a totality of the circumstances framework, without focusing the legal analysis on the perspective of a reasonable woman.[31] In doing so, courts would be at once recognizing that reasonable women are as reasonable as anyone else, and that sexual harassment is recognizable by both men and women.

At bottom, the reasonable woman standard sends a message to women that they are inherently unreasonable. If they were objectively reasonable, a separate legal standard would not be necessary. Further, it minimizes the objective severity of a legally cognizable claim of sexual harassment. Male judges, however, are saying that the harassment is "trivial and isolated" *to them*. Nonetheless, the courts extend a paternalistic hand to protect the victim. In sum, the reasonable woman standard moves courts and women onto shaky ground. For the courts, it undermines the analytical integrity of sexual harassment law and it threatens to spill over into other legal areas. For women, the result is to relegate them into a new, different, and ill-defined status.

NOTES

1 This article is not intended to provide an academic treatment of sexual harassment law and the reasonable woman standard. Instead, the author presents a critical analysis of the reasonable woman standard and examines the impact of such a standard on both sexual harassment claims and women in general. This essay discusses the reasonable woman standard as applied to hostile work environment cases brought pursuant to title VII of the Civil Rights Act of 1964, as amended, 42 USC § 2000e (1982). For a general discussion of sexual harassment and the reasonable woman standard, see Steven H. Winterbauer, "Sexual Harassment – The Reasonable Woman Standard," 7 Lab Lawyer 811 (1991).

2 *Ellison v. Brady*, 924 F2d 872, 879 (9th Cir. 1991) (footnotes and citations omitted).

3 The reasonable woman standard has been adopted in at least three federal appellate jurisdictions: *Yates v. Avco Corp.*, 819 F2d 630, 637 (6th Cir. 1087); *Andrews v. City of Philadelphia*, 895 F2d 1469, 1482 (3d Cir. 1989); *Ellison*, 924 F2d 872.

4 *Ellison*, 924 F2d at 879. Thus, "[i]f we only examined whether a reasonable person would engage in allegedly harassing conduct, we would run the risk of reinforcing the prevailing level of discrimination." Id at 878. This is curious reasoning which appears to suggest that, because sexual harassment is considered normal and indeed reasonable by many men, courts are powerless to intervene. However, "[i]f the pervasiveness of an abuse makes it nonactionable, no inequality sufficiently institutionalized to merit a law against it would be actionable." *Robinson v. Jacksonville Shipyards, Inc.*, 760 F Supp 1486, 1526 (MD Fla 1991), quoting C. MacKinnon, *Feminism Unmodified*, 115 (1987).

5 See, for example, *Chicago Tribune*, Dec 1, 1991, at 25 (fears surrounding affirmative action are not always justified); *Washington Post*, May 21, 1991, at B1 (Georgetown law student accuses school of admitting unqualified applicants based on racial quotas).

6 See, for example, C. MacKinnon, *Sexual Harassment of Working Women* (1979), "women are sexually harassed by men because they are women, that is, because of the social meaning of female sexuality ..." Id at 174.

7 *Yates*, 819 F2d at 637 n2.

8 But see *Robinson*, 760 F Supp at 1623, recognizing that sexual harassment claims recognize such intentions: "This third category describes behavior that creates a barrier to the progress of women in the workplace because it conveys the message that they do not belong, that they are welcome in the workplace only if they will subvert their identities to the sexual stereotypes prevalent in that environment."

9 This is not a new idea. See, for example, Simone De Beauvior, *The Second Sex* (1974) ("She has no grasp, even in thought, on the reality around her. It is opaque to her eyes.") Id at 665.

10 924 F2d at 884 (Stephens, J. dissenting).

11 The tort standard of the reasonable man, now often referred to as the reasonable person, "refers to the average adult person, regardless of gender, and the conduct that can reasonably be expected of him or her." Id.

12 Some, if not most, feminist scholars have rejected this position. See, for example, Christine A. Littleton, "Book Review: Feminist Jurisprudence:

The Difference Method Makes," 41 Stan L Rev 751, 770–71 (1989) ("Retreating to some hypothetical 'neutral' viewpoint is, in practice if not theory, capitulation to make ideology.")

13 Keeton, Dobbs, Keeton & Owen, eds, *Prosser and Keeton on Torts,* 32 (5th ed. 1984).

14 See *Ellison,* 924 F2d at 878. ("Conduct that many men consider unobjectionable may offend many women.") It is also true that conduct offensive to Jewish persons is not offensive to anti-Semites. But courts do not assert that it is thus necessary to resort to a special standard of reasonableness in order to recognize crimes when they occur.

15 Id at 880.

16 Id.

17 See, for example, Susan Estrich, "Sex at Work," 43 Stan L Rev 813 (1991) (discussing and comparing, *inter alia,* the focus on the victim in both sexual harassment law and rape law).

18 *Ellison*; 924 F2d at 880.

19 Id.

20 Id.

21 Id at 878. ("We believe Gray's conduct was sufficiently severe and pervasive to alter the conditions of Ellison's employment and create an abusive working environment.")

22 Id at 879.

23 W. Seavey, "Negligence – Subjective or Objective," 41 Harv L Rev 1, 27 (1927). Although this statement of the reasonable person standard is applicable to negligence, there seems no reason that it could not apply in sexual harassment litigation.

24 *Ellison,* 924 F2d at 884 (Stephens, J. dissenting).

25 *Vance v. Southern Bell Telephone,* 863 F2d 1503, 1510 (11th Cir. 1989).

26 760 F Supp 1486, 1526 (MD Fla 1991), quoting, Note, "The Aftermath of Meritor: A Search for Standards in the Law of Sexual Harassment," 98 Yale LJ 1717, 1737–38 (1989). One wonders: acceptable to whom?

27 This is unlike tort law, for example, where the reasonableness standard measures the conduct of the one charged.

28 *Ellison,* 924 F2d at 879, quoting Abrams, "Gender Discrimination and the Transformation of Workplace Norms," 42 Vand L Rev 1183, 1205 (1989) (emphasis added).

29 Focusing on the victim also removes sexism and sexual harassment from the realm of a societal (indeed global) problem and converts it into a women's issue. "Because women are disproportionately victims of rape

and sexual assault, women have a stronger incentive to be concerned with sexual behavior." *Ellison*, 924 F2d at 879.
30 Id at 877.
31 In discrimination cases, the EEOC Guidelines direct the court to consider "the record as a whole and ... the totality of the circumstances, such as the nature of the sexual advances and the context in which the alleged incidents occurred." 29 CFR 1604.11(b) (1986).

READING QUESTIONS ON KENEALY

1 Why, in Kenealy's view, does the "reasonable woman" standard misconstrue and trivialize the nature of sexual harassment? Is she right?
2 What is the alternative standard that Kenealy proposes, and is it any different from the traditional standard of the "reasonable person"? What do you think MacKinnon would say about it? Do you think there is any version of the "reasonable person" standard that could escape her objection that the law "views women's situation from the standpoint of male dominance"?

Ellison v. Brady, 924 F.2d 872 (U.S.A. 9th Circuit, 1991)

Kerry Ellison, a revenue agent for the IRS in California, brought a complaint against her employer under Title VII of the *Civil Rights Act*. She argued that she had been subjected to hostile-environment sexual harassment as a result of another employee, Sterling Gray. One of the issues before the court was the appropriate test for hostile-environment sexual harassment.

Beezer, Circuit Judge: –

The parties ask us to determine if Gray's conduct, as alleged by Ellison, was sufficiently severe or pervasive to alter the conditions of Ellison's employment and create an abusive working environment. The district court, with the Ninth Circuit case law to look to for guidance, held that

Ellison did not state a prima facie case of sexual harassment due to a hostile working environment. It believed that Gray's conduct was "isolated and trivial." We disagree.

... The EEOC guidelines describe hostile environment harassment as "conduct [which] has the purpose or effect of unreasonably interfering with an individual's work performance or creating an intimidating, hostile or offensive working environment" ...

We have closely examined *Meritor* and our previous cases, and we believe Gray's conduct was sufficiently severe and pervasive to alter the conditions of Ellison's employment and create an abusive working environment ...

Next, we believe that in evaluating the severity and pervasiveness of sexual harassment, we should focus on the perspective of the victim ... If we only examined whether a reasonable person would engage in allegedly harassing conduct, we would run the risk of reinforcing the prevailing level of discrimination. Harassers could continue to harass merely because a particular discriminatory practice was common, and victims of harassment would have no remedy.

We therefore prefer to analyze harassment from the victim's perspective. A complete understanding of the victim's view requires, among other things, an analysis of the different perspectives of men and women. Conduct that many men consider unobjectionable may offend many women. See, e.g., *Lipsett v. University of Puerto Rico*, 864 F.2d. 881, 898 (1st Cir. 1988) ("A male supervisor may believe, for example, that it is legitimate for him to tell a female subordinate that she has a 'great figure' or 'nice legs.' The female subordinate, however, may find such comments offensive") ...

We realize that there is a broad range of viewpoints among women as a group, but we believe that many women share common concerns which men do not necessarily share. For example, because women are disproportionately victims of rape and sexual assault, women have a stronger incentive to be concerned with sexual behaviour. Women who are victims of mild forms of sexual harassment may understandably worry whether a harasser's conduct is merely a prelude to violent sexual assault. Men, who are rarely victims of sexual assault, may view sexual conduct in a vacuum without a full apprehension of the social setting or the underlying threat of violence that a woman may perceive ...

We adopt the perspective of a reasonable woman primarily because we believe that a sex-blind reasonable person standard tends to be male-biased and tends to systematically ignore the experiences of real women. The reasonable woman standard does not establish a higher level of protection for women than for men. Instead, a gender-conscious examination of sexual harassment enables women to participate in the workplace on an equal footing with men. By acknowledging and not trivializing the effects of sexual harassment on reasonable women, courts can work towards ensuring that neither men nor women will have to "run a gauntlet of sexual abuse in return for the privilege of being allowed to work and make a living" ...

We note that the reasonable victim standard we adopt today classifies conduct as unlawful sexual harassment even when harassers do not realize that their conduct creates a hostile working environment. Well-intentioned compliments by co-workers and supervisors can form the basis of a sexual harassment cause of action if a reasonable victim of the same sex as the plaintiff would consider the comments sufficiently severe or pervasive to alter a condition of employment or create an abusive working environment ...

The facts of this case illustrate the importance of considering the victim's perspective. Analyzing the facts from the alleged harasser's viewpoint, Gray could be portrayed as a modern-day Cyrano de Bergerac, wishing no more than to woo Ellison with his words. There is no evidence that Gray harbored ill will toward Ellison. He even offered in his "love letter" to leave her alone if she wished. Examined in this light, it is not difficult to see why the district court characterized Gray's conduct as isolated and trivial.

Ellison, however, did not consider the acts to be trivial. Gray's first note shocked and frightened her. After receiving the three page letter, she became really upset and frightened again. She immediately requested that she or Gray be transferred. Her supervisor's prompt response suggests that she too did not consider the conduct trivial. When Ellison learned that Gray arranged to return to San Mateo, she immediately asked to transfer, and she immediately filed an official complaint.

We cannot say as a matter of law that Ellison's reaction was idiosyncratic or hyper-sensitive. We believe that a reasonable woman could have had a similar reaction. After receiving her first bizarre note from Gray, a person she barely knew, Ellison asked a co-worker to tell Gray to leave her alone. Despite her request, Gray sent her a long, passionate, disturbing letter. He told her he had been "watching" and "experiencing" her; he made repeated references to sex; he said he would write again. Ellison had no way of knowing what Gray would do next. A reasonable woman would consider Gray's conduct, as alleged by

Ellison, sufficiently severe and pervasive to alter a condition of employment and create an abusive working environment.

Sexual harassment is a major problem in the workplace. Adopting the victim's perspective ensures that courts will not "sustain ingrained notions of reasonable behavior fashioned by the offenders." We hope that over time both men and women will learn what conduct offends reasonable members of the other sex. When employers and employees internalize the standards of workplace conduct we establish today, the current gap in perception between the sexes will be bridged.

READING QUESTIONS ON *ELLISON V. BRADY*

1 Is Beezer, J. correct to assume that the ideal of the "reasonable person" is flawed, in the context of sexual harassment law? Does it inevitably reinforce prevailing forms of discrimination, as he suggests?
2 Do you think the standard of "the reasonable woman" is an improvement? Why, or why not?

R. v. S. (RD) [1997] 3 SCR 484

R.D.S. was a 15-year-old African Canadian charged with unlawfully assaulting a white police officer. The police officer and R.D.S. were the only witnesses at trial, and their accounts differed widely. The trial judge, Justice Sparks, weighed the evidence and determined that R.D.S. should be acquitted. While delivering her oral reasons, Justice Sparks remarked that police officers have been known to overreact, particularly with non-white groups, and that this raised a doubt in her mind about the state of mind of the officer. The Crown challenged these comments, arguing that Justice Sparks failed to base her decision on the evidence presented at trial and that she violated the requirement that courts proceed in a manner that is free from a reasonable apprehension of bias. The majority of the Supreme Court held that the decision had been based on evidence, and that there was no reasonable apprehension of bias.

Major, J. dissenting (writing for himself and Lamer, C.J.C. and Sopinka, J.) –

I have read the reasons of Justices L'Heureux-Dubé and McLachlin and those of Justice Cory [judgment not included] and respectfully disagree with the conclusion they reach.

The appellant (accused) R.D.S. was a young person charged with assault on a peace officer. At trial, the Crown's only evidence came from the police officer allegedly assaulted. The appellant testified as the only witness in his defence. The testimony of the two witnesses differed in material respects. The trial judge gave judgment immediately after closing arguments and acquitted the appellant.

This appeal should not be decided on questions of racism but instead on how courts should decide cases. In spite of the submissions of the appellant and interveners on his behalf, the case is primarily about the conduct of the trial. A fair trial is one that is based on the law, the outcome of which is determined by the evidence, free of bias, real or apprehended. Did the trial judge here reach her decision on the evidence presented at the trial or did she rely on something else?

In the course of her judgment the trial judge said:

The Crown says, well, why would the officer say that events occurred the way in which he has relayed them to the Court this morning. I am not saying *that the Constable has misled the court, although police officers have been known to do that in the past*. I am not saying that the officer overreacted, *but certainly police officers do overreact, particularly when they are dealing with non-white groups. That to me indicates a state of mind right there that is questionable.* I believe that probably the situation in this particular case is the case of a young police officer who overreacted. I do accept the evidence of [R.D.S.] that he was told to shut up or he would be under arrest. *It seems to be in keeping with the prevalent attitude of the day.*

At any rate, *based upon my comments and based upon all the evidence before the court I have no other choice but to acquit.* [emphasis added]

In view of the manner in which this appeal was argued, it is necessary to consider two points. First, we should consider whether the trial judge in her reasons, properly instructed herself on the evidence or was an error of law committed by her. The second, and somewhat intertwined question, is whether her comments above could cause a reasonable observer to apprehend bias. The offending comments in the statement are:

(i) "police officers have been known to [mislead the court] in the past";

(ii) "police officers do overreact, particularly when they are dealing with non-white groups";

(iii) "[t]hat to me indicates a state of mind right there that is questionable";

(iv) "[i]t seems to be in keeping with the prevalent attitude of the day"; and,

(v) "based upon my comments and based upon all the evidence before the court I have no other choice but to acquit."

The trial judge stated that "police officers have been known to [mislead the court] in the past" and that "police officers do overreact, particularly when they are dealing with non-white groups" and went on to say "[t]hat to me indicates a state of mind right there that is questionable." She in effect was saying, "sometimes police lie and overreact in dealing with non-whites, therefore I have a suspicion that this police officer may have lied and overreacted in dealing with this non-white accused." This was stereotyping all police officers as liars and racists, and applied this stereotype to the police officer in the present case. The trial judge might be perceived as assigning less weight to the police officer's evidence because he is testifying in the prosecution of an accused who is of a different race. Whether racism exists in our society is not the issue. The issue is whether there was evidence before the court upon which to base a finding that *this* particular police officer's actions were motivated by racism. There was no evidence of this presented at the trial ...

In addition to not being based on the evidence, the trial judge's comments have been challenged as giving rise to a reasonable apprehension of bias. The test for finding a reasonable apprehension of bias has challenged courts in the past. It is interchangeably expressed as a "real danger of bias," a "real likelihood of bias," a "reasonable suspicion of bias" and in several other ways. An attempt at a new definition will not change the test. Lord Denning MR captured the essence of the inquiry in his judgment in *Metropolitan Properties Co. v. Lannon*, [1969] 1 QB 577 (CA), at p. 599:

[I]n considering whether there was a real likelihood of bias, the court does not look at the mind of the justice himself or at the mind of the chairman of the tribunal, or whoever it may be, who sits in a judicial capacity. It does not look to see if there was a real likelihood that he would, or did, in fact favour one side at the expense of the other. The court looks at the impression which would be given to other people. Even if he was as impartial as could be, nevertheless if right-minded persons would think that, in the circumstances, there was a real likelihood of bias on his part, then he should not sit ... The reason is plain enough. Justice must be rooted in confidence: and confidence is destroyed when right-minded people go away thinking: "The judge was biased."

The appellant and the interveners argued that the trial judge's statements were simply a review of the evidence and were her reasons for judgment. They said she was relying on her life experience and to deny that is to deny reality. I disagree.

The life experience of this trial judge, as with all trial judges, is an important ingredient in the ability to understand human behaviour, to weigh the evidence, and to determine credibility. It helps in making a myriad of decisions arising during the course of most trials. It is of no value, however, in reaching conclusions for which there is no evidence. The fact that on some other occasions police officers have lied or overreacted is irrelevant. Life experience is not a substitute for evidence. There was no evidence before the trial judge to support the conclusions she reached.

The trial judge could not decide this case based on what some police officers did in the past without deciding that all police officers are the same. As stated, the appellant was entitled to call evidence of the police officer's conduct to show that there was in fact evidence to support either his bias or racism. No such evidence was called. The trial judge presumably called upon her life experience to decide the issue. This she was not entitled to do.

The bedrock of our jurisprudence is the adversary system. Criminal prosecutions are less adversarial because of the Crown's duty to present all the evidence fairly. The system depends on each side's producing facts by way of evidence from which the court decides the issues. Our system, unlike some others, does not permit a judge to become an independent investigator to seek out the facts.

Canadian courts have, in recent years, criticized the stereotyping of people into what is said to be predictable behaviour patterns. If a judge in a sexual assault case instructed the jury or him- or herself that because the complainant was a prostitute he or she probably consented, or that prostitutes are likely to lie about such things as sexual assault, that decision would be reversed. Such presumptions have no place in a system of justice that treats all witnesses equally. Our jurisprudence prohibits tying credibility to something as irrelevant as gender, occupation or perceived group predisposition ...

In my opinion the comments of the trial judge fall into stereotyping the police officer. She said, among other things, that police officers have been known to mislead the courts, and that police officers overreact when dealing with non-white groups. She then held, in her evaluation of this particular police officer's evidence, that these factors led her to "a state of mind right there that is questionable." The trial judge erred in law by failing to base her conclusions on evidence.

Judges, as arbiters of truth, cannot judge credibility based on irrelevant witness characteristics. All witnesses must be placed on equal footing before the court ...

L'Heureux-Dubé and McLachlin, JJ. [These two judges found that the trial judge's comments were based upon the evidence, and that even if they had not been, they would not have given rise to a reasonable apprehension of bias. What follows is an extract from their analysis of the test for a reasonable apprehension of bias.]

In our view, the test for reasonable apprehension of bias established in the jurisprudence is reflective of the reality that while judges can never be neutral, in the sense of purely objective, they can and must strive for impartiality. It therefore recognizes as inevitable and appropriate that the differing experiences of judges assist them in their decision-making process and will be reflected in their judgments, so long as those experiences are relevant to the cases, are not based on inappropriate stereotypes, and do not prevent a fair and just determination of the cases based on the facts in evidence ...

... [I]t is necessary to distinguish between the impartiality which is required of all judges, and the concept of judicial neutrality. The distinction we would draw is that reflected in the insightful words of Benjamin N. Cardozo in *The Nature of the Judicial Process* (1921), at pp. 12–13 and 167, where he affirmed the importance of impartiality, while at the same time recognizing the fallacy of judicial neutrality:

There is in each of us a stream of tendency, whether you choose to call it philosophy or not, which gives coherence and direction to thought and action. Judges cannot escape that current any more than other mortals. All their lives, forces which they do not recognize and cannot name, have been tugging at them – inherited instincts, traditional beliefs, acquired convictions; and the resultant is an outlook on life, a conception of social needs ... In this mental background every problem finds its setting. We may try to see things as objectively as we please. None the less, we can never see them with any eyes except our own ...

Cardozo recognized that objectivity was an impossibility because judges, like all other humans, operate from their own perspectives. As the Canadian Judicial Council noted in *Commentaries on Judicial Conduct* (1991), at p. 12, "[t]here is no human being who is not the product of every social experience, every process of education, and every human contact." What is possible and desirable, they note, is impartiality:

... the wisdom required of a judge is to recognize, consciously allow for, and perhaps to question, all the baggage of past attitudes and sympathies that fellow citizens are free to carry, untested, to the grave. True impartiality does not require that the judge have no sympathies or opinions; it requires that the judge nevertheless be free to entertain and act upon different points of view with an open mind.

The presence or absence of an apprehension of bias is evaluated through the eyes of the reasonable, informed, practical and realistic person who considers the matter in some detail (*Committee for Justice and Liberty, supra*). The person postulated is not a "very sensitive or scrupulous" person, but rather a right-minded person familiar with the circumstances of the case.

It follows that one must consider the reasonable person's knowledge and understanding of the judicial process and the nature of judging as well as of the community in which the alleged crime occurred.

As discussed above, judges in a bilingual, multiracial and multicultural society will undoubtedly approach the task of judging from their varied perspectives. They will certainly have been shaped by, and have gained insight from, their different experiences, and cannot be expected to divorce themselves from these experiences on the occasion of their appointment to the bench. In fact, such a transformation would deny society the benefit of the valuable knowledge gained by the judiciary while they were members of the Bar. As well, it would preclude the achievement of a diversity of backgrounds in the judiciary ...

A reasonable person[,] far from being troubled by this process, would see it as an important aid to judicial impartiality.

The reasonable person ... is an informed and right-minded member of the community, a community which, in Canada, supports the fundamental principles entrenched in the Constitution by the *Canadian Charter of Rights and Freedoms*. Those fundamental principles include the principles of equality set out in s. 15 of the *Charter* and endorsed in nation-wide quasi-constitutional provincial and federal human rights legislation. The reasonable person must be taken to be aware of the history of discrimination faced by disadvantaged groups in Canadian society protected by the *Charter*'s equality provisions. These are matters of which judicial notice may be taken. In *Parks, supra*, at p. 342, Doherty, J.A., did just this, stating:

Racism, and in particular anti-black racism, is a part of our community's psyche. A significant segment of our community holds overtly racist views. A much larger segment subconsciously operates on the basis of negative racial stereotypes. Furthermore, our institutions, including the criminal justice system, reflect and perpetuate those negative stereotypes.

The reasonable person is not only a member of the Canadian community, but also, more specifically, is a member of the local communities in which the case at issue arose (in this case, the Nova Scotian and Halifax communities). Such a person must be taken to possess knowledge of the local population and its racial dynamics, including the existence in the community of a history of widespread and systemic discrimination against black and aboriginal people, and high profile clashes between the police and the visible minority population over policing issues: *Royal Commission on the Donald Marshall Jr. Prosecution* (1989); *R. v. Smith* (1991), 109 NSR (2d) 394 (Co. Ct.). The reasonable person must thus be deemed to be cognizant of the existence of racism in Halifax, Nova Scotia. It follows that judges may take notice of actual racism known to exist in a particular society. Judges have done so with respect to racism in Nova Scotia. In *Nova Scotia (Minister of Community Services) v. S.M.S.* (1992), 110 NSR (2d) 91 (Fam. Ct.), it was stated at p. 108:

[Racism] is a pernicious reality. The issue of racism existing in Nova Scotia has been well documented in the Marshall Inquiry Report (sub. nom. *Royal Commission on the Donald Marshall, Jr., Prosecution*). A person would have to be stupid, complacent or ignorant not to acknowledge its presence, not only individually, but also systemically and institutionally.

... While it seems clear that Judge Sparks *did not in fact* relate the officer's probable overreaction to the race of the appellant R.D.S., it should be noted that if Judge Sparks *had* chosen to attribute the behaviour of Constable Stienburg to the racial dynamics of the situation, she would not necessarily have erred. As a member of the community, it was open to her to take into account the well-known presence of racism in that community and to evaluate the evidence as to what occurred against that background.

That Judge Sparks recognized that police officers *sometimes* overreact when dealing with non-white groups simply demonstrates that in making her determination in this case, she was alive to the well-known racial dynamics that may exist in interactions between police officers and visible minorities. As found by Freeman, J.A. in his dissenting judgment at the Court of Appeal (1995), 145 NSR (2d) 284, at p. 294:

The case was racially charged, a classic confrontation between a white police officer representing the power of the state and a black youth charged with an offence. Judge Sparks was under a duty to be sensitive to the nuances and implications, and to rely on her own common sense which is necessarily informed by her own experience and understanding.

Given these facts, the question is whether a reasonable and right-minded person, informed of the circumstances of this case, and knowledgeable about the local community and about Canadian *Charter* values, would perceive that the reasons of Judge Sparks would give rise to a reasonable apprehension of bias. In our view, they would not. The clear evidence of prejudgment required to sustain a reasonable apprehension of bias is nowhere to be found.

Judge Sparks' oral reasons show that she approached the case with an open mind, used her experience and knowledge of the community to achieve an understanding of the reality of the case, and applied the fundamental principle of proof beyond a reasonable doubt. Her comments were based entirely on the case before her, were made after a consideration of the conflicting testimony of the two witnesses and in response to the Crown's submissions, and were entirely supported by the evidence. In alerting herself to the racial dynamic in the case, she was simply engaging in the process of contextualized judging which, in our view, was entirely proper and conducive to a fair and just resolution of the case before her.

1 What is the distinction that McLachlin and L'Heureux-Dubé JJ. are attempting to draw between "neutrality" or "objectivity," on the one hand, and "impartiality," on the other? Do you think it is sustainable?
2 McLachlin and L'Heureux-Dubé JJ. imply that, in adjudicating any type of case, Canadian judges ought to reason in light of their own experiences and also in light of the broad values underlying the *Charter*. What would the different authors we examined in chapter 1 say about this? Would they regard such adjudication as appropriate or inappropriate?
3 Does it make a difference to your evaluation of Justice Sparks's comments to know that she is herself non-white? Should it make a difference?

Lavallee v. The Queen (1990) 55 CCC (3d) 97

Lyn Lavallee killed her abusive spouse and successfully argued that she was defending herself. The case, decided by the Supreme Court of Canada, reveals ways in which the law has attempted to integrate the sort of concerns raised by MacKinnon.

Wilson, J.: – The narrow issue raised on this appeal is the adequacy of a trial judge's instructions to the jury regarding expert evidence. The broader issue concerns the utility of expert evidence in assisting a jury confronted by a plea of self-defence to a murder charge by a common law wife who had been battered by the deceased.

1 THE FACTS

The appellant, who was 22 years old at the time, had been living with Kevin Rust for some three to four years. Their residence was the scene of a boisterous party on August 30, 1986. In the early hours of August 31st, after most of the guests had departed, the appellant and Rust had an argument in the upstairs bedroom which was used by the appellant. Rust was killed by a single shot in the back of the head from a .303 calibre rifle fired by the appellant as he was leaving the room.

The appellant did not testify but her statement made to police on the night of the shooting was put in evidence. Portions of it read as follows:

Me and Wendy argued as usual and I ran in the house after Kevin pushed me. I was scared, I was really scared. I locked the door. Herb was downstairs with Joanne and I called for Herb but I was crying when I called him. I said, "Herb come up here please." Herb came up to the top of the stairs and I told him that Kevin was going to hit me actually beat on me again. Herb said he knew and that if I was his old lady things would be different, he gave me a hug. OK, we're friends, there's nothing between us. He said, "Yeah, I know" and he went outside to talk to Kevin leaving the door unlocked. I went upstairs and hid in my closet from Kevin. I was so scared ... My window was open and I could hear Kevin asking questions about what I was doing and what I was saying. Next thing I know he was coming up the stairs for me. He came into my bedroom and said, "Wench, where are you?" And he turned on my light and he said, "Your purse is on the floor," and he kicked it. OK then he turned and he saw me in the closet. He wanted me to come out but I didn't want to come out because I was scared. I was so scared. [The officer who took the statement then testified that the appellant started to cry at this point and stopped after a minute or two.] He grabbed me by the arm right there. There's a bruise on my face also where he slapped me. He didn't slap me right then. First he yelled at me then he pushed me and I pushed him back and he hit me twice on the right-hand side of my head. I was scared. All I thought about was all the other times he used to beat me, I was scared, I was shaking as usual. The rest is a blank, all I remember is he gave me the gun and a shot was fired through my screen. This is all so fast. And then the guns were in another room, and he loaded it the second shot and gave it to me. And I was going to shoot myself. I pointed it to myself, I was so upset. OK and then he went and I was sitting on the bed and he started going like this with his finger [the appellant made a shaking motion with an index finger] and said something like "You're my old lady and you do as you're told" or something like that. He said, "Wait till everybody leaves, you'll get it then," and he said something to the effect of "either you kill me or I'll get you" that was what it was. He kind of smiled and then he turned around. I shot him but I aimed out. I thought I aimed above him and a piece of his head went that way.

The relationship between the appellant and Rust was volatile and punctuated by frequent arguments and violence. They would apparently fight for two or three days at a time or several times a week. Considerable evidence was led at trial indicating that the appellant was frequently a victim of physical abuse at the hands of Rust. Between 1983 and 1986, the appellant made several trips to hospital for injuries including severe bruises, a fractured nose, multiple contusions and a black eye. One of the attending physicians, Dr Dirks, testified that he disbelieved the appellant's explanation on one such occasion that she had sustained her injuries by falling from a horse.

A friend of the deceased, Robert Ezako, testified that he had witnessed several fights between the appellant and the deceased and that he had seen the appellant point a gun at the deceased twice and threaten to kill him if he ever touched her again. Under cross-examination Ezako admitted to seeing or hearing the deceased beat up the appellant on several occasions and, during the preliminary inquiry, described her screaming during one such incident like "a pig being butchered"...

At one point on the night of his death Rust chased the appellant outside the house and a mutual friend, Norman Kolish, testified that the appellant pleaded with Rust to "leave me alone" and sought Kolish's protection by trying to hide behind him. A neighbour overheard Rust and the appellant arguing and described the tone of the former as "argumentative" and the latter as "scared." Later, between the first and second gunshot, he testified that he could hear that "somebody was beating up somebody" and the screams were female. Another neighbour testified to hearing noises like gunshots and then a woman's voice sounding upset saying, "Fuck. He punched me in the face. He punched me in the face." He looked out the window and saw a woman matching the description of the appellant.

... [T]he appellant was seen visibly shaken and upset and was heard to say, "Rooster [the deceased] was beating me so I shot him," and, "You know how he treated me, you've got to help me." The arresting officer testified that en route to the police station the appellant made various comments in the police car, including, "He said if I didn't kill him first he would kill me. I hope he lives. I really love him," and, "He told me he was gonna kill me when everyone left."

The police officer who took the appellant's statement testified to seeing a red mark on her arm where she said the deceased had grabbed her. When the coroner who performed an autopsy on the deceased was shown pictures of the appellant (who had various bruises), he testified that it was "entirely possible" that bruises on the deceased's left hand were occasioned by an assault on the appellant. Another doctor noted an injury to the appellant's pinkie finger consistent with those sustained by the adoption of a defensive stance.

The expert evidence which forms the subject matter of the appeal came from Dr Fred Shane, a psychiatrist with extensive professional experience in the treatment of battered wives. At the request of defence counsel Dr Shane prepared a psychiatric assessment of the appellant. The substance of Dr Shane's opinion was that the appellant had been terrorized by Rust to the point of feeling trapped, vulnerable, worthless, and unable to escape the relationship despite the violence. At the same time, the continuing pattern of abuse put her life in danger. In Dr Shane's opinion the appellant's shooting of the deceased was a final desperate act by a woman who sincerely believed that she would be killed that night:

... I think she felt, she felt in the final tragic moment that her life was on the line, that unless she defended herself, unless she reacted in a violent way that she would die. I mean he made it very explicit to her, from what she told me and from the information I have from the material that you forwarded to me, that she had, I think, to defend herself against his violence.

Dr Shane stated that his opinion was based on four hours of formal interviews with the appellant, a police report of the incident (including the appellant's statement), hospital reports documenting eight of her visits to emergency departments between 1983 and 1985, and an interview with the appellant's mother. In the course of his testimony Dr Shane related many things told to him by the appellant for which there was no admissible evidence. They were not in the appellant's statement to the police, and she did not testify at trial. For example, Dr Shane mentioned several episodes of abuse described by the appellant for which there were no hospital reports. He also related the appellant's disclosure to him that she had lied to doctors about the cause of her injuries. Dr Shane testified that such fabrication was typical of battered women. The appellant also recounted to Dr Shane occasions on which Rust would allegedly beat her, then beg her forgiveness, and ply her with flowers and temporary displays of kindness. Dr Shane was aware of the incidents described by Ezako about the appellant's pointing a gun at Rust on two occasions and explained it as "an issue for trying to defend herself. She was afraid that she would be assaulted." The appellant denied to Dr Shane that she had homicidal fantasies about Rust and mentioned that she had smoked some marijuana on the night in question. These facts were related by Dr Shane in the course of his testimony.

The appellant was acquitted by a jury but the verdict was overturned by a majority of the Manitoba Court of Appeal and the case sent back for retrial ...

3 RELEVANT LEGISLATION

Criminal Code, RSC 1985, c. C-46:

34(2) Every one who is unlawfully assaulted and who causes death or grievous bodily harm in repelling the assault is justified if
(a) he causes it under reasonable apprehension of death or grievous bodily harm from the violence with which the assault was originally made or with which the assailant pursues his purposes, and
(b) he believes on reasonable and probable grounds, that he cannot otherwise preserve himself from death or grievous bodily harm.

4 ISSUES ON APPEAL

It should be noted that two bases for ordering a new trial are implicit in the reasons of the majority of the Court of Appeal. In finding that "absent the evidence of Dr Shane, it is unlikely that the jury, properly instructed, would have accepted the accused's plea of self-defence" the Court of Appeal suggests that the evidence of Dr Shane ought to have been excluded entirely. The alternative ground for allowing the Crown's appeal was that Dr Shane's testimony was properly admitted but the trial judge's instructions with respect to it were deficient. Thus, the issues before this court are as follows:

1 Did the majority of the Manitoba Court of Appeal err in concluding that the jury should have considered the plea of self-defence absent the expert evidence of Dr Shane?
2 Did the majority of the Manitoba Court of Appeal err in holding that the trial judge's charge to the jury with respect to Dr Shane's expert evidence did not meet the requirements set out by this court in *Abbey*, thus warranting a new trial?

5 ANALYSIS

(i) Admissibility of Expert Evidence

In *Kelliher v. Smith*, this court adopted the principle that in order for expert evidence to be admissible "the subject-matter of the inquiry must be such that ordinary people are unlikely to form a correct judgment about it, if unassisted by persons with special knowledge." More recently, this court addressed the admissibility of expert psychiatric evidence in criminal cases in *R. v. Abbey, supra*. At p. 409 of the unanimous judgment Dickson, J. (as he then was) stated the rule as follows:

With respect to matters calling for special knowledge, an expert in the field may draw inferences and state his opinion. An expert's function is precisely this: to provide the judge and jury with a ready-made inference which the judge and jury, due to the technical nature of the facts, are unable to formulate ...

Where expert evidence is tendered in such fields as engineering or pathology, the paucity of the layperson's knowledge is uncontentious. The long-standing recognition that psychiatric or psychological testimony also falls within the realm of expert evidence is predicated on the realization that in some circumstances the average person may not have sufficient knowledge of or experience with human behaviour to draw an appropriate inference from the facts before him or her ...

The need for expert evidence in these areas can, however, be obfuscated by the belief that judges and juries are thoroughly knowledgeable about "human nature" and that no more is needed. They are, so to speak, their own experts on human behaviour. This, in effect, was the primary submission of the Crown to this court.

The bare facts of this case, which I think are amply supported by the evidence, are that the appellant was repeatedly abused by the deceased but did not leave him (although she twice pointed a gun at him), and ultimately shot him in the back of the head as he was leaving her room. The Crown submits that these facts disclose all the information a jury needs in order to decide whether or not the appellant acted in self-defence. I have no hesitation in rejecting the Crown's submission.

Expert evidence on the psychological effect of battering on wives and common law partners must, it seems to me, be both relevant and necessary in the context of the present case. How can the mental state of the appellant be appreciated without it? The average member of the public (or of the jury) can be forgiven for asking: Why would a woman put up with this kind of treatment? Why should she continue to live with such a man? How could she love a partner who beat her to the point of requiring hospitalization? We would expect the woman to pack her bags and go. Where is her self-respect? Why does she not cut loose and make a new life for herself? Such is the reaction of the average person confronted with the so-called battered wife syndrome. We need help to understand it and help is available from trained professionals.

The gravity, indeed, the tragedy of domestic violence can hardly be overstated. Greater media attention to this phenomenon in recent years has revealed both its prevalence and its horrific impact on women from all walks of life ...

Laws do not spring out of a social vacuum. The notion that a man has a right to "discipline" his wife is deeply rooted in the history of our society. The woman's duty was to serve her husband and to stay in the marriage at all costs "till death do us part" and to accept as her due any "punishment" that was meted out for failing to please her husband. One consequence of this attitude was that "wife battering" was rarely spoken of, rarely reported, rarely prosecuted, and even more rarely punished. Long after society abandoned its formal approval of spousal abuse, tolerance of it continued and continues in some circles to this day.

Fortunately, there has been a growing awareness in recent years that no man has a right to abuse any woman under any circumstances. Legislative initiatives designed to educate police, judicial officers, and the public, as well as more aggressive investigation and charging policies all signal a concerted effort by the criminal justice system to take spousal abuse seriously. However, a woman who comes before a judge or jury with the claim that she has been battered and suggests that this may be a relevant factor in evaluating her subsequent actions still faces the prospect of being condemned by popular mythology about domestic violence. Either she was not as badly beaten as she claims or she would have left the man long ago. Or, if she was battered that severely, she must have stayed out of some masochistic enjoyment of it ...

(ii) The Relevance of Expert Testimony to the Elements of Self-Defence

In my view, there are two elements of the defence under s. 34(2) of the *Code* which merit scrutiny for present purposes. The first is the temporal connection in s. 34(2)(a) between the apprehension of death or grievous bodily harm and the act allegedly taken in self-defence. Was the appellant "under reasonable apprehension of death or grievous bodily harm" from Rust as he was walking out of the room? The second is the assessment in s. 34(2)(b) of the magnitude of the force used by the accused. Was the accused's belief that she could not "otherwise preserve herself from death or grievous bodily harm" except by shooting the deceased based "on reasonable grounds"?

The feature common to both s. 34(2)(a) and s. 34(2)(b) is the imposition of an objective standard of reasonableness on the apprehension of death and the need to repel the assault with deadly force ...

If it strains credulity to imagine what the "ordinary man" would do in the position of a battered spouse, it is probably because men do not typically find themselves in that situation. Some women do, however. The definition of what is reasonable must be adapted to circumstances which are, by and large, foreign to the world inhabited by the hypothetical "reasonable man."

... I turn now to a consideration of the specific components of self-defence under s. 34(2) of the *Criminal Code*.

A Reasonable Apprehension of Death

Section 34(2)(a) requires that an accused who intentionally causes death or grievous bodily harm in repelling an assault is justified if he or she does so "under reasonable apprehension of death or grievous bodily harm." In the present case, the assault precipitating the appellant's alleged defensive act was Rust's threat to kill her when everyone else had gone.

It will be observed that s. 34(2)(a) does not actually stipulate that the accused apprehend *imminent* danger when he or she acts. Case law has, however, read that requirement into the defence ... The sense in which "imminent" is used conjures up the image of "an uplifted knife" or a pointed gun. The rationale for the imminence rule seems obvious. The law of self-defence is designed to ensure that the use of defensive force is really necessary. It justifies the act because the defender reasonably believed that he or she had no alternative but to take the attacker's life. If there is a significant time interval between the original unlawful assault and the accused's response, one tends to suspect that the accused was motivated by revenge rather than self-defence. In the paradigmatic case of a one-time bar-room brawl between two men of equal size and strength, this inference makes sense. How can one feel endangered to the point of firing a gun at an unarmed man who utters a death threat, then turns his back and walks out of the room? One cannot be certain of the gravity of the threat or his capacity to carry it out. Besides, one can always take the opportunity to flee or to call the police. If he comes back and raises his fist, one can respond in kind if need be. These are the tacit assumptions that underlie the imminence rule.

... According to the testimony of Dr Shane these assaults [by the deceased] were not entirely random in their occurrence ... Dr Shane acknowledged his debt to Dr [Lenore] Walker in the course of establishing his credentials as an expert at trial. Dr Walker first describes the cycle in the book *The Battered Woman* (1979). In her 1984 book, *The Battered Woman Syndrome,* Dr Walker reports the results of a study involving 400 battered women. Her research was designed to test empirically the theories expounded in her earlier book. At pp. 95-6 of *The Battered Woman Syndrome,* she summarizes the Cycle Theory as follows:

A second major theory that was tested in this project is the Walker Cycle Theory of Violence (Walker, 1979). This tension reduction theory states that there are three distinct phases associated in a recurring battering cycle: (1) tension building, (2) the acute battering incident, and (3) loving contrition. During the first phase, there is a gradual escalation of tension displayed by discrete acts causing increased friction such as name-calling, other mean intentional behaviors, and/or physical abuse. The batterer expresses dissatisfaction and hostility but not in an extreme or maximally explosive form. The woman attempts to placate the batterer, doing what she thinks might please him, calm him down, or at least, what will not further aggravate him. She tries not to respond to his hostile actions and uses general anger reduction techniques. Often she succeeds for a little while which reinforces her unrealistic belief that she can control this man ...

The tension continues to escalate and eventually she is unable to continue controlling his angry response pattern. "Exhausted from the constant stress, she usually withdraws from the batterer, fearing she will inadvertently set off an explosion. He begins to move more oppressively toward her as he observes her withdrawal ... Tension between the two becomes unbearable" (Walker, 1979, p. 59). The second phase, the acute battering incident, becomes inevitable without intervention. Sometimes, she precipitates the inevitable explosion so as to control where and when it occurs, allowing her to take better precautions to minimize her injuries and pain.

"Phase two is characterized by the uncontrollable discharge of the tensions that have built up during phase one" (p. 59). The batterer typically unleashes a barrage of verbal and physical aggression that can leave the woman severely shaken and injured. In fact, when injuries do occur it usually happens during this second phase. It is also the time police become involved, if they are called at all. The acute battering phase is concluded when the batterer stops, usually bringing with its cessation a sharp physiological reduction in tension. This in itself is naturally reinforcing. Violence often succeeds because it does work.

In phase three which follows, the batterer may apologize profusely, try to assist his victim, show kindness and remorse, and shower her with gifts and/or promises. The batterer himself may believe at this point that he will never allow himself to be violent again. The woman wants to believe the batterer and, early in the relationship at least, may renew her hope in his ability to change. This third phase provides the positive reinforcement for remaining in the relationship, for the woman. In fact, our results showed that phase three could also be characterized by an absence of tension or violence, and no observable loving-contrition behaviour, and still be reinforcing for the woman.

... Given the relational context in which the violence occurs, the mental state of an accused at the critical moment she pulls the trigger cannot be understood except in terms of the cumulative effect of months or years of brutality. As Dr Shane explained in his testimony, the deterioration of the relationship between the appellant and Rust in the period immediately preceding the killing led to feelings of escalating terror on the part of the appellant:

But their relationship some weeks to months before was definitely escalating in terms of tension and in terms of the discordant quality about it. They were sleeping in separate bedrooms. Their intimate relationship was lacking and things were building and building and to a point, I think, where it built to that particular point where she couldn't – she felt so threatened and so overwhelmed that she had to – that she reacted in a violent way because of her fear of survival and also because, I think because of her, I guess, final sense that she was – that she had to defend herself and her own sense of violence towards this man who had really desecrated her and damaged her for so long.

Another aspect of the cyclical nature of the abuse is that it begets a degree of predictability to the violence that is absent in an isolated violent encounter between two strangers. This also means that it may in fact be possible for a battered spouse to accurately predict the onset of violence before the first blow is struck, even if an outsider to the relationship cannot. Indeed, it has been suggested that a battered woman's knowledge of her partner's violence is so heightened that she is able to anticipate the nature and extent (though not the onset) of the violence by his conduct beforehand ...

Where evidence exists that an accused is in a battering relationship, expert testimony can assist the jury in determining whether the accused had a "reasonable" apprehension of death when she acted by explaining the heightened sensitivity of a battered woman to her partner's acts. Without such testimony I am skeptical that the average fact-finder would be capable of appreciating why her subjective fear may have been reasonable in the context of the relationship. After all, the hypothetical "reasonable man" observing only the final incident may have been unlikely to recognize the batterer's threat as potentially lethal. Using the case at bar as an example, the "reasonable man" might have thought, as the majority of the Court of Appeal seemed to, that it was unlikely that Rust would make good on his threat to kill the appellant that night because they had guests staying overnight.

The issue is not, however, what an outsider would have reasonably perceived but what the accused reasonably perceived, given her situation and her experience.

Even accepting that a battered woman may be uniquely sensitized to danger from her batterer, it may yet be contended that the law ought to require her to wait until the knife is uplifted, the gun pointed, or the fist clenched before her apprehension is deemed reasonable. This would allegedly reduce the risk that the woman is mistaken in her fear, although the law does not require her fear to be correct, only reasonable. In response to this contention, I need only point to the observation made by Huband J.A. that the evidence showed that when the appellant and Rust physically fought, the appellant "invariably got the worst of it." I do not think it is an unwarranted generalization to say that due to their size, strength, socialization, and lack of training, women are typically no match for men in hand-to-hand combat. The requirement imposed in *Whynot* that a battered woman wait until the physical assault is "under way" before her apprehensions can be validated in law would, in the words of an American court, be tantamount to sentencing her to "murder by installment" ...

B Lack of Alternatives to Self-Help

Section 34(2) requires an accused who pleads self-defence to believe "on reasonable grounds" that it is not possible to otherwise preserve him or herself from death or grievous bodily harm. The obvious question is if the violence was so intolerable, why did the appellant not leave her abuser long ago? This question does not really go to whether she had an alternative to killing the deceased at the critical moment. Rather, it plays on the popular myth already referred to that a woman who says she was battered yet stayed with her batterer was either not as badly beaten as she claimed or else she liked it. Nevertheless, to the extent that her failure to leave the abusive relationship earlier may be used in support of the proposition that she was free to leave at the final moment, expert testimony can provide useful insights. Dr Shane attempted to explain in his testimony how and why, in the case at bar, the appellant remained with Rust:

She had stayed in this relationship, I think, because of the strange, almost unbelievable, but yet it happens, relationship that sometimes develops between people who develop this very disturbed, I think, very disturbed quality of a relationship. Trying to understand it, I think, isn't always easy and there's been a lot written about it recently, in the recent years, in psychiatric literature. But basically it involves two people who are involved in what appears to be an attachment which may have sexual or romantic or affectionate overtones.

And the one individual, and it's usually the women in our society, but there have been occasions where it's been reversed, but what happens is the spouse who becomes battered, if you will, stays in the relationship probably because of a number of reasons.

One is that the spouse gets beaten so badly – so badly – that he or she loses the motivation to react and becomes helpless and becomes powerless. And it's also been shown sometimes, you know, in – not that you can compare animals to human beings, but in laboratories, what you do if you shock an animal, after a while it can't respond to a threat of its life. It becomes just helpless and lies there in an amotivational state, if you will, where it feels there's no power and there's no energy to do anything.

So in a sense it happens in human beings as well. It's almost like a concentration camp, if you will. You get paralyzed with fear.

The other thing that happens often in these types of relationships with human beings is that the person who beats or assaults, who batters, often tries – he makes up and begs for forgiveness. And this individual, who basically has a very disturbed or damaged self-esteem, all of a sudden feels that he or she – we'll use women in this case because it's so much more common – the spouse feels that she again can do the spouse a favour and it can make her feel needed and boost her self-esteem for a while and make her feel worthwhile and the spouse says he'll forgive her and whatnot.

...

The account given by Dr Shane comports with that documented in the literature. Reference is often made to it as a condition of "learned helplessness," a phrase coined by Dr Charles Seligman, the psychologist who first developed the theory by experimenting on animals in the manner described by Dr Shane in his testimony. A related theory used to explain the failure of women to leave battering relationships is described by psychologist and lawyer Charles Patrick Ewing, in his book *Battered Women Who Kill* (1987). Ewing describes a phenomenon labelled "traumatic bonding" that has been observed between hostages and captors, battered children and their parents, concentration camp prisoners and guards, and batterers and their spouses ...

The situation of the battered woman as described by Dr Shane strikes me as somewhat analogous to that of a hostage. If the captor tells her that he will kill her in three days' time, is it potentially reasonable for her to seize an opportunity presented on the first day to kill the captor or must she wait until he makes the attempt on the third day? I think the question the jury must ask itself is whether, given the history, circumstances and perceptions of the appellant, her belief that she could not preserve herself from being killed by Rust that night except by killing him first was reasonable. To the extent that expert evidence can assist the jury in making that determination, I would find such testimony to be both relevant and necessary.

In light of the foregoing discussion I would summarize as follows the principles upon which expert testimony is properly admitted in cases such as this:

1 Expert testimony is admissible to assist the fact-finder in drawing inferences in areas where the expert has relevant knowledge or experience beyond that of the layperson.
2 It is difficult for the layperson to comprehend the battered-wife syndrome. It is commonly thought that battered women are not really beaten as badly as they claim; otherwise they would have

left the relationship. Alternatively, some believe that women enjoy being beaten, that they have a masochistic strain in them. Each of these stereotypes may adversely affect consideration of a battered woman's claim to have acted in self-defence in killing her mate.

3 Expert evidence can assist the jury in dispelling these myths.

4 Expert testimony relating to the ability of an accused to perceive danger from her mate may go to the issue of whether she "reasonably apprehended" death or grievous bodily harm on a particular occasion.

5 Expert testimony pertaining to why an accused remained in the battering relationship may be relevant in assessing the nature and extent of the alleged abuse.

6 By providing an explanation as to why an accused did not flee when she perceived her life to be in danger, expert testimony may also assist the jury in assessing the reasonableness of her belief that killing her batterer was the only way to save her own life.

... In my view, the trial judge did not err in admitting Dr Shane's expert testimony in order to assist the jury in determining whether the appellant had a reasonable apprehension of death or grievous bodily harm and believed on reasonable grounds that she had no alternative but to shoot Kevin Rust on the night in question.

Obviously the fact that the appellant was a battered woman does not entitle her to an acquittal. Battered women may well kill their partners other than in self-defence. The focus is not on who the woman is, but on what she did ...

(iii) Adequacy of Trial Judge's Charge to the Jury

The second issue raised in this case is the adequacy of the trial judge's charge to the jury with respect to the expert evidence furnished by Dr Shane. It appears that Dr Shane relied on various sources in formulating his opinion – his series of interviews with the appellant, an interview with her mother, a police report of the incident (including information regarding her statement to the police), and hospital records documenting eight of her visits to emergency departments between 1983 and 1986. Neither the appellant nor her mother testified at trial. The contents of their statements to Dr Shane were hearsay ...

Where the factual basis of an expert's opinion is a melange of admissible and inadmissible evidence the duty of the trial judge is to caution the jury that the weight attributable to the expert testimony is directly related to the amount and quality of admissible evidence on which it relies. The trial judge openly acknowledged to counsel the inherent difficulty in discharging such a duty in the case at bar. In my view, the trial judge performed his task adequately in this regard. A new trial is not warranted on the basis of the trial judge's charge to the jury.

I would accordingly allow the appeal, set aside the order of the Court of Appeal, and restore the acquittal.

Appeal allowed; acquittal restored.

READING QUESTIONS ON *LAVALLEE*

1 Madame Justice Wilson compares Lavallee's situation to that of a hostage. In what ways are the situations parallel? Do you see any disanalogies?

2 Are there dangers connected to the idea of a "battered woman syndrome"? Does the defensibility of Lavallee's acts turn on her suffering from a condition, or can it be justified purely in light of the situation in which she finds herself?

3 Johnny Frank Buggs was attacked and threatened by members of the Crips gang, who were notorious for carrying grudges and using guns. When he saw them again shortly after the attack, he shot them. Can he claim self-defence? *(State v. Buggs*, 806 P. 2d 1381)

4 Nellie Eyapaise, who had been in a variety of abusive relationships, stabbed a man she barely knew when he made advances at her. Can she claim self-defence? (*R. v. Eyapaise* (1993), 20 CR (4th) 246 (Alta. QB))

5 In the movie *Cape Fear*, a lawyer is harassed by a recently released former client. The client threatens to kill the lawyer's family. The audience knows the convict will eventually do something terrible. Although the police tell the lawyer that he can only kill the convict during a confrontation, they cannot guarantee that they will be able to protect him. Compare this lawyer's situation to those of Lavallee, Eyapaise, and Buggs. Should the lawyer be allowed to act pre-emptively?

4

Law and Values: Liberty, Democracy, and the Rule of Law

This chapter looks at a series of questions revolving around the tensions between the role of law as a protector of individual liberty and as a tool of democratic self-rule. Law has been defended as each of these, yet they are in constant tension. Individual rights are sometimes endangered by policies chosen by majorities. As a result, almost everyone supposes that some limits should be placed on majority rule. Still, profound disagreements arise about how to think about the appropriate limits. Some defenders of the rule of law insist on severe limits. They argue that the law can only protect liberty if it has clear and readily identifiable rules that enable people to plan their own affairs. This understanding of liberty has been criticized on a number of fronts. From one direction, critics have suggested that such a view of liberty sets appropriate limits to the reach of the law, but that more than the protection of liberty is needed if a society is to survive. Defenders of such views may disagree about what more is needed. Some of them suppose that what is important is that the members of the society share some conception of the good life, while others may insist that the material conditions for the meaningful exercise of liberty be guaranteed. Others argue that the very idea of negative liberty is flawed, resting on an unrealistic view of the importance of choice. From still another direction, difficulties with the idea of negative liberty have led some critics to question the very idea of the rule of law. Sometimes this criticism takes the form of a rejection of the distinction between making law and applying it, and concludes that the idea of law as a rule-governed activity makes no sense. In the eyes of these critics, law is always an exercise of power, and at best bears a contingent relation to justice and democracy.

John Stuart Mill
On Liberty (1859)

In the classic work of nineteenth-century liberalism, Mill argues that the only legitimate restrictions on individual liberty are those that will prevent harms to others.

CHAPTER I: INTRODUCTORY

The Subject of this Essay is not the so-called Liberty of the Will, so unfortunately opposed to the misnamed doctrine of Philosophical Necessity; but Civil, or Social Liberty: the nature and limits of the power which can be legitimately exercised by society over the individual. A question seldom stated, and hardly ever discussed, in general terms, but which profoundly influences the practical controversies of the age by its latent presence, and is likely soon to make itself recognised as the vital question of the future. It is so far from being new, that, in a certain sense, it has divided mankind, almost from the remotest ages; but in the stage of progress into which the more civilized portions of the species have now entered, it presents itself under new conditions, and requires a different and more fundamental treatment.

The struggle between Liberty and Authority is the most conspicuous feature in the portions of history with which we are earliest familiar, particularly in that of Greece, Rome, and England. But in old times this contest was between subjects, or some classes of subjects, and the Government. By liberty, was meant protection against the tyranny of the political rulers. The rulers were conceived (except in some of the popular governments of Greece) as in a necessarily antagonistic position to the people whom they ruled. They consisted of a governing One, or a governing tribe or caste, who derived their authority from inheritance or conquest, who, at all events, did not hold it at the pleasure of the governed, and whose supremacy men did not venture, perhaps did not desire, to contest, whatever precautions might be taken against its oppressive exercise. Their power was regarded as necessary, but also as highly dangerous; as a weapon which they would attempt to use against their subjects, no less than against external enemies. To prevent the weaker members of the community from being preyed upon by innumerable vultures, it was needful that there should be an animal of prey stronger than the rest, commissioned to keep them down. But as the king of the vultures would be no less bent upon preying on the flock than any of the minor harpies, it was indispensable to be in a perpetual attitude of defence against his beak and claws. The aim, therefore, of patriots was to set limits to the power which the ruler should be suffered to exercise over the community; and this limitation was what they meant by liberty. It was attempted in two ways. First, by obtaining a recognition of certain immunities, called political liberties or rights, which it was to be regarded as a breach of duty in the ruler to infringe, and which, if he did infringe, specific resistance, or general rebellion, was held to be justifiable. A second, and generally a later expedient, was the establishment of constitutional checks, by which the consent of the community, or of a body of some sort, supposed to represent its interests, was made a necessary condition to some of the more important acts of the governing power. To the first of these modes of limitation, the ruling power, in most European countries, was compelled, more or less, to submit. It was not so with the second; and, to attain this, or when already in some degree possessed, to attain it more completely, became everywhere the principal object of the lovers of liberty. And so long as mankind were content to combat one enemy by another, and to be ruled by a master, on condition of being guaranteed more or less efficaciously against his tyranny, they did not carry their aspirations beyond this point.

A time, however, came, in the progress of human affairs, when men ceased to think it a necessity of nature that their governors should be an independent power, opposed in interest to themselves. It appeared to them much better that the various magistrates of the State should be their tenants or delegates, revocable at their pleasure. In that way alone, it seemed, could they have complete security that the powers of government would never be abused to their disadvantage. By degrees this new demand for elective and temporary rulers became the prominent object of the exertions of the popular party, wherever any such party existed; and superseded, to a considerable extent, the previous efforts to limit the power of rulers. As the struggle proceeded for making the ruling power emanate from the periodical choice of the ruled, some persons began to think that too much importance had been attached to the limitation of the power itself. *That* (it might seem) was a resource against rulers whose interests were habitually opposed to those of the people. What was now wanted was, that the rulers should be identified with the people; that their interest and will should be the interest and will of the nation. The nation did not need to be protected against its own will. There was no fear of its tyrannizing over itself. Let the rulers be effectually responsible to it, promptly removable by it, and it could afford to trust them with power of which it could itself dictate the use to be made. Their power was but the nation's own power, concentrated, and in a form convenient for exercise. This mode of thought, or rather perhaps of feeling, was common among the last generation of European liberalism, in the Continental section of which it still apparently predominates. Those who admit any limit to what a government may do, except in the case of such governments as they think ought not to exist, stand out as brilliant exceptions among the political thinkers of the Continent. A similar tone of sentiment might by this time have been prevalent in our own country, if the circumstances which for a time encouraged it, had continued unaltered.

But, in political and philosophical theories, as well as in persons, success discloses faults and infirmities which failure might have concealed from observation. The notion, that the people have no need to limit their power over themselves, might seem axiomatic, when popular government was a thing only dreamed about, or read of as having existed at some distant period of the past. Neither was that notion necessarily disturbed by such temporary aberrations as those of the French Revolution, the worst of which were the work of an usurping few, and which, in any case, belonged, not to the permanent working of popular institutions, but to a sudden and convulsive outbreak against monarchical and aristocratic despotism. In time, however, a democratic republic came to occupy a large portion of the earth's surface, and made itself felt as one of the most powerful members of the community of nations; and elective and responsible government became subject to the observations and criticisms which wait upon a great existing fact. It was now perceived that such phrases as "self-government," and "the power of the people over themselves," do not express the true state of the case. The "people" who exercise the power are not always the same people with those over whom it is exercised; and the "self-government" spoken of is not the government of each by himself, but of each by all the rest. The will of the people, moreover, practically means the will of the most numerous or the most active *part* of the people; the majority, or those who succeed in making themselves accepted as the majority; the people, consequently, *may* desire to oppress a part of their number; and precautions are as much needed against this as against any other abuse of power. The limitation, therefore, of the power of government over individuals loses none of its importance when the holders of power are regularly accountable to the community, that is, to the strongest party therein. This view of things, recommending itself equally to the intelligence of thinkers and to the inclination of those important classes in European society to whose real or supposed interests democracy is adverse, has had no difficulty in establishing itself; and in political speculations "the tyranny of the majority" is now generally included among the evils against which society requires to be on its guard.

Like other tyrannies, the tyranny of the majority was at first, and is still vulgarly, held in dread, chiefly as operating through the acts of the public authorities. But reflecting persons perceived that when society is itself the tyrant – society collectively, over the separate individuals who compose it – its means of tyrannizing are not restricted to the acts which it may do by the hands of its political functionaries. Society can and does execute its own mandates: and if it issues wrong mandates instead of right, or any mandates at all in things with which it ought not to meddle, it practises a social tyranny more formidable than many kinds of political oppression, since, though not usually upheld by such extreme penalties, it leaves fewer means of escape, penetrating much more deeply into the details of life, and enslaving the soul itself. Protection, therefore, against the tyranny of the magistrate is not enough: there needs protection also against the tyranny of the prevailing opinion and feeling; against the tendency of society to impose, by other means than civil penalties, its own ideas and practices as rules of conduct on those who dissent from them; to fetter the development, and, if possible, prevent the formation, of any individuality not in harmony with its ways, and compel all characters to fashion themselves upon the model of its own. There is a limit to the legitimate interference of collective opinion with individual independence: and to find that limit, and maintain it against encroachment, is as indispensable to a good condition of human affairs, as protection against political despotism.

But though this proposition is not likely to be contested in general terms, the practical question, where to place the limit – how to make the fitting adjustment between individual independence and social control – is a subject on which nearly everything remains to be done. All that makes existence valuable to any one, depends on the enforcement of restraints upon the actions of other people. Some rules of conduct, therefore, must be imposed, by law in the first place, and by opinion on many things which are not fit subjects for the operation of law. What these rules should be, is the principal question in human affairs; but if we except a few of the most obvious cases, it is one of those which least progress has been made in resolving. No two ages, and scarcely any two countries, have decided it alike; and the decision of one age or country is a wonder to another. Yet the people of any given age and country no more suspect any difficulty in it, than if it were a subject on which mankind had always been agreed. The rules which obtain among themselves appear to them self-evident and self-justifying. This all but universal illusion is one of the examples of the magical influence of custom, which is not only, as the proverb says, a second nature, but is continually mistaken for the first. The effect of custom, in preventing any misgiving respecting the rules of conduct which mankind impose on one another, is all the more complete because the subject is one on which it is not generally considered necessary that reasons should be given, either by one person to others, or by each to himself. People are accustomed to believe, and have been encouraged in the belief by some who aspire to the character of philosophers, that their feelings, on subjects of this nature, are better than reasons, and render reasons unnecessary. The practical principle which guides them to their opinions on the regulation of human conduct, is the feeling in each person's mind that everybody should be required to act as he, and those with whom he sympathizes, would like them to act. No one, indeed, acknowledges to himself that his standard of judgment is his own liking; but an opinion on a point of conduct, not supported by reasons, can only count as one person's preference; and if the reasons, when given, are a mere appeal to a similar preference felt by other people, it is still only many people's liking instead of one. To an ordinary man, however, his own preference, thus supported, is not only a perfectly satisfactory reason, but the only one he generally has for any of his notions of morality, taste, or propriety, which are not expressly written in his religious creed; and his chief guide in the interpretation even of that. Men's opinions, accordingly, on what is laudable or blameable, are affected by all the multifarious causes which influence their wishes in regard to the conduct of others, and which are as numerous as those which determine their wishes on any other subject. Sometimes their reason – at other times their prejudices or superstitions: often their social affections, not seldom their antisocial ones, their envy or jealousy, their arrogance or contemptuousness: but most commonly, their desires or fears for themselves – their legitimate or illegitimate self-interest. Wherever there is

an ascendant class, a large portion of the morality of the country emanates from its class interests, and its feelings of class superiority. The
morality between Spartans and Helots, between planters and negroes,
between princes and subjects, between nobles and roturiers, between
men and women, has been for the most part the creation of these class
interests and feelings: and the sentiments thus generated, react in turn
upon the moral feelings of the members of the ascendant class, in their
relations among themselves. Where, on the other hand, a class, formerly
ascendant, has lost its ascendancy, or where its ascendancy is unpopular, the prevailing moral sentiments frequently bear the impress of an
impatient dislike of superiority. Another grand determining principle
of the rules of conduct, both in act and forbearance, which have been
enforced by law or opinion, has been the servility of mankind towards
the supposed preferences or aversions of their temporal masters, or of
their gods. This servility, though essentially selfish, is not hypocrisy; it
gives rise to perfectly genuine sentiments of abhorrence; it made men
burn magicians and heretics. Among so many baser influences, the
general and obvious interests of society have of course had a share, and
a large one, in the direction of the moral sentiments: less, however, as
a matter of reason, and on their own account, than as a consequence of
the sympathies and antipathies which grew out of them: and sympathies and antipathies which had little or nothing to do with the interests
of society, have made themselves felt in the establishment of moralities
with quite as great force.

The likings and dislikings of society, or of some powerful portion of
it, are thus the main thing which has practically determined the rules
laid down for general observance, under the penalties of law or opinion. And in general, those who have been in advance of society in
thought and feeling, have left this condition of things unassailed in
principle, however they may have come into conflict with it in some of
its details. They have occupied themselves rather in inquiring what
things society ought to like or dislike, than in questioning whether its
likings or dislikings should be a law to individuals. They preferred
endeavouring to alter the feelings of mankind on the particular points
on which they were themselves heretical, rather than make common
cause in defence of freedom, with heretics generally. The only case in
which the higher ground has been taken on principle and maintained
with consistency, by any but an individual here and there, is that of
religious belief: a case instructive in many ways, and not least so as
forming a most striking instance of the fallibility of what is called the

moral sense: for the *odium theologicum,* in a sincere bigot, is one of the most unequivocal cases of moral feeling. Those who first broke the yoke of what called itself the Universal Church, were in general as little willing to permit difference of religious opinion as that church itself. But when the heat of the conflict was over, without giving a complete victory to any party, and each church or sect was reduced to limit its hopes to retaining possession of the ground it already occupied; minorities, seeing that they had no chance of becoming majorities, were under the necessity of pleading to those whom they could not convert, for permission to differ. It is accordingly on this battle field, almost solely, that the rights of the individual against society have been asserted on broad grounds of principle, and the claim of society to exercise authority over dissentients openly controverted. The great writers to whom the world owes what religious liberty it possesses, have mostly asserted freedom of conscience as an indefeasible right, and denied absolutely that a human being is accountable to others for his religious belief. Yet so natural to mankind is intolerance in whatever they really care about, that religious freedom has hardly anywhere been practically realized, except where religious indifference, which dislikes to have its peace disturbed by theological quarrels, has added its weight to the scale. In the minds of almost all religious persons, even in the most tolerant countries, the duty of toleration is admitted with tacit reserves. One person will bear with dissent in matters of church government, but not of dogma; another can tolerate everybody, short of a Papist or an Unitarian; another, every one who believes in revealed religion; a few extend their charity a little further, but stop at the belief in a God and in a future state. Wherever the sentiment of the majority is still genuine and intense, it is found to have abated little of its claim to be obeyed.

In England, from the peculiar circumstances of our political history, though the yoke of opinion is perhaps heavier, that of law is lighter, than in most other countries of Europe; and there is considerable jealousy of direct interference, by the legislative or the executive power, with private conduct; not so much from any just regard for the independence of the individual, as from the still subsisting habit of looking on the government as representing an opposite interest to the public. The majority have not yet learnt to feel the power of the government their power, or its opinions their opinions. When they do so, individual liberty will probably be as much exposed to invasion from the government, as it already is from public opinion. But, as yet, there is a considerable amount of feeling ready to be called forth against any attempt of the law to control individuals in things in which they have not hitherto been accustomed to be controlled by it; and this with very little discrimination as to whether the matter is, or is not, within the legitimate sphere of legal control; insomuch that the feeling, highly salutary on the whole, is perhaps quite as often misplaced as well grounded in the particular instances of its application. There is, in fact, no recognised principle by which the propriety or impropriety of government interference is customarily tested. People decide according to their personal preferences. Some, whenever they see any good to be done, or evil to be remedied, would willingly instigate the government to undertake the business; while others prefer to bear almost any amount of social evil, rather than add one to the departments of human interests amenable to governmental control. And men range themselves on one or the other side in any particular case, according to this general direction of their sentiments; or according to the degree of interest which they feel in the particular thing which it is proposed that the government should do, or according to the belief they entertain that the government would, or would not, do it in the manner they prefer; but very rarely on account of any opinion to which they consistently adhere, as to what things are fit to be done by a government. And it seems to me that in consequence of this absence of rule or principle, one side is at present as often wrong as the other; the interference of government is, with about equal frequency, improperly invoked and improperly condemned.

The object of this Essay is to assert one very simple principle, as entitled to govern absolutely the dealings of society with the individual in the way of compulsion and control, whether the means used be physical force in the form of legal penalties, or the moral coercion of public opinion. That principle is, that the sole end for which mankind are warranted, individually or collectively, in interfering with the liberty of action of any of their number, is self-protection. That the only purpose for which power can be rightfully exercised over any member of a civilized community, against his will, is to prevent harm to others. His own good, either physical or moral, is not a sufficient warrant. He cannot rightfully be compelled to do or forbear because it will be better for him to do so, because it will make him happier, because, in the opinions of others, to do so would be wise, or even right. These are good reasons for remonstrating with him, or reasoning with him, or persuading him, or entreating him, but not for compelling him, or visiting him with any evil in case he do otherwise. To justify that, the conduct from which it is desired to deter him, must be calculated to produce evil to some one else. The only part of the conduct of any one, for which he is amenable to society, is that which concerns others. In the part which merely concerns himself, his independence is, of right, absolute. Over himself, over his own body and mind, the individual is sovereign.

It is, perhaps, hardly necessary to say that this doctrine is meant to apply only to human beings in the maturity of their faculties. We are not speaking of children, or of young persons below the age which the law may fix as that of manhood or womanhood. Those who are still in a state to require being taken care of by others, must be protected against their own actions as well as against external injury. For the same reason, we may leave out of consideration those backward states of society in which the race itself may be considered as in its nonage. The early difficulties in the way of spontaneous progress are so great, that there is seldom any choice of means for overcoming them; and a ruler full of the spirit of improvement is warranted in the use of any expedients that will attain an end, perhaps otherwise unattainable. Despotism is a legitimate mode of government in dealing with barbarians, provided the end be their improvement, and the means justified by actually effecting that end. Liberty, as a principle, has no application to any state of things anterior to the time when mankind have become capable of being improved by free and equal discussion. Until then, there is nothing for them but implicit obedience to an Akbar or a Charlemagne, if they are so fortunate as to find one. But as soon as mankind have attained the capacity of being guided to their own improvement by conviction or persuasion (a period long since reached in all nations with whom we need here concern ourselves), compulsion, either in the direct form or in that of pains and penalties for non-compliance, is no longer admissible as a means to their own good, and justifiable only for the security of others.

It is proper to state that I forego any advantage which could be de-rived to my argument from the idea of abstract right, as a thing inde-pendent of utility. I regard utility as the ultimate appeal on all ethical questions; but it must be utility in the largest sense, grounded on the permanent interests of man as a progressive being. Those interests, I contend, authorize the subjection of individual spontaneity to external control, only in respect to those actions of each, which concern the interests of other people. If any one does an act hurtful to others, there is a *prima facie* case for punishing him, by law, or, where legal penalties are not safely applicable, by general disapprobation. There are also many positive acts for the benefit of others, which he may rightfully be compelled to perform; such as, to give evidence in a court of justice; to bear his fair share in the common defence, or in any other joint work necessary to the interest of the society of which he enjoys the protection; and to perform certain acts of individual beneficence, such as saving a fellow-creature's life, or interposing to protect the defenceless against ill-usage, things which whenever it is obviously a man's duty to do, he may rightfully be made responsible to society for not doing. A person may cause evil to others not only by his actions, but by his inaction, and in either case he is justly accountable to them for the injury. The latter case, it is true, requires a much more cautious exercise of compulsion than the former. To make any one answerable for doing evil to others, is the rule; to make him answerable for not preventing evil, is, comparatively speaking, the exception. Yet there are many cases clear enough and grave enough to justify that exception. In all things which regard the external relations of the individual, he is *de jure* amenable to those whose interests are concerned, and if need be, to society as their protector. There are often good reasons for not holding him to the responsibility; but these reasons must arise from the special expediencies of the case: either because it is a kind of case in which he is on the whole likely to act better, when left to his own discretion, than when controlled in any way in which society have it in their power to control him; or because the attempt to exercise control would produce other evils, greater than those which it would prevent. When such reasons as these preclude the enforcement of responsibility, the conscience of the agent himself should step into the vacant judgment seat, and protect those interests of others which have no external protection; judging himself all the more rigidly, because the case does not admit of his being made accountable to the judgment of his fellow-creatures.

But there is a sphere of action in which society, as distinguished from the individual, has, if any, only an indirect interest; comprehending all that portion of a person's life and conduct which affects only himself, or if it also affects others, only with their free, voluntary, and undeceived consent and participation. When I say only himself, I mean directly, and in the first instance: for whatever affects himself, may affect others through himself; and the objection which may be grounded on this contingency, will receive consideration in the sequel. This, then, is the appropriate region of human liberty. It comprises, first, the inward domain of consciousness; demanding liberty of conscience, in the most comprehensive sense; liberty of thought and feeling; absolute freedom of opinion and sentiment on all subjects, practical or speculative, scientific, moral, or theological. The liberty of expressing and publishing opinions may seem to fall under a different principle, since it belongs to that part of the conduct of an individual which concerns other people; but, being almost of as much importance as the liberty of thought itself, and resting in great part on the same reasons, is practically inseparable from it. Secondly, the principle requires liberty of tastes and pursuits; of framing the plan of our life to suit our own character; of doing as we like, subject to such consequences as may follow: without impediment from our fellow-creatures, so long as what we do does not harm them, even though they should think our conduct foolish, perverse, or wrong. Thirdly, from this liberty of each individual, follows the liberty, within the same limits, of combination among individuals; freedom to unite, for any purpose not involving harm to others: the persons combining being supposed to be of full age, and not forced or deceived.

No society in which these liberties are not, on the whole, respected, is free, whatever may be its form of government; and none is completely free in which they do not exist absolute and unqualified. The only freedom which deserves the name, is that of pursuing our own good in our own way, so long as we do not attempt to deprive others of theirs, or impede their efforts to obtain it. Each is the proper guardian of his own health, whether bodily, or mental and spiritual. Mankind are greater gainers by suffering each other to live as seems good to themselves, than by compelling each to live as seems good to the rest.

Though this doctrine is anything but new, and, to some persons, may have the air of a truism, there is no doctrine which stands more directly opposed to the general tendency of existing opinion and practice. Society has expended fully as much effort in the attempt (according to its lights) to compel people to conform to its notions of personal, as of social excellence. The ancient commonwealths thought themselves entitled to practise, and the ancient philosophers countenanced, the regulation of every part of private conduct by public authority, on the ground that the State had a deep interest in the whole bodily and mental discipline of every one of its citizens; a mode of thinking which may have been admissible in small republics surrounded by powerful enemies, in constant peril of being subverted by foreign attack or internal commotion, and to which even a short interval of relaxed energy and self-command might so easily be fatal, that they could not afford to wait for the salutary permanent effects of freedom. In the modern world, the greater size of political communities, and above all, the separation between spiritual and temporal authority (which placed the direction of men's consciences in other hands than those which controlled their worldly affairs), prevented so great an interference by law in the details of private life; but the engines of moral repression have been wielded more strenuously against divergence from the reigning opinion in self-regarding, than even in social matters; religion, the most powerful of the elements which have entered into the formation of moral feeling, having almost always been governed either by the ambition of a hierarchy, seeking control over every department of human conduct, or by the spirit of Puritanism. And some of those modern reformers who have placed themselves in strongest opposition to the religions of the past, have been noway behind either churches or sects in their assertion of the right of spiritual domination: M. Comte, in particular, whose social system, as unfolded in his *Système de Politique Positive,* aims at establishing (though by moral more than by legal appliances) a despotism of society over the individual, surpassing anything contemplated in the political ideal of the most rigid disciplinarian among the ancient philosophers.

Apart from the peculiar tenets of individual thinkers, there is also in the world at large an increasing inclination to stretch unduly the powers of society over the individual, both by the force of opinion and even by that of legislation; and as the tendency of all the changes taking place in the world is to strengthen society, and diminish the power of the individual, this encroachment is not one of the evils which tend spontaneously to disappear, but, on the contrary, to grow more and more formidable. The disposition of mankind, whether as rulers or as fellow-citizens, to impose their own opinions and inclinations as a rule of conduct on others, is so energetically supported by some of the best and by some of the worst feelings incident to human nature, that it is hardly ever kept under restraint by anything but want of power; and as the power is not declining, but growing, unless a strong barrier of moral conviction can be raised against the mischief, we must expect, in the present circumstances of the world, to see it increase.

It will be convenient for the argument, if, instead of at once entering upon the general thesis, we confine ourselves in the first instance to a single branch of it, on which the principle here stated is, if not fully, yet to a certain point, recognised by the current opinions. This one branch is the Liberty of Thought: from which it is impossible to separate the cognate liberty of speaking and of writing. Although these liberties, to some considerable amount, form part of the political morality of all countries which profess religious toleration and free institutions, the grounds, both philosophical and practical, on which they rest, are perhaps not so familiar to the general mind, nor so thoroughly appreciated by many even of the leaders of opinion, as might have been expected. Those grounds, when rightly understood, are of much wider application than to only one division of the subject, and a thorough consideration of this part of the question will be found the best introduction to the remainder. Those to whom nothing which I am about to say will be new, may therefore, I hope, excuse me, if on a subject which for now three centuries has been so often discussed, I venture on one discussion more.

CHAPTER II: OF THE LIBERTY OF THOUGHT AND DISCUSSION

The time, it is to be hoped, is gone by, when any defence would be necessary of the "liberty of the press" as one of the securities against corrupt or tyrannical government. No argument, we may suppose, can now be needed, against permitting a legislature or an executive, not identified in interest with the people, to prescribe opinions to them, and determine what doctrines or what arguments they shall be allowed to hear. This aspect of the question, besides, has been so often and so triumphantly enforced by preceding writers, that it needs not be specially insisted on in this place. Though the law of England, on the subject of the press, is as servile to this day as it was in the time of the Tudors, there is little danger of its being actually put in force against political discussion, except during some temporary panic, when fear of insurrection drives ministers and judges from their propriety; and, speaking generally, it is not, in constitutional countries, to be apprehended, that the government, whether completely responsible to the people or not, will often attempt to control the expression of opinion, except when in doing so it makes itself the organ of the general intolerance of the public. Let us suppose, therefore, that the government is entirely at one with the people, and never thinks of exerting any power of coercion unless in agreement with what it conceives to be their voice. But I deny the right of the people to exercise such coercion, either by themselves or by their government. The power itself is illegitimate. The best government has no more title to it than the worst. It is as noxious, or more noxious, when exerted in accordance with public opinion, than when in opposition to it. If all mankind minus one, were of one opinion, and only one person were of the contrary opinion, mankind would be no more justified in silencing that one person, than he, if he had the power, would be justified in silencing mankind. Were an opinion a personal possession of no value except to the owner; if to be obstructed in the enjoyment of it were simply a private injury, it would make some difference whether the injury was inflicted only on a few persons or on many. But the peculiar evil of silencing the expression of an opinion is, that it is robbing the human race; posterity as well as the existing generation; those who dissent from the opinion, still more than those who hold it. If the opinion is right, they are deprived of the opportunity of exchanging error for truth: if wrong, they lose, what is almost as great a benefit, the clearer perception and livelier impression of truth, produced by its collision with error.

It is necessary to consider separately these two hypotheses, each of which has a distinct branch of the argument corresponding to it. We can never be sure that the opinion we are endeavouring to stifle is a false opinion; and if we were sure, stifling it would be an evil still.

First: the opinion which it is attempted to suppress by authority may possibly be true. Those who desire to suppress it, of course deny its truth; but they are not infallible. They have no authority to decide the question for all mankind, and exclude every other person from the means of judging. To refuse a hearing to an opinion, because they are sure that it is false, is to assume that *their* certainty is the same thing as *absolute* certainty. All silencing of discussion is an assumption of infallibility. Its condemnation may be allowed to rest on this common argument, not the worse for being common.

Unfortunately for the good sense of mankind, the fact of their fallibility is far from carrying the weight in their practical judgment, which is always allowed to it in theory; for while every one well knows himself to be fallible, few think it necessary to take any precautions against their own fallibility, or admit the supposition that any opinion, of which they feel very certain, may be one of the examples of the error to which they acknowledge themselves to be liable. Absolute princes, or others who are accustomed to unlimited deference, usually feel this complete confidence in their own opinions on nearly all subjects. People more happily situated, who sometimes hear their opinions disputed, and are not wholly unused to be set right when they are wrong, place the same unbounded reliance only on such of their opinions as are shared by all who surround them, or to whom they habitually defer: for in proportion to a man's want of confidence in his own solitary judgment, does he usually repose, with implicit trust, on the infallibility of "the world" in general. And the world, to each individual, means the part of it with which he comes in contact; his party, his sect, his church, his class of society: the man may be called, by comparison, almost liberal and large-minded to whom it means anything so comprehensive as his own country or his own age. Nor is his faith in this collective authority at all shaken by his being aware that other ages, countries, sects, churches, classes, and parties have thought, and even now think, the exact reverse. He devolves upon his own world the responsibility of being in the right against the dissentient worlds of other people; and it never troubles him that mere accident has decided which of these numerous worlds is the object of his reliance, and that the same causes which make him a Churchman in London, would have made him a Buddhist or a Confucian in Pekin. Yet it is as evident in itself, as any amount of argument can make it, that ages are no more infallible than individuals; every age having held many opinions which subsequent ages have deemed not only false but absurd; and it is as certain that many opinions, now general, will be rejected by future ages, as it is that many, once general, are rejected by the present.

The objection likely to be made to this argument, would probably take some such form as the following. There is no greater assumption of infallibility in forbidding the propagation of error, than in any other thing which is done by public authority on its own judgment and responsibility. Judgment is given to men that they may use it. Because it may be used erroneously, are men to be told that they ought not to use it at all? To prohibit what they think pernicious, is not claiming exemption from error, but fulfilling the duty incumbent on them, although fallible, of acting on their conscientious conviction. If we were never to act on our opinions, because those opinions may be wrong, we should leave all our interests uncared for, and all our duties unperformed. An objection which applies to all conduct, can be no valid objection to any conduct in particular. It is the duty of governments, and of individuals, to form the truest opinions they can; to form them carefully, and never impose them upon others unless they are quite sure of being right. But when they are sure (such reasoners may say), it is not conscientiousness but cowardice to shrink from acting on their opinions, and allow doctrines which they honestly think dangerous to the welfare of mankind, either in this life or in another, to be scattered abroad without restraint, because other people, in less enlightened times, have persecuted opinions now believed to be true. Let us take care, it may be said, not to make the same mistake: but governments and nations have made mistakes in other things, which are not denied to be fit subjects for the exercise of authority: they have laid on bad taxes, made unjust wars. Ought we therefore to lay on no taxes, and, under whatever provocation, make no wars? Men, and governments, must act to the best of their ability. There is no such thing as absolute certainty, but there is assurance sufficient for the purposes of human life. We may, and must, assume our opinion to be true for the guidance of our own conduct: and it is assuming no more when we forbid bad men to pervert society by the propagation of opinions which we regard as false and pernicious.

I answer, that it is assuming very much more. There is the greatest difference between presuming an opinion to be true, because, with every opportunity for contesting it, it has not been refuted, and assuming its truth for the purpose of not permitting its refutation. Complete liberty of contradicting and disproving our opinion, is the very condition which justifies us in assuming its truth for purposes of action; and on no other terms can a being with human faculties have any rational assurance of being right ...

Let us now pass to the second division of the argument, and dismissing the supposition that any of the received opinions may be false, let us assume them to be true, and examine into the worth of the manner in which they are likely to be held, when their truth is not freely and openly canvassed. However unwillingly a person who has a strong opinion may admit the possibility that his opinion may be false, he ought to be moved by the consideration that however true it may be, if it is not fully, frequently, and fearlessly discussed, it will be held as a dead dogma, not a living truth.

There is a class of persons (happily not quite so numerous as formerly) who think it enough if a person assents undoubtingly to what they think true, though he has no knowledge whatever of the grounds of the opinion, and could not make a tenable defence of it against the most superficial objections. Such persons, if they can once get their creed taught from authority, naturally think that no good, and some harm, comes of its being allowed to be questioned. Where their influence prevails, they make it nearly impossible for the received opinion to be rejected wisely and considerately, though it may still be rejected rashly and ignorantly; for to shut out discussion entirely is seldom possible, and when it once gets in, beliefs not grounded on conviction are apt to give way before the slightest semblance of an argument. Waving, however, this possibility – assuming that the true opinion abides in the mind, but abides as a prejudice, a belief independent of and proof against, argument – this is not the way in which truth ought to be held by a rational being. This is not knowing the truth. Truth, thus held, is but one superstition the more, accidentally clinging to the words which enunciate a truth.

If the intellect and judgment of mankind ought to be cultivated, a thing which Protestants at least do not deny, on what can these faculties be more appropriately exercised by any one, than on the things which concern him so much that it is considered necessary for him to hold opinions on them? If the cultivation of the understanding consists in one thing more than in another, it is surely in learning the grounds of one's own opinions. Whatever people believe, on subjects on which it is of the first importance to believe rightly, they ought to be able to defend against at least the common objections. But, some one may say, "Let them be *taught* the grounds of their opinions. It does not follow that opinions must be merely parroted because they are never heard controverted. Persons who learn geometry do not simply commit the theorems to memory, but understand and learn likewise the demonstrations; and it would be absurd to say that they remain ignorant of the grounds of geometrical truths, because they never hear any one deny, and attempt to disprove them." Undoubtedly: and such teaching suffices on a subject like mathematics, where there is nothing at all to be said on the wrong side of the question. The peculiarity of the evidence of mathematical truths is, that all the argument is on one side. There are no objections, and no answers to objections. But on every subject on which difference of opinion is possible, the truth depends on a balance to be struck between two sets of conflicting reasons. Even in natural philosophy, there is always some other explanation possible of the same facts; some geocentric theory instead of heliocentric, some phlogiston instead of oxygen; and it has to be shown why that other theory cannot be the true one: and until this is shown, and until we know how it is shown, we do not understand the grounds of our opinion. But when we turn to subjects infinitely more complicated, to morals, religion, politics, social relations, and the business of life, three-fourths of the arguments for every disputed opinion consist in dispelling the appearances which favour some opinion different from it. The greatest orator, save one, of antiquity, has left it on record that he always studied his adversary's case with as great, if not with still greater, intensity than even his own.

What Cicero practised as the means of forensic success, requires to be imitated by all who study any subject in order to arrive at the truth. He who knows only his own side of the case, knows little of that. His reasons may be good, and no one may have been able to refute them. But if he is equally unable to refute the reasons on the opposite side; if he does not so much as know what they are, he has no ground for preferring either opinion. The rational position for him would be suspension of judgment, and unless he contents himself with that, he is either led by authority, or adopts, like the generality of the world, the side to which he feels most inclination. Nor is it enough that he should hear the arguments of adversaries from his own teachers, presented as they state them, and accompanied by what they offer as refutations. That is not the way to do justice to the arguments, or bring them into real contact with his own mind. He must be able to hear them from persons who actually believe them; who defend them in earnest, and do their very utmost for them. He must know them in their most plausible and persuasive form; he must feel the whole force of the difficulty which the true view of the subject has to encounter and dispose of; else he will never really possess himself of the portion of truth which meets and removes that difficulty. Ninety-nine in a hundred of what are called educated men are in this condition; even of those who can argue fluently for their opinions. Their conclusion may be true, but it might be false for anything they know: they have never thrown themselves into the mental position of whose who think differently from them, and considered what such persons may have to say; and consequently they do not, in any proper sense of the word, know the doctrine which they themselves profess. They do not know those parts of it which explain and justify the remainder; the considerations which show that a fact which seemingly conflicts with another is reconcilable with it, or that, of two apparently strong reasons, one and not the other ought to be preferred. All that part of the truth which turns the scale, and decides the judgment of a completely informed mind, they are strangers to; nor is it ever really known, but to those who have attended equally and impartially to both sides, and endeavoured to see the reasons of both in the strongest light. So essential is this discipline to a real understanding of moral and human subjects, that if opponents of all important truths do not exist, it is indispensable to imagine them, and supply them with the strongest arguments which the most skilful devil's advocate can conjure up.

...

CHAPTER III: OF INDIVIDUALITY, AS ONE OF THE ELEMENTS OF WELL-BEING

Such being the reasons which make it imperative that human beings should be free to form opinions, and to express their opinions without reserve; and such the baneful consequences to the intellectual, and through that to the moral nature of man, unless this liberty is either conceded, or asserted in spite of prohibition; let us next examine whether the same reasons do not require that men should be free to act upon their opinions – to carry these out in their lives, without hindrance, either physical or moral, from their fellow-men, so long as it is at their own risk and peril. This last proviso is of course indispensable. No one pretends that actions should be as free as opinions. On the contrary, even opinions lose their immunity, when the circumstances in which they are expressed are such as to constitute their expression a positive instigation to some mischievous act. An opinion that corn-dealers are starvers of the poor, or that private property is robbery, ought to be unmolested when simply circulated through the press, but may justly incur punishment when delivered orally to an excited mob assembled before the house of a corn-dealer, or when handed about among the same mob in the form of a placard. Acts, of whatever kind, which, without justifiable cause, do harm to others, may be, and in the more important cases absolutely require to be, controlled by the unfavourable sentiments, and, when needful, by the active interference of mankind. The liberty of the individual must be thus far limited; he must not make himself a nuisance to other people. But if he refrains from molesting others in what concerns them, and merely acts according to his own inclination and judgment in things which concern himself, the same reasons which show that opinion should be free, prove also that he should be allowed, without molestation, to carry his opinions into practice at his own cost. That mankind are not infallible; that their truths, for the most part, are only half-truths; that unity of opinion, unless resulting from the fullest and freest comparison of opposite opinions, is not desirable, and diversity not an evil, but a good, until mankind are much more capable than at present of recognising all sides of the truth, are principles applicable to men's modes of action, not less than to their opinions. As it is useful that while mankind are imperfect there should be different opinions, so is it that there should be different experiments of living; that free scope should be given to varieties of character, short of injury to others; and that the worth of different modes of life should be proved practically, when any one thinks fit to try them. It is desirable, in short, that in things which do not primarily concern others, individuality should assert itself. Where, not the person's own character, but the traditions or customs of other people are the rule of conduct, there is wanting one of the principal ingredients of human happiness, and quite the chief ingredient of individual and social progress ...

CHAPTER IV: OF THE LIMITS TO THE AUTHORITY OF SOCIETY OVER THE INDIVIDUAL

What, then, is the rightful limit to the sovereignty of the individual over himself? Where does the authority of society begin? How much of human life should be assigned to individuality, and how much to society?

Each will receive its proper share, if each has that which more particularly concerns it. To individuality should belong the part of life in which it is chiefly the individual that is interested; to society, the part which chiefly interests society.

Though society is not founded on a contract, and though no good purpose is answered by inventing a contract in order to deduce social obligations from it, every one who receives the protection of society owes a return for the benefit, and the fact of living in society renders it indispensable that each should be bound to observe a certain line of conduct towards the rest. This conduct consists first, in not injuring the interests of one another; or rather certain interests, which, either by express legal provision or by tacit understanding, ought to be considered as rights; and secondly, in each person's bearing his share (to be fixed on some equitable principle) of the labours and sacrifices incurred for defending the society or its members from injury and molestation. These conditions society is justified in enforcing at all costs to those who endeavour to withhold fulfilment. Nor is this all that society may do. The acts of an individual may be hurtful to others, or wanting in due consideration for their welfare, without going the length of violating any of their constituted rights. The offender may then be justly punished by opinion, though not by law. As soon as any part of a person's conduct affects prejudicially the interests of others, society has jurisdiction over it, and the question whether the general welfare will or will not be promoted by interfering with it, becomes open to discussion. But there is no room for entertaining any such question when a person's conduct affects the interests of no persons besides himself, or needs not affect them unless they like (all the persons concerned being of full age, and the ordinary amount of understanding). In all such cases there should be perfect freedom, legal and social, to do the action and stand the consequences ...

READING QUESTIONS ON MILL

1 How broadly or narrowly must harm be construed for Mill's view to provide a defence of liberty?
2 What implications does Mill's focus on social injustice, rather than the injustice of the state, have for the liberal claim that the state should be neutral?
3 How are Mill's views about freedom of expression related to his understanding of individual autonomy?

R. v. Malmo-Levine; R. v. Caine [2003] 3 SCR 571

This case raised the issue of whether the criminalization of the simple possession of marihuana for personal use violates s. 7 of the *Charter*.

Gonthier and Binnie, JJ. writing for the majority:

In these appeals, the Court is required to consider whether Parliament has the legislative authority to criminalize simple possession of marihuana and, if so, whether that power has been exercised in a manner that is contrary to the *Canadian Charter of Rights and Freedoms*. The appellant Caine argues in particular that it is a violation of the principles of fundamental justice for Parliament to provide for a term of imprisonment as a sentence for conduct which he says results in little or no harm to other people. The appellant Malmo-Levine puts in issue the constitutional validity of the prohibition against possession for the purpose of trafficking in marihuana ...

The evidentiary issue at the core of the appellants' constitutional challenge is the "harm principle," and the contention that possession of marihuana for personal use is a "victimless crime." The appellants say that even with respect to the user himself or herself there is no cogent evidence of "significant" or "non-trivial" harm ...

There is no doubt that Canadian society has become much more sceptical about the alleged harm caused by the use of marihuana since the days when Emily Murphy, an Edmonton magistrate, warned that persons under the influence of marihuana "los[e] all sense of moral responsibility ... are immune to pain ... becom[ing] raving maniacs ... liable to kill ... using the most savage methods of cruelty" (*The Black Candle* (1922), at pp. 332–33). However, to exonerate marihuana from such extreme forms of denunciation is not to say it is harmless ...

The trial judge noted that the 1994 Hall Report identified three traditional "high risk groups" (at para. 46):

(1) Adolescents with a history of poor school performance;
(2) Women of childbearing age; and
(3) Persons with pre-existing diseases such as cardiovascular diseases, respiratory diseases, schizophrenia or other drug dependencies.

The inclusion of "women of childbearing age" may have to be reconsidered in light of more recent studies casting doubt on marihuana as a potential source of birth defects. However, given the immense importance of potential birth defects for all concerned, and the widely recognized need for further research, we have to accept that on this point as on many others "the jury is still out." ...

SECTION 7 OF THE *CHARTER*

The appellant Malmo-Levine argues that smoking marihuana is integral to his preferred lifestyle, and that the criminalization of marihuana in both its possession and trafficking aspects is an unacceptable infringement of his personal liberty.

The appellant Caine, on the other hand, takes aim at the potential for imprisonment for conviction of possession of marihuana, and argues that imprisonment for such an offence is not in accordance with the principles of fundamental justice. If the penalty falls, he says, the substantive offence must fall with it.

These "liberty" interests are, of course, very different. We propose therefore first to identify the s. 7 "interest" properly at stake, then secondly to discuss the applicable principles of fundamental justice. Thirdly we will examine whether the deprivation of the s. 7 interest thus identified is in accordance with the principles of fundamental justice relevant to these appeals. As will be seen, we find no s. 7 infringement.

It will therefore not be necessary to move to s. 1 to determine if an infringement would be justified in a free and democratic society.

We say at once that the availability of imprisonment for the offence of simple possession is sufficient to trigger s. 7 scrutiny: *Re B.C. Motor Vehicle Act*, [1985] 2 SCR 486. However, Malmo-Levine's position (which is supported by the intervener British Columbia Civil Liberties Association) requires us to address whether broader considerations of personal autonomy, short of imprisonment, are also sufficient to invoke s. 7 protection ...

While we accept Malmo-Levine's statement that smoking marihuana is central to his lifestyle, the Constitution cannot be stretched to afford protection to whatever activity an individual chooses to define as central to his or her lifestyle. One individual chooses to smoke marihuana; another has an obsessive interest in golf; a third is addicted to gambling. The appellant Caine invokes a taste for fatty foods. A society that extended constitutional protection to any and all such lifestyles would be ungovernable. Lifestyle choices of this order are not, we think, "basic choices going to the core of what it means to enjoy individual dignity and independence" (*Godbout, supra,* at para. 66).

In our view, with respect, Malmo-Levine's desire to build a lifestyle around the recreational use of marihuana does not attract *Charter* protection. There is no free-standing constitutional right to smoke "pot" for recreational purposes.

The appellants also invoke their s. 7 interest in "security of the person." In *Morgentaler, supra,* Dickson, C.J. accepted that "serious *state-imposed* psychological stress" (p. 56 [emphasis added]) would suffice to infringe this interest. The appellants, however, contend that use of marihuana is non-addictive. Prohibition would not therefore lead to a level of stress that is constitutionally cognizable. A very different issue would arise if the marihuana was required for medical purposes, but neither appellant uses marihuana for such a purpose.

The availability of imprisonment is a different matter. We have no doubt that the risk of being sent to jail engages the appellants' liberty interest. Accordingly, it is necessary to move to the next stage of the s. 7 analysis to determine what are the relevant principles of fundamental justice and whether this risk of deprivation of liberty is in accordance with the principles of fundamental justice.

The appellants accept that Parliament may act to avoid harm to others without violating principles of fundamental justice. They focus on the alleged absence of such harm, and contend that it is a denial of fundamental justice to deprive them of their liberty where such denial does not enhance a legitimate interest of the state. To hold otherwise, they say, would require the courts to endorse the arbitrary or irrational use of the criminal law power, contrary to the principles of fundamental justice. As Sopinka, J. stated in *Rodriguez, supra,* at p. 594:

Where the deprivation of the right in question does little or nothing to enhance the state's interest (whatever it may be), it seems to me that a breach of fundamental justice will be made out, as the individual's rights will have been deprived for no valid purpose.

The appellants' s. 7 arguments have several branches predicated on the requirement of harm. First, they argue that the only permissible target of the criminal law is harm to others; in their view, the criminal law cannot prohibit conduct that harms only the accused. Second, they argue that, in any event, marihuana is not a harmful substance, so that the prohibition of simple possession is arbitrary or irrational. Third, they argue that the criminalization of cannabis possession has adverse consequences, both for those users who are charged and convicted and, because of the disrespect engendered by the law, for the administration of justice generally, that are wholly disproportionate to the societal interests sought to be served by the prohibition ...

The appellant Malmo-Levine further submits that any harm-based analysis should focus on the healthy user who engages in harm-reduction strategies. He argues that the Court of Appeal erred "when they characterized the harms that may come with cannabis use as inherent, instead of a product of mis-cultivation, mis-distribution and mis-use" ...

We wish to be clear that we do not accept Malmo-Levine's argument that Parliament should proceed on the assumption that users will use marihuana "responsibly." We accept his point that careful use can mitigate the harmful effects, but it is open to Parliament to proceed on the more reasonable assumption that psychoactive drugs will to some extent be misused. Indeed, the evidence indicates the existence of both use and misuse by chronic users and by vulnerable groups who cause harm to themselves.

Malmo-Levine's related argument, that the pleasure of a large number of people should not be curtailed because of (he says) relatively minor harm to a minority, is similarly misplaced under s. 7. Utilitarian arguments that urge a cost-benefit calculation of alleged benefit to the many versus alleged harm to the few, to the extent such arguments are relevant under the *Charter*, belong in s. 1. The appellants must first of all establish a violation of their s. 7 rights. Only if they are able to do so is the government then required to show that the purported limitation is demonstrably justified in a free and democratic society.

The appellants contend that unless the state can establish that the use of marihuana is harmful to others, the prohibition against simple possession cannot comply with s. 7. Our colleague Arbour, J. accepts this proposition as correct to the extent that "the state resorts to imprisonment" (para. 244). Accordingly, a closer look at the alleged "harm principle" is called for.

... It is agreed by all parties that the *existence* of harm, especially harm to others, is a state interest sufficient to ground the exercise of the criminal law power. The appellants' contention, however, is that the *absence* of demonstrated harm to others deprives Parliament of the power to impose criminal liability. That is what they call the "harm principle" ...

What is the "harm principle"? The appellants rely, in particular, on the writings of the liberal theorist, J.S. Mill, who attempted to establish clear boundaries for the permissible intrusion of the state into private life:

The object of this Essay is to assert one very simple principle, as entitled to govern absolutely the dealings of society with the individual in the way of compulsion and control, whether the means used be physical force in the form of legal penalties, or the moral coercion of public opinion. That principle is, that the sole end for which mankind are warranted, individually or collectively, in interfering with the liberty of action of any of their number, is self-protection. That the only purpose for which power can be rightfully exercised over any member of a civilised community, against his will, is to prevent harm to others. His own good, either physical or moral, is not a sufficient warrant ...

Thus Mill's principle has two essential features. First, it rejects paternalism – that is, the prohibition of conduct that harms only the actor. Second, it excludes what could be called "moral harm." Mill was of the view that such moral claims are insufficient to justify use of the criminal law. Rather, he required clear and tangible harm to the rights and interests of others ...

Mill's statement has the virtues of insight and clarity but he was advocating certain general philosophic principles, not interpreting a constitutional document. Moreover, even his philosophical supporters have tended to agree that justification for state intervention cannot be reduced to a single factor – harm – but is a much more complex matter. One of Mill's most distinguished supporters, Professor H.L.A. Hart, wrote:

> Mill's formulation of the liberal point of view may well be too simple. The grounds for interfering with human liberty are more various than the single criterion of "harm to others" suggests: cruelty to animals or organizing prostitution for gain do not, as Mill himself saw, fall easily under the description of harm to others. Conversely, even where there is harm to others in the most literal sense, there may well be other principles limiting the extent to which harmful activities should be repressed by law. So there are multiple criteria, not a single criterion, determining when human liberty may be restricted.

... The appellants submit that the harm principle is a principle of fundamental justice for the purposes of s. 7 that operates to place limits on the type of conduct the state may criminalize ... However, we do not agree with the attempted elevation of the harm principle to a principle of fundamental justice. That is, in our view the harm principle is not the constitutional standard for what conduct may or may not be the subject of the criminal law for the purposes of s. 7.

In *Re B.C. Motor Vehicle Act, supra,* Lamer, J. (as he then was) explained that the principles of fundamental justice lie in "the basic tenets of our legal system. They do not lie in the realm of general public policy but in the inherent domain of the judiciary as guardian of the justice system" (p. 503). This Court provided further guidance as to what constitutes a principle of fundamental justice for the purposes of s. 7, in *Rodriguez, supra, per* Sopinka, J. (at pp. 590–91 and 607):

> A mere common law rule does not suffice to constitute a principle of funda-mental justice, rather, as the term implies, principles upon which there is some consensus that they are vital or fundamental to our societal notion of justice are required. Principles of fundamental justice must not, however, be so broad as to be no more than vague generalizations about what our society considers to be ethical or moral. They must be capable of being identified

with some precision and applied to situations in a manner which yields an understandable result. They must also, in my view, be legal principles.

...

While the principles of fundamental justice are concerned with more than process, reference must be made to principles which are "fundamental" in the sense that they would have general acceptance among reasonable people.

The requirement of "general acceptance among reasonable people" enhances the legitimacy of judicial review of state action, and ensures that the values against which state action is measured are not just fundamental "in the eye of the beholder *only*": *Rodriguez*, at pp. 607 and 590 (emphasis in original). In short, for a rule or principle to constitute a principle of fundamental justice for the purposes of s. 7, it must be a legal principle about which there is significant societal consensus that it is fundamental to the way in which the legal system ought fairly to operate, and it must be identified with sufficient precision to yield a manageable standard against which to measure deprivations of life, liberty or security of the person.

(a) Is the Harm Principle a Legal Principle?

In our view, the "harm principle" is better characterized as a description of an important state interest rather than a normative "legal" principle. Be that as it may, even if the harm principle could be characterized as a legal principle, we do not think that it meets the other requirements, as explained below.

(b) There Is No Sufficient Consensus That the Harm Principle Is Vital or Fundamental to Our Societal Notion of Criminal Justice

Contrary to the appellants' assertion, we do not think there is a consensus that the harm principle is the sole justification for criminal prohibition. There is no doubt that our case law and academic commentary are full of statements about the criminal law being aimed at conduct that "affects the public," or that constitutes "a wrong against the public welfare," or is "injurious to the public," or that "affects the community." No doubt, as stated, the *presence* of harm to others may justify legislative action under the criminal law power. However, we do not think that the *absence* of proven harm creates the unqualified barrier to legislative action that the appellants suggest. On the contrary, the state may sometimes be justified in criminalizing conduct that is either not harmful (in the sense contemplated by the harm principle), or that causes harm only to the accused ...

Several instances of crimes that do not cause harm to others are found in the *Criminal Code*, RSC 1985, c. C-46. Cannibalism is an offence (s. 182) that does not harm another sentient being, but that is nevertheless prohibited on the basis of fundamental social and ethical considerations. Bestiality (s. 160) and cruelty to animals (s. 446) are examples of crimes that rest on their offensiveness to deeply held social values rather than on Mill's "harm principle" ...

The appellants also rely on a 1982 report by the Law Reform Commission of Canada entitled *The Criminal Law in Canadian Society* which concludes, at p. 45, that the criminal law "ought to be reserved for reacting to conduct that is seriously harmful." This seems, on its face, to support the harm principle. However, the report goes on to state, at p. 45, that such harm

... may be caused or threatened to the collective safety or integrity of society through the infliction of direct damage or the undermining of what the Law Reform Commission terms fundamental or essential values – those values or interests necessary for social life to be carried on, or for the maintenance of the kind of society cherished by Canadians.

Such a definition of "harm" is clearly contrary to Mill's harm principle as endorsed by the appellants.

(c) Nor Is There Any Consensus That the Distinction between Harm to Others and Harm to Self Is of Controlling Importance

... [W]e do not accept the proposition that there is a general prohibition against the criminalization of harm to self. Canada continues to have paternalistic laws. Requirements that people wear seatbelts and motorcycle helmets are designed to "save people from themselves." There is no consensus that this sort of legislation offends our societal notions of justice. Whether a jail sentence is an appropriate penalty for such an offence is another question. However, the objection in that aspect goes to the validity of an assigned punishment – it does not go to the validity of prohibiting the underlying conduct ...

(d) The Harm Principle Is Not a Manageable Standard Against Which to Measure Deprivation of Life, Liberty or Security of the Person

Even those who agree with the "harm principle" as a regulator of the criminal law frequently disagree about what it means and what offences will meet or offend the harm principle. In the absence of any agreed definition of "harm" for this purpose, allegations and counter-allegations of non-trivial harm can be marshalled on every side of virtually every criminal law issue ...

... In the present appeal, for example, the respondents put forward a list of "harms" which they attribute to marihuana use. The appellants put forward a list of "harms" which they attribute to marihuana prohibition. Neither side gives much credence to the "harms" listed by the other. Each claims the "net" result to be in its favour.

In the result, we do not believe that the content of the "harm" principle as described by Mill and advocated by the appellants provides a manageable standard under which to review criminal or other laws under s. 7 of the *Charter*. Parliament, we think, is entitled to act under the criminal law power in the protection of legitimate state interests other than the avoidance of harm to others, subject to *Charter* limits such as the rules against arbitrariness, irrationality and gross disproportionality, discussed below ...

Arbour, J. (dissenting in Caine):

... We are asked to address, directly for the first time, whether the *Charter* requires that harm to others or to society be an essential element of an offence punishable by imprisonment. In a landmark 1985 case, Lamer, J. (as he then was) said : "A law that has the potential to convict a person who has not really done anything wrong offends the principles of fundamental justice and, if imprisonment is available as a penalty, such a law then violates a person's right to liberty under s. 7 of the *Charter*" (*Re B.C. Motor Vehicle Act*, [1985] 2 SCR 486, at p. 492 ("*Motor Vehicle Reference*")). In my view, a "person who has not really done anything wrong" is a person whose conduct caused little or no reasoned risk of harm or whose harmful conduct was not his or her fault. Therefore, for the reasons that follow, I am of the view that s. 7 of the *Charter* requires not only that some minimal mental element be an essential element of any offence punishable by imprisonment, but also that the prohibited act be harmful or pose a risk of harm to others. A law that has the potential to convict a person whose conduct causes little or no reasoned risk of harm to others offends the principles of fundamental justice and, if imprisonment is available as a penalty, such a law then violates a person's right to liberty under s. 7 of the *Charter*. Imprisonment can only be used to punish blameworthy conduct that is harmful to others ...

It is a fundamental substantive principle of criminal law that there should be no criminal responsibility without an act or omission accompanied by some sort of fault. The Latin phrase is *actus non facit reum, nisi mens sit rea* or "[t]he intent and the [a]ct must both concur to constitute the crime" ... Legal causation, which seeks to link the prohibited consequences to a culpable act of the accused, also reflects the fundamental principle that the morally innocent should not be punished (see *R. v. Nette*, [2001] 3 SCR 488, 2001 SCC 78, at para. 45). In determining whether legal causation is established, the inquiry is directed at the question of whether the accused person should be held criminally responsible for the consequences that occurred from his or her conduct. As I said in *Nette, supra*, at para. 47, "[w]hile causation is a distinct issue from *mens rea*, the proper standard of causation expresses an element of fault that is in law sufficient, in addition to the requisite mental element, to base criminal responsibility." This inquiry seeks in fact to determine whether blame can be attributed to the accused and is illustrative of criminal law's preoccupation that both the physical and mental elements of an offence coincide to reflect the blameworthiness attached to the offence and the offender ...

What exactly is wrong or blameworthy in a given criminal offence is rarely an object of debate and is usually described by the harm or risk of harm associated with the conduct. Indeed, harm is so intrinsic to most offences that few would contest, for example, the harm to others associated with murder, assault, or theft. Murder affects the fundamental right to life; assault affects the victim's security and dignity; and theft affects the victim's material comfort and, in certain circumstances, his or her right to security, dignity and privacy ...

... [H]arm or the risk of harm is a determinative factor in the assessment of the seriousness or wrongfulness of prohibited conduct. Harm associated with victimizing conduct, i.e., conduct which infringes on the rights and freedoms of identifiable persons, is the most obvious, and the concern usually is with how much the person has been harmed. This, in turn, is likely to dictate the extent of punishment or the difference in the labelling of an offence, as well as the level of *mens rea* necessary to establish culpability. Other forms of conduct cause harm that is more diffuse, where no identifiable persons have had their rights or freedoms infringed by the conduct; the harm there is collective and it is the public interest that is adversely affected. Finally, other conduct is even more distant from this notion of harm, and the prohibition of that conduct is aimed at advancing public interests distinct from the protection of individuals or society ...

I am of the view that the principles of fundamental justice require that whenever the state resorts to imprisonment, a minimum of harm to others must be an essential part of the offence. The state cannot resort to imprisonment as a punishment for conduct that causes little or no reasoned risk of harm to others. Prohibited conduct punishable by imprisonment cannot be harmless conduct or conduct that only causes harm to the perpetrator. As Braidwood, J.A. said in Caine, "it is common sense that you don't go to jail unless there is a potential that your activities will cause harm to others" (para. 134) ...

READING QUESTIONS ON *MALMO-LEVINE*

1 What are the Majority's reasons for rejecting the harm principle as a principle of fundamental justice? How does Arbour, J. respond? What do you think she might say in answer to the Majority's objection that the harm principle is not a manageable legal standard?

2 Would the Majority really disagree with Arbour, J.'s claim that "a person who has not really done anything wrong" cannot justly be imprisoned? How might they understand the idea of a legal "wrong," in such a way as to accept this claim and yet reject the harm principle? Do you think we should understand the idea of a legal wrong in this way, or in the way that Arbour, J. conceives of it?

R. v. Labaye [2005] 3 SCR 728, 2005 SCC 80

This case examines the relevance of consent to the state's power to criminalize conduct.

The judgment of McLachlin, C.J. and Major, Binnie, Deschamps, Fish, Abella and Charron, JJ. was delivered by THE CHIEF JUSTICE –

2 FACTS

The appellant operated a club in Montréal, called L'Orage. The purpose of the club was to permit couples and single people to meet each other for group sex. Only members and their guests were admitted to the club. Prospective members were interviewed to ensure that they were aware of the nature of the activities of the club and to exclude applicants who did not share the same views on group sex. Members paid an annual membership fee.

6   At the time of the events giving rise to the charge against the appellant, the club L'Orage had three floors. The first floor was occupied by a bar, the second a salon, and the third the "apartment" of the appellant. A doorman manned the main door of the club, to ensure that only members and their guests entered. Two doors separated access to the third floor apartment from the rest of the club ...

Entry to the club and participation in the activities were voluntary. No one was forced to do anything or watch anything. No one was paid for sex. While men considerably outnumbered women on the occasions when the police visited, there is no suggestion that any of the women were there involuntarily or that they did not willingly engage in the acts of group sex.

...

4 ANALYSIS

13   Section 210(1) of the *Criminal Code* makes it an offence, punishable by two years in prison, to keep a common bawdy-house. A bawdy-house is defined in s. 197(1) of the *Code* as a place kept, occupied, or resorted to "by one or more persons for the purpose of prostitution or the practice of acts of indecency." The only question in this case is whether what went on at L'Orage constituted "acts of indecency." ...

21   The shift to a harm-based rationale was completed by this Court's decisions in *R. v. Butler*, [1992] 1 SCR 452, and *Little Sisters Book and Art*

Emporium v. Canada (Minister of Justice), [2000] 2 SCR 1120, 2000 SCC 69. In *Butler*, the two-part test for obscenity of *Towne Cinema* was resolved into a single test, in which the community standard of tolerance was determined by reference to the risk of harm entailed by the conduct:

The courts must determine as best they can what the community would tolerate others being exposed to on the basis of the degree of harm that may flow from such exposure. Harm in this context means that it predisposes persons to act in an anti-social manner as, for example, the physical or mental mistreatment of women by men, or, what is perhaps debatable, the reverse. Anti-social conduct for this purpose is conduct which society formally recognizes as incompatible with its proper functioning. The stronger the inference of a risk of harm the lesser the likelihood of tolerance. [p. 485, *per* Sopinka, J].

22 The Court in *Little Sisters* confirmed that harm is an essential ingredient of obscenity. As Binnie J. pointed out, "the phrase 'degrading or dehumanizing' in *Butler* is qualified immediately by the words 'if the risk of harm is substantial' ..."

23 In *Mara*, the Court affirmed that in cases of indecency, like obscenity, the community standard of tolerance test amounts to a test of harm incompatible with society's proper functioning.

24 Grounding criminal indecency in harm represents an important advance in this difficult area of the law. Harm or significant risk of harm is easier to prove than a community standard. Moreover, the requirement of a risk of harm incompatible with the proper functioning of society brings this area of the law into step with the vast majority of criminal offences, which are based on the need to protect society from harm.

25 However, it is not always clear precisely how the harm test for indecency applies in particular circumstances ...

30 ... [T]he analysis to be performed in a particular case involves two steps. The first step is concerned with the *nature* of the harm ... The second step is concerned with the *degree* of the harm. It asks whether the harm in its degree is incompatible with the proper functioning of society. Both elements must be proved beyond a reasonable doubt before acts can be considered indecent under the *Criminal Code* ...

35 The requirement of formal endorsement ensures that people will not be convicted and imprisoned for transgressing the rules and beliefs of particular individuals or groups. To incur the ultimate criminal sanc-

tion, they must have violated values which Canadian society as a whole has formally endorsed.

36   Three types of harm have thus far emerged from the jurisprudence as being capable of supporting a finding of indecency: (1) harm to those whose autonomy and liberty may be restricted by being confronted with inappropriate conduct; (2) harm to society by predisposing others to anti-social conduct; and (3) harm to individuals participating in the conduct. Each of these types of harm is grounded in values recognized by our Constitution and similar fundamental laws. The list is not closed; other types of harm may be shown in the future to meet the standards for criminality established by *Butler*. But thus far, these are the types of harm recognized by the cases ...

4.1.5 *Summary of the Test*

62   Indecent criminal conduct will be established where the Crown proves beyond a reasonable doubt the following two requirements:

1   That, by its *nature*, the conduct at issue causes harm or presents a significant risk of harm to individuals or society in a way that undermines or threatens to undermine a value reflected in and thus formally endorsed through the Constitution or similar fundamental laws by, for example:
    (a)   confronting members of the public with conduct that significantly interferes with their autonomy and liberty; or
    (b)   predisposing others to anti-social behaviour; or
    (c)   physically or psychologically harming persons involved in the conduct, and
2   That the harm or risk of harm is of a *degree* that is incompatible with the proper functioning of society.

As the above makes clear, the categories of harm capable of satisfying the first branch of the inquiry are not closed, nor is any one of the listed categories in itself an integral part of the definition of harm. For example, predisposition to anti-social behaviour, while central to this Court's analysis in *Butler*, is but one illustration of the type of harm that undermines or threatens to undermine one of society's formally recognized values.

63   This test, applied objectively and on the basis of evidence in successive cases as they arise, is directed to articulating legal standards that

enhance the ability of persons engaged in or facilitating sexual activities to ascertain the boundary between non-criminal conduct and criminal conduct. In this way, the basic requirements of the criminal law of fair notice to potential offenders and clear enforcement standards to police will, it is hoped, be satisfied.

4.2 Application of the Test

64 The first question is whether the conduct at issue harmed, or presented a significant risk of harm to individuals or society.

65 The sexual acts at issue were conducted on the third floor of a private club, behind doors marked "*Privé*" and accessed only by persons in possession of the proper numerical code. The evidence establishes that a number of steps were taken to ensure that members of the public who might find the conduct inappropriate did not see the activities. Pre-membership interviews were conducted to advise of the nature of the activities and screen out persons not sharing the same interests. Only members and guests were admitted to the premises. A doorman controlled access to the principal door.

66 On these facts, none of the kinds of harm discussed above was established. The autonomy and liberty of members of the public was not affected by unwanted confrontation with the sexual conduct in question. On the evidence, only those already disposed to this sort of sexual activity were allowed to participate and watch.

67 Nor was there evidence of the second type of harm, the harm of predisposing people to anti-social acts or attitudes. Unlike the material at issue in *Butler*, which perpetuated abusive and humiliating stereotypes of women as objects of sexual gratification, there is no evidence of anti-social attitudes toward women, or for that matter men. No one was pressured to have sex, paid for sex, or treated as a mere sexual object for the gratification of others. The fact that L'Orage is a commercial establishment does not in itself render the sexual activities taking place there commercial in nature. Members do not pay a fee and check consent at the door; the membership fee buys access to a club where members can meet and engage in consensual activities with other individuals who have similar sexual interests. The case proceeded on the uncontested premise that all participation was on a voluntary and equal basis.

68   Finally, there is no evidence of the third type of harm – physical or psychological harm to persons participating. The only possible danger to participants on the evidence was the risk of catching a sexually transmitted disease. However, this must be discounted as a factor because, as discussed above, it is conceptually and causally unrelated to indecency.

69   As stated above, the categories of harm are not closed; in a future case other different harms may be alleged as a basis for criminal indecency. However, no other harms are raised by the evidence in this case. All that is raised, in the final analysis, is the assessment that the conduct amounted to "an orgy" and that Canadian society does not tolerate orgies (Rochon, J.A., at para. 133). This reasoning erroneously harks back to the community standard of tolerance test, which has been replaced, as discussed, by the harm-based test developed in *Butler*.

READING QUESTIONS ON *R. V. LABAYE*

1   How is the account of harm developed in *R. v. Labaye* related to Mill's "harm principle"? How is it related to the criticisms of the harm principle considered in *R. v. Malmo-Levine*, above?

2   In considering the second type of harm, the court points out that the activities were consensual. Read *R. v. Malmo-Levine*, above. Can the court distinguish between the different ways in which it treats the significance of consent in these two cases?

3   The third type of harm mentioned is "physical or psychological harm to persons participating." How does the court assess the presence or absence of this type of harm? How should it assess it? Do you think Mill would regard it as a legitimate object of criminalization?

4   Malmo-Levine also argued that Parliament should proceed on the assumption that users will use marihuana "responsibly." The court accepted that the dangers of marihuana use can be mitigated, but held that Parliament may proceed on "the more reasonable assumption that psychoactive drugs will to some extent be misused." Would a similar assumption have brought about a different result in *Labaye*?

Isaiah Berlin
"Two Concepts of Liberty" (1969)

I

To coerce a man is to deprive him of freedom – freedom from what? Almost every moralist in human history has praised freedom. Like happiness and goodness, like nature and reality, the meaning of this term is so porous that there is little interpretation that it seems able to resist. I do not propose to discuss either the history or the more than two hundred senses of this protean word recorded by historians of ideas. I propose to examine no more than two of these senses – but those central ones, with a great deal of human history behind them, and, I dare say, still to come. The first of these political senses of freedom or liberty (I shall use both words to mean the same), which (following much precedent) I shall call the "negative" sense, is involved in the answer to the question "What is the area within which the subject – a person or group of persons – is or should be left to do or be what he is able to do or be, without interference by other persons?" The second, which I shall call the positive sense, is involved in the answer to the question "What, or who, is the source of control or interference that can determine someone to do, or be, this rather than that?" The two questions are clearly different, even though the answers to them may overlap.

The Notion of "Negative" Freedom

I am normally said to be free to the degree to which no man or body of men interferes with my activity. Political liberty in this sense is simply the area within which a man can act unobstructed by others. If I am prevented by others from doing what I could otherwise do, I am to that degree unfree; and if this area is contracted by other men beyond a certain minimum, I can be described as being coerced, or, it may be, enslaved. Coercion is not, however, a term that covers every form of inability. If I say that I am unable to jump more than ten feet in the air, or cannot read because I am blind, or cannot understand the darker pages of Hegel, it would be eccentric to say that I am to that degree enslaved or coerced. Coercion implies the deliberate interference of other human beings within the area in which I could otherwise act. You lack political liberty or freedom only if you are prevented from attaining a goal by human beings.[1] Mere incapacity to attain a goal is not lack of political freedom.[2] This is brought out by the use of such modern expressions as "economic freedom" and its counterpart, "economic slavery." It is argued, very plausibly, that if a man is too poor to afford something on which there is no legal ban – a loaf of bread, a journey round the world, recourse to the law courts – he is as little free to have it as he would be if it were forbidden him by law. If my poverty were a kind of disease, which prevented me from buying bread, or paying for the journey round the world or getting my case heard, as lameness prevents me from running, this inability would not naturally be described as a lack of freedom, least of all political freedom. It is only because I believe that my inability to get a given thing is due to the fact that other human beings have made arrangements whereby I am, whereas others are not, prevented from having enough money with which to pay for it, that I think myself a victim of coercion or slavery. In other words, this use of the term depends on a particular social and economic theory about the causes of my poverty or weakness. If my lack of material means is due to my lack of mental or physical capacity, then I begin to speak of being deprived of freedom (and not simply about poverty) only if I accept the theory.[3] If, in addition, I believe that I am being kept in want by a specific arrangement which I consider unjust or unfair, I speak of economic slavery or oppression. "The nature of things does not madden us, only ill will does," said Rousseau. The criterion of oppression is the part that I believe to be played by other human beings, directly or indirectly, with or without the intention of doing so, in frustrating my wishes. By being free in this sense I mean not being interfered with by others. The wider the area of non-interference the wider my freedom.

This is what the classical English political philosophers meant when they used this word.[4] They disagreed about how wide the area could or should be. They supposed that it could not, as things were, be unlimited, because if it were, it would entail a state in which all men could boundlessly interfere with all other men; and this kind of "natural" freedom would lead to social chaos in which men's minimum needs would not be satisfied; or else the liberties of the weak would be suppressed by the strong. Because they perceived that human purposes and activities do not automatically harmonize with one another, and because (whatever their official doctrines) they put high value on other goals, such as justice, or happiness, or culture, or security, or varying degrees of equality, they were prepared to curtail freedom in the interests of other values and, indeed, of freedom itself. For, without this, it was impossible to create the kind of association that they thought desirable. Consequently, it is assumed by these thinkers that the area of men's free action must be limited by law. But equally it is assumed, especially by such libertarians as Locke and Mill in England, and Constant and Tocqueville in France, that there ought to exist a certain minimum area of personal freedom which must on no account be violated; for if it is overstepped, the individual will find himself in an area too narrow for even that minimum development of his natural faculties which alone makes it possible to pursue, and even to conceive, the various ends which men hold good or right or sacred. It follows that a frontier must be drawn between the area of private life and that of public authority. Where it is to be drawn is a matter of argument, indeed of haggling. Men are largely interdependent, and no man's activity is so completely private as never to obstruct the lives of others in any way. "Freedom for the pike is death for the minnows"; the liberty of some must depend on the restraint of others. "Freedom for an Oxford don," others have been known to add, "is a very different thing from freedom for an Egyptian peasant."

This proposition derives its force from something that is both true and important, but the phrase itself remains a piece of political claptrap. It is true that to offer political rights, or safeguards against intervention by the state, to men who are half-naked, illiterate, underfed, and diseased is to mock their condition; they need medical help or education before they can understand, or make use of, an increase in their freedom. What is freedom to those who cannot make use of it? Without adequate conditions for the use of freedom, what is the value of freedom? First things come first: there are situations, as a nineteenth-century Russian radical writer declared, in which boots are superior to the works of Shakespeare; individual freedom is not everyone's primary need. For freedom is not the mere absence of frustration of whatever kind; this would inflate the meaning of the word until it meant too much or too little. The Egyptian peasant needs clothes or medicine before, and more than, personal liberty, but the minimum freedom that he needs today, and the greater degree of freedom that he may need tomorrow, is not some species of freedom peculiar to him, but identical with that of professors, artists, and millionaires.

What troubles the consciences of Western liberals is not, I think, the belief that the freedom that men seek differs according to their social or economic conditions, but that the minority who possess it have gained it by exploiting, or, at least, averting their gaze from, the vast majority who do not. They believe, with good reason, that if individual liberty is an ultimate end for human beings, none should be deprived of it by others; least of all that some should enjoy it at the expense of others. Equality of liberty; not to treat others as I should not wish them to treat me; repayment of my debt to those who alone have made possible my liberty or prosperity or enlightenment; justice, in its simplest and most universal sense – these are the foundations of liberal morality. Liberty is not the only goal of men. I can, like the Russian critic Belinsky, say that if others are to be deprived of it – if my brothers are to remain in poverty, squalor, and chains – then I do not want it for myself, I reject it with both hands and infinitely prefer to share their fate. But nothing is gained by a confusion of terms. To avoid glaring inequality or widespread misery I am ready to sacrifice some, or all, of my freedom: I may do so willingly and freely: but it is freedom that I am giving up for the sake of justice or equality or the love of my fellow men. I should be guilt-stricken, and rightly so, if I were not, in some circumstances, ready to make this sacrifice. But a sacrifice is not an increase in what is being sacrificed, namely freedom, however great the moral need or the compensation for it. Everything is what it is: liberty is liberty, not equality or fairness or justice or culture, or human happiness or a quiet conscience. If the liberty of myself or my class or nation depends on the misery of a number of other human beings, the system which promotes this is unjust and immoral. But if I curtail or lose my freedom, in order to lessen the shame of such inequality, and do not thereby materially increase the individual liberty of others, an absolute loss of liberty occurs. This may be compensated for by a gain in justice or in happiness or in peace, but the loss remains, and it is a confusion of values to say that although my "liberal," individual freedom may go by the board, some other kind of freedom – "social" or "economic" – is increased. Yet it remains true that the freedom of some must at times be curtailed to secure the freedom of others. Upon what principle should this be done? If freedom is a sacred, untouchable value, there can be no such principle. One or other of these conflicting rules or principles must, at any rate in practice, yield: not always for reasons which can be clearly stated, let alone generalized into rules or universal maxims. Still, a practical compromise has to be found.

Philosophers with an optimistic view of human nature and a belief in the possibility of harmonizing human interests, such as Locke or Adam Smith and, in some moods, Mill, believed that social harmony and progress were compatible with reserving a large area for private life over which neither the state nor any other authority must be allowed to trespass. Hobbes, and those who agreed with him, especially conservative or reactionary thinkers, argued that if men were to be prevented from destroying one another and making social life a jungle or a wilderness, greater safeguards must be instituted to keep them in their places; he wished correspondingly to increase the area of centralized control and decrease that of the individual. But both sides agreed that some portion of human existence must remain independent of the sphere of social control. To invade that preserve, however small, would be despotism. The most eloquent of all defenders of freedom and privacy, Benjamin Constant, who had not forgotten the Jacobin dictatorship, declared that at the very least the liberty of religion, opinion, expression, property, must be guaranteed against arbitrary invasion. Jefferson, Burke, Paine, Mill, compiled different catalogues of individual liberties, but the argument for keeping authority at bay is always substantially the same. We must preserve a minimum area of personal freedom if we are not to "degrade or deny our nature." We cannot remain absolutely free, and must give up some of our liberty to preserve the rest. But total self-surrender is self-defeating. What then must the minimum be? That which a man cannot give up without offending against the essence of his human nature. What is this essence? What are the standards which it entails? This has been, and perhaps always will be, a matter of infinite debate. But whatever the principle in terms of which the area of non-interference is to be drawn, whether it is that of natural law or natural rights, or of utility or the pronouncements of a categorical imperative, or the sanctity of the social contract, or any other concept with which men have sought to clarify and justify their convictions, liberty in this sense means liberty *from*; absence of interference beyond the shifting, but always recognizable, frontier. "The only freedom which deserves the name is that of pursuing our own good in our own way," said the most celebrated of its champions. If this is so, is compulsion ever justified? Mill had no doubt that it was. Since justice demands that all individuals be entitled to a minimum of freedom, all other individuals were of necessity to be restrained, if need be by force, from depriving anyone of it. Indeed, the whole function of law was the prevention of just such collisions: the state was reduced to what Lassalle contemptuously described as the functions of a nightwatchman or traffic policeman.

What made the protection of individual liberty so sacred to Mill? In his famous essay he declares that, unless men are left to live as they wish "in the path which merely concerns themselves," civilization cannot advance; the truth will not, for lack of a free market in ideas, come to light; there will be no scope for spontaneity, originality, genius, for mental energy, for moral courage. Society will be crushed by the weight of "collective mediocrity." Whatever is rich and diversified will be crushed by the weight of custom, by men's constant tendency to conformity, which breeds only "withered capacities," "pinched and hidebound," "cramped and warped" human beings. "Pagan self-assertion is as worthy as Christian self-denial." "All the errors which a man is likely to commit against advice and warning are far outweighed by the evil of allowing others to constrain him to what they deem is good." The defence of liberty consists in the "negative" goal of warding off interference. To threaten a man with persecution unless he submits to a life in which he exercises no choices of his goals; to block before him every door but one, no matter how noble the prospect upon which it opens, or how benevolent the motives of those who arrange this, is to sin against the truth that he is a man, a being with a life of his own to live. This is liberty as it has been conceived by liberals in the modern world from the days of Erasmus (some would say of Occam) to our own. Every plea for civil liberties and individual rights, every protest against exploitation and humiliation, against the encroachment of public authority, or the mass hypnosis of custom or organized propaganda, springs from this individualistic, and much disputed, conception of man.

Three facts about this position may be noted. In the first place Mill confuses two distinct notions. One is that all coercion is, in so far as it frustrates human desires, bad as such, although it may have to be applied to prevent other, greater evils; while non-interference, which is the opposite of coercion, is good as such, although it is not the only good. This is the "negative" conception of liberty in its classical form. The other is that men should seek to discover the truth, or to develop a certain type of character of which Mill approved – critical, original, imaginative, independent, non-conforming to the point of eccentricity, and so on – and that truth can be found, and such character can be bred, only in conditions of freedom. Both these are liberal views, but they are not identical, and the connexion between them is, at best, empirical. No one would argue that truth or freedom of self-expression could flourish where dogma crushes all thought. But the evidence of history tends to show (as, indeed, was argued by James Stephen in his formidable attack on Mill in his *Liberty, Equality, Fraternity*) that integrity, love of truth, and fiery individualism grow at least as often in severely disciplined communities among, for example, the puritan Calvinists of Scotland or New England, or under military discipline, as in more tolerant or indifferent societies; and if this is so, Mill's argument for liberty as a necessary condition for the growth of human genius falls to the ground. If his two goals proved incompatible, Mill would be faced with a cruel dilemma, quite apart from the further difficulties created by the inconsistency of his doctrines with strict utilitarianism, even in his own humane version of it.[5]

In the second place, the doctrine is comparatively modern. There seems to be scarcely any discussion of individual liberty as a conscious political ideal (as opposed to its actual existence) in the ancient world. Condorcet had already remarked that the notion of individual rights was absent from the legal conceptions of the Romans and Greeks; this seems to hold equally of the Jewish, Chinese, and all other ancient civilizations that have since come to light.[6] The domination of this ideal has been the exception rather than the rule, even in the recent history of the West. Nor has liberty in this sense often formed a rallying cry for the great masses of mankind. The desire not to be impinged upon, to be left to oneself, has been a mark of high civilization both on the part of individuals and communities. The sense of privacy itself, of the area of personal relationships as something sacred in its own right, derives from a conception of freedom which, for all its religious roots, is scarcely older, in its developed state, than the Renaissance or the Reformation.[7] Yet its decline would mark the death of a civilization, of an entire moral outlook.

The third characteristic of this notion of liberty is of greater importance. It is that liberty in this sense is not incompatible with some kinds of autocracy, or at any rate with the absence of self-government. Liberty in this sense is principally concerned with the area of control, not with its source. Just as a democracy may, in fact, deprive the individual citizen of a great many liberties which he might have in some other form of society, so it is perfectly conceivable that a liberal-minded despot would allow his subjects a large measure of personal freedom. The despot who leaves his subjects a wide area of liberty may be unjust, or encourage the wildest inequalities, care little for order, or virtue, or knowledge; but provided he does not curb their liberty, or at least curbs it less than many other régimes, he meets with Mill's specification.[8] Freedom in this sense is not, at any rate logically, connected with democracy or self-government. Self-government may, on the whole, provide a better guarantee of the preservation of civil liberties than other régimes, and has been defended as such by libertarians. But there is no necessary connexion between individual liberty and democratic rule. The answer to the question "Who governs me?" is logically distinct from the question "How far does government interfere with me?" It is in this difference that the great contrast between the two concepts of negative and positive liberty, in the end, consists.[9] For the "positive" sense of liberty comes to light if we try to answer the question, not "What am I free to do or be?," but "By whom am I ruled?" or "Who is to say what I am, and what I am not, to be or do?" The connexion between democracy and individual liberty is a good deal more tenuous than it seemed to many advocates of both. The desire to be governed by myself, or at any rate to participate in the process by which my life is to be controlled, may be as deep a wish as that of a free area for action, and perhaps historically older. But it is not a desire for the same thing. So different is it, indeed, as to have led in the end to the great clash of ideologies that dominates our world. For it is this – the "positive" conception of liberty: not freedom from, but freedom to – to lead one prescribed form of life – which the adherents of the "negative" notion represent as being, at times, no better than a specious disguise for brutal tyranny.

II

The Notion of Positive Freedom

The "positive" sense of the word "liberty" derives from the wish on the part of the individual to be his own master. I wish my life and decisions to depend on myself, not on external forces of whatever kind. I wish to be the instrument of my own, not of other men's, acts of will. I wish to be a subject, not an object; to be moved by reasons, by conscious purposes, which are my own, not by causes which affect me, as it were, from outside. I wish to be somebody, not nobody; a doer – deciding, not being decided for, self-directed and not acted upon by external nature or by other men as if I were a thing, or an animal, or a slave incapable of playing a human role, that is, of conceiving goals and policies of my own and realizing them. This is at least part of what I mean when I say that I am rational, and that it is my reason that distinguishes me as a human being from the rest of the world. I wish, above all, to be conscious of myself as a thinking, willing, active being, bearing responsibility for my choices and able to explain them by references to my own ideas and purposes. I feel free to the degree that I believe this to be true, and enslaved to the degree that I am made to realize that it is not.

The freedom which consists in being one's own master, and the freedom which consists in not being prevented from choosing as I do by other men, may, on the face of it, seem concepts at no great logical distance from each other – no more than negative and positive ways of saying much the same thing. Yet the "positive" and "negative" notions of freedom historically developed in divergent directions not always by logically reputable steps, until, in the end, they came into direct conflict with each other.

One way of making this clear is in terms of the independent momentum which the, initially perhaps quite harmless, metaphor of self-mastery acquired. "I am my own master"; "I am slave to no man"; but may I not (as Platonists or Hegelians tend to say) be a slave to nature? Or to my own "unbridled" passions? Are these not so many species of the identical genus "slave" – some political or legal, others moral or spiritual? Have not men had the experience of liberating themselves from spiritual slavery, or slavery to nature, and do they not in the course of it become aware, on the one hand, of a self which dominates, and, on the other, of something in them which is brought to heel? This dominant self is then variously identified with reason, with my "higher nature," with the self which calculates and aims at what will satisfy it in the long run, with my "real," or "ideal," or "autonomous" self, or with my self "at its best"; which is then contrasted with irrational impulse, uncontrolled desires, my "lower" nature, the pursuit of immediate pleasures, my "empirical" or "heteronomous" self, swept by every gust of desire and passion, needing to be rigidly disciplined if it is ever to rise to the full height of its "real" nature. Presently the two selves may be represented as divided by an even larger gap: the real self may be conceived as something wider than the individual (as the term is normally understood), as a social "whole" of which the individual is an element or aspect: a tribe, a race, a church, a state, the great society of the living and the dead and the yet unborn. This entity is then identified as being the "true" self which, by imposing its collective, or "organic," single will upon its recalcitrant "members," achieves its own, and therefore their, "higher" freedom. The perils of using organic metaphors to justify the coercion of some men by others in order to raise them to a "higher" level of freedom have often been pointed out. But what gives such plausibility as it has to this kind of language is that we recognize that it is possible, and at times justifiable, to coerce men in the name of some goal (let us say, justice or public health) which they would, if they were more enlightened, themselves pursue, but do not, because they are blind or ignorant or corrupt. This renders it easy for me to conceive of myself as coercing others for their own sake, in their, not my, interest. I am then claiming that I know what they truly need better than they know it themselves. What, at most, this entails is that they would not resist me if they were rational and as wise as I and understood their interests as I do. But I may go on to claim a good deal more than this. I may declare that they are actually aiming at what in their benighted state they consciously resist, because there exists within them an occult entity – their latent rational will, or their "true" purpose – and that this entity, although it is belied by all that they overtly feel and do and say, is their "real" self, of which the poor empirical self in space and time may know nothing or little; and that this inner spirit is the only self that deserves to have its wishes taken into account.[10] Once I take this view, I am in a position to ignore the actual wishes of men or societies, to bully, oppress, torture them in the name, and on behalf, of their "real" selves, in the secure knowledge that whatever is the true goal of man (happiness, performance of duty, wisdom, a just society, self-fulfilment) must be identical with his freedom – the free choice of his "true," albeit often submerged and inarticulate, self.

This paradox has been often exposed. It is one thing to say that I know what is good for X, while he himself does not; and even to ignore his wishes for its – and his – sake; and a very different one to say that he has *eo ipso* chosen it, not indeed consciously, not as he seems in everyday life, but in his role as a rational self which his empirical self may not know – the "real" self which discerns the good, and cannot help choosing it once it is revealed. This monstrous impersonation, which consists in equating what X would choose if he were something he is not, or at least not yet, with what X actually seeks and chooses, is at the heart of all political theories of self-realization. It is one thing to say that I may be coerced for my own good which I am too blind to see: this may, on occasion, be for my benefit; indeed it may enlarge the scope of my liberty. It is another to say that if it is my good, then I am not being coerced, for I have willed it, whether I know this or not, and am free (or "truly" free) even while my poor earthly body and foolish mind bitterly reject it, and struggle against those who seek however benevolently to impose it, with the greatest desperation.

This magical transformation, or sleight of hand (for which William James so justly mocked the Hegelians), can no doubt be perpetrated just as easily with the "negative" concept of freedom, where the self that should not be interfered with is no longer the individual with his actual wishes and needs as they are normally conceived, but the "real" man within, identified with the pursuit of some ideal purpose not dreamed of by his empirical self. And, as in the case of the "positively" free self, this entity may be inflated into some super-personal entity – a state, a class, a nation, or the march of history itself, regarded as a more "real" subject of attributes than the empirical self. But the "positive" conception of freedom, as self-mastery, with its suggestion of a man divided against himself, has, in fact, and as a matter of history, of doctrine and of practice, lent itself more easily to this splitting of personality into two: the transcendent, dominant controller, and the empirical bundle of desires and passions to be disciplined and brought to heel. It is this historical fact that has been influential. This demonstrates (if demonstration of so obvious a truth is needed) that conceptions of freedom directly derive from views of what constitutes a self, a person, a man. Enough manipulation with the definition of man, and freedom can be made to mean whatever the manipulator wishes.

...

III [VIII in original]

The One and the Many

One belief, more than any other, is responsible for the slaughter of individuals on the altars of the great historical ideals – justice or progress or the happiness of future generations, or the sacred mission or emancipation of a nation or race or class, or even liberty itself, which demands the sacrifice of individuals for the freedom of society. This is the belief that somewhere, in the past or in the future, in divine revelation or in the mind of an individual thinker, in the pronouncements of history or science, or in the simple heart of an uncorrupted good man, there is a final solution. This ancient faith rests on the conviction that all the positive values in which men have believed must, in the end, be compatible, and perhaps even entail one another. "Nature binds truth, happiness, and virtue together as by an indissoluble chain," said one of the best men who ever lived, and spoke in similar terms of liberty, equality, and justice.[11] But is this true? It is a commonplace that neither political equality nor efficient organization nor social justice is compatible with more than a modicum of individual liberty, and certainly not with unrestricted *laissez-faire;* that justice and generosity, public and private loyalties, the demands of genius and the claims of society, can conflict violently with each other. And it is no great way from that to the generalization that not all good things are compatible, still less all the ideals of mankind. But somewhere, we shall be told, and in some way, it must be possible for all these values to live together, for unless this is so, the universe is not a cosmos, not a harmony; unless this is so, conflicts of values may be an intrinsic, irremovable element in human life. To admit that the fulfilment of some of our ideals may in principle make the fulfilment of others impossible is to say that the notion of total human fulfilment is a formal contradiction, a metaphysical chimaera. For every rationalist metaphysician, from Plato to the last disciples of Hegel or Marx, this abandonment of the notion of a final harmony in which all riddles are solved, all contradictions reconciled, is a piece of crude empiricism, abdication before brute facts, intolerable bankruptcy of reason before things as they are, failure to explain and to justify, to reduce everything to a system, which "reason" indignantly rejects. But if we are not armed with an *a priori* guarantee of the proposition that a total harmony of true values is somewhere to be found – perhaps in some ideal realm the characteristics of which we can, in our finite state, not so much as conceive – we must fall back on the ordinary resources of empirical observation and ordinary human knowledge. And these certainly give us no warrant for supposing (or even understanding what would be meant by saying) that all good things, or all bad things for that matter, are reconcilable with each other. The world that we encounter in ordinary experience is one in which we are faced with choices between ends equally ultimate, and claims equally absolute, the realization of some of which must inevitably involve the sacrifice of others. Indeed, it is because this is their situation that men place such immense value upon the freedom to choose; for if they had assurance that in some perfect state, realizable by men on earth, no ends pursued by them would ever be in conflict, the necessity and agony of choice would disappear, and with it the central importance of the freedom to choose. Any method of bringing this final state nearer would then seem fully justified, no matter how much freedom were sacrificed to forward its advance. It is, I have no doubt, some such dogmatic certainty that has been responsible for the deep, serene, unshakeable conviction in the minds of some of the most merciless tyrants and persecutors in history that what they did was fully justified by its purpose. I do not say that the ideal of self-perfection – whether for individuals or nations or churches or classes – is to be condemned in itself, or that the language which was used in its defence was in all cases the result of a confused or fraudulent use of words, or of moral or intellectual perversity. Indeed, I have tried to show that it is the notion of freedom in its "positive" sense that is at the heart of the demands for national or social self-direction which animate the most powerful and morally just public movements of our time, and that not to recognize this is to misunderstand the most vital facts and ideas of our age. But equally it seems to me that the belief that some single formula can in principle be found whereby all the diverse ends of men can be harmoniously realized is demonstrably false. If, as I believe, the ends of men are many, and not all of them are in principle compatible with each other, then the possibility of conflict – and of tragedy – can never wholly be eliminated from human life, either personal or social. The necessity of choosing between absolute claims is then an inescapable characteristic of the human condition. This gives its value to freedom as Acton had conceived of it – as an end in itself, and not as a temporary need, arising out of our confused notions and irrational and disordered lives, a predicament which a panacea could one day put right.

I do not wish to say that individual freedom is, even in the most liberal societies, the sole, or even the dominant, criterion of social action. We compel children to be educated, and we forbid public executions. These are certainly curbs to freedom. We justify them on the ground that ignorance, or a barbarian upbringing, or cruel pleasures and excitements are worse for us than the amount of restraint needed to repress them. This judgment in turn depends on how we determine good and evil, that is to say, on our moral, religious, intellectual, economic, and aesthetic values; which are, in their turn, bound up with our conception of man, and of the basic demands of his nature. In other words, our solution of such problems is based on our vision, by which we are consciously or unconsciously guided, of what constitutes a fulfilled human life, as contrasted with Mill's "cramped and warped," "pinched and hidebound" natures. To protest against the laws governing censorship or personal morals as intolerable infringements of personal liberty presupposes a belief that the activities which such laws forbid are fundamental needs of men as men, in a good (or, indeed, any) society. To defend such laws is to hold that these needs are not essential, or that they cannot be satisfied without sacrificing other values which come higher – satisfy deeper needs – than individual freedom, determined by some standard that is not merely subjective, a standard for which some objective status – empirical or *a priori* – is claimed.

The extent of a man's, or a people's, liberty to choose to live as they desire must be weighed against the claims of many other values, of which equality, or justice, or happiness, or security, or public order are perhaps the most obvious examples. For this reason, it cannot be unlimited. We are rightly reminded by R.H. Tawney that the liberty of the strong, whether their strength is physical or economic, must be restrained. This maxim claims respect, not as a consequence of some *a priori* rule, whereby the respect for the liberty of one man logically entails respect for the liberty of others like him; but simply because respect for the principles of justice, or shame at gross inequality of treatment, is as basic in men as the desire for liberty. That we cannot have everything is a necessary, not a contingent, truth. Burke's plea for the constant need to compensate, to reconcile, to balance; Mill's plea for novel "experiments in living" with their permanent possibility of error, the knowledge that it is not merely in practice but in principle impossible to reach clear-cut and certain answers, even in an ideal world of wholly good and rational men and wholly clear ideas – may madden those who seek for final solutions and single, all-embracing systems, guaranteed to be eternal. Nevertheless, it is a conclusion that cannot be escaped by those who, with Kant, have learnt the truth that out of the crooked timber of humanity no straight thing was ever made.

There is little need to stress the fact that monism, and faith in a single criterion, has always proved a deep source of satisfaction both to the intellect and to the emotions. Whether the standard of judgment derives from the vision of some future perfection, as in the minds of the *philosophes* in the eighteenth century and their technocratic successors in our own day, or is rooted in the past – *la terre et les morts* – as maintained by German historicists or French theocrats, or neo-Conservatives in English-speaking countries, it is bound, provided it is inflexible enough, to encounter some unforeseen and unforeseeable human development, which it will not fit; and will then be used to justify the *a priori* barbarities of Procrustes – the vivisection of actual human societies into some fixed pattern dictated by our fallible understanding of a largely imaginary past or a wholly imaginary future. To preserve our absolute categories or ideals at the expense of human lives offends equally against the principles of science and of history; it is an attitude found in equal measure on the right and left wings in our days, and is not reconcilable with the principles accepted by those who respect the facts.

Pluralism, with the measure of "negative" liberty that it entails, seems to me a truer and more humane ideal than the goals of those who seek in the great, disciplined, authoritarian structures the ideal of "positive" self-mastery by classes, or peoples, or the whole of mankind. It is truer, because it does, at least, recognize the fact that human goals are many, not all of them commensurable, and in perpetual rivalry with one another. To assume that all values can be graded on one scale, so that it is a mere matter of inspection to determine the highest, seems to me to falsify our knowledge that men are free agents, to represent moral decision as an operation which a slide-rule could, in principle, perform. To say that in some ultimate, all-reconciling, yet realizable synthesis, duty *is* interest, or individual freedom *is* pure democracy or an authoritarian state, is to throw a metaphysical blanket over either self-deceit or deliberate hypocrisy. It is more humane because it does not (as the system builders do) deprive men, in the name of some remote, or incoherent, ideal, of much that they have found to be indispensable to their life as unpredictably self-transforming human beings.[12] In the end, men choose between ultimate values; they choose as they do, because their life and thought are determined by fundamental moral categories and concepts that are, at any rate over large stretches of time and space, a part of their being and thought and sense of their own identity; part of what makes them human.

It may be that the ideal of freedom to choose ends without claiming eternal validity for them, and the pluralism of values connected with this, is only the late fruit of our declining capitalist civilization: an ideal which remote ages and primitive societies have not recognized, and one which posterity will regard with curiosity, even sympathy, but little comprehension. This may be so; but no sceptical conclusions seem to me to follow. Principles are not less sacred because their duration cannot be guaranteed. Indeed, the very desire for guarantees that our values are eternal and secure in some objective heaven is perhaps only a craving for the certainties of childhood or the absolute values of our primitive past. "To realise the relative validity of one's convictions," said an admirable writer of our time, "and yet stand for them unflinchingly, is what distinguishes a civilised man from a barbarian." To demand more than this is perhaps a deep and incurable metaphysical need; but to allow it to determine one's practice is a symptom of an equally deep, and more dangerous, moral and political immaturity.

NOTES

1 I do not, of course, mean to imply the truth of the converse.

2 Helvétius made this point very clearly: "The free man is the man who is not in irons, nor imprisoned in a gaol, nor terrorized like a slave by the fear of punishment ... it is not lack of freedom not to fly like an eagle or swim like a whale."

3 The Marxist conception of social laws is, of course, the best-known version of this theory, but it forms a large element in some Christian and utilitarian, and all socialist, doctrines.

4 "A free man," said Hobbes, "is he that ... is not hindered to do what he hath the will to do." Law is always a "fetter," even if it protects you from being bound in chains that are heavier than those of the law, say, some more repressive law or custom, or arbitrary despotism or chaos. Bentham says much the same.

5 This is but another illustration of the natural tendency of all but a very few thinkers to believe that all the things they hold good must be intimately connected, or at least compatible, with one another. The history of thought, like the history of nations, is strewn with examples of inconsistent, or at least disparate, elements artificially yoked together in a despotic system, or held together by the danger of some common enemy. In due course the danger passes, and conflicts between the allies arise, which often disrupt the system, sometimes to the great benefit of mankind.

6 See the valuable discussion of this in Michel Villey, *Leçons d'histoire de la philosophie du droit*, who traces the embryo of the notion of subjective rights to Occam.

7 Christian (and Jewish or Moslem) belief in the absolute authority of divine or natural laws, or in the equality of all men in the sight of God, is very different from belief in freedom to live as one prefers.

8 Indeed, it is arguable that in the Prussia of Frederick the Great or in the Austria of Josef II men of imagination, originality, and creative genius, and, indeed, minorities of all kinds, were less persecuted and felt the pressure, both of institutions and custom, less heavy upon them than in many an earlier or later democracy.

9 "Negative liberty" is something the extent of which, in a given case, it is difficult to estimate. It might, prima facie, seem to depend simply on the power to choose between at any rate two alternatives. Nevertheless, not

all choices are equally free, or free at all. If in a totalitarian state I betray my friend under threat of torture, perhaps even if I act from fear of losing my job, I can reasonably say that I did not act freely. Nevertheless, I did, of course, make a choice, and could, at any rate in theory, have chosen to be killed or tortured or imprisoned. The mere existence of alternatives is not, therefore, enough to make my action free (although it may be voluntary) in the normal sense of the word. The extent of my freedom seems to depend on (*a*) how many possibilities are open to me (although the method of counting these can never be more than impressionistic. Possibilities of action are not discrete entities like apples, which can be exhaustively enumerated); (*b*) how easy or difficult each of these possibilities is to actualize; (*c*) how important in my plan of life, given my character and circumstances, these possibilities are when compared with each other; (*d*) how far they are closed and opened by deliberate human acts; (*e*) what value not merely the agent, but the general sentiment of the society in which he lives, puts on the various possibilities. All these magnitudes must be "integrated," and a conclusion, necessarily never precise, or indisputable, drawn from this process. It may well be that there are many incommensurable kinds and degrees of freedom, and that they cannot be drawn up on any single scale of magnitude. Moreover, in the case of societies, we are faced by such (logically absurd) questions as "Would arrangement X increase the liberty of Mr. A more than it would that of Messrs. B, C, and D between them, added together?" The same difficulties arise in applying utilitarian criteria. Nevertheless, provided we do not demand precise measurement, we can give valid reasons for saying that the average subject of the King of Sweden is, on the whole, a good deal freer today than the average citizen of Spain or Albania. Total patterns of life must be compared directly as wholes, although the method by which we make the comparison, and the truth of the conclusions, are difficult or impossible to demonstrate. But the vagueness of the concepts, and the multiplicity of the criteria involved, is an attribute of the subject-matter itself, not of our imperfect methods of measurement, or incapacity for precise thought.

10 "The ideal of true freedom is the maximum of power for all the members of human society alike to make the best of themselves," said T.H. Green in 1881. Apart from the confusion of freedom with equality, this entails that if a man chose some immediate pleasure – which (in whose view?) would not enable him to make the best of himself (what self?) – what he was exercising was not "true" freedom: and if deprived of it, would not

lose anything that mattered. Green was a genuine liberal: but many a tyrant could use this formula to justify his worst acts of oppression.

11 Condorcet, from whose *Esquisse* these words are quoted, declares that the task of social science is to show "by what bonds Nature has united the progress of enlightenment with that of liberty, virtue, and respect for the natural rights of man; how these ideals, which alone are truly good, yet so often separated from each other that they are even believed to be incompatible, should, on the contrary, become inseparable, as soon as enlightenment has reached a certain level simultaneously among a large number of nations." He goes on to say that: "Men still preserve the errors of their childhood, of their country, and of their age long after having recognized all the truths needed for destroying them." Ironically enough, his belief in the need and possibility of uniting all good things may well be precisely the kind of error he himself so well described.

12 On this also Bentham seems to me to have spoken well: "Individual interests are the only real interests ... can it be conceived that there are men so absurd as to ... prefer the man who is not to him who is; to torment the living, under pretence of promoting the happiness of them who are not born, and who may never be born?" This is one of the infrequent occasions when Burke agrees with Bentham; for this passage is at the heart of the empirical, as against the metaphysical, view of politics.

Charles Taylor
"What's Wrong with Negative Liberty" (1985)

Taylor criticizes the coherence of the idea of negative liberty. In particular, he questions its usefulness to liberalism's aim of enabling individuals to flourish.

... Doctrines of positive freedom are concerned with a view of freedom which involves essentially the exercising of control over one's life. On this view, one is free only to the extent that one has effectively determined oneself and the shape of one's life. The concept of freedom here is an exercise-concept.

By contrast, negative theories can rely simply on an opportunity-concept, where being free is a matter of what we can do, of what it is open to us to do, whether or not we do anything to exercise these options. This certainly is the case of the crude, original Hobbesian concept. Freedom consists just in there being no obstacle. It is a sufficient condition of one's being free that nothing stand in the way.

But we have to say that negative theories *can* rely on an opportunity-concept, rather than that they necessarily do so rely, for we have to allow for that part of the gamut of negative theories mentioned above which incorporates some notion of self-realization. Plainly this kind of view cannot rely simply on an opportunity-concept. We cannot say that someone is free, on a self-realization view, if he is totally unrealized, if for instance he is totally unaware of his potential, if fulfilling it has never even arisen as a question for him, or if he is paralysed by the fear of breaking with some norm which he has internalized but which does not authentically reflect him. Within this conceptual scheme, some degree of exercise is necessary for a man to be thought free. Or if we want to think of the internal bars to freedom as obstacles on all fours with the external ones, then being in a position to exercise freedom, having the opportunity, involves removing the internal barriers; and this is not possible without having to some extent realized myself. So that with the freedom of self-realization, having the opportunity to be free requires that I already be exercising freedom. A pure opportunity-concept is impossible here.

But if negative theories can be grounded on either an opportunity- or an exercise-concept, the same is not true of positive theories. The view that freedom involves at least partially collective self-rule is essentially grounded on an exercise-concept. For this view (at least partly) identifies freedom with self-direction, that is, the actual exercise of directing control over one's life.

But this already gives us a hint towards illuminating the above paradox, that while the extreme variant of positive freedom is usually pinned on its protagonists by their opponents, negative theorists seem prone to embrace the crudest versions of their theory themselves. For if an opportunity-concept is not combinable with a positive theory, but either it or its alternative can suit a negative theory, then one way of ruling out positive theories in principle is by firmly espousing an opportunity-concept. One cuts off the positive theories by the root, as it were, even though one may also pay a price in the atrophy of a wide range of negative theories as well. At least by taking one's stand firmly on the crude side of the negative range, where only opportunity-concepts are recognized, one leaves no place for a positive theory to grow.

Taking one's stand here has the advantage that one is holding the line around a very simple and basic issue of principle, and one where the negative view seems to have some backing in common sense. The basic intuition here is that freedom is a matter of being able to do something or other, of not having obstacles in one's way, rather than being a capacity that we have to realize. It naturally seems more prudent to fight the Totalitarian Menace at this last-ditch position, digging in behind the natural frontier of this simple issue, rather than engaging the enemy on the open terrain of exercise-concepts, where one will have to fight to discriminate the good from the bad among such concepts; fight, for instance, for a view of individual self-realization, against various notions of collective self-realization, of a nation, or a class. It seems easier and safer to cut all the nonsense off at the start by declaring all self-realization views to be metaphysical hog-wash. Freedom should just be tough-mindedly defined as the absence of external obstacles.

Of course, there are independent reasons for wanting to define freedom tough-mindedly. In particular there is the immense influence of the anti-metaphysical, materialist, natural-science-oriented temper of thought in our civilization. Something of this spirit at its inception induced Hobbes to take the line that he did, and the same spirit goes marching on today. Indeed, it is because of the prevalence of this spirit that the line is so easy to defend, forensically speaking, in our society.

Nevertheless, I think that one of the strongest motives for defending the crude Hobbes-Bentham concept, that freedom is the absence of external obstacles, physical or legal, is the strategic one above. For most of those who take this line thereby abandon many of their own intuitions, sharing as they do with the rest of us in a post-Romantic civilization which puts great value on self-realization, and values freedom largely because of this. It is fear of the Totalitarian Menace, I would argue, which has led them to abandon this terrain to the enemy.

I want to argue that this not only robs their eventual forensic victory of much of its value, since they become incapable of defending liberalism in the form we in fact value it, but I want to make the stronger claim that this Maginot Line mentality actually ensures defeat, as is often the case with Maginot Line mentalities. The Hobbes-Bentham view, I want to argue, is indefensible as a view of freedom.

To see this, let us examine the line more closely, and the temptation to stand on it. The advantage of the view that freedom is the absence of external obstacles is its simplicity. It allows us to say that freedom is being able to do what you want, where what you want is unproblematically understood as what the agent can identify as his desires. By contrast an exercise-concept of freedom requires that we discriminate among motivations. If we are free in the exercise of certain capacities, then we are not free, or less free, when these capacities are in some way unfulfilled or blocked. But the obstacles can be internal as well as external. And this must be so, for the capacities relevant to freedom must involve some self-awareness, self-understanding, moral discrimination and self-control, otherwise their exercise could not amount to freedom in the sense of self-direction; and this being so, we can fail to be free because these internal conditions are not realized. But where this happens, where, for example, we are quite self-deceived, or utterly fail to discriminate properly the ends we seek, or have lost self-control, we can quite easily be doing what we want in the sense of what we can identify as our wants, without being free; indeed, we can be further entrenching our unfreedom.

Once one adopts a self-realization view, or indeed any exercise-concept of freedom, then being able to do what one wants can no longer be accepted as a sufficient condition of being free. For this view puts certain conditions on one's motivation. You are not free if you are motivated, through fear, inauthentically internalized standards, or false consciousness, to thwart your self-realization.

...

There are some considerations one can put forward straight off to show that the pure Hobbesian concept will not work, that there are some discriminations among motivations which are essential to the concept of freedom as we use it. Even where we think of freedom as the absence of external obstacles, it is not the absence of such obstacles *simpliciter*. For we make discriminations between obstacles as representing more or less serious infringements of freedom. And we do this, because we deploy the concept against a background understanding that certain goals and activities are more significant than others.

Thus we could say that my freedom is restricted if the local authority puts up a new traffic light at an intersection close to my home; so that where previously I could cross as I liked, consistently with avoiding collision with other cars, now I have to wait until the light is green. In a philosophical argument, we might call this a restriction of freedom, but not in a serious political debate. The reason is that it is too trivial, the activity and purposes inhibited here are not really significant. It is not just a matter of our having made a trade-off, and considered that a small loss of liberty was worth fewer traffic accidents, or less danger for the children; we are reluctant to speak here of a loss of liberty at all; what we feel we are trading off is convenience against safety.

By contrast a law which forbids me from worshipping according to the form I believe in is a serious blow to liberty; even a law which tried to restrict this to certain times (as the traffic light restricts my crossing of the intersection to certain times) would be seen as a serious restriction. Why this difference between the two cases? Because we have a background understanding, too obvious to spell out, of some activities and goals as highly significant for human beings and others as less so. One's religious belief is recognized, even by atheists, as supremely important, because it is that by which the believer defines himself as a moral being. By contrast my rhythm of movement through the city traffic is trivial. We do not want to speak of these two in the same breath. We do not even readily admit that liberty is at stake in the traffic light case. For *de minimis non curat libertas.*

But this recourse to significance takes us beyond a Hobbesian scheme. Freedom is no longer just the absence of external obstacle *tout court,* but the absence of external obstacle to significant action, to what is important to man. There are discriminations to be made; some restrictions are more serious than others, some are utterly trivial. About many, there is of course controversy. But what the judgement turns on is some sense of what is significant for human life. Restricting the expression of people's religious and ethical convictions is more significant than restricting their movement around uninhabited parts of the country; and both are more significant than the trivia of traffic control.

But the Hobbesian scheme has no place for the notion of significance. It will allow only for purely quantitative judgements. On the toughest-minded version of his conception, where Hobbes seems to be about to define liberty in terms of the absence of physical obstacles, one is presented with the vertiginous prospect of human freedom being measurable in the same way as the degrees of freedom of some physical object, say a lever. Later we see that this will not do, because we have to take account of legal obstacles to my action. But in any case, such a quantitative conception of freedom is a non-starter.

Consider the following diabolical defence of Albania as a free country. We recognize that religion has been abolished in Albania, whereas it hasn't been in Britain. But on the other hand there are probably far fewer traffic lights per head in Tirana than in London. (I haven't checked for myself, but this is a very plausible assumption.) Suppose an apologist for Albanian socialism were nevertheless to claim that this country was freer than Britain, because the number of acts restricted was far smaller. After all, only a minority of Londoners practise some religion in public places, but all have to negotiate their way through traffic. Those who do practise a religion generally do so on one day of the week, while they are held up at traffic lights every day. In sheer quantitative terms, the number of acts restricted by traffic lights must be greater than that restricted by a ban on public religious practice. So if Britain is considered a free society, why not Albania?

Thus the application even of our negative notion of freedom requires a background conception of what is significant, according to which some restrictions are seen to be without relevance for freedom altogether, and others are judged as being of greater and lesser importance. So some discrimination among motivations seems essential to our concept of freedom. A minute's reflection shows why this must be so. Freedom is important to us because we are purposive beings. But then there must be distinctions in the significance of different kinds of freedom based on the distinction in the significance of different purposes.

But of course, this still does not involve the kind of discrimination mentioned above, the kind which would allow us to say that someone who was doing what he wanted (in the unproblematic sense) was not really free, the kind of discrimination which allows us to put conditions on people's motivations necessary to their being free, and hence to second-guess them. All we have shown is that we make discriminations between more or less significant freedoms, based on discriminations among the purposes people have.

This creates some embarrassment for the crude negative theory, but it can cope with it by simply adding a recognition that we make judgements of significance. Its central claim that freedom just is the absence of external obstacles seems untouched, as also its view of freedom as an opportunity-concept. It is just that we now have to admit that not all opportunities are equal.

But there is more trouble in store for the crude view when we examine further what these qualitative discriminations are based on. What lies behind our judging certain purposes/feelings as more significant than others? One might think that there was room here again for another quantitative theory; that the more significant purposes are those we want more. But this account is either vacuous or false.

It is true but vacuous if we take wanting more just to mean being more significant. It is false as soon as we try to give wanting more an independent criterion, such as, for instance, the urgency or force of a desire, or the prevalence of one desire over another, because it is a matter of the most banal experience that the purposes we know to be more significant are not always those which we desire with the greatest urgency to encompass, nor the ones that actually always win out in cases of conflict of desires.

When we reflect on this kind of significance, we come up against what I have called elsewhere the fact of strong evaluation, the fact that we human subjects are not only subjects of first-order desires, but of second-order desires, desires about desires. We experience our desires and purposes as qualitatively discriminated, as higher or lower, noble or base, integrated or fragmented, significant or trivial, good and bad. This means that we experience some of our desires and goals as intrinsically more significant than others: some passing comfort is less important than the fulfilment of our life-time vocation, our *amour propre* less important than a love relationship; while we experience some others as bad, not just comparatively but absolutely: we desire not to be moved by spite, or some childish desire to impress at all costs. And these judgements of significance are quite independent of the strength of the respective desires: the craving for comfort may be overwhelming at this moment, we may be obsessed with our *amour propre,* but the judgement of significance stands.

But then the question arises whether this fact of strong evaluation doesn't have other consequences for our notion of freedom, than just that it permits us to rank freedoms in importance. Is freedom not at stake when we find ourselves carried away by a less significant goal to over-ride a highly significant one? Or when we are led to act out of a motive we consider bad or despicable?

The answer is that we sometimes do speak in this way. Suppose I have some irrational fear, which is preventing me from doing something I very much want to do. Say the fear of public speaking is preventing me from taking up a career that I should find very fulfilling, and that I should be quite good at, if I could just get over this "hangup." It is clear that we experience this fear as an obstacle, and that we feel we are less than we would be if we could overcome it.

Or again, consider the case where I am very attached to comfort. To go on short rations, and to miss my creature comforts for a time, makes me very depressed. I find myself making a big thing of this. Because of this reaction I cannot do certain things that I should like very much to do, such as going on an expedition over the Andes, or a canoe trip in the Yukon. Once again, it is quite understandable if I experience this attachment as an obstacle, and feel that I should be freer without it.

Or I could find that my spiteful feelings and reactions which I almost cannot inhibit are undermining a relationship which is terribly important to me. At times, I feel as though I am almost assisting as a helpless witness at my own destructive behaviour, as I lash out again with my unbridled tongue at her. I long to be able not to feel this spite. As long as I feel it, even control is not an option, because it just builds up inside until it either bursts out, or else the feeling somehow communicates itself, and queers things between us. I long to be free of this feeling.

These are quite understandable cases, where we can speak of freedom or its absence without strain. What I have called strong evaluation is essentially involved here. For these are not just cases of conflict, even cases of painful conflict. If the conflict is between two desires with which I have no trouble identifying, there can be no talk of lesser freedom, no matter how painful or fateful. Thus if what is breaking up my relationship is my finding fulfilment in a job which, say, takes me away from home a lot, I have indeed a terrible conflict, but I would have no temptation to speak of myself as less free.

Even seeing a great difference in the significance of the two terms doesn't seem to be a sufficient condition of my wanting to speak of freedom and its absence. Thus my marriage may be breaking up because I like going to the pub and playing cards on Saturday nights with the boys. I may feel quite unequivocally that my marriage is much more important than the release and comradeship of the Saturday night bash. But nevertheless I would not want to talk of my being freer if I could slough off this desire.

The difference seems to be that in this case, unlike the ones above, I still identify with the less important desire, I still see it as expressive of myself, so that I could not lose it without altering who I am, losing something of my personality. Whereas my irrational fear, my being quite distressed by discomfort, my spite – these are all things which I can easily see myself losing without any loss whatsoever to what I am. This is why I can see them as obstacles to my purposes, and hence to my freedom, even though they are in a sense unquestionably desires and feelings of mine.

Before exploring further what is involved in this, let us go back and keep score. It would seem that these cases make a bigger breach in the crude negative theory. For they seem to be cases in which the obstacles to freedom are internal; and if this is so, then freedom cannot simply be interpreted as the absence of *external* obstacles; and the fact that I am doing what I want, in the sense of following my strongest desire, is not sufficient to establish that I am free. On the contrary, we have to make discriminations among motivations, and accept that acting out of some motivations, for example irrational fear or spite, or this too great need for comfort, is not freedom, is even a negation of freedom ...

Thus we can experience some desires as fetters, because we can experience them as not ours. And we can experience them as not ours because we see them as incorporating a quite erroneous appreciation of our situation and of what matters to us. We can see this again if we contrast the case of spite with that of another emotion which partly overlaps, and which is highly considered in some societies, the desire for revenge. In certain traditional societies this is far from being considered a despicable emotion. On the contrary, it is a duty of honour on a male relative to avenge a man's death. We might imagine that this too might give rise to conflict. It might conflict with the attempts of a new regime to bring some order to the land. The government would have to stop people taking vengeance, in the name of peace.

But short of a conversion to a new ethical outlook, this would be seen as a trade-off, the sacrifice of one legitimate goal for the sake of another. And it would seem monstrous were one to propose reconditioning people so that they no longer felt the desire to avenge their kin. This would be to unman them.[1]

Why do we feel so different about spite (and for that matter also revenge)? Because the desire for revenge for an ancient Icelander was his sense of a real obligation incumbent on him, something it would be dishonourable to repudiate; while for us, spite is the child of a distorted perspective on things.

We cannot therefore understand our desires and emotions as all brute, and in particular we cannot make sense of our discrimination of some desires as more important and fundamental, or of our repudiation of others, unless we understand our feelings to be import-attributing. This is essential to there being what we have called strong evaluation. Consequently the half-way position which admits strong evaluation, admits that our desires may frustrate our deeper purposes, admits therefore that there may be inner obstacles to freedom, and yet will not admit that the subject may be wrong or mistaken about these purposes

– this position does not seem tenable. For the only way to make the subject's assessment incorrigible in principle would be to claim that there was nothing to be right or wrong about here; and that could only be so if experiencing a given feeling were a matter of the qualities of brute feeling. But this it cannot be if we are to make sense of the whole background of strong evaluation, more significant goals, and aims that we repudiate. This whole scheme requires that we understand the emotions concerned as import-attributing, as, indeed, it is clear that we must do on other grounds as well.

But once we admit that our feelings are import-attributing, then we admit the possibility of error, or false appreciation. And indeed, we have to admit a kind of false appreciation which the agent himself detects in order to make sense of the cases where we experience our own desires as fetters. How can we exclude in principle that there may be other false appreciations which the agent does not detect? That he may be profoundly in error, that is, have a very distorted sense of his fundamental purposes? Who can say that such people cannot exist? All cases are, of course, controversial; but I should nominate Charles Manson and Andreas Baader for this category, among others. I pick them out as people with a strong sense of some purposes and goals as incomparably more fundamental than others, or at least with a propensity to act the having such a sense so as to take in even themselves a good part of the time, but whose sense of fundamental purpose was shot through with confusion and error. And once we recognize such extreme cases, how avoid admitting that many of the rest of mankind can suffer to a lesser degree from the same disabilities?

What has this got to do with freedom? Well, to resume what we have seen: our attributions of freedom make sense against a background sense of more and less significant purposes, for the question of freedom/unfreedom is bound up with the frustration/fulfilment of our purposes. Further, our significant purposes can be frustrated by our own desires, and where these are sufficiently based on misappreciation, we consider them as not really ours, and experience them as fetters. A man's freedom can therefore be hemmed in by internal, motivational obstacles, as well as external ones. A man who is driven by spite to jeopardize his most important relationships, in spite of himself, as it were, or who is prevented by unreasoning fear from taking up the career he truly wants, is not really made more free if one lifts the external obstacles to his venting his spite or acting on his fear. Or at best he is liberated into a very impoverished freedom ...

NOTE

1   Compare the unease we feel at the reconditioning of the hero of Anthony
    Burgess's *A Clockwork Orange.*

READING QUESTION ON TAYLOR

1   Does Taylor's argument give us any basis for choosing between
    legal positivism and Dworkin's or Fuller's alternatives to it?

Patrick Devlin
"Morals and the Criminal Law" (1965)

Devlin advocates a vision of democracy in which justice is determined by
the will of the majority. He argues that a society is no less entitled to protect
itself against moral decay than against treason.

I MORALS AND THE CRIMINAL LAW

The Report of the Committee on Homosexual Offences and Prostitution,
generally known as the Wolfenden Report, is recognized to be an
excellent study of two very difficult legal and social problems. But it has
also a particular claim to the respect of those interested in jurisprudence; it does what law reformers so rarely do; it sets out clearly and
carefully what in relation to its subjects it considers the function of the
law to be. Statutory additions to the criminal law are too often made on
the simple principle that "there ought to be a law against it." The
greater part of the law relating to sexual offences is the creation of
statute and it is difficult to ascertain any logical relationship between it
and the moral ideas which most of us uphold. Adultery, fornication,
and prostitution are not, as the Report points out, criminal offences:
homosexuality between males is a criminal offence, but between
females it is not. Incest was not an offence until it was declared so by
statute only fifty years ago. Does the legislature select those offences
haphazardly or are there some principles which can be used to determine what part of the moral law should be embodied in the criminal?
There is, for example, being now considered a proposal to make A.I.D.,

that is, the practice of artificial insemination of a woman with the seed of a man who is not her husband, a criminal offence; if, as is usually the case, the woman is married, this is in substance, if not in form, adultery. Ought it to be made punishable when adultery is not? This sort of question is of practical importance, for a law that appears to be arbitrary and illogical, in the end and after the wave of moral indignation that has put it on the statute book subsides, forfeits respect. As a practical question it arises more frequently in the field of sexual morals than in any other, but there is no special answer to be found in that field. The inquiry must be general and fundamental. What is the connexion between crime and sin and to what extent, if at all, should the criminal law of England concern itself with the enforcement of morals and punish sin or immorality as such?

The statements of principle in the Wolfenden Report provide an admirable and modern starting-point for such an inquiry. In the course of my examination of them I shall find matter for criticism. If my criticisms are sound, it must not be imagined that they point to any shortcomings in the Report. Its authors were not, as I am trying to do, composing a paper on the jurisprudence of morality; they were evolving a working formula to use for reaching a number of practical conclusions. I do not intend to express any opinion one way or the other about these; that would be outside the scope of a lecture on jurisprudence. I am concerned only with general principles; the statement of these in the Report illuminates the entry into the subject and I hope that its authors will forgive me if I carry the lamp with me into places where it was not intended to go.

Early in the Report the Committee put forward:

Our own formulation of the function of the criminal law so far as it concerns the subjects of this enquiry. In this field, its function, as we see it, is to preserve public order and decency, to protect the citizen from what is offensive or injurious, and to provide sufficient safeguards against exploitation and corruption of others, particularly those who are specially vulnerable because they are young, weak in body or mind, inexperienced, or in a state of special physical, official or economic dependence.

It is not, in our view, the function of the law to intervene in the private lives of citizens, or to seek to enforce any particular pattern of behaviour, further than is necessary to carry out the purposes we have outlined.

The Committee preface their most important recommendation

that homosexual behaviour between consenting adults in private should no longer be a criminal offence, [by stating the argument] which we believe to be decisive, namely, the importance which society and the law ought to give to individual freedom of choice and action in matters of private morality. Unless a deliberate attempt is to be made by society, acting through the agency of the law, to equate the sphere of crime with that of sin, there must remain a realm of private morality and immorality which is, in brief and crude terms, not the law's business. To say this is not to condone or encourage private immorality.

Similar statements of principle are set out in the chapters of the Report which deal with prostitution. No case can be sustained, the Report says, for attempting to make prostitution itself illegal. The Committee refer to the general reasons already given and add: "We are agreed that private immorality should not be the concern of the criminal law except in the special circumstances therein mentioned." They quote with approval the report of the Street Offences Committee, which says: "As a general proposition it will be universally accepted that the law is not concerned with private morals or with ethical sanctions." It will be observed that the emphasis is on *private* immorality. By this is meant immorality which is not offensive or injurious to the public in the ways defined or described in the first passage which I quoted. In other words, no act of immorality should be made a criminal offence unless it is accompanied by some other feature such as indecency, corruption, or exploitation. This is clearly brought out in relation to prostitution: "It is not the duty of the law to concern itself with immorality as such ... it should confine itself to those activities which offend against public order and decency or expose the ordinary citizen to what is offensive or injurious."

These statements of principle are naturally restricted to the subject matter of the Report. But they are made in general terms and there seems to be no reason why, if they are valid, they should not be applied to the criminal law in general. They separate very decisively crime from sin, the divine law from the secular, and the moral from the criminal. They do not signify any lack of support for the law, moral or criminal, and they do not represent an attitude that can be called either religious or irreligious. There are many schools of thought among those who may think that morals are not the law's business. There is first of all the agnostic or free-thinker. He does not of course disbelieve in morals, nor in sin if it be given the wider of the two meanings assigned to it in the *Oxford English Dictionary* where it is defined as "transgression against divine law or the principles of morality." He cannot accept the divine law; that does not mean that he might not view with suspicion any departure from moral principles that have for generations been accepted by the society in which he lives; but in the end he judges for himself. Then there is the deeply religious person who feels that the criminal law is sometimes more of a hindrance than a help in the sphere of morality, and that the reform of the sinner – at any rate when he injures only himself – should be a spiritual rather than a temporal work. Then there is the man who without any strong feeling cannot see why, where there is freedom in religious belief, there should not logically be freedom in morality as well. All these are powerfully allied against the equating of crime with sin.

I must disclose at the outset that I have as a judge an interest in the result of the inquiry which I am seeking to make as a jurisprudent. As a judge who administers the criminal law and who has often to pass sentence in a criminal court, I should feel handicapped in my task if I thought that I was addressing an audience which had no sense of sin or which thought of crime as something quite different. Ought one, for example, in passing sentence upon a female abortionist to treat her simply as if she were an unlicensed midwife? If not, why not? But if so, is all the panoply of the law erected over a set of social regulations? I must admit that I begin with a feeling that a complete separation of crime from sin (I use the term throughout this lecture in the wider meaning) would not be good for the moral law and might be disastrous for the criminal. But can this sort of feeling be justified as a matter of jurisprudence? And if it be a right feeling, how should the relationship between the criminal and the moral law be stated? Is there a good theoretical basis for it, or is it just a practical working alliance, or is it a bit of both? That is the problem which I want to examine, and I shall begin by considering the standpoint of the strict logician. It can be supported by cogent arguments, some of which I believe to be unanswerable and which I put as follows.

Morals and religion are inextricably joined – the moral standards generally accepted in Western civilization being those belonging to Christianity. Outside Christendom other standards derive from other religions. None of these moral codes can claim any validity except by virtue of the religion on which it is based. Old Testament morals differ in some respects from New Testament morals. Even within Christianity there are differences. Some hold that contraception is an immoral practice and that a man who has carnal knowledge of another woman while his wife is alive is in all circumstances a fornicator; others, including most of the English-speaking world, deny both these propositions. Between the great religions of the world, of which Christianity is only one, there are much wider differences. It may or may not be right for the State to adopt one of these religions as the truth, to found itself upon its doctrines, and to deny to any of its citizens the liberty to practise any other. If it does, it is logical that it should use the secular law wherever it thinks it necessary to enforce the divine. If it does not, it is illogical that it should concern itself with morals as such. But if it leaves matters of religion to private judgement, it should logically leave matters of morals also. A State which refuses to enforce Christian beliefs has lost the right to enforce Christian morals.

If this view is sound, it means that the criminal law cannot justify any of its provisions by reference to the moral law. It cannot say, for example, that murder and theft are prohibited because they are immoral or sinful. The State must justify in some other way the punishments which it imposes on wrongdoers and a function for the criminal law independent of morals must be found. This is not difficult to do. The smooth functioning of society and the preservation of order require that a number of activities should be regulated. The rules that are made for that purpose and are enforced by the criminal law are often designed simply to achieve uniformity and convenience and rarely involve any choice between good and evil. Rules that impose a speed limit or prevent obstruction on the highway have nothing to do with morals. Since so much of the criminal law is composed of rules of this sort, why bring morals into it at all? Why not define the function of the criminal law in simple terms as the preservation of order and decency and the protection of the lives and property of citizens, and elaborate those terms in relation to any particular subject in the way in which it is done in the Wolfenden Report? The criminal law in carrying out these objects will undoubtedly overlap the moral law. Crimes of violence are morally wrong and they are also offences against good order; therefore they offend against both laws. But this is simply because the two laws in pursuit of different objectives happen to cover the same area. Such is the argument.

Is the argument consistent or inconsistent with the fundamental principles of English criminal law as it exists today? That is the first way of testing it, though by no means a conclusive one. In the field of jurisprudence one is at liberty to overturn even fundamental conceptions if they are theoretically unsound. But to see how the argument fares under the existing law is a good starting-point.

It is true that for many centuries the criminal law was much concerned with keeping the peace and little, if at all, with sexual morals. But it would be wrong to infer from that that it had no moral content or that it would ever have tolerated the idea of a man being left to judge for himself in matters of morals. The criminal law of England has from the very first concerned itself with moral principles. A simple way of testing this point is to consider the attitude which the criminal law adopts towards consent.

Subject to certain exceptions inherent in the nature of particular crimes, the criminal law has never permitted consent of the victim to be used as a defence. In rape, for example, consent negatives an essential element. But consent of the victim is no defence to a charge of murder. It is not a defence to any form of assault that the victim thought his punishment well deserved and submitted to it; to make a good defence the accused must prove that the law gave him the right to chastise and that he exercised it reasonably. Likewise, the victim may not forgive the aggressor and require the prosecution to desist; the right to enter a *nolle prosequi* belongs to the Attorney-General alone.

Now, if the law existed for the protection of the individual, there would be no reason why he should avail himself of it if he did not want it. The reason why a man may not consent to the commission of an offence against himself beforehand or forgive it afterwards is because it is an offence against society. It is not that society is physically injured; that would be impossible. Nor need any individual be shocked, corrupted, or exploited; everything may be done in private. Nor can it be explained on the practical ground that a violent man is a potential danger to others in the community who have therefore a direct interest in his apprehension and punishment as being necessary to their own protection. That would be true of a man whom the victim is prepared to forgive but not of one who gets his consent first; a murderer who acts only upon the consent, and maybe the request, of his victim is no menace to others, but he does threaten one of the great moral principles upon which society is based, that is, the sanctity of human life. There is only one explanation of what has hitherto been accepted as the basis of the criminal law and that is that there are certain standards of behaviour or moral principles which society requires to be observed; and the breach of them is an offence not merely against the person who is injured but against society as a whole.

Thus, if the criminal law were to be reformed so as to eliminate from it everything that was not designed to preserve order and decency or to protect citizens (including the protection of youth from corruption), it would overturn a fundamental principle. It would also end a number of specific crimes. Euthanasia or the killing of another at his own request, suicide, attempted suicide and suicide pacts, duelling, abortion, incest between brother and sister, are all acts which can be done in private and without offence to others and need not involve the corruption or exploitation of others. Many people think that the law on some of these subjects is in need of reform, but no one hitherto has gone so far as to suggest that they should all be left outside the criminal law as matters of private morality. They can be brought within it only as a matter of moral principle. It must be remembered also that although there is much immorality that is not punished by the law, there is none that is condoned by the law. The law will not allow its processes to be used by those engaged in immorality of any sort. For example, a house may not be let for immoral purposes; the lease is invalid and would not be enforced. But if what goes on inside there is a matter of private morality and not the law's business, why does the law inquire into it at all?

I think it is clear that the criminal law as we know it is based upon moral principle. In a number of crimes its function is simply to enforce a moral principle and nothing else. The law, both criminal and civil, claims to be able to speak about morality and immorality generally. Where does it get its authority to do this and how does it settle the moral principles which it enforces? Undoubtedly, as a matter of history, it derived both from Christian teaching. But I think that the strict logician is right when he says that the law can no longer rely on doctrines in which citizens are entitled to disbelieve. It is necessary therefore to look for some other source.

In jurisprudence, as I have said, everything is thrown open to discussion and, in the belief that they cover the whole field, I have framed three interrogatories addressed to myself to answer:

1 Has society the right to pass judgement at all on matters of morals? Ought there, in other words, to be a public morality, or are morals always a matter for private judgement?

2 If society has the right to pass judgement, has it also the right to use the weapon of the law to enforce it?
3 If so, ought it to use that weapon in all cases or only in some; and if only in some, on what principles should it distinguish?

I shall begin with the first interrogatory and consider what is meant by the right of society to pass a moral judgement, that is, a judgement about what is good and what is evil. The fact that a majority of people may disapprove of a practice does not of itself make it a matter for society as a whole. Nine men out of ten may disapprove of what the tenth man is doing and still say that it is not their business. There is a case for a collective judgement (as distinct from a large number of individual opinions which sensible people may even refrain from pronouncing at all if it is upon somebody else's private affairs) only if society is affected. Without a collective judgement there can be no case at all for intervention. Let me take as an illustration the Englishman's attitude to religion as it is now and as it has been in the past. His attitude now is that a man's religion is his private affair; he may think of another man's religion that it is right or wrong, true or untrue, but not that it is good or bad. In earlier times that was not so; a man was denied the right to practise what was thought of as heresy, and heresy was thought of as destructive of society.

The language used in the passages I have quoted from the Wolfenden Report suggests the view that there ought not to be a collective judgement about immorality *per se*. Is this what is meant by "private morality" and "individual freedom of choice and action"? Some people sincerely believe that homosexuality is neither immoral nor unnatural. Is the "freedom of choice and action" that is offered to the individual, freedom to decide for himself what is moral or immoral, society remaining neutral; or is it freedom to be immoral if he wants to be? The language of the Report may be open to question, but the conclusions at which the Committee arrive answer this question unambiguously. If society is not prepared to say that homosexuality is morally wrong, there would be no basis for a law protecting youth from "corruption" or punishing a man for living on the "immoral" earnings of a homosexual prostitute, as the Report recommends. This attitude the Committee make even clearer when they come to deal with prostitution. In truth, the Report takes it for granted that there is in existence a public morality which condemns homosexuality and prostitution. What the

Report seems to mean by private morality might perhaps be better described as private behaviour in matters of morals.

This view – that there is such a thing as public morality – can also be justified by *a priori* argument. What makes a society of any sort is community of ideas, not only political ideas but also ideas about the way its members should behave and govern their lives; these latter ideas are its morals. Every society has a moral structure as well as a political one: or rather, since that might suggest two independent systems, I should say that the structure of every society is made up both of politics and morals. Take, for example, the institution of marriage. Whether a man should be allowed to take more than one wife is something about which every society has to make up its mind one way or the other. In England we believe in the Christian idea of marriage and therefore adopt monogamy as a moral principle. Consequently the Christian institution of marriage has become the basis of family life and so part of the structure of our society. It is there not because it is Christian. It has got there because it is Christian, but it remains there because it is built into the house in which we live and could not be removed without bringing it down. The great majority of those who live in this country accept it because it is the Christian idea of marriage and for them the only true one. But a non-Christian is bound by it, not because it is part of Christianity but because, rightly or wrongly, it has been adopted by the society in which he lives. It would be useless for him to stage a debate designed to prove that polygamy was theologically more correct and socially preferable; if he wants to live in the house, he must accept it as built in the way in which it is.

We see this more clearly if we think of ideas or institutions that are purely political. Society cannot tolerate rebellion; it will not allow argument about the rightness of the cause. Historians a century later may say that the rebels were right and the Government was wrong and a percipient and conscientious subject of the State may think so at the time. But it is not a matter which can be left to individual judgement.

The institution of marriage is a good example for my purpose because it bridges the division, if there is one, between politics and morals. Marriage is part of the structure of our society and it is also the basis of a moral code which condemns fornication and adultery. The institution of marriage would be gravely threatened if individual judgements were permitted about the morality of adultery; on these points there must be a public morality. But public morality is not to be confined to those moral principles which support institutions such as marriage. People do not think of monogamy as something which has to be supported because our society has chosen to organize itself upon it; they think of it as something that is good in itself and offering a good way of life and that it is for that reason that our society has adopted it. I return to the statement that I have already made, that society means a community of ideas; without shared ideas on politics, morals, and ethics no society can exist. Each one of us has ideas about what is good and what is evil; they cannot be kept private from the society in which we live. If men and women try to create a society in which there is no fundamental agreement about good and evil they will fail; if, having based it on common agreement, the agreement goes, the society will disintegrate. For society is not something that is kept together physically; it is held by the invisible bonds of common thought. If the bonds were too far relaxed the members would drift apart. A common morality is part of the bondage. The bondage is part of the price of society; and mankind, which needs society, must pay its price ...

You may think that I have taken far too long in contending that there is such a thing as public morality, a proposition which most people would readily accept, and may have left myself too little time to discuss the next question which to many minds may cause greater difficulty: to what extent should society use the law to enforce its moral judgements? But I believe that the answer to the first question determines the way in which the second should be approached and may indeed very nearly dictate the answer to the second question. If society has no right to make judgements on morals, the law must find some special justification for entering the field of morality: if homosexuality and prostitution are not in themselves wrong, then the onus is very clearly on the law-giver who wants to frame a law against certain aspects of them to justify the exceptional treatment. But if society has the right to make a judgement and has it on the basis that a recognized morality is as necessary to society as, say, a recognized government, then society may use the law to preserve morality in the same way as it uses it to safeguard anything else that is essential to its existence. If therefore the first proposition is securely established with all its implications, society has a prima facie right to legislate against immorality as such.

The Wolfenden Report, notwithstanding that it seems to admit the right of society to condemn homosexuality and prostitution as immoral, requires special circumstances to be shown to justify the intervention of the law. I think that this is wrong in principle and that any attempt to approach my second interrogatory on these lines is bound to break down. I think that the attempt by the Committee does break down and that this is shown by the fact that it has to define or describe its special circumstances so widely that they can be supported only if it is accepted that the law *is* concerned with immorality as such.

The widest of the special circumstances are described as the provision of "sufficient safeguards against exploitation and corruption of others, particularly those who are specially vulnerable because they are young, weak in body or mind, inexperienced, or in a state of special physical, official or economic dependence." The corruption of youth is a well-recognized ground for intervention by the State and for the purpose of any legislation the young can easily be defined. But if similar protection were to be extended to every other citizen, there would be no limit to the reach of the law. The "corruption and exploitation of others" is so wide that it could be used to cover any sort of immorality which involves, as most do, the co-operation of another person. Even if the phrase is taken as limited to the categories that are particularized as "specially vulnerable," it is so elastic as to be practically no restriction. This is not merely a matter of words. For if the words used are stretched almost beyond breaking-point, they still are not wide enough to cover the recommendations which the Committee make about prostitution.

Prostitution is not in itself illegal and the Committee do not think that it ought to be made so. If prostitution is private immorality and not the law's business, what concern has the law with the ponce or the brothel-keeper or the householder who permits habitual prostitution? The Report recommends that the laws which make these activities criminal offences should be maintained or strengthened and brings them (so far as it goes into principle; with regard to brothels it says simply that the law rightly frowns on them) under the head of exploitation. There may be cases of exploitation in this trade, as there are or used to be in many others, but in general a ponce exploits a prostitute no more than an impresario exploits an actress. The Report finds that "the great majority of prostitutes are women whose psychological makeup is such that they choose this life because they find in it a style of living which is to them easier, freer and more profitable than would be provided by any other occupation ... In the main the association between prostitute and ponce is voluntary and operates to mutual advantage." The Committee would agree that this could not be called exploitation in the ordinary sense. They say: "It is in our view an over-simplification to think that those who live on the earnings of prostitution are exploiting the prostitute as such. What they are really exploiting is the whole complex of the relationship between prostitute and customer; they are, in effect, exploiting the human weaknesses which cause the customer to seek the prostitute and the prostitute to meet the demand."

All sexual immorality involves the exploitation of human weaknesses. The prostitute exploits the lust of her customers and the customer the moral weakness of the prostitute. If the exploitation of human weaknesses is considered to create a special circumstance, there is virtually no field of morality which can be defined in such a way as to exclude the law.

I think, therefore, that it is not possible to set theoretical limits to the power of the State to legislate against immorality. It is not possible to settle in advance exceptions to the general rule or to define inflexibly areas of morality into which the law is in no circumstances to be allowed to enter. Society is entitled by means of its laws to protect itself from dangers, whether from within or without. Here again I think that the political parallel is legitimate. The law of treason is directed against aiding the king's enemies and against sedition from within. The justification for this is that established government is necessary for the existence of society and therefore its safety against violent overthrow must be secured. But an established morality is as necessary as good government to the welfare of society. Societies disintegrate from within more frequently than they are broken up by external pressures. There is disintegration when no common morality is observed and history shows that the loosening of moral bonds is often the first stage of disintegration, so that society is justified in taking the same steps to preserve its moral code as it does to preserve its government and other essential institutions.[1] The suppression of vice is as much the law's business as the suppression of subversive activities; it is no more possible to define a sphere of private morality than it is to define one of private subversive activity. It is wrong to talk of private morality or of the law not being concerned with immorality as such or to try to set rigid bounds to the part which the law may play in the suppression of vice. There are no theoretical limits to the power of the State to legislate against treason and sedition, and likewise I think there can be no theoretical limits to legislation against immorality. You may argue that if a man's sins affect only himself it cannot be the concern of society. If he chooses to get drunk every night in the privacy of his own home, is any one except himself the worse for it? But suppose a quarter or a half of the population got drunk every night, what sort of society would it be? You cannot set a theoretical limit to the number of people who can get drunk before society is entitled to legislate against drunkenness. The same may be said of gambling. The Royal Commission on Betting, Lotteries, and Gaming took as their test the character of the citizen as a member of society. They said: "Our concern with the ethical significance of gambling is confined to the effect which it may have on the character of the gambler as a member of society. If we were convinced that whatever the degree of gambling this effect must be harmful we should be inclined to think that it was the duty of the state to restrict gambling to the greatest extent practicable."

In what circumstances the State should exercise its power is the third of the interrogatories I have framed. But before I get to it I must raise a point which might have been brought up in any one of the three. How are the moral judgements of society to be ascertained? By leaving it until now, I can ask it in the more limited form that is now sufficient for my purpose. How is the law-maker to ascertain the moral judgements of society? It is surely not enough that they should be reached by the opinion of the majority; it would be too much to require the individual assent of every citizen. English law has evolved and regularly uses a standard which does not depend on the counting of heads. It is that of the reasonable man. He is not to be confused with the rational man. He is not expected to reason about anything and his judgement may be largely a matter of feeling. It is the viewpoint of the man in the street or to use an archaism familiar to all lawyers – the man in the Clapham omnibus. He might also be called the right-minded man. For my purpose I should like to call him the man in the jury box, for the moral judgement of society must be something about which any twelve men or women drawn at random might after discussion be expected to be unanimous. This was the standard the judges applied in the days before Parliament was as active as it is now and when they laid down rules of public policy. They did not think of themselves as making law but simply as stating principles which every right-minded person would accept as valid. It is what Pollock called "practical morality," which is based not on theological or philosophical foundations but "in the mass of continuous experience half-consciously or unconsciously accumulated and embodied in the morality of common sense." He called it also "a certain way of thinking on questions of morality which we expect to find in a reasonable civilized man or a reasonable Englishman, taken at random."[2]

Immorality then, for the purpose of the law, is what every right-minded person is presumed to consider to be immoral. Any immorality is capable of affecting society injuriously and in effect to a greater or lesser extent it usually does; this is what gives the law its *locus standi*. It cannot be shut out. But – and this brings me to the third question – the individual has a *locus standi* too; he cannot be expected to surrender to the judgement of society the whole conduct of his life. It is the old and familiar question of striking a balance between the rights and interests of society and those of the individual. This is something which the law is constantly doing in matters large and small. To take a very down-to-earth example, let me consider the right of the individual whose house adjoins the highway to have access to it; that means in these days the right to have vehicles stationary in the highway, sometimes for a considerable time if there is a lot of loading or unloading. There are many cases in which the courts have had to balance the private right of access against the public right to use the highway without obstruction. It cannot be done by carving up the highway into public and private areas. It is done by recognizing that each have rights over the whole; that if each were to exercise their rights to the full, they would come into conflict; and therefore that the rights of each must be curtailed so as to ensure as far as possible that the essential needs of each are safeguarded.

I do not think that one can talk sensibly of a public and private morality any more than one can of a public or private highway. Morality is a sphere in which there is a public interest and a private interest, often in conflict, and the problem is to reconcile the two. This does not mean that it is impossible to put forward any general statements about how in our society the balance ought to be struck. Such statements cannot of their nature be rigid or precise; they would not be designed to circumscribe the operation of the law-making power but to guide those who have to apply it. While every decision which a court of law makes when it balances the public against the private interest is an *ad hoc* decision, the cases contain statements of principle to which the court should have regard when it reaches its decision. In the same way it is possible to make general statements of principle which it may be thought the legislature should bear in mind when it is considering the enactment of laws enforcing morals.

I believe that most people would agree upon the chief of these elastic principles. There must be toleration of the maximum individual freedom that is consistent with the integrity of society. It cannot be said that this is a principle that runs all through the criminal law. Much of the criminal law that is regulatory in character – the part of it that deals with *malum prohibitum* rather than *malum in se* – is based upon the opposite principle, that is, that the choice of the individual must give way to the convenience of the many. But in all matters of conscience the principle I have stated is generally held to prevail. It is not confined to thought and speech; it extends to action, as is shown by the recognition of the right to conscientious objection in war-time; this example shows also that conscience will be respected even in times of national danger. The principle appears to me to be peculiarly appropriate to all questions of morals. Nothing should be punished by the law that does not lie beyond the limits of tolerance. It is not nearly enough to say that a majority dislike a practice; there must be a real feeling of reprobation. Those who are dissatisfied with the present law on homosexuality often say that the opponents of reform are swayed simply by disgust. If that were so it would be wrong, but I do not think one can ignore disgust if it is deeply felt and not manufactured. Its presence is a good indication that the bounds of toleration are being reached. Not everything is to be tolerated. No society can do without intolerance, indignation, and disgust; they are the forces behind the moral law, and indeed it can be argued that if they or something like them are not present, the feelings of society cannot be weighty enough to deprive the individual of freedom of choice. I suppose that there is hardly anyone nowadays who would not be disgusted by the thought of deliberate cruelty to animals. No one proposes to relegate that or any other form of sadism to the realm of private morality or to allow it to be practised in public or in private. It would be possible no doubt to point out that until a comparatively short while ago nobody thought very much of cruelty to animals and also that pity and kindliness and the unwillingness to inflict pain are virtues more generally esteemed now than they have ever been in the past. But matters of this sort are not determined by rational argument. Every moral judgement, unless it claims a divine source, is simply a feeling that no right-minded man could behave in any other way without admitting that he was doing wrong. It is the power of a common sense and not the power of reason that is behind the judgements of society. But before a society can put a practice beyond the limits of tolerance there must be a deliberate judgement that the practice is injurious to society. There is, for example, a general abhorrence of homosexuality. We should ask ourselves in the first instance whether, looking at it calmly and dispassionately, we regard it as a vice so abominable that its mere presence is an offence. If that is the genuine feeling of the society in which we live, I do not see how society can be denied the right to eradicate it. Our feeling may not be so intense as that. We may feel about it that, if confined, it is tolerable, but that if it spread it might be gravely injurious; it is in this way that most societies look upon fornication, seeing it as a natural weakness which must be kept within bounds but which cannot be rooted out. It becomes then a question of balance, the danger to society in one scale and the extent of the restriction in the other. On this sort of point the value of an investigation by such a body as the Wolfenden Committee and of its conclusions is manifest.

The limits of tolerance shift. This is supplementary to what I have been saying but of sufficient importance in itself to deserve statement as a separate principle which law-makers have to bear in mind. I suppose that moral standards do not shift; so far as they come from divine revelation they do not, and I am willing to assume that the moral judgements made by a society always remain good for that society. But the extent to which society will tolerate – I mean tolerate, not approve – departures from moral standards varies from generation to generation. It may be that over-all tolerance is always increasing. The pressure of the human mind, always seeking greater freedom of thought, is outwards against the bonds of society forcing their gradual relaxation. It may be that history is a tale of contraction and expansion and that all developed societies are on their way to dissolution. I must not speak of things I do not know; and anyway as a practical matter no society is willing to make provision for its own decay. I return therefore to the simple and observable fact that in matters of morals the limits of tolerance shift. Laws, especially those which are based on morals, are less easily moved. It follows as another good working principle that in any new matter of morals the law should be slow to act. By the next generation the swell of indignation may have abated and the law be left without the strong backing which it needs. But it is then difficult to alter the law without giving the impression that moral judgement is being weakened. This is now one of the factors that is strongly militating against any alteration to the law on homosexuality.

A third elastic principle must be advanced more tentatively. It is that as far as possible privacy should be respected. This is not an idea that has ever been made explicit in the criminal law. Acts or words done or said in public or in private are all brought within its scope without distinction in principle. But there goes with this a strong reluctance on the part of judges and legislators to sanction invasions of privacy in the detection of crime. The police have no more right to trespass than the ordinary citizen has; there is no general right of search; to this extent an Englishman's home is still his castle. The Government is extremely careful in the exercise even of those powers which it claims to be undisputed. Telephone tapping and interference with the mails afford a good illustration of this. A Committee of three Privy Councillors who recently inquired into these activities found that the Home Secretary and his predecessors had already formulated strict rules governing the exercise of these powers and the Committee were able to recommend that they should be continued to be exercised substantially on the same terms. But they reported that the power was "regarded with general disfavour."

This indicates a general sentiment that the right to privacy is something to be put in the balance against the enforcement of the law. Ought the same sort of consideration to play any part in the formation of the law? Clearly only in a very limited number of cases. When the help of the law is invoked by an injured citizen, privacy must be irrelevant; the individual cannot ask that his right to privacy should be measured against injury criminally done to another. But when all who are involved in the deed are consenting parties and the injury is done to morals, the public interest in the moral order can be balanced against the claims of privacy. The restriction on police powers of investigation goes further than the affording of a parallel; it means that the detection of crime committed in private and when there is no complaint is bound to be rather haphazard and this is an additional reason for moderation. These considerations do not justify the exclusion of all private immorality from the scope of the law. I think that, as I have already suggested, the test of "private behaviour" should be substituted for "private morality" and the influence of the factor should be reduced from that of a definite limitation to that of a matter to be taken into account. Since the gravity of the crime is also a proper consideration, a distinction might well be made in the case of homosexuality between the lesser acts of indecency and the full offence, which on the principles of the Wolfenden Report it would be illogical to do.

The last and the biggest thing to be remembered is that the law is concerned with the minimum and not with the maximum; there is much in the Sermon on the Mount that would be out of place in the Ten Commandments. We all recognize the gap between the moral law and the law of the land. No man is worth much who regulates his conduct with the sole object of escaping punishment, and every worthy society sets for its members standards which are above those of the law. We recognize the existence of such higher standards when we use expressions such as "moral obligation" and "morally bound." The distinction was well put in the judgement of African elders in a family dispute: "We have power to make you divide the crops, for this is our law, and we will see this is done. But we have not power to make you behave like an upright man."[3]

It can only be because this point is so obvious that it is so frequently ignored. Discussion among law-makers, both professional and amateur, is too often limited to what is right or wrong and good or bad for society. There is a failure to keep separate the two questions I have earlier posed – the question of society's right to pass a moral judgement and the question of whether the arm of the law should be used to enforce the judgement. The criminal law is not a statement of how people ought to behave; it is a statement of what will happen to them if they do not behave; good citizens are not expected to come within reach of it or to set their sights by it, and every enactment should be framed accordingly.

The arm of the law is an instrument to be used by society, and the decision about what particular cases it should be used in is essentially a practical one. Since it is an instrument, it is wise before deciding to use it to have regard to the tools with which it can be fitted and to the machinery which operates it. Its tools are fines, imprisonment, or lesser forms of supervision (such as Borstal and probation) and – not to be ignored – the degradation that often follows upon the publication of the crime. Are any of these suited to the job of dealing with sexual immorality? The fact that there is so much immorality which has never been brought within the law shows that there can be no general rule. It is a matter for decision in each case; but in the case of homosexuality the Wolfenden Report rightly has regard to the views of those who are experienced in dealing with this sort of crime and to those of the clergy who are the natural guardians of public morals.

The machinery which sets the criminal law in motion ends with the verdict and the sentence; and a verdict is given either by magistrates or by a jury. As a general rule, whenever a crime is sufficiently serious to justify a maximum punishment of more than three months, the accused has the right to the verdict of a jury. The result is that magistrates administer mostly what I have called the regulatory part of the law. They deal extensively with drunkenness, gambling, and prostitution, which are matters of morals or close to them, but not with any of the graver moral offences. They are more responsive than juries to the ideas of the legislature; it may not be accidental that the Wolfenden Report, in recommending increased penalties for solicitation, did not go above the limit of three months. Juries tend to dilute the decrees of Parliament with their own ideas of what should be punishable. Their province of course is fact and not law, and I do not mean that they often deliberately disregard the law. But if they think it is too stringent, they sometimes take a very merciful view of the facts. Let me take one example out of many that could be given. It is an offence to have carnal knowledge of a girl under the age of sixteen years. Consent on her part is no defence; if she did not consent, it would of course amount to rape. The law makes special provision for the situation when a boy and girl are near in age. If a man under twenty-four can prove that he had reasonable cause to believe that the girl was over the age of sixteen years, he has a good defence. The law regards the offence as sufficiently serious to make it one that is triable only by a judge at assizes. "Reasonable cause" means not merely that the boy honestly believed that the girl was over sixteen but also that he must have had reasonable grounds for his belief. In theory it ought not to be an easy defence to make out but in fact it is extremely rare for anyone who advances it to be convicted. The fact is that the girl is often as much to blame as the boy. The object of the law, as judges repeatedly tell juries, is to protect young girls against themselves; but juries are not impressed.

The part that the jury plays in the enforcement of the criminal law, the fact that no grave offence against morals is punishable without their verdict, these are of great importance in relation to the statements of principle that I have been making. They turn what might otherwise be pure exhortation to the legislature into something like rules that the law-makers cannot safely ignore. The man in the jury box is not just an expression; he is an active reality. It will not in the long run work to make laws about morality that are not acceptable to him.

This then is how I believe my third interrogatory should be answered – not by the formulation of hard and fast rules, but by a judgement in each case taking into account the sort of factors I have been mentioning. The line that divides the criminal law from the moral is not determinable by the application of any clear-cut principle. It is like a line that divides land and sea, a coastline of irregularities and indentations. There are gaps and promontories, such as adultery and fornication, which the law has for centuries left substantially untouched. Adultery of the sort that breaks up marriage seems to be just as harmful to the social fabric as homosexuality or bigamy. The only ground for putting it outside the criminal law is that a law which made it a crime would be too difficult to enforce; it is too generally regarded as a human weakness not suitably punished by imprisonment. All that the law can do with fornication is to act against its worst manifestations; there is a general abhorrence of the commercialization of vice, and that sentiment gives strength to the law against brothels and immoral earnings. There is no logic to be found in this. The boundary between the criminal law and the moral law is fixed by balancing in the case of each particular crime the pros and cons of legal enforcement in accordance with the sort of considerations I have been outlining. The fact that adultery, fornication, and lesbianism are untouched by the criminal law does not prove that homosexuality ought not to be touched. The error of jurisprudence in the Wolfenden Report is caused by the search for some single principle to explain the division between crime and sin. The Report finds it in the principle that the criminal law exists for the protection of individuals; on this principle fornication in private between consenting adults is outside the law and thus it becomes logically indefensible to bring homosexuality between consenting adults in private within it. But the true principle is that the law exists for the protection of society. It does not discharge its function by protecting the individual from injury, annoyance, corruption, and exploitation; the law must protect also the institutions and the community of ideas, political and moral, without which people cannot live together. Society cannot ignore the morality of the individual any more than it can his loyalty; it flourishes on both and without either it dies.

I have said that the morals which underly the law must be derived from the sense of right and wrong which resides in the community as a whole; it does not matter whence the community of thought comes, whether from one body of doctrine or another or from the knowledge of good and evil which no man is without. If the reasonable man believes that a practice is immoral and believes also – no matter whether the belief is right or wrong, so be it that it is honest and dispassionate – that no right-minded member of his society could think otherwise, then for the purpose of the law it is immoral. This, you may say, makes immorality a question of fact – what the law would consider as self-evident fact no doubt, but still with no higher authority than any other doctrine of public policy. I think that this is so, and indeed the law does not distinguish between an act that is immoral and one that is contrary to public policy. But the law has never yet had occasion to inquire into the differences between Christian morals and those which every right-minded member of society is expected to hold. The inquiry would, I believe, be academic. Moralists would find differences; indeed they would find them between different branches of the Christian faith on subjects such as divorce and birth-control. But for the purpose of the limited entry which the law makes into the field of morals, there is no practical difference. It seems to me therefore that the free-thinker and the non-Christian can accept, without offence to his convictions, the fact that Christian morals are the basis of the criminal law and that he can recognize, also without taking offence, that without the support of the churches the moral order, which has its origin in and takes its strength from Christian beliefs, would collapse.

This brings me back in the end to a question I posed at the beginning. What is the relationship between crime and sin, between the Church and the Law? I do not think that you can equate crime with sin. The divine law and the secular have been disunited, but they are brought together again by the need which each has for the other. It is not my function to emphasize the Church's need of the secular law; it can be put tersely by saying that you cannot have a ceiling without a floor. I am very clear about the law's need for the Church. I have spoken of the criminal law as dealing with the minimum standards of human conduct and the moral law with the maximum. The instrument of the criminal law is punishment; those of the moral law are teaching, training, and exhortation. If the whole dead weight of sin were ever to be allowed to fall upon the law, it could not take the strain. If at any point there is a lack of clear and convincing moral teaching, the administration of the law suffers. Let me take as an illustration of this the law on abortion. I believe that a great many people nowadays do not understand why abortion is wrong. If it is right to prevent conception, at what point does it become sinful to prevent birth and why? I doubt if anyone who has not had a theological training would give a satisfactory answer to that question. Many people regard abortion as the next step when by accident birth-control has failed; and many more people are deterred from abortion not because they think it sinful or illegal but because of the difficulty which illegality puts in the way of obtaining it. The law is powerless to deal with abortion *per se*; unless a tragedy occurs or a "professional" abortionist is involved – the parallel between the "professional" in abortions and the "professional" in fornication is quite close – it has to leave it alone. Without one or other of these features the crime is rarely detected; and when detected, the plea *ad misericordiam* is often too strong. The "professional" abortionist is usually the unskilled person who for a small reward helps girls in trouble; the man and the girl involved are essential witnesses for the prosecution and therefore go free; the paid abortionist generally receives a very severe sentence, much more severe than that usually given to the paid assistant in immorality, such as the ponce or the brothel-keeper. The reason is because unskilled abortion endangers life. In a case in 1949[4] Lord Chief Justice Goddard said: "It is because the unskilful attentions of ignorant people in cases of this kind often result in death that attempts to produce abortion are regarded by the law as very serious offences." This gives the law a twist which disassociates it from morality and, I think, to some extent from sound sense. The act is being punished because it is dangerous, and it is dangerous largely because it is illegal and therefore performed only by the unskilled.

The object of what I have said is not to criticise theology or law in relation to abortion. That is a large subject and beyond my present scope. It is to show what happens to the law in matters of morality about which the community as a whole is not deeply imbued with a sense of sin; the law sags under a weight which it is not constructed to bear and may become permanently warped.

I return now to the main thread of my argument and summarize it. Society cannot live without morals. Its morals are those standards of conduct which the reasonable man approves. A rational man, who is also a good man, may have other standards. If he has no standards at all he is not a good man and need not be further considered. If he has standards, they may be very different; he may, for example, not disapprove of homosexuality or abortion. In that case he will not share in the common morality; but that should not make him deny that it is a social necessity. A rebel may be rational in thinking that he is right but he is irrational if he thinks that society can leave him free to rebel.

A man who concedes that morality is necessary to society must support the use of those instruments without which morality cannot be maintained. The two instruments are those of teaching, which is doctrine, and of enforcement, which is the law. If morals could be taught simply on the basis that they are necessary to society, there would be no social need for religion; it could be left as a purely personal affair. But morality cannot be taught in that way. Loyalty is not taught in that way either. No society has yet solved the problem of how to teach morality without religion. So the law must base itself on Christian morals and to the limit of its ability enforce them, not simply because they are the morals of most of us, nor simply because they are the morals which are taught by the established Church – on these points the law recognizes the right to dissent – but for the compelling reason that without the help of Christian teaching the law will fail.

NOTES

1 It is somewhere about this point in the argument that Professor Hart in *Law, Liberty and Morality* discerns a proposition which he describes as central to my thought. He states the proposition and his objection to it as follows (p. 51). "He appears to move from the acceptable proposition that *some* shared morality is essential to the existence of any society [this I take to be the proposition on p. 12] to the unacceptable proposition that a society is identical with its morality as that is at any given moment of its history, so that a change in its morality is tantamount to the destruction of a society. The former proposition might be even accepted as a neces-sary rather than an empirical truth depending on a quite plausible definition of society as a body of men who hold certain moral views in common. But the latter proposition is absurd. Taken strictly, it would prevent us saying that the morality of a given society had changed, and would compel us instead to say that one society had disappeared and another one taken its place. But it is only on this absurd criterion of what it is for the same society to continue to exist that it could be asserted without evidence that any deviation from a society's shared morality threatens its existence." In conclusion (p. 82) Professor Hart condemns the whole thesis in the lecture as based on "a confused definition of what a society is."

I do not assert that *any* deviation from a society's shared morality threatens its existence any more than I assert that *any* subversive activity threatens its existence. I assert that they are both activities which are capable in their nature of threatening the existence of society so that neither can be put beyond the law.

For the rest, the objection appears to me to be all a matter of words. I would venture to assert, for example, that you cannot have a game without rules and that if there were no rules there would be no game. If I am asked whether that means that the game is "identical" with the rules, I would be willing for the question to be answered either way in the belief that the answer would lead to nowhere. If I am asked whether a change in the rules means that one game has disappeared and another has taken its place, I would reply probably not, but that it would depend on the extent of the change.

Likewise I should venture to assert that there cannot be a contract without terms. Does this mean that an "amended" contract is a "new" contract in the eyes of the law? I once listened to an argument by an ingenious counsel that a contract, because of the substitution of one clause for another, had "ceased to have effect" within the meaning of a statutory provision. The judge did not accept the argument; but if most of the fundamental terms had been changed, I daresay he would have done.

The proposition that I make in the text is that if (as I understand Professor Hart to agree, at any rate for the purposes of the argument) you cannot have a society without morality, the law can be used to enforce morality as something that is essential to a society. I cannot see why this proposition (whether it is right or wrong) should mean that morality can never be changed without the destruction of society. If morality is changed, the law can be changed. Professor Hart refers (p. 72) to the proposition as "the use of legal punishment to freeze into immobility the morality dominant at a particular time in a society's existence." One might as well say that the inclusion of a penal section into a statute prohibiting certain acts freezes the whole statute into immobility and prevents the prohibitions from ever being modified.

2   *Essays in Jurisprudence and Ethics* (1882), Macmillan, pp. 278 and 353.
3   A case in the Saa-Katengo Kuta at Lialiu, August 1942, quoted in *The Judicial Process among the Barotse of Northern Rhodesia* by Max Gluckman, Manchester University Press, 1955, 172.
4   *R. v. Tate, The Times*, 22 June 1949.

READING QUESTIONS ON DEVLIN

1   Why does Devlin suppose that "intolerance, indignation, and disgust" are important?
2   Does the toleration of things that disgust many people carry the risks that Devlin suggests?
3   In Phoenix, Arizona, it is against the law to kill a pony within the city limits. There is a Tongan tradition of roasting a pony to celebrate weddings. Should the law be enforced against Tongans living in Phoenix? What would Devlin say?
4   Does Devlin provide a way of replacing the gap left by negative liberty if Taylor is right about its incoherence?

Ronald Dworkin
"Liberty and Moralism" (1977)

Dworkin examines the relation between law and democracy, arguing that democracy requires certain limits on the types of argument that can be put forward. He challenges Devlin's understanding of a moral position.

My purpose is not to settle issues of political morality by the fiat of a dictionary, but to exhibit what I believe to be mistakes in Lord Devlin's moral sociology. I shall try to show that our conventional moral practices are more complex and more structured than he takes them to be, and that he consequently misunderstands what it means to say that the criminal law should be drawn from public morality. This is a popular and appealing thesis, and it lies near the core not only of Lord Devlin's, but of many other, theories about law and morals. It is crucial that its implications be understood.

THE CONCEPT OF A MORAL POSITION

We might start with the fact that terms like "moral position" and "moral conviction" function in our conventional morality as terms of justification and criticism, as well as of description. It is true that we sometimes speak of a group's "morals," or "morality," or "moral beliefs," or "moral positions" or "moral convictions," in what might be called an anthropological sense, meaning to refer to whatever attitudes the group displays about the propriety about human conduct, qualities or goals. We say, in this sense, that the morality of Nazi Germany was based on prejudice, or was irrational. But we also use some of these terms, particularly "moral position" and "moral conviction," in a discriminatory sense, to contrast the positions they describe with prejudices, rationalizations, matters of personal aversion or taste, arbitrary stands, and the like. One use – perhaps the most characteristic use – of this discriminatory sense is to offer a limited but important sort of justification for an act, when the moral issues surrounding that act are unclear or in dispute.

Suppose I tell you that I propose to vote against a man running for a public office of trust because I know him to be a homosexual and because I believe that homosexuality is profoundly immoral. If you disagree that homosexuality is immoral, you may accuse me of being about to cast my vote unfairly, acting on prejudice or out of a personal repugnance which is irrelevant to the moral issue. I might then try to convert you to my position on homosexuality, but if I fail in this I shall still want to convince you of what you and I will both take to be a separate point – that my vote was based on *a* moral position, in the discriminatory sense, even though one which differs from yours. I shall want to persuade you of this, because if I do I am entitled to expect that you will alter your opinion of me and of what I am about to do. Your judgment of my character will be different – you might still think me eccentric (or puritanical or unsophisticated) but these are types of character and not faults of character. Your judgment of my act will also be different, in this respect. You will admit that so long as I hold my moral position, I have a moral right to vote against the homosexual, because I have a right (indeed a duty) to vote my own convictions. You would not admit such a right (or duty) if you were still persuaded that I was acting out of a prejudice or a personal taste.

I am entitled to expect that your opinion will change in these ways, because these distinctions are a part of the conventional morality you and I share, and which forms the background for our discussion. They enforce the difference between positions we must respect, although we think them wrong, and positions we need not respect because they offend some ground rule of moral reasoning. A great deal of debate about moral issues (in real life, although not in philosophy texts) consists of arguments that some position falls on one or the other side of this crucial line.

It is this feature of conventional morality that animates Lord Devlin's argument that society has the right to follow its own lights. We must therefore examine that discriminatory concept of a moral position more closely, and we can do so by pursuing our imaginary conversation. What must I do to convince you that my position is a moral position?

(a) I must produce some reasons for it. This is not to say that I have to articulate a moral principle I am following or a general moral theory to which I subscribe. Very few people can do either, and the ability to hold a moral position is not limited to those who can. My reason need not be a principle or theory at all. It must only point out some aspect or feature of homosexuality which moves me to regard it as immoral: the fact that the Bible forbids it, for example, or that one who practices homosexuality becomes unfit for marriage and parenthood. Of course, any such reason would presuppose my acceptance of some general principle or theory, but I need not be able to state what it is, or realize that I am relying upon it.

Not every reason I might give will do, however. Some will be excluded by general criteria stipulating sorts of reasons which do not count. We might take note of four of the most important such criteria:

1 If I tell you that homosexuals are morally inferior because they do not have heterosexual desires, and so are not "real men," you would reject that reason as showing one type of prejudice. Prejudices, in general, are postures of judgment that take into account considerations our conventions exclude. In a structured context, like a trial or a contest, the ground rules exclude all but certain considerations, and a prejudice is a basis of judgment which violates these rules. Our conventions stipulate some ground rules of moral judgment which obtain even apart from such special contexts, the most important of which is that a man must not be held morally inferior on the basis of some physical, racial or other characteristic he cannot help having. Thus a man whose moral judgements about Jews, or Negroes, or Southerners, or women, or effeminate men are based on his belief that any member of these classes automatically deserves less respect, without regard to anything he himself has done, is said to be prejudiced against that group.

2 If I base my view about homosexuals on a personal emotional reaction ("they make me sick") you would reject that reason as well. We distinguish moral positions from emotional reactions, not because moral positions are supposed to be unemotional or dispassionate – quite the reverse is true – but because the moral position is supposed to justify the emotional reaction, not vice versa. If a man is unable to produce such reasons, we do not deny the fact of his emotional involvement, which may have important social or political consequences, but we do not take this involvement as demonstrating his moral conviction. Indeed, it is just this sort of

position – a severe emotional reaction to a practice or a situation for which one cannot account – that we tend to describe, in lay terms, as a phobia or an obsession.

3 If I base my position on a proposition of fact ("homosexual acts are physically debilitating") which is not only false, but is so implausible that it challenges the minimal standards of evidence and argument I generally accept and impose upon others, then you would regard my belief, even though sincere, as a form of rationalization, and disqualify my reason on that ground. (Rationalization is a complex concept, and also includes, as we shall see, the production of reasons which suggest general theories I do not accept.)

4 If I can argue for my own position only by citing the beliefs of others ("everyone knows homosexuality is a sin") you will conclude that I am parroting and not relying on a moral conviction of my own. With the possible (though complex) exception of a deity, there is no moral authority to which I can appeal and so automatically make my position a moral one. I must have my own reasons, though of course I may have been taught these reasons by others.

No doubt many readers will disagree with these thumbnail sketches of prejudice, mere emotional reaction, rationalization and parroting. Some may have their own theories of what these are. I want to emphasize now only that these are distinct concepts, whatever the details of the differences might be, and that they have a role in deciding whether to treat another's position as a moral conviction. They are not merely epithets to be pasted on positions we strongly dislike.

(b) Suppose I do produce a reason which is not disqualified on one of these (or on similar) grounds. That reason will presuppose some general moral principle or theory, even though I may not be able to state that principle or theory, and do not have it in mind when I speak. If I offer, as my reason, the fact that the Bible forbids homosexual acts, or that homosexual acts make it less likely that the actor will marry and raise children, I suggest that I accept the theory my reason presupposes, and you will not be satisfied that my position is a moral one if you believe that I do not. It may be a question of my sincerity – do I in fact believe that the injunctions of the Bible are morally binding as such, or that all men have a duty to procreate? Sincerity is not, however, the only issue, for consistency is also in point. I may believe that I accept one of these general positions, and be wrong, because my other beliefs, and my own conduct on other occasions, may be inconsistent with it. I may reject certain Biblical injunctions, or I may hold that men have a right to remain bachelors if they please or use contraceptives all their lives.

Of course, my general moral positions may have qualifications and exceptions. The difference between an exception and an inconsistency is that the former can be supported by reasons which presuppose other moral positions I can properly claim to hold. Suppose I condemn all homosexuals on Biblical authority, but not all fornicators. What reason can I offer for the distinction? If I can produce none which supports it, I cannot claim to accept the general position about Biblical authority. If I do produce a reason which seems to support the distinction, the same sorts of question may be asked about that reason as were asked about my original reply. What general position does the reason for my exception presuppose? Can I sincerely claim to accept that further general position? Suppose my reason, for example, is that fornication is now very common, and has been sanctioned by custom. Do I really believe that what is immoral becomes moral when it becomes popular? If not, and if I can produce no other reason for the distinction, I cannot claim to accept the general position that what the Bible condemns is immoral. Of course, I may be persuaded, when this is pointed out, to change my views on fornication. But you would be alert to the question of whether this is a genuine change of heart, or only a performance for the sake of the argument.

In principle there is no limit to these ramifications of my original claim, though of course no actual argument is likely to pursue very many of them.

(c) But do I really have to have a reason to make my position a matter of moral conviction? Most men think that acts which cause unnecessary suffering, or break a serious promise with no excuse, are immoral, and yet they could give no reason for these beliefs. They feel that no reason is necessary, because they take it as axiomatic or self-evident that these are immoral acts. It seems contrary to common sense to deny that a position held in this way can be a moral position.

Yet there is an important difference between believing that one's position is self-evident and just not having a reason for one's position. The former presupposes a positive belief that no further reason is necessary, that the immorality of the act in question does not depend upon its social effects, or its effects on the character of the actor, or its proscription by a deity, or anything else, but follows from the nature of the act itself. The claim that a particular position is axiomatic, in other words, does supply a reason of a special sort, namely that the act is immoral in and of itself, and this special reason, like the others we considered, may be inconsistent with more general theories I hold.

The moral arguments we make presuppose not only moral principles, but also more abstract positions about moral reasoning. In particular, they presuppose positions about what kinds of acts can be immoral in and of themselves. When I criticize your moral opinions, or attempt to justify my own disregard of traditional moral rules I think are silly, I will likely proceed by denying that the act in question has any of the several features that can make an act immoral – that it involves no breach of an undertaking or duty, for example, harms no one including the actor, is not proscribed by any organized religion, and is not illegal. I proceed in this way because I assume that the ultimate grounds of immorality are limited to some such small set of very general standards. I may assert this assumption directly or it may emerge from the pattern of my argument. In either event, I will enforce it by calling positions which can claim no support from any of these ultimate standards *arbitrary*, as I should certainly do if you said that photography was immoral, for instance, or swimming. Even if I cannot articulate this underlying assumption, I shall still apply it, and since the ultimate criteria I recognize are among the most abstract of my moral standards, they will not vary much from those my neighbors recognize and apply. Although many who despise homosexuals are unable to say why, few would claim affirmatively that one needs no reason, for this would make their position, on their own standards, an arbitrary one.

(d) This anatomy of our argument could be continued, but it is already long enough to justify some conclusions. If the issue between us is whether my views on homosexuality amount to a moral position, and hence whether I am entitled to vote against a homosexual on that ground, I cannot settle the issue simply by reporting my feelings. You will want to consider the reasons I can produce to support my belief, and whether my other views and behavior are consistent with the theories these reasons presuppose. You will have, of course, to apply your own understanding, which may differ in detail from mine, of what a prejudice or a rationalization is, for example, and of when one view is inconsistent with another. You and I may end in disagreement over whether my position is a moral one, partly because of such differences in understanding, and partly because one is less likely to recognize these illegitimate grounds in himself than in others.

We must avoid the skeptical fallacy of passing from these facts to the conclusion that there is no such thing as a prejudice or a rationalization or an inconsistency, or that these terms mean merely that the one who uses them strongly dislikes the positions he describes this way. That would be like arguing that because different people have different understandings of what jealousy is, and can in good faith disagree about whether one of them is jealous, there is no such thing as jealousy, and one who says another is jealous merely means he dislikes him very much.

LORD DEVLIN'S MORALITY

We may now return to Lord Devlin's second argument. He argues that when legislators must decide a moral issue (as by his hypothesis they must when a practice threatens a valued social arrangement), they must follow any consensus of moral position which the community at large has reached, because this is required by the democratic principle, and because a community is entitled to follow its own lights. The argument would have some plausibility if Lord Devlin meant, in speaking of the moral consensus of the community, those positions which are moral positions in the discriminatory sense we have been exploring.

But he means nothing of the sort. His definition of a moral position shows he is using it in what I called the anthropological sense. The ordinary man whose opinion we must enforce, he says, "is not expected to reason about anything and his judgment may be largely a matter of feeling." "If the reasonable man believes," he adds, "that a practice is immoral and believes so – no matter whether the belief is right or wrong, so be it that it is honest and dispassionate – that no right-minded member of his society could think otherwise, then for the purpose of the law it is immoral." Elsewhere he quotes with approval Dean Rostow's attribution to him of the view that "the common morality of a society at any time is a blend of custom and conviction, of reason and feeling, of experience and prejudice." His sense of what a moral conviction is emerges most clearly of all from the famous remark about homosexuals. If the ordinary man regards homosexuality "as a vice so abominable that its mere presence is an offence," this demonstrates for him that the ordinary man's feelings about homosexuals are a matter of moral conviction.

His conclusions fail because they depend upon using "moral position" in this anthropological sense. Even if it is true that most men think homosexuality an abominable vice and cannot tolerate its presence, it remains possible that this common opinion is a compound of prejudice (resting on the assumption that homosexuals are morally inferior creatures because they are effeminate), rationalization (based on assumptions of fact so unsupported that they challenge the community's own standards of rationality), and personal aversion (representing no conviction but merely blind hate rising from unacknowledged self-suspicion). It remains possible that the ordinary man could produce no reason for his view, but would simply parrot his neighbor who in turn parrots him, or that he would produce a reason which presupposes a general moral position he could not sincerely or consistently claim to hold. If so, the principles of democracy we follow do not call for the enforcement of the consensus, for the belief that prejudices, personal aversions and rationalizations do not justify restricting another's freedom itself occupies a critical and fundamental position in our popular morality. Nor would the bulk of the community then be entitled to follow its own lights, for the community does not extend that privilege to one who acts on the basis of prejudice, rationalization, or personal aversion. Indeed, the distinction between these and moral convictions, in the discriminatory sense, exists largely to mark off the former as the sort of positions one is not entitled to pursue.

A conscientious legislator who is told a moral consensus exists must test the credentials of that consensus. He cannot, of course, examine the beliefs or behavior of individual citizens; he cannot hold hearings on the Clapham omnibus. That is not the point.

The claim that a moral consensus exists is not itself based on a poll. It is based on an appeal to the legislator's sense of how his community reacts to some disfavored practice. But this same sense includes an awareness of the grounds on which that reaction is generally supported. If there has been a public debate involving the editorial columns, speeches of his colleagues, the testimony of interested groups, and his own correspondence, these will sharpen his awareness of what arguments and positions are in the field. He must sift these arguments and positions, trying to determine which are prejudices or rationalizations, which presuppose general principles or theories vast parts of the population could not be supposed to accept, and so on. It may be that when he has finished this process of reflection he will find that the claim of a moral consensus has not been made out. In the case of homosexuality, I expect, it would not be, and that is what makes Lord Devlin's undiscriminating hypothetical so serious a misstatement. What is shocking and wrong is not his idea that the community's morality counts, but his idea of what counts as the community's morality.

Of course the legislator must apply these tests for himself. If he shares the popular views he is less likely to find them wanting, though if he is self-critical the exercise may convert him. His answer, in any event, will depend upon his own understanding of what our shared morality requires. That is inevitable, for whatever criteria we urge him to apply, he can apply them only as he understands them.

A legislator who proceeds in this way, who refuses to take popular indignation, intolerance and disgust as the moral conviction of his community, is not guilty of moral elitism. He is not simply setting his own educated views against those of a vast public which rejects them. He is doing his best to enforce a distinct, and fundamentally important, part of his community's morality, a consensus more essential to society's existence in the form we know it than the opinion Lord Devlin bids him follow.

No legislator can afford to ignore the public's outrage. It is a fact he must reckon with. It will set the boundaries of what is politically feasible, and it will determine his strategies of persuasion and enforcement within these boundaries. But we must not confuse strategy with justice, nor facts of political life with principles of political morality. Lord Devlin understands these distinctions, but his arguments will appeal most, I am afraid, to those who do not.

READING QUESTION ON DWORKIN

1   Does Dworkin's view give judges too much power? Alternatively, does he give democratic assemblies too much power?

Hofer v. Hofer (1970) 13 DLR 3d 1

Members of a Hutterite colony were expelled when they converted to another religion. They sued, claiming that they were entitled to their proportionate share of the colony's land. The colony insisted that their freedom of religion entitled them to hold all land in common. The decision, by the Supreme Court of Canada, provides a clear illustration of the debate between the two models of freedom that the earlier readings in this section explore. If religious freedom is construed as a negative liberty, the community has no say over the activities of its members. As a result, a certain way of life may prove to be impossible to sustain. By contrast, if freedom of religion is seen as a positive liberty, the community will have power over its members, but the negative liberty of individuals will suffer.

Ritchie, J.: – ... It will be seen from the above that, in my view, adherence to the Hutterite faith was a prerequisite to membership in the Colony which by its very nature was required to be composed exclusively of Hutterian Brethren and their families. I am also of opinion that the decision as to whether or not any individual was a Hutterian Brethren so as to be entitled to continue as a member of the community was a decision which could only be made by the Hutterite Church. In the present case, as I have indicated, the decision to expel the appellants from the Colony was made by the Church, but it had the effect of making the appellants ineligible for continued membership in the Colony. It follows from this that the appellants' contention to the effect that the articles of association were not properly complied with in regard to expulsion is without merit, and in my view the alternative plea with respect to the unlimited power and control of the ministers of the Church over the personal life and property, being contrary to public policy, is equally invalid.

I am also of opinion, as I have indicated, that the Interlake Colony was not a partnership in the accepted legal sense of that term.

There is no doubt that the Hutterian way of life is not that of the vast majority of Canadians, but it makes manifest a form of religious philosophy to which any Canadian can subscribe and it appears to me that if any individual either through birth within the community or by choice wishes to subscribe to such a rigid form of life and to subject himself to the harsh disciplines of the Hutterian Church, he is free to do so. I can see nothing contrary to public policy in the continued existence of these communities, living as they do in accordance with their own rules and beliefs, and as I have indicated, I think it is for the Church to determine who is and who is not an acceptable member of any of its communities.

For all these reasons, as well as for those so fully expressed by the learned trial Judge and the Court of Appeal, I would dismiss this appeal with costs ...

Pigeon, J. (dissenting): – The appellants and the respondents were all Hutterian Brethren. They lived at and were members of the Rock Lake Colony. In 1960, the Rock Lake Colony had grown to such size that it was decided, in accordance with established practice, to split the

Colony and form a "daughter" colony at Interlake, Manitoba. The members of Rock Lake Colony divided into two groups, neither of which knew whether it would go to the new colony or stay at Rock Lake Colony. This was decided by lot. The assets of Rock Lake Colony were then divided roughly in proportion to membership and 2,080 acres of land were purchased for the new Colony at $76 per acre.

The seven parties to this action formed the group moving to the new Colony. In May, 1961, they signed a document entitled "Articles of Association of the Interlake Colony of Hutterian Brethren of the Post Office of Teulon in the Province of Manitoba, Dominion of Canada." Those articles of association include the following provisions:

2. The purposes for which the said Colony is formed are: To promote, engage in and carry on the Christian religion, Christian worship, and religious education and teachings, and to worship God according to the religious belief of the members thereof; and to engage in and carry on farming, stock-raising, milling, and all branches of these industries, and to manufacture and deal in such products and by-products as may be considered by the Directors to be in the best interests of the Colony and for the purposes aforesaid, to hold, own, and possess such real and personal property as may be necessary.

3. The Colony shall be comprised of all persons who sign these Articles. No person shall become a member of the Colony and be permitted to sign these Articles, until he or she shall have:

(a) Attained the full age of seventeen years.

(b) Become a member and communicant of the Hutterian Brethren Church.

(c) Been chosen and elected to Membership upon a majority vote of all the male members of the Colony present at any annual, general, or special meeting of the Colony.

30. All the property, real and personal, of said Colony from whomsoever, whensoever and howsoever it may have been obtained, shall forever be owned, used, occupied, controlled and possessed by the said Colony for the common use, interest, and benefit of each and all members thereof, for the purposes of said Colony ...

31. All the property both real and personal, that each and every member of the said Colony has or may have, own, possess or may be entitled to at the time that he or she joins such Colony, or becomes a member thereof, and all the property both real and personal, that each and every member of the said Colony may have, obtain, inherit, possess or be entitled to, after he or she

becomes a member of the said Colony, shall be and become the property of the said Colony for the common use, interest, and benefit of each and all of the members thereof as aforesaid.

32. None of the property, either real or personal, of the said Colony shall ever be taken, held, owned, removed or withdrawn from the said Colony, or be granted, sold, transferred or conveyed otherwise than by the Board of Directors, and if any member of the said Colony shall be expelled therefrom, or cease to be a member thereof, he or she shall not have, take, withdraw, grant, sell, transfer or convey, or be entitled to any of the property of the said Colony, or any interest therein; and if any member of the said Colony shall die, be expelled therefrom, or cease to be a member thereof, he or she, or his or her representatives, heirs-at-law, legatees or devisees or creditors or any other person shall not be entitled to, or have any of the property of the said Colony, or interest therein, whether or not he or she owned, possessed or had any interest in or to any of the property of the said Colony at the time he or she became member thereof, or at any time thereafter, or had given, granted, conveyed or transferred any property or property interest to the said Colony at any time.

33. Each and every member of the said Colony shall give and devote all his or her time, labor, services, earnings and energies to the said Colony, and the purposes for which it is formed, freely, voluntarily, and without compensation or reward of any kind whatsoever, other than as herein expressed.

34. The members of the said Colony shall be entitled to have their husbands, wives and children, who are not members thereof, reside with them, and be supported, maintained, instructed and educated by the said Colony, according to the rules, regulations and requirements of the said Colony, and the Christian religion, Christian worship, religious education, teachings and belief promoted, engaged in and carried on by the said Colony, during the time and so long as they obey, abide by and conform to the rules, regulations, instructions, and requirements of the said Colony.

35. Whenever any member of the said Colony shall die then his or her husband, wife and children who are not members thereof, shall have the right to remain with, and be supported, instructed and educated by the said Colony, during the time and so long as they give and devote all of their time, labor, services, earnings, and energies to the said Colony, and the purposes thereof, and obey and conform to the rules, regulations and requirements of the said Colony, the same as if the said member had lived ...

37. The Community, or Association, or Colony hereby created shall not be dissolved without the consent of all of the members thereof.

The parties with their families moved to the Interlake Colony on December 20, 1961. Benjamin Hofer, one of the appellants, had by that time begun to be attracted by the teachings of the Radio Church of God and by March, 1964, he and David Hofer, another appellant, had both become converted to the beliefs of that Church. These differed from those of the Hutterite Church in many respects. For instance, the Radio Church of God did not regard community of property as a part of its faith. It did not believe in the Christian festivals as observed by the Hutterian Brethren and it condemned the eating of pork. The two dissidents became subscribers to a monthly magazine published by the Radio Church of God and entitled *The Plain Truth*.

On March 3, 1964, no less than 20 ministers of the Hutterite Church came from other colonies to Interlake and talked to the two dissidents in an attempt to re-establish their faith. A second and unavailing effort was made on March 13th, when 24 ministers came from other colonies and the two dissidents were asked if they did accept a Church penalty of "unfrieden." Both dissidents refused and challenged the authority of the ministers to impose it. The penalty was, however, imposed and meant that the two dissidents were shunned by the rest of the Colony and their families were subjected to various indignities.

On June 13, 1964, the two dissidents, Benjamin and David Hofer, were expelled.

A year later, it became apparent that the other two appellants, John Hofer and Joseph Hofer, had also abandoned the Hutterite faith in favour of the Radio Church of God. Attempts to bring them back to the Hutterian faith were unsuccessful and in the end they were also expelled.

By their action, the appellants sought a declaration that they were still members of the Interlake Colony together with an order for the winding-up of its affairs, the appointment of a receiver, an accounting of its assets and liabilities, and a direction that its assets should be distributed equally among each of the appellants and respondents. The respondents counter-claimed for a declaration that the appellants are no longer members of the Colony, and are not entitled to any portion of its property and directing them to vacate the real property owned by the Colony and deliver up possession of all personal property owned by it which may have come into their possession.

Appellants' action was dismissed and respondents' counter-claim was allowed by Dickson, J. [59 DLR (2d) 723], and this judgment was affirmed by the Court of Appeal of Manitoba [65 DLR (2d) 607].

In my view, the first question to be considered is the legal nature of the Colony. Having heard a great deal of evidence respecting the beliefs of the Hutterian Brethren Church, the trial Judge found as a fact that the Interlake Colony is a congregation of that Church. I have no doubt that if the question is approached as the trial Judge did, namely, by looking at how the matter is considered according to the teachings of the Hutterians, this is the correct conclusion. However, it appears to me that this is not the manner in which the question must be approached for legal purposes. What is religion, what is a church in the eyes of the law, does not depend on the religious beliefs of any confession, at least under a regime of freedom of religion.

In Walter et al. v. A.-G. Alta., 3 DLR (3d) 1, [1969] SCR 383, 66 WWR 513, this Court decided that the fact that Hutterites consider as part of their religion the holding of land as communal property does not mean that legislation controlling such holding is in relation to religion. Martland, J., said for the Court (at p. 9):

... The fact that a religious group upholds tenets which lead to economic views in relation to land holding does not mean that a provincial legislature, enacting land legislation which may run counter to such views, can be said, in consequence, to be legislating in respect of religion and not in respect of property.

Religion, as the subject-matter of legislation, wherever the jurisdiction may lie, must mean religion in the sense that it is generally understood in Canada. It involves matters of faith and worship, and freedom of religion involves freedom in connection with the profession and dissemination of religious faith and the exercise of religious worship.

In *Robertson and Rosetanni v. The Queen,* 41 DLR (2d) 485, [1964] 1 CCC 1, [1963] SCR 651, Ritchie, J., said for the majority (at p. 494):

It is said on behalf of the appellants that freedom of religion means "freedom to enjoy the freedom which my own religion allows without being confined by restrictions imposed by Parliament for the purpose of enforcing the tenets of a faith to which I do not subscribe." It is further pointed out that Orthodox Jews observe Saturday as the Sabbath and as a day of rest from their labours, whereas Friday is the day so observed by the members of the Mohammedan faith, and it is said that the *Lord's Day Act* imposes an aspect of the Christian faith, namely, the observance of Sunday on some citizens who do not subscribe to that faith.

My own view is that the *effect* of the *Lord's Day Act* rather than its *purpose* must be looked to in order to determine whether its application involves the abrogation, abridgment or infringement of religious freedom, and I can see nothing in that statute which in any way affects the liberty of religious thought and practice of any citizen of this country. Nor is the "untrammelled affirmations of religious belief and its propagation" in any way curtailed.

The practical result of this law on those whose religion requires them to observe a day of rest other than Sunday, is a purely secular and financial one in that they are required to refrain from carrying on or conducting their business on Sunday as well as on their own day of rest. In some cases this is no doubt a business inconvenience, but it is neither an abrogation nor an abridgment nor an infringement of religious freedom, and the fact that it has been brought about by reason of the existence of a statute enacted for the purpose of preserving the sanctity of Sunday, cannot, in my view, be construed as attaching some religious significance to an effect which is purely secular in so far as non-Christians are concerned.

If the evidence respecting the operations of the Colony is considered on the basis that the legal nature of that association is to be determined by reference to generally accepted principles and not by reference to the tenets of the Hutterians, it becomes evident that it is a commercial undertaking, not a church. The land is used essentially for growing crops and raising livestock and while some part of the production is consumed by the members of the Colony and their families, the major part is sold in the same manner as the product of any similar undertaking whether owned by an individual, a joint stock company or a cooperative association. Of course, some small part of the land is used for a place of worship but it is clear that looking at the matter according to ordinary principles, this is only an extremely minor part. For legal purposes, it can no more be controlling than the use of two small rooms, one for the chaplain's office, the other for board meetings, in a large building otherwise occupied for commercial purposes could be considered as putting a property in the class of "properties occupied by a youth association" in *L'Association Catholique de la Jeunesse Canadienne - Française v. Chicoutimi*, [1940] 4 DLR 348, [1940] SCR 510.

It must also be noted that if the articles of association rather than the teachings and theories of the Hutterian Church are examined, it becomes apparent that two distinct purposes are enumerated in art. 2, religion and industry, the industrial purpose being described in the following way:

to engage in and carry on farming, stock-raising, milling, and all branches of these industries, and to manufacture and deal in such products and by-products as may be considered by the Directors to be in the best interest of the Colony ...

It is therefore contrary to the articles of association to say that the Colony was set up as a church. The articles of association as well as the facts properly considered show that the Colony was set up both for a religious purpose and the object of operating a communal farm. In respect of the agricultural operations, the Colony cannot be considered otherwise than as a secular undertaking; it is not a charitable undertaking. Because it has among its purposes an object that cannot be classified as charitable, it follows that it must in law be treated as a commercial undertaking.

With great deference to the trial Judge and the Judges of the Court of Appeal, it was wrong to decide the case by the application of rules of law governing churches. In my view, the situation from the point of view of religion must be said to be that the members of the Colony and their families formed a congregation of the Hutterian Brethren Church. This distinction between the Church and the Colony is fully recognized in the articles of association. One of the qualifications for becoming a member of the Colony is to have "(b) Become a member and communicant of the Hutterian Brethren Church." It is clear that the Church in this provision of the articles means the unincorporated religious community. This is not to be identified with the Hutterian Brethren Church, a corporation incorporated by the Parliament of Canada (1950–51 (Can.), c. 77).

From a religious point of view, the dissenting tendencies of Benjamin and David Hofer were obviously of concern to the whole church and not merely to the Interlake congregation and that may explain why a large number of ministers of other congregations together with the local minister concerned themselves with the situation, and in fact made the decision first to impose a Church penalty and ultimately, when the appellants did not repent from their dissent, to expel them from the Church.

Before considering the effect of that decision with respect to the subsequent expulsion from the Colony, it seems convenient to examine the status of churches in Canada. It is clear that the basic principle is freedom of religion. I see no reason for not applying in Manitoba the following statement of the legal situation in Quebec that was made by the Privy Council in *Despatie v. Tremblay*, 58 DLR 27 at pp. 37–8, [1921] 1 AC 702, 47 Que. KB 305:

The religious position in the Province of Quebec in 1774, was therefore that every individual had the right to profess and practise the Catholic religion without let or hindrance. But it must be borne in mind that this is a privilege granted to the individual. There is no legislative compulsion of any kind whatever. He may change his religion at will. If he remains in the Roman Catholic community he may, so far as the law is concerned, choose to be orthodox or not, subject to the inherent power of any voluntary community, such as the Roman Catholic Church, to decide the conditions on which he may remain a member of that community unless that power has been limited in some way by the past acts of the community itself. In other words, each member of the Roman Catholic community in Quebec possessed the same privileges as any other citizen so far as religious freedom is concerned, save that he was not subject to any of the disabilities which then and, for a long time after, attached to Protestant dissenters. The Legislature did not put over him as a citizen any ecclesiastical jurisdiction. The decisions of the ecclesiastical Courts that existed in the Roman Church bound him solely as a matter of conscience. The Legislature gave to their decrees no civil effect nor bound any of its subjects to obey them. Indeed, the Act in art. 17 expressly reserves to His Majesty the power to set up Courts of ecclesiastical jurisdiction in the Province and to appoint Judges thereof, although that power seems never to have been acted upon. But what has just been said must not be misunderstood. The law did not interfere in any way with the jurisdiction of any ecclesiastical Courts of the Roman Catholic religion over the members of that communion so far as questions of conscience were concerned. But it gave to them no civil operation. Whether the persons affected chose to recognize those decrees or not was a matter of individual choice which might, or might not, affect their continuance as members of that religious communion. But that was a matter which concerned themselves alone.

It will be noted that freedom of religion includes the right for each individual to change his religion at will. While churches are otherwise free like other voluntary associations to establish whatever rules they may see fit, freedom of religion means that they cannot make rules having the effect of depriving their members of this fundamental freedom. In my view, this is precisely what these Hutterians have been attempting to do. With respect to the indignities suffered by appellants and their families, the learned trial Judge said [59 DLR (2d) 723 at p. 731]:

> The application of pressures upon a deviant, through shunning, deprivation of privileges, and the like, follows Hutterian custom and was intended to make the non-conforming deviant once more conform. Some of the indignities and mistreatment suffered by plaintiffs and members of their families appear strange and repellant, and on occasion excessive, although there can be no doubt that within a religious community stern discipline must be observed if the community is to survive.

With deference, it appears to me that the learned Judge's comments are based on a misconception of the extent of the power that may properly be exercised by Church authorities on communicants. He is clearly assuming that this may be whatever the rules of a church provide for. In other words, the decision in the Courts below proceeds on the assumption that religion extends to whatever a particular congregation may choose to include in it and that the religious authority is coextensive with such definition. This is contrary to the proper legal conception of religion whereby its scope is limited to what is commonly so considered and the extent of religious authority is limited to what is consistent with freedom of religion as properly understood, that is freedom for the individual not only to adopt a religion but also to abandon it at will.

The evidence shows that the rules and practices of this religious group make it as nearly impossible as can be for those who are born in it to do otherwise than embrace its teachings and remain forever within it. As the trial Judge has noted, it is unusual for Hutterian children to be allowed to go beyond Grade 8 education. They have no right at any time in their life to leave the Colony where they are living unless they abandon literally everything. Even the clothes they are wearing belong to the Colony and, according to the judgments below, they are to be returned to it as its property by anyone who ceases to be a member of the Church.

Such a construction of the contractual relationship between the members of the Colony means that they really cannot exercise their right of freedom of religion. If the rights of the Church and of the Colony are fully enforceable as the Courts below have held them to be, it is really legally impossible for them to leave because to do so they must do what the respondents did not hesitate to characterize as "stealing from the Church," in other words committing a crime (*Criminal Code*, ss. 2, 37, 269, 280). It does not seem to me that it is a proper answer to say that these rights will not be enforced to the limit. This is precisely what the British Court of Appeal refused to admit with respect to a contract with a money-lender that was not nearly as harsh as the contract embodied in the articles of association: *Horwood v. Millar's Timber & Trading Co. Ltd.*, [1917] 1 KB 305. In that case, the Master of the Rolls [Lord Cozens-Hardy] said (at p. 311):

... Is it open for a man in consideration of a sum of cash to bind himself not to leave the house where he is, not to sell any of his furniture and effects in the house or in any future house he may move into, which furniture is not the subject of any charge in favour of the mortgagee; is it open to him to say "Whatever property I may have I will not give any kind of security upon it for any sum of money or for any debt which legally or morally I may desire to pay"? Such a covenant would prevent the man from employing a doctor or a surgeon in the case of illness in his family, and would prevent him from raising money for the maintenance of his wife and children, or for the education of the latter. I think this is a deed which the law must recognize as bad on grounds of public policy of the most well-established kind.

He had previously stated the applicable principle in the following words (at p. 311):

... It seems to me that if as a matter of construction I come to the conclusion that the contract is one which puts the covenanter in the position – I cannot think of a better word at the moment to express my view – of *adscriptus glebae*, as the villein used to be called in mediaeval times, on the ground of public policy the law will not recognize such a thing. No one has a right so to deal with a man's liberty of action as well as his property, and the law says it is contrary to public policy.

In the present case, through the articles of association if construed and applied as embodying therein the rules of the Hutterian Church, each of the appellants was literally made *adscriptus glebae* and, in my view, such a result is contrary to public policy ...

I cannot agree that on their proper construction the articles of association provide for automatic expulsion of any member who is expelled from the Church. Such expulsion would be in the nature of a forfeiture of the whole of appellants' worldly possessions and would divest them without compensation of an important share in very valuable assets. Under ordinary rules of construction this could not be inferred; explicit words would be required which I cannot find. In any event, I am of the opinion that such a provision would be unenforceable as contrary to freedom of religion and also contrary to public policy in the context of such an association or partnership as these colonies existing for commercial purposes as opposed to church bodies or other religious or charitable organizations that may be subject to the rules applicable to churches and as to which no opinion is expressed.

In the Court of Appeal, Freedman, J.A., said [65 DLR (2d) at p. 613]:

Here, however, the vital point is that Benjamin and his brothers had by their own free and voluntary act precluded themselves, so long as they continued to be members of the Colony, from the luxury of adopting or espousing doctrines alien to Hutterianism. Outside the Hutterian Brethren Church, and not as members of the Colony, they possessed (and still possess) the ordinary rights of free citizens to follow any religious beliefs they might desire, or indeed no religious beliefs, if that should be their inclination. But within the Colony they were Hutterites, pledged by solemn obligation and specific covenants to adhere to the religion of the Hutterian Brethren Church. Their rejection of that religion and their acceptance in its place of the doctrines of the Church of God could only be a disruptive influence in a close-knit and united Colony.

With respect, I fail to see on what basis freedom of religion can be so circumscribed. Of course, inside a church no one can be allowed to disrupt services by challenging the tenets of the religion according to which they are conducted. But, as this Court in effect held in the *Barickman Colony* case, the Colony is a farm, not a Church. No one can contract out of freedom of religion, no one can by acquiring a large tract of land establish one religion over that area and exclude freedom of religion therefrom. The authorities already cited make it abundantly clear that such freedom is a matter of public policy.

It is of some significance that in Manitoba the *Religious Societies' Lands Act*, RSM 1940, c. 180 [RSM 1954, c. 225], limits the land that a religious society may hold to a maximum area that is small by comparison with that which is held by the Interlake Colony. The following provisions of that Act are to be noted:

2   (1) In this Act,

...

(c) "religious society" means a religious society, church, or congregation, of Christians or Jews in Manitoba.

...

3   (1) A religious society may, in the name of trustees subject to this Act hold

(a) land not exceeding three hundred acres to be used for the site of a church, chapel, meeting house, residence of a minister, or for the support of public worship and the propagation of Christian knowledge or for other like religious or congregational purposes;

(b) lands not exceeding twenty acres to be used subject to subsection (2) for a cemetery.

Those provisions show that if the Colony was considered as a church it would be holding land largely in excess of the maximum area fixed by law. I do not find it necessary to consider what the legal consequences would be in that view because I agree with Freedman, J.A., that the proper rule to apply in the instant case is that which was enunciated by Wynn-Parry, J., in the case of *Re Hartley Baird Ltd.*, [1955] Ch. 143 at p. 146, as follows:

In the interpretation of such a commercial document as articles of association, the maxim ut res magis valeat quam pereat [it is better for a thing to have effect than to be made void] should certainly be applied, and I propose to interpret these articles in the light of that maxim.

It appears to me that the application of that rule supports the view already expressed that the Colony is a farmers' association, not a church, and that members are not subject to expulsion for the reason that they cease to be members of the Hutterian Church. It follows that the resolutions whereby the appellants were expelled should be declared void and they should be declared to be members.

Because, in the opinion of the majority, this appeal fails, it becomes unnecessary to consider what further remedies should be allowed.

As to costs, this is a case where all parties throughout appear to have acted in accordance with their sincere view of what their respective religious beliefs required. I would therefore order the costs of all parties in all Courts to be paid out of the assets of the Colony.

Appeal dismissed.

1 Do you think that the court reaches the right balance between individual and group freedoms?
2 Suppose that the Hutterites, like many agrarian religious communities, held land individually. Would the tension between the two understandings of freedom of religion still arise? To what extent is the tension between competing views of property, rather than about religious freedom?

Jean Hampton
"Democracy and the Rule of Law" (1994)

Hampton argues that a combination of Hobbes and Hart yields a democratic account of the rule of law.

Prominent Soviet supporters of Boris Yeltsin who defeated the coup of August 1991, when questioned by Western reporters, argued that its defeat vindicated the Soviet people's commitment to two important ideals: first, the ideal of democracy, and second, the ideal of the "rule of law." The thesis of this paper is that these two ideals are connected, and that we should understand contemporary democracy as a style of government quite unlike the ancient Greek democracies heavily criticized by early modern political theorists, insofar as it is based on the idea of the rule of law and not, as ancient Greek democracies were, on the rule of human will. Indeed, as I shall explain in what follows, it is because James Madison identified democracy as a species of will-directed human government that he was so concerned to deny that a United States under the Constitution would be an instance of it.

I shall explicate and defend my thesis in part by arguing against Thomas Hobbes's contention that all political societies must be founded on human will in order properly to be considered political societies. Hobbes maintained that it was logically impossible to have something called a government that was founded on a rule, or set of precepts, put forward in some kind of constitution or contract between the people and the ruler. Ironically, I will argue that implicit in Hobbes's own contract method is the idea not only that law can be the ultimate governor in a political society but also that the ruling law can and should have what I will call a certain "democratic" content. In a strange way, one might even consider Hobbes the father of modern democracy, although he would have been horrified to have received such a title.

I THE TRADITIONAL DEFINITION OF DEMOCRACY

Consider Hobbes's definition of democracy, the main lines of which would be approved by political theorists of ancient Greece and Rome and the Middle Ages:

The difference of Common-wealths, consisteth in the difference of the Soveraign or the Person representative of all and every one of the Multitude. And because the Soveraignty is either in one Man, or in an Assembly either every man hath right to enter, or not every one, but Certain men distinguished from the rest; it is manifest, there can be but Three kinds of Common-wealth. For the Representative must needs be One man, or More: and if more, then it is the Assembly of All, or but of a Part. When the Representative is One man, then is the Common-wealth a MONARCHY: when an Assembly of All that will come together, then it is a DEMOCRACY, or Popular Common-wealth: when an Assembly of a Part onely, then it is called an ARISTOCRACY. Other kind of Common-wealth there can be none: for either One, or More, or All must have the Soveraign Power (which I have shewn to be indivisible) entire.[1]

Note that Hobbes's categorization assumes that political authority is ultimately a human-directed phenomenon: the three kinds of political authority are merely three ways in which human beings can rule over others. Either all of them can rule, or only some of them, or only one of them. And when all of them rule, the resulting government is defined as a democracy. Thus for Hobbes, *democracy is a species of government based on human will – and in this case, the human will is constituted by all the people.*

Hobbes's definition of governments in terms of *how many humans are doing the ruling* is consciously based upon an argument to the effect that there cannot be a nonhuman, rule-based political authority. The best statement of this argument is to be found in *De Cive*, in the following passage:

It is therefore manifest, that in every city there is some one man, or council, or court, who by right hath as great a power over each single citizen, as each man hath over himself considered out of that civil state; that is, supreme and absolute, to be limited only by the strength and forces of the city itself, and by nothing else in the world. For if his power were limited, that limitation must necessarily proceed from some greater power. For he that prescribes limits, must have a greater power than he who is confined by them. Now that confining power is either without limit, or is again restrained by some other greater than itself; and so we shall at length arrive to a power, which hath no other limit but that which is the *terminus ultimus* of the forces of all the citizens together. That same is called the supreme command; and if it be committed to a council, a supreme council, but if to one man, the supreme lord of the city.[2]

This "regress argument" is briefly summarized in a passage in *Leviathan*:

[W]hosoever thinking Soveraign Power too great, will seek to make it lesse, must subject himselfe, to the Power, that can limit it; that is to say, to a greater.[3]

The conclusion of this argument is that in a political society there is a single source of power, beyond which no subject can appeal, and which is authorized to decide any question, resolve any dispute, no matter the content, the history, or the parties involved. This single source of power, called the "Sovereign," must be a kind of human will: either it is a single human will or a collective of human wills acting as one.

But hasn't Hobbes made an obvious mistake here? Even if we grant that a political society must be a "closed" system, with an ultimate authority, must that ultimate authority be human? Why can't it also be a constitution or set of laws, as Kelsen or H.L.A. Hart have argued, which acts as the "final decider" in the regime?[4]

In his expansion of the regress argument in *Leviathan*, Hobbes attempts to show that a final non-human decider is impossible. The problems of conflict and disorder that the political society is supposed to cure cannot be cured unless that political society rests on an ultimate and undivided *human* will. After all, argues Hobbes, in any controversy between human beings, only another human being is in a position to decide it, and to enforce that decision. A rule is inherently powerless; it only takes on life if it is interpreted, applied, and enforced by individuals. That set of human beings that has final say over what the rules are, how they should be applied, and how they should be enforced has ultimate control over what these rules actually *are*. *So human beings control the rules*, and not vice versa. Hence, if we agree with Hobbes that the central reason for having a political society is to resolve conflict, and if we agree with his observation that laws alone are unable to resolve anything because their meaning and their power over us are entirely a function of how they are defined, applied, and enforced, then we must accept the conclusion of the regress argument that only a regime with a final human decider who (either directly or through delegates) defines, applies, and enforces these laws is in a position to effect peace, and thus actually *be* a political society. And so, to those who propose that a constitution (limiting the power of a ruler) could be the final decider in a regime, Hobbes insists that this is not a viable form of polity because

to be subject to Laws, is to be subject to the Common-wealth, that is to the Soveraign Representative, that is, to himselfe; which is not subjection, but freedom from the Lawes. Which errour, because it setteth the Lawes above the Soveraign, setteth also a *Judge* above him, and *a power to punish him*; which is to make a new Soveraign; and again for the same reason a third, to punish the second; and so continually without end, to the Confusion, and Dissolution of the Common-wealth.[5]

Note that Hobbes assumes that a political regime is only in place when one has an authority established that has the potential power to resolve all controversies that could potentially threaten the union. And he argues that laws cannot do this because their nature is such that they are just as able to generate conflict as to resolve it.

In part 2 of *Leviathan*, Hobbes elaborates on why he regards all laws, no matter their content, as worthless as an ultimate foundation of any political unit. Hobbes's position on the inefficacy of laws as governors is based on the following three beliefs:

1 Laws can never be rendered so completely clear that it is obvious to every human being what they mean. Hence they can themselves be the source of conflict unless there is a human being authorized to give the definitive interpretation of them. And if such a human being exists, then *he* is the ultimate authority, and not the laws he interprets, because he has control over them, rather than vice versa.

2 Laws can never be written so that their application to every situation is obvious to every human being. Thus, the question of how they are to be applied can generate controversy, which can only be resolved if a human being is authorized to decide their application in a definitive fashion.
3 Even if it were possible to define laws in a completely clear way, such that their application to any situation would be obvious, Hobbes would still maintain that human nature is such that those who stood to be disadvantaged by their application would be motivated by self-love to insist on defining them in some other, more advantageous way. So laws are often the source of conflict because of the way human nature responds to normative rules that get in the way of self-interest.

Relying on these three assumptions, Hobbes responds to opponents who argue, as Locke was to do later in the century, on behalf of rule-based (and sometimes morally motivated) limits on government power over the people it rules. First, to those who insist that there can and should be a contract between ruler and people, or else some sort of overarching constitution that defines and potentially limits the ruler's power, Hobbes replies in chapter 18 of *Leviathan* that this is merely an attempt to establish a set of rules as ultimate deciders in a regime, and is therefore doomed to fail because it does not incorporate into a political regime the kind of solution to the problem that such regimes are supposed to solve, namely, a final decider. Indeed, it not only neglects to incorporate that solution but also contributes to the social problem of disorder by interjecting into the social fabric yet another source of controversy.

Second, to those who want to divide sovereignty – for example, between a king and a parliament, or between a king, a parliament, and a court – Hobbes points out that sovereignty can only be divided via laws or rules setting out the division and the relative jurisdiction of each branch of government. So, argues Hobbes, if someone were to propose that, for example, sovereignty be divided into judicial, executive, and legislative units, he would be advocating, in effect,

not government ... not one independent Common-wealth, but three independent Factions; not one Representative Person, but three. In the Kingdome of God, there may be three Persons independent, without breach of unity in God that Reigneth, but where men Reigne, *that be subject to a diversity of opinion*, it cannot be so.[6]

So if the point of creating a political regime is to create an institution that will resolve all union-threatening controversy in a society, then one simply fails to create such an institution if one sets about to divide sovereignty, because such division must be accomplished by laws that are inevitably conflict generating.

Third and finally, if constitutional laws cannot be the final deciders of a political regime, this is even more true of moral laws. While Hobbes is willing to admit the existence of "laws of nature" that he regards as hypothetical imperatives dictating various forms of peaceful behavior that, when performed in concert with others, will promote peaceful and commodious living, once again he argues that, insofar as those laws are the subject of great controversy, they cannot be the final solution of conflict.

All Laws, written, and unwritten, have need of Interpretation. The unwritten Law of Nature, though it be easy to such, as without partiality, and passion, make use of their naturall reason, and therefore leave the violators thereof without excuse; yet considering there be few, perhaps none, that in some cases are not blinded by self love, or some other passion, it is now become of all Laws the most obscure; and has consequently the greatest need of able Interpreters.[7]

So Hobbes would think it fruitless to try to amend or clarify moral rules intended as fundamental legal rules in a society so as to minimize conflict over how they are to be understood and applied because human nature makes the obvious response to them impossible when self-interest is at stake.

Let me restate Hobbes's regress argument so that we understand exactly what assumptions about laws and about human nature that argument rests upon:

1 A political institution exists if and only if it has the ability to re-solve or forestall all conflict among human beings who interact in a certain territory.
2 An institution, purporting to be political, whose ultimate authority is some set of rules, whether moral rules, rules dividing power among branches of government, or rules limiting the power of political officials, cannot resolve conflict among human beings because these rules will themselves be the source of conflict, and this is because
   a) it is virtually impossible to define such rules clearly enough to eliminate all controversies about what they mean;

b) it is virtually impossible to define rules clearly enough to eliminate all controversies about how and when they should be applied;

c) human nature is such that, even if a rule is clear and easy to apply, if its application to one's own case is disadvantageous, one will strive to argue for a different application, thereby coming into conflict with those who are intent on understanding and applying it properly.

3 A political institution will be able to resolve all conflict only if total power (or sovereignty) is invested in a human will – the will of either one person or a group of persons or all the people.

4 Therefore, only those institutions in which total power is invested in a human will (in any of these three ways) can count as political institutions.

II WHO SHALL JUDGE?

Hobbes's argument is best understood as one salvo in a theoretical war waged in many sectors of European life during the seventeenth century concerning what kinds of government are possible. This was a frequent topic of discussion in the pamphlets written by politically interested people, from clergyman to lords, in seventeenth-century England. One pamphlet, written by Philip Hunton, which argued in favor of divided sovereignty, is particularly interesting because of the way it struggles with the issues raised by Hobbes's regress argument. Hunton maintained that England should divide powers between the king and the Parliament, with the king's power limited by the latter. However, he was aware that this position was attacked by royalists convinced that it was a recipe for anarchy. If the king is in effect a servant of the people insofar as he is subject to the power of Parliament, how can he hope to rule over them? Won't they ignore those of his rulings that they dislike, or remove him from power altogether if their self-interest so dictates? Hunton replies to this objection as follows:

[I]f I convey an estate of Land to another, it doth not hold that after such conveyance I have a better estate remayning in me then that other, but rather the contrary; because what was in one is passed to the other: The servant who at the year of *Jubile* would ... give his master a full Lordship over him: can we argue, that he had afterward more power over himselfe then his

Master, because he gave his Master that power over him, by that act of Oeconomical Contract[?][8]

Hunton's idea seems to be that although the people are responsible for the king's power, nonetheless, when they create that power the people *give up* their right to govern themselves, and pass it entirely on to him. Nonetheless Hunton also wants to argue that the king's power is limited and subject, in part, to the control of Parliament. So what will happen if the king's behavior is perceived as extending beyond the legal prerogatives of his power? *Who decides* whether or not he has over-stepped his bounds? Note that this last question asks for the person or persons entitled to apply what is in effect a rule defining the king's jurisdiction of power.

Hunton struggles mightily to answer the question. The decider, he notes, cannot be any foreign power, because if it were, the autonomy of the state would be destroyed. And one cannot grant the right to decide to the king himself, because that would, in effect, make the monarch absolute in power. Finally, he considers whether or not the people should judge the rule, *and he rejects this option also*, because this would turn the people into the ruler and make the king their servant, who could only govern them subject to their whims and pleasures (which are sufficiently dangerous to justify the creation of a ruling power over them in the first place). So in the end, Hunton says that in the kind of regime he would install in England, *no one* has the right to judge whether the monarch is abusing his powers! This is a remarkable example of intellectual honesty but seems so foolish as to indirectly make Hobbes's own case for him. The royalist Robert Filmer ridicules Hunton's position as follows: "Thus our Author hath caught himself in a plaine *dilemma*: if the King be judge, then he is no limited Monarch. If the people be judge, then he is no Monarch at all. So farewell *limited Monarchy*, nay farewell *all government* if there be no Judge."[9]

Hunton realized the unsatisfactory nature of this position, and thus tacked on the following codicil to it, maintaining that while the people cannot judge the ruler in any legal sense, they do have the *moral* right to judge him:

And this power of judging argues not a superiority of those who Judge, over him who is Judged; for it is not Authoritative and Civill, but morall, residing in reasonable Creatures and lawfull for them to execute, because never de-vested and put off by any act in the constitution of a legall Government, but rather the reservation of it intended: For when they define the Superiour to a Law, and constitute no Power to Judge of his Excesses from that Law, it is evident they reserve to themselves, not a Formall Authoritative Power but a morall Power, such as they had originally before the Constitution of the Government; which must needs remaine, being not conveyed away in the Constitution.[10]

But the reader is puzzled: at first Hunton describes the king as the *master* of the people, who are his slaves, and now he is granting these slaves the moral right not only to judge the king's performance but also to depose him if they think it necessary! Filmer attacks Hunton's position: "Thus at the last, every man is brought by this Doctrine of our Authors, to be his owne judge. And I also appeal to the consciences of mankinde, whether the end of this be not utter confusion, and Anarchy."[11]

Hobbes would argue that all of Hunton's problems stem from the fact that he would make government rest on a law defining and limiting a king's power. With any such government, one must ask the question, "Who shall judge the law?", and as the regress argument shows, either the answer to this question will establish who the *real* (human) authority in the regime is, insofar as it is the law's deciders who establish what will prevail in the regime, or it will show that there are no deciders of these laws, in which case the regime is doomed to collapse and thus cannot count as a genuine government. Note that if the decider is the king, then it is his will that is the foundation of the regime. But if the decider is the people, Hobbes would insist that the king can't be the ultimate ruler, since it is not he, but the people, who effectively constitute the human will calling the shots in the society. Hobbes has a dim view of the viability of democratic rule so understood, given that the people's tendency to misbehave or fail to coordinate effectively is the very reason for creating a political society in the first place. I suspect he would agree with James Madison, who maintained, in the context of explaining why the United States Constitution did not establish a democracy in the style of the Greeks, that "[d]emocracies have ever been spectacles of turbulence and contention: have ever been found incompatible with personal security or the rights of property; and have in general been as short in their lives, as they have been violent in their deaths."[12]

After the seventeenth century many theorists took Hobbes to be right. For example, it was commonplace in the nineteenth century to analyze modern regimes in the Hobbesian manner, by identifying the sovereign. Many believed this was easy to do in the case of Britain, insofar as Parliament by that time had become, to all intents and purposes, the sole legislative body in the country. But it was not easy to do for countries such as the United States, where the Supreme Court, the Congress, and the president are supposed to "share" power by performing separate (but equal) governmental functions. Indeed, the United States seems to be an example of a regime that Hobbes thought was impossible: namely, a regime in which the sovereignty is divided according to an ultimate rule, which acts as a "final decider." If Hobbes is right that such a regime is impossible and that laws cannot rule, there must be an ultimate human decider somewhere in this country. Indeed, perhaps in this regime it would make sense to say that the decider is the will of the entire people. (And this may be the correct analysis of countries such as Britain, in which most of the members of Parliament are, after all, popularly elected.)

But if the people are continually called "sovereign" in these regimes, how does it make sense to consider the people "ruled"? Hunton's dilemma returns. If babysitters are hired to supervise a bunch of unruly children, and in reality the babysitters turn out to *be* the unruly children, the supervision is useless. And similarly, if the reason for creating a political institution is that people cannot govern themselves satisfactorily, and the political regime that is created is one in which the people rule, the exercise appears useless. James Buchanan, whose own contractarian analysis of the state gives the people the last word in government, calls this "the paradox of sovereignty":

Man's universal thirst for freedom is a fact of history, and his ubiquitous reluctance to "be governed" insures that his putative masters, who are also men, face never-ending threats of rebellion against and disobedience to any rules that attempt to direct and order individual behavior.[13]

But the idea that each of us lives in a political regime under a master whom the people believe they are both able and right to master themselves when he gets out of line is not a benign paradox for theorists such as Hobbes; it is a straightforward inconsistency. We who live in regimes in which this seems to be true dismiss the charges of inconsistency without, however, understanding why we are justified in doing so, or indeed, why these regimes work, despite their paradoxical character. The fact that we have so little to say to defend our regimes against Hobbesian attack suggests that we don't yet understand how they work, why they cohere so well, and why they are capable of being highly stable, despite the force of Hobbes's attacks. In a curious way, we are in the same position as Philip Hunton: we know what polity we like, but we don't know how to defend it coherently against Hobbesian attacks.

III A HOBBESIAN RULE OF RECOGNITION

So we must understand the polity of the contemporary modern democracy better. To do so, let us begin with H.L.A. Hart's famous argument that a political society must have at least one rule, namely, the rule of recognition, which identifies what counts as law in that society. Hart's charge against Austin's positivist theory of law, namely, that it neglected to recognize the existence of the rule of recognition, is also an argument against Hobbes's entirely will-based analysis of government. Hobbes had hoped to avoid laws at the foundation of a regime, but in Hart's view, such an attempt is futile, because in each of the types of political regime Hobbes recognizes, there must be at least one law prevailing in order to identify who the sovereign is, and thus who has the power to decide all conflicts in a regime. That rule authorizes either one person or a group of persons or every person to make the law. Upon that rule rests the very fact that there is a political regime, and not simply a group of hoodlums with superior might ordering around a population.

To accommodate Hart's conclusion, therefore, we might amend the Hobbesian argument as follows:

In order for a group of people to be considered to constitute a political society, there must be a rule of recognition identifying as law whatever arises from some kind of human will, whether that be a single person's will, or the will of some group less than the entire population, or the population. No other rule of recognition will result in the creation of a legal system, and therefore of genuinely effective law.

This revision attributes to Hobbes the position that the rule of recognition, in order to be understood to define a political regime, must have a certain content. His regress argument is therefore reinterpreted as a thesis about how the socially recognized and followed rule of recognition must identify law if government is to be created: namely, that it must specify the law as the product of some kind of human will.

But can we reconcile Hobbes's attack on governments founded in law with this revised position's reliance on the rule of recognition? Perhaps. Although Hobbes takes a dim view of the possibility of human beings cooperating in the interpretation of a rule, if the rule of recognition is as simple and straightforward as the revised position above would make it, then even Hobbes might think it possible for human beings to agree on what it means. This is particularly true in the case of monarchical government, where the rule might simply specify one individual as ruler.[14]

But must a rule of recognition have this form in order to define government effectively? And even if our post-Hartian Hobbes isn't right that a legal society *must* be so defined, is he right that it *ought* to be so defined if the ends of political society are to be effectively achieved?

IV THE STRATIFICATION SOLUTION

In order to begin the process of finding answers to these questions, I want to return to Buchanan's "paradox of being governed." I shall offer a solution to that paradox here,[15] and then go on to use it to evaluate the effectiveness of Hobbes's arguments against rules of recognition that rely either entirely or in part on something other than human will to define law. That evaluation will then allow us to analyze and defend an interpretation of the structure of modern democratic regimes.

This paradox should be solved in the same way that linguistic paradoxes are standardly solved: namely, by differentiating levels of inquiry and analysis. Consider the famous "liar's paradox," which one can illustrate with the sentence "This sentence is false." The sentence cannot be true when it tells us it is false; but if it is false, then given the assertion it is making, it would seem to be true. Tarski resolved this paradox by distinguishing two kinds of language, which he called the "object" language and the "meta" language. The meta language is used to talk about the object language but is not itself part of that language. By understanding the predicates "is true" and "is false" to belong only to the meta language, one avoids the paradox. An assertion in the object language may not involve these words, which are properly employed only as part of evaluations at the meta level.

We can employ the same "stratification" solution to the paradox of being governed. Let us start by distinguishing two levels of government, the object level and the meta level. The object level is the level of laws made by those with legislative power in a regime: call this the level of the "legal system." That which defines this system is the rule of recognition – a rule that is part of the meta level, not the object level. Hart himself calls the rule of recognition a "secondary" rule, one that is about the "primary rules." So, as Hart noted, there are two kinds of laws in the legal system, the kind that defines what the system is, that is, the rule of recognition, and the kind that is created in the system, as specified by the system-defining rule. As I've discussed, if we revise Hobbes's regress argument along Hartian lines, that argument concludes that the system-defining rule must operate by identifying who the makers, interpreters, and enforcers of the primary (or "object") law are. Those who are not authorized by the rule of recognition to perform some aspect of governing would be appropriately considered "the ruled," pure and simple.

But how does such a rule of recognition, even if it has the kind of content Hobbes would recommend, get to be authoritative? And who is the person or group that shall judge whether those who are ruling have respected their role as defined by the rule of recognition? These are twentieth-century versions of the questions that troubled Hobbes and Hunton.

In a recent article, Jules Coleman argues that the rule of recognition is "authoritative only if there is a social practice in regard to it among relevant officials."[16] That is, it isn't authoritative insofar as it derives its validity from some higher law: "It is not valid or in some other sense correct; it just is."[17] Instead, to use Coleman's phrase, its authoritativeness is a "social fact," and he refers to the rule as a kind of social "convention."

Now surely Coleman is right that a rule of recognition is a social fact, one that sociologists or anthropologists or historians would be concerned to discover were they trying to understand the political society that it defined. But how is it that this social fact comes into existence, and how does that generation explain the authority of this social convention? Coleman's language above (which he takes to be suggested by Hart) seems to support the thesis that this fact is generated and maintained by the officials who are operating according to the rule of recognition. But surely this is to get the cart before the horse. The person who is identified as having a certain role in government by the rule of recognition doesn't make that law authoritative over her by obeying it; quite the contrary – it is *because* she understands it as authoritative over her that she obeys it as she performs that role. Of course, were she to fail to do so, she might be contributing to a weakening of that rule's authority. But whether or not this is true, if she does not obey it, she is flouting a law whose authority derives from something other than her prior obedience to it. This is only to say that, as Hart himself noted, the rule of recognition is a genuine *rule*, not a mere custom or social regularity but a normative requirement, and one that those who are empowered by it are obligated to respect.[18] So where does its normativity come from?

Hart himself suggests that its normativity comes from those who make up the regime when he discusses the source of the "acceptance" of the rule of recognition in a legal society: "Plainly, general acceptance [of the rule of recognition] is here a complex phenomenon, in a sense divided between official and ordinary citizens, who contribute to it in different ways."[19] Hart goes on to say that whereas the officials contribute by explicitly acknowledging what this law is, and what it means, as they play their roles in the system, in contrast, "The ordinary citizen manifests his acceptance largely by acquiescence in the results of these official operations."[20]

Now this last passage grants the people a role in maintaining the rule of recognition that appears to be quite passive – that is, acquiescence as opposed to active interpretation of its meaning. But elsewhere Hart suggests that "acquiescence" must be understood in a more active way, when he relates what is, in essence, a contractarian story to explain the origination and legitimacy of a legal system.[21] If a group of people were in a prelegal state, argues Hart, they would agree that, as a way of promoting order, instituting a government was desirable, and they would therefore create it by specifying a secondary rule – the rule of recognition – defining what would count as the primary rules in the legal society. This story essentially makes people the ultimate source of the legal system itself, and therefore the party that not only maintains it but also ultimately decides whether or not it will continue (and if so, under what form). The people's "acquiescence" is therefore analogous to the "acquiescence" of someone who has hired a lawyer to look after her affairs. The lawyer decides what to do, and acts under this person's authority, and as long as he does so satisfactorily, his client will be prepared to "acquiesce" in his decisions. But just as he holds his office only as long as she retains him in her service, so too does the ruler maintain his power only as long as the people retain him in their service (and indeed retain the very definition of the office he holds). So Hart's answer is that of a contractarian: the secondary rule has its source in and derives its authority from the people – including not only the officials who are rulers but also the people who are being ruled.

If the people are the source of the rules, mustn't they also be the ones who should judge it? Here we must beware: to say that "[t]he people who are ruled are also the ones who rule" is just as misleading as to say, "This sentence is false." To answer this question, we must specify *which* rules we're talking about. The people in most societies don't have the job of interpreting any of the primary or object rules. That job is performed by someone who occupies a certain legal office. But the people *do* decide the rule of recognition, and as they do so they are performing a meta-level action – that is, they are engaged in an action that is about the operation of the object level.

But have I solved the paradox of being governed by a mere verbal trick? I would insist that I have not, because the analysis I have just given doesn't merely generate labels, but does so in a way that allows us to *describe and understand the relationship between fundamentally different kinds of political activity.* Imagine a group of children who are playing a game of baseball in a vacant lot and who periodically stop the game to argue about the rules (they might want to make up new rules, argue about the interpretation of existing rules, or object to the application of the existing rules by the person they've appointed umpire). We know the difference between "playing baseball" and "arguing about the rules of baseball." And similarly, this analysis helps us to see the difference between "being subject to primary rules" and "participating in activities that seek to change how such rules are generated" in political societies. We are engaged in "being ruled" when we follow the law and experience sanctions set by legal authorities. And we are engaged in "interpreting the rule of recognition" either when we participate in activities that "create and maintain" our governments, or when we do what we can to overthrow them. I have discussed at length elsewhere the particular activities that constitute "creation and maintenance" of political structures: they can include everything from voting to doing jury duty to assisting in the punishment of those who have violated the primary laws to attempting to make constitutional changes (a process in which we behave most like the children arguing over the baseball rules in the vacant lot) to, perhaps most important, refraining from performing, advocating, or assisting in violent activities designed to overthrow the government.[22]

In a curious way, I think that this analysis might be what Philip Hunton was trying to get at in his remarks. He was right that no one in a political regime has the *legal* right to judge the fundamental rule of recognition defining the powers of government – that is, no one has that right in the "object legal system" itself, because at this level the rules are the foundation of government. But he was also right that the people have the "moral" right – or better, the "extralegal right" – to decide these rules in the sense that they have a right *outside* the legal system itself as they scrutinize the government at the meta level.

Why does the stratification analysis assume that the people are the ones who decide how well the object game is going at the meta level? Why doesn't it allow the possibility that it could be a right held only by a few individuals, or a small group? The answer to this question is, I would argue, implicit in the contractarian's methodology. One of the covert messages being sent by those, such as Hobbes, who justify the existence of the state on the basis of what we "could agree to," is that – in fact – a state exists *only* because enough of the people who constitute it either have created it and/or continue to maintain it, which means they behave such that the rule of recognition does not change, or changes only minimally. Creating a political system is like creating a game: the creators set out the rules that provide for the roles each person will play in the game (and most of us play the role of "ruled" in the political system), and everyone plays his or her part for as long as a sufficient number are satisfied with how it's going. So, contractarians are saying that, in fact, a political system is the "people's game" because (whether or not rulers wish to acknowledge this fact) the people will decide how well the game is going, and in particular, how well any ruler is adhering to the rules defining the extent of his jurisdiction and power. And this is not a normative thesis, but *a descriptive thesis*. A political system isn't something built into nature, created by God, or designed and maintained by only a few individuals, who naturally rule other human beings in the way that a farmer rules over the animals in his herds. It is a thoroughly human institution, whose existence depends, in a variety of ways, on the behavior of those who constitute it.

This thesis was highly radical in the seventeenth century because it essentially insists that, as a matter of *fact*, the authority of the state is not something that can be derived from some sort of natural or innate authority possessed by some set of supposedly superior persons, nor is it something that is derived solely from the word of God. Instead, it maintains that the authority of the state is the creation of the people who constitute it (albeit perhaps also a creation that God endorses). The creation of the state is the creation of rules, or authoritative norms, that define the legal system and establish the obligations of those who would serve in it. Only officials who are empowered by this set of norms are correctly known as "legal authorities." Although no contractarian believes that *all* authorities are human creations (Locke maintained that parental authority was natural; and even Hobbes accepted that God's authority is natural and not a human creation), the thrust of their argument is that the authority of a *legal* system is a human invention – and yet one to which we nonetheless believe we owe great allegiance.

The issue of how far Hobbes should be understood to endorse the conception of the state I have just described is complicated. I've been representing the contractarian methodology in a very Lockean way – a way that Hobbes himself tried self-consciously not to endorse. Hobbes wanted to say that when the people create the government they *give up* their right to rule themselves, so that they can never get it back, which means that they can never be justified in staging a revolution to replace the ruler. Or, in other words, he perceived the people as *alienating* their right to govern themselves.[23] In contrast, Locke saw people not as giving up their right to rule to the persons they named rulers, but rather as *entrusting* that right to the rulers, fully prepared to take it back if they were not satisfied with their rulers' use of it. On Locke's view, the people make the rulers their *agents*.[24] Clearly Hart's contract argument is in the Lockean tradition. But remarkably, at a number of points in *Leviathan* Hobbes himself cannot resist an agency conception of political rule, at one point claiming,

The obligation of Subjects to the Sovereign is understood to last as long, and no longer, [sic] than the power lasteth, by which he is able to protect them. For the right men have by Nature to protect themselves, when none else can protect them, can by no Covenant be relinquished.[25]

Such passages caused conservative royalists such as Bishop Bramhall to label Hobbes's *Leviathan* a "rebel's catechism."[26] But how can a philosopher who has maintained that the people *give up* their right to govern themselves slip into language that is supportive of rebellion? In my book I argue at length that an alienation interpretation of the contract argument cannot be consistently maintained by Hobbes, given his psychological assumptions – particularly the assumption that we will and ought to do whatever we need to do to insure our preservation (which, as Hobbes recognizes in the quotation above, might conceivably require deposing the sovereign in certain circumstances).[27]

So both the premises of his argument and the contractarian assumption that the state is the people's creation push Hobbes in the direction of the main outlines of an agency approach. The royalist Robert Filmer was surely right that if Hobbes wanted to defend an absolutist government, his contractarian method was exactly the wrong one to use to do it.[28] That method suggests not only a new descriptive account of the nature of a state but also a new understanding of the source of government's legitimacy. Indeed, it may even be the case, as I shall now explain, that these two implications of the contract method played a role in the development of the new concept of democratic polity in the eighteenth century.

V THE STRUCTURE OF A MODERN DEMOCRACY

Let us now turn to the analysis of the structure of a modern democracy. What does the rule of recognition in a political society with this kind of polity look like? I will argue that it is substantially different from the kind of rule a post-Hartian Hobbes would endorse. In this section I will set out the central components of this rule, relying on the stratification analysis just developed. And in the next section, I will defend the analysis against Hobbesian attack.

In the old days, those theorists, such as Hobbes, Hunton, or John Locke, who maintained, contra the divine rights theorists, that it was the people, and not God, who established and legitimized political power, also assumed that, as a matter of fact (albeit perhaps not of right), what the people did when they didn't like a regime was to stage a revolution, preferably bloodless, in which rulers were overthrown and, if necessary (as in 1688), the political rules changed. But what if one could design a political system in which "revolution" was an organized and regular part of the political process? This is the idea that inspired the founders of modern democratic societies (and particularly the founders of the American polity); it is at the heart of the structure of contemporary democratic states.

Defenders of modern democracy self-consciously recognize that *political societies are created and maintained by the people who are ruled in them*. And as I've discussed, this creation-and-maintenance process involves the creation and maintenance of a set of authoritative norms that define the legal system and the obligations of the officials who work within it. However, *democracies operate so that the people have continual control over the process of creating and maintaining the regime*. In modern democracies, the people have created not only the "legal game" but also another game that defines how to play the "creation and maintenance" game. Let me explain.

Consider the standard coup: Ruler X has power because there is a rule, accepted by the people, that he is authorized to have it. But when some or all of the people no longer accept that rule, they engage in various power-retracting activities, and if enough people (or enough of the people who have most control over the present rulership convention) engage in these activities, Ruler X is gone. (So, for example, in the case of the Soviet coup, when too many people in powerful positions refused to obey orders – for example, Russian and Baltic soldiers in the army, political officers in various Soviet states, and various people involved in the economic life of the nation – the coup collapsed.) How such activities can come to be possible, and even coordinated despite the opposition of rulers, is a fascinating story; communication among opponents of a ruler is critical (and thus some pundits argued that one of the reasons the Soviet coup failed was the existence of the FAX machine). In another place I have described this kind of revolutionary activity at length and labeled it "convention-dissolving," in virtue of the fact that it unravels the convention defining who is to hold power – which is just to say that it destroys the society's rule of recognition.[29]

The experience of England in the seventeenth century was that political convention-dissolving could be difficult, lengthy, and even dangerous for those involved in it. This lesson was not lost on the American revolutionaries. But what the framers essentially asked themselves was this: what if the people could get control of convention-dissolving activity – establishing rules that would actually allow it to occur on a periodic basis if the people so decided, and that would regulate it so that the dissolution would be as peaceful and orderly as possible? If there could be a "system of revolution" that was attached to the legal system, both rules and rulers could be changed quickly with minimal cost and disruption to the people. And the possibility of replacing them peacefully and painlessly would increase the people's control over the shape of their political game and thus allow them to better supervise their leaders (who would know that their being fired was not a particularly costly action for the people, and who would thus be under pressure, if they wanted to retain their jobs, to perform them as the people required). By and large, this "controlled convention-dissolving activity" involves what is commonly referred to as "voting," as I shall now explain.

Consider how the American Constitution works. This document not only sets up a certain kind of government, with offices that involve distinctive kinds of power and jurisdiction, but it also sets up rules for creating and dissolving conventions about *who* holds these offices. Through these rules our various government officials are empowered; but through these rules they can also be peacefully and effectively deprived of power. *Voting is therefore a form of controlled revolutionary activity.* Socialist radicals of the early twentieth century were right when they referred to votes as "paper stones."[30] Our elected "representatives" don't represent us in any literal sense – as if we were doing the ruling "through them." This is nonsense. They rule and we don't. But it is because we can easily deprive them of power – depose them, if you will – at certain regular intervals that they have (at least theoretically) the incentive to rule in a way responsive to our interests. Just like any other employee, if they want to keep their jobs they must work to the satisfaction of their employer. They therefore "represent" us in the way that any agent represents those who authorize her. In modern democratic regimes, representation is actually a form of agency.[31] Thus, those who would rule us are, in a democracy, in a continual competition with one another, attempting to gather votes that will, each hopes, be sufficient, according to the rules, to hire him or her as ruler. In democracies, more than in any other kind of regime, rulers don't have tenure.[32]

So our government is by the people, for the people, and of the people – except that this last preposition is misleading. Unlike in ancient Athens, most of us aren't actually in the government – only a few of us are. What makes this a government of the people is the fact that built into the rule of recognition are not only the rules that define the object political game but also rules that grant the people the power to create and dissolve portions of that object political game if they choose to do so with relatively little cost. Creating these rules is a novel way of extending the activity involved in creating and maintaining government. Such rules allow the people to play their "meta" role as definers of their political society in a more effective and controlled way. Those who fashioned modern democracies came to see that not only such activities as criminal punishment and tort litigation but also the very process of adding to or changing the political game itself could be made part of a large conception of the "political game." Or, to put it another way, they discovered that revolutionary activity could be an everyday part of the operation of a political society. (Other democracies besides the United States might be better exemplars of this point; one thinks for example of Italy.)

To appreciate the precise structure of these regimes, we need to examine more closely the content of the rules of recognition that define them. As Hart appreciated, any rule of recognition is a *type* of rule – that is, it is a rule about rules, or what Hart calls a "secondary" rule. Now Hart notes that there are other secondary rules (about rules) that operate *within* a legal system, for example, contract rules (which are rules about how to create "private" transactional rules between two or more parties), or rules about how to make wills (which define rules about the distribution of property). The rule of recognition is not only a rule about rules, but more generally a rule about how to recognize and/or produce *any* rule in the legal system defined by it.

However, I will now argue that in a democracy, this rule is actually a *set* of rules that can be divided into types, as follows:

First, as Hart noted, this set of rules includes those rules that identify what is to count as the law in the object political regime. In democratic societies, these rules operate by defining offices that perform legislative, executive, and judicial functions, offices that, taken together, generate the primary laws in this society. Let me call such rules "structural" in virtue of the way they set out the institutions that perform these functions. They are, as Hart notes, a type of secondary (or meta) rule.

However, there is a second type of rule that Hart failed to explicitly recognize, and whose addition transforms any regime into a modern democracy. This type of rule defines how it is that the people control and/or change the operation of the political regime as defined by the first type of rule, and it does so in two ways. First, these rules dictate how the people install or replace those who hold the offices defined by the structural type of rule just discussed, through either direct or indirect voting procedures. Second, these rules set out the procedures for changing the rules that define these offices and the procedures for filling them. (For example, the U.S. Constitution sets out an elaborate process for constitutional amendment.) By including these rules in the rule of recognition, the people not only define the object political game but also determine the system by which the people can revise that game, and under what circumstances they will be warranted to do so.

So with the addition of these latter rules, the overall rule of recognition now contains components that are *tertiary* as well as secondary: that is, it contains rules about rules about rules (i.e., "meta meta rules") insofar as it defines not merely the object political game and the primary rules generated in that game, but also the game of changing the object political game. Politics becomes a three-tier, not merely a two-tier, activity.

Now all political societies have a three-tiered structure. What makes democratic societies different is that *the way one engages in third-tier activities is now governed by rules.* That is, in a nondemocratic regime, the citizen's role as member of the population that creates, maintains, or destroys the rule of recognition defining this object game is ill defined, often little understood, often thwarted by the ruler to any extent possible, and something she and her fellow citizens "make up as they go along." In a modern democracy, the citizen not only plays a role in the object game and not only plays a role as a member of the population that creates, maintains, and changes the rule of recognition defining the first game but also performs the latter role according to well-defined procedures laid out in other parts of the rule of recognition, procedures that can involve elections, plebiscites, constitutional conventions, and so forth. And indeed, in some democracies, she plays the fourth-tier role of creating, maintaining, or changing those rules that define these election procedures, and that also define how to create, maintain, or destroy any other part of the rule of recognition. And when she plays either of these last two roles, she is part of a population that has taken it upon itself to structure and abide by rules that it uses to "revolutionize" the government.

Disgruntled members of a democratic regime are supposed to follow the procedures laid down by the rule of recognition for changing their rulers, or the offices they hold, or these procedures themselves. But they might not do so; and if they attempt to change the rule of recognition – including those rules that tell the population how to change rulers or offices in the regime – by taking certain actions (including violent actions) or by following procedures not laid down in that rule, they are engaging in what might be called "extralegal revolution." Such "old-fashioned" revolution is still possible in modern democratic states and occurs whenever the citizenry strives to revise or destroy the rule of recognition *without* respecting the rules it contains for carrying out a revision process. But insofar as the rule of recognition's procedures for revision are perceived as reasonable and are endorsed by most of the population, such revolutionaries will appear as opponents not only of the present rulers of the regime but also of the vast majority who support and maintain the way the rule of recognition defines the process of overseeing the regime's operation. Such a position makes their revolutionary activity seem unlikely to succeed, and contributes to what many see as the remarkable stability of modern democratic states.

There is one other type of rule that can be a constituent of a rule of recognition in modern democracies – but this type of rule need not be present in order for the regime to be appropriately called a democracy. It requires those who are to govern to do so in conformity to certain moral requirements. This type of rule is morally loaded to the extent that it partially articulates or partially points to a moral theory as the proper source of the content of object law created by the legislature. Coleman has rightly pointed out that there is no reason such rules cannot be part of (or even all of) the rule of recognition, and Randy Barnett argues that the presence of the Bill of Rights, and particularly the ninth amendment, indicates that the framers of the U.S. Constitution were convinced that moral reality was sufficiently clear to enable the American people to recognize and operate from that part of it circumscribed by these amendments.[33] Modern democracies do not have to incorporate such moral rules in order to be democracies, since their democratic structure is basically created by the tertiary rules discussed above. Nor do they need these rules to be explicitly written down in order for them to play an operational role in defining the nature of the object political society established by the rule of recognition. But they are a common part of many such societies, especially in written form, because they help to provide a moral yardstick that the people can use to judge the performance of those whom they are able to peacefully depose at the voting booth.

In my judgement the contribution of social contract arguments to the development of this modern conception of democracy is enormous. Historical documentation must await another paper, but consider that even though the image of an explicit social contract as the basis of government is make-believe, nonetheless that image must surely have generated in the minds of those who constructed modern democracies the idea that a well-run polity is one that recognizes and allows for the control of the people over that which is their creation – the political regime.

VI THE STABILITY OF MODERN DEMOCRACIES

Hobbes would certainly question how a rule of recognition with the democratic structure I have outlined could be either long lived or stable. After all, his regress argument establishes that the law alone, uninterpreted and unenforced, cannot rule. In a sense he would be right – the types of rules that together constitute the rule of recognition in modern democracies can govern only because the people of the political society understand them in more or less the same fashion and are prepared to do what is required to ensure that they are followed. So human will is behind the democratic rule of recognition, and the kinds of law making it up.

But one of the most important lessons we learn from the stratification analysis is that the particular kinds of behavior that human beings must perform to insure that a modern democratic political system survives are ones that all human beings – even the "bad" ones – are capable of performing. As I've described, these behaviors all come under the rubric "maintaining the rule of recognition," and as people engage in these behaviors, they are engaged in a meta game of controlling the political game, which, in modern democracies, now includes procedures for revolution itself.[34] The people's control over this political game need not be tight; if the political system (and those who rule within it) is/are perceived as performing satisfactorily, public apathy is likely. This is Hart's "acquiescence." After all, why participate actively in meta activities if the political game is going well and the officials are performing (in the people's view) ably in interpreting the rule of recognition? However, such apathy can encourage power-hungry or incompetent government officials to make changes in the operation of that game and/or in the interpretation of that rule in ways that benefit them or the interest groups that they represent, and thus damage the people's ability to supervise them. (This can involve everything from trying to pack the Supreme Court to manipulating rules about campaign contributions in order to make incumbents' reelection highly likely.) As anyone who has been hurt by a bad lawyer will recognize, if the people fail to supervise their agents properly, they may wind up at their agents' mercy. Nonetheless, the object political game is the people's to lose.

But Hobbes would wonder why that loss wouldn't be inevitable, given that effective control of these agents is only possible when the population of the democratic regime by and large share a common understanding of what these normative conventions mean, so that they are able to reach a consensus on whether they are being followed and when they are being flouted. Despite the stratification analysis, this may seem problematic. Even assuming that the people are playing a meta role when they judge the officials of the regimes in which they live, nonetheless, as they play this role they will have to cooperate and agree with one another to a large degree about what components of the rule of recognition mean and how well the officials are playing the roles that this rule sets out. But this means the rule will have to be interpreted and enforced by the very people whose inability to cooperate and agree with one another is the fundamental reason for installing a government in the first place. So how can such a regime last for any length of time?

We can reply to these Hobbesian worries by pointing out that a modern democracy is explicitly designed to deal with and resolve the sort of disagreements about the performance of the rulers that Hobbes thought were inevitable. A democracy controls these disagreements, channels them into peaceful political paths, and makes the deposing of leaders rather easy if dissatisfaction is great. Rather than rely on a sovereign to banish such disagreement (a solution that post-Hobbesians thought unlikely to work, and in any case, unacceptable), the framers of modern democracies set up rules that would resolve disagreements about the performance of rulers through the use of various voting procedures. And although there is no voting procedure that can by itself persuade everyone that the outcome of the vote is the correct one, voting can provide a means of evaluating the operation of various parts of the object game that can strike people as "fair" in the sense that it grants everyone a say, and thus allows the opposition to state its case – even while leading in the end to a decision. And the opposition knows that this decision is reversible (in their favor) if they can garner enough votes for their side in the future, a fact that encourages them to remain supportive of the system that nonetheless produced, in their eyes, a bad outcome. Moreover, a society has a *democratic culture* when every citizen, including those with large differences in political outlook, can nonetheless follow and agree on the interpretation of those tertiary (or quaternary) constituents of the rule of recognition that set out procedures for resolving that controversy in favor of only one party.

Granted, in order for this style of government to work, the people must be in rough agreement about the correct interpretation of the meta rules defining these voting procedures. And even if the interpretation of these rules is, by and large, relegated to "expert" officials, the people must generally support their interpretive practices if the regime is to be stable and peaceful. Of course, one must remember that creating an object political game involves (as I've argued at length elsewhere[35]) the creation of a coercive policing power that, once installed, may be difficult to remove. (After all, those who govern are supposed to have more force than you, so that they will be able to prevail upon you were you to break the law. But such an advantage can also be used to undermine revolutionary activity against them.) So even considerable unhappiness in the population about how the tertiary rules are being interpreted may still be consistent with the stable and peaceful operation of the regime. Nonetheless, because even the policing power of a state relies on people either being actively involved in policing activities or else refraining from interfering with the operation of this policing power, the continued health of even this institution relies on the people's support of it and their ability to create and sustain at least some rough conventions about what rules mean and how rulers are doing. However, the success and stability of this style of government in the modern world is proof that at least this minimal cooperation is something human beings are quite capable of, contra Hobbes's cynical assertions to the contrary.

So, to summarize, modern democracies are highly successful in today's world because the remedy they propose for the disagreements that will inevitably accompany publicity about the private citizenry's evaluations of their government's performance is not the use of political coercion to try to banish all but one point of view, as Hobbes proposed, but the creation of (meta) rules that allow the people to reconcile their differing points of view, and to build those rules into the political process. And perhaps the increasing capacity of human beings to communicate and thus coordinate with one another has made this type of regime not only possible but also inevitable, given that governments based upon unconstrained human will cannot survive in a society where it is commonly known that dissatisfaction among the people is rampant. There is, of course, no guarantee that all such governments will remain stable and unified indefinitely, in part because there is no guarantee that the people will be able to maintain a commitment to following and commonly interpreting the meta rules defining how to reconcile their disagreements over its operation. But the fact that such highly stratified states are both possible and surprisingly robust permits us to be optimistic about both the future of fledgling democracies and the continued health of older ones, in the face of Hobbes's "proof" that such regimes fall quickly and inevitably into ruins.

NOTES

1 *Leviathan*, ch. 19, par. 1, p. 94 of 1651 ed. (Henceforth, all page references in *Leviathan* will be to the 1651 ed., but I will also give the number of the paragraph of the chapter in which the passage occurs, to assist those whose editions do not preserve the pagination of the 1651 ed.)
2 See *The English Works of Thomas Hobbes*, vol. 2, *De Cive*, ed. W. Molesworth (London: Bohn, 1840), ch. 6, par. 18, p. 88.
3 *Leviathan*, 20, 18, 107.
4 H.L.A. Hart, *The Concept of Law* (Oxford: Clarendon, 1961), 97–107; and Hans Kelsen, *The General Theory of Law and the State*, trans. Anders Wedberg (Cambridge, MA: Harvard University Press, 1945), 110–16.
5 *Leviathan*, 29, 9, 169.
6 Ibid., 29, 16, 172.
7 Ibid., 26, 21, 143.
8 Philip Hunton, *A Treatise of Monarchy* (London, 1643), 15–16.
9 Robert Filmer, *The Anarchy of a Limited or Mixed Monarchy* (London, 1648), 20; reprinted in *Patriarcha and other Political Works by Robert Filmer*, ed. Peter Laslett (Oxford: Blackwell, 1949).
10 Hunton, *Treatise*, 18.
11 Filmer, *Anarchy*, 22.
12 From *The Federal Papers*, Paper No. 10, written by Madison. (Quotation from Mentor ed. [New York: New American Library, 1961], 81.)
13 James Buchanan, *The Limits of Liberty* (Chicago: University of Chicago Press, 1975), 92.
14 However, if this were all the rule did, then the political regime would last only as long as this ruler lived. There would be no rule requiring a certain procedure for transferring power. Moreover, if the rule established a democracy or aristocracy, the problem of succession would be removed, but we would now face the problem of defining how the aristocratic group or the entire population of citizenry must cooperate internally to create law. Rules would certainly be necessary to clarify how this would be done; and such rules would be open to interpretive controversy. Hobbes fails to realize that democracies and aristocracies require rules of recognition with substantial content.

15 This solution is based on the one that I offered in ch. 9 of my *Hobbes and the Social Contract Tradition* (Cambridge: Cambridge University Press, 1986).

16 Jules Coleman, "Rules and Social Facts," *Harvard Journal of Law and Public Policy* 14, no. 3 (Summer 1991), 721.

17 Randy Barnett, "Unenumerated Constitutional Rights and the Rule of Law," *Harvard Journal of Law and Public Policy* 14, no. 3 (Summer 1991), 719.

18 Coleman himself sometimes characterizes the rule as a social "convention," but conventions are often normative in character (and indeed called "rules"), e.g., traffic conventions, conventions about constructing a legal document such as a will or a contract.

19 Hart, *Concept of Law*, 59.

20 Hart, *Concept of Law*, 60.

21 See ibid., *Concept of Law*, 89ff.

22 See my "The Contractarian Explanation of the State," in *Midwest Studies in Philosophy: The Philosophy of the Social Sciences*, ed. T. Ueling (Minneapolis: University of Minnesota Press, 1990).

23 I discuss the many passages in which Hobbes uses language suggesting alienation in chapter 5 of my *Hobbes and the Social Contract Tradition*.

24 Locke actually uses the metaphor of trust rather than of agency, but from the legal point of view, the latter relationship better captures Locke's own understanding of the ruler/subject relationship than the former. For more on this, see note 31 below.

25 *Leviathan*, 21, 21, 272.

26 Bishop John Bramhall, *The Catching of Leviathan ... Appendix to Castigations of Mister Hobbes ... Concerning Liberty and Universal Necessity* (London, 1658), 515.

27 See my *Hobbes and the Social Contract Tradition*, esp. chs. 6–8.

28 As Filmer himself puts it, "I consent with him about the Rights of exercising government, but I cannot agree to his meanes of acquiring it ... [I] praise his building, and yet mislike his Foundation." From preface to *Observations concerning the Original of Government* (London, 1652); reprinted in Laslett, *Patriarcha* (see note 9 above).

29 See my "Contractarian Explanation of the State."

30 See the book *Paper Stones* by Adam Przeworski and John Sprague for a discussion of this term.

31 This is not unlike Hannah Pitkin's view of the nature of representation in modern democratic societies, as put forth in her book *The Concept of Representation* (Berkeley: University of California Press, 1967). However,

Pitkin tends to use the metaphor of trust, and that metaphor is problematic. A trustor does not own that which is used on his behalf by the trustee. Moreover, unlike in an agent/client relationship, the trustee/trustor relationship is one in which the trustor does not have sufficient standing to fire the trustee, and is generally regarded as inferior to or less competent than the trustee, such that he must be subject to the trustee's care. (So children are assigned trustees; and in nineteenth-century England women could only hold property in trust, in virtue of what was taken to be their inferior reasoning abilities.) The assumptions of the rights of citizens in modern democratic societies are at odds with the presumption of the trustor's incompetence.

32 I am grateful to Pasquale Pasquino for the tenure metaphor here.

33 See Coleman and R. Barnett, notes 16 and 17 above.

34 So members of Western democracies can never be considered subjects; the word is misused because at best one could say that they are subjects not to any political office holder but to rules that they have made, some of which give them control over the office holder.

35 See my "Contractarian Explanation of the State."

READING QUESTIONS ON HAMPTON

1 How do you think Hobbes and Hart would react to Hampton's use of their theories?
2 Are Dworkin's and Devlin's accounts of the rule of law in tension with Hampton's?

PART TWO

SOME CONTEMPORARY ISSUES

5

Equality

Most of us agree that the state ought to treat people as equals. But we disagree over what this requires. This chapter explores some of the different answers that have been given to this question, particularly in connection with the equality rights contained in s. 15 of the *Charter*.

Section 15(1) states that "[e]very individual is equal before and under the law and has the right to the equal protection and equal benefit of the law without discrimination and, in particular, without discrimination based on race, national or ethnic origin, colour, religion, sex, age or mental or physical disability." Canadian courts have interpreted this as a general right to non-discrimination; and in the seminal 1999 case of *Law v. Canada*, the Supreme Court identified discrimination with distinctions that violate an individual's dignity. The idea of dignity is of course quite broad and susceptible of numerous interpretations; so one interesting feature of this analysis of s. 15 is that it leaves the judiciary in a rather different position with respect to s. 15 than they are in with respect to other *Charter* rights. In the case of other rights, such as the rights to liberty and security in s. 7 or the right to freedom of speech in s. 2(b), it is at least clear what concept is under discussion, even though there are different views of how best to interpret that concept. But in the case of equality rights, it is still unclear what concept we are aiming to capture.

Is dignity an inherent and immutable feature of each of us, a type of worth that we have by virtue of possessing certain capacities? And does it require that the same set of opportunities or goods be made available to all? If so, s. 15 may look like what Charles Taylor, in the extract from *Multiculturalism and the Politics of Recognition*, calls "the politics of equal dignity." As Taylor mentions, this view of equality has been criticized as being insufficiently sensitive to the differences between individuals and groups, and to their need to determine for themselves what constitutes their identity and what they therefore require by way of equal treatment. Perhaps the same criticism can be made of the Supreme Court's decision in *Gosselin v. Quebec*, which relied heavily on appeals to the government's legislative purpose in determining whether a certain distinction amounted to a violation of dignity, rather than looking to the effects on the claimant and her own self-respect.

Such criticisms can make what Taylor calls "the politics of recognition" seem an attractive alternative approach to equality rights. This different approach treats the purpose of equality rights as that of supporting the unique, self-defined identity of each individual or group. An understanding of "dignity" that accords with this approach might focus more closely on each individual's own sense of self-respect; and there are moments in the s. 15 jurisprudence, particularly in the case of *Halpern v. Canada*, where "dignity" seems to be understood in this light. These two approaches outlined by Taylor are not, of course, exhaustive; and the discussions of the different "contextual factors" relevant to the *Law* test in *Halpern* are useful in suggesting alternative approaches.

A further set of controversial issues that arises in the interpretation of equality rights is raised by Nitya Iyer in her article "Categorical Denials: Equality Rights and the Shaping of Social Identities" and also by Justice L'Heureux-Dubé in her judgment in *Egan*. In order to assert her equality rights, a person must present her situation in terms of certain fixed categories, which are not of her choosing and which may distort both her identity and the true nature of the problem that has been foisted on her. A claimant must base her claim on one of the recognized grounds, even though this ground may fail fully to capture the constellation of factors that have resulted in her exclusion, and even though the ground may be more a reflection of other groups' priorities than of her situation; and she must show that she has been treated differently than some other group or individual, even though this forces her to define herself in relation to these others and their norms. In her judgment in *Egan*, L'Heureux-Dubé suggests that these difficulties could be avoided by abandoning a grounds-based approach in favour of a group-based approach. But it is unclear whether her proposed alternative does not simply replicate the problems she seeks to avoid. Moreover, it is unclear whether any approach to equality rights could fully avoid these difficulties, since it is unclear whether we can make and adjudicate claims to equal treatment without engaging in some categorization.

A further question raised by all of the s. 15 cases in this chapter, and also raised by L'Heureux-Dubé's group-based approach, is whether equality rights protect individuals *qua* members of groups or simply *qua* individuals. Discussions of equality often slip between talk of individuals and talk of groups. But it matters whether we think the aim of equality rights is to protect individuals simply by virtue of some capacity or need of theirs, or to protect them because they are members of valuable groups, which we have reason to preserve. The framework for equality-rights analysis that L'Heureux-Dubé proposes in *Egan* is very similar to what later came to be adopted as the authoritative test in *Law*, except that L'Heureux-Dubé rejects the idea that discrimination must occur on a recognized "ground" and asks us to look instead for membership in an "identifiable group." Is this appeal to groups helpful; or does it unduly narrow the scope of equality rights, protecting the wrong thing for the wrong reasons?

Underlying all of these questions about the substance of equality rights is a set of questions about the role of the judiciary in interpreting these rights. Some of these questions are related to debates in chapters 1, 2, and 7 concerning the nature of law and its relation to morality, and the aims and legitimacy of judicial review; some are also related to issues we considered in chapter 4. Is it appropriate for judges to theorize about what equal respect for dignity requires, if these theories are not already a part of positive law? What role, if any, should judges accord to society's core moral values and institutions in interpreting s. 15? If a certain person's or group's claim to equality threatens the integrity of a certain core social institution, is this a fact that courts can or should give weight to? These questions are raised by all of the cases in this chapter, but come into particularly sharp focus in *Vriend* and *Lawrence v. Texas*.

Charles Taylor
"Multiculturalism and the Politics of Recognition" (1992)

I want to concentrate here on the public sphere, and try to work out what a politics of equal recognition has meant and could mean.

In fact, it has come to mean two rather different things, connected, respectively, with the two major changes I have been describing. With the move from honor to dignity has come a politics of universalism, emphasizing the equal dignity of all citizens, and the content of this politics has been the equalization of rights and entitlements. What is to be avoided at all costs is the existence of "first-class" and "second-class" citizens. Naturally, the actual detailed measures justified by this principle have varied greatly, and have often been controversial. For some, equalization has affected only civil rights and voting rights; for others, it has extended into the socioeconomic sphere. People who are systematically handicapped by poverty from making the most of their citizenship rights are deemed on this view to have been relegated to second-class status, necessitating remedial action through equalization. But through all the differences of interpretation, the principle of equal citizenship has come to be universally accepted. Every position, no matter how reactionary, is now defended under the colors of this principle. Its greatest, most recent victory was won by the civil rights movement of the 1960s in the United States. It is worth noting that even the adversaries of extending voting rights to blacks in the southern states found some pretext consistent with universalism, such as "tests" to be administered to would-be voters at the time of registration.

By contrast, the second change, the development of the modern notion of identity, has given rise to a politics of difference. There is, of course, a universalist basis to this as well, making for the overlap and confusion between the two. *Everyone* should be recognized for his or her unique identity. But recognition here means something else. With the politics of equal dignity, what is established is meant to be universally the same, an identical basket of rights and immunities; with the politics of difference, what we are asked to recognize is the unique identity of this individual or group, their distinctness from everyone else. The idea is that it is precisely this distinctness that has been ignored, glossed over, assimilated to a dominant or majority identity. And this assimilation is the cardinal sin against the ideal of authenticity.[1]

Now underlying the demand is a principle of universal equality. The politics of difference is full of denunciations of discrimination and refusals of second-class citizenship. This gives the principle of universal equality a point of entry within the politics of dignity. But once inside, as it were, its demands are hard to assimilate to that politics. For it asks that we give acknowledgment and status to something that is not universally shared. Or, otherwise put, we give due acknowledgment only to what is universally present – everyone has an identity – through recognizing what is peculiar to each. The universal demand powers an acknowledgment of specificity.

The politics of difference grows organically out of the politics of universal dignity through one of those shifts with which we are long familiar, where a new understanding of the human social condition imparts a radically new meaning to an old principle. Just as a view of human beings as conditioned by their socioeconomic plight changed the understanding of second-class citizenship, so that this category came to include, for example, people in inherited poverty traps, so here the understanding of identity as formed in interchange, and as possibly so malformed, introduces a new form of second-class status into our purview. As in the present case, the socioeconomic redefinition justified social programs that were highly controversial. For those who had not gone along with this changed definition of equal status, the various redistributive programs and special opportunities offered to certain populations seemed a form of undue favoritism.

Similar conflicts arise today around the politics of difference. Where the politics of universal dignity fought for forms of nondiscrimination that were quite "blind" to the ways in which citizens differ, the politics of difference often redefines nondiscrimination as requiring that we make these distinctions the basis of differential treatment. So members of aboriginal bands will get certain rights and powers not enjoyed by other Canadians, if the demands for native selfgovernment are finally agreed on, and certain minorities will get the right to exclude others in order to preserve their cultural integrity, and so on.

To proponents of the original politics of dignity, this can seem like a reversal, a betrayal, a simple negation of their cherished principle. Attempts are therefore made to mediate, to show how some of these measures meant to accommodate minorities can after all be justified on the original basis of dignity. These arguments can be successful up to a point. For instance, some of the (apparently) most flagrant departures from "difference-blindness" are reverse discrimination measures, affording people from previously unfavored groups a competitive advantage for jobs or places in universities. This practice has been justified on the grounds that historical discrimination has created a pattern within which the unfavored struggle at a disadvantage. Reverse discrimination is defended as a temporary measure that will eventually level the playing field and allow the old "blind" rules to come back into force in a way that doesn't disadvantage anyone. This argument seems cogent enough – wherever its factual basis is sound. But it won't justify some of the measures now urged on the grounds of difference, the goal of which is not to bring us back to an eventual "difference-blind" social space but, on the contrary, to maintain and cherish distinctness, not just now but forever. After all, if we're concerned with identity, then what is more legitimate than one's aspiration that it never be lost?[2]

So even though one politics springs from the other, by one of those shifts in the definition of key terms with which we're familiar, the two diverge quite seriously from each other. One basis for the divergence comes out even more clearly when we go beyond what each requires that we acknowledge – certain universal rights in one case, a particular identity on the other – and look at the underlying intuitions of value.

The politics of equal dignity is based on the idea that all humans are equally worthy of respect. It is underpinned by a notion of what in human beings commands respect, however we may try to shy away from this "metaphysical" background. For Kant, whose use of the term *dignity* was one of the earliest influential evocations of this idea, what commanded respect in us was our status as rational agents, capable of directing our lives through principles.[3] Something like this has been the basis for our intuitions of equal dignity ever since, though the detailed definition of it may have changed.

Thus, what is picked out as of worth here is a *universal human potential*, a capacity that all humans share. This potential, rather than anything a person may have made of it, is what ensures that each person deserves respect. Indeed, our sense of the importance of potentiality reaches so far that we extend this protection even to people who through some circumstance that has befallen them are incapable of realizing their potential in the normal way – handicapped people, or those in a coma, for instance.

In the case of the politics of difference, we might also say that a universal potential is at its basis, namely, the potential for forming and defining one's own identity, as an individual, and also as a culture. This potentiality must be respected equally in everyone. But at least in the intercultural context, a stronger demand has recently arisen: that one accord equal respect to actually evolved cultures. Critiques of European or white domination, to the effect that they have not only suppressed but failed to appreciate other cultures, consider these depreciatory judgments not only factually mistaken but somehow morally wrong. When Saul Bellow is famously quoted as saying something like, "When the Zulus produce a Tolstoy we will read him,"[4] this is taken as a quintessential statement of European arrogance, not just because Bellow is allegedly being *de facto* insensitive to the value of Zulu culture, but frequently also because it is seen to reflect a denial in principle of human equality. The possibility that the Zulus, while having the same potential for culture formation as anyone else, might nevertheless have come up with a culture that is less valuable than others is ruled out from the start. Even to entertain this possibility is to deny human equality. Bellow's error here, then, would not be a (possibly insensitive) particular mistake in evaluation, but a denial of a fundamental principle.

To the extent that this stronger reproach is in play, the demand for equal recognition extends beyond an acknowledgment of the equal value of all humans potentially, and comes to include the equal value of what they have made of this potential in fact. This creates a serious problem, as we shall see below.

These two modes of politics, then, both based on the notion of equal respect, come into conflict. For one, the principle of equal respect requires that we treat people in a difference-blind fashion. The fundamental intuition that humans command this respect focuses on what is the same in all. For the other, we have to recognize and even foster particularity. The reproach the first makes to the second is just that it violates the principle of nondiscrimination. The reproach the second makes to the first is that it negates identity by forcing people into a homogeneous mold that is untrue to them. This would be bad enough if the mold were itself neutral – nobody's mold in particular. But the complaint generally goes further. The claim is that the supposedly neutral set of difference-blind principles of the politics of equal dignity is in fact a reflection of one hegemonic culture. As it turns out, then, only the minority or suppressed cultures are being forced to take alien form. Consequently, the supposedly fair and difference-blind society is not only inhuman (because suppressing identities) but also, in a subtle and unconscious way, itself highly discriminatory.[5]

This last attack is the cruelest and most upsetting of all. The liberalism of equal dignity seems to have to assume that there are some universal, difference-blind principles. Even though we may not have defined them yet, the project of defining them remains alive and essential. Different theories may be put forward and contested – and a number have been proposed in our day[6] but the shared assumption of the different theories is that one such theory is right.

The charge leveled by the most radical forms of the politics of difference is that "blind" liberalisms are themselves the reflection of particular cultures. And the worrying thought is that this bias might not just be a contingent weakness of all hitherto proposed theories, that the very idea of such a liberalism may be a kind of pragmatic contradiction, a particularism masquerading as the universal.

NOTES

1 A prime example of this charge from a feminist perspective is Carol
Gilligan's critique of Lawrence Kohlberg's theory of moral development,
for presenting a view of human development that privileges only one
facet of moral reasoning, precisely the one that tends to predominate in
boys rather than girls. See Gilligan, *In a Different Voice* (Cambridge,
Mass.: Harvard University Press, 1982).

2 Will Kymlicka, in his very interesting and tightly argued book *Liberalism,
Community and Culture* (Oxford: Clarendon Press, 1989), tries to argue for
a kind of politics of difference, notably in relation to aboriginal rights in
Canada, but from a basis that is firmly within a theory of liberal neutrality. He wants to argue on the basis of certain cultural needs – minimally,
the need for an integral and undamaged cultural language with which
one can define and pursue his or her own conception of the good life. In
certain circumstances, with disadvantaged populations, the integrity of
the culture may require that we accord them more resources or rights
than others. The argument is quite parallel to that made in relation to
socioeconomic inequalities that I mentioned above.

But where Kymlicka's interesting argument fails to recapture the actual
demands made by the groups concerned – say Indian bands in Canada,
or French-speaking Canadians – is with respect to their goal of survival.
Kymlicka's reasoning is valid (perhaps) for *existing* people who find
themselves trapped within a culture under pressure, and can flourish
within it or not at all. But it doesn't justify measures designed to ensure
survival through indefinite future generations. For the populations
concerned, however, that is what is at stake. We need only think of the
historical resonance of "la survivance" among French Canadians.

3 See Kant, *Grundlegung der Metaphysik der Sitten* (Berlin: Gruyter, 1968;
reprint of the Berlin Academy edition), 434.

4 I have no idea whether this statement was actually made in this form by
Saul Bellow, or by anyone else. I report it only because it captures a
widespread attitude, which is, of course, why the story had currency in
the first place.

5 One hears both kinds of reproach today. In the context of some modes of
feminism and multiculturalism, the claim is the strong one, that the
hegemonic culture discriminates. In the Soviet Union, however, alongside a similar reproach leveled at the hegemonic Great Russian culture,
one also hears the complaint that Marxist-Leninist communism has been
an alien imposition on all equally, even on Russia itself. The communist

mold, on this view, has been truly nobody's. Solzhenitsyn has made this claim, but it is voiced by Russians of a great many different persuasions today, and has something to do with the extraordinary phenomenon of an empire that has broken apart through the quasi-secession of its metropolitan society.

6   See John Rawls, *A Theory of Justice* (Cambridge, Mass.: Harvard University Press, 1971); Ronald Dworkin, *Taking Rights Seriously* (London: Duckworth, 1977) and *A Matter of Principle* (Cambridge, Mass.: Harvard University Press, 1985); and Jürgen Habermas, *Theories des kommunikativen Handelns* (Frankfurt: Suhrkamp, 1981).

READING QUESTIONS ON TAYLOR

1   Does the "politics of equal dignity" really require that we treat people in a difference-blind fashion? If not, is there a more subtle way of explaining the difference between this view of equality and "the politics of difference"?

2   What does it mean to say that the politics of equal dignity is "a reflection of one hegemonic culture"? Is this right? If it is accurate as a factual description of the cultural origins of this view, does anything follow from this about the correctness of this view of equality, as a moral view?

3   Can you think of any ways of conceiving of equality other than in terms of "the politics of equal dignity" or "the politics of difference"?

Halpern v. Canada (Attorney General) [2003] OJ No. 2268 (June 10, 2003)

In this case, the Ontario Court of Appeal held that the common-law definition of marriage violates the equality rights of same-sex couples under s. 15 of the *Charter*, and is not saved by s. 1. The Divisional Court (the lower court whose decision was on appeal) had given the government two years to modify the definition, after which a court-formulated definition would replace it. The Court of Appeal went farther, declaring the reformulated definition to be effective immediately.

McMurtry C.J.O., Macpherson and Gillese JJ.A.

BY THE COURT: –

A INTRODUCTION

The definition of marriage in Canada, for all of the nation's 136 years, has been based on the classic formulation of Lord Penzance in *Hyde v. Hyde and Woodmansee* (1866), LR 1 P. & D. 130, [1861–73] All ER Rep. 175 at p. 177 All ER, p. 133 P. & D.: "I conceive that marriage, as understood in Christendom, may for this purpose be defined as the voluntary union for life of one man and one woman, to the exclusion of all others." The central question in this appeal is whether the exclusion of same-sex couples from this common law definition of marriage breaches ss. 2(a) or 15(1) of the *Canadian Charter of Rights and Freedoms* (the "*Charter*") in a manner that is not justified in a free and democratic society under s. 1 of the *Charter*.

This appeal raises significant constitutional issues that require serious legal analysis. That said, this case is ultimately about the recognition and protection of human dignity and equality in the context of the social structures available to conjugal couples in Canada.

In *Law v. Canada (Minister of Employment and Immigration)*, [1999] 1 SCR 497, 170 DLR (4th) 1, at p. 530 SCR, Iacobucci J., writing for a unanimous court, described the importance of human dignity:

Human dignity means that an individual or group feels self-respect and self-worth. It is concerned with physical and psychological integrity and empowerment. Human dignity is harmed by unfair treatment premised upon personal traits or circumstances which do not relate to individual needs, capacities, or merits. It is enhanced by laws which are sensitive to the needs, capacities, and merits of different individuals, taking into account the context underlying their differences. Human dignity is harmed when individuals and groups are marginalized, ignored, or devalued, and is enhanced when laws recognize the full place of all individuals and groups within Canadian society ...

Marriage is, without dispute, one of the most significant forms of personal relationships. For centuries, marriage has been a basic element of social organization in societies around the world. Through the institution of marriage, individuals can publicly express their love and commitment to each other. Through this institution, society publicly recognizes expressions of love and commitment between individuals, granting them respect and legitimacy as a couple. This public recognition and sanction of marital relationships reflect society's approbation of the personal hopes, desires and aspirations that underlie loving, committed conjugal relationships. This can only enhance an individual's sense of self-worth and dignity.

The ability to marry, and to thereby participate in this fundamental societal institution, is something that most Canadians take for granted. Same-sex couples do not; they are denied access to this institution simply on the basis of their sexual orientation.

Sexual orientation is an analogous ground that comes under the umbrella of protection in s. 15(1) of the *Charter*: see *Egan v. Canada*, [1995] 2 SCR 513, 124 DLR (4th) 609, and *M. v. H.*, [1999] 2 SCR 3, 171 DLR (4th) 577. As explained by Cory, J. in *M. v. H.* at pp. 52–53 SCR:

> In *Egan* ... this Court unanimously affirmed that sexual orientation is an analogous ground to those enumerated in s. 15(1). Sexual orientation is "a deeply personal characteristic that is either unchangeable or changeable only at unacceptable personal costs" (para. 5). In addition, a majority of this Court explicitly recognized that gays, lesbians and bisexuals, "whether as individuals or couples, form an identifiable minority who have suffered and continue to suffer serious social, political and economic disadvantage" (para. 175, *per* Cory, J.; see also para. 89, *per* L'Heureux-Dubé, J.).

Historically, same-sex equality litigation has focused on achieving equality in some of the most basic elements of civic life, such as bereavement leave, health care benefits, pensions benefits, spousal support, name changes and adoption. The question at the heart of this appeal is whether excluding same-sex couples from another of the most basic elements of civic life – marriage – infringes human dignity and violates the Canadian Constitution.

B FACTS

(1) The Parties and the Events

Seven gay and lesbian couples (the "Couples") want to celebrate their love and commitment to each other by getting married in civil ceremonies. In this respect, they share the same goal as countless other Canadian couples. Their reasons for wanting to engage in a formal civil ceremony of marriage are the same as the reasons of heterosexual couples. By way of illustration, we cite the affidavits of three of the persons who seek to be married:

Aloysius Edmund Pittman
I ask only to be allowed the right to be joined together by marriage the same as my parents and my heterosexual friends.

Julie Erbland
I understand marriage as a defining moment for people choosing to make a life commitment to each other. I want the family that Dawn and I have created to be understood by all of the people in our lives and by society. If we had the freedom to marry, society would grow to understand our commitment and love for each other. We are interested in raising children. We want community recognition and support. I doubt that society will support us and our children, if our own government does not afford us the right to marry.

Carolyn Rowe
We would like the public recognition of our union as a "valid" relationship and would like to be known officially as more than just roommates. Married spouse is a title that one chooses to enter into while common-law spouse is something that a couple happens into if they live together long enough. We want our families, relatives, friends, and larger society to know and understand our relationship for what it is, a loving committed relationship between two people. A traditional marriage would allow us the opportunity to enter into such a commitment. The marriage ceremony itself provides a time for family and friends to gather around a couple in order to recognise the love and commitment they have for each other.

The Couples applied for civil marriage licences from the Clerk of the City of Toronto. The Clerk did not deny the licences but, instead, indicated that she would apply to the court for directions, and hold the licences in abeyance in the interim. The Couples commenced their own application. By order dated August 22, 2000, Lang, J. transferred the Couples' application to the Divisional Court. The Clerk's application was stayed on consent.

In roughly the same time frame, the Metropolitan Community Church of Toronto ("MCCT"), a Christian church that solemnizes marriages for its heterosexual congregants, decided to conduct mar-

riages for its homosexual members. Previously, MCCT had felt constrained from performing marriages for same-sex couples because it
understood that the municipal authorities in Toronto would not issue
a marriage licence to same-sex couples. However, MCCT learned that
the ancient Christian tradition of publishing the banns of marriage was
a lawful alternative under the laws of Ontario to a marriage licence
issued by municipal authorities: see *Marriage Act*, RSO 1990, c. M.3, s.
5(1).

Two couples, Kevin Bourassa and Joe Varnell and Elaine and Anne
Vautour, decided to be married in a religious ceremony at MCCT. In an
affidavit, Elaine and Anne Vautour explained their decision:

We love one another and are happy to be married. We highly value the love
and commitment to our relationship that marriage implies. Our parents
were married for over 40 and 50 years respectively, and we value the
tradition of marriage as seriously as did our parents.

The pastor at MCCT, Rev. Brent Hawkes, published the banns of
marriage for the two couples during services on December 10, 17 and 24,
2000. On January 14, 2001, Rev. Hawkes presided at the weddings at
MCCT. He registered the marriages in the Church Register and issued
marriage certificates to the couples.

In compliance with the laws of Ontario, MCCT submitted the
requisite documentation for the two marriages to the Office of the
Registrar General: see *Vital Statistics Act*, RSO 1990, c. V.4, s. 19(1) and
the Regulations under the *Marriage Act*, RRO 1990, Reg. 738, s. 2(3). The
Registrar refused to accept the documents for registration, citing an
alleged federal prohibition against same-sex marriages. As a result,
MCCT launched its application to the Divisional Court.

By order dated January 25, 2001, Lang, J. consolidated the Couples'
and MCCT's applications ...

C ISSUES

We frame the issues as follows:

1 What is the common law definition of marriage? Does it prohibit
   same-sex marriages?
2 Is a constitutional amendment required to change the common law
   definition of marriage, or can a reformulation be accomplished by
   Parliament or the courts?

3 Does the common law definition of marriage infringe MCCT's rights under ss. 2(a) and 15(1) of the *Charter*?
4 Does the common law definition of marriage infringe the Couples' equality rights under s. 15(1) of the *Charter*?
5 If the answer to question 3 or 4 is 'Yes', is the infringement saved by s. 1 of the *Charter*?
6 If the common law definition of marriage is unconstitutional, what is the appropriate remedy and should it be suspended for any period of time?

D ANALYSIS

Before turning to the issues raised by the appeal, we make ... preliminary observations.

First, the definition of marriage is found at common law. The only statutory reference to a definition of marriage is found in s. 1.1 of the *Modernization of Benefits and Obligations Act*, SC 2000, c. 12, which provides:

For greater certainty, the amendments made by this Act do not affect the meaning of the word "marriage," that is, the lawful union of one man and one woman to the exclusion of all others.

The *Modernization of Benefits and Obligations Act* is the federal government's response to the Supreme Court of Canada's decision in *M. v. H.* The Act extends federal benefits and obligations to all unmarried couples that have cohabited in a conjugal relationship for at least one year, regardless of sexual orientation. As recognized by the parties, s. 1.1 does not purport to be a federal statutory definition of marriage. Rather, s. 1.1 simply affirms that the Act does not change the common law definition of marriage.

Second, it is clear and all parties accept that, the common law is subject to *Charter* scrutiny where government action or inaction is based on a common law rule: see *British Columbia Government Employees' Union v. British Columbia (Attorney General)*, [1988] 2 SCR 214, 53 DLR (4th) 1; *R. v. Swain*, [1991] 1 SCR 933, 63 CCC (3d) 481; *R. v. Salituro*, [1991] 3 SCR 654, 8 CRR (2d) 173; and *Hill v. Church of Scientology of Toronto*, [1995] 2 SCR 1130, 126 DLR (4th) 129. Accordingly, there is no dispute that the AGC was the proper respondent in the applications brought by the Couples and MCCT, and that the common law definition of marriage is subject to *Charter* scrutiny ...

The intervenor, The Association for Marriage and the Family in Ontario (the "Association"), takes the position that the word "marriage," as used in the *Constitution Act, 1867*, is a constitutionally entrenched term that refers to the legal definition of marriage that existed at Confederation. The Association argues that the legal definition of marriage at Confederation was the "union of one man and one woman." As a constitutionally entrenched term, this definition of marriage can be amended only through the formal constitutional amendment procedures. As a consequence, neither the courts nor Parliament have jurisdiction to reformulate the meaning of marriage ...

In our view, the Association's constitutional amendment argument is without merit for two reasons. First, whether same-sex couples can marry is a matter of capacity. There can be no issue, nor was the contrary argued before us, that Parliament has authority to make laws regarding the capacity to marry. Such authority is found in s. 91(26) of the *Constitution Act, 1867*.

Second, to freeze the definition of marriage to whatever meaning it had in 1867 is contrary to this country's jurisprudence of progressive constitutional interpretation. This jurisprudence is rooted in Lord Sankey's words in *Edwards v. A.G. Canada*, [1930] AC 124, [1929] All ER Rep. 571 (PC) at p. 136 AC: "The British North America Act planted in Canada a living tree capable of growth and expansion within its natural limits" ...

In its cross-appeal, MCCT takes the position that the common law definition of marriage breaches its freedom of religion under s. 2(a) of the *Charter* and its right to be free from religious discrimination under s. 15(1). MCCT argues that the common law definition of marriage is rooted in Christian values, as propounded by the Anglican Church of England, which has never recognized same-sex marriages. MCCT contends that this definition, therefore, has the unconstitutional purpose of enforcing a particular religious view of marriage and excluding other religious views of marriage. MCCT also contends that the common law definition of marriage, which provides legal recognition and legitimacy to marriage ceremonies that accord with one religious view of marriage, has the effect of diminishing the status of other religious marriages ...

In our view, this case does not engage religious rights and freedoms. Marriage is a legal institution, as well as a religious and a social institution. This case is solely about the legal institution of marriage. It is not about the religious validity or invalidity of various forms of marriage. We do not view this case as, in any way, dealing or interfering with the religious institution of marriage ...

SECTION 15(1) OF THE *CHARTER*

Section 15(1) of the *Charter* provides that "[e]very individual is equal before and under the law and has the right to the equal protection and equal benefit of the law without discrimination and, in particular, without discrimination based on race, national or ethnic origin, colour, religion, sex, age or mental or physical disability."

In *Law*, Iacobucci, J., writing for a unanimous court, described the purpose of s. 15(1) in the following terms, at p. 529 SCR:

It may be said that the purpose of s. 15(1) is to prevent the violation of essential human dignity and freedom through the imposition of disadvantage, stereotyping, or political or social prejudice, and to promote a society in which all persons enjoy equal recognition at law as human beings or as members of Canadian society, equally capable and equally deserving of concern, respect and consideration.

Iacobucci, J. emphasized that a s. 15(1) violation will be found to exist only where the impugned law conflicts with the purpose of s. 15(1). The determination of whether such a conflict exists must be approached in a purposive and contextual manner: *Law* at p. 525 SCR. To that end, Iacobucci, J. articulated a three-stage inquiry, at pp. 548–49 SCR:

(A) Does the impugned law (a) draw a formal distinction between the claimant and others on the basis of one or more personal characteristics, or (b) fail to take into account the claimant's already disadvantaged position within Canadian society resulting in substantively differential treatment between the claimant and others on the basis of one or more personal characteristics?
(B) Is the claimant subject to differential treatment based on one or more enumerated and analogous grounds?

and

(C) Does the differential treatment discriminate, by imposing a burden upon or withholding a benefit from the claimant in a manner which reflects the stereotypical application of presumed group or personal characteristics, or which otherwise has the effect of perpetuating or promoting the view that the individual is less capable or worthy of recognition or value as a human being or as a member of Canadian society, equally deserving of concern, respect, and consideration?

The claimant has the burden of establishing each of these factors on a balance of probabilities.

(b) The existence of differential treatment

The first stage of the s. 15(1) inquiry requires the court to determine whether the impugned law: (a) draws a formal distinction between the claimant and others on the basis of one or more personal characteristics; or (b) fails to take into account the claimant's already disadvantaged position within Canadian society resulting in substantively differential treatment between the claimant and others on the basis of one or more personal characteristics.

This stage of the inquiry recognizes that the equality guarantee in s. 15(1) of the *Charter* is a comparative concept. As explained by Iacobucci, J. in *Law* at p. 531 SCR:

The object of a s. 15(1) analysis is not to determine equality in the abstract; it is to determine whether the impugned legislation creates differential treatment between the claimant and others on the basis of enumerated or analogous grounds, which results in discrimination.

Accordingly, it is necessary to identify the relevant comparator group in order to determine whether the claimants are the subject of differential treatment. Generally speaking, the claimants choose the group with whom they wish to be compared for the purpose of the discrimination inquiry: *Law* at p. 532 SCR.

In this case, the Couples submit that the common law definition of marriage draws a formal distinction between opposite-sex couples and same-sex couples on the basis of their sexual orientation. Opposite-sex couples have the legal capacity to marry; same-sex couples do not.

The AGC submits that marriage, as an institution, does not produce a distinction between opposite-sex and same-sex couples. The word "marriage" is a descriptor of a unique opposite-sex bond that is common across different times, cultures and religions as a virtually universal norm. Marriage is not a common law concept; rather, it is a historical and worldwide institution that pre-dates our legal framework. The Canadian common law captured the definition of marriage by attaching benefits and obligations to the marriage relationship. Accordingly, it is not the definition of marriage itself that is the source of the differential treatment. Rather, the individual pieces of legislation that provide the authority for the distribution of government benefits and obligations are the source of the differential treatment. Moreover, since the enactment of the *Modernization of Benefits and Obligations Act*, same-sex couples receive substantive equal benefit and protection of the federal law.

In our view, the AGC's argument must be rejected for several reasons.

First, the only issue to be decided at this stage of the s. 15(1) analysis is whether a distinction is made. The fact that the common law adopted, rather than invented, the opposite-sex feature of marriage is irrelevant ...

Second, Canadian governments chose to give legal recognition to marriage. Parliament and the provincial legislatures have built a myriad of rights and obligations around the institution of marriage. The provincial legislatures provide licensing and registration regimes so that the marriages of opposite-sex couples can be formally recognized by law. Same-sex couples are denied access to those licensing and registration regimes. That denial constitutes a formal distinction between opposite-sex and same-sex couples ...

Third, whether a formal distinction is part of the definition itself or derives from some other source does not change the fact that a distinction has been made. If marriage were defined as "a union between one man and one woman of the Protestant faith," surely the definition would be drawing a formal distinction between Protestants and all other persons. Persons of other religions and persons with no religious affiliation would be excluded. Similarly, if marriage were defined as "a union between two white persons," there would be a distinction between white persons and all other racial groups. In this respect, an analogy can be made to the anti-miscegenation laws that were declared unconstitutional in *Loving v. Virginia*, 388 U.S. 1 (1967) because they distinguished on racial grounds.

Fourth, an argument that marriage is heterosexual because it "just is" amounts to circular reasoning. It sidesteps the entire s. 15(1) analysis. It is the opposite-sex component of marriage that is under scrutiny ...

The second stage of the s. 15(1) inquiry asks whether the differential treatment identified under stage one of the inquiry is based on an enumerated or analogous ground.

In *Egan* at p. 528 SCR, the Supreme Court of Canada recognized sexual orientation as an analogous ground, observing that sexual orientation is a "deeply personal characteristic that is either unchangeable or changeable only at unacceptable personal costs."

In this case, the AGC properly conceded that, if this court determined that marriage imposes differential treatment, then sexual orientation, as an analogous ground, is the basis for such differential treatment.

Accordingly, stage two of the s. 15(1) inquiry has been met ...

The third stage of the s. 15(1) inquiry requires the court to determine whether the differential treatment imposes a burden upon, or withholds a benefit from, the claimants in a manner that reflects the stereotypical application of presumed group or personal characteristics, or that otherwise has the effect of perpetuating or promoting the view that the individual is less capable or worthy of recognition or value as a human being or as a member of Canadian society, equally deserving of concern, respect, and consideration ...

The assessment of whether a law has the effect of demeaning a claimant's dignity should be undertaken from a subjective-objective perspective. The relevant point of view is not solely that of a "reasonable person," but that of a "reasonable person, dispassionate and fully apprised of the circumstances, possessed of similar attributes to, and under similar circumstances as, the group of which the rights claimant is a member": *Egan* at p. 553 SCR; *Law* at pp. 533–34 SCR. This requires a court to consider the individual's or group's traits, history, and circumstances in order to evaluate whether a reasonable person, in circumstances similar to the claimant, would find that the impugned law differentiates in a manner that demeans his or her dignity: *Law* at p. 533 SCR ...

In *Law* at pp. 550–52 SCR, Iacobucci, J. identified four contextual factors that a claimant may reference in order to demonstrate that the impugned law demeans his or her dignity in purpose or effect. The list of factors is not closed and not all of the factors will be relevant in every case. The four factors identified by Iacobucci, J. are examined below.

(i) Pre-existing disadvantage, stereotyping or vulnerability of the claimants

The first contextual factor to be examined is the existence of a pre-existing disadvantage, stereotyping, prejudice or vulnerability experienced by the individual or group at issue ...

The AGC acknowledges that gay men and lesbians have been recognized as a disadvantaged group in Canada. It emphasizes, however, that historical disadvantage is not presumed to embody discrimination. It points to the Supreme Court of Canada's recent decision in *Nova Scotia (Attorney General) v. Walsh*, 2002 SCC 83, 221 DLR (4th) 1, where, despite the fact that cohabiting common law couples have been recognized as a historically disadvantaged group, the court found that the impugned law was not discriminatory.

We agree that the existence of historical disadvantage is not presumptive of discrimination ...

However, as previously stated, Iacobucci, J. also made it clear that historical disadvantage is a strong indicator of discrimination: see *Law* at pp. 534–35 SCR. Therefore, the historical disadvantage suffered by same-sex couples favours a finding of discrimination in this case ...

(ii) Correspondence between the grounds and the claimant's actual needs, capacities or circumstances

The second contextual factor is the correspondence, or lack thereof, between the grounds on which the claim is based and the actual needs, capacities or circumstances of the claimant or others with similar traits: *Law* at pp. 537, 551 SCR. As illustrated in *Eaton v. Brant County Board of Education*, [1997] 1 SCR 241, 142 DLR (4th) 385, legislation that accommodates the actual needs, capacities and circumstances of the claimants is less likely to demean dignity.

The AGC submits that marriage relates to the capacities, needs and circumstances of opposite-sex couples. The concept of marriage – across time, societies and legal cultures – is that of an institution to facilitate, shelter and nurture the unique union of a man and woman who, together, have the possibility to bear children from their relationship and shelter them within it.

We cannot accept the AGC's argument for several reasons.

First, it is important to remember that the purpose and effects of the impugned law must at all times be viewed from the perspective of the claimant. The question to be asked is whether the law takes into account the actual needs, capacities and circumstances of same-sex couples, not whether the law takes into account the needs, capacities and circumstances of opposite-sex couples. In *Law* at p. 538 SCR, Iacobucci, J. cautioned that "[t]he fact that the impugned legislation may achieve a valid social purpose for one group of individuals cannot function to deny an equality claim where the effects of the legislation upon another person or group conflict with the purpose of the s. 15(1) guarantee."

Second, the AGC's argument on this point is more appropriately considered in the context of a s. 1 justification analysis ...

Third, a law that prohibits same-sex couples from marrying does not accord with the needs, capacities and circumstances of same-sex couples. While it is true that, due to biological realities, only opposite-sex couples can "naturally" procreate, same-sex couples can choose to have children by other means, such as adoption, surrogacy and donor insemination. An increasing percentage of children are being conceived and raised by same-sex couples: *M. v. H.* at p. 75 SCR.

Importantly, no one, including the AGC, is suggesting that procreation and childrearing are the only purposes of marriage, or the only reasons why couples choose to marry. Intimacy, companionship, societal recognition, economic benefits, the blending of two families, to name a few, are other reasons that couples choose to marry. As recognized in *M. v. H.* at p. 50 SCR, same-sex couples are capable of forming "long, lasting, loving and intimate relationships." Denying same-sex couples the right to marry perpetuates the contrary view, namely, that same-sex couples are not capable of forming loving and lasting relationships, and thus same-sex relationships are not worthy of the same respect and recognition as opposite-sex relationships.

Accordingly, in our view, the common law requirement that marriage be between persons of the opposite sex does not accord with the needs, capacities and circumstances of same-sex couples. This factor weighs in favour of a finding of discrimination.

(iii) Ameliorative purpose or effects on more disadvantaged individuals or groups in society

The third contextual factor to be considered is whether the impugned law has an ameliorative purpose or effect upon a more disadvantaged person or group in society. The question to be asked is whether the group that has been excluded from the scope of the ameliorative law is in a more advantaged position than the person coming within the scope of the law. In *Law* at p. 539 SCR, Iacobucci, J. emphasized that "[u]nderinclusive ameliorative legislation that excludes from its scope the members of a historically disadvantaged group will rarely escape the charge of discrimination."

The AGC cites La Forest, J. in *Egan* at p. 539 SCR for the proposition that, since opposite-sex couples raise the vast majority of children, supporting opposite-sex relationships "does not exacerbate an historic disadvantage; rather it ameliorates an historic economic disadvantage."

We do not accept the AGC's submission. The critical question to be asked in relation to this contextual factor is whether opposite-sex couples are in a more disadvantaged position than same-sex couples. As previously stated, same-sex couples are a group who have experienced historical discrimination and disadvantages. There is no question that opposite-sex couples are the more advantaged group.

In our view, any economic disadvantage that may arise from raising children is only one of many factors to be considered in the context of marriage. Persons do not marry solely for the purpose of raising children. Furthermore, since same-sex couples also raise children, it cannot be assumed that they do not share that economic disadvantage. Accordingly, if alleviating economic disadvantages for opposite-sex couples due to childrearing were to be considered an ameliorative purpose for the opposite-sex requirement in marriage, we would find the law to be underinclusive ...

(iv) Nature of the interest affected

The fourth contextual factor to be examined is the nature of the interest affected by the impugned law. The more severe and localized the effect of the law on the affected group, the greater the likelihood that the law is discriminatory ...

The AGC submits that the existence of the *Modernization of Benefits and Obligations Act* precludes a finding of discrimination. With this Act, Parliament amended 68 federal statutes in order to give same-sex couples the same benefits and obligations as opposite-sex couples. The AGC also points to recent amendments to provincial legislation that similarly extended benefits to same-sex couples. As a result, same-sex couples are afforded equal treatment under the law.

In our view, the AGC's submission must be rejected.

First, we do not agree that same-sex couples are afforded equal treatment under the law with respect to benefits and obligations. In many instances, benefits and obligations do not attach until the same-sex couple has been cohabiting for a specified period of time. Conversely, married couples have instant access to all benefits and obligations ... Second, the AGC's submission takes too narrow a view of the s. 15(1) equality guarantee. As the passage cited from *Egan* indicates, s. 15(1) guarantees more than equal access to economic benefits. One must also consider whether persons and groups have been excluded from fundamental societal institutions ...

In this case, same-sex couples are excluded from a fundamental societal institution – marriage. The societal significance of marriage, and the corresponding benefits that are available only to married persons, cannot be overlooked. Indeed, all parties are in agreement that marriage is an important and fundamental institution in Canadian society. It is for that reason that the claimants wish to have access to the institution. Exclusion perpetuates the view that same-sex relationships are less worthy of recognition than opposite-sex relationships. In doing so, it offends the dignity of persons in same-sex relationships.

(v) Conclusion

Based on the foregoing analysis, it is our view that the dignity of persons in same-sex relationships is violated by the exclusion of same-sex couples from the institution of marriage. Accordingly, we conclude that the common-law definition of marriage as "the voluntary union for life of one man and one woman to the exclusion of all others" violates s. 15(1) of the *Charter*. The next step is to determine whether this violation can be justified under s. 1 of the *Charter*.

REASONABLE LIMITS UNDER SECTION 1 OF THE *CHARTER*

(a) The necessity of a s. 1 analysis

Section 1 of the *Charter* provides:

1. The *Canadian Charter of Rights and Freedoms* guarantees the rights and freedoms set out in it subject only to such reasonable limits prescribed by law as can be demonstrably justified in a free and democratic society ...

In *R. v. Oakes*, [1986] 1 SCR 103, 26 DLR (4th) 200, at pp. 138–39 SCR., Dickson, C.J.C. formulated the test for determining whether a law is a reasonable limit on a *Charter* right or freedom in a free and democratic society. The party seeking to uphold the impugned law has the burden of proving on a balance of probabilities that:

(1) The objective of the law is pressing and substantial; and
(2) The means chosen to achieve the objective are reasonable and demonstrably justifiable in a free and democratic society. This requires:

(A) The rights violation to be rationally connected to the objective of the law;
(B) The impugned law to minimally impair the *Charter* guarantee; and
(C) Proportionality between the effect of the law and its objective so that the attainment of the objective is not outweighed by the abridgement of the right ...

The AGC submits that marriage, as a core foundational unit, benefits society at large in that it has proven itself to be one of the most durable institutions for the organization of society. Marriage has always been understood as a special kind of monogamous opposite-sex union, with spiritual, social, economic and contractual dimensions, for the purposes of uniting the opposite sexes, encouraging the birth and raising of children of the marriage, and companionship.

No one is disputing that marriage is a fundamental societal institution. Similarly, it is accepted that, with limited exceptions, marriage has been understood to be a monogamous opposite-sex union. What needs to be determined, however, is whether there is a valid objective to maintaining marriage as an exclusively heterosexual institution. Stating that marriage is heterosexual because it always has been heterosexual is merely an explanation for the opposite-sex requirement of marriage; it is not an objective that is capable of justifying the infringement of a *Charter* guarantee.

We now turn to the more specific purposes of marriage advanced by the AGC: (i) uniting the opposite sexes; (ii) encouraging the birth and raising of children of the marriage; and (iii) companionship.

The first purpose, which results in favouring one form of relationship over another, suggests that uniting two persons of the same sex is of lesser importance ... [A] purpose that demeans the dignity of same-sex couples is contrary to the values of a free and democratic society and cannot be considered to be pressing and substantial. A law cannot be justified on the very basis upon which it is being attacked: *Big M Drug Mart* at p. 352 SCR.

The second purpose of marriage, as advanced by the AGC, is encouraging the birth and raising of children. Clearly, encouraging procreation and childrearing is a laudable goal that is properly regarded as pressing and substantial. However, the AGC must demonstrate that the objective of maintaining marriage as an exclusively heterosexual institution is pressing and substantial: see *Vriend* at pp. 554–57 SCR.

We fail to see how the encouragement of procreation and childrearing is a pressing and substantial objective of maintaining marriage as an exclusively heterosexual institution. Heterosexual married couples will not stop having or raising children because same-sex couples are permitted to marry. Moreover, an increasing percentage of children are being born to and raised by same-sex couples.

The AGC submits that the union of two persons of the opposite sex is the only union that can "naturally" procreate. In terms of that biological reality, same-sex couples are different from opposite-sex couples. In our view, however, "natural" procreation is not a sufficiently pressing and substantial objective to justify infringing the equality rights of same-sex couples. As previously stated, same-sex couples can have children by other means, such as adoption, surrogacy and donor insemination. A law that aims to encourage only "natural" procreation ignores the fact that same-sex couples are capable of having children.

Similarly, a law that restricts marriage to opposite-sex couples, on the basis that a fundamental purpose of marriage is the raising of children, suggests that same-sex couples are not equally capable of childrearing. The AGC has put forward no evidence to support such a proposition. Neither is the AGC advocating such a view; rather, it takes the position that social science research is not capable of establishing the proposition one way or another. In the absence of cogent evidence, it is our view that the objective is based on a stereotypical assumption that is not acceptable in a free and democratic society that prides itself on promoting equality and respect for all persons.

The third purpose of marriage advanced by the AGC is companionship. We consider companionship to be a laudable goal of marriage. However, encouraging companionship cannot be considered a pressing and substantial objective of the *omission* of the impugned law ...

[The fact that the omission of same-sex couples from the definition of marriage served no appropriate purpose is sufficient to impugn it, on the *Oakes* test. But the Court went on, for the sake of completeness, to apply the other parts of the test.]

... [T]he AGC has not shown that the opposite-sex requirement in marriage is rationally connected to the encouragement of procreation and childrearing. The law is both overinclusive and underinclusive. The ability to "naturally" procreate and the willingness to raise children are not prerequisites of marriage for opposite-sex couples. Indeed, many opposite-sex couples that marry are unable to have children or choose not to do so. Simultaneously, the law is underinclusive because it excludes same-sex couples that have and raise children ...

With respect to minimal impairment, the AGC submits that there is no other way to achieve Parliament's objectives than to maintain marriage as an opposite-sex institution. Changing the definition of marriage to incorporate same-sex couples would profoundly change the very essence of a fundamental societal institution. The AGC points to no-fault divorce as an example of how changing one of the essential features of marriage, its permanence, had the unintended result of destabilizing the institution with unexpectedly high divorce rates. This, it is said, has had a destabilizing effect on the family, with adverse effects on men, women and children. Tampering with another of the core features, its opposite-sex nature, may also have unexpected and unintended results. Therefore, a cautious approach is warranted.

We reject the AGC's submission as speculative. The justification of a *Charter* infringement requires cogent evidence. In our view, same-sex couples and their children should be able to benefit from the same stabilizing institution as their opposite-sex counterparts ...

Allowing same-sex couples to choose their partners and to celebrate their unions is not an adequate substitute for legal recognition. This is not a case of the government balancing the interests of competing groups. Allowing same-sex couples to marry does not result in a corresponding deprivation to opposite-sex couples.

Nor is this a case of balancing the rights of same-sex couples against the rights of religious groups who oppose same-sex marriage. Freedom of religion under s. 2(a) of the *Charter* ensures that religious groups have the option of refusing to solemnize same-sex marriages. The equality guarantee, however, ensures that the beliefs and practices of various religious groups are not imposed on persons who do not share those views.

In our view, the opposite-sex requirement in the definition of marriage does not minimally impair the rights of the claimants. Same-sex couples have been completely excluded from a fundamental societal institution. Complete exclusion cannot constitute minimal impairment ...

Accordingly, we conclude that the violation of the Couples' equality rights under s. 15(1) of the *Charter* is not justified under s. 1 of the *Charter*. The AGC has not demonstrated that the objectives of excluding same-sex couples from marriage are pressing and substantial. The AGC has also failed to show that the means chosen to achieve its objectives are reasonable and justified in a free and democratic society ...

Having found that the common law definition of marriage violates the Couples' equality rights under s. 15(1) of the *Charter* in a manner that is not justified under s. 1 of the *Charter*, we turn to consider the appropriate remedy ...

We reject the AGC's submission that the only remedy we should order is a declaration of invalidity, and that this remedy should be suspended to permit Parliament to respond. A declaration of invalidity alone fails to meet the court's obligation to reformulate a common law rule that breaches a *Charter* right. Lamer, C.J.C. highlighted this obligation in *Swain* at p. 978 SCR:

[B]ecause this appeal involves a *Charter* challenge to a common law, judge-made rule, the *Charter* analysis involves somewhat different considerations than would apply to a challenge to a legislative provision ...

Given that the common law rule was fashioned by judges and not by Parliament or a legislature, judicial deference to elected bodies is not an issue. If it is possible to reformulate a common law rule so that it will not conflict with the principles of fundamental justice, such a reformulation should be undertaken ...

There is no evidence before this court that a declaration of invalidity without a period of suspension will pose any harm to the public, threaten the rule of law, or deny anyone the benefit of legal recognition of their marriage. We observe that there was no evidence before us that the reformulated definition of marriage will require the volume of legislative reform that followed the release of the Supreme Court of Canada's decision in *M. v. H.* In our view, an immediate declaration will simply ensure that opposite-sex couples and same-sex couples immediately receive equal treatment in law in accordance with s. 15(1) of the *Charter.*

Accordingly, we would allow the cross-appeal by the Couples on remedy. We would reformulate the common law definition of marriage as "the voluntary union for life of two persons to the exclusion of all others." We decline to order a suspension of the declaration of invalidity or of the reformulated common law definition of marriage. We would also make orders, in the nature of *mandamus*, requiring the Clerk of the City of Toronto to issue marriage licences to the Couples, and requiring the Registrar General of the Province of Ontario to accept for registration the marriage certificates of Kevin Bourassa and Joe Varnell and of Elaine and Anne Vautour ...

READING QUESTIONS ON *HALPERN*

1 What do you think of the *Law* test for violations of s. 15, as it is discussed here? Does its appeal to "dignity" seem close to what Taylor called "the politics of equal dignity," or does it differ in certain respects?

2 Some same-sex couples oppose the institution of marriage, partly on the grounds that it purports to define the essence of committed relationships while doing so in light of certain arguably oppressive features of traditional heterosexual relationships. Do you think that the Court of Appeal makes this mistake, in the way that it presents marriage? If so, does this decision really recognise same-sex couples for what they are and wish to be; or is it, in its own way, discriminatory?

3 The issue of whether it is constitutional to prohibit same-sex couples from marrying has also been litigated in the United States. In one such case, *Goodridge v. Department of Public Health*, 798 NE 2d 941 (Mass. 2003), the Massachussets Court of Appeal held 4–3 that the Massachussets prohibition on same-sex marriage was unconstitutional. The three dissenting judges argued that the issue was not whether the prohibition on same-sex marriage was constitutional (since, they argued, there is no explicit constitutional protection against discrimination on the grounds of sexual orientation). Rather, the issue in their view was simply whether there was

some rational basis for the prohibition. On this point, Madam Justice Sosman had this to say:

In considering whether the Legislature has a rational reason for postponing a dramatic change to the definition of marriage, it is surely pertinent to the inquiry to recognize that this proffered change affects not just a load-bearing wall of our social structure but the very cornerstone of that structure. Before making a fundamental alteration to that cornerstone, it is eminently rational for the Legislature to require a high degree of certainty as to the precise consequences of that alteration, to make sure that it can be done safely ...

More importantly, it is not our confidence in the lack of adverse consequences that is at issue, or even whether that confidence is justifiable. The issue is whether it is rational to reserve judgment on whether this change can be made at this time without damaging the institution of marriage or adversely affecting the critical role it has played in our society. Absent consensus on the issue (which obviously does not exist), or unanimity among scientists studying the issue (which also does not exist), or a more prolonged period of observation of this new family structure (which has not yet been possible), it is rational for the Legislature to postpone any redefinition of marriage that would include same-sex couples until such time as it is certain that redefinition will not have unintended and undesirable social consequences. Through the political process, the people may decide when the benefits of extending civil marriage to same-sex couples have been shown to outweigh whatever risks – be they palpable or ephemeral – are involved. However minimal the risks of that redefinition of marriage may seem to us from our vantage point, it is not up to us to decide what risks society must run, and it is inappropriate for us to abrogate that power to ourselves merely because we are confident that "it is the right thing to do."

Is Justice Sosman relying here on an idea similar to Lord Devlin's – namely, that society is entitled to protect its core moral values and institutions from subversion? If so, is this just a reactionary position? Or is it a legitimate attempt to defer to the Legislature in a case where the constitution is not explicit? Does it matter to Lord Devlin whether the people's core value judgments are reasonable or not? Should it matter to Sosman whether the Legislature's judgment is reasonable? Should the Ontario Court of Appeal in *Halpern* have considered any of the kinds of arguments which Sosman makes, when it assessed whether the violation of s. 15 was "reasonably and demonstrably justified in a free and democratic society," under s. 1?

Reference Re Same Sex Marriage [2004] 3 SCR 698

This case was a Reference – that is, an advisory opinion issued by the Supreme Court at the request of Parliament on a particular legal matter. The questions posed by Parliament concerned the legality of same-sex marriage.

THE COURT: –

On July 16, 2003, the Governor in Council issued Order in Council PC 2003-1055 asking this Court to hear a reference on the federal government's *Proposal for an Act respecting certain aspects of legal capacity for marriage for civil purposes* ("*Proposed Act*"). The operative sections of the *Proposed Act* read as follows:

1. Marriage, for civil purposes, is the lawful union of two persons to the exclusion of all others.
2. Nothing in this Act affects the freedom of officials of religious groups to refuse to perform marriages that are not in accordance with their religious beliefs.

It will be noted that s. 1 of the *Proposed Act* deals only with civil marriage, not religious marriage.

The Order in Council sets out the following questions:

1   Is the annexed *Proposal for an Act respecting certain aspects of legal capacity for marriage for civil purposes* within the exclusive legislative authority of the Parliament of Canada? If not, in what particular or particulars, and to what extent?
2   If the answer to question 1 is yes, is section 1 of the proposal, which extends capacity to marry to persons of the same sex, consistent with the *Canadian Charter of Rights and Freedoms*? If not, in what particular or particulars, and to what extent?

3 Does the freedom of religion guaranteed by paragraph 2(a) of the *Canadian Charter of Rights and Freedoms* protect religious officials from being compelled to perform a marriage between two persons of the same sex that is contrary to their religious beliefs?

On January 26, 2004, the Governor in Council issued Order in Council PC 2004-28 asking a fourth question, namely:

4 Is the opposite-sex requirement for marriage for civil purposes, as established by the common law and set out for Quebec in section 5 of the *Federal Law–Civil Law Harmonization Act, No. 1*, consistent with the *Canadian Charter of Rights and Freedoms*? If not, in what particular or particulars and to what extent?

With respect to Question 1, we conclude that s. 1 of the *Proposed Act* is within the exclusive legislative competence of Parliament, while s. 2 is not.

With respect to Question 2, we conclude that s. 1 of the *Proposed Act*, which defines marriage as the union of two persons, is consistent with the *Canadian Charter of Rights and Freedoms*.

With respect to Question 3, we conclude that the guarantee of freedom of religion in the *Charter* affords religious officials protection against being compelled by the state to perform marriages between two persons of the same sex contrary to their religious beliefs.

For reasons to be explained, the Court declines to answer Question 4 ...

[The Court's discussion of Question 1 has been omitted.]

Question 2: Is section 1 of the *Proposed Act*, which extends capacity to marry to persons of the same sex, consistent with the *Charter*? ...

The purpose of s. 1 of the *Proposed Act* is to extend the right to civil marriage to same-sex couples. The course of events outlined below in relation to Question 4 suggests that the provision is a direct legislative response to the findings of several courts that the opposite-sex requirement for civil marriage violates the equality guarantee enshrined in s. 15(1) of the *Charter*: see *EGALE Canada Inc. v. Canada (Attorney General)* (2003), 225 DLR (4th) 472, 2003 BCCA 251 ; *Halpern v. Canada (Attorney General)* (2003), 65 O.R. (3d) 161 (CA); and *Hendricks v. Québec (Procureure-générale)*, [2002] RJQ 2506 (Sup. Ct.) ...

Turning to the substance of the provision itself, we note that s. 1 embodies the government's policy stance in relation to the s. 15(1) equality concerns of same-sex couples. This, combined with the circumstances giving rise to the *Proposed Act* and with the preamble thereto, points unequivocally to a purpose which, far from violating the *Charter*, flows from it ...

Some interveners submit that the mere legislative recognition of the right of same-sex couples to marry would have the effect of discriminating against (1) religious groups who do not recognize the right of same-sex couples to marry (religiously) and/or (2) opposite-sex married couples. No submissions have been made as to how the *Proposed Act*, in its effect, might be seen to draw a distinction for the purposes of s. 15, nor can the Court surmise how it might be seen to do so. It withholds no benefits, nor does it impose burdens on a differential basis. It therefore fails to meet the threshold requirement of the s. 15(1) analysis laid down in *Law v. Canada (Minister of Employment and Immigration)*, [1999] 1 SCR 497.

The mere recognition of the equality rights of one group cannot, in itself, constitute a violation of the rights of another. The promotion of *Charter* rights and values enriches our society as a whole and the furtherance of those rights cannot undermine the very principles the *Charter* was meant to foster.

... It is argued that the effect of the *Proposed Act* may violate freedom of religion in three ways: (1) the *Proposed Act* will have the effect of imposing a dominant social ethos and will thus limit the freedom to hold religious beliefs to the contrary; (2) the *Proposed Act* will have the effect of forcing religious officials to perform same-sex marriages; and (3) the *Proposed Act* will create a "collision of rights" in spheres other than that of the solemnization of marriages by religious officials.

The first allegation of infringement says in essence that equality of access to a civil institution like marriage may not only conflict with the views of those who are in disagreement, but may also violate their legal rights. This amounts to saying that the mere conferral of rights upon one group can constitute a violation of the rights of another. This argument was discussed above in relation to s. 15(1) and was rejected.

The second allegation of infringement, namely the allegation that religious officials would be compelled to perform same-sex marriages contrary to their religious beliefs, will be addressed below in relation to Question 3.

This leaves the issue of whether the *Proposed Act* will create an impermissible collision of rights. The potential for a collision of rights does not necessarily imply unconstitutionality. The collision between rights must be approached on the contextual facts of actual conflicts. The first question is whether the rights alleged to conflict can be reconciled: *Trinity Western University v. British Columbia College of Teachers*, [2001] 1 SCR 772, 2001 SCC 31, at para. 29. Where the rights cannot be reconciled, a true conflict of rights is made out. In such cases, the Court will find a limit on religious freedom and go on to balance the interests at stake under s. 1 of the *Charter*: *Ross v. New Brunswick School District No. 15*, [1996] 1 SCR 825, at paras. 73–74. In both steps, the Court must proceed on the basis that the Charter does not create a hierarchy of rights (*Dagenais v. Canadian Broadcasting Corp.*, [1994] 3 SCR 835, at p. 877) and that the right to religious freedom enshrined in s. 2(a) of the *Charter* is expansive.

Here, we encounter difficulty at the first stage. The *Proposed Act* has not been passed, much less implemented. Therefore, the alleged collision of rights is purely abstract. There is no factual context. In such circumstances, it would be improper to assess whether the *Proposed Act*, if adopted, would create an impermissible collision of rights in as yet undefined spheres ...

Question 3: Does the freedom of religion guaranteed by section 2(a) of the *Charter* protect religious officials from being compelled to perform same-sex marriages contrary to their religious beliefs?

The *Proposed Act* is limited in its effect to marriage for civil purposes: see s. 1. It cannot be interpreted as affecting religious marriage or its solemnization. However, Question 3 is formulated broadly and without reference to the *Proposed Act*. We therefore consider this question as it applies to the performance, by religious officials, of both religious and civil marriages ... The concern here is that if the *Proposed Act* were adopted, religious officials could be required to perform same-sex marriages contrary to their religious beliefs. Absent state compulsion on religious officials, this conjecture does not engage the *Charter*. If a promulgated statute were to enact compulsion, we conclude that such compulsion would almost certainly run afoul of the *Charter* guarantee of freedom of religion, given the expansive protection afforded to religion by s. 2(a) of the *Charter* ...

The question we are asked to answer is confined to the performance of same-sex marriages by religious officials. However, concerns were raised about the compulsory use of sacred places for the celebration of such marriages and about being compelled to otherwise assist in the celebration of same-sex marriages. The reasoning that leads us to conclude that the guarantee of freedom of religion protects against the compulsory celebration of same-sex marriages, suggests that the same would hold for these concerns ...

Question 4: Is the opposite-sex requirement for marriage for civil purposes, as established by the common law and set out for Quebec in section 5 of the *Federal Law–Civil Law Harmonization Act, No. 1*, consistent with the *Charter*? ...

A unique set of circumstances is raised by Question 4, the combined effect of which persuades the Court that it would be unwise and inappropriate to answer the question.

The first consideration on the issue of whether this Court should answer the fourth question is the government's stated position that it will proceed by way of legislative enactment, regardless of what answer we give to this question. In oral argument, counsel reiterated the government's unequivocal intention to introduce legislation in relation to same-sex marriage, regardless of the answer to Question 4. The government has clearly accepted the rulings of lower courts on this question and has adopted their position as its own. The common law definition of marriage in five provinces and one territory no longer imports an opposite-sex requirement. In addition, s. 5 of the *Federal Law–Civil Law Harmonization Act, No. 1*, SC 2001, c. 4, no longer imports an opposite-sex requirement. Given the government's stated commitment to this course of action, an opinion on the constitutionality of an opposite-sex requirement for marriage serves no legal purpose. On the other hand, answering this question may have serious deleterious effects, which brings us to our next point.

The second consideration is that the parties to previous litigation have now relied upon the finality of the judgments they obtained through the court process. In the circumstances, their vested rights outweigh any benefit accruing from an answer to Question 4. Moreover, other same-sex couples acted on the finality of *EGALE, Halpern* and *Hendricks* to marry, relying on the Attorney General of Canada's adoption of the result in those cases. While the effects of the *EGALE* and *Hendricks* decisions were initially suspended, the suspensions were lifted with the consent of the Attorney General. As a result of these developments, same-sex marriages have generally come to be viewed as legal and have been regularly taking place in British Columbia, Ontario and Quebec. Since this reference was initiated, the opposite-sex requirement for marriage has also been struck down in the Yukon,

Manitoba, Nova Scotia and Saskatchewan ... In each of those instances, the Attorney General of Canada conceded that the common law definition of marriage was inconsistent with s. 15(1) of the *Charter* and was not justifiable under s. 1, and publicly adopted the position that the opposite-sex requirement for marriage was unconstitutional.

As noted by this Court in *Nova Scotia (Attorney General) v. Walsh*, [2002] 4 SCR 325, 2002 SCC 83, at para. 43:

The decision to marry or not is intensely personal and engages a complex interplay of social, political, religious, and financial considerations by the individual.

The parties in *EGALE*, *Halpern* and *Hendricks* have made this intensely personal decision. They have done so relying upon the finality of the judgments concerning them. We are told that thousands of couples have now followed suit. There is no compelling basis for jeopardizing acquired rights, which would be a potential outcome of answering Question 4 ...

The final consideration is that answering this question has the potential to undermine the government's stated goal of achieving uniformity in respect of civil marriage across Canada. There is no question that uniformity of the law is essential. This is the very reason that Parliament was accorded legislative competence in respect of marriage under s. 91(26) of the *Constitution Act, 1867*. However, as discussed, the government has already chosen to address the question of uniformity by means of the *Proposed Act*, which we have found to be within Parliament's legislative competence and consistent with the *Charter*. Answering the fourth question will not assist further. Given that uniformity is to be addressed legislatively, this rationale for answering Question 4 fails to compel.

On the other hand, consideration of the fourth question has the potential to undermine the uniformity that would be achieved by the adoption of the proposed legislation. The uniformity argument succeeds only if the answer to Question 4 is "no." By contrast, a "yes" answer would throw the law into confusion. The decisions of the lower courts in the matters giving rise to this reference are binding in their respective provinces. They would be cast into doubt by an advisory opinion which expressed a contrary view, even though it could not overturn them. The result would be confusion, not uniformity ...

READING QUESTIONS ON SAME-SEX MARRIAGE REFERENCE

1 The Court held, in response to Question 2, that the mere recognition of the equality rights of one group cannot, in itself, constitute
   a violation of the equality rights of another. Do you agree?
2 What do you think of the Court's reasons for declining to answer
   Question 4? Is the fact that the government is committed to a
   certain course of action, and that a contrary advisory opinion from
   the court would therefore not sway the government, a good reason
   for not answering Question 4? Is the fact that an advisory opinion
   contrary to the lower court rulings would cast them in doubt
   without strictly overruling them a good reason for not answering
   the question? What would Dworkin say? What would Hart say?

Nitya Iyer
"Categorical Denials: Equality Rights and the Shaping of Social Identity" (1993–4)

INTRODUCTION

Legal rights to equality in Canada today derive from multiple sources:
they are found in human rights codes and acts,[1] in statutory bills of
rights,[2] and in the *Constitution*.[3] Legal writers have criticized aspects of
the interaction of the various rights,[4] the jurisdictional limitations of
particular sources of rights,[5] and the substantive scope and efficacy of
each of the rights. My focus in this paper is more general. It concerns a
structural feature that I believe is common to all equality rights in
Canadian law: the conception of equality as no more than protection
from discrimination on specific grounds. For example, s. 15 of the
Charter provides:

Every individual is equal before and under the law and has the right to the
equal protection and equal benefit of the law without discrimination and, in
particular, without discrimination based on race, national or ethnic origin,
colour, religion, sex, age or mental or physical disability.

While there are significant differences between the various kinds of
rights – for example, the rights in human rights legislation are consid-

ered absolute, in contrast to the balancing that occurs under s. 1 of the *Charter* after a s. 15 violation has been found[6] – I believe that their common premise, the definition of equality as protection from discrimination on a particular list of characteristics, deserves critical examination.

In this paper, I argue that, no matter how long or inclusive the list of protected grounds or characteristics, the mechanical, categorical, or category-based, approach to equality embedded in such a structure obscures the complexity of social identity in ways that are damaging both to particular rights claimants, and to the larger goal of redressing relations of inequality. The categorical approach to equality fails to comprehend complex social identities. It therefore cannot accurately describe relationships of inequality, which is a precondition both for redressing particular rights violations, and for succeeding with the larger project of social reform. In essence, the categorical structure of equality rights requires those injured through relations of inequality to *caricaturize* both themselves and their experiences of inequality, in order to succeed with a legal claim. Because law perceives and accepts this caricature of social identity and social relations, it cannot properly address inequality.

In Part I of the paper, I describe categories and categorical reasoning, emphasizing their implications for anti-discrimination law.[7] In this Part, I further develop some of the theoretical conclusions of an earlier study, in which I examined whether laws prohibiting sex and race discrimination respond adequately to the experiences of women of colour in Canada.[8]

In Part II, I develop a model of our current anti-discrimination law, and illustrate two sets of problems which arise from this model by examining two recent equality cases. The first, *Canada (Attorney-General) v. Mossop*,[9] is a challenge to provisions of a collective agreement on the basis of the *Canadian Human Rights Act*; the second, *Symes v. Minister of National Revenue*,[10] is a challenge to the *Income Tax Act* on the basis of s. 15 of the *Charter*.

I CATEGORIES, SIMILARITY, AND DIFFERENCE

Categories are inherent in language and are therefore essential to the way we think.[11] Inevitably, categorizing involves making assignments of similarity and difference: things within a category are relevantly similar; they are collectively differentiated from things outside the category. Categorizing would not be troublesome if the formation of categories and assignment of membership in them remained elastic so that categories and their content could be constantly revised as contexts changed – and if there was a fair sharing of who got to do the revisions. However, categorical thinking, especially in legal contexts, tends to be rigid, so that existing categories and their content tend *not* to be revised.[12] When the categories in question are legal categories, and especially when they purport to sort people on the basis of characteristics which carry particular social weight, such as "race," "sex," and "disability," this rigidity, coupled with the fact that categorizing turns on *assignments* of difference, takes on special significance. In particular, two senses of difference – difference as distinction, and difference as hierarchy – have been conflated, and then entrenched at the core of anti-discrimination law.

A Difference as Distinction

Categorizing necessarily implies that elements within a category are relevantly similar and, at the same time, collectively different from things outside the category. Therefore, placing elements in a category tends to suppress differences and emphasize similarities among those elements. At the same time, it heightens differences between members and non-members of a category, while suppressing any similarities that some members might share with non-members. For example, placing Claire, Gwen, and myself[13] in the category "woman" tends to suppress differences of racialization,[14] age, sexuality, and height, among us, and to underscore our collective difference from Joel. We are perceived as female in comparison to his maleness at the same time that characteristics such as occupation (Joel, Claire, and I are law professors; Gwen is not), or skin colour (Joel, Claire, and Gwen are white; I am not) which group us differently, are suppressed. Thus, the assignment of differences is a function of the categorizer's perceptions – of the characteristics which Gwen, Claire, Joel, and I possess and which group us in different ways, it is femaleness/maleness that I as categorizer have noticed rather than anything else. The way that I sort people is partially a function of my conscious choice (as when I perceive a set of characteristics such as "sex," "race," "disability," and "age," and then select one of them to sort people by), and partly unconscious (as when I tend to perceive only certain characteristics,[15] or to perceive that some are more fundamental than others). If I sort people unconsciously, I will always sort people into the same groups. Further, my categorization of people is elastic to the extent that it responds to changes in context. To the extent that I rely on conventions or stereotypes when defining categories, instead of inquiring into what groupings are most relevant in a particular context and for a particular purpose, my categorizations will be rigid.

Understanding categorization as a process of distinction involves the important insight that difference is necessarily a comparative concept. It does not inhere in people or things; it expresses a relationship. A thing cannot be different in isolation. Moreover, difference always expresses relationships from a particular perspective: Joel might sort our group according to Jewishness rather than whiteness. Thus, differences are neither natural nor immutable. They are always contingent and dynamic.

B Difference as Hierarchy

Difference is not only about distinction, however, and categories don't just distinguish. Assignments of difference, or categorizations, are also expressions of hierarchies, assertions of power. When characteristics such as race and sex are perceived as differences, and are used to categorize people, they rarely merely distinguish among them. They are much more likely to be said and understood hierarchically. For example, I tend not to say, "Gwen and I differ from each other in that we have different colours of skin." I am much more likely to say, "Gwen is white." The comparative element is suppressed and, along with it, the existence of the characteristic in the comparison-maker. Gwen becomes her difference: "Gwen is white." The racial aspect of her identity overwhelms. It overwhelms both all of the other aspects of her social identity, and any other similarities and differences between us.

It is evident that to be in the speaker's position, to be the categorizer or comparison-maker, is to occupy a position of power.[16] It is empowering in two ways. First, doing the categorizing allows you to draw comparisons between yourself and others on the basis of *your* choice of characteristics: what Gwen might have chosen as relevant differences between us is immaterial; her point of view is entirely absent (except to the extent that I choose to solicit it, and reflect it, in my comparison-making). Second, as categorizer, I can make myself absent from the process: I can create one side of the comparison as "a difference" inherent in the person or group labelled by that difference, while constituting my particular constellation of attributes as the invisible background norm. Thus, Gwen is white, Claire is tall, and Joel is male. Regardless of what feature each of them might have chosen to distinguish them from me, the differences I choose become part of them,[17] and my brown-ness, short-ness and female-ness, which are the points of comparison from which these differences emerge, disappear.

C Categories and the Background Norm

In essence, the conflation of difference as distinction with difference as hierarchy and the consequences which flow from this, are what I think is entailed by and wrong with a legal approach which defines equality as protection against discrimination on various grounds. It is not just anyone who gets to do the categorizing. The categorizer in anti-discrimination law has a particular social identity shared, in varying degrees, by members of the dominant group in Canadian society. This social identity is historically and geographically specific. While characteristics of the dominant social identity are largely congruent with those of the dominant social group, the latter is not exhaustive of the former. The dominant social identity is embedded in the basic social structures so that it remains white and male and heterosexual even though not all members of the dominant group possess all of these characteristics. This ensures that the dominant social identity can resist change.

The particular set of social characteristics of the dominant social identity and its ideology constitute the invisible background norm against which categorizations of difference are made in anti-discrimination law. Two consequences follow. First, the choice of categories (what is and is not included in the list of grounds which attract protection from discrimination) reflects the dominant perspective about what social characteristics are relevant when differentiating among people.[18] For example, according to our anti-discrimination law, it is generally not acceptable to treat people adversely on the basis of sex, race, or disability, but it is acceptable to differentiate on the basis of class/socioeconomic status, intelligence,[19] and height. Denial of employment on the basis of one of the former characteristics would clearly give rise to a legal claim; denial of employment on the basis of one of the latter characteristics would not.[20] To the extent that the dominant perspective (which is the perspective of the categorizer) represents the "common sense" of society, these choices will not be controversial: members of marginalized as well as dominant groups are socialized within an ideology which leads all of us to accept that only some characteristics deserve protection under anti-discrimination law.[21] Further, once a list of characteristics has been set out in legislation, the list itself begins to appear neutral and permanent, particularly if the lists in various anti-discrimination laws are similar. It becomes part of the way things are; it appears as though everyone would agree with this list, and no other, for all time.[22] To the extent, however, that a marginalized group is able to acquire some social power with which to challenge the hegemony of the dominant social identity, the continued exclusion of characteristics associated with that group may become controversial or politicized, resulting in the addition of these characteristics to the list of protected grounds.[23]

Arguing that previously unlisted characteristics should be included in the list of protected grounds requires individuals or groups to draw analogies between listed and unlisted grounds. The doctrines developed to guide such arguments elucidate the ideological rationales underlying anti-discrimination law. This can be seen in the judicial tests developed to determine when a characteristic not listed in s. 15 of the *Charter* should be added to the list of protected grounds.[24] While the doctrine is not settled, many consider "immutability" to be a critical consideration.[25] According to the immutability test, characteristics alleged to be analogous must be *"personal characteristics of* individuals [and] ... all but one ... are *immutable,* at least in the sense that they cannot be changed by the choice of the individual [emphasis in original]."[26] Such a test reflects a particular understanding of the characteristics in s. 15, and of what is wrong with using them as reasons for differential treatment. By focusing on immutability, the test reinforces an understanding of ascribed social characteristics as intrinsic to individuals, rather than comparative or relational; as inevitable, rather than historically and geographically variable; and as neutral, rather than reflecting a particular pattern of social relations.[27]

Under this approach, a claimant who seeks inclusion of a new ground in s. 15 (which is a prerequisite for a legal remedy), must present the unincluded social characteristic as if it were immutable. The argument for inclusion will be more or less convincing depending on the dominant ideological understanding of what social characteristics cannot be changed by the choice of the individual. For example, "socioeconomic status" or "poverty" will be hard to present as analogous because, within a capitalist liberal ideology, this is understood to be a product of individual choice and merit.[28] Moreover, in asserting the immutability of a social characteristic, a claimant is forced to deny his or her subjective agency with respect to the characteristic, and to present him or herself as possessing an "unfortunate" social attribute. The requirement of immutability entails that the claimant cannot simply assert a particular social identity and show that his or her oppression arises from the hierarchical relationship between the dominant social identity and this identity.[29]

The second consequence of the fact that the dominant social identity expresses the background norm is that the content, or meaning, of each listed category is determined by reference to the particular expression of the listed characteristics which comprise the dominant social identity. This is because the dominant group categorizer constitutes its own characteristics as the background norm against which assignments of difference are made. The differentiation ceases to be an explicit comparison, and the non-dominant expression of the characteristic appears to inhere in the "other," the non-dominant group.[30] Thus, we can ascertain the social characteristics of the dominant social identity by contemplating what we do *not* imagine when we think about the superficially neutral characteristics listed in anti-discrimination laws:[31] race is "not white," sex is "not male," sexual orientation is "not heterosexual," disability is "not able-bodied," and so on. It is those characteristics which we tend *not* to perceive as noteworthy or "different" about ourselves that we share with the dominant social identity.[32]

Once a characteristic is created as intrinsic to a group, and becomes its identifier, it is regarded as wholly constitutive of that group's social identity. For example, people of colour are racialized, obscuring differences of class, gender, and disability among them. Further, the social identity constructed on the basis of this now "intrinsic" difference is *exactly the same* for every member of the group: East Asians, South Asians, Africans, First Nations are all "non-white."

II A MODEL OF ANTI-DISCRIMINATION LAW AND HOW IT WORKS

The categorical approach to equality upon which our current anti-discrimination law is based can be graphically conceptualized as a central sphere representing the dominant social identity, surrounded by little pockets of "difference." Each pocket bears a label which designates the particular attribute by which it is distinguished from the dominant social identity. The label is written in the neutral form of the characteristic; the pocket actually contains the instances of the characteristic which differ from its expression in the dominant social identity. For example, "race" is the label, "non-white" is the content.[33] In order to succeed in an anti-discrimination claim in law, an individual or group must first convince a decision-maker, who is usually a member of the dominant social group, that the individual or group belongs in a pocket.[34] This means that the claimant must present a caricature of the individual or group's social identity, distorting the individual and communal experience of a social characteristic (one that is historically specific and contingent, and which interacts in complex ways with other characteristics), into a static and oversimplified image of the claimant's "difference."[35] In this cartoon drawn from the perspective of the categorizer not from that of the subject of categorization, one social characteristic assumes gigantic proportions while other aspects of social identity are rendered indistinguishable from the background norm. If this distortion is accepted by the court, the claimant can then go on to show a causal link between this image and the harm suffered.

At least two sets of problems arise from this model of anti-discrimination law. The first arises from the fact that each pocket is isolated from the others. That is, it is assumed that it is possible and appropriate in the context of redressing relations of inequality to consider the social characteristic each pocket represents in isolation. Although it is useful to maintain analytic distinctions between race and gender and all of the other grounds, I believe that it is rarely, if ever, possible to arrive at socially just outcomes by treating rights claimants as if they *are* one (and only one) particular social characteristic.[36] Further, because pockets are isolated, the definition of the characteristic each represents is similarly isolated and static. The definition of the characteristic is what, in the dominant group's view (necessarily a perspective external to those in the pocket) the meaning of that characteristic is, what it considers to be the "difference" from the dominant social identity. As categorizer, I choose what I see as different about Gwen and what that means. Regardless of how she would describe her racialization, I can decide that she is "white" and, by extension, what "whiteness" is. Therefore, there is no guarantee that someone whose subjective experience of adverse treatment corresponds to the label on one or more pockets will actually succeed in her or his claim. The claim will fail unless the claimant's experience of discrimination can be made to accord with how the dominant group imagines discrimination on the basis of a given characteristic. I call these kinds of situations problems of falling through the cracks.

The second set of problems arises from the fact that the content of each pocket is homogeneous. Since it is assumed that everyone in a particular pocket has no other relevant characteristics, it is not possible to articulate differences between those within a pocket – differences with respect to other social characteristics and even with respect to the social characteristic under discussion. If Joel and Claire are both "white" then differences of age and gender between them disappear, as does the fact that one is Jewish (arguably a racial characteristic in that anti-semitism is considered to be race discrimination), and one is not. This has disturbing implications. For example, when a claimant wins an anti-discrimination case, the law assumes that the remedy is appropriate for all members in the group; differences among those within the group (or pocket) which might make the remedy unhelpful, or even harmful for some, are not perceived. I call these kinds of situations problems of pushing others through the cracks.

...

B Problems of Pushing Others Through the Cracks: Symes[37]

Elizabeth Symes worked as a partner in a Toronto law firm and there-fore earned "income from a business" as defined in s. 9 of the *Income Tax Act (ITA)*.[38] Under s. 63 of the *ITA*, a deduction for child care expenses is available to all taxpayers, regardless of their source of income. However, the actual cost of child care to most families greatly exceeds the s. 63 deduction.[39] Symes wanted to claim the portion of her actual child care expenses that exceeded the amount deductible under s. 63 as a business expense.[40] She argued that to interpret the *ITA* so as to preclude her from claiming her non-deductible child care expenses as business expenses would constitute sex discrimination under s. 15 of the *Charter*.[41] She claimed that because women are primarily responsible for child care, disallowing the deduction of child care expenses as business expenses has a greater adverse impact on self-employed women than on self-employed men, a difference which constitutes sex discrimination.

Cullen, J. heard Symes' case in the Federal Court and held in her favour. On appeal, Decary, J., writing for the Federal Court of Appeal, overturned the lower court decision. The case is currently before the Supreme Court of Canada.

For Symes to win her *Charter* argument in the Supreme Court, she must show that the *ITA* discriminates against her on the basis of her sex. If the Court holds that the provision preventing her from deducting the full amount of her child care expenses is not discriminatory, it will be saying that Symes does not belong in the sex pocket, despite her experience of the treatment as sex-related.[42] Essentially, this was what Decary, J. in the Federal Court of Appeal said when he held that as a "professional woman," Symes was not a member of a group protected by s. 15 of the *Charter*.[43] From this perspective, Symes is not in the sex pocket because she cannot make herself fit the caricaturized and homogeneous image of women that the pocket represents. She is an atypical woman. If the Supreme Court wishes to mitigate the harshness of this ruling, along the lines of Lamer, C.J.'s suggestion to Mossop that the correct pocket for him was "sexual orientation" (a ground not included in the *CHRA*), it might say to Symes that the correct pocket for her is "entrepreneur;" however, unfortunately, this pocket is not available to her under s. 15.[44] Should the Court take this approach, Symes will have fallen through the cracks just as Brian Mossop did.

If the Court agrees with Cullen, J., in the Federal Court that Symes has suffered sex discrimination and awards her a remedy,[45] a different problem arises. If Symes wins, she succeeds as a *woman*. In that case, the differences between Symes and other women – women employees, the woman she employs – are of no account, and have no legal existence. Rather than being excluded from the sex pocket because she does not fit its image of woman, Symes will become the woman on the pocket's label – she will represent women, regardless of the many other characteristics which differentiate women from each other. Obviously, Symes is very different from many women, notably along class lines. But, in law, Symes' win will have no class. The doctrine's inability to recognize this means that Symes' success in her case, which *would* address her experience of sex discrimination as a "working mother" actually worsens the position of many other working mothers.[46] Because of her class location, if Symes wins her sex equality case, the effect will actually be to disadvantage most women. Further, the women who will be disadvantaged by the case will be disadvantaged in respect of the same constellation of social factors – motherhood, participation in the paid labour force, and class – that advantages Symes.

The decisions of both of the lower courts, although they come to opposite conclusions, reveal the same inadequacy in the doctrine: it cannot address differences among members of a group who share a common expression of one social characteristic. Whether or not Symes can win her case depends on whether she fits into the "sex" pocket, which, in turn, depends on whether she fits the dominant group's image of that characteristic. Implicit in the reasons of Decary, J. in the Federal

Court of Appeal is the view that Symes is not a "typical" woman because she is a "professional" woman – he compares her to other women and finds she is relatively privileged.[47] Implicit in the reasons of Cullen, J. in the Federal Court is the view that Symes *is* a typical woman because she bears primary responsibility for child care. He compares her to "businessmen" and finds she is relatively disadvantaged.[48] Neither result is just: either Symes' real experience of the sex-specific, discriminatory burden of child care responsibilities is ignored because she is relatively economically privileged, or the same burden borne by less economically privileged women is worsened, because Symes is economically disadvantaged relative to economically privileged men.

This puts the Supreme Court of Canada in a difficult position: either it "sacrifices" Symes in order to ensure that the position of women employees who are restricted to the s. 63 deduction is not worsened, or it "sacrifices" these women in order to rectify the adverse impact of the restricted business expense deduction on Symes.[49] The doctrine requires one or the other of these unsatisfactory outcomes because its conception of sex discrimination is homogeneous. It presumes the existence of a typical woman, which means that it cannot recognize that there are differences among women that are relevant to their experiences of sex discrimination[50] There is no doctrinal space within which to recognize that the adverse impact of primary responsibility for child care is something which Symes shares with all other women who are mothers, *and* that this impact differs between women, in this particular case, because tax treatment differs according to source of income. The doctrine necessarily pushes someone through the cracks.

CONCLUSION

A brief analysis of *Mossop* and *Symes* shows that the current model of anti-discrimination law has serious drawbacks. It fails to address the unequal treatment of some claimants, and, in the process of vindicating the rights of some members of a group possessing a protected characteristic, it can harm other members of that group. My criticism of this model is not that it openly endorses a vision of social justice in which, for example, it is explicitly found appropriate to extend benefits to heterosexual families and not gay or lesbian families, or to subsidize entrepreneurial mothers but not mothers who are employees.[51] My concern in this paper has been to show that a categorical model of anti-discrimination law entails such outcomes quite unintentionally: it is structured so that decision-makers are not required to advert to these issues. Law and legal actors remain conveniently innocent of the injustices entailed by legal doctrine and legal cases. People do not fit in pockets, or they are overly representative of a pocket, simply because of the way the doctrine is organized. Because the doctrine is based on an oversimplified, caricaturized conception of social identity, it does not recognize and redress complex relations of inequality.[52]

Some suggestions about how to move towards an improved model of anti-discrimination law are therefore in order.[53] I think that we need to struggle against both the pockets and the centre in the current model. We need to open up the pockets and permit them to intersect. All of the listed characteristics should be used as touchstones in all cases, and they should be considered with respect to the claimant as well as the respondent (and other parties) in the case.[54] Those involved in an equality rights case – decision-makers, lawyers, and investigators, etc. – should proceed from the premise that redressing a claim of inequality entails complex alterations to the existing web of social relations, and that it is therefore imperative that everyone involved be as attentive as possible to all the relationships implicated in the particular claim.[55] We must also displace the dominant group's hold on the centre. We need to generate a self-consciousness about the location of the dominant group, to make visible the invisible norms against which claimants are measured. Respect for the complexity of social identity and social relations requires an ongoing struggle against the centralizing tendencies of categorical thought. This is neither easy to imagine, nor to implement. For example, in *Mossop,* the groups intervening in favour of Mossop and the Canadian Human Rights Commission[56] worked hard to define "family" in such a way that the Court would have a basis to find that Mossop, his partner, and his partner's father were a family, and therefore that to deny the benefit was discrimination on the basis of family status. However, every definition seemed to exclude some groups that would consider themselves to be families. Finally, it occurred to us[57] to redirect the enquiry, and to ask instead about the purpose of the benefit, and the concerns motivating a desire to limit it. In this context, it became possible to conceive of a less categorical approach to providing bereavement leave. Thus, the intervener's factum submitted:[58]

There are alternative ways to provide for bereavement leave in a collective agreement. For example, the family relationship qualification could be eliminated so that leave is granted for bereavement purposes regardless of the relationship between the employee and the deceased. Alternatively, the definition of immediate family could be open-ended, allowing employees to determine for themselves who is immediate family for the purposes of the benefit. The lack of precision associated with subjective determinations should not be held up as a justification for continued discrimination. Concerns about administrative workability and possible abuse could be addressed by imposing a cap on the number of days of leave available, within a prescribed time frame, for each employee.

This example is not intended to show that there is a relatively easy way to solve the kinds of problems I have identified in the current model of anti-discrimination law, nor that the Court erred in failing to accept the intervenors' submission. Rather it illustrates the limitations of the categorical approach to equality. Despite their creative suggestions, the intervenors could only request that the appeal be allowed "on the basis that excluding same sex partners from a family based employment benefit ... constitutes discrimination on the basis of family status."[59] The remedy asked for was inclusion in the pocket; it could not and did not challenge the pocket's existence. It was not open to the intervenors to ask the Supreme Court of Canada to rewrite the collective agreement so as to restructure the bereavement leave provision in a less categorical way. Similarly, it is not open to the Supreme Court of Canada in *Symes* to rewrite the *ITA* and restructure the subsidization of child care expenses in a less categorical way. The Court will not be able to make an order that recognizes Symes' position as a typical woman in some respects (bearing primary responsibility for child care), and not in others (enjoying the benefit of preferential tax treatment for business income). The categorical approach to equality that I have criticized is embedded within a legal system with rules and procedures governing such matters as jurisdiction and institutional competence that preclude such results. Judges, for very good reasons, are prevented from sudden and radical departures from fundamental legal concepts such as the current model of equality.

Although the power of the courts is limited, legal arguments based on a reconceptualization of equality, even in as narrow a context as a bereavement leave benefit, do serve an important purpose. At the hearing of the appeal in *Mossop,* the suggestion by counsel that it was not necessary to define "family" at all for the purposes of a bereavement leave benefit caused consternation to some judges.[60] Calling into question the inevitability of the categorical approach and illustrating concrete instances of the injustices it can produce in cases such as *Mossop* goes some way to opening the door to change. It makes the current conception of equality a little less self-evident, a little less comfortable. Adopting an approach which explicitly displaces the dominant categories is necessarily unsettling to those whose field of expertise is categorical thought, and discomfort is a stimulus for change.[61]

Attempting to move away from the current legal model of equality is unsettling because it reveals the poverty of our underlying vision of equality. Even for a benefit as particular and narrow as a bereavement leave, it is hard, and even disturbing, to think of ways to structure an egalitarian benefit – one that is not premised on an exclusive, or caricaturized, image of family. But this is precisely where we must direct our imaginations. Law necessarily reflects the poverty of our social vision. The virtue of its categorical approach is that it allows some people to feel as if Canadian society is becoming more egalitarian by presenting oversimplified depictions of social relations as conflicts for judges to resolve. In this way, law achieves legal equality while preserving social inequality. Real change requires us to engage directly, creatively, and politically in conceptions of, and struggles for, social justice.

NOTES

1 *The Saskatchewan Human Rights Code*, SS 1979, c. S-24.1: *The Human Rights Code*, SM 1987, c. 45, CCSM H175; *Human Rights Code*, RSO 1990, c. H-19; *Human Rights Code*, RSNB 1973, c. H-11; *Human Rights Code*, SN 1988, c. 62; *Canadian Human Rights Act*, RSC 1985, c. H-6 [hereinafter *CHRA*]; *Fair Practices Act*, RSNWT 1988, c. F-2; *Human Rights Act*, SBC 1984, c. 22; *Individual's Rights Protection Act*, RSA 1980, c. I-2; *Human Rights Act*, RSNS 1989, c. 214; *Human Rights Act*, RSPEI 1988, c. H-12.

2 Canadian Bill of Rights, S.C. 1960, c. 44; *Charter of Human Rights and Freedoms*, RSQ c. C-12.

3 *Canadian Charter of Rights and Freedoms*, Part I of the *Constitution Act, 1982.* [hereinafter *Charter*].

4 Commentators have addressed the interaction between rights in human rights legislation and the *Charter*, as well as interactions among the various substantive rights.

5 Perhaps the most well-known critique concerns the limitation of the *Charter* to governmental activity laid down in *R.W.D.S.U., Local 580 v.*

Dolphin Delivery, [1986] 2 SCR 573. See: Joel Bakan, "Constitutional Interpretation and Social Change: You Can't Always Get What You Want (Nor What You Need)" (1991) 70 Can. Bar Rev. 307 at 315–318; David Beatty, "Constitutional Conceits: The Coercive Authority of Courts" (1987) 37 U.T.L.J. 183; and Allan Hutchinson and Andrew Petter, "Private Rights/Public Wrongs: The Liberal Lie of the Charter" (1988) 38 U.T.L.J. 278. For criticism of the jurisdictional limitations of human rights legislation see e.g.: William W. Black, "Human Rights in British Columbia: Equality Postponed" [1984–85] Can. Hum. Rts. Y.B. 219; Donna Greschner, "Why *Chambers* is Wrong: A Purposive Interpretation of 'Offered to the Public'" (1988) 52 Sask. L. Rev. 161.

6 *Andrews v. Law Society of British Colubia,* [1989] 1 SCR 143 at 176 [hereinafter *Andrews*]. Some lists are more explicit than others: s. 15 of the *Charter* contains both enumerated grounds, whereas each protected characteristic in the *Canadian Human Rights Act, supra* note 1, is explicitly listed in s. 3. My point is that, wheter explicitly or implicitly, the definition of equality in both the *Charter* and human rights statutes is "protection from discrimination," and specifically, a category- or grounds-based approach to such protection.

7 I use "anti-discrimination law" as a comprehensive term which includes both the rights in s. 15 of the *Charter* (often called "the equality rights"), and the rights in human rights legislation (often called "human rights"). Anti-discrimination law is a useful term for my purposes, because it emphasizes the structural similarity between equality rights and human rights, and underscores my contention that the egalitarian liberal conception of equality in such legislation defines equality as neither more nor less than anti-discrimination.

8 See Nitya Duclos, "Disappearing Women: Racial Minority Women in Human Rights Cases" (1993) 6 C.J.W.L. 25. This work draws upon analyses of equality and discrimination which focus on race and gender, and contains references to some of the related literature; see especially notes 8 and 9.

9 See *infra* note 37.

10 See *infra* note 51.

11 I agree with the postmodernist insight that language is an important determinant of perception, and I believe that understanding its function as an organizing principle is necessary to critical analysis. However, I also find that ideology is an invaluable analytical tool. For useful critical discussion of postmodernism and ideology, see Susan Boyd, "Some Postmodernist Challenges to Feminist Analyses of Law, Family and State:

Ideology and Discourse in Child Custody Law" (1991) 10 Can. J. Fam. L. 79; Yuezhi Zhao, "The 'End of Ideology' Again? The Concept of Ideology in the Era of Postmodern Theory" (1993) 18(1) Can. J. of Sociology 70.

12 For a useful analysis of libraries as a metaphor for, and site of, the hierarchies embedded in categorization, see Nicholas Packwood, "Browsing the Apparatus: Homosexuality, classification, power/knowledge" (1993) 28 Border/Lines 19.

13 I use Gwen Brodsky, Claire Young, Joel Bakan, and myself as illustrations throughout this paper. (Gwen, Claire, and Joel became my examples because we sat together on the panel at which I presented an earlier version of this paper.) I have chosen real people rather than hypothetical beings as examples, and have described our actual characteristics because it is important that my arguments hold for real people in real relationships. This device is helpful in that it personalizes an otherwise abstract analysis (and can make it fun to read). However, getting personal also has an unwelcome tendency to underplay the role of social context and power in the analysis, even while bringing it to bear on four very real people: Gwen, Claire, Joel, and I are inevitably reduced to the categories I use us to illustrate.

14 "Race" is a difficult term, in that its very status as a characteristic is in doubt. See for example, Vic Satzewich, "The Political Economy of Race and Ethnicity" in Peter Li, ed., *Race and Ethnic Relations in Canada* (Toronto: Oxford University Press, 1990) at 251–65, where he argues that "race" has been reified, and that it lacks scientific meaning but that analysis of racialization, which is the process of attaching social significance to "race" is vital. Many other commonly used social characteristics, for example, "disability" and "sexual orientation," are similarly controversial.

15 For example, I have noticed that Claire, Gwen, and I are female, but I have overlooked the fact that Claire and Gwen are lesbian.

16 I do not suggest that this power is absolute: collectively, listeners exercise power over who they will listen to – the voices of the disempowered are not always heard.

17 It is worth noting that the list of possible distinguishing characteristics is lengthy. Other attributes which differentiate Claire, Gwen, Joel, and myself which I (or one of them) might have chosen include sexuality, religion, marital status, parental status, occupation, age, beauty ...

18 As I suggested above, if I am doing the categorizing, what Gwen would have chosen as a relevant differentiating characteristic between us is irrelevant.

19 By intelligence, I mean the restricted set of variations in mental ability that are considered indicative of intelligence, and which would not be considered to be mental disability.

20 If the claim is brought under s. 15 of the *Charter*, an unlisted ground might be recognized and added to the list of characteristics which give rise to legal claims. This point is discussed in detail below.

21 There are important differences in usage of a characteristic by those who are and those who are not marginalized on the basis of the characteristic. Disability, gender, and sexual orientation, for example, are important political rallying cries for members of disempowered groups. But even in this usage, the labels tend to overemphasize the homogeneity of the group in ways that can be destructive for some members. Moreover, the need to rely on these labels may be derived from the dominant social construction of some people as disempowered because of these "intrinsic" differences. When all that is perceived is your "difference," it may well become an important source of strength and resistance for you.

22 This is what Eagleton refers to as the universalizing and naturalizing functions of ideologies: Terry Eagleton, *Ideology: An Introduction* (London: Verso, 1991) at 51–61.

23 Since the list in s. 15 of the *Charter* is not exhaustive, the addition may be accomplished judicially. In the case of human rights legislation, it is usually accomplished legislatively: for example, *Equality Rights Statute Law*, SO 1986, c. 64, s. 18 (adding sexual orientation as a protected ground under the Ontario *Human Rights Code*); although it can also be done by means of a *Charter* challenge: for example, *Haig v. Canada (Minister of Justice)* (1992), 9 OR (3d) 495 (Ont CA) [hereinafter *Haig*] (*Charter* s. 15 requires that "sexual orientation" be read into the *Canadian Human Rights Act* as a protected ground).

24 See generally: *Andrews, supra* note 6; *R. v. Turpin*, [1989] 1 SCR 1296; *Reference Re Workers' Compensation Act*, 1983 (Nfld.), [1989] 1 SCR 922.

25 See: *Andrews, supra* note 6 at 195, La Forest, J; *Veysey v. Canada (Commissioner, Correctional Service)* (1989), [1990] 1 FC 321, 29 FTR 74, 44 CRR 364 (FCTD), aff'd on other grounds (1990), 109 NR 300 (FCA); *Leroux v. Cooperators General Insurance Co.* (1991), 83 DLR (4th) 694 (Ont. CA), rev'g on other grounds (1990), 65 DLR (4th) 702 (Ont. HCJ); Peter W. Hogg, *Constitutional Law of Canada*, 3d ed. (Toronto: Carswell, 1992) at 1167–71. But see Joel Bakan's review of Hogg's text (The Advocate, 1993, forthcoming), arguing that Wilson J.'s "historical disadvantage/social prejudice" test stated in *Turpin, supra* note 24, is at least as accepted as

immutability. Other suggested tests include "a personal characteristic" (in which immutability is sometimes a factor), and "a discrete and insular minority." See generally: William Black and Lynn Smith, "Constitutional Law – Charter of Rights and Freedoms, Sections 15 and 1 – Canadian Citizenship and the Right to Practice Law: *Andrews v. Law Society of British Columbia*" (1989) 68 Can Bar Rev. 591 at 605–608; A. Wayne Mac-Kay and Dianne Pothier, "Developments in Constitutional Law: The 1988–89 Term" (1990) 1 (2d) Supreme Court LR 81 at 92–93; Richard Moon, "A Discrete and Insular Right to Equality: Comment on *Andrews v. Law Society of British Columbia*" (1989) 21 Ottawa L. Rev. 563 at 575–578; N. Colleen Sheppard, "Recognition of the Disadvantaging of Women: The Promise of *Andrews v. Law Society of British Columbia*" (1989) 35 McGill L.J. 207 at 226–228.

26 Hogg, *supra* note 25 at 1167.

27 Although this point is particularly obvious in the case of immutability, I believe it is also true of the other suggested tests and, in particular, of the historical disadvantage/social prejudice test. What courts understand as a pattern of historic disadvantage and social prejudice will also reflect dominant ideology, although there is perhaps more room to challenge that understanding under this test than the others.

28 For a thorough recent review of the very low success rates of challenges to inadequacies in social welfare legislation under ss. 7 and 15 of the *Charter*, see Martha Jackman, "Poor Rights: Using the Charter to Support Social Welfare Claims" (1993) 19 Queens L.J. 65. For a socialist analysis of social welfare cases under the *Charter*, see Reuben Hasson, "What's Your Favourite Right? The Charter and Income Maintenance Legislation" (1989) 5 J.L. & Social Pol'y 1.

29 Some lesbian writers have criticized the presentation of sexual orientation as an immutable characteristic in gay rights cases: Didi Herman, "Are We Family? Lesbian Rights and Women's Liberation" (1990) 28 Osgoode Hall L.J. 789 at 811–813. Disability rights activists have trenchantly observed that disability issues which result in legal cases arise far more from society's treatment of various individuals rather than from any characteristic inherent in the "disabled" person: for example, see Susan Lonsdale, *Women and Disability: The Experience of Physical Disability Among Women* (Basingstoke, England: Macmillan, 1990) at 142.

30 As noted above, if I am doing the categorizing, Gwen *is* white. My racial characteristic becomes the invisible measure against which her difference is judged. For a similar analysis with respect to sex (maleness as the measure, femaleness the "difference"), see Catharine MacKinnon,

Feminism Unmodified: Discourses on Life and Law (Cambridge: Harvard University Press, 1987) at 34.

31 Barbara Findlay, in *With All of Who We Are: A Discussion of Oppression and Dominance* (Vancouver: Lazara Press, 1991), calls the tendency to over-look privileged characteristics "internalized dominance." See also Patricia Cain, "Teaching Feminist Legal Theory at Texas: Listening to Difference and Exploring Connections" (1988) 38 J. of Legal Education 165 at 168–169; Elizabeth Spelman, *Inessential Woman: Problems of Exclusion in Feminist Thought* (Boston: Beacon Press, 1988) at 80–113.

32 As Didi Herman pointed out to me, the apparent neutrality of the norm is actually sustained by the suppressed comparison with what is "different." There is no norm without an "other."

33 For a critique of this model in the context of lesbian and gay rights campaigns, see Didi Herman, "The Politics of Law Reform: Lesbian and Gay Rights Struggles into the 90s" in J. Bristow and A. Woslon, eds, *Activating Theory* (London: Lawrence & Wishert, 1993).

34 I do not mean to suggest that white people, or men, or others who share dominant social characteristics are formally precluded from advancing anti-discrimination claims on the basis of those characteristics. The formal egalitarianism embedded in our equality rights guarantees the superficial neutrality of these categories. For examples of how men have used the s. 15 sex equality guarantee, see Gwen Brodsky and Shelagh Day, *Canadian Charter Equality Rights for Women: One Step Forward or Two Steps Back?* (Ottawa: Canadian Advisory Council on the Status of Women, 1989) at 56–61.

35 For example, a white, working-class, lesbian mother's experiences of sexual orientation is likely different from a wealthy, childless, East Asian gay man's experiences of sexual orientation.

36 I think it is a mistake to assume that the various social characteristics have the same or parallel effects on social identity. Experiences of racism for people of colour should not be assumed to be analogous to experiences of sexism for women. In limited contexts, and for limited purposes, the analogy may be appropriate, but this requires careful investigation before the parallel is drawn. Neither should it be assumed that the various characteristics are so different that groups marginalized on the basis of different characteristics have nothing to learn from each other. We all possess the full list of characteristics; our particular constellation of attributes proclaims our membership in multiple overlapping groups: I am simultaneously brown and female and short and a mother and heterosexual and a law professor ... My quarrel with anti-discrimination law is that it suppresses this obvious fact.

37 *Symes v. M.N.R.*, [1991] 3 FC 507, [1991] 2 CTC 1 (FCA), rev'g (sub nom. *Symes v. M.N.R.*), [1989] 1 CTC 476 (FCTD) [hereinafter *Symes* cited to CTC]. The case was argued before the Supreme Court of Canada on 2 March 1993.

38 R.S.C. 1952, c. 148, as am. by S.C. 1970–71–72, c. 63.

39 In the 1993 taxation year, the deduction is $5000 for children aged 0–6 and $3000 for those aged 7–13. In January, 1993, the average group daycare fee for toddlers (18 months–3 years) in Vancouver was $631/month or $7572 annually. Infant care is more expensive, as is care for more than one pre-schooler. (Figures provided by Westcoast Child Care Resource Centre, communication of June 9, 1993, on file with author.) In 1985, s. 63 permitted Symes to deduct only 30% of her actual outlay that year for child care: Audrey Macklin, "*Symes v. M.N.R.*: Where Sex Meets Class" (1992) 5 C.J.W.L. 498–499; see also Claire Young, "Child Care and the Charter: Privileging the Privileged" (1994) 2 Rev. of Constitutional Studies at 9–10 [forthcoming].

40 Business expenses are defined as "expense[s] made or incurred by the taxpayer for the purpose of gaining or producing income from a business." See *ITA, supra* note 52, ss. 9 and 18.

41 *Supra* note 51 at 6 (FCA). My comments are restricted to the s. 15 sex equality aspect of Symes' case.

42 See CBA factum, para. 13, p. 7, and Appendix A, Factum of Elizabeth Symes, paras. 6, 15, 19–21.

43 Decary, J. stated, *supra* note 51 at 13–14 (FCA): "I am not prepared to concede that professional women make up a disadvantaged group against whom a form of discrimination recognized by s. 15 has been perpetrated."

44 Symes also argued that the disallowance of her child care expenses as business expenses discriminated against her as a "parent/employer." See *supra* note 51 at 478 (FCTD). Cullen, J. found for Symes on this point, although his reasons why "parent" is an analogous ground, at 489–490, are very brief and unclear, and, in his conclusion, he does not clearly separate the two claims. On appeal, Decary, J. rejected outright the claim that Symes suffered discrimination of any kind: *supra* note 51 at 11 (FCA). Since his reasons, at 13, focus on "*professional* women or parents" [emphasis added], it is still unclear whether "parent" constitutes a separate head of discrimination, or whether it is part of the sex discrimination claim.

45 For the purposes of this argument, I am assuming that the Supreme Court does not decide that the provision is justified under s. 1 of the *Charter*.

46 In the sense that women employees, and anyone else who cannot claim child care expenses as business expenses, will pay proportionately more tax. They will have to pay any child care expenses in excess of the s. 63 deduction out of after-tax dollars, whereas entrepreneurial women, and perhaps men, will no longer be taxed on these amounts. Further, if taxes are subsequently raised to compensate for the loss of revenue flowing from a decision in favour of Symes, women employees (and others) will be worse off in an absolute sense.

   For detailed analysis of the tax inequities resulting from a decision in favour of Symes: see Macklin, *supra* note 53 at 509–10; Faye Woodman, "The *Charter* and the Taxation of Women" 22 Ottawa L. Rev. 625; Young, *supra* note 53 at 13–15; Claire Young, "Child Care – A Taxing Issue?" (Presentation at CLAS/CALT Plenary:The Legal Regulation of Parenting, Learned Societies Conference, Ottawa, 6 June 1993).

47 In the context of this argument, "privilege" refers to the preferential tax treatment of those who gain or produce income from a business or property over those who earn income from employment.

48 Audrey Macklin uses an apt metaphor to make this point: she "imagine[s] the judges peering at Beth Symes through different pairs of glasses." Macklin, *supra* note 53 at 508.

49 This may also be a reason why feminists have been ambivalent about the *Symes* case.

50 That is, according to the doctrine, class is entirely different from sex, so that it is possible to address sex discrimination without regard to class. Finding in favour of Symes is saying that this is a sex discrimination case, and class is irrelevant. Finding against her is saying that this is differentiation on the basis of class (an unprotected characteristic), and sex is irrelevant.

51 Although if it did, I would be critical of this position.

52 I have focused on conceptual and doctrinal inadequacies. However, factors such as lack of access to the legal system, and the unrepresentativeness of the judiciary, are also important causes of the poor response of the legal system to experiences of inequality.

53 My suggestions apply to reform in the context of deciding individual cases, as well as in legislative and policy spheres. In advancing them, I do not imply that concerns about institutional competence to effect such reform are unimportant. Pragmatically, however, I think we need to push for change on all available fronts, since it is very difficult to control either legislative agendas or which cases get taken to court.

54 Further, no list of characteristics should be considered closed. This can be accomplished legislatively, by amending human rights statutes to add a

provision stipulating that the list of protected characteristics is non-exhaustive. Alternatively, it can be accomplished judicially, by invoking s. 15 of the *Charter* to find that the omission of a particular characteristic is unconstitutional, as was done in *Haig, supra* note 23.

55 These ideas are developed in Duclos, *supra* note 8 at 46–51.
56 The groups were: Equality for Gays and Lesbians Everywhere (EGALE), Canadian Rights and Liberties Federation, The National Association of Women and the Law, The Canadian Disability Rights Council, and The National Action Committee on the Status of Women.
57 I participated in some of these discussions.
58 Factum of EGALE *et al.*, at 19, paragraph 58. For a detailed exposition and analysis of the reasoning which led to this approach to family, see: Jody Freeman, "Defining Family in *Mossop v. D.S.S.*: The Challenges of Anti-Essentialism and Interactive Discrimination for Human Rights Litigation" (1993) U.T.L.J. [forthcoming]; Brenda Cossman, "Family Inside/Out" (1993) U.T.L.J. [forthcoming]; Didi Herman, "'Sociologically Speaking': Law, Sexuality, and Social Change" (1991) 2 J. of Hum. Justice 57.
59 Factum of EGALE *et al.*, at 20.
60 Notes from oral hearing, on file with author.
61 By this I mean to include lawyers and legal academics, as well as judges. The more such experts come to feel uncomfortable with the current model, the more likely it is that it will be revised.

READING QUESTIONS ON IYER

1 What is "the categorical approach to equality," and why, in Iyer's view, is it objectionable?
2 Can you think of an approach to equality rights that avoids this objectionable sort of categorization? What is the approach that Iyer herself proposes? Would it completely avoid the problems that she identifies in our current approach?

Egan v. *Canada* [1995] 2 SCR 513

In this case, the Supreme Court of Canada upheld the constitutionality of a law that defined "spouse" in a way which excluded homosexual couples. Three justices dissented, including Justice L'Heureux-Dubé, part of whose judgment is reproduced here.

L'Heureux-Dubé, J.:

This appeal raises the question of whether a legislative distinction that limits eligibility for a spousal supplement under the *Old Age Security Act*, RSC, 1985, c. O-9, to "opposite sex" spouses is discriminatory within the meaning of s. 15 of the *Canadian Charter of Rights and Freedoms* and, if so, whether it is saved by s. 1 of the *Charter*. Although I agree with much of what is said by my colleagues Justices Cory and Iacobucci, as well as with the result they reach, I have some concerns as to the proper approach to be taken to s. 15 of the *Charter*, which I shall outline below ...

I will first discuss why I believe that the current vehicle of choice for fulfilling the purposes of s. 15, the "grounds" approach, is incapable of giving full effect to this purpose. I will then elaborate upon an approach that I believe to be more capable of enabling s. 15 to realize its full potential ...

It is obvious that this Court could not have adopted an enumerated and analogous grounds approach if, instead of there being nine enumerated grounds in s. 15(1), there had been none. Would the absence of "particularities" in s. 15(1) have changed the basic guarantee of equality without discrimination? In the alternative, what would have happened under the "analogous grounds" approach if, instead of setting out nine enumerated grounds, s. 15(1) had set out only three or four? What if, furthermore, religion was not one of them? Most would agree that the common characteristics of all of the enumerated grounds other than religion is that they involve so-called "immutable" character-istics. Religion, on the other hand, has been described as being premised on a "fundamental choice." Does this mean that s. 15, despite being consciously left open-ended by the drafters, could never have encom-passed discrimination on the basis of religion, or any other characteristic which involves a "fundamental choice"? This result seems absurd, yet it seems to flow inevitably from an approach to "discrimination" that relies exclusively on drawing analogies from the essential characteristics of the enumerated grounds ...

... By looking at the grounds for the distinction instead of at the *impact* of the distinction on particular *groups*, we risk undertaking an analysis that is distanced and desensitized from real people's real experiences. To make matters worse, in defining the appropriate categories upon which findings of discrimination may be based, we risk relying on conventions and stereotypes about individuals within these categories that, themselves, further entrench a discriminatory status quo. More often than not, disadvantage arises from the way in which society treats particular individuals, rather than from any characteristic inherent in those individuals.

For all of these reasons, I am led inevitably to the conclusion that a truly purposive approach to s. 15 must place "discrimination" first and foremost in the Court's analysis ...

In my view, for an individual to make out a violation of their rights under s. 15(1) of the *Charter*, he or she must demonstrate the following three things:

1 that there is a legislative distinction;
2 that this distinction results in a denial of one of the four equality rights on the basis of the rights claimant's membership in an identifiable group;
3 that this distinction is "discriminatory" within the meaning of s. 15
...

No one would dispute that two identical projectiles, thrown at the same speed, may nonetheless leave a different scar on two different types of surfaces. Similarly, groups that are more socially vulnerable will experience the adverse effects of a legislative distinction more vividly than if the same distinction were directed at a group which is not similarly socially vulnerable. As such, a distinction may be discriminatory in its impact upon one group yet not discriminatory in its impact upon another group. While it may be discriminatory against women to prohibit female guards from searching male prisoners, it may not be discriminatory against men to prohibit male guards from searching female prisoners: *Weatherall v. Canada (Attorney General), supra*. While it may be discriminatory to define a particular criminal offence as only applying to women, it may not be discriminatory to restrict the applicability of the offence of sexual assault of a minor to men: *R. v. Hess, supra*. In the same way that it does not really matter why the affected surface is soft, it is not necessary that there be a formal nexus between the social vulnerability of the affected group and the prejudice flowing from the impugned distinction in order for that vulnerability to be relevant to determining whether the distinction is discriminatory. Put another way, it is merely admitting reality to acknowledge that members of advantaged groups are generally less sensitive to, and less likely to experience, discrimination than members of disadvantaged, socially vulnerable or marginalized groups. See, by analogy, *Schacht-schneider v. Canada*, [1994] 1 FC 40 (CA), *per* Linden, J.A.

Most of the factors identified in *Andrews* under the "analogous grounds" approach as characteristic of the enumerated grounds in s. 15 are, not surprisingly, integral to evaluating the nature of the group affected by the impugned distinction. It is highly relevant, for instance, to inquire into whether the impugned distinction is based upon fundamental attributes, such as those enumerated in s. 15, that are generally considered to be essential to our popular conception of "personhood" or "humanness." Furthermore, it is important to ask ourselves questions such as "Is the adversely affected group already a victim of historical disadvantage?"; "Is this distinction reasonably capable of aggravating or perpetuating that disadvantage?"; "Are group members currently socially vulnerable to stereotyping, social prejudice and/or marginalization?"; and "Does this distinction expose them to the reasonable possibility of future social vulnerability to stereotyping, social prejudice and/or marginalization?" Membership in a "discrete and insular minority," lacking in political power and thus susceptible to having its interests overlooked, is yet another consideration that may be taken into account.

Consideration of these factors involves the recognition that differently situated groups are starting on different levels of the s. 15 playing field. In my view, our approach to s. 15 must reflect that reality. Indeed, I reiterate McIntyre, J.'s words in *Andrews, supra*, at p. 169, that "for the accommodation of differences, which is the essence of true equality, it will frequently be necessary to make distinctions." Treating historically vulnerable, disadvantaged or marginalized groups in the same manner as groups which do not generally suffer from such vulnerability may not accommodate, or even contemplate, those differences. In fact, ignoring such differences may compound them, by making access to s. 15 relief most difficult for those groups that are the most disempowered of all in Canadian society ...

READING QUESTIONS ON *EGAN*

1 Why does L'Heureux-Dubé substitute "groups" for "grounds" at the second stage of her proposed test? Does this approach really avoid the difficulties that she sees in the grounds-based approach? Does it avoid all of the problems that Iyer identifies?

2 What is the significance of groups in claims for equal treatment? Must an individual be a member of a certain kind of group, in order to suffer discrimination? What kind of group? Does discrimination law protect groups as such? Why, or why not?

Bowers v. Hardwick 478 U.S. 186 (1986)

A case in which the U.S. Supreme Court upheld the Georgia law outlawing consensual sodomy. The majority argues that, because homosexuality has traditionally been judged to be immoral, the state is entitled to prohibit it.

Justice White delivered the opinion of the Court: – In August 1982, respondent Hardwick (hereafter respondent) was charged with violating the Georgia statute criminalizing sodomy[1] by committing that act with another adult male in the bedroom of respondent's home. After a preliminary hearing, the District Attorney decided not to present the matter to the grand jury unless further evidence developed. Respondent then brought suit in the Federal District Court, challenging the constitutionality of the statute insofar as it criminalized consensual sodomy[2] ...

This case does not require a judgment on whether laws against sodomy between consenting adults in general, or between homosexuals in particular, are wise or desirable. It raises no question about the right or propriety of state legislative decisions to repeal their laws that criminalize homosexual sodomy, or of state-court decisions invalidating those laws on state constitutional grounds. The issue presented is whether the Federal Constitution confers a fundamental right upon homosexuals to engage in sodomy and hence invalidates the laws of the many States that still make such conduct illegal and have done so for a very long time. The case also calls for some judgment about the limits of the Court's role in carrying out its constitutional mandate.

We first register our disagreement with the Court of Appeals and with respondent that the Court's prior cases have construed the Constitution to confer a right of privacy that extends to homosexual sodomy and for all intents and purposes have decided this case ...

Precedent aside, however, respondent would have us announce, as the Court of Appeals did, a fundamental right to engage in homosexual sodomy. This we are quite unwilling to do ...

Striving to assure itself and the public that announcing rights not readily identifiable in the Constitution's text involves much more than the imposition of the Justices' own choice of values on the States and the Federal Government, the Court has sought to identify the nature of the rights qualifying for heightened judicial protection. In *Palko v. Connecticut*, it was said that this category includes those fundamental liberties that are "implicit in the concept of ordered liberty," such that "neither liberty nor justice would exist if [they] were sacrificed." A different description of fundamental liberties appeared in *Moore v. East Cleveland*, where they are characterized as those liberties that are "deeply rooted in this Nation's history and tradition" ...

It is obvious that neither of these formulations would extend a fundamental right to homosexuals to engage in acts of consensual sodomy. Proscriptions against that conduct have ancient roots ... Sodomy was a criminal offense at common law and was forbidden by the laws of the original 13 States when they ratified the Bill of Rights. In 1868, when the Fourteenth Amendment was ratified, all but 5 of the 37 States in the Union had criminal sodomy laws.

In fact, until 1961, all 50 States outlawed sodomy, and today, 24 States and the District of Columbia continue to provide criminal penalties for sodomy performed in private and between consenting adults ... Against this background, to claim that a right to engage in such conduct is "deeply rooted in this Nation's history and tradition" or "implicit in the concept of ordered liberty" is, at best, facetious.

... Victimless crimes, such as the possession and use of illegal drugs, do not escape the law where they are committed at home ... And if respondent's submission is limited to the voluntary sexual conduct between consenting adults, it would be difficult, except by fiat, to limit the claimed right to homosexual conduct while leaving exposed to prosecution adultery, incest, and other sexual crimes even though they are committed in the home. We are unwilling to start down that road.

... This is essentially not a question of personal "preferences" but rather of the legislative authority of the State. I find nothing in the Constitution depriving a State of the power to enact the statute challenged here.

Dissent: Justice Blackmun – This case is no more about "a fundamental right to engage in homosexual sodomy," as the Court purports to declare, than *Stanley v. Georgia* was about a fundamental right to watch obscene movies, or *Katz v. United States* was about a fundamental right to place interstate bets from a telephone booth. Rather, this case is about "the most comprehensive of rights and the right most valued by civilized men," namely, "the right to be let alone."

... I believe that "[it] is revolting to have no better reason for a rule of law than that so it was laid down in the time of Henry IV. It is still more revolting if the grounds upon which it was laid down have vanished long since, and the rule simply persists from blind imitation of the past."[3] I believe we must analyze respondent Hardwick's claim in the light of the values that underlie the constitutional right to privacy. If that right means anything, it means that, before Georgia can prosecute its citizens for making choices about the most intimate aspects of their lives, it must do more than assert that the choice they have made is an "abominable crime not fit to be named among Christians."

... I cannot agree that either the length of time a majority has held its convictions or the passions with which it defends them can withdraw legislation from this Court's scrutiny ... That certain, but by no means all, religious groups condemn the behavior at issue gives the State no license to impose their judgments on the entire citizenry. The legitimacy of secular legislation depends instead on whether the State can advance some justification for its law beyond its conformity to religious doctrine ... Thus, far from buttressing his case, petitioner's invocation of Leviticus, Romans, St Thomas Aquinas, and sodomy's heretical status during the Middle Ages undermines his suggestion that s. 16-6-2 represents a legitimate use of secular coercive power ...

NOTES

1 Georgia Code Ann. at 16-6-2 (1984) provides, in pertinent part, as follows: "(a) A person commits the offense of sodomy when he performs or submits to any sexual act involving the sex organs of one person and the mouth or anus of another ... (b) A person convicted of the offense of sodomy shall be punished by imprisonment for not less than one nor more than 20 years ..."

2 John and Mary Doe were also plaintiffs in the action. They alleged that they wished to engage in sexual activity proscribed by 16-6-2 in the privacy of their home, App. 3, and that they had been "chilled and deterred" from engaging in such activity by both the existence of the

statute and Hardwick's arrest. Ibid., at 5. The District Court held, however, that because they had neither sustained, nor were in immediate
danger of sustaining, any direct injury from the enforcement of the
statute, they did not have proper standing to maintain the action. Ibid., at
18. The Court of Appeals affirmed the District Court's judgment dismissing the Does' claim for lack of standing, 760 F.2d 1202, 1206–1207 (CA11
1985), and the Does do not challenge that holding in this Court.

3   Holmes, *The Path of the Law*, 10 Harv L Rev 457, 469 (1897).

Lawrence v. Texas 539 U.S. 558 (2003)

The U.S. Supreme Court revisited its decision in *Bowers*. The majority
decision focuses on the issue of whether the state has a legitimate interest in
regulating sexuality. Justice Scalia's dissent seeks to reposition the issue as
one of the legitimate powers of democratic majorities. The case raises a
number of important issues about adjudication, the nature of the criminal
law power, and the limits on majority rule.

Justice Kennedy [writing for the majority]:

...

The Court began its substantive discussion in *Bowers* as follows: "The
issue presented is whether the Federal Constitution confers a fundamental right upon homosexuals to engage in sodomy and hence invalidates
the laws of the many States that still make such conduct illegal and have
done so for a very long time." *Id.*, at 190. That statement, we now
conclude, discloses the Court's own failure to appreciate the extent of
the liberty at stake. To say that the issue in *Bowers* was simply the right
to engage in certain sexual conduct demeans the claim the individual
put forward, just as it would demean a married couple were it to be said
marriage is simply about the right to have sexual intercourse. The laws
involved in *Bowers* and here are, to be sure, statutes that purport to do
no more than prohibit a particular sexual act. Their penalties and
purposes, though, have more far-reaching consequences, touching upon
the most private human conduct, sexual behavior, and in the most
private of places, the home. The statutes do seek to control a personal
relationship that, whether or not entitled to formal recognition in the

law, is within the liberty of persons to choose without being punished as criminals.

This, as a general rule, should counsel against attempts by the State, or a court, to define the meaning of the relationship or to set its boundaries absent injury to a person or abuse of an institution the law protects. It suffices for us to acknowledge that adults may choose to enter upon this relationship in the confines of their homes and their own private lives and still retain their dignity as free persons. When sexuality finds overt expression in intimate conduct with another person, the conduct can be but one element in a personal bond that is more enduring. The liberty protected by the Constitution allows homosexual persons the right to make this choice ...

The doctrine of *stare decisis* is essential to the respect accorded to the judgments of the Court and to the stability of the law. It is not, however, an inexorable command. *Payne v. Tennessee*, 501 U.S. 808, 828 (1991) ("*Stare decisis* is not an inexorable command; rather, it 'is a principle of policy and not a mechanical formula of adherence to the latest decision'") (quoting *Helvering v. Hallock*, 309 U.S. 106, 119 (1940)). In *Casey* we noted that when a Court is asked to overrule a precedent recognizing a constitutional liberty interest, individual or societal reliance on the existence of that liberty cautions with particular strength against reversing course. 505 U.S., at 855–56; see also *id.*, at 844 ("Liberty finds no refuge in a jurisprudence of doubt"). The holding in *Bowers*, however, has not induced detrimental reliance comparable to some instances where recognized individual rights are involved. Indeed, there has been no individual or societal reliance on *Bowers* of the sort that could counsel against overturning its holding once there are compelling reasons to do so. *Bowers* itself causes uncertainty, for the precedents before and after its issuance contradict its central holding.

The rationale of *Bowers* does not withstand careful analysis ...

Justice Scalia (dissenting):

...

It seems to me that the "societal reliance" on the principles confirmed in *Bowers* and discarded today has been overwhelming. Countless judicial decisions and legislative enactments have relied on the ancient proposition that a governing majority's belief that certain sexual behavior is "immoral and unacceptable" constitutes a rational basis for regulation. See, e.g., *Williams v. Pryor*, 240 F.3d 944, 949 (CA11 2001) (citing *Bowers* in upholding Alabama's prohibition on the sale of sex toys on the ground that "[t]he crafting and safeguarding of public morality ... indisputably is a legitimate government interest under rational basis scrutiny"); *Milner v. Apfel*, 148 F.3d 812, 814 (CA7 1998) (citing *Bowers* for the proposition that "[l]egislatures are permitted to legislate with regard to morality ... rather than confined to preventing demonstrable harms"); *Holmes v. California Army National Guard* 124 F.3d 1126, 1136 (CA9 1997) (relying on *Bowers* in upholding the federal statute and regulations banning from military service those who engage in homosexual conduct); *Owens v. State*, 352 Md. 663, 683, 724 A.2d 43, 53 (1999) (relying on *Bowers* in holding that "a person has no constitutional right to engage in sexual intercourse, at least outside of marriage"); *Sherman v. Henry*, 928 S. W. 2d 464, 469–73 (Tex. 1996) (relying on *Bowers* in rejecting a claimed constitutional right to commit adultery). We ourselves relied extensively on *Bowers* when we concluded, in *Barnes v. Glen Theatre, Inc.*, 501 U.S. 560, 569 (1991), that Indiana's public indecency statute furthered "a substantial government interest in protecting order and morality," *ibid.*, (plurality opinion); see also *id.*, at 575 (Scalia, J., concurring in judgment). State laws against bigamy, same-sex marriage, adult incest, prostitution, masturbation, adultery, fornication, bestiality, and obscenity are likewise sustainable only in light of *Bowers'* validation of laws based on moral choices. Every single one of these laws is called into question by today's decision; the Court makes no effort to cabin the scope of its decision to exclude them from its holding ...

I turn now to the ground on which the Court squarely rests its holding: the contention that there is no rational basis for the law here under attack. This proposition is so out of accord with our jurisprudence – indeed, with the jurisprudence of *any* society we know – that it requires little discussion.

The Texas statute undeniably seeks to further the belief of its citizens that certain forms of sexual behavior are "immoral and unacceptable," *Bowers, supra*, at 196 – the same interest furthered by criminal laws against fornication, bigamy, adultery, adult incest, bestiality, and obscenity. *Bowers* held that this *was* a legitimate state interest. The Court today reaches the opposite conclusion. The Texas statute, it says, "furthers *no legitimate state interest* which can justify its intrusion into the personal and private life of the individual," *ante*, at 18 (emphasis added). The Court embraces instead Justice Stevens' declaration in his *Bowers* dissent, that "the fact that the governing majority in a State has traditionally viewed a particular practice as immoral is not a sufficient reason for upholding a law prohibiting the practice," *ante*, at 17. This effectively decrees the end of all morals legislation. If, as the Court asserts, the promotion of majoritarian sexual morality is not even a *legitimate* state interest, none of the above-mentioned laws can survive rational-basis review ...

One of the most revealing statements in today's opinion is the Court's grim warning that the criminalization of homosexual conduct is "an invitation to subject homosexual persons to discrimination both in the public and in the private spheres." *Ante,* at 14. It is clear from this that the Court has taken sides in the culture war, departing from its role of assuring, as neutral observer, that the democratic rules of engagement are observed. Many Americans do not want persons who openly engage in homosexual conduct as partners in their business, as scoutmasters for their children, as teachers in their children's schools, or as boarders in their home. They view this as protecting themselves and their families from a lifestyle that they believe to be immoral and destructive. The Court views it as "discrimination" which it is the function of our judgments to deter ...

Let me be clear that I have nothing against homosexuals, or any other group, promoting their agenda through normal democratic means ... But persuading one's fellow citizens is one thing, and imposing one's views in absence of democratic majority will is something else. I would no more *require* a State to criminalize homosexual acts – or, for that matter, display *any* moral disapprobation of them – than I would *forbid* it to do so. What Texas has chosen to do is well within the range of traditional democratic action, and its hand should not be stayed through the invention of a brand-new "constitutional right" by a Court that is impatient of democratic change ...

One of the benefits of leaving regulation of this matter to the people rather than to the courts is that the people, unlike judges, need not carry things to their logical conclusion. The people may feel that their disapprobation of homosexual conduct is strong enough to disallow homosexual marriage, but not strong enough to criminalize private homosexual acts – and may legislate accordingly. The Court today pretends that it possesses a similar freedom of action, so that we need not fear judicial imposition of homosexual marriage, as has recently occurred in Canada (in a decision that the Canadian Government has chosen not to appeal). See *Halpern v. Toronto,* 2003 WL 34950 (Ontario Ct. App.). At the end of its opinion ... the Court says that the present case "does not involve whether the government must give formal recognition to any relationship that homosexual persons seek to enter." *Ante,* at 17. Do not believe it. More illuminating than this bald, unreasoned disclaimer is the progression of thought displayed by an earlier passage in the Court's opinion, which notes the constitutional protections afforded to "personal decisions relating to *marriage*, procreation, contraception, family relationships, child rearing, and education," and then declares that "[p]ersons in a homosexual relationship may seek autonomy for these purposes, just as heterosexual persons do." *Ante*, at 13 (emphasis added). Today's opinion dismantles the structure of constitutional law that has permitted a distinction to be made between heterosexual and homosexual unions, insofar as formal recognition in marriage is concerned. If moral disapprobation of homosexual conduct is "no legitimate state interest" for purposes of proscribing that conduct, *ante*, at 18; and if, as the Court coos (casting aside all pretense of neutrality), "[w]hen sexuality finds overt expression in intimate conduct with another person, the conduct can be but one element in a personal bond that is more enduring," *ante*, at 6; what justification could there possibly be for denying the benefits of marriage to homosexual couples exercising "[t]he liberty protected by the Constitution," *ibid.*? ... This case "does not involve" the issue of homosexual marriage only if one entertains the belief that principle and logic have nothing to do with the decisions of this Court. Many will hope that, as the Court comfortingly assures us, this is so ...

READING QUESTIONS ON *LAWRENCE*

1 Has the Court adopted a version of Mill's "harm principle" in this case?
2 Scalia, J. contends that *Lawrence* opens the door to same-sex marriage. Do you agree? Do you think Justice Kennedy agrees?
3 Read the discussion of adjudication and judicial review in chapter 6. Which of the writers encountered there comes closer to Kennedy's approach? Scalia's?
4 Read the Supreme Court of Canada's decision in *Malmo-Levine*, above. Compare and contrast their approaches to the significance of social morality with the court in *Lawrence*.

Vriend v. Alberta [1998] 1 SCR 493

Vriend was dismissed from his job in a private religious school on the basis of his sexual orientation. The *Charter of Rights and Freedoms* only limits state action, so he could not bring a case against his employers under the *Charter*. He sought to bring a complaint under Alberta's *Individual's Rights Protections Act*, but the Alberta Human Rights Commission (a government body) refused to hear his complaint because sexual orientation was not among the enumerated grounds of discrimination it was charged with prohibiting. Vriend argued that failure to include sexual orientation among the prohibited grounds of discrimination was a violation of his equality rights under the *Charter*.

Cory, J.: – The *Individual's Rights Protection Act*, RSA 1980, c I-2 ("*IRPA*" or the "Act"), prohibits discrimination in a number of areas of public life, and establishes the Human Rights Commission to deal with complaints of discrimination ... In 1990, the Act included the following list of prohibited grounds of discrimination: race, religious beliefs, colour, gender, physical disability, mental disability, age, ancestry and place of origin. At the present time it also includes marital status, source of income and family status.

Despite repeated calls for its inclusion sexual orientation has never been included in the list of those groups protected from discrimination ... The reasons given for declining to take this action include the assertions that sexual orientation is a "marginal" ground; that human rights legislation is powerless to change public attitudes; and that there have only been a few cases of sexual orientation discrimination in employment brought to the attention of the Minister.

In 1992, the Human Rights Commission decided to investigate complaints of discrimination on the basis of sexual orientation. This decision was immediately vetoed by the Government and the Minister directed the Commission not to investigate the complaints.

...

B Vriend's Dismissal From King's College and Complaint to the Alberta Human Rights Commission

In December 1987 the appellant Delwin Vriend was employed as a laboratory coordinator by King's College in Edmonton, Alberta. He was given a permanent, full-time position in 1988. Throughout his term of employment he received positive evaluations, salary increases and promotions for his work performance. On February 20, 1990, in response to an inquiry by the President of the College, Vriend disclosed that he was homosexual. In early January 1991, the Board of Governors of the College adopted a position statement on homosexuality, and shortly thereafter, the President of the College requested Vriend's resignation. He declined to resign, and on January 28, 1991, Vriend's employment was terminated by the College. The sole reason given for his termination was his non-compliance with the policy of the College on homosexual practice. Vriend appealed the termination and applied for reinstatement, but was refused.

On June 11, 1991, Vriend attempted to file a complaint with the Alberta Human Rights Commission on the grounds that his employer discriminated against him because of his sexual orientation. On July 10, 1991, the Commission advised Vriend that he could not make a complaint under the *IRPA*, because the Act did not include sexual orientation as a protected ground.

...

II RELEVANT STATUTORY PROVISIONS

Since the time the appellant made his claim in 1992, the relevant statute was amended (*Individual's Rights Protection Amendment Act, 1996*, S.A. 1996, c. 25). The Act is now known as the *Human Rights, Citizenship and Multiculturalism Act*. In these reasons, however, we refer to the statute, as amended, as the *Individual's Rights Protection Act* or *IRPA*, since that is how the legislation was most often referred to by the parties on this appeal. For the sake of convenience, the provisions are set out below first as they existed at the time the action commenced, and then as they currently stand.

Individual's Rights Protection Act, RSA 1980, c I-2, am. SA 1985, c 33, SA 1990, c. 23

Preamble

Whereas recognition of the inherent dignity and the equal and inalienable rights of all persons is the foundation of freedom, justice and peace in the world; and

Whereas it is recognized in Alberta as a fundamental principle and as a matter of public policy that all persons are equal in dignity and rights without regard to race, religious beliefs, colour, gender, physical disability, mental disability, age, ancestry or place of origin; and

Whereas it is fitting that this principle be affirmed by the Legislature of

Alberta in an enactment whereby those rights of the individual may be protected ...

7(1) No employer or person acting on behalf of an employer shall
(a) refuse to employ or refuse to continue to employ any person, or
(b) discriminate against any person with regard to employment or any term or condition of employment,
because of the race, religious beliefs, colour, gender, physical disability, mental disability, marital status, age, ancestry or place of origin of that person or of any other person.
(2) Subsection (1) as it relates to age and marital status does not affect the operation of any bona fide retirement or pension plan or the terms or conditions of any bona fide group or employee insurance plan.
(3) Subsection (1) does not apply with respect to a refusal, limitation, specification or preference based on a bona fide occupational requirement.
8(1) No person shall use or circulate any form of application for employment or publish any advertisement in connection with employment or prospective employment or make any written or oral inquiry of an applicant
(a) that expresses either directly or indirectly any limitation, specification or preference indicating discrimination on the basis of the race, religious beliefs, colour, gender, physical disability, mental disability, marital status, age, ancestry or place of origin of any person, or
(b) that requires an applicant to furnish any information concerning race, religious beliefs, colour, gender, physical disability, mental disability, marital status, age, ancestry or place of origin.
(2) Subsection (1) does not apply with respect to a refusal, limitation, specification or preference based on a bona fide occupational requirement ...

Canadian Charter of Rights and Freedoms

1. The *Canadian Charter of Rights and Freedoms* guarantees the rights and freedoms set out in it subject only to such reasonable limits prescribed by law as can be demonstrably justified in a free and democratic society.

15. (1) Every individual is equal before and under the law and has the right to the equal protection and equal benefit of the law without discrimination and, in particular, without discrimination based on race, national or ethnic origin, colour, religion, sex, age or mental or physical disability.

24. (1) Anyone whose rights or freedoms, as guaranteed by this Charter, have been infringed or denied may apply to a court of competent jurisdic-

tion to obtain such remedy as the court considers appropriate and just in the circumstances.

32. (1) This Charter applies
(a) to the Parliament and government of Canada in respect of all matters within the authority of Parliament including all matters relating to the Yukon Territory and Northwest Territories; and
(b) to the legislature and government of each province in respect of all matters within the authority of the legislature of each province.

Constitution Act, 1982

52.(1) The Constitution of Canada is the supreme law of Canada, and any law that is inconsistent with the provisions of the Constitution is, to the extent of the inconsistency, of no force or effect.

III DECISIONS BELOW

A Alberta Court of Queen's Bench (1994), 152 A.R. 1

The appellants applied to Russell, J., as she then was, for an order (1) declaring that ss. 2(1), 3, 4 and 7(1) of the *IRPA* are inconsistent with s. 15(1) of the *Charter* and infringe the appellants' rights, as a result of the absence of sexual orientation from the list of proscribed grounds of discrimination; (2) that Vriend has the right to file a complaint under the *IRPA* alleging discrimination on the grounds of sexual orientation; and (3) that lesbians and gays have the right to the protections of the *IRPA*.

Russell, J. noted also that discrimination does not depend on a finding of invidious intent ...

B Alberta Court of Appeal (1996), 181 A.R. 16

McClung, J.A. held that the first question to be resolved was whether the *IRPA* is "answerable, as it stands" to the *Charter* (at p. 22). He was of the opinion that the omission of "sexual orientation" from the discrimination provisions of the *IRPA* does not amount to governmental action for the purpose of s. 32(1) of the *Charter*.

...

IV ISSUES

The constitutional questions which have been stated by this Court are:

1 Do (a) decisions not to include sexual orientation or (b) the non-inclusion of sexual orientation, as a prohibited ground of discrimination in the preamble and ss. 2(1), 3, 4, 7(1), 8(1), 10 and 16(1) of the *Individual's Rights Protection Act*, R.S.A. 1980, c. I-2, as am., now called the *Human Rights, Citizenship and Multiculturalism Act*, R.S.A. 1980, c. H-11.7, infringe or deny the rights guaranteed by s. 15(1) of the *Canadian Charter of Rights and Freedoms*?
2 If the answer to Question 1 is "yes," is the infringement or denial demonstrably justified as a reasonable limit pursuant to s. 1 of the *Canadian Charter of Rights and Freedoms*?

The parties have also raised issues with respect to standing, the application of the *Charter* and the appropriate remedy.

V ANALYSIS

...

1 Application of the Charter to a Legislative Omission

Does s. 32 of the *Charter* prohibit consideration of a s. 15 violation when that issue arises from a legislative omission? ...

[C]onfusion results when arguments concerning the respective roles of the legislature and the judiciary are introduced into the s. 32 analysis. These arguments put forward the position that courts must defer to a decision of the legislature not to enact a particular provision, and that the scope of *Charter* review should be restricted so that such decisions will be unchallenged. I cannot accept this position. Apart from the very problematic distinction it draws between legislative action and inaction, this argument seeks to substantially alter the nature of considerations of legislative deference in *Charter* analysis. The deference very properly due to the choices made by the legislature will be taken into account in deciding whether a limit is justified under s. 1 and again in determining the appropriate remedy for a *Charter* breach. My colleague Iacobucci, J. deals with these considerations at greater length more fully in his reasons.

The notion of judicial deference to legislative choices should not, however, be used to completely immunize certain kinds of legislative decisions from *Charter* scrutiny. McClung, J.A. in the Alberta Court of Appeal criticized the application of the *Charter* to a legislative omission as an encroachment by the courts on legislative autonomy. He objected to what he saw as judges dictating provincial legislation under the pretext of constitutional scrutiny. In his view, a choice by the legislature not to legislate with respect to a particular matter within its jurisdiction, especially a controversial one, should not be open to review by the judiciary: "When they choose silence provincial legislatures need not march to the *Charter* drum. In a constitutional sense they need not march at all ... The *Canadian Charter of Rights and Freedoms* was not adopted by the provinces to promote the federal extraction of subsidiary legislation from them but only to police it once it is proclaimed – if it is proclaimed" (pp. 25 and 28).

There are several answers to this position. The first is that in this case, the constitutional challenge concerns the *IRPA*, legislation that has been proclaimed ...

It is suggested that this appeal represents a contest between the power of the democratically elected legislatures to pass the laws they see fit, and the power of the courts to disallow those laws, or to dictate that certain matters be included in those laws. To put the issue in this way is misleading and erroneous. Quite simply, it is not the courts which limit the legislatures. Rather, it is the Constitution, which must be interpreted by the courts, that limits the legislatures. This is necessarily true of all constitutional democracies. Citizens must have the right to challenge laws which they consider to be beyond the powers of the legislatures. When such a challenge is properly made, the courts must, pursuant to their constitutional duty, rule on the challenge ...

The respondents contend that a deliberate choice not to legislate should not be considered government action and thus does not attract *Charter* scrutiny. This submission should not be accepted ...

The relevant subsection, s. 32(1)(b), states that the *Charter* applies to "the legislature and government of each province in respect of all matters within the authority of the legislature of each province." There is nothing in that wording to suggest that a *positive act* encroaching on rights is required; rather the subsection speaks only of *matters within the authority of the legislature* ...

The *IRPA* is being challenged as unconstitutional because of its failure to protect *Charter* rights, that is to say its underinclusiveness. The mere fact that the challenged aspect of the Act is its underinclusiveness should not necessarily render the *Charter* inapplicable. If an omission were not subject to the *Charter*, underinclusive legislation which was worded in such a way as to simply omit one class rather than to explicitly exclude it would be immune from *Charter* challenge. If this position was accepted, the form, rather than the substance, of the legislation would determine whether it was open to challenge. This result would be illogical and more importantly unfair ...

It might also be possible to say in this case that the deliberate decision to omit sexual orientation from the provisions of the *IRPA* is an "act" of the Legislature to which the *Charter* should apply.

2 *Application of the Charter to Private Activity*

The respondents further argue that the effect of applying the *Charter* to the *IRPA* would be to regulate private activity ...

The respondents' submission has failed to distinguish between "private activity" and "laws that regulate private activity." The former is not subject to the *Charter*, while the latter obviously is. It is the latter which is at issue in this appeal ...

Section 15(1)

1. Approach to Section 15(1). The rights enshrined in s. 15(1) of the *Charter* are fundamental to Canada. They reflect the fondest dreams, the highest hopes and finest aspirations of Canadian society. When universal suffrage was granted it recognized to some extent the importance of the individual. Canada by the broad scope and fundamental fairness of the provisions of s. 15(1) has taken a further step in the recognition of the fundamental importance and the innate dignity of the individual. That it has done so is not only praiseworthy but essential to achieving the magnificent goal of equal dignity for all. It is the means of giving Canadians a sense of pride. In order to achieve equality the intrinsic worthiness and importance of every individual must be recognized regardless of the age, sex, colour, origins, or other characteristics of the person. This in turn should lead to a sense of dignity and worthiness for every Canadian and the greatest possible pride and appreciation in being a part of a great nation ...

Yet, if any enumerated or analogous group is denied the equality provided by s. 15 then the equality of every other minority group is threatened. That equality is guaranteed by our constitution. If equality rights for minorities had been recognized, the all too frequent tragedies of history might have been avoided. It can never be forgotten that discrimination is the antithesis of equality and that it is the recognition of equality which will foster the dignity of every individual.

How then should the analysis of s. 15 proceed? ... The essential requirements of all these cases will be satisfied by enquiring first, whether there is a distinction which results in the denial of equality before or under the law, or of equal protection or benefit of the law; and second, whether this denial constitutes discrimination on the basis of an enumerated or analogous ground.

2. The IRPA Creates a Distinction Between the Claimant and Others Based on a Personal Characteristic, and Because of That Distinction, It Denies the Claimant Equal Protection or Equal Benefit of the Law.

(a) Does the IRPA Create a Distinction? The respondents have argued that because the *IRPA* merely omits any reference to sexual orientation, this "neutral silence" cannot be understood as creating a distinction. They contend that the *IRPA* extends full protection on the grounds contained within it to heterosexuals and homosexuals alike, and therefore there is no distinction and hence no discrimination. It is the respondents' position that if any distinction is made on the basis of sexual orientation that distinction exists because it is present in society and not because of the *IRPA*.

These arguments cannot be accepted ... It has been repeatedly held that identical treatment will not always constitute equal treatment (see for example *Andrews, supra*, at p. 164). It is also clear that the way in which an exclusion is worded should not disguise the nature of the exclusion so as to allow differently drafted exclusions to be treated differently ...

The respondents concede that if homosexuals were excluded altogether from the protection of the *IRPA* in the sense that they were not protected from discrimination on any grounds, this would be discriminatory. Clearly that would be discrimination of the most egregious kind. It is true that gay and lesbian individuals are not entirely excluded from the protection of the *IRPA*. They can claim protection on some grounds. Yet that certainly does not mean that there is no discrimination present. For example, the fact that a lesbian and a heterosexual woman are both entitled to bring a complaint of discrimination on the basis of gender does not mean that they have *equal* protection under the Act ...

If the mere silence of the legislation was enough to remove it from s. 15(1) scrutiny then any legislature could easily avoid the objects of s. 15(1) simply by drafting laws which omitted reference to excluded groups ...

It is clear that the *IRPA*, by reason of its underinclusiveness, does create a distinction. The distinction is simultaneously drawn along two different lines. The first is the distinction between homosexuals, on one hand, and other disadvantaged groups which are protected under the Act, on the other. Gays and lesbians do not even have formal equality with reference to other protected groups, since those other groups are explicitly included and they are not.

The second distinction, and, I think, the more fundamental one, is between homosexuals and heterosexuals. This distinction may be more difficult to see because there is, on the surface, a measure of formal equality: gay or lesbian individuals have the same access as heterosexual individuals to the protection of the *IRPA* in the sense that they could complain to the Commission about an incident of discrimination on the basis of any of the grounds currently included. However, the exclusion of the ground of sexual orientation, considered in the context of the social reality of discrimination against gays and lesbians, clearly has a disproportionate impact on them as opposed to heterosexuals. Therefore the *IRPA* in its underinclusive state denies substantive equality to the former group ...

Finally, the respondents' contention that the distinction is not created by law, but rather exists independently of the *IRPA* in society, cannot be accepted. It is, of course, true that discrimination against gays and lesbians exists in society. The reality of this cruel and unfortunate discrimination was recognized in *Egan*. Indeed it provides the context in which the legislative distinction challenged in this case must be analysed. The reality of society's discrimination against lesbians and gay men demonstrates that there is a distinction drawn in the *IRPA* which denies these groups equal protection of the law by excluding lesbians and gay men from its protection, the very protection they so urgently need because of the existence of discrimination against them in society. It is not necessary to find that the legislation *creates* the discrimination existing in society in order to determine that it creates a potentially discriminatory distinction.

Although the respondents try to distinguish this case from *Bliss v. Attorney General of Canada*, [1979] 1 SCR 183, the reasoning they put forward is very much reminiscent of the approach taken in that case ... There it was held that a longer qualifying period for unemployment benefits relating to pregnancy was not discriminatory because it applied to all pregnant individuals, and that if this category happened only to include women, that was a distinction created by nature, not by law. This reasoning has since been emphatically rejected (see, e.g., *Brooks*) ...

The omission of sexual orientation as a protected ground in the *IRPA* creates a distinction on the basis of sexual orientation. The "silence" of the *IRPA* with respect to discrimination on the ground of sexual orientation is not "neutral." Gay men and lesbians are treated differently from other disadvantaged groups and from heterosexuals. They, unlike gays and lesbians, receive protection from discrimination on the grounds that are likely to be relevant to them.

(b) Denial of Equal Benefit and Protection of the Law. It is apparent that the omission from the *IRPA* creates a distinction. That distinction results in a denial of the equal benefit and equal protection of the law. It is the exclusion of sexual orientation from the list of grounds in the *IRPA* which denies lesbians and gay men the protection and benefit of the Act in two important ways. They are excluded from the government's statement of policy against discrimination, and they are also denied access to the remedial procedures established by the Act.

Therefore, the *IRPA*, by its omission or underinclusiveness, denies gays and lesbians the equal benefit and protection of the law on the basis of a personal characteristic, namely sexual orientation.

3. The Denial of Equal Benefit and Equal Protection Constitutes Discrimination Contrary to Section 15(1). In *Egan*, it was said that there are two aspects which are relevant in determining whether the distinction created by the law constitutes discrimination. First, "whether the equality right was denied on the basis of a personal characteristic which is either enumerated in s. 15(1) or which is analogous to those enumerated." Second "whether that distinction has the effect on the claimant of imposing a burden, obligation or disadvantage not imposed upon others or of withholding or limiting access to benefits or advantages which are available to others" (para. 131) ...

(a) The Equality Right is Denied on the Basis of a Personal Characteristic Which Is Analogous to Those Enumerated in Section 15(1). In *Egan*, it was held, on the basis of "historical social, political and economic disadvantage suffered by homosexuals" and the emerging consensus among legislatures (at para. 176), as well as previous judicial decisions (at para. 177), that sexual orientation is a ground analogous to those listed in s. 15(1). Sexual orientation is "a deeply personal characteristic that is either unchangeable or changeable only at unacceptable personal costs" (para. 5). It is analogous to the other personal characteristics enumerated in s. 15(1); and therefore this step of the test is satisfied ...

It may at first be difficult to recognize the significance of being excluded from the protection of human rights legislation. However it imposes a heavy and disabling burden on those excluded ...

Apart from the immediate effect of the denial of recourse in cases of discrimination, there are other effects which, while perhaps less obvious, are at least as harmful. In *Haig*, the Ontario Court of Appeal based its finding of discrimination on both the "failure to provide an avenue for redress for prejudicial treatment of homosexual members of society" and "the possible inference from the omission that such treatment is acceptable" (p. 503). It can be reasonably inferred that the absence of any legal recourse for discrimination on the ground of sexual orientation perpetuates and even encourages that kind of discrimination. The respondents contend that it cannot be assumed that the "silence" of the *IRPA* reinforces or perpetuates discrimination, since governments "cannot legislate attitudes." However, this argument seems disingenuous in light of the stated purpose of the *IRPA*, to prevent discrimination. It cannot be claimed that human rights legislation will help to protect individuals from discrimination, and at the same time contend that an exclusion from the legislation will have no effect.

However, let us assume, contrary to all reasonable inferences, that exclusion from the *IRPA*'s protection does not actually contribute to a greater incidence of discrimination on the excluded ground. Nonetheless that exclusion, deliberately chosen in the face of clear findings that discrimination on the ground of sexual orientation does exist in society, sends a strong and sinister message ... to all Albertans that it is permissible, and perhaps even acceptable, to discriminate against individuals on the basis of their sexual orientation. The effect of that message on gays and lesbians is one whose significance cannot be underestimated ...

Fear of discrimination will logically lead to concealment of true identity and this must be harmful to personal confidence and self-esteem. Compounding that effect is the implicit message conveyed by the exclusion, that gays and lesbians, unlike other individuals, are not worthy of protection. This is clearly an example of a distinction which demeans the individual and strengthens and perpetrates the view that gays and lesbians are less worthy of protection as individuals in Canada's society. The potential harm to the dignity and perceived worth of gay and lesbian individuals constitutes a particularly cruel form of discrimination.

...

4. "Mirror" Argument. The respondents take the position that if the appellants are successful, the result will be that human rights legislation will always have to "mirror" the *Charter* by including all of the enumerated and analogous grounds of the *Charter*. This would have the undesirable result of unduly constraining legislative choice and allowing the *Charter* to indirectly regulate private conduct, which should be left to the legislatures.

... However, the notion of "mirroring" is too simplistic. Whether an omission is unconstitutional must be assessed in each case, taking into account the nature of the exclusion, the type of legislation, and the context in which it was enacted. The determination of whether a particular exclusion complies with s. 15 of the *Charter* would not be made through the mechanical application of any "mirroring" principle, but rather, as in all other cases, by determining whether the exclusion was proven to be discriminatory in its specific context and whether the discrimination could be justified under s. 1. If a provincial legislature chooses to take legislative measures which do not include all of the enumerated and analogous grounds of the *Charter*, deference may be shown to this choice, so long as the tests for justification under s. 1, including rational connection, are satisfied.

5. Conclusion Regarding Section 15. In summary, this Court has no choice but to conclude that the *IRPA*, by reason of the omission of sexual orientation as a protected ground, clearly violates s. 15 of the *Charter*. The *IRPA* in its underinclusive state creates a distinction which results in the denial of the equal benefit and protection of the law on the basis of sexual orientation, a personal characteristic which has been found to be analogous to the grounds enumerated in s. 15 ... It is therefore necessary to determine whether this violation can be justified under s. 1. This analysis will be undertaken by my colleague.

Iacobucci, J.: – Section 1 of the *Charter* guarantees the rights and freedoms set out therein, but allows for *Charter* infringements provided that the state can establish that they are reasonably justifiable in a free and democratic society. The analytical framework for determining whether a statutory provision is a reasonable limit on a *Charter* right or freedom has been set out many times since it was first established in *R. v. Oakes*, [1986] 1 SCR 103. It was recently restated in *Egan, supra*, at para. 182, which was quoted with approval in *Eldridge, supra*, at para. 684:

A limitation to a constitutional guarantee will be sustained once two conditions are met. First, the objective of the legislation must be press-ing and substantial. Second, the means chosen to attain this legislative end must be reasonable and demonstrably justifiable in a free and democratic society. In order to satisfy the second requirement, three criteria must be satisfied: (1) the rights violation must be rationally connected to the aim of the legislation; (2) the impugned provision must minimally impair the *Charter* guarantee; and (3) there must be a proportionality between the effect of the measure and its objective so that the attainment of the legislative goal is not outweighed by the abridgement of the right. In all s. 1 cases the burden of proof is with the government to show on a balance of probabilities that the violation is justifiable.

1. Pressing and Substantial Objective ... In my view, where, as here, a law has been found to violate the *Charter* owing to underinclusion, the legislation as a whole, the impugned provisions, and the omission itself are all properly considered.

Section 1 of the *Charter* states that it is the *limits* on *Charter* rights and freedoms that must be demonstrably justified in a free and democratic society. It follows that under the first part of the *Oakes* test, the analysis must focus upon the objective of the impugned limitation, or in this case, the omission ...

However, in my opinion, the objective of the omission cannot be fully understood in isolation. It seems to me that some consideration must also be given to both the purposes of the Act as a whole and the specific impugned provisions so as to give the objective of the omission the context that is necessary for a more complete understanding of its operation in the broader scheme of the legislation.

Applying these principles to the case at bar, the preamble of the *IRPA* suggests that the object of the Act in its entirety is the recognition and protection of the inherent dignity and inalienable rights of Albertans through the elimination of discriminatory practices. Clearly, the protection of human rights in our society is a laudable goal and is aptly described as pressing and substantial. As to the impugned provisions, their objective can generally be described as the protection against discrimination for Albertans belonging to specific groups in various settings, for example, employment and accommodation. This too is properly regarded as a pressing and substantial objective.

Against this backdrop, what can be said of the objective of the omission? The respondents submit that only the overall goal of the Act need be examined and offer no direct submissions in answer to this question. In the Court of Appeal, absent any evidence on this point, Hunt, J.A. relied on the factum of the respondents from which she gleaned several possible reasons why, when the matter was debated by the Alberta Legislature in 1985 and considered at various other times, a decision was made not to add sexual orientation to the *IRPA*. Some of these same reasons appear in the factum that the respondents have submitted to this Court and include the following:

- The *IRPA* is inadequate to address some of the concerns expressed by the homosexual community (e.g., parental acceptance) (para. 57);
- Attitudes cannot be changed by order of the Human Rights Commission (para. 57);
- Despite the Minister asking for examples which would be ameliorated by the inclusion of sexual orientation in the *IRPA* (e.g., employment), only a few illustrations were provided (para. 57);
- Codification of marginal grounds which affect few persons raises objections from larger numbers of others, adding to the number of exemptions that would have been needed to satisfy both groups (para. 66).

In my view, although these statements go some distance toward explaining the Legislature's choice to exclude sexual orientation from the *IRPA*, this is not the type of evidence required under the first step of the *Oakes* test. At the first stage of that test, the government is asked to demonstrate that the "objective" of the omission is pressing and substantial. An "objective," being a goal or a purpose to be achieved, is a very different concept from an "explanation" which makes plain that which is not immediately obvious. In my opinion, the above statements fall into the latter category and hence are of little help.

In his reasons for judgment, McClung, J.A. alludes to "moral" considerations that likely informed the Legislature's choice. However, even if such considerations could be said to amount to a pressing and substantial objective (a position which I find difficult to accept in this case), I note that it is well established that the onus of justifying a *Charter* infringement rests on the government (see, e.g., *Andrews v. Law Society of British Columbia, supra*). In the absence of any submissions regarding the pressing and substantial nature of the objective of the omission, the respondents have failed to discharge their evidentiary burden, and thus, I conclude that their case must fail at this first stage of the s. 1 analysis.

... Even if I were to put the evidentiary burden aside in an attempt to discover an objective for the omission from the provisions of the *IRPA*, in my view, the result would be the same. As I noted above, the overall goal of the *IRPA* is the protection of the dignity and rights of all persons living in Alberta. The exclusion of sexual orientation from the Act effectively denies gay men and lesbians such protection ...

2. Proportionality Analysis

(a) Rational Connection. On the basis of my conclusion above, it is not necessary to analyse the second part of the *Oakes* test to dispose of this appeal. However, to deal with this matter more fully, I will go on to consider the remainder of the test. I will assume, solely for the sake of the analysis, that the respondents correctly argued that where the objective of the whole of the legislation is pressing and substantial, this is sufficient to satisfy the first stage of the inquiry under s. 1 of the *Charter*.

At the second stage of the *Oakes* test, the preliminary inquiry is a consideration of the rationality of the impugned provisions (*Oakes, supra*, at p. 141). The party invoking s. 1 must demonstrate that a rational connection exists between the objective of the provisions under attack and the measures that have been adopted. Thus, in the case at bar, it falls to the Legislature to show that there is a rational connection between the goal of protection against discrimination for Albertans belonging to specific groups in various settings, and the exclusion of gay men and lesbians from the impugned provisions of the *IRPA*.

Far from being rationally connected to the objective of the impugned provisions, the exclusion of sexual orientation from the Act is antithetical to that goal ...

(b) Minimal Impairment. The respondents contend that an *IRPA* which is silent as to sexual orientation minimally impairs the appellants' s. 15 rights. The *IRPA* is alleged to be the type of social policy legislation that requires the Alberta Legislature to mediate between competing groups. It is suggested that the competing interests in the present case are religious freedom and homosexuality. Relying upon Sopinka, J.'s reasons in *Egan*, the respondents advocate judicial deference in these circumstances. I reject these submissions for several reasons.

To begin, I cannot accede to the suggestion that the Alberta Legislature has been cast in the role of mediator between competing groups. To the extent that there may be a conflict between religious freedom and the protection of gay men and lesbians, the *IRPA* contains internal mechanisms for balancing these rival concerns. Section 11.1 of the *IRPA* provides a defence where the discrimination was "reasonable and justifiable in the circumstances." In addition, ss. 7(3) and 8(2) excuse discrimination which can be linked to a *bona fide* occupational requirement. The balancing provisions ensure that no conferral of rights is absolute. Rather, rights are recognized in tandem, with no one right being automatically paramount to another ... Thus, in the present case it is no answer to say that rights cannot be conferred upon one group because of a conflict with the rights of others. A complete solution to any such conflict already exists within the legislation.

In any event, although this Court has recognized that the Legislatures ought to be accorded some leeway when making choices between competing social concerns ... judicial deference is not without limits ...

(c) Proportionality Between the Effect of the Measure and the Objective of the Legislation. The respondents did not address this third element of the proportionality requirement. However, in my view, the deleterious effects of the exclusion of sexual orientation from the *IRPA*, as noted by Cory, J., are numerous and clear. As the Alberta Government has failed to demonstrate any salutary effect of the exclusion in promoting and protecting human rights, I cannot accept that there is any proportionality between the attainment of the legislative goal and the infringement of the appellants' equality rights. I conclude that the exclusion of sexual orientation from the *IRPA* does not meet the requirements of the *Oakes* test and accordingly, it cannot be saved under s. 1 of the *Charter*.

II REMEDY

A Introduction: The Relationship Between the Legislatures and the Courts Under the Charter

Having found the exclusion of sexual orientation from the *IRPA* to be an unjustifiable violation of the appellants' equality rights, I now turn to the question of remedy under s. 52 of the *Constitution Act, 1982*. Before discussing the jurisprudence on remedies, I believe it might be helpful to pause to reflect more broadly on the general issue of the relationship between legislatures and the courts in the age of the *Charter*.

Much was made in argument before us about the inadvisability of the Court interfering with or otherwise meddling in what is regarded as the proper role of the legislature, which in this case was to decide whether or not sexual orientation would be added to Alberta's human rights legislation. Indeed, it seems that hardly a day goes by without some comment or criticism to the effect that under the *Charter* courts are wrongfully usurping the role of the legislatures. I believe this allegation misunderstands what took place and what was intended when our country adopted the *Charter* in 1981–82.

When the *Charter* was introduced, Canada went, in the words of former Chief Justice Brian Dickson, from a system of Parliamentary supremacy to constitutional supremacy ("Keynote Address," in *The Cambridge Lectures 1985* (1985), at pp. 3–4). Simply put, each Canadian was given individual rights and freedoms which no government or legislature could take away. However, as rights and freedoms are not absolute, governments and legislatures could justify the qualification or infringement of these constitutional rights under s. 1 as I previously discussed. Inevitably disputes over the meaning of the rights and their justification would have to be settled and here the role of the judiciary enters to resolve these disputes. Many countries have assigned the important role of judicial review to their supreme or constitutional courts ...

We should recall that it was the deliberate choice of our provincial and federal legislatures in adopting the *Charter* to assign an interpretive role to the courts and to command them under s. 52 to declare unconstitutional legislation invalid ...

The leading case on constitutional remedies is *Schachter, supra.* Writing on behalf of the majority in *Schachter*, Lamer, C.J. stated that the first step in selecting a remedial course under s. 52 is to define the extent of the *Charter* inconsistency which must be struck down ...

Because the *Charter* violation in the instant case stems from an omission, the remedy of reading down is simply not available. Further, I note that given the considerable number of sections at issue in this case and the important roles they play in the scheme of the *IRPA* as a whole, severance of these sections from the remainder of the Act would be akin to striking down the entire Act ...

As I discussed above, the purpose of the *IRPA* is the recognition and protection of the inherent dignity and inalienable rights of Albertans through the elimination of discriminatory practices. It seems to me that the remedy of reading in would minimize interference with this clearly legitimate legislative purpose and thereby avoid excessive intrusion into the legislative sphere whereas striking down the *IRPA* would deprive all Albertans of human rights protection and thereby unduly interfere with the scheme enacted by the Legislature.

... I agree with K. Roach who noted that the legislature "can always subsequently intervene on matters of detail that are not dictated by the Constitution" (*Constitutional Remedies in Canada* (1994, loose-leaf), at p. 14–64.1). I therefore conclude on this point that, in the present case, there is sufficient remedial precision to justify the remedy of reading in.

Turning to budgetary repercussions, in the circumstances of the present appeal, such considerations are not sufficiently significant to warrant avoiding the reading in approach ...

Where a statute has been found to be unconstitutional, whether the court chooses to read provisions into the legislation or to strike it down, legislative intent is necessarily interfered with to some extent. Therefore, the closest a court can come to respecting the legislative intention is to determine what the legislature would likely have done if it had known that its chosen measures would be found unconstitutional. As I see the matter, a deliberate choice of means will not act as a bar to reading in save for those circumstances in which the means chosen can be shown to be of such centrality to the aims of the legislature and so integral to the scheme of the legislation, that the legislature would not have enacted the statute without them.

... When a court remedies an unconstitutional statute by reading in provisions, no doubt this constrains the legislative process and therefore should not be done needlessly, but only after considered examination.

However, in my view, the "parliamentary safeguards" remain. Governments are free to modify the amended legislation by passing exceptions and defences which they feel can be justified under s. 1 of the *Charter* ...

III CONCLUSIONS AND DISPOSITION

I would answer the constitutional questions as follows:

1 Do (a) decisions not to include sexual orientation or (b) the non-inclusion of sexual orientation, as a prohibited ground of discrimination in the preamble and ss. 2(1), 3, 4, 7(1), 8(1), 10 and 16(1) of the *Individual's Rights Protection Act*, R.S.A. 1980, c. I-2, as am., now called the *Human Rights, Citizenship and Multiculturalism Act*, R.S.A. 1980, c. H-11.7, infringe or deny the rights guaranteed by s. 15(1) of the *Canadian Charter of Rights and Freedoms*? Answer: Yes.
2 If the answer to Question 1 is "yes," is the infringement or denial demonstrably justified as a reasonable limit pursuant to s. 1 of the *Canadian Charter of Rights and Freedoms*? Answer: No.

L'Heureux-Dubé, J.: – I am in general agreement with the results reached by my colleagues, Cory and Iacobucci, JJ. ...

I do not agree with the centrality of enumerated and analogous grounds in Cory, J.'s approach to s. 15(1). Although the presence of enumerated or analogous grounds may be indicia of discrimination, or may even raise a presumption of discrimination, it is in the appreciation of the nature of the individual or group who is being negatively affected that they should be examined. Of greatest significance to a finding of discrimination is the effect of the legislative distinction on that individual or group ...

This being said, I agree with Cory and Iacobucci, JJ. to allow the appeal and dismiss the cross-appeal with costs.

Major, J. (dissenting in part): – ... Reading in may be appropriate where it can be safely assumed that the legislature itself would have remedied the underinclusiveness by extending the benefit or protection to the previously excluded group. That assumption cannot be made in this appeal.

The issue may be that the Legislature would prefer no human rights Act over one that includes sexual orientation as a prohibited ground of discrimination, or the issue may be *how* the legislation ought to be amended to bring it into conformity with the *Charter* ...

There are numerous ways in which the legislation could be amended to address the underinclusiveness. Sexual orientation may be added as a prohibited ground of discrimination to each of the impugned provisions. In so doing, the Legislature may choose to define the term "sexual orientation," or it may devise constitutional limitations on the scope of protection provided by the *IRPA*. As an alternative, the Legislature may choose to override the *Charter* breach by invoking s. 33 of the *Charter*, which enables Parliament or a legislature to enact a law that will operate notwithstanding the rights guaranteed in s. 2 and ss. 7 to 15 of the *Charter*. Given the persistent refusal of the Legislature to protect against discrimination on the basis of sexual orientation, it may be that it would choose to invoke s. 33 in these circumstances. In any event it should lie with the elected Legislature to determine this issue. They are answerable to the electorate of that province and it is for them to choose the remedy whether it is changing the legislation or using the notwithstanding clause. That decision in turn will be judged by the voters ...

READING QUESTIONS ON *VRIEND*

1 What is the "mirror" argument that Cory, J. rejects? Is there more to be said for the worry than he allows?

2 Iacobucci, J. rejects the contention that the Alberta legislature made its decision on moral grounds, saying that the onus is on the legislature to explain its grounds. How do you think he would have decided the s. 1 issue if Alberta had made an explicit Devlin-style argument?

3 L'Heureux-Dubé, J. says that a *Charter* finding of discrimination does not require showing that the situation of the individual or group discriminated against is analogous to that of others receiving legal protection. How else might one identify discrimination?

4 The Court decides to "read in" the missing provisions of the *Individual's Rights Protection Act*. What does this mean? Why does Major, J. object? What would the Court do if the legislature decided to repeal the Act? Would Vriend have any recourse against his employer or the government?

6

Judicial Review

In Canada and elsewhere, the issue of judicial authority to review legislation for its compliance with constitutional commitments is highly contentious, as is, naturally, the issue of whether it is appropriate to have an entrenched bill of rights. Critics of judicial review and of such bills from the right and left wings of politics unite to argue that judges are an unelected elite who should have no authority to second-guess the wisdom of statutes enacted by the democratically chosen legislators. Often this position is associated with legal positivism, though most contemporary positivists would say that legal positivism takes no stand on the issue of what kind of power judges should have.

Wil Waluchow
"Constitutions as Living Trees: An Idiot Defends" (2005)

Waluchow presents a version of legal positivism that is consistent with a defence of judicial review and criticizes positivists who regard such review as undemocratic.

I SETTING THE STAGE

For a variety of fairly well known reasons, Charters (or Bills) of Rights are often heralded as good things to have. For example, they are often applauded for the protections they are said to afford minorities, or for their help in securing certain fundamental liberal rights thought essential to a thriving democracy. But Charters are not without their detractors. My principal aim in this paper is to defend Charters, and the practices of judicial review to which they normally give rise, against a variety of objections that have been made in both popular and academic discourse. In defending a practice, the best strategy is usually to address the arguments of its strongest critic, and it is for this reason that I will be concentrating, though not exclusively, on Jeremy Waldron who, in two important books, *The Dignity of Legislation* and *Law and Disagreement*, argues strenuously against Charters and their enforcement by judges. Waldron's formidable critique represents the most serious challenge in the literature to the intelligibility and desirability of Charters. In focusing on Waldron's arguments, I will address what I believe to be some of their vulnerable points (some of which have already been noted by others). But more importantly, I will try to take some initial steps towards developing an alternative to the conception of Charters which I think underlies both his critique and the views of those (or at least many of them) he is attacking.[1] In particular, I want to challenge what I think is their shared picture of the role a Charter plays in the realms of law and politics. That role is one of providing a (more or less) stable, fixed point of agreement on and pre-commitment to moral limits to government power; these are limits found, paradigmatically in moral rights upon which valid government action may not infringe. Typically the relevant government powers are exercised in legislative actions, but of course they can be exercised in other ways as well, e.g., in executive or judicial orders or in decisions by administrative bodies empowered by legislation to develop standards or render decisions within particular domains of competence. The Advocates argue that such a stable fixed point is not only possible, despite some acknowledged measure of disagreement and controversy about the moral limits enshrined, and despite the inevitable changes to them which are inadvertently brought about through interpretations of a Charter's provisions. They also argue that this stable framework is, for a variety of different reasons (e.g., protection from majority tyranny, from mass hysteria in times of national crisis, or from simple moral blindness) morally and politically desirable, perhaps even essential. Some Advocates think of Charters as representing a regrettable, but on balance warranted, compromise of democratic principle (if everyone were always fully enlightened, impartial, could be trusted always to bear fundamental rights in mind, etc., then it would be right to empower the majority, or its representatives, always to decide, but ...) while others think of them as the very embodiment of democratic principle (the fundamental ideas of democracy are respect for individual autonomy and self-government; majority rule is warranted only if, and to the extent that, it respects these ideas, but, in fact, it systematically fails to do so. Hence the need for Charters ...).

Waldron, for his part, challenges (a) the very *intelligibility* of this fixed point conception of Charters; (b) the moral and political *desirability* of attempting to have them play the assigned role; and (c) the various *arguments* and *analogies* put forward in defense of (b). The agreement and pre-commitment presupposed by the Advocates' conception and its defense simply do not exist within what Waldron aptly calls "the circumstances of politics." These circumstances consist in the "felt need among the members of a certain group for a common framework or decision or course of action on some matter, even in the face of disagreement about what that framework, decision or action should be."[2] They include, not only the desire to act in concert politically and in ways that do not infringe the fundamental rights of individuals. They also include radical disagreement about how we should go about achieving these results; that is, there are deep disagreements about what our rights actually are and how they are to be understood and applied. These disagreements extend to questions concerning whether to adopt a Charter, then what rights to include within it, and how these rights are to be applied in the concrete circumstances of every day life and politics, and, perhaps most importantly for our purposes, in the Charter disputes which these inevitably bring to light. According to Waldron, "it looks as though it is disagreement all the way down, so far as constitutional choice is concerned."[3] Yet if "the people" cannot agree, at any particular moment in time, let alone across generations, on the nature and content of the moral rights enshrined in their Charters, they cannot intelligibly pre-commit to the stable, fixed point of constitutional limits within which government power is supposed to be exercised on their behalf. Instead of a relatively stable, fixed point of pre-commitment, imposed by the people themselves and enforced by judges on their behalf, they will, in adopting a Charter, have offered an ill advised, open-ended invitation to judges to impose unprincipled and arbitrary constraints upon their right to self-determination; and whatever else might be said about them, such impositions cannot possibly be squared with the ideals of democracy. And even if, at some moment in time when the decision is taken to enshrine a set of Charter rights, we were to have complete agreement on which rights to include and how these are to be inter-preted and applied, the fact of the matter is that citizens in a few years time will inevitably disagree with some or all of the previously agreed answers. Why, then, should "the people *now*" be bound by what "the people *then*" agreed were appropriate constraints on the powers of government? How can this possibly be squared with the ideals of autonomy and self-government at the heart of our democratic commit-ments?

If this shared picture of the role Charters are supposed to play is accepted, then it seems to me that it's pretty much game over and Waldron is entitled to take home the Cup. One might attempt to establish a temporally extended, perhaps even cross-generational, basis of rational, implicit or hypothetical agreement upon which some notion of democratically legitimate, pre-commitment could be based by offering a philosophical theory which, in one's view, no reasonable person, then or now, could possibly dispute. But it is not clear that this strategy will, in the end, work. The main problem is one which Waldron highlights to great effect: no theory of political morality has ever stood the "no-reasonable-disagreement test," and there is little hope that one ever will.[4] Rawlsian "burdens of judgment" apply to philosophers as much as legislators, judges and ordinary citizens, leading to the inevitable conclusion that we will all continue to disagree about rights so long as we remain human beings with an interest in politics, political theory and the pursuit of what we judge to be the good life.[5] One might alternatively seek a basis for agreement in something less ambitious than sound moral philosophy. One might, for example, attempt to base it on an "overlapping consensus" of moral judgments held within the community over time, even if that overlapping consensus fails, in the view of some at least, to stand the test of philosophical scrutiny. Perhaps one could discover something like Rawls' "free standing" political conception of justice which could serve as the basis of a kind of shared "public reason" which naturally finds expression in Charters. But as many have pointed out, even here the prospects do not look very promising. Supposing that some such consensus could be found, (itself, perhaps, an unreasonable assumption) it is not clear that it could ever be stable over time. Whatever overlapping consensus about racial equality might have existed two hundred years ago in Western democracies, it is pretty clear that it is significantly different from any consensus that might exist at the present time. In Canada, any overlap-ping consensus that might have existed as little as five years ago on the idea of gay marriage would have been plainly against the practice. At present no such consensus exists, or if it does, it has shifted in favour of the idea. But if this kind of shift occurs, as it appears to do on a fairly regular basis, then we are left wondering, once again, about the very intelligibility of the notion that Charters can, to any extent, be thought to represent stable, fixed points of agreement and pre-commitment which renders them not only helpful in securing fundamental rights, but helpful in ways which are consistent with, or an embodiment of, democratic ideals.

So instead of attempting to discover a basis upon which the notion of rational pre-commitment to a stable, fixed point of moral agreement could be based, I am going to offer an alternative account of the role Charters aspire to play. On this conception, Charters are far from aspiring to set fixed points, and importantly, they do not presuppose the level of confidence in the rectitude of our moral judgment presupposed by Waldron and (I think) most of the Advocates. I am going to suggest that we instead view Charters as representing a mixture of only very modest pre-commitment combined with a considerable measure of humility. The latter stems from the recognition that we do *not* in fact have all the answers when it comes to moral rights, and that we should do all we can to ensure that our moral short sightedness does not, in the circumstances of politics, lead to morally questionable government action. Far from being based on the (unwarranted) assumption that we have the right answers to the controversial issues of political morality arising under Charter challenges, the alternative conception stems from the exact opposite: from a recognition that we do *not* have all the answers, and that we are better off designing our political and legal institutions in ways which are sensitive to this feature of our predicament. Contra Waldron and other Critics, Charters need not be seen as embodying a naïve confidence in our judgments about which rights count, how they are to be interpreted, and which political actions (including legislative acts) are consistent with fundamental rights. Charters can and should be viewed as representing a concession to our inability fully to understand both the nature of fundamental rights and how these might be infringed by government action – and this includes, paradigmatically, government actions premised on the relatively blunt instrument of binding general legislation. Once we see Charters in this very different light, we can see not only why they could well be good things to have, we can see our way clear to answering the various arguments offered by Waldron and other Critics against their adoption.

The structure of my argument will be as follows. I will begin, in Section II, by analytically separating four questions concerning Charters. I will then outline some of the more popular, standard objections to Charters that one encounters in academic and popular discourse. Many of these are taken up and defended by Waldron. I will attempt to highlight how each of the objections and its underlying argument relies on the view of Charters sketched above: that they aspire to serve as fixed points of moral agreement and pre-commitment. In Section III, I will begin to sketch my alternative conception of Charters which, for reasons which will become clear later, I propose to call "the common law conception." In Sections IV and V, I will discuss briefly Hart's thoughts on the competing needs at play whenever we attempt to implement the rule of law. Sections VI and VII will bring Hart's thoughts to bear on the common law conception and, more broadly, fundamental questions of constitutional design. Finally, in Section VIII I will attempt to answer Waldron's spirited case against judicial review.

II ANTI-CHARTER ARGUMENTS

In discussing the nature and merits (or lack thereof) of Charters, one needs, analytically, to separate at least four questions: (1) What role does a Charter play in a constitutional democracy?[6] (2) Is a Charter (serving that particular role) a good thing to have in a constitutional democracy (and if so why)? (3) Is judicial review on the basis of a Charter a good thing to have in a constitutional democracy (and if so, what form should that take)?[7] and (4) How should judges go about interpreting and applying Charters in the context of the judicial review of legislation? These questions, though different, are undeniably related to one another. For instance, how one answers (4) will depend crucially on how one answers (2) and (3). The reasons why Charters are (or are not) good things to have, and the type of judicial review they license, are all factors which are bound, in some way or other, to have a bearing on how they should be interpreted. For instance, a court whose decisions do not have the effect of striking down a legislative act, or whose decision can be overridden by a special legislative initiative as in Canada, might well feel much freer to interpret a Charter's moral provisions according to moral views not widely shared within the legislature or the general population than would be the case were the court's decision to have the effect of rendering the law invalid or inoperable. In the former case, there is a kind of built-in safety valve which can serve to relieve the burden of final judgment which is bound to felt by the latter. If no such safety valve is built into the process of judicial review because, for example, the court's decision has the effect of overruling the legislature's judgment and is binding, the judges may feel (perhaps justifiably) hesitant to offer unorthodox interpretations, preferring instead to be far more deferential to the legislature's moral views and intentions or the views widely shared within the community. Their deferential attitude – which they might reasonably believe to be fully justified given the nature of the Charter and the power it provides them – could well lead judges to seek refuge in factors like "legislative intent" or "settled meanings" factors which will appear to relieve them of the responsibility of expressing and enforcing their own moral views.

In a similar vein, the way in which one answers questions (2) and (3) is going to depend on how one conceives the role served by a Charter, i.e., on how one answers question (1). The standard answer to (1), advanced by most Advocates, goes something like this. All constitutions, written or unwritten, include norms which create and structure the organs of government, i.e., the fundamental executive, legislative and judicial powers which together give shape to political and legal systems. But constitutions which include Charters go well beyond this; they entrench certain basic moral rights as fixed points which the organs of government created by the constitution are forbidden from infringing when they exercise their constitutionally licensed powers, at least till such time as a formal constitutional amendment is introduced, something that happens very rarely and requires levels of political will, commitment and agreement which can be very difficult to marshal. Most other substantive issues of policy and principle are up for grabs in the everyday thrust and parry of political decision making, but Charters set fixed moral limits upon which (ideally at least) everyone is in agreement and which all have pre-committed to observe. They represent agreed moral boundaries for the legally valid exercise of government power.

There are many standard reasons offered both in public discourse and in the philosophical literature for this kind of arrangement. Charters are heralded as useful or essential vehicles for the protection of minorities from Mill's tyranny of the majority. They are sometimes viewed as embodying the "rational pre-commitment" of the community to observe certain fundamental rights essential to (a) enlightened democratic rule, and (b) the free and equal exercise of individual autonomy. (a) is thought to require such things as the right to vote and freedom of the press, while (b) is thought to require artistic freedom, equality before and under the law, the right to privacy, and so on. These are all stressed, to varying degrees by philosophers such as Rawls, Dworkin and Samuel Freeman.[8] Although the factor is seriously underplayed in arguments surrounding their merits or drawbacks, Charters are also applauded for the symbolic value they are capable of embodying. They can help define and reinforce the character of the nation as one publicly committed, in its legal and moral practices, to the fundamental rights and values it includes. As such they help establish the identity of the community, and serve as the moral and conceptual backdrop within which public policy debates take place.

Despite their intuitive appeal, Charters face many points of criticism from a wide range of sources. Among the more common complaints are the following.

1 The Argument from Democracy

Charters are sometimes condemned as affronts to the ideals of democratic self-rule. One often encounters the following kind of argument: If one is to have an effective Charter of Rights, the courts must play a central role in its enforcement, including its enforcement against otherwise valid legislative initiatives. But this arrangement only serves to thwart the will of the people as expressed through their elected representatives. It is not enough to say that "the people" have themselves chosen to impose these judicially enforced, entrenched limits on legislative power, because quite often the limits in question were set years, perhaps generations, ago when the Charter was first adopted. Why should "the people now" be restricted in their current choices by what "the people then" decided were appropriate limits to entrench in a constitutional document, especially given the bias against change which constitutional amending formulae typically, perhaps even essentially, build right into constitutions? All this seems, on the surface at least, inconsistent with the notion of ongoing self-government which lies as the heart of democratic ideals. And even leaving aside the problems associated with temporally extended constraints upon current expressions of popular will, we are faced with the following serious difficulty: allowing (largely) unelected judges to overrule the considered views of responsible, representative legislators represents the complete abandonment of self-government. It represents an unflattering admission that we are better off allowing a small cadre of judicial elites to make our decisions of political morality for us than we are making those decisions ourselves, if only through the agency of our elected representatives. Why, it is asked, should we not feel slighted by this kind of admission? Have we not here conceded that we are incapable of the exercise of self-government?[9] 求从;咄

> ... if A is ... excluded from [a] decision (for example because the final decision has been assigned to an aristocratic elite), A will feel slighted: he will feel that his own sense of justice has been denigrated as inadequate to the task of deciding not only something important, but something important in which he, A, has a stake as well as others. To feel this insult does not require him to think that his vote – if he had it – would give him substantial and palpable power. He knows that if he [or his elected representative] has the right to participate, so do millions [or hundreds] of others. All he asks – so far as participation is concerned – is that he and all others be treated as equals in matters affecting their interests, their rights, and their duties.[10]
>
> To think that a constitutional immunity is called for is to think oneself justified in disabling legislators in this respect (and thus, indirectly, in disabling the citizens whom they represent). It is ... worth pondering the attitudes that lie behind the enthusiasm for imposing such disabilities.[11]

2 Hobbsean Predators and Respect for Persons

The attitude to which Waldron makes reference in the preceding quotation serves as the basis for a second, fundamental objection. There is, Waldron thinks, a deep inconsistency built right into Charters. On the one hand, we have the standard picture of Charters as providing stable or transient minorities with vital protections against mistaken, overzealous, or perhaps even irrational, stable or transient majorities; yet these are protections which we believe, with utmost confidence, to be not only important but essential and therefore worthy of constitutional entrenchment. On the other hand, we have the liberal view of individual citizens as agents worthy of exercising, in an ongoing and responsible manner, the fundamental rights enunciated in a Charter, a view which underlies both democratic ideals and the view that we are creatures with dignity, deserving of the rights accorded us in liberal democratic theory and society. To adopt a Charter is to combine self assurance and mistrust: self assurance in the proponent's conviction that what he is putting forward really *is* a matter of fundamental right and that he has captured it adequately in the particular formulation he is propounding; and mistrust, implicit in his view that any alterative conception that might be conceived by elected legislators next year or in ten years' time is so likely to be wrong-headed or ill-motivated that *his own* formulation is to be elevated immediately beyond the reach of ordinary legislative revision.[12]

Yet constraining future majorities by putting constitutionally entrenched roadblocks in their way

does not sit particularly well with the aura of respect for their autonomy and responsibility that is conveyed by the substance of the rights which are being entrenched ... If the desire for entrenchment is motivated by a predatory view of human nature and of what people will do to one another when let loose in the arena of democratic politics, it will be difficult to explain how or why people are to be viewed as essentially bearers of rights.[13]

So there is a deep inconsistency in the very idea of a Charter. On the one hand, we say that people are autonomous moral agents worthy of the possession and informed, responsible exercise of the moral rights we (typically) enshrine in Charters. We view them as responsible moral agents fully capable of pursuing their own conceptions of the good life on an ongoing basis, and willing and able to contribute meaningfully and responsibly to collective efforts of self-government through participation in democratic politics. This status, this inherent human dignity, deems them not only worthy of rights, and to whatever protections are necessary for their securing (including the adoption of a Charter of Rights) it also deems them worthy of helping to determine, on an ongoing and continual basis, what those rights entail or amount to, and how public policy should be shaped so as not to infringe those rights so understood. This they do by participating in democratic politics, if only through the vehicle of electing responsible and accountable legislators, empowered to make decisions on their behalf. On the other hand, we also view them (and their agents in the legislature) as predators, unable to constrain themselves if "let loose in the arena of democratic politics." They cannot be trusted to exercise their rights responsibly without undermining the rights of others. Nor can they be trusted, in hard cases, to provide balanced views about the concrete implications of the rights they trumpet. They are lacking in both self-restraint and knowledge – areas in which, by comparison, the authors of Charters excel. Hence the need for Charter constraint of democratic power – and the saving grace of judges. Waldron is right: these two views of human agents cannot possibly be reconciled.

3 Judges as Platonic Kings

A third popular objection to Charters is that a very small group of judges sitting in chambers are no more competent than legislators, or the citizens they represent, to deal sensitively and effectively with the deeply controversial, complex issues of morality and public policy typically at stake in Charter cases. And yet this is precisely what Charters presuppose – else why have Charters and why assign their interpretation and enforcement to judges? But reality suggests a far different picture. Judges, though well schooled in the law, are in no sense of the term "moral authorities" – if such a notion even makes sense. Nor are they experts in the various fields of social policy with which government action typically deals. They most certainly do not exhibit levels of moral and public policy understanding superior to the levels enjoyed by the government authorities whose actions they are called on to sit in moral judgment. They are no more able than these others to discern the content of the fixed points of moral agreement and pre-commitment that Charters are (supposedly) designed to represent. They most certainly are not, nor will they ever be, philosopher kings with the insight of Dworkin's Hercules or Rawls' ideal contractors. Why then should the people and their representatives bow to the no less authoritative moral decisions of this handful of judges on matters of common concern? Indeed, if we accept the plausible hypothesis that the greater the number of people of varying backgrounds, knowledge bases, perspectives and so on that we have working on a complex social problem, the greater our chances of arriving at well thought out, reasonable solutions upon which agreement can be based, then we should eschew a system under which a few weathered heads in chambers are allowed to substitute their judgments for those of a great many representative heads, elected by the people to serve their interests, advance their perspectives, and so and are accountable to the people on that score.

It is particularly insulting when [citizens and their elected representatives] discover that the judges disagree among themselves along exactly the same lines as the citizens and representatives do, and that the judges make their decisions, too, in the courtroom by majority voting. The citizens may well feel that if disagreements on these matters are to be settled by counting heads, then it is their heads or those of their accountable representatives that should be counted.[14]

4 Judges and the Elites of Society

A closely related objection goes beyond questioning the superiority of judges' moral and public policy judgments. Many theorists, far more critical of legal practices than Waldron, point to the inevitable bias which is introduced into our political and legal cultures when judges are allowed to decide the kinds of questions raised by Charters. As many Critical Legal Scholars point out, judges tend to originate from the social, political and financial elites within society and share their perspectives on the issues of morality and public policy around which Charter cases revolve. The consequence, it is said, is suppression of those – women, minority racial groups, the poor, and so on – whose interests are not adequately recognized or supported by the dominant, mainstream ideologies to which judges have an affinity. Instead of the curbing of unwarranted, arbitrary government power for which Charters are thought to stand, we have political suppression disguised in a cloak of false constitutional legitimacy. The inevitable result is not tyranny of the majority but tyranny of powerful minority elites. Does this too not fly in the face of any sane conception of democracy?

5 The Threat of Moral Nihilism

A fifth common objection to Charters[15] is that their appeal stems from discredited, naïve views of morality and rationality, and the moral limits which Charters are meant to enshrine. More particularly, it stems from a naïve view concerning the possibility of "objectively right" answers to the moral, and otherwise evaluative, questions which typically arise in Charter cases. Many critics espouse utter skepticism about the "objectivity" of moral reasoning. Morality, including the political morality at stake in most Charter disputes, is wholly "subjective" and/or "relative." As a result, Charters license judges' unbridled pursuit of their own personal moral preferences. And since elitist judges cannot help but impose their own, purely subjective moral understandings on the workings of the political process, the inevitable result once again is the total discrediting of Charters. The bulwark against the unwarranted exercise of government power and oppression which Charters are meant to establish is nothing but a sham – and a harmful one at that.

6 The Threat of Radical Dissensus: An Idiot's Search for Ulysses' Mast

In explaining the nature and appeal of Charters, Advocates sometimes cite the metaphor of Ulysses' decision to be tied to the mast of his ship so as not to succumb to the tempting call of the Sirens. Just as Ulysses knows, in advance, and in a moment of cool reflection, that he is justified in arranging now for a restriction on his freedom to choose and act later, we, as a people, can know, in advance, and in a moment of cool reflection (a moment of constitutional choice) that we are justified in tying ourselves to the mast of entrenched Charter rights and their enforcement, on our behalf, by the judiciary. Just as Ulysses knows that he will descend into madness when he hears the call of the Sirens, we can know that at some point we will inevitably succumb to the siren call of self-interest, prejudice, fear, hatred or simple moral blindness, and be led, in the course of everyday politics, to violate the rights of some of our fellow citizens. In Waldron's view, however, radical dissensus undermines this image entirely.

Leaving aside the nest of thorny questions introduced by the possibility of moral nihilism and skepticism about the "objectivity" of moral judgments, the fact of the matter is that we live in a pluralistic world of significant moral dissensus. People's moral and political views differ dramatically – and for all we can tell, reasonably – in ways which are not easily subject to mutual accommodation and efforts to achieve consensus. So even if there are right answers to questions about moral rights, we cannot agree on what these are or on what they entail for the questions of law, morality and public policy which Charters bring to the fore. As Waldron insists, "even if there is an objectively right answer to the question of what rights we have, still people disagree implacably about what that right answer is."[16] Yet if we cannot agree on the rights we have, let alone what these entail for the questions of law and public policy which Charters being to the fore, then it is sheer folly to believe that we – and this includes judges – could ever agree on what a Charter's provisions mean and on the limits they supposedly impose on legislative and executive power. And if we cannot agree on the limits established by a Charter, we can hardly pre-commit to them. We cannot tie ourselves to the mast of entrenched moral rights, if we cannot locate the mast, let alone agree on what it might look like. "My theme in all this is reasonable disagreement, but I cannot restrain myself from saying that anyone who thinks a narrative like this is appropriately modeled by the story of Ulysses and the sirens is an idiot."[17]

7 The Futility of "Results Driven" Arguments for Charters

託偽

Radical dissensus about rights has, Waldron believes, a further important consequence for Charters and the arguments usually put forward in their defense. Dissensus rules out the validity of defenses premised on any kind of "results-driven" standard. According to Advocates, Charters result in stronger and more consistent rights enforcement. That they achieve these results serves not only to explain their nature and appeal, it also serves to show why they are essential components of thriving democracies and fully justified if for that reason alone. Dworkin, for instance, has argued as follows:

I see no alternative but to use a result-driven rather than a procedure-driven standard ... The best institutional structure is one best calculated to produce the best answers to the essentially moral question of what the democratic conditions actually are, and to secure stable compliance with those conditions.[18]

On this standard, Dworkin suggests, the adoption of a Charter is fully warranted because it secures better understanding and enforcement of moral rights. Waldron's response is to challenge both the truth of Dworkin's premises and the validity of the argument in which they figure. In rejecting Dworkin's premises, he falls in line with other critics who are keen to contrast the *Lochner* era (Bill of Rights exists but rights thwarted by the courts) with the long standing tradition of civil rights protection evident in the United Kingdom (no Charter and yet the courts have consistently contributed to successful efforts to secure respect for fundamental rights.) As for the question of validity, the fact of disagreement renders the argument invalid.

Even if they agree that democracy implicates certain rights, citizens will surely disagree what these rights are and what in detail they commit us to ... But a citizenry who disagree about what would count as the right results are not in a position to construct their constitution on this basis.[19]

在 right 的意見上有分坡, 自然不同意 result driven 的 Charte

We seem, then, to be in a bind. It looks as though it is disagreement all the way down, so far as constitutional choice is concerned ... [W]e cannot use a results-driven test, because we disagree about which results would count in favour of and which against a given decision-procedure ... [W]e cannot appeal to any procedural criterion either, since procedural questions are at the very nub of the disagreements we are talking about.[20]

8 Charters and the Level of Public Debate

Advocates often defend Charters as a valuable means for focusing and improving the level of public debate. Waldron once again cites Dworkin:

When an issue is seen as constitutional ... and as one that will ultimately be resolved by courts applying general constitutional principles, the quality of public argument is often improved, because the argument concentrates from the start on questions of political morality ... When a constitutional issue has been decided by the Supreme Court, and is important enough so that it can be expected to be elaborated, expanded, contracted, or even reversed by future decisions, a sustained national debate begins, in newspapers and other media, in law schools and classrooms, in public meetings and around dinner tables. That debate better matches [the] conception of republican government, in its emphasis on matters of principle, than almost anything the legislative process on its own is likely to produce.[21]

Waldron's response? "I am afraid I do not agree with any of this."[22] Contra Dworkin and his fellow Advocates, transforming debates of political morality into constitutional disputes is as likely to reduce the level of public debate as improve it. In support of this indictment, Waldron cites two factors: history and the artificiality of constitutional debate under Charters.

My experience is that national debates about abortion are as robust and well-informed in countries like the United Kingdom and New Zealand, where they are not constitutionalized, as they are in the United States – the more so perhaps because they are uncontaminated by quibbling about how to interpret the text of an eighteenth century document. It is sometimes liberating to be able to discuss issues like abortion directly, on the principles that ought to be engaged, rather than having to scramble around constructing those principles out of scraps of some sacred text, in a tendentious exercise of constitutional calligraphy.[23]

Further points of comparison are drawn by Waldron: debates about capital punishment in countries free to focus on the general aims of penal policy, as compared with American debates centred on questions about the extent to which the practice is "cruel and unusual;" the lack of depth and sophistication of the decision in *Bowers v. Hardwick* as compared with the debate about homosexuality initiated in the UK by the Wolfenden Report and sustained in the comparatively sophisticated (and sensitive) exchange between H.L.A. Hart and Lord Patrick Devlin. In summing up the judgment of history, Waldron writes: "If the debate that actually takes place in American society and American legislatures is as good as that in other countries, it is so *despite* the Supreme Court's framing of the issues, not because of it."[24]

Among the central reasons for this difference in the quality of the debates Waldron suggests is the "verbal rigidity" (often) introduced by the choice to "constitutionalize" fundamental moral rights in a Charter.

A legal right that finds protection in a Bill of Rights finds it under the auspices of some canonical form of words in which the provisions of the charter are enunciated. One lesson of American constitutional experience is that the words of each provision in the Bill of Rights tend to take on a life of their own, becoming the obsessive catch-phrase for expressing everything one might want to say about the right in question. For example, First Amendment doctrine in America is obsessed to the point of scholasticism with the question of whether some problematic form of behaviour [e.g., flag burning, pornography, topless dancing] that the state has an interest in regulating is to be regarded as "speech" or not.[25]

Yet, Waldron adds, this is surely not the way to argue about fundamental rights. We can, he says, use phrases like "freedom of speech" to "pick out the sort of concerns we have in mind in invoking a particular right; but that is not the same as saying that the *word* 'speech' ... is the key to our concerns in the area."[26] If instead we allow our evolving understandings of moral rights to be reflected in more flexible and less verbally constrained common law principles and precedents, "and easier still if rights take the form of 'conventional understandings' subscribed to the political community at large, as they have in Britain for many years," we will have a public discourse less constrained by verbal formulas and semantic obsessions and more able to ask the questions of moral substance that should really be our principal focus.

Charter 的 verbalism 限制了人们的思维, 使 讨论更像 嚼 解字 而非辩论

What we need are institutional mechanisms for protecting rights which are "free from the obsessive verbalism of a particular written charter."[27]

III AN ALTERNATIVE CONCEPTION?

The preceding section contained some of the strongest and most common objections to Charters one encounters in both public and academic discourse. The list is by no means exhaustive, and it may not fully reflect the full spectrum of critical views. It does, however, provide what I believe to be a fair picture of the kinds of objections on offer. In each instance there are, of course, responses to be made, some of which already exist in the literature spawned by Waldron's critique.[28] But instead of pursuing these here, I would like to focus on one of the agreed, basic premises upon which much of the debate between the Advocates and Critics has been based. Consider again the various objections outlined. In each case we can see that the criticism is premised on the following critical assumption: Charters aspire to embody fixed points of agreement on and pre-commitment to moral limits on government power. With this unstated assumption in place, the Critic then goes on to argue that, for one reason or another, Charters so conceived either (a) fail to live up to this aspiration; or (b) are unworthy of our allegiance in a democratic society even if they do so. The supposed fact of radical dissensus, employed to such powerful effect by Waldron, underlies conclusion (a), that Charters simply cannot do the work their Advocates would have them do and cannot possibly be explained in the terms they suggest. The Ulysses metaphor, for instance, cannot sensibly serve to explain the nature and effect of Charters. Only an idiot would think that we can intelligibly pre-commit to limits upon which we cannot agree in advance. At best we can pre-commit to a practice which licenses other people, viz., judges, to make our decisions for us on issues and questions upon which we ourselves cannot reach agreement, and which we, as individuals whose self-image includes the honorific title "rights bearer," really should be making. If, despite acknowledged worries that disagreement just might go all the way down, we continue to hold on to the idea that Charters really can and do embody fixed points, then we will inevitably be led to serious concerns about their democratic pedigree, and to the unflattering picture of human beings (as *Hobbesean* predators) which that picture seems to suggest. We will be led to ask why the people now should be hamstrung in their pursuit of sound, morally responsible public policy by decisions made earlier by "the people then" and entrenched by *them*, not *us*, against efforts to change those decisions in light of the new and evolving understandings of a self-governing people characterized by its commitment to rights and the fundamental human dignity they pre-suppose. One might valiantly try, as Jed Rubenfeld does, to diminish the force of this objection by invoking the possibility of community identity across time, so that "the people then" are really one and the same as "the people now."[29] But whether in the end this kind of strategy will work is highly questionable, and not only because of the inevitable metaphysical questions which invariably accompany theories of group identity and agency. However these latter questions are answered, we will be faced with the following difficulty. Just as individuals often change their beliefs and commitments, sometimes in fundamental ways,[30] there is little reason to deny the very real possibility that one and the same "people" might, on many important issues, change their mind from one year to the next, let alone one generation to the next. If so, then the Critics' question remains valid: Why should "the people's" ability to change their mind about rights be denied or curtailed? Why should they be hamstrung in their ability to make those changes of mind effective in their everyday political decisions? True, there is always the process of constitutional amendment, but it would be difficult to overestimate the practical difficulties associated with such a process. We must ask whether, in light of this fact, it is defensible to place such impediments in our way. Can they be made consistent with the picture we like to paint of ourselves, viz., of a responsible, self-governing people who can be trusted *on an ongoing basis* with decisions about justice and rights?

So an Advocate who accepts the assumption that Charters aspire to embody fixed points of agreement and pre-commitment, will inevitably be met with powerful objections. She seems left, then, with three options: (a) she can either continue to seek the means to answer Waldron and other Critics in the terms they have established;[31] (b) she can succumb to the force of their arguments and agree that Charters and their implementation via judicial review is a bad idea; or (c) she can seek an alterative understanding of Charters, one which sees their aspirations as different. In the remainder of this paper I want to explore option (c). I will do so by proposing an alternative understanding of a Charter according to which neither its coherence nor its legitimacy is under-mined by the circumstances of politics. On the contrary, a Charter can be a quite sensible response to such circumstances. Its legitimacy can be

主要困境：人们对正义的观点会改变

explained by the role it plays in helping to overcome difficulties we inevitably encounter whenever we seek to govern ourselves by law, difficulties which are only exacerbated by the circumstances of politics. This alternative conception takes its inspiration from two sources: Hart's thoughts on the move from the pre-legal to legal world, and an idea articulated long ago by Lord Sankey in *Edwards*,[32] a landmark Canadian constitutional case, decided by the Privy Council in 1930, and now commonly referred to as "The Persons Case." *Edwards* is famous for two reasons: (1) it established, for the first time in Canadian legal history, that women are indeed "persons" for purposes of appointment to the Senate; and (2) it introduced into Canadian constitutional law what is now called the "living tree" metaphor of the constitution, a conception repeatedly endorsed by the Canadian courts in a string of important Charter cases.[33] On this conception constitutions, and hence those Charters which enjoy constitutional status, in no way represent fixed points of agreement and pre-commitment. By its nature, a Charter is "a living tree capable of growth and expansion within its natural limits."[34] It is an instrument which must, within limits inherent in its nature as part of a constitution, be allowed to grow and adapt to new contemporary circumstances and evolving beliefs about justice. Waldron claims that with Charters we loose "our ability to evolve a free and flexible discourse of politics," a discourse which can easily evolve if, instead of introducing Charters, we rely for rights protection on "legal recognition in the form of common law principles and precedents" or "'conventional' understandings subscribed to in the political community at large." The living tree conception brings these two approaches together into a kind of "common law understanding" of Charters; this is one which seeks to combine both the relative fixity of entrenched, written law and the relative adaptability characteristic of the common law. If this option truly is open, then our choice is not simply between having a Charter or eschewing one altogether. We can also choose *how* our Charters are to function in constitutional democracies. My argument will be that, in choosing a living tree, common law conception, we are able to reap the many of the benefits for which Charters are promoted by the Advocates, while avoiding most, if not all, of the difficulties cited by the Critics. In particular, we avoid the hubris, and the insult to democratic ideals and human dignity, which the fixed view and many of its underlying arguments seem to entail. Whether this is a case of an idiot tying to have his cake and eat it too, you'll have to answer for yourself.

IV HART AND LAW BY RULE

Much as Hobbes did when he asked us to ponder our emergence from the state of nature, H.L.A. Hart asks us to consider life without law, and how the introduction of a rudimentary legal system can help overcome a number of "defects" inherent in a hypothetical, pre-legal society.[35] Among these are uncertainty about the identity of the rules governing social behaviour, their immunity from deliberate change, and the inefficiency of diffuse social pressure as a means of enforcing the rules. The defect of uncertainty can be overcome by the introduction of a rule of recognition. Overcoming this defect is by no means guaranteed, of course, but the potential is there; this is a potential which is much more difficult to realize absent a rule of recognition. Similar points can be made about rules of change and adjudication. Success is not guaranteed here either; indeed, it will be highly unlikely when, e.g., the rules governing the introduction or elimination of legislative rules are cumbersome, vague or ambiguous, or require an unattainable level of consensus among legislative bodies. But again, the potential is there when both the rules and the social conditions are right. In having us consider, in this way, the emergence of law from a pre-legal society, Hart hoped not only to illuminate the distinctive features of modern, domestic legal systems, but to illustrate their social significance and potential value. The union of primary rules with fundamental secondary rules of recognition, change and adjudication not only transforms society, it does so in a way which creates the potential radically to improve the social condition.

Yet Hart was all too aware that the promise of law is purchased at a potentially heavy cost. The very features of law by which it can achieve its promise also create the worrisome possibility that a community's law will war with its morality or with the demands of reason, critical morality, or common sense.[36] Hart's reflections on the "pathology of a legal system" are a salutary reminder of the ever present dangers inherent in the structures introduced by law. Once accepted social rules – which cannot exist absent widespread acceptance among those to whom they apply – are replaced with rules satisfying a rule of recognition, the distinct possibility emerges of a complete divorce between validity and acceptance, between the rules which are to be applied because they are valid and those which are acceptable to those over whom they govern. This is because a rule of recognition can require, for legal validity, nothing more than, e.g., formal enactment by the appropriate person or bodies of persons. If so, then there is nothing to guarantee that the rules adopted will be ones which citizens will find acceptable. Nor is there anything to guarantee that the rules will in any way serve the real or perceived interests of justice, fairness, or utility. In extreme cases, the community's governing rules might be ones which no one, save the officials who adopt and enforce them, actually accepts or believes to be justified. In such a situation we may end up no better than sheep led to the slaughterhouse. So the emergence from a pre-legal society to one with law is, at best, a mixed blessing.

Yet another hazard of legal regulation highlighted by Hart arises from the means by which law characteristically communicates its expectations. Factors such as ignorance of fact, indeterminacy of aim, evolving technologies, changing social contexts, and so on, combine to create the ever present possibility that general legal rules will lead, upon application to specific cases, to absurd or otherwise highly undesirable results. These are often results which most everyone, including those who introduced the rules in the first place, would have wished to avoid had they foreseen them in advance. Think here of Hart's toy motor car in the park. The example shows, of course, the empty promise of legal formalism, but its real power, I suggest, lies in highlighting the moral shortcomings of the formalist ideal. Rules so tightly crafted that they leave, at point of application, no room for informed judgment and discretion, quite often represent a thoroughly unworthy ideal. Fortunately, Hart suggests, we have ways of avoiding the pitfalls of formalism. For example, the open texture of natural language permits some measure of the desired leeway. Sometimes this leeway arises by accident, as when a hard case just happens to fall within the "penumbra of uncertainty" and this fact can be seized upon to decide on the merits of the case without (undue) concern about observing the letter of the law. But open texture can also be put to use deliberately, and in advance, in a wide range of scenarios. Sometimes we can foresee that situations are very likely to arise in which blind pre-commitment to a particular legal result would have been foolish or morally problematic. We can know this *general* fact, even though we cannot foresee the particular unwanted results that are bound to arise.[37] In such scenarios, Hart counsels, legislators are wise deliberately to frame open-textured rules and standards incorporating terms like `reasonable' and 'fair.' These provide some level of antecedent guidance while allowing both judge and citizen to address, at point of application, questions which could not reasonably have been settled in advance.[38] Whether or not some such device is employed, however, one fact remains: we cannot always foresee the results to which our general rules will lead, a point it would be foolish to ignore in thinking about how best to design our legal institutions. These are points well understood, if not always fully appreciated, within the realms of ordinary law. Yet they seem to have been largely ignored in the debates between Advocates and Critics. I want to rectify this problem by feeding Hart's insights into the mix and seeing what results. The result, I submit, is an alternative conception of Charters and their legitimacy which is in no way undermined by the circumstances of politics. On the contrary, Charters can be seen to be a quite sensible response to them.

V LESSONS TO BE LEARNED

Among the most important lessons to be drawn from Hart's thoughts on these matters is this: despite its undeniable potential for good, law is an inherently dangerous and often unwieldy social tool. By its very nature, it has the potential to separate the validity of a norm both from its moral and rational merit, and from its general acceptance among the society over whom it governs. And given that legal norms are (typically) general in nature – they deal with general classes of individuals, actions, situations and so on – laws also have the potential to be either over- or under-inclusive, and to lead to unforeseen, troublesome results in concrete cases.[39] Fair enough. But now an important question comes to the fore: are these not risks which we simply must bear if we are to reap the benefits of the rule of law? Is not the very point of law to assume these risks by separating the validity and application of legal norms from contestable questions of reason, morality and common sense?[40] If so, then do we not just have to live with the attendant risks in order to realize the promise of law? Not necessarily, a point sometimes stressed not only by defenders of Inclusive Positivism but by others, like Fred Schauer, who are concerned to understand the wide variety of ways in which the rule of law can be achieved. Schauer writes:

> [T]o the extent that legal systems embrace rule-based decision-making, they embrace as well those values of intertemporal consistency ... stability for stability's sake, unwillingness to trust decision-makers to depart too dramatically from the past, and a conservatism committed to the view that changes from the past as more likely to be for the worse than for the better.... [N]othing inherent in the idea of a legal system mandates that it serves these values.[41]

This, of course, is a sentiment shared by Hart:

[A]ll systems, in different ways, compromise between two social needs: the need for certain rules which can, over great areas of conduct, safely be applied by private individuals to themselves without fresh official guidance or weighing up of social interests, and the need to leave open, for later settlement by an informed official choice, issues which can only be properly appreciated and settled when they arise in a concrete case ... [W]e need to remind ourselves that human inability to anticipate the future, which is at the root of this indeterminacy, varies in degree in different fields of conduct, and that legal systems cater for this inability by a corresponding variety of techniques.[42]

That law should serve what Scott Shapiro calls its "essential guidance function" is undeniably true.[43] But as Hart correctly notes, there are always competing considerations at play, and ignoring these may leave us vulnerable to the temptations of formalism and to a system in which we strive to ensure that our binding legal rules are identified, interpreted and fixed exclusively, decisively and in advance, possibly by source-based considerations alone. There is no doubt that a society might in some scenarios have ample reason to pursue this line of action vigorously. One needn't contemplate a Hobbsean state of nature to recognize the wisdom, in some social settings, of employing relatively hard and fast rules whose validity and concrete requirements leave little room for judgment (moral or otherwise) at point of application. The wisdom of such a move is evident in far less brutish but narrowly circumscribed, stable, and well understood situations (e.g., situations defining offer and acceptance in contract law, or the familiar signing of wills and the two-witnesses requirement) where the need for and possibility of relative certainty about the identity, requirements and satisfaction of the relevant legal rules is at a premium. In such situations, an appropriate level of the kind of guidance highlighted by Hart and invoked by Shapiro may be well nigh impossible should controversial factors, particularly contestable moral norms, play a *prominent* role in determining the validity and application of the relevant rules. But two further points, crucial to our understandings of Charters, must be stressed at this stage: (1) that moral factors should not play too great a role in such situations in no way entails that they should play no role whatsoever, as they arguably did, for example, in *Riggs v. Palmer*.[44] Nor does it entail: (2) that situations cannot arise in which the acknowledged value of antecedent guidance by relatively fixed rules is trumped by our concern that those rules do not infringe, in cases which could not have been anticipated and in ways which could not have been foreseen or appreciated, important norms of morality or practical rationality.[45] We might not have foreseen some such conflict for any number of reasons. For example, unforeseen developments in our ability to communicate electronically can render rules which were, in the age of the telegraph, well designed and morally unproblematic, highly problematic in the age of the Internet with its ever increasing threat to our privacy. In this kind of case, we might have been, and continue to be, in agreement about how to understand the moral value(s) at stake. What we have not been able to foresee, however, is how the rules in question would later impact on the agreed value(s). At other times, the problematic case will arise, not because of evolving social circumstances in a context of relatively stable moral values, but because the relevant values, or our understanding of them, have for some reason changed.[46] Our understanding of "moral equality" for instance, has clearly changed in such a way that the "separate but equal" treatment, which was at one time in the racial history of the United States thought perfectly consistent with that value, is now generally agreed not to be so. I suspect that a time will soon come when it will be generally realized that the option of disallowing gay marriage, but providing for "civil unions" with legal rights more or less equivalent to those associated with the former institution, is just another form of "separate but equal treatment" and equally condemned, on that account, by the norms of moral equality. It is with these factors in mind that we should consider the possibilities open to us when the decision is taken to contemplate the adoption of a Charter.[47]

One possibility, of course, is to avoid Charters altogether; this is the option urged by Waldron and other critics. Recall Waldron's objection that Charters artificially constrain our ability to respond to changing views about rights.[48] Such responses will be easier, we are told, if, instead of adopting a Charter, we allow our evolving understandings of moral rights to be reflected in more flexible and less verbally constrained common law principles and precedents, "and easier still if rights take the form of 'conventional understandings' subscribed to the political community at large, as they have in Britain for many years." Eschewing a Charter, we are told, will create the possibility of a public discourse less constrained by verbal formulas and semantic obsessions and more able to ask the questions of moral substance that should really be our principal focus. What we need are institutional mechanisms for protecting rights which are "free from the obsessive verbalism of a particular written charter."⁴⁹ But this really is a case of throwing the baby out with the bath water. One can agree with the need for institutional mechanisms which are free from "obsessive verbalism" (and, importantly, from obsession with finding fixed points of agreement and pre-commitment which "original meanings or understandings" and the "intentions of the framers" are sometimes said to express) without thereby rejecting written Charters altogether. One will be led to reject the latter for the sake of the former only if one views Charters as the choice of a society obsessed, for misguided normative or conceptual reasons, with the first of Hart's two needs: "the need for certain rules which can, over great areas of conduct, safely be applied by private individuals to themselves without fresh official guidance or weighing up of social interests," and unable to see the force of Hart's second need: "to leave open, for later settlement by an informed official choice, issues which can only be properly appreciated and settled when they arise in a concrete case." But there is nothing in the nature of law, or a Charter, which prevents us from bearing this second need firmly in mind. In particular, we can bear in mind the human inability to anticipate the future, to possess certain knowledge of moral truth both in the abstract and in the concrete circumstances of life and politics. There is also nothing which forces us to deny the important fact that all "legal systems cater for [these] inability[ies] by a corresponding variety of techniques." One of the available techniques, I submit, is the adoption of a Charter understood and applied as the "living tree" metaphor suggests. Charters both can and should be seen to represent a mixture of only very modest pre-commitment and confidence, combined with a considerable measure of humility. The latter stems from the recognition that we – and this includes our legislators – do *not* in fact have all the answers when it comes to moral rights and the impact of our actions on them, and that we should do all we can to ensure that our moral short sightedness does not, in the circumstances of politics, lead us to morally unworthy government action, understood, once again, as encompassing legislative, executive and judicial acts. Far from being based on the unwarranted assumption that we can have, in advance, all the right answers to the controversial issues of political morality which might arise under Charter challenges to government action, and that we are warranted in imposing these answers on those by whom we are succeeded, the living tree conception stems from the *exact opposite* sentiment: from a recognition that we do not have all the answers, and that we are best off designing our political and legal institutions in ways which are sensitive to this feature of our predicament. Contra Waldron and other Critics, Charters need not be seen as embodying a naïve over-confidence in our judgments of political morality. Charters represent a *concession* to our inability to understand fully the nature of fundamental rights and how these might be infringed by government action, including, paradigmatically, actions invoking the relatively blunt instrument of binding general legislation. Once we see Charters in this different light, as (among other things) protections against the unforeseen impact of government action on moral rights and values, we can then begin to see not only why they might be good things to have, we can also see our way clear to answering the various arguments offered by Waldron and other Critics against their adoption.

VI THE LIVING TREE CONCEPTION: FLESHING OUT A METAPHOR

So a Charter need not be viewed as attempting to establish stable fixed points of agreement and pre-commitment, but as planting a "living tree." So understood, a Charter has a kind of flexibility that renders it sensitive to the second of Hart's two fundamental needs. But what about the first need: the need for certain rules which can safely be applied without fresh official guidance or weighing up of social interests? How can Charters, as living trees, be made consistent with this fundamental requirement of the rule of law? One promising, and familiar answer, lies in the approach to legal regulation exemplified by the common law, viz., system which, in various ways and with different emphases, manages to satisfy both of Hart's needs. As Schauer notes,

> ... not only does the common law as it actually exists appear willing to sacrifice some of the goals of predictability and efficiency on the alter of perfectability, but it seems also, much to Bentham's disgust, to be willing to entrust considerable decision-making to the judiciary ... By ameliorating rule-based decision-making, the common law allocates power to its judges, treating the risks consequent to that empowerment as less dangerous than those flowing from the application of crude canonical rules to circumstances their makers might not have imagined and producing results the society might not be willing to tolerate.[50]

Despite its well-known adaptability, which is either celebrated or condemned depending on the theorist's jurisprudential leanings, it is important not to underestimate the capacity of the common law to cater to the need for antecedent guidance. Hart again: "Notwithstanding [the ability of courts to avoid precedents] the result of the English system of precedent has been to produce, by its use, a body of rules of which a vast number, of both major and minor importance, are as determinate as any statutory rule. They can now only be altered where the 'merits' seem to run counter to the requirements of the established precedents."[51] The degree of fixity Hart ascribes to the English common law system has, of course, been challenged, most notably by Brian Simpson.[52] And even if Hart's characterization of (the then current) state of English law is correct, it remains true that a common law system might cater to the element of adaptability to a far greater extent than envisaged by Hart. In fact, it might do so to the point where one could reasonably ask whether it has, in effect, abandoned the rule of law entirely by providing its judges with unbridled discretion.[53] More liberal powers of overruling and distinguishing than Hart describes are always possible, depending on the demands placed on judges by the norms of adjudication circumscribing their powers of decision. But whatever blend a system embodies, the point remains that the common law has a long established history with which we are all familiar, of successfully combining (in various ways) fixity with adaptability. If so, then we have reason to look to the common law as a model for understanding Charters and the roles they are capable of playing. Why should we not view Charters as setting the stage for a kind of common-law jurisprudence of the moral rights cited in the Charter?[54] I'll begin with some of the advantages of this approach, and finish with some final thoughts on how this conception allows us to address the various worries raised by Waldron and his fellow Critics.

VII SOME OF THE ADVANTAGES?

One might, at this point, raise the following concern about the argument thus far. Suppose it's true that we can graft common law methodology onto a living tree conception of Charters. Suppose further that this possibility reveals an important fact about much of the current dispute between Advocates (such as Freeman and Rawls) and Critics (such as Waldron). They all assume that Charters aspire to embody fixed points of agreement and disagreement, and on that basis they are either celebrated or condemned. This we have now seen to be an unwarranted assumption given that the common law conception is a live option.[55] The fact remains, however, that we have yet to see any positive reason to take this third option. What would we gain were we to adopt a written Charter whose role is to set the stage for the development of a common law jurisprudence of moral rights? Would we gain anything more than we could were we instead to pursue the option favoured by Waldron, viz., adopting institutional mechanisms for protecting rights which are "free from the obsessive verbalism of a particular written charter"?[56] A thorough answer to this question requires considerable discussion of what these other "institutional mechanisms" would be. If we "are talking about legal recognition in the form of common law principles and precedents," then presumably we are still talking about judicial review and the supposed insult to democracy and moral agency that Waldron envisages.[57] If instead we are talking about rights taking "the form of 'conventional' understandings subscribed to in the political community at large" then at least two replies are possible. First, we might reasonably ask how Waldron could appeal to such understandings if the circumstances of politics truly are as he envisages. "Conventional understandings" are unlikely to exist if, in fact, *disagreement goes all the way down*.[58] Second, there is absolutely nothing in the common law conception which rules out conventional understandings as a possible source of guidance for the courts. Indeed, the community's values, considered judgments and moral commitments, to the extent that these can be identified, will figure in most every Charter case involving a moral norm. We are, after all, talking about a form of law which is supposed, at least in part, to embody the common beliefs, practices and commitments of the community.[59] Leaving these criticisms aside, however, I hazard the following as tentative reasons for preferring the common law Charter option.

Among the standard arguments in favour of Charters, the most compelling is that Charters serve as vehicles for the protection of entrenched or transitory minorities against the majoritarian biases and excesses of democratic legislatures. They are applauded as embodying the "rational pre-commitment" of the community to work against these biases and excesses by tying itself to the mast of a chosen set of fundamental rights. Paradigmatically, these are rights thought essential to enlightened democratic rule, and to the free and equal exercise of individual autonomy. These are all stressed, to varying degrees in public discourse and by philosophers such as Rawls, Dworkin and Freeman. We have now seen that there are serious problems with this picture; the (apparently) presupposed level of pre-commitment seems lacking, giving rise to the myriad objections raised by Waldron and his fellow Critics. So the picture we paint will need to be modified. But there is no reason to think that its essential details cannot remain. We can, for example, retain the notion of pre-commitment, so long as we are careful to acknowledge the inherent limitations. Recall, for example, the complaint that Charter pre-commitment allows the "dead hand of the past" to determine our choices today, a situation which is thought to undermine the very notion of a self-governing people. A modicum of truth remains in this point since Charters do entrench prior decisions about which rights deserve constitutional protection. And if common law reasoning is brought to bear on how, for purposes of constitutional practices, these rights are to be understood and applied, then the force of precedent (whatever that force happens to be in the particular jurisdiction in question) will always be a factor with which we will have to reckon. The dead hand of precedent has the potential to be as constraining as the dead hand of the "founders." But a number of countervailing considerations should be borne in mind. First, there is the ever present possibility of constitutional amendment, difficult as it might be to marshal the political will and consensus required to exercise this power. Second, though there is often deep disagreement about the content of the rights enshrined in Charters, there is seldom serious disagreement over the legitimacy of the rights actually chosen. Most everyone, including those who preceded us decades or generations ago, would agree that rights to "equality," "freedom of expression (or speech)," "due process" or "fundamental justice" are worthy of inclusion in a Charter. Reasonable people might wish, if we could start with a clean slate, for a slightly different collection of rights than those settled upon, but few would deny the legitimacy of the choice made.[60] There is always a range of morally acceptable Charters, just as there is a range of morally acceptable institutional designs each of which is consonant with the ideals of democracy. Each is fully deserving of respect and allegiance if adopted by the relevant community.[61] Third, though precedent is always to some extent constraining on future decision makers, the usual common law powers of avoidance are always available. These, as noted earlier, come in a variety of forms and with a variety of conditions under which they may be exercised. But under no sensible theory of common law reasoning would a contemporary Supreme Court be completely barred from overruling a constitutional precedent which was confidently believed (by the Court or the political community) to have outlived its usefulness or its moral merit.[62]

① constitutional amendment

② 大型分歧少见 (虽然 right 不范认同)

③ "usual common law power of avoidance?"

The common law approach ... does not suppose that there is some independent value in adhering to past judgments that are by hypothesis wrong, which is to be compared to the value of making the right judgments .... [W]e should think twice about our judgments of right and wrong when they are inconsistent with what has gone before. We adhere to [precedents] not despite their wrongness, but because we might be mistaken to think them wrong. It follows that if, on reflection, we are sufficiently confident that we are right, and if the stakes are high enough, then we can reject even long-standing [precedent.][63]

So if the dead hand of the past constrains us when we have a common law Charter, it will seldom do so in a way which seriously threatens the autonomy of a self-governing people.

Fair enough, Charters can be to some degree flexible. And the extent to which they enable the dead hand of the past to constrain our choices need not overly concern us. But we are still faced with Waldron's question: why opt for a *written* Charter instead of allowing public discourse, legislative debate – and, to some degree perhaps, judicial decisions framed within a common law of moral rights but "free from the obsessive verbalism of a particular written charter"[64] – to serve as our vehicle for rights protection within the public domain? If flexibility is important, then why not go for the most flexible option?

One reason is that Waldron's option really isn't any more flexible – or at least it needn't be so. True, with Charters we are constrained to frame our debates in the abstract terms chosen to express its commitments. Americans, for example, have had to frame their discussions of expressive freedom in terms of "speech" not "expression." And this has on occasion proved somewhat awkward. As Waldron notes, it stretches linguistic propriety to think of flag-burning and nude dancing as forms of speech, whereas it is quite natural to describe these as expressive acts. But there are a number of reasons why this need not be seen as posing a significant problem for the proposal under consideration. First, American Courts seem to have managed, in their own ways, to come to much the same judgments as they would have done had the more general of the two terms been employed. Only those obsessed with the idea that Charters embody fixed points, established (in a way that is simply not possible) by the plain, literal meaning of the abstract terms employed, would reject the idea that it's the moral values behind the linguistic expression chosen that are of paramount importance. In this instance, these are the individual and political values that argue for the

for verbalism

need to recognize expressive freedom, of which freedom of speech is a species. In other words, the words constrain, but they need not do so to the point where the underlying values are ignored or sacrificed. And if, at some point, the constraint becomes unwieldy and too limiting, perhaps even irrational, there is always the option of constitutional amendment. Waldron complains that American debates concerning the death penalty have been unduly and needlessly hampered by the necessity that they be framed in terms of whether the practice is both cruel and unusual. Perhaps this is an unfortunate fact of American legal and political history. But if so, it is one which could have been rectified by a constitutional amendment were the difficulties truly insurmountable. In short, the fact that drafters sometimes chose the wrong language doesn't show that we should abandon Charters altogether. It only shows that a better choice could have been, and perhaps still can be, made. So Charters need not be hampered by the need "to scramble around constructing ... principles out of scraps of some sacred text, in a tendentious exercise of constitutional calligraphy.[65] But once again, we must ask: why even run a slightest risk of this kind of unsatisfactory constitutional practice? Why not just abandon written Charters altogether and leave it to the courts, legislatures, and the general public, to develop a flexible jurisprudence of rights? One important reason is that, notwithstanding the dangers of allowing words to constrain us in undesirable ways, we almost always do need, as Hart noted, to combine the desired flexibility with some measure of fixity. And with Charters we can have an acceptable mix. Charters are, after all, formally entrenched, written constitutional documents which solidify the commitments they represent in ways not always possible with less formal means. They also tend to be very well known among the general population. The average Canadian on the street, for example, might not know many of the intricate details of how the Canadian Charter's provisions have been dealt with by the courts, but he often knows some of this legal history, and he is certainly aware of the Charter's more prominent sections, e.g., sections [1]5 (equality) and 33 (the "override" provision). Unwritten rules used to decide cases are, on the other hand, often more difficult to state and grasp, and are more subject to controversy as to content than those embodied in written texts, particularly formally entrenched, canonical texts. For these reasons, they can also, in some cases, be more easily avoided and finessed.

So there can be a kind of fixity in written Charters that is not always present with unwritten rules. Though there is much truth in this observation, it would be wrong to overstate it. Well established unwritten rules and conventions, particularly those with constitutional status, are often as rigid and entrenched as written rules, if only because their elimination, alteration or re-interpretation typically require widespread changes in traditional attitudes, beliefs and behaviour on the part of a wide range of political actors. And such changes can be as difficult to bring about as a formal constitutional amendment. They can also, given the right set of circumstances, be just as well known as written rules. Canadians, for example, are probably as aware of the unwritten constitutional convention instructing the Governor General to appoint, as Prime Minister, the leader of the party with the most seats in the House of Commons as they are aware of the requirement that no law shall abridge the right to life, liberty and security of the person except in accordance with the principles of fundamental justice.[66] So if the case for Charters rested solely on the potential for a desired degree of fixity, we might agree with Waldron that we are better off without one.

Fortunately, there are other considerations in play. A second, perhaps more important reason for a written Charter, is its symbolic value. This factor, though often cited in passing, is, I believe, under appreciated. Charters help define and reinforce the character of the nation as one publicly committed, in its legal and moral practices, to the fundamental rights and values it includes. These public commitments can, of course, be expressed in other ways, e.g., in the informal pronouncements of public authorities, or in legislative or judicial decisions which are sometimes publicly defended as a means of protecting the relevant rights. But Charters, as entrenched, foundational documents widely known, cited and understood as embodying the nation's fundamental commitments to its constituent members, are a far more powerful means of expressing these commitments than most any other institutional or conventional vehicle. Ask an American for one feature of the American political culture of which she is most proud, and the answer will likely be the Bill of Rights. Ask a Canadian to name the one thing which publicly expresses the identity and commitments of the Canadian people, and the answer will likely be Hockey Night in Canada and the Stanley Cup playoffs. But the second most popular answer will be the Charter of Rights and Freedoms. The latter is seen, not only as embodying Canada's commitment to rights protection, it is seen as expressing, in its commitments to such things as multi-culturalism, group rights, equality before and under the law, and the mediating effect of Section

1 limitations, an identity which distinguishes Canada, as a nation, from its more powerful neighbour to the South.

So Charters represent a potent, publicly accessible means for helping to establish the identity of the community and for solidifying its promise to each of its members – especially its minority members – that their rights count in fundamental ways. But they do so, under the common law, living tree conception, in a way which expresses the requisite degree of humility which underpins clear recognition of Hart's second fundamental need: the need to leave open, for later settlement by an informed (or at least better informed) choice, decisions which could not reasonably have been made in advance without the knowledge, moral and otherwise, which the unanticipated case brings to the fore. A Charter need not be conceived as saying the following:

The Hubristic Message:

"We know *which* moral rights count, *why* they count, and *the many complex ways* they count in the myriad circumstances of politics. Furthermore, we agree to tie our selves and future generations of citizens and legislators to the mast of these commitments. We do this so as to counteract our (and their) natural tendency to become Hobbsean predators consumed with prejudice, greed, blind passion, fear and hysteria, and a willingness and desire to violate the moral rights of fellow minority members."

In fact, the message can be quite the opposite. A Charter conceived as the common law conception suggests, says this:

The Humble Message:

"We do *not* know, with certainty, which moral rights count, why they count, and in what ways and to what degree they count in the myriad circumstances of politics. What we do know, however, is the following. We know that the constellation of moral rights chosen for inclusion in our Charter constitutes, at least for the time being, a *reasonable* answer to the question of which moral rights deserve constitutional protection against government power. We further know that a reasonable answer to the question of why we should choose these and not some other collection of rights is that the chosen set contributes, in ways consistent with (though certainly not determined by) the demands of reason and morality, to the workings of a reasonably free and democratic society which aspires to respect its members as rights bearers deserving of equal concern and respect. We further know that we are somewhat in the dark concerning the many concrete questions of rights which will inevitably, and in unforeseen ways, come to the fore when government power is exercised, principally, though not exclusively, through the introduction of general legislation. Although we do not know in advance what these questions will be or how they should be answered, we commit ourselves to asking them, and to acting on the answers arrived at by the relevant Court(s) in whose hands we agree to place the decision."

VIII THE CASE FOR JUDICIAL REVIEW

Recall that at the outset we distinguished, analytically, among four different questions: (1) What role does a Charter play in a constitutional democracy? (2) Is a Charter (serving that particular role) a good thing to have in a constitutional democracy? (3) Is judicial review on the basis of a Charter a good thing to have in a constitutional democracy? and (4) How should judges go about interpreting and applying Charters in the context of the judicial review of legislation? The Humble Message displays how the common law conception provides a plausible framework within which to answer questions (1) and (2). And if we answer question (3) in the affirmative, we have a promising framework in which to begin developing an answer to question (4).[67] But we have yet to see a convincing reason for answering "yes" to question (3). One can imagine Waldron and his fellow Critics accepting Charters as the inspirational, symbolic, and yet humility-presupposing entities presupposed by the Humble Message. One can even imagine them adding that Charters can serve as a useful moral and conceptual backdrop within which public policy debates take place both inside and outside legislative chambers.[68] Again, there is nothing in the nature of a Charter which demands its enforcement through the practice(s) of judicial review. New Zealand stands as an obvious counter-example to that assertion.[69] In short, there is nothing here to support the practice of judicial review, even if the Charter is treated as a living tree. Are there any good reasons for thinking that advantages would accrue were judges handed the job of dealing with the complex, morally charged issues which arise under the common law conception instead of a legislative body, such as Parliament or Congress? In this final section, I will begin building a case, some of it on familiar ground, for thinking that we might indeed be well served by the judiciary.

In order that we might better appreciate the case for judicial review, we need to return to Waldron and consider a crucial feature of his position which has, to this point, been ignored. Waldron's attack on Charters, judicial review, and the reasons usually offered in their defense, combines a *stark realism,* concerning the prospects of agreement and pre-commitment in the circumstances of politics, with a professed *idealism* concerning the under-appreciated possibilities of majoritarian self-government. The realism comes out, for example, in his rejection of Rawls' attempt to find a basis for agreement in an overlapping consensus of public reason.[70] The idealism comes out in his decision, early in his critique, deliberately to set aside or bracket many of the unattractive features of majoritarian rule to which Advocates tend to draw our attention, and which serve as central elements in their case for Charters and judicial review. Advocates are fond of pointing out, for example, that majorities can often, in pursuit of self-interest, either ignore or undervalue the competing interests and rights of stable and transient minorities, and that they are easily swayed by factors like fear, insecurity, bias and prejudice, and the pernicious effects of campaign advertising dollars. They are also fond of noting that political decision making in most every constitutional democracy in existence today often amounts to nothing more than an exercise of pure partisan politics. Waldron deliberately brackets such factors in developing his argument in favour of majoritarian decision-making in order to counteract the undeniable tendency in much legal and jurisprudential scholarship to denigrate politics and legislative assemblies on the one hand and sanctify judicial reasoning and courts on the other. The former are often characterized as nothing more than a forum for the unprincipled clash of "deal-making, logrolling, interest-pandering, pork-barrelling, horse-trading, and Arrovian cycling – as anything, indeed, except principled political decision-making,"[71] while the latter is sanctified as the "forum of principle," the domain of cool, rational, objective, and impartial deliberation where reason rules and all are treated with the dignity and respect owed the holders of rights. Bias in favour of Courts, and hence Charters is, he thinks, the inevitable result, together with skewed jurisprudential theories and bad political philosophy. In order to counteract this imbalance in perspective, Waldron asks us to imagine what could be said in favour of politics and legislatures were they to *function well,* that is, were they to exemplify the ideals expressed by early modem democrats like Locke and Rousseau. We are asked to imagine a legislature, not as the forum of pork barrel politics but as a forum in which free and equal people (or their representatives) come together, in common cause and the spirit of reciprocity, and bearing in mind the competing, contentious demands of justice and equality, to decide how they are to be governed in the circumstances of politics.

What I want to do is apply the canon of symmetry in the opposite direction. I want to ask: "What would it be like to develop a rosy picture of legislatures and their structures and processes that matched in its normativity and perhaps its naivety, the picture of courts – 'the forum of principle' ... etc. – that we present in the more elevated moments of our constitutional jurisprudence?"[72]

Viewed in this light, he thinks, we'll begin to see not only the possibilities of democratic politics, but the hubris and unwarranted optimism involved in Charters and the insult to democracy and moral autonomy they represent.

So there purports to be both an element of realism and an element of idealism in Waldron's approach. He refuses to allow Advocates to rest their case for institutional design on unwarranted assumptions concerning the possibilities of rational agreement and pre-commitment and the ability of courts, in the forum of principle, to hold us to these commitments. Here he stresses the stark reality of the circumstances of politics, the fact that it's disagreement all the way down. But when it comes to considering the possibilities of majoritarian politics as a means of dealing with these very same circumstances, we are asked to park our cynicism at the door and share, at least for the time being, in a kind of idealism. But one can't help but ask: is this a sound basis for addressing questions of basic institutional design? Should the same element of realism not apply to both sides of the argument? There is perhaps nothing amiss in considering how things might be in an ideal setting, but when the hard questions of institutional design are addressed, we had better re-introduce a good measure of realism into the mixture. And what do we find when we re-introduce these elements of realism? We discover, not only a serious difficulty in Waldron's own argument in favour of majoritarian decision-making, we also find a number of factors which add up to a pretty strong case for thinking that Charters may well be good things to have, despite Waldron's welcome warnings about not pushing that case too far.

Let's begin with the serious difficulty. As noted above, Waldron takes Rawls and others to task for pre-supposing a seemingly non-existent consensus of judgments on fundamental questions of justice and equality. Here we are urged to be realistic in light of the circumstances of politics. But as many commentators have pointed out, the deep disagreements of which Waldron's arguments make such heavy weather apply no less to the principles underlying his own case for majoritarian solutions. As a result, Waldron has given us no convincing reason to prefer *his* solution to the circumstances of politics over those offered by Advocates like Rawls, Dworkin and Freeman. We might now add to that list the solution being proposed here: the common law conception combined with some form of judicial review. Tom Christiano, David Estlund and Aileen Kavanagh each press this point home by noting the internal inconsistency which seems to underlie Waldron's argument in favour of majoritarian solutions. As we have seen, Waldron's critique of the Advocates' position rests on the key premise that there is "disagreement all the way down." From this, we are told, it follows that we cannot agree on fixed points of pre-commitment which enable us to avoid the many objections to which Charters and judicial review are said to be susceptible. It further follows, according to Waldron, that we have no plausible option but to allow those with a stake in decisions about rights a continuous say in their interpretation and application. We must, that is, affirm the fundamental "right of rights," to participate in decisions affecting ones salient interests. And this we are further told, rules out Charters and judicial review. Yet if disagreement truly does go all the way down, then there is nothing in Waldron's account which rules out reasonable disagreement about "the legitimacy of the collective decision-procedures themselves in addition to the disagreement that animates the call for those procedures."[73]

Contrary to Waldron's claim that the right of participation demands that those whose fundamental interests are directly at stake should always be the ones to make the decisions affecting those interests, the opposing sentiment can enjoy considerable plausibility. Natural justice and the desire for sound, balanced decision-making often combine to condemn situations in which individuals – reasonable and well intentioned as they might be – are permitted to serve as judge of their own cause. In many such situations, it is thought quite appropriate to assign the task of decision-making to persons or institutions whose interests are *not* directly at stake. Independent arbitrators and judges are often appealed to in situations of this kind. And it is arguable that this is just what we have here. There is considerable plausibility in the suggestion that we should turn to judges to help us avoid the injustice and lack of wisdom of permitting unfettered stable or transient majorities to determine whether the government acts they support unjustifiably infringe important minority interests and rights, contestable as these might be. We do not denigrate the right of participation if we recognize that the most conscientious, reasonable and well intentioned members of majorities, concerned to assign fair weight to the contestable interests and rights of their fellow minority members, will sometimes fail, in light of the burdens of judgment, to achieve the desired balance. In light of this fact, they might reasonably support a practice which allows judges to re-evaluate their decisions in light of an evolving understanding of constitutionally recognized moral rights.[74] It would be foolish, however, to push this point too far, as Critical Theorists of all stripes would no doubt insist. After all, judges are members of society too, and they are often, perhaps usually, members of the very majority whose interests are at stake. Yet even so, the requirement that judgments be publicly defended in light of constitutional principle, can sometimes work against any political biases to which judges might be subject.[75]

So Waldron must surely admit that the reasonable disagreement he finds inherent in the circumstances of politics extends to his right of participation and the majoritarian practices he defends by invoking that right. Reasonable disagreement is to be found here too, leaving us, it seems, in a bit of a quandary. How are we to choose among the possible modes of decision-making open to us without begging the question? If the response is that we can dissolve the paradox by utilizing "higher order procedures that give everyone an equal say," then Waldron seems threatened by an infinite regress.[76] Why should we assume that there will be no reasonable disagreement about this higher-order procedure, that no one will dispute the claim that the higher order decision-procedure must be majoritarian?[77] Indeed, the fact that there are many Advocates who put forward reasonable arguments in favour of a system incorporating Charters and judicial review suggests that we would be ill advised to make this assumption. Yet if there is reasonable disagreement even at this very elementary stage – which seems inevitable if disagreement truly does go all the way down – then how are we, ultimately, to decide? By fiat? In virtue of traditional practice? By an argument which suggests that we have to decide some way or other, and so it might just as well be by a procedure that gives everyone an equal say? By way of a philosophical argument which has, as its conclusion, the one which Waldron seeks to defend? But of course none of these strategies will work for Waldron. If one of these options is pursued, then sheer consistency (and fairness, if we could ever agree on what that means!) entail that it must be open to the Advocates as well. If unbridled majoritarianism is to be grounded in one of these ways, despite reasonable disagreement about its soundness as a foundational principle, then there is nothing to disqualify others from positing their preferred starting points, despite the acknowledged fact of reasonable disagreement. There is nothing to prevent them from asserting, as their starting point, a "constitutional conception of democracy" which "takes the defining aim of democracy to be a different one: that collective decisions be made by political institutions whose structure, composition, and practices treat all members of the community, as individuals, with equal concern and respect.... Democracy means government subject to conditions – we might call these 'democratic' conditions – of equal status for all citizens."[78] And there is nothing to rule out judges as a good choice for the task of helping to ensure that those particular conditions are met.

Waldron seems to have landed himself in a fix somewhat reminiscent of the one in which Descartes finds himself at the end of the first Mediation. Having pursued his method of doubt – which bars any proposition with respect to which there is any ground for doubt, however implausible that ground might be – to the point where even the rules of reason and logic must be rejected, Descartes turns around, in Mediation Two, and attempts to reason himself out of his predicament. He fashions arguments for the existence of a God whose benevolence guarantees Descartes' clear and distinct perceptions, including his perceptions of the rules of reason and logic. In other words, he uses the very methods – logic and reason – he is attempting to validate. But as Arnauld famously pointed out, this strategy is doomed from the beginning. The resulting circle robs Descartes' project of its foundation and its promised legitimacy. The moral of Descartes' story is that one cannot reject everything about which some meager ground of doubt can be entertained, including the rules of reason and logic, and then try to *reason* oneself out of this fix. Something must be presupposed, something must be given before we can begin to reason about the world and what we can know of it. At the very least, we must accept, as a reasonable starting point, propositions about which there are logically possible grounds for doubt. And this is so even if an objector could reasonably

立法者的民主更多时候是少数服从多数，即使大家都承认有disagreement
多数人的一方可以颁布法律

judge 和 Charter 的政原则却保证了 individual 都被平等对待，没有的基 treated equally

本权力会得不到中联

disagree with ones starting point(s). An analogous point seems appropriate in response to Waldron's valiant attempt to base his theory of institutional design on a solid foundation, one which is somehow invulnerable to the threat of reasonable dissensus upon which all other positions are said to founder? In Descartes' case, everything was subject to doubt, and nothing, as a result, could be proved beyond all doubt; this was the standard Descartes had imposed upon himself and by which he attempted, miserably, to adhere. In Waldron's case, everything in politics is subject to reasonable disagreement, and nothing, as a result, can be established which meets the no-reasonable-disagreement criterion, the standard which Waldron has set for himself and others, and which cannot possibly be met. In short, Waldron's theory falls victim to his own standard of acceptable argument and institutional design. If, in response, he is willing, at some level, to privilege the supposed, but undeniably disputed, virtues of unadulterated majority rule, then he is in no position to reject similar attempts by Advocates, who embrace Charters and their interpretation and enforcement via judicial review, on the ground that they all founder on the rock of reasonable dissensus.[79]

So the element of realism at play in Waldron's critique seems to threaten the very foundation upon which he attempts to establish his own position. But the element of idealism at work is no less troublesome. Waldron is no doubt correct that philosophers tend to glamorize judging and denigrate ordinary politics. And he is certainly right that our theories should be sensitive to this tendency. But in attempting to correct the imbalance, he seems to have rigged the debate in the opposite direction. Waldron does us a great service in stressing both the circumstances of politics and the unreasonableness of the ideal pictures often painted of judges and their capacity to exemplify the ideals of Hercules. He also does a marvelous job reminding us of the possibilities contemplated by the democratic ideals associated with majoritarian decision-making. But in attempting to restore reality to the judicial side of the equation and re-institute the "dignity of legislation" by deliberately stressing the positive potential of the legislative process, he has left out many of the not-so-desirable features of the latter, features with which the former might be well suited to deal. He has, in short, ignored important aspects of the circumstances of politics, over and above the fact of reasonable disagreement, and he has conveniently underplayed the ability of the courts to deal with those aspects effectively. Yet all those troublesome, unflattering elements of everyday politics which

Waldron has us eliminate from the picture, so as to develop a more flattering picture of the possibilities of legislative politics and the workings of democracy, are as much a part of the circumstances of politics as the dissensus he cautions us not to forget. Let's put them back into the picture and see what results. Let's see what results from a comparison between judging and legislating in which these elements are kept clearly in view.

We can begin by agreeing with Waldron that judges are not Platonic Kings. They aren't smarter than the rest of us, nor do they possess a degree of moral insight and sophistication surpassing that of the average citizen or legislator. So we must completely agree that any attempt to justify a preference for judicial review over legislative supremacy premised on these idealistic assumptions is doomed from the start. If the role of the courts were simply to substitute, *under identical conditions of deliberation,* the judgments of a few heads (the court's) for those of a greater number of heads (the legislature), then there is no reason to think that the results would be any better. Indeed, if we accept Condorcet's jury theorem and Aristotle's arguments concerning the "wisdom of the multitudes" there is every reason to think, again as Waldron rightly points out, that we would probably end up with far worse results.[80] But all this rests on the key assumption that the contexts of decision are, in all relevant respects, identical with one another. But this is far from being true. For instance, there is the familiar point that judges are relatively insulated from the pressures to which legislators are inevitably subject.

A host of practical considerations are relevant, and many of these may argue forcefully for allowing an elected legislature itself to decide on the moral limits of its power. But other considerations argue in the opposite direction, including the fact that legislators are vulnerable to political pressures of manifold kinds, both financial and political, so that a legislature is not the safest vehicle for protecting rights of politically unpopular groups.[81]

True, things would be different if, when votes are cast, the following were the case: (a) members of legislative assemblies could be counted on to bear in mind the constraints of justice and equality and not just vote in terms of the special interests or wishes of their constituents; (b) members also continued to bear in mind the 'general good' of the wider community when deciding whether to support a bill which disfavours the interests or wishes of their own constituents; (c) members were not concerned to curry favour with special interest groups upon whose support, financial or otherwise, their re-election depends; (d) members had the courage, sometimes, to break the bonds of party discipline when, in the member's best judgment, the party's measure is for some reason unjust or in violation of some other important moral right;[82] (e) members were willing to take a stand upon an issue of principle upon which, in the member's best judgment, her constituents or backers are simply mistaken, perhaps because they have not thought through the issues in sufficient depth and are relying instead on "knee-jerk" reactions;[83] (f) members were willing to stand up for the interests of oppressed minorities even when prejudice, self-interest, or ignorance have led constituents to oppose a measure which protects the fundamental interests and rights (on any reasonable conception of those rights) of some minority group;[84] and so on. Under these ideal conditions of deliberation, there is considerable power in Waldron's arguments that the people, through the voice of their representatives, should be the ones to settle together, through majority vote, the hard questions of justice and equality which touch them all and upon which reasonable people of good faith and integrity disagree. But this is to ignore the wider circumstances of politics which Waldron's arguments have conveniently bracketed. Once those circumstances are re-introduced, the case for Charters of Rights coupled with some form of judicial review, begins to emerge with strength.

So one crucial element of the circumstances of politics (bracketed by Waldron in his attempt to resurrect the "dignity of legislation") is that judges are largely removed from the financial and political pressures which often bias legislative members toward decisions favouring powerful majority opinion (however misguided) or toward opinions sanctioned by powerful elites. It would of course be unwise to discount entirely the courage sometimes exhibited by legislative members, just as it would be unwise to ignore the powerful, all-too human desires for conformity and approval which no doubt inclines many judges toward maintaining the status quo. It would also be foolish to ignore the views of those Critics who note the "elite" social backgrounds from which judges tend to be drawn. All this must be borne in mind, and factored into decisions about the concrete details of how courts operate[85] and how judges are selected. And we should no doubt bear such factors in mind when addressing equally important questions about how to correct what many now see as a "democratic deficit" in many modern constitutional democracies. Canada's Prime Minister has, for example,

法官不受 政治权力斗争的影响 （不要工资）

called for changes to legislative practices which will, he thinks, provide back-bench MPs with greater ability to contribute meaningfully to the drafting of legislation and the freedom to break party discipline. There has also been much talk of introducing some form of proportional representation to offset the perils of the first-past-the-post system which has, in contemporary Canada, resulted in the inability of minority points of view to have much influence on the course of government policy. And there are the calls for changes to the rules governing campaign financing, access by marginal parties to public air time during election campaigns and so on. Such changes may well have the effect of raising the level of legislative (and public) debate. But they may equally have the opposite effect. For instance, we must weigh against the virtue of allowing members of the legislative majority to vote against government policy, the fact that there is strength in numbers, especially when a government's decision on a controversial, heated topic like the legal recognition of same-sex marriages, meets with significant resistance within the general population. A legislative member, no longer able to cite the imperatives of party discipline to escape the accountability which inevitably accompanies the liberty to vote one's own conscience, might well feel more pressured to fall in line with the misguided views of constituents. So the questions of institutional design are numerous and complex, and the answers uncertain, difficult, and significantly dependent on empirical questions it is beyond my abilities to address here. But, at the end of the day, when all had been said and done, were I forced to bet on which group, judges or legislators, is more likely to stand up to the relevant political forces at play in deciding the contentious issues surrounding Charter rights, my money would be on the judges.

Let's return now to the common law conception and to Hart's thoughts on the choices we face when attempting to implement the rule of law. As we saw earlier, we face two competing needs whenever we contemplate the possible forms of legal regulation. On the one hand, there is the need for general rules which can be applied, at point of application, without fresh judgments about relevant background considerations; these considerations are now commonly referred to as "dependent reasons.[86] On the other hand, there is the need to leave room, at point of application, for further consideration of dependent reasons. This is largely because unforeseen situations will inevitably arise, and these will bring into relief issues and questions which could not possibly have been appreciated and intelligently settled in advance.

Hart goes on to suggest that there are a variety of techniques we can use to find an acceptable balance between these two fundamental needs. These include the employment, in drafting general legislation, of "open-textured" terms like "fair" and "reasonable." Yet another technique, one which Hart thought inevitable, is the exercise of discretion by judges. Now one reply which could be made to Hart's suggestions is that it is neither desirable nor necessary that decisions in hard cases generally be left to judges. Whenever we do so, we face many of the difficulties cited by the Critics in their case against Charters: judges are not philosopher kings; decisions about what our rules should be should always rest with the people, or with their elected, and accountable representatives, and so on. In light of such concerns, one might urge an approach embodied in the French law of 16–24 August, 1790, title 2, article 12, which (in rough translation) reads: "Courts will address themselves to the legislature every time they believe it necessary to interpret a law," or in the French Constitution of 1790, article 256, which (again in very rough translation) reads: "When, after the Supreme Court of Appeal has quashed the decision of a lower court, a second decision on the merits is appealed on the same grounds, the issue cannot be discussed in the Supreme Court on Appeal until it has been submitted to the legislature, which enacts a law binding on the Supreme Court of Appeal." Further appeal to the enacting body is always a logical possibility to deal with any hard case which arises when laws are applied to concrete situations. There is obviously very good reason, however, why no contemporary system (of which I am aware) actually pursues this model in dealing generally with cases in which constitutional rights or values are not at stake. Hard cases calling for discretion are so numerous, and complex in their particularity, that an already over-loaded legislature would likely be swamped were it to assume the responsibility to decide all such cases. This is one very good reason why we opt for a division of labour and assign judges the task of dealing with the unforeseeable difficulties which come to the fore in typical hard cases.[87] But if this is true in cases where no constitutional right is at stake, why should we think things are different when the hard case does involve an unforeseen potential violation of some such right?

One reason might be the limited range and heightened significance of a typical Charter challenge. What is at stake here is not just the wisdom of government action in light garden variety, dependent reasons, but a much more limited range of *constitutional* rights and values of deep significance, and more often than not, political and moral

如果立法机关 elected，怎么保证立法的公正性？立法人应该对法的哲学理论有充分的研究 which the most of citizens don't have；这就是为什么中国立法权在"judge"手上而非普通市民或在公民手上

disagreement. It would be completely unreasonable were we to send back every hard case to the legislature, but less so if we restricted ourselves to cases involving constitutional norms. Surely, it might be said, legislatures can find the time to deal with *these* issues. I'm not so sure, however. The number of cases in which, e.g., the Canadian Charter figures is enormous. These include, not only those landmark decisions which make the headlines and generate all the controversy. They also include, in far greater numbers, all those cases in which judges, carefully and deliberately, and without much fanfare, interpret the Charter, and the rules and precedents developed by the Courts in deciding Charter conflicts to decide the particular case before them. Were all these cases, with their complex array of particular facts and circumstances, and in which some degree of moral controversy is *always* possible, returned to the legislature for decision, I suspect that the wheels of government truly would grind to a halt.

Yet another relevant consideration is the question whether legislatures really are in a position to display the same degree of competence as the Courts in deciding hard Charter cases. Here we return, one final time, to an earlier point: that if the decisional contexts are identical, there is little reason to prefer the decisions of a few unrepresentative and [un]accountable heads to those arrived at by a great many accountable heads who are able to represent, in their joint deliberations, the full range of reasonable views about the relevant considerations at stake in a Charter case. But are the decisional contexts the same? I doubt it. Setting aside, for the sake of argument, the important points made earlier about the powerful forces working against responsible decision-making by legislators (these are forces to which judges are largely immune thanks to the doctrine of judicial independence), we should bear in mind the following points. Legislatures, of practical necessity, must utilize the blunt instrument of *general legislation.* Whatever solution a legislature were to propose, it would likely meet with the same fate as the original legislation. That is, it would find its way back to the legislature where a still further attempt to map out, in canonical general terms, a solution to the complex array of questions the Charter challenge brought to the fore would have to be made. It is not easy to imagine intelligible, general legislation which could somehow sensibly cover the variety of different kinds of particular cases and issues which have been decided under the equality provision of the Canadian Charter, or the due process clause of the U.S. Bill of Rights. One rightfully celebrated virtue of the common law is its ability, owing to its inherent adaptability

中国对此 *违数直理* *舆论影响*

因： *受行政侵害走上刑引线在哲法院中*

精英的 *怎样得林协商得到协议* *与英美相应的问题* *即精英制* *（如果抛弃精英）* *振而轻视英美，这些问题的本性是问公平性而非限度*

有太多复杂的case，组成并被Chater 解释，如果抛弃Chater 和法官，这些全交给 legislature，可能会误于处理

宪政，不可能抛弃精英

politics and law committee 包括司法 非elected elite

The chinese people's congress 合宪性审查 elected

and facility for incremental change via case by case reasoning, to escape these often troublesome features of statutory regimes. Precedents do not have the status of fixed canonical texts, nor do they represent attempts to settle issues once and for all by way of general rules whose exceptions are only those included within the rules themselves. On the contrary, a precedent is typically said to stand only for the actual decision made on the concrete issue(s) raised, and is recognized as provisional and revisable in light of developing case law and the new cases brought to our attention. Through such incremental, piece by piece changes, what often emerges, over time, is a body of law which, Bentham's hostility notwithstanding, exemplifies a level of practical reasonableness which statutory regimes struggle to achieve. This, the life blood of the common law, is something which the common law conception of Charters both allows and celebrates at the level of constitutional practice. It is also something which judges are perhaps better trained than legislators to embody.

Obviously, on any theory of rights, decisions about rights are better if they are based on more rather than less information about a variety of facts. But I know of no reason why a legislator is more likely to have accurate beliefs about the sort of fact that, under any plausible conception of rights, would be relevant in determining what people's rights are. On any plausible theory of rights, moreover, *questions of speculative consistency* – questions that test a theory of rights by imagining circumstances in which that theory would produce unacceptable results – are likely to be of importance in an argument about particular rights, because no claim of right is sound if it cannot stand the test of hypothetical counter-example. But the technique of examining a claim of right for speculative consistency is a technique far more developed in judges than in legislators or in the bulk of the citizens who elect legislators.[88]

Furthermore, there is reason to think, contra Waldron's skepticism about 'results-driven' tests, that allowing courts a prominent role in shaping Charter norms through the process of case-by-case development of a common law of moral rights, may well result, not only in better decisions, but in raising the level of public debate. "Even when the debate is illuminating ... the majoritarian process encourages compromises that may subordinate important issues of principle. Constitutional cases, by contrast, can and do provide a widespread public discussion that focuses on political morality."[89]

It would be foolish to push these last points too far. With Dworkin, "I put the suggestion that judicial review may provide a superior kind of ... deliberation about [Charter] issues tentatively, as a possibility, because [like him] I do not believe that we have enough information for much confidence either way."[90] But perhaps enough has been said here to warrant one final tentative conclusion: We may, in the end, be very well served by a Charter understood as the common law model supposes, and developed and applied by judges in partnership with other government bodies."[91] If we reject the view of Charters as confident, hubristic attempts to establish (illusory) fixed points of agreement and pre-commitment, and view them instead as the living trees whose roots are fixed (by precedent and the terms chosen to express the Charter's moral commitments) but whose branches can develop over time through a developing common law jurisprudence of moral rights, we stand a better chance of satisfying both of Hart's two fundamental needs, and of reconciling Charters with our self-image as self-governing, autonomous rights holders who, alas, don't have all the answers.

NOTES

An earlier version of this paper was presented at the 2004 Analytic Legal Philosophy Conference at New York University Law School. I wish to thank the participants of that conference for their many helpful comments and suggestions.

1 Henceforth, I will refer to these latter individuals as "the Advocates," with the understanding that this class of defenders includes a range of authors whose arguments for Charters are not all the same. Advocates within the philosophical literature include Dworkin, Rawls and Samuel Freeman. Those, like Waldron, who argue against practices of judicial review under Charters will be referred to as "the Critics," with the same understanding applying.

2 Jeremy Waldron, *Law and Disagreement* (Oxford: Oxford University Press, 1999) at 102.

3 Ibid. at 295.

4 This indictment extends to Waldron's own theory. The significance of this fact will be addressed below in Section VIII.

5 In *Political Liberalism* (New York: Columbia University Press, 1996), Rawls writes that "the idea of reasonable disagreement involves an account of the sources, or causes, of disagreement between reasonable persons so defined. These sources I refer to as the burdens of judgment

.... [They are] the many hazards involved in the correct (and conscientious) exercise of our powers of reason and judgment in the ordinary
course of political life" (55–56). The burdens of judgment include things
like conflicting evidence, disagreements about the proper weighting of
evidence, vague and indeterminate concepts and conceptions, differences
in individual backgrounds that influence individual interpretation of
evidence, and so on. These burdens can result in different judgments
based on the same "evidence," differing judgments which are nevertheless "compatible with those judging being fully reasonable" (58).

6 Charters can, of course, exist alongside other forms of government. But
we will restrict ourselves to constitutional democracies such as one finds
in Canada, the US, New Zealand, and the UK. I include the UK even
though it is often said to contain no written constitution and Parliament
is often said to be constitutionally unlimited. But it is clear that the UK
has long recognized constitutional limits on Parliament; some of these are
statutory in origin, while others have emerged as part of the common law
or are matters of constitutional convention.

7 It is usually assumed that the form of judicial review under discussion is
the strong American form. But there are alternatives. For example, in
New Zealand courts rule on the constitutionality of legislation even
though they are barred from striking it down. New Zealand Bill of Rights
Act 1990, section 4 states: "No court shall, in relation to any enactment
(whether passed or made before or after the commencement of this Bill of
Rights), – (a) [h]old any provision of the enactment to be impliedly
repealed or revoked, or to be in any way invalid or ineffective; or (b)
[d]ecline to apply any provision of the enactment – by reason only that
the provision is inconsistent with any provision of this Bill of Rights."
Furthermore, section 7 provides for the Attorney-General to intervene in
legislative debate to warn of a possible infringement of the Bill of Rights.
"Where any Bill is introduced into the House of Representatives, the
Attorney-General shall, (a) [i]n the case of a Government Bill, on the
introduction of that Bill; or (b) [i]n any other case, as soon as practicable
after the introduction of the Bill, bring to the attention of the House of
Representatives any provision in the Bill that appears to be inconsistent
with any of the rights and freedoms contained in this Bill of Rights." (I
owe these references to a paper ("Some Models of Dialogue between
Judges and Legislators") delivered by Waldron at a conference at the
University of Western Ontario in September of 2003. In Canada, the legislative override included in Section 33 of *The Constitution Act* empowers
Parliament or a provincial legislature to introduce, for a period of time
and subject to renewal every five years, legislation which it acknowl-

edges either infringes a right enshrined in the *Charter of Rights and Freedoms*, or is inconsistent with a judicial ruling – in the view of the legislature, an incorrect ruling – on what that right means or entails for legal purposes.

8 See John Rawls, *A Theory of Justice* (Cambridge, MA: Harvard University Press, 1971), *Political Liberalism* (New York: Columbia University Press, 1993); Ronald Dworkin, *Taking Rights Seriously* (London: Duckworth, 1977), *A Matter of Principle* (Cambridge, MA: Harvard University Press, 1985), *Law's Empire* (Cambridge, MA: Harvard University Press, 1986), *A Bill of Rights for Britain* (London: Chatto and Windrus, 1990), *Freedom's Law: The Moral Reading of the American Constitution* (Cambridge, MA: Harvard University Press, 1996); Samuel Freeman, "Constitutional Democracy and the Legitimacy of Judicial Review" (1990) 9 L. & Phil. 9.

9 It is seldom noted that the real question in play is not whether we should, as responsible agents, be making our own decisions on the relevant matters, or assigning this task to judges. In a representative democracy, the question is *to whom* the task of deciding should be assigned: judges or elected representatives.

10 *Law and Disagreement, supra* note 2 at 239.

11 Ibid. at 221.

12 Ibid. at 221–22.

13 Ibid. at 222.

14 Ibid. at 15. The sting of this insult was experienced by the many Americans who were utterly dismayed by the U.S. Supreme Court's decision in *Bush v. Gore.*

15 Few philosophers endorse this objection; Waldron certainly does not. It is, however, often encountered in popular discourse and in some philosophical circles.

16 *Law and Disagreement, supra* note 2 at 244.

17 Ibid. at 268. 1 am going to run the risk of having Waldron think me an idiot by suggesting later that there is considerable truth in the Ulysses metaphor, despite deep disagreements about many of the concrete implications of Charter rights. Perhaps he will want to say that this only goes to show that there is considerable truth in the charge that Waluchow really is an idiot.

18 *Freedom's Law, supra* note 8 at 34.

19 *Law and Disagreement, supra* note 2 at 294.

20 Ibid. at 295.

21 Dworkin, *Freedom's Law, supra* note 8 at 345, cited by Waldron in *Law and Disagreement, supra* note 2 at 289.

22 *Law and Disagreement, supra* note 2 at 290.

23 Ibid.

24 Ibid.

25 Ibid. at 220.

26 Ibid.

27 Ibid. at 221.

28 See, for example, Joseph Raz, "Disagreement in Politics" (1998) 43 Am. J. Juris.; Thomas Christiano, "Waldron on *Law and Disagreement*" in (2000) 19 L. & Phil. 513; David Estlund, "Waldron on *Law and Disagreement*" (2000) 99:1 Phil. Stud. 111; and Aileen Kavanagh, "Participation and Judicial Review: A Reply to Waldron" (2003) 22 L. & Phil. 451.

29 See Jed Rubenfeld, "Legitimacy and Interpretation" in Larry Alexander, ed., *Constitutionalism: Philosophical Foundations* (Cambridge: Cambridge University Press, 1998) at 194.

30 Think, for example, of a religious conversion, or how radical youths often turn out to be the among the most committed middle aged conservatives.

31 One might, for example, attempt to undermine the claim of radical dissensus. Alternatively, one might question the Hobbsean predator element of Waldron's picture of Charters. Our concern to protect minorities from majority excesses need not be premised on such an unflattering picture of ourselves and the burdens of judgment and action under which we operate in public life. This is a point to which we will return in the final section.

32 *Edwards v. A.-G. Canada*, [1930] AC 124.

33 See, e.g., *A.-G. Que. v. Blaikie*, [1979] 2 SCR 1016, 1029 (language rights); *A.-G. B.C. v. Canada Trust Co.*, [1980] 2 SCR 466, 478 (powers of taxation); *Law Society of Upper Canada v. Shapinker*, [1984] 1 SCR 357, 365 (mobility rights). The idea of the constitution as a "living tree" is, of course, not unique to Canadian legal practice. Elsewhere the idea is expressed in theories which speak of a constitution as a "living thing" or as capable of "organic growth." For further exploration of the notion of a constitution as a living entity, see Aileen Kavanagh, "The Idea of a Living Constitution" (2003) 16 Can. J. L. & Juris. 55; Laurence Sager, "The Incorrigible Constitution" (1990) 65 N.Y.U.L. Rev. 893; and William Rehnquist, "The Notion of a Living Constitution" (1976) 54 Texas L. Rev. 693.

34 Edwards, *supra* note 32 at 136.

35 I say 'hypothetical' because Hart's argument in no way rests on the historical claim that pre-legal societies ever did exist. Pre-legal society serves as an analytical device, not an historical reality.

36 One of the most thoughtful and illuminating discussions of this element of Hart's thinking is found in Waldron's "All We Like Sheep" (1999) 12 Can. J. L. & Juris. 169.

37 Consider scenarios involving the use of rapidly changing technologies like the Internet. Or scenarios in which significant, individuating factors are likely to be present in most every case arising under a rule, e.g., situations involving the use of force in warding off perceived threats to person and property.

38 By "legislators" I mean anyone charged with the responsibility of creating or developing a legal norm. This can include members of legislative assemblies, administrative bodies, or a court called upon to decide a case whose precedent-setting ratio decidendi might function as a legal norm.

39 The most developed and insightful analysis of this feature of general rules is Fred Schauer's *Playing by the Rules* (Oxford: Clarendon Press, 1991).

40 This issue, and what it entails for our understanding of the nature of law, is one which has held centre stage in contemporary disputes among Inclusive and Exclusive Positivists.

41 Schauer, *supra* note 39 at 174. According to Schauer, all we need for a legal system to exist are "jurisdictional rules," which empower authoritative decision-making by individuals who may or may not be bound (completely or to some degree) to decide according to pre-established legal rules. Weber's "qadi legal system" is a conceptual possibility. Cf. Raz's related suggestion that only norm-applying institutions are necessary for law.

42 *The Concept of Law,* 2nd ed. (Oxford: Clarendon Press, 1994) at 130–31.

43 See "On Hart's Way Out" (1998) 4 Legal Theory 46 and "Law, Morality, and the Guidance of Conduct" (2000) 6 Legal Theory 127.

44 *Riggs v. Palmer* 115 N.Y. 506, 22 NE 188 (1889).

45 Again, think of *Riggs,* as well as the vast array of legal norms which make use of terms like "reasonable," "fair" and so on.

46 A widespread change in the understanding of a moral value can be described as a change in social circumstances. By the latter phrase I mean to exclude that kind of change. I have in mind factors like technological development, changes in the basic structure of the work place or the family unit, and so on.

47 Many Canadian courts have held that the opposite-sex requirement for civil marriage violates the equality guarantee enshrined in s. 15(1) of the *Charter*. As a result, same-sex marriages have generally come to be viewed as legal and have been regularly taking place in British Columbia, Ontario, Quebec, the Yukon, Manitoba, Nova Scotia and Saskatchewan. See *EGALE Canada Inc. v. Canada (Attorney General)* (2003), 225 DLR (4th) 472, 2003 BCCA 251; *Halpern v. Canada (Attorney General)* (2003), 65 OR

(3d) 161 (CA); and *Hendricks v. Quebec (Procureur général)*, [2002] RJQ 2506 (Sup. Ct.); *Dunbar v. Yukon*, [2004] YJ No. 61 (QL), 2004 YKSC 54, *Vogel v. Canada (Attorney General)*, [2004] M.J. No. 418 (QL) (Q.B.), *Boutilier v. Nova Scotia (Attorney General)*, [2004] NSJ No. 357 (QL) (SC), and *N.W. v. Canada (Attorney General)*, [2004] SJ No. 669 (QL), 2004 SKQB 434. In each of those instances, the Attorney General of Canada conceded that the common law definition of marriage was inconsistent with s. 15(1) of the *Charter* and was not justifiable under s. 1, and publicly adopted the position that the opposite-sex requirement for marriage was unconstitutional. In its recent *Reference re Same-Sex Marriage,* the Supreme Court of Canada declined to rule on the constitutionality of the opposite-sex requirement, ruling that the burden of establishing the requirements of marriage in Canada lies, at present, on the shoulders of Parliament – subject, of course, to Charter review should a test case later be brought to the Court for decision. See *Reference re Same-Sex Marriage* (2004) SCC 79.

48 And because of this they also threaten the ideals of democracy by artificially constraining "the people now" by entrenching decisions taken by "the people then."

49 *Law and Disagreement, supra* note 2 at 221.

50 Schauer, *supra* note 39 at 179.

51 *The Concept of Law,* 2nd ed. (Oxford: Clarendon Press, 1994) at 135.

52 See A.W.B. Simpson, "The Common Law and Legal Theory" in A.W.B. Simpson, ed., *Oxford Essays in Jurisprudence,* 2nd series (Oxford: Clarendon Press, 1973) at 77. Simpson's major criticism is that it is wrong to view the common law as comprised of highly adaptable *rules,* a view to which, he thinks, Hart is led owing to his commitment to positivist legal theory and "the model of rules."

53 Many who decry the history of recent Canadian Supreme Court's decisions assert that the Courts have employed the Charter to rationalize what is, in reality, a naked "discretionary power grab." This sort of complaint is often accompanied by appeal to many of the objections canvassed in Section II above: e.g., the threat of moral nihilism and the dangers inherent in rule by judicial elites putting themselves forward as Philosopher Kings. Dworkin's theory of constitutional law has met with many similar objections, e.g., that his "moral reading" grants judges unbridled power to decide constitutional decisions according to their own moral lights, a power perhaps safe in the hands of Hercules, but dangerous in the hands of his lesser acolytes. Yet these criticisms either ignore or seriously underplay the dimension of "fit" in Dworkin's account. See, for example, *A Matter of Principle* (Cambridge, MA: Harvard

University Press, 1985) where Dworkin writes: "[C]onstitutional interpretation is disciplined, under the moral reading, by the requirement of constitutional *integrity* ... Judges may not read their own convictions into the Constitution. They may not read the abstract moral clauses as expressing any particular moral judgment, no matter how much that judgment appeals to them, unless they find it consistent in principle with the structural design of the Constitution as a whole, and also with the dominant line of past constitutional interpretation by other judges" (10). They must seek an interpretation which "fits the broad story of America's historical record ... Our constitution is law, and like all law it is anchored in history, practice and integrity" (11). Similar points apply if we conceive of Charters as embodying a common law jurisprudence of rights.

54 I have neither the space (nor the legal competence) to argue this point, but it would appear as though Charter adjudication in the United States and Canada are, in fact, modeled on the common law. As Schauer notes in a review essay, "I sneak in a constitutional example only to remind the reader that American constitutional adjudication in the Supreme Court seems a central case of common law methodology." F. Schauer, "Is the Common Law Law?" (1989) 77 Cal. L. Rev. at 455 (a review of Melvin Eisenberg, *The Nature of the Common Law* (Cambridge, MA: Harvard University Press, 1988)).

55 This is not to say, of course, that there are not other options as well. Dworkin's constitutional theory, which might well be a variation of the common law conception, is yet another possibility.

56 *Law and Disagreement, supra* note 2 at 221.

57 Ibid.

58 Many positivists, particularly Jules Coleman, have spent considerable time and effort attempting to determine how much disagreement is compatible with the existence of conventional rules or understandings. But wherever the limit is set, it's pretty clear that a disagreement "which goes all the way down" goes well beyond it. See Coleman's *The Practice of Principle* (Oxford: Oxford University Press, 2001) at esp. Lectures 7 and 8.

59 I attempt to develop a conception of the "community's constitutional morality" which can serve as the source of the norms invoked by a Charter in "From Pre-Legal Society to Constitutional Morality," presented at the IVR conference in August, 2003 in Lund, Sweden. Draft copy available from the author.

60 For instance, some in Canada believe that the "right to property" should have been included in the Canadian *Charter of Rights and Freedoms* (as it

now is in the Chinese constitution). Few, if any, believe, that the *Charter* is, for this reason, illegitimate.

61 On this see Joseph Raz, "On the Authority and Interpretation of Constitutions" in *Constitutionalism: Philosophical Foundations, supra* note 29 especially at 171–74. As Raz observes, "Constitutions, at least old ones, do not derive their authority from the authority of their authors. But there is no need to worry as to the source of their authority. They are self-validating. They are valid just because they are there, enshrined in the practices of their countries.... A most important qualification should be added ... *As long as they remain within the boundaries set by moral principles* ...." (173). Raz adds a further important qualification: that this conclusion follows only "*if morality underdetermines* the principles concerning the form of government and the content of individual rights enshrined in constitutions." This "underdetermination thesis" is one to which both Raz and I subscribe and with which even a natural lawyer like Aquinas would, I suspect, be in agreement. Recall his theory of "determination of common notions." *Summa Theologica,* Question XCV (Human Law), 2nd Article (Whether Every Human Law Is Derived from the Natural Law).

62 Even the House of Lords, in its infamous "Practice Statement" formally rejected the practice of considering itself absolutely bound by its previous decisions.

63 David A. Strauss, "Common Law Constitutional Interpretation" (1996) 63 U. Chi. L. Rev. 877 at 896–97. Note the appeal to humility in the face of limited knowledge implicit in Strauss's characterization, a humility which is part and parcel of the living tree, common law theory of Charters for which this paper argues.

64 *Law and Disagreement, supra* note 2 at 221.

65 Ibid. at 290.

66 Paraphrasing the *Charter of Rights and Freedoms* at s. 7.

67 For example, we will be inclined to reject various forms of interpretive strategy, such as originalism, which presuppose fixed pre-commitments.

68 Of course the symbolism can prove hollow if the political, legal and social cultures of the society in question fail to reflect the norms formally expressed in their Charter. And there is nothing to rule out the possibility of a society without a Charter possessing a strong culture of respecting the rights typically included in written Charters. The former Soviet Union is often cited as an example of the former, the UK an example of the latter. The only claim I make here, is that within the context of a culture of rights recognition, the powerful symbolism of a Charter can enhance that practice.

69 And even if judicial review is chosen, there is, once again, no reason why it has to be a form which provides the judiciary with final say on all questions raised by the *Charter of Rights and Freedoms law.* Canada's section 33 "notwithstanding" or override clause, for example, allows Parliament sometimes to substitute its own judgment for that of the Courts.

70 This realism also underpins his critique of a range of other authors, including Dworkin, Freeman, and those who champion the ideals of "deliberative democracy" and "consensus politics."

71 *Law and Disagreement, supra* note 2 at 30.

72 Ibid. at 32.

73 Christiano, *supra* note 28 at 520. Advocates, such as Freeman and Dworkin, presumably have reasonable arguments to the effect that simple majoritarianism is inconsistent with democracy. Waldron of course disagrees, but surely he is not willing to say that the views of Freeman and Dworkin are "unreasonable." At this stage it is worth remembering Waldron's claim, *supra* note 20 that "We seem, then, to be in a bind. It looks as though it is disagreement all the way down, so far as constitutional choice is concerned ... [W]e cannot use a results-driven test, because we disagree about which results would count in favour of and which against a given decision-procedure ... [W]e cannot appeal to any procedural criterion either, since procedural questions are at the very nub of the disagreements we are talking about."

74 I say re-evaluate since, as Waldron notes, there is nothing in the nature of majoritarian, legislative processes which suggests that legislators do not themselves often evaluate their proposed legislative measures to ensure that they do not violate constitutionally entrenched moral rights. Notice further that there is nothing in the thoughts being developed here which presupposes the self-image of a Hobbesean predator. There is nothing amiss in the idea of morally responsible holders of rights recognizing their own burdens of judgment, and welcoming the possibility of assigning the power to review their decisions to a body of persons less encumbered by those particular burdens. There is nothing at all unflattering, or contrary to the legacy of human rights theory, in this alternative picture.

75 But again, one should be careful not to push this point too far, as evidenced by the decision in *Bush v. Gore.*

76 Christiano, *supra* note 28 at 520–21.

77 Ibid. at 521.

78 Dworkin, *Freedom's Law, supra* note 8 at 17.

79 There might also be a parallel between Waldron's position and the claim that if there is no moral truth, then we ought to allow each individual to

decide questions of personal morality according to his own moral lights. Under such conditions, it is sometimes said, no one has the moral right to impose his own views on anyone else. Of course, if there is no moral truth, then there is no sound moral basis for this latter claim. Likewise, if we cannot agree on issues of political morality, then presumably one of the issues upon which we cannot agree is the question whether we should, as a matter of sound political morality, allow the people affected by public decisions to decide for themselves. If we cannot agree on issues of political morality, then presumably there is no sound basis for this particular moral claim either.

80 See *Law and Disagreement, supra* note 2 at ch. 6.

81 Dworkin, *Freedom's Law, supra* note 8 at 34.

82 In Canada many House members are now facing this kind of dilemma on the issue of same-sex marriages.

83 Ditto.

84 A glaring example of this situation is legislation governing the rights of inmates to vote in elections. Courts and legislators who affirm such democratic rights for prisoners are often pilloried in the press and in public discourse.

85 For example, these factors are relevant in determining which groups, including those whose voice may have been overwhelmed or marginalized in public discourse and legislative debates, are to be granted intervener status in Charter cases. This raises yet another respect in which the decisional contexts of judge and legislator are often relevantly different: for a variety of reasons, minority voices are often unheard or ignored in legislative contexts. Courts are often the best, indeed only, institutional forum in which those voices can successfully be heard and the expressed interests considered and given due measure.

86 The phrase was first introduced by Raz. See, e.g., "Authority, Law and Morality" (1985) 68 The Monist at 295.

87 Of relevance here is the fact that legislatures, for similar reasons, frequently create and empower (the unelected) members of administrative bodies to enact, interpret and apply specific rules on their behalf. One can easily conceive judges as serving an analogous role. Indeed, this is the role theorists often have in mind when they refer to judicial discretion as representing a kind of delegated, "quasi-legislative" power.

88 Dworkin, A *Matter of Principle, supra* note 8 at 30. Emphasis added.

89 Dworkin, *Freedom's Law, supra* note 8 at 30–31.

90 Ibid. at 31. Much of the argument would turn on complex empirical questions which are well beyond the scope of this paper.

91 The idea of partnership is worth stressing when considering the role of judges in constitutionally limited democracies. Far too often judges who strike down or otherwise change legislation on moral grounds specified in a Charter are criticized for claiming superior authority over legislatures. But this need not be so. The role of legislating general rules (whose moral consequences are sometimes unforeseeable) is fully compatible with the role (served by another body) of deciding what must be done in unforeseeable cases of potential conflict with the norms of constitutional morality. Seen in this light, judges and legislators are not – at least not always – in *competition* with each other over who has the better moral vision. On the contrary, they can each contribute, in their own unique ways, and from their own unique perspectives and contexts of decision, to the achievement of a morally sensitive and enlightened rule of law.

READING QUESTION ON WALUCHOW

1   Is Waluchow's defence of judicial review better supported by Dworkin's account of law than by legal positivism?

Kent Roach
"Dialogic Judicial Review and Its Critics" (2005)

Roach responds to the critics of judicial review in Canada by trying to show that Canada's constitution is a productive reconciliation of democracy and liberalism, or, to put things differently, of legislative supremacy and constitutionalism. His main example is the same-sex marriage issue, encountered in the previous chapter.

The idea that judicial review can produce a dialogue between courts and legislatures has been getting much scrutiny in Canada. This attention can be explained by the structure of the *Canadian Charter of Rights and Freedoms*.[1] By allowing ordinary legislation to place limits on rights as interpreted by the courts and even to override them, the *Charter* contemplates and invites dialogue between courts, legislatures and the larger society about the treatment of rights in a free and democratic society. The *Charter* is a prototype of a dialogic bill of rights because it allows legislatures to prescribe by law and justify limits on all rights without restricting the range of legislative objectives that can justify a limit on the right. The *Charter*'s most famous dialogic instrument allows the enactment of legislation notwithstanding most *Charter* rights for a renewable five-year period.

The dialogic structure of the *Charter* has influenced other modern bills of rights. New Zealand and the United Kingdom have opted for a weaker form of dialogic judicial review that allows courts to presume compliance with rights in the absence of clear statements to the contrary. Courts can declare laws to be incompatible with rights and invite legislative reconsideration, but they cannot strike laws down.[2] South Africa has opted for a stronger form of dialogic judicial review that allows laws to be struck down and does not allow the legislature, except in emergency situations, to derogate from rights as interpreted by the courts. South Africa has also followed Canadian practice with respect to allowing legislatures to justify reasonable limits on rights and allowing courts to suspend declarations of invalidity to allow legislative as opposed to judicial correction of a matter.[3] From this constitutional perspective, the future of dialogic judicial review looks bright. The design differences are significant and should be studied, but the idea that there should be dialogue between courts and legislatures with respect to the treatment of rights seems to be gaining ground.

But there are clouds on the horizon. The judges on the Supreme Court of Canada have invoked the metaphor of dialogue to attempt to justify some of their more controversial constitutional decisions in recent years. The results have been mixed if not muddled, with judges using the dialogue metaphor to justify both judicial revision and invalidation of legislation and judicial deference to legislation. At first, the Court argued that the possibility of dialogue through the use of the override helped to justify its decision to read sexual orientation as a prohibited ground of discrimination into Alberta's Human Rights Code.[4] A year later, however, the Court used dialogue as a justification for upholding an "in your face" Parliamentary reply to a previous controversial decision about the accused's right to full answer and defence in sexual assault cases.[5] More recently, judges have disagreed about the meaning of dialogue, with some stressing that it cannot be an excuse for an abdication of an anti-majoritarian judicial role even when evaluating a Parliamentary reply to a previous Supreme Court decision,[6] and others suggesting that it requires judges to defer when Parliament expresses reasonable disagreement with the Court's reconciliation of individual and social interests.[7] From this judicial perspective, the future of dialogic judicial review does not look bright. Inconsistency and indeterminacy in the use of the dialogue metaphor[8] suggest that it will be no more a satisfactory theory of judicial review than its predecessors, whether they be based on originalism, the re-enforcement of democracy or the protection of fundamental rights.[9]

In the first part of this article, I will outline the major features of dialogic judicial review in Canada as a political or constitutional theory about how both courts and legislatures can contribute to debates about controversies about rights and freedoms. These key features include both sections 1 and 33 of the *Charter*, the exercise of remedial discretion to allow legislatures to select among a range of constitutional options and cabinet-dominated Parliamentary government. I will argue that dialogue theory is not a theory of judicial review that will tell judges how to decide hard cases. Judges do not dialogue with legislatures. They decide cases according to their view of the law. Dialogue theorists should be addressing their arguments as much to the public and legislators as to the judges. One positive impact of dialogue theory is that the recent debate about judicial activism in Canada on issues such as gay marriage and decriminalization of marijuana seems to be slowly shifting focus from criticisms of the Court for doing its job to criticisms of Parliament for failing to do its job.

A conclusion that dialogue theory is not in itself a theory of judicial review, however, begs the more difficult question of what, if anything, justifies giving the unelected judiciary any role in the political dialogue about rights and freedoms. Some critics of dialogue argue that "dialogue theory lacks normative content ... The fact that one institution can escape the consequences of another's actions says nothing about the latter's legitimacy."[10] In the second part of this article, I will respond to this important critique by acknowledging that there is a need to articulate what courts can uniquely contribute to political debates about rights. Courts should play a role that will not otherwise be played by legislatures. Such a judicial role includes good faith interpretation of the constitutional text, fair hearings of claims about rights and injustice and the protection of minorities and fundamental values that are vulnerable to hostility or neglect in the legislative process.[11] On such issues, defenders of dialogic judicial review may appear to be getting too close to traditional theorists of judicial review, but they only bear the burden of justifying judicial contributions to political debates about rights, and not judicial supremacy.

But what about the argument that although the *Charter* does not contemplate judicial supremacy, it can result in judicial supremacy when the courts seem to have the last word on controversial matters such as abortion and perhaps gay marriage?[12] Concerns have been expressed that the *Charter* gives judges a privileged and unwarranted place, if not a monopoly, in articulating constitutional values.[13] In the third part of this article, I will attempt to disentangle empirical and normative strands in this important critique of dialogue theory. At an empirical level, we need a better understanding of when and why legislatures accept certain judicial decisions. This will increasingly take those interested in dialogic judicial review into the realm of case studies of the interaction of the judicial and legislative processes.[14] Comparative studies may also assist in a better understanding of the importance of the placement of the burden of legislative inertia and the conditions that are necessary to surmount various burdens. The focus should be on how particular bills of rights and judicial decisions influence the process of dialogue between courts and legislature, and also the influence of other actors in civil society such as the media, advocacy groups, and international organizations in influencing legislative priorities. In addition, the role of popular perceptions of both rights and courts should be examined. One hypothesis is that popular perceptions of judicial review may still be rooted in an older vision of judicial supremacy and may not have caught up to new understandings of dialogic judicial review. Another is that legislatures require increased capacity to engage in their own independent interpretation of the *Charter*.

Increased study of dialogue in practice will provide valuable insights, but it will not end the normative controversy about whether dialogue between courts and legislatures contributes to democracy. There is a danger that empirical accounts of dialogue will run at cross purposes if their normative premises are not made clear and debated. For some, there is genuine dialogue even when legislatures fail to revise or reverse *Charter* decisions.[15] A government is democratically accountable for such decisions because it has ample tools under the *Charter* and in Parliament to revise or reverse *Charter* decisions and because dialogue may result in agreement. Parliament has been able to reverse and revise unpopular decisions about the rights of the accused,[16] perhaps the most unpopular group in our democracy. On matters such as abortion and gay rights, however, public opinion is more divided and the political benefits of challenging the Court less certain. Hence, the Court's decisions have had more sticking power. When the legislature fails to revise a *Charter* decision, the people may still be getting what they want or at least, not being stuck with a state of affairs that they clearly do not want.

Others, however, argue that there is no genuine dialogue unless the legislature acts on its own interpretation of the *Charter*.[17] This raises the question of whether legislatures are suited to interpreting the rights of minorities and the accused and long-term fundamental values. The track record of legislatures on *Charter* issues is not strong. The dangers are not only that legislatures will gang up on the unpopular and act as a judge in their own majoritarian causes, but also that they will avoid or finesse issues of principle. Courts may have a legitimate role in slowing down majorities and sending signals to them about the consequences of their actions for minorities and fundamental values. Courts may also have a legitimate role in provoking legislatures to confront issues of principle and exclusion that they would rather ignore. Dialogic judicial review may serve as a means of placing important and uncomfortable issues on the legislative agenda. The government will then have to decide whether it is prepared to expend limited political capital and energy in enacting ordinary legislation to revise or reverse the relevant *Charter* decision. Under this view of dialogic judicial review, the people should not always get what they immediately want or be allowed to enjoy the comfort of a status quo that may infringe rights. Their preferences should be tested by allowing the courts to consider claims of rights and injustice in a way that is procedurally different from the way that such issues are discussed on the floor of the legislature. Popular preferences can still be vindicated through legislation revising or reversing *Charter* decisions, but the process will be characterized by fuller deliberation and debate and better awareness of the consequences because of the court's contribution to the dialogue about rights and freedoms.

Even if one accepts that legislatures can revise or reject *Charter* decisions, this begs the question of the legitimacy of such legislative actions. Here the worry is that dialogic judicial review may place both fundamental rights and vulnerable minorities, as protected by courts, at risk from legislatures. This criticism of dialogic judicial review has largely been nascent, but it will increase in the years to come as dialogical judicial review gains greater prominence.[18] Conventional theorists of judicial review, whether they are attracted to Bork, Ely or Dworkin, will surely challenge dialogue theory as too willing to sacrifice judicial attempts to reach right answers through the vagaries of politics. There are also concerns that dialogue theory will give judges an excuse to back away from constitutional commitments especially when legislatures have responded negatively to previous court decisions. In other words, dialogue theory may send a message to minorities that courts are not truly committed to rights and to legislatures that "if at first you do not succeed, try, try again."[19] In Canada, the possibility that the override could be used to prevent gay marriages is disconcerting for many and Quebec has already used the override to limit the rights of its non-francophone minorities. Here defenders of dialogic judicial review will need assistance from the very theorists who have criticized them for leaving too little room for legislatures. In other words, proponents of dialogue will need to justify legislative participation in societal debates about the treatment of rights and freedoms. On these issues, dialogue theorists may appear to be getting too close to traditional theories of legislative supremacy, but it is important for defenders of dialogic judicial review to explain why elected legislatures, as well as courts, are important and legitimate interlocutors in societal dialogues about rights. Dialogue theorists must defend a vision of constitutional democracy that avoids either judicial or legislative supremacy.

I WHAT IS DIALOGIC JUDICIAL REVIEW?

Dialogic judicial review refers to any constitutional design that allows rights, as contained in a bill of rights and as interpreted by the courts, to be limited or overridden by the ordinary legislation of a democratically enacted legislature. This definition of dialogic judicial review focuses on issues of constitutional design and the constitutional rejection of both judicial and legislative supremacy. It does not capture all the dialogue that actually occurs between courts, legislatures and the broader society. For example, it would exclude Bruce Ackerman's theory of constitutional moments even though that theory provides an interesting account of how the United States Supreme Court at crucial times in its history has been checked by society and the elected branches of government. The reason why Ackerman's theory would not qualify is that the dialogue that he outlines was achieved not by ordinary legislation, but by a Civil War and consequent constitutional amendments prohibiting slavery and by threats to pack the Court before its acceptance of New Deal legislation.[20] Attempting to change the Court or the Constitution are drastic and desperate forms of dialogue that accept judicial supremacy as the condition of ordinary politics. Similarly a variety of sophisticated sub-constitutional devices used in the United States to encourage dialogue between courts and legislatures in the shadow of constitutional norms would not qualify under the above definition of dialogic judicial review.[21] Although these devices allow the legislature to respond to the court's decision with ordinary legislation, they fail to produce a full constitutional decision by the courts on the merits.[22] Dialogic judicial review combines constitutional decisions of courts with legislative revision or rejection of those decisions by means of ordinary legislation.

The key to understanding dialogue under the *Charter* or other modern bills of rights is that those constitutional documents allow court decisions about rights to be revised or rejected by ordinary legislation. It is not necessary for courts to avoid or minimize constitutional decisions in order to leave room for legislative replies. It is also not necessary to gain the extraordinary consensus necessary to amend the formal constitution to revise court decisions or to use the appointment process as an indirect device to encourage the Court to alter its decisions. Under dialogic judicial review, constitutional decisions of the Court can be addressed by the legislature on their merits and through ordinary legislation.

Drawing on the work of Guido Calabresi,[23] I have suggested elsewhere that the ability of Canadian legislatures to respond to *Charter* decisions through ordinary legislation means that there are important continuities between common law and dialogic constitutionalism.[24] Long before the *Charter*, the courts enforced a common law bill of rights in many fields of public law. The courts' common law decisions to allow judicial review or require hearings in administrative law or to require proof of subjective fault in criminal law were often quite controversial. Nevertheless, they could be revised or rejected should the legislature be prepared to clearly displace the common law. Under the *Charter*, legislatures can similarly use ordinary legislation to accept, revise or reject a judicial decision defining rights. As Peter Hogg and Allison Bushell note in their important and influential article about *Charter* dialogue, "[w]here a judicial decision is open to legislative reversal, modification, or avoidance, then it is meaningful to regard the relationship between the Court and the competent legislative body as a dialogue."[25]

The structure of both the *Charter* and Canadian legislatures are key to understanding the process of dialogue between these two institutions.

Section 1 of the *Charter* allows legislatures to prescribe by law reasonable limits on all *Charter* rights in the name of any pressing and substantial governmental objective. The "prescribed by law" requirement is an important dialogic feature of the *Charter* that has frequently been neglected. It continues the common law tradition of requiring clear statements by the legislature when they infringe rights, a device that should promote democratic deliberation and accountability for the limitation of rights. This is especially important given that much *Charter* litigation is directed against actions taken by state officials such as the police. The prescribed-by-law requirement forces these officials to demonstrate that their actions in limiting rights have in fact been authorized and contemplated by the people's elected representatives. The German Constitutional Court has recognized the need for legislation to authorize executive action, not only to respect the rule of law, but so that "official action [will] be comprehensible and to a certain extent predictable for the citizen." The Israeli Supreme Court has drawn the link between the rule of law and democracy even more clearly, concluding that "the legislature may not refer the critical and difficult decisions to the executive without giving it guidance" because the legislature "is elected by the people to enact its laws."[26] Unfortunately, the Supreme Court of Canada has been fairly lax in enforcing the prescribed-by-law requirement. It has often allowed officials to take shelter in broad legislative grants of discretion without requiring clear statements that the legislature has considered and authorized its officials to place limits on *Charter* rights.[27] The requirement that limits on rights be prescribed-by-law can play an important role in prompting democratic debates in the legislature about the treatment of rights and freedoms.

In order to justify a limit on *Charter* rights, however, the government must do more than clearly state in legislation its intent to limit rights. The legislation must also be justified on the basis of a legitimate and important governmental objective. Section 1 differs from comparable limitations provisions in the European Convention on Human Rights or the International Covenant on Civil and Political Rights because it does not attempt to limit the range of objectives for legislative limits on rights and because it applies to all rights. Canadian legislatures can define the terms of the justification process by articulating in litigation and through devices such as preambles the particular legislative objectives that in their view justify restrictions on *Charter* rights. To be sure, the Supreme Court has in relatively rare cases rejected some objectives as not important enough to limit *Charter* rights. For example, attempts to impose a state religion through Sunday closing laws or attempts to explain rather than justify a legislature's neglect of gays and lesbians have been held not to be sufficiently important objectives to limit *Charter* rights.[28] As Hogg and Bushell note, dialogue may be precluded in the relatively rare cases where the courts rule the legislative objective not to be worthy enough to limit the *Charter* right.[29] At the same time, however, this is a relatively rare restriction on dialogue[30] and one that can be overcome if the legislature re-formulates its objective for limiting the relevant *Charter* right. For example, legislatures were able to successfully defend Sunday closing laws on the basis of the secular objective of imposing a common pause day.[31] The generality of section 1 of the *Charter* means that legislatures have considerable scope to place limits on rights as interpreted by the Court.

Once the legislative objective is determined, the courts apply a proportionality analysis that inquires into the fit between the objective and the particular rights violation, as well as the overall balance between the ability of the impugned law to accomplish the objective and the effect on the *Charter* right. The courts exercise considerable discretion in this analysis, but the legislature also plays an important role. The government has the burden under section 1 and may introduce a wide range of evidence to justify a limit on a *Charter* right. It can clarify its precise objective through the use of preambles and other devices. It can also commission and introduce evidence to demonstrate why a policy alternative that the court might see as less restrictive of rights will not be feasible or effective in achieving the legislature's policy objective. Judges should not conduct section 1 analysis in the abstract; they should listen and learn from the government and respond to the government's arguments. Although section 1 analysis can be contentious, the terms of the debate can be shaped by the legislature. In its more rigid guises, section 1 analysis can seem constrained by what Jeremy Waldron has criticized as the "obsessive verbalism of a particular written *Charter*." From its inception and increasingly in recent years, however, section 1 analysis has proven to be relatively flexible and attentive to context. At all times, it avoids the one step formula of American constitutional law in determining whether the government has infringed "speech," "religion," "cruel and unusual punishment" or "due process" in favour of a more "free and flexible discourse of politics."[32] Of course, Professor Waldron's desire is not to encourage an even more flexible discourse of politics in the courtroom. My point is only to illustrate how the legislature can help shape the terms of justification under section 1 of the *Charter*.

The other main structural device for dialogue under the *Charter* is section 33. It allows legislatures to enact legislation notwithstanding the fundamental freedoms, legal and equality rights of the *Charter* for a renewable five-year period. The courts have deferred to legislative uses of the override upholding Quebec's omnibus use of the override and have only have struck down retroactive uses of the override.[33] Thus the legislature can override *Charter* rights for whatever objective it selects. It is not necessary for the legislature to declare a state of emergency. Section 33(1) echoes clear statement rules by requiring the legislature to "expressly declare" that the specific act will operate notwithstanding specified parts of the *Charter*. Section 33, like derogation provisions in other modern bills of rights, contemplates continued democratic dialogue over rights and freedoms because the override must be renewed every five years, a time that dovetails with the maximum duration of a legislature under section 4 of the *Charter*.[34] The use of the override can potentially be an issue in the next election.

There are several contentious design features of section 33. One is that it can and often has been used in a pre-emptive fashion before a court has issued a *Charter* decision. A pre-emptive use of the override shuts up the dialogue before the judges have even uttered a word on the matter. If all other governments had followed Alberta's lead in 2000 and used the override to preclude challenges to traditional definitions of marriage, the courts would have been unable to hear claims of discrimination by gays and lesbians and society would have been deprived of judicial decisions deciding whether the traditional definition of marriage discriminates against gays and lesbians and whether it can be justified as a reasonable limit in a free and democratic society. Pre-emptive uses of section 33 are problematic from a dialogic perspective.

Another contentious issue is that the wording of section 33 requires a legislature to state that it is overriding rights. Jeremy Waldron has argued that section 33 forces the legislature into declaring misgivings about rights whereas there is most often only a reasonable disagreement about rights.[35] It might well have been preferable to have followed Christopher Manfredi's suggestion that section 33 be worded in a manner that only allows a legislature to override judicial interpretations of rights.[36] Nevertheless, the wording of section 33 is not fatal to the dialogue model. When the override is used to reverse a court decision, it is likely that people will realize that the legislature is not really overriding the relevant *Charter* right, but rather the court's interpretation of the right. On the other hand, when the legislature uses the override preemptively to shut down dialogue with the courts about the meaning of the right, it is not unreasonable for the legislature to be required to take the heat for overriding the right. The legislature is effectively saying that it does not care how the court interprets the right. On this view, Quebec's omnibus use of the override in 1982 could reasonably be portrayed as misgivings about *Charter* rights[37] but Quebec's use of the override after the Supreme Court's signs decision could not reasonably be seen as a misgiving about freedom of expression as such, but rather as an objection about how the Supreme Court in a particular case balanced its broad interpretation of free expression against Quebec's interest in promoting French as its official public language. Although section 33 required Quebec to state it was legislating notwithstanding section 2 of the *Charter*, the people should be given some credit for knowing the true nature of the dispute between the court and the legislature.

Another design issue is why some rights in the *Charter* – democratic, mobility and language rights – are exempted from the override. In the *Sauvé*[38] case about prisoner voting, the majority concluded that the exemption of the right to vote from the override underlined the prime importance of this democratic right. The right to vote and the right to have periodic elections can indeed be seen as the most basic rights in a democracy. Minority language rights may also have been exempted from the override because of a concern about the tyranny of large linguistic majorities over small linguistic minorities. This may also explain why Aboriginal and treaty rights protected under section 35 of the *Constitution Act, 1982* are exempted from both section 1 and from section 33.[39] At the same time, it is less clear why mobility rights are not subject to the override. It could be argued that the dialogic structure of the *Charter* would be improved if the override were available for all rights.

In some cases, courts can fashion their decisions to keep open the option of using the override. In 1998, the Supreme Court struck down an election law as an unreasonable violation of freedom of expression and avoided deciding the case under the right to vote in part to preserve Parliament's right to override the decision.[40] Such an approach could also have been used in *Sauvé* because the case was argued on the alternative grounds that it violated the equality rights of prisoners. In my view, little would have been lost in terms of judicial reasoning had the Court taken this approach. Restrictions on the franchise in Canada are intimately connected with the struggle of the poor, women, racial minorities, and Aboriginal people for equality.[41] To be sure, deciding *Sauvé* only on section 15 grounds would have left a very vulnerable minority – prisoners serving federal time, nearly a fifth of whom are Aboriginal – open to denial of their rights by a majority, an issue that raises serious normative questions that will be examined in the final part of this article. At the same time, it would have allowed Parliament an opportunity to re-evaluate its policy in light of the Supreme Court's conclusion that prisoner disenfranchisement was an ineffective means to punish offenders or to signal the importance of the franchise and the rule of law in a democracy. The exemption of some rights from the override may frustrate some forms of dialogue, but the fact remains that by far the most litigated provisions of the *Charter* remain subject to the override.

Sections 1 and 33 are the main instruments of dialogue under the *Charter*. From a democratic perspective, what is noteworthy about both provisions is that they require legislation to prescribe limits on *Charter* rights or to expressly override such rights. In this sense, both sections enhance democracy as represented by the process of the people's elected representatives deliberating and voting on some piece of legislation. Both sections 1 and 33 provide a direct vehicle to engage the merits of particular court decisions and can be contrasted favourably to the epic political battles and current deadlock over the appointment of judges that presently beset the American system and constitute, at best, an indirect means to respond to and to anticipate judicial decisions. Under the Canadian system, legislators are allowed to address specific court decisions directly. They can discuss the merits and shortcomings of such decisions and in most cases can enact legislation to revise or reverse those decisions. In the American system, legislators are often limited to speculating about the possible future voting patterns of this or that judicial nominee. I agree whole-heartedly with Jeremy Waldron that "impotent debating" about what "a few black-robed celebrities" might decide in the future "is hardly the essence of democratic citizenship."[42] Enacting ordinary legislation that revises or rejects a court's constitutional decision, however, is a very significant act of democracy.

Another important feature of dialogic review in Canada has been the courts' exercise of their remedial discretion in such a way as to leave governments room to revise their judgments and to select from a range of constitutional options. The most important remedy[43] in this respect has been the delayed or suspended declaration of invalidity which has developed as an important and innovative remedy since it was first used by the Supreme Court of Canada in the *Manitoba Language Reference*.[44] Although the Court in *Schachter v. Canada*[45] attempted to limit the use of suspended declarations of invalidity and to reject the dialogic idea that they can be justified on the basis of concerns about the relative role of courts and legislatures, the Supreme Court has in many subsequent cases suspended declarations of invalidity in order to allow legislatures an opportunity to pre-empt the court's blunt remedy of a declaration of invalidity.[46] The delayed declaration of invalidity, a novel remedial instrument that is now specifically contemplated in South Africa's constitution,[47] is an instrument of dialogue because it allows the legislature to enact ordinary legislation to revise the court's remedy before that remedy takes effect. To be sure, the legislature may not always be able to act in the six- to 18-month periods that the courts generally allow and sometimes the reply legislation may follow the court's judgment fairly closely. Nevertheless, the suspended declaration of invalidity allows the legislature an important opportunity to select among a range of constitutional options and pre-empt the court's remedy. Moreover, there have been legislative replies in the majority of cases in which suspended declarations of invalidity have been used.[48] As will be discussed below, the Ontario Court of Appeal's immediate and mandatory remedy in the gay marriage case has been controversial[49] and reduced the range of dialogue available between courts and legislatures on the same-sex marriage issue.

There is a final feature of the Canadian Constitution that is important in facilitating dialogue between courts and legislation. That feature is the nature of Canadian parliamentary government. Canadian parliamentary government is characterized by Cabinet and even prime ministerial domination, a first past the post system that encourages majority governments and tight party discipline. To be sure, all of these features of Canadian governance are controversial. Many argue that they produce a democratic deficit that diminishes the accountability of governments to the people. There are many calls to increase the power of backbenchers and committees, increase the power of the Senate through election, diminish the hold of party discipline and to introduce devices such as proportional representation and referenda. Leaving aside the merits of such proposals, as well as claims that the defects of the present system are so great that Canada's elected governments themselves lack democratic legitimacy,[50] the present system has the virtue of generally ensuring that a government can quickly enact legislation to respond to a *Charter* decision.[51] In other words, even if the American Bill of Rights was amended to included dialogic devices such as sections 1 and 33 of the *Charter* and judicial remands of issues to legislatures, it would still be more difficult to enact effective legislative replies to court decisions under the American Congressional system of internal checks and balances than under the Canadian parliamentary system of Cabinet domination.

To summarize, dialogue theory in Canada is a constitutional or political theory that explains how the Court's *Charter* decisions can be reversed or revised by ordinary legislation under sections 1 or 33 of the *Charter*, legislative selection among a broad range of constitutional options, and by the type of quick legislative activism that is presently available in Canada's system of parliamentary government. Dialogue theory does not claim to provide judges with the right answers to the difficult questions that come before the courts in *Charter* cases. Somewhat ironically given its frequent invocation by Justices of the Supreme Court in a number of *Charter* cases, the original Hogg and Bushell article conceded that "judges have a great deal of discretion in `interpreting' the law of the constitution, and the process of interpretation inevitably remakes the constitution into the likeness favoured by the judges."[52] This is a fairly robust concession – indeed one that I will suggest in the next part is a bit too robust – to legal realism and judicial discretion in interpreting the *Charter*. It may only feed concerns that unelected judges will "inevitably" use the *Charter* to impose their own personal values on the polity and that dialogue theory is lacking in moral content and fails to justify the judicial role in dialogues with the legislatures. Hogg and Bushell are, however, certainly right to concede that dialogue theory does not provide judges with right answers to hard cases. Dialogue theory departs from the preoccupation of much contemporary constitutional theory because it does not focus on finding the right answers to difficult cases. In turn, it is not set back or shattered by a conclusion that people can reasonably disagree with a particular court's decision about rights.

Dialogue theory represents a concession that the conventional theories of judicial review have reached something of a dead end. The mythical judge – Dworkin's Hercules – who can reach reliably right answers is just that: a myth. Reasonable disagreement about how judicial review should be practiced has led dialogue theorists to examine a different question: the options available for legislatures and society to respond and revise the court's perhaps flawed decisions. There is no guarantee that the judges will find reliably right answers to the difficult questions that they face and for that reason, dialogic judicial review allows legislatures room to debate and to revise and even to reject judicial decisions.

Although dialogue theory does not claim to provide judges with the right answers to hard cases, I believe it is a mistake for dialogue theorists to accept that judges have a strong form of discretion to decide *Charter* cases that is not informed by their views about the law. The positivistic idea that judicial decision-making under the *Charter* is in hard cases a matter of unguided discretion leaves dialogue theory vulnerable to Andrew Petter's criticism that "dialogue theory lacks normative content, and exerts no moral claim to support judges involvement in *Charter* decision-making ... The fact that one institution can escape the consequences of another's actions says nothing about the latter's legitimacy."[53] Keith Ewing in his recent contribution to the *Oxford Handbook of Legal Studies* made a similar point, namely that "if judicial review is to be justified, it must be for reasons of principle which are intrinsic to the process itself, and not because the process is not as intrusive or as expansive in practice as might otherwise be claimed by the opponents of judicial review of legislation."[54] Dialogue theorists bear the burden of justifying the judicial role in the dialogue about rights and freedoms.

There is some mischief in criticisms that dialogue theorists have not justified judicial review. Dean Petter, for one, believes that any attempt to justify the judicial role is a "futile search for legitimacy" and he is somewhat nostalgic for the days when supporters of the *Charter* justified it on the basis of conventional theories of judicial review based on the intent of the framers, Ely's theory of democracy or Dworkin's theory of rights. To the extent that dialogue theory moves in the direction of the legitimacy debate, it can be criticized for being not only unoriginal, but more importantly undemocratic. In other words, conventional theories of judicial review are open to criticism for being too substantive. As my colleague David Dyzenhaus has argued, they contain a vision of "liberal constitutionalism" based on rights as trumps that can be contrasted with a more open-ended vision of "democratic constitutionalism" based on governments justifying their actions.[55] There is a democratic justification for dialogue theory focusing more on the ability of the legislature to revise or reverse court decisions than on how a judge should decide a hard case under the *Charter*.

At the same time, however, Petter and Ewing have a valid point when they argue that dialogue theorists need to justify the judicial contribution to the dialogue. For my own part, I am reluctant to go as far as Hogg and Bushell seem to do in conceding that constitutional interpretation is a matter of judicial discretion. The judicial role in the dialogue would not be justified if judges were flipping coins, making decisions without reasons or simply imposing their own vision of the good society in their decisions. Dialogue theorists need to pay more attention to the legitimacy of judicial contributions to societal debates about rights and freedoms. This process will bring them closer to the conventional debate about judicial review, albeit with the important caveat that dialogue theorists do not have to justify judicial supremacy. The dialogic structure of the *Charter* makes it possible to have Dworkin's Hercules as a judge, but to harness Hercules by ordinary legislation that revises or reverses his decisions.

Even though Hercules' decisions may be revised or reversed by the legislature, Hercules' role must still be justified. Dialogic judicial review is derived from a legal process tradition that is concerned with the unique attributes of courts as compared to legislatures or the executive. Following Bickel and Fuller and others in the legal process tradition, dialogic judicial review must account for the unique institutional role of the judiciary and of the process of adjudication. As Bickel recognized, the role of the courts in a democracy can only be defined in relation to the role of the legislature and the executive:

The search must be for a function which might (indeed, must) involve the making of policy, yet which differs from the legislative and executive functions; which is peculiarly suited to the capabilities of courts; which will not likely be performed elsewhere if the courts do not assume it ...[56]

Other unique attributes of courts include their commitment to allowing structured and guaranteed participation from aggrieved parties; their independence from the executive, and their commitment to giving reasons for their decisions.[57] In addition, courts have a special commitment to make sense of legal texts that were democratically enacted as foundational documents. It is important that judges have to make some effort to engage in a good faith interpretation of the constitutional text, even though the fact of reasonable disagreement is evident to all.

Critics of judicial review love to focus on 5:4 decisions to reveal the contingency of judicial reasoning about rights. If judges are so closely divided, so the argument goes, why should their views prevail over larger groups of elected representatives who are also divided and who also vote? Judges, however, do not vote simply by standing when their names are called. They are not subject to coercion from the party whip. Judges write reasons, sometimes overly long reasons, but reasons nevertheless to explain their vote. The reasons should respond to the arguments and evidence submitted by the parties who have a guaranteed ability to marshal their case and the ability to define the issues and present evidence and argument in support of their case. Pleaders in court do not have to lobby for some face time with the decision-maker and they do not have to worry about other pleaders making secret submissions or having disproportionate time to influence the decision-maker. The pleader in court has a guaranteed right of participation and a right to a reasoned decision that addresses the arguments made in court, as well as the relevant text of the democratically enacted law. The fair process of adjudication and the requirement for reasons help justify why unelected judges should play an important role in our debates about rights and freedoms.

The differences between how issues concerning rights and freedoms are debated and decided in legislatures and courts can be revealed by comparing the legislative debates when Parliament enacted a law denying the vote to prisoners serving sentences of two years' imprisonment or more and the debates within the Supreme Court when it decided in a 5:4 decision that the law was an unjustified violation of the right to vote. To be sure, some of the same arguments made by the majority in the Supreme Court about the importance of the right to vote in a democracy, prisoners' legitimate claims to citizenship and the inability of disenfranchisement to serve valid penal ends and its tension with the goal of rehabilitation and re-integration were made by a minority in Parliament.[58] An important difference between the legislative and the court debates, however, was the those defending the restriction on the vote did not really have to answer these arguments. Only a few members and no minister even bothered to defend the law in Parliament. One with reference to Clifford Olson, a notorious mass murderer, argued that he "just cannot get excited about such people losing their right to vote for the period they are incarcerated"[59] and another argued that the denial of the vote to offenders was "simple common sense."[60] The government was not required, as it was in court, to marshal its arguments about its precise objectives in limiting the vote of prisoners. Finally, the procedure used to resolve differences of opinion in Parliament and the Supreme Court were also quite different, even though both involved voting. A motion to give prisoners the right to vote was defeated in Parliament on a yelled voice vote despite objections that there was no quorum in the House,[61] while all nine Justices were present and signed lengthy reasons when the issue was decided in the Supreme Court.

Judges can add value to societal debates about justice by listening to claims of injustice and by promoting values and perspectives that may not otherwise be taken seriously in the legislative process. This means embracing an anti-majoritarian judicial role so that courts do what they can to protect minorities who are vulnerable to discrimination in the legislative and administrative processes of government. Thus a judge at a minimum should be influenced by the work of John Hart Ely and the *Carolene Products* footnote.[62] As non-elected officials with tenure, judges have a special role to look out for vulnerable minorities. As Wilson, J. recognized, this judicial role is a dynamic one as the outcasts of today may not be the outcasts of tomorrow.[63] Indeed, I would go further and suggest that judges in a dialogic system should be concerned not only with the protection of vulnerable minorities, but also with the protection of fundamental values in a manner similar to that contemplated by Dworkin.[64] The fact that their decisions under the *Charter* can be revised or reversed by the legislature suggests that judges can afford to err on the side of more robust approaches to judicial review. This does not mean that they can afford to be irresponsible or simply impose their own personal views of the good society. They must still make a good faith effort to offer a reasonable interpretation, of the text and the purposes of the *Charter* and to respond to the arguments of the parties, including the section 1 justification offered by the government.

There may be concerns that dialogic forms of judicial review can undercut the judicial role by giving judges an incentive to defer to the legislature whenever it revises or reverses a *Charter* decision. The record here is mixed with cases such as *Mills*[65] and to a lesser extent *Hall*[66] suggesting that the court may use the dialogue metaphor as a ground to defer to legislative replies to its previous decisions, but decisions such as *Sauvé*[67] reject the idea that the legislature should always succeed on its second try. Although it is possible that judges may use the dialogue metaphor as a justification for deference, such deference may betray the deeper dialogic structure of the *Charter*. In *Mills* for example, the Court could have struck down Parliament's reversal of its prior decision, but still left the door open to dialogue through the use of the override. Alternatively, the Court could have engaged in an internal form of dialogue and overruled its prior decision in *O'Connor*[68] on the basis that it did not give adequate weight to the equality interests of female complainants in sexual assault cases. There is nothing inherent in the dialogic structure of the *Charter* that counsels judicial deference.[69]

Dialogue theory allows for the possibility that judges may select the wrong minorities or values to protect or that they may go too far in protecting such minorities and such values.[70] If, as critics on the left have claimed, judges protect corporations and the wealthy too much, legislatures can respond with better justifications of why the rights of these entities should be limited. If, as critics on the right have claimed, judges protect criminals and unpopular minorities too much, legislatures can respond with better justifications of why the rights of these people should be limited. In all cases, legislatures also have the right to attempt to mobilize society to support the use of the override. There is nothing under the *Charter* that prevents a political party from running against the Court and committing itself to more frequent or even omnibus uses of the override. In Quebec, the Parti Quebecois government employed this strategy in the early 1980s and in the late 1990s, the neo-conservative Reform Party adopted such a strategy before retreating from it as part of an attempt to gain a broader base of support. A Canadian political party could mould much of its legislative agenda on opposition to the Court. It would not have to content itself with cranky and futile proposals to change the Constitution or the Court, but rather could introduce ordinary legislation to revise or reverse specific judicial decisions. The fact that an anti-Court platform would not at present appeal to a majority of Canadians can be explained by their moderate political preferences and their perceptions of rights and courts. Such attitudes could, however, change. In any event, they are not dictated by the structure of the *Charter*.

Although dialogue theorists do not have to bear the burden of justifying judicial supremacy, they do have to bear the burden of justifying the ability of the judiciary to place issues on the legislative agenda – issues that the government of the day may often prefer to avoid. Before the Supreme Court entered the fray, Parliament was content to leave its 1969 abortion law in place. The law provided that women could obtain a legal abortion if a committee of doctors concluded that the continuation of the pregnancy would endanger the women's life and health.[71] By invalidating the abortion law, the Supreme Court disturbed the status quo and perhaps even the policy preferences of our elected representatives to avoid the abortion issue so as not to alienate people on both sides of the debate. But this policy preference was a fraudulent one in the sense that Parliament had not taken responsibility for legislation that specifically authorized a "local option" system in which abortions were not available in some provinces or which gave committees arbitrary discretion to apply different standards to married and unmarried women. Parliament had enacted a national law that promised that all women could obtain an abortion if the continuation of a pregnancy would endanger their life or health. The pre-*Charter* status quo ante on abortion was also an unprincipled one in the sense that it had not been challenged by those who argued that it violated the rights of either women or the foetus. In its abortion decisions, the Supreme Court was able to cast light on the low visibility decisions made by hospitals and therapeutic abortion committees and to test the legislation against various rights claims. The Court found the 1969 abortion law to be unconstitutional, but it did not assert any particular solution for the abortion issue as the final word. Only one judge came close to a *Roe v. Wade*[72] trimester approach and all the judges recognized that Parliament could justifiably limit a woman's rights in order to protect the foetus. The Court's decision striking the law down required Parliament to take responsibility for what individual officials acting in its name actually did when they denied women access to abortions. The Court's decision did not prevent Parliament from justifying restrictions on abortions under section 1 or even exempting a new law from the *Charter*.

F.L. Morton and Rainer Knopff have argued that court decisions on abortion and gay rights are undemocratic because they disturb the policy preferences of democratically elected legislatures.[73] For example, the Court's decision reading in protection against discrimination on the basis of sexual orientation into the human rights code disturbed Alberta's decision not to include it and placed the province in a position where it was effectively forced to go along with the Court's decision or use the section 33 override to reverse the Court's decision. In the gay marriage cases, the courts' decisions have similarly disturbed Parliament's policy preference to affirm the traditional understanding of marriage as a union between a man and a woman both in a 1999 resolution and in legislation enacted in 2000 that extended benefits to same-sex couples. The courts' decisions have placed the issue of gay marriage on the agenda of a legislature that was content with maintaining the traditional status quo even when it recognized that in other respects same-sex couples were entitled to the same state recognition and benefits as other couples. The courts' ability to set part of the legislative agenda is a considerable power, but in my view can be justified on the basis of the guarantees in the *Charter* and its dialogic structure. What the *Charter* does is allow individuals to challenge the status quo on the basis of claims of principle as articulated in *Charter* rights. The *Charter* and the courts can force governments to confront issues of principle that they may well be inclined to ignore or finesse, but in most cases they cannot force a committed legislature to accept the court's resolution of the larger matter of policy. *Charter* decisions can be seen in a mature democracy as a means to manufacture disagreement[74] and to turn complacent majoritarian monologues into democratic and, at times, divisive dialogues. As a result of controversial court decisions on issues such as gay marriage, we have more not less democratic debate and disputation in Canada and the debate has a sharper and clearer edge. Regardless of whether one agrees with the outcome of the dialogue between courts and legislatures, the *Charter* has placed issues such as abortion, gay rights, and the rights of the accused on the legislative agenda, and by doing so has improved democracy.

III WHEN COURTS APPEAR TO HAVE THE LAST WORD IN THE DIALOGUE

Even if one accepts the argument that the *Charter* and the parliamentary system give elected governments the power to revise and reject *Charter* decisions, concerns have been raised that on some issues the Court has had or shaped the last word. Fears have been expressed that whatever its potential, dialogic judicial review can degenerate into judicial monologue and supremacy. This critique has both empirical and normative dimensions. Empirically, the concern is that the court's assignment of the burden of legislative inertia can be decisive.

In order to explore the empirical issue, the conditions under which legislatures have successfully revised or rejected court decisions and the conditions under which they have failed to do so should be studied and compared. Acceptance of a judicial decision may in the real world of politics simply reflect the fact that reply legislation was not enough of a priority to get on a limited legislative agenda. A failure to reply or alter a court decision may also reflect the way the issue was packaged by the litigants, the courts or the media. What may be more helpful than quantitative approaches that depend on debatable and norm driven classification schemes are case studies of actual court decisions and the subsequent reply or lack of reply by the legislature.[75] Such case studies will have the beneficial effect of making constitutional scholarship less centered on the courts. Even popular discourse in Canada about judicial activism seems to be evolving in a less court-centred direction. For example, in recent debates about gay marriage and the decriminalization of marijuana, there seems to be somewhat less of a focus on criticizing the judges than in past debates and more on how Parliament has exercised or failed to exercise its policy-making role. All of this is healthy and suggests dialogic theories of judicial review may be playing some role in reviving interest in the legislative process and its reform. At the same time, however, even an enriched empirical debate about dialogue will likely not resolve the debate about whether dialogue under modern bills of rights contributes to democracy. The empirical debate is often driven by normative assumptions about what constitutes genuine dialogue and the proper role of legislatures and courts in a democracy.

One of the most famous examples of the Court having the last word under the *Charter* is with respect to abortion. In its 1988 decision in *R. v. Morgentaler*, the Supreme Court struck down the 1969 abortion law that allowed abortions when approved by a hospital committee as necessary to prevent danger to the life or health of the woman. The majority of the Court was careful to invalidate the law mainly on procedural grounds relating to the committee structure and to indicate that the protection of the foetus was a legitimate objective to limit the rights of pregnant women under section 1 of the *Charter*. There seemed to be a fairly broad range of possible legislative responses to the Court's decision, but the government of the day was not eager to take on the issue. It allowed a free vote on a series of propositions, all of which were defeated. The government eventually prepared a new law which allowed legal abortions whenever a single doctor was of the opinion that the health or life of the woman would be threatened. This law was passed by a vote of 140 to 131 in the House of Commons with party discipline only being applied to the *Cabinet*. It was subsequently defeated by a tied 43–43 vote in the Senate, the first defeat of a government bill in the unelected Senate in 30 years. This case demonstrates how relaxation of party discipline could make it more difficult for the government effectively to respond to a court decision. It also suggests that the Court is more likely to have the final word when public opinion is polarized and the government is unwilling or unable to make a strong case for a compromise. This observation may be of more than historical interest in light of divided opinion on the gay marriage issue.[76]

The case of gay marriage is a moving topic, but it has provoked some commentators to argue that the courts are routinely having the last word on policy matters. Indeed, Jeffrey Simpson used the gay marriage cases as support for a provocative argument that Parliament should simply relinquish the job of developing policy to the courts.[77] Even Simpson, however, was forced to admit that Parliament still had some options if it was prepared to use the notwithstanding clause to stop gay marriages.[78] A closer look at the gay rights issue reveals some of the complexities of dialogue between courts, Parliament and society. Although many may share Simpson's concerns that the courts are calling the shots on this issue, elected governments have already made some important decisions and may do so in the future.

As Alexander Bickel recognized, there will be false starts and delays in the recognition of the rights of unpopular minorities and the court "interacts with other institutions, with whom it is engaged in an endlessly renewed educational conversation ... And it is a conversation, not a monologue."[79] When the *Charter* was drafted in the early 1980s, Parliament was not prepared to list sexual orientation as a prohibited ground of discrimination. At the same time, however, it was not prepared to make the nine enumerated grounds of discrimination exclusive and left room in the drafting of section 15 of the *Charter* for the courts to add new grounds of discrimination to the list.[80] In 1995, the Court recognized sexual orientation as an analogous ground of discrimination. At the same time, however, a majority of the Court rejected the case for extending benefits to same-sex couples. Four judges saw couples as essentially heterosexual while the fifth judge believed that Parliament and society should be given more time to recognize same-sex partnerships.[81] Four years later, however, the Court was prepared in a 8:1 decision to recognize that same-sex couples should generally have the same burdens and benefits as opposite sex couples.[82] The Court, however, allowed the legislature an opportunity to develop its precise response to the issue and went out of its way to indicate that its decision did not cover marriage. Legislatures responded to this decision in a variety of ways with Ontario taking a separate but equal approach, Alberta using the section 33 override in an attempt to preserve the traditional definition of marriage, British Columbia making moves to accepting gay marriage, and Nova Scotia and Quebec developing registered partnership schemes.[83] The federal structure of Canada is a sometimes neglected feature of dialogic judicial review. It allows space for multiple governments to develop their own responses to court decisions, but as will be seen, in areas of exclusive federal jurisdiction, it may constrain the ability of governments to fashion their own responses to court decisions.

The federal Parliament also addressed the definition of marriage. In 1999, a motion that "marriage is and should remain the union of one man and one woman to the exclusion of all others, and that Parliament will take all necessary steps to preserve this definition of marriage in Canada" was passed.[84] A year later, a provision defining marriage as the union of a man and a woman to the exclusion of all others was added to a bill providing equal benefits to same-sex couples. It is instructive to compare the nature of the debate about marriage in Parliament with the debate in the courts. In both the 1999 and 2000 debates in Parliament, proponents of the traditional definition of marriage stressed over and over that they had received numerous phone calls, letters and petitions from their constituents in favour of retaining the traditional definition of marriage. The dominant idea was that the majority of Canadians believed that marriage was and should be limited to opposite sex couples. Leaving aside the question of whether this was an accurate perception of public opinion on this matter, it does illustrate how Parliament regards itself as an institution that is accountable to the majority and can justify its actions simply on the basis of the desires of the majority. As Eric Lowther, who moved the 1999 motion, explained:

Our job is to represent our constituents and Canadians on issues that are important to them. We believe that marriage should remain the union of a man and a woman. It is foundational to family and foundational to the strength of the nation. We believe that strong families make strong nations and marriage is part of that.[85]

John Bryden, a Liberal member who supported the motion and the subsequent amendment, similarly argued that "many Canadians still believe ... absolutely in the sanctity of marriage. We owe those Canadians an obligation to respect their feelings on this issue."[86] As was the case with respect to the law denying the right to vote to federal prisoners, supporters of the motion and the amendment made radically underarticulated and question-begging arguments. For example, Tom Wappel argued that the amendment "simply restated what most people in this country know to be the definition of marriage. ... This is exactly what marriage is and that is what I would argue marriage should remain."[87]

Debate in Parliament on the marriage issue was also very undisciplined compared to debate in the courts. Proponents of the traditional definition of marriage would frequently explore side issues by accusing the government of being "anti-family" on a wide variety of unrelated matters such as young offenders and pornography. Some members also made arguments that appealed to prejudice against gay men.[88] In contrast, intervenors supporting the traditional definition of marriage in the courts could not make such veiled appeals to prejudice and stereotype, but rather were required to make more detailed arguments relating to the applicability of the *Charter* and the justifications for restricting marriage to heterosexual couples. In turn, the minority in Parliament who opposed the motion and the amendment affirming the traditional definition of marriage also engaged in some name calling that would not go far in court.[89] Overall, there was little debate in Parliament about the central issues that would occupy the courts; namely the objectives of marriage and whether these were related to and justified the exclusion of gays and lesbians from the institution of marriage.

The formal procedures and conventions of adjudication – equal time to make arguments, structured arguments, professional traditions of respect and courtesy – focused and disciplined debate in court. The argument from tradition was filtered into an argument that the 1867 Constitution incorporated the common law definition of marriage by giving Parliament jurisdiction over "marriage and divorce" and that the 1982 *Charter* could not apply to such a definition of marriage. It was also channeled into arguments that any changes to the common law definition of marriage must be incremental. These arguments were more articulate than the refrain in Parliament that marriage must remain as it had been. Arguments under section 15 of the *Charter* required the lawyers and judges to address the effects of the traditional definition of marriage on gays and lesbians. The issue was not examined on the basis of the feelings of either the majority or the minority, but rather on the basis of what a reasonable person with the same characteristics and history as the *Charter* applicants would conclude about the effects of the impugned provision. The analysis was also contextual because it paid attention to the actual circumstances, needs and capacities of same-sex couples. Section 1 of the *Charter* allowed the government to make its best case for the traditional definition of marriage. The government had the burden of fleshing out the rationales for excluding same-sex couples from the institution of marriage and it introduced expert evidence to support its case. The analysis under section 1 of the *Charter* was more rigorous than the debate in Parliament because it went beyond the invocation of general objectives such as the promotion of families and companionship to explore questions about whether there was a rational connection between these objectives and the exclusion of same-sex couples and a comparison of the proportionality between the benefits and harms of excluding same-sex couples. The tests for determining whether there was a violation of equality rights and whether any such violations could be justified as reasonable limits were fairly settled,[90] so that all parties could marshal their best arguments and not be diverted by surprises, side issues, and appeals to pure emotions.

The judges who heard the gay marriage cases, unlike the parliamentarians who considered the issue, were not deluged with phone calls and faxes from their constituents. They did not have to worry about opinion polls and re-election. They did, however, have to worry about fairly listening to the parties and responding to their arguments. Both the British Columbia and Ontario Courts of Appeal responded with detailed reasons about why the *Charter* applied to the traditional common law definition of marriage despite the fact that the Attorney General of Canada conceded this issue on appeal. In doing so, they were respectfully responding to the arguments made by interveners who supported the traditional definition of marriage, as well as the reasons given by the one trial judge who found that the *Charter* did not apply. The judges then went on to examine the effects of the traditional definition of marriage on the *Charter* applicants, same-sex couples who wanted their relationships recognized as marriages. The judges then responded to each of the objectives presented by the Attorney General of Canada as justifying the exclusion of same-sex couples. The adjudicative process can itself be seen as a form of dialogue in which the parties have a guaranteed and meaningful ability to participate and the judges are obliged to respond to the arguments and give reasons for accepting or rejecting the arguments.

Most of the judges were careful to preserve some space for legislatures to respond to their decisions recognizing same-sex relationships as marriages. They suggested that the path of principle and equality led to reformulation of the definition of marriage to include same-sex couples, but they delayed the implementation of this remedy for a two-year period.[91] To be sure, delayed or suspended remedies are a departure from the traditional ideal of adjudication which stresses the close and immediate connection between the recognition of rights and the provision of retroactive remedies. At the same time, however, delayed or suspended constitutional remedies are an important instrument of dialogue because they give the legislature a finite period of time to select among constitutional options while articulating what the court's remedy will be should the legislature not intervene. As discussed above, suspended remedies have become quite routine in Canada and are now specifically contemplated under the South African Constitution.[92]

The Ontario Court of Appeal's decision in the summer of 2003 altered this dialogic balance by providing that judicial recognition of same-sex marriages should apply immediately and by imposing a mandatory order that the government allow the successful *Charter* applicants to marry. In quick order, a significant number of gay marriages have been solemnized in Ontario, "facts on the ground" that may constrain the approach eventually taken by federal and provincial legislatures. The Ontario Court of Appeal's immediate and mandatory remedy is difficult to justify from a dialogic perspective. The immediate remedy may preclude the federal government, perhaps in concert with the provinces, from trying to devise an alternative to gay marriage that could perhaps be justified under section 1 of the *Charter* as a reasonable limit on the equality rights of gays and lesbians. Any new regime would create horizontal inequities between same-sex couples who have had an opportunity to be married and those, either under any new regime or in other provinces, who have not had such an opportunity. Even if the Ontario Court of Appeal had concluded, and it is not clear from its judgment that it had, that no alternative to same-sex marriages could be justified under section 1 of the *Charter*, they also should have recognized the possibility that Parliament might be prepared to use the override to prevent same-sex marriages. In fact, a motion that seemed to authorize the use of the override was defeated by a narrow 137–132 vote in Parliament a few months after the Court of Appeal's decision.[93] Even if the Court of Appeal was firmly of the view that nothing short of the override could justify any departure from same-sex marriage, they should have respected Parliament's ability to use the override as part of the *Charter*.[94] The Court of Appeal also should have known that legislatures cannot use the override in a retroactive fashion.[95] Should Parliament have been prepared to use the override to back up its commitment to the traditional definition of marriage, the Ontario Court of Appeal's immediate remedy would again have created horizontal inequities between the successful *Charter* applicants and other same-sex couples who had become married pursuant to the court's immediate remedy and those who could not become married after Parliament had employed the override.

To be sure, the Ontario Court of Appeal had some justifications for its immediate and mandatory remedy. The Supreme Court's leading decision on remedies can be read as limiting suspended remedies to emergency situations where an immediate remedy would threaten the rule of law, public safety or benefits received by others, factors that were not present in the gay marriage cases. Moreover, some statements in that case suggest that courts should not use suspended declarations of invalidity for dialogic reasons relating to the respective role of courts and legislatures.[96] Nevertheless, the fact remains that the Supreme Court itself has routinely not observed these restrictions and has frequently suspended its own remedy to allow legislatures an opportunity to intervene and pre-empt the Court's remedy. The Court of Appeal may have followed the letter of the Supreme Court's judgment in *Schachter*, but it did not follow the Supreme Court's practice of routinely suspending declarations to allow the legislature time to select among the range of constitutional options.

The Court of Appeal may also have been moved by the equity of the case, the fact that the successful *Charter* applicants wanted their right to marry recognized now. Suspending the court's remedy but exempting the successful applicants from the period of suspension was not an option because this would have created inequities with respect to other similarly situated same-sex couples who wanted to be married, but who might have to wait a year or more and who might find themselves precluded from marrying if Parliament and the provinces had pre-empted the court's remedy with a different regime. The Ontario Court of Appeal acted on the traditional corrective ideal that successful litigants should receive immediate remedies from the courts. Nevertheless, the Court of Appeal's immediate and mandatory remedy limited the range of possible legislative responses to its ruling. It also produced anger and frustration among some Parliamentarians who believed that the court had deliberately pre-empted the work of a committee that was holding public hearings and examining the marriage issue.[97]

Even the Ontario Court of Appeal's strong actions, however, have not stopped the federal government from playing an important role on the gay marriage issue. The government could have appealed the decision and even have sought a stay of the court's remedy pending the hearing of an appeal before the Supreme Court. A decision was made by the Cabinet, however, not to appeal the ruling but rather to draft legislation recognizing gay marriages but exempting religions from recognizing such marriages. The Cabinet made a conscious decision to balance state acceptance of gay marriage with state acceptance of religious freedom not to recognize gay marriage. Although this policy has not satisfied some opponents of gay marriage, it was a significant act of accommodation and statecraft. It broadened the debate beyond the issue being litigated; namely whether traditional restrictions on marriage were a justified restriction on the equality rights of gays and lesbians.[98] Leaving aside for the moment the fact that the government made a decision not to have the draft legislation debated or enacted in Parliament, the draft legislation is an example of dialogue between courts and elected governments in which the two institutions play distinct and complementary roles. The courts have responded to claims by same-sex couples that they have been unjustly excluded from the institution of marriage. The government seems to have accepted the injustice of that exclusion but has broadened the debate beyond the civil definition of marriage to include the freedom of religions to decide on their own whether to recognize same-sex marriages.

The Cabinet also decided to direct a reference on the constitutionality of the draft legislation to the Supreme Court. The reference procedure is an important dialogic instrument that allows governments to refer draft pieces of legislation to the court and can be contrasted with the prohibition of references under the non-dialogic American Bill of Rights. The government made a controversial decision not to refer the question of whether something short of same-sex marriage could be justified under the *Charter*. Unfortunately, Cabinet decisions, unlike judicial decisions, are made with a high degree of confidentiality and are not always accompanied with formal reasons. One Cabinet Minister, Steve Mahoney, is reported to have urged "some kind of `compromise' at the cabinet table, such as civil unions for gays and lesbians, but said the government's legal advice is that it would create a two-tiered system of marriage likely to be struck down by the court." Another Cabinet Minister, Solicitor General Wayne Easter, has expressed reservations about the plan adding "It would be nice to know what the Supreme Court would say if we didn't use the word "marriage." That's what I would like to know."[99] Martin Cauchon, the Attorney General of Canada, has made a strong argument that civil unions or registered partnerships would fall "short of true equality. Clearly, we must do better than almost equal."[100] The decision to limit the range of options before the court was a decision of the government of the day. Nevertheless, it may change, especially because Prime Minister Paul Martin has made comments that suggest openness to alternatives to same-sex marriages provided they are consistent with the *Charter*.[101]

The eventual resolution of the same-sex marriage issue remains uncertain, but the important point from a dialogic perspective is that it has remained a matter of continued political controversy and debate. Although the courts have provoked this debate, they do not own it. In the aftermath of the Ontario Court of Appeal decision, there has been more interest about how Members of Parliament will vote than how the Supreme Court will decide the reference.[102] The official opposition was able to force a vote on a motion re-affirming the 1999 resolution in favour of the traditional definition of marriage. It was defeated by a narrow 137–132 vote, even though the resolution could be read as authorizing Parliament to use all its powers, including the notwithstanding clause, to preserve the traditional definition of marriage. The excitement surrounding the vote belies extravagant claims that Parliament is dead in the age of the *Charter*. It remains unclear whether and when the draft legislation will be introduced into Parliament or whether it will be introduced in its current form. The government has committed itself to a free vote on the issue. Legislation recognizing same-sex marriages could be defeated in Parliament, especially if the controversial use of the override is taken off the table. The defeat of the bill would, however, not alter the new status quo in Ontario and British Columbia where courts have now recognized gay marriages with immediate effect. A new legislative majority would have to be formed either to develop a third option other than traditional or gay marriage and that option would likely be tested under the *Charter*. Yet another majority would have to be formed to use the override to affirm the exclusion of gays and lesbians from marriage notwithstanding the equality rights of the *Charter*. The gay marriage controversy is far from over and it could well be an issue in the next election. The conservative opposition may make opposition to same-sex marriage a key element of its platform. It could present a third option, offer to use the override and/or promise to hold a referendum on the issue. These various scenarios, all of which depend in part on what elected Members of Parliament are prepared to do, belie Jeffrey Simpson's arguments that "Parliament could vote 301–0 against same-sex marriage and it wouldn't matter, because the courts have decided what the definition should be."[103]

Even if the draft legislation is approved by the Court and enacted by Parliament, the elected government will have played a significant role in the debate both by ratifying the Court's decision on the principle of gay marriage and by balancing that with concerns about freedom of religion. The draft legislation provides that "marriage, for civil purposes, is the lawful union of two persons to the exclusion of others" but that "nothing in this Act affects the freedom of officials of religious groups to refuse to perform marriages that are not in accordance with their religious beliefs." The government has made an important policy decision to accept gay marriage[104] and to introduce a competing principle of religious freedom into the debate. In this sense, the draft law lives up to the Minister of Justice's press release announcing the reference that concluded with the statement that:

The Government of Canada believes that a strong, effective democratic system depends on a dynamic dialogue between Parliament and the courts. This dialogue enhances the democratic process by ensuring that our laws reflect the fundamental values of the *Charter*. That is why the Government chose this course of action.[105]

Some of the government's actions are more questionable from a dialogic perspective. Although the government has ensured that Members of Parliament will be able not only to vote on the draft bill, but to do so in a free vote without party discipline, it may have been preferable for the bill to have been introduced and debated in Parliament. Some have questioned whether a reference to the Supreme Court is necessary, but it is probably advisable given that the government has chosen not to appeal the Court of Appeal's ruling. Nevertheless, it should be clear that the government as represented by the Cabinet has made a policy decision to accept gay marriage but to balance that with the religious freedom clause. Even more debatable from a dialogic perspective is the government's decision to invite the Court to rule that the draft act defining marriage "for civil purposes" as "the lawful union of two persons to the exclusion of all others" is within the exclusive legislative authority of the federal Parliament. The federal division of powers provides Parliament with jurisdiction over "marriage and divorce" and, unlike the *Charter*, is not subject to either reasonable limits or an override. Some provinces such as Alberta will argue that provincial jurisdiction over the "solemnization of marriage in the province" provides them with some jurisdiction to reply to the courts' decision, if not the federal legislation. Federalism, combined with dialogic structure of the *Charter*, can allow a range of reasonable policy alternatives to be recognized. Nevertheless a ruling that marriage is the exclusive preserve of the federal Parliament, combined with the determination of the present federal government never to use the override, could inhibit the range of possible legislative replies to the gay marriage decisions. Dialogue will be precluded not so much by the *Charter* but by the division of powers, which does not have the same dialogic structure as the *Charter*.

My point in this discussion of the gay marriage cases is not to attempt to read the political tea leaves, but only to show that even on an issue where the courts have been quite bold, elected governments have already played an important role and could play an even more important role in the future. Democracy should be measured not only by the possibility of legislative reply, but also by the tenor of democratic debate. In large part because of the courts' bold decisions, gay marriage is headline news and the subject of much debate. The courts have provoked a more vigorous and open political debate on the issue than occurred either when Parliament affirmed the traditional definition of marriage or Alberta used the override to preclude *Charter* litigation of the issue. The current debate is in no way limited to speculation about what the Supreme Court will decide in the reference. Much of the debate is about what Members of Parliament and the Prime Minister will do now that they have been forced by the courts to confront this issue. The legislative agenda on gay marriage has largely been set by *Charter* litigation and the courts, but its outcome remains in the hands of our elected governments.

Close empirical examinations of legislative decisions to accept, revise or reject court decisions will enrich our understanding of dialogue, but at the same time, they will not resolve the normative controversy about whether dialogic judicial review is a more democratic and acceptable alternative to either judicial or legislative supremacy. One normative issue that looms large in the empirical debate about the frequency and quality of legislative replies to court decisions is the true meaning of dialogue. Different understandings of dialogue lie at the heart of the disagreement between Hogg and Thornton on the one hand and Manfredi and Kelly on the other about the true extent of dialogue under the *Charter*. Hogg and Thorton classify legislative acceptance of a judicial decision as a form of dialogue:

remembering that the legislature nearly always has a range of choice, it is difficult to maintain that the legislature is not exercising any of that choice when it implements the court's decision. After all, in common experience, dialogue does sometimes lead to agreement ... if a new law is slow to materialize, that is just one of the consequences of a democratic system of government, not a failing of judicial review under the *Charter*.[106]

In contrast, Manfredi and Kelly characterize genuine dialogue in a much more restrictive manner that requires that the legislature interpret the *Charter* differently than the majority and perhaps even the minority of the Court. They argue that "[g]enuine dialogue only exists when legislatures are recognized as legitimate interpreters of the constitution and have an *effective* means to assert that interpretation."[107] Behind their empirical dispute about the number of legislative replies to *Charter* decisions lies a normative debate about what constitutes dialogue between courts and legislatures.

Hogg's and Thornton's argument that dialogue occurs even when a legislature accepts or fails to reverse or revise a *Charter* decision is supported by the nature of parliamentary government in Canada. As discussed above, governments in Canada generally do not have significant problems implementing their legislative agenda. Power is concentrated in the Cabinet and increasingly the Prime Minister. This concentration of power focuses democratic responsibility for the acceptance or rejection of *Charter* decisions. If Canadians do not like the way the federal government is responding to the gay marriage cases, they can blame the Prime Minister. They can, of course, blame the judges and increased criticism of the courts are legitimate in a democracy. Nevertheless such criticisms are in a sense futile because of the independence of the judiciary. What should not be futile, however, is criticism of the elected government that allowed the Court decision to stand. As Jeffrey Goldsworthy has argued, democrats should accept responsibility for the legislature not responding to a judicial decision and not using the override because it is the "electorate's democratic right" to prefer a judicial decision to a legislative decision to override that right as interpreted by the courts.[108] I do not discount, however, the possibility that Canadians may increasingly feel that their criticisms and engagement with democratic governments are impotent, but this should not count as a strong criticism of dialogic judicial review. If anything, dialogic judicial review provides citizens with one more lever for articulating grievances against their government.

Manfredi and Kelly dispute the idea that legislative acceptance or failure to reverse a *Charter* decision constitutes genuine dialogue between the court and the legislature. They argue that such dialogue only occurs when the legislature interprets the constitution for itself and they express skepticism about whether this occurs even when the legislature reverses a *Charter* decision by adopting the legal position of a minority on the Court. In the United States, Mark Tushnet has recently argued that legislatures should be encouraged to act on their own interpretation of the "thin" constitution.[109] Co-ordinate construction has impressive democratic credentials going back at least to the thought of Thomas Jefferson and James Madison at the time of the founding of the American Republic. It is being reclaimed by scholars and has emerged as a strong theory of dialogue that challenges conventional theories of judicial review on the basis that they give the courts a privileged role in interpreting constitutional values.

A number of responses are available to the proponents of coordinate construction. One is that regardless of its desirability, legislatures in Canada have not appeared overly able or eager to interpret the *Charter* for themselves. Even when Parliament has been prepared to reverse a *Charter* decision, it has been attracted to the legal opinion produced by dissenting judges and unprepared to generate a genuinely novel interpretation of the Constitution.[110] Parliament and its legal advisers have also fastened with perhaps undue haste on policy suggestions that the courts have made about less drastic alternatives.[111] Some legislative replies to *Charter* decisions have been accompanied by little debate. For example, there was little discussion in Parliament when it resurrected a public interest criteria for denying bail in response to a *Charter* decision and one judge has characterized legislative debate about the reasons for denying prisoners the vote as "more fulmination than illumination."[112] One hypothesis advanced by Professor Hiebert is that legislatures lack the capacity to engage in their own interpretation of the Constitution and this should be augmented through increased use of legislative committees and devices such as preambles.[113]

It is not clear that even with increased capacity and incentives that legislatures will want to produce their own interpretations of the *Charter*.[114] There already is extensive capacity within the executive branch of government to engage in *Charter* interpretation.[115] The Attorney General who sits in Parliament bears responsibility for ensuring that all public bills are consistent with the *Charter*, but has so far not once exercised the statutory duty to report to Parliament that a bill is inconsistent with the *Charter*.[116] This suggests that legislators may be unwilling to interpret the *Charter* in a manner that is more generous than the courts. The fact that legislatures have made infrequent use of section 33 also suggests that legislatures may be reluctant to develop and take responsibility for alternative interpretations of the Constitution. This may suggest that many in our democracy associate rights with courts and that the possibility of legislatures reasonably interpreting rights may lack popular support. American ideas of judicial supremacy may be as common in Canada as American-style critiques of judicial activism or American popular culture.[117] On this argument, the problem of courts having the last word in the interpretation of rights lies less with the structure of the *Charter* or the idea of dialogue and more with the people's faith in courts and the unwillingness or inability of legislatures to provide compelling alternative interpretations of the *Charter*.

Another response to the proponents of co-ordinate construction is at a more normative level. Should legislatures concerned with re-election be encouraged to define the rights of minorities, the rights of the accused or the treatment of fundamental values that are threatened by crises such as post–September 11 fears about terrorism? My concern is that Parliament may interpret the constitution to impose extreme costs on either *de jure* or *de facto* non-citizens who do not have either the legal right to vote or a meaningful right to vote in the sense that they are not the marginal voters that political parties worry about. When Parliament limited the voting rights of prisoners, it imposed costs on an unpopular and feared minority that, if it had its way, could not even vote. Even now that prisoners can vote, they and their families lie outside the mainstream of marginal voters. Once a minority is outside of the range of potential and influential voters of the governing party, it can be dismissed by the elected government and any party that hopes to become the elected government. Although it is possible to design the legislative process to maximize the power of minorities, the Canadian legislative process does not do so. The interests of rural residents and smaller provinces are somewhat overrepresented on the electoral map and representational concerns play a role in the formation of the Cabinet and appointments to the Senate, but there is little attempt to guarantee a voice for disadvantaged minorities in the legislative process. It would take a strong faith in the very limited checks and balances of Canadian representative democracy[118] to trust legislatures to address the rights of minorities in a fair and open manner. In my view, there are enough reservations about co-ordinate construction that it should generally be limited to those cases in which the legislature is prepared to use the override. Hopefully, this will encourage legislatures to give full reasons for their interpretation of the *Charter*[119] and in any event will require them to re-evaluate their reasons in five years' time.

A more restrained approach to co-ordinate construction is to give legislatures a role in defining reasonable limits on rights as opposed to defining the rights of minorities and fundamental values themselves. Professor Hiebert has argued that the dialogue metaphor "does not differentiate between the rights-oriented dimension of defining normative values in the *Charter* and the more policy-laden task of assessing the reasonableness of complex policy objectives."[120] She seems less comfortable than Professors Manfredi or Tushnet with judicial interpretation of *Charter* rights – or at least what she believes are "core rights"[121] – but argues that Parliament's interpretation of policy under section 1 of the *Charter* deserves greater respect from the court. There is something to be said for the idea that co-ordinate construction is more acceptable under section 1 of the *Charter*. In a sense, section 1 is the government's turf and it may have some advantages over the courts in determining its true purposes in limiting rights, the alternatives available and the overall balance struck.

But there are problems in courts deferring to Parliament's interpretation of section 1. Parliament will have an incentive to define the purpose of the legislation strategically in order to maximize its chance of survival under section 1. In many cases, it may focus on the broad objectives of the law as opposed to the more limited objectives of limiting *Charter* rights. Although Parliament should be in a good position to speak to the proportionality of the means used to pursue its objectives, it has often failed to address the tough issues of section 1 analysis. For example, the legislative reply to *Daviault*[122] did not explain why Parliament concluded it was necessary to reverse the Court's *Charter* decision as opposed to creating a new intoxication-based offence as suggested by the Court.[123] It may well be that Parliament has some good reasons for not adopting this widely discussed option, but they are not found in the reply legislation or in the preamble to the reply legislation. Similarly, the Court's oft-criticized decision striking down restrictions on tobacco advertising was in large part driven by the Court's perception that the government was hiding the ball by failing to disclose its own studies about the effectiveness of less restrictive regulations on tobacco advertising.[124] If the government's interpretation of what constitutes a reasonable limit on rights is to receive more deference from the courts, it must not avoid the more difficult questions. One of the virtues of judicial review is that judges often ask the difficult and uncomfortable questions that politicians too frequently avoid or gloss over. Should political debate become more searching and candid, then Parliament's claim to respect for its interpretation of section 1 will be much stronger.

Although there is room for improvement in the legislative contributions to section 1 analysis, I remain skeptical that courts should defer to even new and improved legislative interpretations of section 1. Even when legislatures bolster their interpretative capacity through the use of legislative preambles,[125] courts still will need to conduct an independent evaluation of the objective for limiting *Charter* rights. Moreover, the independent judiciary still has an important role in determining the overall balance between the social objectives of limiting the right and the harm caused by the violation of a right. Even though legislatures should become more adept at articulating the purposes of the limitation and the harmful consequences for society of not limiting a *Charter* right, there is still a danger that they will undervalue the harms of violating some *Charter* rights. Even if Parliament takes the *Charter* seriously, it may still be inclined to ignore or neglect the rights of minorities and the unpopular because of its nature as an elected institution. This is particularly a danger in the field of criminal justice which empirically consumes a significant majority of all *Charter* cases. In my view, it is no coincidence that the two pieces of legislation that Professor Hiebert praises as based on Parliament's "alternative interpretation of the *Charter*"[126] were laws that diminished the rights of those accused of committing sexual violence. The accused will always be less popular than the victim. There will always be more votes in appearing tough on crime and sympathetic to victims than in appearing to be soft on crime and unsympathetic to victims.[127] Thus in criminal justice, which lies at the heart of *Charter* litigation, there will be a continued need for the independent judiciary to rigorously scrutinize Parliament's claim to have enacted new criminal laws based on its own interpretation of the *Charter*.

In summary, cases where legislatures fail to revise or reject court decisions raise interesting issues for dialogue theory. There is a need for continued empirical research to better understand the complexities of dialogue between courts and legislatures. It is possible that popular understandings of rights and court rulings are more absolute than contemplated under dialogic theories of judicial review. Thus one of the goals of dialogue theory should be to explain the range of options open to legislatures after *Charter* decisions. Legislatures may not have the necessary capacity to generate interpretations of the *Charter* that are independent from those of the courts. Should this capacity become enhanced and in those cases in which it is exercised, however, normative questions about co-ordinate construction remain. In my view, it is not wise to think that a legislature elected by the majority and concerned with re-election is the best institution to interpret the rights of minorities, the rights of the accused and fundamental and long-term values such as freedom of expression and procedural fairness that may be neglected in times of perceived crisis. In any event, legislatures can help shape section 1 analysis and they can act on their own interpretations of the *Charter* if they are prepared to use the override. Governments can also be held democratically accountable for their acceptance of *Charter* decisions. For example, if a majority of Canadians are strongly opposed to gay marriage, they will be able to punish the government for its acceptance of the courts' decision on that topic in the next election.

IV WHEN LEGISLATURES APPEAR TO HAVE THE LAST WORD IN THE DIALOGUE

The above reservations about the ability of legislatures to interpret the Constitution lead to the question of why trust legislatures to play any role in dialogues about the rights of minorities and fundamental freedoms. In other words are the flaws in the legislative process so great as to justify judicial supremacy on such issues? Most conventional theories of judicial review answer yes, but that option is not open to theories of dialogic judicial review. Although most critiques of dialogue theory have been made by supporters of either legislative supremacy or co-ordinate construction, conventional theorists of judicial review should not be far behind in criticizing dialogue theory. Their concern will not be that dialogic judicial review gives judges too strong and privileged a role, but rather that it sacrifices their right answers, whether they be based on framers' intent, the protection of minorities vulnerable in democracy or fundamental values, to the vagaries of politics. Dialogue theorists who now find themselves defending the role of courts from charges that they are engaged in undemocratic judicial activism may someday find themselves defending bills of rights that allow legislatures to derogate from rights through ordinary legislation. Defenders of conventional judicial review will ask dialogue theorists why they are prepared to place the rights of minorities and fundamental values at risk from legislative majorities. This will not be an easy question to answer.

What are the justifications for allowing legislative revisions and re-jections of court decisions about rights? The justifications are found both in democracy and in a pragmatic appreciation of the limits of con-stitutional adjudication. One justification is found in the dangers that courts may over-enforce certain rights. The history of judicial review in the 20th century suggests that courts may over-enforce various rights at various times. Dialogic judicial review allows elected governments an opportunity to correct such judicial errors. Note that such corrections will generally only occur when courts are perceived to have gone too far in enforcing rights. It is only then that sections 1 and 33 of the *Charter* can be used to limit or override rights as interpreted by the courts. If courts under-enforce *Charter* rights, perhaps by strategically trimming their sails to avoid criticism or the possibility of a legislative override, legislative correction is still possible, but less likely. In the 1970s, Par-liament corrected widely criticized judicial decisions that under-enforced the *Canadian Bill of Rights* by refusing to invalidate capital punishment, wiretapping without a judicial warrant, reversals of jury acquittals by an appellate court and discrimination against women when they were pregnant. In the *Charter* era, however, there are far fewer examples of legislatures correcting judicial decisions that were seen to under-enforce rights.[128] Judicial review may be most harmful to democracy not when it provokes a noisy "in your face" legislative reply or an override of a court decision, but rather when courts quietly accept dubious laws and practices as consistent with the *Charter* and such laws can be enacted and applied with little or no controversy or debate.

Even when legislatures do accept court decisions, there is a value to knowing that the decision could have been revised or reversed if the legislature so desired. Such knowledge can provide increased democ-ratic legitimacy for court decisions and might help avoid the sort of defiance of court orders that has sometimes occurred under the Ameri-can Bill of Rights. Even if the court plays the role of Socrates in teaching legislators and the people about the importance of long-term values, the lessons are better learned by the knowledge that the students and the electorate could overpower the Socratic Court if they really desired to do so. The polity may be more willing to consider the merits of the courts' decisions if it knows it can reject them. This argument is in a sense the flip side of Jeremy Waldron's argument that even assuming that courts would reach the right answers to difficult questions involving rights, something would be lost if correction came from outside and from the wisdom of unelected judges. My argument is that something is gained when citizens debate controversial court decisions knowing that their government could, if it wanted, take formal action and responsibility for limiting or overriding the decision.

The debate about gay marriage is improved by the fact that Parliament could override the courts' decisions and prevent gay marriage. I want to be clear that this is not a result that I as a citizen desire. Nevertheless, I think it is both democratic and educational for citizens to think through the possibility that their government could override the court decisions through the use of the override. This thinking through of all the options is better for society than sullen acceptance of a court decision or exploration of extra-legislative means to nullify or disobey the court decision. A democratically debated and enacted override of the gay marriage decisions would be regrettable and embarrassing in the future, but it would not make the controversy go away. The courts' argument that equality requires gay marriage would be preserved and held in abeyance for five years when we as a society would have to debate whether the override should be renewed.

It is unfortunate in my view that some defences of gay marriage have been premised on rhetoric that seems to assume judicial supremacy. For example, one of the lawyers for the successful applicants in *Halpern* has been reported as stating "the government doesn't really have a choice in the matter and the courts have clearly spoken, that equality requires that this be done." One of the successful applicants in *Halpern* similarly declared "it's done, it's over with ... No Supreme Court is going to say we're unmarried. That's un-Canadian,"[129] These comments may simply reflect the understandable thrill of a hard-fought court-room victory and the fact that the Ontario Court of Appeal provided an immediate and mandatory remedy that resolved the matter in the applicants' favour. Nevertheless, as suggested above, the larger political issue is still very much in play. Backbenchers and candidates in the next election, not to mention the voters, need to be convinced of the merits of the case for gay marriage. The fact that advocates of same-sex marriage have won in court is not enough to convince these people. Parliament could use either sections 1 or 33 to limit or override the judicial decisions that equality requires the recognition of same-sex marriage. Even if the draft legislation in enacted, the debate about same-sex marriages will shift from the legislature to religious organizations and people will still have to be convinced of the justness of the case for gay marriage. It is always short-sighted in a democracy not to engage fellow citizens about the justice of your cause. The bonds of community in our society can also be strengthened by the possibility of legislative revision or reversal of court decisions. In a democracy, a win in court should not be enough.

The gay marriage issue may be somewhat unique because it is so symbolic and because court decisions such as the Ontario Court of Appeal's appear to be self-executing. In contrast, rights advocates on issues such as abortion, free speech, police powers, Aboriginal rights and prison reform cannot generally afford to stop after court victories because both public and governmental support is required to make the rights recognized by the courts real and effective. A win in court is often only the start of a difficult process of achieving reform. Members of the so-called Court Party of civil libertarians, feminists and minorities understand that they must work with legislators, administrators and citizens, as well as judges, to achieve meaningful reform. As Bickel recognized even under the American Bill of Rights "the effectiveness of the judgment universalized depends on consent and administration."[130] Under a dialogic bill of rights, the need to engage the government and the public after court decisions is even greater.

If one is inclined to take a pessimistic view of democracy, it can be argued that the override will be used in those cases in which society would in any event resist and refuse to obey a highly controversial court decision about the rights of the unpopular. An override to prevent gay marriage would on this view simply represent attitudes in society that would have provoked an extra-legal backlash and have made the legal recognition of gay marriage something of a "hollow hope."[131] In this sense, dialogic judicial review accommodates a tragic sense of human nature. It recognizes that rights will be violated and minorities ganged up on regardless of whether there is judicial review or not. The least dangerous branch will not save us from the worst sides of our nature. What the courts can do, however, is make society more aware of the consequences of its actions and require sober second thoughts and perhaps extraordinary majorities before the override is used. It also recognizes the potential for moral growth and evolution by requiring continued debates about whether the override should be renewed.

But dialogic judicial review also appeals to a more optimistic view of democracy and human nature. The gamble here is that majorities will frequently decide that they can live with judicial decisions proclaiming the rights of the unpopular. Left to their own devices, legislatures may avoid divisive issues such as abortion or gay rights and cling to the comforts of the status quo. On this view, legislative majorities are not inherently malevolent, but happy to pursue the route of least resistance. When courts disturb the status quo and make decisions applying principles such as equality and fairness, legislative majorities will often accept such decisions and avoid being held accountable for new legislation that authorizes treatment that the courts have held is unequal or unfair. There is a history of legislatures acting in this very fashion. Many common law presumptions prevailed before the *Charter* because legislators were unwilling to make clear statements that people should be denied hearings or convicted in the absence of fault.

It was an optimistic take on democracy that led my colleague Sujit Choudhry and me to urge that Parliament address the issue of racial and religious profiling in its *Anti-terrorism Act*[132] enacted in the wake of the September 11 terrorist attacks. The legislation avoided the profiling issue even though it was very much on the public's mind. Our argument was that Parliament should either take responsibility for profiling and authorize it in the legislation or it should clearly prohibit it as unacceptable in a democracy committed to equality. The gamble was that Parliament would select the latter course and we were optimistic that "an express policy of profiling could not withstand the scrutiny of legislative and public debate. Canada is now a very different country than when it turned against its residents of Japanese descent." Parliament, however, continued to duck the issue, as it often does on divisive issues. The result is that the *Anti-terrorism Act* does not prohibit or specifically authorize racial profiling and any remedy for specific acts of profiling would likely be limited to requests by individuals for some form of compensation. This state of affairs is undesirable in part because it diminished democratic debate and accountability on the profiling issue. Some could "argue that our preference for provoking a democratic debate on profiling, as well as for theories of judicial review which promote dialogue between courts and legislatures, leaves vulnerable minorities at risk" to an explicit Parliamentary authorization of profiling.[133] But this would at least have been more candid than allowing the issue to go underground by being delegated to the Executive. Specific legislative authorization of profiling would have prompted more democratic debate about the subject. Parliament would have been forced to contemplate whether it wanted to take responsibility for clear statements authorizing profiling. Such clear legislative statements would have facilitated *Charter* challenges to profiling, perhaps requiring Parliament to consider whether it was prepared to enact legislation notwithstanding equality rights in order to authorize profiling.[134] If Parliament was truly prepared to override equality rights in order to authorize profiling, little would be lost by such legislation particularly if the legislation would expire in five years' time after which hopefully the injustice and the inefficiency of profiling would be better known to the people. A society that was so determined to single people out because they were of Arab descent or the Muslim religion that it would authorize profiling, perhaps by means of the override, would be a society that would practise discriminatory profiling regardless of what the law said. The override would, at least, make society more aware of what it was doing and would require the legislature to re-visit the matter in five years' time, when calmer heads would hopefully prevail.

A dialogic bill of rights such as the *Charter* allows the legislature to revise or reverse judicial decisions that seem as manifestly wrong-headed as *Lochner v. New York*[135] or as manifestly right as *Brown v. Board of Education*.[136] A society that is prepared to override its *Brown* would not, however, be a society that would live its justice even in the absence of an override. On the other hand, a society that could seriously debate whether it should override *Brown* and decide that it should not might become a society that accepts and internalizes the decision in a way that might not occur under a regime of judicial supremacy in which citizens have the limited options of disobeying court decisions or futilely attempting to change the Court and the Constitution.

V CONCLUSION

Dialogic judicial review is a theory that rejects the idea that either the judges or the legislators are infallible. Dialogic judicial review is prompted by a concern that legislators may ignore fundamental long-term values or gang up on the unpopular in the absence of independent courts having the ability to apply a bill of rights. Dialogic judicial review can place justice issues on the legislative agenda and can counter the tendency of legislators to duck divisive issues or defer to the status quo. Judicial activism on issues such as abortion and gay marriage should increase rather than decrease meaningful democratic deliberation. At the same time, dialogic judicial review does not set the judges up as infallible Platonic guardians. Section 1 and 33 of the *Charter*, combined with the government's ability to implement its legislative agenda, mean that in most cases, the legislature should be able to revise and reverse most *Charter* decisions. Although legislators may frequently accept court decisions through explicit legislation or simply by not revisiting the issue, they still bear democratic responsibility for their decisions not to enact ordinary legislation that revises or reverses the *Charter* decision. In short, accountable legislators have ample ability under the *Charter* and parliamentary government to say no to the Court. Dialogic bills of rights trust citizens to make responsible and just decisions about rights as interpreted by the courts.

In the end dialogic judicial review seems destined to be attacked from both sides: from the defenders of rights as declared once and for all by the judiciary and from defenders of democracy who are suspicious of judicial fetters on the legislature. In response to the first line of critics, dialogue theorists will have to justify a strong legislative role in debates about rights while not going all the way to legislative supremacy. In response to the latter, dialogue theorists will have to justify a strong judicial role in debates about rights while not going all the way to judicial supremacy. The future of dialogic judicial review will be a continued rejection of the extremes of legislative or judicial supremacy and continued interest in both what the courts and legislatures have to say about justice issues. Defending dialogic judicial review as a halfway house between legislative and judicial supremacy will not be easy given that many commentators are committed to judicial or legislative supremacy and have suspected that dialogic judicial review leans towards the position that they oppose. Dialogue theorists should make clear that their theories will not tell judges how to decide hard cases, but are directed more at how society should struggle together for the best answers to controversies about justice. The normative and empirical premises of dialogue will continue to be contested, but dialogic judicial review will survive and hopefully thrive as a theory that makes sense of the *Charter* and other modern bills of rights which allow rights as defined by the courts to be limited or overridden by ordinary legislation.

NOTES

[All references in these notes to articles "in this volume" refer to its original publication source, (2004) 23 S.C.L.R. (2d).]

1 Being Part I of the *Constitution Act, 1982,* being Schedule B of the *Canada Act 1982 (U.K.,* 1982, c. 11 [hereinafter "*Charter*"].

2 *New Zealand Bill of Rights Act (N.Z.),* 1990/109; *Human Rights Act 1998 (U.K.),* 1998, c. 42.

3 *Constitution of the Republic of South Africa 1996,* No. 108 of 1996, ss. 36, 172(1).

4 *Vriend v. Alberta*, [1998] 1 SCR 493, at 562–67.

5 *R. v. Mills*, [1999] 3 SCR 668, at 711–13 [hereinafter "*Mills*"].

6 *R. v. Hall*, [2002] 3 SCR 309, at paras. 127–28, Iacobucci, J., dissenting [hereinafter "*Hall*"]; *Sauvé v. Canada (Chief Electoral Officer)* [2002] 3 SCR 519, at para. 17, McLachlin, C.J.C. [hereinafter "*Sauvé*"].

7 *Mills, supra,* note 5, at paras. 56–60, Iacobucci and McLachlin, JJ.; *Sauvé, supra,* note 6, at para. 98, Gonthier J dissenting.

8 For more discussion of inconsistency in the Court's use of the dialogue metaphor see Manfredi, "The Life of a Metaphor: Dialogue in the Supreme Court, 1998–2003," in this volume.

9 The critical literature on these conventional theories of judicial review is vast. See e.g., Tushnet, *Red, White and Blue: A Critical Analysis of Constitutional Law* (1988).

10 Petter, "Rip Van Winkle in Charterland" in Bazowski, ed., *The Charter at Twenty* (forthcoming); Ewing, "Human Rights" in Cane and Tushnet, eds., *The Oxford Handbook of Legal Studies* (2003).

11 See generally Roach, *The Supreme Court on Trial: Judicial Activism or Democratic Dialogue* (2001), at ch. 12.

12 Tushnet, "Judicial Activism or Restraint in a Section 33 World" (2003) 53 U.T.L.J. 89.

13 Manfredi, *Judicial Power and the Charter: Canada and the Paradox of Liberal Constitutionalism* (2nd ed., 2001).

14 See e.g., Hiebert, *Charter Conflicts: What is Parliament's Role?* (2002) [hereinafter "*Charter Conflicts*"].

15 Hogg and Thornton, "Reply to 'Six Degrees of Dialogue'" (1999) 37 Osgoode Hall L.J. 529.

16 Parliament's robust responses to the Supreme Court's decisions about the *Charter* rights of the accused in *R. v. Seaboyer*, [1991] 2 SCR 577 [hereinafter "*Seaboyer*"]; *R. v. Daviault*, [1994] 3 SCR 63 [hereinafter "*Daviault*"]; and *R. v. O'Connor*, [1995] 4 SCR 411 [hereinafter "*O'Connor*"] are discussed in Hiebert, *supra,* note 14, at ch. 5, and Roach, *supra,* note 11, at ch. 10.

17 Manfredi and Kelly, "Six Degrees of Dialogue: A Response to Hogg and Bushell" (1999) 37 Osgoode Hall L.J. 513.

18 For some such criticisms of dialogue see Cameron, "The Charter's Legislative Override: Feat or Figment of the Constitutional Imagination?," in this volume (criticizing the override); Ryder, "Suspending the Charter" (2003) 21 S.C.L.R. (2d) 267 (criticizing the use of suspended declarations of invalidity); Leclair, "Réflexions critiques au sujet de la métaphore du dialogue en droit constitutionnel canadien" (2002) R. du B. 379; Weinrib, "The Canadian Charter's Transformative

Aspirations" (2003) 19 S.C.L.R. (2d) 17, at 19 (more general critique of dialogue).

19 *Sauvé, supra,* note 6, at para. 17, *per* McLachlin, C.J.C. (in the context of dismissing such an argument).

20 Ackerman, *We the People: Foundations* (1993).

21 Bickel, *The Least Dangerous Branch: The Supreme Court at the Bar of Politics* (2nd ed., 1986) at ch. 4; Eskridge, *Dynamic Statutory Interpretation* (1994); Sunstein, *One Case at a Time: Judicial Minimalism on the Supreme Court* (1999).

22 On the state of dialogue in the United States with comparison to Canada see Mathen, "Constitutional Dialogues in Canada and the United States" (2003) 14 N.J.C.L. 403.

23 Calabresi, *A Common Law for our Age of Statutes* (1982); Calabresi, "Foreword: Anti-discrimination and Constitutional Accountability (What the Bork-Brennan Debate Ignores)" (1991) 105 Harv. L. Rev. 80.

24 See Roach, *The Supreme Court on Trial, supra,* note 11, and Roach "Constitutional and Common Law Dialogues Between the Supreme Court and Canadian Legislatures" (2001) 80 Can. Bar Rev. 481.

25 Hogg and Bushell, "The Charter Dialogue Between Courts and Legislatures" (1997) 35 Osgoode Hall L.J. 75, at 79.

26 Quoted in Barak, "Foreward: A Judge on Judging: The Role of a Supreme Court in a Democracy" (2002) 116 Harv. L. Rev. 16, at 137. For arguments that judicial supervision of police practices do not detract from liberal constitutionalism or result in judicial supremacy see Kelly, "The Supreme Court of Canada and the Complexity of Judicial Activism" in James, Abelson, and Lusztig, eds., *The Myth of the Sacred: The Charter, the Courts and the Politics of the Constitution in Canada* (2002), at 97.

27 *Slaight Communications Inc. v. Davidson,* [1989] 1 SCR *1038; R. v. Ladouceur,* [1990] 1 SCR 1257; *Little Sisters Book and Art Emporium v. Canada (Minister of Justice),* [2000] 2 SCR 1120. For further argument relating the prescribed-by-law requirement to democratic dialogue between courts and legislatures, see Choudhry and Roach, "Racial and Ethnic Profiling: Statutory Discretion, Constitutional Remedies and Democratic Accountability" (2003) 41 Osgoode Hall L.J. 1.

28 *R. v. Big M Drug Mart Ltd.,* [1985] 1 SCR *295; Vriend v. Alberta,* [1998] 1 SCR 493.

29 Hogg and Bushell, *supra,* note 25, at 92–95. The legislature may also have a diminished role in cases such as *R. v. Mills,* [1999] 3 SCR 668, where the Court reconciles competing *Charter* rights for itself without

reaching s. 1 and in cases such as *United States v. Burns*, [2001] 1 SCR 283, in which the Court indicates that s. 1 limits on s. 7 rights can only be justified in an emergency situation.

30 One study of Supreme Court decisions found that the Court accepted the legitimacy of the legislative objective in 97 per cent of cases. Trakman, Cole-Hamilton, and Gatien, "*R. v. Oakes*, 1986–1997: Back to the Drawing Board" (1998) 36 Osgoode Hall L.J 83.

31 *R. v. Edwards Books and Art Ltd.*, [1986] 2 SCR 713. In some important recent cases, however, the courts have indicated some serious reservations about whether the government's objectives were important enough to justify a limitation on a *Charter* right, but have assumed so and gone on to determine whether the limitation was proportionate to the objective. See *Sauvé v. Canada*, [2002] 3 SCR 519 (denial of voting rights to prisoners to promote the rule of law and punish prisoners); *EGALE v. Canada* (2003), 225 DLR (4th) 472 (BCCA); *Halpern v. Canada* (2003), 65 OR (3d) 161 (CA) (denial of marriage to gays and lesbians to promote procreation and recognize companionship).

32 Waldron, *Law and Disagreement* (1999) at 221. This flexibility is significantly diminished however to the extent that the Supreme Court has indicated that it would rarely, if ever, accept a violation of s. 7 or s. 12 of the *Charter* as a reasonable limit under s. 1 of the *Charter*, and also when the Court rejects the objective offered by the legislature.

33 *Ford v. Quebec (Attorney General)*, [1988] 2 SCR 712.

34 For example, s. 17 of the *Human Rights Act, 1998 (U.K.), 1998,* c. 42, follows s. 33 of the *Charter* by requiring that derogations from Convention rights be reviewed at least every five years.

35 Waldron, "Some Models of Dialogue Between Judges and Legislators," in this volume.

36 See the proposal made in Manfredi, *supra*, note 13, at 192–94 for requiring that the override be used only after a final judicial decision.

37 Even in that case, the people knew that Quebec's use of the override was largely an objection to the patriation process as most of the *Charter*'s rights were already contained and protected under Quebec's own *Charter*.

38 *Sauvé, supra,* note 31.

39 The Supreme Court, has, however read in a s. 1 type justification process into the adjudication of existing Aboriginal and treaty rights. The dialogue model may require some modification when applied to Aboriginal rights so as to encourage not only dialogue between courts and legislatures but also dialogue and negotiation between Canadian gov-

ernments and the representatives of Canada's various Aboriginal peoples. See Schneiderman, "Review" [2003] W.Y.B. Access to Justice. For judicial statements about the importance of such negotiations see *Delgamuukw v. British Columbia*, [1997] 3 SCR 1010; *R. v. Powley*, [2003] 2 SCR 207. For discussion of how judicial remedies for violations of Aboriginal rights may facilitate negotiation between governments and Aboriginal peoples see Roach, "Remedies for Violations of Aboriginal Rights" (1992) 21 Man. L.J. 498 and "Remedies in Aboriginal Litigation" in Magnet and Dorey, eds., *Aboriginal Rights Litigation* (2003).

40 *Thomson Newspapers Co. v. Canada (Attorney General)*, [1998] 1 SCR 877, at 935.

41 I represented an intervener in that case, Aboriginal Legal Services of Toronto, who argued that the law should be struck down as an unreasonable violation of the equality rights of prisoners and Aboriginal prisoners. The four dissenting judges found no violation of these equality rights and the five judges in the majority did not decide the equality rights issue.

42 Waldron, *Law and Disagreement* (1999), at 291. See Roach, *The Supreme Court on Trial: Judicial Activism or Democratic Dialogue* (2001), at 295.

43 General declarations as opposed to specific injunctions can also be seen as dialogic remedies because they allow the executive considerable discretion to determine the exact means to be used to comply with the court's general articulation of constitutional entitlement. In *Eldridge v. British Columbia (Attorney General)*, [1997] 3 SCR 624, at para. 96, the Supreme Court justified the use of a declaration on the dialogic basis that there were "myriad options available to the government that may rectify the unconstitutionality of the current system. It is not this Court's role to dictate how this is to be accomplished." For an evaluation of the strength and weaknesses of reliance on declaratory relief see Roach, "Remedial Consensus and Dialogue under the *Charter*: General Declarations and Delayed Declarations of Invalidity" (2002) 35 U.B.C. L. Rev. 211.

44 *Reference re Manitoba Language Rights*, [1985] 1 SCR 721.

45 [1992] 2 SCR 679.

46 See most recently *Nova Scotia (Workers' Compensation Board) v. Martin*, [2003] 2 SCR 504, at paras. 119–21. For contrasting views about the use of delayed or suspended declarations of invalidity compare Choudhry and Roach, "Putting the Past Behind Us" (2003) 21 S.C.L.R. (2d) 205 and Ryder, "Suspending the Charter" (2003) 21 S.C.L.R. (2d) 267. For an assessment of the various uses of delayed declarations of invalidity and

how many of these do fit into the *Schachter* categories see Roach, *Constitutional Remedies in Canada* (Aurora: Canada Law Book, as updated), at ch. 14.

47 Section 172(1) of the South African Constitution provides that:

When deciding a constitutional matter within its power, a court

(a) must declare that any law or conduct that is inconsistent with the Constitution is invalid to the extent of its inconsistency; and

(b) may make any order that is just and equitable, including

(i) an order limiting the retrospective effect of the declaration of invalidity; and

(ii) an order suspending the declaration of invalidity for any period and on any conditions, to allow the competent authority to correct the defect.

48 There has been reply legislation in 11 of 14 cases in which the Supreme Court of Canada has used a delayed declaration of invalidity. See Choudhry and Roach, "Putting the Past Behind Us," *supra*, note 46, at table B.

49 *Halpern v. Canada, supra,* note 31, at paras. 151–53.

50 Andrew Petter, who has returned to academe from a decade of distinguished service in British Columbia's Cabinet, has written that "my political experiences have persuaded me that the major threats to Canadian democracy lie in the undemocratic character of our democratic institutions ... Unlike dialogue theorists, I do not believe these institutions, as currently structured, can claim legitimacy for themselves, let alone for judicial review. Nor do I see how the interplay between unaccountable legislatures and elected judges qualifies as 'democratic dialogue'": "Rip Van Winkle in Charterland," id., Bazowski, ed., *The Charter at Twenty* (forthcoming).

51 When I referred to strong legislatures in *The Supreme Court on Trial* some reviewers took me to task on the grounds that legislatures are not strong under the present system of Cabinet domination. See Kelly, "Review" (2002) 17 Can. J. of Law and Society 174, at 179. My point was and remains that legislatures are strong under the *Charter* in the sense that they can quickly respond to court decisions should the political will in Cabinet be present.

52 Hogg and Bushell, "The Charter Dialogue Between Courts and Legislatures" (1997) 35 Osgoode Hall L.J. 75, at 77.

53 Petter, "Rip Van Winkle in Charterland," *supra*, note 50.

54 Ewing, "Human Rights," in Cane and Tushnet, eds., *The Oxford Handbook of Legal Studies* (2003), at 309.

55 Dyzenhaus, "Law as Justification: Etienne Mureinik's Conception of Legal Culture" (1998) 14 S.A.J.H.R., at 31–33.

56 Bickel, *The Least Dangerous Branch: The Supreme Court at the Bar of Politics* (2nd ed., 1986), at 24.

57 See e.g., Fuller, "The Forms and Limits of Adjudication" (1978) 92 Harv. L. Rev. 353; Bickel, *supra,* note 56.

58 Peter Milliken, an opposition member from a riding containing a large number of federal penitentiaries, moved a motion to allow prisoners to vote and criticized the restriction on the vote as "harsh and unfair." He argued that punishment for crime did not result in an offender "being stripped of his or her citizenship" and that the Charter required prisoners to be able to vote. Hansard, April 2, 1993, at 18012. Milliken also argued that "It does not aid in the punishment that the person not have a right to vote." Id., at 18013. Another opposition member, Louis Plamondon, argued that the restriction on the vote "would limit prisoners' rights as though they were perpetual outcasts from society and did not deserve consideration because they had made a mistake." Id., at 18019.

59 Id., at 18016, *per* Pat Nowlan.

60 Id., at 18018, *per* John Reimer.

61 The bells were, however, rung and a quorum obtained before a second motion, restricting the right to vote to those serving sentences of five years' imprisonment or more, was also defeated by a voice vote: id., at 18019.

62 Ely, *Democracy and Distrust: A Theory of Judicial Review* (1980); *United States v. Carolene Products Co.,* 304 U.S. 144, at 152 (1938).

63 *Andrews v. Law Society of British Columbia,* [1989] 1 SCR 143.

64 Dworkin, *Law's Empire* (1986). Here I am indebted to Guido Calabresi, who argues that courts should enforce both anti-discrimination norms and hold legislatures accountable for their treatment of a wider range of constitutional values. See Calabresi, "Foreword: Antidiscrimination and Constitutional Accountability" (1991) 105 Harv. L. Rev. 80.

65 *R. v. Mills,* [1999] 3 SCR 668. In this case, the majority of the Court accepted Parliament's reply even though it was largely based on the dissenting judgment in *R. v. O'Connor,* [1995] 4 SCR 411. In my view, an "in your face" reply to a Court's decision should generally be accompanied by the use of the override. Other options might include a reference to ask the Court to re-consider or overrule its prior decisions.

66 *R. v. Hall,* [2002] 3 SCR 309. In this case, the majority of the Court did accept most of Parliament's reply to its previous *Charter* decision, but

did sever the denial of bail on the basis of any just cause as excessively vague.

67 *Sauvé v. Canada (Chief Electoral Officer)*, [2002] 3 SCR 519.

68 *O'Connor, supra,* note 65.

69 For a similar conclusion see Mathen, "Constitutional Dialogues in Canada and the United States" (2003) 14 N.J.C.L. 403, at 461.

70 For a provocative argument that discrete and insular minorities may often have enough political clout to look after themselves see Ackerman, "Beyond Carolene Products" (1985) 98 Harv. L. Rev. 713.

71 *R. v. Morgentaler*, [1988] 1 SCR 30.

72 410 U.S. 113 (1973).

73 Morton and Knopff, *The Charter Revolution and the Court Party* (2000), at 157ff.

74 Waldron, *Law and Disagreement* (1999), at 311. Professor Waldron might argue, however, that judicial decisions are not necessary because there is already enough disagreement about many of the issues confronted by the courts under the *Charter*. But this may underestimate the difficulty that unpopular minorities and especially the criminally accused may have being heard in political debates were it not for their ability to claim *Charter* rights or engage in *Charter* litigation.

75 See, e.g., Hiebert, *Charter Conflicts: What Is Parliament's Role?* (2002).

76 See Parkin, "A Country Evenly Divided on Gay Marriage," *Policy Options* (October 2003), 39.

77 The federal government's reference to the Supreme Court of Canada of a draft bill on same-sex marriages underscores the need to change Canadian democracy. Parliament, in the Age of the *Charter of Rights and Freedoms*, is increasingly an institution of secondary importance ... So the political system should adapt to new circumstances. It should bring the Supreme Court and other higher courts fully into the political process, where the courts are anyway, by letting them decide much earlier what should or should not be done in public policy. The legislatures could rubberstamp or fine-tune what the courts decide, and all Canadians would understand who's making the important decisions.

Simpson, "Why don't we just turn policy over to courts," *Globe and Mail* (22 July 2003).

78 Simpson, "Heed the courts or change the Constitution," *Globe and Mail* (9 August 2003). He subsequently predicted that the override would never be used because of the Liberal pledge not to use the notwithstanding clause. As Simpson noted, however, Prime Minister Chretien helped negotiate s. 33, casting some doubts on the argument that "the use of

one perfectly legitimate, negotiated *Charter* provision will destroy the entire document." Simpson "Same-sex debate: Irrelevancy is Parliament's fate," *Globe and Mail* (17 September 2003).

79 Bickel, *The Morality of Consent* (1975), at 111. See also Bickel, *The Supreme Court and the Idea of Progress* (1970).

80 Fraser, "What the Framers of the Charter Intended," *Policy Options* (October, 2003), 78.

81 *Egan v. Canada,* [1995] 2 SCR 513.

82 *M. v. H.,* [1999] 2 SCR 3.

83 Murphy, "Dialogic Responses to *M. v. H.*: From Compliance to Defiance" (2001) 59 U.T. Fac. L. Rev. 299.

84 Hansard, June 8, 1999, at 15960.

85 Id., at 15963.

86 Id., at 15992.

87 Hansard, April 3, 2000, at 5567.

88 Id., at 5577, *per* Garry Breitkreuz, expressing concerns that those who practised "buggery" received benefits from the state and stressing the need to protect children.

89 Svend Robinson criticized the amendment as "a shameful collapse by the Minister of Justice to the pressure of her own backbenchers, the so-called family caucus in the Liberal Party, which some have called the dinosaur wing of the Liberal caucus" and based on a "campaign of fear, of distortion, of lies by too many people in the public and those, in some cases, in the House." Hansard, April 3, 2000, at 5565.

90 *Law v. Canada (Minister of Employment and Immigration),* [1999] 1 SCR 497; *R. v. Oakes,* [1986] 1 SCR 103.

91 *Halpern v. Canada (Attorney General)* (2002), 60 OR (3d) 321 (Div. Ct.); *EGALE v. Canada* (2003), 225 DLR (4th) 472 (BCCA) (remedies suspended until July 12, 2004). The Quebec trial decisions gave a slightly longer period to September 2004. *Hendricks v. Quebec,* [2002] J.Q. No. 3816 (SC).

92 See *supra,* note 47.

93 Lurman and Fagan, "Marriage divides the house," *Globe and Mail* (17 September 2003).

94 As Christopher Manfredi has argued: "The notwithstanding clause is part of the *Charter,* the *Charter* would not exist without it, and the Supreme Court has on several occasions recognized the legitimacy of its use." Manfredi, "Same-Sex Marriage and the Notwithstanding Clause," *Policy Options* (October, 2003), 21, at 24.

95 *Ford v. Quebec (Attorney General),* [1988] 2 SCR 712.

96 *Schachter v. Canada*, [1992] 2 SCR 679. For my criticisms of this limited approach see Roach, *Constitutional Remedies in Canada* (as updated), at 14.1640–14.1670.

97 For example, Janet Hiebert has argued that "the judicial decision to change the law before Parliament had completed its deliberations demonstrates contempt for Parliament." Hiebert, "From Equality Rights to Same-Sex Marriage – Parliament and the Courts in the Age of the Charter," *Policy Options* (October, 2003) 10, at 14.

98 Both Courts of Appeal did mention that their decisions did not affect the freedom of religions, but these comments can be seen as *obiter dicta* that went beyond the case as pleaded and argued by the parties. See *EGALE v. Canada* (2003), 225 DLR (4th) 472, at paras. 133, 181 (BCCA); *Halpern v. Canada* (2003), 65 OR (3d) 161, at para. 138 (CA).

99 MacCharles, "Faith can be reconciled with gay bill, Liberals say," *Toronto Star* (8 August 2003) A7.

100 Cauchon, Notes for an Address to the Canadian Bar Association *(18* August 2003).

101 Clark, "'Civil union' is an option on same-sex, Martin says," *Globe and Mail* (20 August 2003).

102 Laghi, Lunman and Clark, "Liberals facing defeat in same-sex free vote," *Globe and Mail* (14 August 2003); "Where the MPs Stand," id.

103 Simpson, "Heed the courts or change the Constitution," *Globe and Mail* (9 August 2003).

104 The government in the reference has switched the terms of the debate from the question in previous court cases of whether the traditional definition of marriage violates the *Charter* to the question of whether the draft bill "which extends capacity to marry to persons of the same-sex" is "consistent with the Canadian Charter of Rights and Freedoms?" See Department of Justice Reference to the Supreme Court Backgrounder (17 July 2003).

105 Press Release Minister of Justice Announces Reference to the Supreme Court of Canada (17 July 2003).

106 Hogg and Thornton, "Reply to 'Six Degrees of Dialogue'" (1999) 37 Osgoode Hall L.J. 529, at 536; Hogg and Bushell, "The Charter Dialogue Between Courts and Legislatures" (1997) 35 Osgoode Hall L.J. 75, at 96.

107 Manfredi and Kelly, "Six Degrees of Dialogue" (1999) 37 Osgoode Hall L.J. 513, at 524; Manfredi and Kelly, "Dialogue, Deference and Restraint: Judicial Independence and Trial Procedures" (2001) 64 Sask. L. Rev. 323, at 336.

108 Goldsworthy, "Legislation, Interpretation and Judicial Review" (2001) 51 U.T.L.J. 75, at 81. See also Goldsworthy, "Judicial Review, Legislative Override, and Democracy" (2003) 38 Wake Forest L. Rev. 451.

109 Tushnet, *Taking the Constitution Away from the Courts* (1999).

110 The legislative response to both *R. v. Daviault*, [1994] 3 SCR 63 and *R. v. O'Connor*, [1995] 4 SCR 411 were based on the logic of the dissenting judges. The legislative response to *R. v. Seaboyer*, [1991] 2 SCR 577 was in my view more complex because it expanded the debate beyond the rape shield issue, but on the rape shield issue, it was influenced by the Court's majority opinion.

111 See the response to *RJR-MacDonald v. Canada (Attorney General)*, [1995] 3 SCR 199 as discussed in Hiebert, *Charter Conflicts* (2002).

112 *Sauvé v. Canada (Chief Electoral Officer)*, [2002] 3 SCR 519, at para 21.

113 Hiebert, *supra*, note 111.

114 Mandel, "Against Constitutional Law (Populist or Otherwise)" (2000) 34 U. Rich. L. Rev. 443.

115 See Kelly, "Bureaucratic Activism and the Charter of Rights and Freedoms: The Department of Justice and its Entry into the Centre of Government" (1999) 42 Can. Public Admin. 476; Sossin "Review" Osgoode Hall L.J. (forthcoming).

116 *Department of Justice Act*, RSC 1985, c. J-2, s. 4.1.

117 In opinion polls 71 per cent of respondents "say that if the Supreme Court declares a law unconstitutional because it conflicts with the *Charter*, the Court – not Parliament – should have the final say. Only 24 per cent would give Parliament the final say." Parkin, "A Country Evenly Divided on Gay Marriage," *Policy Options* (October 2003), 39, at 40.

118 For arguments that his opposition to judicial activism is based on a defence of representative government as opposed to populism see Knopff, "How Democratic Is the Charter? And Does It Matter?" (2003) 19 S.C.L.R. 199, at 216–18. Professor Knopff may be right that I have misunderstood his invocation of Lord Durham, but I remain skeptical that the representative and responsible government that he advocates will provide adequate protection for minorities in the absence of judicial protection. For example in the work which invokes Lord Durham for the proposition that "parliamentary sovereignty was the key to protecting rights," he also candidly explains the decision of the Alberta government not to protect gays and lesbians from discrimination was made on the basis that "the Klein government could safely ignore this issue, upsetting only a small coalition of activists, few of whom were Tory

supporters in any case." Morton and Knopff, *The Charter Revolution and the Court Party* (2000), at 153, 165. So much for the idea that "parliamentary sovereignty was the key to protecting rights" or that political opponents should be treated as "fellow citizens" as opposed to "activists" not relevant to the governing coalition.

For an interesting account of how checks and balances such as disallowance, defeat of bills in the Senate and even federalism have declined in Canada and how the Court has emerged as a new check on Cabinet domination see Flanagan, "Canada's Three Constitutions: Protecting, Overturning, and Reversing the Status Quo," in James, Abelson, and Lusztig, *The Myth of the Sacred: The Charter, the Courts and the Politics of the Constitution in Canada* (2002), at 127–33. For a populist call for the use of referenda as a means of "transferring the decision to invoke the notwithstanding clause from the politicians to the people," see Morton, "Can Judicial Supremacy Be Stopped?" *Policy Options* (October 2003) 25, at 29.

119 But see Kahana, "The Notwithstanding Mechanism and Public Discussion: Lessons from the Ignored Practice of Section 33 of the *Charter*" (2001) 44 Can. Public Admin. 255 for examples of the override being used without public engagement.

120 Hiebert, *supra*, note 111, at 51. In other words, a "judge's expertise lies more in defining rights than in suggesting appropriate ways to pursue complex legislative initiatives." Id., at 223.

121 Id., at 57. Her definition of core rights is somewhat unhelpful and selective. She writes that core rights "include the conditions necessary to ensure the just treatment of individuals in their encounters with the coercive powers of the state, such as due process and freedom from arbitrary arrest and detention" (id., at 57), but then writes approvingly of Parliament's rejection of the Court's approach to the accused's right to full answer and defence in *O'Connor*, suggesting that this right is not core, or at least not immune from rebalancing by Parliament. Id., at 110–17. In other places, Professor Hiebert suggests that Parliament should re-evaluate the court's interpretation of "extremely marginal rights claim" which she believes includes commercial advertising. Id., at 90.

122 *Supra*, note 110.

123 *Criminal Code*, RSC 1985, c. C-46, s. 33.1, as amended by SC 1995, c. 32, s. 1.

124 *RJR-MacDonald Inc. v. Canada (Attorney General)*, [1995] 3 SCR 199.

125 On the increased use of preambles in legislation, most of which only speak to issues of legislative purpose and not proportionality, see Roach, "The Uses and Audiences of Preambles in Legislation" (2001) 47 McGill L.J. 129.

126 Hiebert, *supra,* note 111, at 224.

127 Dripps, "Criminal Procedure, Footnote Four, and the Theory of Public Choice; Or, Why Don't Legislatures Give a Damn About the Rights of the Accused?" (1993) 44 Syracuse L. Rev. 1079; Cameron, "Dialogue and Hierarchy in *Charter* Interpretation: A Comment on *R. v. Mills"* (2001) 38 Alta. L. Rev. 1051.

128 See, however, the legislative revision of tax laws even after they were found to be consistent with the Charter in *Thibaudeau v. Canada,* [1995] 2 SCR 627 as discussed in Hogg and Bushell, "The Charter Dialogue Between Courts and Legislatures" (1997) 35 Osgoode Hall L.J. 75, at 104–105.

129 The first quote is from Joanna Radbord and the second from Michael Leshner. See www.cbc.ca/stories/2003/06/10/ont_samesex030610. See also Tibbetts, "Minister mulls creating new marriage law," *National Post* (12 June 2003).

130 Bickel, *The Supreme Court and the Idea of Progress* (1970), at 91.

131 On the resistance to Supreme Court decisions on desegregation, voting rights and police powers see Rosenberg, *The Hollow Hope: Can Courts Bring about Social Change?* (1991).

132 S.C. 2001, c. 41.

133 Choudhry and Roach, "Racial and Ethnic Profiling: Statutory Discretion, Constitutional Remedies and Democratic Accountability" (2003) 41 Osgoode Hall L.J. 1, at 35–36.

134 There would be a strong case that racial or religious profiling violated s. 15 of the *Charter* and could not be justified as a proportionate means to prevent terrorism. If profiling had been authorized by legislation, the appropriate remedy would be a declaration that the statute was invalid under s. 52 of the *Constitution Act, 1982.* The same arguments can be made against profiling that is not specifically authorized by legislation, but the available remedy would be damages under s. 24(1) of the *Charter* and the exclusion of evidence under s. 24(2). These remedies would be less likely to trigger democratic debate and accountability about profiling.

135 198 U.S. 45 (1905).

136 347 U.S. 483 (1954).

Mark Tushnet
"Weak-Form Judicial Review: Its Implications for Legislatures" (2005)

Tushnet argues that the kind of constitutional order praised by both Waluchow and Roach is in substance no different from that of the United States of America, where there is judicial rather than legislative supremacy on constitutional issues.

I INTRODUCTION

We can – for convenience – identify three important intellectual or theoretical issues of concern to students of comparative constitutional law.[1] First, how do different constitutional systems deal with federalism, the allocation of legislative competence between or among different levels of government? For a scholar from the United States, the primary interlocutor on this question is the European Union, precisely because the issue there is framed as whether the European Union is, is not, or is on the way to becoming, a federal state.

Second, what substantive rights do, should, or can constitutions guarantee? Here the interlocutor is the international human rights community, and the issues concern the identification and enforceability (in various venues) of first-generation classical liberal political rights, second-generation social and economic rights, and third-generation cultural and environmental rights.

The third important issue is the one on which I focus here – the question of judicial review, the role of courts in constitutional systems that generally comply with rule-of-law requirements. Here the interlocutor is what Stephen Gardbaum has called the "new Commonwealth model" of judicial review.[2] In that model, courts assess legislation against constitutional norms, but do not have the final word on whether statutes comply with those norms. In some versions the courts are directed to interpret legislation to make it consistent with constitutional norms if doing so is fairly possible according to (previously) accepted standards of statutory interpretation. In other versions the courts gain the additional power to declare statutes inconsistent with constitutional norms, but not to enforce such judgments coercively against a losing party.[3] In still others, the courts can enforce the judgment coercively, but the legislature may respond by reinstating the original legislation by some means other than a cumbersome amendment process.[4]

Proponents of this new model of judicial review describe it as an attractive way to reconcile democratic self-governance with constitutionalism. As Jeffrey Goldsworthy puts it, the new model:

offer[s] the possibility of a compromise that combines the best features of both the traditional models, by conferring on courts constitutional responsibility to review the consistency of legislation with protected rights, while preserving the authority of legislatures to have the last word.[5]

This new model of judicial review gives rise to a new set of questions for comparative constitutional law.[6] Despite the recency of the invention of weak-form review, we can identify some of its structural features and, in particular, some of the ways in which institutional incentives might push weak-form review in one or another direction.

The issues I address here, in a quite preliminary way, are these. Proponents of weak-form review treat it as an attractive way to reconcile democratic self-governance with the constraints that constitutionalism necessarily places on self-governance. The people get a chance to enact the policies they prefer, to consider the views of expert judges about whether those policies are consistent with constitutional constraints, and then to consider whether they agree with the judges about whether the policies do transgress constitutional constraints.[7] This defence places a lot of weight on the ability of legislative bodies to evaluate questions of constitutionality independent of their evaluation of policy questions. The first issue, then, is whether legislatures in systems with weak-form judicial review are likely to do a decent job of constitutional evaluation.[8]

Second, is weak-form review likely to be stable? The question here is whether the distinction between weak-form and strong-form systems (in one direction), or the distinction between weak-form systems of judicial review and systems of parliamentary supremacy (in another), is illusory. Proponents of weak-form review typically assert that they anticipate that legislatures will accept the courts' rulings – that, confronted with a judicial decision that arguably distorts a statute to ensure that it is consistent with constitutional constraints, the legislature will not enact the same statute again, this time with a pellucid statement that it wants to do what the courts have said would be inconsistent with constitutional constraint, or that, confronted with a declaration of incompatibility, the legislature will repair the defects the courts have identified. Yet, if those assertions are credited, it is not entirely clear how weak-form systems differ from strong-form ones, except in the purely formal sense that the legislature has the (never-to-be-exercised) power to disregard the courts. And, on the other side, if legislatures regularly disregard the courts' actions, as they are entitled to do in a weak-form system, it becomes hard to distinguish such a system from the system of parliamentary supremacy it was designed to replace.

II THE QUESTION OF LEGISLATIVE RESPONSIBILITY

The arguments in favor of some form of judicial review are familiar and, to many, compelling.[9] Constitutions are supposed to place constraints on the policies representative legislatures enact because, constitution-makers fear, the values they identify provide benefits in the long run while imposing costs in the short run, and elected representatives concerned about re-election are likely to focus on the short run. Elected representatives will therefore undervalue (if not ignore) constitutional values when they enact statutes. Committing the protection of constitutional values to elected representatives is, in the familiar phrase, like setting the fox to guard the chicken-coop. And yet, weak-form judicial review does just that – or, at least, it relies on the fox to guard the chickens effectively most of the time. We can call this a *public-choice* skepticism about the likelihood that legislatures will respect constitutional values, and so, indirectly, about the value of weak-form review.

There is an additional difficulty, which we can call a *legalist* skepticism. Constitutionalism involves enforcing *pre-existing* constraints on policy-making, constraints that are typically embodied in canonical texts ("the constitution," in short hand).[10] Participants in constitutional systems orient themselves to the interpretation of those canonical texts, using them to identify the constraints on legislative power. But, the legalist skepticism goes, legislatures may be quite good at determining what would be good policy for the future, but they have few incentives to engage in the interpretive activity associated with constitutional law, and little expertise in that activity either.

I believe that the public-choice skepticism is overstated, and that well-designed constitutional systems do give legislators incentives to take constitutional values into account as they legislate. The legalist skepticism is, I think, more substantial, although far less emphasized in the literature on constitutionalism.[11]

Elected legislators can develop concern for constitutional values when their electoral prospects depend on their having such concern. James Madison's famous argument about the way in which relatively large electoral districts limit the effects of faction offers some insights into why elected legislators might be concerned about avoiding actions that transgress constitutional limits. Some of the factions Madison identifies want to do things that violate the constitutional rights of others, or that exceed the power affirmatively granted the legislature. But, Madison argues, a large enough jurisdiction will have enough factions that a person seeking to be elected cannot secure election by promising to satisfy any single faction's demands. Faction A wants to violate the rights of faction B, and faction B wants to violate the rights of faction A. And, even if neither one of them likes faction C, still faction C has some bargaining power, residing in its ability to throw its votes to the candidate preferred by either A or B depending on whether that candidate promises to protect faction C from its enemies. In the end, in a large enough jurisdiction, according to Madison, a candidate cannot get votes by promising to violate rights. In effect, the factions' competing demands cancel each other out.

The Madisonian argument works reasonably well with respect to issues of public policy.[12] It works, but I think less well, with respect to questions of constitutional constraints on public policy. I personally think the residuum of public-choice skepticism that remains after the Madisonian argument is taken into account ought to be dealt with by rejecting the strongest assumptions that animate public-choice skepticism. In addition, I can identify one mechanism that would *allow* an elected representative to vote (ordinarily) only for proposals that, in the representative's view, are consistent with constitutional values, and another that would *encourage* him or her to do so.[13]

The first mechanism is this: suppose that a representative does an exceptionally good job of advancing the (factional) interests of the constituency, and that, generally speaking, those interests, while narrow and not in the nation's overall interest, do not conflict with constitutional values. That kind of performance will give the representative freedom to act on his or her conscientious views about what the constitution requires or prohibits – at least as long as those views do not conflict with the constituency's special interest or with extremely strongly held views among the constituency. The idea here is that the representative can get a free pass on most constitutional issues as long as he or she provides exceptionally good constituency services, including advancing narrow or special-interest legislation of particular concern to the constituency. And, by the Madisonian argument, different representatives will get free passes on different constitutional issues, so that, in the aggregate, the legislature will enact only legislation consistent with the constraints the constitution places on it.[14]

The second mechanism is that constituents themselves might have principled views about what the constitution requires or prohibits.[15] A representative responsive to the constituency would then seek votes by acting in conformity with the constituency's constitutional – not merely policy – preferences. This effect need not be strong in individual districts for it to have a significant effect on legislative output. Consider a weakened version of the Madisonian argument, in which factional interests do not completely offset each other, but merely reduce the net impulse toward factional legislation. A mild constitutional view in the constituency might induce a representative to act in accord with that view, and, even though small, the effect might be enough to offset the (diminished) factional impulse.

So far I have focused on the individual legislator and his or her incentives to comply with the constitution. But legislators act in institutions, and ordinary institutional arrangements may give the legislature as a whole an incentive to comply with constitutional norms. The basic mechanism here is separation of powers. Consider first the American style of separation of powers, with the executive elected independently of the legislature. As Madison said, separation of powers sets ambition to counter ambition. The legislature will be alert to executive encroachments, and *vice versa*. Neither branch will yield when the other proposes to violate the constitution, and the product of their competition and resistance is compliance with the constitution.

Madison was particularly concerned about one branch's encroachments on the other, and the metaphor of competition and combat pretty clearly works most effectively in that setting. Yet, it is not irrelevant where one branch proposes action that might violate constitutional rights outside the separation of powers scheme. The reason is that a party with substantial support in the legislature, say, can use the executive's proposed constitutional violation as a weapon in its electoral battles against the executive and the executive's supporters in the legislature – if constituents have some concern for ensuring that legislation conforms to the constitution. Even when the same party controls the executive and the legislature, the risk of electoral defeat because of proposals that can effectively be portrayed as unconstitutional will exercise some constraint on the party's behaviour.[16]

The next question, then, is whether similar effects can be achieved in Westminster-like parliamentary systems of party government, where the chief executive can command legislative majorities by insisting on party discipline.[17] That such effects can *sometimes* be achieved seems obvious; one need only note the possibility that the executive will allow a free vote, releasing all members from party discipline. And, indeed, one observes serious constitutional debate on some proposals – notably, abortion – when party discipline has been lifted. It would be convenient were there reasons to believe that governments would allow free votes generally when legislative proposals raised important constitutional concerns, but I know of no such reasons.

Rather, the mechanism in systems of party government that parallels separation of powers in other systems is the creation of an analogue to separation of powers *within* party government. We can see the analogue in operation when there is a coalition government. The parties negotiating the coalition agreement stand in relation to each other as the legislature stands to the executive in a separation of powers system. And, for the same reason that separation of powers conduces to respect for constitutional norms, so will coalition government.

Not all party governments are coalition governments,[18] yet something *like* a coalition government can exist within an apparently unified government. The reason is that an apparently unified party is, quite often, a coalition of informal (sometimes formal) factions. The coalition is formed before the election rather than after it, and within a single party rather than in forming a government. Still, the unified party's platform can be seen as the analogue of the coalition agreement.[19] So, to the extent that coalition governments can reproduce the effects of separation of powers on inducing sensitivity to constitutional norms, so can single-party governments.

So far I have dealt with the incentives individual representatives have to consider constitutional questions seriously with respect to particular proposals. That, though, can be time-consuming. Representatives who know – because of the incentives I have described – that they will (sometimes) want to deal seriously with constitutional questions can ease the burden of decision by delegating some portion of the task to a committee within their institution.[20]

A committee on constitutional matters can amplify the institution's consideration of constitutional questions. As a general matter, those who staff any relatively permanent body become invested in the body's mission: set up a committee on constitutional matters, and its members will take their mission more seriously than they would were they simply members of the house.[21] Assignment to such a committee might not be particularly attractive, because service is unlikely to provide constituents with any specific benefits, in the way that assignment to more substantive committees (such as those dealing with agriculture or shipping) might.[22] Still, those assigned to the committee will be marginally more invested in the mission than others. Some will take the constitution as their area of specialization within the House. And, of course, anyone who volunteers for such a committee is likely to be particularly alert to constitutional matters. Finally, there are at least some representatives who see themselves as good institutional citizens. They have no aspirations beyond service in the House, and take their personal mission to be protecting the House – and, perhaps, the constitution more generally – from the erosion of its power.[23] And, those institutional citizens who are lawyers may have a particularly strong sense of a duty to protect the constitution.

None of this is to say, of course, that legislatures will *always* respect constitutional norms. I have identified mechanisms that give rise to the possibility that legislatures will be sensitive to constitutional norms, but nothing in my arguments establishes how large those possibilities are. Some of the mechanisms seem to me clearly much stronger than others, and some seem to me rather weak taken in themselves. My argument is only that we have a number of reasons for thinking that public choice skepticism about the possibility of responsible legislative consideration of constitutional norms is overstated. Weak-form judicial review might work well when legislatures are moderately responsive to constitutional norms, as my arguments suggest – but do not establish – that they might be.[24]

What of the legalist skepticism? Recall that it arises because constitutional responsibility means respect for canonical texts, by means of some sort of interpretive activity. But, the legalist skeptic suggests, legislators – even when acting with the advice of a specialized committee – are unlikely to engage in a serious interpretive enterprise.

In an earlier study I examined a small practice in the U.S. Senate in which Senators formally debate constitutional questions.[25] I found that the Senators generally *were* attempting to interpret the Constitution (and, sometimes, the Supreme Court's decisions interpreting the Constitution). The legalist skeptic, though, wonders what incentives legislators have for such behaviour.[26] One, I think, is obvious: efficiency. The responses I have sketched to the public-choice skeptic suggest that legislators have incentives to *address* constitutional questions. But, how are they to do so? They could rethink constitutional values from the bottom up. That would be time-consuming. Casting their discussions in already existing terms – that is, addressing constitutional issues by referring to the language of the constitution, judicial decisions interpreting it, and the like – cuts down on the effort legislators must expend. If legislators are to address constitutional questions, then, their concern for disposing of their work efficiently gives them an incentive to do so by means of interpretation.

Interpretation of pre-existing constitutional texts may enter a legislator's deliberations in a more subtle way. The idea here is that constitutional documents can become embedded in a nation's constitutional culture and self-understanding, to the point where major legislation, at least, comes to be understood as embodying the nation's constitutional commitments. Legislators (at least when dealing with major legislation) then can see themselves as carrying forward the nation's constitutional commitments – that is, as interpreting the nation's constitution as embedded in its traditions. A legislator taking this approach may refer to specific constitutional provisions or judicial opinions, particularly those that have deep cultural resonance such as the Equal Protection Clause and *Brown v. Board of Education*[27] in the United States. More often, perhaps, such a legislator will refer generically to traditions of equality or, to use another example from the United States, the *Declaration of Independence* or the Constitution's Preamble. The latter are indeed documents, but as a formal matter they have no legal status. And yet, a legislator who refers to them is, I think, engaged in a constitutional *and* an interpretive enterprise.

The practice I have just described invokes the constitution in a highly abstract form. As it turns out, the question of what level of abstraction we think appropriate in constitutional analysis has some bearing on the second topic I address here, the stability of weak-form judicial review.

III THE QUESTION OF STABILITY

Weak-form judicial review is interesting because it offers a new way of reconciling democratic self-government with constitutionalism. It does so by recognizing that the general or abstract terms of the constitution can be specified in numerous reasonable ways, and that legislatures might sometimes adopt unreasonable specifications or, more likely, fail to attend to constitutional considerations in enacting legislation. Weak-form systems allow the courts to remind legislatures of their constitutional obligations, without making the courts' specification unrevisable except by constitutional amendment. Legislatures and courts interact on questions of the constitution's meaning, and proponents of weak-form review suggest that the outcome of the process will advance both self-governance and constitutionalism, as legislators, instructed but not compelled by the courts, modify the policies they adopt to conform to constitutional limits on their power, and – importantly – as courts, instructed but not compelled by legislators, modify their views of what the constitution requires.

The question of stability is this: can weak-form review be sustained over a long term, or will it become such a weak institution that the constitutional system is, for all practical purposes, indistinguishable from a system of parliamentary supremacy or such a strong institution that the courts' decisions will be taken as conclusive and effectively coercive on the legislature? Experience with weak-form systems is, as I have indicated, thin, but I think there is some evidence, mostly from Canada but some from New Zealand, that weak-form systems do become strong-form ones.

The evidence, such as it is, is that judicial interpretations generally "stick." That is, legislatures have the *formal* power to respond to a judicial interpretation with which its members disagree through legislation rather than constitutional amendment, but they exercise that power so rarely that a natural inference is that the political-legal cultures in nations with weak-form review have come to treat judicial interpretations as authoritative and final.

The evidence of practice is hard to analyze, though. The basic problem lies in distinguishing between *agreement* with the courts' result, and mere resigned *acceptance* of it. An example of the difficulty is provided by *Simpson v. Attorney General (Baigent's Case)*.[28] The case involved a search conducted by police relying on a warrant that had been issued based on false factual assumptions, where it was alleged that the police continued to search even after they knew that they were searching the wrong house. The targets of the search sued for damages, alleging that their rights under the *New Zealand Bill of Rights Act*[29] had been violated. Their difficulty was two-fold. The *Bill of Rights Act* is declaratory and interpretive; although it tells courts to interpret legislation to be consistent with its provisions, it provides no remedies for violations of the rights it identifies. It seemed, then, that the plaintiffs had to rely on their common-law remedies against the police officers. But, the second difficulty was that the police officers were immunized by a statute from liability under the common law.

The Court of Appeal held in favour of the plaintiffs nonetheless. It held that the *Bill of Rights Act* authorized the courts to create a new "public-law" remedy. Such a remedy was different from common-law remedies. In particular, the statutory immunity Parliament provided was, the court held, directed solely at common-law tort actions. As a result, the plaintiffs could pursue their new cause of action and the police officers could not assert a statutory immunity from damages.

The government then asked the New Zealand Law Commission to consider whether a legislative response to *Baigent's Case* should be developed. The Commission endorsed the Court of Appeal's analysis and told the government that it should not introduce legislation to eliminate the "public-law" remedy, the contours of which, the Commission said, should be fleshed out by further *judicial* action. The government agreed with that recommendation. *Baigent's Case* has been the object of substantial criticism – and admiration – in the New Zealand legal literature. At the end of the day, though, does the government's non-response represent agreement with the decision or simple acquiescence in it?[30]

Baigent's Case illustrates another way in which the difficulty of distinguishing between agreement and acceptance can arise. Weak-form systems have focused on human rights protections, as in the *Canadian Charter of Rights and Freedoms*[31] and the British *Human Rights Act*.[32] But, human rights are *also* protected by international human rights norms, which are themselves sometimes enforceable coercively and which, in any event, have deep cultural resonance. To the extent that a weak-form court enforces a domestic right that tracks an international human rights norm, a legislature's failure to respond might result not from agreement with the court but from recognition that some international institution may enforce the international norm directly or from acceptance of the fact that the courts' invocation of international human rights norms creates a new political impediment to the enactment of purely domestic legislation.[33]

In *Baigent's Case*, one judge referred to the *International Covenant on Civil and Political Rights*, which mentions the power of courts to "develop the possibilities of ... remedy," as a justification for the creation of the public-law remedy.[34] He continued by observing that it would be "strange" to say that Parliament expected New Zealand citizens to be able to complain to the United Nations Human Rights Committee, as authorized by the government's agreement to the Optional Protocol authorizing individual complaints to the Committee, but did not want the very same citizens to be able to get a domestic remedy under the *Bill of Rights Act*, which, he said, was one means of implementing the *Covenant*.[35] But, with the threat of intervention from outside in the background, is the government's acquiescence in the case's outcome properly taken to represent acceptance of the Court of Appeal's approach to enforcing fundamental rights?

A second difficulty arises from the way in which weak-form review is conceptualized, as expressed in the provisions creating it. Constitutions describe limits on government power in general terms, which have to be applied to particular statutes. A court (weak- or strong-form) can find a statute unconstitutional for basically two reasons. It might think that the legislature overlooked some constitutional value, or it might think that the legislature disregarded such a value, or gave it less weight than the constitution requires that it be given. Consider the legislature's response after a weak-form court finds a statute unconstitutional.[36] Where invalidation is based on a judgment that the legislature overlooked a constitutional value, the legislature might take the overlooked value into account now that it has been brought to its attention, and it might agree with the court. Or, it might take the overlooked value into account and conclude that, on balance, the legislation remains desirable. At that point, the first type of invalidation blends into the second. The court has specified what the constitution means, and the legislature simply disagrees with that specification.

In such a situation, the conceptualization of weak-form review becomes important. Recall that weak-form systems reconcile democratic self-governance with constitutionalism by recognizing that the general or abstract terms of the constitution can be specified in numerous reasonable ways. Legislatures might overlook constitutional values and might need to be reminded of them. But, once legislatures are so reminded, weak-form systems should conceptualize the legislature's action as offering an alternative specification of the meaning of the constitution's general or abstract terms.

Some verbal formulations of weak-form review can interfere with such a conceptualization. This is notably true of Canada's version, which requires the legislature to declare that it wishes its legislation to take effect notwithstanding *Charter* rights. The notwithstanding clause has been invoked so rarely that I cannot provide a real example of the difficulty, but a stylized one can make the point. Parliament enacts a statute, which the Supreme Court of Canada finds to violate a *Charter* right. Parliament then invokes the notwithstanding clause, declaring that the statute should take effect notwithstanding the fact that it violates the *Charter* right. But, in Parliament's view, the statute does *not* violate the *Charter* right. What it wishes is that the statute take effect notwithstanding the Supreme Court's mistaken (though reasonable) specification of the *Charter* right's meaning. It is not hard to imagine that it is politically more difficult to enact a statute notwithstanding the fact that it violates the *Charter* than to enact one notwithstanding the views expressed about the *Charter* by the courts. In this way, the terms used in creating Canada's system of weak-form review make it more difficult to determine when legislative action consistent with the courts' decision expresses agreement with the courts or mere acquiescence in the near-inevitable.[37]

Weak-form systems that direct courts to interpret statutes in a manner consistent with fundamental rights present the problem of conceptualizing weak-form systems in a slightly different form. Interpretive directives typically carve out an exception for statutes that cannot be fairly interpreted to be consistent with fundamental rights. So, for example, the British *Human Rights Act* reserves the possibility of a declaration of incompatibility for such statutes. The interpretive directive, though, is likely to induce judges to strive hard to find interpretations that make the statutes compatible with fundamental rights. In doing so, the judges will inevitably run the risk of opening themselves to charges that they are distorting rather than interpreting the statutes. The language of distortion versus faithful interpretation is language that can obscure the underlying question, which is whether the courts are rejecting a reasonable specification of fundamental rights.

A recent British case offers an instructive example.[38] The case involved the process by which income support for asylum applicants would be terminated when their applications for asylum were rejected. The relevant regulation provided that support would be ended when the applicant ceased to be an asylum seeker, which occurred "on the date on which it is ... recorded" by the Secretary of State "as having been determined." The Secretary of State rejected the application for asylum on November 20, and the rejection was recorded within the Secretary's internal system on that date. The applicant did not receive notice of the denial for another four or five months. She claimed that she was entitled to income support for the period between the denial and her receipt of notice of the denial. One judge in the House of Lords thought that the applicant's claim was barred by the regulation's plain language: she ceased to be an asylum applicant when her application was denied and recorded, which occurred in November. The other Law Lords disagreed. Invoking what he called fundamental principles of the rule of law, Lord Steyn "interpreted" the regulation to mean that the denial had to be *properly* recorded, and that rule-of-law principles meant that the denial could not be properly recorded until the applicant received notice that her application had been denied. At the least, this is creative interpretation. More important for present purposes, calling what Lord Steyn did *interpretation* may obscure the more basic question: Were the government's procedures for ending income support to those whose applications for asylum had been rejected a reasonable approach to providing fair procedures? Lord Steyn made a powerful case that they were not,[39] which suggests that decisions that purport to interpret statutes can openly address the underlying question. In other cases, though, the form of "interpretation" may make less apparent the disagreement between the courts and the government on what a reasonable specification of fundamental rights is.

A related conceptual difficulty arises from what might be called the myth of objective rights.[40] Suppose we have a political-legal culture in which two beliefs are widespread: first, that there *are* objective rights (or, more generally, objective limits placed on government power in the constitution), and second, that courts have some comparative advantage over legislatures in specifying the content of general or abstract rights. In such a culture, one would expect legislatures never to override a court's invalidation, because legislators would believe both that there were rights and that the courts were more likely than they to identify what those rights are. That is, weak-form review does not make sense in such a culture. Perhaps the transformation of weak- into strong-form review, if it occurs, indicates only that the nations that have adopted weak-form review actually have political-legal cultures more suitable for strong-form review.

Yet, judicial review in any form makes no sense unless courts have *some* comparative advantage over legislatures in specifying the constitution's meaning. So, the two conditions for the stability of weak-form review seem to be these: first, the nation's political-legal culture accepts the possibility of a range of reasonable specifications of general or abstract rights. Second, the courts' comparative advantage over legislatures in specifying the constitution's meaning is relatively modest.[41] I have my doubts about whether the first condition can ever be satisfied. Many legal academics in the United States are comfortable with the idea of a range of reasonable specifications, but, I believe, most academics, judges, lawyers, and non-lawyers think that there are, in Ronald Dworkin's terms, right answers to questions about rights.

If my belief is correct, the dynamics of weak-form review's transformation into strong-form review are straightforward. The courts specify the meaning of the constitutional right. This is taken to identify the correct meaning of the right. The constitution authorizes legislatures to respond to that specification. But, in the political-legal culture I am considering, the legislature can respond only by overriding, not the specification on the ground that the legislature disagrees with the court's evaluation, but the very right itself. Overriding a right, while authorized, is politically costly – beyond the political costs associated with the underlying policy. Legislators therefore must expend political capital to overcome the incremental cost of overriding a right. Doing so reduces the political capital available for other policy proposals.

Weak-form review affects public policy even if the cost of overriding a right is relatively small. It re-orders the government's legislative priorities by taking political capital away from alternative proposals. Observing a legislature failing to respond to a weak-form invalidation thus tells us little about whether the legislature accepts the courts' decision on the merits. It could be that the legislature disagrees with the decision on the merits, but believes that expressing its disagreement would preclude it from adopting some other policy that seems more important than the invalidated one.

And, if the cost of overriding a right is high, as I suspect it is likely to be, a legislative response is extremely unlikely. The cost of doing so would be too high, in terms of other policies forgone. At least in this case, which I think is likely to be the common one, weak-form review becomes strong-form review because of the political costs – not with respect to the invalidated statute, but with respect to other policies forgone – of invoking the mechanisms of response authorized by the constitution.

IV CONCLUSION

The promise held out by proponents of weak-form systems of judicial review is that they reconcile constitutionalism and self-governance in a particularly attractive way. I have suggested that this promise can be fulfilled only under some (I believe) rather restrictive conditions. Legislators, and their constituents, must be committed to some degree to advancing constitutional values even when those values conflict with immediate interests. They must believe that courts have some advantage over legislators in interpreting what the constitution means, but that the courts' advantage is not too large. Weak-form systems with legislators not committed to constitutional values might override judicial interventions too readily, re-establishing a system of parliamentary supremacy. Weak-form systems whose legislators believe that courts have a large advantage over them will defer to the courts' interpretations too often, transforming the system into one of strong-form review.

Weak-form judicial review is an extremely interesting innovation in constitutional design. Whether it will endure and fulfil the promises of its proponents remains to be seen.

NOTES

1 A fourth issue – the choice between parliamentary and separation-of-powers systems – is sometimes of concern to scholars of comparative constitutional law. See, e.g., Ackerman, "The New Separation of Powers" (2000) 113 Harv. L. Rev. 633. More commonly, though, that issue is the domain of political scientists.

2 Gardbaum, "The New Commonwealth Model of Constitutionalism" (2001) 49 Am. J. Comp. L. 707.

3 Ordinarily, of course, the government.

4 In these versions, the degree to which the courts are likely to prevail depends in part on the formalities of the process of reinstating the legislation found by the courts to be inconsistent with constitutional norms. A court could have full power to invalidate legislation and yet the system of judicial review would conform to the "new Commonwealth model" if the process of constitutional amendment were extremely easy, for example, one that authorized amendment by simple parliamentary majority in a single session. As the requirements for amendment increase – to require

a 60 per cent or two-thirds majority in a single session, or to require parliamentary majorities in successive sessions, for example – the more the system resembles older forms of judicial review.

5 Goldsworthy, "Homogenizing Constitutions" (2003) 23 Oxford J. Leg. Stud. 483, at 484.

6 Another question is whether this new model should indeed be called a "Commonwealth" model. That is, is there something that connects the new model of judicial review to the common-law tradition shared by Commonwealth nations? Gardbaum properly observes that the new model was invented in and propagated among Commonwealth nations, although it is worth noting as well that South Africa and some other former Commonwealth nations adopted the old form of judicial review. The connection between the Commonwealth and the new form of judicial review therefore cannot be a strong one. (One possibility is that the nations of the Commonwealth are the ones in which the idea of parliamentary sovereignty, or its practice, was most strongly developed.)

Still, it might be that something about the common-law law-making process conduces to adoption of the new model of judicial review. One possibility is that texts play a different role in common-law systems than they do in civilian systems, and that perhaps this different role makes it easier to adopt the new form of judicial review in Commonwealth nations. The civil law's emphasis on the role of courts in enforcing written texts might make the old model of review particularly attractive to lawyers trained in that tradition. Yet, precedents – and, in the modern world, statutes – play the role in common-law systems that the code plays in civil law systems. It is unclear to me that anything in the common-law tradition is distinctively conducive to the new model of judicial review. For that reason, I prefer to call the new model one of "weak-form" judicial review, distinguishing it from the older "strong-form" system and making no claims about its relation to the Commonwealth or to the common-law tradition. Perhaps as we gain experience with weak-form judicial review we will be able to figure out whether it does have some connection to the common-law tradition.

7 Formally, the sequence could vary, with the experts weighing in early – through an advisory opinion rendered on a reference as can occur in Canada, or through post-enactment, pre-promulgation review as in the French system – or later, through immediate review on request or through review in the course of adjudicating ordinary cases.

8 This issue implicates intertwined issues of incentives and expertise. I want to be clear that strong- and weak-form systems do not necessarily

differ in the degree to which courts are aggressive in enforcing their views of fundamental rights, or in whether courts defer or refuse to defer to legislative judgments about whether legislation is consistent with constitutional guarantees. The differences between the systems reside in the relative ease or difficulty of a legislative response to judicial determinations. So, for example, a court in a weak-form system could say, "We hereby hold the statute at issue unconstitutional, exercising our own independent judgment about the constitution's meaning and giving no weight whatever to the legislature's judgment. But, of course, we acknowledge that the legislature can reinstate its own judgment by overriding our decision or by making it clear as crystal that it wishes to enforce a statute that we judges believe to be unconstitutional." And, similarly, a court in a strong-form system could say, "We refuse to hold this statute unconstitutional because it embodies the legislature's judgment that the statute is consistent with the constitution, even though, were we to examine the question anew, we might well disagree."

9 My perspective is of course that of a scholar of U.S. constitutional law, and my initial comments are framed with reference to the U.S. experience, but eventually I broaden the frame so that it incorporates parliamentary systems as well.

10 Particular systems may have a number of texts that, taken together, are the nation's constitution. And, I would not rule out the creation of a constitution by judicial decision, in which case the canonical texts would be the court's precedents.

11 I note an additional complication, associated with the transition from a system without judicial review to one with it. The very fact of transition is likely to bring home to legislators their responsibility to assess policy proposals in light of constitutional constraints. As a result, in the immediate aftermath of the transition, legislators are likely to be particularly alert to constitutional norms. That effect, though, will dissipate over time. I ignore the transition effect because I want to concentrate on the more permanent structures and incentives associated with weak-form judicial review.

12 It has to be supplemented by the obvious point that a representative who wants to be re-elected has to do something. Because the representative cannot enact the program favoured by either faction A or faction B, the representative will enact good, that is, non-factional public policy.

13 I note, but put aside as analytically irrelevant, the fact that representatives are likely to develop views of the constitution according to which the policy proposals they favour on policy grounds are constitutional,

and that they might often hold those views in good faith because of the openness of constitutions to alternative reasonable interpretations. I believe this observation is analytically irrelevant because I see nothing normatively problematic about adopting a tenable position on the constitution's meaning for the reason that that position is compatible with one's policy preferences.

14 This mechanism can have some effect even if some constituents affirmatively want to violate constitutional rights, if this preference is localized – that is, if only the constituents in a particular district want to violate a specific constitutional right and constituents in other districts do not (or want to violate some other constitutional right).

15 The pervasiveness and strength of such preferences will of course vary, and perhaps weak-form systems of judicial review are particularly well adapted to political-legal cultures in which citizens are especially alert to constitutional values. Or, in a slightly different variant, such systems might be well adapted to cultures in which citizens trust their representatives to be constitutionally responsible (even if the citizens themselves are not themselves that responsible).

16 Separation of powers need not take the relatively strong form it does in the United States for it to provide the opportunity I have described. In particular, a separately elected and effective upper house may be enough. My thinking about this issue has been influenced by Martens, "Reconsidering Republican Institutions as Guardians of Rights: Lessons from Australia," prepared for delivery at the 2003 Annual Meeting of the American Political Science Association. Martens describes how an effective parliamentary committee on the constitution was created in Australia when the Senate came to see itself as what Martens describes as a "Senate of Opposition."

17 The question is particularly pressing because weak-form review has been adopted in such systems.

18 Duverger's Law holds that constitution-designers can induce a tendency to coalition government by establishing proportional representation as the electoral scheme. Perhaps, then, we ought to think of weak-form judicial review in party-government systems as forming a package with proportional representation.

19 Debate over constitutional matters can occur in the party caucus, even if it does not occur in the legislature itself.

20 That is, representatives have incentives both to consider constitutional questions seriously and to delegate that consideration to a sub-unit of the institution of which they are members.

21 As will the professional staff assigned to such a committee.

22 Committee members might have an advantage in obtaining a judicial appointment, and so membership might attract those who see themselves as potential judges.

23 In conversation, Janet Hiebert pointed out that these institutional citizens may play a particularly important role in party government systems. These are permanent backbench members, who have no hope of ever becoming a member of the executive government. They continue to serve in part because of their concern for their constituents, but also in part because of their concern for their institution.

24 I believe that nothing in my analysis so far turns on whether the system is weak- or strong-form, but I have not thought through the issue enough to be confident in that belief.

25 Tushnet, "Non-Judicial Review" (2003) 40 Harv. J. Legis. 453.

26 Without incentives, the activity I described could simply be the result of an essentially random set of decisions by senators.

27 347 U.S. 483 (1954).

28 [1994] 3 NZLR 667 [hereinafter "*Simpson*"].

29 109 NZ Stat. 1687 (1990).

30 My sense is that, in accepting the Law Commission's "do nothing" recommendation, the government at least came quite close to accepting the decision as an appropriate one.

31 Part I of the *Constitution Act, 1982,* being Schedule B to the *Canada Act 1982* (U.K.), 1982, c. 11.

32 (UK), 1998, c. 42.

33 In Great Britain, for example, the *Human Rights Act* authorizes the highest court to declare legislation incompatible with the *European Convention for the Protection of Human Rights and Fundamental Freedoms,* Nov. 4, 1950, 312 UNTS 221. Commentators have observed that, under such circumstances, Parliament would be ill-advised to refuse to modify the legislation, because the European Court of Human Rights is likely to take the domestic courts' declaration of incompatibility as strong evidence that the legislation does violate the Convention (and, in particular, that the legislation does not fall within the margin of appreciation accorded laws that respond to peculiar local conditions). For a discussion, see Tushnet, *supra,* note 25, at 482–83.

34 *Simpson, supra,* note 28, at 691, *per* Casey, J. (citing art. 2(3)(b) of the *International Covenant on Civil and Political Rights*), 999 UNTS 171 (1966).

35 Id., at 691.

36 I use this as a shorthand formulation to encompass all weak-form sys-

tems. In some, the form of the court's judgment is a statement that the statute would violate constitutional norms were it to be interpreted in one way rather than another.

37 A parallel problem might emerge under the British *Human Rights Act*, although here it would depend on the language courts use in making declarations of incompatibility. In my view, British judges should avoid flat statements to the effect that legislation is incompatible with Convention rights, and adopt more circumspect formulations, such as statements that legislation is "in my view" incompatible.

38 *R. (on the application of Anufrijeva) v. Secretary of State for the Home Department*, 2003 UKHL 36, [2003] 3 All ER 827 (HL).

39 He wrote, for example, "There simply is no rational explanation for such a policy," id., at para. 24, and referred to Kafka in describing the system as one involving "hole in the corner decisions," id., at para. 28.

40 Janet Hiebert suggested this line of argument to me.

41 The second condition matters because a weak-form system properly becomes a strong-form one when the courts' comparative advantage is large.

Reference re Secession of Quebec [1998] 2 SCR 217

The *Quebec Secession Reference* concerned the legality of any secession from Canada by Quebec. The matter came to Court through a special process known as the reference procedure. The essence of a reference is that it asks the Court to give an advisory opinion on important legal questions that may or may not have arisen in the context of concrete disputes between interested parties, without the benefit of findings of fact made at trial. Quebec refused to appear in the proceedings before the Court, alleging that the Court lacked the jurisdiction to consider a matter that was fundamentally political in nature, and that was for the population of Quebec to decide itself. The Court did wish to hear all sides of the legal argument and so took the unusual step of appointing a lawyer to make arguments on Quebec's behalf. It also rejected in its judgment the argument that the issue was too political in nature to be adjudicated by a Court.

The Court (Lamer, C.J.C. and L'Heureux-Dubé, Gonthier, Cory, McLachlin, Iacobucci, Major, Bastarache and Binnie, JJ.): –

I INTRODUCTION

[1] This Reference requires us to consider momentous questions that go to the heart of our system of constitutional government. The observation we made more than a decade ago in *Reference re Manitoba Language Rights*, [1985] 1 SCR 721 (*Manitoba Language Rights Reference*), at p. 728, applies with equal force here: as in that case, the present one "combines legal and constitutional questions of the utmost subtlety and complexity with political questions of great sensitivity." In our view, it is not possible to answer the questions that have been put to us without a consideration of a number of underlying principles. An exploration of the meaning and nature of these underlying principles is not merely of academic interest. On the contrary, such an exploration is of immense practical utility. Only once those underlying principles have been examined and delineated may a considered response to the questions we are required to answer emerge.

[2] The questions posed by the Governor in Council by way of Order in Council P.C. 1996-1497, dated September 30, 1996, read as follows:

1 Under the Constitution of Canada, can the National Assembly, legislature or government of Quebec effect the secession of Quebec from Canada unilaterally?
2 Does international law give the National Assembly, legislature or government of Quebec the right to effect the secession of Quebec from Canada unilaterally? In this regard, is there a right to self-determination under international law that would give the National Assembly, legislature or government of Quebec the right to effect the secession of Quebec from Canada unilaterally?
3 In the event of a conflict between domestic and international law on the right of the National Assembly, legislature or government of Quebec to effect the secession of Quebec from Canada unilaterally, which would take precedence in Canada?

...

III REFERENCE QUESTIONS

A Question 1

Under the Constitution of Canada, can the National Assembly, legislature or government of Quebec effect the secession of Quebec from Canada unilaterally?

(1) Introduction

[32] As we confirmed in *Reference re Objection by Quebec to a Resolution to amend the Constitution*, [1982] 2 SCR 793, at p. 806, "The *Constitution Act, 1982* is now in force. Its legality is neither challenged nor assailable." The "Constitution of Canada" certainly includes the constitutional texts enumerated in s. 52(2) of the *Constitution Act, 1982*. Although these texts have a primary place in determining constitutional rules, they are not exhaustive. The Constitution also "embraces unwritten, as well as written rules," as we recently observed in the *Provincial Judges Reference*, [1997] 3 SCR 3, at para. 92. Finally, as was said in the *Patriation Reference*, [1981] 1 SCR 753, at p. 874, the Constitution of Canada includes

the global system of rules and principles which govern the exercise of constitutional authority in the whole and in every part of the Canadian state.

These supporting principles and rules, which include constitutional conventions and the workings of Parliament, are a necessary part of our Constitution because problems or situations may arise which are not expressly dealt with by the text of the Constitution. In order to endure over time, a constitution must contain a comprehensive set of rules and principles which are capable of providing an exhaustive legal framework for our system of government. Such principles and rules emerge from an understanding of the constitutional text itself, the historical context, and previous judicial interpretations of constitutional meaning. In our view, there are four fundamental and organizing principles of the Constitution which are relevant to addressing the question before us (although this enumeration is by no means exhaustive): federalism; democracy; constitutionalism and the rule of law; and respect for minorities. The foundation and substance of these principles are addressed in the following paragraphs. We will then turn to their specific application to the first reference question before us.

(2) Historical Context: The Significance of Confederation

[33] In our constitutional tradition, legality and legitimacy are linked. The precise nature of this link will be discussed below. However, at this stage, we wish to emphasize only that our constitutional history de-

monstrates that our governing institutions have adapted and changed to reflect changing social and political values. This has generally been accomplished by methods that have ensured continuity, stability and legal order.

[34] Because this Reference deals with questions fundamental to the nature of Canada, it should not be surprising that it is necessary to review the context in which the Canadian union has evolved. To this end, we will briefly describe the legal evolution of the Constitution and the foundational principles governing constitutional amendments. Our purpose is not to be exhaustive, but to highlight the features most relevant in the context of this Reference.

[35] Confederation was an initiative of elected representatives of the people then living in the colonies scattered across part of what is now Canada. It was not initiated by Imperial fiat. In March 1864, a select committee of the Legislative Assembly of the Province of Canada, chaired by George Brown, began to explore prospects for constitutional reform. The committee's report, released in June 1864, recommended that a federal union encompassing Canada East and Canada West, and perhaps the other British North American colonies, be pursued. A group of Reformers from Canada West, led by Brown, joined with Étienne P. Taché and John A. Macdonald in a coalition government for the purpose of engaging in constitutional reform along the lines of the federal model proposed by the committee's report.

[36] An opening to pursue federal union soon arose. The leaders of the maritime colonies had planned to meet at Charlottetown in the fall to discuss the perennial topic of maritime union. The Province of Canada secured invitations to send a Canadian delegation. On September 1, 1864, 23 delegates (five from New Brunswick, five from Nova Scotia, five from Prince Edward Island, and eight from the Province of Canada) met in Charlottetown. After five days of discussion, the delegates reached agreement on a plan for federal union.

[37] The salient aspects of the agreement may be briefly outlined. There was to be a federal union featuring a bicameral central legislature. Representation in the Lower House was to be based on population, whereas in the Upper House it was to be based on regional equality, the regions comprising Canada East, Canada West and the Maritimes. The significance of the adoption of a federal form of government cannot be exaggerated. Without it, neither the agreement of the delegates from Canada East nor that of the delegates from the maritime colonies could have been obtained.

[38] Several matters remained to be resolved, and so the Charlotte-town delegates agreed to meet again at Quebec in October, and to invite Newfoundland to send a delegation to join them. The Quebec Conference began on October 10, 1864. Thirty-three delegates (two from Newfoundland, seven from New Brunswick, five from Nova Scotia, seven from Prince Edward Island, and twelve from the Province of Canada) met over a two and a half week period. Precise consideration of each aspect of the federal structure preoccupied the political agenda. The delegates approved 72 resolutions, addressing almost all of what subsequently made its way into the final text of the *Constitution Act, 1867*. These included guarantees to protect French language and culture, both directly (by making French an official language in Quebec and Canada as a whole) and indirectly (by allocating jurisdiction over education and "Property and Civil Rights in the Province" to the provinces). The protection of minorities was thus reaffirmed.

[39] Legally, there remained only the requirement to have the Quebec Resolutions put into proper form and passed by the Imperial Parliament in London. However, politically, it was thought that more was required. Indeed, Resolution 70 provided that "The Sanction of the Imperial and *Local Parliaments* shall be sought for the Union of the Provinces, on the principles adopted by the Conference." (Cited in J. Pope, ed., *Confederation: Being a Series of Hitherto Unpublished Documents Bearing on the British North America Act* (1895), at p. 52 (emphasis added).)

[40] Confirmation of the Quebec Resolutions was achieved more smoothly in central Canada than in the Maritimes. In February and March 1865, the Quebec Resolutions were the subject of almost six weeks of sustained debate in both houses of the Canadian legislature. The Canadian Legislative Assembly approved the Quebec Resolutions in March 1865 with the support of a majority of members from both Canada East and Canada West. The governments of both Prince Edward Island and Newfoundland chose, in accordance with popular sentiment in both colonies, not to accede to the Quebec Resolutions. In New Brunswick, a general election was required before Premier Tilley's pro-Confederation party prevailed. In Nova Scotia, Premier Tupper ultimately obtained a resolution from the House of Assembly favouring Confederation.

[41] Sixteen delegates (five from New Brunswick, five from Nova Scotia, and six from the Province of Canada) met in London in December 1866 to finalize the plan for Confederation. To this end, they agreed to some slight modifications and additions to the Quebec

Resolutions. Minor changes were made to the distribution of powers, provision was made for the appointment of extra senators in the event of a deadlock between the House of Commons and the Senate, and certain religious minorities were given the right to appeal to the federal government where their denominational school rights were adversely affected by provincial legislation. The British North America Bill was drafted after the London Conference with the assistance of the Colonial Office, and was introduced into the House of Lords in February 1867. The Act passed third reading in the House of Commons on March 8, received royal assent on March 29, and was proclaimed on July 1, 1867. The Dominion of Canada thus became a reality.

[42] There was an early attempt at secession. In the first Dominion election in September 1867, Premier Tupper's forces were decimated: members opposed to Confederation won 18 of Nova Scotia's 19 federal seats, and in the simultaneous provincial election, 36 of the 38 seats in the provincial legislature. Newly-elected Premier Joseph Howe led a delegation to the Imperial Parliament in London in an effort to undo the new constitutional arrangements, but it was too late. The Colonial Office rejected Premier Howe's plea to permit Nova Scotia to withdraw from Confederation. As the Colonial Secretary wrote in 1868:

The neighbouring province of New Brunswick has entered into the union in reliance on having with it the sister province of Nova Scotia; and vast obligations, political and commercial, have already been contracted on the faith of a measure so long discussed and so solemnly adopted. . . . I trust that the Assembly and the people of Nova Scotia will not be surprised that the Queen's government feel that they would not be warranted in advising the reversal of a great measure of state, attended by so many extensive consequences already in operation ... (Quoted in H. Wade MacLauchlan, "Accounting for Democracy and the Rule of Law in the Quebec Secession Reference," [1997], 76 *Can Bar Rev* 155, at p. 168.)

The interdependence characterized by "vast obligations, political and commercial," referred to by the Colonial Secretary in 1868, has, of course, multiplied immeasurably in the last 130 years.

[43] Federalism was a legal response to the underlying political and cultural realities that existed at Confederation and continue to exist today. At Confederation, political leaders told their respective communities that the Canadian union would be able to reconcile diversity with unity. It is pertinent, in the context of the present Reference, to mention

the words of George-Étienne Cartier (cited in the *Parliamentary Debates on the subject of the Confederation* (1865), at p. 60):

Now, when we [are] united, if union [is] attained, we [shall] form a political nationality with which neither the national origin, nor the religion of any individual, [will] interfere. It was lamented by some that we had this diversity of races, and hopes were expressed that this distinctive feature would cease. The idea of unity of races [is] utopian – it [is] impossible. Distinctions of this kind [will] always exist. Dissimilarity, in fact, appear[s] to be the order of the physical world and of the moral world, as well as in the political world. But with regard to the objection based on this fact, to the effect that a great nation [can]not be formed because Lower Canada [is] in great part French and Catholic, and Upper Canada [is] British and Protestant, and the Lower Provinces [are] mixed, it [is] futile and worthless in the extreme ... In our own Federation we [will] have Catholic and Protestant, English, French, Irish and Scotch, and each by his efforts and his success [will] increase the prosperity and glory of the new Confederacy ... [W]e [are] of different races, not for the purpose of warring against each other, but in order to compete and emulate for the general welfare.

The federal-provincial division of powers was a legal recognition of the diversity that existed among the initial members of Confederation, and manifested a concern to accommodate that diversity within a single nation by granting significant powers to provincial governments. The *Constitution Act, 1867* was an act of nation-building. It was the first step in the transition from colonies separately dependent on the Imperial Parliament for their governance to a unified and independent political state in which different peoples could resolve their disagreements and work together toward common goals and a common interest. Federalism was the political mechanism by which diversity could be reconciled with unity.

[44] A federal-provincial division of powers necessitated a written constitution which circumscribed the powers of the new Dominion and Provinces of Canada. Despite its federal structure, the new Dominion was to have "a Constitution similar in Principle to that of the United Kingdom" (*Constitution Act, 1867*, preamble). Allowing for the obvious differences between the governance of Canada and the United Kingdom, it was nevertheless thought important to thus emphasize the continuity of constitutional principles, including democratic institutions and the rule of law; and the continuity of the exercise of sovereign

power transferred from Westminster to the federal and provincial capitals of Canada.

[45] After 1867, the Canadian federation continued to evolve both territorially and politically. New territories were admitted to the union and new provinces were formed. In 1870, Rupert's Land and the Northwest Territories were admitted and Manitoba was formed as a province. British Columbia was admitted in 1871, Prince Edward Island in 1873, and the Arctic Islands were added in 1880. In 1898, the Yukon Territory and in 1905, the provinces of Alberta and Saskatchewan were formed from the Northwest Territories. Newfoundland was admitted in 1949 by an amendment to the *Constitution Act, 1867*. The new territory of Nunavut was carved out of the Northwest Territories in 1993 with the partition to become effective in April 1999.

[46] Canada's evolution from colony to fully independent state was gradual. The Imperial Parliament's passage of the *Statute of Westminster*, 1931 (U.K.), 22 & 23 Geo. 5, c. 4, confirmed in law what had earlier been confirmed in fact by the Balfour Declaration of 1926, namely, that Canada was an independent country. Thereafter, Canadian law alone governed in Canada, except where Canada expressly consented to the continued application of Imperial legislation. Canada's independence from Britain was achieved through legal and political evolution with an adherence to the rule of law and stability. The proclamation of the *Constitution Act, 1982* removed the last vestige of British authority over the Canadian Constitution and re-affirmed Canada's commitment to the protection of its minority, aboriginal, equality, legal and language rights, and fundamental freedoms as set out in the *Canadian Charter of Rights and Freedoms*.

[47] Legal continuity, which requires an orderly transfer of authority, necessitated that the 1982 amendments be made by the Westminster Parliament, but the legitimacy as distinguished from the formal legality of the amendments derived from political decisions taken in Canada within a legal framework which this Court, in the *Patriation Reference*, had ruled was in accordance with our Constitution. It should be noted, parenthetically, that the 1982 amendments did not alter the basic division of powers in ss. 91 and 92 of the *Constitution Act, 1867*, which is the primary textual expression of the principle of federalism in our Constitution, agreed upon at Confederation. It did, however, have the important effect that, despite the refusal of the government of Quebec to join in its adoption, Quebec has become bound to the terms of a Constitution that is different from that which prevailed previously, par-

ticularly as regards provisions governing its amendment, and the *Canadian Charter of Rights and Freedoms.* As to the latter, to the extent that the scope of legislative powers was thereafter to be constrained by the *Charter,* the constraint operated as much against federal legislative powers as against provincial legislative powers. Moreover, it is to be remembered that s. 33, the "notwithstanding clause," gives Parliament and the provincial legislatures authority to legislate on matters within their jurisdiction in derogation of the fundamental freedoms (s. 2), legal rights (ss. 7 to 14) and equality rights (s. 15) provisions of the *Charter.*

[48] We think it apparent from even this brief historical review that the evolution of our constitutional arrangements has been characterized by adherence to the rule of law, respect for democratic institutions, the accommodation of minorities, insistence that governments adhere to constitutional conduct and a desire for continuity and stability. We now turn to a discussion of the general constitutional principles that bear on the present Reference.

(3) Analysis of the Constitutional Principles

(a) Nature of the Principles.
[49] What are those underlying principles? Our Constitution is primarily a written one, the product of 131 years of evolution. Behind the written word is an historical lineage stretching back through the ages, which aids in the consideration of the underlying constitutional principles. These principles inform and sustain the constitutional text: they are the vital unstated assumptions upon which the text is based. The following discussion addresses the four foundational constitutional principles that are most germane for resolution of this Reference: federalism, democracy, constitutionalism and the rule of law, and respect for minority rights. These defining principles function in symbiosis. No single principle can be defined in isolation from the others, nor does any one principle trump or exclude the operation of any other.

[50] Our Constitution has an internal architecture, or what the majority of this Court in *OPSEU v. Ontario (Attorney General),* [1987] 2 SCR 2, at p. 57, called a "basic constitutional structure." The individual elements of the Constitution are linked to the others, and must be interpreted by reference to the structure of the Constitution as a whole. As we recently emphasized in the *Provincial Judges Reference,* certain underlying principles infuse our Constitution and breathe life into it. Speaking of the rule of law principle in the *Manitoba Language Rights Reference, supra,* at p. 750, we held that "the principle is clearly implicit

in the very nature of a Constitution." The same may be said of the other three constitutional principles we underscore today.

[51] Although these underlying principles are not explicitly made part of the Constitution by any written provision, other than in some respects by the oblique reference in the preamble to the *Constitution Act, 1867*, it would be impossible to conceive of our constitutional structure without them. The principles dictate major elements of the architecture of the Constitution itself and are as such its lifeblood.

[52] The principles assist in the interpretation of the text and the delineation of spheres of jurisdiction, the scope of rights and obligations, and the role of our political institutions. Equally important, observance of and respect for these principles is essential to the ongoing process of constitutional development and evolution of our Constitution as a "living tree," to invoke the famous description in *Edwards v. Attorney-General for Canada*, [1930] AC 124 (PC), at p. 136. As this Court indicated in *New Brunswick Broadcasting Co. v. Nova Scotia (Speaker of the House of Assembly)*, [1993] 1 SCR 319, Canadians have long recognized the existence and importance of unwritten constitutional principles in our system of government.

[53] Given the existence of these underlying constitutional principles, what use may the Court make of them? In the *Provincial Judges Reference, supra*, at paras. 93 and 104, we cautioned that the recognition of these constitutional principles (the majority opinion referred to them as "organizing principles" and described one of them, judicial independence, as an "unwritten norm") could not be taken as an invitation to dispense with the written text of the Constitution. On the contrary, we confirmed that there are compelling reasons to insist upon the primacy of our written constitution. A written constitution promotes legal certainty and predictability, and it provides a foundation and a touchstone for the exercise of constitutional judicial review. However, we also observed in the *Provincial Judges Reference* that the effect of the preamble to the *Constitution Act, 1867* was to incorporate certain constitutional principles by reference, a point made earlier in *Fraser v. Public Service Staff Relations Board*, [1985] 2 SCR 455, at pp. 462–3. In the *Provincial Judges Reference*, at para. 104, we determined that the preamble "invites the courts to turn those principles into the premises of a constitutional argument that culminates in the filling of gaps in the express terms of the constitutional text."

[54] Underlying constitutional principles may in certain circumstances give rise to substantive legal obligations (have "full legal force," as we described it in the *Patriation Reference, supra*, at p. 845), which

constitute substantive limitations upon government action. These principles may give rise to very abstract and general obligations, or they may be more specific and precise in nature. The principles are not merely descriptive, but are also invested with a powerful normative force, and are binding upon both courts and governments. "In other words," as this Court confirmed in the *Manitoba Language Rights Reference, supra,* at p. 752, "in the process of Constitutional adjudication, the Court may have regard to unwritten postulates which form the very foundation of the Constitution of Canada." It is to a discussion of those underlying constitutional principles that we now turn.

(b) Federalism.

[55] It is undisputed that Canada is a federal state. Yet many commentators have observed that, according to the precise terms of the *Constitution Act, 1867,* the federal system was only partial. See, e.g., K.C. Wheare, *Federal Government* (4th ed. 1963), at pp. 18–20. This was so because, on paper, the federal government retained sweeping powers which threatened to undermine the autonomy of the provinces. Here again, however, a review of the written provisions of the Constitution does not provide the entire picture. Our political and constitutional practice has adhered to an underlying principle of federalism, and has interpreted the written provisions of the Constitution in this light. For example, although the federal power of disallowance was included in the *Constitution Act, 1867,* the underlying principle of federalism triumphed early. Many constitutional scholars contend that the federal power of disallowance has been abandoned (e.g., P.W. Hogg, *Constitutional Law of Canada* (4th ed. 1997), at p. 120).

[56] In a federal system of government such as ours, political power is shared by two orders of government: the federal government on the one hand, and the provinces on the other. Each is assigned respective spheres of jurisdiction by the *Constitution Act, 1867.* See, e.g., *Liquidators of the Maritime Bank of Canada v. Receiver-General of New Brunswick,* [1892] AC 437 (PC), at pp. 441–2. It is up to the courts "to control the limits of the respective sovereignties": *Northern Telecom Canada Ltd. v. Communication Workers of Canada,* [1983] 1 SCR 733, at p. 741. In interpreting our Constitution, the courts have always been concerned with the federalism principle, inherent in the structure of our constitutional arrangements, which has from the beginning been the lodestar by which the courts have been guided.

[57] This underlying principle of federalism, then, has exercised a role of considerable importance in the interpretation of the written

provisions of our Constitution. In the *Patriation Reference, supra,* at pp. 905–9, we confirmed that the principle of federalism runs through the political and legal systems of Canada. Indeed, Martland and Ritchie, JJ., dissenting in the *Patriation Reference,* at p. 821, considered federalism to be "the dominant principle of Canadian constitutional law." With the enactment of the *Charter,* that proposition may have less force than it once did, but there can be little doubt that the principle of federalism remains a central organizational theme of our Constitution. Less obviously, perhaps, but certainly of equal importance, federalism is a political and legal response to underlying social and political realities.

[58] The principle of federalism recognizes the diversity of the component parts of Confederation, and the autonomy of provincial governments to develop their societies within their respective spheres of jurisdiction. The federal structure of our country also facilitates democratic participation by distributing power to the government thought to be most suited to achieving the particular societal objective having regard to this diversity. The scheme of the *Constitution Act, 1867,* it was said in *Re the Initiative and Referendum Act,* [1919] AC 935 (PC), at p. 942, was

> not to weld the Provinces into one, nor to subordinate Provincial Governments to a central authority, but to establish a central government in which these Provinces should be represented, entrusted with exclusive authority only in affairs in which they had a common interest. Subject to this each Province was to retain its independence and autonomy and to be directly under the Crown as its head.

More recently, in *Haig v. Canada,* [1993] 2 SCR 995, at p. 1047, the majority of this Court held that differences between provinces "are a rational part of the political reality in the federal process." It was referring to the differential application of federal law in individual provinces, but the point applies more generally. A unanimous Court expressed similar views in *R. v. S. (S.),* [1990] 2 SCR 254, at pp. 287–8.

[59] The principle of federalism facilitates the pursuit of collective goals by cultural and linguistic minorities which form the majority within a particular province. This is the case in Quebec, where the majority of the population is French-speaking, and which possesses a distinct culture. This is not merely the result of chance. The social and demographic reality of Quebec explains the existence of the province of Quebec as a political unit and indeed, was one of the essential reasons for establishing a federal structure for the Canadian union in 1867. The

experience of both Canada East and Canada West under the *Union Act, 1840* (U.K.), 3–4 Vict., c. 35, had not been satisfactory. The federal structure adopted at Confederation enabled French-speaking Canadians to form a numerical majority in the province of Quebec, and so exercise the considerable provincial powers conferred by the *Constitution Act, 1867* in such a way as to promote their language and culture. It also made provision for certain guaranteed representation within the federal Parliament itself.

[60] Federalism was also welcomed by Nova Scotia and New Brunswick, both of which also affirmed their will to protect their individual cultures and their autonomy over local matters. All new provinces joining the federation sought to achieve similar objectives, which are no less vigorously pursued by the provinces and territories as we approach the new millennium.

(c) Democracy.

[61] Democracy is a fundamental value in our constitutional law and political culture. While it has both an institutional and an individual aspect, the democratic principle was also argued before us in the sense of the supremacy of the sovereign will of a people, in this case potentially to be expressed by Quebecers in support of unilateral secession. It is useful to explore in a summary way these different aspects of the democratic principle.

[62] The principle of democracy has always informed the design of our constitutional structure, and continues to act as an essential interpretive consideration to this day. A majority of this Court in *OPSEU v. Ontario, supra*, at p. 57, confirmed that "the basic structure of our Constitution, as established by the *Constitution Act, 1867*, contemplates the existence of certain political institutions, including freely elected legislative bodies at the federal and provincial levels." As is apparent from an earlier line of decisions emanating from this Court, including *Switzman v. Elbling*, [1957] SCR 285, *Saumur v. City of Quebec*, [1953] 2 SCR 299, *Boucher v. The King*, [1951] SCR 265, and *Reference re Alberta Statutes*, [1938] SCR 100, the democracy principle can best be understood as a sort of baseline against which the framers of our Constitution, and subsequently, our elected representatives under it, have always operated. It is perhaps for this reason that the principle was not explicitly identified in the text of the *Constitution Act, 1867* itself. To have done so might have appeared redundant, even silly, to the framers. As explained in the *Provincial Judges Reference, supra*, at para.

100, it is evident that our Constitution contemplates that Canada shall be a constitutional democracy. Yet this merely demonstrates the importance of underlying constitutional principles that are nowhere explicitly described in our constitutional texts. The representative and democratic nature of our political institutions was simply assumed.

[63] Democracy is commonly understood as being a political system of majority rule. It is essential to be clear what this means. The evolution of our democratic tradition can be traced back to the *Magna Carta* (1215) and before, through the long struggle for Parliamentary supremacy which culminated in the English *Bill of Rights* of 1689, the emergence of representative political institutions in the colonial era, the development of responsible government in the 19th century, and eventually, the achievement of Confederation itself in 1867. "[T]he Canadian tradition," the majority of this Court held in *Reference re Provincial Electoral Boundaries (Sask.)*, [1991] 2 SCR 158, at p. 186, is "one of evolutionary democracy moving in uneven steps toward the goal of universal suffrage and more effective representation." Since Confederation, efforts to extend the franchise to those unjustly excluded from participation in our political system – such as women, minorities, and aboriginal peoples – have continued, with some success, to the present day.

[64] Democracy is not simply concerned with the process of government. On the contrary, as suggested in *Switzman v. Elbling, supra,* at p. 306, democracy is fundamentally connected to substantive goals, most importantly, the promotion of self-government. Democracy accommodates cultural and group identities: *Reference re Provincial Electoral Boundaries,* at p. 188. Put another way, a sovereign people exercises its right to self-government through the democratic process. In considering the scope and purpose of the *Charter*, the Court in *R. v. Oakes*, [1986] 1 SCR 103, articulated some of the values inherent in the notion of democracy (at p. 136):

The Court must be guided by the values and principles essential to a free and democratic society which I believe to embody, to name but a few, respect for the inherent dignity of the human person, commitment to social justice and equality, accommodation of a wide variety of beliefs, respect for cultural and group identity, and faith in social and political institutions which enhance the participation of individuals and groups in society.

[65] In institutional terms, democracy means that each of the provincial legislatures and the federal Parliament is elected by popular

franchise. These legislatures, we have said, are "at the core of the system of representative government": *New Brunswick Broadcasting, supra*, at p. 387. In individual terms, the right to vote in elections to the House of Commons and the provincial legislatures, and to be candidates in those elections, is guaranteed to "Every citizen of Canada" by virtue of s. 3 of the *Charter*. Historically, this Court has interpreted democracy to mean the process of representative and responsible government and the right of citizens to participate in the political process as voters (*Reference re Provincial Electoral Boundaries, supra*) and as candidates (*Harvey v. New Brunswick (Attorney General)*, [1996] 2 SCR 876). In addition, the effect of s. 4 of the *Charter* is to oblige the House of Commons and the provincial legislatures to hold regular elections and to permit citizens to elect representatives to their political institutions. The democratic principle is affirmed with particular clarity in that s. 4 is not subject to the notwithstanding power contained in s. 33.

[66] It is, of course, true that democracy expresses the sovereign will of the people. Yet this expression, too, must be taken in the context of the other institutional values we have identified as pertinent to this Reference. The relationship between democracy and federalism means, for example, that in Canada there may be different and equally legitimate majorities in different provinces and territories and at the federal level. No one majority is more or less "legitimate" than the others as an expression of democratic opinion, although, of course, the consequences will vary with the subject matter. A federal system of government enables different provinces to pursue policies responsive to the particular concerns and interests of people in that province. At the same time, Canada as a whole is also a democratic community in which citizens construct and achieve goals on a national scale through a federal government acting within the limits of its jurisdiction. The function of federalism is to enable citizens to participate concurrently in different collectivities and to pursue goals at both a provincial and a federal level.

[67] The consent of the governed is a value that is basic to our understanding of a free and democratic society. Yet democracy in any real sense of the word cannot exist without the rule of law. It is the law that creates the framework within which the "sovereign will" is to be ascertained and implemented. To be accorded legitimacy, democratic institutions must rest, ultimately, on a legal foundation. That is, they must allow for the participation of, and accountability to, the people, through public institutions created under the Constitution. Equally,

however, a system of government cannot survive through adherence to the law alone. A political system must also possess legitimacy, and in our political culture, that requires an interaction between the rule of law and the democratic principle. The system must be capable of reflecting the aspirations of the people. But there is more. Our law's claim to legitimacy also rests on an appeal to moral values, many of which are imbedded in our constitutional structure. It would be a grave mistake to equate legitimacy with the "sovereign will" or majority rule alone, to the exclusion of other constitutional values.

[68] Finally, we highlight that a functioning democracy requires a continuous process of discussion. The Constitution mandates government by democratic legislatures, and an executive accountable to them, "resting ultimately on public opinion reached by discussion and the interplay of ideas" (*Saumur v. City of Quebec, supra*, at p. 330). At both the federal and provincial level, by its very nature, the need to build majorities necessitates compromise, negotiation, and deliberation. No one has a monopoly on truth, and our system is predicated on the faith that in the marketplace of ideas, the best solutions to public problems will rise to the top. Inevitably, there will be dissenting voices. A democratic system of government is committed to considering those dissenting voices, and seeking to acknowledge and address those voices in the laws by which all in the community must live.

[69] The *Constitution Act, 1982* gives expression to this principle, by conferring a right to initiate constitutional change on each participant in Confederation. In our view, the existence of this right imposes a corresponding duty on the participants in Confederation to engage in constitutional discussions in order to acknowledge and address democratic expressions of a desire for change in other provinces. This duty is inherent in the democratic principle which is a fundamental predicate of our system of governance.

(d) Constitutionalism and the Rule of Law.

[70] The principles of constitutionalism and the rule of law lie at the root of our system of govern-ment. The rule of law, as observed in *Roncarelli v. Duplessis*, [1959] SCR 121, at p. 142, is "a fundamental postulate of our constitutional structure." As we noted in the *Patriation Reference, supra*, at pp. 805–6, "[t]he 'rule of law' is a highly textured expression, importing many things which are beyond the need of these reasons to explore but conveying, for example, a sense of orderliness, of subjection to known legal rules and of executive accountability to legal

authority." At its most basic level, the rule of law vouchsafes to the citizens and residents of the country a stable, predictable and ordered society in which to conduct their affairs. It provides a shield for individuals from arbitrary state action.

[71] In the *Manitoba Language Rights Reference, supra,* at pp. 747–52, this Court outlined the elements of the rule of law. We emphasized, first, that the rule of law provides that the law is supreme over the acts of both government and private persons. There is, in short, one law for all. Second, we explained, at p. 749, that "the rule of law requires the creation and maintenance of an actual order of positive laws which preserves and embodies the more general principle of normative order." It was this second aspect of the rule of law that was primarily at issue in the *Manitoba Language Rights Reference* itself. A third aspect of the rule of law is, as recently confirmed in the *Provincial Judges Reference, supra,* at para. 10, that "the exercise of all public power must find its ultimate source in a legal rule." Put another way, the relationship between the state and the individual must be regulated by law. Taken together, these three considerations make up a principle of profound constitutional and political significance.

[72] The constitutionalism principle bears considerable similarity to the rule of law, although they are not identical. The essence of constitutionalism in Canada is embodied in s. 52(1) of the *Constitution Act, 1982,* which provides that "[t]he Constitution of Canada is the supreme law of Canada, and any law that is inconsistent with the provisions of the Constitution is, to the extent of the inconsistency, of no force or effect." Simply put, the constitutionalism principle requires that all government action comply with the Constitution. The rule of law principle requires that all government action must comply with the law, including the Constitution. This Court has noted on several occasions that with the adoption of the *Charter,* the Canadian system of government was transformed to a significant extent from a system of Parliamentary supremacy to one of constitutional supremacy. The Constitution binds all governments, both federal and provincial, including the executive branch (*Operation Dismantle Inc. v. The Queen,* [1985] 1 SCR 441, at p. 455). They may not transgress its provisions: indeed, their sole claim to exercise lawful authority rests in the powers allocated to them under the Constitution, and can come from no other source.

[73] An understanding of the scope and importance of the principles of the rule of law and constitutionalism is aided by acknowledging

explicitly why a constitution is entrenched beyond the reach of simple majority rule. There are three overlapping reasons.

[74] First, a constitution may provide an added safeguard for fundamental human rights and individual freedoms which might otherwise be susceptible to government interference. Although democratic government is generally solicitous of those rights, there are occasions when the majority will be tempted to ignore fundamental rights in order to accomplish collective goals more easily or effectively. Constitutional entrenchment ensures that those rights will be given due regard and protection. Second, a constitution may seek to ensure that vulnerable minority groups are endowed with the institutions and rights necessary to maintain and promote their identities against the assimilative pressures of the majority. And third, a constitution may provide for a division of political power that allocates political power amongst different levels of government. That purpose would be defeated if one of those democratically elected levels of government could usurp the powers of the other simply by exercising its legislative power to allocate additional political power to itself unilaterally.

[75] The argument that the Constitution may be legitimately circumvented by resort to a majority vote in a province-wide referendum is superficially persuasive, in large measure because it seems to appeal to some of the same principles that underlie the legitimacy of the Constitution itself, namely, democracy and self-government. In short, it is suggested that as the notion of popular sovereignty underlies the legitimacy of our existing constitutional arrangements, so the same popular sovereignty that originally led to the present Constitution must (it is argued) also permit "the people" in their exercise of popular sovereignty to secede by majority vote alone. However, closer analysis reveals that this argument is unsound, because it misunderstands the meaning of popular sovereignty and the essence of a constitutional democracy.

[76] Canadians have never accepted that ours is a system of simple majority rule. Our principle of democracy, taken in conjunction with the other constitutional principles discussed here, is richer. Constitutional government is necessarily predicated on the idea that the political representatives of the people of a province have the capacity and the power to commit the province to be bound into the future by the constitutional rules being adopted. These rules are "binding" not in the sense of frustrating the will of a majority of a province, but as defining

the majority which must be consulted in order to alter the fundamental balances of political power (including the spheres of autonomy guaranteed by the principle of federalism), individual rights, and minority rights in our society. Of course, those constitutional rules are themselves amenable to amendment, but only through a process of negotiation which ensures that there is an opportunity for the constitutionally defined rights of all the parties to be respected and reconciled.

[77] In this way, our belief in democracy may be harmonized with our belief in constitutionalism. Constitutional amendment often requires some form of substantial consensus precisely because the content of the underlying principles of our Constitution demand it. By requiring broad support in the form of an "enhanced majority" to achieve constitutional change, the Constitution ensures that minority interests must be addressed before proposed changes which would affect them may be enacted.

[78] It might be objected, then, that constitutionalism is therefore incompatible with democratic government. This would be an erroneous view. Constitutionalism facilitates – indeed, makes possible – a democratic political system by creating an orderly framework within which people may make political decisions. Viewed correctly, constitutionalism and the rule of law are not in conflict with democracy; rather, they are essential to it. Without that relationship, the political will upon which democratic decisions are taken would itself be undermined.

(e) Protection of Minorities.
[79] The fourth underlying constitutional principle we address here concerns the protection of minorities. There are a number of specific constitutional provisions protecting minority language, religion and education rights. Some of those provisions are, as we have recognized on a number of occasions, the product of historical compromises. As this Court observed in *Reference re Bill 30, An Act to amend the Education Act (Ont.)*, [1987] 1 SCR 1148, at p. 1173, and in *Reference re Education Act (Que.)*, [1993] 2 SCR 511, at pp. 529–30, the protection of minority religious education rights was a central consideration in the negotiations leading to Confederation. In the absence of such protection, it was felt that the minorities in what was then Canada East and Canada West would be submerged and assimilated. See also *Greater Montreal Protestant School Board v. Quebec (Attorney General)*, [1989] 1 SCR 377, at

pp. 401–2, and *Adler v. Ontario*, [1996] 3 SCR 609. Similar concerns animated the provisions protecting minority language rights, as noted in *Société des Acadiens du Nouveau-Brunswick Inc. v. Association of Parents for Fairness in Education*, [1986] 1 SCR 549, at p. 564.

[80] However, we highlight that even though those provisions were the product of negotiation and political compromise, that does not render them unprincipled. Rather, such a concern reflects a broader principle related to the protection of minority rights. Undoubtedly, the three other constitutional principles inform the scope and operation of the specific provisions that protect the rights of minorities. We emphasize that the protection of minority rights is itself an independent principle underlying our constitutional order. The principle is clearly reflected in the *Charter's* provisions for the protection of minority rights. See, e.g., *Reference re Public Schools Act (Man.), s. 79(3), (4) and (7)*, [1993] 1 SCR 839, and *Mahe v. Alberta*, [1990] 1 SCR 342.

[81] The concern of our courts and governments to protect minorities has been prominent in recent years, particularly following the enactment of the *Charter*. Undoubtedly, one of the key considerations motivating the enactment of the *Charter*, and the process of constitutional judicial review that it entails, is the protection of minorities. However, it should not be forgotten that the protection of minority rights had a long history before the enactment of the *Charter*. Indeed, the protection of minority rights was clearly an essential consideration in the design of our constitutional structure even at the time of Confederation: *Senate Reference*, [1980] 1 SCR 54, at p. 71. Although Canada's record of upholding the rights of minorities is not a spotless one, that goal is one towards which Canadians have been striving since Confederation, and the process has not been without successes. The principle of protecting minority rights continues to exercise influence in the operation and interpretation of our Constitution.

[82] Consistent with this long tradition of respect for minorities, which is at least as old as Canada itself, the framers of the *Constitution Act, 1982* included in s. 35 explicit protection for existing aboriginal and treaty rights, and in s. 25, a non-derogation clause in favour of the rights of aboriginal peoples. The "promise" of s. 35, as it was termed in *R. v. Sparrow*, [1990] 1 SCR 1075, at p. 1083, recognized not only the ancient occupation of land by aboriginal peoples, but their contribution to the building of Canada, and the special commitments made to them by successive governments. The protection of these rights, so recently and

arduously achieved, whether looked at in their own right or as part of the larger concern with minorities, reflects an important underlying constitutional value.

(4) The Operation of the Constitutional Principles in the Secession Context

[83] Secession is the effort of a group or section of a state to withdraw itself from the political and constitutional authority of that state, with a view to achieving statehood for a new territorial unit on the international plane. In a federal state, secession typically takes the form of a territorial unit seeking to withdraw from the federation. Secession is a legal act as much as a political one. By the terms of Question 1 of this Reference, we are asked to rule on the legality of unilateral secession "[u]nder the Constitution of Canada." This is an appropriate question, as the legality of unilateral secession must be evaluated, at least in the first instance, from the perspective of the domestic legal order of the state from which the unit seeks to withdraw. As we shall see below, it is also argued that international law is a relevant standard by which the legality of a purported act of secession may be measured.

[84] The secession of a province from Canada must be considered, in legal terms, to require an amendment to the Constitution, which perforce requires negotiation. The amendments necessary to achieve a secession could be radical and extensive. Some commentators have suggested that secession could be a change of such a magnitude that it could not be considered to be merely an amendment to the Constitution. We are not persuaded by this contention. It is of course true that the Constitution is silent as to the ability of a province to secede from Confederation but, although the Constitution neither expressly authorizes nor prohibits secession, an act of secession would purport to alter the governance of Canadian territory in a manner which undoubtedly is inconsistent with our current constitutional arrangements. The fact that those changes would be profound, or that they would purport to have a significance with respect to international law, does not negate their nature as amendments to the Constitution of Canada.

[85] The Constitution is the expression of the sovereignty of the people of Canada. It lies within the power of the people of Canada, acting through their various governments duly elected and recognized under the Constitution, to effect whatever constitutional arrangements are desired within Canadian territory, including, should it be so

desired, the secession of Quebec from Canada. As this Court held in the *Manitoba Language Rights Reference, supra,* at p. 745, "[t]he Constitution of a country is a statement of the will of the people to be governed in accordance with certain principles held as fundamental and certain prescriptions restrictive of the powers of the legislature and government." The manner in which such a political will could be formed and mobilized is a somewhat speculative exercise, though we are asked to assume the existence of such a political will for the purpose of answering the question before us. By the terms of this Reference, we have been asked to consider whether it would be constitutional in such a circumstance for the National Assembly, legislature or government of Quebec to effect the secession of Quebec from Canada unilaterally.

[86] The "unilateral" nature of the act is of cardinal importance and we must be clear as to what is understood by this term. In one sense, any step towards a constitutional amendment initiated by a single actor on the constitutional stage is "unilateral." We do not believe that this is the meaning contemplated by Question 1, nor is this the sense in which the term has been used in argument before us. Rather, what is claimed by a right to secede "unilaterally" is the right to effectuate secession without prior negotiations with the other provinces and the federal government. At issue is not the legality of the first step but the legality of the final act of purported unilateral secession. The supposed juridical basis for such an act is said to be a clear expression of democratic will in a referendum in the province of Quebec. This claim requires us to examine the possible juridical impact, if any, of such a referendum on the functioning of our Constitution, and on the claimed legality of a unilateral act of secession.

[87] Although the Constitution does not itself address the use of a referendum procedure, and the results of a referendum have no direct role or legal effect in our constitutional scheme, a referendum undoubtedly may provide a democratic method of ascertaining the views of the electorate on important political questions on a particular occasion. The democratic principle identified above would demand that considerable weight be given to a clear expression by the people of Quebec of their will to secede from Canada, even though a referendum, in itself and without more, has no direct legal effect, and could not in itself bring about unilateral secession. Our political institutions are premised on the democratic principle, and so an expression of the democratic will of the people of a province carries weight, in that it would confer legitimacy on the efforts of the government of Quebec to initiate the Constitution's

amendment process in order to secede by constitutional means. In this context, we refer to a "clear" majority as a qualitative evaluation. The referendum result, if it is to be taken as an expression of the democratic will, must be free of ambiguity both in terms of the question asked and in terms of the support it achieves.

[88] The federalism principle, in conjunction with the democratic principle, dictates that the clear repudiation of the existing constitutional order and the clear expression of the desire to pursue secession by the population of a province would give rise to a reciprocal obligation on all parties to Confederation to negotiate constitutional changes to respond to that desire. The amendment of the Constitution begins with a political process undertaken pursuant to the Constitution itself. In Canada, the initiative for constitutional amendment is the responsibility of democratically elected representatives of the participants in Confederation. Those representatives may, of course, take their cue from a referendum, but in legal terms, constitution-making in Canada, as in many countries, is undertaken by the democratically elected representatives of the people. The corollary of a legitimate attempt by one participant in Confederation to seek an amendment to the Constitution is an obligation on all parties to come to the negotiating table. The clear repudiation by the people of Quebec of the existing constitutional order would confer legitimacy on demands for secession, and place an obligation on the other provinces and the federal government to acknowledge and respect that expression of democratic will by entering into negotiations and conducting them in accordance with the underlying constitutional principles already discussed.

[89] What is the content of this obligation to negotiate? At this juncture, we confront the difficult inter-relationship between substantive obligations flowing from the Constitution and questions of judicial competence and restraint in supervising or enforcing those obligations. This is mirrored by the distinction between the legality and the legitimacy of actions taken under the Constitution. We propose to focus first on the substantive obligations flowing from this obligation to negotiate; once the nature of those obligations has been described, it is easier to assess the appropriate means of enforcement of those obligations, and to comment on the distinction between legality and legitimacy.

[90] The conduct of the parties in such negotiations would be governed by the same constitutional principles which give rise to the duty to negotiate: federalism, democracy, constitutionalism and the rule of law, and the protection of minorities. Those principles lead us to reject

two absolutist propositions. One of those propositions is that there would be a legal obligation on the other provinces and federal government to accede to the secession of a province, subject only to negotiation of the logistical details of secession. This proposition is attributed either to the supposed implications of the democratic principle of the Constitution, or to the international law principle of self-determination of peoples.

[91] For both theoretical and practical reasons, we cannot accept this view. We hold that Quebec could not purport to invoke a right of self-determination such as to dictate the terms of a proposed secession to the other parties: that would not be a negotiation at all. As well, it would be naive to expect that the substantive goal of secession could readily be distinguished from the practical details of secession. The devil would be in the details. The democracy principle, as we have emphasized, cannot be invoked to trump the principles of federalism and rule of law, the rights of individuals and minorities, or the operation of democracy in the other provinces or in Canada as a whole. No negotiations could be effective if their ultimate outcome, secession, is cast as an absolute legal entitlement based upon an obligation to give effect to that act of secession in the Constitution. Such a foregone conclusion would actually undermine the obligation to negotiate and render it hollow.

[92] However, we are equally unable to accept the reverse proposition, that a clear expression of self-determination by the people of Quebec would impose no obligations upon the other provinces or the federal government. The continued existence and operation of the Canadian constitutional order cannot remain indifferent to the clear expression of a clear majority of Quebecers that they no longer wish to remain in Canada. This would amount to the assertion that other constitutionally recognized principles necessarily trump the clearly expressed democratic will of the people of Quebec. Such a proposition fails to give sufficient weight to the underlying constitutional principles that must inform the amendment process, including the principles of democracy and federalism. The rights of other provinces and the federal government cannot deny the right of the government of Quebec to pursue secession, should a clear majority of the people of Quebec choose that goal, so long as in doing so, Quebec respects the rights of others. Negotiations would be necessary to address the interests of the federal government, of Quebec and the other provinces, and other participants, as well as the rights of all Canadians both within and outside Quebec.

[93] Is the rejection of both of these propositions reconcilable? Yes, once it is realized that none of the rights or principles under discussion is absolute to the exclusion of the others. This observation suggests that other parties cannot exercise their rights in such a way as to amount to an absolute denial of Quebec's rights, and similarly, that so long as Quebec exercises its rights while respecting the rights of others, it may propose secession and seek to achieve it through negotiation. The negotiation process precipitated by a decision of a clear majority of the population of Quebec on a clear question to pursue secession would require the reconciliation of various rights and obligations by the representatives of two legitimate majorities, namely, the clear majority of the population of Quebec, and the clear majority of Canada as a whole, whatever that may be. There can be no suggestion that either of these majorities "trumps" the other. A political majority that does not act in accordance with the underlying constitutional principles we have identified puts at risk the legitimacy of the exercise of its rights.

[94] In such circumstances, the conduct of the parties assumes primary constitutional significance. The negotiation process must be conducted with an eye to the constitutional principles we have outlined, which must inform the actions of all the participants in the negotiation process.

[95] Refusal of a party to conduct negotiations in a manner consistent with constitutional principles and values would seriously put at risk the legitimacy of that party's assertion of its rights, and perhaps the negotiation process as a whole. Those who quite legitimately insist upon the importance of upholding the rule of law cannot at the same time be oblivious to the need to act in conformity with constitutional principles and values, and so do their part to contribute to the maintenance and promotion of an environment in which the rule of law may flourish.

[96] No one can predict the course that such negotiations might take. The possibility that they might not lead to an agreement amongst the parties must be recognized. Negotiations following a referendum vote in favour of seeking secession would inevitably address a wide range of issues, many of great import. After 131 years of Confederation, there exists, inevitably, a high level of integration in economic, political and social institutions across Canada. The vision of those who brought about Confederation was to create a unified country, not a loose alliance of autonomous provinces. Accordingly, while there are regional economic interests, which sometimes coincide with provincial bound-

aries, there are also national interests and enterprises (both public and private) that would face potential dismemberment. There is a national economy and a national debt. Arguments were raised before us regarding boundary issues. There are linguistic and cultural minorities, including aboriginal peoples, unevenly distributed across the country who look to the Constitution of Canada for the protection of their rights. Of course, secession would give rise to many issues of great complexity and difficulty. These would have to be resolved within the overall framework of the rule of law, thereby assuring Canadians resident in Quebec and elsewhere a measure of stability in what would likely be a period of considerable upheaval and uncertainty. Nobody seriously suggests that our national existence, seamless in so many aspects, could be effortlessly separated along what are now the provincial boundaries of Quebec. As the Attorney General of Saskatchewan put it in his oral submission:

A nation is built when the communities that comprise it make commitments to it, when they forego choices and opportunities on behalf of a nation, ... when the communities that comprise it make compromises, when they offer each other guarantees, when they make transfers and perhaps most pointedly, when they receive from others the benefits of national solidarity. The threads of a thousand acts of accommodation are the fabric of a nation ...

[97] In the circumstances, negotiations following such a referendum would undoubtedly be difficult. While the negotiators would have to contemplate the possibility of secession, there would be no absolute legal entitlement to it and no assumption that an agreement reconciling all relevant rights and obligations would actually be reached. It is foreseeable that even negotiations carried out in conformity with the underlying constitutional principles could reach an impasse. We need not speculate here as to what would then transpire. Under the Constitution, secession requires that an amendment be negotiated.

[98] The respective roles of the courts and political actors in discharging the constitutional obligations we have identified follows ineluctably from the foregoing observations. In the *Patriation Reference*, a distinction was drawn between the law of the Constitution, which, generally speaking, will be enforced by the courts, and other constitutional rules, such as the conventions of the Constitution, which carry only political sanctions. It is also the case, however, that judicial inter-

vention, even in relation to the law of the Constitution, is subject to the Court's appreciation of its proper role in the constitutional scheme.

[99] The notion of justiciability is, as we earlier pointed out in dealing with the preliminary objection, linked to the notion of appropriate judicial restraint. We earlier made reference to the discussion of justiciability in *Reference re Canada Assistance Plan*, [1991] 2 SCR 525, at p. 545:

> In exercising its discretion whether to determine a matter that is alleged to be non-justiciable, the Court's primary concern is to retain its proper role within the constitutional framework of our democratic form of government.

In *Operation Dismantle, supra*, at p. 459, it was pointed out that justiciability is a "doctrine ... founded upon a concern with the appropriate role of the courts as the forum for the resolution of different types of disputes." An analogous doctrine of judicial restraint operates here. Also, as observed in *Canada (Auditor General) v. Canada (Minister of Energy, Mines and Resources)*, [1989] 2 SCR 49 (the *Auditor General's* case), at p. 91:

> There is an array of issues which calls for the exercise of judicial judgment on whether the questions are properly cognizable by the courts. Ultimately, such judgment depends on the appreciation by the judiciary of its own position in the constitutional scheme.

[100] The role of the Court in this Reference is limited to the identification of the relevant aspects of the Constitution in their broadest sense. We have interpreted the questions as relating to the constitutional framework within which political decisions may ultimately be made. Within that framework, the workings of the political process are complex and can only be resolved by means of political judgments and evaluations. The Court has no supervisory role over the political aspects of constitutional negotiations. Equally, the initial impetus for negotiation, namely a clear majority on a clear question in favour of secession, is subject only to political evaluation, and properly so. A right and a corresponding duty to negotiate secession cannot be built on an alleged expression of democratic will if the expression of democratic will is itself fraught with ambiguities. Only the political actors would have the information and expertise to make the appropriate judgment as to the point at which, and the circumstances in which, those ambiguities are resolved one way or the other.

[101] If the circumstances giving rise to the duty to negotiate were to arise, the distinction between the strong defence of legitimate interests and the taking of positions which, in fact, ignore the legitimate interests of others is one that also defies legal analysis. The Court would not have access to all of the information available to the political actors, and the methods appropriate for the search for truth in a court of law are ill-suited to getting to the bottom of constitutional negotiations. To the extent that the questions are political in nature, it is not the role of the judiciary to interpose its own views on the different negotiating positions of the parties, even were it invited to do so. Rather, it is the obligation of the elected representatives to give concrete form to the discharge of their constitutional obligations which only they and their electors can ultimately assess. The reconciliation of the various legitimate constitutional interests outlined above is necessarily committed to the political rather than the judicial realm, precisely because that reconciliation can only be achieved through the give and take of the negotiation process. Having established the legal framework, it would be for the democratically elected leadership of the various participants to resolve their differences.

[102] The non-justiciability of political issues that lack a legal component does not deprive the surrounding constitutional framework of its binding status, nor does this mean that constitutional obligations could be breached without incurring serious legal repercussions. Where there are legal rights there are remedies, but as we explained in the *Auditor General*'s case, *supra*, at p. 90, and *New Brunswick Broadcasting*, *supra*, the appropriate recourse in some circumstances lies through the workings of the political process rather than the courts ...

[104] Accordingly, the secession of Quebec from Canada cannot be accomplished by the National Assembly, the legislature or government of Quebec unilaterally, that is to say, without principled negotiations, and be considered a lawful act. Any attempt to effect the secession of a province from Canada must be undertaken pursuant to the Constitution of Canada, or else violate the Canadian legal order. However, the continued existence and operation of the Canadian constitutional order cannot remain unaffected by the unambiguous expression of a clear majority of Quebecers that they no longer wish to remain in Canada. The primary means by which that expression is given effect is the constitutional duty to negotiate in accordance with the constitutional principles that we have described herein. In the event secession negotiations are initiated, our Constitution, no less than our history, would

call on the participants to work to reconcile the rights, obligations and legitimate aspirations of all Canadians within a framework that emphasizes constitutional responsibilities as much as it does constitutional rights.

[105] It will be noted that Question 1 does not ask how secession could be achieved in a constitutional manner, but addresses one form of secession only, namely unilateral secession. Although the applicability of various procedures to achieve lawful secession was raised in argument, each option would require us to assume the existence of facts that at this stage are unknown. In accordance with the usual rule of prudence in constitutional cases, we refrain from pronouncing on the applicability of any particular constitutional procedure to effect secession unless and until sufficiently clear facts exist to squarely raise an issue for judicial determination.

(5) Suggested Principle of Effectivity

[106] In the foregoing discussion we have not overlooked the principle of effectivity, which was placed at the forefront in argument before us. For the reasons that follow, we do not think that the principle of effectivity has any application to the issues raised by Question 1. A distinction must be drawn between the right of a people to act, and their power to do so. They are not identical. A right is recognized in law: mere physical ability is not necessarily given status as a right. The fact that an individual or group can act in a certain way says nothing at all about the legal status or consequences of the act. A power may be exercised even in the absence of a right to do so, but if it is, then it is exercised without legal foundation. Our Constitution does not address powers in this sense. On the contrary, the Constitution is concerned only with the rights and obligations of individuals, groups and governments, and the structure of our institutions. It was suggested before us that the National Assembly, legislature or government of Quebec could unilaterally effect the secession of that province from Canada, but it was not suggested that they might do so as a matter of law: rather, it was contended that they simply could do so as a matter of fact. Although under the Constitution there is no right to pursue secession unilaterally, that is secession without principled negotiation, this does not rule out the possibility of an unconstitutional declaration of secession leading to a de facto secession ...

[107] In our view, the alleged principle of effectivity has no constitutional or legal status in the sense that it does not provide an *ex ante* explanation or justification for an act. In essence, acceptance of a principle of effectivity would be tantamount to accepting that the National Assembly, legislature or government of Quebec may act without regard to the law, simply because it asserts the power to do so. So viewed, the suggestion is that the National Assembly, legislature or government of Quebec could purport to secede the province unilaterally from Canada in disregard of Canadian ... law. It is further suggested that if the secession bid was successful, a new legal order would be created in that province, which would then be considered an independent state.

[108] Such a proposition is an assertion of fact, not a statement of law. It may or may not be true; in any event it is irrelevant to the questions of law before us. If, on the other hand, it is put forward as an assertion of law, then it simply amounts to the contention that the law may be broken as long as it can be broken successfully. Such a notion is contrary to the rule of law, and must be rejected ...

READING QUESTIONS ON QUEBEC SECESSION REFERENCE

1 What do you make of the fact that no judge's name is affixed to the judgment, that is, that it purports to be the judgment of an impersonal Court?
2 Do you think the judgment is firmly based on principles of Canadian law or do you think the judges merely cloaked their political stance, one supportive of the Federal Government's political aims, in legal language?
3 If you are dealing with the Supreme Court's judgment in *Vriend*, ask yourself whether in both this decision and *Vriend* the judges went beyond their legitimate role.

7

Terrorism, States of Emergency, and the Rule of Law

Since 9/11, the democracies of the West have been confronted with the question of how to respond effectively to the threat of international terrorism. One way of responding is to declare a state of emergency, if the legal order permits this; that is, to suspend the ordinary legal protections of rights and freedoms for the duration of a confined period of emergency. The idea is that it is impossible to deal with certain threats through ordinary legal mechanisms, so one should suspend the ordinary law for a brief period until the threat has been countered. However, this response might not seem appropriate if a state of emergency is by definition temporary in nature and international terrorism has brought about a "new normal" – a threat of potentially indefinite duration. A second response is that a Western democracy has to fight, as Aharon Barak, former president of the Supreme Court of Israel put it in a judgment reproduced in this chapter, with "one hand tied behind its back." That is, if we want to continue to maintain our commitments to the rule of law, we have to accept its constraints. One concern about this response is that because extraordinary measures are required to respond to terrorism, governments will do what they need to in secret if they cannot procure the necessary legal powers. A third response is that the ordinary law has to be adapted, but should be adapted in a way that complies as far as possible with the rule of law. Concerns about this response include that the protections given by the rule of law risk becoming so insubstantial that law is abused as a cloak for arbitrary government power, which then brings the rule of law into disrepute. A fourth response is that one should not change the ordinary law to give government officials power to deal with threats in ways that would ordinarily be illegal, for example, torturing an individual to get information about a "ticking bomb." Rather, officials should act illegally but publicly and then society can decide whether they should be punished or whether some legal mechanism, for example, a pardon, should be used to immunize them against punishment. The concern here is that officials might come to expect immunity and the government might be able to manipulate public opinion to meet that expectation. You should keep in mind these issues as you read through the cases and the essay by David Cole in this chapter.

David Cole
"Judging the Next Emergency: Judicial Review and Individual Rights in Times of Crisis" (2002)

INTRODUCTION

As virtually every law student who studies *Marbury v. Madison*[1] learns, Chief Justice John Marshall's tactical genius was to establish judicial review in a case where the result could not be challenged. As a technical matter, Marbury lost, and the executive branch won. As furious as President Jefferson reportedly was with the decision, there was nothing he could do about it, for there was no mandate to defy. The Court's decision offered no remedy for Marbury himself, whose rights were directly at issue, and whose rights the Court found had indeed been violated. But over time, it became clear that the decision was a landmark victory for those who consider judicial review of political-branch action a critical element of a constitutional system.

Judicial review on matters of national security frequently follows the *Marbury* model. It rarely provides relief to the individuals before the Court when the national-security crisis is at its height. As in *Marbury* itself, the challengers generally lose, and the government generally wins. As a result, the conventional wisdom is that courts function poorly as guardians of liberty in times of crisis. *Schenck*,[2] *Korematsu*,[3] and *Dennis*,[4] from World War I, World War II, and the Cold War, respectively, are a few of the more notorious examples. In those cases, the Court authorized the criminalization of speech during World War I, detention based on race during World War II, and guilt by association during the Cold War.

The traditional view, based on these and other examples, holds that judicial review has largely failed to protect individual rights when their protection is most needed. There are good reasons to suspect that this would be so, and, as the examples cited above illustrate, there is plenty of evidence to support the conventional wisdom. But the conventional wisdom is too pessimistic. It is akin to arguing that *Marbury* demonstrates the weakness of the judiciary because the Court failed to afford Marbury himself relief for the violation of his rights.

Considered over time, judicial review of emergency and national-security measures can and has established important constraints on the exercise of emergency powers and has restricted the scope of what is acceptable in future emergencies. Because emergency measures frequently last well beyond the de facto end of the emergency, and because the wheels of justice move slowly, courts often have an opportunity to assess the validity of emergency measures after the emergency has passed, when passions have been reduced and reasoned judgment is more attainable. In doing so, courts have at least sometimes been able to take advantage of hindsight to pronounce certain emergency measures invalid for infringing constitutional rights. And because courts, unlike the political branches or the political culture more generally, must explain their reasons in a formal manner that then has precedential authority in future disputes, judicial decisions offer an opportunity to set the terms of the *next* crisis, even if they often come too late to be of much assistance in the immediate term. Thus, the Court has over time developed a highly protective test for speech advocating illegal activity,[5] subjected all racial discrimination since *Korematsu* to exacting scrutiny,[6] and prohibited guilt by association.[7] These decisions, among others, impose important limits on what the government can do in the current, post–September 11th crisis.

Since *Marbury,* scholars have devoted thousands of pages to debating the issue of judicial review, offering critiques of Chief Justice Marshall's reasoning, proposing alternative defenses of judicial review, and, more recently, questioning the value of judicial review altogether. One of the most familiar, and in my view still the strongest, defenses of judicial review is that first advanced in footnote four of *Carolene Products,*[8] implemented by the Warren Court and given its definitive academic elaboration in Professor John Hart Ely's *Democracy and Distrust.*[9] This is the notion that as an institution insulated from everyday politics, the Court is best suited to protect the interests of those who cannot protect themselves through the political process, whether they be members of discrete and insular minorities, dissidents, noncitizens, or other vulnerable individuals. As others have shown, the Court does not always live up to its responsibility.[10] But it is nonetheless an important ideal to which courts should be held accountable.

How should we judge judicial review from the standpoint of protecting the constitutional rights and liberties of the vulnerable in times of crisis? It is in times of crisis that constitutional rights and liberties are most needed, because the temptation to sacrifice them in the name of national security will be at its most acute. To government officials, civil rights and liberties often appear to be mere obstacles to effective protection of the national interest. As Bush-administration supporters frequently intone when defending their post–September 11th initiatives, "the Constitution is not a suicide pact."[11] Judicial protection is also critical because crisis measures are typically targeted at the most vulnerable among us, especially noncitizens, who have little or no voice in the political process.[12] We have been in such a crisis period since September 11th and will be for the foreseeable future. So now is a particularly propitious time to assess the value of judicial review in times of crisis.[13]

Part I of this Article will set forth the traditional view that the judiciary is inadequate in times of crisis, along with the evidence that supports it and the reasons that might explain it. Part II maintains that the traditional view overstates the case, because over time judicial decisions have had more of a constraining influence on emergency measures than appears when one looks only at the courts' performance in the midst of a crisis. Part III surveys judicial performance since September 11th on matters of national security and argues that while the record is far from exemplary, courts have actually been more willing to stand up to the government in this period than in many prior crises. Part IV responds to a recent proposal by two leading scholars that courts and the Constitution ought to play less of a role in assessing emergency measures.[14] Professors Oren Gross and Mark Tushnet have both recently argued that the poor performance of courts during emergency periods and the need for extraordinary emergency powers should impel us to acknowledge explicitly the validity of extraconstitutional emergency measures and leave judgment of such measures to the political rather than the judicial process. In my view, this proposal is fundamentally misguided, both because it fails to acknowledge the valuable role that courts have played, when viewed over time, in constraining emergency powers, and because the alternative of relying on the political process would almost certainly provide even less protection for individual rights than the courts have. To paraphrase Winston Churchill, judicial review is the worst protector of liberty in times of crisis, with the exception of all the others.

I THE CONVENTIONAL WISDOM

The conventional wisdom is that courts are ineffective as guardians of liberty when the general public is clamoring for security. Clinton Rossiter, in an influential study of the Supreme Court in wartime, concluded that:

the courts of the United States, from the highest to the lowest, can do nothing to restrain and next to nothing to mitigate an arbitrary presidential military program suspending the liberties of some part of the civilian population ... Whatever relief is afforded, and however ringing the defense of liberty that goes with it, will be precious little and far too late.[15]

Judge Learned Hand similarly concluded that one cannot rely on the courts in times when the people do not fight for their own rights:

I often wonder whether we do not rest our hopes too much upon constitutions, upon laws and upon courts. These are false hopes ... Liberty lies in the hearts of men and women; when it dies there, no constitution, no law, nor court can save it; no constitution, no law, no court can even do much to help it. While it lies there it needs no constitution, no law, no court to save it.[16]

Justice Robert Jackson took this view so far as to advocate in dissent in *Korematsu* that the civil courts should simply refuse to enforce military orders. Jackson famously wrote:

Of course the existence of a military power resting on force, so vagrant, so centralized, so necessarily heedless of the individual, is an inherent threat to liberty. But I would not lead people to rely on this Court for a review that seems to me wholly delusive ... If the people ever let command of the war power fall into irresponsible and unscrupulous hands, the courts wield no power equal to its restraint. The chief restraint upon those who command the physical forces of the country, in the future as in the past, must be their responsibility to the political judgments of their contemporaries and to the moral judgments of history.[17]

Finally, George Bernard Shaw gave the critique his own inimitable flair in offering the following evaluation of the courts during World War I:

[D]uring the war the courts in France, bleeding under German guns, were very severe; the courts in England, hearing but the echoes of those guns, were grossly unjust; but the courts in the United States, knowing naught save censored news of those guns, were stark, staring, raving mad.[18]

There is a wealth of evidence to support this conventional wisdom. During the Civil War, apart from Chief Justice Taney's ineffectual solo intervention in *Ex parte Merryman*[19] – in which he declared invalid President Lincoln's suspension of habeas corpus, only to have Lincoln ignore him – the Supreme Court as a whole largely stayed out of the war. During World War I, the Court failed to overturn a single one of the more than one thousand convictions handed down for speaking out against the war or the draft.[20] It chose to review only a handful of the convictions, and affirmed them all, most by a unanimous vote.[21] In World War II, the Court upheld the Japanese internment and unanimously affirmed the military-tribunal convictions of several German saboteurs,[22] with Justice Frankfurter playing a lead role in crafting the majority decision despite having personally played a critical advisory role in creating the tribunals in the first place.[23] In the early years of the Cold War, as well, the Court either denied review or affirmed anti-Communist measures, thereby allowing guilt by association to operate largely unchecked.[24]

There are at least four reasons why courts are likely to fare poorly on matters of national security, especially in times of crisis. First, their independence notwithstanding, judges are part of the government and are likely to identify with the government's interests when matters of national security are at stake. The populace as a whole generally rallies around the executive branch in times of crisis, and courts are likely to do so as well. As history has shown, judges cannot stand above the crisis, precisely because the threat at least presumably implicates them as well – both as part of the government and as part of the society.

Second, assessing claims of national security, especially during times of crisis, is inherently difficult, and judges are likely to feel ill-equipped to do so. Most questions of constitutional rights and liberties present a question of balancing. Even the prohibition on race discrimination can be overcome by a sufficiently compelling justification and narrowly tailored means.[25] But how does one accurately measure the risk that Al

Qaeda might gain critical information enabling it to attack us, or that an individual, if set free, might endanger the national security?

Such decisions must inevitably rest on incomplete information, and the courts' information is often even more incomplete than that of the executive. The executive branch frequently has a monopoly on the information because so much of it is classified, the challengers are often unable to respond, and, absent adversarial testing, it is difficult for a court to know whether the government has been fully candid in its assessment. The Supreme Court's decision in *Korematsu*, in which it deferred to military claims of necessity as justification for the Japanese internment, was later shown to be based on an inaccurate record; the executive branch concealed from the Court critical information about its own doubts concerning the reality of the threat posed by the Japanese population. Indeed, the executive branch's misrepresentations were so fundamental that years later courts overturned the convictions on writs of coram nobis.[26]

Third, courts must worry that if they rule against the government on a matter of national security, they may face a potential test of their credibility and legitimacy. If the President truly believes that the security of the nation is at stake, it is entirely possible that he will defy any decision against him.[27] During the Civil War, for example, when Chief Justice Taney in *Ex parte Merryman*[28] ruled that President Lincoln's suspension of the writ of habeas corpus was unconstitutional and granted a writ of habeas corpus, the military refused to produce the petitioner. Justice Taney then issued an attachment for contempt, but the military refused to accept service of that order. President Lincoln simply ignored Justice Taney's decision altogether.

Fourth, and perhaps most significantly, judges must worry that if they rule against the government, their decisions might be *followed*, at some subsequent cost to national security. Just as no judge wants to be the one who has freed a defendant to commit violent crime again, so no judge wants to issue an order that actually causes serious harm to the national security. And since prognostications about security risks are just that, and one can never really be certain, judges may be inclined to err on the side of caution and the government. At the oral argument before the Third Circuit in *North Jersey Media Group v. Ashcroft*,[29] a case challenging the constitutionality of the Attorney General's decision to close to the public all immigration proceedings involving hundreds of detainees labeled of "special interest" to the September 11th investigation, Judge Morton Greenberg told the ACLU lawyer arguing the case,

"We could make a decision here ... and people could die. Lots of people ... I saw the second hit [during the World Trade Center attack of September 11th], and I can't erase it from my mind."[30]

II A REVISIONIST VIEW

While there are undoubtedly good reasons and plenty of evidence to support the conventional wisdom that courts perform poorly on matters of national security, that judgment ultimately rests on too narrow a focus – namely, an assessment of how the courts have performed in the midst of particular crises for the particular litigants before them. When one asks instead what role judicial decisions have played over time in framing the options available to the executive branch in emergency periods, a less pessimistic evaluation is warranted. The Supreme Court's decisions during the waning of emergencies, or after the emergencies have ended, have not infrequently called into question or reversed its earlier rulings and have created precedents that impose a degree of restraint on the government's actions during the *next* emergency.

After the Civil War ended and President Lincoln was buried, for example, the Supreme Court issued *Ex parte Milligan*,[31] in which it declared that, as long as the civil courts remained open for business, the President did not have constitutional authority to try a United States citizen by military tribunal for allegedly conspiring with the enemy. The Court broadly insisted that the Constitution applies equally in peacetime and wartime:

The Constitution of the United States is a law for rulers and people, equally in war and in peace, and covers with the shield of its protection all classes of men, at all times, and under all circumstances. No doctrine, involving more pernicious consequences, was ever invented by the wit of man than that any of its provisions can be suspended during any of the great exigencies of government. Such a doctrine leads directly to anarchy or depotism, but the theory of necessity on which it is based is false; for the government, within the Constitution, has all the powers granted to it, which are necessary to preserve its existence; as has been happily proved by the result of the great effort to throw off its just authority.[32]

At the close of World War II, the Court decided *Duncan v. Kohana-moku*,[33] which, like *Ex parte Milligan*, imposed limits on martial law by invalidating a conviction of a civilian in a military tribunal in Hawaii.

The Court reasoned, as in *Milligan,* that trial by military tribunal was barred as long as the civil courts were open. Notably, however, the Court delayed issuing a decision in *Kohanamoku* until more than a year after it agreed to hear the case, leading one contemporaneous commentator to speculate that the Court had purposefully waited until it was clear that martial law would not have to be reimposed in Hawaii.[34]

Similarly, while the Court consistently upheld the harsh suppression of antiwar speech during World War I,[35] it subsequently developed increasingly stronger versions of the "clear and present danger" test for protecting subversive speech. In *Yates v. United States,*[36] decided two and one-half years after Senator Joseph McCarthy had been censured, the Court required the government to prove advocacy of action, not merely advocacy of abstract doctrine. That ruling put an end to the ongoing use of the 1940 Smith Act[37] to criminalize Communist Party leaders for their advocacy.[38] Still later, in 1969, the Court adopted an even more speech-protective test in *Brandenburg v. Ohio,* holding that speech advocating illegal conduct is constitutionally protected unless it is "directed to inciting or producing imminent lawless action and is likely to incite or produce such action."[39] That test forecloses virtually any prosecution for speech advocating crime short of an actual conspiracy to commit crime. With these rulings, the Court's First Amendment doctrine now imposes significant limits on the government's ability to restrict speech in times of emergency or as a matter of national security. Thus, even though the Court did little to help antiwar activists Schenck, Debs, Frohwerk, and Abrams during World War I,[40] or to stand up to McCarthyism at its height, the Court ultimately adopted an interpretation of the First Amendment that protects the rights of latter-day Schencks and Communists to speak as they wish, so much so that outright censorship of antiwar speech is no longer a plausible option for the government in wartime.

Supreme Court decisions have also largely barred another common tactic of emergency government – guilt by association. In emergencies, authorities seeking to prevent future harm often resort to guilt by association because it permits the imposition of guilt without proof that an individual has committed a specific violent act.[41] When the Court in *Yates* effectively foreclosed prosecutions of Communists under the Smith Act's advocacy provisions, federal prosecutors turned to that statute's "membership" provisions. But in *Scales v. United States,*[42] the Court interpreted the membership provisions to require proof not merely of membership, but of "specific intent" to further the organization's illegal ends.[43] Driven by concerns that guilt by association violates both the First and Fifth Amendments, the Court ruled that individuals could not be prosecuted for mere membership in the Communist Party, nor even for active membership supporting its lawful ends. Instead, the Court held that the government must prove that an individual's Party activities were specifically intended to further criminal conduct – in effect, that he had conspired to commit or support crime. The Court subsequently extended that principle broadly, ruling that absent proof of specific intent, the state could not use association to deny security clearances for work in defense facilities, passports for travel abroad, teaching positions, admission to the bar, or even the use of campus meeting rooms by student groups.[44] Thus, while the Court did little to block the imposition of guilt by association during the early years of the Cold War, its later decisions stemming from that period largely prohibit that tactic today.[45]

The Vietnam War era also resulted in important judicial decisions limiting or rejecting claims of national security. The Vietnam War did not present the same sort of direct threat to national security that was felt during the World Wars and the Cold War. But it nonetheless prompted substantial government incursions on liberties and also produced two landmark national-security cases, both of which resulted in decisions against the government. In *New York Times Co. v. United States*,[46] the Court in 1971 permitted the publication of the Pentagon Papers over the government's claim that disclosure of this secret account of the Vietnam War would harm national security. The following year, in *United States v. United States District Court*,[47] the Court held that the Attorney General lacked power under the Constitution to authorize warrantless "domestic security" wiretaps. Both cases reflected a skepticism about claims of national security and executive prerogative, and created significant constraints on the government's ability to enforce secrecy and to conduct searches and wiretaps without probable cause of criminal activity.

The Court's decision in *Korematsu* provides the most conspicuous counterexample to this more optimistic take on the Court's role in reviewing national-security measures. By the time that case was decided, according to Clinton Rossiter, "the military areas had been disestablished and the relocation centers were being broken up."[48] Yet the Court upheld the internment by a vote of six to three and has never reversed the decision. Pessimists might well point to *Korematsu* as an example of a judicial decision having the opposite effect from that which I have been emphasizing – as Justice Jackson warned at the time, *Korematsu* might well have paved the way for future inroads on civil rights and liberties in times of crisis.[49] But *Korematsu*'s legacy suggests that Jackson's concern may have been overstated. While the decision has not been formally overruled, eight of the Supreme Court's sitting Justices have said that the case was wrongly decided.[50] Justice Scalia, perhaps the Court's most conservative member, has compared the decision to *Dred Scott*.[51] In short, *Korematsu* has not proved to be the "loaded weapon" that Justice Jackson feared. To the contrary, it has served as an object lesson in what the Court and the government ought *not* do in future crises.

Thus, when one takes a longer view of the role of courts in constraining emergency powers, the picture is less bleak than the conventional account admits. While most of the developments discussed above came too late to forestall civil rights and civil liberties violations when they were initially undertaken, they have the prophylactic effect of forestalling the same or similar measures in future emergencies. The judicial process is especially conducive to playing this role for several reasons. First, since emergency powers, and the disputes to which they give rise, tend to outlast the actual emergency, those powers can be reviewed by courts when the worst of the crisis is over. Thus, the Court's liberty-protective decisions in *Milligan* and *Kahanamoku* came when the wars were effectively over, and the Court's protective decisions from the Cold War period began after McCarthy had been censured and the height of anticommunist fervor had passed. The ability (and obligation) of courts to assess the legality of measures long after they have been adopted means that courts may bring more perspective to the question than those acting in the midst of the emergency.

Second, the fact that legal decisions must offer a statement of reasons that then binds future cases contributes to the judiciary's ability to exert control over the next emergency. The obligation to create and to follow precedent means that judicial decisions are likely to have a longer "shelf life" than those of other branches of government. The lawyers' ability to distinguish the current emergency from prior ones, and the current emergency measure from those previously invalidated, means that the obligation to state reasons is no guarantee of future effectiveness in protecting rights, but precedents do tend to take certain options off the table. The government could not punish antiwar speech today, for example.

Third, the common-law method facilitates a measured development of rules in the context of specific cases and permits the incorporation of lessons learned from the early and often most overreactive stages of emergencies. Once those lessons are learned and instantiated in Supreme Court decisions, they play an important role in precluding certain measures that were part of the government's arsenal in the prior emergency. In this sense, just as in *Marbury*, the Court's emergency-powers decisions may not help the parties immediately before it at the height of the controversy, but in the long run these decisions establish principles that are critical to checking future government abuse.

Fourth, the formalities of the judicial process mandate the creation of an official record that may facilitate reaching a just result. The conviction in *Korematsu* was ultimately overturned on a writ of coram nobis because Korematsu was able to show, through access to government records, that the Justice Department had misled the courts about the strength of the evidence underlying its national-security concerns. As the warrant requirement demonstrates, record-keeping requirements permit evaluation of government actions after the fact. While judicial proceedings are not necessary to impose record-keeping requirements, the highly formalized judicial process itself creates a record that may make subsequent assessments, beyond the heat of the moment, more reliable.

Fifth, and perhaps most important, federal courts are independent of the political process, and their institutional self-definition turns in significant part on that independence, especially when it comes to the interpretation and enforcement of constitutional rights. As a result, they are better suited to entertain claims challenging executive action than are Congress or the executive branch itself, and more likely to take politically unpopular positions than the political branches. While, as noted above, judges, like other government officials, are likely to defer to the executive branch on matters of national security, complete deference is likely to clash with their understanding of their role as judges.

To be sure, judicial decisions are not the only forces that may constrain government actors in the next emergency. Developing cultural norms may also play a role. As noted above, *Korematsu* has never been formally overruled, but it is nonetheless highly unlikely that anything on the scale of the Japanese internment would happen again. The cultural condemnation of that initiative, reflected in Congress's issuance of a formal apology and restitution,[52] has been so powerful that the option is a nonstarter even without controlling Supreme Court law. But even here, the legislative apology followed judicial decisions nullifying the convictions on writs of coram nobis.[53] In addition, the formal requirements that judges give reasons that are binding on future judges means that judicial decisions are likely to play a more specific constraining function than the development of cultural norms. Indeed, John Finn has argued that the obligation to give reasons is constitutive of constitutionalism and underscores the necessity of judicial review to any meaningful system of constitutional law.[54] Cultural norms and political initiatives are rarely as clear-cut as a legal prohibition, and their very contestability means that they are likely to exert less restraining force than a judicial holding. Court decisions are, of course, also contestable, but generally along a narrower range of alternatives.

Thus, the conventional wisdom that courts perform poorly in crises should be qualified by the important proviso that, when viewed over time, judicial decisions do exert a constraining effect on what the government may do in the next emergency.

III SEPTEMBER 11TH AND THE COURTS

How have the courts fared since September 11th? As Judge Greenberg's comments at the oral argument in *North Jersey Media Group* illustrate,[55] the attacks of that day and the threat of future catastrophes place tremendous pressure on judges. Nonetheless, a surprising number of judicial decisions initially upheld claims of constitutional rights against official antiterrorist measures. As time went on, the picture began to look more familiar, as courts increasingly deferred to government claims of national security. As of this writing, the Supreme Court has yet to weigh in, and therefore all judgments are necessarily preliminary.

Nonetheless, given the history of judicial deference in times of crisis, the early decisions were quite stunning. In *Center for National Security Studies v. United States Department of Justice*,[56] a federal district court ruled that the Justice Department's secret arrests of hundreds of persons detained in a preventive detention campaign after September 11th violated the *Freedom of Information Act* ("FOIA"), and ordered the government to disclose the detainees' names.

In several cases challenging the government's related practice of closing to the public all immigration proceedings involving detainees connected to the September 11th investigations, two district courts ruled that this practice violated the First Amendment right of access of the public,[57] and one court ruled that it also violated a detainee's Fifth Amendment due process right to a public hearing.[58] The United States Court of Appeals for the Sixth Circuit unanimously affirmed one of the First Amendment rulings, writing that "democracies die behind closed doors."[59]

A federal district judge in New York reviewing the government's treatment of a September 11th suspect, Osama Awadallah, issued a pair of rulings lambasting the government's tactics.[60] The judge ruled that the government had abused the "material witness" statute[61] by employing it to hold a witness for a grand jury proceeding rather than for a criminal trial, had lied to obtain the material witness warrant, and had physically abused Awadallah while in custody. The court dismissed all charges against Awadallah, and ordered his release.

A district court ruled in October 2001 that a federal statute making it a crime to provide "personnel" and "training" to designated "foreign terrorist organizations"[62] was unconstitutionally vague, reasoning that these terms appear to prohibit clearly protected First Amendment activity on behalf of disfavored organizations.[63] In December 2003, the Court of Appeals for the Ninth Circuit unanimously affirmed that decision and also ruled, by a two to one vote, that in order to satisfy due process, a mens rea requirement must be read into the material support statute.[64] In January 2004, a district court in a related case declared unconstitutional a *USA PATRIOT Act* provision criminalizing the provision of "expert advice and assistance" to terrorist groups.[65] These provisions have proved to be the linchpin of the government's domestic war on terrorism.[66] In August 2003, another federal judge declared unconstitutional the ban on providing "personnel" and "communications" to terrorist organizations, in one of the Justice Department's most highly publicized post–September 11th antiterrorist prosecutions, against the lawyer and translators for Sheikh Omar Abdel Rahman.[67]

In May 2002, the federal judges authorized to issue warrants for searches and electronic wiretaps under the *Foreign Intelligence Surveillance Act* ("FISA"),[68] sitting as one court, ruled that the minimization provisions of that statute barred criminal prosecutors from directing foreign intelligence investigations and applications for warrants.[69] The court cited numerous problems it had experienced under the statute, including the fact that the government had on seventy-five prior occasions provided the court with misleading or inaccurate information.[70]

The district courts hearing challenges to the detentions of American citizens Yaser Hamdi and Jose Padilla, who were being held as "enemy combatants," also rejected sweeping assertions that the detainees had no right to see a lawyer or to obtain judicial review of their detentions. In *Hamdi*, District Judge Robert G. Doumar rejected the government's position that habeas corpus review was unavailable, insisted that judicial review was required, and sharply dismissed the government's submission of a two-page declaration from a government bureaucrat based on unidentified hearsay as insufficient to establish the propriety of detaining Hamdi.[71] In an early appeal, the United States Court of Appeals for the Fourth Circuit, the most conservative federal appellate court in the nation, similarly rejected the government's "sweeping contention" that the President could, without judicial review, designate citizens as enemy combatants and hold them indefinitely.[72]

The district court hearing a habeas action on behalf of Padilla similarly ruled that it could review the legality of the detention. And over strong objections from the military, the court also ordered that Padilla, who has been held incommunicado, must be granted access to his attorney for purposes of challenging his detention.[73] On appeal, the U.S. Court of Appeals for the Second Circuit went even further, ruling that the President lacked any authority to hold citizens as enemy combatants absent express authorization from Congress.[74]

In December 2003, the United States Court of Appeals for the Ninth Circuit ruled that the foreign nationals held as enemy combatants in Guantanamo Bay, Cuba, have a right to seek habeas corpus review in federal court of the legality of their detentions.[75] Several other lower courts had previously held to the contrary, but in November 2003, the Supreme Court granted review of two such lower court decisions over the opposition of the executive branch.[76] In January 2004, the Court also agreed to hear Yaser Hamdi's claims that he was being held unlawfully as an enemy combatant, again over the opposition of the executive branch, which had urged the Court to deny certiorari.[77] Thus, in an area where the administration initially asserted unilateral authority to detain, unreviewable by the courts, the Supreme Court has now agreed to exercise review. What that review will consist of remains to be seen, of course. But the very fact that the Court agreed to hear the cases over the executive branch's opposition is significant.

In two of the most prominent prosecutions in the war on terrorism, those charging French citizen Zacarias Moussaoui with involvement in the September 11th conspiracy and American citizen John Walker Lindh with aiding Al Qaeda and conspiring to kill Americans, federal courts ruled, again over strenuous objections from the government, that the defendants must be granted access to enemy combatant detainees who allegedly had exculpatory evidence about the defendants.[78] Shortly after the district court in the *Lindh* case issued that ruling, the government agreed to drop all terrorism charges in exchange for a plea of guilty to a lesser charge.[79] In the *Moussaoui* case, the government has appealed the district court's ruling and has suggested that if it does not prevail, it may remove Moussaoui's case from the criminal process to a military tribunal.[80]

Four federal judges have declared unconstitutional a regulation issued shortly after September 11th that gives immigration "prosecutors," or district directors, the power to keep a foreign national in custody when the immigration judge presiding over the case has found no basis for detention and ordered release on bond.[81] All four courts found that the regulation violated due process by permitting preventive detention where no showing of flight risk or danger to the community had been made.

These decisions suggest an increasing willingness on the part of judges to question broad assertions of national security. At the same time, other decisions, including subsequent decisions in several of the same cases, fit the more traditional model of deference. The Court of Appeals for the Third Circuit upheld the blanket closure of immigration hearings,[82] and the Supreme Court denied a petition for certiorari.[83] A specially convened court of appeals, after entertaining a one-sided secret appeal by the government, reversed the unanimous decision of the FISA judges imposing limits on criminal prosecutors' role in FISA investigations and also ruled that the *USA PATRIOT Act*'s expansion of FISA posed no Fourth Amendment problems.[84] Again, the Supreme Court denied review.[85]

The Fourth Circuit in a later appeal in the *Hamdi* case essentially gave the government what the court earlier said it would not countenance – the power to detain without any meaningful judicial review. The Fourth Circuit upheld Hamdi's detention on the basis of nothing more than what it characterized as the "undisputed" fact that Hamdi had been captured on the battlefield abroad and refused to allow Hamdi to participate in the review.[86] (The court did not explain how the circumstances of Hamdi's capture could be disputed or undisputed when Hamdi was unable to participate in the proceeding, and the lawyers representing his interests had no basis for knowing where he was captured).

And with the exception of the Ninth Circuit's decision in *Gherebi*, federal courts have refused even to consider habeas corpus petitions challenging the detention of foreign enemy combatants at Guantanamo

Bay, although the Supreme Court has agreed to review the threshold jurisdictional question on whether the courts have any power to entertain the habeas claims.[87]

After the *Awadallah* decision,[88] another judge in the same federal district ruled that the material witness statute was properly employed to detain witnesses to testify in grand jury proceedings and was not limited to criminal cases.[89] The Court of Appeals for the Second Circuit subsequently reversed the lower court decision in *Awadallah* and reinstated the perjury charges against Awadallah.[90]

The Court of Appeals for the D.C. Circuit reversed the FOIA decision requiring disclosure of the names of the September 11th detainees, over a spirited dissent by Judge David Tatel.[91] Finally, the federal courts have uniformly dismissed constitutional concerns raised by two Muslim charities whose assets have been frozen on vague charges of support for terrorism under the *International Emergency Economic Powers Act*.[92]

It is too early to draw firm conclusions regarding the role of courts in the war on terrorism; we are, after all, still in the initial stages of this crisis, when courts are historically deferential, and the Supreme Court has not yet weighed in. The lower courts' greater willingness to challenge the government's national-security assertions may reflect the fact that the buck does not stop with those courts; any ruling against the government in this area is likely to be but one stop along the road to appeal. The Supreme Court was able to reach the result it did in *Marbury* in part because it left the President with nothing to defy, and thereby created the space to announce its doctrine of judicial supremacy. So, too, a district court decision on a matter of national security is unlikely to be the judiciary's last word, and therefore it may be easier for a district court to rule against the government's national-security assertions. The further up the appellate chain, the more likely a judicial decision will be determinative, and consequently, the more pressure judges may feel to uphold the government's actions.

Cultural factors may also play a role in the marginally increased willingness of courts to question the government's national-security initiatives. As Jack Goldsmith and Cass Sunstein have argued, President Bush's order authorizing military tribunals sparked a much more critical public reaction than did President Franklin Delano Roosevelt's use of military tribunals during World War II.[93] They attribute the change to an increasing distrust of government in the wake of Vietnam and Watergate, and to a "massively strengthened commitment to individual rights" in our constitutional law.[94]

Without a doubt, the Vietnam era, and especially the revelations of FBI abuses targeted at antiwar and civil rights protesters during that period, effected a seismic shift in public and judicial attitudes toward executive power and national-security claims.[95] Before Vietnam, J. Edgar Hoover was a national hero; today his name is shorthand for politically motivated government repression. The abuses of COINTELPRO, including extensive wiretapping of Dr. Martin Luther King, Jr., infiltration and disruption of lawful political organizations through "dirty tricks," secret warrantless searches, and the compiling of extensive records on the Bureau's critics, all undertaken under the rubric of "national security," have given the public and the media good reason to be skeptical about assertions of unchecked executive power.

Significantly, the Supreme Court itself took part in that transformation, as it permitted the publication of the Pentagon Papers,[96] held unconstitutional warrantless "domestic security" wiretaps,[97] and rejected President Nixon's broad assertions of executive privilege in connection with the Watergate prosecutions.[98] In each of these cases, the Court stood up to the government, and its public reputation was enhanced as a result. That experience may well play a role in the courts' apparently greater willingness to challenge the government in the current era.[99]

A third factor may be the dramatically increased presence of human rights, civil rights, civil liberties, and immigrants' rights groups. During the Cold War, for example, the American Civil Liberties Union, the organization one might expect to be defending the Communists, was busy purging itself of Communists.[100] The National Lawyers Guild was one of the few legal organizations to defend Communists' rights, and the Attorney General and the Director of the FBI targeted it as a Communist front organization for its efforts.[101]

Today, by contrast, the ACLU has been a vigorous defender of civil liberties, and it stands among a broad spectrum of organizations and institutions that have spoken out for the need to respect civil liberties in the war on terrorism. These include human rights organizations such as Amnesty International, Human Rights Watch, and the Lawyers' Committee for Human Rights; civil liberties and civil rights groups such as the Center for Constitutional Rights, the National Lawyers Guild, the National Committee to Protect Political Freedom, and the Center for National Security Studies; immigrants' rights and ethnicity-based groups such as the American-Arab Anti-Discrimination Committee, the American Immigration Lawyers' Association, the Asian American Legal

Defense Fund, the National Immigration Forum, and the Japanese American Citizens League; grassroots organizing groups such as the Bill of Rights Defense Committees; religious groups such as the Muslim Public Affairs Council and the Council on American Islamic Relations; electronic privacy-focused groups such as the Center for Democracy and Technology and the Electronic Privacy Information Center; and libertarian organizations such as the Cato Institute. Most of these groups did not even exist during the Cold War. Their active and vocal presence today creates opportunities for grassroots involvement and education; generates reports and press releases on civil liberties abuses; gives voice to those who would otherwise be voiceless; and brings both domestic and international media attention to the government's excesses.[102] That in turn affects the broader culture of concern about rights, which may lead courts to be more attentive than they might otherwise be to concerns on the liberty side of the security-liberty balance.

In short, while courts remain no panacea, we ought not dismiss them too quickly, as they have the potential to play a critical role in checking emergency powers.

IV AN UNTIMELY PROPOSAL

Despite these developments, some commentators have recently argued that the Constitution and, by extension, the courts ought not play much of a role at all in restricting the government's emergency powers. Professors Oren Gross and Mark Tushnet have each proposed that in light of the failure of constitutional constraints to limit executive action during emergencies, it might be better to recognize explicitly the validity of extraconstitutional measures during emergencies, or put differently, to acknowledge that emergency powers are not governed by the Constitution.[103] Both do so in large part to avoid tainting constitutional law for ordinary times with decisions rendered on the exercise of emergency authorities. Justice Jackson warned of precisely such danger in his dissent in *Korematsu*. He maintained that as threatening to liberty as the military order establishing Japanese internment was, "a judicial construction of the due process clause that will sustain this order is a far more subtle blow to liberty than the promulgation of the order itself."[104] He reasoned that the military order would last only so long as the emergency and could be lifted by a subsequent commander, but that

once a judicial opinion rationalizes such an order to show that it conforms to the Constitution, or rather rationalizes the Constitution to show that the

Constitution sanctions such an order, the Court for all time has validated the principle of racial discrimination in criminal procedure and of transplanting American citizens.[105]

Justice Jackson's proposal was in fact far more modest than his critique. He argued that the civil courts ought not play a role in *enforcing* military orders.[106] Korematsu's case arose from a criminal prosecution in civil court for violating the military's exclusion order, and Justice Jackson would have reversed the conviction on the ground that civilian courts ought not dirty their hands with the military's business. But Jackson's proposal is as ineffectual as it is modest. It would have resolved Korematsu's case, but it would not have removed civilian courts from the business of reviewing the legality of military detention. Other detainees might well have filed habeas corpus actions challenging the validity of their detention. Unless Justice Jackson was prepared to say that the courts could unilaterally suspend the writ of habeas corpus for any military detention, he could not have avoided the necessity of passing judgment on the military's actions.

Mark Tushnet, in a thoughtful article provocatively titled *Defending Korematsu?*[107] cites Jackson's observations but takes them one step further. Not content with Jackson's prescription, Tushnet argues much more broadly for affirmative recognition of extraconstitutional emergency powers: "it is better to have emergency powers exercised in an extraconstitutional way, so that everyone understands that the actions are extraordinary, than to have the actions rationalized away as consistent with the Constitution and thereby normalized."[108] In his view, this is justified in order "to avoid normalizing the exception."[109]

Oren Gross advocates a similar approach in much more detail in *Chaos and Rules: Should Responses to Violent Crises Always Be Constitutional?*[110] Gross contends, like Tushnet, that as a matter of reality we should candidly acknowledge that executive officials in times of crisis will act extraconstitutionally, and that we should do so in order to avoid "contaminat[ing]" the ordinary legal system with emergency powers.[111] Gross would "inform public officials that they may act extralegally when they believe that such action is necessary for protecting the nation and the public in the face of calamity provided that they openly and publicly acknowledge the nature of their actions."[112] Because on this view extralegal authority is expressly permitted, the courts would not play a role in restraining such authority. Instead, it would "be up to the people to decide, either directly or indirectly (e.g., through their elected representatives in the legislature), how to respond to such actions."[113]

Like Tushnet, Gross insists that his approach is aimed at "the preservation of the constitutional order and of its most fundamental principles and tenets."[114] He argues that the requirement that officials seeking to exercise such powers must act openly in defiance of the law and throw themselves on the judgment of the people would serve as an important deterrent to executive abuse of emergency powers.

These proposals are misguided. While I share to some extent the authors' skepticism about the ability of courts to protect the individual rights of those before them in national-security emergencies, both authors ignore the long-term benefits that judicial decisions in the national-security area have had in narrowing the range of rights-violative options available to the government in the next emergency. Were courts to adopt the Gross-Tushnet notion that extraconstitutional measures are appropriate during emergencies, and that the only real check is political, much would be lost and little gained in the protection of civil liberties.

I would hesitate to adopt the Gross-Tushnet position for several reasons. First, it is predicated on a distinction between "emergency" periods and "normal" periods that, as Gross himself has convincingly shown, simply cannot be maintained. As Gross argues, "the belief in our ability to separate emergency from normalcy, counter-terrorism measures from the ordinary set of legal rules and norms," is a dangerous illusion.[115] The United States has been under one state of emergency or another since 1933; by the mid-1970s, there were more than 470 "emergency" laws on the books.[116] Israel has been under an emergency regime since it was established as a state more than fifty years ago.[117] And Great Britain has been under a state of emergency for most of the last thirty years, occasioned first by the IRA and later by the attacks of September 11th.[118] Thus, emergency powers have a way of surviving long after the emergency has passed, and emergencies themselves may last decades. Emergency measures adopted in the United States today are especially likely to be long-lasting, given the nature of the war on terrorism, which is more like the war on drugs than a traditional war between nations.[119] When Donald Rumsfeld was asked when the war on terrorism would be over (and therefore when the Guantanamo enemy combatant detainees would be freed), he answered that the war would not be over until there were no longer any "effective global terrorist networks functioning in the world."[120] Vice President Richard Cheney has been even more candid, arguing that we should consider the current period not an emergency at all, but "the new normalcy."[121]

If the line between emergency and normal is evanescent, a doctrine of extraconstitutional authority cannot be safely cabined to emergency times. Far from protecting the Constitution in normal times, then, a doctrine expressly authorizing extralegal actions during emergencies would be at least as likely to contaminate the norm by expanding the realm of available government measures across the board as would insistence on a continuing role for courts and the Constitution in checking emergency and nonemergency government action.

Second, the Gross-Tushnet proposal to acknowledge extraconstitutional power would be likely to undermine the protection of rights during emergencies (and by extension, during normal times that officials call emergencies). Gross claims that his proposal would have a salutary deterrent effect on official abuse of emergency powers, because officials could never be certain that their actions would in fact be ratified after the fact. And he argues that shifting the locus of justification and judgment from the judiciary to a political forum – the people or their elected representatives – would avoid the problem identified by Justice Jackson of formally authorizing emergency measures through judicial approval.

There are substantial reasons, however, to doubt both of Gross's claims. Even if acknowledging the legitimacy of extralegal measures would avoid formal judicial approval, it would not avoid the creation of less formal precedents that could be pointed to later to justify further incursions on liberties. The post hoc political rationalization process that Gross envisions, while lacking the attributes of the formal legal process, would nonetheless generate a more informal common law of extralegal emergency authorities. Once the political process has ratified a particular extralegal emergency action, officials will be able to point to that precedent as justification for their own subsequent actions. "Illegal" measures deemed permissible after the fact will no longer be clearly illegal, so long as a subsequent emergency can be analogized to the emergency found to warrant the illegal action previously.[122]

Nor is it clear that the Gross-Tushnet proposal would have the effect of avoiding formal judicial approval of emergency measures. Even if we were to adopt such a scheme, public officials would be exceedingly unlikely to admit that their actions were extralegal. Rather, they would almost invariably argue first that their measures were constitutional and argue only in the alternative that their actions were justified even if illegal.[123] As a result, courts would continue to have to address the legality of emergency measures, and the drive to accommodate the

Constitution to emergency conditions would continue to exert pressure on constitutional jurisprudence. Given the open-ended character of the Constitution and the fact that few of the liberties it protects are absolute, there will rarely be an emergency measure that government lawyers cannot defend with some constitutional argument. And while an open acknowledgment of the propriety of extralegal measures might reduce the hydraulic forces inducing courts to uphold emergency actions, the extent to which this would "save" normal constitutional law or deter abuse of emergency powers seems likely to be minimal. For the reasons stated above, courts would presumably still be reticent to rule against the government in emergency periods. And the open acknowledgment of the validity of extraconstitutional authority would seriously undercut the force of judicial decisions that now constrain emergency measures.

From the standpoint of deterring the abuse of emergency authority, the Gross-Tushnet proposal is not very different from what already exists. If a government official today adopts an extraconstitutional response to an emergency and his actions are later declared unconstitutional, he may in theory be subject to civil or criminal sanctions. But the likelihood that criminal or civil sanctions will be imposed is, in fact, virtually nil, and in any event the state nearly always indemnifies its officials from such liability.[124] Moreover, such an official could always seek political post hoc ratification, in the form of immunity or indemnity from Congress or a pardon from the President. Thus, under the status quo, elected officials who act extraconstitutionally already face some, albeit limited, risk of liability, and have some political recourse to avoid liability.

Third, there is little reason to trust the political process to do the job of judging that Gross and Tushnet would assign to it. The real difference under a Gross-Tushnet approach would be that the principal job of judging emergency measures would presumptively fall not on the courts but on the political process. But this seems the most dubious aspect of the proposal. If courts are not particularly reliable in imposing limits on executive action during emergencies, the political process would almost certainly be worse. As Gross himself argues, the public and their elected representatives are especially prone to overreaction during times of crisis.[125] The public is easily scared, and quick to approve of security measures launched in its name, especially if the measures do not directly affect the rights of the majority. Their elected representatives know that, and vote accordingly. Indeed, the very reason that we adopted a Constitution was that we understood that the people and their representatives would be tempted to violate basic principles in times of stress. In the words of Senator John Stockton in 1871: "Constitutions are chains with which men bind themselves in their sane moments that they may not die by a suicidal hand in the day of their frenzy."[126]

Moreover, emergency measures almost always selectively target vulnerable groups and individuals, and foreign nationals in particular, making the political process an especially unreliable check on emergency powers.[127] This fact apparently does not concern Tushnet;[128] but for those concerned with the human rights of the most vulnerable, proposals that point to political rather than judicial processes for assessing the validity of emergency measures are fatally flawed.

Finally, Gross and Tushnet's proposal rests on the conventional wisdom that courts cannot be trusted to perform well in times of crisis. But the real question to be asked when assessing the courts' performance is: Compared to what? The courts are undoubtedly highly imperfect; but the alternatives are worse. One cannot rely on the executive branch to police itself in times of crisis. As Francis Biddle, Franklin Delano Roosevelt's Attorney General, candidly acknowledged, "The Constitution has not bothered any wartime President."[129] Executive officials after September 11th knew that they would take a much bigger "hit" politically if there were another terrorist act than if they locked up thousands of foreign nationals unconnected to terrorism. In such periods, executive officials ask for untrammeled authority, and assure the public that they will not abuse it. History shows that such trust is not warranted.

Congress is also unlikely to be a guardian of civil liberties. Its overwhelming approval of the *Smith Act*[130] and the *Internal Security Act*[131] during the McCarthy era and of the *Antiterrorism and Effective Death Penalty Act*[132] and the *Patriot Act*[133] in the current era, coupled with its appropriation of funds for the Japanese internment in World War II, illustrate that legislators are exceedingly unlikely to stand up against executive power in the name of civil liberties during emergencies. The need to be seen as "doing something" about the threat often translates into legislation that delegates sweeping powers to the executive branch.

Only the courts have an *obligation* to entertain claims of rights violations. The executive and legislative branches can simply choose to ignore such claims, and are likely to do so when those claims are not backed by substantial political power or influence. By contrast, assuming standing and justiciability, courts must adjudicate any claim that a government initiative violates constitutional rights. As a result, courts are often the only forum realistically available. For more than two years, the President has asserted the unilateral power to detain anyone he labels as an enemy combatant. Congress has done nothing to check or limit or even seriously address this assertion of power. The courts, by contrast, have addressed the question and issued multiple opinions, all of which are as of this writing headed for Supreme Court review.

To cite another example, over the past decade and a half, I have represented thirteen foreign nationals whom the government accused of having ties to terrorist organizations and sought to detain or deport using classified evidence that the foreign nationals had no opportunity to confront or rebut.[134] The government maintained that the individuals' presence in the United States threatened national security, and that revealing the evidence that proved that contention would itself endanger national security. All thirteen were eventually released without undermining national security, but only when we challenged the government's actions *in court* as a violation of due process. Of the thirteen, twelve were Arab and/or Muslim. The thirteenth was a Kenyan woman married to a Palestinian and accused of being associated with a Palestinian organization.

What were our options in seeking to protect these individuals' constitutional rights? Congress would not help them. The issue of secret evidence in immigration proceedings had been raised in Congress, but far from providing a remedy, in 1996 Congress expressly expanded and authorized its use in a number of immigration settings.[135] The executive branch was equally unresponsive. It was the executive branch, after all, that invoked the tactic in the first place. Even under the administration of President Bill Clinton, the executive branch was not a source of relief. And the public and the press, with a few exceptions, by and large paid little attention. When a court ordered an individual released, its decision would often receive coverage in the print media. But I received countless phone calls from television news producers over the years looking for legal stories, all of whom ultimately determined that the secret evidence story would not sell because it involved foreign nationals rather than citizens.[136] For my clients, it was court or nothing, court or more years of detention based on evidence they could not see. And to their credit, the courts were uniformly skeptical of the government's claims, and protective of the foreign nationals' right to see the evidence being used to deprive them of their liberty.[137] Even immigration judges, who as administrative judges ultimately reviewable by the Attorney General lack the independence of the federal courts, were highly skeptical of the government's claims.[138]

Because courts are the only realistic option available to those targeted by emergency measures, and precisely because judges are all too human and already face substantial pressure to avoid fulfilling their responsibility, it seems especially misguided to *advocate* that they do so. The formal guarantees and ethical obligation of independence do not mean that judges are in fact always impartial and courageous, but the insistence that it is their obligation to be independent is critical to the enterprise of judging. We should not let judges off the hook when it comes to emergency matters, because they are the only real option for most persons targeted by emergency measures. As Fred Schauer has eloquently argued in a different setting, "The mere fact that courts will fold under pressure, however, does not dictate that they should be *told* that they may fold under pressure, because the effect of the message may be to increase the likelihood of folding even when the pressure is less."[139] Schauer continued, "Resisting the inevitable is not to be desired because it will prevent the inevitable, but because it may be the best strategy for preventing what is less inevitable but more dangerous."[140]

In my view, the historical record does not demonstrate that courts will inevitably fold under the pressure of emergencies, but only that they will *often* do so. The historical developments reviewed above suggest that at least some judges may have learned from history to demand more narrowly tailored responses to emergencies. But more important, the record also shows that by exercising their responsibility to decide cases pitting individual rights against emergency executive power, the courts have over time developed rules that do constrain the executive in the next emergency. The danger of Gross and Tushnet's proposal is that we would be sacrificing even that for benefits that seem evanescent at best.

CONCLUSION

Courts, like every other institution of human governance, are imperfect. Tasked with the job of enforcing individual constitutional rights against the majority's will, judges remain prone to the same fears and anxieties that afflict us all during times of crisis. Thus, it should not be a surprise that courts have all too often deferred to unfounded assertions of government power on issues of national security; when the executive claims that the fate of the nation is at stake, it takes real courage to stand up to that assertion and subject it to careful scrutiny.

At the same time, the conventional wisdom that courts have failed during times of crisis is itself overstated. It is based both on a snapshot view of the courts' decisions, and on an overly idealized vision of what is in fact possible. When considered over time, courts have played a valuable role in reviewing and ultimately restraining some of the more egregious rights violations undertaken in the name of saving the country. Judicial decisions, while rarely providing relief to the initial victims of a crisis mentality, have played a role in restricting the options available to the government in the *next* emergency. Like *Marbury v. Madison* itself, these decisions may well be more important over the long run than their bottom lines would make them appear in the short run.

Given the salutary role that courts have played in enforcing constitutional limits on emergency responses, and given the paucity of credible alternatives, we should be reluctant to let judges off the hook. There seems to be little reason to trust the political branches to be more attentive to constitutional rights concerns than courts, even if courts themselves do not always perform as we might hope they would. As Eugene Rostow argued in assessing the Japanese internment cases shortly after they were decided, "It is hard to imagine what courts are for if not to protect people against unconstitutional arrest ... It is essential to every democratic value in society that official action taken in the name of the war power be held to standards of responsibility."[141]

NOTES

1 *Marbury v. Madison*, 5 U.S. (1 Cranch) 137, 177 (1803).

2 *Schenck v. United States*, 249 U.S. 47 (1919).

3 *Korematsu v. United States*, 323 U.S. 214 (1944).

4 *Dennis v. United States*, 341 U.S. 494 (1951).

5 *Brandenburg v. Ohio*, 395 U.S. 444 (1969).

6 See, e.g., *Grutter v. Bollinger*, 123 S. Ct. 2325 (2003).

7 See, e.g., *NAACP v. Claiborne Hardware Co.*, 458 U.S. 886, 932 (1982).

8 *Carolene Prods. v. United States*, 304 U.S. 144, 152 n.4 (1944).

9 John Hart Ely, *Democracy and Distrust* (1980).

10 See, e.g., Gerald N. Rosenberg, *The Hollow Hope* (1991).

11 See, e.g., Bruce Fein, "Narrow, Prudent, and Impeccable," *Wash. Times*, Dec. 10, 2002. The quote comes from *Kennedy v. Mendoza-Martinez*, 372 U.S. 144, 160 (1963).

12 I develop this point in David Cole, *Enemy Aliens: Double Standards and Constitutional Freedoms in the War on Terrorism* (2003) [hereinafter Cole, *Enemy Aliens*].

13 I will resist offering broad generalizations about judicial review. Generalizing about judicial review from the standpoint of how courts act in national emergencies is, to me, as invalid as judging the propriety of judicial review on the basis of the Supreme Court's performance in *Bush v. Gore*, 531 U.S. 98 (2000). The fact that courts, like all other institutions, are susceptible to political pressure in times of high crisis does not warrant a rejection of judicial review in general or of the ideals that animate it. I address only the somewhat more specific question of how judicial review works in emergencies and on matters of national security.

14 Oren Gross," Chaos and Rules: Should Responses to Violent Crises Always Be Constitutional?" 112 Yale L.J. 1011 (2003); Mark Tushnet, "Defending Korematsu?: Reflections on Civil Liberties in Wartime," 2003 Wis. L. Rev. 273.

15 Clinton Rossiter & R. Longaker, *The Supreme Court and the Commander in Chief* (expanded ed. 1976), 52.

16 *Learned Hand, The Spirit of Liberty: Papers and Addresses of Learned Hand*, ed. Irving Dullard (1960), 89–90

17 *Korematsu v. United States*, 323 U.S. 214, 248 (1944) (Jackson J, dissenting).

18 See *Ex parte* Starr, 263 F. 145, 147 (D. Mont. 1920). Justice Brennan has advanced much the same evaluation. See William J. Brennan, Jr, "The Quest to Develop a Jurisprudence of Civil Liberties in Times of Security Crises," 18 Isr. Y.B. Hum. Rts. 11, 11 (1988) ("There is ... a good deal to be embarrassed about, when one reflects on the shabby treatment civil liberties have received in the United States during times of perceived threats to its national security").

19 17 F. Cas. 144 (1861) (No. 9487).

20 Cole, *Enemy Aliens, supra* note 12, at 12–13.

21 Id.

22 *Ex Parte Quirin*, 317 U.S. 1 (1942).

23 Melvin I. Urofsky, "Inter Arma Silent Leges: Extrajudicial Activity, Patriotism and the Rule of Law," in *Total War and the Law: The American Home Front in World War II*, ed. Daniel R. Ernst and Victor Jew (2002), 27.

24 Arthur J. Sabin, in *Calmer Times: The Supreme Court and Red Monday* (1999), 90–105; William M. Wiecek, "The Legal Foundations of Domestic Anticommunism: The Background of *Dennis v. United States*," 2001 Sup. Ct. Rev. 375, 428–34.

25 See, e.g., *Grutter v. Bollinger*, 123 S. Ct. 2325 (2003).

26 *Hirabayashi v. United States*, 828 F.2d 591, 604–08 (9th Cir. 1987); *Korematsu v. United States*, 584 F. Supp. 1406, 1419 (ND Cal. 1984). See generally Peter Irons, *Justice at War* (1983).

27 See Louis Smith, *American Democracy and Military Power* (1951), 266.

28 17 F. Cas. 144 (1861).

29 308 F.3d 198 (3d Cir. 2002).

30 "Arguments Made on Deportation Hearing Regs", PA. L. Wkly., Sept. 23, 2002, at 9 (quoting Judge Greenberg).

31 71 U.S. (4 Wall.) 2 (1866).

32 *Ex parte Milligan*, 71 U.S. at 120–21; see also *Home Bldg. & Loan Ass'n v. Blaisdell*, 290 U.S. 398, 425–26 (1934) ("[The Constitution's] grants of power to the Federal Government and its limitations of the power of the States were determined in the light of emergency and they are not altered by emergency ... even the war power does not remove constitutional limitations safeguarding essential liberties").

33 327 U.S. 304 (1946).

34 Edwin Corwin, *Total War and the Constitution* (1947), 104–5.

35 See, e.g., *Gilbert v. Minnesota*, 254 U.S. 325, 332–33 (1920); *Abrams v. United States*, 250 U.S. 616, 629 (1919); *Frohwerk v. United States*, 249 U.S. 204, 209–10 (1919); *Schenck v. United States*, 249 U.S. 47, 52 (1919).

36 354 U.S. 298 (1957).

37 *Alien Registration Act* of 1940, Pub. L. No. 76–670, 54 Stat. 670.

38 See Sabin, *supra* note 24, at 169–70 (discussing the effect of the *Yates* decision).

39 395 U.S. 444, 447 (1969).

40 See *supra* note 35.

41 See David Cole, "The New McCarthyism: Repeating History in the War on Terrorism," 38 Harv. C.R.–C.L. L. Rev. 1, 6–8 (2003) (discussing reliance on guilt by association in preventive law enforcement).

42 367 U.S. 203 (1961).

43 *Scales v. United States*, 367 U.S. 203, 220 (1961).

44 See *NAACP v. Claiborne Hardware Co.*, 458 U.S. 886, 932 (1982) (holding membership in NAACP insufficient basis for tort liability absent proof of specific intent); *Healy v. James*, 408 U.S. 169, 186–87 (1972) (finding association with Students for Democratic Socialism insufficient basis for denying use of campus meeting rooms); *United States v. Robel*, 389 U.S. 258, 262 (1967) (holding government could not deny Communist Party members security clearances for work in defense facilities absent proof that they had specific intent to further the Party's unlawful ends);

Keyishian v. Bd. of Regents, 385 U.S. 589, 606 (1967) ("[m]ere knowing membership without a specific intent to further the unlawful aims of an organization is not a constitutionally adequate basis" for barring employment in state university system to Communist Party members); *Apatheker v. Sec'y of State*, 378 U.S. 500, 514 (1964) (finding Communist Party membership insufficient basis for denying passport).

45 This claim is subject to an important qualification. While the war on terrorism has not thus far led to the direct criminalization of membership per se in political groups, the government has resurrected the tactic of "guilt by association" in the name of cutting off terrorist financing. Under a 1996 antiterrorism statute, it is a crime to provide "material support" to designated "terrorist organizations," without regard to the intent, purpose, or effect of one's support. *Antiterrorism and Effective Death Penalty Act* of 1996 § 303(a), 18 U.S.C. § 2339B (2003). Under this statute, it is no defense to show that one's support was in fact intended to support only nonviolent humanitarian activities, nor even to show that one's support was designed to and did in fact *reduce* a recipient group's reliance on violence. One court of appeals has held that this statute does not violate the prohibition on guilt by association because it punishes not membership per se, but acts of material support. *Humanitarian Law Project v. Reno*, 205 F.3d 1130 (9th Cir. 2000). In my view, this exalts form over substance. What good is the right of association if one has no right to provide any kind of support to the group with which one associates? See generally David Cole, "Hanging with the Wrong Crowd: Of Gangs, Terrorists, and the Right of Association," 1999 Sup. Ct. Rev. 203. At the same time, the existence of Supreme Court precedents strongly condemning guilt by association preclude punishing membership itself and provide strong arguments against this new version of associational guilt.

46 403 U.S. 713 (1971).

47 407 U.S. 232 (1972).

48 Clinton Rossiter and Richard P. Longaker, *The Supreme Court and the Commander in Chief* (1976).

49 *Korematsu v. United States*, 323 U.S. 214, 246 (1944) (Jackson, J., dissenting) (arguing that the principle underlying the *Korematsu* decision "lies about like a loaded weapon ready for the hand of any authority that can bring forward a plausible claim of an urgent need").

50 See Cole, *Enemy Aliens*, *supra* note 12, at 99, 261 n.42 (citing cases).

51 *Stenberg v. Carhart*, 530 U.S. 914, 953 (2000) (Scalia J, dissenting).

52 See *Civil Liberties Act* of 1988, Pub. L. No. 100–383, 102 Stat. 903.

53 See *supra* note 26.

54 John E. Finn, *Constitutions in Crisis: Political Violence and the Rule of Law* (1991), 33 ("Some type of constitutional review is a constitutive element of constitutionalism, for the activity of review, the very possibility of review, is predicated upon the necessity to produce reasons in support of action taken").

55 See "Arguments Made on Deportation Hearing Regs," *supra* note 30.

56 215 F. Supp. 2d 94 (DDC 2002), modified, 331 F.3d 918 (DC Cir. 2003).

57 *Detroit Free Press v. Ashcroft*, 195 F. Supp. 2d 948 (ED Mich. 2002), *aff'd,* 303 F.3d 681 (6th Cir. 2002); *N. Jersey Media Group v. Ashcroft*, 205 F. Supp. 2d 288 (DNJ 2002), *rev'd,* 308 F.3d 198 (3d Cir. 2002).

58 *Haddad v. Ashcroft*, 221 F. Supp. 2d 799 (ED Mich. 2002).

59 *Detroit Free Press v. Ashcroft*, 303 F.3d 681 (6th Cir. 2002).

60 *United States v. Awadallah*, 202 F. Supp. 2d 55 (SDNY 2002), *rev'd,* 349 F.3d 42 (2d Cir. 2003); *United States v. Awadallah*, 202 F. Supp. 2d 82 (SDNY 2002), *rev'd,* 349 F.3d 42 (2d Cir. 2003).

61 18 USC § 3144 (2000).

62 18 USC § 2339B (2000).

63 *Humanitarian Law Project v. Reno*, No. CV 98-1971 ABC (BQRx), 2001 U.S. Dist. LEXIS 16729 (CD Cal. Oct. 3, 2001), modified *sub nom. Humanitarian Law Project v. U.S. Dep't of Justice*, No. 02-55082, 2003 U.S. App. LEXIS 24305 (9th Cir. Dec. 3, 2003).

64 *Humanitarian Law Project v. U.S. Dep't of Justice*, No. 02-55082, 2003 U.S. App. LEXIS 24305 (9th Cir. Dec. 3, 2003).

65 *Humanitarian Law Project v. Ashcroft*, No. CV-03-6107, 2004 U.S. Dist. LEXIS 926 (U.S. Jan. 22, 2004).

66 See Cole, *Enemy Aliens, supra* note 12, at 75–76, 256 n.11.

67 *United States v. Sattar*, No. 02 Cr. 395 (JGK), 2003 U.S. Dist. LEXIS 12531 (SDNY July 22, 2003).

68 50 USC §§ 1801–1863 (2000).

69 *In re* All Matters Submitted to the Foreign Intelligence Surveillance Court, 218 F. Supp. 2d 611 (U.S. Foreign Intelligence Surveillance Ct. 2002).

70 Id. at 620.

71 *Hamdi v. Rumsfeld*, 243 F. Supp. 2d 527 (ED Va. 2002), *rev'd,* 316 F.3d 450 (4th Cir. 2002).

72 *Hamdi v. Rumsfeld*, 296 F.3d 278, 283 (4th Cir. 2002).

73 *Padilla v. Bush*, 233 F. Supp. 2d 564 (SDNY 2002); see also *Padilla v. Rumsfeld*, 243 F. Supp. 2d 42 (SDNY 2003) (reaffirming earlier decision and denying motion for reconsideration).

74 *Padilla v. Rumsfeld*, 352 F.3d 695 (2d Cir. 2003).

75 *Gherebi v. Bush*, No. 03-55785, 2003 U.S. App. LEXIS 25625 (9th Cir. Dec. 18, 2003).

76 *Al Odah v. United States*, No. 03-343, 124 S. Ct. 534, 2003 WL 22070725 (U.S. Nov. 10, 2003) (granting certiorari).

77 *Hamdi v. Rumsfeld*, No. 03-6696, 124 S. Ct. 981, 2004 WL 42546 (U.S. Jan. 9, 2004) (granting certiorari).

78 See *United States v. Moussaoui*, 333 F.3d 509 (4th Cir. 2003); Katherine Q. Seelye, "War on Terror Makes for Odd Twists in Justice System," N.Y. Times, June 23, 2002, at A16.

79 *United States v. Lindh*, 227 F. Supp. 2d 565 (ED Va. 2002); Jane Mayer, "Lost in the Jihad: Why Did the Government's Case against John Walker Lindh Collapse?" New Yorker, Mar. 10, 2003, at 50.

80 Toni Locy, "Moussaoui Clash Tests Future of Terror Trials," USA Today, July 21, 2003, at 2A; Susan Schmidt, "Prosecution of Moussaoui Nears a Crossroad: Facing Demands for Witness Testimony, Government May Turn Suspect Over to U.S. Military," Wash. Post, Jan. 21, 2003, at A8.

81 *Ashley v. Ridge*, 288 F. Supp. 2d 662 (DNJ 2003); *Uritsky v. Ridge*, 286 F. Supp. 2d 842 (ED Mich. 2003); *Bezmen v. Ashcroft*, 245 F. Supp. 2d 446 (D. Conn. 2003); *Almonte-Vargas v. Elwood*, No. 02-CV-2666, 2002 U.S. Dist. LEXIS 12387 (ED Pa. June 28, 2002).

82 *N. Jersey Media Group, Inc. v. Ashcroft*, 308 F.3d 198 (3d Cir. 2002), *cert. denied*, 123 S. Ct. 2215 (2003).

83 123 S. Ct. 2215 (2003).

84 *In re* Sealed Case No. 02-001, 310 F.3d 717 (U.S. Foreign Intelligence Surveillance Ct. of Review 2002).

85 *ACLU v. United States*, 538 U.S. 920 (2003).

86 *Hamdi v. Rumsfeld*, 316 F.3d 450 (4th Cir. 2002), *cert. granted*, 124 S. Ct. 981 (2004).

87 See, e.g., *Al Odah v. United States*, 321 F.3d 1134 (DC Cir. 2003), *cert. granted*, 124. S. Ct. 534 (2003); *Coalition of Clergy v. Bush*, 310 F.3d 1153 (9th Cir. 2002), *cert. denied*, 123 S. Ct. 2073 (2003).

88 *United States v. Awadallah*, 202 F. Supp. 2d 17 (SDNY 2002), *rev'd* 349 F.3d 42 (2d Cir. 2003).

89 *In re* the Application of the United States for a Material Witness Warrant, 213 F. Supp. 2d 287 (SDNY 2002).

90 *Awadallah*, 349 F.3d 42 (2d Cir. 2003).

91 *Ctr. for Nat'l Sec. Studies v. U.S. Dep't of Justice*, 331 F.3d 918 (DC Cir. 2003), *cert. denied*, 124 S. Ct. 1041 (2004).

92 *See Holy Land Found. for Relief & Dev. v. Ashcroft*, 219 F. Supp. 2d 57 (DDC 2002), *aff'd*, 333 F.3d 156 (DC Cir. 2003); *Global Relief Found., Inc. v. O'Neill*, 207 F. Supp. 2d 779 (ND Ill. 2002), *aff'd*, 315 F.3d 748 (7th Cir. 2002), *cert. denied sub nom. Global Relief Found., Inc. v. Snow*, 124 S. Ct. 531 (2003).

93 Jack Goldsmith and Cass R. Sunstein, "Military Tribunals and Legal Culture: What a Difference Sixty Years Makes," 19 Const. Comm. 261 (2003).

94 Id. at 282.

95 See generally *Supplementary Detailed Staff Reports on Intelligence Activities and the Rights of Americans, Book III, Final Report of the Select Comm. to Study Governmental Operations with Respect to Intelligence Activities*, S. Rep. No. 94-755 (1976); Frank Donner, *The Age of Surveillance: The Aims and Methods of America's Political Intelligence System* (1980).

96 *New York Times Co. v. United States*, 403 U.S. 713 (1971).

97 *United States v. U.S. District Court*, 407 U.S. 232 (1972).

98 *United States v. Nixon*, 418 U.S. 683 (1974).

99 Coincidentally, the district court judge who initially barred the use of "domestic security" wiretaps, Judge Damon Keith, also wrote the decision for the Court of Appeals for the Sixth Circuit declaring unconstitutional John Ashcroft's blanket closure of immigration hearings.

100 *See* Samuel Walker, *In Defense of American Liberties: A History of the ACLU* (1990), 173–216.

101 Id. at 177, 264–65; see also Robert Justin Goldstein, *Political Repression in Modern America: from 1870 to the Present* (1978), 364; Athan G. Theoharis and John Stuart Cox, *The Bull: J. Edgar Hoover and the Great American Inquisition* (1988), 218–19.

102 One initiative in particular has appeared to be especially influential. Soon after the *USA PATRIOT* Act was enacted, the Bill of Rights Defense Committee formed to pursue a grassroots strategy of getting local towns and counties to adopt resolutions condemning the civil liberties abuses of the Patriot Act. As of February 2004, 242 jurisdictions had adopted such resolutions, including three states – Hawaii, Alaska, and Vermont – and several major cities, including Chicago, Philadelphia, Detroit, Baltimore, San Francisco, and Albuquerque. See Bill of Rights Def. Comm., http://www.bordc.org (last updated Feb. 6, 2004). The initiative appears to have shifted public views toward the Patriot Act, prompting the Attorney General to launch an unprecedented speaking tour to seek to defend the Act. See David Cole, "On the Road with Ashcroft," Nation, Sept. 22, 2003, at 22.

103 Gross, *supra* note 14; Tushnet, *supra* note 14. Professor George Alexander before them made a similar argument, contending that because courts perform poorly in emergencies, they should not get involved at all, and "redress must be achieved politically if it is to be effective." George J. Alexander, "The Illusory Protection of Human Rights by National Courts during Periods of Emergency," 5 Hum. Rts. L.J. 1, 27, 65 (1984).

104 *Korematsu v. United States*, 323 U.S. 214, 245–46 (1944) (Jackson, J., dissenting).

105 Id. at 246 (Jackson, J., dissenting).

106 Id. at 247 (Jackson, J., dissenting).

107 Tushnet, *supra* note 14.

108 Id. at 306.

109 Id. at 307.

110 Gross, *supra* note 14.

111 Id. at 1133.

112 Id. at 1023.

113 Id.

114 Id. at 1024.

115 Gross, *supra* note 14, at 1022, 1069–96.

116 Glenn E. Fuller, Note, "The National Emergency Dilemma: Balancing the Executive's Crisis Powers with the Need for Accountability," 52 S. Cal. L. Rev. 1453, 1453 (1979). When the Senate considered a balanced budget amendment in 1995, Senator Howell Heflin proposed a "national security" exception and implied that it would have been appropriately invoked some 200 times in the 220 years of the republic. See Theodore P. Seto, "Drafting a Federal Balanced Budget Amendment That Does What It Is Supposed to Do (and No More)," 106 Yale L.J. 1449, 1533 (1997).

117 Gross, *supra* note 14, at 1073.

118 Id. at 1074.

119 Tushnet concedes that the war on terrorism is more like a "condition" than an "emergency," but he does not explain how or even whether judges in his model would distinguish between the two. See Tushnet, *supra* note 14, at 297.

120 News Transcript, "Dept of Defense News Briefing: Secretary Rumsfeld and General Myers" (Mar. 28, 2002), available at http://www.defense link.mil/transcripts/2002/_t03282002_t0328sd.html.

121 Lynn Ludlow, "Paper Tigers," S.F. Chronicle, Nov. 4, 2001, at C2; Bob Woodward, "CIA Told to Do 'Whatever Necessary' to Kill Bin Laden;

Agency and Military Collobarating at 'Unprecedented' Level; Cheney Says War Against Terror 'May Never End,'" Wash. Post, Oct. 21, 2001, at A1.

122 The 1988 statute offering restitution and an apology to the victims of the Japanese internment program suggests that at some point the political process may repudiate prior emergency measures. But that is almost certainly the exception that proves the rule. It took forty years to achieve and came only *after* the federal courts had themselves repudiated the convictions arising from the exclusion and internment programs. See *supra* note 26. Had the political process been asked to ratify the internment at the time, or in the decade or so that followed it, there is *no* evidence to suggest the result would have been repudiation rather than ratification.

123 See Finn, *supra* note 54, at 9 (1991) ("Even public officials who propose action that is arguably extraconstitutional typically seek to justify their actions on constitutional grounds").

124 Cornelia T.L. Pillard, "Taking Fiction Seriously: The Strange Results of Public Officials' Individual Liability Under *Bivens*," 88 Geo. L.J. 65 (1999) (critiquing the breadth of immunity doctrines and noting that indemnification of government officials is nearly universal).

125 Gross, *supra* note 14, at 1035–42.

126 Cong. Globe, 42d Cong., 1st Sess. 574 (1871).

127 Cole, *Enemy Aliens, supra* note 12; David Cole, "Enemy Aliens," 54 Stan. L. Rev. 953 (2002); Gross, *supra* note 14, at 1037, 1082–85.

128 Tushnet, *supra* note 14, at 296–97 (arguing that the Justice Department's selective targeting of Arab and Muslim foreign nationals for questioning, secret detentions and trials, and selective deportation "does not seem to be a violation of civil liberties," and if so, are only "violations of the rights of residents who are not U.S. citizens"). In my view, these actions violated a wide range of constitutional rights, and the fact that they specifically affected foreign nationals, the most vulnerable and voiceless among us, only exacerbates the wrongs. See generally Cole, *Enemy Aliens, supra* note 12.

129 Francis Biddle, in *Brief Authority* (1962), 219.

130 *Alien Registration Act*, Pub. L. No. 76–670, 54 Stat. 670 (1940).

131 *Internal Security Act* of 1950, Pub. L. No. 81–831, 64 Stat. 987.

132 *Antiterrorism and Effective Death Penalty Act* of 1996, Pub. L. No. 104–132, 110 Stat. 1214.

133 *Uniting and Strengthening America by Providing Appropriate Tools Required to Intercept and Obstruct Terrorism* (USA Patriot) *Act* of 2001, Pub. L. No. 107–56, 115 Stat. 272.

134 See generally David Cole, "Secrecy, Guilt by Association, and the Terrorist Profile," 15 J.L. & Religion 267 (2000–2001).

135 *Antiterrorism and Effective Death Penalty Act* § 401 (codified at 8 USC § 1531 (2000)).

136 I am aware of only one exception. CBS's *60 Minutes* covered the story of the government's use of secret evidence to deny entry to a group of Iraqis who had been involved in a failed CIA–backed coup attempt against Saddam Hussein, had been airlifted out of Iraq by the United States, but had then been determined at the border to have been double agents based on classified evidence. *60 Minutes:* "Unfinished Business: Six Iraqis Brought to the United States by the US Government for Help Against Saddam Hussein Are Imprisoned on Undisclosed Charges by the INS" (CBS television broadcast, July 25, 1999). But it is likely that *60 Minutes'* interest in the story stemmed as much from the identity of the Iraqis' pro bono lawyer – former CIA Director James Woolsey – as from their predicament.

137 See, e.g., *American-Arab Anti-Discrimination Comm. v. Reno*, 70 F.3d 1045, 1070 (9th Cir. 1995); *Rafeedie v. INS*, 880 F.2d 506, 512–13, 516 (DC Cir. 1989); *Al Najjar v. Reno*, 97 F. Supp. 2d 1329, 1356 (SD Fla. 2000), *vacated on other grounds*, 273 F.3d 1330 (11th Cir. 2001); *Kiareldeen v. Reno*, 71 F. Supp. 2d 402 (DNJ 1999).

138 See Cole, *supra* note 134, at 272–75. The immigration judges' skepticism suggests that relief was sometimes available within the executive branch. But it is significant that the relief came only from *judges* within the executive branch.

139 Frederick Schauer, "May Officials Think Religiously," 27 Wm. & Mary L. Rev. 1075, 1084 n. 11 (1986).

140 Id. at 1085.

141 Eugene V. Rostow, "The Japanese American Cases – A Disaster," 54 Yale L.J. 489, 511, 514 (1945).

Public Commission Against Torture in Israel v. Government of Israel (1999)

Here the Israeli Supreme Court had to decide whether interrogations by the General Security Service which involved physical force of varying degrees and which were supposedly authorized by secret regulations were legal. These regulations had been put in place on the basis of an argument that has resurfaced after 9/11 in the United States. Those who put forward the argument say that they do not condone torture, but that it has to be recognized that torture will be used in extreme situations. They conclude that it is better that torture be regulated, rather than happen illegally in secret, since then it can be controlled. In addition, they usually argue that controlled torture is not really torture properly so called, but severe interrogation.

Supreme Court Decision on GSS Practices (September 6, 1999), Judgment

President A. Barak:

The General Security Service (hereinafter, the "GSS") investigates individuals suspected of committing crimes against Israel's security. Is the GSS authorized to conduct these interrogations? The interrogations are conducted on the basis of directives regulating interrogation methods. These directives equally authorize investigators to apply physical means against those undergoing interrogation (for instance, shaking the suspect and the "Shabach" position). The basis for permitting such methods is that they are deemed immediately necessary for saving human lives. Is the sanctioning of these interrogation practices legal? – These are the principal issues presented by the applicants before us.

BACKGROUND

1. The State of Israel has been engaged in an unceasing struggle for both its very existence and security, from the day of its founding. Terrorist organizations have established as their goal Israel's annihilation. Terrorist acts and the general disruption of order are their means of choice. In employing such methods, these groups do not distinguish between civilian and military targets. They carry out terrorist attacks in which scores are murdered in public areas, public transportation, city squares and centers, theaters and coffee shops. They do not distinguish between men, women and children. They act out of cruelty and without mercy. (For an in depth description of this phenomenon see the Report of the Commission of Inquiry Regarding the GSS' Interrogation Practices with Respect to Hostile Terrorist Activities headed by (ret.) Justice M. Landau, 1987 – hereinafter, "Commission of Inquiry Report," published in the Landau Book 269, 276 (Volume 1, 1995).)

The facts presented before this Court reveal that one hundred and twenty one people died in terrorist attacks between 1.1.96 to 14.5.98. Seven hundred and seven people were injured. A large number of those killed and injured were victims of harrowing suicide bombings in the heart of Israel's cities. Many attacks – including suicide bombings, attempts to detonate car bombs, kidnappings of citizens and soldiers, attempts to highjack buses, murders, the placing of explosives, etc. – were prevented due to the measures taken by the authorities responsible for fighting the above described hostile terrorist activities on a daily basis. The main body responsible for fighting terrorism is the GSS.

In order to fulfill this function, the GSS also investigates those suspected of hostile terrorist activities. The purpose of these interrogations is, among others, to gather information regarding terrorists and their organizing methods for the purpose of thwarting and preventing them from carrying out these terrorist attacks. In the context of these interrogations, GSS investigators also make use of physical means. The legality of these practices is being examined before this Court in these applications.

THE APPLICATIONS

2. These applications are entirely concerned with the GSS' interrogation methods. They outline several of these methods, in detail, before us. Two of the applications are of a public nature. One of these (H.C. 5100/94) is brought by the Public Committee Against Torture in Israel. It submits that GSS investigators are not authorized to investigate those suspected of hostile terrorist activities. Moreover, they claim that the GSS is not entitled to employ those pressure methods approved by the Commission of Inquiry's Report ("the application of non-violent psychological pressure" and the application of "a moderate degree of physical pressure"). The second application (hereafter 4054/95), is brought by the Association for Citizen's Rights in Israel (ACRI). It argues that the GSS should be instructed to refrain from shaking suspects during interrogations.

Five of the remaining applications involve specific applicants who turned to the Court individually. They each petitioned the Court to hold that the methods used against them by the GSS are illegal. Who are these applicants?

3. The applicants in H.C. 5188/96 (Wa'al Al Kaaqua and Ibrahim Ab-d'alla Ganimat) were arrested at the beginning of June 1996. They were interrogated by GSS investigators. They appealed to this Court (on 21-7-96) via the Center for the Defence of the Individual, founded by Dr. Lota Saltzberger. Their attorney petitioned the Court for an order nisi prohibiting the use of physical force against the applicants during their interrogation. The Court granted the order. The two applicants were released from custody prior to the hearing. As per their attorney's request, we have elected to continue hearing their case, in light of the importance of the issues they raise in principle.

4. The applicant in H.C. 6536/96 (Hat'm Abu Zayda), was arrested (on 21-9-95) and interrogated by GSS investigators. He turned to this Court (on 22-10-95) via of the Center for the Defence of the Individual, founded by Dr. Lota Saltzberger. His attorney complained about the interrogation methods allegedly used against his client (deprivation of sleep, shaking, beatings, and use of the "Shabach" position). We immediately instructed the application be heard. The Court was informed that the applicant's interrogation had ended (as of 19-10-95). The information provided to us indicates that the applicant in question was subsequently convicted of activities in the military branch of the Hamas terrorist organization. He was sentenced to seventy four months in prison. The convicting Court held that the applicant both recruited and constructed the Hamas' infrastructure, for the purpose of kidnapping Israeli soldiers and carrying out terrorist attacks against security forces. It has been argued before us that the information provided by the applicant during the course of his interrogation led to the thwarting of an actual plan to carry out serious terrorist attacks, including the kidnapping of soldiers.

5. The applicant in H.C. 7563/97 (Abd al Rahman Ismail Ganimat) was arrested (on 13-11-97) and interrogated by the GSS. He appealed to this Court (24-12-97) via the Public Committee Against Torture in Israel. He claimed to have been tortured by his investigators (through use of the "Shabach" position, excessive tightening of handcuffs and sleep deprivation). His interrogation revealed that he was involved in numerous terrorist activities in the course of which many Israeli citizens were killed. He was instrumental in the kidnapping and murder of IDF soldier (Sharon Edry, of blessed memory); additionally, he was involved in the bombing of the Cafe "Appropo" in Tel Aviv, in which three

women were murdered and thirty people were injured. He was charged with all these crimes and convicted at trial. He was sentenced to five consecutive life sentences plus an additional twenty years of prison.

A powerful explosive device, identical to the one detonated at Cafe "Appropo" in Tel Aviv, was found in the applicant's village (Tzurif) subsequent to the dismantling and interrogation of the terrorist cell to which he belonged. Uncovering this explosive device thwarted an attack similar to the one at Cafe "Appropo." According to GSS investigators, the applicant possessed additional crucial information which he only revealed as a result of their interrogation. Revealing this information immediately was essential to safeguarding state and regional security and preventing danger to human life.

6. The applicant in H.C. 7628/97 (Fouad Awad Quran) was arrested (on 10-12-97) and interrogated. He turned to this Court (on 25-12-97) via the Public Committee against Torture in Israel. Before the Court, he claimed that he was being deprived of sleep and was being seated in the "Shabach" position. The Court issued an order nisi and held an immediate hearing of the application. During the hearing, the State informed the Court that "at this stage of the interrogation the GSS is not employing the methods alleged by the applicant against him." For this reason, no interim order was granted.

7. The applicant in H.C.1043/99 (Issa Ali Batat) was arrested (on 22-2-99) and interrogated by GSS investigators. The application, brought via the Public Committee Against Torture in Israel, argued that physical force was used against the applicant during the course of the interrogation. The Court issued an order nisi. While hearing the application, it came to the Court's attention that the applicant's interrogation had ended and that he was being detained pending trial; the indictment alleges his involvement in hostile activities, the purpose of which was to harm the "area's" (Judea, Samaria and the Gaza strip) security and public safety.

THE PHYSICAL MEANS

8. The physical means employed by the GSS investigators were presented before this Court by the GSS investigators. The State's attorneys were prepared to present them for us behind closed doors (in camera). The applicants' attorneys were opposed to this proposal. Thus,

the information at the Court's disposal was provided by the applicants and was not tested in each individual application. This having been said, the State's position, which failed to deny the use of these interrogation methods, and even offered these and other explanations regarding the rationale justifying the use of an interrogation methods or another, provided the Court with a picture of the GSS' interrogation practices.

The decision to utilize physical means in a particular instance is based on internal regulations, which requires obtaining permission from various ranks of the GSS hierarchy. The regulations themselves were approved by a special Ministerial Committee on GSS interrogations. Among other guidelines, the Committee set forth directives pertaining to the rank authorized to allow these interrogation practices. These directives were not examined by this Court. Different interrogation methods are employed depending on the suspect, both in relation to what is required in that situation and to the likelihood of obtaining authorization. The GSS does not resort to every interrogation method at its disposal in each case.

Shaking

9. A number of applicants (H.C. 5100/94; H.C. 4054/95; H.C. 6536/95) claimed that the shaking method was used against them. Among the investigation methods outlined in the GSS' interrogation regulations, shaking is considered the harshest. The method is defined as the forceful shaking of the suspect's upper torso, back and forth, repeatedly, in a manner which causes the neck and head to dangle and vacillate rapidly. According to an expert opinion submitted in one of the applications (H.C. (motion) 5584/95 and H.C. 5100/95), the shaking method is likely to cause serious brain damage, harm the spinal cord, cause the suspect to lose consciousness, vomit and urinate uncontrollably and suffer serious headaches.

The State entered several countering expert opinions into evidence. It admits the use of this method by the GSS. To its contention, there is no danger to the life of the suspect inherent to shaking; the risk to life as a result of shaking is rare; there is no evidence that shaking causes fatal damage; and medical literature has not to date listed a case in which a person died directly as a result of having been only shaken. In any event, they argue, doctors are present in all interrogation compounds, and instances where the danger of medical damage presents itself are investigated and researched.

All agree that in one particular case (H.C. 4054/95) the suspect in question expired after being shaken. According to the State, that case constituted a rare exception. Death was caused by an extremely rare complication resulting in the atrophy of the neurogenic lung. In addition, the State argues in its response that the shaking method is only resorted to in very particular cases, and only as a last resort. The interrogation directives define the appropriate circumstances for its application and the rank responsible for authorizing its use. The investigators were instructed that in every case where they consider resorting to shaking, they must probe the severity of the danger that the interrogation is intending to prevent; consider the urgency of uncovering the information presumably possessed by the suspect in question; and seek an alternative means of preventing the danger. Finally, the directives respecting interrogation state, that in cases where this method is to be used, the investigator must first provide an evaluation of the suspect's health and ensure that no harm comes to him. According to the respondent, shaking is indispensable to fighting and winning the war on terrorism. It is not possible to prohibit its use without seriously harming the GSS' ability to effectively thwart deadly terrorist attacks. Its use in the past has lead to the thwarting of murderous attacks.

Waiting in the "Shabach" Position

10. This interrogation method arose in numerous applications (H.C. 6536/95, H.C. 5188/96, H.C. 7628/97). As per applicants' submission, a suspect investigated under the "Shabach" position has his hands tied behind his back. He is seated on a small and low chair, whose seat is tilted forward, towards the ground. One hand is tied behind the suspect, and placed inside the gap between the chair's seat and back support. His second hand is tied behind the chair, against its back support. The suspect's head is covered by an opaque sack, falling down to his shoulders. Powerfully loud music is played in the room. According to the affidavits submitted, suspects are detained in this position for a prolonged period of time, awaiting interrogation at consecutive intervals.

The aforementioned affidavits claim that prolonged sitting in this position causes serious muscle pain in the arms, the neck and headaches. The State did not deny the use of this method before this Court. They submit that both crucial security considerations and the investigators' safety require tying up the suspect's hands as he is being interrogated. The head covering is intended to prevent contact between the suspect in question and other suspects. The powerfully loud music is played for the same reason.

The "Frog Crouch"

11. This interrogation method appeared in one of the applications (H.C. 5188/96). According to the application and the attached corresponding affidavit, the suspect being interrogated was found in a "frog crouch" position. This refers to consecutive, periodical crouches on the tips of one's toes, each lasting for five minute intervals. The State did not deny the use of this method, thereby prompting the Court to issue an order nisi in the application where this method was alleged. Prior to hearing the application, however, this interrogation practice ceased.

Excessive Tightening of Handcuffs

12. In a number of applications before this Court (H.C. 5188/96; H.C. 7563/97), various applicants have complained of excessive tightening of hand or leg cuffs. To their contention, this practice results in serious injuries to the suspect's hands, arms and feet, due to the length of the interrogations. The applicants invoke the use of particularly small cuffs, ill fitted in relation to the suspect's arm or leg size. The State, for its part, denies any use of unusually small cuffs, arguing that those used were both of standard issue and properly applied. They are, nonetheless, prepared to admit that prolonged hand or foot cuffing is likely to cause injuries to the suspect's hands and feet. To the State's contention, however, injuries of this nature are inherent to any lengthy interrogation.

Sleep Deprivation

13. In a number of applications (H.C. 6536/96; H.C. 7563/97; H.C. 7628/97) applicants have complained of being deprived of sleep as a result of being tied in the "Shabach" position, being subjected to the playing of powerfully loud music, or intense non-stop interrogations without sufficient rest breaks. They claim that the purpose of depriving them of sleep is to cause them to break from exhaustion. While the State agrees that suspects are at times deprived of regular sleep hours, it argues that this does not constitute an interrogation method aimed at

causing exhaustion, but rather results from the prolonged amount of time necessary for conducting the interrogation.

APPLICANTS' ARGUMENTS

14. Before us lie a number of applications. Different applicants raise different arguments. In principle, all the applications raise two essential arguments: First, they submit that the GSS is never authorized to conduct interrogations. Second, they argue that the physical means employed by GSS investigators not only infringe upon the human dignity of the suspect undergoing interrogation, but in fact constitute criminal offences. These methods, argue the applicants, are in violation of International Law as they constitute "Torture," which is expressly prohibited under International Law. Thus, the GSS investigators are not authorized to conduct these interrogations. Furthermore, the "necessity" defence which, according to the State, is available to the investigators, is not relevant to the circumstances in question. In any event, the doctrine of "necessity" at most constitutes an exceptional post factum defence, exclusively confined to criminal proceedings against investigators. It cannot, however, by any means, provide GSS investigators with the preemptory authorization to conduct interrogations ab initio. GSS investigators are not authorized to employ any physical means, absent unequivocal authorization from the Legislator pertaining to the use of such methods and conforming to the requirements of the Basic Law: Human Dignity and Liberty. There is no purpose in engaging in a bureaucratic set up of the regulations and authority, as suggested by the Commission of Inquiry's Report, since doing so would merely regulate the torture of human beings.

We asked the applicants' attorneys whether the "ticking time bomb" rationale was not sufficiently persuasive to justify the use of physical means, for instance, when a bomb is known to have been placed in a public area and will undoubtedly explode causing immeasurable human tragedy if its location is not revealed at once. This question elicited a variety of responses from the various applicants before the Court. There are those convinced that physical means are not to be used under any circumstances; the prohibition on such methods to their mind is absolute, whatever the consequences may be. On the other hand, there are others who argue that even if it is perhaps acceptable to employ physical means in most exceptional "ticking time bomb" circumstances, these methods are in practice used even in absence of the "ticking time bomb" conditions. The very fact that, in most cases, the use of such means is illegal provides sufficient justification for banning their use altogether, even if doing so would inevitably absorb those rare cases in which physical coercion may have been justified. Whatever their particular views, all applicants unanimously highlight the distinction between the ability to potentially escape criminal liability post factum and the granting of permission to use physical means for interrogation purposes ab initio.

THE STATE'S ARGUMENTS

15. The position of the State is as follows: The GSS investigators are duly authorized to interrogate those suspected of committing crimes against Israel's security. This authority emanates from the government's general and residual (prerogative) powers (Article 40 of the Basic Law: the Government). Similarly, the authority to investigate is equally bestowed upon every individual investigator by virtue of article 2(1) of the Criminal Procedure Statute (Testimony) and the relevant accessory powers. With respect to the physical means employed by the GSS, the State argues that these do not violate International Law. Indeed, it is submitted that these methods cannot be qualified as "torture," "cruel and inhuman treatment" or "degrading treatment," [which] are strictly prohibited under International Law. Instead, the practices of the GSS do not cause pain and suffering, according to the State's position.

Moreover, the State argues that these means are equally legal under Israel's internal (domestic) law. This is due to the "necessity" defence outlined in article 34(11) of the Penal Law (1977). Hence, in the specific cases bearing the relevant conditions inherent to the "necessity" defence, GSS investigators are entitled to use "moderate physical pressure" as a last resort in order to prevent real injury to human life and well being. Such "moderate physical pressure" may include shaking, as the "necessity" defence provides in specific instances. Resorting to such means is legal, and does not constitute a criminal offence. In any case, if a specific method is not deemed to be a criminal offence, there is no reason not to employ it even for interrogation purposes. As per the State's submission, there is no reason for prohibiting a particular act, in specific circumstances, ab initio if it does not constitute a crime. This is particularly true with respect to the GSS investigators' case, who, according to the State, are after all responsible for the protection of lives and public safety. In support of their position, the State notes that the use of physical means by GSS investigators is most unusual and is only employed as a last resort in very extreme cases. Moreover, even in these rare cases, the application of such methods is subject to the strictest of scrutiny and supervision, as per the conditions and restrictions set forth in the Commission of Inquiry's Report. This having been said, when the exceptional conditions requiring the use of these means are in fact present, the above described interrogation methods are fundamental to saving human lives and safeguarding Israel's security.

THE COMMISSION OF INQUIRY'S REPORT

16. The GSS' authority to employ particular interrogation methods, and the relevant law respecting these matters were examined by the Commission of Inquiry (whose report was published, as mentioned, in the Landau Book (1995) Volume 1 at 269). The Commission, appointed by the government by virtue of the Commission of Inquiry Statute (1968), considered the GSS' legal status [among other issues]. Following a prolonged deliberation, the Commission concluded that the GSS is authorized to investigate those suspected of hostile terrorist acts, even in absence of express statutory regulation of its activities, in light of the powers granted to it by specific legislation and the government's residual (prerogative) powers, outlined in the Basic Law: the Government (article 29 of the old statute and article 40 of the new version). In addition, the power to investigate suspects, granted to investigators by the Minister of Justice as per article 2(1) of the Statute of Criminal Procedure [Testimony], equally endows the GSS with the authority to investigate (*supra*, p. 301 and following). Another part of the Commission of Inquiry's Report deals with "the investigator's potential defences" (defences available to the investigator). With regards to this matter, the Commission concluded that in cases where the saving of human lives necessarily requires obtaining certain information, the investigator is entitled to apply both psychological pressure and "a moderate degree of physical pressure" (*supra*, at 328). Thus, an investigator who, in the face of such danger, applies that specific degree of physical pressure, which does not constitute abuse or torture of the suspect, but is instead proportional to the danger to human life, can avail himself of the "necessity" defence, in the face of potential criminal liability. The Commission was convinced that its conclusions to this effect were not in conflict with International Law, but instead reflect an

approach consistent with both the Rule of Law and the need to effectively safeguard the security of Israel and its citizens.

The Commission approved the use of "a moderate degree of physical pressure" with various stringent conditions including directives that were set out in the second (and secret) part of the Report, and for the supervision of various elements both internal and external to the GSS. The Commission's recommendations were duly approved by the government.

THE APPLICATIONS

17. A number of applications dealing with the application of physical force by the GSS for interrogation purposes have made their way to this Court throughout the years (See, for example, H.C. 7964/95 *Billbissi v. The GSS* (unpublished); H.C. 8049/96 *Hamdan v. The GSS* (unpublished); H.C. 3123/94 *Atun v. The Head of the GSS* (unpublished); H.C. 3029/95 *Arquan v. The GSS* (unpublished); H.C. 5578/95 *Hajazi v. The GSS* (unpublished)). An immediate hearing was ordered in each of these cases. In most, the State declared that the GSS does not employ physical means. As a result, the applicants requested to withdraw their applications. The Court accepted these motions and informed the applicants of their right to set forth a complaint if physical means were or are in fact being used against them (see H.C. 3029/95 *supra*.). Only in a minority of complaints did the State not issue the above mentioned notice. In other instances, an interim order was issued. At times, the Court noted that, "we (the Court) did not receive any information regarding the interrogation methods which the respondent (generally the GSS) seeks to employ and we did not take any position with respect to these methods" (see H.C. 8049/96 *Hamdan v. The GSS* (unpublished). In a different case, the Court noted that, "[T]he annulment of the interim order does not in any way constitute permission to employ methods that do not conform to the law and binding directives" (In H.C. 336/96; In H.C. 7954/95 *Billbissi v. The GSS* (unpublished)).

Until now, therefore, the Court did not actually decide the issue of whether the GSS is permitted to employ physical means for interrogation purposes in circumstances outlined by the defence of "necessity." Essentially, we did not do so due to the fact that it was not possible for the Court to hear the sort of arguments that would provide a complete normative picture, in all its complexity. At this time, by contrast, a number of applications before us have properly laid out (both orally and in writing) complete arguments from the sides' respective attorneys. For this we thank them.

Although the various applications are somewhat distinct in that some are rather general or theoretical while others are quite specific, we have decided to deal with them, since above all we seek to clarify (uncover) the state of the law in this most complicated question. To this end, we shall begin by addressing the first issue – namely, are GSS investigators generally authorized to conduct interrogations. We shall then proceed to examine whether a general power to investigate would potentially sanction the use of physical means – including mental suffering – the likes of which the GSS employs. Finally, we shall probe the circumstances under which the above mentioned methods are immediately necessary to rescue human lives and whether these circumstances justify endowing GSS investigators with the authority to employ physical interrogation methods.

THE AUTHORITY TO INTERROGATE

18. The term "interrogation" takes on various meanings in different contexts. For the purposes of the applications before the Court at present, we refer to the asking of questions which seek to elicit a truthful answer (subject to the limitations respecting the privilege against self-incrimination; see article 2 of the Criminal Procedure Statute [Testimony]). Generally, the investigation of a suspect is conducted at the suspect's place of detention. An interrogation inevitably infringes upon the suspect's freedom, even if physical means are not used. Indeed, undergoing an interrogation infringes on both the suspect's dignity and his individual privacy. In a state adhering to the Rule of Law, interrogations are therefore not permitted in absence of clear statutory authorization, be it through primary legislation or secondary legislation, the latter being explicitly rooted in the former. This essential principle is expressed by the Legislator in the Criminal Procedure Statute (Powers of Enforcement – Detention – 1996) which states as follows:

Detentions and arrests shall be conducted only by law or by virtue of express statutory authorization for this purpose (article 1(a)). Hence, the statute and regulations must adhere to the requirements of the Basic Law: Human Dignity and Liberty (see article 8 of the Basic Law). The same principle applies to interrogations. Thus, an administrative body, seeking to interrogate an individual – an interrogation being defined as an exercise seeking to elicit truthful answers, as opposed to the mere asking of questions as in the context of an ordinary conversation – must point to the explicit statutory provision which legally empowers it. This is required by the Rule of Law (both formally and substantively). Moreover, this is required by the principle of administrative legality.

If an authority (government body) cannot point to a statute from which it derives its authority to engage in certain acts, that act is ultra vires (beyond its competence) and illegal. (See I. Zamir, Administrative Authority (1996) at 50; see also B. Bracha, Administrative Law (Vol. 1, 1987) at 25.)

19. Does a statute, authorizing GSS investigators to carry out interrogations (as we defined this term above) exist? A specific instruction, dealing with GSS agents, in their investigating capacity was not found. "The Service's status, its function and powers are not in fact outlined in any statute addressing this matter" (Commission of Inquiry's Report, *supra*, at 302). This having been said, the GSS constitutes an integral part of the executive branch. The fact that the GSS forms part of the executive branch is not in itself sufficient to invest it with the authority to interrogate. It is true that the government does possess residual or prerogative powers, defined as follows:

The Government is authorized to perform in the name of the State and subject to any law, all actions which are not legally incumbent on another authority. (Article 40, Basic Law: The Government)

However, we are not to conclude from this provision the authority to investigate, for our purposes. As mentioned, the power to investigate infringes on a person's individual liberty. The government's residual (prerogative) powers authorize it to act whenever there is an "administrative vacuum" (see H.C. 2918/93 *The City of Kiryat Gatt v. The State of Israel and others*, 37(5) P.D. 832 at 843).

A so called "administrative vacuum" of this nature does not appear in the case at bar, as the relevant field is entirely occupied by the principle of individual freedom. Infringing upon this liberty therefore requires specific directives, as insisted upon by President Shamgar:

There are activities which do not fall within the government's powers or scope. Employing them, absent statutory authorization, runs contrary to our most basic normative understanding, an understanding which emanates from our system's very [democratic] character. Thus, it is respecting basic rights that forms part of our positive law, whether they have been spelled out in a Basic Law or whether this has yet to be done. Thus, the government is not endowed with the capacity to, for example, shut down a newspaper on the basis of an administrative decision, absent explicit statutory authorization to this effect, irrespective of whether a Basic Law expressly protects freedom of expression; an act of this sort would undoubtedly run contrary to our basic understanding regarding human liberty and the [democratic] nature of our regime, which provides that liberty may only be infringed upon by virtue of explicit statutory authorization ... Hence, freedom of expression, a basic right, forms an integral part of our positive law, creates an exception binding the executive (branch) and does not allow it to stray from the prohibition respecting guaranteed human liberty, absent statutory authorization. (In H.C. 5128/94 *Federman v. The Minister of Police*, 48(5) P.D. 647 at 652.)

In a similar vein, Professor Zamir has noted:

While allowing the government to act, article 40 of the Basic Law: The Government (article 29 to the old Basic Law) simultaneously subjects it to the law. Clearly, this exception precludes the government from acting in a manner contrary to statutory directives. Moreover, it prevents the government from infringing upon individuals' basic rights. This is of course all the more true respecting specific rights protected explicitly by the Basic Laws Human Dignity and Liberty and Freedom of Occupation. Notwithstanding, this is also the case for human rights not specifically enumerated in the Basic Laws. For instance, article 29 (now article 40) does not in any way authorize the government to limit freedom of expression ... Indeed, article 29 (now 40) merely endows the administrative authority with general executive powers that cannot serve to directly infringe upon human rights, unless there is explicit or implicit statutory authorization for doing so. (I. Zamir, Administrative Authority (vol. 1, 1996) at 337).

This is the law relevant to the case at bar. An individual's liberty is not to be the object of an interrogation – this is a basic liberty under our constitutional regime. There are to be no infringements on this liberty absent statutory provisions which successfully pass constitutional muster. The government's general administrative powers fail to fulfill these requirements. Indeed, when the Legislator sought to endow the GSS with the power to infringe upon a person's individual liberty, he proceeded to legislate specific provisions accordingly. Thus, for instance, it is stipulated that the head of a security service, under special circumstances, is authorized to allow for the secret monitoring of telephone conversations (see article 5 of the Secret Interception of Communication Statute –1979; compare article 19(3)(4) of the Protection of Privacy Statute – 1981). This requires that the following question be asked: Does there exist a special statutory instruction endowing GSS investigators with interrogating powers?

20. A specific statutory provision authorizing GSS investigators to conduct interrogations does not exist. While it is true that various interrogation directives, some with ministerial approval, followed the Commission of Inquiry's Report, these do not satisfy the requirement that the authority flow directly from statute or from explicit statutory authorization. The directives set out following the Inquiry Commission's Report merely constitute internal regulations. Addressing these directives, Justice Levin opined:

Clearly, these directives are not to be understood as being tantamount to a "statute," as defined in article 8 of the Basic Law: Human Dignity. They are to therefore be struck down if they are found not to conform to it. (H.C. 2581/91 *Salhat v. The State of Israel*, 47(4) P.D. 837, at 845).

From where then, do the GSS investigators derive their interrogation powers? The answer is found in article 2(1) of the Criminal Procedure Statute [Testimony] which provides (in its 1944 version, as amended):

A police officer, of or above the rank of inspector, or any other officer or class of officers generally or specially authorized in writing by the Chief Secretary to the Government, to hold enquiries into the commission of offences, may examine orally any person supposed to be acquainted with the facts and circumstances of any offence in respect whereof such officer or police or other authorized officer as aforesaid is enquiring, and may reduce into writing any statement by a person so examined.

It is by virtue of the above provision that the Minister of Justice particularly authorized the GSS investigators to conduct interrogations regarding the commission of hostile terrorist activities. It has been brought to the Court's attention that in the authorizing decree, the Minister of Justice took care to list the names of those GSS investigators who were authorized to conduct secret interrogations with respect to crimes committed under the Penal Law – 1977, the Prevention of Terrorism Statute – 1948, the (Emergency) Defence Regulations – 1945, The Prevention of Infiltration Statute (Crimes and Judging) – 1954, and crimes which are to be investigated as per the Emergency Defence Regulations (Judea, Samaria and the Gaza strip – Judging in Crimes and Judicial Assistance – 1967). It appears to us – and we have heard no arguments to the contrary – that the question of the GSS' authority to conduct interrogations can thus be resolved. By virtue of this authorization, GSS investigators are tantamount to police officers in the eyes of the law. If this solution is appropriate, is there not place for regulating the GSS investigators' powers by statute? We shall express an opinion on the matter at this time.

THE MEANS EMPLOYED FOR INTERROGATION PURPOSES

21. As we have seen, the GSS investigators are endowed with the authority to conduct interrogations (see par. 20, supra). What is the scope of these powers and do they encompass the use of physical means in the course of the interrogation in order to advance it? Can use be made of the physical means presently employed by GSS investigators (such as shaking, the "Shabach" position, and sleep deprivation) by virtue of the investigating powers given the GSS investigators? Let us note that the State did not argue before us that all the means employed by GSS investigators are permissible by virtue of the "law of interrogation" per se. Thus, for instance, the State did not make the argument that shaking is permitted simply because it is an "ordinary" investigator's method in Israel. Notwithstanding, it was argued before this Court that some of the physical means employed by the GSS investigators are permitted by the "law of interrogation" itself. For instance, this is the case with respect to some of the physical means applied in the context of waiting in the "Shabach" position: the placing of the head covering (for preventing communication between the suspects); the playing of powerfully loud music (to prevent the passing of information between suspects); the tying of the suspect's hands to a chair (for the investigators' protection) and the deprivation of sleep, as deriving from the needs of the interrogation. Does the "law of interrogation" sanction the use of physical means, the like used in GSS interrogations?

22. An interrogation, by its very nature, places the suspect in a difficult position. "The criminal's interrogation," wrote Justice Vitkon over

twenty years ago, "is not a negotiation process between two open and fair vendors, conducting their business on the basis of maximum mutual trust" (Cr. A 216/74 *Cohen v. The State of Israel*) 29(1) P.D. 340 at 352). An interrogation is a "competition of minds," in which the investigator attempts to penetrate the suspect's thoughts and elicit from him the information the investigator seeks to obtain. Quite accurately, it was noted that:

Any interrogation, be it the fairest and most reasonable of all, inevitably places the suspect in embarrassing situations, burdens him, intrudes his conscience, penetrates the deepest crevices of his soul, while creating serious emotional pressure. (Y. Kedmi, On Evidence, Part A, 1991, at 25)

Indeed, the authority to conduct interrogations, like any administrative power, is designed for a specific purpose, which constitutes its foundation, and must be in conformity with the basic principles of the [democratic] regime. In crystallizing the interrogation rules, two values or interests clash. On the one hand, lies the desire to uncover the truth, thereby fulfilling the public interest in exposing crime and preventing it. On the other hand, is the wish to protect the dignity and liberty of the individual being interrogated. This having been said, these interests and values are not absolute. A democratic, freedom-loving society does not accept that investigators use any means for the purpose of uncovering the truth. "The interrogation practices of the police in a given regime," noted Justice Landau, "are indicative of a regime's very character" (Cr. A. 264/65 *Artzi v. The Government's Legal Advisor*, 20(1) P.D. 225 at 232). At times, the price of truth is so high that a democratic society is not prepared to pay it (see Barak, On Law, Judging and Truth, 27 Mishpatim (1997) 11 at 13). To the same extent however, a democratic society, desirous of liberty seeks to fight crime and to that end is prepared to accept that an interrogation may infringe upon the human dignity and liberty of a suspect provided it is done for a proper purpose and that the harm does not exceed that which is necessary. Concerning the collision of values, with respect to the use of evidence obtained in a violent police interrogation, Justice H. Cohen opined as follows:

On the one hand, it is our duty to ensure that human dignity be protected; that it not be harmed at the hands of those who abuse it, and to do all that we can to restrain police investigators from fulfilling the object of their interrogation through prohibited and criminal means; on the other hand, it is (also) our duty to fight the increasingly growing crime rate which destroys the positive aspects of our country, and to prevent the disruption of public peace to the caprices of violent criminals that were beaten by police investigators. (Cr. A. 183/78 *Abu Midjim v. The State of Israel*, 34(4) P.D. 533 at 546)

Our concern, therefore, lies in the clash of values and the balancing of conflicting values. The balancing process results in the rules for a "reasonable interrogation" (see Bein, The Police Investigation – Is There Room for Codification of the "Laws of the Hunt," 12 Iyunei Mishpat (1987) 129). These rules are based, on the one hand, on preserving the "human image" of the suspect (see Cr. A. 115/82 *Mouadi v. The State of Israel*, 35(1) P.D. 197 at 222–4) and on preserving the "purity of arms" used during the interrogation (Cr. A. 183/78, *supra*, ibid.). On the other hand, these rules take into consideration the need to fight the phenomenon of criminality in an effective manner generally, and terrorist attacks specifically. These rules reflect "a degree of reasonableness, straight thinking (right mindedness) and fairness" (Kedmi, *supra*, at 25). The rules pertaining to investigations are important to a democratic state. They reflect its character. An illegal investigation harms the suspect's human dignity. It equally harms society's fabric.

23. It is not necessary for us to engage in an in-depth inquiry into the "law of interrogation" for the purposes of the applications before us. These vary from one matter to the next. For instance, the law of interrogation differs as it appears in the context of an investigator's potential criminal liability, as opposed to the purpose of admitting evidence obtained by questionable means. Here, by contrast, we deal with the "law of interrogation" as a power activated by an administrative authority (see Bein *supra*.). The "law of interrogation" by its very nature, is intrinsically linked to the circumstances of each case. This having been said, a number of general principles are nonetheless worth noting: First, a reasonable investigation is necessarily one free of torture, free of cruel, inhuman treatment of the subject and free of any degrading handling whatsoever. There is a prohibition on the use of "brutal or inhuman means" in the course of an investigation (F.H. 3081/91 *Kozli v. The State of Israel*, 35(4) P.D. 441 at 446). Human dignity also includes the dignity of the suspect being interrogated (compare H.C. 355/59 *Catlan v. Prison Security Services*, 34(3) P.D. 293 at 298 and C.A. 4463/94 *Golan v. Prison Security Services*, 50(4) P.D. 136). This conclusion is in

perfect accord with (various) International Law treaties – to which Israel is a signatory – which prohibit the use of torture, "cruel, inhuman treatment" and "degrading treatment" (see M. Evans and R. Morgan, Preventing Torture (1998) at 61; N.S. Rodley, The Treatment of Prisoners under International Law (1987) at 63). These prohibitions are "absolute." There are no exceptions to them and there is no room for balancing. Indeed, violence directed at a suspect's body or spirit does not constitute a reasonable investigation practice. The use of violence during investigations can potentially lead to the investigator being held criminally liable (see, for example, article 277 of the Penal Law: Pressure on a Public Servant; *supra* at 130, 134; Cr. A. 64/86 *Ashash v. The State of Israel* (unpublished)). Second, a reasonable investigation is likely to cause discomfort; it may result in insufficient sleep; the conditions under which it is conducted risk being unpleasant. Indeed, it is possible to conduct an effective investigation without resorting to violence. Within the confines of the law, it is permitted to resort to various machinations and specific sophisticated activities which serve investigators today (both for Police and GSS); similar investigations – accepted in the most progressive of societies – can be effective in achieving their goals. In the end result, the legality of an investigation is deduced from the propriety of its purpose and from its methods. Thus, for instance, sleep deprivation for a prolonged period, or sleep deprivation at night when this is not necessary to the investigation time wise may be deemed a use of an investigation method which surpasses the least restrictive means.

FROM THE GENERAL TO THE PARTICULAR

24. We shall now turn from the general to the particular. Plainly put, shaking is a prohibited investigation method. It harms the suspect's body. It violates his dignity. It is a violent method which does not form part of a legal investigation. It surpasses that which is necessary. Even the State did not argue that shaking is an "ordinary" investigation method which every investigator (in the GSS or police) is permitted to employ. The submission before us was that the justification for shaking is found in the "necessity" defence. That argument shall be dealt with below. In any event, there is no doubt that shaking is not to be resorted to in cases outside the bounds of "necessity" or as part of an "ordinary" investigation.

25. It was argued before the Court that one of the investigation methods employed consists of the suspect crouching on the tips of his toes for

five minute intervals. The State did not deny this practice. This is a prohibited investigation method. It does not serve any purpose inherent to an investigation. It is degrading and infringes upon an individual's human dignity.

26. The "Shabach" method is composed of a number of cumulative components: the cuffing of the suspect, seating him on a low chair, covering his head with an opaque sack (head covering) and playing powerfully loud music in the area. Are any of the above acts encompassed by the general power to investigate? Our point of departure is that there are actions which are inherent to the investigation power (compare C.A. 4463/94, *supra*, ibid.). Therefore, we accept that the suspect's cuffing, for the purpose of preserving the investigators' safety, is an action included in the general power to investigate (compare H.C. 8124/96 *Mubarak v. The GSS* (unpublished)). Provided the suspect is cuffed for this purpose, it is within the investigator's authority to cuff him. The State's position is that the suspects are indeed cuffed with the intention of ensuring the investigators' safety or to prevent fleeing from legal custody. Even the applicants agree that it is permissible to cuff a suspect in similar circumstances and that cuffing constitutes an integral part of an interrogation. Notwithstanding, the cuffing associated with the "Shabach" position is unlike routine cuffing. The suspect is cuffed with his hands tied behind his back. One hand is placed inside the gap between the chair's seat and back support, while the other is tied behind him, against the chair's back support. This is a distorted and unnatural position. The investigators' safety does not require it. Similarly, there is no relevant justification for handcuffing the suspect's hands with particularly small handcuffs, if this is in fact the practice. The use of these methods is prohibited. As was noted, "Cuffing causing pain is prohibited" (see the Mubarak affair *supra*). Moreover, there are other ways of preventing the suspect from fleeing from legal custody which do not involve causing the suspect pain and suffering.

27. This is the law with respect to the method involving seating the suspect in question in the "Shabach" position. We accept that seating a man is inherent to the investigation. This is not the case when the chair upon which he is seated is a very low one, tilted forward facing the ground, and when he is sitting in this position for long hours. This sort of seating is not encompassed by the general power to interrogate. Even if we suppose that the seating of the suspect on a chair lower than that of his investigator can potentially serve a legitimate investigation

objective (for instance, to establish the "rules of the game" in the contest of wills between the parties, or to emphasize the investigator's superiority over the suspect), there is no inherent investigative need for seating the suspect on a chair so low and tilted forward towards the ground, in a manner that causes him real pain and suffering. Clearly, the general power to conduct interrogations does not authorize seating a suspect on a forward tilting chair, in a manner that applies pressure and causes pain to his back, all the more so when his hands are tied behind the chair, in the manner described. All these methods do not fall within the sphere of a "fair" interrogation. They are not reasonable. They impinge upon the suspect's dignity, his bodily integrity and his basic rights in an excessive manner (or beyond what is necessary). They are not to be deemed as included within the general power to conduct interrogations.

28. We accept that there are interrogation related considerations concerned with preventing contact between the suspect under interrogation and other suspects and his investigators, which require means capable of preventing the said contact. The need to prevent contact may, for instance, flow from the need to safeguard the investigators' security, or that of the suspects and witnesses. It can also be part of the "mind game" which pits the information possessed by the suspect, against that found in the hands of his investigators. For this purpose, the power to interrogate – in principle and according to the circumstances of each particular case – includes preventing eye contact with a given person or place. In the case at bar, this was the explanation provided by the State for covering the suspect's head with an opaque sack, while he is seated in the "Shabach" position. From what was stated in the declarations before us, the suspect's head is covered with an opaque sack throughout his "wait" in the "Shabach" position. It was argued that the sack (head covering) is entirely opaque, causing the suspect to suffocate. The edges of the sack are long, reaching the suspect's shoulders. All these methods are not inherent to an interrogation. They do not confirm the State's position, arguing that they are meant to prevent eye contact between the suspect being interrogated and other suspects. Indeed, even if such contact should be prevented, what is the purpose of causing the suspect to suffocate? Employing this method is not connected to the purpose of preventing the said contact and is consequently forbidden. Moreover, the statements clearly reveal that the suspect's head remains covered for several hours, throughout his wait. For these purposes, less harmful means must be employed, such as letting the suspect wait in a detention

cell. Doing so will eliminate any need to cover the suspect's eyes. In the alternative, the suspect's eyes may be covered in a manner that does not cause him physical suffering. For it appears that at present, the suspect's head covering – which covers his entire head, rather than eyes alone – for a prolonged period of time, with no essential link to the goal of preventing contact between the suspects under investigation, is not part of a fair interrogation. It harms the suspect and his (human) image. It degrades him. It causes him to lose sight of time and place. It suffocates him. All these things are not included in the general authority to investigate. In the cases before us, the State declared that it will make an effort to find a "ventilated" sack. This is not sufficient. The covering of the head in the circumstances described, as distinguished from the covering of the eyes, is outside the scope of authority and is prohibited.

29. Cutting off the suspect from his surroundings can also include preventing him from listening to what is going on around him. We are prepared to assume that the authority to investigate an individual equally encompasses precluding him from hearing other suspects under investigation or voices and sounds that, if heard by the suspect, risk impeding the interrogation's success. Whether the means employed fall within the scope of a fair and reasonable interrogation warrant examination at this time. In the case at bar, the detainee is found in the "Shabach" position while listening to the consecutive playing of powerfully loud music. Do these methods fall within the scope or the general authority to conduct interrogations? Here too, the answer is in the negative. Being exposed to powerfully loud music for a long period of time causes the suspect suffering. Furthermore, the suspect is tied (in place) in an uncomfortable position with his head covered (all the while). The use of the "Shabach" method is prohibited. It does not fall within the scope of the authority to conduct a fair and effective interrogation. Powerfully loud music is a prohibited means for use in the context described before us.

30. To the above, we must add that the "Shabach" position includes all the outlined methods employed simultaneously. Their combination, in and of itself gives rise to particular pain and suffering. This is a harmful method, particularly when it is employed for a prolonged period of time. For these reasons, this method does not form part of the powers of interrogation. It is an unacceptable method. "The duty to safeguard the detainee's dignity includes his right not to be degraded and not to

be submitted to sub-human conditions in the course of his detention, of the sort likely to harm his health and potentially his dignity" (In Cr. A. 7223/95 *The State of Israel v. Rotenstein* (not yet published)).

A similar – though not identical – combination of interrogation methods were discussed in the case of *Ireland v. United Kingdom* (1978) 2 EHRR 25. In that case, the Court probed five interrogation methods used by England for the purpose of investigating detainees suspected of terrorist activities in Northern Ireland. The methods were as follows: protracted standing against the wall on the tip of one's toes; covering of the suspect's head throughout the detention (except during the actual interrogation); exposing the suspect to powerfully loud noise for a prolonged period and deprivation of sleep, food and drink. The Court held that these methods did not constitute "torture." However, since they treated the suspect in an "inhuman and degrading" manner, they were nonetheless prohibited.

31. The interrogation of a person is likely to be lengthy, due to the suspect's failure to cooperate or due to the information's complexity or in light of the imperative need to obtain information urgently and immediately (for instance, see the Mubarak affair, *supra*; H.C. 5318/95 *Hajazi v. GSS* (unpublished)). Indeed, a person undergoing interrogation cannot sleep as does one who is not being interrogated. The suspect, subject to the investigators' questions for a prolonged period of time, is at times exhausted. This is often the inevitable result of an interrogation, or one of its side effects. This is part of the "discomfort" inherent to an interrogation. This being the case, depriving the suspect of sleep is, in our opinion, included in the general authority of the investigator (compare H.C. 3429/94 *Shbana v. GSS* (unpublished)). So noted Justice Shamgar, in a similar instance:

The interrogation of crimes and in particular, murder or other serious crimes – cannot be accomplished within the confines of an ordinary public servant's work day ... The investigation of crime is essentially a game of mental resistance ... For this reason, the interrogation is often carried out at consecutive intervals. This, as noted, causes the investigation to drag on ... and requires diligent insistence on its momentum and consecutiveness. (Cr. A. 485/76 *Ben Loulou v. The State of Israel* (unpublished))

The above described situation is different from those in which sleep deprivation shifts from being a "side effect" inherent to the interrogation, to an end in itself. If the suspect is intentionally deprived of sleep for a prolonged period of time, for the purpose of tiring him out or "breaking" him – it shall not fall within the scope of a fair and reasonable investigation. Such means harm the rights and dignity of the suspect in a manner surpassing that which is required.

32. All that was stated regarding the limitations pertinent to an interrogation, flowing from the requirement that an interrogation be fair and reasonable, is the accepted law with respect to a regular police interrogation. The power to interrogate given to the GSS investigator by law is the same interrogation powers the law bestows upon the ordinary police force investigator. It appears that the restrictions applicable to the police investigations are equally applicable to GSS investigations. There is no statutory instruction endowing a GSS investigator with special interrogating powers that are either different or more serious than those given the police investigator. From this we conclude that a GSS investigator, whose duty is to conduct the interrogation according to the law, is subject to the same restrictions applicable to a police interrogation.

PHYSICAL MEANS AND THE "NECESSITY" DEFENCE

33. We have arrived at the conclusion that the GSS personnel who have received permission to conduct interrogations (as per the Criminal Procedure Statute [Testimony]) are authorized to do so. This authority – like that of the police investigator – does not include most of the physical means of interrogation which are the subject of the application before us. Can the authority to employ these interrogation methods be anchored in a legal source beyond the authority to conduct an interrogation? This question was answered by the State's attorneys in the affirmative. As noted, an explicit authorization permitting GSS to employ physical means is not to be found in our law. An authorization of this nature can, in the State's opinion, be obtained in specific cases by virtue of the criminal law defense of "necessity," prescribed in the Penal Law. The language of the statute is as follows: (Article 34 (1)):

A person will not bear criminal liability for committing any act immediately necessary for the purpose of saving the life, liberty, body or property, of either himself or his fellow person, from substantial danger of serious harm, imminent from the particular state of things [circumstances], at the requisite timing, and absent alternative means for avoiding the harm.

The State's position is that by virtue of this "defence" to criminal liability, GSS investigators are also authorized to apply physical means, such as shaking, in the appropriate circumstances, in order to prevent serious harm to human life or body, in the absence of other alternatives. The State maintains that an act committed under conditions of "necessity" does not constitute a crime. Instead, it is deemed an act worth committing in such circumstances in order to prevent serious harm to a human life or body. We are therefore speaking of a deed that society has an interest in encouraging, as it is deemed proper in the circumstances. It is choosing the lesser evil. Not only is it legitimately permitted to engage in the fighting of terrorism, it is our moral duty to employ the necessary means for this purpose. This duty is particularly incumbent on the state authorities – and for our purposes, on the GSS investigators – who carry the burden of safeguarding the public peace. As this is the case, there is no obstacle preventing the investigators' superiors from instructing and guiding them with regard to when the conditions of the "necessity" defence are fulfilled and the proper boundaries in those circumstances. From this flows the legality of the directives with respect to the use of physical means in GSS interrogations. In the course of their argument, the State's attorneys submitted the "ticking time bomb" argument. A given suspect is arrested by the GSS. He holds information respecting the location of a bomb that was set and will imminently explode. There is no way to defuse the bomb without this information. If the information is obtained, however, the bomb may be defused. If the bomb is not defused, scores will be killed and maimed. Is a GSS investigator authorized to employ physical means in order to elicit information regarding the location of the bomb in such instances? The State's attorneys answer in the affirmative. The use of physical means shall not constitute a criminal offence, and their use is sanctioned, to the State's contention, by virtue of the "necessity" defence.

34. We are prepared to assume that – although this matter is open to debate (see A. Dershowitz, Is It Necessary to Apply "Physical Pressure" to Terrorists – And to Lie About It? [1989] 23 Israel L. Rev. 193; Bernsmann, Private Self-Defence and Necessity in German Penal Law and in the Penal Law Proposal – Some Remarks, [1998] 30 Israel L. Rev. 171, 208–10) – the "necessity" defence is open to all, particularly an investigator, acting in an organizational capacity of the State in interrogations of that nature. Likewise, we are prepared to accept –

although this matter is equally contentious – (see M. Kremnitzer, The Landau Commission Report – Was the Security Service Subordinated to the Law or the Law to the Needs of the Security Service? [1989] 23 Israel L. Rev. 216, 244–47) – that the "necessity" exception is likely to arise in instances of "ticking time bombs," and that the immediate need ("necessary in an immediate manner" for the preservation of human life) refers to the imminent nature of the act rather than that of the danger. Hence, the imminence criteria is satisfied even if the bomb is set to explode in a few days, or perhaps even after a few weeks, provided the danger is certain to materialize and there is no alternative means of preventing its materialization. In other words, there exists a concrete level of imminent danger of the explosion's occurrence (see Kremnitzer and Segev, The Application of Force in the Course of GSS Interrogations – A Lesser Evil? [1998] 4 Mishpat U' Mimshal 667 at 707; see also Feller, Not Actual "Necessity" but Possible "Justification"; Not "Moderate Pressure," but Either "Unlimited" or "None at All" [1989] 23 Israel L. Rev. 201, 207).

Consequently we are prepared to presume, as was held by the Inquiry Commission's Report, that if a GSS investigator – who applied physical interrogation methods for the purpose of saving human life – is criminally indicted, the "necessity" defence is likely to be open to him in the appropriate circumstances (see Cr. A. 532/91 *Anonymous v. The State of Israel* (unpublished)). A long list of arguments, from both the fields of Ethics and Political Science, may be raised for and against the use of the "necessity" defence (see Kremnitzer and Segev, *supra*, at 696; M.S. Moor, Torture and the Balance of Evils, [1989] 23 Israel L. Rev. 280; L. Shelf, The Lesser Evil and the Lesser Good – On the Landau Commission's Report, Terrorism and Torture, [1990] 1 Plilim 185; W.L. & P.E. Twining, Bentham on Torture, [1973] 24 Nothern Ireland Legal Quarterly 305; D. Stetman, The Question of Absolute Morality Regarding the Prohibition on Torture, [1997] 4 Mishpat U' Mimshal 161 at 175; A. Zuckerman, Coercion and the Judicial Ascertainment of Truth, [1989] 23 Israel L. Rev. 357). This matter, however, has already been decided under Israeli law. Israel's Penal Law recognizes the "necessity" defence.

35. Indeed, we are prepared to accept that in the appropriate circumstances, GSS investigators may avail themselves of the "necessity" defence, if criminally indicted. This however, is not the issue before this Court. We are not dealing with the potential criminal liability of a GSS investigator who employed physical interrogation methods in circum-

stances of "necessity." Moreover, we are not addressing the issue of admissibility or probative value of evidence obtained as a result of a GSS investigator's application of physical means against a suspect. We are dealing with a different question. The question before us is whether it is possible to infer the authority to, in advance, establish permanent directives setting out the physical interrogation means that may be used under conditions of "necessity." Moreover, we are asking whether the "necessity" defence constitutes a basis for the GSS investigator's authority to investigate, in the performance of his duty. According to the State, it is possible to imply from the "necessity" defence, available (post factum) to an investigator indicted of a criminal offence, an advance legal authorization endowing the investigator with the capacity to use physical interrogation methods. Is this position correct?

36. In the Court's opinion, a general authority to establish directives respecting the use of physical means during the course of a GSS interrogation cannot be implied from the "necessity" defence. The "necessity" defence does not constitute a source of authority, allowing GSS investigators to make use of physical means during the course of interrogations. The reasoning underlying our position is anchored in the nature of the "necessity" defence. This defence deals with deciding those cases involving an individual reacting to a given set of facts; it is an ad hoc endeavour, in reaction to a event. It is the result of an improvisation given the unpredictable character of the events (see Feller, ibid. at 209). Thus, the very nature of the defence does not allow it to serve as the source of a general administrative power. The administrative power is based on establishing general, forward looking criteria, as noted by Professor Enker:

Necessity is an after-the-fact judgment based on a narrow set of considerations in which we are concerned with the immediate consequences, not far-reaching and long-range consequences, on the basis of a clearly established order of priorities of both means and ultimate values ... The defence of necessity does not define a code of primary normative behaviour. Necessity is certainly not a basis for establishing a broad detailed code of behaviour such as how one should go about conducting intelligence interrogations in security matters, when one may or may not use force, how much force may be used and the like. (Enker, "The Use of Physical Force in Interrogations and the Necessity Defense," in Israel and International Human Rights Law: The Issue of Torture 61, 62 (1995))

In a similar vein, Kremnitzer and Segev note:

The basic rationale underlying the necessity defence is the absence of the possibility to establish accurate rules of behaviour in advance, appropriate in concrete emergency situations, whose circumstances are varied and unexpected. From this it follows, that the necessity defence is not well suited for regulation of a general situation, the circumstances of which are known and (often) repeat themselves. In similar cases, there is no reason for not setting the rules of behaviour in advance, in order that their content be determined in a thought out and well-planned manner, in advance, permitting them to apply in a uniform manner to all." (*supra*, at 705)

Moreover, the "necessity" defence has the effect of allowing one who acts under the circumstances of "necessity" to escape criminal liability. The "necessity" defence does not possess any additional normative value. In addition, it does not authorize the use of physical means for the purposes of allowing investigators to execute their duties in circumstances of necessity. The very fact that a particular act does not constitute a criminal act (due to the "necessity" defence) does not in itself authorize the administration to carry out this deed, and in doing so infringe upon human rights. The Rule of Law (both as a formal and substantive principle) requires that an infringement on a human right be prescribed by statute, authorizing the administration to this effect. The lifting of criminal responsibility does not imply authorization to infringe upon a human right. It shall be noted that the Commission of Inquiry did not hold that the "necessity" defence is the source of authority for employing physical means by GSS investigators during the course of their interrogations. All that the Commission of Inquiry determined is that if an investigator finds himself in a situation of "necessity," constraining him to choose the "lesser evil" – harming the suspect for the purpose of saving human lives – the "necessity" defence shall be available to him. Indeed, the Commission of Inquiry noted that, "the law itself must ensure a proper framework governing the [security] service's actions with respect to the interrogation of hostile terrorist activities and the related problems particular to it" (ibid. at 328).

37. In other words, general directives governing the use of physical means during interrogations must be rooted in an authorization prescribed by law and not from defences to criminal liability. The principle of "necessity" cannot serve as a basis of authority (see

Kremnitzer, ibid. at 236). If the State wishes to enable GSS investigators to utilize physical means in interrogations, they must seek the enactment of legislation for this purpose. This authorization would also free the investigator applying the physical means from criminal liability. This release would flow not from the "necessity" defence but from the "justification" defense which states: "A person shall not bear criminal liability for an act committed in one of the following cases:(1) He was obliged or authorized by law to commit it" (Article 34(13) of the Penal Law). The defence to criminal liability by virtue of the "justification" is rooted in an area outside of the criminal law. This "external" law serves as a defence to criminal liability. This defence does not rest upon the "necessity," which is "internal" to the Penal Law itself. Thus, for instance, where the question of when an officer is authorized to apply deadly force in the course of detention arises, the authority is found in a provision of the Law of Detention, external to the Penal Law. If a man is killed as a result of the application of force, the provision is likely to give rise to a defence, by virtue of the "Justification" (see Cr. A. 486/88, *Ankonina v. The Chief Army Prosecutor*, 34(2) P.D. 353). The "necessity" defence cannot constitute the basis for the determination of rules respecting the needs of an interrogation. It cannot constitute a source of authority on which the individual investigator can rely for the purpose of applying physical means in an investigation that he is conducting. The power to enact rules and to act according to them requires legislative authorization, by legislation whose object is the power to conduct interrogations. Within the boundaries of this legislation, the Legislator, if he so desires, may express his views on the social, ethical and political problems, connected to authorizing the use of physical means in an interrogation. These considerations did not, from the nature of things, arise before the Legislature at the time when the "necessity" defence was enacted (see Kremnitzer, *supra*, at 239–40). The "necessity" defence is not the appropriate place for laying out these considerations (see Enker, *supra*, at 72). Endowing GSS investigators with the authority to apply physical force during the interrogation of suspects suspected of involvement in hostile terrorist activities, thereby harming the latter's dignity and liberty, raise basic questions of law and society, of ethics and policy, and of the Rule of Law and security. These questions and the corresponding answers must be determined by the Legislative branch. This is required by the principle of the Separation of Powers and the Rule of Law, under our very understanding of democracy (see H.C. 3267/97 *Rubinstein v. Minister of Defence* (has yet to be published)).

38. Our conclusion is therefore the following: According to the existing state of the law, neither the government nor the heads of security services possess the authority to establish directives and bestow authorization regarding the use of liberty infringing physical means during the interrogation of suspects suspected of hostile terrorist activities, beyond the general directives which can be inferred from the very concept of an interrogation. Similarly, the individual GSS investigator – like any police officer – does not possess the authority to employ physical means which infringe upon a suspect's liberty during the interrogation, unless these means are inherently accessory to the very essence of an interrogation and are both fair and reasonable.

An investigator who insists on employing these methods, or does so routinely, is exceeding his authority. His responsibility shall be fixed according to law. His potential criminal liability shall be examined in the context of the "necessity" defence, and according to our assumptions (see paragraph 35 *supra*), the investigator may find refuge under the "necessity" defence's wings (so to speak), provided this defence's conditions are met by the circumstances of the case. Just as the existence of the "necessity" defence does not bestow authority, so too the lack of authority does not negate the applicability of the necessity defence or that of other defences from criminal liability. The Attorney General can instruct himself regarding the circumstances in which investigators shall not stand trial, if they claim to have acted from a feeling of "necessity." Clearly, a legal statutory provision is necessary for the purpose of authorizing the government to instruct in the use of physical means during the course of an interrogation, beyond what is permitted by the ordinary "law of investigation," and in order to provide the individual GSS investigator with the authority to employ these methods. The "necessity" defence cannot serve as a basis for this authority.

A FINAL WORD

39. This decision opens with a description of the difficult reality in which Israel finds herself security wise. We shall conclude this judgment by re-addressing that harsh reality. We are aware that this decision does not ease dealing with that reality. This is the destiny of democracy, as not all means are acceptable to it, and not all practices employed by its enemies are open before it. Although a democracy must often fight with one hand tied behind its back, it nonetheless has the upper hand. Preserving the Rule of Law and recognition of an individual's liberty

constitutes an important component in its understanding of security. At the end of the day, they strengthen its spirit and allow it to overcome its difficulties. This having been said, there are those who argue that Israel's security problems are too numerous, thereby requiring the authorization to use physical means. If it will nonetheless be decided that it is appropriate for Israel, in light of its security difficulties to sanction physical means in interrogations (and the scope of these means which deviate from the ordinary investigation rules), this is an issue that must be decided by the legislative branch which represents the people. We do not take any stand on this matter at this time. It is there that various considerations must be weighed. The pointed debate must occur there. It is there that the required legislation may be passed, provided, of course, that a law infringing upon a suspect's liberty "befit[s] the values of the State of Israel," is enacted for a proper purpose, and to an extent no greater than is required (Article 8 to the Basic Law: Human Dignity and Liberty).

40. Deciding these applications weighed heavily on this Court. True, from the legal perspective, the road before us is smooth. We are, however, part of Israeli society. Its problems are known to us and we live its history. We are not isolated in an ivory tower. We live the life of this country. We are aware of the harsh reality of terrorism in which we are, at times, immersed. Our apprehension is that this decision will hamper the ability to properly deal with terrorists and terrorism disturbs us. We are, however, judges. Our brethren require us to act according to the law. This is equally the standard that we set for ourselves. When we sit to judge, we are being judged. Therefore, we must act according to our purest conscience when we decide the law. The words of the Deputy President of the Supreme Court, Justice Landau, speak well to our purposes:

We possess proper sources upon which to construct our judgments and have no need, and while judging, are forbidden from, involving our personal views as citizens of this country in our decisions. Still, great is the fear that the Court shall be perceived as though it had abandoned its proper place and descended to the midst of public debate, and that its decision making will be obstructed by one side of the population's uproar and by the other side's absolute and emotional rejection. In that sense, I see myself here as someone whose duty is to decide according to the law in all cases legally brought before the Court. I am strictly bound by this duty. As I am well aware in advance that the public at large will not pay attention to the legal reasoning, but to the end result alone. And that the Court's proper status, as an institution above partisan debates, risks being harmed. What can we do, as this is our function and role as judges. (H.C. 390/79 *Dawikat v. The State of Israel*, 34(1) P.D. 1 at 4)

The Commission of Inquiry pointed to the "difficult dilemma between the imperative need to safeguard the State of Israel's very existence and the lives of its citizens, and preserving its character – that of a country subject to the Rule of Law and holding basic moral values" (*supra*, p. 326). The Commission rejected an approach suggesting that the actions of security services in the context of fighting terrorism, shall take place in the recesses of the law. The Commission equally rejected the "ways of the hypocrites, who remind us of their adherence to the Rule of Law, while ignoring (being willfully blind) to what is being done in practice" (ibid., at 327). The Commission elected to follow a third route, "the way of Truth and the Rule of Law" (ibid., at 328). In so doing, the Commission of Inquiry outlined the dilemma faced by Israel in a manner both transparent and open to inspection by Israeli society.

Consequently, it is decided that the order nisi be made absolute, as we declare that the GSS does not have the authority to "shake" a man, hold him in the "Shabach" position (which includes the combination of various methods, as mentioned in paragraph 30), force him into a "frog crouch" position and deprive him of sleep in a manner other than that which is inherently required by the interrogation. Likewise, we declare that the "necessity" defence, found in the Penal Law, cannot serve as a basis of authority for the use of these interrogation practices, or for the existence of directives pertaining to GSS investigators, allowing them to employ interrogation practices of this kind. Our decision does not negate the possibility that the "necessity" defence be available to GSS investigators, be within the discretion of the Attorney General, if he decides to prosecute, or if criminal charges are brought against them, as per the Court's discretion.

READING QUESTIONS ON THE TORTURE DECISION

1 Do you think that the Security Service stopped torturing because of the decision? If your answer is "no," how does this affect your evaluation of the decision?

2   One of the arguments put by the Security Service is that the regulations were valid because an official who tortures in order to
prevent a calamity can rely on the defence of necessity if he is
brought to trial. The Court rejected this argument, but seemed to
suggest that the legislature could enact a set of regulations based
on its interpretation of the elements of the defence of necessity.
One could interpret this suggestion as the Court's willingness to
uphold such regulations as long as they were authorized by the
legislature or as a kind of dare to the legislature that the Court
could safely bet the legislature would not take up. Which do you
think is the better interpretation? Note that Israel does not have an
entrenched bill of rights, but only a statute that protects rights, the
Basic Law. Does the Court's position provide another illustration
of the argument encountered in the last chapter that weak-form
judicial review is likely to turn into strong-form judicial review?

Hamdi v. Rumsfeld (2004)

Here the majority of the U.S. Supreme Court dismissed the government's
argument that the President had inherent constitutional authority – that is,
he did not have to have legislative authorization – to establish a class of
"enemy combatants" who could be detained without any check by an
independent tribunal to ensure that they were in fact enemy combatants.
However, Justice O'Connor for the plurality of the Court found that a
vaguely worded Congressional Resolution provided the authorization, and
the procedural safeguards she thought the detainees would be entitled to
seem rather meagre. Notice how Justices Souter and Ginsburg are concerned
about these aspects of the plurality's judgment, but concur in it because they
thought it was important that there be a majority opinion which rejected the
government's argument. Contrast the approach of the two most conservative judges on the court: Justice Scalia's approach is all or nothing – either
suspend habeas corpus by statute or let the detaineees have their full procedural rights – while Justice Thomas accepted the government's arguments.

Justice O'CONNOR announced the judgment of the Court and
delivered an opinion, in which THE CHIEF JUSTICE, Justice KEN-
NEDY, and Justice BREYER join:

At this difficult time in our Nation's history, we are called upon to consider the legality of the Government's detention of a United States citizen on United States soil as an "enemy combatant" and to address the process that is constitutionally owed to one who seeks to challenge his classification as such. The United States Court of Appeals for the Fourth Circuit held that petitioner's detention was legally authorized and that he was entitled to no further opportunity to challenge his enemy-combatant label. We now vacate and remand. We hold that although Congress authorized the detention of combatants in the narrow circumstances alleged here, due process demands that a citizen held in the United States as an enemy combatant be given a meaningful opportunity to contest the factual basis for that detention before a neutral decisionmaker.

I

On September 11, 2001, the al Qaeda terrorist network used hijacked commercial airliners to attack prominent targets in the United States. Approximately 3,000 people were killed in those attacks. One week later, in response to these "acts of treacherous violence," Congress passed a resolution authorizing the President to "use all necessary and appropriate force against those nations, organizations, or persons he determines planned, authorized, committed, or aided the terrorist attacks" or "harbored such organizations or persons, in order to prevent any future acts of international terrorism against the United States by such nations, organizations or persons." Authorization for Use of Military Force ("the AUMF"), 115 Stat. 224. Soon thereafter, the President ordered United States Armed Forces to Afghanistan, with a mission to subdue al Qaeda and quell the Taliban regime that was known to support it.

This case arises out of the detention of a man whom the Government alleges took up arms with the Taliban during this conflict. His name is Yaser Esam Hamdi. Born an American citizen in Louisiana in 1980, Hamdi moved with his family to Saudi Arabia as a child. By 2001, the parties agree, he resided in Afghanistan. At some point that year, he was seized by members of the Northern Alliance, a coalition of military groups opposed to the Taliban government, and eventually was turned over to the United States military. The Government asserts that it initially detained and interrogated Hamdi in Afghanistan before transferring him to the United States Naval Base in Guantanamo Bay in January 2002. In April 2002, upon learning that Hamdi is an American citizen, authorities transferred him to a naval brig in Norfolk, Virginia, where he remained until a recent transfer to a brig in Charleston, South Carolina. The Government contends that Hamdi is an "enemy combatant," and that this status justifies holding him in the United States indefinitely – without formal charges or proceedings – unless and until it makes the determination that access to counsel or further process is warranted.

In June 2002, Hamdi's father, Esam Fouad Hamdi, filed the present petition for a writ of habeas corpus under 28 U.S.C. § 2241 in the Eastern District of Virginia, naming as petitioners his son and himself as next friend. The elder Hamdi alleges in the petition that he has had no contact with his son since the Government took custody of him in 2001, and that the Government has held his son "without access to legal counsel or notice of any charges pending against him." App. 103, 104. The petition contends that Hamdi's detention was not legally authorized. Id., at 105. It argues that, "[a]s an American citizen, ... Hamdi enjoys the full protections of the Constitution," and that Hamdi's detention in the United States without charges, access to an impartial tribunal, or assistance of counsel "violated and continue[s] to violate the Fifth and Fourteenth Amendments to the United States Constitution." Id., at 107. The habeas petition asks that the court, among other things, (1) appoint counsel for Hamdi; (2) order respondents to cease interrogating him; (3) declare that he is being held in violation of the Fifth and Fourteenth Amendments; (4) "[t]o the extent Respondents contest any material factual allegations in this Petition, schedule an evidentiary hearing, at which Petitioners may adduce proof in support of their allegations"; and (5) order that Hamdi be released from his "unlawful custody." Id., at 108–109. Although his habeas petition provides no details with regard to the factual circumstances surrounding his son's capture and detention, Hamdi's father has asserted in documents found elsewhere in the record that his son went to Afghanistan to do "relief work," and that he had been in that country less than two months before September 11, 2001, and could not have received military training. Id., at 188–189. The 20-year-old was traveling on his own for the first time, his father says, and "[b]ecause of his lack of experience, he was trapped in Afghanistan once that military campaign began." Id., at 188–189 ...

On remand, the Government filed a response and a motion to dismiss the petition. It attached to its response a declaration from one Michael Mobbs (hereinafter "Mobbs Declaration"), who identified himself as Special Advisor to the Under Secretary of Defense for Policy. Mobbs indicated that in this position, he has been "substantially involved with matters related to the detention of enemy combatants in the current war against the al Qaeda terrorists and those who support and harbor them (including the Taliban)." App. 148. He expressed his "familiar[ity]" with Department of Defense and United States military policies and procedures applicable to the detention, control, and transfer of al Qaeda and Taliban personnel, and declared that "[b]ased upon my review of relevant records and reports, I am also familiar with the facts and circumstances related to the capture of ... Hamdi and his detention by U.S. military forces." Ibid.

Mobbs then set forth what remains the sole evidentiary support that the Government has provided to the courts for Hamdi's detention. The declaration states that Hamdi "traveled to Afghanistan" in July or August 2001, and that he thereafter "affiliated with a Taliban military unit and received weapons training." Ibid. It asserts that Hamdi "remained with his Taliban unit following the attacks of September 11" and that, during the time when Northern Alliance forces were "engaged in battle with the Taliban," "Hamdi's Taliban unit surrendered" to those forces, after which he "surrender[ed] his Kalishnikov assault rifle" to them. Id., at 148–149. The Mobbs Declaration also states that, because al Qaeda and the Taliban "were and are hostile forces engaged in armed conflict with the armed forces of the United States," "individuals associated with" those groups "were and continue to be enemy combatants." Id., at 149. Mobbs states that Hamdi was labeled an enemy combatant "[b]ased upon his interviews and in light of his association with the Taliban." Ibid. According to the declaration, a series of "U.S. military screening team[s]" determined that Hamdi met "the criteria for enemy combatants," and "a subsequent interview of Hamdi has confirmed that he surrendered and gave his firearm to Northern Alliance forces, which supports his classification as an enemy combatant." Id., at 149–150 ...

II

The threshold question before us is whether the Executive has the authority to detain citizens who qualify as "enemy combatants." There is some debate as to the proper scope of this term, and the Government has never provided any court with the full criteria that it uses in classifying individuals as such. It has made clear, however, that, for purposes of this case, the "enemy combatant" that it is seeking to detain is an individual who, it alleges, was "'part of or supporting forces hostile to the United States or coalition partners'" in Afghanistan and who "'engaged in an armed conflict against the United States'" there. Brief for Respondents 3. We therefore answer only the narrow question before us: whether the detention of citizens falling within that definition is authorized.

The Government maintains that no explicit congressional authorization is required, because the Executive possesses plenary authority to detain pursuant to Article II of the Constitution. We do not reach the question whether Article II provides such authority, however, because we agree with the Government's alternative position, that Congress has in fact authorized Hamdi's detention, through the AUMF.

Our analysis on that point, set forth below, substantially overlaps with our analysis of Hamdi's principal argument for the illegality of his detention. He posits that his detention is forbidden by 18 U.S.C. § 4001(a). Section 4001(a) states that "[n]o citizen shall be imprisoned or otherwise detained by the United States except pursuant to an Act of Congress" ... [F]or the reasons that follow, we conclude that the AUMF is explicit congressional authorization for the detention of individuals in the narrow category we describe (assuming, without deciding, that such authorization is required), and that the AUMF satisfied § 4001(a)'s requirement that a detention be "pursuant to an Act of Congress" (assuming, without deciding, that § 4001(a) applies to military detentions).

The AUMF authorizes the President to use "all necessary and appropriate force" against "nations, organizations, or persons" associated with the September 11, 2001, terrorist attacks. 115 Stat. 224. There can be no doubt that individuals who fought against the United States in Afghanistan as part of the Taliban, an organization known to have supported the al Qaeda terrorist network responsible for those attacks, are individuals Congress sought to target in passing the AUMF. We conclude that detention of individuals falling into the limited category we are considering, for the duration of the particular conflict in which they were captured, is so fundamental and accepted an incident to war as to be an exercise of the "necessary and appropriate force" Congress has authorized the President to use.

The capture and detention of lawful combatants and the capture, detention, and trial of unlawful combatants, by "universal agreement and practice," are "important incident[s] of war." *Ex parte Quirin*, 317

U.S., at 28, 63 S.Ct. 2. The purpose of detention is to prevent captured individuals from returning to the field of battle and taking up arms once again. Naqvi, Doubtful Prisoner-of-War Status, 84 Int'l Rev. Red Cross 571,572 (2002) ("[C]aptivity in war is 'neither revenge, nor punishment, but solely protective custody, the only purpose of which is to prevent the prisoners of war from further participation in the war'") (quoting decision of Nuremberg Military Tribunal, reprinted in 41 Am. J. Int'l L. 172, 229 (1947)); W. Winthrop, Military Law and Precedents 788 (rev. 2d ed. 1920) ("The time has long passed when 'no quarter' was the rule on the battlefield ... It is now recognized that 'Captivity is neither a punishment nor an act of vengeance,' but 'merely a temporary detention which is devoid of all penal character' ... 'A prisoner of war is no convict; his imprisonment is a simple war measure.'" (citations omitted)); cf. *In re Territo*, 156 F.2d 142, 145 (C.A.9 1946) ("The object of capture is to prevent the captured individual from serving the enemy. He is disarmed and from then on must be removed as completely as practicable from the front, treated humanely, and in time exchanged, repatriated, or otherwise released" (footnotes omitted)).

There is no bar to this Nation's holding one of its own citizens as an enemy combatant. In *Quirin*, one of the detainees, Haupt, alleged that he was a naturalized United States citizen. 317 U.S., at 20, 63 S.Ct. 2. We held that "[c]itizens who associate themselves with the military arm of the enemy government, and with its aid, guidance and direction enter this country bent on hostile acts, are enemy belligerents within the meaning of ... the law of war." Id., at 37–38, 63 S.Ct. 2 ...

In light of these principles, it is of no moment that the AUMF does not use specific language of detention. Because detention to prevent a combatant's return to the battlefield is a fundamental incident of waging war, in permitting the use of "necessary and appropriate force," Congress has clearly and unmistakably authorized detention in the narrow circumstances considered here.

Hamdi objects, nevertheless, that Congress has not authorized the *indefinite* detention to which he is now subject. The Government responds that "the detention of enemy combatants during World War II was just as 'indefinite' while that war was being fought." Id., at 16. We take Hamdi's objection to be not to the lack of certainty regarding the date on which the conflict will end, but to the substantial prospect of perpetual detention. We recognize that the national security underpinnings of the "war on terror," although crucially important, are broad and malleable. As the Government concedes, "given its unconventional nature, the current conflict is unlikely to end with a formal cease-fire agreement." Ibid. The prospect Hamdi raises is therefore not far-fetched. If the Government does not consider this unconventional war won for two generations, and if it maintains during that time that Hamdi might, if released, rejoin forces fighting against the United States, then the position it has taken throughout the litigation of this case suggests that Hamdi's detention could last for the rest of his life.

It is a clearly established principle of the law of war that detention may last no longer than active hostilities. See Article 118 of the Geneva Convention (III) Relative to the Treatment of Prisoners of War, Aug. 12, 1949, [1955] 6 U.S.T. 3316, 3406, T.I.A.S. no. 3364 ("Prisoners of war shall be released and repatriated without delay after the cessation of active hostilities") ...

Hamdi contends that the AUMF does not authorize indefinite or perpetual detention. Certainly, we agree that indefinite detention for the purpose of interrogation is not authorized. Further, we understand Congress' grant of authority for the use of "necessary and appropriate force" to include the authority to detain for the duration of the relevant conflict, and our understanding is based on longstanding law-of-war principles. If the practical circumstances of a given conflict are entirely unlike those of the conflicts that informed the development of the law of war, that understanding may unravel. But that is not the situation we face as of this date. Active combat operations against Taliban fighters apparently are ongoing in Afghanistan ... The United States may detain, for the duration of these hostilities, individuals legitimately determined to be Taliban combatants who "engaged in an armed conflict against the United States." If the record establishes that United States troops are still involved in active combat in Afghanistan, those detentions are part of the exercise of "necessary and appropriate force," and therefore are authorized by the AUMF ...

III

Even in cases in which the detention of enemy combatants is legally authorized, there remains the question of what process is constitutionally due to a citizen who disputes his enemy-combatant status. Hamdi argues that he is owed a meaningful and timely hearing ... The Government counters that any more process than was provided below would be both unworkable and "constitutionally intolerable." Brief for Respondents 46. Our resolution of this dispute requires a careful examination both of the writ of habeas corpus, which Hamdi now seeks to employ as a mechanism of judicial review, and of the Due Process Clause, which informs the procedural contours of that mechanism in this instance.

A

Though they reach radically different conclusions on the process that ought to attend the present proceeding, the parties begin on common ground. All agree that, absent suspension, the writ of habeas corpus remains available to every individual detained within the United States. U.S. Const., Art. I, § 9, cl. 2 ("The Privilege of the Writ of Habeas Corpus shall not be suspended, unless when in Cases of Rebellion or Invasion the public Safety may require it"). Only in the rarest of circumstances has Congress seen fit to suspend the writ ... All agree suspension of the writ has not occurred here. Thus, it is undisputed that Hamdi was properly before an Article III court to challenge his detention under 28 U.S.C. § 2241. Brief for Respondents 12. Further, all agree that § 2241 and its companion provisions provide at least a skeletal outline of the procedures to be afforded a petitioner in federal habeas review. Most notably, § 2243 provides that "the person detained may, under oath, deny any of the facts set forth in the return or allege any other material facts," and § 2246 allows the taking of evidence in habeas proceedings by deposition, affidavit, or interrogatories.

The simple outline of § 2241 makes clear both that Congress envisioned that habeas petitioners would have some opportunity to present and rebut facts and that courts in cases like this retain some ability to vary the ways in which they do so as mandated by due process. The Government recognizes the basic procedural protections required by the habeas statute, Id., at 37–38, but asks us to hold that, given both the flexibility of the habeas mechanism and the circumstances presented in this case, the presentation of the Mobbs Declaration to the habeas court completed the required factual development. It suggests two separate reasons for its position that no further process is due.

B

First, the Government urges ... that because it is "undisputed" that Hamdi's seizure took place in a combat zone, the habeas determination can be made purely as a matter of law, with no further hearing or factfinding necessary. This argument is easily rejected ... [T]he circumstances surrounding Hamdi's seizure cannot in any way be characterized as "undisputed," as "those circumstances are neither conceded in fact, nor susceptible to concession in law, because Hamdi has not been permitted to speak for himself or even through counsel as to those circumstances." 337 F.3d 335, 357 (C.A.4 2003) (Luttig, J., dissenting from denial of rehearing en banc); see also id., at 371–372 (Motz, J., dissenting from denial of rehearing en banc). Further, the "facts" that constitute the alleged concession are insufficient to support Hamdi's detention. Under the definition of enemy combatant that we accept today as falling within the scope of Congress' authorization, Hamdi would need to be "part of or supporting forces hostile to the United States or coalition partners" and "engaged in an armed conflict against the United States" to justify his detention in the United States for the duration of the relevant conflict. Brief for Respondents 3. The habeas petition states only that "[w]hen seized by the United States Government, Mr. Hamdi resided in Afghanistan." App. 104. An assertion that one resided in a country in which combat operations are taking place is not a concession that one was "captured in a zone of active combat operations in a foreign theater of war," 316 F.3d, at 459 ..., and certainly is not a concession that one was "part of or supporting forces hostile to the United States or coalition partners" and "engaged in an armed conflict against the United States." Accordingly, we reject any argument that Hamdi has made concessions that eliminate any right to further process.

C

The Government's second argument requires closer consideration. This is the argument that further factual exploration is unwarranted and inappropriate in light of the extraordinary constitutional interests at stake. Under the Government's most extreme rendition of this argument, "[r]espect for separation of powers and the limited institutional capabilities of courts in matters of military decision-making in connection with an ongoing conflict" ought to eliminate entirely any individual process, restricting the courts to investigating only whether legal authorization exists for the broader detention scheme. Brief for Respondents 26. At most, the Government argues, courts should review its determination that a citizen is an enemy combatant under a very deferential "some evidence" standard ... Under this review, a court would assume the accuracy of the Government's articulated basis for Hamdi's detention, as set forth in the Mobbs Declaration, and assess only whether that articulated basis was a legitimate one ...

In response, Hamdi emphasizes that this Court consistently has recognized that an individual challenging his detention may not be held at the will of the Executive without recourse to some proceeding before a neutral tribunal to determine whether the Executive's asserted justifications for that detention have basis in fact and warrant in law. See, e.g., *Zadvydas v. Davis*, 533 U.S. 678, 690, 121 S.Ct. 2491, 150 L.Ed.2d 653 (2001); *Addington v. Texas*, 441 U.S. 418, 425–427, 99 S.Ct. 1804, 60 L.Ed.2d 323 (1979). He argues that the Fourth Circuit inappropriately "ceded power to the Executive during wartime to define the conduct for which a citizen may be detained, judge whether that citizen has engaged in the proscribed conduct, and imprison that citizen indefinitely," Brief for Petitioners 21, and that due process demands that he receive a hearing in which he may challenge the Mobbs Declaration and adduce his own counter evidence ...

Both of these positions highlight legitimate concerns. And both emphasize the tension that often exists between the autonomy that the Government asserts is necessary in order to pursue effectively a particular goal and the process that a citizen contends he is due before he is deprived of a constitutional right. The ordinary mechanism that we use for balancing such serious competing interests, and for determining the procedures that are necessary to ensure that a citizen is not "deprived of life, liberty, or property, without due process of law," U.S. Const., Amdt. 5, is the test that we articulated in *Mathews v. Eldridge*, 424 U.S. 319, 96 S.Ct. 893, 47 L.Ed.2d 18 (1976) ... *Mathews* dictates that the process due in any given instance is determined by weighing "the private interest that will be affected by the official action" against the Government's asserted interest, "including the function involved" and the burdens the Government would face in providing greater process. 424 U.S., at 335, 96 S.Ct. 893. The *Mathews* calculus then contemplates a judicious balancing of these concerns, through an analysis of "the risk of an erroneous deprivation" of the private interest if the process were reduced and the "probable value, if any, of additional or substitute safeguards." Ibid. We take each of these steps in turn.

1

It is beyond question that substantial interests lie on both sides of the scale in this case. Hamdi's "private interest ... affected by the official action," ibid., is the most elemental of liberty interests – the interest in being free from physical detention by one's own government ... [O]ur starting point for the *Mathews v. Eldridge* analysis is unaltered by the allegations surrounding the particular detainee or the organizations with which he is alleged to have associated. We reaffirm today the fundamental nature of a citizen's right to be free from involuntary confinement by his own government without due process of law, and we weigh the opposing governmental interests against the curtailment of liberty that such confinement entails.

2

On the other side of the scale are the weighty and sensitive governmental interests in ensuring that those who have in fact fought with the enemy during a war do not return to battle against the United States. As discussed above, *supra*, at 2640, the law of war and the realities of combat may render such detentions both necessary and appropriate, and our due process analysis need not blink at those realities. Without doubt, our Constitution recognizes that core strategic matters of warmaking belong in the hands of those who are best positioned and most politically accountable for making them ...

The Government also argues at some length that its interests in reducing the process available to alleged enemy combatants are heightened by the practical difficulties that would accompany a system of trial-like process. In its view, military officers who are engaged in the serious work of waging battle would be unnecessarily and dangerously distracted by litigation half a world away, and discovery into military operations would both intrude on the sensitive secrets of national defense and result in a futile search for evidence buried under the rubble of war. Brief for Respondents 46–49. To the extent that these burdens are triggered by heightened procedures, they are properly taken into account in our due process analysis.

3

Striking the proper constitutional balance here is of great importance to the Nation during this period of ongoing combat. But it is equally vital that our calculus not give short shrift to the values that this country holds dear or to the privilege that is American citizenship. It is during our most challenging and uncertain moments that our Nation's commitment to due process is most severely tested; and it is in those times that we must preserve our commitment at home to the principles for which we fight abroad ...

With due recognition of these competing concerns, we believe that neither the process proposed by the Government nor the process apparently envisioned by the District Court below strikes the proper constitutional balance when a United States citizen is detained in the United States as an enemy combatant. That is, "the risk of erroneous deprivation" of a detainee's liberty interest is unacceptably high under the Government's proposed rule, while some of the "additional or substitute procedural safeguards" suggested by the District Court are unwarranted in light of their limited "probable value" and the burdens they may impose on the military in such cases. *Mathews*, 424 U.S., at 335, 96 S.Ct. 893.

We therefore hold that a citizen-detainee seeking to challenge his classification as an enemy combatant must receive notice of the factual basis for his classification, and a fair opportunity to rebut the Government's factual assertions before a neutral decisionmaker. See *Cleveland Bd. of Ed. v. Loudermill*, 470 U.S. 532, 542, 105 S.Ct. 1487, 84 L.Ed.2d 494 (1985) ("An essential principle of due process is that a deprivation of life, liberty, or property 'be preceded by notice and opportunity for hearing appropriate to the nature of the case'") ... These essential constitutional promises may not be eroded.

At the same time, the exigencies of the circumstances may demand that, aside from these core elements, enemy combatant proceedings may be tailored to alleviate their uncommon potential to burden the Executive at a time of ongoing military conflict. Hearsay, for example, may need to be accepted as the most reliable available evidence from the Government in such a proceeding. Likewise, the Constitution would not be offended by a presumption in favor of the Government's evidence, so long as that presumption remained a rebuttable one and fair opportunity for rebuttal were provided. Thus, once the Government puts forth credible evidence that the habeas petitioner meets the enemy-combatant criteria, the onus could shift to the petitioner to rebut that evidence with more persuasive evidence that he falls outside the criteria. A burden-shifting scheme of this sort would meet the goal of ensuring that the errant tourist, embedded journalist, or local aid worker has a chance to prove military error while giving due regard to the Executive once it has put forth meaningful support for its conclusion that the detainee is in fact an enemy combatant. In the words of

Mathews, process of this sort would sufficiently address the "risk of erroneous deprivation" of a detainee's liberty interest while eliminating certain procedures that have questionable additional value in light of the burden on the Government. 424 U.S., at 335, 96 S.Ct. 893 ...

We think it unlikely that this basic process will have the dire impact on the central functions of warmaking that the Government forecasts. The parties agree that initial captures on the battlefield need not receive the process we have discussed here; that process is due only when the determination is made to continue to hold those who have been seized. The Government has made clear in its briefing that documentation regarding battlefield detainees already is kept in the ordinary course of military affairs. Brief for Respondents 3–4. Any factfinding imposition created by requiring a knowledgeable affiant to summarize these records to an independent tribunal is a minimal one. Likewise, arguments that military officers ought not have to wage war under the threat of litigation lose much of their steam when factual disputes at enemy-combatant hearings are limited to the alleged combatant's acts. This focus meddles little, if at all, in the strategy or conduct of war, inquiring only into the appropriateness of continuing to detain an individual claimed to have taken up arms against the United States. While we accord the greatest respect and consideration to the judgments of military authorities in matters relating to the actual prosecution of a war, and recognize that the scope of that discretion necessarily is wide, it does not infringe on the core role of the military for the courts to exercise their own time-honored and constitutionally mandated roles of reviewing and resolving claims like those presented here. Cf. *Korematsu v. United States*, 323 U.S. 214, 233–234, 65 S.Ct. 193, 89 L.Ed. 194 (1944) (Murphy J, dissenting) ("[L]ike other claims conflicting with the asserted constitutional rights of the individual, the military claim must subject itself to the judicial process of having its reasonableness determined and its conflicts with other interests reconciled"); *Sterling v. Constantin*, 287 U.S. 378, 401, 53 S.Ct. 190, 77 L.Ed. 375 (1932) ("What are the allowable limits of military discretion, and whether or not they have been overstepped in a particular case, are judicial questions").

In sum, while the full protections that accompany challenges to detentions in other settings may prove unworkable and inappropriate in the enemy-combatant setting, the threats to military operations posed by a basic system of independent review are not so weighty as to trump a citizen's core rights to challenge meaningfully the Government's case and to be heard by an impartial adjudicator.

D

In so holding, we necessarily reject the Government's assertion that separation of powers principles mandate a heavily circumscribed role for the courts in such circumstances. Indeed, the position that the courts must forgo any examination of the individual case and focus exclusively on the legality of the broader detention scheme cannot be mandated by any reasonable view of separation of powers, as this approach serves only to condense power into a single branch of government. We have long since made clear that a state of war is not a blank check for the President when it comes to the rights of the Nation's citizens. *Youngstown Sheet & Tube*, 343 U.S., at 587, 72 S.Ct. 863. Whatever power the United States Constitution envisions for the Executive in its exchanges with other nations or with enemy organizations in times of conflict, it most assuredly envisions a role for all three branches when individual liberties are at stake. *Mistretta v. United States*, 488 U.S. 361, 380, 109 S.Ct. 647, 102 L.Ed.2d 714 (1989) (It was "the central judgment of the Framers of the Constitution that, within our political scheme, the separation of governmental powers into three coordinate Branches is essential to the preservation of liberty"); *Home Building & Loan Assn. v. Blaisdell*, 290 U.S. 398, 426, 54 S.Ct. 231, 78 L.Ed. 413 (1934) (The war power "is a power to wage war successfully, and thus it permits the harnessing of the entire energies of the people in a supreme cooperative effort to preserve the nation. But even the war power does not remove constitutional limitations safeguarding essential liberties"). Likewise, we have made clear that, unless Congress acts to suspend it, the Great Writ of habeas corpus allows the Judicial Branch to play a necessary role in maintaining this delicate balance of governance, serving as an important judicial check on the Executive's discretion in the realm of detentions. See *St. Cyr*, 533 U.S., at 301, 121 S.Ct. 2271 ("At its historical core, the writ of habeas corpus has served as a means of reviewing the legality of Executive detention, and it is in that context that its protections have been strongest"). Thus, while we do not question that our due process assessment must pay keen attention to the particular burdens faced by the Executive in the context of military action, it would turn our system of checks and balances on its head to suggest that a citizen could not make his way to court with a challenge to the factual basis for his detention by his government, simply because the Executive opposes making available such a challenge. Absent suspension of the writ by Congress, a citizen detained as an enemy combatant is entitled to this process.

Because we conclude that due process demands some system for a citizen detainee to refute his classification, the proposed "some evidence" standard is inadequate. Any process in which the Executive's factual assertions go wholly unchallenged or are simply presumed correct without any opportunity for the alleged combatant to demonstrate otherwise falls constitutionally short ...

Aside from unspecified "screening" processes, Brief for Respondents 3–4, and military interrogations in which the Government suggests Hamdi could have contested his classification, Tr. of Oral Arg. 40, 42, Hamdi has received no process. An interrogation by one's captor, however effective an intelligence-gathering tool, hardly constitutes a constitutionally adequate factfinding before a neutral decisionmaker. Compare Brief for Respondents 42–43 (discussing the "secure interrogation environment," and noting that military interrogations require a controlled "interrogation dynamic" and "a relationship of trust and dependency" and are "a critical source" of "timely and effective intelligence") with *Concrete Pipe*, 508 U.S., at 617–618, 113 S.Ct. 2264 ("[o]ne is entitled as a matter of due process of law to an adjudicator who is not in a situation which would offer a possible temptation to the average man as a judge ... which might lead him not to hold the balance nice, clear and true" (internal quotation marks omitted)). That even purportedly fair adjudicators "are disqualified by their interest in the controversy to be decided is, of course, the general rule." *Tumey v. Ohio*, 273 U.S. 510, 522, 47 S.Ct. 437, 71 L.Ed. 749 (1927). Plainly, the "process" Hamdi has received is not that to which he is entitled under the Due Process Clause.

There remains the possibility that the standards we have articulated could be met by an appropriately authorized and properly constituted military tribunal. Indeed, it is notable that military regulations already provide for such process in related instances, dictating that tribunals be made available to determine the status of enemy detainees who assert prisoner-of-war status under the Geneva Convention. See Enemy Prisoners of War, Retained Personnel, Civilian Internees and Other Detainees, Army Regulation 190-8, § 1–6 (1997). In the absence of such process, however, a court that receives a petition for a writ of habeas corpus from an alleged enemy combatant must itself ensure that the minimum requirements of due process are achieved ... As we have discussed, a habeas court in a case such as this may accept affidavit evidence like that contained in the Mobbs Declaration, so long as it also permits the alleged combatant to present his own factual case to rebut the Government's return. We anticipate that a District Court would proceed with the caution that we have indicated is necessary in this setting, engaging in a factfinding process that is both prudent and incremental. We have no reason to doubt that courts faced with these sensitive matters will pay proper heed both to the matters of national security that might arise in an individual case and to the constitutional limitations safeguarding essential liberties that remain vibrant even in times of security concerns.

IV

Hamdi asks us to hold that the Fourth Circuit also erred by denying him immediate access to counsel upon his detention and by disposing of the case without permitting him to meet with an attorney. Brief for Petitioners 19. Since our grant of certiorari in this case, Hamdi has been appointed counsel, with whom he has met for consultation purposes on several occasions, and with whom he is now being granted unmonitored meetings. He unquestionably has the right to access to counsel in connection with the proceedings on remand. No further consideration of this issue is necessary at this stage of the case.

...

The judgment of the United States Court of Appeals for the Fourth Circuit is vacated, and the case is remanded for further proceedings. It is so ordered.

Justice SOUTER, with whom Justice GINSBURG joins, concurring in part, dissenting in part, and concurring in the judgment:

... The Government [argues] that Hamdi's incommunicado imprisonment as an enemy combatant seized on the field of battle falls within the President's power as Commander in Chief under the laws and usages of war, and is in any event authorized by two statutes. Accordingly, the Government contends that Hamdi has no basis for any challenge by petition for habeas except to his own status as an enemy combatant; and even that challenge may go no further than to enquire whether "some evidence" supports Hamdi's designation, see Brief for Respondents 34–36; if there is "some evidence," Hamdi should remain locked up at the discretion of the Executive. At the argument of this case, in fact, the Government went further and suggested that as long as long as a prisoner could challenge his enemy combatant designation when responding to interrogation during incommunicado detention he was accorded sufficient process to support his designation as an enemy combatant. See Tr. of Oral Arg. 40; id., at 42 ("[H]e has an opportunity to explain it in his own words" "[d]uring interrogation"). Since on either view judicial enquiry so limited would be virtually worthless as a way to contest detention, the Government's concession of jurisdiction to hear Hamdi's habeas claim is more theoretical than practical, leaving the assertion of Executive authority close to unconditional.

The plurality rejects any such limit on the exercise of habeas jurisdiction and so far I agree with its opinion. The plurality does, however, accept the Government's position that if Hamdi's designation as an enemy combatant is correct, his detention (at least as to some period) is authorized by an Act of Congress as required by § 4001(a), that is, by the Authorization for Use of Military Force, 115 Stat. 224 (hereinafter Force Resolution). *Ante*, at 2639–2642. Here, I disagree and respectfully dissent. The Government has failed to demonstrate that the Force Resolution authorizes the detention complained of here even on the facts the Government claims. If the Government raises nothing further than the record now shows, the *Non-Detention Act* entitles Hamdi to be released ...

The threshold issue is how broadly or narrowly to read the *Non-Detention Act*, the tone of which is severe: "No citizen shall be imprisoned or otherwise detained by the United States except pursuant to an Act of Congress." Should the severity of the Act be relieved when the Government's stated factual justification for incommunicado detention is a war on terrorism, so that the Government may be said to act "pursuant" to congressional terms that fall short of explicit authority to imprison individuals? With one possible though important qualification, see infra, at 2640, the answer has to be no. For a number of reasons, the prohibition within § 4001(a) has to be read broadly to accord the statute a long reach and to impose a burden of justification on the Government.

First, the circumstances in which the Act was adopted point the way to this interpretation. The provision superseded a cold-war statute, the *Emergency Detention Act* of 1950 (formerly 50 U.S.C. § 811 et seq. (1970 ed.)), which had authorized the Attorney General, in time of emergency, to detain anyone reasonably thought likely to engage in espionage or sabotage. That statute was repealed in 1971 out of fear that it could authorize a repetition of the World War II internment of citizens of

Japanese ancestry; Congress meant to preclude another episode like the one described in *Korematsu v. United States*, 323 U.S. 214, 65 S.Ct. 193, 89 L.Ed. 194 (1944). See H.R.Rep. No. 92–116, pp. 2, 4–5 (1971), U.S. Code Cong. & Admin.News 1971, 1435, 1435–1436, 1437–1438. While Congress might simply have struck the 1950 statute, in considering the repealer the point was made that the existing statute provided some express procedural protection, without which the Executive would seem to be subject to no statutory limits protecting individual liberty. See id., at 5, U.S. Code Cong. & Admin. News 1971, 1435, 1438 (mere repeal "might leave citizens subject to arbitrary executive action, with no clear demarcation of the limits of executive authority"); 117 Cong. Rec. 31544 (1971) (*Emergency Detention Act* "remains as the only existing barrier against the future exercise of executive power which resulted in" the Japanese internment); cf. id., at 31548 (in the absence of further procedural provisions, even § 4001(a) "will virtually leave us stripped naked against the great power ... which the President has"). It was in these circumstances that a proposed limit on Executive action was expanded to the inclusive scope of § 4001(a) as enacted.

The fact that Congress intended to guard against a repetition of the World War II internments when it repealed the 1950 statute and gave us § 4001(a) provides a powerful reason to think that § 4001(a) was meant to require clear congressional authorization before any citizen can be placed in a cell. It is not merely that the legislative history shows that § 4001(a) was thought necessary in anticipation of times just like the present, in which the safety of the country is threatened. To appreciate what is most significant, one must only recall that the internments of the 1940's were accomplished by Executive action. Although an Act of Congress ratified and confirmed an Executive order authorizing the military to exclude individuals from defined areas and to accommodate those it might remove, see *Ex parte Endo*, 323 U.S. 283, 285–288, 65 S.Ct. 208, 89 L.Ed. 243 (1944), the statute said nothing whatever about the detention of those who might be removed, id., at 300–301, 65 S.Ct. 208; internment camps were creatures of the Executive, and confinement in them rested on assertion of Executive authority, see id., at 287–293, 65 S.Ct. 208. When, therefore, Congress repealed the 1950 Act and adopted § 4001(a) for the purpose of avoiding another *Korematsu*, it intended to preclude reliance on vague congressional authority (for example, providing "accommodations" for those subject to removal) as authority for detention or imprisonment at the discretion of the Executive (maintaining detention camps of American citizens, for example). In requiring that any Executive detention be "pursuant to an Act of Congress," then, Congress necessarily meant to require a congressional enactment that clearly authorized detention or imprisonment.

Second, when Congress passed § 4001(a) it was acting in light of an interpretive regime that subjected enactments limiting liberty in wartime to the requirement of a clear statement and it presumably intended § 4001(a) to be read accordingly. This need for clarity was unmistakably expressed in *Ex parte Endo, supra*, decided the same day as *Korematsu*. *Endo* began with a petition for habeas corpus by an interned citizen claiming to be loyal and law-abiding and thus "unlawfully detained." 323 U.S., at 294, 65 S.Ct. 208. The petitioner was held entitled to habeas relief in an opinion that set out this principle for scrutinizing wartime statutes in derogation of customary liberty:

In interpreting a wartime measure we must assume that [its] purpose was to allow for the greatest possible accommodation between ... liberties and the exigencies of war. We must assume, when asked to find implied powers in a grant of legislative or executive authority, that the law makers intended to place no greater restraint on the citizen than was clearly and unmistakably indicated by the language they used. (Id., at 300, 65 S.Ct. 208)

Congress's understanding of the need for clear authority before citizens are kept detained is itself therefore clear, and § 4001(a) must be read to have teeth in its demand for congressional authorization.

Finally, even if history had spared us the cautionary example of the internments in World War II, even if there had been no *Korematsu*, and *Endo* had set out no principle of statutory interpretation, there would be a compelling reason to read § 4001(a) to demand manifest authority to detain before detention is authorized. The defining character of American constitutional government is its constant tension between security and liberty, serving both by partial helpings of each. In a government of separated powers, deciding finally on what is a reasonable degree of guaranteed liberty whether in peace or war (or some condition in between) is not well entrusted to the Executive Branch of Government, whose particular responsibility is to maintain security. For reasons of inescapable human nature, the branch of the Government asked to counter a serious threat is not the branch on which to rest the Nation's entire reliance in striking the balance between the will to win and the cost in liberty on the way to victory; the responsibility for security will naturally amplify the claim that security legitimately raises. A reasonable balance is more likely to be reached on the judgment of a different branch, just as Madison said in remarking that "the constant aim is to divide and arrange the several offices in such a manner as that each may be a check on the other – that the private interest of every individual may be a sentinel over the public rights." The Federalist no. 51, p. 349 (J. Cooke ed. 1961). Hence the need for an assessment by Congress before citizens are subject to lockup, and likewise the need for a clearly expressed congressional resolution of the competing claims.

III

Under this principle of reading § 4001(a) robustly to require a clear statement of authorization to detain, none of the Government's arguments suffices to justify Hamdi's detention.

A

First, there is the argument that § 4001(a) does not even apply to wartime military detentions, a position resting on the placement of § 4001(a) in Title 18 of the United States Code, the gathering of federal criminal law. The text of the statute does not, however, so limit its reach, and the legislative history of the provision shows its placement in Title 18 was not meant to render the statute more restricted than its terms ... Congress was aware that § 4001(a) would limit the Executive's power to detain citizens in wartime to protect national security, and it is fair to say that the prohibition was thus intended to extend not only to the exercise of power to vindicate the interests underlying domestic criminal law, but to statutorily unauthorized detention by the Executive for reasons of security in wartime, just as Hamdi claims ...

B

Next, there is the Government's claim, accepted by the Court, that the terms of the Force Resolution are adequate to authorize detention of an enemy combatant under the circumstances described, ... a claim the Government fails to support sufficiently to satisfy § 4001(a) as read to require a clear statement of authority to detain. Since the Force Resolution was adopted one week after the attacks of September 11, 2001, it naturally speaks with some generality, but its focus is clear, and that is on the use of military power. It is fairly read to authorize the use of armies and weapons, whether against other armies or individual terrorists. But, like the statute discussed in *Endo*, it never so much as uses the word detention, and there is no reason to think Congress might have perceived any need to augment Executive power to deal with dangerous citizens within the United States, given the well-stocked statutory arsenal of defined criminal offenses covering the gamut of actions that a citizen sympathetic to terrorists might commit ...

C

Even so, there is one argument for treating the Force Resolution as sufficiently clear to authorize detention of a citizen consistently with § 4001(a). Assuming the argument to be sound, however, the Government is in no position to claim its advantage.

Because the Force Resolution authorizes the use of military force in acts of war by the United States, the argument goes, it is reasonably clear that the military and its Commander in Chief are authorized to deal with enemy belligerents according to the treaties and customs known collectively as the laws of war. Brief for Respondents 20–22; see ante, at 2639–2642 (accepting this argument). Accordingly, the United States may detain captured enemies, and *Ex parte Quirin*, 317 U.S. 1, 63 S.Ct. 2, 87 L.Ed. 3 (1942), may perhaps be claimed for the proposition that the American citizenship of such a captive does not as such limit the Government's power to deal with him under the usages of war. Id., at 31, 37–38, 63 S.Ct. 2. Thus, the Government here repeatedly argues that Hamdi's detention amounts to nothing more than customary detention of a captive taken on the field of battle: if the usages of war are fairly authorized by the Force Resolution, Hamdi's detention is authorized for purposes of § 4001(a).

There is no need, however, to address the merits of such an argument in all possible circumstances. For now it is enough to recognize that the Government's stated legal position in its campaign against the Taliban (among whom Hamdi was allegedly captured) is apparently at odds with its claim here to be acting in accordance with customary law of war and hence to be within the terms of the Force Resolution in its detention of Hamdi. In a statement of its legal position cited in its brief, the Government says that "the Geneva Convention applies to the Taliban detainees." Office of the White House Press Secretary, Fact Sheet, Status of Detainees at Guantanamo (Feb. 7, 2002), www.whitehouse.gov/

news/releases/2002/ 02/20020207-13.html (as visited June 18, 2004, and available in Clerk of Court's case file) (hereinafter White House Press Release) (cited in Brief for Respondents 24, n. 9). Hamdi presumably is such a detainee, since according to the Government's own account, he was taken bearing arms on the Taliban side of a field of battle in Afghanistan. He would therefore seem to qualify for treatment as a prisoner of war under the Third Geneva Convention, to which the United States is a party. Article 4 of the Geneva Convention (III) Relative to the Treatment of Prisoners of War, Aug. 12, 1949, [1955] 6 U.S. T. 3316, 3320, T.I.A.S. no. 3364.

By holding him incommunicado, however, the Government obviously has not been treating him as a prisoner of war, and in fact the Government claims that no Taliban detainee is entitled to prisoner of war status. See Brief for Respondents 24; White House Press Release. This treatment appears to be a violation of the Geneva Convention provision that even in cases of doubt, captives are entitled to be treated as prisoners of war "until such time as their status has been determined by a competent tribunal." Art. 5, 6 U.S. T., at 3324. The Government answers that the President's determination that Taliban detainees do not qualify as prisoners of war is conclusive as to Hamdi's status and removes any doubt that would trigger application of the Convention's tribunal requirement. See Brief for Respondents 24. But reliance on this categorical pronouncement to settle doubt is apparently at odds with the military regulation, Enemy Prisoners of War, Retained Personnel, Civilian Internees and Other Detainees, Army Reg. 190–8, §§ 1–5, 1–6 (1997), adopted to implement the Geneva Convention, and setting out a detailed procedure for a military tribunal to determine an individual's status. See, e.g., id., § 1–6 ("A competent tribunal shall be composed of three commissioned officers"; a "written record shall be made of proceedings"; "[p]roceedings shall be open" with certain exceptions; "[p]ersons whose status is to be determined shall be advised of their rights at the beginning of their hearings," "allowed to attend all open sessions," "allowed to call witnesses if reasonably available, and to question those witnesses called by the Tribunal," and to "have a right to testify"; and a tribunal shall determine status by a "[p]reponderance of evidence"). One of the types of doubt these tribunals are meant to settle is whether a given individual may be, as Hamdi says he is, an "[i]nnocent civilian who should be immediately returned to his home or released." Id., 1–6e (10)(c). The regulation, jointly promulgated by the Headquarters of the Departments of the Army, Navy, Air Force, and

Marine Corps, provides that "[p]ersons who have been determined by a competent tribunal not to be entitled to prisoner of war status may not be executed, imprisoned, or otherwise penalized without further proceedings to determine what acts they have committed and what penalty should be imposed." Id., § 1–6g. The regulation also incorporates the Geneva Convention's presumption that in cases of doubt, "persons shall enjoy the protection of the ... Convention until such time as their status has been determined by a competent tribunal." Id., § 1–6a. Thus, there is reason to question whether the United States is acting in accordance with the laws of war it claims as authority.

Whether, or to what degree, the Government is in fact violating the Geneva Convention and is thus acting outside the customary usages of war are not matters I can resolve at this point. What I can say, though, is that the Government has not made out its claim that in detaining Hamdi in the manner described, it is acting in accord with the laws of war authorized to be applied against citizens by the Force Resolution. I conclude accordingly that the Government has failed to support the position that the Force Resolution authorizes the described detention of Hamdi for purposes of § 4001(a).

It is worth adding a further reason for requiring the Government to bear the burden of clearly justifying its claim to be exercising recognized war powers before declaring § 4001(a) satisfied. Thirty-eight days after adopting the Force Resolution, Congress passed the statute entitled *Uniting and Strengthening America by Providing Appropriate Tools Required to Intercept and Obstruct Terrorism Act* of 2001 (*USA PATRIOT Act*), 115 Stat. 272; that Act authorized the detention of alien terrorists for no more than seven days in the absence of criminal charges or deportation proceedings, 8 U.S.C. § 1226a(a)(5) (2000 ed., Supp. I). It is very difficult to believe that the same Congress that carefully circumscribed Executive power over alien terrorists on home soil would not have meant to require the Government to justify clearly its detention of an American citizen held on home soil incommunicado.

D

Since the Government has given no reason either to deflect the application of § 4001(a) or to hold it to be satisfied, I need to go no further; the Government hints of a constitutional challenge to the statute, but it presents none here. I will, however, stray across the line between statutory and constitutional territory just far enough to note the weakness of the Government's mixed claim of inherent, extrastatutory authority under a combination of Article II of the Constitution and the usages of war. It is in fact in this connection that the Government developed its argument that the exercise of war powers justifies the detention, and what I have just said about its inadequacy applies here as well. Beyond that, it is instructive to recall Justice Jackson's observation that the President is not Commander in Chief of the country, only of the military. *Youngstown Sheet & Tube Co. v. Sawyer*, 343 U.S. 579, 643–644, 72 S.Ct. 863, 96 L.Ed. 1153 (1952) (concurring opinion) ...

There may be room for one qualification to Justice Jackson's statement, however: in a moment of genuine emergency, when the Government must act with no time for deliberation, the Executive may be able to detain a citizen if there is reason to fear he is an imminent threat to the safety of the Nation and its people (though I doubt there is any want of statutory authority, see *supra*, at 2656–2657). This case, however, does not present that question, because an emergency power of necessity must at least be limited by the emergency; Hamdi has been locked up for over two years. Cf. *Ex parte Milligan*, 4 Wall. 2, 127, 18 L.Ed. 281 (1866) (martial law justified only by "actual and present" necessity as in a genuine invasion that closes civilian courts).

Whether insisting on the careful scrutiny of emergency claims or on a vigorous reading of § 4001(a), we are heirs to a tradition given voice 800 years ago by Magna Carta, which, on the barons' insistence, confined executive power by "the law of the land."

IV

Because I find Hamdi's detention forbidden by § 4001(a) and unauthorized by the Force Resolution, I would not reach any questions of what process he may be due in litigating disputed issues in a proceeding under the habeas statute or prior to the habeas enquiry itself. For me, it suffices that the Government has failed to justify holding him in the absence of a further Act of Congress, criminal charges, a showing that the detention conforms to the laws of war, or a demonstration that § 4001(a) is unconstitutional. I would therefore vacate the judgment of the Court of Appeals and remand for proceedings consistent with this view.

Since this disposition does not command a majority of the Court, however, the need to give practical effect to the conclusions of eight members of the Court rejecting the Government's position calls for me to join with the plurality in ordering remand on terms closest to those

I would impose ... Although I think litigation of Hamdi's status as an enemy combatant is unnecessary, the terms of the plurality's remand will allow Hamdi to offer evidence that he is not an enemy combatant, and he should at the least have the benefit of that opportunity.

It should go without saying that in joining with the plurality to produce a judgment, I do not adopt the plurality's resolution of constitutional issues that I would not reach. It is not that I could disagree with the plurality's determinations (given the plurality's view of the Force Resolution) that someone in Hamdi's position is entitled at a minimum to notice of the Government's claimed factual basis for holding him, and to a fair chance to rebut it before a neutral decision-maker, see *ante*, at 2648; nor, of course, could I disagree with the plurality's affirmation of Hamdi's right to counsel, see *ante*, at 2652. On the other hand, I do not mean to imply agreement that the Government could claim an evidentiary presumption casting the burden of rebuttal on Hamdi, see *ante*, at 2649, or that an opportunity to litigate before a military tribunal might obviate or truncate enquiry by a court on habeas, see *ante*, at 2651–2652.

Subject to these qualifications, I join with the plurality in a judgment of the Court vacating the Fourth Circuit's judgment and remanding the case.

Justice SCALIA, with whom Justice STEVENS joins, dissenting:

... This case brings into conflict the competing demands of national security and our citizens' constitutional right to personal liberty. Although I share the Court's evident unease as it seeks to reconcile the two, I do not agree with its resolution.

Where the Government accuses a citizen of waging war against it, our constitutional tradition has been to prosecute him in federal court for treason or some other crime. Where the exigencies of war prevent that, the Constitution's Suspension Clause, Art. I, § 9, cl. 2, allows Congress to relax the usual protections temporarily. Absent suspension, however, the Executive's assertion of military exigency has not been thought sufficient to permit detention without charge. No one contends that the congressional Authorization for Use of Military Force, on which the Government relies to justify its actions here, is an implementation of the Suspension Clause. Accordingly, I would reverse the decision below.

I

The very core of liberty secured by our Anglo-Saxon system of separated powers has been freedom from indefinite imprisonment at the will of the Executive. Blackstone stated this principle clearly:

Of great importance to the public is the preservation of this personal liberty: for if once it were left in the power of any, the highest, magistrate to imprison arbitrarily whomever he or his officers thought proper ... there would soon be an end of all other rights and immunities ... To bereave a man of life, or by violence to confiscate his estate, without accusation or trial, would be so gross and notorious an act of despotism, as must at once convey the alarm of tyranny throughout the whole kingdom. But confinement of the person, by secretly hurrying him to gaol, where his sufferings are unknown or forgotten; is a less public, a less striking, and therefore a more dangerous engine of arbitrary government ...

To make imprisonment lawful, it must either be, by process from the courts of judicature, or by warrant from some legal officer, having authority to commit to prison; which warrant must be in writing, under the hand and seal of the magistrate, and express the causes of the commitment, in order to be examined into (if necessary) upon a habeas corpus. If there be no cause expressed, the gaoler is not bound to detain the prisoner. For the law judges in this respect, ... that it is unreasonable to send a prisoner, and not to signify withal the crimes alleged against him. 1 W. Blackstone, Commentaries on the Laws of England 132–133 (1765); hereinafter Blackstone.

... The two ideas central to Blackstone's understanding – due process as the right secured, and habeas corpus as the instrument by which due process could be insisted upon by a citizen illegally imprisoned – found expression in the Constitution's Due Process and Suspension Clauses. See Amdt. 5; Art. I, § 9, cl. 2. The gist of the Due Process Clause, as understood at the founding and since, was to force the Government to follow those common-law procedures traditionally deemed necessary before depriving a person of life, liberty, or property. When a citizen was deprived of liberty because of alleged criminal conduct, those procedures typically required committal by a magistrate followed by indictment and trial. See, e.g., 2 & 3 Phil. & M., c. 10 (1555); 3 J. Story, Commentaries on the Constitution of the United States § 1783, p. 661 (1833) (hereinafter Story) (equating "due process of law" with "due presentment or indictment, and being brought in to answer thereto by due process of the common law"). The Due Process Clause "in effect affirms the right of trial according to the process and proceedings of the common law." Ibid. See also T. Cooley, General Principles of Constitutional Law 224 (1880) ("When life and liberty are in question, there must in every instance be judicial proceedings; and that requirement implies an accusation, a hearing before an impartial tribunal, with proper jurisdiction, and a conviction and judgment before the punishment can be inflicted" (internal quotation marks omitted)).

To be sure, certain types of permissible *non* criminal detention – that is, those not dependent upon the contention that the citizen had committed a criminal act – did not require the protections of criminal procedure. However, these fell into a limited number of well-recognized exceptions – civil commitment of the mentally ill, for example, and temporary detention in quarantine of the infectious. See Opinion on the Writ of Habeas Corpus, 97 Eng. Rep. 29, 36-37 (H.L.1758) (Wilmot J). It is unthinkable that the Executive could render otherwise criminal grounds for detention noncriminal merely by disclaiming an intent to prosecute, or by asserting that it was incapacitating dangerous offenders rather than punishing wrongdoing. Cf. *Kansas v. Hendricks*, 521 U.S. 346, 358, 117 S.Ct. 2072, 138 L.Ed.2d 501 (1997) ("A finding of dangerousness, standing alone, is ordinarily not a sufficient ground upon which to justify indefinite involuntary commitment").

These due process rights have historically been vindicated by the writ of habeas corpus. In England before the founding, the writ developed into a tool for challenging executive confinement. It was not always effective. For example, in *Darnel's Case*, 3 How. St. Tr. 1 (K.B. 1627), King Charles I detained without charge several individuals for failing to assist England's war against France and Spain. The prisoners sought writs of habeas corpus, arguing that without specific charges, "imprisonment shall not continue on for a time, but for ever; and the subjects of this kingdom may be restrained of their liberties perpetually." Id., at 8. The Attorney General replied that the Crown's interest in protecting the realm justified imprisonment in "a matter of state ... not ripe nor timely" for the ordinary process of accusation and trial." Id., at 37. The court denied relief, producing widespread outrage, and Parliament responded with the Petition of Right, accepted by the King in 1628, which expressly prohibited imprisonment without formal charges, see 3 Car. 1, c. 1, §§ 5, 10.

The struggle between subject and Crown continued, and culminated in the *Habeas Corpus Act* of 1679, 31 Car. 2, c. 2, described by Blackstone as a "second *magna charta*, and stable bulwark of our liberties." 1 Blackstone 133. The Act governed all persons "committed or detained ... for any crime." § 3. In cases other than felony or treason plainly expressed in the warrant of commitment, the Act required release upon appropriate sureties (unless the commitment was for a nonbailable offense). Ibid. Where the commitment was for felony or high treason, the Act did not require immediate release, but instead required the Crown to commence criminal proceedings within a specified time. § 7. If the prisoner was not "indicted some Time in the next Term," the judge was "required ... to set at Liberty the Prisoner upon Bail" unless the King was unable to produce his witnesses. Ibid. Able or no, if the prisoner was not brought to trial by the next succeeding term, the Act provided that "he shall be discharged from his Imprisonment." Ibid. English courts sat four terms per year, see 3 Blackstone 275–277, so the practical effect of this provision was that imprisonment without indictment or trial for felony or high treason under § 7 would not exceed approximately three to six months.

The writ of habeas corpus was preserved in the Constitution – the only common-law writ to be explicitly mentioned. See Art. I, § 9, cl. 2. Hamilton lauded "the establishment of the writ of habeas corpus" in his Federalist defense as a means to protect against "the practice of arbitrary imprisonments ... in all ages, [one of] the favourite and most formidable instruments of tyranny." The Federalist no. 84, *supra*, at 444. Indeed, availability of the writ under the new Constitution (along with the requirement of trial by jury in criminal cases, see Art. III, § 2, cl. 3) was his basis for arguing that additional, explicit procedural protections were unnecessary. See The Federalist no. 83, at 433.

II

The allegations here, of course, are no ordinary accusations of criminal activity. Yaser Esam Hamdi has been imprisoned because the Government believes he participated in the waging of war against the United States. The relevant question, then, is whether there is a different, special procedure for imprisonment of a citizen accused of wrongdoing by *aiding the enemy in wartime.*

A

Justice O'CONNOR, writing for a plurality of this Court, asserts that captured enemy combatants (other than those suspected of war crimes) have traditionally been detained until the cessation of hostilities and then released. *Ante*, at 2640. That is probably an accurate description of wartime practice with respect to enemy aliens. The tradition with respect to American citizens, however, has been quite different. Citizens aiding the enemy have been treated as traitors subject to the criminal process.

... The Constitution provides: "Treason against the United States, shall consist only in levying War against them, or in adhering to their Enemies, giving them Aid and Comfort"; and establishes a heightened proof requirement (two witnesses) in order to "convic[t]" of that offense. Art. III, § 3, cl. 1 ...

The modern treason statute is 18 U.S.C. § 2381; it basically tracks the language of the constitutional provision. Other provisions of Title 18 criminalize various acts of warmaking and adherence to the enemy. See, e.g., § 32 (destruction of aircraft or aircraft facilities), § 2332a (use of weapons of mass destruction), § 2332b (acts of terrorism transcending national boundaries), § 2339A (providing material support to terrorists), § 2339B (providing material support to certain terrorist organizations), § 2382 (misprision of treason), § 2383 (rebellion or insurrection), § 2384 (seditious conspiracy), § 2390 (enlistment to serve in armed hostility against the United States). See also 31 CFR § 595.204 (2003) (prohibiting the "making or receiving of any contribution of funds, goods, or services" to terrorists); 50 U.S.C. § 1705(b) (criminalizing violations of 31 CFR § 595.204). The only citizen other than Hamdi known to be imprisoned in connection with military hostilities in Afghanistan against the United States was subjected to criminal process and convicted upon a guilty plea. See *United States v. Lindh*, 212 F.Supp.2d 541 (E.D.Va.2002) (denying motions for dismissal); Seelye, N.Y. Times, Oct. 5, 2002, p. A1, col. 5.

B

There are times when military exigency renders resort to the traditional criminal process impracticable. English law accommodated such exigencies by allowing legislative suspension of the writ of habeas corpus for brief periods. Blackstone explained:

And yet sometimes, when the state is in real danger, even this [i.e., executive detention] may be a necessary measure. But the happiness of our constitution is, that it is not left to the executive power to determine when the danger of the state is so great, as to render this measure expedient. For the parliament only, or legislative power, whenever it sees proper, can authorize the crown, by suspending the habeas corpus act for a short and limited time, to imprison suspected persons without giving any reason for so doing ... In like manner this experiment ought only to be tried in case of extreme emergency; and in these the nation parts with it[s] liberty for a while, in order to preserve it for ever. 1 Blackstone 132

Where the Executive has not pursued the usual course of charge, committal, and conviction, it has historically secured the Legislature's explicit approval of a suspension ... Our Federal Constitution contains a provision explicitly permitting suspension, but limiting the situations in which it may be invoked: "The privilege of the Writ of Habeas Corpus shall not be suspended, unless when in Cases of Rebellion or Invasion the public Safety may require it." Art. I, § 9, cl. 2. Although this provision does not state that suspension must be effected by, or authorized by, a legislative act, it has been so understood, consistent with English practice and the Clause's placement in Article I. See *Ex parte Bollman*, 4 Cranch 75, 101, 2 L.Ed. 554 (1807); *Ex parte Merryman*, 17 F. Cas. 144, 151–152 (C.D.Md. 1861) (Taney C.J., rejecting Lincoln's unauthorized suspension); 3 Story § 1336, at 208–209.

The Suspension Clause was by design a safety valve, the Constitution's only "express provision for exercise of extraordinary authority because of a crisis," *Youngstown Sheet & Tube Co. v. Sawyer*, 343 U.S. 579, 650, 72 S.Ct. 863, 96 L.Ed. 1153 (1952) (Jackson, J., concurring). Very early in the Nation's history, President Jefferson unsuccessfully sought a suspension of habeas corpus to deal with Aaron Burr's conspiracy to overthrow the Government. See 16 Annals of Congress 402–425 (1807). During the Civil War, Congress passed its first Act authorizing Executive suspension of the writ of habeas corpus, see Act of Mar. 3, 1863, 12 Stat. 755, to the relief of those many who thought President Lincoln's unauthorized proclamations of suspension (e.g., Proclamation no. 1, 13 Stat. 730 (1862)) unconstitutional. Later Presidential proclamations of suspension relied upon the congressional authorization, e.g., Proclamation no. 7, 13 Stat. 734 (1863). During Reconstruction, Congress passed the *Ku Klux Klan Act*, which included a provision authorizing suspension of the writ, invoked by President Grant in quelling a rebellion in nine South Carolina counties ...

III

Of course the extensive historical evidence of criminal convictions and habeas suspensions does not necessarily refute the Government's position in this case. When the writ is suspended, the Government is entirely free from judicial oversight. It does not claim such total liberation here, but argues that it need only produce what it calls "some evidence" to satisfy a habeas court that a detained individual is an enemy combatant. See Brief for Respondents 34. Even if suspension of the writ on the one hand, and committal for criminal charges on the other hand, have been the only traditional means of dealing with citizens who levied war against their own country, it is theoretically possible that the Constitution does not require a choice between these alternatives.

I believe, however, that substantial evidence does refute that possibility. First, the text of the 1679 *Habeas Corpus Act* makes clear that indefinite imprisonment on reasonable suspicion is not an available option of treatment for those accused of aiding the enemy, absent a suspension of the writ. In the United States, this Act was read as "enforc[ing] the common law," *Ex parte Watkins*, 3 Pet. 193, 202, 7 L.Ed. 650 (1830), and shaped the early understanding of the scope of the writ ...

The absence of military authority to imprison citizens indefinitely in wartime – whether or not a probability of treason had been established by means less than jury trial – was confirmed by three cases decided during and immediately after the War of 1812. In the first, *In re Stacy*, 10 Johns. *328 (N.Y.1813), a citizen was taken into military custody on suspicion that he was "carrying provisions and giving information to the enemy." Id., at *330. Stacy petitioned for a writ of habeas corpus, and, after the defendant custodian attempted to avoid complying, Chief Justice Kent ordered attachment against him. Kent noted that the military was "without any color of authority in any military tribunal to try a citizen for that crime" and that it was "holding him in the closest confinement, and contemning the civil authority of the state." Id., at *333–334.

Two other cases, later cited with approval by this Court in *Ex parte Milligan*, 4 Wall. 2, 128–129, 18 L.Ed. 281 (1866), upheld verdicts for false imprisonment against military officers. In *Smith v. Shaw*, 12 Johns. *257

(N.Y. 1815), the court affirmed an award of damages for detention of a citizen on suspicion that he was, among other things, "an enemy's spy in time of war." Id., at *265. The court held that "[n]one of the offences charged against Shaw were cognizable by a court-martial, except that which related to his being a spy; and if he was an American citizen, he could not be charged with such an offence. He might be amenable to the civil authority for treason; but could not be punished, under martial law, as a spy." Ibid. "If the defendant was justifiable in doing what he did, every citizen of the United States would, in time of war, be equally exposed to a like exercise of military power and authority." Id., at *266. Finally, in *M'Connell v. Hampton*, 12 Johns. *234 (N.Y. 1815), a jury awarded $9,000 for false imprisonment after a military officer confined a citizen on charges of treason; the judges on appeal did not question the verdict but found the damages excessive, in part because "it does not appear that [the defendant] ... knew [the plaintiff] was a citizen." Id., at *238 (Spencer, J.) ...

Further evidence comes from this Court's decision in *Ex parte Milligan*, supra. There, the Court issued the writ to an American citizen who had been tried by military commission for offenses that included conspiring to overthrow the Government, seize munitions, and liberate prisoners of war. Id., at 6–7. The Court rejected in no uncertain terms the Government's assertion that military jurisdiction was proper "under the 'laws and usages of war,'"id., at 121:

It can serve no useful purpose to inquire what those laws and usages are, whence they originated, where found, and on whom they operate; they can never be applied to citizens in states which have upheld the authority of the government, and where the courts are open and their process unobstructed. Ibid.

Milligan is not exactly this case, of course, since the petitioner was threatened with death, not merely imprisonment. But the reasoning and conclusion of *Milligan* logically cover the present case. The Government justifies imprisonment of Hamdi on principles of the law of war and admits that, absent the war, it would have no such authority. But if the law of war cannot be applied to citizens where courts are open, then Hamdi's imprisonment without criminal trial is no less unlawful than Milligan's trial by military tribunal.

Milligan responded to the argument, repeated by the Government in this case, that it is dangerous to leave suspected traitors at large in time of war:

If it was dangerous, in the distracted condition of affairs, to leave Milligan unrestrained of his liberty, because he 'conspired against the government, afforded aid and comfort to rebels, and incited the people to insurrection,' the law said arrest him, confine him closely, render him powerless to do further mischief; and then present his case to the grand jury of the district, with proofs of his guilt, and, if indicted, try him according to the course of the common law. If this had been done, the Constitution would have been vindicated, the law of 1863 enforced, and the securities for personal liberty preserved and defended. Id., at 122.

Thus, criminal process was viewed as the primary means – and the only means absent congressional action suspending the writ – not only to punish traitors, but to incapacitate them.

The proposition that the Executive lacks indefinite wartime detention authority over citizens is consistent with the Founders' general mistrust of military power permanently at the Executive's disposal. In the Founders' view, the "blessings of liberty" were threatened by "those military establishments which must gradually poison its very fountain." The Federalist no. 45, p. 238 (J. Madison) ... A view of the Constitution that gives the Executive authority to use military force rather than the force of law against citizens on American soil flies in the face of [this] mistrust ...

V

It follows from what I have said that Hamdi is entitled to a habeas decree requiring his release unless (1) criminal proceedings are promptly brought, or (2) Congress has suspended the writ of habeas corpus. A suspension of the writ could, of course, lay down conditions for continued detention, similar to those that today's opinion prescribes under the Due Process Clause. Cf. Act of Mar. 3, 1863, 12 Stat. 755. But there is a world of difference between the people's representatives' determining the need for that suspension (and prescribing the conditions for it), and this Court's doing so.

The plurality finds justification for Hamdi's imprisonment in the Authorization for Use of Military Force, 115 Stat. 224, which provides:

That the President is authorized to use all necessary and appropriate force against those nations, organizations, or persons he determines planned, authorized, committed, or aided the terrorist attacks that occurred on

September 11, 2001, or harbored such organizations or persons, in order to prevent any future acts of international terrorism against the United States by such nations, organizations or persons. § 2(a)

This is not remotely a congressional suspension of the writ, and no one claims that it is. Contrary to the plurality's view, I do not think this statute even authorizes detention of a citizen with the clarity necessary to satisfy the interpretive canon that statutes should be construed so as to avoid grave constitutional concerns, see *Edward J. DeBartolo Corp. v. Florida Gulf Coast Building & Constr.* ...; or with the clarity necessary to overcome the statutory prescription that "[n]o citizen shall be imprisoned or otherwise detained by the United States except pursuant to an Act of Congress." 18 U.S.C. § 4001(a). But even if it did, I would not permit it to overcome Hamdi's entitlement to habeas corpus relief. The Suspension Clause of the Constitution, which carefully circumscribes the conditions under which the writ can be withheld, would be a sham if it could be evaded by congressional prescription of requirements other than the common-law requirement of committal for criminal prosecution that render the writ, though available, unavailing. If the Suspension Clause does not guarantee the citizen that he will either be tried or released, unless the conditions for suspending the writ exist and the grave action of suspending the writ has been taken; if it merely guarantees the citizen that he will not be detained unless Congress by ordinary legislation says he can be detained; it guarantees him very little indeed.

It should not be thought, however, that the plurality's evisceration of the Suspension Clause augments, principally, the power of Congress. As usual, the major effect of its constitutional improvisation is to increase the power of the Court. Having found a congressional authorization for detention of citizens where none clearly exists; and having discarded the categorical procedural protection of the Suspension Clause; the plurality then proceeds, under the guise of the Due Process Clause, to prescribe what procedural protections it thinks appropriate. It "weigh[s] the private interest ... against the Government's asserted interest," *ante*, at 2646 (internal quotation marks omitted), and – just as though writing a new Constitution – comes up with an unheard-of system in which the citizen rather than the Government bears the burden of proof, testimony is by hearsay rather than live witnesses, and the presiding officer may well be a "neutral" military officer rather than judge and jury. See *ante*, at 2648–2649. It claims authority to engage in this sort of "judicious balancing" from *Mathews v. Eldridge*, 424 U.S. 319, 96 S.Ct. 893, 47 L.Ed.2d 18 (1976), a case involving ... the withdrawal of disability benefits! Whatever the merits of this technique when newly recognized property rights are at issue (and even there they are questionable), it has no place where the Constitution and the common law already supply an answer.

Having distorted the Suspension Clause, the plurality finishes up by transmogrifying the Great Writ – disposing of the present habeas petition by remanding for the District Court to "engag[e] in a factfinding process that is both prudent and incremental," *ante*, at 2652. "In the absence of [the Executive's prior provision of procedures that satisfy due process], ... a court that receives a petition for a writ of habeas corpus from an alleged enemy combatant must itself ensure that the minimum requirements of due process are achieved." *Ante*, at 2651–2652. This judicial remediation of executive default is unheard of. The role of habeas corpus is to determine the legality of executive detention, not to supply the omitted process necessary to make it legal ... It is not the habeas court's function to make illegal detention legal by supplying a process that the Government could have provided, but chose not to. If Hamdi is being imprisoned in violation of the Constitution (because without due process of law), then his habeas petition should be granted; the Executive may then hand him over to the criminal authorities, whose detention for the purpose of prosecution will be lawful, or else must release him.

There is a certain harmony of approach in the plurality's making up for Congress's failure to invoke the Suspension Clause and its making up for the Executive's failure to apply what it says are needed procedures – an approach that reflects what might be called a Mr. Fix-it Mentality. The plurality seems to view it as its mission to Make Everything Come Out Right, rather than merely to decree the consequences, as far as individual rights are concerned, of the other two branches' actions and omissions. Has the Legislature failed to suspend the writ in the current dire emergency? Well, we will remedy that failure by prescribing the reasonable conditions that a suspension should have included. And has the Executive failed to live up to those reasonable conditions? Well, we will ourselves make that failure good, so that this dangerous fellow (if he is dangerous) need not be set free. The problem with this approach is not only that it steps out of the courts' modest and limited role in a democratic society; but that by repeatedly doing what it thinks the political branches ought to do it encourages their lassitude and saps the vitality of government by the people.

VI

Several limitations give my views in this matter a relatively narrow compass. They apply only to citizens, accused of being enemy combatants, who are detained within the territorial jurisdiction of a federal court. This is not likely to be a numerous group; currently we know of only two, Hamdi and Jose Padilla. Where the citizen is captured outside and held outside the United States, the constitutional requirements may be different. Cf. *Johnson v. Eisentrager*, 339 U.S. 763, 769–771, 70 S.Ct. 936, 94 L.Ed. 1255 (1950); *Reid v. Covert*, 354 U.S. 1, 74–75, 77 S.Ct. 1222, 1 L.Ed.2d 1148 (1957) (Harlan, J., concurring in result); *Rasul v. Bush, ante*, — U.S. —, 124 S.Ct. 2686, 2708-2709, 159 L.Ed.2d 548, 2004 WL 1432134 (2004) (SCALIA, J., dissenting). Moreover, even within the United States, the accused citizen-enemy combatant may lawfully be detained once prosecution is in progress or in contemplation. See, e.g., *County of Riverside v. McLaughlin*, 500 U.S. 44, 111 S.Ct. 1661, 114 L.Ed.2d 49 (1991) (brief detention pending judicial determination after warrantless arrest); *United States v. Salerno*, 481 U.S. 739, 107 S.Ct. 2095, 95 L.Ed.2d 697 (1987) (pretrial detention under the *Bail Reform Act*). The Government has been notably successful in securing conviction, and hence long-term custody or execution, of those who have waged war against the state.

I frankly do not know whether these tools are sufficient to meet the Government's security needs, including the need to obtain intelligence through interrogation. It is far beyond my competence, or the Court's competence, to determine that. But it is not beyond Congress's. If the situation demands it, the Executive can ask Congress to authorize suspension of the writ – which can be made subject to whatever conditions Congress deems appropriate, including even the procedural novelties invented by the plurality today. To be sure, suspension is limited by the Constitution to cases of rebellion or invasion. But whether the attacks of September 11, 2001, constitute an "invasion," and whether those attacks still justify suspension several years later, are questions for Congress rather than this Court ... If civil rights are to be curtailed during wartime, it must be done openly and democratically, as the Constitution requires, rather than by silent erosion through an opinion of this Court.

...

The Founders well understood the difficult tradeoff between safety and freedom. "Safety from external danger," Hamilton declared,

is the most powerful director of national conduct. Even the ardent love of liberty will, after a time, give way to its dictates. The violent destruction of life and property incident to war; the continual effort and alarm attendant on a state of continual danger, will compel nations the most attached to liberty, to resort for repose and security to institutions which have a tendency to destroy their civil and political rights. To be more safe, they, at length, become willing to run the risk of being less free. (The Federalist no. 8, p. 33)

The Founders warned us about the risk, and equipped us with a Constitution designed to deal with it. Many think it not only inevitable but entirely proper that liberty give way to security in times of national crisis – that, at the extremes of military exigency, *inter arma silent leges*. Whatever the general merits of the view that war silences law or modulates its voice, that view has no place in the interpretation and application of a Constitution designed precisely to confront war and, in a manner that accords with democratic principles, to accommodate it. Because the Court has proceeded to meet the current emergency in a manner the Constitution does not envision, I respectfully dissent.

Justice THOMAS, dissenting:

The Executive Branch, acting pursuant to the powers vested in the President by the Constitution and with explicit congressional approval, has determined that Yaser Hamdi is an enemy combatant and should be detained. This detention falls squarely within the Federal Government's war powers, and we lack the expertise and capacity to second-guess that decision. As such, petitioners' habeas challenge should fail, and there is no reason to remand the case. The plurality reaches a contrary conclusion by failing adequately to consider basic principles of the constitutional structure as it relates to national security and foreign affairs and by using the balancing scheme of *Mathews v. Eldridge*, 424 U.S. 319, 96 S.Ct. 893, 47 L.Ed.2d 18 (1976). I do not think that the Federal Government's war powers can be balanced away by this Court. Arguably, Congress could provide for additional procedural protections, but until it does, we have no right to insist upon them. But even if I were to agree with the general approach the plurality takes, I could not accept the particulars. The plurality utterly fails to account for the Government's compelling interests and for our own institutional inability to weigh competing concerns correctly. I respectfully dissent ...

I agree with the plurality that the Federal Government has power to detain those that the Executive Branch determines to be enemy combatants ... But I do not think that the plurality has adequately explained the breadth of the President's authority to detain enemy combatants, an authority that includes making virtually conclusive factual findings. In my view, ... we lack the capacity and responsibility to second-guess this determination ...

In a case strikingly similar to this one, the Court addressed a Governor's authority to detain for an extended period a person the executive believed to be responsible, in part, for a local insurrection. Justice Holmes wrote for a unanimous Court:

When it comes to a decision by the head of the State upon a matter involving its life, the ordinary rights of individuals must yield to what *he deems* the necessities of the moment. Public danger warrants the substitution of executive process for judicial process. This was admitted with regard to killing men in the actual clash of arms, and we think it obvious, although it was disputed, that the same is true of temporary detention to prevent apprehended harm. (*Moyer*, 212 U.S., at 85, 29 S.Ct. 235; citation omitted; emphasis added)

The Court answered Moyer's claim that he had been denied due process by emphasizing that

it is familiar that what is due process of law depends on circumstances. It varies with the subject-matter and the necessities of the situation. Thus summary proceedings suffice for taxes, and executive decisions for exclusion from the country ... Such arrests are not necessarily for punishment, but are by way of precaution to prevent the exercise of hostile power. (Id., at 84–85, 90 S.Ct. 1068; citations omitted).

In this context, due process requires nothing more than a good-faith executive determination ...

The Government's asserted authority to detain an individual that the President has determined to be an enemy combatant, at least while hostilities continue, comports with the Due Process Clause ... The

Executive's decision that a detention is necessary to protect the public need not and should not be subjected to judicial second-guessing. Indeed, at least in the context of enemy-combatant determinations, this would defeat the unity, secrecy, and dispatch that the Founders believed to be so important to the warmaking function ...

Accordingly, I conclude that the Government's detention of Hamdi as an enemy combatant does not violate the Constitution. By detaining Hamdi, the President, in the prosecution of a war and authorized by Congress, has acted well within his authority. Hamdi thereby received all the process to which he was due under the circumstances. I therefore believe that this is no occasion to balance the competing interests, as the plurality unconvincingly attempts to do ...

...

For these reasons, I would affirm the judgment of the Court of Appeals.

READING QUESTIONS ON *HAMDI*

1   Does the approach of the majority make things worse by placing a thin veneer of legality over what is in substance an exercise of arbitrary power? Would it have made a difference if the majority had required that there be explicit legislative authorization for such detentions and had said that the legislature must devise appropriate procedural protections for the detainees, but without telling the legislature what the Court thought was minimally appropriate?
2   Do you think that Justice Scalia's or Justice Thomas's approaches might reflect better the realities of the "new normal"?

A and others v. Secretary of State for the Home Department [2005] 2 AC 68

The House of Lords had to respond to the British government's decision to derogate from its commitments to the right to liberty in terms of Article 15 of the *European Convention on Human Rights* in order to detain aliens – non-British individuals – who were suspected of being threats to national security. In terms of the *Human Rights Act* (1998), a court may not invalidate legislation that is incompatible with human rights but simply makes a declaration to that effect. Here the derogation had been from the right to liberty, but the majority of the Court found that the detention of aliens violated commitments to equality and also was disproportionate. However, the majority (Lord Bingham) thought it appropriate to defer to the government on the issue of whether there was an emergency. Lord Hoffmann found that the derogation was invalid because in his view there was no public emergency threatening the life of the nation, as required by Article 15. A lone dissenting judge reasoned that the Court had to defer to the government on both the issue that there was an emergency and on how best to respond to the emergency.

HOUSE OF LORDS
Lord Bingham of Cornhill:

[3] The appellants share certain common characteristics which are central to their appeals. All are foreign (non–United Kingdom) nationals. None has been the subject of any criminal charge. In none of their cases is a criminal trial in prospect. All challenge the lawfulness of their detention. More specifically, they all contend that such detention was inconsistent with obligations binding on the United Kingdom under the European Convention for the Protection of Human Rights and Fundamental Freedoms 1950 (Rome, 4 November 1950; TS 71 (1953); Cmd 8969), given domestic effect by the *Human Rights Act 1998*; that the United Kingdom was not legally entitled to derogate from those obligations; that, if it was, its derogation was none the less inconsistent with the convention and so ineffectual to justify the detention; and that the statutory provisions under which they have been detained are incompatible with the convention. The duty of the House, and the only duty of the House in its judicial capacity, is to decide whether the appellants' legal challenge is soundly based.

THE BACKGROUND

[5] In July 2000 Parliament enacted the *Terrorism Act 2000*. This was a substantial measure, with 131 sections and 16 schedules, intended to overhaul, modernise and strengthen the law relating to the growing problem of terrorism ...

[6] On 11 September 2001 terrorists launched concerted attacks in New York, Washington DC and Pennsylvania. The main facts surrounding those attacks are too well known to call for recapitulation here. It is enough to record that they were atrocities on an unprecedented scale, causing many deaths and destroying property of immense value. They were intended to disable the governmental and commercial power of the United States. The attacks were the product of detailed planning. They were committed by terrorists fired by ideological hatred of the United States and willing to sacrifice their own lives in order to injure the leading nation of the western world. The mounting of such attacks against such targets in such a country inevitably caused acute concerns about their own security in other western countries, particularly those which, like the United Kingdom, were particularly prominent in their support for the United States and its military response to Al-Qa'ida, the organisation quickly identified as responsible for the attacks. Before and after 11 September Usama bin Laden, the moving spirit of Al-Qa'ida, made threats specifically directed against the United Kingdom and its people.

[7] Her Majesty's government reacted to the events of 11 September in two ways directly relevant to these appeals. First, it introduced (and Parliament, subject to amendment, very swiftly enacted) what became Pt 4 of the *Anti-terrorism, Crime and Security Act 2001*. Second, it made the *Human Rights Act 1998* (Designated Derogation) Order 2001, SI 2001/3644 (the derogation order). Before summarising the effect of these measures it is important to understand their underlying legal rationale.

[8] First, it was provided by para 2(2) of Sch. 3 to the *Immigration Act 1971* that the Secretary of State might detain a non-British national pending the making of a deportation order against him. Paragraph 2(3) of the same schedule authorised the Secretary of State to detain a person against whom a deportation order had been made "pending his removal or departure from the United Kingdom." *In R. v. Governor of Durham Prison, ex p Singh*, [1984] 1 All ER 983, [1984] 1 WLR 704 it was held, in a decision which has never been questioned (and which was followed by the Privy Council in *Tan Te Lam v. Superintendent of Tai A Chau Detention Centre*, [1996] 4 All ER 256, [1997] AC 97), that such detention was permissible only for such time as was reasonably necessary for the process of deportation to be carried out. Thus there was no warrant for the long-term or indefinite detention of a non–United Kingdom national whom the Home Secretary wished to remove. This ruling was wholly consistent with the obligations undertaken by the United Kingdom in

the convention, the core articles of which were given domestic effect by the 1998 Act. Among these articles is art. 5(1) which guarantees the fundamental human right of personal freedom: "Everyone has the right to liberty and security of person." This must be read in the context of art 1, by which contracting states undertake to secure the convention rights and freedoms to "everyone within their jurisdiction." But the right of personal freedom, fundamental though it is, cannot be absolute and art. 5(1) of the convention goes on to prescribe certain exceptions. One exception is crucial to these appeals:

"(1) Everyone has the right to liberty and security of person. No one shall be deprived of his liberty save in the following cases and in accordance with a procedure prescribed by law ... (f) the lawful arrest or detention of ... a person against whom action is being taken with a view to deportation ..."

Thus there is, again, no warrant for the long-term or indefinite detention of a non–United Kingdom national whom the Home Secretary wishes to remove. Such a person may be detained only during the process of deportation. Otherwise, the convention is breached and the convention rights of the detainee are violated.

[9] Second, reference must be made to the important decision of the European Court of Human Rights in *Chahal v. UK* (1996) 1 BHRC 405. Mr Chahal was an Indian citizen who had been granted indefinite leave to remain in this country but whose activities as a Sikh separatist brought him to the notice of the authorities both in India and here. The Home Secretary of the day decided that he should be deported from this country because his continued presence here was not conducive to the public good for reasons of a political nature, namely the international fight against terrorism. He resisted deportation on the ground (among others) that, if returned to India, he faced a real risk of death, or of torture in custody contrary to art. 3 of the European convention which provides that "No one shall be subjected to torture or to inhuman or degrading treatment or punishment." Before the European Court the United Kingdom contended that the effect of art. 3 should be qualified in a case where a state sought to deport a non-national on grounds of national security. This was an argument which the court, affirming a unanimous decision of the European Commission of Human Rights, rejected. It said (at 422):

"79. Article 3 enshrines one of the most fundamental values of democratic society. The Court is well aware of the immense difficulties faced by states in modern times in protecting their communities from terrorist violence. However, even in these circumstances, the convention prohibits in absolute terms torture or inhuman or degrading treatment or punishment, irrespective of the victim's conduct. Unlike most of the substantive clauses of the convention and of Protocols Nos. 1 and 4, art. 3 makes no provision for exceptions and no derogation from it is permissible under art. 15 even in the event of a public emergency threatening the life of the nation.

"80. The prohibition provided by art. 3 against ill-treatment is equally absolute in expulsion cases. Thus, whenever substantial grounds have been shown for believing that an individual would face a real risk of being subjected to treatment contrary to art. 3 if removed to another state, the responsibility of the contracting state to safeguard him or her against such treatment is engaged in the event of expulsion ... In these circumstances, the activities of the individual in question, however undesirable or dangerous, cannot be a material consideration. The protection afforded by art. 3 is thus wider than that provided by arts. 32 and 33 of the [United Nations Convention on the Status of Refugees (Geneva, 28 July 1951; TS 39 (1954); Cmnd 9171)]."

The court went on to consider whether Mr Chahal's detention, which had lasted for a number of years, had exceeded the period permissible under art. 5(1)(f). On this question the court, differing from the unanimous decision of the commission, held that it had not. But it reasserted (at 430 (para 113)) that "any deprivation of liberty under art. 5(1)(f) will be justified only for as long as deportation proceedings are in progress." In a case like Mr Chahal's, where deportation proceedings are precluded by art. 3, art. 5(1)(f) would not sanction detention because the non-national would not be "a person against whom action is being taken with a view to deportation." A person who commits a serious crime under the criminal law of this country may of course, whether a national or a non-national, be charged, tried and, if convicted, imprisoned. But a non-national who faces the prospect of torture or inhuman treatment if returned to his own country, and who cannot be deported to any third country and is not charged with any crime, may not under art. 5(1)(f) of the convention and Sch. 3 to the 1971 Act be detained here even if judged to be a threat to national security.

[10] The convention gives member states a limited right to derogate from some articles of the convention (including art. 5, although not art. 3). The governing provision is art. 15, which so far as relevant provides:

"Derogation in time of emergency

1. In time of war or other public emergency threatening the life of the nation any High Contracting Party may take measures derogating from

its obligations under this Convention to the extent strictly required by the exigencies of the situation, provided that such measures are not inconsistent with its other obligations under international law."

A member state availing itself of the right of derogation must inform the Secretary General of the Council of Europe of the measures it has taken and the reasons for them. It must also tell the Secretary General when the measures have ceased to operate and the provisions of the convention are again being fully executed. Article 15 of the convention is not one of the articles expressly incorporated by the 1998 Act, but s. 14 of that Act makes provision for prospective derogations by the United Kingdom to be designated for the purposes of the Act in an order made by the Secretary of State. It was in exercise of his power under that section that the Home Secretary, on 11 November 2001, made the derogation order, which came into force two days later, although relating to what was at that stage a proposed derogation.

THE DEROGATION ORDER

[11] The derogation related to art. 5(1), in reality art. 5(1)(f), of the convention. The proposed notification by the United Kingdom was set out in a schedule to the order. The first section of this, entitled "Public emergency in the United Kingdom," referred to the attacks of 11 September and to United Nations Security Council resolutions recognising those attacks as a threat to international peace and security and requiring all states to take measures to prevent the commission of terrorist attacks, "including by denying safe haven to those who finance, plan, support or commit terrorist attacks." It was stated in the schedule:

"There exists a terrorist threat to the United Kingdom from persons suspected of involvement in international terrorism. In particular, there are foreign nationals present in the United Kingdom who are suspected of being concerned in the commission, preparation or instigation of acts of international terrorism, of being members of organisations or groups which are so concerned or of having links with members of such organisations or groups, and who are a threat to the national security of the United Kingdom."

The next section summarised the effect of what was to become the 2001 Act ... In a section entitled "Article 5(1)(f) of the Convention" the effect of the court's decision in *Chahal v. UK* was summarised. In the next section it was recognised that the extended power in the new legislation to detain a person against whom no action was being taken with a view to deportation might be inconsistent with art. 5(1)(f). Hence the need for derogation. Formal notice of derogation was given to the Secretary General on 18 December 2001 ...

THE 2001 ACT

[12] The 2001 Act is a long and comprehensive statute. Only Pt 4 ("Immigration and Asylum") has featured in argument in these appeals, because only Pt 4 contains the power to detain indefinitely on reasonable suspicion without charge or trial of which the appellants complain, and only Pt 4 is the subject of the United Kingdom derogation ...

The appellants' challenge in these proceedings was brought under this section ...

PUBLIC EMERGENCY

[16] The appellants repeated before the House a contention rejected by both the SIAC and the Court of Appeal, that there neither was nor is a "public emergency threatening the life of the nation" within the meaning of art. 15(1). Thus, they contended, the threshold test for reliance on art. 15 has not been satisfied ...

[20] The appellants did not seek to play down the catastrophic nature of what had taken place on 11 September 2001 nor the threat posed to western democracies by international terrorism. But they argued that there had been no public emergency threatening the life of the British nation, for three main reasons: if the emergency was not (as in all the decided cases) actual, it must be shown to be imminent, which could not be shown here; the emergency must be of a temporary nature, which again could not be shown here; and the practice of other states, none of which had derogated from the convention, strongly suggested that there was no public emergency calling for derogation. All these points call for some explanation.

[21] The requirement of imminence is not expressed in art. 15 of the convention or art. 4 of the ICCPR but it has, as already noted, been treated by the European Court of Human Rights as a necessary condition of a valid derogation. It is a view shared by the distinguished academic authors of the Siracusa Principles, who in 1985 formulated the rule (applying to the ICCPR):

"54. The principle of strict necessity shall be applied in an objective manner. Each measure shall be directed to an actual, clear, present, or imminent danger and may not be imposed merely because of an apprehension of potential danger."

In submitting that the test of imminence was not met, the appellants pointed to ministerial statements in October 2001 and March 2002: "There is no immediate intelligence pointing to a specific threat to the United Kingdom, but we remain alert, domestically as well as internationally"; and "[I]t would be wrong to say that we have evidence of a particular threat (see 372 HC official Report (6th series) col 925 and HC Paper 348-I (2001–2002) para 13)."

[22] The requirement of temporariness is again not expressed in art. 15 or art. 4 unless it be inherent in the meaning of "emergency." But the United Nations Human Rights Committee on 24 July 2001, in General Comment no 29 on art. 4 of the ICCPR (UN Doc CCPR/C/21/Rev 1/Add 11 (2001)), observed in para 2 that: "Measures derogating from the provisions of the Covenant must be of an exceptional and temporary nature." This view was also taken by the Parliamentary Joint Committee on Human Rights, which in its Eighteenth Report of the Session 2003–2004 (HL paper 158, HC paper 713), p 6 (para 4), observed:

"Derogations from human rights obligations are permitted in order to deal with emergencies. They are intended to be temporary. According to the Government and the Security Service, the UK now faces a near-permanent emergency."

It is indeed true that official spokesmen have declined to suggest when, if ever, the present situation might change.

[23] No state other than the United Kingdom has derogated from art. 5. In Resolution 1271 adopted on 24 January 2002, the Parliamentary Assembly of the Council of Europe resolved (para 9) that: "In their fight against terrorism, Council of Europe member states should not provide for any derogations to the European Convention on Human Rights." It also called on all member states (para 12.v) to "refrain from using Article 15 of the European Convention on Human Rights (derogation in time of emergency) to limit the rights and liberties guaranteed under its Article 5 (right to liberty and security)" ...

[24] The appellants submitted that detailed information pointing to a real and imminent danger to public safety in the United Kingdom had not been shown. In making this submission they were able to rely on a series of reports by the Joint Committee on Human Rights ...

[25] The Attorney General, representing the Home Secretary, answered these points. He submitted that an emergency could properly be regarded as imminent if an atrocity was credibly threatened by a body such as Al-Qa'ida which had demonstrated its capacity and will to carry out such a threat, where the atrocity might be committed without warning at any time. The government, responsible as it was and

is for the safety of the British people, need not wait for disaster to strike before taking necessary steps to prevent it striking. As to the requirement that the emergency be temporary, the Attorney General did not suggest that an emergency could ever become the normal state of affairs, but he did resist the imposition of any artificial temporal limit to an emergency of the present kind, and pointed out that the emergency which had been held to justify derogation in Northern Ireland in 1988 had been accepted as continuing for a considerable number of years (see *Marshall v. UK*, App no 41571/98 (10 July 2001, unreported), at [18], above). Little help, it was suggested, could be gained by looking at the practice of other states. It was for each national government, as the guardian of its own people's safety, to make its own judgment on the basis of the facts known to it. In so far as any difference of practice as between the United Kingdom and other Council of Europe members called for justification, it could be found in this country's prominent role as an enemy of Al-Qa'ida and an ally of the United States. The Attorney General also made two more fundamental submissions. First, he submitted that there was no error of law in the SIAC's approach to this issue and accordingly, since an appeal against its decision lay only on a point of law, there was no ground upon which any appellate court was entitled to disturb its conclusion. Second, he submitted that the judgment on this question was pre-eminently one within the discretionary area of judgment reserved to the Secretary of State and his colleagues, exercising their judgment with the benefit of official advice, and to Parliament.

[26] The appellants have in my opinion raised an important and difficult question, as the continuing anxiety of the Joint Committee on Human Rights, the observations of the Commissioner for Human Rights and the warnings of the United Nations Human Rights Committee make clear. In the result, however, not without misgiving (fortified by reading the opinion of my noble and learned friend Lord Hoffmann), I would resolve this issue against the appellants, for three main reasons.

[27] First, it is not shown that the SIAC or the Court of Appeal misdirected themselves on this issue. The SIAC considered a body of closed material, that is, secret material of a sensitive nature not shown to the parties. The Court of Appeal was not asked to read this material. The Attorney General expressly declined to ask the House to read it. From this I infer that while the closed material no doubt substantiates and strengthens the evidence in the public domain, it does not alter its essential character and effect. But this is in my view beside the point. It

is not shown that the SIAC misdirected itself in law on this issue, and the view which it accepted was one it could reach on the open evidence in the case.

[28] My second reason is a legal one. The European Court of Human Rights decisions in *Ireland v. UK* (1978) 2 EHRR 25; *Brannigan v. UK* (1993) 17 EHRR 539; *Aksoy v. Turkey* (1996) 1 BHRC 625; and *Marshall v. UK* seem to me to be, with respect, clearly right. In each case the member state had actually experienced widespread loss of life caused by an armed body dedicated to destroying the territorial integrity of the state. To hold that the art. 15 test was not satisfied in such circumstances, if a response beyond that provided by the ordinary course of law was required, would have been perverse. But these features were not, on the facts found, very clearly present in *Lawless v. Ireland* (No 3) (1961) 1 EHRR 15. That was a relatively early decision of the European Court of Human Rights, but it has never to my knowledge been disavowed and the House is required by s. 2(1) of the 1998 Act to take it into account. The decision may perhaps be explained as showing the breadth of the margin of appreciation accorded by the court to national authorities. It may even have been influenced by the generous opportunity for release given to Mr Lawless and those in his position. If, however, it was open to the Irish government in *Lawless v. Ireland* (No 3) to conclude that there was a public emergency threatening the life of the Irish nation, the British government could scarcely be faulted for reaching that conclusion in the much more dangerous situation which arose after 11 September.

[29] Third, I would accept that great weight should be given to the judgment of the Home Secretary, his colleagues and Parliament on this question, because they were called on to exercise a pre-eminently political judgment. It involved making a factual prediction of what various people around the world might or might not do, and when (if at all) they might do it, and what the consequences might be if they did. Any prediction about the future behaviour of human beings (as opposed to the phases of the moon or high water at London Bridge) is necessarily problematical. Reasonable and informed minds may differ, and a judgment is not shown to be wrong or unreasonable because that which is thought likely to happen does not happen. It would have been irresponsible not to err, if at all, on the side of safety. As will become apparent, I do not accept the full breadth of the Attorney General's argument on what is generally called the deference owed by the courts to the political authorities. It is perhaps preferable to approach this

question as one of demarcation of functions or what Liberty in its written case called "relative institutional competence." The more purely political (in a broad or narrow sense) a question is, the more appropriate it will be for political resolution and the less likely it is to be an appropriate matter for judicial decision. The smaller, therefore, will be the potential role of the court. It is the function of political and not judicial bodies to resolve political questions. Conversely, the greater the legal content of any issue, the greater the potential role of the court, because under our constitution and subject to the sovereign power of Parliament it is the function of the courts and not of political bodies to resolve legal questions. The present question seems to me to be very much at the political end of the spectrum ... The appellants recognised this by acknowledging that the Home Secretary's decision on the present question was less readily open to challenge than his decision (as they argued) on some other questions. This reflects the unintrusive approach of the European Court of Human Rights to such a question. I conclude that the appellants have shown no ground strong enough to warrant displacing the Secretary of State's decision on this important threshold question.

PROPORTIONALITY

[30] Article 15 requires that any measures taken by a member state in derogation of its obligations under the convention should not go beyond what is "strictly required by the exigencies of the situation." Thus the convention imposes a test of strict necessity or, in convention terminology, proportionality ... In determining whether a limitation is arbitrary or excessive, the court must ask itself

"whether: (i) the legislative objective is sufficiently important to justify limiting a fundamental right; (ii) the measures designed to meet the legislative objective are rationally connected to it; and (iii) the means used to impair the right or freedom are no more than is necessary to accomplish the objective" ...

[31] The appellants' argument under this head can, I hope fairly, be summarised as involving the following steps:

(1) Part 4 of the 2001 Act reversed the effect of the decisions in *R. v. Governor of Durham Prison, ex p Singh*, [1984] 1 All ER 983, [1984] 1 WLR 704 and *Chahal v. UK* (1996) 1 BHRC 405 and was apt to address the problems of immigration control caused to the United Kingdom by art. 5(1)(f) of the convention read in the light of those decisions.

(2) The public emergency on which the United Kingdom relied to derogate from the convention right to personal liberty was the threat to

the security of the United Kingdom presented by Al-Qa'ida terrorists and their supporters.

(3) While the threat to the security of the United Kingdom derived predominantly and most immediately from foreign nationals, some of whom could not be deported because they would face torture or inhuman or degrading treatment or punishment in their home countries and who could not be deported to any third country willing to receive them, the threat to the United Kingdom did not derive solely from such foreign nationals.

(4) Sections 21 and 23 did not rationally address the threat to the security of the United Kingdom presented by Al-Qa'ida terrorists and their supporters because (a) it did not address the threat presented by United Kingdom nationals, (b) it permitted foreign nationals suspected of being Al-Qa'ida terrorists or their supporters to pursue their activities abroad if there was any country to which they were able to go, and (c) the sections permitted the certification and detention of persons who were not suspected of presenting any threat to the security of the United Kingdom as Al-Qa'ida terrorists or supporters.

(5) If the threat presented to the security of the United Kingdom by United Kingdom nationals suspected of being Al-Qa'ida terrorists or their supporters could be addressed without infringing their right to personal liberty, it is not shown why similar measures could not adequately address the threat presented by foreign nationals.

(6) Since the right to personal liberty is among the most fundamental of the rights protected by the convention, any restriction of it must be closely scrutinised by the national court and such scrutiny involves no violation of democratic or constitutional principle.

(7) In the light of such scrutiny, neither the derogation order nor ss. 21 and 23 of the 2001 Act can be justified.

[32] It is unnecessary to linger on the first two steps of this argument, neither of which is controversial and both of which are clearly correct. The third step calls for closer examination. The evidence before the SIAC was that the Home Secretary considered "that the serious threats to the nation emanated predominantly (albeit not exclusively) and more immediately from the category of foreign nationals." The SIAC held ([2002] HRLR 1274 at 1313 (para 95)):

"But the evidence before us demonstrates beyond argument that the threat is not so confined [i.e. is not confined to the alien section of the population]. There are many British nationals already identified – mostly in detention abroad – who fall within the definition of 'suspected international terrorists,' and it was clear from the submissions made to us that in the opinion of the [Home Secretary] there are others at liberty in the United Kingdom who could be similarly defined."

This finding has not been challenged, and since the SIAC is the responsible fact-finding tribunal it is unnecessary to examine the basis of it. There was however evidence before the SIAC that "upwards of a thousand individuals from the UK are estimated on the basis of intelligence to have attended training camps in Afghanistan in the last five years," that some British citizens are said to have planned to return from Afghanistan to the United Kingdom and that "The backgrounds of those detained show the high level of involvement of British citizens and those otherwise connected with the United Kingdom in the terrorist networks." It seems plain that the threat to the United Kingdom did not derive solely from foreign nationals or from foreign nationals whom it was unlawful to deport. Later evidence, not before the SIAC or the Court of Appeal, supports that conclusion. The Newton Committee recorded the Home Office argument that the threat from Al-Qa'ida terrorism was predominantly from foreigners but drew attention (HC Paper 100 (2003–2004) p 54 (para 193)) to "accumulating evidence that this is not now the case. The British suicide bombers who attacked Tel Aviv in May 2003, Richard Reid ('the Shoe Bomber'), and recent arrests suggest that the threat from UK citizens is real. Almost 30% of Terrorism Act 2000 suspects in the past year have been British. We have been told that, of the people of interest to the authorities because of their suspected involvement in international terrorism, nearly half are British nationals."

[33] The fourth step in the appellants' argument is of obvious importance to it. It is plain that ss. 21 and 23 of the 2001 Act do not address the threat presented by United Kingdom nationals since they do not provide for the certification and detention of United Kingdom nationals. It is beside the point that other sections of the 2001 Act and the 2000 Act do apply to United Kingdom nationals, since they are not the subject of derogation, are not the subject of complaint and apply equally to foreign nationals. Yet the threat from United Kingdom nationals, if quantitatively smaller, is not said to be qualitatively different from that from foreign nationals. It is also plain that ss. 21 and 23 do permit a person certified and detained to leave the United Kingdom and go to any other country willing to receive him, as two of the appellants did when they left for Morocco and France respectively (see [2], above). Such freedom to leave is wholly explicable in terms of immigration control: if the British authorities wish to deport a foreign national but cannot deport him to country "A" because of *Chahal v. UK*

their purpose is as well served by his voluntary departure for country "B." But allowing a suspected international terrorist to leave our shores and depart to another country, perhaps a country as close as France, there to pursue his criminal designs, is hard to reconcile with a belief in his capacity to inflict serious injury to the people and interests of this country. It seems clear from the language of s. 21 of the 2001 Act, read with the definition of terrorism in s. 1 of the 2000 Act, that s 21 is capable of covering those who have no link at all with Al-Qa'ida (they might, for example, be members of the Basque separatist organisation ETA), or who, although supporting the general aims of Al-Qa'ida, reject its cult of violence. The Attorney General conceded that ss. 21 and 23 could not lawfully be invoked in the case of suspected international terrorists other than those thought to be connected with Al-Qa'ida, and undertook that the procedure would not be used in such cases. A restrictive reading of the broad statutory language might in any event be indicated (see *Padfield v. Minister of Agriculture Fisheries and Food*, [1968] 1 All ER 694, [1968] AC 997). The appellants were content to accept the Attorney General's concession and undertaking. It is not however acceptable that interpretation and application of a statutory provision bearing on the liberty of the subject should be governed by implication, concession and undertaking ...

[35] The fifth step in the appellants' argument permits of little elaboration. But it seems reasonable to assume that those suspected international terrorists who are United Kingdom nationals are not simply ignored by the authorities. When G, one of the appellants, was released from prison by SIAC on bail (see *G v. Secretary of State for the Home Dept* (20 May 2004, unreported), it was on condition (among other things) that he wear an electronic monitoring tag at all times; that he remain at his premises at all times; that he telephone a named security company five times each day at specified times; that he permit the company to install monitoring equipment at his premises; that he limit entry to his premises to his family, his solicitor, his medical attendants and other approved persons; that he make no contact with any other person; that he have on his premises no computer equipment, mobile telephone or other electronic communications device; that he cancel the existing telephone link to his premises; and that he install a dedicated telephone link permitting contact only with the security company. The appellants suggested that conditions of this kind, strictly enforced, would effectively inhibit terrorist activity. It is hard to see why this would not be so.

[36] In urging the fundamental importance of the right to personal

freedom, as the sixth step in their proportionality argument, the appellants were able to draw on the long libertarian tradition of English law, dating back to Ch 39 of *Magna Carta 1215* (9 Hen 3), given effect in the ancient remedy of habeas corpus, declared in the *Petition of Right 1627* (3 Car 1c1), upheld in a series of landmark decisions down the centuries and embodied in the substance and procedure of the law to our own day ...

[37] While the Attorney General challenged and resisted the third, fourth and fifth steps in the appellants' argument, he directed the weight of his submission to challenging the standard of judicial review for which the appellants contended in this sixth step. He submitted that as it was for Parliament and the executive to assess the threat facing the nation, so it was for those bodies and not the courts to judge the response necessary to protect the security of the public. These were matters of a political character calling for an exercise of political and not judicial judgment. Just as the European Court of Human Rights allowed a generous margin of appreciation to member states, recognising that they were better placed to understand and address local problems, so should national courts recognise, for the same reason, that matters of the kind in issue here fall within the discretionary area of judgment properly belonging to the democratic organs of the state. It was not for the courts to usurp authority properly belonging elsewhere. The Attorney General drew attention to the dangers identified by Richard Ekins in "Judicial Supremacy and the Rule of Law" (2003) 119 LQR 127. This is an important submission, properly made, and it calls for careful consideration.

[38] Those conducting the business of democratic government have to make legislative choices which, notably in some fields, are very much a matter for them, particularly when (as is often the case) the interests of one individual or group have to be balanced against those of another individual or group or the interests of the community as a whole ...

Where the conduct of government is threatened by serious terrorism, difficult choices have to be made and the terrorist dimension cannot be overlooked ...

[39] While any decision made by a representative democratic body must of course command respect, the degree of respect will be conditioned by the nature of the decision. As the European Court of Human Rights observed in *Frett v. France*, [2003] 2 FCR 39 at 57–58 (para 40):

"... the contracting states enjoy a margin of appreciation in assessing whether and to what extent differences in otherwise similar situations

justify a different treatment in law. The scope of the margin of appreciation will vary according to the circumstances, the subject matter and its
background; in this respect, one of the relevant factors may be the
existence or non-existence of common ground between the laws of the
contracting states."

...

Another area in which the court was held to be qualified to make its
own judgment is the requirement of a fair trial ... The Supreme Court
of Canada took a similar view in *Libman v. A-G of Quebec* (1997) 3 BHRC
269 at 288-89 (para 59). In his dissenting judgment (cited with approval
in *Libman v. A-G of Quebec*) in *RJR-MacDonald Inc v. A-G of Canada*, [1995]
3 LRC 653 at 697, La Forest J, sitting in the same court, said:

"Courts are specialists in the protection of liberty and the interpretation of legislation and are, accordingly, well placed to subject criminal
justice legislation to careful scrutiny. However, courts are not specialists
in the realm of policy-making, nor should they be"

...

[40] The convention regime for the international protection of human
rights requires national authorities, including national courts, to exercise
their authority to afford effective protection ...

[41] Even in a terrorist situation the convention organs have not been
willing to relax their residual supervisory role ... In *Aksoy v. Turkey*
(1996) 1 BHRC 625 at 643 (para 76), the court, clearly referring to
national courts as well as the convention organs, held:

"The Court would stress the importance of art. 5 in the convention
system: it enshrines a fundamental human right, namely the protection
of the individual against arbitrary interference by the state with his or
her right to liberty. Judicial control of interferences by the executive
with the individual's right to liberty is an essential feature of the
guarantee embodied in art. 5(3), which is intended to minimise the risk
of arbitrariness and to ensure the rule of law."

...

[42] It follows from this analysis that the appellants are in my
opinion entitled to invite the courts to review, on proportionality
grounds, the derogation order and the compatibility with the convention of s. 23 and the courts are not effectively precluded by any doctrine
of deference from scrutinising the issues raised. It also follows that I do
not accept the full breadth of the Attorney General's submissions. I do
not in particular accept the distinction which he drew between

democratic institutions and the courts. It is of course true that the judges in this country are not elected and are not answerable to Parliament. It is also of course true, as pointed out at [29], above, that Parliament, the executive and the courts have different functions. But the function of independent judges charged to interpret and apply the law is universally recognised as a cardinal feature of the modern democratic state, a cornerstone of the rule of law itself. The Attorney General is fully entitled to insist on the proper limits of judicial authority, but he is wrong to stigmatise judicial decision-making as in some way undemocratic. It is particularly inappropriate in a case such as the present in which Parliament has expressly legislated in s. 6 of the 1998 Act to render unlawful any act of a public authority, including a court, incompatible with a convention right, has required courts (in s. 2) to take account of relevant Strasbourg jurisprudence, has (in s. 3) required courts, so far as possible, to give effect to convention rights and has conferred a right of appeal on derogation issues. The effect is not, of course, to override the sovereign legislative authority of the Queen in Parliament, since if primary legislation is declared to be incompatible the validity of the legislation is unaffected (s. 4(6)) and the remedy lies with the appropriate minister (s. 10), who is answerable to Parliament. The 1998 Act gives the courts a very specific, wholly democratic, mandate. As Professor Jowell has put it: "The courts are charged by Parliament with delineating the boundaries of a rights-based democracy." (See "Judicial deference: servility, civility or institutional capacity?" [2003] PL 592, p. 597. See also Clayton, "Judicial deference and 'democratic dialogue': the legitimacy of judicial intervention under the Human Rights Act 1998" [2004] PL 33.)

[43] The appellants' proportionality challenge to the order and s. 23 is, in my opinion, sound, for all the reasons they gave and also for those given by the European Commissioner for Human Rights and the Newton Committee. The Attorney General could give no persuasive answer. In a discussion paper Counter-Terrorism Powers: Reconciling Security and Liberty in an Open Society (2004) (Cm 6147) the Secretary of State replied to one of the Newton Committee's criticisms in this way (p. 8):

"32. It can be argued that as suspected international terrorists their departure for another country could amount to exporting terrorism: a point made in the Newton Report at paragraph 195. But that is a natural consequence of the fact that Part 4 powers are immigration powers: detention is permissible only pending deportation and there is no other power available to detain (other than for the purpose of police enquiries) if a foreign national chooses voluntarily to leave the UK. (Detention in those circumstances is limited to 14 days after which the person must be either charged or released.) Deportation has the advantage moreover of disrupting the activities of the suspected terrorist."

This answer, however, reflects the central complaint made by the appellants: that the choice of an immigration measure to address a security problem had the inevitable result of failing adequately to address that problem (by allowing non–United Kingdom suspected terrorists to leave the country with impunity and leaving British suspected terrorists at large) while imposing the severe penalty of indefinite detention on persons who, even if reasonably suspected of having links with Al-Qa'ida, may harbour no hostile intentions towards the United Kingdom. The conclusion that the order and s. 23 are, in convention terms, disproportionate is in my opinion irresistible ...

DISCRIMINATION

[45] As part of their proportionality argument, the appellants attacked s. 23 as discriminatory. They contended that, being discriminatory, the section could not be "strictly required" within the meaning of art. 15 and so was disproportionate. The courts below found it convenient to address this discrimination issue separately, and I shall do the same.

[46] The appellants complained that in providing for the detention of suspected international terrorists who were not United Kingdom nationals but not for the detention of suspected international terrorists who were United Kingdom nationals, s. 23 unlawfully discriminated against them as non–United Kingdom nationals in breach of art. 14 of the convention. That article provides:

"Prohibition of discrimination

The enjoyment of the rights and freedoms set forth in this Convention shall be secured without discrimination on any ground such as sex, race, colour, language, religion, political or other opinion, national or social origin, association with a national minority, property, birth or other status."

It is well established that the obligation on the state not to discriminate applies only to rights which it is bound to protect under the convention. The appellants claim that s. 23 discriminates against them in their enjoyment of liberty under art. 5. Article 14 is of obvious importance ...

[47] The United Kingdom did not derogate from art. 14 of the convention (or from art. 26 of the ICCPR, which corresponds to it). The Attorney General did not submit that there had been an implied derogation, an argument advanced to the SIAC but not to the Court of Appeal or the House.

[48] The foreign nationality of the appellants does not preclude them from claiming the protection of their convention rights. By art. 1 of the convention (which has not been expressly incorporated) the contracting states undertook to secure the listed convention rights "to everyone within their jurisdiction." That includes the appellants. The European Court of Human Rights has recognised the convention rights of non-nationals (see, for a recent example, *Conka v. Belgium* (2002) 11 BHRC 555). This accords with domestic authority. In *Khawaja v. Secretary of State for the Home Dept*, [1983] 1 All ER 765 at 782, [1984] AC 74 at 111–12:

"Habeas corpus protection is often expressed as limited to 'British subjects.' Is it really limited to British nationals? Suffice it to say that the case law has given an emphatic 'No' to the question. Every person within the jurisdiction enjoys the equal protection of our laws. There is no distinction between British nationals and others. He who is subject to English law is entitled to its protection. This principle has been in the law at least since Lord Mansfield freed 'the black' in *Sommersett's Case* (1772) 20 State Tr 1 at 20. There is nothing here to encourage in the case of aliens or non-patrials the implication of words excluding the judicial review our law normally accords to those whose liberty is infringed."

[49] It was pointed out that nationality is not included as a forbidden ground of discrimination in art. 14. The Strasbourg court has however treated nationality as such. In *Gaygusuz v. Austria* (1997) 23 EHRR 364 at 381 (para 42), it said:

"However, very weighty reasons would have to be put forward before the Court could regard a difference of treatment based exclusively on the ground of nationality as compatible with the Convention."

The Attorney General accepted that "or other status" would cover the appellants' immigration status, so nothing turns on this point. Nationality is a forbidden ground of discrimination within s. 3(1) of the *Race Relations Act 1976* and the Secretary of State is bound by that Act by virtue of s. 19B(1). It was not argued that in the present circumstances he was authorised to discriminate by s. 19D.

[50] The first important issue between the parties was whether, in the present case, the Secretary of State had discriminated against the

appellants on the ground of their nationality or immigration status. The Court of Human Rights gave guidance on the correct approach in the *Belgian Linguistics Case* (No 2) (1968) 1 EHRR 252 at 284 (para 10):

"In spite of the very general wording of the French version ('*sans distinction aucune*'), Article 14 does not forbid every difference in treatment in the exercise of the rights and freedoms recognised. This version must be read in the light of the more restrictive text of the English version ('without discrimination'). In addition, and in particular, one would reach absurd results were one to give Article 14 an interpretation as wide as that which the French version seems to imply. One would, in effect, be led to judge as contrary to the Convention every one of the many legal or administrative provisions which do not secure to everyone complete equality of treatment in the enjoyment of the rights and freedoms recognised. The competent national authorities are frequently confronted with situations and problems which, on account of differences inherent therein, call for different legal solutions; moreover, certain legal inequalities tend only to correct factual inequalities. The extensive interpretation mentioned above cannot consequently be accepted.

"It is important, then, to look for the criteria which enable a determination to be made as to whether or not a given difference in treatment, concerning of course the exercise of one of the rights and freedoms set forth, contravenes Article 14. On this question, the Court, following the principles which may be extracted from the legal practice of a large number of democratic States, holds that the principle of equality of treatment is violated if the distinction has no objective and reasonable justification. The existence of such a justification must be assessed in relation to the aim and effects of the measure under consideration, regard being had to the principles which normally prevail in democratic societies. A difference of treatment in the exercise of a right laid down in the Convention must not only pursue a legitimate aim: Article 14 is likewise violated when it is clearly established that there is no reasonable relationship of proportionality between the means employed and the aim sought to be realised."

The question is whether persons in an analogous or relevantly similar situation enjoy preferential treatment, without reasonable or objective justification for the distinction, and whether and to what extent differences in otherwise similar situations justify a different treatment in law ... The parties were agreed that in domestic law, seeking to give effect to the convention, the correct approach is to pose the questions formulated by Grosz, Beatson and Duffy, Human Rights: The 1998 Act and the European Convention (2000), pp. 326–327 ... As expressed in this last case (at [42]) the questions are:

"(1) Do the facts fall within the ambit of one or more of the convention rights? (2) Was there a difference in treatment in respect of that right between the complainant and others put forward for comparison? (3) If so, was the difference in treatment on one or more of the proscribed grounds under art. 14? (4) Were those others in an analogous situation? (5) Was the difference in treatment objectively justifiable in the sense that it had a legitimate aim and bore a reasonable relationship of proportionality to that aim?"

[51] It is plain that the facts fall within the ambit of art. 5. That is why the United Kingdom thought it necessary to derogate. The Attorney General reserved the right to argue in another place at another time that it was not necessary to derogate, but he accepted for the purpose of these proceedings that it was. The appellants were treated differently from both suspected international terrorists who were not United Kingdom nationals but could be removed and also from suspected international terrorists who were United Kingdom nationals and could not be removed. There can be no doubt but that the difference of treatment was on grounds of nationality or immigration status (one of the proscribed grounds under art. 14). The problem has been treated as an immigration problem.

[52] The Attorney General submitted that the position of the appellants should be compared with that of non–United Kingdom nationals who represented a threat to the security of the United Kingdom but who could be removed to their own or to safe third countries. The relevant difference between them and the appellants was that the appellants could not be removed. A difference of treatment of the two groups was accordingly justified and it was reasonable and necessary to detain the appellants. By contrast, the appellants' chosen comparators were suspected international terrorists who were United Kingdom nationals. The appellants pointed out that they shared with this group the important characteristics (a) of being suspected international terrorists and (b) of being irremovable from the United Kingdom. Since these were the relevant characteristics for purposes of the comparison, it was unlawfully discriminatory to detain non–United Kingdom nationals while leaving United Kingdom nationals at large.

[53] Were suspected international terrorists who were United

Kingdom nationals, the appellants' chosen comparators, in a relevantly analogous situation to the appellants? ...

[54] Following the guidance given in the *Belgian Linguistics Case* (No 2) (1968) 1 EHRR 252 (see [50], above) it is then necessary to assess the justification of the differential treatment of non–United Kingdom nationals "in relation to the aim and effects of the measure under consideration." The undoubted aim of the relevant measure, s. 23 of the 2001 Act, was to protect the United Kingdom against the risk of Al-Qa'ida terrorism. As noted above (at [32]) that risk was thought to be presented mainly by non–United Kingdom nationals but also and to a significant extent by United Kingdom nationals. The effect of the measure was to permit the former to be deprived of their liberty but not the latter. The appellants were treated differently because of their nationality or immigration status. The comparison contended for by the Attorney General might be reasonable and justified in an immigration context, but cannot in my opinion be so in a security context, since the threat presented by suspected international terrorists did not depend on their nationality or immigration status. It is noteworthy that in *Ireland v. UK* (1978) 2 EHRR 25 the court was considering legislative provisions which were, unlike s. 23, neutral in their terms, in that they provided for internment of Loyalist as well as Republican terrorists. Even so, the court was gravely exercised whether the application of the measures had been even handed as between the two groups of terrorists. It seems very unlikely that the measures could have been successfully defended had they only been capable of application to Republican terrorists, unless it were shown that they alone presented a threat.

[55] The Attorney General also made a more far-reaching submission. He relied on the old-established rule that a sovereign state may control the entry of aliens into its territory and their expulsion from it. He submitted that the convention permits the differential treatment of aliens as compared with nationals. He also submitted that international law sanctions the differential treatment, including detention, of aliens in times of war or public emergency ...

[63] The materials I have cited are not legally binding on the United Kingdom. But there is no European or other authority to support the Attorney General's submission. On the other hand, the Council of Europe is the body to which the states parties to the convention belong. The Attorney General in his written case accepted that art. 14 of the convention and art. 26 of the ICCPR are to the same effect. And the

United Kingdom has ratified the International Convention on the Elimination of All Forms of Racial Discrimination. These materials are inimical to the submission that a state may lawfully discriminate against foreign nationals by detaining them but not nationals presenting the same threat in a time of public emergency ...

[68] I must respectfully differ from this analysis. Article 15 requires any derogating measures to go no further than is strictly required by the exigencies of the situation and the prohibition of discrimination on grounds of nationality or immigration status has not been the subject of derogation. Article 14 remains in full force. Any discriminatory measure inevitably affects a smaller rather than a larger group, but cannot be justified on the ground that more people would be adversely affected if the measure were applied generally. What has to be justified is not the measure in issue but the difference in treatment between one person or group and another. What cannot be justified here is the decision to detain one group of suspected international terrorists, defined by nationality or immigration status, and not another. To do so was a violation of art. 14 ...

...

[73] I would allow the appeals. There will be a quashing order in respect of the derogation order. There will also be a declaration under s. 4 of the 1998 Act that s. 23 of the 2001 Act is incompatible with arts. 5 and 14 of the convention in so far as it is disproportionate and permits detention of suspected international terrorists in a way that discriminates on the ground of nationality or immigration status. The Secretary of State must pay the appellants' costs in the House and below.

Lord Hoffmann:

[86] My Lords, I have had the advantage of reading in draft the speech of my noble and learned friend Lord Bingham of Cornhill and I gratefully adopt his statement of the background to this case and the issues which it raises. This is one of the most important cases which the House has had to decide in recent years. It calls into question the very existence of an ancient liberty of which this country has until now been very proud: freedom from arbitrary arrest and detention. The power which the Home Secretary seeks to uphold is a power to detain people indefinitely without charge or trial. Nothing could be more antithetical to the instincts and traditions of the people of the United Kingdom.

[87] At present, the power cannot be exercised against citizens of this country. First, it applies only to foreigners whom the Home Secretary would otherwise be able to deport. But the power to deport foreigners is extremely wide. Second, it requires that the Home Secretary should reasonably suspect the foreigners of a variety of activities or attitudes in connection with terrorism, including supporting a group influenced from abroad whom the Home Secretary suspects of being concerned in terrorism. If the finger of suspicion has pointed and the suspect is detained, his detention must be reviewed by the Special Immigration Appeals Commission. They can decide that there were no reasonable grounds for the Home Secretary's suspicion. But the suspect is not entitled to be told the grounds upon which he has been suspected. So he may not find it easy to explain that the suspicion is groundless. In any case, suspicion of being a supporter is one thing and proof of wrongdoing is another. Someone who has never committed any offence and has no intention of doing anything wrong may be reasonably suspected of being a supporter on the basis of some heated remarks overheard in a pub. The question in this case is whether the United Kingdom should be a country in which the police can come to such a person's house and take him away to be detained indefinitely without trial.

[88] The technical issue in this appeal is whether such a power can be justified on the ground that there exists a "war or other public emergency threatening the life of the nation" within the meaning of art. 15 of the European Convention for the Protection of Human Rights and Fundamental Freedoms 1950 (Rome, 4 November 1950; TS 71 (1953); Cmnd 8969). But I would not like anyone to think that we are concerned with some special doctrine of European law. Freedom from arbitrary arrest and detention is a quintessentially British liberty, enjoyed by the inhabitants of this country when most of the population of Europe could be thrown into prison at the whim of their rulers. It was incorporated into the convention in order to entrench the same liberty in countries which had recently been under Nazi occupation. The United Kingdom subscribed to the convention because it set out the rights which British subjects enjoyed under the common law.

[89] The exceptional power to derogate from those rights also reflected British constitutional history. There have been times of great national emergency in which habeas corpus has been suspended and powers to detain on suspicion conferred on the government. It happened during the Napoleonic Wars and during both World Wars in the twentieth century. These powers were conferred with great misgiving

and, in the sober light of retrospect after the emergency had passed, were often found to have been cruelly and unnecessarily exercised. But the necessity of draconian powers in moments of national crisis is recognised in our constitutional history. Article 15 of the convention, when it speaks of "war or other public emergency threatening the life of the nation," accurately states the conditions in which such legislation has previously been thought necessary.

[90] Until the *Human Rights Act 1998*, the question of whether the threat to the nation was sufficient to justify suspension of habeas corpus or the introduction of powers of detention could not have been the subject of judicial decision. There could be no basis for questioning an Act of Parliament by court proceedings. Under the 1998 Act, the courts still cannot say that an Act of Parliament is invalid. But they can declare that it is incompatible with the human rights of persons in this country. Parliament may then choose whether to maintain the law or not. The declaration of the court enables Parliament to choose with full knowledge that the law does not accord with our constitutional traditions.

[91] What is meant by "threatening the life of the nation"? The "nation" is a social organism, living in its territory (in this case, the United Kingdom) under its own form of government and subject to a system of laws which expresses its own political and moral values. When one speaks of a threat to the "life" of the nation, the word life is being used in a metaphorical sense. The life of the nation is not coterminous with the lives of its people. The nation, its institutions and values, endure through generations. In many important respects, England is the same nation as it was at the time of the first Elizabeth or the Glorious Revolution. The Armada threatened to destroy the life of the nation, not by loss of life in battle, but by subjecting English institutions to the rule of Spain and the Inquisition. The same was true of the threat posed to the United Kingdom by Nazi Germany in the Second World War. This country, more than any other in the world, has an unbroken history of living for centuries under institutions and in accordance with values which show a recognisable continuity.

[92] This, I think, is the idea which the European Court of Human Rights was attempting to convey when it said (in *Lawless v. Ireland* (No 3) (1961) 1 EHRR 15 at 31 (para 28)) that it must be a "threat to the organised life of the community of which the State is composed," although I find this a rather desiccated description. Nor do I find the European cases particularly helpful. All that can be taken from them is

that the Strasbourg court allows a wide "margin of appreciation" to the national authorities in deciding "both on the presence of such an emergency and on the nature and scope of derogations necessary to avert it" (see *Ireland v. UK* (1978) 2 EHRR 25 at 91–92 (para 207)). What this means is that we, as a United Kingdom court, have to decide the matter for ourselves.

[93] Perhaps it is wise for the Strasbourg court to distance itself from these matters. The institutions of some countries are less firmly based than those of others. Their communities are not equally united in their loyalty to their values and system of government. I think that it was reasonable to say that terrorism in Northern Ireland threatened the life of that part of the nation and the territorial integrity of the United Kingdom as a whole. In a community riven by sectarian passions, such a campaign of violence threatened the fabric of organised society. The question is whether the threat of terrorism from Muslim extremists similarly threatens the life of the British nation.

[94] The Home Secretary has adduced evidence, both open and secret, to show the existence of a threat of serious terrorist outrages. The Attorney General did not invite us to examine the secret evidence, but despite the widespread scepticism which has attached to intelligence assessments since the fiasco over Iraqi weapons of mass destruction, I am willing to accept that credible evidence of such plots exist. The events of 11 September 2001 in New York and Washington and 11 March 2003 in Madrid make it entirely likely that the threat of similar atrocities in the United Kingdom is a real one.

[95] But the question is whether such a threat is a threat to the life of the nation. The Attorney General's submissions and the judgment of the Special Immigration Appeals Commission ([2002] HRLR 1274) treated a threat of serious physical damage and loss of life as necessarily involving a threat to the life of the nation. But in my opinion this shows a misunderstanding of what is meant by "threatening the life of the nation." Of course the government has a duty to protect the lives and property of its citizens. But that is a duty which it owes all the time and which it must discharge without destroying our constitutional freedoms. There may be some nations too fragile or fissiparous to withstand a serious act of violence. But that is not the case in the United Kingdom. When Milton urged the government of his day not to censor the press even in time of civil war, he said: "Lords and Commons of England, consider what nation it is whereof ye are, and whereof ye are the governours."

[96] This is a nation which has been tested in adversity, which has survived physical destruction and catastrophic loss of life. I do not underestimate the ability of fanatical groups of terrorists to kill and destroy, but they do not threaten the life of the nation. Whether we would survive Hitler hung in the balance, but there is no doubt that we shall survive Al-Qa'ida. The Spanish people have not said that what happened in Madrid, hideous crime as it was, threatened the life of their nation. Their legendary pride would not allow it. Terrorist violence, serious as it is, does not threaten our institutions of government or our existence as a civil community.

[97] For these reasons I think that the Special Immigration Appeals Commission made an error of law and that the appeal ought to be allowed. Others of your Lordships who are also in favour of allowing the appeal would do so, not because there is no emergency threatening the life of the nation, but on the ground that a power of detention confined to foreigners is irrational and discriminatory. I would prefer not to express a view on this point. I said that the power of detention is at present confined to foreigners and I would not like to give the impression that all that was necessary was to extend the power to United Kingdom citizens as well. In my opinion, such a power in any form is not compatible with our constitution. The real threat to the life of the nation, in the sense of a people living in accordance with its traditional laws and political values, comes not from terrorism but from laws such as these. That is the true measure of what terrorism may achieve. It is for Parliament to decide whether to give the terrorists such a victory.

READING QUESTIONS ON *A*

1 In response to the House of Lords, the British government released the detainees, but then placed them under a control-order regime, a system which allows for virtual house arrest, with severe restrictions on contact with the outside world, visitors, and so on. Some of those subject to the control-order regime have said that it is so much worse than prison that they would prefer to go to their home countries, where they likely face torture or death. At the same time, the government is trying to negotiate with these countries to secure assurances that these people can be deported there without them facing the risk of torture or death. But since all of these countries deny that they either torture or murder, it is not

clear what the worth of the assurances would be. Do you think that these events show that human rights have no role in controlling the "war" against terrorism?

2 Do you think the majority was consistent in deciding to defer to the government on the issue of whether there was an emergency while refusing to defer on the issue of whether the response to the emergency was appropriate?

3 Are there any similarities between Lord Hoffmann's approach and Justice Scalia's in *Hamdi*?

"Authorisation to shoot down aircraft in the *Aviation Security Act* void" (2006)

This press release contains a brief report of the German Constitutional Court's decision invalidating a provision in the *Aviation Security Act*. In evaluating the reasoning, you should look back to the brief description of bills of attainder in question 2 following the Head Tax case in chapter 2.

§ 14.3 of the *Aviation Security Act* (*Luftsicherheitsgesetz – LuftSiG*), which authorizes the armed forces to shoot down aircraft that are intended to be used as weapons in crimes against human lives, is incompatible with the Basic Law and hence void. This was decided by the First Senate of the Federal Constitutional Court in its judgment of 15 February 2006. The Federal Constitutional Court held that the Federation lacks legislative competence to issue such regulation in the first place. According to the Court, Article 35.2 sentence 2 and 35.3 sentence 1 of the Basic Law (*Grundgesetz – GG*), which regulates the employment of the armed forces for the control of natural disasters or in the case of especially grave accidents, does not permit the Federation to order missions of the armed forces with specifically military weapons. Moreover, § 14.3 of the *Aviation Security Act* is incompatible with the fundamental right to life and with the guarantee of human dignity to the extent that the use of armed force affects persons on board the aircraft who are not participants in the crime. By the state's using their killing as a means to save others, they are treated as mere objects, which denies them the value that is due to a human being for his or her own sake.

Thus, the constitutional complaint lodged by four lawyers, a patent attorney and a flight captain, who had directly challenged § 14.3 of the *Aviation Security Act*, was successful.

The decision is essentially based on the following considerations:

1. The Federation lacks the legislative competence to issue the regulation laid down in § 14.3 of the *Aviation Security Act*. It is true that Article 35.2 sentence 2 and 35.3 sentence 1 of the Basic Law directly provides the Federation with the right to issue regulations that provide the details concerning the use of the armed forces for the control of natural disasters and in the case of especially grave accidents in accordance with these provisions and concerning the cooperation with the Länder (states) affected. The armed forces' authorization to use direct armed force against an aircraft which is contained in § 14.3 of the *Aviation Security Act* is, however, not in harmony with Article 35.2 sentence 2 and 35.3 of the Basic Law.

a) The incompatibility of § 14.3 of the *Aviation Security Act* with Article 35.2 sentence 2 of the Basic Law (regional emergency situation) does, however, not result from the mere fact that the operation is intended to be ordered and carried out at a point-time in which a major aerial incident (hijacking of an aircraft) has already happened but in which the especially grave accident (intended air crash) itself has not yet occurred. For the concept of an "especially grave accident" within the meaning of Article 35.2 sentence 2 of the Basic Law also comprises events in which a disaster can be expected to happen with near certainty. The reason why an operation involving the direct use of armed force against an aircraft does not respect the boundaries of Article 35.2 sentence 2 of the Basic Law is, however, that this provision does not permit an operational mission of the armed forces with specifically military weapons for the control of natural disasters or in the case of especially grave accidents. The "assistance" referred to in Article 35.2 sentence 2 of the Basic Law is rendered to the *Länder* to enable them to effectively fulfil the task, which is incumbent on them in the context of their police power, to deal with natural disasters or especially grave accidents. Because the assistance is oriented towards this task which falls under the police power of the *Länder* this also necessarily determines the kind of resources that can be used where the armed forces are employed for rendering assistance. They cannot be of a kind which is, with regard to their quality, completely different from those which are originally at the disposal of the *Länder* police forces for performing their duties.

b) § 14.3 of the *Aviation Security Act* is also not compatible with Article 35.3 sentence 1 of the Basic Law. This provision explicitly authorizes only the Federal Government to order the employment of the armed forces in the case of an interregional emergency situation. The regulations in the *Aviation Security Act* do not take sufficient account of this. They provide that the Minister of Defence, in agreement with the Federal Minister of the Interior, shall decide in cases in which a decision of the Federal Government is not possible in time. In view of the fact that generally, the time available in such a context will only be very short, the Federal Government will, pursuant to this provision, be substituted not only in exceptional cases but regularly by individual government ministers when it comes to deciding on the employment of the armed forces in interregional emergency situations. This clearly shows that as a general rule, it will not be possible to deal with measures of the kind regulated in § 14.3 of the *Aviation Security Act* in the manner that is provided under Article 35.3 sentence 1 of the Basic Law. Moreover, the boundaries of constitutional law relating to the armed forces under Article 35.3 sentence 1 of the Basic Law have been overstepped above all because also in the case of an interregional emergency situation, a mission of the armed forces with typically military weapons is constitutionally impermissible.

2. § 14.3 of the *Aviation Security Act* is also not compatible with the right to life (Article 2.2 sentence 1 of the Basic Law) in conjunction with the guarantee of human dignity (Article 1.1 of the Basic Law) to the extent that the use of armed force affects persons on board the aircraft who are not participants in the crime.

The passengers and crew members who are exposed to such a mission are in a desperate situation. They can no longer influence the circumstances of their lives independently from others in a self-determined manner. This makes them objects not only of the perpetrators of the crime. Also the state which in such a situation resorts to the measure provided by § 14.3 of the *Aviation Security Act* treats them as mere objects of its rescue operation for the protection of others. Such a treatment ignores the status of the persons affected as subjects endowed with dignity and inalienable rights. By their killing being used as a means to save others, they are treated as objects and at the same time deprived of their rights; with their lives being disposed of unilaterally by the state, the persons on board the aircraft, who, as victims, are themselves in need of protection, are denied the value which is due to a human being for his or her own sake. In addition, this happens under circumstances in which it cannot be expected that at the moment in which a decision concerning an operation pursuant to § 14.3 of the *Aviation Security Act* is taken, there is always a complete picture of the factual situation and that the factual situation can always be assessed correctly then.

Under the applicability of Article 1.1 of the Basic Law (guarantee of human dignity) it is absolutely inconceivable to intentionally kill persons who are in such a helpless situation on the basis of a statutory authorization. The assumption that someone boarding an aircraft as a crew member or as a passenger will presumably consent to its being shot down, and thus in his or her own killing, in the case of the aircraft becoming involved in an aerial incident is an unrealistic fiction. Also the assessment that the persons affected are doomed anyway cannot remove from the killing of innocent people in the situation described its nature of an infringement of these people's right to dignity. Human life and human dignity enjoy the same constitutional protection regardless of the duration of the physical existence of the individual human being. The opinion, which has been advanced on some occasions, that the persons who are held on board have become part of a weapon and must bear being treated as such, expresses in a virtually undisguised manner that the victims of such an incident are no longer perceived as human beings. The idea that the individual is obliged to sacrifice his or her life in the interest of the state as a whole in case of need if this is the only possible way of protecting the legally constituted body politic from attacks which are aimed at its breakdown and destruction also does not lead to a different result. For in the area of application of § 14.3 of the *Aviation Security Act* the issue is not the defence against attacks aimed at abolishing the body politic and at eliminating the state's legal and constitutional system. Finally, § 14.3 of the *Aviation Security Act* also cannot be justified by invoking the state's duty to protect those against whose lives the aircraft that is abused as a weapon for a crime is intended to be used. Only such means may be used to comply with the state's obligations to protect as are in harmony with the constitution. This is not the case in the case at hand.

3. § 14.3 of the *Aviation Security Act* is, however, compatible with Article 2.2 sentence 1 in conjunction with Article 1.1 of the Basic Law to the extent that the direct use of armed force is aimed at a pilotless aircraft or exclusively at persons who want to use the aircraft as a weapon of a crime against the lives of people on the ground. It corresponds to the attacker's position as a subject if the consequences of his or her self-determined conduct are attributed to him or her personally, and if the attacker is held responsible for the events that he or she started. The principle of proportionality is also complied with. The objective to save human lives which is pursued by § 14.3 of the *Aviation Security Act* is of such weight that it can justify the grave encroachment on the perpetrators' fundamental right to life. Moreover, the gravity of the encroachment upon their fundamental rights is reduced by the fact that the perpetrators themselves brought about the necessity of state intervention and that they can avert such intervention at any time by refraining from realizing their criminal plan.

All the same, the regulation is void also in this respect because the Federation lacks legislative competence in the first place.

8

Speech, Hate Propaganda, and Pornography

Freedom of expression is a central value in a free and democratic society. Indeed, it is so important that some people have suggested that it is entirely without exceptions. Despite its high-minded tone, such a view is probably unrealistic. As the American judge Oliver Wendell Holmes famously put it, even the most stringent protection of free speech will not extend to the person falsely shouting "fire" in a crowded theatre. There are plainly exceptions to free expression; the problem for philosophers is to come up with a principled way of thinking about them. Unfortunately, much of the public debate about free expression consists in exaggerated claims about the harmful effects of either speech or censorship. The readings in this section offer some more sophisticated accounts of the basis and limits of the protection of expression.

Joel Feinberg
"Pornography and the Criminal Law" (1979)

Feinberg argues that offensive material should be treated as a private matter. As a result, regulations are only legitimate if they aim to protect those who are offended from materials that bother them.

When the possession, use, or display of sexually explicit materials is prohibited by law, and violations are punished by fine or imprisonment, many thousands of persons are prevented from doing what they would otherwise freely choose to do. Such forceful interference in private affairs seems morally outrageous, unless, of course, it is supported by special justifying reasons. In the absence of appropriate reasons, the coercive use of governmental power, based ultimately on guns and clubs, is merely arbitrary and as such is always morally illegitimate. Criminal prohibitions, of course, are sometimes backed by appropriate reasons, and when that is the case, they are not morally illicit uses of force but rather reasonable regulations of our social activities.

What then are "appropriate reasons" for criminal prohibitions? Surely the need to prevent harm or injury to persons other than the one interfered with is one kind of legitimate reason. Some actions, however, while harmless in themselves, are great nuisances to those who are affected by them, and the law from time immemorial has provided remedies, some civil and some criminal, for actions in this category. So a second kind of legitimate reason for prohibiting conduct is the need to protect others from certain sorts of offensive, irritating, or inconveniencing experiences. Extreme nuisances can actually reach the threshold of harm, as when noises from the house next door prevent a student from studying at all on the evening before an examination, or when an obstructed road causes a person to be late for an important appointment. But we are not very happy with nuisances even when they do not harm our interests, but only cause irritations to our senses, or inconvenient detours from our normal course. The offending conduct produces unpleasant or uncomfortable experiences – affronts to sense or sensibility, disgust, shock, shame, embarrassment, annoyance, boredom, anger, or humiliation – from which one cannot escape without unreasonable inconvenience or even harm.

We demand protection from nuisances when we think of ourselves as *trapped* by them, and we think it unfair that we should pay the cost in inconvenience that is required to escape them. In extreme cases, the offending conduct commandeers our attention from the outside, forcing us to relinquish control of our inner states, and drop what we were doing in order to cope, when it is greatly inconvenient to do so. That is why laws prohibiting nuisances are sometimes said to protect our interest in "privacy."

What distinguishes the "liberal position" on this question is the insistence that the need to prevent harm to others and the need to prevent offensive nuisances to others between them exhaust all the types of reasons which may appropriately support criminal prohibitions. Insofar as a criminal statute is unsupported by reasons of either of these two kinds, it tends to be arbitrary and hence morally illicit. In this respect certain commonly proffered reasons are no better than no reasons at all. The need to protect either the interests or the character of the actor himself from his own folly, does not, according to the liberal, confer moral legitimacy on a criminal statute, nor does the need to prevent inherently sinful or immoral conduct as such. Liberalism so construed does not purport to be a guide to useful public policy for the utilitarian legislator, nor does it claim to provide a key to the interpretation of the American, or any other, constitution. (It is entirely possible that the moral restrictions liberalism would place on legislative discretion are not always socially useful, and also that the Constitution itself allows some morally illegitimate statutes to remain as valid laws.) Instead liberalism purports to indicate to the legislator where the moral limits to government coercion are located.

Let me state from the outset that I am a committed liberal, in this sense, on the question of the legal regulation of pornography. Like the late Herbert Packer, I believe that pornography, at its worst, is not so much a menace as a nuisance, and that the moral right of legislatures to restrict it derives from, and is limited by, the same principles that morally entitle the state to command owners of howling dogs to stop their racket, to punish owners of fertilizing plants for letting odors escape over a whole town, to prohibit indecent exposure and public defecation, and so on. It is absurd to punish nuisances as severely as harmful or injurious conduct, however, and unless certain well-understood conditions are satisfied, it may be illegitimate to punish a given nuisance at all. For that reason it may be useful, before looking at the pornography problem, to examine the restrictions recognized by legislatures and courts on the proper regulation of harmless but offensive nuisances.

I

The most interesting aspect of the law of nuisance is its version of the unavoidable legal balancing act. Both legislatures, when they formulate statutes that define public nuisances, and courts, when they adjudicate conflicts between neighboring landowners in "private nuisance" cases, must weigh opposing considerations. Establishing that one person's conduct is or would be a nuisance to someone else is by no means sufficient to warrant legal interference. First one must compare carefully the magnitude of the nuisance to the one against the reasonableness of the conduct of the other, and the necessity "that all may get on together."[1]

William Prosser, describing the various factors that weigh on one side of the scale, tells us that the magnitude of the nuisance (or "seriousness of the inconvenience") to the plaintiff in a private nuisance action depends upon (1) the extent, duration, and character of the interference, (2) the social value of the use the plaintiff makes of his land, and (3) the extent to which the plaintiff can, without undue burden or hardship, avoid the offense by taking precautions against it.[2] These three factors yield the weight to be assigned to the "seriousness" of the inconvenience. They must be weighed against the reasonableness of the defendant's conduct, which is determined by (1) "the social value of its ultimate purpose, (2) the motive of the defendant [in particular its character as innocent or spiteful], and (3) whether the defendant by taking reasonable steps can avoid or reduce the inconvenience to the plaintiff without undue burden or inconvenience to himself."[3] Finally Prosser would have us throw on to the scale the interests of the "public at large," in particular its interest in "the nature of the locality" where the nuisance occurred – to "what paramount use it is already devoted" and given that background, "the suitability of the use made of the land by both plaintiff and defendant."[4] In sum, the more extended, durable, and severe the inconvenience to the plaintiff, and the greater the social value of the land uses interfered with, then the greater is the magnitude of the nuisance, while the greater the ease with which the plaintiff can avoid the nuisance, the smaller its magnitude. Similarly, the greater the social value of the defendant's conduct[5] and the freer his motives of spite toward the plaintiff, the more reasonable is his conduct, despite its inconvenience to the plaintiff, while the easier it is for him to achieve his goals by means that do not inconvenience the plaintiff, the less reasonable is his offending conduct. Finally, the prevalent character of the neighborhood weighs heavily, so that a householder who takes up residence in a manufacturing district cannot complain, as a plaintiff in a private nuisance suit, of the noise, dust, or vibration, whereas the same amount of disturbance caused by a factory in a primarily residential district, will be declared a nuisance to the landowners in its vicinity.

If, as I recommend, we think of pornographic exhibitions and publications as nuisances which may properly be controlled by the law under certain very strict conditions, we shall have to posit a similar set of conflicting considerations to be weighed carefully, not only by juries in private tort suits, but also by legislatures in their deliberations over the wording of criminal statutes designed to prohibit and punish pornography. Let me suggest that legislators who are impressed by the model of "public nuisance" should weigh, in the case of each main category and context of pornography, the seriousness of the offense caused to unwilling witnesses against the reasonableness of the offender's conduct. The magnitude of the offensiveness would be determined by (1) the intensity and durability of the repugnance the material produces, and the extent to which repugnance could be anticipated to be the general reaction of strangers to the conduct displayed or represented (conduct offensive only to persons with an abnormal susceptibility to offense would not count as *very* offensive), (2) the ease with which unwilling witnesses can avoid the offensive displays, and (3) whether or not the witnesses have willingly assumed the risk of being offended either through curiosity or the anticipation of pleasure. (The maxim *volenti non fit injuria* applies to offense as well as to harm.) We can refer to these norms, in order, as "the extent of offense standard" (with its "exclusion of abnormal susceptibility corollary"), "the reasonable avoidability standard," and "the *volenti* standard."

These factors would be weighed as a group against the reasonableness of the pornographers' conduct as determined by (1) its personal importance to the exhibitors themselves and its social value generally, remembering always the enormous social utility of unhampered expression (in those cases where expression is involved), (2) the availability of alternative times and places where the conduct in question would cause less offense, and (3) the extent if any to which the offense is caused by spiteful motives. In addition, the legislature would examine the prior established character of various neighborhoods, and consider establishing licensed zones in areas where the conduct in question is known to be already prevalent, so that people inclined to be offended are not likely to stumble on it to their surprise.

A legislature, of course, does not concern itself with judging specific actions and specific offended states after they have occurred. Rather its eyes are to the future, and it must weigh against one another, or authorize courts to weigh against one another, generalized *types* of conduct and offense. In hard cases this balancing procedure can be very complex and uncertain, but there are some cases that fall clearly within one or another standard in such a way as to leave no doubt how they must be decided. Thus, the *volenti* standard, for example, preempts all the others when it clearly applies. Film exhibitors cannot reasonably be charged with criminally offensive conduct when they have seen to it that the only people who witness their films are those adults who voluntarily purchased tickets to do so, knowing full well what sort of film they were about to see. One cannot be *wrongfully* offended by that to which one fully consents. Similarly, bans on *books* must fail to be morally legitimate in view of the ease with which offense at printed passages can be avoided. Since potential readers are not "captive audiences," here the reasonable avoidability standard is preemptive. So also do inoffensively expressed political or theological opinions fail to qualify as "criminal nuisances," by virtue of their personal and social importance as "free expression." On the other side, purely spiteful motives in the offender can be a preemptive consideration weighting the balance scale decisively on the side of unreasonableness.

In some cases, no one standard is preemptive, but nevertheless all applicable standards pull together towards one inevitable decision. The public eating of excrement (coprophagia) fully and unambiguously satisfies the extent of offense standard. One doesn't have to be abnormally squeamish to be offended by the very sight of it. If it is done (say) on a public bus, it definitely fails to win the support of the reasonable avoidability and *volenti* standards, which is to say that it causes intense disgust to captive observers. Hence, by *all* the relevant criteria, it is seriously offensive. By all the criteria for weighing reasonableness, public coprophagia does poorly too. It cannot be very important to the neurotic person who does it (not as important, for example, as earning a living, or eating fresh food); it has a definitely limited social utility; it is not the expression in language of an opinion, nor does it fall into a recognized genre of aesthetic expression; and it could as well be done in private. Hence it is both seriously offensive and unredeemed by independent "reasonableness." It would not of course be called "pornography," but its criminal proscription under another name would be morally legitimate in principle, even though in practice it might be unwise, uneconomical, or unnecessary.

...

NOTES

1 Practically all human activities, unless carried on in a wilderness, interfere to some extent with others or involve some risk of interference, and these interferences range from mere trifling annoyances to serious harms. It is an obvious truth that each individual in a community must put up with a certain amount of annoyance, inconvenience and interference, and must take a certain amount of risk in order that all may get on together. The very existence of organized society depends upon the principle of

"give and take, live and let live," and therefore the law of torts does not attempt to impose liability or shift the loss in every case where one person's conduct has some detrimental effect on another. Liability is imposed only in those cases where the harm or risk [or inconvenience or offense] to one is greater than he ought to be required to bear under the circumstances ... Restatement of Torts s. 822, comment j (1939).

2 W. Prosser, *Handbook of the Law of Torts* 597 (4th ed. 1971).

3 Ibid., at 597–9.

4 Ibid., at 599–600.

5 "The world must have factories, smelters, oil refineries, noisy machinery, and blasting, as well as airports, even at the expense of some inconvenience to those in the vicinity, and the plaintiff may be required to accept and tolerate some not unreasonable discomfort for the general good ... On the other hand, a foul pond, or a vicious or noisy dog, will have little if any social value, and relatively slight annoyance from it may justify relief." Ibid. at 597–8 (footnotes omitted).

READING QUESTIONS ON FEINBERG

1 Feinberg seems to suppose that the liberal commitment to individual autonomy survives confining one's expression of important aspects of one's personality to the private. Is this adequate, or do you suppose that public expression is sometimes important to autonomy?

2 As you go through the readings below, think about the implications of Feinberg's distinction between offence and harm. How should such a distinction be drawn in particular cases?

T.M. Scanlon
"A Theory of Freedom of Expression" (1972)

Scanlon argues that the need to protect freedom of expression follows from the importance of individual autonomy. The state must treat citizens as capable of making up their own minds. As a result, it cannot hold one person responsible for something that others do because of reasons they have offered them.

... Typically, the acts of expression with which a theory of "free speech" is concerned are addressed to a large (if not the widest possible) audience, and express propositions or attitudes thought to have a certain generality of interest. This accounts, I think, for our reluctance to regard as an act of expression in the relevant sense the communication between the average bank robber and the teller he confronts. This reluctance is diminished somewhat if the note the robber hands the teller contains, in addition to the usual threat, some political justification for his act and an exhortation to others to follow his example. What this addition does is to broaden the projected audience and increase the generality of the message's interest. The relevance of these features is certainly something which an adequate theory of freedom of expression should explain, but it will be simpler at present not to make them part of the definition of the class of acts of expression.

Almost everyone would agree, I think, that the acts which are protected by a doctrine of freedom of expression will all be acts of expression in the sense I have defined. However, since acts of expression can be both violent and arbitrarily destructive, it seems unlikely that anyone would maintain that as a class they were immune from legal restrictions. Thus the class of protected acts must be some proper subset of this class. It is sometimes held that the relevant subclass consists of those acts of expression which are instances of "speech" as opposed to "action." But those who put forward such a view have generally wanted to include within the class of protected acts some which are not speech in any normal sense of the word (for instance, mime and certain forms of printed communication) and to exclude from it some which clearly are speech in the normal sense (talking in libraries, falsely shouting "fire" in crowded theatres etc.). Thus if acts of speech are the relevant subclass of acts of expression, then "speech" is here functioning as a term of art which needs to be defined. To construct a theory following these traditional lines we might proceed to work out a technical correlate to the distinction between speech and action which seemed to fit our clearest intuitions about which acts do and which do not qualify for protection.[1]

To proceed in this way seems to me, however, to be a serious mistake. It seems clear that the intuitions we appeal to in deciding whether a given restriction infringes freedom of expression are not intuitions about which things are properly called speech as opposed to action, even in some refined sense of "speech." The feeling that we must look for a definition of this kind has its roots, I think, in the view that since any adequate doctrine of freedom of expression must extend to some acts a privilege not enjoyed by all, such a doctrine must have its theoretical basis in some difference between the protected acts and others, i.e., in some definition of the protected class. But this is clearly wrong. It could be, and I think is, the case that the theoretical bases of the doctrine of freedom of expression are multiple and diverse, and while the net effect of these elements taken together is to extend to some acts a certain privileged status, there is no theoretically interesting (and certainly no simple and intuitive) definition of the class of acts which enjoys this privilege. Rather than trying at the outset to carve out the privileged subset of acts of expression, then, I propose to consider the class as a whole and to look for ways in which the charge of irrationality brought against the doctrine of freedom of expression might be answered without reference to a single class of privileged acts.

As I mentioned at the start, this charge arises from the fact that under any nontrivial form of the doctrine there will be cases in which acts of expression are held to be immune from legal restriction despite the fact that they give rise to undoubted harms which would in other cases be sufficient to justify such restriction. (The "legal restriction" involved here may take the form either of the imposition of criminal sanctions or of the general recognition by the courts of the right of persons affected by the acts to recover through civil suits for damages.) Now it is not in general sufficient justification for a legal restriction on a certain class of acts to show that certain harms will be prevented if this restriction is enforced. It might happen that the costs of enforcing the restriction outweigh the benefits to be gained, or that the enforcement of the restriction infringes some right either directly (e.g., a right to the unimpeded performance of exactly those acts to which the restriction applies) or indirectly (e.g., a right which under prevailing circumstances can be secured by many only through acts to which the restriction applies). Alternatively, it may be that while certain harms could be prevented by placing legal restrictions on a class of acts, those to whom the restriction would apply are not responsible for those harms and hence cannot be restricted in order to prevent them.

Most defences of freedom of expression have rested upon arguments of the first two of these three forms. In arguments of both these forms factors which taken in isolation might have been sufficient to justify restrictions on a given class of acts are held in certain cases to be overridden by other considerations. As will become clear later, I think that appeals both to rights and to the balancing of competing goals are essential components of a complete theory of freedom of expression. But I want to begin by considering arguments which, like disclaimers of responsibility, have the effect of showing that what might at first seem to be reasons for restricting a class of acts cannot be taken as such reasons at all.

My main reason for beginning in this way is this: it is easier to say what the classic violations of freedom of expression have in common than it is to define the class of acts which is protected by that doctrine. What distinguishes these violations from innocent regulation of expression is not the character of the acts they interfere with but rather what they hope to achieve – for instance, the halting of the spread of heretical notions. This suggests that an important component of our intuitions about freedom of expression has to do not with the illegitimacy of certain restrictions but with the illegitimacy of certain justifications for restrictions. Very crudely, the intuition seems to be something like this: those justifications are illegitimate which appeal to the fact that it would be a bad thing if the view communicated by certain acts of expression were to become generally believed; justifications which are legitimate, though they may sometimes be overridden, are those that appeal to features of acts of expression (time, place, loudness) other than the views they communicate.

As a principle of freedom of expression this is obviously unsatisfactory as it stands. For one thing, it rests on a rather unclear notion of "the view communicated" by an act of expression; for another, it seems too restrictive, since, for example, it appears to rule out any justification for laws against defamation. In order to improve upon this crude formulation, I want to consider a number of different ways in which acts of expression can bring about harms, concentrating on cases where these harms clearly can be counted as reasons for restricting the acts that give rise to them. I will then try to formulate the principle in a way which accommodates these cases. I emphasize at the outset that I am not maintaining in any of these cases that the harms in question are always sufficient justification for restrictions on expression, but only that they can always be taken into account.

1 Like other acts, acts of expression can bring about injury or damage as a direct physical consequence. This is obviously true of the more bizarre forms of expression mentioned above, but no less true of more pedestrian forms: the sound of my voice can break

glass, wake the sleeping, trigger an avalanche, or keep you from paying attention to something else you would rather hear. It seems clear that when harms brought about in this way are intended by the person performing an act of expression, or when he is reckless or negligent with respect to their occurrence, then no infringement of freedom of expression is involved in considering them as possible grounds for criminal penalty or civil action.

2   It is typical of the harms just considered that their production is in general quite independent of the view which the given act of expression is intended to communicate. This is not generally true of a second class of harms, an example of which is provided by the common-law notion of assault. In at least one of the recognized senses of the term, an assault (as distinct from a battery) is committed when one person intentionally places another in apprehension of imminent bodily harm. Since assault in this sense involves an element of successful communication, instances of assault may necessarily involve expression. But assaults and related acts can also be part of larger acts of expression, as for example when a guerrilla theatre production takes the form of a mock bank robbery which starts off looking like the real thing, or when a bomb scare is used to gain attention for a political cause. Assault is sometimes treated as inchoate battery, but it can also be viewed as a separate offence which consists in actually bringing about a specific kind of harm. Under this analysis, assault is only one of a large class of possible crimes which consist in the production in others of harmful or unpleasant states of mind, such as fear, shock, and perhaps certain kinds of offence. One may have doubts as to whether most of these harms are serious enough to be recognized by the law or whether standards of proof could be established for dealing with them in court. In principle, however, there seems to be no alternative to including them among the possible justifications for restrictions on expression.

3   Another way in which an act of expression can harm a person is by causing others to form an adverse opinion of him or by making him an object of public ridicule. Obvious examples of this are defamation and interference with the right to a fair trial.

4   As Justice Holmes said, "The most stringent protection of free speech would not protect a man in falsely shouting fire in a theatre and causing a panic."[2]

5 One person may through an act of expression contribute to the production of a harmful act by someone else, and at least in some cases the harmful consequences of the latter act may justify making the former a crime as well. This seems to many people to be the case when the act of expression is the issuance of an order or the making of a threat or when it is a signal or other communication between confederates.

6 Suppose some misanthropic inventor were to discover a simple method whereby anyone could make nerve gas in his kitchen out of gasoline, table salt, and urine. It seems just as clear to me that he could be prohibited by law from passing out his recipe on handbills or broadcasting it on television as that he could be prohibited from passing out free samples of his product in aerosol cans or putting it on sale at Abercrombie and Fitch. In either case his action would bring about a drastic decrease in the general level of personal safety by radically increasing the capacity of most citizens to inflict harm on each other. The fact that he does this in one case through an act of expression and in the other through some other form of action seems to me not to matter.

It might happen, however, that a comparable decrease in the general level of personal safety could be just as reliably predicted to result from the distribution of a particularly effective piece of political propaganda which would undermine the authority of the government, or from the publication of a theological tract which would lead to a schism and a bloody civil war. In these cases the matter seems to me to be entirely different, and the harmful consequence seems clearly not to be a justification for restricting the acts of expression.

What I conclude from this is that the distinction between expression and other forms of action is less important than the distinction between expression which moves others to act by pointing out what they take to be good reasons for action and expression which gives rise to action by others in other ways, e.g., by providing them with the means to do what they wanted to do anyway. This conclusion is supported, I think, by our normal views about legal responsibility.

If I were to say to you, an adult in full possession of your faculties, "What you ought to do is rob a bank," and you were subsequently to act on this advice, I could not be held legally responsible for your act, nor could my act legitimately be made a separate crime. This remains true if I supplement my advice with a battery of arguments about why banks should be robbed or even about why a certain bank in particular should be robbed and why you in particular are entitled to rob it. It might become false – what I did might legitimately be made a crime – if certain further conditions held: for example, if you were a child, or so weak-minded as to be legally incompetent, and I knew this or ought to have known it; or if you were my subordinate in some organization and what I said to you was not advice but an order, backed by the discipline of the group; or if I went on to make further contributions to your act, such as aiding you in preparations or providing you with tools or giving you crucial information about the bank.

The explanation for these differences seems to me to be this. A person who acts on reasons he has acquired from another's act of expression acts on what *he* has come to believe and has judged to be a sufficient basis for action. The contribution to the genesis of his action made by the act of expression is, so to speak, superseded by the agent's own judgment. This is not true of the contribution made by an accomplice, or by a person who knowingly provides the agent with tools (the key to the bank) or with technical information (the combination of the safe) which he uses to achieve his ends. Nor would it be true of my contribution to your act if, instead of providing you with reasons for thinking bank robbery a good thing, I issued orders or commands backed by threats, thus changing your circumstances so as to *make* it a (comparatively) good thing for you to do.

It is a difficult matter to say exactly when legal liability arises in these cases, and I am not here offering any positive thesis about what constitutes being an accessory, inciting, conspiring, etc. I am interested only in maintaining the negative thesis that whatever these crimes involve, it has to be something more than merely the communication of persuasive reasons for action (or perhaps some special circumstances, such as diminished capacity of the person persuaded).

I will now state the principle of freedom of expression which was promised at the beginning of this section. The principle, which seems to me to be a natural extension of the thesis Mill defends in Chapter II of *On Liberty,* and which I will therefore call the Millian Principle, is the following:

There are certain harms which, although they would not occur but for certain acts of expression, nonetheless cannot be taken as part of a justification for legal restrictions on these acts. There harms are: (a) harms to certain individuals which consist in their coming to have false beliefs as a result of those acts of expression; (b) harmful consequences of acts performed as a result of those acts of expression, where the connection between the acts of expression and the subsequent harmful acts consists merely in the fact that the act of expression led the agents to believe (or increased their tendency to believe) these acts to be worth performing.

I hope it is obvious that this principle is compatible with the examples of acceptable reasons for restricting expression presented in 1 through 6 above. (One case in which this may not be obvious, that of the man who falsely shouts "fire," will be discussed more fully below.) The preceding discussion, which appealed in part to intuitions about legal responsibility, was intended to make plausible the distinction on which the second part of the Millian Principle rests and, in general, to suggest how the principle could be reconciled with cases of the sort included in 5 and 6. But the principle itself goes beyond questions of responsibility. In order for a class of harms to provide a justification for restricting a person's act it is not necessary that he fulfil conditions for being legally responsible for any of the individual acts which actually produce those harms. In the nerve-gas case, for example, to claim that distribution of the recipe may be prevented one need not claim that a person who distributed it could be held legally responsible (even as an accessory) for any of the particular murders the gas is used to commit. Consequently, to explain why this case differs from sedition it would not be sufficient to claim that providing means involves responsibility while providing reasons does not.

I would like to believe that the general observance of the Millian Principle by governments would, in the long run, have more good consequences than bad. But my defence of the principle does not rest on this optimistic outlook. I will argue in the next section that the Millian Principle, as a general principle about how governmental restrictions on the liberty of citizens may be justified, is a consequence of the view, coming down to us from Kant and others, that a legitimate government is one whose authority citizens can recognize while still regarding themselves as equal, autonomous, rational agents. Thus, while it is not a principle about legal responsibility, the Millian Principle has its origins in a certain view of human agency from which many of our ideas about responsibility also derive.

Taken by itself, the Millian Principle obviously does not constitute an adequate theory of freedom of expression. Much more needs to be said about when the kinds of harmful consequences which the principle allows us to consider can be taken to be sufficient justification for restrictions on expression. Nonetheless, it seems to me fair to call the Millian Principle the basic principle of freedom of expression. This is so, first, because a successful defence of the principle would provide us with an answer to the charge of irrationality by explaining why certain of the most obvious consequences of acts of expression cannot be appealed to as a justification for legal restrictions against them. Second, the Millian Principle is the only plausible principle of freedom of expression I can think of which applies to expression in general and makes no appeal to special rights (e.g., political rights) or to the value to be attached to expression in some particular domain (e.g., artistic expression or the discussion of scientific ideas). It thus specifies what is special about acts of expression as opposed to other acts and constitutes in this sense the usable residue of the distinction between speech and action.

I will have more to say in Section IV about how the Millian Principle is to be supplemented to obtain a full account of freedom of expression. Before that, however, I want to consider in more detail how the principle can be justified.

III

As I have already mentioned, I will defend the Millian Principle by showing it to be a consequence of the view that the powers of a state are limited to those that citizens could recognize while still regarding themselves as equal, autonomous, rational agents. Since the sense of autonomy to which I will appeal is extremely weak, this seems to me to constitute a strong defence of the Millian Principle as an exceptionless restriction on governmental authority. I will consider briefly in section V, however, whether there are situations in which the principle should be suspended.

To regard himself as autonomous in the sense I have in mind a person must see himself as sovereign in deciding what to believe and in weighing competing reasons for action. He must apply to these tasks his own canons of rationality, and must recognize the need to defend his beliefs and decisions in accordance with these canons. This does not mean, of course, that he must be perfectly rational, even by his own standard of rationality, or that his standard of rationality must be exactly ours. Obviously the content of this notion of autonomy will vary according to the range of variation we are willing to allow in canons of rational decision. If just anything counts as such a canon then the requirements I have mentioned will become mere tautologies: an autonomous man believes what he believes and decides to do what he decides to do. I am sure I could not describe a set of limits on what can count as canons of rationality which would secure general agreement, and I will not try, since I am sure that the area of agreement on this question extends far beyond anything which will be relevant to the applications of the notion of autonomy that I intend to make. For present purposes what will be important is this. An autonomous person cannot accept without independent consideration the judgment of others as to what he should believe or what he should do. He may rely on the judgment of others, but when he does so he must be prepared to advance independent reasons for thinking their judgment likely to be correct, and to weigh the evidential value of their opinion against contrary evidence.

The requirements of autonomy as I have so far described them are extremely weak. They are much weaker than the requirements Kant draws from essentially the same notion,[3] in that being autonomous in my sense (like being free in Hobbes's) is quite consistent with being subject to coercion with respect to one's actions. A coercer merely changes the considerations which militate for or against a certain course of action; weighing these conflicting considerations is still up to you.

An autonomous man may, if he believes the appropriate arguments, believe that the state has a distinctive right to command him. That is, he may believe that (within certain limits, perhaps) the fact that the law requires a certain action provides him with a very strong reason for performing that action, a reason which is quite independent of the consequences, for him or others, of his performing it or refraining. How strong this reason is – what, if anything, could override it – will depend on his view of the arguments for obedience to law. What is essential to the person's remaining autonomous is that in any given case his mere recognition that a certain action is required by law does not settle the question of whether he will do it. That question is settled only by his own decision, which may take into account his current assessment of the general case for obedience and the exceptions it admits, consideration of his other duties and obligations, and his estimate of the consequences of obedience and disobedience in this particular case.[4]

Thus, while it is not obviously inconsistent with being autonomous to recognize a special obligation to obey the commands of the state, there are limits on the *kind* of obligation which autonomous citizens could recognize. In particular, they could not regard themselves as being under an "obligation" to believe the decrees of the state to be correct, nor could they concede to the state the right to have its decrees obeyed without deliberation. The Millian Principle can be seen as a refinement of these limitations.

The apparent irrationality of the doctrine of freedom of expression derives from its apparent conflict with the principle that it is the prerogative of a state – indeed, part if its duty to its citizens – to decide when the threat of certain harms is great enough to warrant legal action, and when it is, to make laws adequate to meet this threat. (Thus Holmes's famous reference to "substantive evils that Congress has a right to prevent."[5]) Obviously this principle is not acceptable in the crude form in which I have just stated it; no one thinks that Congress can do *anything* it judges to be required to save us from "substantive evils." The Millian Principle specifies two ways in which this prerogative must be limited if the state is to be acceptable to autonomous subjects. The argument for the first part of the principle is as follows.

The harm of coming to have false beliefs is not one that an autonomous man could allow the state to protect him against through restrictions on expression. For a law to provide such protection it would have to be in effect and deterring potential misleaders while the potentially misled remained susceptible to persuasion by them. In order to be protected by such a law a person would thus have to concede to the state the right to decide that certain views were false and, once it had so decided, to prevent him from hearing them advocated even if he might wish to. The conflict between doing this and remaining autonomous would be direct if a person who authorized the state to protect him in this way necessarily also bound himself to accept the state's judgment about which views were false. The matter is not quite this simple, however, since it is conceivable that a person might authorize the state to act for him in this way while still reserving to himself the prerogative of deciding, on the basis of the arguments and evidence left available to him, where the truth was to be found. But such a person would be "deciding for himself" only in an empty sense, since in any case where the state exercised its prerogative he would be "deciding" on the basis of evidence preselected to include only that which supported one conclusion. While he would not be under an obligation to accept the state's judgment as correct, he would have conceded to the state the right to deprive him of grounds for making an independent judgement.

The argument for the second half of the Millian Principle is parallel to this one. What must be argued against is the view that the state, once it has declared certain conduct to be illegal, may when necessary move to prevent that conduct by outlawing its advocacy. The conflict between this thesis and the autonomy of citizens is, just as in the previous one, slightly oblique. Conceding to the state the right to use this means to secure compliance with its laws does not immediately involve conceding to it the right to require citizens to believe that what the law says ought not to be done ought not to be done. None the less, it is a concession that autonomous citizens could not make, since it gives the state the right to deprive citizens of the grounds for arriving at an independent judgement as to whether the law should be obeyed.

These arguments both depend on the thesis that to defend a certain belief as reasonable a person must be prepared to defend the grounds of his belief as not obviously skewed or otherwise suspect. There is a clear parallel between this thesis and Mill's famous argument that if we are interested in having truth prevail we should allow all available arguments to be heard.[6] But the present argument does not depend, as Mill's may appear to, on an empirical claim that the truth is in fact more likely to win out if free discussion is allowed. Nor does it depend on the perhaps more plausible claim that, given the nature of people and governments, to concede to governments the power in question would be an outstandingly poor strategy for bringing about a situation in which true opinions prevail.

It is quite conceivable that a person who recognized in himself a fatal weakness for certain kinds of bad arguments might conclude that everyone would be better off if he were to rely entirely on the judgment of his friends in certain crucial matters. Acting on this conclusion, he might enter into an agreement, subject to periodic review by him, empowering them to shield him from any sources of information likely to divert him from their counsel on the matters in question. Such an agreement is not obviously irrational, nor, if it is entered into voluntarily, for a limited time, and on the basis of the person's own knowledge of himself and those he proposes to trust, does it appear to be inconsistent with his autonomy. The same would be true if the proposed trustees were in fact the authorities of the state. But the question we have been considering is quite different: Could an autonomous individual regard the state as having, not as part of a special voluntary agreement with him but as part of its normal powers *qua* state, the power to put such an arrangement into effect without his consent whenever *it* (i.e., the legislative authority) judged that to be advisable? The answer to this question seems to me to be quite clearly no.

Someone might object to this answer on the following grounds. I have allowed for the possibility that an autonomous man might accept a general argument to the effect that the fact that the state commands a certain thing is in and of itself a reason why that thing should be done. Why couldn't he also accept a similar argument to the effect that the state *qua* state is in the best position to decide when certain counsel is best ignored?

I have already argued that the parallel suggested here between the state's right to command action and a right to restrict expression does not hold. But there is a further problem with this objection. What saves temporary, voluntary arrangements of the kind considered above from being obvious violations of autonomy is the fact that they can be based on a firsthand estimation of the relative reliability of the trustee's judgment and that of the "patient." Thus the person whose information is restricted by such an arrangement has what he judges to be good grounds for thinking the evidence he does receive to be a sound basis for judgment. A principle which provided a corresponding basis for relying on the state *qua* state would have to be extremely general, applying to all states of a certain kind, regardless of who occupied positions of authority in them, and to all citizens of such states. Such a principle would have to be one which admitted variation in individual cases and rested its claim on what worked out best "in the long run." Even if some generalization of this kind were true, it seems to me altogether implausible to suppose that it could be rational to rely on such a general principle when detailed knowledge of the individuals involved in a particular case suggested a contrary conclusion.

A more limited case for allowing states the power in question might rest not on particular virtues of governments but on the recognized fact that under certain circumstances individuals are quite incapable of acting rationally. Something like this may seem to apply in the case of the man who falsely shouts "fire" in a crowded theatre. Here a restriction on expression is justified by the fact that such acts would lead others (give them reason) to perform harmful actions. Part of what makes the restriction acceptable is the idea that the persons in the theatre who react to the shout are under conditions that diminish their capacity for rational deliberation. This case strikes us as a trivial one. What makes it trivial is, first, the fact that only in a very far-fetched sense is a person who is prevented from hearing the false shout under such circumstances prevented from making up his own mind about some question. Second, the diminished capacity attributed to those in the theatre is extremely brief, and applies equally to anyone under the relevant conditions. Third, the harm to be prevented by the restriction is not subject to any doubt or controversy, even by those who are temporarily "deluded." In view of all these facts, the restriction is undoubtedly one which would receive unanimous consent if that were asked.[7]

This is not true, however, of most of the other exceptions to the Millian Principle that might be justified by appeal to "diminished rationality." It is doubtful, for example, whether any of the three conditions I have mentioned would apply to a case in which political debate was to be suspended during a period of turmoil and impending revolution. I cannot see how nontrivial cases of this kind could be made compatible with autonomy.

The arguments I have given may sound like familiar arguments against paternalism, but the issue involved is not simply that. First, a restriction on expression justified on grounds contrary to the Millian Principle is not necessarily paternalistic, since those who are to be protected by such a restriction may be other than those (the speaker and his audience) whose liberty is restricted. When such a restriction is paternalistic, however, it represents a particularly strong form of paternalism, and the arguments I have given are arguments against paternalism only in this strong form. It is quite consistent with a person's autonomy, in the limited sense I have employed, for the law to restrict his freedom of action "for his own good," for instance by requiring him to wear a helmet while riding his motorcycle. The conflict arises only if compliance with this law is then promoted by forbidding, for example, expression of the view that wearing a helmet isn't worth it, or is only for sissies.

It is important to see that the argument for the Millian Principle rests on a limitation of the authority of states to command their subjects rather than on a right of individuals. For one thing, this explains why this particular principle of freedom of expression applies to governments rather than to individuals, who do not have such authority to begin with. There are surely cases in which individuals have the right not to have their acts of expression interfered with by other individuals, but these rights presumably flow from a general right to be free from arbitrary interference, together with considerations which make certain kinds of expression particularly important forms of activity.

If the argument for the Millian Principle were thought to rest on a right, "the right of citizens to make up their own minds," then that argument might be thought to proceed as follows. Persons who see themselves as autonomous see themselves as having a right to make up their own minds, hence also a right to whatever is necessary for them to do this; what is wrong with violations of the Millian Principle is that they infringe this right.

A right of this kind would certainly support a healthy doctrine of freedom of expression, but it is not required for one. The argument given above was much more limited. Its aim was to establish that the authority of governments to restrict the liberty of citizens in order to prevent certain harms does not include authority to prevent these harms by controlling people's sources of information to ensure that they will maintain certain beliefs. It is a long step from this conclusion to a right which is violated whenever someone is deprived of information necessary for him to make an informed decision on some matter that concerns him.

There are clearly cases in which individuals have a right to the information necessary to make informed choices and can claim this right against the government. This is true in the case of political decisions, for example, when the right flows from a certain conception of the relation between a democratic government and its citizens. Even where there is no such right, the provision of information and other conditions for the exercise of autonomy is an important task for states to pursue. But these matters take us beyond the Millian Principle.

IV

The Millian Principle is obviously incapable of accounting for all of the cases that strike us as infringements of freedom of expression. On the basis of this principle alone we would raise no objection against a government that banned all parades or demonstrations (they interfere with traffic), outlawed posters and handbills (too messy), banned public meetings of more than 10 people (likely to be unruly), and restricted newspaper publication to one page per week (to save trees). Yet such policies surely strike us as intolerable. That they so strike us is a reflection of our belief that free expression is a good which ranks above the maintenance of absolute peace and quiet, clean streets, smoothly flowing traffic, and rock-bottom taxes.

Thus there is a part of our intuitive view of freedom of expression which rests upon a balancing of competing goods. By contrast with the Millian Principle, which provides a single defence for all kinds of expression, here it does not seem to be a matter of the value to be placed on expression (in general) as opposed to other goods. The case seems to be different for, say, artistic expression than for the discussion of scientific matters, and different still for expression of political views.

Within certain limits, it seems clear that the value to be placed on having various kinds of expression flourish is something which should be subject to popular will in the society in question. The limits I have in mind here are, first, those imposed by considerations of distributive justice. Access to means of expression for whatever purposes one may have in mind is a good which can be fairly or unfairly distributed among the members of a society, and many cases which strike us as violations of freedom of expression are in fact instances of distributive injustice. This would be true of a case where, in an economically inegalitarian society, access to the principal means of expression was controlled by the government and auctioned off by it to the highest bidders, as is essentially the case with broadcasting licences in the United States today. The same might be said of a parade ordinance which allowed the town council to forbid parades by unpopular groups because they were too expensive to police.

But to call either of these cases instances of unjust distribution tells only part of the story. Access to means of expression is in many cases a necessary condition for participation in the political process of the country, and therefore something to which citizens have an independent right. At the very least the recognition of such rights will require governments to ensure that means of expression are readily available through which individuals and small groups can make their views on political issues known, and to ensure that the principal means of expression in the society do not fall under the control of any particular segment of the community. But exactly what rights of access to means of expression follow in this way from political rights will depend to some extent on the political institutions in question. Political participation may take different forms under different institutions, even under equally just institutions.

The theory of freedom of expression which I am offering, then, consists of at least four distinguishable elements. It is based upon the Millian Principle, which is absolute but serves only to rule out certain justifications for legal restrictions on acts of expression. Within the limits set by this principle the whole range of governmental policies affecting opportunities for expression, whether by restriction, positive intervention, or failure to intervene, are subject to justification and criticism on a number of diverse grounds. First, on grounds of whether they reflect an appropriate balancing of the value of certain kinds of expression relative to other social goods; second, whether they ensure equitable distribution of access to means of expression throughout the society; and third, whether they are compatible with the recognition of certain special rights, particularly political rights.

This mixed theory is somewhat cumbersome, but the various parts seem to me both mutually irreducible and essential if we are to account for the full range of cases which seem intuitively to constitute violations of "free speech."

V

The failure of the Millian Principle to allow certain kinds of exceptions may seem to many the most implausible feature of the theory I have offered. In addition to the possibility mentioned earlier, that exceptions should be allowed in cases of diminished rationality, there may seem to be an obvious case for allowing deviations from the principle in time of war or other grave emergency.

It should be noticed that because the Millian Principle is much narrower than, say, a blanket protection of "speech," the theory I have offered can already accommodate some of the restrictions on expression which wartime conditions may be thought to justify. The Millian Principle allows one, even in normal times, to consider whether the publication of certain information might present serious hazards to public safety by giving people the capacity to inflict certain harms. It seems likely that risks of this kind which are worth taking in time of peace in order to allow full discussion of, say, certain scientific questions, might be intolerable in wartime.

But the kind of emergency powers that governments feel entitled to invoke often go beyond this and include, for example, the power to cut off political debate when such debate threatens to divide the country or otherwise to undermine its capacity to meet a present threat. The obvious justification for such powers is clearly disallowed by the Millian Principle, and the theory I have offered provides for no exceptions of this kind.

It is hard for me at the present moment to conceive of a case in which I would think the invocation of such powers by a government right. I am willing to admit that there might be such cases, but even if there are I do not think that they should be seen as "exceptions" to be incorporated within the Millian Principle.

That principle, it will be recalled, does not rest on a right of citizens but rather expresses a limitation on the authority governments can be supposed to have. The authority in question here is that provided by a particular kind of political theory, one which has its starting point in the question: How could citizens recognize a right of governments to command them while still regarding themselves as equal, autonomous, rational agents? The theory is normally thought to yield the answer that this is possible if, but only if, that right is limited in certain ways, and if certain other conditions, supposed to ensure citizen control over government, are fulfilled. I have argued that one of the necessary limitations is expressed by the Millian Principle. If I am right, then the claim of a government to rule by virtue of this particular kind of authority is undermined, I think completely, if it undertakes to control its citizens in the ways that the Millian Principle is intended to exclude.

This does not mean, however, that it could not in an extreme case be right for certain people, who normally exercised the kind of authority held to be legitimate by democratic political theory, to take measures which this authority does not justify. These actions would have to be justified on some other ground (e.g., utilitarian), and the claim of their agents to be obeyed would not be that of a legitimate government in the usual (democratic) sense. None the less most citizens might, under the circumstances, have good reason to obey.

There are a number of different justifications for the exercise of coercive authority. In a situation of extreme peril to a group, those in the group who are in a position to avert disaster by exercising a certain kind of control over the others may be justified in using force to do so, and there may be good reason for their commands to be obeyed. But this kind of authority differs both in justification and extent from that which, if democratic political theory is correct, a legitimate democratic government enjoys. What I am suggesting is that if there are situations in which a general suspension of civil liberties is justified – and, I repeat, it is not clear to me that there are such – these situations constitute a shift from one kind of authority to another. The people involved will probably continue to wear the same hats, but this does not mean that they still rule with the same title.

It should not be thought that I am here giving governments licence to kick over the traces of constitutional rule whenever this is required by the "national interest." It would take a situation of near catastrophe to justify a move of the kind I have described, and if governments know what they are doing it would take such a situation to make a move of this sort inviting. For a great deal is given up in such a move, including any notion that the commands of government have a claim to be obeyed which goes beyond the relative advantages of obedience and disobedience.

When the situation is grave and the price of disorder enormous, such utilitarian considerations may give the government's commands very real binding force. But continuing rule on this basis would be acceptable only for a society in permanent crisis or for a group of people who, because they could see each other only as obedient servants or as threatening foes, could not be ruled on any other.

NOTES

1 This task is carried out by Thomas Emerson in *Toward a General Theory of the First Amendment* (New York, 1966). See esp. pp. 60–2.
2 In *Schenck v. United States*, 249 US 47 (1919).
3 Kant's notion of autonomy goes beyond the one I employ in that for him there are special requirements regarding the reasons which an autonomous being can act on. (See the second and third sections of *Foundations of the Metaphysics of Morals*.) While his notion of autonomy is stronger than mine, Kant does not draw from it the same limitations on the authority of states (see *Metaphysical Elements of Justice*, sections 46–9).
4 I am not certain whether I am here agreeing or disagreeing with Robert Paul Wolff (*In Defense of Anarchism*, New York, 1970). At any rate I would not call what I am maintaining anarchism. The limitation on state power I have in mind is that described by John Rawls in the closing paragraphs of 'The Justification of Civil Disobedience," in *Civil Disobedience: Theory and Practice*, ed. Hugo Bedau (New York, 1969).
5 In *Schenck v. United States*.
6 In Ch. II of *On Liberty*.
7 This test is developed as a criterion for justifiable paternalism by Gerald Dworkin in his essay "Paternalism," in *Morality and the Law*, ed. Richard Wasserstrom (Belmont, Calif., 1971).

READING QUESTIONS ON SCANLON

1 Does Scanlon's argument apply to all types of speech that claims to offer reasons?
2 Do all forms of speech purport to offer reasons to be evaluated? Think about pornography and hate speech.
3 Reread Mill's discussion of speech, above. How is Scanlon's view related to Mill's?

R. v. Keegstra [1990] 3 SCR 697

The Supreme Court of Canada upheld the section of the *Criminal Code* outlawing the incitement of hatred. Writing for the majority, Dickson, C.J.C. argued that the reasons for limiting expression in this case were the same as the reasons for protecting it more generally.

Dickson, C.J.C.: – This appeal ... raises a delicate and highly controversial issue as to the constitutional validity of s. 319(2) of the *Criminal Code*, RSC, 1985, c. C-46, a legislative provision which prohibits the wilful promotion of hatred, other than in private conversation, towards any section of the public distinguished by colour, race, religion or ethnic origin. In particular, the court must decide whether this section infringes the guarantee of freedom of expression found in s. 2(b) of the *Canadian Charter of Rights and Freedoms* in a manner that cannot be justified under s. 1 of the *Charter*. A secondary issue arises as to whether the presumption of innocence protected in the *Charter's* s. 11(d) is unjustifiably breached by reason of s. 319(3)(a) of the *Code*, which affords a defence of "truth" to the wilful promotion of hatred, but only where the accused proves the truth of the communicated statements on the balance of probabilities.

FACTS

Mr James Keegstra was a high school teacher in Eckville, Alberta, from the early 1970s until his dismissal in 1982. In 1984, Mr Keegstra was charged under s. 319(2) (then 281.2(2)) of the *Criminal Code* with unlawfully promoting hatred against an identifiable group by communicating anti-Semitic statements to his students. He was convicted by a jury in a trial before McKenzie, J. of the Alberta Court of Queen's Bench.

Mr Keegstra's teachings attributed various evil qualities to Jews. He thus described Jews to his pupils as "treacherous," "subversive," "sadistic," "money-loving," "power hungry," and "child killers." He taught his classes that Jewish people seek to destroy Christianity and are responsible for depressions, anarchy, chaos, wars, and revolution. According to Mr Keegstra, Jews "created the Holocaust to gain sympathy" and, in contrast to the open and honest Christians, were said to be deceptive, secretive, and inherently evil. Mr Keegstra expected his students to reproduce his teachings in class and on exams. If they failed to do so, their marks suffered.

Prior to his trial, Mr Keegstra applied to the Court of Queen's Bench in Alberta for an order quashing the charge on a number of grounds, the primary one being that s. 319(2) of the *Criminal Code* unjustifiably infringed his freedom of expression as guaranteed by s. 2(b) of the *Charter*. Among the other grounds of appeal was the allegation that the defence of truth found in s. 319(3)(a) of the *Code* violates the *Charter's* presumption of innocence. The application was dismissed by Quigley, J., and Mr Keegstra was thereafter tried and convicted. He then appealed his conviction to the Alberta Court of Appeal, raising the same *Charter* issues. The Court of Appeal unanimously accepted his argument, and it is from this judgment that the Crown appeals.

RELEVANT STATUTORY AND CONSTITUTIONAL PROVISIONS

The relevant legislative and Charter provisions are set out below:

Criminal Code
319(2) Every one who, by communicating statements, other than in private conversation, wilfully promotes hatred against any identifiable group is guilty of
(a) an indictable offence and is liable to imprisonment for a term not exceeding two years; or
(b) an offence punishable on summary conviction.

(3) No person shall be convicted of an offence under subsection (2)
(a) if he establishes that the statements communicated were true;
(b) if, in good faith, he expressed or attempted to establish by argument an opinion upon a religious subject;
(c) if the statements were relevant to any subject of public interest, the discussion of which was for the public benefit, and if on reasonable grounds he believed them to be true; or
(d) if, in good faith, he intended to point out, for the purpose of removal, matters producing or tending to produce feelings of hatred towards an identifiable group in Canada.

(6) No proceeding for an offence under subsection (2) shall be instituted without the consent of the Attorney General.

(7) In this section,
"communicating" includes communicating by telephone, broadcasting or other audible or visible means;
"identifiable group" has the same meaning as in section 318;
"public place" includes any place to which the public have access as of right or by invitation, express or implied;
"statements" includes words spoken or written or recorded electronically or electromagnetically or otherwise, and gestures, signs or other visible representations.

318(4) In this section, "identifiable group" means any section of the public distinguished by colour, race, religion or ethnic origin.

Canadian Bill of Rights, RSC 1985, App. III

1. It is hereby recognized and declared that in Canada there have existed and shall continue to exist without discrimination by reason of race, national origin, colour, religion or sex, the following human rights and fundamental freedoms, namely, ...
(d) freedom of speech;

Canadian Charter of Rights and Freedoms

1. *The Canadian Charter of Rights and Freedoms* guarantees the rights and freedoms set out in it subject only to such reasonable limits prescribed by law as can be demonstrably justified in a free and democratic society.

2. Everyone has the following fundamental freedoms:
(b) freedom of thought, belief, opinion and expression, including freedom of the press and other media of communication;

11. Any person charged with an offence has the right
(d) to be presumed innocent until proven guilty according to law in a fair and public hearing by an independent and impartial tribunal;

15(1) Every individual is equal before and under the law and has the right to the equal protection and equal benefit of the law without discrimination and, in particular, without discrimination based on race, national and ethnic origin, colour, religion, sex, age or mental or physical disability.

27. This *Charter* shall be interpreted in a manner consistent with the preservation and enhancement of the multicultural heritage of Canadians.

THE HISTORY OF HATE PROPAGANDA CRIMES IN CANADA

...

While the history of attempts to prosecute criminally the libel of groups is lengthy, the *Criminal Code* provisions discussed so far do not focus specifically upon expression propagated with the intent of causing hatred against racial, ethnic, or religious groups. Even before the Second World War, however, fears began to surface concerning the inadequacy of Canadian criminal law in this regard. In the 1930s, for example, Manitoba passed a statute combatting a perceived rise in the dissemination of Nazi propaganda. Following the Second World War and revelation of the Holocaust, in Canada and throughout the world a desire grew to protect human rights, and especially to guard against discrimination. Internationally, this desire led to the landmark *Universal Declaration of Human Rights* in 1948, and, with reference to hate propaganda, was eventually manifested in two international human rights instruments ...

The Special Committee on Hate Propaganda in Canada, usually referred to as the Cohen Committee ... released [its] unanimous report ...

The tenor of the report is reflected in the opening paragraph of its preface, which reads:

This Report is a study in the power of words to maim, and what it is that a civilized society can do about it. Not every abuse of human communication can or should be controlled by law or custom. But every society from time to time draws lines at the point where the intolerable and the impermissible coincide. In a free society such as our own, where the privilege of speech can induce ideas that may change the very order itself, there is bias weighted heavily in favour of the maximum of rhetoric whatever the cost and consequences. But that bias stops this side of injury to the community itself and to individual members or identifiable groups innocently caught in verbal crossfire that goes beyond legitimate debate.

In keeping with these remarks, the recurrent theme running throughout the report is the need to prevent the dissemination of hate propaganda without unduly infringing the freedom of expression ...

SECTION 2(B) OF THE *CHARTER* – FREEDOM OF EXPRESSION

...

Obviously, one's conception of the freedom of expression provides a crucial backdrop to any s. 2(b) inquiry; the values promoted by the freedom help not only to define the ambit of s. 2(b), but also come to the forefront when discussing how competing interests might co-exist with the freedom under s. 1 of the *Charter*.

In the recent past, this court has had the opportunity to hear and decide a number of freedom of expression cases ... Together, the judgments in these cases provide guidance as to the values informing the freedom of expression, and additionally indicate the relationship between ss. 2(b) and 1 of the *Charter* ...

[I]t was argued before this court that the wilful promotion of hatred is an activity the form and consequences of which are analogous to those associated with violence or threats of violence. This argument contends that Supreme Court of Canada precedent excludes violence and threats of violence from the ambit of s. 2(b), and that the reason for such exclusion must lie in the fact that these forms of expression are inimical to the values supporting freedom of speech. Indeed, in support of this view it was pointed out to us that the court in *Irwin Toy* stated that "freedom of expression ensures that we can convey our thoughts and feelings in non-violent ways without fear of censure" (p. 607). Accordingly, we were urged to find that hate propaganda of the type caught by s. 319(2), insofar as it imperils the ability of target group members themselves to convey thoughts and feelings in non-violent ways without fear of censure, is analogous to violence and threats of violence and hence does not fall within s. 2(b) ...

Turning specifically to the proposition that hate propaganda should be excluded from the coverage of s. 2(b), I begin by stating that the communications restricted by s. 319(2) cannot be considered as violence, which on a reading of *Irwin Toy* I find to refer to expression communicated directly through physical harm. Nor do I find hate propaganda to be analogous to violence, and through this route exclude it from the protection of the guarantee of freedom of expression. As I have explained, the starting proposition in *Irwin Toy* is that all activities conveying or attempting to convey meaning are considered expression for the purposes of s. 2(b); the content of expression is irrelevant in determining the scope of this *Charter* provision. Stated at its highest, an exception has been suggested where meaning is communicated directly via physical violence, the extreme repugnance of this form to free expression values justifying such an extraordinary step. Section 319(2) of the *Criminal Code* prohibits the communication of meaning that is repugnant, but the repugnance stems from the content of the message as opposed to its form. For this reason, I am of the view that hate propaganda is to be categorized as expression so as to bring it within the coverage of s. 2(b).

As for threats of violence, *Irwin Toy* spoke only of restricting s. 2(b) to certain forms of expression, stating at p. 607 that,

While the guarantee of free expression protects all content of expression, certainly violence as a form of expression receives no such protection. It is not necessary here to delineate precisely when and on what basis a form of expression chosen to convey a meaning falls outside the sphere of the guarantee. But it is clear, for example, that a murderer or rapist cannot invoke the freedom of expression in justification of the form of expression he has chosen.

While the line between form and content is not always easily drawn, in my opinion threats of violence can only be so classified by reference to the content of their meaning. As such, they do not fall within the exception spoken of in *Irwin Toy*, and their suppression must be justified under s. 1. As I do not find threats of violence to be excluded from the definition of expression envisioned by s. 2(b), it is unnecessary to determine whether the threatening aspects of hate propaganda can be seen as threats of violence, or analogous to such threats, so as to deny it protection under s. 2(b).

The second matter which I wish to address before leaving the s. 2(b) inquiry concerns the relevance of other *Charter* provisions and international agreements to which Canada is a party in interpreting the coverage of the freedom of expression guarantee. It has been argued in support of excluding hate propaganda from the coverage of s. 2(b) that the use of ss. 15 and 27 of the *Charter* – dealing respectively with equality and multiculturalism – and Canada's acceptance of international agreements requiring the prohibition of racist statements make s. 319(2) incompatible with even a large and liberal definition of the freedom ... The general tenor of this argument is that these interpretive aids inextricably infuse each constitutional guarantee with values supporting equal societal participation and the security and dignity of all persons. Consequently, it is said that s. 2(b) must be curtailed so as not to extend to communications which seriously undermine the equality, security, and dignity of others ...

I thus conclude on the issue of s. 2(b) by finding that s. 319(2) of the *Criminal Code* constitutes an infringement of the *Charter* guarantee of freedom of expression, and turn to examine whether such an infringement is justifiable under s. 1 as a reasonable limit in a free and democratic society.

SECTION 1 ANALYSIS OF SECTION 319(2)

General Approach to Section 1

Though the language of s. 1 appears earlier in these reasons, it is appropriate to repeat its words:

1. *The Canadian Charter of Rights and Freedoms* guarantees the rights and freedoms set out in it subject only to such reasonable limits prescribed by law as can be demonstrably justified in a free and democratic society.

In *R. v. Oakes* (1986), 24 CCC (3d) 321, this court offered a course of analysis to be employed in determining whether a limit on a right or freedom can be demonstrably justified in a free and democratic society. Under the approach in *Oakes*, it must first be established that impugned state action has an objective of pressing and substantial concern in a free and democratic society. Only such an objective is of sufficient stature to warrant overriding a constitutionally protected right or freedom. The second feature of the *Oakes* test involves assessing the proportionality between the objective and the impugned measure. The inquiry as to proportionality attempts to guide the balancing of individual and group interests protected in s. 1, and in *Oakes* was broken down into the following three segments:

First, the measures adopted must be carefully designed to achieve the objective in question. They must not be arbitrary, unfair or based on irrational considerations. In short, they must be rationally connected to the objective. Secondly, the means, even if rationally connected to the objective in this first sense, should impair "as little as possible" the right or freedom in question ... Thirdly, there must be a proportionality between the effects of the measures which are responsible for limiting the *Charter* right or freedom, and the objective which has been identified as of "sufficient importance."

The analytical framework of *Oakes* has been continually reaffirmed by this court, yet it is dangerously misleading to conceive of s. 1 as a rigid and technical provision, offering nothing more than a last chance for the state to justify incursions into the realm of fundamental rights. From a crudely practical standpoint, *Charter* litigants sometimes may perceive s. 1 in this manner, but in the body of our nation's constitutional law it plays an immeasurably richer role, one of great magnitude and sophistication ... As this court has said before, the premier article of the *Charter* has a dual function, operating both to activate *Charter* rights and freedoms and to permit such reasonable limits as a free and democratic society may have occasion to place upon them (*Oakes*, at pp. 343–4). What seems to me to be of significance in this dual function is the commonality that links the guarantee of rights and freedoms to their limitation. This commonality lies in the phrase "free and democratic society" ...

Obviously, a practical application of s. 1 requires more than an incantation of the words "free and democratic society." These words require some definition, an elucidation as to the values that they invoke. To a large extent, a free and democratic society embraces the very values and principles which Canadians have sought to protect and further by entrenching specific rights and freedoms in the Constitution, although the balancing exercise in s. 1 is not restricted to values expressly set out in the *Charter*. With this guideline in mind, in *Oakes* I commented upon some of the ideals that inform our understanding of a free and democratic society, saying (at p. 346):

The court must be guided by the values and principles essential to a free and democratic society which I believe embody, to name but a few, respect for the inherent dignity of the human person, commitment to social justice and equality, accommodation of a wide variety of beliefs, respect for cultural and group identity, and faith in social and political institutions which enhance the participation of individuals and groups in society. The underlying values and principles of a free and democratic society are the genesis of the rights and freedoms guaranteed by the *Charter* and the ultimate standard against which a limit on a right or freedom must be shown, despite its effect, to be reasonable and demonstrably justified.

Undoubtedly these values and principles are numerous, covering the guarantees enumerated in the *Charter* and more. Equally, they may well deserve different emphases, and certainly will assume varying degrees of importance depending upon the circumstances of a particular case.

It is important not to lose sight of factual circumstances in undertaking a s. 1 analysis, for these shape a court's view of both the right or freedom at stake and the limit proposed by the state; neither can be surveyed in the abstract. As Wilson, J. said in *Edmonton Journal, supra*, referring to what she termed the "contextual approach" to *Charter* interpretation (at p. 584):

... a particular right or freedom may have a different value depending on the context. It may be, for example, that freedom of expression has greater value in a political context than it does in the context of disclosure of the details of a matrimonial dispute ...

Though Wilson, J. was speaking with reference to the task of balancing enumerated rights and freedoms, I see no reason why her view should not apply to all values associated with a free and democratic society. Clearly, the proper judicial perspective under s. 1 must be derived from an awareness of the synergetic relation between two elements: the values underlying the *Charter* and the circumstances of the particular case ...

The Use of American Constitutional Jurisprudence

Having discussed the unique and unifying role of s. 1, I think it appropriate to address a tangential matter, yet one nonetheless crucial to the disposition of this appeal: the relationship between Canadian and American approaches to the constitutional protection of free expression, most notably in the realm of hate propaganda. Those who attack the constitutionality of s. 319(2) draw heavily on the tenor of First Amendment jurisprudence in weighing the competing freedoms and interests in this appeal, a reliance which is understandable given the prevalent opinion that the criminalization of hate propaganda violates the Bill of Rights ... In response to the emphasis placed upon this jurisprudence, I find it helpful to summarize the American position and to determine the extent to which it should influence the s. 1 analysis in the circumstances of this appeal.

A myriad of sources – both judicial and academic – offer reviews of First Amendment jurisprudence as it pertains to hate propaganda. Central to most discussions is the 1952 case of *Beauharnais v. Illinois*, 343 US 250, where the Supreme Court of the United States upheld as constitutional a criminal statute forbidding certain types of group defamation. Though never overruled, *Beauharnais* appears to have been weakened by later pronouncements of the Supreme Court ... The trend reflected in many of these pronouncements is to protect offensive, public invective as long as the speaker has not knowingly lied and there exists no clear and present danger of violence or insurrection.

In the wake of subsequent developments in the Supreme Court, on several occasions *Beauharnais* has been distinguished and doubted by lower courts ...

The question that concerns us in this appeal is not, of course, what the law is or should be in the United States. But it is important to be explicit as to the reasons why or why not American experience may be useful in the s. 1 analysis of s. 319(2) of the *Criminal Code*. In the United States, a collection of fundamental rights has been constitutionally protected for over 200 years. The resulting practical and theoretical experience is immense, and should not be overlooked by Canadian courts. On the other hand, we must examine American constitutional law with a critical eye, and in this respect La Forest, J. has noted ...:

While it is natural and even desirable for Canadian courts to refer to American constitutional jurisprudence in seeking to elucidate the meaning of *Charter* guarantees that have counterparts in the United States Constitution, they should be wary of drawing too ready a parallel between constitutions born to different countries in different ages and in very different circumstances ...

Having examined the American cases relevant to First Amendment jurisprudence and legislation criminalizing hate propaganda, I would be adverse to following too closely the line of argument that would overrule *Beauharnais* on the ground that incursions placed upon free expression are only justified where there is a clear and present danger of imminent breach of peace. Equally, I am unwilling to embrace various categorizations and guiding rules generated by American law without careful consideration of their appropriateness to Canadian constitutional theory. Though I have found the American experience tremendously helpful in coming to my own conclusions regarding this appeal, and by no means reject the whole of the First Amendment doctrine, in a number of respects I am thus dubious as to the applicability of this doctrine in the context of a challenge to hate propaganda legislation.

... [A]pplying the *Charter* to the legislation challenged in this appeal reveals important differences between Canadian and American constitutional perspectives. I have already discussed in some detail the special role of s. 1 in determining the protective scope of *Charter* rights and freedoms. Section 1 has no equivalent in the United States, a fact previously alluded to by this court in selectively utilizing American constitutional jurisprudence. Of course, American experience should never be rejected simply because the *Charter* contains a balancing provision, for it is well known that American courts have fashioned compromises between conflicting interests despite what appears to be the absolute guarantee of constitutional rights. Where s. 1 operates to accentuate a uniquely Canadian vision of a free and democratic society, however, we must not hesitate to depart from the path taken in the United States. Far from requiring a less solicitous protection of *Charter* rights and freedoms, such independence of vision protects these rights and freedoms in a different way. As will be seen below, in my view the international commitment to eradicate hate propaganda and, most importantly, the special role given equality and multiculturalism in the Canadian Constitution necessitate a departure from the view, reasonably prevalent in America at present, that the suppression of hate propaganda is incompatible with the guarantee of free expression ...

Most importantly, the nature of the s. 1 test as applied in the context of a challenge to s. 319(2) may well demand a perspective particular to Canadian constitutional jurisprudence when weighing competing interests. If values fundamental to the Canadian conception of a free and democratic society suggest an approach that denies hate propaganda the highest degree of constitutional protection, it is this approach which must be employed.

Objective of Section 319(2)

I now turn to the specific requirements of the *Oakes* approach in deciding whether the infringement of s. 2(b) occasioned by s. 319(2) is justifiable in a free and democratic society. According to *Oakes*, the first aspect of the s. 1 analysis is to examine the objective of the impugned legislation. Only if the objective relates to concerns which are pressing and substantial in a free and democratic society can the legislative limit on a right or freedom hope to be permissible under the *Charter*. In examining the objective of s. 319(2), I will begin by discussing the harm caused by hate propaganda as identified by the Cohen Committee and subsequent study groups, and then review in turn the impact upon this objective of international human rights instruments and ss. 15 and 27 of the *Charter*.

Harm Caused by Expression Promoting the Hatred of Identifiable Groups

Looking to the legislation challenged in this appeal, one must ask whether the amount of hate propaganda in Canada causes sufficient harm to justify legislative intervention of some type. The Cohen Committee, speaking in 1965, found that the incidence of hate propaganda in Canada was not insignificant (at p. 24):

... there exists in Canada a small number of persons and a somewhat larger number of organizations, extremist in outlook and dedicated to the preaching and spreading of hatred and contempt against certain identifiable minority groups in Canada. It is easy to conclude that because the number of persons and organizations is not very large, they should not be taken too seriously. The Committee is of the opinion that this line of analysis is no longer tenable after what is known to have been the result of hate propaganda in other countries, particularly in the 1930s when such material and ideas played a significant role in the creation of a climate of malice, destructive to the central values of Judaic-Christian society, the values of our civilization. The Committee believes, therefore, that the actual and potential danger caused by present hate activities in Canada cannot be measured by statistics alone.

Even the statistics, however, are not unimpressive, because while activities have centered heavily in Ontario, they nevertheless have extended from Nova Scotia to British Columbia and minority groups in at least eight Provinces have been subjected to these vicious attacks.

In 1984, the House of Commons Special Committee on Participation of Visible Minorities in Canadian Society in its report, entitled *Equality Now!*, observed that increased immigration and periods of economic difficulty "have produced an atmosphere that may be ripe for racially motivated incidents" (p. 69). With regard to the dissemination of hate propaganda, the Special Committee found that the prevalence and scope of such material had risen since the Cohen Committee made its report, stating (at p. 69):

There has been a recent upsurge in hate propaganda. It has been found in virtually every part of Canada. Not only is it anti-semitic and anti-black, as in the 1960s, but it is also now anti-Roman Catholic, anti-East Indian, anti-aboriginal people and anti-French. Some of this material is imported from the United States but much of it is produced in Canada. Most worrisome of all is that in recent years Canada has become a major source of supply of hate propaganda that finds its way to Europe, and especially to West Germany.

As the quotations above indicate, the presence of hate propaganda in Canada is sufficiently substantial to warrant concern. Disquiet caused by the existence of such material is not simply the product of its offensiveness, however, but stems from the very real harm which it causes. Essentially, there are two sorts of injury caused by hate propaganda. First, there is harm done to members of the target group. It is indisputable that the emotional damage caused by words may be of grave psychological and social consequence. In the context of sexual harassment, for example, this court has found that words can in themselves constitute harassment: *Janzen v. Platy Enterprises Ltd* (1989), 59 DLR (4th) 352. In a similar manner, words and writings that wilfully promote hatred can constitute a serious attack on persons belonging to a racial or religious group, and in this regard the Cohen Committee noted that these persons are humiliated and degraded (p. 214).

In my opinion, a response of humiliation and degradation from an individual targeted by hate propaganda is to be expected. A person's sense of human dignity and belonging to the community at large is closely linked to the concern and respect accorded the groups to which he or she belongs. The derision, hostility and abuse encouraged by hate propaganda therefore have a severely negative impact on the individual's sense of self-worth and acceptance. This impact may cause target group members to take drastic measures in reaction, perhaps avoiding activities which bring them into contact with non-group members or adopting attitudes and postures directed towards blending in with the majority. Such consequences bear heavily in a nation that prides itself on tolerance and the fostering of human dignity through, among other things, respect for the many racial, religious, and cultural groups in our society.

A second harmful effect of hate propaganda which is of pressing and substantial concern is its influence upon society at large. The Cohen Committee noted that individuals can be persuaded to believe "almost anything" (p. 30) if information or ideas are communicated using the right technique and in the proper circumstances (at p. 8):

... we are less confident in the 20th century that the critical faculties of individuals will be brought to bear on the speech and writing which is directed at them. In the 18th and 19th centuries, there was a widespread belief that man was a rational creature, and that if his mind was trained and liberated from superstition by education, he would always distinguish truth from falsehood, good from evil. So Milton, who said "let truth and falsehood grapple: who ever knew truth put to the worse in a free and open encounter."

We cannot share this faith today in such a simple form. While holding that over the long run, the human mind is repelled by blatant falsehood and seeks the good, it is too often true, in the short run, that emotion displaces reason and individuals perversely reject the demonstrations of truth put before them and forsake the good they know. The successes of modern advertising, the triumphs of impudent propaganda such as Hitler's, have qualified sharply our belief in the rationality of man. We know that under the strain and pressure in times of irritation and frustration, the individual is swayed and even swept away by hysterical, emotional appeals. We act irresponsibly if we ignore the way in which emotion can drive reason from the field.

It is thus not inconceivable that the active dissemination of hate propaganda can attract individuals to its cause, and in the process create serious discord between various cultural groups in society. Moreover, the alteration of views held by the recipients of hate propaganda may occur subtly, and is not always attendant upon conscious acceptance of the communicated ideas. Even if the message of hate propaganda is outwardly rejected, there is evidence that its premise of racial or religious inferiority may persist in a recipient's mind as an idea that holds some truth, an incipient effect not to be entirely discounted.

The threat to the self-dignity of target group members is thus matched by the possibility that prejudiced messages will gain some credence, with the attendant result of discrimination, and perhaps even violence, against minority groups in Canadian society. With these dangers in mind, the Cohen Committee made clear in its conclusions that the presence of hate propaganda existed as a baleful and pernicious element, and hence a serious problem, in Canada (at p. 59):

We believe that, given a certain set of socioeconomic circumstances, such as a deepening of the emotional tensions or the setting in of a severe business recession, public susceptibility might well increase significantly. Moreover, the potential psychological and social damage of hate propaganda, both to a desensitized majority and to sensitive minority target groups, is incalculable.

As noted previously, in articulating concern about hate propaganda and its contribution to racial and religious tension in Canada, the Cohen

Committee recommended that Parliament use the *Criminal Code* in order to prohibit wilful, hate-promoting expression and underline Canada's commitment to end prejudice and intolerance ...

International Human Rights Instruments

There is a great deal of support, both in the submissions made by those seeking to uphold s. 319(2) in this appeal and in the numerous studies of racial and religious hatred in Canada, for the conclusion that the harm caused by hate propaganda represents a pressing and substantial concern in a free and democratic society. I would also refer to international human rights principles, however, for guidance with respect to assessing the legislative objective.

Generally speaking, the international human rights obligations taken on by Canada reflect the values and principles of a free and democratic society, and thus those values and principles that underlie the *Charter* itself ...

No aspect of international human rights has been given attention greater than that focused upon discrimination ... In 1966, the United Nations adopted the international *Convention on the Elimination of All Forms of Racial Discrimination*, 1970, Can. TS, No. 28 (hereinafter CERD). The convention, in force since 1969 and including Canada among its signatory members, contains a resolution that states parties agree to:

... adopt all necessary measures for speedily eliminating racial discrimination in all its forms and manifestations, and to prevent and combat racist doctrines and practices in order to promote understanding between races and to build an international community free from all forms of racial segregation and racial discrimination ...

Article 4 of the *CERD* is of special interest, providing that:

States Parties condemn all propaganda and all organizations which are based on ideas or theories of superiority of one race or group of persons of one colour or ethnic origin, or which attempt to justify or promote racial hatred and discrimination in any form, and undertake to adopt immediate and positive measures designed to eradicate all incitement to, or acts of, such discrimination and, to this end, with due regard to the principles embodied in the *Universal Declaration of Human Rights* and the rights expressly set forth in article 5 of this *Convention*, inter alia:

(a) Shall declare an offence punishable by law all dissemination of ideas based on racial superiority or hatred, incitement to racial discrimination, as well as all acts of violence or incitement to such acts against any race or group of persons of another colour or ethnic origin, and also the provision of any assistance to racist activities, including the financing thereof;

Further, the *International Covenant on Civil and Political Rights*, 1966, 999 UNTS 171 (hereinafter *ICCPR*) , adopted by the United Nations in 1966 and in force in Canada since 1976, in the following two articles guarantees the freedom of expression while simultaneously prohibiting the advocacy of hatred.

It appears that the protection provided freedom of expression by *CERD* and ICCPR does not extend to cover communications advocating racial or religious hatred ...

Other Provisions of the *Charter*

Significant indicia of the strength of the objective behind s. 319(2) are gleaned not only from the international arena, but are also expressly evident in various provisions of the *Charter* itself. As Wilson, J. noted in *Singh v. Canada (Minister of Employment and Immigration)* (1985), 17 DLR (4th) 422 at p. 468, [1985] 1 SCR 177, 14 CRR 13:

... it is important to bear in mind that the rights and freedoms set out in the *Charter* are fundamental to the political structure of Canada and are guaranteed by the *Charter* as part of the supreme law of our nation. I think that in determining whether a particular limitation is a reasonable limit prescribed by law which can be "demonstrably justified in a free and democratic society" it is important to remember that the courts are conducting this inquiry in light of a commitment to uphold the rights and freedoms set out in other sections of the *Charter*.

Most importantly for the purposes of this appeal, ss. 15 and 27 represent a strong commitment to the values of equality and multiculturalism, and hence underline the great importance of Parliament's objective in prohibiting hate propaganda.

... [T]he effects of entrenching a guarantee of equality in the *Charter* are not confined to those instances where it can be invoked by an individual against the state. Insofar as it indicates our society's dedication to promoting equality, s. 15 is also relevant in assessing the aims of s.

319(2) of the *Criminal Code* under s. 1. In *Andrews v. Law Society of British Columbia* (1989), 56 DLR (4th) 1 at p. 15, this court examined the equality guarantee of s. 15, McIntyre, J. noting:

It is clear that the purpose of s. 15 is to ensure equality in the formulation and application of the law. The promotion of equality entails the promotion of a society in which all are secure in the knowledge that they are recognized at law as human beings equally deserving of concern, respect and consideration. It has a large remedial component.

... The principles underlying s. 15 of the *Charter* are thus integral to the s. 1 analysis.

In its written submission to the court, the intervenor LEAF [Women's Legal Education and Action Fund (*eds.*)] made the following comment in support of the view that the public and wilful promotion of group hatred is properly understood as a practice of inequality:

Government sponsored hatred on group grounds would violate section 15 of the *Charter*. Parliament promotes equality and moves against inequality when it prohibits the wilful public promotion of group hatred on these grounds. It follows that government action against group hate, because it promotes social equality as guaranteed by the *Charter*, deserves special constitutional consideration under section 15.

I agree with this statement. In light of the *Charter* commitment to equality, and the reflection of this commitment in the framework of s. 1, the objective of the impugned legislation is enhanced insofar as it seeks to ensure the equality of all individuals in Canadian society. The message of the expressive activity covered by s. 319(2) is that members of identifiable groups are not to be given equal standing in society, and are not human beings equally deserving of concern, respect, and consideration. The harms caused by this message run directly counter to the values central to a free and democratic society, and in restricting the promotion of hatred Parliament is therefore seeking to bolster the notion of mutual respect necessary in a nation which venerates the equality of all persons.

Section 15 is not the only *Charter* provision which emphasizes values both important to a free and democratic society and pertinent to the disposition of this appeal under s. 1. Section 27 states that:

27. This *Charter* shall be interpreted in a manner consistent with the preservation and enhancement of the multicultural heritage of Canadians.

This court has where possible taken account of s. 27 and its recognition that Canada possesses a multicultural society in which the diversity and richness of various cultural groups is a value to be protected and enhanced ... The value expressed in s. 27 cannot be casually dismissed in assessing the validity of s. 319(2) under s. 1, and I am of the belief that s. 27 and the commitment to a multicultural vision of our nation bears notice in emphasizing the acute importance of the objective of eradicating hate propaganda from society.

Hate propaganda seriously threatens both the enthusiasm with which the value of equality is accepted and acted upon by society and the connection of target group members to their community. I thus agree with the sentiments of Cory, J.A. who, in writing to uphold s. 319(2) in *R. v. Andrews* (1988), 43 CCC (3d) 193 at p. 213, said: "Multiculturalism cannot be preserved let alone enhanced if free rein is given to the promotion of hatred against identifiable cultural groups." When the prohibition of expressive activity that promotes hatred of groups identifiable on the basis of colour, race, religion, or ethnic origin is considered in light of s. 27, the legitimacy and substantial nature of the government objective is therefore considerably strengthened.

Conclusion Respecting Objective of Section 319(2)

In my opinion, it would be impossible to deny that Parliament's objective in enacting s. 319(2) is of the utmost importance ...

Proportionality

The second branch of the *Oakes* test – proportionality – poses the most challenging questions with respect to the validity of s. 319(2) as a reasonable limit on freedom of expression in a free and democratic society. It is therefore not surprising to find most commentators, as well as the litigants in the case at bar, agreeing that the objective of the provision is of great importance, but to observe considerable disagreement when it comes to deciding whether the means chosen to further the objective are proportional to the ends ...

Relation of the Expression at Stake to Free Expression Values

In discussing the nature of the government objective, I have commented at length upon the way in which the suppression of hate propaganda furthers values basic to a free and democratic society. I have said little, however, regarding the extent to which these same values, including the freedom of expression, are furthered by *permitting* the exposition of such expressive activity. This lacuna is explicable when one realizes that the interpretation of s. 2(b) under *Irwin Toy, supra,* gives protection to a very wide range of expression. Content is irrelevant to this interpretation, the result of a high value being placed upon freedom of expression in the abstract. This approach to s. 2(b) often operates to leave unexamined the extent to which the expression at stake in a particular case promotes freedom of expression principles. In my opinion, however, the s. 1 analysis of a limit upon s. 2(b) cannot ignore the nature of the expressive activity which the state seeks to restrict. While we must guard carefully against judging expression according to its popularity, it is equally destructive of free expression values, as well as the other values which underlie a free and democratic society, to treat all expression as equally crucial to those principles at the core of s. 2(b).

In *Rocket v. Royal College of Dental Surgeons of Ontario, supra,* McLachlin, J. recognized the importance of context in evaluating expressive activity under s. 1, stating with regard to commercial speech (at p. 78):

While the Canadian approach does not apply special tests to restrictions on commercial expression, our method of analysis does permit a sensitive, case-oriented approach to the determination of their constitutionality. Placing the conflicting values in their factual and social context when performing the s. 1 analysis permits the courts to have regard to special features of the expression in question.

...

Royal College dealt with provincial limitations upon the freedom of dentists to impart information to patients and potential patients via advertisements. In these circumstances, the court found that the expression regulated was of a nature that made its curtailment something less than a most serious infringement of the freedom of expression, the limitation affecting neither participation in the political process nor the ability of the individual to achieve spiritual or artistic self-fulfilment ...

Applying the *Royal College* approach to the context of this appeal is a key aspect of the s. 1 analysis. One must ask whether the expression prohibited by s. 319(2) is tenuously connected to the values underlying s. 2(b) so as to make the restriction "easier to justify than other infringements." In this regard, let me begin by saying that, in my opinion, there can be no real disagreement about the subject-matter of the messages and teachings communicated by the respondent, Mr Keegstra: it is deeply offensive, hurtful and damaging to target group members, misleading to his listeners, and antithetical to the furtherance of tolerance and understanding in society. Furthermore, as will be clear when I come to discuss in detail the interpretation of s. 319(2), there is no doubt that all expression fitting within the terms of the offence can be similarly described. To say merely that expression is offensive and disturbing, however, fails to address satisfactorily the question of whether, and to what extent, the expressive activity prohibited by s. 319(2) promotes the values underlying the freedom of expression. It is to this difficult and complex question that I now turn.

From the outset, I wish to make clear that in my opinion the expression prohibited by s. 319(2) is not closely linked to the rationale underlying s. 2(b). Examining the values identified in *Ford* and *Irwin Toy* as fundamental to the protection of free expression, arguments can be made for the proposition that each of these values is diminished by the suppression of hate propaganda. While none of these arguments is spurious, I am of the opinion that expression intended to promote the hatred of identifiable groups is of limited importance when measured against free expression values.

At the core of freedom of expression lies the need to ensure that truth and the common good are attained, whether in scientific and artistic endeavours or in the process of determining the best course to take in our political affairs. Since truth and the ideal form of political and social organization can rarely, if at all, be identified with absolute certainty, it is difficult to prohibit expression without impeding the free exchange of potentially valuable information. Nevertheless, the argument from truth does not provide convincing support for the protection of hate propaganda. Taken to its extreme, this argument would require us to permit the communication of all expression, it being impossible to know with absolute certainty which factual statements are true, or which ideas obtain the greatest good. The problem with this extreme position, however, is that the greater the degree of certainty that a statement is erroneous or mendacious, the less its value in the quest for truth. Indeed, expression can be used to the detriment of our search for truth; the state should not be the sole arbiter of truth, but neither should we overplay the view that rationality will overcome all falsehoods in the unregulated market-place of ideas. There is very little chance that statements intended to promote hatred against an identifiable group are true, or that their vision of society will lead to a better world. To portray such statements as crucial to truth and the betterment of the political and social milieu is therefore misguided.

Another component central to the rationale underlying s. 2(b) concerns the vital role of free expression as a means of ensuring individuals the ability to gain self-fulfilment by developing and articulating thoughts and ideas as they see fit. It is true that s. 319(2) inhibits this process among those individuals whose expression it limits, and hence arguably works against freedom of expression values. On the other hand, such self-autonomy stems in large part from one's ability to articulate and nurture an identity derived from membership in a cultural or religious group. The message put forth by individuals who fall within the ambit of s. 319(2) represents a most extreme opposition to the idea that members of identifiable groups should enjoy this aspect of the s. 2(b) benefit. The extent to which the unhindered promotion of this message furthers free expression values must therefore be tempered insofar as it advocates with inordinate vitriol an intolerance and prejudice which views as execrable the process of individual self-development and human flourishing among all members of society.

Moving on to a third strain of thought said to justify the protection of free expression, one's attention is brought specifically to the political realm. The connection between freedom of expression and the political process is perhaps the linchpin of the s. 2(b) guarantee, and the nature of this connection is largely derived from the Canadian commitment to democracy. Freedom of expression is a crucial aspect of the democratic commitment, not merely because it permits the best policies to be chosen from among a wide array of proffered options, but additionally because it helps to ensure that participation in the political process is open to all persons. Such open participation must involve to a substantial degree the notion that all persons are equally deserving of respect and dignity. The state therefore cannot act to hinder or condemn a political view without to some extent harming the openness of Canadian democracy and its associated tenet of equality for all.

The suppression of hate propaganda undeniably muzzles the participation of a few individuals in the democratic process, and hence detracts somewhat from free expression values, but the degree of this limitation is not substantial. I am aware that the use of strong language in political and social debate – indeed, perhaps even language intended to promote hatred – is an unavoidable part of the democratic process. Moreover, I recognize that hate propaganda is expression of a type which would generally be categorized as "political," thus putatively placing it at the very heart of the principle extolling freedom of expression as vital to the democratic process. Nonetheless, expression can work to undermine our commitment to democracy where employed to propagate ideas anathemic to democratic values. Hate propaganda works in just such a way, arguing as it does for a society in which the democratic process is subverted and individuals are denied respect and dignity simply because of racial or religious characteristics. This brand of expressive activity is thus wholly inimical to the democratic aspirations of the free expression guarantee.

Indeed, one may quite plausibly contend that it is through rejecting hate propaganda that the state can best encourage the protection of values central to freedom of expression, while simultaneously demonstrating dislike for the vision forwarded by hate-mongers. In this regard, the reaction to various types of expression by a democratic government may be perceived as meaningful expression on behalf of the vast majority of citizens. I do not wish to be construed as saying that an infringement of s. 2(b) can be justified under s. 1 merely because it is the product of a democratic process; the *Charter* will not permit even the democratically elected legislature to restrict the rights and freedoms crucial to a free and democratic society. What I do wish to emphasize, however, is that one must be careful not to accept blindly that the suppression of expression must always and unremittingly detract from values central to freedom of expression.

I am very reluctant to attach anything but the highest importance to expression relevant to political matters. But given the unparalleled vigour with which hate propaganda repudiates and undermines democratic values, and in particular its condemnation of the view that all citizens need be treated with equal respect and dignity so as to make participation in the political process meaningful, I am unable to see the protection of such expression as integral to the democratic ideal so central to the s. 2(b) rationale ... In my view, hate propaganda should not be accorded the greatest of weight in the s. 1 analysis.

As a caveat, it must be emphasized that the protection of extreme statements, even where they attack those principles underlying the freedom of expression, is not completely divorced from the aims of s. 2(b) of the *Charter*. As noted already, suppressing the expression covered by s. 319(2) does to some extent weaken these principles. It can also be argued that it is partly through a clash with extreme and erroneous views that truth and the democratic vision remain vigorous and alive. In this regard, judicial pronouncements strongly advocating the importance of free expression values might be seen as helping to expose prejudiced statements as valueless even while striking down legislative restrictions that proscribe such expression. Additionally, condoning a democracy's collective decision to protect itself from certain types of expression may lead to a slippery slope on which encroachments on expression central to s. 2(b) values are permitted. To guard against such a result, the protection of communications virulently unsupportive of free expression values may be necessary in order to ensure that expression more compatible with these values is never unjustifiably limited.

None of these arguments is devoid of merit, and each must be taken into account in determining whether an infringement of s. 2(b) can be justified under s. 1. It need not be, however, that they apply equally or with the greatest of strength in every instance ... While I cannot conclude that hate propaganda deserves only marginal protection under the s. 1 analysis, I can take cognizance of the fact that limitations upon hate propaganda are directed at a special category of expression which strays some distance from the spirit of s. 2(b), and hence conclude that "restrictions on expression of this kind might be easier to justify than other infringements of s. 2(b)": *Royal College, supra,* at p. 79.

As a final point, it should be stressed that in discussing the relationship between hate propaganda and freedom of expression values I do not wish to be taken as advocating an inflexible "levels of scrutiny" categorization of expressive activity. The contextual approach necessitates an open discussion of the manner in which s. 2(b) values are engaged in the circumstances of an appeal. To become transfixed with categorization schemes risks losing the advantage associated with this sensitive examination of free expression principles, and I would be loath to sanction such a result.

Having made some preliminary comments as to the nature of the expression at stake in this appeal, it is now possible to ask whether s. 319(2) is an acceptably proportional response to Parliament's valid objective. As stated above, the proportionality aspect of the *Oakes* test requires the court to decide whether the impugned state action: (i) is rationally connected to the objective; (ii) minimally impairs the *Charter* right or freedom at issue, and (iii) does not produce effects of such severity so as to make the impairment unjustifiable.

Rational Connection

... Doubts have been raised, however, as to whether the actual effect of s. 319(2) is to undermine any rational connection between it and Parliament's objective. As stated in the reasons of McLachlin, J., there are three primary ways in which the effect of the impugned legislation might be seen as an irrational means of carrying out the Parliamentary purpose. First, it is argued that the provision may actually promote the cause of hate-mongers by earning them extensive media attention. In this vein, it is also suggested that persons accused of intentionally promoting hatred often see themselves as martyrs, and may actually generate sympathy from the community in the role of underdogs engaged in battle against the immense powers of the state. Secondly, the public may view the suppression of expression by the government with suspicion, making it possible that such expression – even if it be hate propaganda – is perceived as containing an element of truth. Finally, it is often noted ... that Germany of the 1920s and 1930s possessed and used hate propaganda laws similar to those existing in Canada, and yet these laws did nothing to stop the triumph of a racist philosophy under the Nazis.

If s. 319(2) can be said to have no impact in the quest to achieve Parliament's admirable objectives, or in fact works in opposition to these objectives, then I agree that the provision could be described as "arbitrary, unfair or based on irrational considerations": (*Oakes, supra,* at p. 348). I recognize that the effect of s. 319(2) is impossible to define with exact precision – the same can be said for many laws, criminal or otherwise. In my view, however, the position that there is no strong and evident connection between the criminalization of hate propaganda and its suppression is unconvincing. I come to this conclusion for a number of reasons, and will elucidate these by answering in turn the three arguments just mentioned.

It is undeniable that media attention has been extensive on those occasions when s. 319(2) has been used. Yet from my perspective, s. 319(2) serves to illustrate to the public the severe reprobation with which society holds messages of hate directed towards racial and religious groups. The existence of a particular criminal law, and the process of holding a trial when that law is used, is thus itself a form of expression, and the message sent out is that hate propaganda is harmful to target group members and threatening to a harmonious society ... The many, many Canadians who belong to identifiable groups surely gain a great deal of comfort from the knowledge that the hate-monger is criminally prosecuted and his or her ideas rejected. Equally, the community as a whole is reminded of the importance of diversity and multiculturalism in Canada, the value of equality and the worth and dignity of each human person being particularly emphasized.

In this context, it can also be said that government suppression of hate propaganda will not make the expression attractive and hence increase acceptance of its content. Similarly, it is very doubtful that Canadians will have sympathy for either propagators of hatred or their ideas. Governmental disapproval of hate propaganda does not invariably result in dignifying the suppressed ideology. Pornography is not dignified by its suppression, nor are defamatory statements against individuals seen as meritorious because the common law lends its support to their prohibition. Again, I stress my belief that hate propaganda legislation and trials are a means by which the values beneficial to a free and democratic society can be publicized. In this context, no dignity will be unwittingly foisted upon the convicted hate-monger or his or her philosophy, and that a hate-monger might see him or herself as a martyr is of no matter to the content of the state's message.

As for the use of hate propaganda laws in pre–World War Two Germany, I am skeptical as to the relevance of the observation that legislation similar to s. 319(2) proved ineffective in curbing the racism of the Nazis. No one is contending that hate propaganda laws can in themselves prevent the tragedy of a Holocaust; conditions particular to Germany made the rise of Nazi ideology possible despite the existence and use of these laws. Rather, hate propaganda laws are one part of a free and democratic society's bid to prevent the spread of racism, and their rational connection to this objective must be seen in such a context. Certainly West Germany has not reacted to the failure of pre-war laws by seeking their removal, a new set of criminal offences having been implemented as recently as 1985 ... In sum, having found that the purpose of the challenged legislation is valid, I also find that the means chosen to further this purpose are rational in both theory and operation, and therefore conclude that the first branch of the proportionality test has been met.

Minimal Impairment of the Section 2(b) Freedom

The criminal nature of the impugned provision, involving the associated risks of prejudice through prosecution, conviction, and the imposition of up to two years' imprisonment, indicates that the means embodied in hate propaganda legislation should be carefully tailored so as to minimize impairment of the freedom of expression. It therefore must be shown that s. 319(2) is a measured and appropriate response to the phenomenon of hate propaganda, and that it does not overly circumscribe the s. 2(b) guarantee.

The main argument of those who would strike down s. 319(2) is that it creates a real possibility of punishing expression that is not hate propaganda. It is thus submitted that the legislation is overbroad, its terms so wide as to include expression which does not relate to Parliament's objective, and also unduly vague, in that a lack of clarity and precision in its words prevents individuals from discerning its meaning with any accuracy. In either instance, it is said that the effect of s. 319(2) is to limit the expression of merely unpopular or unconventional communications. Such communications may present no risk of causing the harm which Parliament seeks to prevent, and will perhaps be closely associated with the core values of s. 2(b). This overbreadth and vagueness could consequently allow the state to employ s. 319(2) to infringe excessively the freedom of expression or, what is more likely, could have a chilling effect whereby persons potentially within s. 319(2) would exercise self-censorship. Accordingly, those attacking the validity of s. 319(2) contend that vigorous debate on important political and social issues, so highly valued in a society that prizes a diversity of ideas, is unacceptably suppressed by the provision.

The question to be answered, then, is whether s. 319(2) indeed fails to distinguish between low value expression that is squarely within the focus of Parliament's valid objective and that which does not invoke the need for the severe response of criminal sanction ...

Terms of Section 319(2). In assessing the constitutionality of s. 319(2), especially as concerns arguments of overbreadth and vagueness, an immediate observation is that statements made "in private conversation" are not included in the criminalized expression. The provision thus does not prohibit views expressed with an intention to promote hatred if made privately, indicating Parliament's concern not to intrude upon the privacy of the individual. Indeed, that the legislation excludes private conversation, rather than including communications made in a public forum, suggests that the expression of hatred in a place accessible to the public is not sufficient to activate the legislation. This observation is supported by comparing the words of s. 319(2) with those of the prohibition against the incitement of hatred likely to lead to a breach of peace in s. 319(1). Section 319(1) covers statements communicated "in a public place," suggesting that a wider scope of prohibition was intended where the danger occasioned by the statements was of an immediate nature, while the wording of s. 319(2) indicates that private conversations taking place in public areas are not prohibited. Moreover, it is reasonable to infer a subjective *mens rea* requirement regarding the type of conversation covered by s. 319(2), an inference supported by the definition of "private communications" contained in s. 183 of the *Criminal Code*. Consequently, a conversation or communication intended to be private does not satisfy the requirements of the provision if through accident or negligence an individual's expression of hatred for an identifiable group is made public.

Is s. 319(2) nevertheless overbroad because it captures *all* public expression intended to promote hatred? It would appear not, for the harm which the government seeks to prevent is not restricted to certain mediums and/or locations. To attempt to distinguish between various forms and fora would therefore be incongruent with Parliament's legitimate objective ...

The way in which I have defined the s. 319(2) offence, in the context of the objective sought by society and the value of the prohibited expression, gives me some doubt as to whether the *Charter* mandates that truthful statements communicated *with an intention to promote hatred* need be excepted from criminal condemnation. Truth may be used for widely disparate ends, and I find it difficult to accept that circumstances exist where factually accurate statements can be used for no other purpose than to stir up hatred against a racial or religious group. It would seem to follow that there is no reason why the individual who intentionally employs such statements to achieve harmful ends must under the *Charter* be protected from criminal censure.

Nevertheless, it is open to Parliament to make a concession to free expression values, whether or not such is required by the *Charter*. Deference to truth as a value central to free expression has thus led Parliament to include the defence in s. 319(3)(a), even though the accused has used truthful statements to cause harm of the type falling squarely within the objective of the legislation. When the statement contains no truth, however, this flicker of justification for the intentional promotion of hatred is extinguished, and the harmful malice of the disseminator stands alone. The relationship between the value of hate propaganda as expression and the parliamentary objective of eradicating harm, slightly altered so as to increase the magnitude of the former where the statement of the accused is truthful, thus returns to its more usual condition, a condition in which it is permissible to suppress the expression.

Because the presence of truth, though legally a defence to a charge under s. 319(2), does not change the fact that the accused has intended to promote the hatred of an identifiable group, I cannot find excessive impairment of the freedom of expression merely because s. 319(3)(a) does not cover negligent or innocent error. Whether or not a statement is susceptible to classification as true or false, my inclination is therefore to accept that such error should not excuse an accused who has wilfully used a statement in order to promote hatred against an identifiable group ...

That s. 319(2) may in the past have led authorities to restrict expression offering valuable contributions to the arts, education, or politics in Canada is surely worrying. I hope, however, that my comments as to the scope of the provision make it obvious that only the most intentionally extreme forms of expression will find a place within s. 319(2). In this light, one can safely say that the incidents mentioned above illustrate not over-expansive breadth and vagueness in the law, but rather actions by the state which cannot be lawfully taken pursuant to s. 319(2). The possibility of illegal police harassment clearly has minimal bearing on the proportionality of hate propaganda legislation to legitimate parliamentary objectives, and hence the argument based on such harassment can be rejected.

Alternative Modes of Furthering Parliament's Objective ... Given the stigma and punishment associated with a criminal conviction and the presence of other modes of government response in the fight against intolerance, it is proper to ask whether s. 319(2) can be said to impair minimally the freedom of expression. With respect to the efficacy of criminal legislation in advancing the goals of equality and multicultural tolerance in Canada, I agree that the role of s. 319(2) will be limited. It is important, in my opinion, not to hold any illusions about the ability of this one provision to rid our society of hate propaganda and its associated harms. Indeed, to become overly complacent, forgetting that there are a great many ways in which to address the problem of racial and religious intolerance, could be dangerous. Obviously, a variety of measures need be employed in the quest to achieve such lofty and important goals.

In assessing the proportionality of a legislative enactment to a valid governmental objective, however, s. 1 should not operate in every instance so as to force the government to rely upon only the mode of intervention least intrusive of a *Charter* right or freedom. It may be that a number of courses of action are available in the furtherance of a pressing and substantial objective, each imposing a varying degree of restriction upon a right or freedom. In such circumstances, the government may legitimately employ a more restrictive measure, either alone or as part of a larger program of action, if that measure is not redundant, furthering the objective in ways that alternative responses could not, and is in all other respects proportionate to a valid s. 1 aim.

Analysis of Section 319(2) under Section 1 of the Charter: *Conclusion*

I find that the infringement of the respondent's freedom of expression as guaranteed by s. 2(b) should be upheld as a reasonable limit pre-scribed by law in a free and democratic society. Furthering an im-mensely important objective and directed at expression distant from the core of free expression values, s. 319(2) satisfies each of the components of the proportionality inquiry. I thus disagree with the Alberta Court of Appeal's conclusion that this criminal prohibition of hate propaganda violates the *Charter,* and would allow the appeal in this respect ...

McLachlin, J. (dissenting): – ...

Hate Propaganda and Freedom of Speech – An Overview

Before entering upon the analysis of whether s. 319(2) of the *Criminal Code* is inconsistent with the *Charter* and must be struck down, it may be useful to consider the conflicting values underlying the question of the prohibition of hate literature and how the issue has been treated in other jurisdictions.

Hate literature presents a great challenge to our conceptions about the value of free expression. Its offensive content often constitutes a direct attack on many of the other principles which are cherished by our society. Tolerance, the dignity and equality of all individuals; these and other values are all adversely affected by the propagation of hateful sentiment. The problem is not peculiarly Canadian; it is universal. Wherever racially or culturally distinct groups of people live together, one finds people, usually a small minority of the population, who take it upon themselves to denigrate members of a group other than theirs. Canada is no stranger to this conduct. Our history is replete with ex-amples of discriminatory communications. In their time, Canadians of Asian and East Indian descent, black, and native people have been the objects of communications tending to foster hate. In the case at bar it is the Jewish people who have been singled out as objects of calumny.

The evil of hate propaganda is beyond doubt. It inflicts pain and indignity upon individuals who are members of the group in question. Insofar as it may persuade others to the same point of view, it may threaten social stability. And it is intrinsically offensive to people – the majority in most democratic countries – who believe in the equality of all people regardless of race or creed.

For these reasons, governments have legislated against the dissemination of propaganda directed against racial groups, and in some cases this legislation has been tested in the courts. Perhaps the experience most relevant to Canada is that of the United States, since its Constitution, like ours, places a high value on free expression, raising starkly the conflict between freedom of speech and the countervailing values of individual dignity and social harmony. Like s. 2(b), the First Amendment guarantee is conveyed in broad, unrestricted language, stating that "Congress shall make no law ... abridging the freedom of speech, or of the press." The relevance of aspects of the American experience to this case is underlined by the factums and submissions, which borrowed heavily from ideas which may be traced to the United States.

The protections of the First Amendment to the U.S. Constitution, and in particular free speech, have always assumed a particular importance within the U.S. constitutional scheme, being regarded as the cornerstone of all other democratic freedoms. As expressed by Jackson, J., in *West Virginia State Board of Education v. Barnette,* 319 US 624 (1943), "[i]f there is any fixed star in our constitutional constellation, it is that no official, high or petty, can prescribe what shall be orthodox in politics, nationalism, religion, or other matters of opinion or force citizens to confess by word or act their faith therein" (p. 642). The U.S. Supreme Court, particularly in recent years, has pronounced itself strongly on the need to protect speech even at the expense of other worthy competing values ...

In the United States, a provision similar to s. 319(2) of the *Criminal Code* was struck down in *Collin v. Smith, supra,* on the ground that is was fatally overbroad. In addition, the Seventh Circuit Court of Appeals hinted that the provision might also be void for vagueness. The ordinance in *Collin* prohibited "[t]he dissemination of any materials within the Village of Skokie which promotes and incites hatred against persons by reason of their race, national origin, or religion, and is intended to do so." The court found that the activity in question in the case – a proposed neo-Nazi demonstration in Skokie, Illinois – was a form of expression entitled to protection under the First Amendment. The ordinance, it found, was overbroad in that it "could conceivably be applied to criminalize dissemination of *The Merchant of Venice* or a vigorous discussion of the merits of reverse racial discrimination in Skokie" (p. 1207) ...

The *Charter* follows the American approach in method, affirming freedom of expression as a broadly defined and fundamental right, and contemplating balancing the values protected by and inherent in freedom of expression against the benefit conferred by the legislation limiting that freedom under s. 1 of the *Charter*. This is in keeping with the strong liberal tradition favouring free speech in this country – a tradition which had led to conferring quasi-constitutional status on free expression in this country prior to any bill of rights or *Charter*. At the same time, the tests are not necessarily the same as in the United States ...

The Construction Arguments

These submissions urge that s. 2(b) of the *Charter* should not be construed as extending to statements which offend s. 319(2) of the *Criminal Code*. The arguments are founded on three distinct considerations: s. 15 of the *Charter*, s. 27 of the *Charter*; and Canada's international obligations.

The Argument Based on Section 15 of the *Charter*

The first argument is that the scope of s. 2(b) is diminished by s. 15 of the *Charter*. This argument is based on the principle of construction that where possible, the provisions of a statute should be read together so as to avoid conflict. The guarantee of equality in s. 15, it is submitted, is offended by speech which denigrates a particular ethnic or religious group. The competing values reflected by the two sections might therefore be reconciled by informing the content of s. 2(b) with the values of s. 15. Accordingly, the freedom of expression guarantee should be read down to exclude from protected expression statements whose content promotes such inequality.

It is important initially to define the nature of the potential conflict between s. 2(b) and s. 15 of the *Charter*. This is not a case of the collision of two rights which are put into conflict by the facts of the case. There is no violation of s. 15 in the case at bar, since there is no law or state action which puts the guarantee of equality into issue. The right granted by s. 15 is the right to be free from inequality and discrimination effected by the state. That right is not violated in the case at bar. The conflict, then, is not between *rights*, but rather between philosophies.

There are two significant considerations which militate against an acceptance of the argument based on s. 15. First, it is important to consider the nature of the two guarantees in question. On the one hand, s. 2(b) confers on each individual freedom of expression, unconstrained by state regulation or action, and subject only to a possible limitation under s. 1. On the other hand s. 15 grants the right to be free from inequality and discrimination effected by the state. Given that the protection under s. 2(b) is aimed at protecting individuals from having their expression infringed by the government, it seems a misapplication of *Charter* values to thereby limit the scope of that individual guarantee with an argument based on s. 15, which is also aimed at circumscribing the power of the state ...

This conclusion is supported by a second factor which weighs against limiting the scope of freedom of expression on the basis of the guarantee of s. 15. The cases where this court has considered the meaning of s. 2(b) have expressly rejected the suggestion that certain statements should be denied the protection of the guarantee on the basis of their content. This court has repeatedly affirmed that no matter how offensive or disagreeable the content of the expression, it cannot on that account be denied protection under s. 2(b) of the *Charter*: see *Irwin Toy* and *Reference re ss. 193 and 195.1(1)(c) of the Criminal Code* (Man.), *supra*. The argument based on s. 15 is clearly opposed to this principle, as it suggests that protection be denied expression whose content conflicts with the values underlying the s. 15 guarantee.

Even if these difficulties could be surmounted, one would be faced with the prospect of cutting back a freedom guaranteed by the *Charter* on the basis that the exercise of the freedom may run counter to the philosophy behind another section of the *Charter*. The alleged breach of s. 2(b) can be placed in a factual context. But since there is no breach of s. 15, the value to be weighed on that side of the balance cannot be placed in a factual context. This would render the exercise of balancing the conflicting values extremely difficult ...

I conclude that this court should not reduce the scope of expression protected by s. 2(b) of the *Charter* because of s. 15 of the *Charter*.

The Argument Based on Section 27 of the *Charter*

Section 27 states that the *Charter* shall be interpreted in a manner consistent with the preservation and enhancement of the multicultural heritage of Canadians. Similar considerations apply here as applied to the argument based on s. 15 of the *Charter*. As in the case of the s. 15 argument, there is no conflict of rights, s. 27 embodying not a right or freedom but a principle of construction. As in the case of the s. 15 argument, the submission under s. 27 amounts to advocating that certain statements be denied protection under s. 2(b) because of their content, an approach which this court has rejected. Using s. 27 to limit the protection guaranteed by s. 2(b) is likewise subject to the objection that it would leave unprotected a large area of arguably legitimate social and political debate. All this is not to mention the difficulty of weighing abstract values such as multiculturalism in the balance against freedom of speech.

Further difficulties are not hard to conjure up. Different people may have different ideas about what undermines multiculturalism. The issue is inherently vague and to some extent a matter of personal opinion. For example, it might be suggested that a statement that Canada should not permit immigration from a certain part of the world is inconsistent with the preservation and enhancement of multiculturalism. Is s. 2(b) to be cut back to eliminate protection for such a statement, given the differing opinions one might expect on such a matter? It may be argued, moreover, that a certain latitude for expression of derogatory opinion about other groups is a necessary correlative of a multicultural society, where different groups compete for limited resources ...

Before leaving this point I would add that there is no evidence that the impugned legislation in fact contributes to the enhancement and preservation of multiculturalism in Canada. Reliance, therefore, on s. 27 to tailor or otherwise cut back the protection afforded by s. 2(b) risks undercutting the fundamental freedom with no guarantee of a tangible benefit in return. In my opinion, the weighing of interests and values implicit in questions such as these is better accomplished under s. 1 of the *Charter*.

The Argument Based on International Law

... Canada's international obligations, and the accords negotiated between international governments may well be helpful in placing *Charter* interpretation in a larger context. Principles agreed upon by free and democratic societies may inform the reading given to certain of its guarantees. It would be wrong, however, to consider these obligations as determinative of or limiting the scope of those guarantees. The provisions of the *Charter*, though drawing on a political and social philosophy shared with other democratic societies, are uniquely Canadian. As a result, considerations may point, as they do in this case, to a conclusion regarding a rights violation which is not necessarily in accord with those international covenants.

I should add that I am not of the view that any measures taken to implement Canada's international obligations to combat racial discrimination and hate propaganda must necessarily be unconstitutional. The obligations expressed in the *International Covenant on Civil and Political Rights* (to prohibit by law "[a]ny advocacy of national, racial or religious hatred that constitutes incitement to discrimination, hostility or violence") and the *International Convention on the Elimination of All Forms of Racial Discrimination* (to "declare an offence punishable by law all dissemination of ideas based on racial superiority or hatred") are general in nature. Details of methods to be used are not specified. Nothing in those instruments compels enactment of s. 319(2), as opposed to other provisions combating racism.

I conclude that none of the arguments which are advanced for construing s. 2(b) of the *Charter* narrowly to exclude from its protection statements offending s. 319(2) of the *Criminal Code* can prevail.

...

THE ANALYSIS UNDER SECTION 1

Section 1 and the Infringement of Freedom of Expression

The court's function under s. 1 of the *Charter* is that of weighing and balancing. Before reaching s. 1, the court must already have determined that the law in question infringes a right or freedom guaranteed by the *Charter*. The infringement alone, however, does not mandate that the law must fall. If the limit the law imposes on the right infringed is "reasonable" and "can be demonstrably justified in a free and democratic society," the law is valid. The demonstration of this justification, the burden of which lies on the state, involves proving that there are other rights or interests which outweigh the right infringed in the context of that case ...

The Objective of Section 319(2) of the *Criminal Code*

...

The objective of s. 319(2) of the *Criminal Code* is to prevent the promotion of hatred towards identifiable groups within our society. As the

Attorney General of Canada puts it, the objective of the legislation is, "among other things, to protect racial, religious and other groups from the wilful promotion of hatred against them, to prevent the spread of hatred and the breakdown of racial and social harmony," and "to prevent the destruction of our multicultural society." These aims are subsumed in the twin values of social harmony and individual dignity ...

Given the problem of racial and religious prejudice in this country, I am satisfied that the objective of the legislation is of sufficient gravity to be capable of justifying limitations on constitutionally protected rights and freedoms.

Proportionality

General Considerations. The real question in this case, as I see it, is whether the means – the criminal prohibition of wilfully promoting hatred – are proportional and appropriate to the ends of suppressing hate propaganda in order to maintain social harmony and individual dignity. The objective of the legislation is one of great significance, such significance that it is capable of outweighing the fundamental values protected by the *Charter.* The ultimate question is whether this objective is of sufficient importance to justify the limitation on free expression effected by s. 319(2) of the *Criminal Code.* In answering this question, the court must consider not only the importance of the right or freedom in question and the significance of its limitation, but whether the way in which the limitation is imposed is justifiable. How serious is the infringement of the constitutionally guaranteed freedom, in this case freedom of expression? Is the limiting measure likely to further the objective in practice? Is the limiting measure overbroad or unnecessarily invasive? In the final analysis, bearing all these things in mind, does the benefit to be derived from the legislation outweigh the seriousness of the infringement? These are the considerations relevant to the question of the proportionality of the limiting law.

I have said that the contest in this case lies between the fundamental right of free expression on the one hand, and the values of social harmony and individual liberty on the other. In approaching the difficult task of determining where the balance lies in the context of this case, it is important not to be diverted by the offensive content of much of the speech in question. As this court has repeatedly stated, even the most reprehensible or disagreeable comments are prima facie entitled to the protection of s. 2(b). It is not the statements of Mr Keegstra which are at issue in this case, but rather the constitutionality of s. 319(2) of the *Criminal Code*. That must be our focus.

Another general consideration relevant to the balancing of values involved in the proportionality test in this case relates peculiarly to the nature of freedom of expression. Freedom of expression is unique among the rights and freedoms guaranteed by the *Charter* in two ways.

The first way in which freedom of expression may be unique was alluded to earlier in the context of the philosophical underpinnings of freedom of expression. The right to fully and openly express one's views on social and political issues is fundamental to our democracy and hence to all the other rights and freedoms guaranteed by the *Charter*. Without free expression, the vigorous debate on policies and values that underlies participatory government is lacking. Without free expression, rights may be trammelled with no recourse in the court of public opinion. Some restrictions on free expression may be necessary and justified and entirely compatible with a free and democratic society. But restrictions which touch the critical core of social and political debate require particularly close consideration because of the dangers inherent in state censorship of such debate. This is of particular importance under s. 1 of the *Charter* which expressly requires the court to have regard to whether the limits are reasonable and justified in a free and democratic society.

A second characteristic peculiar to freedom of expression is that limitations on expression tend to have an effect on expression other than that which is their target. In the United States this is referred to as the chilling effect. Unless the limitation is drafted with great precision, there will always be doubt about whether a particular form of expression offends the prohibition. There will always be limitations inherent in the use of language, but that must not discourage the pursuit of the greatest drafting precision possible. The result of a failure to do so may be to deter not only the expression which the prohibition was aimed at, but legitimate expression. The law-abiding citizen who does not wish to run afoul of the law will decide not to take the chance in a doubtful case. Creativity and the beneficial exchange of ideas will be adversely affected. This chilling effect must be taken into account in performing the balancing required by the analysis under s. 1. It mandates that in weighing the intrusiveness of a limitation on freedom of expression our consideration cannot be confined to those who may ultimately be convicted under the limit, but must extend to those who may be deterred from legitimate expression by uncertainty as to whether they might be convicted.

I make one final point before entering on the specific tests for proportionality proposed in *Oakes*. In determining whether the particular limitation of a right or freedom is justified under s. 1, it is important to consider not only the proportionality and effectiveness of the particular law in question, but alternative ways of furthering the objective. This is particularly important at stages two (minimum impairment) and three (balancing the infringement against the objective) of the proportionality analysis proposed in *Oakes*.

Against this background, I turn to the three considerations critical to determining whether the limitation on freedom of expression effected by s. 319(2) of the *Criminal Code* is reasonably and demonstrably justifiable in a free and democratic society.

Rational Connection. The first question is whether s. 319(2) of the *Criminal Code* may be seen as carefully designed or rationally connected to the objectives which it is aimed at promoting. This may be viewed in two ways.

The first is whether Parliament carefully designed s. 319(2) to meet the objectives it is enacted to promote.

Although some evidence of care in linking s. 319(2) to its objectives is clear, it has been argued that it is overbroad, an allegation which I will consider in greater detail in discussing whether s. 319(2) represents a "minimum impairment" of the right of free speech guaranteed by s. 2(b) of the *Charter*. Nevertheless it is clear that the legislation does, at least at one level, further Parliament's objectives. Prosecutions of individuals for offensive material directed at a particular group may bolster its members' beliefs that they are valued and respected in their community, and that the views of a malicious few do not reflect those of the population as a whole. Such a use of the criminal law may well affirm certain values and priorities which are of a pressing and substantial nature.

It is necessary, however, to go further, and consider not only Parliament's intention, but whether, given the actual effect of the legislation, a rational connection exists between it and its objectives. Legislation designed to promote an objective may in fact impede that objective ...

Section 319(2) may well have a chilling effect on defensible expression by law-abiding citizens. At the same time, it is far from clear that it provides an effective way of curbing hate-mongers. Indeed, many have suggested it may promote their cause. Prosecutions under the *Criminal Code* for racist expression have attracted extensive media coverage. Zundel, prosecuted not under s. 319(2), but for the crime of spreading false news (s. 181), claimed that his court battle had given him "a million dollars worth of publicity" (*Globe and Mail*, March 1, 1985, p. 1) ...

Not only does the criminal process confer on the accused publicity for his dubious causes – it may even bring him sympathy. The criminal process is cast as a conflict between the accused and the state, a conflict in which the accused may appear at his most sympathetic. Franz Kafka was not being entirely whimsical when he wrote, "If you have the right eye for these things, you can see that accused men are often attractive" (*The Trial*, 1976, p. 203).

The argument that criminal prosecutions for this kind of expression will reduce racism and foster multiculturalism depends on the assumption that some listeners are gullible enough to believe the expression if exposed to it. But if this assumption is valid, these listeners might be just as likely to believe that there must be some truth in the racist expression because the government is trying to suppress it. Theories of a grand conspiracy between government and elements of society wrongly perceived as malevolent can become all too appealing if government dignifies them by completely suppressing their utterance. It is therefore not surprising that the criminalization of hate propaganda and prosecutions under such legislation have been subject to so much controversy in this country ...

Minimum Impairment. The second matter which must be considered in determining whether the infringement represented by the legislation is proportionate to its ends is whether the legislation impairs the right to the minimum extent possible.

Those supporting s. 319(2) of the *Criminal Code* point to the fact that it applies only to wilful promotion of hatred, and not to promotion of any lesser emotion. Hatred, they argue, is the most extreme and reprehensible of human emotions. They also point out that s. 319(2) provides a number of defences, including the truth of the statements made, discussion for public benefit of a subject of public importance (provided the statements were believed to be true on reasonable grounds), and good faith opinion on a religious subject. They add that s. 319(2) does no more than fulfil Canada's international obligations and that similar provisions apply in other Western democracies ...

Despite the limitations found in s. 319(2), a strong case can be made that it is overbroad in that its definition of offending speech may catch many expressions which should be protected. The first difficulty lies in the different interpretations which may be placed on the word "hatred." The *Shorter Oxford English Dictionary* defines "hatred" as: "The condition or state of relations in which one person hates another; the emotion of hate; active dislike, detestation; enmity, ill-will, malevolence." The wide range of diverse emotions which the word "hatred" is capable of denoting is evident from this definition. Those who defend its use in s. 319(2) of the *Criminal Code* emphasize one end of this range – hatred, they say, indicates the most powerful of virulent emotions lying beyond the bounds of human decency and limiting s. 319(2) to extreme materials. Those who object to its use point to the other end of the range, insisting that "active dislike" is not an emotion for the promotion of which a person should be convicted as a criminal. To state the arguments is to make the case; "hatred" is a broad term capable of catching a wide variety of emotion.

It is not only the breadth of the term "hatred" which presents dangers; it is its subjectivity. "Hatred" is proved by inference – the inference of the jury or the judge who sits as trier of fact – and inferences are more likely to be drawn when the speech is unpopular. The subjective and emotional nature of the concept of promoting hatred compounds the difficulty of ensuring that only cases meriting prosecution are pursued and that only those whose conduct is calculated to dissolve the social bonds of society are convicted ...

The absence of any requirement that actual harm or incitement to hatred be shown further broadens the scope of s. 319(2) of the *Criminal Code*. This, in the view of the Court of Appeal, was the section's main defect. In effect, the provision makes a crime not only of actually inciting others to hatred, but also of attempting to do so. The Court of Appeal accepted the argument that this made the crime, at least potentially, a victimless one. In the view of Kerans, J.A., while a prohibition on expression that actually spread hatred would be justified, a prohibition on attempts to spread hatred was not ...

Not only is the category of speech caught by s. 319(2) defined broadly. The application of the definition of offending speech, i.e., the circumstances in which the offending statements are prohibited, is virtually unlimited. Only private conversations are exempt from state scrutiny. Section 319(2) is calculated to prevent absolutely expression of the offending ideas in any and all public forums through any and all mediums. Speeches are caught. The corner soap-box is no longer open. Books, films, and works of art – all these fall under the censor's scrutiny because of s. 319(2) of the *Criminal Code*.

The real answer to the debate about whether s. 319(2) is overbroad is provided by the section's track record. Although the section is of relatively recent origin, it has provoked many questionable actions on the part of the authorities. There have been no reported convictions, other than the instant appeals. But the record amply demonstrates that intemperate statements about identifiable groups, particularly if they represent an unpopular viewpoint, may attract state involvement or calls for police action ...

The combination of overbreadth and criminalization may well lead people desirous of avoiding even the slightest brush with the criminal law to protect themselves in the best way they can – by confining their expression to non-controversial matters. Novelists may steer clear of controversial characterizations of ethnic characteristics, such as Shakespeare's portrayal of Shylock in *The Merchant of Venice*. Scientists may well think twice before researching and publishing results of research suggesting difference between ethnic or racial groups. Given the serious consequences of criminal prosecution, it is not entirely speculative to suppose that even political debate on crucial issues such as immigration, educational language rights, foreign ownership, and trade may be tempered. These matters go to the heart of the traditional justifications for protecting freedom of expression.

This brings me to the second aspect of minimum impairment. The examples I have just given suggest that the very fact of criminalization itself may be argued to represent an excessive response to the problem of hate propagation. The procedures and sanctions associated with the criminal law are comparatively severe. Given the stigma that attaches and the freedom which is at stake, the contest between the individual and the state imposed by a criminal trial must be regarded as difficult and harrowing in the extreme. The seriousness of the imprisonment which may follow conviction requires no comment. Moreover, the chilling effect of prohibitions on expression is at its most severe where they are effected by means of the criminal law. It is this branch of the law more than any other which the ordinary, law-abiding citizen seeks to avoid. The additional sanction of the criminal law may pose little deterrent to a convinced hate-monger who may welcome the publicity it brings; it may, however, deter the ordinary individual.

Moreover, it is arguable whether criminalization of expression calculated to promote racial hatred is necessary. Other remedies are perhaps more appropriate and more effective. Discrimination on grounds of race and religion is worthy of suppression. Human rights legislation, focusing on reparation rather than punishment, has had considerable success in discouraging such conduct ...

Finally, it can be argued that greater precision is required in the criminal law than, for example, in human rights legislation because of the different character of the two types of proceedings. The consequences of alleging a violation of s. 319(2) of the *Criminal Code* are direct and serious in the extreme. Under the human rights process a tribunal has considerable discretion in determining what messages or conduct should be banned and by its order may indicate more precisely their exact nature, all of which occurs before any consequences inure to the alleged violator.

In summary, s. 319(2) of the *Criminal Code* catches a broad range of speech and prohibits it in a broad manner, allowing only private conversations to escape scrutiny. Moreover, the process by which the prohibition is effected – the criminal law – is the severest our society can impose and is arguably unnecessary given the availability of alternate remedies. I conclude that the criminalization of hate statements does not impair free speech to the minimum extent permitted by its objectives ...

READING QUESTIONS ON *KEEGSTRA*

1   What does Dickson, C.J.C. mean in saying that the reasons for limiting expression in this case are the same as those for protecting it more generally?
2   Both the majority and the dissent appeal to the consequences of the law. How are considerations of equality and consequences related in the competing arguments?
3   How are McLachlin, J.'s arguments about statutory construction related to libertarian views about the rule of law?

R.A.V. v. City of St Paul 112 S.Ct. 2538 (1992)

The U.S. Supreme Court overturned a Minnesota ordinance prohibiting displays of racial hatred on the grounds that it advocated a particular viewpoint. In the instant case, the law would have punished white youths for burning a cross on the lawn of an African American family.

Justice Scalia delivered the opinion of the Court.

In the predawn hours of June 21, 1990, petitioner and several other teenagers allegedly assembled a crudely made cross by taping together broken chair legs. They then allegedly burned the cross inside the fenced yard of a black family that lived across the street from the house where petitioner was staying. Although this conduct could have been punished under any of a number of laws, one of the two provisions under which respondent city of St. Paul chose to charge petitioner (then a juvenile) was the St. Paul Bias-Motivated Crime Ordinance, St. Paul, Minn., Legis.Code § 292.02 (1990), which provides:

Whoever places on public or private property a symbol, object, appellation, characterization or graffiti, including, but not limited to, a burning cross or Nazi swastika, which one knows or has reasonable grounds to know arouses anger, alarm or resentment in others on the basis of race, color, creed, religion or gender commits disorderly conduct and shall be guilty of a misdemeanor.

Petitioner moved to dismiss this count on the ground that the St. Paul ordinance was substantially overbroad and impermissibly content based and therefore facially invalid under the First Amendment ...

In construing the St. Paul ordinance, we accept the Minnesota Supreme Court's authoritative statement that the ordinance reaches only those expressions that constitute "fighting words" within the meaning of *Chaplinsky*. 464 N.W.2d, at 510–11. Petitioner and his amici urge us to modify the scope of the *Chaplinsky* formulation, thereby invalidating the ordinance as "substantially overbroad," *Broadrick v. Oklahoma*, 413 U.S. 601, 610, 93 S.Ct. 2908, 2914–15, 37 L.Ed.2d 830 (1973). We find it unnecessary to consider this issue. Assuming, *arguendo*, that all of the expression reached by the ordinance is proscribable under the "fighting words" doctrine, we nonetheless conclude that the ordinance is facially unconstitutional in that it prohibits otherwise permitted speech solely on the basis of the subjects the speech addresses.

The First Amendment generally prevents government from proscribing speech ... Content-based regulations are presumptively invalid ... From 1791 to the present, however, our society, like other free but civilized societies, has permitted restrictions upon the content of speech in a few limited areas, which are "of such slight social value as a step to truth that any benefit that may be derived from them is clearly outweighed by the social interest in order and morality." ... We have recognized that "the freedom of speech" referred to by the First Amendment does not include a freedom to disregard these traditional limitations. Our decisions since the 1960's have narrowed the scope of the traditional categorical exceptions for defamation ... but a limited categorical approach has remained an important part of our First Amendment jurisprudence.

We have sometimes said that these categories of expression are "not within the area of constitutionally protected speech," ... or that the "protection of the First Amendment does not extend" to them ... Such statements must be taken in context, however, and are no more literally true than is the occasionally repeated shorthand characterizing obscenity "as not being speech at all," ... What they mean is that these areas of speech can, consistently with the First Amendment, be regulated *because of their constitutionally proscribable content* (obscenity, defamation, etc.) – not that they are categories of speech entirely invisible to the Constitution, so that they may be made the vehicles for content discrimination unrelated to their distinctively proscribable content. Thus, the government may proscribe libel; but it may not make the further content discrimination of proscribing only libel critical of the government. We recently acknowledged this distinction ... where, in upholding New York's child pornography law, we expressly recognized that there was no "question here of censoring a particular literary theme ..."

Our cases surely do not establish the proposition that the First Amendment imposes no obstacle whatsoever to regulation of particular instances of such proscribable expression, so that the government "may regulate [them] freely," ... That would mean that a city council could enact an ordinance prohibiting only those legally obscene works that contain criticism of the city government or, indeed, that do not include endorsement of the city government. Such a simplistic, all-or- nothing-at-all approach to First Amendment protection is at odds with common sense and with our jurisprudence as well. It is not true that "fighting words" have at most a *"de minimis "* expressive content, ibid., or that their content is *in all respects* "worthless and undeserving of constitutional protection," ... sometimes they are quite expressive indeed. We have not said that they constitute "no part of the expression of ideas," but only that they constitute "no *essential* part of any exposition of ideas" ...

The proposition that a particular instance of speech can be proscribable on the basis of one feature (e.g., obscenity) but not on the basis of another (e.g., opposition to the city government) is commonplace and has found application in many contexts. We have long held, for example, that nonverbal expressive activity can be banned because of the action it entails, but not because of the ideas it expresses – so that burning a flag in violation of an ordinance against outdoor fires could be punishable, whereas burning a flag in violation of an ordinance against dishonoring the flag is not. Similarly, we have upheld reasonable "time, place, or manner" restrictions, but only if they are "justified without reference to the content of the regulated speech." ... And just as the power to proscribe particular speech on the basis of a noncontent element (e.g., noise) does not entail the power to proscribe the same speech on the basis of a content element; so also, the power to proscribe it on the basis of one content element (e.g., obscenity) does not entail the power to proscribe it on the basis of other content elements.

In other words, the exclusion of "fighting words" from the scope of the First Amendment simply means that, for purposes of that Amendment, the unprotected features of the words are, despite their verbal character, essentially a "nonspeech" element of communication. Fighting words are thus analogous to a noisy sound truck: Each is, as Justice Frankfurter recognized, a "mode of speech," ... both can be used to convey an idea; but neither has, in and of itself, a claim upon the First Amendment. As with the sound truck, however, so also with fighting words: The government may not regulate use based on hostility – or favoritism – towards the underlying message expressed ...

Even the prohibition against content discrimination that we assert the First Amendment requires is not absolute. It applies differently in the context of proscribable speech than in the area of fully protected speech. The rationale of the general prohibition, after all, is that content discrimination "raises the specter that the Government may effectively drive certain ideas or viewpoints from the marketplace," ... But content discrimination among various instances of a class of proscribable speech often does not pose this threat.

When the basis for the content discrimination consists entirely of the very reason the entire class of speech at issue is proscribable, no significant danger of idea or viewpoint discrimination exists. Such a reason, having been adjudged neutral enough to support exclusion of the entire class of speech from First Amendment protection, is also neutral enough to form the basis of distinction within the class. To illustrate: A State might choose to prohibit only that obscenity which is the most patently offensive in its prurience – i.e., that which involves the most lascivious displays of sexual activity. But it may not prohibit, for example, only that obscenity which includes offensive political messages. And the Federal Government can criminalize only those threats of violence that are directed against the President, see 18 U.S.C. § 871 – since the reasons why threats of violence are outside the First Amendment (protecting individuals from the fear of violence, from the disruption that fear engenders, and from the possibility that the threatened violence will occur) have special force when applied to the person of the President. But the Federal Government may not criminalize only those threats against the President that mention his policy on aid to inner cities. And to take a final example ... a State may choose to regulate price advertising in one industry but not in others, because the risk of fraud (one of the characteristics of commercial speech that justifies depriving it of full First Amendment protection) but it may not prohibit only that commercial advertising that depicts men in a demeaning fashion.

Another valid basis for according differential treatment to even a content-defined subclass of proscribable speech is that the subclass happens to be associated with particular "secondary effects" of the speech, so that the regulation is "justified without reference to the content of the ... speech," ... A State could, for example, permit all obscene live performances except those involving minors. Moreover, since words can in some circumstances violate laws directed not against speech but against conduct (a law against treason, for example, is violated by telling the enemy the Nation's defense secrets), a particular content-based subcategory of a proscribable class of speech can be swept up incidentally within the reach of a statute directed at conduct rather than speech ... Thus, for example, sexually derogatory "fighting words," among other words, may produce a violation of Title VII's general prohibition against sexual discrimination in employment practices ... Where the government does not target conduct on the basis of its expressive content, acts are not shielded from regulation merely because they express a discriminatory idea or philosophy.

These bases for distinction refute the proposition that the selectivity of the restriction is "even arguably 'conditioned upon the sovereign's agreement with what a speaker may intend to say.'" ... There may be other such bases as well. Indeed, to validate such selectivity (where totally proscribable speech is at issue) it may not even be necessary to identify any particular "neutral" basis, so long as the nature of the content discrimination is such that there is no realistic possibility that official suppression of ideas is afoot. (We cannot think of any First Amendment interest that would stand in the way of a State's prohibiting only those obscene motion pictures with blue-eyed actresses.) Save for that limitation, the regulation of "fighting words," like the regulation of noisy speech, may address some offensive instances and leave other, equally offensive, instances alone.

Applying these principles to the St. Paul ordinance, we conclude that, even as narrowly construed by the Minnesota Supreme Court, the ordinance is facially unconstitutional. Although the phrase in the ordinance, "arouses anger, alarm or resentment in others," has been limited by the Minnesota Supreme Court's construction to reach only those symbols or displays that amount to "fighting words," the remaining, unmodified terms make clear that the ordinance applies only to "fighting words" that insult, or provoke violence, "on the basis of race, color, creed, religion or gender." Displays containing abusive invective, no matter how vicious or severe, are permissible unless they are addressed to one of the specified disfavored topics. Those who wish to use "fighting words" in connection with other ideas – to express hostility, for example, on the basis of political affiliation, union membership, or homosexuality – are not covered. The First Amendment does not permit St. Paul to impose special prohibitions on those speakers who express views on disfavored subjects.

In its practical operation, moreover, the ordinance goes even beyond mere content discrimination, to actual viewpoint discrimination. Displays containing some words – odious racial epithets, for example – would be prohibited to proponents of all views. But "fighting words" that do not themselves invoke race, color, creed, religion, or gender – aspersions upon a person's mother, for example – would seemingly be usable *ad libitum* in the placards of those arguing *in favor* of racial, color, etc., tolerance and equality, but could not be used by those speakers' opponents. One could hold up a sign saying, for example, that all "anti-Catholic bigots" are misbegotten; but not that all "papists" are, for that would insult and provoke violence "on the basis of religion." St. Paul has no such authority to license one side of a debate to fight freestyle, while requiring the other to follow Marquis of Queensberry rules.

What we have here, it must be emphasized, is not a prohibition of fighting words that are directed at certain persons or groups (which would be *facially* valid if it met the requirements of the Equal Protection

Clause); but rather, a prohibition of fighting words that contain (as the Minnesota Supreme Court repeatedly emphasized) messages of "bias-motivated" hatred and in particular, as applied to this case, messages "based on virulent notions of racial supremacy." One must wholeheartedly agree with the Minnesota Supreme Court that "[i]t is the responsibility, even the obligation, of diverse communities to confront such notions in whatever form they appear," ... but the manner of that confrontation cannot consist of selective limitations upon speech. St. Paul's brief asserts that a general "fighting words" law would not meet the city's needs because only a content-specific measure can communicate to minority groups that the "group hatred" aspect of such speech "is not condoned by the majority." The point of the First Amendment is that majority preferences must be expressed in some fashion other than silencing speech on the basis of its content ...

The content-based discrimination reflected in the St. Paul ordinance comes within neither any of the specific exceptions to the First Amendment prohibition we discussed earlier nor a more general exception for content discrimination that does not threaten censorship of ideas. It assuredly does not fall within the exception for content discrimination based on the very reasons why the particular class of speech at issue (here, fighting words) is proscribable. As explained earlier ... the reason why fighting words are categorically excluded from the protection of the First Amendment is not that their content communicates any particular idea, but that their content embodies a particularly intolerable (and socially unnecessary) mode of expressing whatever idea the speaker wishes to convey. St. Paul has not singled out an especially offensive mode of expression – it has not, for example, selected for prohibition only those fighting words that communicate ideas in a threatening (as opposed to a merely obnoxious) manner. Rather, it has proscribed fighting words of whatever manner that communicate messages of racial, gender, or religious intolerance. Selectivity of this sort creates the possibility that the city is seeking to handicap the expression of particular ideas. That possibility would alone be enough to render the ordinance presumptively invalid, but St. Paul's comments and concessions in this case elevate the possibility to a certainty ...

Finally, St. Paul and its *amici* defend the conclusion of the Minnesota Supreme Court that, even if the ordinance regulates expression based on hostility towards its protected ideological content, this discrimination is nonetheless justified because it is narrowly tailored to serve compelling state interests. Specifically, they assert that the ordinance helps to ensure the basic human rights of members of groups that have historically been subjected to discrimination, including the right of such group members to live in peace where they wish. We do not doubt that these interests are compelling, and that the ordinance can be said to promote them. But the "danger of censorship" presented by a facially content-based statute ... requires that that weapon be employed only where it is "necessary to serve the asserted [compelling] interest." The existence of adequate content-neutral alternatives thus "undercut[s] significantly" any defense of such a statute ... The dispositive question in this case, therefore, is whether content discrimination is reasonably necessary to achieve St. Paul's compelling interests; it plainly is not. An ordinance not limited to the favored topics, for example, would have precisely the same beneficial effect. In fact the only interest distinctively served by the content limitation is that of displaying the city council's special hostility towards the particular biases thus singled out. That is precisely what the First Amendment forbids. The politicians of St. Paul are entitled to express that hostility – but not through the means of imposing unique limitations upon speakers who (however benightedly) disagree.

* * *

Let there be no mistake about our belief that burning a cross in someone's front yard is reprehensible. But St. Paul has sufficient means at its disposal to prevent such behavior without adding the First Amendment to the fire.

The judgment of the Minnesota Supreme Court is reversed, and the case is remanded for proceedings not inconsistent with this opinion.

It is so ordered.

Justice White, (concurring)

...

Although I disagree with the Court's analysis, I do agree with its conclusion: The St. Paul ordinance is unconstitutional. However, I would decide the case on overbreadth grounds.

We have emphasized time and again that overbreadth doctrine is an exception to the established principle that "a person to whom a statute may constitutionally be applied will not be heard to challenge that statute on the ground that it may conceivably be applied unconstitutionally to others, in other situations not before the Court" ... A defendant being prosecuted for speech or expressive conduct may challenge the law on its face if it reaches protected expression, even when that person's activities are not protected by the First Amendment. This is because "the possible harm to society in permitting some unprotected speech to go unpunished is outweighed by the possibility that protected speech of others may be muted" ...

The St. Paul antibias ordinance is such a law. Although the ordinance reaches conduct that is unprotected, it also makes criminal expressive conduct that causes only hurt feelings, offense, or resentment, and is protected by the First Amendment ... The ordinance is therefore fatally overbroad and invalid on its face.

Justice Stevens, with whom Justice White and Justice Blackmun join as to Part I, concurring in the judgment.

Conduct that creates special risks or causes special harms may be prohibited by special rules. Lighting a fire near an ammunition dump or a gasoline storage tank is especially dangerous; such behavior may be punished more severely than burning trash in a vacant lot. Threatening someone because of her race or religious beliefs may cause particularly severe trauma or touch off a riot, and threatening a high public official may cause substantial social disruption; such threats may be punished more severely than threats against someone based on, say, his support of a particular athletic team. There are legitimate, reasonable, and neutral justifications for such special rules.

This case involves the constitutionality of one such ordinance. Because the regulated conduct has some communicative content – a message of racial, religious, or gender hostility – the ordinance raises two quite different First Amendment questions. Is the ordinance "overbroad" because it prohibits too much speech? If not, is it "underbroad" because it does not prohibit enough speech?

In answering these questions, my colleagues today wrestle with two broad principles: first, that certain "categories of expression [including 'fighting words'] are 'not within the area of constitutionally protected speech,'" ... and second, that "[c]ontent-based regulations [of expression] are presumptively invalid." Although in past opinions the Court has repeated both of these maxims, it has – quite rightly – adhered to neither with the absolutism suggested by my colleagues. Thus, while I agree that the St. Paul ordinance is unconstitutionally overbroad for the reasons stated in Part II of Justice White's opinion, I write separately to suggest how the allure of absolute principles has skewed the analysis of both the majority and Justice White's opinions.

Fifty years ago, the Court articulated a categorical approach to First Amendment jurisprudence ... The Court today revises this categorical approach. It is not, the Court rules, that certain "categories" of expression are "unprotected," but rather that certain "elements" of expression are wholly "proscribable." To the Court, an expressive act, like a chemical compound, consists of more than one element. Although the act may be regulated because it contains a proscribable element, it may not be regulated on the basis of another (nonproscribable) element it also contains. Thus, obscene antigovernment speech may be regulated because it is obscene, but not because it is antigovernment. ... It is this revision of the categorical approach that allows the Court to assume that the St. Paul ordinance proscribes only fighting words, while at the same time concluding that the ordinance is invalid because it imposes a content-based regulation on expressive activity.

As an initial matter, the Court's revision of the categorical approach seems to me something of an adventure in a doctrinal wonderland, for the concept of "obscene anti-government" speech is fantastical. The category of the obscene is very narrow; to be obscene, expression must be found by the trier of fact to "appea[l] to the prurient interest, ... depic[t] or describ[e], in a patently offensive way, sexual conduct, [and], taken as a whole, lac[k] serious literary, artistic, political, or scientific value." *Miller v. California*, 413 U.S. 15, 24. "Obscene antigovernment" speech, then, is a contradiction in terms: If expression is antigovernment, it does not "lac[k] serious ... political ... value" and cannot be obscene.

The Court attempts to bolster its argument by likening its novel analysis to that applied to restrictions on the time, place, or manner of expression or on expressive conduct. It is true that loud speech in favor of the Republican Party can be regulated because it is loud, but not because it is pro-Republican; and it is true that the public burning of the American flag can be regulated because it involves public burning and not because it involves the flag. But these analogies are inapposite. In each of these examples, the two elements (e.g., loudness and pro-Republican orientation) can coexist; in the case of "obscene antigovernment" speech, however, the presence of one element ("obscenity") by definition means the absence of the other. To my mind, it is unwise and unsound to craft a new doctrine based on such highly speculative hypotheticals.

I am, however, even more troubled by the second step of the Court's analysis – namely, its conclusion that the St. Paul ordinance is an unconstitutional content-based regulation of speech. Drawing on broadly worded dicta, the Court establishes a near-absolute ban on content-based regulations of expression and holds that the First Amendment prohibits the regulation of fighting words by subject matter. Thus, while the Court rejects the "all-or-nothing-at-all" nature of the categorical approach, ante, at 2543, it promptly embraces an absolutism of its own: Within a particular "proscribable" category of expression, the Court holds, a government must either proscribe all speech or no speech at all. This aspect of the Court's ruling fundamentally misunderstands the role and constitutional status of content-based regulations on speech, conflicts with the very nature of First Amendment jurisprudence, and disrupts well-settled principles of First Amendment law.

Although the Court has, on occasion, declared that content-based regulations of speech are "never permitted," ... such claims are overstated ... [O]ur decisions demonstrate that content-based distinctions, far from being presumptively invalid, are an inevitable and indispensable aspect of a coherent understanding of the First Amendment.

This is true at every level of First Amendment law. In broadest terms, our entire First Amendment jurisprudence creates a regime based on the content of speech. The scope of the First Amendment is determined by the content of expressive activity: Although the First Amendment broadly protects "speech," it does not protect the right to "fix prices, breach contracts, make false warranties, place bets with bookies, threaten, [or] extort" ...

Likewise, whether speech falls within one of the categories of "unprotected" or "proscribable" expression is determined, in part, by its content. Whether a magazine is obscene, a gesture a fighting word, or a photograph child pornography is determined, in part, by its content. Even within categories of protected expression, the First Amendment status of speech is fixed by its content ... Speech about public officials or matters of public concern receives greater protection than speech about other topics. It can, therefore, scarcely be said that the regulation of expressive activity cannot be predicated on its content: Much of our First Amendment jurisprudence is premised on the assumption that content makes a difference.

Consistent with this general premise, we have frequently upheld content-based regulations of speech. For example, in *Young v. American Mini Theatres*, the Court upheld zoning ordinances that regulated movie theaters based on the content of the films shown ... We have long recognized the power of the Federal Trade Commission to regulate misleading advertising and labeling ... It is also beyond question that the Government may choose to limit advertisements for cigarettes, but not for cigars; choose to regulate airline advertising ... but not bus advertising; or choose to monitor solicitation by lawyers ... but not by doctors.

All of these cases involved the selective regulation of speech based on content – precisely the sort of regulation the Court invalidates today. Such selective regulations are unavoidably content based, but they are not, in my opinion, "presumptively invalid" ...

Our First Amendment decisions have created a rough hierarchy in the constitutional protection of speech. Core political speech occupies the highest, most protected position; commercial speech and nonobscene, sexually explicit speech are regarded as a sort of second-class expression; obscenity and fighting words receive the least protection of all. Assuming that the Court is correct that this last class of speech is not wholly "unprotected," it certainly does not follow that fighting words and obscenity receive the same sort of protection afforded core political speech. Yet in ruling that proscribable speech cannot be regulated based on subject matter, the Court does just that. Perversely, this gives fighting words greater protection than is afforded commercial speech. If Congress can prohibit false advertising directed at airline passengers without also prohibiting false advertising directed at bus passengers and if a city can prohibit political advertisements in its buses while allowing other advertisements, it is ironic to hold that a city cannot regulate fighting words based on "race, color, creed, religion or gender" while leaving unregulated fighting words based on "union membership ... or homosexuality." The Court today turns First Amendment law on its head: Communication that was once entirely unprotected (and that still can be wholly proscribed) is now entitled to greater protection than commercial speech – and possibly greater protection than core political speech ...

In a pivotal passage, the Court writes: "[T]he Federal Government can criminalize only those threats of violence that are directed against the President, see 18 U.S.C. § 871 – since the reasons why threats of violence are outside the First Amendment (protecting individuals from the fear of violence, from the disruption that fear engenders, and from the possibility that the threatened violence will occur) have special force when applied to the ... President" ...

As I understand this opaque passage, Congress may choose from the set of unprotected speech (all threats) to proscribe only a subset (threats against the President) because those threats are particularly likely to cause "fear of violence," "disruption," and actual "violence."

Precisely this same reasoning, however, compels the conclusion that St. Paul's ordinance is constitutional. Just as Congress may determine that threats against the President entail more severe consequences than other threats, so St. Paul's City Council may determine that threats based on the target's race, religion, or gender cause more severe harm to both the target and to society than other threats. This latter judgment – that harms caused by racial, religious, and gender-based invective are qualitatively different from that caused by other fighting words – seems to me eminently reasonable and realistic ...

Similarly, it is impossible to reconcile the Court's analysis of the St. Paul ordinance with its recognition that "a prohibition of fighting words that are directed at certain persons or groups ... would be facially valid." Ante, at 2548 (emphasis deleted). A selective proscription of unprotected expression designed to protect "certain persons or groups" (for example, a law proscribing threats directed at the elderly) would be constitutional if it were based on a legitimate determination that the harm created by the regulated expression differs from that created by the unregulated expression (that is, if the elderly are more severely injured by threats than are the nonelderly). Such selective protection is no different from a law prohibiting minors (and only minors) from obtaining obscene publications ... St. Paul has determined – reasonably in my judgment – that fighting-word injuries "based on race, color, creed, religion or gender" are qualitatively different and more severe than fighting-word injuries based on other characteristics. Whether the selective proscription of proscribable speech is defined by the protected target ("certain persons or groups") or the basis of the harm (injuries "based on race, color, creed, religion or gender") makes no constitutional difference: What matters is whether the legislature's selection is based on a legitimate, neutral, and reasonable distinction.

In sum, the central premise of the Court's ruling – that "[c]ontent-based regulations are presumptively invalid" – has simplistic appeal, but lacks support in our First Amendment jurisprudence. To make matters worse, the Court today extends this overstated claim to reach categories of hitherto unprotected speech and, in doing so, wreaks havoc in an area of settled law. Finally, although the Court recognizes exceptions to its new principle, those exceptions undermine its very conclusion that the St. Paul ordinance is unconstitutional. Stated directly, the majority's position cannot withstand scrutiny ...

In sum, the St. Paul ordinance (as construed by the Court) regulates expressive activity that is wholly proscribable and does so not on the basis of viewpoint, but rather in recognition of the different harms caused by such activity. Taken together, these several considerations persuade me that the St. Paul ordinance is not an unconstitutional content-based regulation of speech. Thus, were the ordinance not overbroad, I would vote to uphold it.

READING QUESTIONS ON *R.A.V.*

1 How does the court distinguish between expression and action? Is their distinction tenable?

Virginia v. Black 538 U.S. 343 (2003)

This case revisits *R.A.V.*'s question of the extent to which the U.S. constitution protects symbolic action by characterizing it as speech.

Justice O'Connor (for the Court):

In this case we consider whether the Commonwealth of Virginia's statute banning cross burning with "an intent to intimidate a person or group of persons" violates the First Amendment. Va. Code Ann. §18.2–423 (1996). We conclude that while a State, consistent with the First Amendment, may ban cross burning carried out with the intent to intimidate, the provision in the Virginia statute treating any cross burning as prima facie evidence of intent to intimidate renders the statute unconstitutional in its current form.

Respondents Barry Black, Richard Elliott, and Jonathan O'Mara were convicted separately of violating Virginia's cross-burning statute, §18.2–423. That statute provides:

It shall be unlawful for any person or persons, with the intent of intimidating any person or group of persons, to burn, or cause to be burned, a cross on the property of another, a highway or other public place. Any person who shall violate any provision of this section shall be guilty of a Class 6 felony.

Any such burning of a cross shall be prima facie evidence of an intent to intimidate a person or group of persons.

On August 22, 1998, Barry Black led a Ku Klux Klan rally in Carroll County, Virginia. Twenty-five to thirty people attended this gathering, which occurred on private property with the permission of the owner, who was in attendance ... At the conclusion of the rally, the crowd circled around a 25- to 30-foot cross. The cross was between 300 and 350 yards away from the road. According to the sheriff, the cross "then all of a sudden ... went up in a flame." ...

On May 2, 1998, respondents Richard Elliott and Jonathan O'Mara, as well as a third individual, attempted to burn a cross on the yard of James Jubilee. Jubilee, an African-American, was Elliott's next-door neighbor in Virginia Beach, Virginia ...

To this day, regardless of whether the message is a political one or whether the message is also meant to intimidate, the burning of a cross is a "symbol of hate." *Capitol Square Review and Advisory Bd. v. Pinette*, 515 U.S., at 771 (Thomas, J., concurring). And while cross burning sometimes carries no intimidating message, at other times the intimidating message is the *only* message conveyed. For example, when a cross burning is directed at a particular person not affiliated with the Klan, the burning cross often serves as a message of intimidation, designed to inspire in the victim a fear of bodily harm. Moreover, the history of violence associated with the Klan shows that the possibility of injury or death is not just hypothetical ... We did not hold in *R.A.V.* that the First Amendment prohibits *all* forms of content-based discrimination within a proscribable area of speech ... Similarly, Virginia's statute does not run afoul of the First Amendment insofar as it bans cross burning with intent to intimidate. Unlike the statute at issue in *R.A.V.*, the Virginia statute does not single out for opprobrium only that speech directed toward "one of the specified disfavored topics." *Id.*, at 391. It does not matter whether an individual burns a cross with intent to intimidate because of the victim's race, gender, or religion, or because of the victim's "political affiliation, union membership, or homosexuality." *Ibid.* Moreover, as a factual matter it is not true that cross burners direct their intimidating conduct solely to racial or religious minorities ... Indeed, in the case of Elliott and O'Mara, it is at least unclear whether the respondents burned a cross due to racial animus ...

The Supreme Court of Virginia ruled in the alternative that Virginia's cross-burning statute was unconstitutionally overbroad due to its provision stating that "[a]ny such burning of a cross shall be prima facie evidence of an intent to intimidate a person or group of persons."

The prima facie evidence provision, as interpreted by the jury instruction, renders the statute unconstitutional. Because this jury instruction is the Model Jury Instruction, and because the Supreme Court of Virginia had the opportunity to expressly disavow the jury instruction, the jury instruction's construction of the prima facie provision "is a ruling on a question of state law that is as binding on us as though the precise words had been written into" the statute ... As construed by the jury instruction, the prima facie provision strips away the very reason why a State may ban cross burning with the intent to intimidate. The prima facie evidence provision permits a jury to convict in every cross-burning case in which defendants exercise their constitutional right not to put on a defense. And even where a defendant like Black presents a defense, the prima facie evidence provision makes it more likely that the jury will find an intent to intimidate regardless of the particular facts of the case. The provision permits the Commonwealth to arrest, prosecute, and convict a person based solely on the fact of cross burning itself.

It is apparent that the provision as so interpreted "would create an unacceptable risk of the suppression of ideas."

Justice Thomas, dissenting:

...

That in the early 1950s the people of Virginia viewed cross burning as creating an intolerable atmosphere of terror is not surprising ... [T]he legislature sought to criminalize terrorizing *conduct* ... [A]t the time the statute was enacted, racial segregation was not only the prevailing practice, but also the law in Virginia ... It strains credulity to suggest that a state legislature that adopted a litany of segregationist laws self-contradictorily intended to squelch the segregationist message. Even for segregationists, violent and terroristic conduct, the Siamese twin of cross burning, was intolerable. The ban on cross burning with intent to intimidate demonstrates that even segregationists understood the difference between intimidating and terroristic conduct and racist expression. It is simply beyond belief that, in passing the statute now under review, the Virginia legislature was concerned with anything but penalizing conduct it must have viewed as particularly vicious.

Accordingly, this statute prohibits only conduct, not expression. And, just as one cannot burn down someone's house to make a political point and then seek refuge in the First Amendment, those who hate cannot terrorize and intimidate to make their point. In light of my conclusion that the statute here addresses only conduct, there is no need to analyze it under any of our First Amendment tests.

Even assuming that the statute implicates the First Amendment, in my view, the fact that the statute permits a jury to draw an inference of intent to intimidate from the cross burning itself presents no constitutional problems. Therein lies my primary disagreement with the plurality ...

A presumption is a rule of law that compels the fact finder to draw a certain conclusion or a certain inference from a given set of facts. The primary significance of a presumption is that it operates to shift to the opposing party the burden of producing evidence tending to rebut the presumption. As explained in Part I, *not* making a connection between cross burning and intimidation would be irrational.

The plurality, however, is troubled by the presumption because this is a First Amendment case. The plurality laments the fate of an innocent cross-burner who burns a cross, but does so without an intent to intimidate. The plurality fears the chill on expression because, according to the plurality, the inference permits "the Commonwealth to arrest, prosecute and convict a person based solely on the fact of cross burning itself." Maj. op., at 19. First, it is, at the very least, unclear that the inference comes into play during arrest and initiation of a prosecution, that is, prior to the instructions stage of an actual trial. Second, as I explained above, the inference is rebuttable and, as the jury instructions given in this case demonstrate, Virginia law still requires the jury to find the existence of each element, including intent to intimidate, beyond a reasonable doubt.

...

That the First Amendment gives way to other interests is not a remarkable proposition. What is remarkable is that, under the plurality's analysis, the determination of whether an interest is sufficiently compelling depends not on the harm a regulation in question seeks to prevent, but on the area of society at which it aims. For instance, in *Hill v. Colorado*, 530 U.S. 703 (2000), the Court upheld a restriction on protests near abortion clinics, explaining that the State had a legitimate interest, which was sufficiently narrowly tailored, in protecting those seeking services of such establishments "from unwanted advice" and "unwanted communication," *id.*, at 708; *id.*, at 716; *id.*, at 717; *id.*, at 729. In so concluding, the Court placed heavy reliance on the "vulnerable physical and emotional conditions" of patients. *Id.*, at 729. Thus, when it came to the rights of those seeking abortions, the Court deemed restrictions on "unwanted advice," which, notably, can be given only from a distance of at least 8 feet from a prospective patient, justified by the countervailing interest in obtaining abortion. Yet, here, the plurality strikes down the statute because one day an individual might wish to burn a cross, but might do so without an intent to intimidate anyone ...

QUESTIONS ON *VIRGINIA V. BLACK*

1 Does Thomas, J. think that any freedom of expression interests are implicated in this case? Do you agree? How would he have decided *R.A.V.*, above?
2 O'Connor, J. rules that the presumption of intent to intimidate is unconstitutional. How is this supposed to be related to freedom of expression? What is the relation between intent and expression?

American Booksellers v. Hudnut **771 F.2d 323 (7th Cir. 1985), excerpts**

This American case struck down as unconstitutional an ordinance which dealt with pornography as a violation of civil rights.

... Easterbrook, Circuit Judge: – Indianapolis enacted an ordinance defining "pornography" as a practice that discriminates against women. "Pornography" is to be redressed through the administrative and judicial methods used for other discrimination. The City's definition of "pornography" is considerably different from "obscenity," which the Supreme Court held is not protected by the First Amendment ...

"Pornography" under the ordinance is "the graphic sexually explicit subordination of women, whether in pictures or in words, that also includes one or more of the following:

(1) Women are presented as sexual objects who enjoy pain or humiliation or
(2) Women are presented as sexual objects who experience sexual pleasure in being raped; or
(3) Women are presented as sexual objects tied up or cut up or mutilated or bruised or physically hurt, or as dismembered or truncated or fragmented or severed into body parts; or
(4) Women are presented as being penetrated by objects or animals; or
(5) Women are presented in scenarios of degradation, injury, abasement, torture, shown as filthy or inferior, bleeding, bruised, or hurt in a context that makes these conditions sexual; or
(6) Woman are presented as sexual objects for domination, conquest, violation, exploitation, possession, or use, or through postures or positions of servility or submission or display."

Indianapolis Code s. 16-3(q). The statute provides that the "use of men, children, or transsexuals in the place of women in paragraphs (1) through (6) shall also constitute pornography under this section."

The ordinance as passed in April 1984 defined "sexually explicit" to mean actual or simulated intercourse or the uncovered exhibition of the genitals, buttocks or anus. An amendment in June 1984 deleted this provision, leaving the term undefined.

The Indianapolis ordinance does not refer to the prurient interest, to offensiveness, or to the standards of the community. It demands attention to particular depictions, not to the work judged as a whole. It is irrelevant under the ordinance whether the work has literary, artistic, political, or scientific value. The City and many amici point to these omissions as virtues. They maintain that pornography influences attitudes, and the statute is a way to alter the socialization of men and women rather than to vindicate community standards of offensiveness. And as one of the principal drafters of the ordinance has asserted, "if a woman is subjected, why should it matter that the work has other value?" Catharine A. MacKinnon, *Pornography, Civil Rights, and Speech,* 20 Harv.Civ.Rts. – Civ.Lib.L.Rev. 1, 21 (1985).

Civil rights groups and feminists have entered this case as amici on both sides. Those supporting the ordinance say that it will play an important role in reducing the tendency of men to view women as sexual objects, a tendency that leads to both unacceptable attitudes and discrimination in the workplace and violence away from it. Those opposing the ordinance point out that much radical feminist literature is explicit and depicts women in ways forbidden by the ordinance and that the ordinance would reopen old battles. It is unclear how India-napolis would treat works from James Joyce's *Ulysses* to Homer's *Iliad*; both depict women as submissive objects for conquest and domination.

We do not try to balance the arguments for and against an ordinance such as this. The ordinance discriminates on the ground of the content of the speech. Speech treating women in the approved way – in sexual encounters "premised on equality" (MacKinnon, *supra*, at 22) – is lawful no matter how sexually explicit. Speech treating women in the disap-proved way – as submissive in matters sexual or as enjoying humilia-tion – is unlawful no matter how significant the literary, artistic, or political qualities of the work taken as a whole. The state may not ordain preferred viewpoints in this way. The Constitution forbids the state to declare one perspective right and silence opponents ...

"If there is any fixed star in our constitutional constellation, it is that no official, high or petty, can prescribe what shall be orthodox in politics, nationalism, religion, or other matters of opinion or force citi-zens to confess by word or act their faith therein." *West Virginia State Board of Education v. Barnette*, 319 US 624, 642, 63 S.Ct. 1178, 1187, 87 L.Ed. 1628 (1943). Under the First Amendment the government must leave to the people the evaluation of ideas. Bald or subtle, an idea is as powerful as the audience allows it to be. A belief may be pernicious – the beliefs of Nazis led to the death of millions, those of the Klan to the repression of millions. A pernicious belief may prevail. Totalitarian governments today rule much of the planet, practicing suppression of billions and spreading dogma that may enslave others. One of the things that separates our society from theirs is our absolute right to propagate opinions that the government finds wrong or even hateful ...

Under the ordinance graphic sexually explicit speech is "pornogra-phy" or not depending on the perspective the author adopts. Speech that "subordinates" women and also, for example, presents women as enjoying pain, humiliation, or rape, or even simply presents women in "positions of servility or submission or display" is forbidden, no matter how great the literary or political value of the work taken as a whole. Speech that portrays women in positions of equality is lawful, no mat-ter how graphic the sexual content. This is thought control. It establishes an "approved" view of women, of how they may react to sexual en-counters, of how the sexes may relate to each other. Those who espouse the approved view may use sexual images; those who do not, may not.

Indianapolis justifies the ordinance on the ground that pornography affects thoughts. Men who see women depicted as subordinate are more likely to treat them so. Pornography is an aspect of dominance. It does not persuade people so much as change them. It works by socializing, by establishing the expected and the permissible. In this view pornography is not an idea; pornography is the injury.

There is much to this perspective. Beliefs are also facts. People often act in accordance with the images and patterns they find around them. People raised in a religion tend to accept the tenets of that religion, often without independent examination. People taught from birth that black people are fit only for slavery rarely rebelled against that creed; beliefs coupled with the self-interest of the masters established a social structure that inflicted great harm while enduring for centuries. Words and images act at the level of the subconscious before they persuade at the level of the conscious. Even the truth has little chance unless a statement fits within the framework of beliefs that may never have been subjected to rational study.

Therefore we accept the premises of this legislation. Depictions of subordination tend to perpetuate subordination. The subordinate status of women in turn leads to affront and lower pay at work, insult and injury at home, battery and rape on the streets. In the language of the legislature, "[p]ornography is central in creating and maintaining sex as a basis of discrimination. Pornography is a systematic practice of exploitation and subordination based on sex which differentially harms women. The bigotry and contempt it produces, with the acts of aggression it fosters, harm women's opportunities for equality and rights [of all kinds]." Indianapolis Code s. 16-1(a)(2).

Yet this simply demonstrates the power of pornography as speech. All of these unhappy effects depend on mental intermediation. Pornography affects how people see the world, their fellows, and social relations. If pornography is what pornography does, so is other speech. Hitler's orations affected how some Germans saw Jews. Communism is a world view, not simply a *Manifesto* by Marx and Engels or a set of speeches. Efforts to suppress communist speech in the United States were based on the belief that the public acceptability of such ideas would increase the likelihood of totalitarian government. Religions affect socialization in the most pervasive way...

Many people believe that the existence of television, apart from the content of specific programs, leads to intellectual laziness, to a penchant for violence, to many other ills. The Alien and Sedition Acts passed during the administration of John Adams rested on a sincerely held belief that disrespect for the government leads to social collapse and revolution – a belief with support in the history of many nations. Most governments of the world act on this empirical regularity, suppressing critical speech. In the United States, however, the strength of the support for this belief is irrelevant. Seditious libel is protected speech unless the danger is not only grave but also imminent ...

Sexual responses often are unthinking responses, and the association of sexual arousal with the subordination of women therefore may have a substantial effect. But almost all cultural stimuli provoke unconscious responses ...

Much of Indianapolis's argument rests on the belief that when speech is "unanswerable," and the metaphor that there is a "marketplace of ideas" does not apply, the First Amendment does not apply either. The metaphor is honored; Milton's *Aeropagitica* and John Stuart Mill's *On Liberty* defend freedom of speech on the ground that the truth will prevail, and many of the most important cases under the First Amendment recite this position. The Framers undoubtedly believed it. As a general matter it is true. But the Constitution does not make the dominance of truth a necessary condition of freedom of speech. To say that it does would be to confuse an outcome of free speech with a necessary condition for the application of the amendment.

A power to limit speech on the ground that truth has not yet prevailed and is not likely to prevail implies the power to declare truth. At some point the government must be able to say (as Indianapolis has said): "We know what the truth is, yet a free exchange of speech has not driven out falsity, so that we must now prohibit falsity" ...

At all events, "pornography" is not low value speech within the meaning of these cases. Indianapolis seeks to prohibit certain speech because it believes this speech influences social relations and politics on a grand scale, that it controls attitudes at home and in the legislature. This precludes a characterization of the speech as low value. True, pornography and obscenity have sex in common. But Indianapolis left out of its definition any reference to literary, artistic, political, or scientific value. The ordinance applies to graphic sexually explicit subordination in words great and small.[1] The Court sometimes balances the value of speech against the costs of its restriction, but it does this by category of speech and not by the content of particular works ...

Any rationale we could imagine in support of this ordinance could not be limited to sex discrimination. Free speech has been on balance an ally of those seeking change. Governments that want stasis start by restricting speech. Culture is a powerful force of continuity; Indianapolis paints pornography as part of the culture of power. Change in any complex system ultimately depends on the ability of outsiders to challenge accepted views and the reigning institutions. Without a strong guarantee of freedom of speech, there is no effective right to challenge what is.

The definition of "pornography" is unconstitutional. No construction or excision of particular terms could save it ...

But the ... Indianapolis ordinance is not neutral with respect to viewpoint. The ban on distribution of works containing coerced performances is limited to pornography; coercion is irrelevant if the work is not "pornography," and we have held the definition of "pornography" to be defective root and branch. A legislature might replace "pornography" in s. 16-3(g)(4) with "any film containing explicit sex" or some similar expression, but even the broadest severability clause does not permit a federal court to rewrite as opposed to excise. Rewriting is work for the legislature of Indianapolis ...

Much speech is dangerous. Chemists whose work might help someone build a bomb, political theorists whose papers might start political movements that lead to riots, speakers whose ideas attract violent protesters, all these and more leave loss in their wake. Unless the remedy is very closely confined, it could be more dangerous to speech than all the libel judgments in history. The constitutional requirements for a valid recovery for assault caused by speech might turn out to be too rigorous for any plaintiff to meet.[2] But the Indianapolis ordinance requires the complainant to show that the attack was "directly caused by specific pornography" (s. 16-3(g)(7)), and it is not beyond the realm of possibility that a state court could construe this limitation in a way that would make the statute constitutional. We are not authorized to prevent the state from trying.

Again, however, the assault statute is tied to "pornography," and we cannot find a sensible way to repair the defect without seizing power that belongs elsewhere. Indianapolis might choose to have no ordinance if it cannot be limited to viewpoint-specific harms, or it might choose to extend the scope to all speech, just as the law of libel applies to all speech. An attempt to repair this ordinance would be nothing but a blind guess.

No amount of struggle with particular words and phrases in this ordinance can leave anything in effect. The district court came to the same conclusion. Its judgment is therefore

Affirmed.

NOTES

1   Indianapolis briefly argues that *Beauharnais v. Illinois,* 343 US 250, 72 S.Ct.
    725, 96 L.Ed. 919 (1952), which allowed a state to penalize "group libel,"
    supports the ordinance. In *Colin v. Smith, supra,* 578 F.2d at 1205, we
    concluded that cases such as *New York Times v. Sullivan* had so washed
    away the foundations of *Beauharnais* that it could not be considered
    authoritative. If we are wrong in this, however, the case still does not
    support the ordinance. It is not clear that depicting women as subordi-
    nate in sexually explicit ways, even combined with a depiction of plea-
    sure in rape, would fit within the definition of a group libel. The well
    received film *Swept Away* used explicit sex, plus taking pleasure in rape,
    to make a political statement, not to defame. Work must be an insult or
    slur for its own sake to come within the ambit of *Beauharnais,* and a work
    need not be scurrilous at all to be "pornography" under the ordinance.
2   See, e.g., *Zamora v. CBS,* 480 F.Supp. 199 (S.D.Fla.1979), among the many
    cases concluding that particular plaintiffs could not show a connection
    sufficiently direct to permit liability consistent with the First Amend-
    ment.

READING QUESTIONS ON *HUDNUT*

1   Why does Judge Easterbrook put so much weight on the idea that
    the ordinance is "viewpoint based"? Is it viewpoint based in the
    sense he suggests?
2   Should speech be protected even when it is harmful? How serious
    must the harm be to justify censorship?

Seana Valentine Shiffrin
"Speech, Death, and Double Effect" (2003)
78 N.Y.U.L. Rev. 1135

Shiffrin explains the prohibition on regulating the content of expression in
terms of the difference between speech and action. The point of speech is to
influence the behaviour of others, and any attempt to limit speech based on
its success in doing so would undermine its value. Its secondary effects,
such as noise or littering, can be regulated, because they are merely incidental to the point of expression.

... [R]oughly, the doctrine of double effect states that morally, it may be more permissible to bring about harm as a merely foreseen or foreseeable side effect of an otherwise permissible aim than to intend this harm as a means or an end. I am assuming that when a law punishes activity, this is a way of holding people responsible for their actions. If there is more punishment in virtue of an action's side effects than its intended effects, and if one holds that the degree to which we hold people responsible for actions should be a reflection of an action's permissibility, then this pattern would be in tension with the doctrine of double effect. Here, understood in light of its rationale for denying the right to assisted suicide, the law holds potential suicides responsible only for the foreseeable, but unintended, consequences of their desired activity on intermediary agents; incendiary speakers are protected, however, despite the fact that the relevant intermediary agents' actions are both intended and foreseeable by the speakers. The law here seems to enforce what I will call (for lack of a better term) a reverse pattern of double effect. More precisely, this part of the constitutional law permits a state to hold agents more (legally) responsible for merely foreseeable consequences than for foreseeable and intended consequences.

... [I]t looks as though a speaker may be held responsible for incidental effects of her speech but not (except under special circumstances) for direct, intended effects. The negative or positive effects on an audience from its understanding and directly reacting to the contents of one's speech may not be the grounds for restriction, but the side effects of one's speech may be so used.

... Suppose we want to protect a class of activities because we believe it is valuable, generally, for both its practitioners and, where relevant, for those toward whom the practitioners aim their activities. And suppose that the value of the conduct derives, in large part, from the agents' intentions being expressed and put into action and from the typical, normal consequences of this behavior. This value need not be construed in a consequentialist manner. The agent, or those toward whom the agent's behavior is directed, may have special interests or rights to implement these intentions (or in having these intentions implemented).

Protecting this value may require protecting all agents who engage in this conduct – even those who lack the typically valuable intentions associated with the conduct and who produce harm. If that were so, one might see how one could arrive at a situation in which one's regulations reasonably treated some conduct that intentionally produced harm more leniently than it treated conduct that unintentionally produced the same sort of harm. The former conduct might be part of a generally valuable class of conduct (whose rogue members cannot or should not be differentiated out), whereas the latter may not be. The poorly intentioned conduct might well enjoy greater protection because of the value of the class of intentional action to which it belongs – a value whose achievement and production is inextricably connected to the possibility of producing harmful consequences. The conduct producing unintended harms may not have such compensating virtues (or the way it produces such harms may be unrelated to the operation of its valuable aspect).

It is not so farfetched to think that this abstract description portrays one important aspect of free speech's value. Although there is quite substantial value associated with the pure act of self-articulation and self-expression associated with speech, a predominant value of speech lies in its nature as a communicative enterprise. We prize speech, in large part, because it communicates content to others and stimulates thought, understanding, critical reflection, emotional reactions, subtle and radical changes in self-conception and behavior, and other responses in audiences about that content. Speakers offer visions of what our lives represent and what they should become; that is, how we, as citizens and moral agents, should act. In part, a commitment to free speech manifests a hope and optimism that what a speaker aims or intends to convey will in fact offer or stimulate insights that may catalyze necessary change, on a large or small scale. Alternatively, it may prevent unnecessary change; speech may provide reasons for maintaining or recommitting anew to our prior path or merely may help to understand better our situation. A large part of what we value about speech is located in the speaker's intentions to communicate to an audience and to influence, through the transmission of content and its uptake, that audience's perceptions, beliefs, and plans. Speech is valued, in large part, for the intentions it expresses and the effects that should be reasonably construed as within the scope of that intention.

Our optimism about speech's possibilities is part of what motivates us to make room for the chain of events that follows from the expression of an aim to a responsive audience. Making room for these possibilities, however, may require that we forego efforts to differentiate between truly valuable and misguided speech – for all the standard pessimistic reasons: The state is a poor and deeply biased judge about what visions for stability and change are defective; whether something is a good or a bad vision may often depend on the possibilities for consensus around it – it may depend upon one's degree of success in enlisting audience support and may not be fully determined prior to its communication; our vitality as a democratic collectivity depends on our joint engagement with and evaluation of competing visions; differentiation may fuel worry that one's speech will be perceived as poorly intentioned, thus deterring valuable speech from being delivered; etc. We want speakers to have full freedom in the construction and dissemination of their intent. Our legitimacy depends on it. Protection of the bitter alongside the sweet, then, may be a necessary condition of protecting those valuable processes and outcomes provoked by insightful speech.

Familiar Millian arguments give us reason to venture deeper and toward a deliberate, positive argument for protecting disruptive and misguided intentions alongside insightful ones (whether peaceful or revolutionary). It is not merely that pragmatic constraints counsel us to tolerate the bad alongside the good in order to produce, identify, or protect the good. It is not merely that it is too difficult or too dangerous to attempt to identify poorly intentioned speakers. We also value misguided speech precisely for its communication of a speaker's vision and the effect this has on an audience. Confrontations with misguided views provoke audiences to reconsider their judgments and to reassess the foundations of their convictions. Negative audience reactions to them provoke reconsideration and reassessment by speakers. It is vital to legitimating functions and authentic compliance with the law that audiences have opportunities to be exposed to others' good-faith, but misguided, intention that the former do wrong and that speakers be exposed to the reactions and responses, both positive and negative, of audiences to their visions. Ongoing public confrontation and reaction to other citizens' good-faith visions of how we should live together is central to our way of both discovering and understanding our convictions of how we should go on ... And these ideas may make some more sense of (although not sensitivity out of) Judge Easterbrook's declarations in *Hudnut* that it was the very persuasiveness and effectiveness of pornography that underwrote its basis for protection.

[S]peaker liability is rejected not because there is a sense that the speaker does not directly or indirectly cause the harm. Rather, speaker liability is rejected primarily because the point of the activity and our protection of it depend on a separation of responsibility between speakers and audiences. It depends on a view of the role of audience members that conflicts with assigning a large amount of responsibility to the speaker, namely a view that audience members are, or are able to act as, independent minds who react to the content of speech for themselves and perform their own evaluations of these ideas and their relevance to action. Moreover, pragmatically achieving the ends of a free speech regime requires that speakers float ideas and views for independent evaluation: Holding them responsible for convincing others to act in certain ways will deter speech, the voicing of which the institution's protection is designed to encourage, for independent review, evaluation, and understanding ...

From a political and legal perspective, there may be greater reason to protect speakers with respect to the intended consequences of their speech on others' agency than there is with respect to those that are merely foreseeable. Speech that produces intentional harm by stimulating others into endorsing and acting upon the speech's content is operating as it should – as it is supposed to. It is also operating as it should when listeners consider the content and reject it. That is, it operates as it should when audiences consider and react to its content. A central reason for protecting speech is to permit a variety of ideas to be promulgated to, and evaluated and tested by, independent agents. To restrict or burden speech on the ground that its content motivates some agents to act seems inconsistent with the very grounds for protecting and valuing speech in the first place: Our conception of speech's value depends on the assumption that audiences will have an opportunity to evaluate the speech for themselves and that they may evaluate that speech in a way that affects their agenda for action. If we value speech as a communicative enterprise and we value the voicing of a range of ideas (including mistaken and possibly mistaken ones), we have strong reason not to use the effectiveness of speech qua speech, in the context of its normal mode of operation, as grounds for its suppression. To use speech's effectiveness as grounds for its regulation or restriction would betray an inconsistent attitude toward its value and toward the role and function of audiences.

By contrast, we do not face the same presumption against efforts to control harm that is a byproduct of speech and not the product of those qualities about speech that we value politically and legally. Such efforts do not betray an inconsistent attitude toward the value of speech. This is not to say that there is no presumption at all against such regulation or that indifference to the effects of such regulation on the climate for speech is warranted. One may, quite reasonably, take the view that regulations that burden speech should face a heavy presumption against them, no matter why that speech is burdened ... Even if the rationale for a law that burdened speech (in this case, supposedly incidentally) is a permissible one, the fact that the effect is one that burdens speech itself provides a reason to apply a heightened standard of review, to require a showing that a significant interest is served that outweighs the burden on speech, and to require a showing that the least restrictive means have been adopted. The worry here is that too much speech will be suppressed or deterred and that the cost of this suppression – of the constriction of opportunities for speech – is not outweighed by the harm to be prevented ...

READING QUESTIONS ON *SHIFFRIN*

1 Does Shiffrin provide a persuasive account of Judge Easterbrook's reasoning in *Hudnut*?
2 Does Shiffrin's analysis prevent hate-speech laws, or only increase the burden of justification for them?
3 How is Shiffrin's argument related to Scanlon's, above?
4 How would it apply to a case like *R.A.V.*, or *Virginia v. Black*?

R. v. Butler [1992] 1 SCR 452

A decision of the Canadian Supreme Court upholding Canada's obscenity law.

Sopinka, J. for the majority: – This appeal calls into question the constitutionality of the obscenity provisions of the *Criminal Code*, RSC 1985, c. C-46, s. 163. They are attacked on the ground that they contravene s. 2(b) of the *Canadian Charter of Rights and Freedoms*. The case requires the Court to address one of the most difficult and controversial of contemporary issues, that of determining whether, and to what extent, Parliament may legitimately criminalize obscenity. I propose to begin with a review of the facts which gave rise to this appeal, as well of the proceedings in the lower courts.

FACTS AND PROCEEDINGS

In August, 1987, the appellant, Donald Victor Butler, opened the Avenue Video Boutique located in Winnipeg, Manitoba. The shop sells and rents "hard core" videotapes and magazines as well as sexual paraphernalia. Outside the store is a sign which reads:

Avenue Video Boutique; a private members only adult video/visual club.

Notice: if sex oriented material offends you, please do not enter.

No admittance to persons under 18 years.

On August 21, 1987, the City of Winnipeg Police entered the appellant's store with a search warrant and seized all the inventory. The appellant was charged with 173 counts in the first indictment: three counts of selling obscene material contrary to s. 159(2)(a) of the *Criminal Code*, RSC 1970, c. C-34 (now s. 163(2)(a)), 41 counts of possessing obscene material for the purpose of distribution contrary to s. 159(l)(a) (now s. 163(l)(a)) of the *Criminal Code*, 128 counts of possessing obscene material for the purpose of sale contrary to s. 159(2)(a) of the *Criminal Code*, and one count of exposing obscene material to public view contrary to s. 159(2)(a) of the *Criminal Code*.

On October 19, 1987, the appellant re-opened the store at the same location. As a result of a police operation a search warrant was executed on October 29, 1987, resulting in the arrest of an employee, Norma McCord. The appellant was arrested at a later date.

A joint indictment was laid against the appellant doing business as Avenue Video Boutique and Norma McCord. The joint indictment contains 77 counts under s. 159 (now s. 163) of the *Criminal Code:* two counts of selling obscene material contrary to s. 159(2)(a), 73 counts of possessing obscene material for the purpose of distribution contrary to s. 159(l)(a), one count of possessing obscene material for the purpose of sale contrary to s. 159(2)(a), and one count of exposing obscene material to public view contrary to s. 159(2)(a).

The trial judge convicted the appellant on eight counts relating to eight films. Convictions were entered against the co-accused McCord with respect to two counts relating to two of the films. Fines of $1,000 per offence were imposed on the appellant. Acquittals were entered on the remaining charges.

The Crown appealed the 242 acquittals with respect to the appellant, and the appellant cross-appealed the convictions. The majority of the Manitoba Court of Appeal allowed the appeal of the Crown and entered convictions for the appellant with respect to all of the counts ...

RELEVANT LEGISLATION

Criminal Code, RSC 1985, c. C-46.

163. (1) Everyone commits an offence who,
(a) makes, prints, publishes, distributes, circulates or has in his possession for the purpose of publication, distribution or circulation any obscene written matter, picture, model, phonograph record or other thing whatever; or
(b) makes, prints, publishes, distributes, sells or has in his possession for the purpose of publication, distribution or circulation a crime comic.
(2) Every one commits an offence who knowingly, without lawful justification or excuse,
(a) sells, exposes to public view or has in his possession for such a purpose any obscene written matter, picture, model, phonograph record or other thing whatever;
(b) publicly exhibits a disgusting object or an indecent show;
(c) offers to sell, advertises or publishes an advertisement of, or has for sale or disposal, any means, instructions, medicine, drug or article intended or represented as a method of causing abortion or miscarriage; or
(d) advertises or publishes an advertisement of any means, instructions, medicine, drug or article intended or represented as a method for restoring sexual virility or curing venereal diseases or diseases of the generative organs.
(3) No person shall be convicted of an offence under this section if he establishes that the public good was served by the acts that are alleged to constitute the offence and that the acts alleged did not extend beyond what served the public good.
(4) For the purposes of this section, it is a question of law whether an act served the public good and whether there is evidence that the act alleged went beyond what served the public good, but it is a question of fact whether the acts did or did not extend beyond what served the public good.
(5) For the purposes of this section, the motives of an accused are irrelevant.
(6) Where an accused is charged with an offence under subsection (1), the fact that the accused was ignorant of the nature or presence of the matter, picture, model, phonograph record, crime comic or other thing by means of

or in relation to which the offence was committed is not a defence to the charge.

(7) In this section, "crime comic" means a magazine, periodical or book that exclusively or substantially comprises matter depicting pictorially

(a) the commission of crimes, real or fictitious; or

(b) events connected with the commission of crimes, real or fictitious, whether occurring before of after the commission of the crime.

(8) For the purposes of this Act, any publication a dominant characteristic of which is the undue exploitation of sex, or of sex and any one or more of the following subjects, namely, crime, horror, cruelty and violence, shall be deemed to be obscene.

ISSUES

The following constitutional questions are raised by this appeal:

1 Does s. 163 of the *Criminal Code* of Canada, RSC 1985, c. C-46, violate s. 2(b) of the *Canadian Charter of Rights and Freedoms?*

2 If s. 163 of the *Criminal Code* of Canada, RSC 1985, c. C-46, violates s. 2(b) of the *Canadian Charter of Rights and Freedoms,* can s. 163 of the *Criminal Code* of Canada be demonstrably justified under s. 1 of the *Canadian Charter of Rights and Freedoms* as a reasonable limit prescribed by law?

ANALYSIS

... In my view, in the circumstances, this appeal should be confined to the examination of the constitutional validity of s. 163(8) only.

Before proceeding to consider the constitutional questions, it will be helpful to review the legislative history of the provision as well as the extensive judicial interpretation and analysis which have infused meaning into the bare words of the statute.

Legislative History

...

The *Criminal Code* did not [in the past] provide a definition of any of the operative terms, "obscene," "indecent," or "disgusting." The notion of obscenity embodied in these provisions was based on the test formulated by Cockburn, C.J. in *R. v. Hicklin* (1868), LR 3 QB 360:

I think the test of obscenity is this, whether the tendency of the matter charged as obscenity is to deprave and corrupt those whose minds are open to such immoral influences, and into whose hands a publication of this sort may fall. (At p. 371)

The focus on the "corruption of morals" in the earlier legislation grew out of the English obscenity law which made the Court the "guardian of public morals" ...

The current provision, which is the subject of this appeal, entered into force in 1959 in response to the much criticized former version ... Unlike the previous statutes, s-s. (8) provided a statutory definition of "obscene":

(8) For the purposes of this Act, any publication a dominant characteristic of which is the undue exploitation of sex, or of sex and any one or more of the following subjects, namely, crime, horror, cruelty and violence, shall be deemed to be obscene.

As will be discussed further, the introduction of the statutory definition had the effect of replacing the *Hicklin* test with a series of rules developed by the courts. The provision must be considered in light of these tests.

Judicial Interpretation of Section 163(8)

The first case to consider the current provision was *Brodie v. The Queen*, [1962] SCR 681. The majority of this Court found in that case that D.H. Lawrence's novel, *Lady Chatterley's Lover*, was not obscene within the meaning of the *Code*. The *Brodie* case lay the groundwork for the interpretation of s. 163(8) by setting out the principal tests which should govern the determination of what is obscene for the purposes of criminal prosecution. The first step was to discard the *Hicklin* test.

Section 163(8) to be Exclusive Test

In examining the definition provided by s-s. (8), the majority of this Court was of the view that the new provision provided a clean slate and had the effect of bringing in an "objective standard of obscenity" which rendered all the jurisprudence under the *Hicklin* definition obsolete. In the words of Judson, J.:

I think that the new statutory definition does give the Court an opportunity to apply tests which have some certainty of meaning and are capable of objective application and which do not so much depend as before upon the idiosyncrasies and sensitivities of the tribunal of fact, whether judge or jury. We are now concerned with a Canadian statute which is exclusive of all others. [At p. 702]

...

Tests of "Undue Exploitation of Sex"

In order for the work or material to qualify as "obscene," the exploitation of sex must not only be its dominant characteristic, but such exploitation must be "undue." In determining when the exploitation of sex will be considered "undue," the courts have attempted to formulate workable tests. The most important of these is the "community standard of tolerance" test.

"Community Standard of Tolerance" Test. In *Brodie,* Judson, J. accepted the view espoused notably by the Australian and New Zealand courts that obscenity is to be measured against "community standards." He cited the following passage in the judgment of Fullager, J. in *R. v. Close,* [1948] VLR 445:

There does exist in any community at all times – however the standard may vary from time to time – a general instinctive sense of what is decent and what is indecent, of what is clean and what is dirty, and when the distinction has to be drawn, I do not know that today there is any better tribunal than a jury to draw it ... I am very far from attempting to lay down a model direction, but a judge might perhaps, in the case of a novel, say something like this: "It would not be true to say that any publication dealing with sexual relations is obscene. The relations of the sexes are, of course, legitimate matters for discussion everywhere ... There are certain standards of decency which prevail in the community, and you are really called upon to try this case because you are regarded as representing, and capable of justly applying, those standards. What is obscene is something which offends against those standards." [At pp. 705–6]

The community standards test has been the subject of extensive judicial analysis. It is the standards of the community as a whole which must be considered and not the standards of a small segment of that community such as the university community where a film was shown ... The standard to be applied is a national one ... With respect to expert evidence, it is not necessary and is not a fact which the Crown is obliged to prove as part of its case ... In *R. v. Dominion News & Gifts (1962) Ltd*, [1963] 2 CCC 103 (Man. CA), Freedman, J.A. (dissenting) emphasized that the community standards test must necessarily respond to changing mores:

Community standards must be contemporary. Times change, and ideas change with them. Compared to the Victorian era this is a liberal age in which we live. One manifestation of it is the relative freedom with which the whole question of sex is discussed. In books, magazines, movies, television, and sometimes even in parlour conversation, various aspects of sex are made the subject of comment, with a candour that in an earlier day would have been regarded as indecent and intolerable. We cannot and should not ignore these present-day attitudes when we face the question whether [the subject materials] are obscene according to our criminal law. [At pp. 116–17]

Our Court was called upon to elaborate the community standards test in *Towne Cinema Theatres Ltd v. The Queen*, [1985] 1 SCR 494. Dickson, C.J. reviewed the case law and found:

The cases all emphasize that it is a standard of *tolerance*, not taste, that is relevant. What matters is not what Canadians think is right for themselves to see. What matters is what Canadians would not abide other Canadians seeing because it would be beyond the contemporary Canadian standard of tolerance to allow them to see it. Since the standard is tolerance, I think the audience to which the allegedly obscene material is targeted must be relevant. The operative standards are those of the Canadian community as a whole, but since what matters is what other people may see, it is quite conceivable that the Canadian community would tolerate varying degrees of explicitness depending upon the audience and the circumstances. [Emphasis in original; at pp. 508–9]

Therefore, the community standards test is concerned not with what Canadians would not tolerate being exposed to themselves, but what they would not tolerate other Canadians being exposed to. The minority view was that the tolerance level will vary depending on the manner, time, and place in which the material is presented as well as the audience to whom it is directed. The majority opinion on this point was expressed by Wilson, J. in the following passage:

It is not, in my opinion, open to the courts under s. 159(8) of the *Criminal Code* to characterize a movie as obscene if shown to one constituency but not if shown to another ... In my view, a movie is either obscene under the *Code* based on a national community standard of tolerance or it is not. If it is not, it may still be the subject of provincial regulatory control. [At p. 521]

"Degradation or Dehumanization" Test. There has been a growing recognition in recent cases that material which may be said to exploit sex in a "degrading or dehumanizing" manner will necessarily fail the community standards test ...

Among other things, degrading or dehumanizing materials place women (and sometimes men) in positions of subordination, servile submission, or humiliation. They run against the principles of equality and dignity of all human beings. In the appreciation of whether material is degrading or dehumanizing, the appearance of consent is not necessarily determinative. Consent cannot save materials that otherwise contain degrading or dehumanizing scenes. Sometimes the very appearance of consent makes the depicted acts even more degrading or dehumanizing.

This type of material would, apparently, fail the community standards test not because it offends against morals but because it is perceived by public opinion to be harmful to society, particularly to women. While the accuracy of this perception is not susceptible of exact proof, there is a substantial body of opinion that holds that the portrayal of persons being subjected to degrading or dehumanizing sexual treatment results in harm, particularly to women and therefore to society as a whole ... It would be reasonable to conclude that there is an appreciable risk of harm to society in the portrayal of such material. The effect of the evidence on public opinion was summed up by Wilson, J. in *Towne Cinema, supra*, as follows:

The most that can be said, I think, is that the public has concluded that exposure to material which degrades the human dimensions of life to a sub-human or merely physical dimension and thereby contributes to a process of moral desensitization must be harmful in some way. [At p. 524]

In *Towne Cinema*, Dickson, C.J. considered the "degradation" or "dehumanization" test to be the principal indicator of "undueness" without specifying what role the community tolerance test plays in respect of this issue. He did observe, however, that the community might tolerate some forms of exploitation that caused harm that was nevertheless undue. The relevant passages appear at p. 505:

There are other ways in which exploitation of sex might be "undue." Ours is not a perfect society and it is unfortunate but true that the community may tolerate publications that cause harm to members of society and therefore to society as a whole. Even if, at certain times, there is a coincidence between what is not tolerated and what is harmful to society, there is no necessary connection between these two concepts. Thus, a legal definition of "undue" must also encompass publications harmful to members of society and, therefore, to society as a whole.

Sex related publications which portray persons in a degrading manner as objects of violence, cruelty or other forms of dehumanizing treatment, may be "undue" for the purpose of s. 159(8). No one should be subject to the degradation and humiliation inherent in publications which link sex with violence, cruelty, and other forms of dehumanizing treatment. It is not likely that at a given moment in a society's history, such publications will be tolerated ...

However, as I have noted above, there is no *necessary* coincidence between the undueness of publications which degrade people by linking violence, cruelty or other forms of dehumanizing treatment with sex, and the community standard of tolerance. Even if certain sex related materials were found to be within the standard of tolerance of the community, it would still be necessary to ensure that they were not "undue" in some other sense, for example, in the sense that they portray persons in a degrading manner as objects of violence, cruelty, or other forms of dehumanizing treatment. [Emphasis in original]

In the reasons of Wilson, J. concurring in the result, the line between the mere portrayal of sex and the dehumanization of people is drawn by the "undueness" concept. The community is the arbiter as to what is harmful to it. She states:

As I see it, the essential difficulty with the definition of obscenity is that "undueness" must presumably be assessed in relation to consequences. It is implicit in the definition that at some point the exploitation of sex becomes harmful to the public or at least the public believes that to be so. It is therefore necessary for the protection of the public to put limits on the degree of exploitation and, through the application of the community standard test, the public is made the arbiter of what is harmful to it and what is not. The problem is that we know so little of the consequences we are seeking to avoid. Do obscene movies spawn immoral conduct? Do they degrade women? Do they promote violence? The most that can be said, I think, is that the public has concluded that exposure to material which degrades the human dimensions of life to a subhuman or merely physical dimension and thereby contributes to a process of moral desensitization must be harmful in some way. It must therefore be controlled when it gets out of hand, when it becomes "undue." [At p. 524]

"Internal Necessities Test" or "Artistic Defence." In determining whether the exploitation of sex is "undue," Judson, J. set out the test of "internal necessities" in *Brodie, supra:*

What I think is aimed at is excessive emphasis on the theme for a base purpose. But I do not think that there is undue exploitation if there is no more emphasis on the theme than is required in the serious treatment of the theme of a novel with honesty and uprightness. That the work under attack is a serious work of fiction is to me beyond question. It has none of the characteristics that are often described in judgments dealing with obscenity – dirt for dirt's sake, the leer of the sensualist, depravity in the mind of an author with an obsession for dirt, pornography, an appeal to a prurient interest, etc. The section recognizes that the serious-minded author must have freedom in the production of a work of genuine artistic and literary merit and the quality of the work, as the witnesses point out and common sense indicates, must have real relevance in determining not only a dominant characteristic but also whether there is undue exploitation. [At pp. 704–5]

As counsel for the Crown pointed out in his oral submissions, the artistic defence is the last step in the analysis of whether the exploitation of sex is undue. Even material which by itself offends community standards will not be considered "undue," if it is required for the serious treatment of a theme ...

Accordingly, the "internal necessities" test, or what has been referred to as the "artistic defence," has been interpreted to assess whether the exploitation of sex has a justifiable role in advancing the plot or the theme, and in considering the work as a whole, does not merely represent "dirt for dirt's sake" but has a legitimate role when measured by the internal necessities of the work itself.

The Relationship of the Tests to Each Other. This review of jurisprudence shows that it fails to specify the relationship of the tests one to another. Failure to do so with respect to the community standards test and the degrading or dehumanizing test, for example, raises a serious question as to the basis on which the community acts in determining whether the impugned material will be tolerated. With both these tests being applied to the same material and apparently independently, we do not know whether the community found the material to be intolerable because it was degrading or dehumanizing, because it offended against morals or on some other basis. In some circumstances a finding that the material is tolerable can be overruled by the conclusion by the court that it causes harm and is therefore undue. Moreover, is the internal necessities test dominant so that it will redeem material that would otherwise be undue or is it just one factor? Is this test applied by the community or is it determined by the court without regard for the community? This hiatus in the jurisprudence has left the legislation open to attack on the ground of vagueness and uncertainty. That attack is made in this case. This lacuna in the interpretation of the legislation must, if possible, be filled before subjecting the legislation to *Charter* scrutiny. The necessity to do so was foreseen by Wilson, J. in *Towne Cinema* when she stated:

The test of the community standard is helpful to the extent that it provides a norm against which impugned material may be assessed but it does little to elucidate the underlying question as to why some exploitation of sex falls on the permitted side of the line under s. 159(8) and some on the prohibited side. No doubt this question will have to be addressed when the validity of the obscenity provisions of the *Code* is subjected to attack as an infringement on freedom of speech and the infringement is sought to be justified as reasonable. [At p. 525]

Pornography can be usefully divided into three categories: (1) explicit sex with violence, (2) explicit sex without violence but which subjects people to treatment that is degrading or dehumanizing, and (3) explicit sex without violence that is neither degrading nor dehumanizing. Violence in this context includes both actual physical violence and threats of physical violence. Relating these three categories to the terms of s. 163(8) of the *Code,* the first, explicit sex coupled with violence, is expressly mentioned. Sex coupled with crime, horror, or cruelty will sometimes involve violence. Cruelty, for instance, will usually do so.

But, even in the absence of violence, sex coupled with crime, horror, or cruelty may fall within the second category. As for category (3), subject to the exception referred to below, it is not covered.

Some segments of society would consider that all three categories of pornography cause harm to society because they tend to undermine its moral fibre. Others would contend that none of the categories cause harm. Furthermore, there is a range of opinion as to what is degrading or dehumanizing ... Because this is not a matter that is susceptible of proof in the traditional way and because we do not wish to leave it to the individual tastes of judges, we must have a norm that will serve as an arbiter in determining what amounts to an undue exploitation of sex. That arbiter is the community as a whole.

The courts must determine as best they can what the community would tolerate others being exposed to on the basis of the degree of harm that may flow from such exposure. Harm in this context means that it predisposes persons to act in an anti-social manner as, for example, the physical or mental mistreatment of women by men, or, what is perhaps debatable, the reverse. Anti-social conduct for this purpose is conduct which society formally recognizes as incompatible with its proper functioning. The stronger the inference of a risk of harm the lesser the likelihood of tolerance. The inference may be drawn from the material itself or from the material and other evidence. Similarly evidence as to the community standards is desirable but not essential.

In making this determination with respect to the three categories of pornography referred to above, the portrayal of sex coupled with violence will almost always constitute the undue exploitation of sex. Explicit sex which is degrading or dehumanizing may be undue if the risk of harm is substantial. Finally, explicit sex that is not violent and neither degrading nor dehumanizing is generally tolerated in our society and will not qualify as the undue exploitation of sex unless it employs children in its production.

If material is not obscene under this framework, it does not become so by reason of the person to whom it is or may be shown or exposed nor by reason of the place or manner in which it is shown. The availability of sexually explicit materials in theatres and other public places is subject to regulation by competent provincial legislation. Typically such legislation imposes restrictions on the material available to children ...

The foregoing deals with the inter-relationship of the "community standards test" and "the degrading or dehumanizing" test. How does the "internal necessities" test fit into this scheme? The need to apply this test only arises if a work contains sexually explicit material that by itself would constitute the undue exploitation of sex. The portrayal of sex must then be viewed in context to determine whether that is the dominant theme of the work as a whole. Put another way, is undue exploitation of sex the main object of the work or is this portrayal of sex essential to a wider artistic, literary, or other similar purpose? Since the threshold determination must be made on the basis of community standards, that is, whether the sexually explicit aspect is undue, its impact when considered in context must be determined on the same basis. The court must determine whether the sexually explicit material when viewed in the context of the whole work would be tolerated by the community as a whole. Artistic expression rests at the heart of freedom of expression values and any doubt in this regard must be resolved in favour of freedom of expression.

Does Section 163 Violate Section 2(b) of the Charter?

The majority of the Court of Appeal in this case allowed the appeal of the Crown on the ground that s. 163 does not violate freedom of expression as guaranteed under s. 2(b) of the *Charter* ... [However] [t]he form of activity in this case is the medium through which the meaning sought to be conveyed is expressed, namely, the film, magazine, written matter, or sexual gadget. There is nothing inherently violent in the vehicle of expression, and it accordingly does not fall outside the protected sphere of activity.

In light of our recent decision in *R. v. Keegstra,* [1990] 3 SCR 697, the respondent, and most of the parties intervening in support of the respondent, do not take issue with the proposition that s. 163 of the *Criminal Code* violates s. 2(b) of the *Charter.* In *Keegstra,* we were unanimous in advocating a generous approach to the protection afforded by s. 2(b) of the *Charter.* Our Court confirmed the view ... that activities cannot be excluded from the scope of the guaranteed freedom on the basis of the content or meaning being conveyed ...

With respect, the majority of the Court of Appeal did not sufficiently distance itself from the content of the materials ...

Meaning sought to be expressed need not be "redeeming" in the eyes of the Court to merit the protection of s. 2(b) whose purpose is to ensure that thoughts and feelings may be conveyed freely in non-violent ways without fear of censure.

In this case, both the purpose and effect of s. 163 is specifically to restrict the communication of certain types of materials based on their content. In my view, there is no doubt that s. 163 seeks to prohibit certain types of expressive activity and thereby infringes s. 2(b) of the *Charter* ...

I would conclude that the first constitutional question should be answered in the affirmative.

Is Section 163 Justified under Section 1 of the Charter?

Is Section 163 a Limit Prescribed by Law?

The appellant argues that the provision is so vague that it is impossible to apply it. Vagueness must be considered in relation to two issues in this appeal: (1) is the law so vague that it does not qualify as "a limit prescribed by law"; and (2) is it so imprecise that it is not a reasonable limit ...

In assessing whether s. 163(8) prescribes an intelligible standard, consideration must be given to the manner in which the provision has been judicially interpreted ...

The fact that a particular legislative term is open to varying interpretations by the courts is not fatal ... Therefore the question at hand is whether the impugned sections of the *Criminal Code* can be or have been given sensible meanings by the courts ...

Standards which escape precise technical definition, such as "undue," are an inevitable part of the law. The *Criminal Code* contains other such standards. Without commenting on their constitutional validity, I note that the terms "indecent," "immoral," or "scurrilous," found in ss. 167, 168, 173, and 175, are nowhere defined in the *Code*. It is within the role of the judiciary to attempt to interpret these terms. If such interpretation yields an intelligible standard, the threshold test for the application of s. 1 is met. In my opinion, the interpretation of s. 163(8) in prior judgments which I have reviewed, as supplemented by these reasons, provides an intelligible standard.

Objective

The respondent argues that there are several pressing and substantial objectives which justify overriding the freedom to distribute obscene materials. Essentially, these objectives are the avoidance of harm resulting from antisocial attitudinal changes that exposure to obscene material causes and the public interest in maintaining a "decent society." On the other hand, the appellant argues that the objective of s. 163 is to have the state act as "moral custodian" in sexual matters and to impose subjective standards of morality.

The obscenity legislation and jurisprudence prior to the enactment of s. 163 were evidently concerned with prohibiting the "immoral influences" of obscene publications and safeguarding the morals of individuals into whose hands such works could fall. The *Hicklin* philosophy posits that explicit sexual depictions, particularly outside the sanctioned contexts of marriage and procreation, threatened the morals or the fabric of society ... In this sense, its dominant, if not exclusive, purpose was to advance a particular conception of morality. Any deviation from such morality was considered to be inherently undesirable, independently of any harm to society ... [T]his particular objective is no longer defensible in view of the *Charter*. To impose a certain standard of public and sexual morality, solely because it reflects the conventions of a given community, is inimical to the exercise and enjoyment of individual freedoms, which form the basis of our social contract. D. Dyzenhaus, "Obscenity and the Charter: Autonomy and Equality" (1991), 1 CR (4th) 367, at p. 370, refers to this as "legal moralism," of a majority deciding what values should inform individual lives and then coercively imposing those values on minorities. The prevention of "dirt for dirt's sake" is not a legitimate objective which would justify the violation of one of the most fundamental freedoms enshrined in the *Charter*.

On the other hand, I cannot agree with the suggestion of the appellant that Parliament does not have the right to legislate on the basis of some fundamental conception of morality for the purposes of safeguarding the values which are integral to a free and democratic society. As Dyzenhaus, *supra*, writes:

Moral disapprobation is recognized as an appropriate response when it has its basis in *Charter* values. (At p. 376)

As the respondent and many of the interveners have pointed out, much of the criminal law is based on moral conceptions of right and wrong and the mere fact that a law is grounded in morality does not automatically render it illegitimate. In this regard, criminalizing the proliferation of materials which undermine another basic *Charter* right may indeed be a legitimate objective.

In my view, however, the overriding objective of s. 163 is not moral disapprobation but the avoidance of harm to society. In *Towne Cinema*, Dickson, C.J. stated:

It is harm to society from undue exploitation that is aimed at by the section, not simply lapses in propriety or good taste. (At p. 507)

The harm was described in the following way in the *Report on Pornography by the Standing Committee on Justice and Legal Affairs* (MacGuigan Report) (1978):

The clear and unquestionable danger of this type of material is that it reinforces some unhealthy tendencies in Canadian society. The effect of this type of material is to reinforce male-female stereotypes to the detriment of both sexes. It attempts to make degradation, humiliation, victimization, and violence in human relationships appear normal and acceptable. A society which holds that egalitarianism, non-violence, consensualism, and mutuality are basic to any human interaction, whether sexual or other, is clearly justified in controlling and prohibiting any medium of depiction, description or advocacy which violates these principles.

The appellant argues that to accept the objective of the provision as being related to the harm associated with obscenity would be to adopt the "shifting purpose" doctrine explicitly rejected in *R. v. Big M Drug Mart Ltd*, [1985] 1 SCR 295. This Court concluded in that case that a finding that the *Lord's Day Act* has a secular purpose was not possible given that its religious purpose, in compelling sabbatical observance, has been long-established and consistently maintained by the courts. The appellant relies on the words of Dickson, J. (as he then was):

... the theory of a shifting purpose stands in stark contrast to fundamental notions developed in our law concerning the nature of "Parliamentary intention." Purpose is a function of the intent of those who drafted and enacted the legislation at the time, and not of any shifting variable ...

While the effect of such legislation as the *Lord's Day Act* may be more secular today than it was in 1677 or in 1906, such a finding cannot justify a conclusion that its purpose has similarly changed. In result, therefore, the *Lord's Day Act* must be characterized as it has always been, a law the primary purpose of which is the compulsion of sabbatical observance. [At pp. 335–6]

I do not agree that to identify the objective of the impugned legislation as the prevention of harm to society, one must resort to the "shifting purpose" doctrine. First, the notions of moral corruption and harm to society are not distinct, as the appellant suggests, but are inextricably linked. It is moral corruption of a certain kind which leads to the detrimental effect on society. Second, and more importantly, I am of the view that with the enactment of s. 163, Parliament explicitly sought to address the harms which are linked to certain types of obscene materials. The prohibition of such materials was based on a belief that they had a detrimental impact on individuals exposed to them and consequently on society as a whole. Our understanding of the harms caused by these materials has developed considerably since that time; however, this does not detract from the fact that the purpose of this legislation remains, as it was in 1959, the protection of society from harms caused by the exposure to obscene materials ...

It is the harm to society resulting from the undue exploitation of such matters which is aimed at by the section. The "harm" conceived by Parliament in 1959 may not have been expressed in the same words as one would today. The Court is not limited to a 1959 perspective in the determination of this matter ...

A permissible shift in emphasis was built into the legislation when, as interpreted by the courts, it adopted the community standards test. Community standards as to what is harmful have changed since 1959.

This being the objective, is it pressing and substantial? Does the prevention of the harm associated with the dissemination of certain obscene materials constitute a sufficiently pressing and substantial concern to warrant a restriction on the freedom of expression? In this regard, it should be recalled that in *Keegstra, supra,* this Court unanimously accepted that the prevention of the influence of hate propaganda on society at large was a legitimate objective ...

This Court has thus recognized that the harm caused by the proliferation of materials which seriously offend the values fundamental to our society is a substantial concern which justifies restricting the otherwise full exercise of the freedom of expression. In my view, the harm sought to be avoided in the case of the dissemination of obscene materials is similar ... [I]f true equality between male and female persons is to be achieved, we cannot ignore the threat to equality resulting from exposure to audiences of certain types of violent and degrading material. Materials portraying women as a class as objects for sexual exploitation and abuse have a negative impact on "the individual's sense of self-worth and acceptance."

In reaching the conclusion that legislation proscribing obscenity is a valid objective which justifies some encroachment of the right to freedom of expression, I am persuaded in part that such legislation may be found in most free and democratic societies ...

The advent of the *Charter* did not have the effect of dramatically depriving Parliament of a power which it has historically enjoyed ...

Finally, it should be noted that the burgeoning pornography industry renders the concern even more pressing and substantial than when the impugned provisions were first enacted. I would therefore conclude that the objective of avoiding the harm associated with the dissemination of pornography in this case is sufficiently pressing and substantial to warrant some restriction on full exercise of the right to freedom of expression. The analysis of whether the measure is proportional to the objective must, in my view, be undertaken in light of the conclusion that the objective of the impugned section is valid only insofar as it relates to the harm to society associated with obscene materials. Indeed, the section as interpreted in previous decisions and in these reasons is fully consistent with that objective. The objective of maintaining conventional standards of propriety, independently of any harm to society, is no longer justified in light of the values of individual liberty which underlie the *Charter*. This, then, being the objective of s. 163, which I have found to be pressing and substantial, I must now determine whether the section is rationally connected and proportional to this objective. As outlined above, s. 163(8) criminalizes the exploitation of sex and sex and violence, when, on the basis of the community test, it is undue. The determination of when such exploitation is undue is directly related to the immediacy of a risk of harm to society which is reasonably perceived as arising from its dissemination.

Proportionality

General. The proportionality requirement has three aspects:

1 the existence of a rational connection between the impugned measures and the objective;
2 minimal impairment of the right or freedom; and
3 a proper balance between the effects of the limiting measures and the legislative objective.

In assessing whether the proportionality test is met, it is important to keep in mind the nature of expression which has been infringed ...

The values which underlie the protection of freedom of expression relate to the search for truth, participation in the political process, and individual self-fulfilment. The Attorney General for Ontario argues that of these, only "individual self-fulfilment," and only in its most base aspect, that of physical arousal, is engaged by pornography. On the other hand, the civil liberties groups argue that pornography forces us to question conventional notions of sexuality and thereby launches us into an inherently political discourse. In their factum, the BC Civil Liberties Association adopts a passage from R. West, "The Feminist-Conservative Anti-Pornography Alliance and the 1986 Attorney General's Commission on Pornography Report" (1987), 4 *American Bar Foundation Research Journal* 681, at p. 696:

Good pornography has value because it validates women's will to pleasure. It celebrates female nature. It validates a range of female sexuality that is wider and truer than that legitimated by the non-pornographic culture. Pornography when it is good celebrates both female pleasure and male rationality.

A proper application of the test should not suppress what West refers to as "good pornography." The objective of the impugned provision is not to inhibit the celebration of human sexuality. However, it cannot be ignored that the realities of the pornography industry are far from the picture which the BC Civil Liberties Association would have us paint ...

In my view, the kind of expression which is sought to be advanced does not stand on equal footing with other kinds of expression which directly engage the "core" of the freedom of expression values.

This conclusion is further buttressed by the fact that the targeted material is expression which is motivated, in the overwhelming majority of cases, by economic profit ...

I will now turn to an examination of the three basic aspects of the proportionality test.

Rational Connection. The message of obscenity which degrades and dehumanizes is analogous to that of hate propaganda. As the Attorney General of Ontario has argued in its factum, obscenity wields the power to wreak social damage in that a significant portion of the population is humiliated by its gross misrepresentations.

Accordingly, the rational link between s. 163 and the objective of Parliament relates to the actual causal relationship between obscenity and the risk of harm to society at large. On this point, it is clear that the literature of the social sciences remains subject to controversy ...

While a direct link between obscenity and harm to society may be difficult, if not impossible, to establish, it is reasonable to presume that exposure to images bears a causal relationship to changes in attitudes and beliefs ...

I am in agreement with ... the view that Parliament was entitled to have a "reasoned apprehension of harm" resulting from the desensitization of individuals exposed to materials which depict violence, cruelty, and dehumanization in sexual relations.

Accordingly, I am of the view that there is a sufficiently rational link between the criminal sanction, which demonstrates our community's disapproval of the dissemination of materials which potentially victimize women and which restricts the negative influence which such materials have on changes in attitudes and behaviour, and the objective.

Finally, I wish to distinguish this case from *Keegstra*, in which the minority adopted the view that there was no rational connection between the criminalization of hate propaganda and its suppression. As McLachlin, J. noted, prosecutions under the *Criminal Code* for racist expression have attracted extensive media coverage. The criminal process confers on the accused publicity for his or her causes and succeeds even in generating sympathy. The same cannot be said of the kinds of expression sought to be suppressed in the present case. The general availability of the subject materials and the rampant pornography industry are such that, in the words of Dickson, C.J. in *Keegstra*, "pornography is not dignified by its suppression." In contrast to the hate-monger who may succeed, by the sudden media attention, in gaining an audience, the prohibition of obscene materials does nothing to promote the pornographer's cause.

Minimal Impairment. In determining whether less intrusive legislation may be imagined ... it is not necessary that the legislative scheme be the "perfect" scheme, but that it be appropriately tailored *in the context of the infringed right* ...

There are several factors which contribute to the finding that the provision minimally impairs the freedom which is infringed.

First, the impugned provision does not proscribe sexually explicit erotica without violence that is not degrading or dehumanizing. It is designed to catch material that creates a risk of harm to society. It might be suggested that proof of actual harm should be required. It is apparent from what I have said above that it is sufficient in this regard for Parliament to have a reasonable basis for concluding that harm will result and this requirement does not demand actual proof of harm.

Second, materials which have scientific, artistic, or literary merit are not captured by the provision. As discussed above, the court must be generous in its application of the "artistic defence." For example, in certain cases, materials such as photographs, prints, books, and films which may undoubtedly be produced with some motive for economic profit, may nonetheless claim the protection of the *Charter* insofar as their defining characteristic is that of aesthetic expression, and thus represent the artist's attempt at individual fulfilment. The existence of an accompanying economic motive does not, of itself, deprive a work of significance as an example of individual artistic or self-fulfilment.

Third, in considering whether the provision minimally impairs the freedom in question, it is legitimate for the court to take into account Parliament's past abortive attempts to replace the definition with one that is more explicit ... The attempt to provide exhaustive instances of obscenity has been shown to be destined to fail ... It seems that the only practicable alternative is to strive towards a more abstract definition of obscenity which is contextually sensitive and responsive to progress in the knowledge and understanding of the phenomenon to which the legislation is directed. In my view, the standard of "undue exploitation" is therefore appropriate. The intractable nature of the problem and the impossibility of precisely defining a notion which is inherently elusive makes the possibility of a more explicit provision remote. In this light, it is appropriate to question whether, and at what cost, greater legislative precision can be demanded.

Fourth, while the discussion in this appeal has been limited to the definition portion of s. 163, I would note that the impugned section, with the possible exception of s-s. 1 which is not in issue here, has been held by this Court not to extend its reach to the private use or viewing of obscene materials ...

Accordingly, it is only the public distribution and exhibition of obscene materials which is in issue here.

Finally, I wish to address the arguments of the interveners, Canadian Civil Liberties Association and Manitoba Association for Rights and Liberties, that the objectives of this kind of legislation may be met by alternative, less intrusive measures. First, it is submitted that reasonable time, manner, and place restrictions would be preferable to outright prohibition. I am of the view that this argument should be rejected.

Once it has been established that the objective is the avoidance of harm caused by the degradation which many women feel as "victims" of the message of obscenity, and of the negative impact exposure to such material has on perceptions and attitudes towards women, it is untenable to argue that these harms could be avoided by placing restrictions on access to such material. Making the materials more difficult to obtain by increasing their cost and reducing their availability does not achieve the same objective. Once Parliament has reasonably concluded that certain acts are harmful to certain groups in society and to society in general, it would be inconsistent, if not hypocritical, to argue that such acts could be committed in more restrictive conditions. The harm sought to be avoided would remain the same in either case.

It is also submitted that there are more effective techniques to promote the objectives of Parliament. For example, if pornography is seen as encouraging violence against women, there are certain activities which discourage it – counselling rape victims to charge their assailants, provision of shelter and assistance for battered women, campaigns for laws against discrimination on the grounds of sex, education to increase the sensitivity of law enforcement agencies and other governmental authorities. In addition, it is submitted that education is an under-used response.

It is noteworthy that many of the above-suggested alternatives are in the form of *responses* to the harm engendered by negative attitudes against women. The role of the impugned provision is to control the dissemination of the very images that contribute to such attitudes. Moreover, it is true that there are additional measures which could alleviate the problem of violence against women. However, given the gravity of the harm, and the threat to the values at stake, I do not believe that the measure chosen by Parliament is equalled by the alternatives which have been suggested. Education, too, may offer a means of combating negative attitudes to women, just as it is currently used as a means of addressing other problems dealt with in the *Code*. However, there is no reason to rely on education alone. It should be emphasized that this is in no way intended to deny the value of other educational and counselling measures to deal with the roots and effects of negative attitudes. Rather, it is only to stress the arbitrariness and unacceptability of the claim that such measures represent the sole legitimate means of addressing the phenomenon. Serious social problems such as violence against women require multi-pronged approaches by government. Education and legislation are not alternatives but complements in addressing such problems. There is nothing in the *Charter* which requires Parliament to choose between such complementary measures.

Balance between Effects of Limiting Measures and Legislative Objective. The final question to be answered in the proportionality test is whether the effects of the law so severely trench on a protected right that the legislative objective is outweighed by the infringement. The infringement on freedom of expression is confined to a measure designed to prohibit the distribution of sexually explicit materials accompanied by violence, and those without violence that are degrading or dehumanizing. As I have already concluded, this kind of expression lies far from the core of the guarantee of freedom of expression. It appeals only to the most base aspect of individual fulfilment, and it is primarily economically motivated.

The objective of the legislation, on the other hand, is of fundamental importance in a free and democratic society. It is aimed at avoiding harm, which Parliament has reasonably concluded will be caused directly or indirectly, to individuals, groups such as women and children, and consequently to society as a whole, by the distribution of these materials. It thus seeks to enhance respect for all members of society, and non-violence and equality in their relations with each other. I therefore conclude that the restriction on freedom of expression does not outweigh the importance of the legislative objective.

CONCLUSION

I conclude that while s. 163(8) infringes s. 2(b) of the *Charter*, freedom of expression, it constitutes a reasonable limit and is saved by virtue of the provisions of s. 1. The trial judge convicted the appellant only with respect to materials which contained scenes involving violence or cruelty intermingled with sexual activity or depicted lack of consent to sexual contact or otherwise could be said to dehumanize men or women in a sexual context. The majority of the Court of Appeal, on the other hand, convicted the appellant on all charges.

While the trial judge concluded that the material for which the accused were acquitted was not degrading or dehumanizing, he did so in the context of s. 1 of the *Charter*. In effect, he asked himself whether, if the material was proscribed by s. 163(8), that section would still be supportable under s. 1. In this context, he considered the government objectives of s. 163(8) and measured the material which was the subject of the charges against this objective. The findings at trial were therefore made in a legal framework that is different from that outlined in these reasons. Specifically, in considering whether the materials were degrading or dehumanizing, he did not address the issue of harm. Accordingly, it would be speculation to conclude that the same result would have been obtained if the definition of obscenity contained in these reasons had been applied. The test applied by the majority of the Court of Appeal also differed significantly from these reasons. I therefore cannot accept their conclusion that all of the materials are obscene. Accordingly, I would allow the appeal and direct a new trial on all charges. I note, however, that I am in agreement with Wright, J.'s conclusion that, in the case of material found to be obscene, there should only be one conviction imposed with respect to a single tape.

I would answer the constitutional questions as follows:

Question 1: Does s. 163 of the *Criminal Code* of Canada, RSC 1985, c. C-46, violate s. 2(b) of the *Canadian Charter of Rights and Freedoms?*
Answer: Yes.
Question 2: If s. 163 of the *Criminal Code* of Canada, RSC 1985, c. C-46, violates s. 2(b) of the *Canadian Charter of Rights and Freedoms,* can s. 163 of the *Criminal Code of Canada* be demonstrably justified under s. 1 of the *Canadian Charter of Rights and Freedoms* as a reasonable limit prescribed by law?
Answer: Yes.

READING QUESTION ON *BUTLER*

1 MacKinnon, as you will see below, approves of this decision. Is there a covert legal moralism of the kind Devlin advocates in Sopinka, J.'s reasoning?

Catharine MacKinnon
Only Words (1993)

MacKinnon defends the court's approach in *Butler* against the approach taken in *Hudnut.*

The pornography issue, far more than the political speech cases, has provided the setting for the definitive development of the absolutist approach to speech. First Amendment absolutism did not begin in obscenity cases, but it is in explaining why obscenity should be protected speech, and how it cannot be distinguished from art and literature, that much of the work of absolutism has been done, taking as its point of departure and arrival the position that whatever is expressive should be constitutionally protected. In pornography, absolutism found, gained, and consolidated its ground and hit its emotional nerve. It began as a dissenting position of intellectual extremists and ended by reducing the regulation of obscenity to window dressing on violence against women.

Concretely, observe that it was the prospect of losing access to pornography that impelled the social and legal development of absolutism as a bottom line for the First Amendment, as well as occasioned bursts of passionate eloquence on behalf of speech per se; if we can't have this, they seem to say, what can we have? During the same twenty-year period of struggle over obscenity standards, the Court was watching more and more pornography as its mass-marketed forms became more and more intrusive and aggressive. Observing this process from its end point of state protection of pornography, I have come to think that the main principle at work here is that, once pornography becomes pervasive, speech will be defined so that men can have their pornography. American obscenity law merely illustrates one adaptation of this principle: some men ineffectually prohibit it while others vaunt it openly as the standard for speech as such.

Consider the picture. The law against pornography was not designed to see harm to women in the first place. It is further weakened as pornography spreads, expanding into new markets (such as video and computers) and more legitimate forums and making abuse of women more and more invisible as abuse, as that abuse becomes more and more visible as sex. So the Court becomes increasingly *unable to tell* what is pornography and what is not, a failing it laments not as a consequence of the saturation of society by pornography, but as a specifically judicial failure, then finally as an impossibility of line-drawing. The stage is thus set for the transformation of pornography into political speech: the excluded and stigmatized "ideas" we love to hate. Obscured is the way this protects what pornography says and ignores what it does, or, alternatively, protects what pornography says as a means of protecting what it does. Thus can a law develop which prohibits restricting a film because it advocates adultery, but does not even notice a film that is made from a rape.

Nothing in the American law of obscenity is designed to perceive the rape, sexual abuse of children, battering, sexual harassment, prostitution, or sexual murder in pornography. This becomes insulting upon encountering obscenity law's search for harm and failure to find any. The law of child pornography, by contrast – based as it is on the assumption that children are harmed by having sex pictures made of them – applies a test developed in areas of speech other than the sexual: if the harm of speech outweighs its value, it can be restricted by properly targeted means. Given the history of the law of pornography of adult women, it is tempting to regard this as a miracle. Child pornography is not considered the speech of a sexually dissident minority, which it is, advocating "ideas" about children and sex, which it does. Perhaps the fact that boys were used in the film in the test case has something to do with it. The ability to see that child pornography is harmful has everything to do with a visceral sense of the inequality in power between children and adults, yet inequality is never mentioned.

Now, in this context of speech and equality concerns, consider again the judicial opinion on the law Andrea Dworkin and I wrote and Indianapolis passed. This law defines the documented harms pornography does as violations of equality rights and makes them actionable as practices of discrimination, of second-class citizenship. This ordinance allows anyone hurt through pornography to prove its role in their abuse, to recover for the deprivation of their civil rights, and to stop it from continuing. Judicially, this was rendered as censorship of ideas.

In *American Booksellers v. Hudnut*, the Court of Appeals for the Seventh Circuit found that this law violated the First Amendment. It began by recognizing that the harm pornography does is real, conceding that the legislative finding of a causal link was judicially adequate: "... we accept the premises of this legislation. Depictions of subordination tend to perpetuate subordination. The subordinate status of women in turn leads to affront and lower pay at work, insult and injury at home, battery and rape on the streets. In the language of the legislature, "pornography is central in creating and maintaining sex as a basis of discrimination."[1] Writing for the panel, Judge Easterbrook got, off and on, that "subordination" is something pornography does, not something it just says, and that its active role had to be proven in each case brought under the ordinance. But he kept losing his mental bearings and referring to pornography as an "idea,"[2] finally concluding that the harm it does "demonstrates the power of pornography as speech."[3] This is like saying that the more a libel destroys a reputation, the greater is its power as speech. To say that the more harm speech does, the more protected it is, is legally wrong, even in this country.

Implicitly applying the political speech model, Judge Easterbrook said that the law restricted the marketplace of ideas, the speech of outcast dissenters – referring presumably to those poor heads of organized crime families making ten billion dollars a year trafficking women. He said the law discriminated on the basis of point of view, establishing an approved view of what could be said and thought about women and sex. He failed to note at this point that the invalidated causes of action included coercion, force, and assault, rather a far cry from saying and thinking. He reminded us of *Sullivan*, whose most famous dictum is that to flourish, debate must be "uninhibited, robust, and wide-open."[4] Behind his First Amendment façade, women were being transformed into ideas, sexual traffic in whom was protected as if it were a discussion, the men uninhibited and robust, the women wide-open.

Judge Easterbrook did not say this law was not a sex discrimination law, but he gave the state interest it therefore served – opposition to sex inequality – no constitutional weight. He did this by treating it as if it were a group defamation law, holding that no amount of harm of discrimination can outweigh the speech interests of bigots, so long as they say something while doing it. Besides, if we restrict this, who knows where it will end. He is sure it will end with "Leda and the Swan." He did not suggest that bestiality statutes also had to go, along with obscenity's restrictions on depictions of sex between humans and animals. Both restrict a disapproved sexuality that, no doubt, contains an element of "mental intermediation."[5] Nothing in *Hudnut* explains why, if pornography is protected speech based on its mental elements, rape and sexual murder, which have mental elements, are not as well.

A dissent in a recent case invalidating sentence enhancements for crimes of bias could have been a dissent here: "The majority rationalizes their conclusion [that the statute violates the First Amendment] by insisting that this statute punishes bigoted thought. Not so. The statute does not impede or punish the right of persons to have bigoted thoughts or to express themselves in a bigoted fashion or otherwise, regarding the race, religion, or other status of a person. It does attempt to limit the effects of bigotry. What the statute does punish is acting upon those thoughts. It punishes the act of [discrimination] not the thought or expression of bigotry."[6]

Perhaps it is the nature of legal inequality that was missed by the Seventh Circuit. Discrimination has always been illegal because it is based on a prohibited motive: "an evil eye and an unequal hand,"[7] what the perpetrator is thinking while doing, what the acts mean. Racial classifications are thought illegal because they "supply a reason to infer antipathy."[8] A showing of discriminatory intent is required under the Fourteenth Amendment. Now we are told that this same motive, this same participation in a context of meaning, this same hatred and bigotry, these same purposes and thoughts, presumably this same intent, *protect* this same activity under the First Amendment. The courts cannot have it both ways, protecting discriminatory activity under the First Amendment on the same ground they make a requirement for its illegality under the Fourteenth. To put it another way, it is the "idea" of discrimination in the perpetrator's mind that courts have required be proven before the acts that effectuate it will be considered discriminatory. Surely, if acts that are otherwise legal, like hiring employees or renting rooms or admitting students, are made illegal under the Constitution by being based on race or sex because of what those who engage in this think about race or sex, acts that are otherwise *illegal*, like coercion, force, and assault, do not become constitutionally protected because they are done with the same thoughts in mind ...

That these tortured consequences result from the lack of an equality context in which to interpret expressive freedoms is clear from the fact that the same issues produced exactly the opposite results in Canada. Canada's new constitution, the *Charter of Rights and Freedoms*, includes an expansive equality guarantee and a serious entrenchment of freedom of expression. The Supreme Court of Canada's first move was to define equality in a meaningful way – one more substantive than formal, directed toward changing unequal social relations rather than monitoring their equal positioning before the law. The United States, by contrast, remains in the grip of what I affectionately call the stupid theory of equality. Inequality here is defined as distinction, as differentiation, indifferent to whether dominant or subordinated groups are hurt or helped. Canada, by contrast, following the argument of the Women's Legal Education and Action Fund (LEAF), repudiated this view in so many words, taking as its touchstone the treatment of historically disadvantaged groups and aiming to alter their status. The positive spin of the Canadian interpretation holds the law to promoting equality, projecting the law into a more equal future, rather than remaining rigidly neutral in ways that either reinforce existing social inequality or prohibit changing it, as the American constitutional perspective has increasingly done in recent years.

The first case to confront expressive guarantees with equality requirements under the new constitution came in the case of James Keegstra, an anti-Semite who taught Holocaust revisionism to school-children in Alberta. Prosecuted and convicted under Canada's hate propaganda provision, Keegstra challenged the statute as a violation of the new freedom of expression guarantee. LEAF intervened to argue that the hate propaganda law promoted equality. We argued that group libel, most of it concededly expression, promotes the disadvantage of unequal groups; that group-based enmity, ill will, intolerance, and prejudice are the attitudinal engines of the exclusion, denigration, and subordination that make up and propel social inequality; that without bigotry, social systems of enforced separation, ghettoization, and apartheid would be unnecessary, impossible, and unthinkable; that stereotyping and stigmatization of historically disadvantaged groups through group hate propaganda shape their social image and reputation, which controls their access to opportunities more powerfully than their individual abilities ever do; and that it is impossible for an individual to receive equality of opportunity when surrounded by an atmosphere of group hate.

We argued that group defamation is a verbal form inequality takes, that just as white supremacy promotes inequality on the basis of race, color, and sometimes ethnic or national origin, anti-Semitism promotes the inequality of Jews on the basis of religion and ethnicity. We argued that group defamation in this sense is not a mere expression of opinion but a practice of discrimination in verbal form, a link in systemic discrimination that keeps target groups in subordinated positions through the promotion of terror, intolerance, degradation, segregation, exclusion, vilification, violence, and genocide. We said that the nature of the practice can be understood and its impact measured from the damage it causes, from immediate psychic wounding to consequent physical aggression. Where advocacy of genocide is included in group defamation, we said an equality approach to such speech would observe that to be liquidated because of the group you belong to is the ultimate inequality.

The Supreme Court of Canada agreed with this approach, a majority upholding the hate propaganda provision, substantially on equality grounds. The Court recognized the provision as a content restriction – content that had to be stopped because of its anti-egalitarian meaning and devastating consequences.[9]

Subsequently, the Winnipeg authorities arrested a whole pornography store and prosecuted the owner, Donald Victor Butler, for obscenity. Butler was convicted but said the obscenity law was an unconstitutional restriction on his Charter-based right of freedom of expression. LEAF argued that if Canada's obscenity statute, substantially different from U.S. obscenity law in prohibiting "undue exploitation of sex, or sex and violence, cruelty, horror, or crime," was interpreted to institutionalize some people's views about women and sex over others, it would be unconstitutional. But if the community standards applied were interpreted to prohibit harm to women as harm to the community, it was constitutional because it promoted sex equality.

The Supreme Court of Canada essentially agreed, upholding the obscenity provision on sex equality grounds.[10] It said that harm to women – which the Court was careful to make "contextually sensitive" and found could include humiliation, degradation, and subordination – *was* harm to society as a whole. The evidence on the harm of pornography was sufficient for a law against it. Violent materials always present this risk of harm, the Court said; explicit sexual materials that are degrading or dehumanizing (but not violent) could also unduly exploit sex under the obscenity provision if the risk of harm was substantial. Harm in this context was defined as "predispos[ing] persons to act in an anti-social manner, as, for example, the physical or mental mistreatment of women by men, or, what is perhaps debatable, the reverse." The unanimous Court noted that "if true equality between male and female persons is to be achieved, we cannot ignore the threat to equality resulting from exposure to audiences of certain types of violent and degrading material." The result rested in part on *Keegstra* but also observed that the harms attendant to the production of pornography situated the problem of pornography differently, such that the appearance of consent by women in such materials could exacerbate its injury. Recognizing that education could be helpful in combating this harm, the Court held that that fact did not make the provision unconstitutional.[11]

Although the Canadians considered the U.S. experience on these issues closely in both cases, the striking absence of a U.S.-style political speech litany suggests that taking equality seriously precludes it, or makes it look like the excuse for enforcing inequality that it has become. The decision did not mention the marketplace of ideas. Maybe in

Canada, people talk to each other, rather than buy and sell each other as ideas. In an equality context, it becomes obvious that those with the most power buy the most speech, and that the marketplace rewards the powerful, whose views then become established as truth. We were not subjected to "Let [Truth] and falsehood grapple; who ever knew Truth put to the worse, in a free and open encounter." Milton had not been around for the success of the Big Lie technique, but this Court had.

Nor did the Canadian Court even consider the "slippery slope," a largely phony scruple impossible to sustain under a contextually sensitive equality rule. With inequality, the problem is not where intervention will end, but when it will ever begin. Equality is the law; if the slippery slope worked, the ineluctable logic of principle would have slid us into equality by now. Also, perhaps, because the Canadian law of equality is moored in the world, and knows the difference between disadvantaged groups and advantaged ones, it is less worried about the misfiring of restrictions against the powerless and more concerned about having nothing to fire against abuses of power by the powerful.

Fundamentally, the Supreme Court of Canada recognized the reality of inequality in the issues before it: this was not big bad state power jumping on poor powerless individual citizen, but a law passed to stand behind a comparatively powerless group in its social fight for equality against socially powerful and exploitative groups. This positioning of forces – which makes the hate propaganda prohibition and the obscenity law of Canada (properly interpreted) into equality laws, although neither was called such by Parliament – made the invocation of a tradition designed to keep government off the backs of people totally inappropriate. The Court also did not say that Parliament had to limit its efforts to stop the harm of inequality by talking to it. What it did was make more space for the unequal to find voice.

Nor did the Canadians intone, with Brandeis and nearly every American court that has ruled on a seriously contested speech issue since, that "[f]ear of serious injury cannot alone justify suppression of free speech ... Men feared witches and burnt women."[12] I have never understood this argument, other than as a way of saying that zealots misidentify the causes of their woes and hurt the wrong people. What has to be added to fear of serious injury to justify doing something about the speech that causes it? *Proof* of serious injury? If we can't restrict it then, when can we? Isn't fear of serious injury the concern behind restricting publication of the dates on which troop ships sail? Is it mere "fear" of injury to children that supports the law against the use of children to make pornography? If that isn't enough, why isn't proof of injury required? "Men feared witches and burnt women." Where is the speech here? Promoting the fear? Nobody tried to suppress tracts against witches. If somebody had, would some women not have been burnt? Or was it the witches' writings? Did they write? So burning their writings is part of the witch-hunt aspect of the fear? The women who are being burned as witches these days are the women in the pornography, and their burning is sex and entertainment and protected as speech. Those who are hunted down, stigmatized, excluded, and unpublished are the women who oppose their burning.

Neither Canadian decision reduces the harm of hate propaganda or pornography to its "offensiveness." When you hear the woman next door screaming as she is bounced off the walls by a man she lives with, are you "offended"? Hate speech and pornography do the same thing: enact the abuse. Women's reactions to the presentation of other women being sexually abused in pornography, and the reactions of Jews living in Skokie to having Nazis march through their town, are routinely trivialized in the United States as "being offended." The position of those with less power is equated with the position of those with more power, as if sexual epithets against straight white men were equivalent to sexual epithets against women, as if breaking the window of a Jewish-owned business in the world after Kristallnacht were just so much breaking glass.

In the cases both of pornography and of the Nazi march in Skokie, it is striking how the so-called speech reenacts the original experience of the abuse, and how its defense as speech does as well. It is not only that both groups, through the so-called speech, are forcibly subjected to the spectacle of their abuse, legally legitimized. Both have their response to it trivialized as "being offended," that response then used to support its speech value, hence its legal protection. Both are also told that what they can do about it is avert their eyes, lock their doors, stay home, stay silent, and hope the assault, and the animus it makes tangible, end when the film or the march ends. This is exactly what perpetrators of rape and child sexual abuse tell their victims and what the Jews in Germany were told by the Nazis (and the rest of the world) in the 1930s. Accept the freedom of your abusers. This best protects you in the end. Let it happen. You are not really being hurt. When sexually abused women are told to let the system work and tolerate the pornography, this is what they are being told. The Jews in Germany, and the Jews in Skokie, were told to let the system work. At least this time around, the Jews of Canada were not, nor were sexually abused women.

The final absence in the Canadian decisions, perhaps the most startling, is the failure to mention any equivalent to the notion that, under the First Amendment, there is no such thing as a false idea. Perhaps under equality law, in some sense there is. When equality is recognized as a constitutional value and mandate, the idea that some people are inferior to others on the basis of group membership is authoritatively rejected as the basis for public policy. This does not mean that ideas to the contrary cannot be debated or expressed. It should mean, however, that social inferiority cannot be imposed through any means, including expressive ones.

Because society is made of language, distinguishing talk about inferiority from verbal imposition of inferiority may be complicated at the edges, but it is clear enough at the center with sexual and racial harassment, pornography, and hate propaganda. At the very least, when equality is taken seriously in expressive settings, such practices are not constitutionally insulated from regulation on the ground that the ideas they express cannot be regarded as false. Attempts to address them would not be prohibited – as they were in rejecting the Indianapolis pornography ordinance, for example – on the ground that, in taking a position in favor of equality, such attempts assume that the idea of human equality is true. The legal equality guarantee has already decided that. There is no requirement that the state remain neutral as between equality and inequality – quite the contrary. Equality is a "compelling state interest" that can already outweigh First Amendment rights in certain settings. In other words, expressive means of practicing inequality can be prohibited.

This is not the place to spell out in detail all the policy implications of such a view. Suffice it to say that those who wish to keep materials that promote inequality from being imposed on students – such as academic books purporting to document women's biological inferiority to men, or arguing that slavery of Africans should return, or that Fourteenth Amendment equality should be repealed, or that reports of rape are routinely fabricated – especially without critical commentary, should not be legally precluded from trying on the grounds that the ideas contained in them cannot be assumed false. No teacher should be forced to teach falsehoods as if they must be considered provisionally true, just because bigots who have managed to get published have made their lies part of a debate. Teachers who wish to teach such materials should be prepared to explain what they are doing to avoid creating a hostile learning environment and to provide all students the equal benefit of an education. Wherever equality is mandated, racial and sexual epithets, vilification, and abuse should be able to be prohibited, unprotected by the First Amendment. The current legal distinction between screaming "go kill that nigger" and advocating the view that African-Americans should be eliminated from parts of the United States needs to be seriously reconsidered, if real equality is ever to be achieved. So, too, the current line separating pornography from hate speech and what is done to make pornography from the materials themselves.

Pornography, under current conditions, *is* largely its own context. Many believe that in settings that encourage critical distance, its show-ing does not damage women as much as it sensitizes viewers to the damage it does to women. My experience, as well as all the information available, makes me think that it is naive to believe that anything other words can do is as powerful as what pornography itself does. At the very least, pornography should never be imposed on a viewer who does not choose – then and there, without pressure of any kind – to be exposed to it. Tom Emerson said a long time ago that imposing what he called "erotic material" on individuals against their will is a form of action that "has all the characteristics of a physical assault."[13] Equality on campuses, in workplaces, everywhere, would be promoted if such assaults were actionable. Why any women should have to attend school in a setting stacked against her equality by the showing of pornography – especially when authoritatively permitted by those who are legally obligated to take her equality seriously – is a question that those who support its showing should have to answer. The answer is not that she should have to wait for the resulting abuse or leave.

Where is all this leading? To a new model for freedom of expression in which the free speech position no longer supports social dominance, as it does now; in which free speech does not most readily protect the activities of Nazis, Klansmen, and pornographers, while doing nothing for their victims, as it does now; in which defending free speech is not speaking on behalf of a large pile of money in the hands of a small group of people, as it is now. In this new model, principle will be defined in terms of specific experiences, the particularity of history, substantively rather than abstractly. It will notice who is being hurt and never forget who they are. The state will have as great a role in providing relief from injury to equality through speech and in giving equal access to speech as it now has in disciplining its power to intervene in that speech that manages to get expressed.

In a society in which equality is a fact, not merely a word, words of racial or sexual assault and humiliation will be nonsense syllables. Sex between people and things, human beings and pieces of paper, real men and unreal women, will be a turn-off. Artifacts of these abuses will reside in a glass case next to the dinosaur skeletons in the Smithsonian. When this day comes, silence will be neither an act of power, as it is now for those who hide behind it, nor an experience of imposed power-lessness, as it is now for those who are submerged in it, but a context of repose into which thought can expand, an invitation that gives speech its shape, an opening to a new conversation.

NOTES

1 *Hudnut*, 771 F.2d at 328–9.
2 "... above all else, the First Amendment means that government has no power to restrict expression because of its message [or] ideas ..." Ibid. at 328.
3 *Hudnut*, 771 F.2d at 329.
4 *Sullivan*, 376 US at 270.
5 *Hudnut*, 771 F.2d at 329.
6 *State v. Mitchell*, 485 NW2d at 820 (Bablitch, J., dissenting).
7 *Yick Wo v. Hopkins*, 118 US 356 (1886).
8 *Personnel Administrator v. Feeney*, 442 US 256 at 272 (1979); *Vance v. Bradley*, 440 US 93 at 97 (1979).
9 *R. v. Keegstra*, [1991] 2 WWR 1 (1990) (Can.).
10 *Butler v. Regina*, [1992] 2 WWR 577 (Can.).
11 Ibid. at 594-7, 601, 609.
12 *Whitney v. California*, 274 US 357 at 376 (1927) (Brandeis, J., concurring).
13 Thomas I. Emerson, *The System of Freedom of Expression* 496 (1970): "A communication of this [erotic] nature, imposed upon a person contrary to his wishes, has all the characteristics of a physical assault" and "can therefore realistically be classified as action." A comparison with his preliminary formulation in *Toward a General Theory of the First Amendment* 91 (1963) suggests that his view on this subject became stronger by his 1970 revisiting of the issue.

1   What does MacKinnon mean by "silencing"? What view of freedom of expression does her argument rest on? What view of
equality does her argument rest on, and what is the relation
between equality and freedom of expression on her theory?

Ronald Dworkin,
"Two Concepts of Liberty" (1991)

Dworkin charges that MacKinnon's approach is undemocratic.

When Isaiah Berlin delivered his famous Inaugural Lecture as Chichele
Professor of Social and Political Theory at Oxford, in 1958, he felt it
necessary to acknowledge that politics did not attract the professional
attention of most serious philosophers in Britain and America. They
thought philosophy had no place in politics and *vice versa;* that political
philosophy could be nothing more than a parade of the theorist's own
preferences and allegiances with no supporting argument of any rigour
or respectability. That gloomy picture is unrecognisable now. Political
philosophy thrives as a mature industry; it dominates many distinguished philosophy departments and attracts a large share of the best
graduate students almost everywhere.

Berlin's lecture, "Two Concepts of Liberty," played an important and
distinctive role in this renaissance. It provoked immediate, continuing,
heated and mainly illuminating controversy. It became, almost at once,
a staple of graduate and undergraduate reading lists, as it still is. Its
scope and erudition, its historical sweep and evident contemporary
force, its sheer interest, made political ideas suddenly seem exciting and
fun. Its main polemical message – that it is fatally dangerous for
philosophers to ignore either the complexity or the power of those ideas
– was both compelling and overdue. But chiefly, or so I think, its
importance lay in the force of its central argument. For though Berlin
began by conceding to the disdaining philosophers that political philosophy could not match logic or the philosophy of language as a theatre
for "radical discoveries" in which "talent for minute analyses is likely

to be rewarded," he continued by analysing subtle distinctions that, as it happens, are even more important now, in the Western democracies at least, than when he first called our attention to them.

I must try to describe two central features of his argument, though in this short note I shall have to leave out much that is important to them. The first is the celebrated distinction described in the lecture's title: between two (closely allied) senses of liberty. Negative liberty (as Berlin came later to restate it) means not being obstructed by others in doing whatever one might wish to do. We count some negative liberties – like the freedom to speak our mind without censorship – as very important, and others – like driving at very fast speeds – as trivial. But they are both instances of negative freedom, and though a state may be justified in imposing speed limits, for example, on grounds of safety and convenience, that is nevertheless an instance of restricting negative liberty. Positive liberty, on the other hand, is the power to control or participate in public decisions, including the decision how far to curtail negative liberty. In an ideal democracy, whatever that is, the people govern themselves. Each is master to the same degree, and positive liberty is secured for all.

In the Inaugural Lecture Berlin described the historical corruption of the idea of positive liberty, a corruption that began in the idea that someone's true liberty lies in control by his rational self rather than his empirical self, that is, in control that aims at securing goals other than those the person himself recognises. Freedom, on that conception, is possible only when people are governed, ruthlessly if necessary, by rulers who know their true, metaphysical, will. Only then are people truly free, albeit against their will. That deeply confused and dangerous, but nevertheless potent, chain of argument had in many parts of the world turned positive liberty into the most terrible tyranny. Of course, Berlin did not mean, by calling attention to this corruption of positive liberty, that negative liberty was an unalloyed blessing, and should be protected in all its forms in all circumstances at all costs. He said, later, that on the contrary the vices of excessive and indiscriminate negative liberty were so evident, particularly in the form of savage economic inequality, that he had not thought it necessary much to describe them.

The second feature of Berlin's argument I have in mind is a theme repeated throughout his writing on political topics. He insists on the complexity of political value, and the fallacy of supposing that all the political virtues that are attractive in themselves can be realised in a single political structure. The ancient Platonic ideal, of some master accommodation of all attractive virtues and goals, combined in institutions satisfying each in the right proportion and sacrificing none, is in Berlin's view, for all its imaginative power and historical influence, only a seductive myth.

One freedom may abort another; [he said, summing up later] one freedom may obstruct or fail to create conditions which make other freedoms, or a larger degree of freedom, or freedom for more persons, possible; positive and negative freedom may collide; the freedom of the individual or the group may not be fully compatible with a full degree of participation in a common life, with its demands for cooperation, solidarity, fraternity. But beyond all these there is an acuter issue: the paramount need to satisfy the claims of other, no less ultimate, values: justice, happiness, love, the realisation of capacities to create new things and experiences and ideas, the discovery of the truth. Nothing is gained by identifying freedom proper, in either of its senses, with these values, or with the conditions of freedom, or by confounding types of freedom with one another.[1]

Berlin's warnings about conflating positive and negative liberty, and liberty itself with other values, seemed to students of political philosophy in the great Western democracies in the 1950s to provide important lessons about authoritarian regimes in other times and places. Though cherished liberties were very much under attack in both American and Britain in that decade, the attack was not grounded in or defended through either form of confusion. The enemies of negative liberty were powerful, but they were also crude and undisguised. Joseph McCarthy and his allies did not rely on a Kantian or Hegelian or Marxist concept of metaphysical selves to justify censorship or blacklists. They distinguished liberty not from itself, but from security; they claimed that too much free speech made us vulnerable to spies and intellectual saboteurs and ultimately to conquest. In both Britain and America, in spite of limited reforms, the state still sought to enforce conventional sexual morality about pornography, contraception, prostitution and homosexuality. Conservatives who defended these invasions of negative liberty appealed not to some higher or different sense of freedom, however, but to values that were plainly distinct from and in conflict with freedom: religion, true morality, and traditional and proper family values. The wars over liberty were fought, or so it seemed, by clearly divided armies. Liberals were for liberty, except for the negative liberty of economic entrepreneurs. Conservatives were for that liberty, but against other forms when these collided with security or their view of decency and morality.

But now the political maps have radically changed and some forms of negative liberty have acquired new opponents. Both in America and Britain, though in different ways, racial and gender conflicts have transformed old alliances and divisions. Speech that expresses racial hatred, or a degrading attitude toward women, or that threatens environmental destruction has come to seem intolerable to many people whose convictions are otherwise traditionally liberal. It is hardly surprising that they should try to reduce the conflict between their old liberal ideals and their new acceptance of censorship by some redefinition of what liberty, properly understood, really is. It is hardly surprising, but the result is dangerous confusion, and Berlin's warnings, framed with different problems in mind, are directly in point.

I shall try to illustrate that point with a single example: a lawsuit arising out of the attempt by certain feminist groups in America to outlaw what they consider a particularly objectionable form of pornography. I select this example not because pornography is more important or dangerous or objectionable than racist invective or other highly distasteful kinds of speech, but because the debate over pornography has been the subject of the fullest and most comprehensive scholarly discussion.

Through the efforts of Catharine MacKinnon and other prominent feminists, Indianapolis in Indiana enacted an anti-pornography ordinance. The ordinance defined pornography as "the graphic sexually explicit subordination of women, whether in pictures or words ...," and it specified, as among pornographic materials falling within that definition, those that present women as enjoying pain or humiliation or rape, or as degraded or tortured or filthy, bruised or bleeding, or in postures of servility or submission or display. It included no exception for literary or artistic value, and opponents claimed that applied literally it would outlaw James Joyce's *Ulysses*, John Cleland's *Memoirs*, various works of D.H. Lawrence, and even Yeat's *Leda and the Swan*. But the groups who sponsored the ordinance were anxious to establish that their objection was not to obscenity or indecency, as such, but to the consequences of a particular kind of pornography, and they presumably thought that an exception for artistic value would undermine that claim.

Publishers and members of the public who claimed a desire to read the banned material arranged a prompt constitutional challenge. The federal district court held that the ordinance was unconstitutional because it violated the First Amendment to the United States Constitution, which guarantees the negative liberty of free speech.[2] The Circuit Court for the Seventh Circuit upheld the district court's decision,[3] and the Supreme Court of the United States declined to review that holding. The Circuit Court's decision, in an opinion by Judge Easterbrook, noticed that the ordinance did not outlaw obscene or indecent material generally but only material reflecting the opinion that women are submissive, or enjoy being dominated, or should be treated as if they did. Easterbrook said that the central point of the First Amendment was exactly to protect speech from content-based regulation of that sort. Censorship may on some occasions be permitted if it aims to prohibit directly dangerous speech – crying fire in a crowded theatre or inciting a crowd to violence, for example – or speech particularly and unnecessarily inconvenient – broadcasting from sound trucks patrolling residential streets at night, for instance. But nothing must be censored because the message it seeks to deliver is a bad one, because it expresses ideas that should not be heard at all.

It is by no means universally agreed that censorship should never be based on content. The British Race Relations Act, for example, forbids speech of racial hatred, not only when it is likely to lead to violence, but generally, on the grounds that members of minority races should be protected from racial insults. In America, however, it is a fixed principle of constitutional law that regulation is unconstitutional unless some compelling necessity, not just official or majority disapproval of the message, requires it. Pornography is often grotesquely offensive; it is insulting, not only to women but to men as well. But we cannot consider that a sufficient reason for banning it without destroying the principle that the speech we hate is as much entitled to protection as any other. The essence of negative liberty is freedom to offend, and that applies to the tawdry as well as the heroic.

Lawyers who defend the Indianapolis ordinance argue that society does have a further justification for outlawing pornography: that it causes great harm as well as offence to women. But their arguments mix together claims about different types of kinds of harm, and it is necessary to distinguish these. They argue, first, that some forms of pornography significantly increase the danger that women will be raped or physically assaulted. If that were true, and the danger were clear and present, then it would indeed justify censorship of those forms, unless less stringent methods of control, such as restricting pornographer's audience, would be feasible, appropriate and effective. In fact, however, though there is some evidence that exposure to pornography weakens people's critical attitudes toward sexual violence, there is no persuasive evidence that it causes more actual incidents of assault. The Seventh Circuit cited a variety of studies (including that of the Williams Commission in Britain in 1979) all of which concluded, the Court said, "that it is not possible to demonstrate a direct link between obscenity and rape ..."[4] A recent and guarded report on a year's research in Britain said: "The evidence does not point to pornography as a cause of deviant sexual orientation in offenders. Rather, it seems to be used as part of that deviant sexual orientation."[5]

Some feminist groups argue, however, that pornography causes not just physical violence but a more general and endemic subordination of women. In that way, they say, pornography makes for inequality. But even if it could be shown, as a matter of causal connection, that pornography is in part responsible for the economic structure in which few women attain top jobs or equal pay for the same work, that would not justify censorship under the Constitution. It would plainly be unconstitutional to ban speech directly *advocating* that women occupy inferior roles, or none at all, in commerce and the professions, even if that speech fell on willing male ears and achieved its goals. So it cannot be a reason for banning pornography that it contributes to an unequal economic or social structure, even if we think that it does.

But the most imaginative feminist literature for censorship makes a further and different argument: that negative liberty for pornographers conflicts not just with equality but with positive liberty as well, because pornography leads to women's *political* as well as economic or social subordination. Of course pornography does not take the vote from women, or somehow make their votes count less. But it produces a climate, according to this argument, in which women cannot have genuine political power or authority because they are perceived and understood unauthentically, made over by male fantasy into people very different, and of much less consequence, than the people they really are. Consider, for example, these remarks from the work of the principal sponsor of the Indianapolis ordinance. "[Pornography] institutionalizes the sexuality of male supremacy, fusing the eroticization of dominance and submission with the social construction of male and female ... Men treat women as who they see women as being. Pornography constructs who that is. Men's power over women means that the way men see women defines who women can be."

Pornography, on this view, denies the positive liberty of women; it denies them the right to be their own masters by recreating them, for politics and society, in the shapes of male fantasy. That is a powerful argument, even in constitutional terms, because it asserts a conflict not just between liberty and equality but within liberty itself, that is, a conflict that cannot be resolved simply on the ground that liberty must be sovereign. What shall we make of the argument understood that way? We must notice, first, that it remains a causal argument. It claims not that pornography is a consequence or symptom or symbol of how the identity of women has been reconstructed by men, but an important cause or vehicle of that reconstruction.

That seems strikingly implausible. Sadistic pornography is revolting, but it is not in any general circulation, except for its milder, soft-porn manifestations. It seems unlikely that it has remotely the influence over how women's sexuality or character or talents are conceived by men, and indeed by women, that commercial advertising and soap operas have. Television and other parts of popular culture use sex to sell everything, and they show women as experts in domestic detail and unreasoned intuition and nothing else. The images they create are subtle and ubiquitous, and it would not be surprising to learn, through whatever research might establish this, that they do indeed do great damage to the way women are understood and allowed to be influential in politics. Sadistic pornography, though much more offensive and disturbing, is greatly overshadowed by these dismal cultural influences as a causal force.

Judge Easterbrook's opinion for the Seventh Circuit assumed *arguendo*, however, that pornography did have the consequences the defenders of the ordinance claimed. He said that nevertheless the argument failed because the point of free speech is precisely to allow ideas to have whatever consequences follows from their dissemination, including undesirable consequences for positive liberty. "Under the First Amendment," he said, "the government must leave to the people the evaluation of ideas. Bald or subtle, an idea is as powerful as the audience allows it to be ... [The assumed result] simply demonstrates the power of pornography as speech. All of these unhappy effects depend on mental intermediation."

That is right as a matter of American constitutional law. The Ku Klux Klan and the American Nazi Party are allowed to propagate their ideas in America, and the British Race Relations Act, so far as it forbids abstract speech of racial hatred, would be unconstitutional there. But does the American attitude represent the kind of Platonic absolutism Berlin warned against? No, because there is an important difference between the idea he thinks absurd, that all ideals attractive in themselves can be perfectly reconciled within a single utopian political order, and the different idea he thought essential, that we must, as individuals and nations, choose among possible combinations of ideals a coherent, even though inevitably and regrettably limited, set of these to define our own individual or national way of life. Freedom of speech, conceived and protected as a fundamental negative liberty, is the core of the choice modern democracies have made, a choice we must now honour in finding our own ways to combat the shaming inequalities women still suffer.

This reply depends, however, on seeing the alleged conflict within liberty as a conflict between the negative and positive senses of that virtue. We must consider yet another argument which, if successful, could not be met in the same way, because it claims that pornography presents a conflict within the negative liberty of speech itself. Berlin said that the character, at least, of negative liberty was reasonably clear, that although excessive claims of negative liberty were dangerous, they could at least always be seen for what they were. But the argument I have in mind, which has been offered, among others, by Frank Michelman of the Harvard Law School, expands the idea of the negative liberty in an unanticipated way. He argues that some speech, including pornography, may be itself "silencing," so that its effect is to prevent other people from exercising their negative freedom to speak.

Of course it is fully recognised in First Amendment jurisprudence that some speech is silencing in that way. Government must indeed balance negative liberties when it prevents heckling or other demonstrative speech designed to stop others from speaking or being heard. But Michelman has something different in mind. He says that a woman's speech may be silenced not just by noise intended to drown her out but also by argument and image that change her audience's perceptions of her character, needs, desires and standing, and also, perhaps, change her own sense of who she is and what she wants. Speech with that consequence silences her, Michelman supposes, by making it impossible for her effectively to contribute to the process Judge Easterbrook said the First Amendment protected, the process through which ideas battle for the public's favour. "[I]t is a highly plausible claim," Michelman writes, "[that] pornography [is] a cause of women's subordination and silencing ... It is a fair and obvious question why our society's openness to challenge does not need protection against repressive private as well as public action."[6]

He argues that if our commitment to negative freedom of speech is consequentialist – if we want free speech in order to have a society in which no idea is barred from entry – then we must censor some ideas in order to make entry possible for other ones. He protests that the distinction American constitutional law makes, between the suppression of ideas by the effect of public criminal law and by the consequences of private speech, is arbitrary, and that a sound concern for openness would be equally concerned about both forms of control. But the distinction the law makes is not between public and private power, as such, but between negative liberty and other virtues, including positive liberty. It would indeed be contradictory for a constitution to prohibit official censorship but also to protect the right of private citizens physically to prevent other citizens from publishing or broadcasting specified ideas. That would allow private citizens to violate the negative liberty of other citizens by preventing them from saying what they wish. But there is no contradiction in insisting that every idea must be allowed to be heard, even those whose consequence is that other ideas will be misunderstood, or given little consideration, or even not be spoken at all because those who might speak them are not in control of their own public identities and therefore cannot be understood as they wish to be. These are very bad consequences, and they must be resisted by whatever means our constitution permits. But they are not the same thing as depriving others of their negative liberty to speak, and the distinction, as Berlin insisted, is very far from arbitrary or inconsequential.

It is of course understandable why Michelman and others should want to expand the idea of negative liberty in the way they try to do. Only by characterising certain ideas as themselves "silencing" ideas, only by supposing that censoring pornography is the same thing as stopping people from drowning out other speakers, can they hope to justify censorship within the constitutional scheme that assigns a pre-eminent place to free speech. But the assimilation is nevertheless a confusion, exactly the kind of confusion Berlin warned against in his original lecture, because it obscures the true political choice that must be made. I return to Berlin's lecture, which put the point with that striking combination of clarity and sweep I have been celebrating. "I should be guilt-stricken, and rightly so, if I were not, in some circumstances, ready to make [some] sacrifice [of freedom]. But a sacrifice is not an increase in what is being sacrificed, namely freedom, however great the moral need or the compensation for it. Everything is what it is: liberty is liberty, not equality or fairness or justice or culture, or human happiness or a quiet conscience."

NOTES

1 Berlin, *Four Essays on Liberty*, Oxford Paperbacks, 1969, p. lvi.
2 *American Booksellers Association, Inc et al. v. William Hudnut, III, Mayor, City of Indianapolis et al.,* 598 F. Supp. 1316 (S.D. Ind. 1984).
3 771 F2d 323 (US Court Appeals, Seventh Circuit).
4 That court, in a confused passage, said that it nevertheless accepted "the premises of this legislation, which included the claims about a causal connection with sexual violence. But it seemed to mean that it was accepting the rather different causal claim considered in the next paragraph, about subordination. In any case, it said that it accepted those premises only arguendo, since it thought it had no authority to reject decisions of Indianapolis based on its interpretation of empirical evidence.
5 See *Daily Telegraph,* December 23, 1990.
6 Frank Michelman, "Conceptions of Democracy in American Constitutional Argument: The Case of Pornography Regulation," 57 *Tennessee Law Review* 291, 1989, pp. 303–4.

READING QUESTIONS ON DWORKIN

1 Should the law in a society marked by pervasive inequalities be the same as it would in a society of equals? Can you think of any exceptions to this claim?
2 Can MacKinnon's argument be restated so that it passes the test for an acceptable moral argument that Dworkin outlines in his response to Devlin?
3 Does Dworkin tacitly rely on a positivistic conception of law in this essay?

Brenda Cossman
Bad Attitude/s on Trial: Pornography, Feminism, and the **Butler** *Decision* **(1997)**

Cossman argues that *Butler* serves a conservative agenda, something revealed by a careful analysis of its text. Her argument, though, is that it could not help but serve such an agenda because of the distinction between good and bad sex which it presupposes.

CHAPTER 3: FEMINIST FASHION OR MORALITY IN DRAG? THE SEXUAL SUBTEXT OF THE *BUTLER* DECISION

In *R. v. Butler* (1992), the Supreme Court of Canada upheld the constitutionality of the criminal prohibition of obscenity under section 163 of the *Criminal Code* of Canada (RSC 1985, c. c–46). The Court held that although this provision violated free speech as guaranteed by section 2 of the *Canadian Charter of Rights and Freedoms*, it was a reasonable limit under section 1. In so doing, the Supreme Court tries to tell us that the obscenity laws are no longer concerned with corrupting morals, or with courts as the guardians of public morality. Rather, in the Court's view, the obscenity law is justifiable in its objective of preventing harm, particularly harm towards women, and in promoting the equality and dignity of women.

This has become the official story of *Butler* – it is the story that the Court tries to tell within the text of the decision, and it is the story that feminists who support the obscenity provisions have told before, during, and after the decision (McAllister 1992–3; Busby 1994; Landsberg 1992). But there is another story to be told about the *Butler* decision. *Butler* is also a decision about sex: it is a decision about the role and status of sex, sexuality, and the representation of sexual practices in our society. When we scratch beneath the surface, we find a conservative sexual morality that sees sex as bad, physical, shameful, dangerous, base, guilty until proved innocent, and redeemable only if it transcends its base nature. It is a sexual subtext informed by the basic assumptions that have traditionally informed the dominant ideological discourses of sexuality in Western society: sexual negativity <sex is bad>, sexual essentialism <sex is biological>, sexual monism <there is one way to have sex>, and sexual hierarchy <some sex is better than others>.

In this chapter, I will deconstruct the *Butler* decision in an effort to reveal this sexual subtext. A textual analysis of the decision will reveal the extent to which the discourse of the decision is informed by the same conservative sexual morality that has traditionally framed obscenity law in Canada, with its problematic assumptions about the nature of sex and sexuality. The chapter will argue that, contrary to the claims of anti-pornography feminists, the most significant change in the law represented by the *Butler* decision is one of language alone. Now the law is dressed up in feminist discourse, that of preventing harm towards women, of equality and dignity. The test for obscenity as reviewed and synthesized by the Supreme Court of Canada in *Butler* simply provides a new discourse for what is in fact a very old objective – the legal regulation of sexual morality, and the legal repression of sexual representation. The *Butler* decision and its discourse of harm against women is really just sexual morality in drag.

Further, I will argue that this sexual subtext is essential in understanding how *Butler* has set the discursive stage for the subsequent judicial applications of the *Butler* test, in which gay and lesbian sexual representations have been held to be obscene. The first two obscenity cases to have reached the courts since *Butler* were both against Glad Day Bookshop – a gay and lesbian bookstore in Toronto. While prosecutions have since been brought against heterosexual pornography as well, the particular way in which this law has been used against gay and lesbian sexual representations should alert us to this discursive drag. Yet, feminists who support the *Butler* decision continue to argue that this targeting of gay and lesbian sexual representations constitutes a misapplication of the *Butler* test (Busby 1994, 185). Contrary to these arguments, I will argue that the underlying conservative sexual morality of *Butler* has set the discursive framework for this targeting. The sexual subtext and its good sex / bad sex distinction is particularly dangerous in the context of gay and lesbian sexual representations. The heterosexist assumptions informing this sexual morality operate to locate these representations on the bad side of the dichotomy, and thus pave the road for a particular judicial determination of obscenity.

The Butler *Decision: Sex and the Supreme Court*

The majority decision of the Supreme Court of Canada in the *Butler* case was written by Mr. Justice Sopinka.[1] The decision is divided into two parts. In the first part, the court reviews and clarifies the law of obscenity. In the second part, the court then examines whether this law of obscenity is constitutional, that is, whether it violates the right to freedom of expression guarantees of the *Charter*, and if so, whether it is a reasonable limit on that right. In reviewing the text of both parts of the decision, this section will challenge the dominant representation of the *Butler* decision, by illustrating the sexual subtext of the decision – a sexual subtext informed by the same assumptions of sexual morality that prevailed before the *Butler* decision.

The Law of Obscenity

In the first part of the decision, the Court reviews and clarifies the law of obscenity as set out in s. 163 of the Criminal Code. Obscenity is defined in subsection 163(8) as "any publication a dominant characteristic of which is the undue exploitation of sex, or of sex and any one or more of the following subjects, namely, crime, horror, cruelty and violence." The question of what constitutes the "undue exploitation of sex" has been the subject of considerable judicial analysis. Sopinka J thus begins by reviewing the various tests that have emerged to determine whether the exploitation of sex is undue.

Community Standards. The first and most important test developed by the courts to determine when the exploitation of sex is undue is the community standards of tolerance. The Court begins by quoting a passage from *R. v. Close* (1948), which was first adopted by the Supreme Court in *R. v. Brodie* (1962) and has been cited by the Supreme Court of Canada in its obscenity case law ever since: "There does exist in any community at all times – however the standard may vary from time to time – a general instinctive sense of what is decent and what is indecent, of what is clean and what is dirty" (as cited in *Butler* 1992, 464). Within this passage, which has set the discursive framework within which the Supreme Court of Canada has repeatedly interpreted the undue exploitation of sex, obscenity is cast in the language of indecency and dirt. Not all sexual representations are obscene; only indecent or dirty sexual representations are obscene.[2] Within this framework, there is a distinction made between good and bad sex – a binary opposition between clean and dirty, decent and indecent. Bad sex is dirty sex. There is no positive theory of sexual expression that tells us what makes sex good. The best the courts have been able to do is establish a test of some generality to defer to community standards – that is, to allow "the community" to draw the lines between clean and dirty sex.

Sopinka, J. further observed that this community standard has been found to be a national standard; that expert evidence is not required to establish the community standard, and that the community standard may change over time (*Butler* 1992, 465). Finally, the community-standards test is not based on taste, but tolerance, and the measure of tolerance is not what Canadians would themselves tolerate, but "what they would tolerate other Canadians being exposed to" (ibid., 465–6). It attempts to escape the subjective nature of individual taste by directing attention away from "what Canadians think is right for themselves" to the ostensibly broader standard of "what Canadians would not abide other Canadians seeing because it would be beyond the contemporary Canadian standard of tolerance to allow them to see it[3] (*Towne Cinema* 1985, as cited in *Butler* 1992, 465–6).

According to this test, individual Canadians may have different tastes, but we all subscribe to the same standard of tolerance. Although this standard of tolerance may change over time, at any one moment it is monolithic. In other words, at any moment in time, there is in the eyes of all Canadians a clear and singular distinction between what we will tolerate others seeing and what we will not – between what is clean (good sex) and what is dirty (bad sex) – even though this may not correspond to each of our own personal tastes of good sex and bad sex. And the obviousness of this distinction is underscored by the fact that no expert evidence is required to establish it. The line between good sex and bad sex is an "instinctive" matter – a matter of common sense for a judge who will, presumably, simply recognize it when he sees it.

Degradation and Dehumanization. The Court examines a second and more recent test for determining whether the exploitation of sex is undue. This test emerged in the 1980s, as anti-pornography feminism began to shape the discourse within which pornography was debated, and was first endorsed by the Supreme Court of Canada in *R. v. Towne Cinema* (*Towne Cinema* 1985, 202–3). According to this test, materials that "may be said to exploit sex in a degrading or dehumanizing manner will ... fail the community standards test" (*Butler* 1992, 466). In elaborating on the meaning of this test, the Court tells us that it means materials that harm women: "Among other things, degrading or dehumanizing materials place women (and sometimes men) in positions of subordination, servile submission or humiliation. They run against the principles of equality and dignity" (ibid., 466). According to this approach, material that is degrading and dehumanizing fails the community-standards test, "not because it offends morals," but because these materials are "perceived by public opinion to be harmful to society, particularly to women" (ibid., 467). The Court notes that although "this perception is not susceptible to exact proof," there is nevertheless a body of literature that supports the view that these materials are harmful to women.[4]

In this passage, the Court has begun its attempt to shift the objective of obscenity law from the legal regulation of morality to the legal regulation of material that is harmful to women. It emphasizes that material is obscene not because it offends morals, but because it is harmful to women. The shift in the discourse used to articulate and justify the obscenity provisions obscures the extent to which, as Lise Gotell has argued in chapter 2, the feminist discourse of harm does represent a moral claim. Moreover, this effort to shift the discourse from morality to harm has not displaced the underlying conservative sexual morality that has informed the law before *Butler*. Rather, this sexual morality – its opposition between good and bad sex and its strictly negative theory of sexual expression – continues to inform the Court's approach. According to this degrading and dehumanizing test, any sexual representation involving aspects of dominance is bad sex. But this test does not tell us what is good about sex, or what good sex is. By implication, good sex must be the opposite of bad sex. If bad sex is sex that places any of its subjects "in positions of subordination, servile submission or humiliation," then good sex must be sex that does not place its subjects in such positions. Good sex must be what bad sex is not.

In this good sex/bad sex distinction, the Court tells us that consent is not necessarily determinative. "Consent cannot save materials that otherwise contain degrading or dehumanizing scenes. Sometimes the very appearance of consent makes the depicted acts even more degrading or dehumanizing" (*Butler* 1992, 466–7). Again, the Court does not tell us what good sex is, but, simply, what it is not. Good sex is not necessarily sex with consent. Sex with consent can be really bad sex; in fact, it can make bad sex even worse. There is no positive theory of what makes sex good; only the further articulation of sex that might be bad. The good sex/bad sex distinction continues to appear in even more troubling forms. It is seen in the passage cited from Madam Justice Wilson, in *Towne Cinema*: "the public has concluded that exposure to material which degrades the human dimensions of life to a subhuman or merely physical dimension and thereby contributes to a process of moral desensitization must be harmful in some way" (*Towne Cinema* 1985, 217–18, as quoted in *Butler* 1992, 468). We see in this passage from Wilson, J. as affirmed by Sopinka, J., a particular vision of sex and sexual representation. The merely physical dimension of sex is subhuman. The opposition of good and bad sex reappears in a somewhat different guise. Bad sex is subhuman sex. Bad sex is sex that emphasizes the merely physical dimension of sex.

We begin to see here the underlying binary opposition. It is the distinction between mind and body, between the intellectual and physical, between the emotional and sensual, that has long informed

Western thought.[5] In this opposition, the body, the physical, the sensual, are seen as base, as bad, in need of control and, ultimately, transcendence. Sex is physical, it is about the body and the sensual pleasures of the body. Being of the body, it is natural, essential, and unchanging[6] (Rubin 1989, 275). And, being of the body, it is, by reference to the mind/body opposition, bad. This conflation of sex with the physical operates to sustain what Gayle Rubin describes as sex negativity, that is, the idea deeply rooted in Western culture that sex is "a dangerous, destructive, negative force" (ibid., 278; Weeks 1986). But sex is saved from complete damnation by another opposition. Good sex, then, is sex that is not only physical; it is not only sensual. Good sex must transcend the very nature of sex as physical pleasure. Good sex, then, must be sex with more, it must appeal to the other side of the opposition, and thus be part of the mind, the intellect, the soul.

The interaction between these two oppositions, while saving sex from itself, operates to destabilize the underlying assumptions about sex, and to constitute sex and sexuality as a highly contradictory category. The good sex/bad sex opposition, for example, brings into question the assumption of sex negativity <that sex is always bad>, as well as that of sexual essentialism <that sex is physical, natural, and unchanging>. If sex is, by definition, bad, how can it be made good? If sex is of the body, how can it be made not of the body? And if sex is unchanging, how can it change? The good sex/bad sex opposition introduces all of these possibilities – possibilities that sit awkwardly with the underlying assumptions about the nature of sex. Yet, these assumptions are never completely undermined. Sex continues to be presumed to be bad, unless it can be made good.[7] Sex continues to be of the body, unless it can be made to be of the mind. And sex continues to be natural and unchanging, unless it is changed <that is, made good and of the mind>. According to the good sex/bad sex distinction, sex can now become that which, by definition, it is not. Sex can now become more than sex.

Internal Necessities/Artistic Defence. The theme of "sex with more" is continued in the third and final test reviewed by the Court. Sopinka, J. begins by quoting the internal-necessities test as set out in *Brodie*: "What I think is aimed at is excessive emphasis on the theme for a base purpose. But I do not think that there is undue exploitation if there is no more emphasis on the theme than is required in the serious treatment of the theme of a novel with honesty and uprightness" (*Brodie* 1962, 181, as quoted in *Butler* 1992, 468). The Court in *Brodie*, in evaluating the work in question – D.H. Lawrence's *Lady Chatterley's Lover* – held: "It has none of the characteristics that are often described in judgments dealing with obscenity – dirt for dirt's sake, the leer of the sensualist, depravity of the mind of an author with an obsession for dirt, pornography, an appeal to a prurient interest etc. The section recognizes that the serious-minded author must have freedom in the protection of work of genuine artistic and literary merit and the quality of the work must have real relevance in determining not only a dominant characteristic but also whether there is undue exploitation" (*Brodie* 1962, 181 quoted in *Butler* 1992, 468). According to the Court, this artistic defence has been considered to be the last step in determining whether the exploitation of sex is undue. If sexual material is "required for the serious treatment of a theme," then it will not be held to be "undue." "[T]he internal necessities test ... has been interpreted to assess whether the exploitation of sex has a justifiable role in advancing the plot or the theme, and in considering the work as a whole, does not merely represent 'dirt for dirt's sake' but has a legitimate role when measured by the internal necessities of the work itself" (*Butler* 1992, 469). According to this test, the representation of sex in and of itself constitutes "dirt for dirt's sake."[8] We again see the view that sex is dirt – it is dirty, it is bad. Within this vision, art cannot be sex for sex's sake. By definition, sex is not art. Sex is not a legitimate focus for art. It can at most be part of the larger artistic purpose, but sexuality in and of itself is not art. Within the courts' view, this is one area of human activity (or subhuman activity) that is inappropriate for artistic portrayal.

Art, like good sex, is defined in relation to the mind/body opposition. Art is that which appeals to more than our physical nature. It is, by definition, that which appeals to our higher dimensions – to our intellectual, emotional or spiritual aspirations (Nead 1993a, 145; 1993b, 281–2). Accordingly, only sex with more, sex that appeals to the other side of the mind/body distinction – that is, sex that transcends its physical nature by appealing to the intellect, the emotions, the soul – can become good sex and, thus, be the subject of art. In other words, only sex that is not sex can be a legitimate focus for art.[9]

Relationship between the Tests. Sopinka, J. then attempts to clarify the relationship between these tests, which he acknowledges has been unclear in the case law. He begins by dividing pornography into three categories: "(1) explicit sex with violence (2) explicit sex without violence but which subjects people to treatment that is degrading or dehumanizing and (3) explicit sex without violence that is neither degrading nor dehumanizing" (*Butler* 1992, 470). The Court notes that there is some disagreement in society as to which materials would constitute the undue exploitation of sex. Some would argue that all three categories should be prohibited; others would argue that none of these categories should be prohibited. Sopinka, J. further observes that this is not an issue "that is susceptible to proof in the traditional way" (ibid.). In order to avoid these determinations being made according to the subjective opinions of individual judges, there must be a "norm that will serve as an arbiter in determining what amounts to an undue exploitation of sex. That arbiter is the community as a whole" (ibid.). According to the community-standards test, the courts must decide what "the community would tolerate others being exposed to on the basis of the degree of harm that may flow from such exposure" (ibid.). "Harm in this context means that it predisposes persons to act in an antisocial manner as, for example, the physical or mental mistreatment of women by men, or what is perhaps debatable, the reverse. Antisocial conduct for this purpose is conduct which society formally recognizes as incompatible with its proper functioning" (ibid. 470–1). The com-munity standards test continues to play a central role in the *Butler* test for obscenity, although it is now more carefully articulated in the discourse of harm, avoiding any obvious references to morality. Under the revised test, the guideline of community standards is intended to allow courts to categorize pornography into one of the three discrete categories, according to an objective legal norm. This categorization approach is based on the assumption that the meaning of pornography can be objectively established. We can begin to see in this test the Court's literalist approach to representation. Like the approach of anti-pornography feminism discussed in the previous chapter, in the Court's view, the meaning of sexual images can be determined in isolation from the context of these images; meaning is thus separated from context.

The Court then returns to the three categories of pornography. In Sopinka, J.'s view, the first category <sex with violence> is explicitly mentioned within s. 163(8) and will almost always constitute the undue exploitation of sex. The second category <sex without violence, but that is degrading or dehumanizing> may be undue exploitation of sex if the risk of harm is substantial. The third category <sex without violence, and that is not degrading or dehumanizing> is generally tolerated, and will not, with the exception of the involvement of children, constitute undue exploitation of sex. The Court then turns to the question of the internal-necessities test, and how it fits into this new scheme. Sopinka, J. states that the artistic defence – that is, whether the undue exploitation of sex is the main object of the work, or whether the portrayal of sex is essential to a wider artistic, literary, or other similar purpose – remains the last step in determining if the material is obscene. "The portrayal of sex must then be viewed in context to determine whether that is the dominant theme of the work as a whole. Put another way, is undue exploitation of sex the main object of the work or is this portrayal of sex essential to a wider artistic, literary, or other similar purpose" (*Butler* 1992, 471). The court must determine whether the community would tolerate the sexually explicit materials when seen within the broader context of the work as a whole.

According to this test, not only can pornography be objectively and unequivocally classified into one of three discrete categories, but this categorization becomes determinative as to whether the material will be considered to be obscene. This categorization further underscores the absence of a positive theory of sex and sexual expression in *Butler*. The very definition of good sex – the third category – is framed in purely negative terms. Good sex does *not* involve violence, it does *not* involve children, it is *not* degrading or dehumanizing, and it does *not* create a risk of harm. The Court does not tell us what makes sex good; it only tells us what makes sex bad. Good sex, then, is defined only in opposition to what it is not: bad sex. Within this categorization of pornography, the major contested site of sexual representation is degrading and dehumanizing sex.[10] The courts must determine whether particular sexual representations are degrading and dehumanizing, and if so, whether these degrading and dehumanizing representations are likely to cause harm. This is the dividing line between good and bad sex. Drawing the line between good and bad sex continues to be the job of the community-standards test. Notwithstanding the repeated claims to the contrary, this determination can only be made by reference to an underlying sexual morality. The very exercise of drawing a line between good sex and bad sex presumes an underlying conservative sexual morality in which sex is divided between good and bad, and in which there is a hierarchy of sexual practices.

The use of a community standard in this exercise further presumes an underlying sexual morality in which sex and sexual practices are, or should be, essential and monolithic. It continues to assume that there is a national standard that can judge which sexual practices are acceptable and which are not; a national standard that presumes that there is, or should be, a monolithic view of good and bad sex. Not only is sex simply of the body, but this biological imperative is such that sex always and only ever takes one form. As Gayle Rubin has argued, "sexuality is supposed to conform to a single standard. One of the most tenacious ideas about sex is that there is one best way to do it, and that everyone should do it that way" (Rubin 1989, 283). These assumptions of sexual essentialism and sexual monism – of a single and essential nature of sex, any deviation from which is condemned as "unnatural," and thus bad – continue to operate, barely beneath the surface of the *Butler* test.

Finally, by simply incorporating the artistic defence as the last step in determining whether material is obscene, the Supreme Court has reinscribed the underlying oppositions of sex and art, of good and bad sex, of mind and body, that have long informed the internal-necessities test. Indeed, in articulating the new relationship between these various tests, the Supreme Court can be seen to have rearticulated the sexual subtext, and its underlying oppositions, that has long informed each of these tests. Sex remains a highly contradictory category. Sex is of the body, it is physical, not mental, it is sensual not intellectual, it is pleasure, not pursuit. Sex, being of the body, is bad unless it can be made good, by transcending the body and its physical pleasures. Sex can only be made good by transcending its very nature. Good sex is discursively constituted as a contradictory category – it is sex (which is of the body) that has been made of the mind: it is sex that is not sex. According to the test set out in *Butler*, drawing the line between good sex and bad sex continues to be a determination made by reference to this underlying sexual morality.

The Constitutionality of Obscenity

In the second part of the decision, the Court examines whether s. 163 violates the right to freedom of expression guaranteed by the *Charter*. The Court's discussion of the constitutionality of obscenity is divided into two parts, which will be examined in turn: (1) whether the law violates the right to freedom of expression as guaranteed by s. 2(b) of the *Charter*, and (2) if so, whether the violation is a reasonable limit on the right, as contemplated by section 1 of the *Charter*. In upholding the law from the constitutional challenge, the Court tells us, over and over again, that the objective of the obscenity law is preventing harm, particularly harm towards women. At the same time, in taking a deeper look at why the criminalization of sexual expression is justifiable, the Court continues to expose its views on the value of sex, sexuality, and sexual expression. As I will attempt to illustrate, beneath the official story of preventing harm and promoting equality is the same sexual subtext as found in the first part of the decision, and the same sexual morality that informed the law of obscenity before *Butler*.

Sexual Representation as Expression. The Court first considers whether s. 163 violates freedom of expression as guaranteed by section 2(b) of the *Charter*. Sopinka, J. rejected the argument made by the government that physical activity, such as sexual activity, could not be considered expression. In the Court's view, the fact that the subject matter of the materials was "clearly physical" did not mean that the materials did not "convey or attempt to convey meaning" (*Butler* 1992, 472). In previous decisions, the Supreme Court of Canada has consistently adopted an expansive approach to the protection provided by s. 2(b), holding that the content or meaning cannot exclude the activities or statements from the scope of protection accorded by s. 2(b), no matter how offensive those activities or statements may be to the Court.[11] "Meaning sought to be expressed need not be 'redeeming' in the eyes of the court to merit the protection of s. 2(b) whose purpose is to ensure that thoughts and feelings may be conveyed freely in non-violent ways without fear of censure" (ibid., 473). Sopinka, J. held that both the purpose and effect of s. 163 was to restrict "the communication of certain types of materials based on their content" (ibid.). As a result, the law prohibited expressive activity, and violated s. 2(b) of the Charter.

While the Court rejected the view that "purely physical activity does not convey meaning," implicit in the Court's language is the view that sex constitutes purely physical activity.[12] It is of, and only of, the body. At the same time, however, the Court recognizes that the portrayal of this physical activity "conveys ideas, opinions, or feeling" (*Butler* 1992, 472). For example, the Court notes that the portrayal of this physical activity involves the production of meaning by film-makers: "in creating a film, regardless of its content, the maker of the film is consciously choosing the particular images which together constitute the film. In choosing his or her images, the creator of the film is attempting to convey some meaning" (ibid., 474). In the Court's view, although sex is purely physical, sexual representations are not. Rather, the process of representation necessarily involves the other side of the mind/body distinction, and thus constitutes expression, regardless of the content of that expression.

Obscenity as a Reasonable Limit. The Court then considered whether this violation of s. 2(b) by s. 163 of the *Criminal Code* is a reasonable limit within the meaning of section 1 of the *Charter*. The discussion proceeds along the lines of the well-established *Oakes* test, which requires that there be an objective that is sufficiently pressing and substantial to justify the violation of the *Charter* right, and that the violation of the right be proportional to the objective.[13] In addressing the question of objective, Sopinka, J. observed that, historically, the objective of obscenity legislation was the prohibition of "immoral influences" and the imposition of a "standard of public and sexual morality" (*Butler* 1992, 476). In the Court's view, this objective is no longer sustainable. "The prevention of 'dirt for dirt's sake' is not a legitimate objective which would justify the violation of one of the most fundamental freedoms enshrined in the *Charter*" (ibid.). The Court does not say that Parliament cannot legislate on the basis of morality. However, it does say that the objective of s. 163 "is not moral disapprobation but the avoidance of harm to society" (ibid., 477). The Court cited with approval the description of the harm of pornography in the Report of the Standing Committee on Justice and Legal Affairs (1978, 18:4). "The clear and unquestionable danger of this type of material is that it reinforces some unhealthy tendencies in Canadian society. The effect of this type of material is to reinforce male-female stereotypes to the detriment of both sexes. It attempts to make degradation, humiliation, victimization and violence in human relationships appear normal and acceptable. A society which holds that egalitarian, non-violence, consensualism and mutuality are basic to any human interaction, whether sexual or other, is clearly justified in controlling and prohibiting any medium of de-piction, description or advocacy which violates these principles" (*Butler* 1991, 477). The objective of s. 163 is thus not the imposition of a sexual morality but, rather, the prevention of the harm that pornography causes to women.

Much has been made of these statements of the objective of s. 163, particularly by feminists, who support the *Butler* decision. LEAF, for example, has argued that this represents a fundamental shift in obscenity law, away from the regulation of sexual morality and towards a feminist reformulation of the harm of pornography (Busby 1994, 176). However, the Court's effort to reconceptualize the objective must be read within the framework of the decision as a whole. It must be considered alongside the actual test for obscenity set out by the Court in the first part of the decision, as well as considered in light of the rest of section 1 analysis. When evaluated within the discursive framework of the decision as a whole, and its sexual subtext, the assertion that the statement of objective signifies a radical transformation in the law of obscenity is, at the very least, contestable.

Indeed, even the discussion of the objective of the law itself is contradictory, in so far as the Court is not able to sustain the distinction it is attempting to make between morality <the old law> and harm <the new law>. The sexual morality of the old law is apparent even in the language of the decision. Although the Court specifically states that regulating a standard of public and sexual morality would be inappropriate – that is, it is not an acceptable objective to prohibit "dirt for dirt's sake" – the Court continues to use the term "dirt for dirt's sake" as a synonym for pornography in several places in the decision. Again we see the extent to which, in the eyes of the Court, sexually explicit materials constitute dirt. Of course, according to the official story, the point is that the Court has to find another reason to regulate and prohibit this "dirt."

In attempting to locate the harm as something other than moral disapprobation, the distinction between morality and harm is further disrupted. In previous decisions, the Supreme Court has held that the purpose of a law cannot be seen to change or shift over time.[14] The purpose of a law is, in effect, written in stone at the time that the legislation was drafted and enacted. As a result, the Court in *Butler* was confronted with a problem: did this effort to recast the objective of the law as preventing harm, particularly harm against women, violate this shifting-purpose doctrine – that is, did it constitute an effort to change the purpose of the law from the regulation of morality to the prevention of harm? The Supreme Court of Canada said no. Yet, in so doing, the Court is forced to retreat from its earlier position that morality and harm were distinct. "[T]he notions of moral corruption and harm to society are not distinct ... but are inextricably linked. It is a moral corruption of a certain kind which leads to the detrimental effect on society" (*Butler* 1992, 427). Since the objective of the law cannot change, Sopinka, J. holds that the prevention of harm is intricately related to morality. Now, morality and harm are not different. According to Sopinka, J. the only thing that has changed is our understanding of the harm caused by pornography. "The prohibition of such materials was based on the belief that they had a detrimental impact on individuals exposed to them and consequently on society as a whole. Our understanding of the harms caused by these materials has developed considerably since that time; however, this does not detract from the fact that the purpose of this legislation remains, as it was in 1959, the protection of society from harms caused by the exposure to obscene materials" (ibid., 478). The Court spins around a tautological circle: the harms that are intended to be addressed by obscenity legislation are the harms that are caused by obscenity. If this circular reasoning is valid, we now have a generic objective so broad that it can be applied to virtually any piece of legislation. Just fill in the blank: the objective of the <pornography, traffic congestion, security fraud> law is to prevent the harm that <pornography, traffic congestion, security fraud> causes to society. According to this generic, or "no-name" objective of preventing harm, there will be little difficulty avoiding the net of the shifting-purpose doctrine whenever it is convenient to do so.[15]

Further, in these passages, the Court's views on the relationship between harm and morality is inconsistent. First, Sopinka, J. tells us that the law is not about morality, but about harm (morality is bad, and distinct from harm). But, then he tells us that harm is not actually distinct from morality, so there is no shifting purpose (morality is OK, and related to harm). And, finally, he tells us that the harm intended to be addressed is the harm caused by pornography, which used to be immorality but now is harm to women (morality is bad, and distinct from harm). So morality is bad, except when it is related to harm, in which case it is no longer morality. The Court's effort to cast the objective of s. 163 as something other than moral approbation is, at best, on rather shaky ground.

The sexual morality underlying the decision is made further manifest in the subsequent analysis of the proportionality requirement.[16] This sexual morality is most clearly revealed in the Court's brief discussion of the nature of the expression at stake in the legal regulation of pornography, which in its view is important in deciding whether the proportionality requirement has been met. Sopinka, J. examines whether the nature of the expression at issue in the regulation of pornography is in any way related to the three values that underlie the right to freedom of expression, namely, "the search for truth, participation in the political process, and individual self-fulfilment" (*Butler* 1992, 481). In evaluating the nature of the expression, the Court reviews the contrasting positions of the Ontario Attorney General and the British Columbia Civil Liberties Association. The former argued that "only individual self fulfilment and only at its most base aspect, that of physical arousal, is engaged by pornography" (ibid.). The latter argued that "pornography forces us to question conventional notions of sexuality and thereby launches us into an inherently political discourse" (ibid.). Interestingly, the Court then quotes a passage from Robin West (cited in the BCCLA factum), who argues, "Good pornography has value because it validates women's will to pleasure. It celebrates female nature. It validates a range of female sexuality that is wider and truer than that legitimated by the non-pornographic culture. Pornography when it is good celebrates both female pleasure and male rationality" (Robin West as quoted in *Butler* 1992, 481). The Court seems to adopt West's view of the positive value of sexual expression, in noting that "[a] proper application of the test should not suppress what West refers to as "good pornography." The objective of the impugned provision is not to inhibit the celebration of human sexuality" (*Butler* 1992, 481).

This is as close as the Court comes to articulating a positive theory of sexual expression. Pornography is divided into good pornography and bad pornography (good sex/bad sex). Good pornography is sexual expression that affirms women's agency (*will* to pleasure, not just pleasure). It is the will, the appeal to agency that comes from the intellect, the mind that transforms sex from bad to good. It is good because it has transcended its purely physical nature. It is also good because it "celebrates female nature" – a nature that although unarticulated is more than the body; it is of the whole female person – which must include the mind, the spirit. Female pleasure rooted in female nature seems to be posited as something more than physical self-fulfilment. Finally, sexual expression is good when it affirms "male rationality" – that is, when male sexuality transcends its base and corporeal nature; when it is no longer just of the body, but of the mind. We catch a glimpse of the deeply gendered nature of these oppositions: men are associated with rationality <which is of the mind> and women with pleasure <which is of the body> (Hekman 1990). This articulation of a positive theory of sexual expression is thus firmly rooted in the underlying conservative sexual morality and its good sex/bad sex, mind/body oppositions.

This positive theory of sexual expression is further limited when the Court shifts back, in the next sentence to its focus on the negative value of sexual expression. "[I]t cannot be ignored that the realities of the pornography industry are far from the picture which the B.C. Civil Liberties Association would have us paint" (*Butler* 1992, 481). This assertion of "the realities of the pornography industry" is supported only by reference to another court decision that describes pornographic materials; it is a reality apparently so obvious that the Court does not even have to take judicial notice, nor refer to expert evidence or secondary literature. These "realities of the pornography industry" are such that the Court is compelled to adopt the position of the Ontario Attorney General on the nature of the expression, namely, that it appeals only to the most base aspect of individual self-fulfilment. Sopinka, J. concludes: "the kind of expression which is sought to be advanced does not stand on equal footing with other kinds of expression which directly engage with 'core' of the freedom of expression values" (ibid., 482). While the Court had found that sexual expression was expression within the meaning of s. 2(b) of the *Charter*, it subsequently holds that sexual expression is an inferior form of expression, and thus not entitled to the same degree of protection. While, for the purpose of s. 2(b), all expression is equal, for the purpose of s. 1, the Court appears to be of the view that some expression is more equal than others.[17]

Why is sexual expression a lesser form of expression? All the Court tells us is that it is not related to any of the three core values underlying expression – the pursuit of truth, participation in the political process, or individual self-fulfilment. The Court's answer begs the deeper question – that is, why is sexual expression not related to the pursuit of truth, or to political participation, or to individual self-fulfilment? Sopinka, J. only addresses the third value, that of individual self-fulfilment. In his view, "this kind of expression is far from the core of the guarantee of freedom of expression. It appeals only to the most base aspect of individual fulfilment" (*Butler* 1992, 488). In this passage, Sopinka, J. seems to endorse the position advocated by the Ontario Attorney General, which, as noted, described this most base aspect of self-fulfilment as physical arousal. Sexual expression is a lesser form of expression because it appeals only to our most base – that is, our physical – dimension.

A now familiar subtext emerges: sexual arousal, rather than being an important part of our human dimension, is seen as base. And sexual arousal is seen as purely physical arousal – as a purely physiological reaction devoid of any mental elements. Again, sex is only of the body, not of the mind. Since individual self-fulfilment is valued only when it is promoting arousal of something more than the body – arousal of the mind or the spirit – it does not apply to sexual arousal or fulfilment. And again, we see the mind/body opposition, in which sex is located firmly within the body; it is bad unless it can be made good by transcending its corporeal nature. It is, then, this appeal to the body that makes sexual expression a lesser form of expression. As Linda Williams has argued, we can begin to see the extent to which pornography is "a volatile issue not simply because it represents sexual acts and fantasies, but because in that representation it frankly seeks to arouse viewers. Perhaps more than any other genre its pleasures are aimed at the body" (Williams 1989, 46). It is the very fact that this expression is directed at the pleasures of the body that makes it a lesser form of expression. It is based on an understanding of sex and sexual pleasure as being only of the body. There is no recognition of the role of our minds or our imaginations in sexual arousal and sexual pleasure. Nor is there any recognition of the social construction of sexuality. We again see the assumption of sexual essentialism operating: sex is biological, it is of and only of the body and, as such, unaffected by social relationships or culture.

Ironically, this assumption of sexual essentialism sits in stark contrast to the understanding of sexuality that informs the feminist anti-pornography position. The work of anti-pornography feminists has been based on the idea that sexuality is socially constructed – that sex and sexual desire are a product of the patriarchal society in which we live, and that sexual arousal (particularly, male sexual arousal) is negatively affected by images that represent women as sexual objects. Indeed, the sexual essentialism of the decision sits awkwardly with the Court's own assertion of the relationship between pornography and harm to women. Yet, it is only through this biological essentialism of sex, as of and only of the body, that the Court can sustain the assertion that sex appeals only to the most base aspect of physical fulfilment, and, in turn, the conclusion that sexual expression is a lesser form of expression.

The question of why sexual expression is not related to the other two values of expression – the search for truth and political participation – is not directly addressed by the Court. This silence, however, speaks volumes as to the underlying sexual morality. It is based on an unstated understanding of the truth about pornography – what it is, and what it is not; a "truth" that upon further deconstruction reveals a multiplicity of assumptions about sex and sexuality. In the Court's view, there is a "truth" to pornography, which is asserted to dismiss the idea that it could in any way be related to the values underlying freedom of expression. It was the truth about pornography – that it appeals only to the most base dimension of physical fulfilment – that allowed the Court to reject any connection between sexual expression and individual self-fulfilment. It is similarly this truth about pornography that allows the

Court to implicitly reject any connection between sexual expression and the pursuit of truth.

For example, the efforts of the BC Civil Liberties Association to frame sexual expression as a challenge to conventional sexuality and, in turn, as a political discourse (see Gotell), were simply rejected on the basis of the "realities" of the pornography industry. According to the Court, the realities or truth of the pornography industry are that it is characterized by a particular form of sexual representations of women, that is, of women as sexual objects for men. In this view, there is no possibility of a diversity of sexual representations within the pornography industry. Nor is there any room to admit that these sexual representations may be subject to different interpretations (Williams 1989). Again, we see the Court's literalist approach to representation, according to which pornography is seen to have a single and universal meaning, readily available to any viewer. This reality of the pornography industry, along with the monolithic nature of its representations, the meaning of which is uncontestable, precludes the possibility that pornography could be implicated in what we otherwise value – the search for truth. The "truth" of the pornography industry is in effect asserted to preclude the possibility that pornography could be implicated in the search for truth.

It is similarly the truth about pornography that precludes the possibility that pornography could in any way be involved in promoting the second value of freedom of expression – that is, participation in the political process. Pornography, or more specifically the pornography industry, which by definition undermines women's equality and dignity, becomes the antithesis of participation. The arguments that sexual representation is for some communities part of an inherently political process of forging community identities were not, in the Court's view, even deemed worthy of mention. The question "participation for whom?" thus remains unaddressed, as does the question of participation in relation to what issues.

This rejection of the potential value of sexual expression in promoting participation in the political process also implies that sex is not worthy of the political process – that sex is not a matter for the political process. Yet the very history of the legal regulation of sex demonstrates how extensive this regulation has been. The failure to consider any possible connection between sexual expression and political participation obscures the extent to which sex has long been a subject of legal regulation and repression. Indeed, the sexualities of the very individuals who are now seeking to forge their identities in and through these sexual representations – lesbians and gay men, sex-trade workers, feminist artists – have long been the subject of legal regulation and repression, without their consent.

Contrary to the historical realities of legal regulation, the sexual subtext of the decision is based on the idea that sex is not a matter for politics, or for political debate. Not only is the subject not worthy of politics, but we see again the underlying assumptions of the monolithic nature of sexuality. The truth about sex is that sex is just sex – basically it's bad, unless it's good, and we all know which one it is when we see it. There is no room for disagreement or dissent, or for the possibility that there may be diverse sexualities. Nor is there any room to acknowledge that the exploration of diverse sexualities may have value in and of itself.

Sex, being of the body, cannot be the subject of debate. As a function of biology, of pure physical arousal, there is nothing to debate. This sexual essentialism is further reinforced by the assumption of sexual monism. Because there is only one way to have sex, or at least, one good way to have sex, there is nothing to be gained from sexual expression. It is not a subject that can contribute to or be advanced by political debate. These various assumptions of sexual morality – sexual essentialism, sexual monism, and sexual negativity – combine and interact to produce a truth about the nature of sexual expression, a truth according to which sexual expression is not in any way related to political participation, or to any of the other core values that underlie freedom of expression.

Again, we can begin to see the tensions in this sexual subtext. The assumption of sexual monism sits awkwardly with the good sex/bad sex distinction and the sexual hierarchy implicit in this distinction. The idea that there is only one way to have sex is at odds with the idea that there is good sex and bad sex. The latter suggests that there is in fact more than one way to have sex, although one way is good and the other bad. Notwithstanding this tension, these two assumptions – of sexual monism and sexual negativity – operate together to the effect that there is only one way that we should have sex.

In the context of sexual expression, this sexual subtext operates to reinforce the idea that nothing is to be gained from such expression, and, in fact, much is to be lost. Since there is only one way to have sex, sexual expression may only lead others astray; it may encourage people to have bad sex (which in the Court's view is what pornography does). This view is reinforced by the truth about the pornography industry –

that is, that it only represents bad sex. The very problem with sexual expression, then, is that it will cause people to have sex or sexual desire in ways that they should not. The repression of such expression, by contrast, will ensure that sex will be as it should be, in the natural order of things, which is still bad, unless it can become good, which if left to the natural order of things <marriage, heterosexuality, and reproduction> it can.

In the subsequent discussion of the three dimensions of the proportionality test, the Court continues to articulate its now popular refrain – obscenity laws do not prohibit all sexual materials, only those sexual materials that cause harm, particularly harm towards women. The sexual subtext of this refrain is also articulated again and again. On the question of minimum impairment, for example, the Court finds that s. 163(8) does not proscribe all sexually explicit material, but only that which is violent, degrading, and/or dehumanizing. The provision does not prohibit good sex, that is, "sexually explicit erotica without violence, that is not degrading or dehumanizing" (*Butler* 1992, 485). Nor does the section include sexually explicit materials that have scientific, artistic, or literary merit. The Court here rearticulates the distinction between sex and art, noting that materials that involve "aesthetic expression," and thus "represent the artist's attempt at individual fulfilment" would not be captured by the provision. The same good sex/bad sex, mind/body, art/sex distinctions continue to appear.

Concluding Remarks on the *Butler* Decision

The result of the *Butler* decision was twofold. The Supreme Court reformulated the test for obscenity under s. 163 and subsequently found that although s. 163 violated the right to freedom of expression, it was a reasonable limit on this right, and thus constitutional. The meaning of the decision remains highly contested. Those who take the position that *Butler* represents a feminist victory have argued that the objectives of s. 163 now require that degrading and dehumanizing be read in a new light, and that the meaning of community standards has been so fundamentally transformed as to resemble the previous test in name alone (Busby 1994, 176). I have tried to map out a very different reading of the *Butler* decision, within which the underlying sexual morality, and its assumptions of sexual negativity, sexual essentialism, and sexual monism, can be seen to leave s. 163 transformed in language alone. The classification of sexual representations into one of the three categories of pornography according to the community-standards test of harm can only be done by an implicit reliance on an underlying sexual morality. The very concept of sex that is or could be degrading and dehumanizing only makes sense through the underlying discourses on sexuality – of good sex/bad sex, of mind/body distinctions, and of the assumptions of sexual negativity, essentialism, monism, and hierarchy on which these distinctions are based. Similarly, community standards only make sense in relation to a prevailing, and generally accepted, understanding of sexual morality, in which some sex is good and some sex is not.

In this reading of the *Butler* decision, the sexual subtext can be seen to inform the Court's discussion of the objective of the legislation, and indeed the discussion of the constitutionality of the law as a whole. Notwithstanding the Court's best efforts to cast the objective of the law as the prevention of harm, particularly of harm towards women, the underlying sexual morality continues to infuse and shape the discourse of the decision. We do not have to look very far to find the continued references to morality, to sexual morality, to good sex and bad sex, to sex being of the body and thus bad, unless it can be made something more, and thereby good. Yet, there is no explicit articulation of what makes sex good. Rather, good sex is simply implied as that which bad sex is not: not base, not physical, not violent, not degrading or dehumanizing, not involving children. The sexual subtext of the *Butler* decision is informed by the discourses on sexuality that have dominated Western thought since the nineteenth century: sexual negativity <sex is bad>, sexual essentialism <sex is biological>, sexual monism <sex is singular>, and sexual hierarchy <some sex is better than other>.

These different assumptions informing prevailing understandings of sexuality sit in awkward relationship to one another, and operate to constitute sex as a highly unstable category. For example, the idea that sex is bad sits in awkward juxtaposition to the idea that it can be made good, which in turn does not seem consistent with the idea that sex being of the body can be made good only by becoming that which it is not – of the mind. The very idea of sexual hierarchy – that some sex <marital, heterosexual, reproductive> is better than other <non-marital, non-reproductive, homosexual> sits inconsistently with the idea of sexual monism – that there is only one sexuality. Sexual hierarchy seems to be based on an implicit notion of sexual diversity, and yet operates at the same time to condemn that diversity. The diversity is reduced to a simple binary opposition of good and bad sex. In *Butler*, these assumptions interact in multiple and seemingly contradictory ways to constitute sex as a highly unstable category – yet not so unstable as to be easily displaced. This unstated sexual morality remains powerfully entrenched as the ideologically dominant discourse of sexuality.

Beyond Butler*: Obscenity and the Representation of Gay and Lesbian Sexuality*

Since the *Butler* decision, gay and lesbian sexually explicit materials continue to be targeted by customs officials and police. The continued criminalization of gay and lesbian sexual representations raises some difficult questions around the ostensible rejection of sexual morality in obscenity law. According to *Butler*, the purpose of s. 163 is to prevent harm, particularly harm towards women. The understanding of harm is based on the tenuous, but judicially accepted, link between pornography and violence against women. Men watching pictures in which women are objectified as sex objects is seen to cause men to mistreat women. It is an understanding of harm set in a heterosexual framework. The pornography is male heterosexual pornography, and its harm is that heterosexual men are likely to mistreat women. The feminist literature on which this understanding of harm is based has similarly operated within this heterosexual discursive framework. In the work of its leading exponents, (hetero)sexuality is identified as the site of women's oppression. It is in and through (hetero)sexuality that men are constituted as aggressive and dominant, and women are constituted as passive and subordinate (MacKinnon 1987, Dworkin 1981).

This heterosexual framework raises a serious question about applying the *Butler* test, and its conception of harm, to gay and lesbian materials. Many gay men and lesbians have argued that gay or lesbian sexual representations have absolute nothing to do with the harm towards women associated with heterosexual pornography. Carl Stychin has contended, for example, that the sexually explicit images of gay male pornography do not reinforce patriarchal male sexuality, but, rather, directly challenge dominant constructs of masculinity by displacing the heterosexual norm (Stychin 1992, 857). Lesbian writers, such as Barbara Smith and Lisa Henderson, have similarly resisted the equation of lesbian pornography and heterosexual pornography, insisting instead on the cultural specificity and the cultural transgression of sexually explicit imagery created for, by, and about lesbians (Smith 1988; Henderson 1992). Within this view, since gay and lesbian sexual representations do not operate within a heterosexual framework, these images cannot and should not be measured against a heterosexual norm.

It would therefore not be unreasonable to suggest that the heterosexual framework of the *Butler* test should limit the applicability of this obscenity doctrine to heterosexual pornography. At a minimum, this heterosexual framework would seem to require that courts at least address the question of how the understanding of harm could be applied to gay and lesbian sex. How does men watching pictures of men having sex with men, or women watching pictures of women having sex with women, contribute to the type of harm to women identified in *Butler*? In the case law that followed on the heels of the *Butler* decision, however, the courts have neither limited the *Butler* test to heterosexual materials nor explored how this heterosexually defined concept of harm can be applied to gay and lesbian imagery. The first two obscenity cases after *Butler* involved Glad Day Bookshop (a gay and lesbian bookstore), and the courts used the obscenity test as set out by the Supreme Court of Canada to find sexually explicit gay and lesbian materials to be obscene. Not only was the question of the relationship between gay and lesbian sexual imagery and harm to women not answered in these cases – the question was not even posed.

Indeed, it is in this application of the *Butler* test, and of its model of harm to gay and lesbian sexual representations, that the discursive drag of the *Butler* decision can be most directly challenged. It is within the context of gay and lesbian materials that the distinction between morality and harm is most difficult to sustain, and that we can most clearly see the extent to which obscenity laws are still predicated on the legal regulation of sexual morality. Gay and lesbian sexual representations are not produced within the heterosexual framework of the more mainstream pornography to which the *Butler* decision addressed itself – the images are of gay/lesbian sexuality, produced by gay men/lesbians, to be consumed by gay men/lesbians. Yet, these sexual representations have been charged and found guilty pursuant to the *Butler* test for obscenity. In this section, I will argue that the criminalization of these gay and lesbian sexual materials does, however, make sense within the discursive context of the sexual subtext of the *Butler* decision. I will illustrate the extent to which the sexual morality underlying the *Butler* decision has framed and informed these two obscenity decisions against Glad Day Bookshop. The sexual subtext, and its good sex/bad sex oppositions is particularly dangerous in the context of gay and lesbian sexual representations. The heterosexist and often homophobic discourses of this conservative sexual morality operate to locate these representations on the bad-sex side of the dichotomy.

Glad Day Bookshop v. Canada

In the case of *Glad Day Bookshop* (1992), the dangerous implications of the *Butler* decision, and of its understanding of sex and sexuality, for gay and lesbian sexual representation has begun to come clear. This case arose in the context of a customs seizure of gay male pornography en route to Glad Day Bookshop. Glad Day appealed from a determination of the deputy minister of National Revenue for Customs and Excise, declaring the materials to be obscene and, thus, prohibited from import into Canada.[18]

After reviewing the case in considerable detail (and dismissing the expert evidence called by the defence) and the law of obscenity as established in *Butler*, Hayes, J. turned to the material in question. The Ontario Court (General Division) reviewed each of the seized materials. Hayes, J. briefly described each publication, and concluded that each magazine, story, and comic strip was "degrading and dehumanizing." Throughout the decision, each publication is dealt with in two or three paragraphs: one paragraph describes the sexual representation; the second paragraph is conclusory in nature – that is, the Court concludes that the material is degrading, that the material does violate community standards. For example, in relation to *Oriental Guys* no. 4 (Spring 1989), which contains explicit representations of gay oral and anal sex with no violence, the Court held: "The description in the magazine of this sexual activity is degrading, I am of the opinion that this particular material does indicate a strong inference of a risk of harm that might flow from the community being exposed to this material. I am of the opinion that the community would not tolerate others being exposed to this item. The dominant characteristic is an undue exploitation of sex. It is obscene" (*Glad Day Bookshop* 1992, 15). There is almost no analysis as to why particular materials are degrading. Rather, in each case, the Court simply asserts that the material is degrading, that there is a risk of harm, that the community would not tolerate others being exposed to it.

To the extent that the Court gives any reason as to why the material is degrading, the theme that emerges, in single sentences and passages, is the ostensible absence of "real human relationships." For example, with regard to *Movie Star Confidential*, a sexually explicit comic strip, the Court writes "It does not contain any real human relationship. In its grotesque figures and their sexual activity, it is completely degrading and dehumanizing" (*Glad Day Bookshop* 1992, 16). On *Spartan's Quest*, Hayes, J. writes: "It is a sexual encounter without any real meaningful human relationship" (ibid.). On *Humongous – True Gay Encounters*, a collection of short stories, which includes explicit gay sex with strangers: "The manner in which they express explicit sexual activity is described is degrading [sic] to human beings. *There is no real human relationship*" (ibid., 17; emphasis added). On *Sex Stop*: "The introduction to this book ... clearly indicates the base purpose of the material which has no human dimension and is degrading and dehumanizing" (ibid., 18). On *Advocate Men*, a magazine with explicit representations of oral and anal sex: "The description and activities are degrading and without any human dimension. The dominant characteristic is the undue exploitation of sex" (ibid., 19).

According to Hayes, J. any explicit sexual representation without a "human dimension" or "human relationship" is degrading and dehumanizing, and constitutes the undue exploitation of sex. The implication throughout the decision is that sex is not human – a sexual relationship is not a human relationship. Our sexual dimension is not part of our human dimension – our sexual dimension makes us base, makes us subhuman. This understanding of sex is informed by and reinforces the binary opposition between good and bad sex, in which sex – which in and of itself is bad – gets to become good if it can transcend its subhuman nature and become human. Sex becomes good if it can transcend the purely physical, purely pleasurable, dimension and become something more. Sex becomes good if it can become that which by definition it is not.

In Hayes, J.'s view, sexual representations are bad, unless they can be redeemed by emotional relationships. The *Glad Day Bookshop* decision makes clear that what is needed to make sex (which is inherently bad) good is an intimate, loving, monogamous relationship. However, since even *Advocate Men*, the gay male equivalent to *Playboy*, was found to be obscene, it is difficult to imagine what, if any, representations of gay male sex and sexuality would meet this test. It seems as if it is the representation of gay male sex in and of itself that is without a "human dimension" and thus degrading and dehumanizing.

According to the *Glad Day Bookshop* decision, sex with strangers, group sex, sex with bondage are all degrading and dehumanizing. Not only are the actual sexual practices considered to be inappropriate, but the mere representation of sexual fantasies are also prohibited (such as comic books, which represent the fantastical, not the real). Even the fantastical "without a human dimension" is degrading and dehumanizing. There is, in Hayes, J.'s sexual morality, no distinction between the real and the fantastical, between reality and fantasy. The *Glad Day Bookshop* decision has been argued by some to be a misapplication of the *Butler* test, and it is currently under appeal. There is no question that the Court failed to engage with the *Butler* test. There was no consideration of why particular materials were degrading and dehumanizing, nor why these materials would cause harm. They were simply deemed to be degrading and dehumanizing and, in turn, deemed to cause harm. However, the failure of the Court to engage with the *Butler* test should not be taken as a vindication of the *Butler* test. First, the *Glad Day Bookshop* decision exemplifies what lower courts can do with an inherently vague test like "degrading and dehumanizing," and with a community-standards test that does not require evidence. The vagueness of the test opens the door to, and invites the application of, a subjective determination on the nature of the sexually explicit materials. Second, it is not at all clear that the finding in Hayes is at odds with the sexual subtext of the *Butler* decision. Rather, in its assumptions of sexual negativity and sexual essentialism – sex is of the body and bad, unless it can be made good – the Hayes decision is quite consistent with the sexual morality of *Butler*.

The main point of potential conflict between the *Glad Day Bookshop* decision and the *Butler* decision is in the application of a heterosexist model of harm to gay sexual representations. The Court does not engage with the fundamental question of what the *Butler* model of harm has to do with gay sexual representations. Indeed, the Court makes no reference to harm in terms of harm towards women. The only reference to harm by Hayes, J. is in terms of causing "anti-social conduct." The ostensibly feminist objective of the law evaporates. Rather, the application of the law is simply the application of a conservative sexual morality. The harm, according to the Court, is the harm of sexually explicit materials. The sexual subtext of the *Butler* decision – the good sex/bad sex distinction – is given a particularly homophobic spin in *Glad Day Bookshop*, whereby the representation of explicit gay sexuality becomes, by definition, bad sex.

R. v. Scythes, Glad Day Bookshop

On 30 April 1992, two months after the *Butler* decision, the Toronto police seized the magazine *Bad Attitude* – a magazine of "lesbian erotic fiction" – from Toronto's Glad Day Bookshop, and charged the store and the store's owner, John Scythes, with the possession and sale of obscene material, in contravention of s. 163 of the *Criminal Code*. After a five-day trial in December 1992, Justice Paris of the Ontario Court (Provincial Division) delivered a six page judgement in February 1993, in which he found *Bad Attitude* to be obscene, and the accuseds were convicted of violating s. 163.

At trial, the Crown focused on a number of parts of the magazine: the fictional articles containing accounts of lesbian sadomasochist sex, and the accompanying photographs of explicit lesbian sex. In the decision, however, the Court focused on one article entitled "Wunna My Fantasies," in which writer Trish Thomas tells a story about the sexual practices of two fictional lesbian characters. One lesbian character stalks another in a shower room, and the two women engage in s/m sex.

The brief decision is a journey through heterosexual assumptions and neo-Victorian sexual morality. Interestingly, after briefly reviewing the *Butler* decision, the Court specifically turns to the question of heterosexuality. Paris, J. denies that the "sexual orientation" of the sexual representations have anything to do with his decision.

I have detected during this trial a concern that the Court will find relevant the sexual orientation of Bad Attitude. In recent years, many courts and tribunals have struck down laws and practices held to discriminate against gays. This is an indication that our society has moved beyond tolerance to the actual recognition that homosexuals form an essential part of our community. It follows then that as members of a sexual minority they have the right to communicate publicly on the subject that bind together. That right however will on occasion be curtailed in the public interest. The community tolerance test is blind to sexual orientation or practices. Its only focus is the potential harm to the public. Any consideration given to the sexual orientation of the material would constitute an unwarranted application of the test. (*Scythes* 1993, 4)

In the Court's view, sexual orientation is irrelevant, and the community-standards test must be applied in a formally equal manner. In the name of formal equality – which does not exist for gays and lesbians in Canadian law – the Court has ensured that the particular context of lesbian sexuality and representations will not be considered relevant. The test for community standards is supposed to be formally neutral to sexual orientation. But what this standard of formal neutrality obscures is the extent to which the standard is one deeply informed by heterosexual assumptions. The community standard is a heterosexual standard, and it is this heterosexual standard that becomes the norm by which all representations of sexuality are to be judged.

In the next paragraph, Paris, J. finds that the article contains representations of both sex and violence, and thus falls within the definition of s. 163(8). He then briefly turns his attention to the question of consent: "The consent in this case, far from redeeming the material makes it degrading and dehumanizing" (*Scythes* 1993, 4). In a slick discursive move, provided courtesy of the Supreme Court of Canada in *Butler*, the consensual nature of the sexual practices is not simply rendered irrelevant, but, in the Court's view, actually contributes to making the material degrading and dehumanizing. This discursive shift, in which consent becomes degradation, ensures the erasure of the specificity of lesbian sexual practices.

Consent is a cornerstone in lesbian s/m sexual practices, and in lesbian sexual/cultural production. As Lisa Henderson has argued, consent appears as a subtext throughout lesbian s/m sexual/cultural production.[19] As Becki Ross discusses in greater detail in the next chapter, the defence counsel in the case tried to explain this consensual nature of sex in "Wunna My Fantasies" to the Court. This attempt to explain the importance of consent within lesbian s/m culture, however, proved futile.[20] Even if established, in the reasoning of the *Butler* decision, consent only makes the sexual representation more degrading. After citing the *Butler* decision's passage on consent, Paris, J. writes: "This material flashes every light and blows every whistle of obscenity. Enjoyable sex after subordination by bondage and physical abuse at the hands of a total stranger" (*Scythes* 1993, 5). In Paris, J.'s sexual world, there is no legitimate space for s/m sex, no room for bondage, no room for fantasizing about sex with a stranger. None of these sexual practices and fantasies could or should lead to enjoyable sex. Moreover, Paris, J. seems unable to comprehend the extent to which the story represents a sexual fantasy. In the Court's view, the sexual representations combined too many elements of bad sex: sex with strangers, sex with bondage, sex with submission, or even sexual fantasy.

Paris, J. then commits the ultimate act of judicial heterosexism: "If I replaced the aggressor in this article with a man there would be very few people in the community who would not recognize the potential for harm. The fact that the aggressor is a female is irrelevant because the potential for harm remains" (*Scythes* 1993, 5). To determine whether the text in question is obscene, the Court replaces the woman aggressor with a male aggressor. This substitution is allowed by the framework that the Court sets out at the beginning of the decision, which insists that sexual orientation is not relevant in determining community standards. Since sexual orientation is not relevant, then, in the Court's eyes, it does not matter whether the sex is occurring between two women, or between a woman and a man. The court is able to use its understanding of heterosexual sex to evaluate whether the representation of lesbian sex is obscene.[21] Through this judicial technique of heteroswitching, the specificity of lesbian sexuality, and of lesbian s/m cultural practices, are negated. All the arguments of the defence counsel, on the need to consider the specific cultural and ideological context under which lesbian sexual images are produced and given meaning, are, in a single heterosexual sweep, rendered irrelevant. And the heterosexual norm of the ostensibly neutral community standards is thereby reinforced.

In the final paragraph of the decision, the Court rejects the comparison the defence attempted to make between *Bad Attitude* and Madonna's book *Sex*. Defence counsel argued that the sexually explicit representations in *Sex*, which includes both heterosexual and homosexual s/m practices, demonstrated a shift in community standards. The commercial success of *Sex* in the Canadian market was presented as evidence that these kinds of sexually explicit representations do not violate community standards. The Court, however, was unpersuaded. "Madonna's book called Sex was offered to show the public tolerance to this type of material. One photograph of particular relevance shows a so called playful rape in a school gymnasium. I received very little information on the distribution of this book. I am told however that few were available and were sold immediately. I find the sample too small to be a reliable indication of the public's reaction to is distribution" (*Scythes* 1993, 6). The strongest argument on the nature of community standards, and the challenge to the assumed heterosexism of the standards, was simply rejected on the grounds that there was not enough evidence. The *Butler* test reaffirmed that there is no need to enter evidence of the community standard. Yet, here, the arbitrary and discretionary nature of the community-standards test is used to say that there was not enough evidence to show that the community standard has been changed. In other words, while no evidence is required to prove community standards, evidence is required to prove that these standards have changed.

In *Bad Attitude*, the representation of s/m lesbian sex, which in the Court's view involves explicit sex with violence, is, by the standards laid down by the Supreme Court of Canada, bad sex. There was no need to entertain the question of whether the representation constituted good sex, because the representation "blows every whistle of obscenity." Again, we see the Court expound on the negative values of sexual expression, on what is bad about sex. Sex with bondage, with domination, with strangers, is bad sex. And in order to insulate itself from charges that it was reverting back to the regulation of sexual morality, and not the prevention of harm towards women, the Court simply turned lesbian sex into heterosexual sex. It was only by virtue of this heteroswitching that the Court was able to conclude that the sexual representations harmed women, within the heterosexual framework of the *Butler* decision. Indeed, within this framework, no gay or lesbian sexual representations will be safe from review on the ground that there is no harm towards women. Rather, through this new-found judicial technique of heteroswitching, gay sexual representations can always be transformed by replacing a man with a woman; and lesbian sexual representations transformed by replacing one of the women with a man.[22]

R. v. 931536 Ontario

Gay and lesbian sexual representations have not been the only focus of criminal prosecutions. Heterosexual pornography has also been subject to prosecution under s. 163 in the aftermath of *Butler*. Interestingly, some of the so-called straight porn that has been prosecuted has included scenes of lesbian or gay sexuality.[23] In *R. v. 931536 Ontario*, this lesbian imagery played a central role in the Court's finding of the material to be degrading and dehumanizing. In this case, eight videos were alleged to be obscene. At trial, the court held that seven of the videos did exploit sex, and thus had to determine whether this exploitation was "undue." According to the Court, six of the remaining videos did not fall within the categories proscribed by *Butler*: they did not involve sex with violence, they were not degrading or dehumanizing, and did not create a substantial risk of harm. But one video, entitled *Cherry Tricks*, was held to be obscene on the basis that "its dominant theme is the degrading and demeaning treatment of women, combined with unobjectionable heterosexual and lesbian acts of sex."

While this reference to lesbian acts of sex as unobjectionable might suggest that lesbian sexuality was not a relevant factor in the case, a deeper look at the reasoning brings this claim into at least some doubt.

In reviewing the video, the Court tells us that women are degraded throughout the video in their portrayal as "stupid, with no skills or ability, except sex." The women are "required to and are prepared to have sex with men who are either their employers, acting teachers, or men in positions to give them a job." The Court describes that each sex act begins *after* a scene in which a woman is humiliated. "The only actual overlapping of sex and humiliation occurs when two women are requested to suck and lick each other so that the men can choose the appropriate person for a job (a pun made in the movie), while the men look on. The women in the scene are shown as consenting and enjoying the sex" (*R. v. 931536*). The Court concludes, on the basis of *Butler*, that the "film is degrading and dehumanizing because it places women in positions of subordination or humiliation, and runs against the principles of equality and dignity of all human beings." The Court repeats that "the sexual acts, themselves, taken in isolation, are not degrading.'

It is the lesbian sex act that nevertheless stands out. It is in this sequence that women are humiliated at the same time as they perform an otherwise "unobjectionable sex act." In the Court's view, there is a connection between the degrading mental treatment and the sex act. "There is the false consent, and the sex is always related to the woman's servile and subordinate position in relation to the men. The non-degrading sex taken in isolation is so interwoven with the reasons the women are having sex that it becomes degrading itself (*R. v. 931536*). It is interesting that this ostensibly "false consent" and the depiction of women in subordinate positions is present in other scenes, which the Court describes but does not focus on in finding the video to be an "undue" exploitation of sex. Women are shown as only able to advance in their modelling or acting careers by having sex with their male employers or teachers. There is also the depiction of what the Court describes as "non-violent sexual assault," in which a woman consents to sex with a man on the basis of mistaking his identity. Yet, these are not the images that attract the Court's attention – apparently because the humiliation immediately precedes the sex. The Court does not tell us why humiliating women just before sex (and, presumably, into having sex) is any less degrading and dehumanizing to women than if the act of humiliation continues during the sex.

Nor does the Court tell us why this particular sex act is any more humiliating than the others, in which women are compelled to have sex with their male employers or teachers. The Court insists that it is not because the act is a lesbian act. Lesbian sex is, according to the Court, unobjectionable in isolation. This position is consistent with the Court's conclusion on two of the other videos, which also contain scenes of explicit sex between women, but which were not held to be degrading and dehumanizing. While lesbian sex may be unobjectionable, forcing women to have lesbian sex is, apparently, a different story. Indeed, it appears to be a different story than forcing women to have sex with men. The subtext is difficult to escape: what is particular objectionable is coercing women to have lesbian sex.

Lesbian sexuality is not irrelevant. While it may not be sufficient in itself to make sexual representations bad sex (which is certainly a step forward from the *Glad Day Bookshop* decision), it does operate as a factor that pushes sex across the line into bad sex. Compelling women to have sex with male employers to get a job may not exactly be good sex – in the Court's view, it is clearly sexist – but it is not sufficient to push the sex into the bad-sex category. Compelling women to have sex with other women to get a job, however, is bad sex. This is not to suggest that if the court had focused on the other scenes in *Cherry Tricks*, then the finding that the video was degrading and dehumanizing would have been justified. It is simply an attempt to illustrate the underlying assumptions of sexual morality that continue to operate – assumptions in which sexual orientation is not a neutral factor. Neither the *Butler* test nor the sexual morality within which it is interpreted or applied is neutral on sexual orientation. While the decision in *Cherry Tricks* is evidence that this sexual morality has shifted, in so far as the Court is willing to say that lesbian sexuality is not in and of itself obscene, this is not the end of the story. Underlying the decision is still a sexual morality informed by the assumption of sexual hierarchy, in which some sex is better than others. Lesbian and gay sex may not be bad sex in and of itself, but it is certainly not as good as straight sex.

Good Girls (and Boys) Don't: Gay and Lesbian Sexual Representations as Bad Sex

The question that remains unanswered in these cases is what gay and lesbian sexual representations have to do with harm against women? While in *Cherry Tricks* the sexual representations of women having sex with women were, arguably, not inappropriately interpreted within the heterosexual context of the video, the same does not apply to the first two cases involving specifically gay and lesbian material. In the *Glad Day Bookshop* decision, the Court did not even attempt to answer the question. In *Scythes*, the Court engages with the question, although it hardly provides an acceptable answer. The Court simply falls back on the heterosexual discursive framework of *Butler*, and assumes that the same harms would flow. At this level, it would seem that both of these obscenity charges against Glad Day Bookshop could reasonably be seen as a misapplication of the *Butler* test. And this is the view taken by feminists who support the *Butler* decision: that *Butler* has been misapplied, and that gay and lesbian representations are being unfairly targeted (Busby 1994, 184–7).

At a deeper level, however, it is considerably less clear that these cases can simply be dismissed as a misapplication. The sexual subtexts of the cases is quite consistent with the sexual subtext of the *Butler* decision. Each of these cases is characterized by assumptions of sexual negativity, sexual essentialism, sexual monism, and sexual hierarchy. While these assumptions are troubling enough in a heterosexual context, they are disastrous in a gay or lesbian context. If heterosexual sex is at risk of being bad sex, then gay or lesbian sex is most certain to be bad sex (sexual negativity). If (hetero) sex is a natural force, then gay or lesbian sex is most likely to be unnatural (sexual essentialism). If there is only one way to have (hetero) sex, then it is almost certain that it is not the way of gay or lesbian sex. And in the hierarchy of sexual activity, gay or lesbian sex most certainly ranks well below heterosexual sex.

Gayle Rubin, in her description of the sex hierarchy, observes that some areas of previously contested sex are now "inching across the line of acceptability": "Unmarried couples living together, masturbation, and some forms of homosexuality are moving in the direction of respectability. Most homosexuality is still on the bad side of the line. But if it is coupled and monogamous, the society is beginning to recognize that it includes the full range of human interaction" (Rubin 1989, 283). In the context of representations of gay and lesbian sexuality, sexually explicit representations risk pushing this sex back across the line of bad sex. Sexually explicit materials focus attention on sexual interaction, which, in turn, seems to detract from viewing gay and lesbian sexuality within this fuller "range of human interaction." Good sex for gay men and lesbians must not only be monogamous and loving

– it must also be private and, preferably, in the absence of cameras. The mere representation of gay and lesbian sex risks pushing the new-found acceptability back across the line of bad sex. Gay sexuality can be represented within a higher artistic context – witness films such as *M. Butterfly*, *The Wedding Banquet*, *Torch Song Trilogy*, and *Strawberry and Chocolate*, which illustrate the so-called fuller human dimension of gay men's lives, in which sex is only a small part. But, the representation of gay and lesbian sex for the explicit purpose of sexual arousal is in a different category – a category more likely than not to fall on the side of bad sex. Gay and lesbian sexuality may not be degrading and dehumanizing in and of itself – it is just the *representation* of gay and lesbian sexuality that is degrading and dehumanizing. Gay and lesbian sex is not bad sex, but representations of gay and lesbian sex might be. And the more the representation hints at other forms of traditionally "deviant" sexuality, the more likely it is to be bad sex. Bondage and leather is virtually guaranteed to be bad sex. However, even non-monogamous or non-intimate sex, which abounds in heterosexual pornography, risks becoming bad sex if it is situated in the context of gay and lesbian explicit sexual representations.

As I have tried to argue, the *Butler* decision is not neutral on sexual orientation. The analysis of harm within *Butler* is based on a particular analysis of heterosexual sexuality. Yet, it is being deployed in ways that assume that the analysis of harm can be applied to all sexually explicit representations. And as such, the decisions are beginning to expose this underlying heterosexism of the *Butler* test. In *Glad Day Bookshop*, this heterosexual norm was most notoriously exposed: it was simply the representation of gay sex that made the sex bad. In *Bad Attitude*, the heterosexism was somewhat less visible, but no less significant. Lesbian sex was not in and of itself degrading and dehumanizing. Rather, lesbian sex was turned into heterosexual sex, and then judged by heterosexual norms. Even in *Cherry Tricks*, a "straight porn" video, the heterosexual norm of the degrading and dehumanizing test was again apparent, in so far as "otherwise unobjectionable" lesbian sex was judged by harsher standards than heterosexual sex.

Neither the discursive framework of the *Butler* test, nor the dominant sexual morality within which this test is applied, is neutral on the question of sexual orientation. The relevance of sexual orientation within this sexual morality has shifted over time, to the extent that sexual orientation has now become a contested site. It is a sexual morality in which some courts are willing to state that gay and lesbian sexuality is not in and of itself obscene. This is an important change, but it does not signal the end of sexual orientation's relevance. There is still a conservative sexual morality informed by the assumption of sexual hierarchy, in which some sex is better than others. Lesbian and gay sex may not (always) be bad sex in and of itself, but it is certainly not as good as straight sex. Lesbian and gay sex continues to run a much higher risk of being pushed back across the dividing line between good and bad sex, back from its tenuous legitimacy, into its all-too-familiar condemnation as bad sex.

To return to the argument that some feminists have made that the gay and lesbian community is being unfairly targeted and that these decisions by lower courts are a misapplication of the *Butler* decision, I believe that a different reading is possible. While I agree that these are not particularly exceptional examples of judicial decision-making, I disagree that these decisions represent some fundamental deviation from the principles established in *Butler*. The very argument that gay and lesbian sexual representations have been misclassified by the courts – that these representations should not be bad sex – is based on the tacit acceptance of the good sex/bad sex distinction of the *Butler* test, a distinction that only makes sense when put within the framework of the dominant discourses of sexuality. Further, the *Butler* decision still involves an appeal to a community standard – a standard that is national in scope and can be established without evidence. It is a standard that only makes sense in the context of dominant discourses of sexuality that remain informed by a profoundly conservative sexuality morality, in which heterosexuality, and only certain forms of heterosexuality, remain privileged.

While the discourse of *Butler* justifies the law of obscenity in relation to harm towards women, and the promotion of equality and dignity, the sexual subtext of the decision has provided the lower courts with the arsenal they need to repress sexual representation – particularly, sexual representation by sexual minorities. The anti-sex agenda of the *Butler* decision paved the road for the particular judicial approach to gay and lesbian sexual representation.

At the same time, it is important to recognize that the legal regulation of sexual representations in the post-*Butler* era continues to be a site of contest, conflict, and change. Neither the Supreme Court of Canada nor any of the lower courts has yet had their last word in the development and application of obscenity doctrine. In *R. v. Hawkins*, the Ontario Court of Appeal entered the fray and attempted to correct what it considered to be evidentiary problems in the early application of the *Butler* test.[24] The site of contest in *Hawkins* was, again, the second category of the *Butler* typography of pornography – degrading and dehumanizing. The Court of Appeal revisited the specific requirements set out in *Butler* for this category of materials. The Court emphasized that not all sexually explicit materials that are degrading and dehumanizing are obscene, but rather must also, according to the *Butler* test, create a substantial risk of harm to society. And, like any element in a criminal trial, "such risk must be proved beyond a reasonable doubt and that proof must be found in the evidence adduced at trial." In considering the facts of each case, and whether sufficient evidence has been adduced at trial to conclude that the materials did create a substantial risk of harm, the Court of Appeal dismissed all but one appeal, in which the Court held that the trial court had incorrectly found the materials to be obscene.[25]

Hawkins is an important development in the post-*Butler* obscenity jurisprudence, particularly in its re-emphasis that the Crown must prove that degrading and dehumanizing materials create a substantial risk of harm. In so doing, it may operate to protect against some of the more flagrant abuses of *Butler*, by ensuring that the Crown meets the regular standard of proof in a criminal case. The ruling casts further doubt on the *Glad Day Bookshop* decision, in which there is a strong argument to be made that the trial judge erred in finding the materials to be obscene, without adequate evidence that the materials caused harm.

However, *Hawkins* does not represent a departure from the *Butler* test, nor from its sexual subtext. It simply re-emphasizes the objective elements of the crime that the Crown must establish. And in so doing, the Court of Appeal can be seen to be reinscribing the good sex/bad sex distinctions that underlie *Butler*. For example, in attempting to clarify the degree of proof that is required to establish the material causes harm, the Court held:

In some cases, as, for example, in films portraying necrophilia, bondage or bestiality, or sex associated with crime, horror, cruelty, coercion or children, it may be concluded from the contents of the films themselves, without expert or other evidence, that they may predispose persons to act in the antisocial manner contemplated by *Butler*. In other cases, as, for example, in films in which the participants appear as fully willing participants occupying substantially equal roles in a setting devoid of violence or the other kinds of conducts just noted, the risk of societal harm may not be evident.

Further evidence may be required to prove that exposure to the impugned materials will create a substantial risk of an identifiable harm that may cause persons to act in a manner inimical to the proper functioning of society. (*Hawkins*)

According to the Court of Appeal, some sexual representations are so bad that no further evidence is required to prove that they are bad. Other sexual representations that are not so bad will require further evidence in order to prove that they are bad sex. A new dualism thus arrives on the obscenity scene: bad sex that is really bad, and bad sex that is not really bad. This somewhat recast good sex/bad sex distinction (really bad sex/not really bad sex) is thus deployed to establish the degree of proof required to draw the lines between good and bad sex. In other words, the line between good and bad sex is used to help draw the line between good and bad sex. Ironically, the more the Court attempts to establish objective standards of proof, the more it falls back on it subjective distinctions between good and bad sex.[26]

Hawkins, then, is at best a cause for cautious optimism, in the continuing conflict over the legitimacy of sexual representations. As a legal text, it too is the site of contradictory assumptions about the place and status of sexual representations, assumptions that include instinctive notions about what is good and what is bad. And leave to appeal to the Supreme Court of Canada has been granted in one of the cases included within the *Hawkins* appeal.[27] This appeal means that within the foreseeable future, the Supreme Court of Canada will have another opportunity to address the law of obscenity. And more generally, the appeal is yet another indication that the struggle over the legal representation of sexual representation is far from over. The law of obscenity, along with the place and status of sexual representations in our society, continues to be a site of contest and change.

Conclusion

My efforts in this chapter to reveal and deconstruct the conservative sexual morality of the *Butler* decision should not be seen as a condemnation of any concept of sexual morality. To critique the conservative sexual morality is not necessarily to adopt a position of sexual libertarianism according to which "anything goes." My argument is not that we can transcend sexual morality, and that the Supreme Court of Canada has failed in not doing so. Rather, my concern is with the content of that sexual morality. We delude ourselves with the attempt to cast the legal regulation of sex as something other than what it is. We must, as Carol Smart has argued, recognize that feminism has not transcended moral questions, and begin to address feminism's failure to confront moral questions "sufficiently reflexively" (Smart 1993, 187; see also Gotell in this volume). The legal regulation of sex will necessarily involve a sexual morality – of what is good and what is bad about sex. My point is that the sexual morality of the *Butler* decision is one about which we should be very concerned.

I believe that we need to turn our minds to the question of sexual morality, not away from it. Recognizing and critiquing the deeply problematic nature of the dominant sexual morality that informs the *Butler* decision need not mean that we relinquish the terrain of discursive struggle about sexuality. As feminists and queer theorists have revealed, our sexualities are deeply political. We can and must continue to engage in political argument about the sexual world that we want to inhabit. We need to re-image our sexualities in ways that embrace their deeply political nature and the diversity of human sexual experiences. We need to develop more positive theories of sex and sexual expression; of what makes sex a good and positive dimension to our humanity. We need to move beyond the assumptions of sexual essentialism and sexual monism – to recognize the ways in which our sexualities are products of the communities in which we live, and the ways in which our sexual desires and practices are different. We must transcend the mere denunciation of diversity if we are to construct a sexual morality that is based on respect.

A revisioned sexual morality, based on a radical sexual pluralism, could still allow us to be attentive to the subtle workings of power in sexual discourses. We can still be attentive to the ways in which these subtle workings of power deprive many women from engaging in consensual sex. Yet, we must do so in a way that does not make sweeping generalizations about the way other people engage in consensual sex, including s/m practices of consensual nonconsensuality. Such a sexual morality would further allow us to rethink the legal regulation of sex. Sex laws that seek to impose a conservative sexual morality, in which sex is bad – such as obscenity and the criminalization of prostitution – should be abolished. Sex laws, by contrast that seek to eliminate coercive sex – sexual assault and child sexual abuse – should be retained, and even strengthened. We need not relinquish normative judgment, nor even the drawing of lines between good and bad sex, and, in turn, between good sex laws and bad sex laws. But, we must radically rethink the way in which we do so.

NOTES

1 Lamer, C.J.C., LaForest, Cory, McLachlin, Stevenson, and Iacobucci, JJ. concurred with Sopinka, J. Gonthier, J. wrote a minority decision, in which he agreed in the result of the majority, although he offered different reasons. L'Heureux-Dubé, J. concurred in this minority decision. It is the majority decision that is the focus of this discussion.

2 In this respect, the community-standard test did represent a significant change from the *Hicklin* test. Under *Hicklin*, virtually any sexual representation could be (and was) found to be obscene, since it was sexual images themselves that were bad. With the community-standards test, it was no longer necessarily the case that sexual representations were in and of themselves bad, but only those representations that were dirty, indecent, or illicit. The community-standards test introduced into obscenity law the possibility of distinguishing between good sex and bad sex. See Kendrick 1987.

3 Another assumption underlying this test seems to be that tolerance is not only more objective than taste, but that it is also broader. This distinction flies in the face of the history of the legal regulation of obscenity, where the explicit justification of prohibiting its distribution was that certain particularly vulnerable groups in society – notably, poor, uneducated men, and all women, particularly young women – must not be exposed to its influences. Although pornographic images were acceptable for the educated male elites, they must not be massly distributed. The history of pornography reveals that tolerance was in fact considerably more narrow than taste.

4 The Court cites some of the literature that has been seen to establish a connection between pornography and violence against women, including the U.S. Attorney General's Commission on Pornography (the Meese Commission) of 1986. For a critique of the Meese Commission in particular, see Vance 1993b. For a critique of the literature attempting to find a casual connection between pornography and violence, see Segal 1993 and Thelma McCormack, "Making Sense of the Research on Pornography," in *Women Against Censorship*, ed. V. Burstyn (Vancouver: Douglas and McIntyre 1985).

5 This mind/body opposition, which has formed a cornerstone of Western thought since Descartes, rests on and reinforces a series of founda-

tional dualisms: rational/irrational, culture/nature, subject/object. As feminist theorists have argued, these oppositions are also deeply gendered. "In each of the dualisms on which Enlightenment thought rests, rational/irrational, subject/object, and culture/nature, the male is associated with the first element, the female with the second. And in each case, the male element is privileged over the female" (Hekman 1990, 5). The gendered nature of the mind/body distinction, in which men are associated with the mind, and women with the body, makes several brief, but significant, appearances in the text of the decision.

6   Gayle Rubin describes this assumption of sexual essentialism as "the idea that sex is a natural force that exists prior to social life and shapes institutions ... [it] consider[s] sex to be eternally unchanging, asocial and transhistorical" (Rubin 1989, 275).

7   As Gayle Rubin argues, "[s]ex is presumed guilty until proven innocent. Virtually all erotic behavior is considered bad unless a specific reason to exempt it has been established" (Rubin 1989, 278). And that reason must have something to do with the other side of the mind/body distinction.

8   Some readers might be inclined to dismiss the relevance of this language – since it comes, after all, from an old case, which the Court is only reviewing, not unequivocally adopting. Indeed, some commentators point to the fact that the Court expressly rejects this objective of obscenity law later in the decision. However, I believe that this language is not insignificant. Similar language is deployed through the decision. Sopinka, J. resorts to the language of sex as dirty, of "dirt for dirt's sake," on several occasions in the decision. His use of quotation marks, signalling both the adoption of this language from earlier decisions and, presumably, his distance from this language, is somehow intended to sanitize his deployment of the language. These are not his words, after all. Yet, he chooses to use them – again and again. Even in quotation marks, the effect of the repetition of this phrase is to reinforce the underlying binary opposition between good and bad sex (between dirty and clean sex). This repeated deployment of the discourse of sex as dirty is significant in the production of meaning, and in revealing the sexual subtext of the decision.

9   As Lynda Nead's work has illustrated, pornography and art have been set up as binary oppositions, in which each is defined as that which the other is not. "If art is a reflection of the highest social values, then pornography is a symptom of a rotten society; if art stands for lasting, universal values, then pornography represents disposability, trash. Art

is a sign of cleanliness and licit morality, whereas pornography symbolizes filth and the illicit" (Nead 1993b, 282).

10 This second category is not the only contested site. Rather, the question of what constitutes "sex with violence" within the first category is also a highly contested site, particularly within the context of s/m sex. S/m-sex advocates argue that s/m sex is not violence, and thus ought not to be classified as "sex with violence." Gayle Rubin, for example, writes "S/M materials are aimed at an audience that understand a set of conventions for interpreting them. Sadomasochism is not a form of violence, but is rather a type of ritual and contractual sex play whose aficionados go to great lengths in order to do it and to ensure the safety and enjoyment of one another. S/m fantasy does involve images of coercion and sexual activities that may appear violent to outsiders" (Rubin 1993a, 22). Yet the mere appearance of these images is within the context of the *Butler* test, likely to lead to their classification as "sex with violence." As a result, consensual s/m sex, as well as depictions of sex with bondage, is (mis)classified as "sex with violence."

11 *See R. v. Keegstra* (1990), 61 CCC (3d) 1; *Reference re: ss.193 and 195.1(1)(c) of the Criminal Code* (1990), 56 CCC (3d) 65.

12 There is some inconsistency in the Court's description of sex as physical activity. At 472, the Court distinguishes between purely physical activity, like parking a car, and physical activity, such as sex. However, at 474, the Court again uses the phrase "purely physical activity" as synonymous with "purely sexual activity." The point seems to be that although sex may not be so purely physical as to be devoid of any expression, it is, nevertheless, still physical. In relation to the mind/body distinction, it remains of the body, which foreshadows the Court's subsequent discussion of the "nature of expression."

13 Section 1 of the *Charter* provides that all rights and freedoms are "subject only to such reasonable limits, prescribed by law, as can be demonstrably justified in a free and democratic society." The Supreme Court of Canada has established a test for this section 1 analysis *(R. v. Oakes)*. According to this test, the Government must first establish that there is a pressing and substantial objective that justifies overriding the violation of the *Charter* right. Second, the government must establish that the violation of the *Charter* right is proportional with the objective of the legislation.

14 Although the Court tends to use the words "objective" and "purpose" interchangeably, the word "purpose" is often used specifically in relation to the "shifting purpose doctrine." Shifting-purpose doctrine refers to the idea that the purpose of a law can change over time. This doctrine

was rejected by the Supreme Court in *R. v. Big M Drug Mart Ltd*, [1985] 1 SCR 295. Dickson, J. (as he then was) held that "Purpose is a function of the intent of those who drafted and enacted the legislation at the time and not of any shifting variable." In considering the objective of the legislation, courts are thus not permitted to consider a new purpose, but rather must focus only on the purpose of the drafters of the legislation.

15 It is interesting to note, however, the way in which the shifting-purpose doctrine has been used in other cases by the Supreme Court of Canada. In a subsequent s. 2(b) case, *R. v. Zundel* (1992), in which neo-Nazi Ernst Zundel was charged with the crime of spreading false news for his publication of Holocaust denials, the Supreme Court of Canada struck down s. 181 of the *Criminal Code*, on the basis that it violated freedom of expression and was not justifiable under section 1. The shifting-purpose doctrine was an important factor in the decision. The Court rejected the arguments of the Government that the objective of the legislation could be seen. On the basis of *Butler*, it was open to the Court to cast the objective of the legislation more broadly. Indeed, it is difficult to reconcile the decisions of the Court in *Butler* with its decision in *Zundel* on the shifting-purpose doctrine.

In comparing the use of the shifting-purpose doctrine in these two cases, I do not mean to conflate the regulation of sexual expression with the regulation of hate expression. These two areas, which are often conflated in procensorship arguments <pornography is framed as hate speech>, have very different histories, with very distinct legislative objectives. A position for or against the censorship of sexual representations should be seen and evaluated quite separately from a position for or against the censorship of hate speech. Although there may be similar arguments in terms of the relative legitimacy and efficacy of state censorship, the arguments are otherwise quite distinct. As discussed in the introduction, it is not our intention in this book to evaluate the relative merits of the regulation of hate speech.

16 This proportionality requirement involves a three-step test: (1) there must be a rational connection between the legislative provision violating the right and the objective; (2) there must be a minimum impairment of the right; and (3) there must be proper balance between the effect of the legislative provision and the legislative objective.

17 For a further discussion of this marginalization of the s. 2(b) guarantees through the section 1 analysis, see Jamie Cameron, "Abstract Principle v. Contextual Conceptions of Harm: A Comment on R. v. Butler," (1992) 37 *McGill LJ* 1135.

18 Tariff Code 9956 prohibits the importation of obscene materials, as

defined by s. 163 of the *Criminal Code* into Canada. When materials are seized by Canada Customs, the importer has a right of appeal. The first step involves a request for redetermination, after which ensues an appeal to the deputy minister of National Revenue for Customs and Excise, and, subsequently, to court.

19 Henderson examines the lesbian s/m imagery in *On Our Backs*, a lesbian sex magazine, and Pat Califia's *Macho Sluts*, a collection of short stories about lesbian s/m. She argues that both are filled with references to the consensual nature of the sexual practices of the women. "*Macho Sluts* also addresses a range of readers through its demystifications of s/m practice, particularly around images of consent. Indeed, in her introduction, Califia challenges critics who would argue that amid the sexual coercions of patriarchal society, women cannot truly consent to sadomasochism: "If you don't believe we choose to do s/m, you aren't using the term 'consent' in any meaningful way, but rather, as a synonym for 'mature,' 'socially acceptable' and 'politically correct' ... Virtually all the stories ... make pointed distinctions between sadomasochism and sexual coercion" (Henderson 1992, 184).

20 This issue of consent in lesbian sexual representations is explored more fully by Becki Ross in chapter 4.

21 We are at least partially indebted to LEAF for this heteroswitching technique. In the *Butler* case, LEAF attempted to support their arguments of the degrading and dehumanizing nature of pornography to women with reference to gay male pornography. Kathleen Mahoney, quoted in *MS Magazine*, explained: "We showed them the porn – and among the seized videos were some horrifically violent and degrading gay movies. We made the point that the abused men in these films were being treated like women – and the judges got it. Otherwise, men can't put themselves in our shoes. Porn makes women's subordination look sexy and appealing; it doesn't threaten men's jobs, safety, rights, or credibility" (Landsberg 1992, 14).

Karen Busby, however, denies that LEAF played into homophobic discourses in its arguments, and she specifically takes issue with the allegations that LEAF showed videos of gay sex to the Court, which she insists is categorically untrue, and simply the product of media misrepresentation. It is difficult to know what to make of Mahoney's quote in the Landsberg article, since neither Mahoney, Landsberg, or *MS Magazine* appear to have retracted the comments. While LEAF did not in fact show videos in Court, Mahoney's words suggest that LEAF may have simply tried to make this connection in oral argument. Busby admits that LEAF did refer to gay male pornography, but that the arguments in no way collapsed these materials with the harms-based analysis of heterosexual pornography (Busby 1994, 179–80). It is difficult, however, to reconcile Busby's argument with the submission in LEAF's factum, which Busby herself cites – that is, that "LEAF submits that some of the subject of pornography of men for men, in addition to abusing some men in ways that is more common to abuse women through sex, arguably contributes to abuse and homophobia as it normalizes sexual aggression generally." The submission seems more in line with Mahoney's quote than with Busby's explanation.

22 The technique of heteroswitching can be related to what Eve Sedgwick has described as the trope of "gender inversion," according to which lesbians have long been constructed as virile and masculine (and conversely, gay men as effeminate) in order to maintain "the essential heterosexuality within desire itself" (*Epistemology of the Closet* [Berkeley: University of California Press, 1990] at 87). The construction of sexuality as heterosexuality is thereby not threatened or displaced by the recognition of same-sex sexuality. The heteroswitching is perhaps a particular manifestation of this gender inversion, which within the context of obscenity leaves the heterosexual norm of both sexuality and its model of harm unchallenged.

23 This is hardly a surprising factor, in so far as much straight pornography includes depictions of women having sex with women. The discursive distinction between these sexual representations and the representations of specifically lesbian sexuality is discussed in greater length by Becki Ross in chapter 4.

24 *R. v. Hawkins* involved appeals from five separate criminal charges, in relation to four different accused persons: Hawkins, Ronish, Smeek, and Jorgensen: Jorgenson had two different charges against him – one against his adult video store in Hamilton, and one against his store in Scarborough. The Crown appealed the acquittals of Hawkins and Ronish at trial. The defendants Jorgensen and Smeek appealed their convictions.

25 In *Hawkins*, the Crown had adduced no evidence to establish harmful effects, and the material had been approved by the Ontario Film Review Board for "restricted audiences," which absent any evidence rebutting this finding could be taken as a significant indication of the community standard of tolerance. The Crown's appeal of the acquittal was dismissed.

In *Ronish*, the evidence adduced by the Crown did not prove to the satisfaction of the judge that social harm would result from exposure to the films. The Crown's appeal of the acquittal was dismissed.

In *Jorgensen* (Scarborough), the trial judge correctly concluded that the content of the three videos included the depiction of sex coupled with violence and coercion and created the requisite risk of harm. The approval of the materials by the OFRB was found not to be determinative. Rather, the trial judge had properly treated this evidence as indicative of community standards of tolerance, but concluded that it did not outweigh the evidence before her that the material coupled sex with violence and created a substantial risk of harm. The defendant's appeal was dismissed. In *Jorgensen* (Hamilton), the record in the case did not contain evidence to support the conclusion that community standards require that "sexual activity take place within the context of love, affection, commitment, or emotional involvement." The evidence, including the testimony of the Chair of the OFRB, indicated the opposite – that is, that "explicit depiction of human sexuality in a context devoid of any meaningful relationship does not exceed contemporary national community standards of tolerance." The defendant's appeal was allowed.

In *Smeek*, the violence, vampirism, and necrophilia depicted in the films was, according to the Court of Appeal, "patently such as to bring the films within the second of the *Butler* categories." The depictions were degrading and dehumanizing, and created a risk of harm. The defendant's appeal was dismissed.

26 Further, in this passage, the Court articulates its own view of which particular sexual practices constitute really bad sex. These bad representations include those specifically mentioned in s. 163 – sex with "crime, horror, cruelty," as well as those specifically mentioned in *Butler* – sex with children. But, these representations also include sexual practices that are not explicitly mentioned in s. 163, or by the Supreme court of Canada in the *Butler* test – necrophilia, bondage, bestiality, coercion. There may in fact be a strong argument to be made on the face of the *Butler* reasoning, and its underlying sexual morality, that these practices are within these categories of bad sex. But, these practices were not specifically so designated within the *Butler* decision. Nor does the Court of Appeal articulate its reasoning for including these practices within these proscribed categories. Rather, it simply asserts these practices as obvious examples of really bad sex – so obvious, that no reasoning is required to bring them within the *Butler* categories.

27 The Crown's application for leave to appeal in the acquittals of *Hawkins* and *Ronish* was dismissed, but the defendant's applications for leave to appeal their convictions in *Jorgensen* was allowed.

1   Do Dworkin and Cossman arrive at the same conclusion by very
different routes or do they share more in common than at first
sight appears to be the case?

Little Sisters Book and Art Emporium v. Canada (Minister of Justice) 2000 SCC 69

Little Sisters, a bookstore in Vancouver, challenged the right of Canadian
customs officers to seize gay and lesbian materials at the border. The officers
believed it was their mandate to do so under the *Butler* decision, above.

Binnie, J.: – Little Sisters is a lesbian and gay bookshop ... The store
carried a specialized inventory catering to the gay and lesbian community which consisted largely of books that included, but was not limited
to, gay and lesbian literature, travel information, general interest pe-
riodicals, academic studies related to homosexuality, AIDS/HIV safe
sex advisory material and gay and lesbian erotica. It was not in the
nature of a "XXX Adult" store. It was and is a boutique carrying a fairly
broad range of inventory of interest to a special clientele. It was
considered something of a "community centre" for Vancouver's gay
and lesbian population.

The appellants concede that much of the material imported by Little
Sisters consisted of erotica but have denied throughout that anything it
has imported is obscene ... We are told that Canada produces very little
gay and lesbian erotica, obscene or otherwise, and Little Sisters therefore depends on foreign suppliers, mainly in the United States. The
appeal therefore requires us to consider what limitations may constitutionally be placed on freedom of expression when "expression" crosses
international boundaries, and to what extent the rights of importers
must be balanced against the state's interest in preventing the importation of materials that the state considers to be harmful to society ...

Section 99 of the *Customs Act* authorizes customs officers to examine
imported goods and mail and to open packages that they reasonably

suspect may contain goods referred to in the *Customs Tariff*, RSC 1985, c. 41 (3rd Supp.) ... At the entry level, Customs Inspectors determine the appropriate tariff classification (s. 58). At the relevant time, an item considered "obscene" and thus prohibited was subject to a re-determination upon request, by a specialized Customs unit and upon a further appeal subject to a further re-determination by the Deputy Minister or designate ...

Government interference with freedom of expression in any form calls for vigilance. Where, as here, a trial judge finds that such interference is accompanied "by the systemic targeting" of a particular group in society (in this case individuals who were seen as standard bearers for the gay and lesbian community), the issue takes on a further and even more serious dimension. Sexuality is a source of profound vulnerability, and the appellants reasonably concluded that they were in many ways being treated by Customs officials as sexual outcasts ... In this Court the Crown acknowledged that errors were made in the classification of the appellants' imported materials, but says that such errors were only to be expected given the huge volume of cross-border mail handled at the Vancouver Customs Mail Centre each day ...

I propose first to deal with the relationship between the Customs legislation and the obscenity provisions of the *Criminal Code* as interpreted in *Butler*. My conclusion is that the Customs legislation violates the appellants' freedom of expression, as the Crown is prepared to concede, but with the exception of the reverse onus provision in s. 152(3) of the *Customs Act*, it constitutes a reasonable limit prescribed by law which the Crown has justified under s. 1 of the *Charter*.

The administration of the Act, however, was characterized by conduct of Customs officials that was oppressive and dismissive of the appellants' freedom of expression. Its effect – whether intended or not – was to isolate and disparage the appellants on the basis of their sexual orientation ...

My conclusion on the first branch of the appellants' attack is that the *Butler* analysis does not discriminate against the gay and lesbian community. *Butler* is directed to the prevention of harm, and is indifferent to whether such harm arises in the context of heterosexuality or homosexuality. Nor in my view is the gay and lesbian community discriminated against in the Customs legislation, which is quite capable of being administered in a manner that respects *Charter* rights. The government is entitled to impose border inspections of expressive material. The obstacles experienced by the appellants and detailed at length by the trial judge were not inherent in the statutory scheme. The obstacles were, however, very real and in the end quite unjustified ...

The appellants contend that importing a majoritarian analysis into the definition of obscenity (e.g., what the broader Canadian community will tolerate), inevitably creates prejudice against non-mainstream, minority representations of sex and sexuality. They argue that the "national" community is by definition majoritarian and is more likely than the homosexual community itself to view gay and lesbian imagery as degrading and dehumanizing. The whole idea of a community standards test, they say, is incompatible with *Charter* values that were enacted to protect minority rights. The fact that no particular evidence to define the community standard is required to support a successful prosecution heightens the vulnerability of minorities ... What makes this standard even more problematic in the context of gay and lesbian erotica is that where expression is suppressed on the basis of sexual orientation, so goes the argument, it silences voices that are already suppressed and subject to discrimination ...

This line of argument simply rejects the idea that *Butler* means what it says, i.e., that the community standard of tolerance is based on the reasonable apprehension of harm, not on morality. The arguments assume that any appeal to a national community standard cannot be targeted on harm and will inevitably be overwhelmed by majoritarian taste. This approach presupposes that the arbiter (the broader community) is incapable of being focussed on the task that it is required to address (harm). We have no evidence that the courts are not able to apply the *Butler* test, and the reported decisions seem to confirm that the identification of harm is a well understood requirement ...

The constitutional question challenges the validity of s. 71 of the *Customs Act*, on which the redetermination and court proceedings are based. In part, the challenge relies on the "reverse onus" provision applied in such proceedings by virtue of s. 152(3) of the *Customs Act*, as explained in oral argument by counsel for the appellants:

We challenge the entire scheme, not just the power of the Customs officer at the front line to do that detention and prohibition, but the scheme insofar as it puts the onus on the importer, whether the importer is a bookstore or a regular individual to seek a redetermination, or review, or appeal, would have you through a byzantine bureaucratic process and ultimately to the Courts in order to prove that the material is not obscene.

Section 152(3) is not specific to obscenity or even to prohibited goods generally, but applies to "any proceeding under this Act," including the appeals process authorized by s. 71. Section 152(3) directs the decision-maker to assume that Customs officials are right unless and until the importer proves them to be wrong. It provides:

(3) Subject to subsection (4), in any proceeding under this Act, the burden of proof in any question relating to ...

(d) the compliance with any of the provisions of this Act or the regulations in respect of any goods lies on the person, other than Her Majesty, who is a party to the proceeding or the person who is accused of an offence, and not on Her Majesty.

The appellants did not directly impugn the constitutionality of the reverse onus provision in their application to state the constitutional questions, presumably because they intended to rely on its continued validity as a lever to overturn the rest of the Customs legislation in relation to expressive materials. In my view, however, the appellants' attack on s. 71 and the procedures it authorizes is inextricably bound up with the reverse onus provision, and the Court is not bound to accept the application of the latter as valid when considering the constitutionality of the former. The constitutional question in relation to s. 71 encompasses both aspects of the appellants' argument.

The first step is to identify which of the various remedies afforded by s. 71 attract the s. 152(3) onus. Where applicable, it would put on the importer the burden of establishing a negative, i.e., that the expressive material is more likely than not to be non-obscene.

The word "proceeding" is of course apt to apply to any court action that may follow an in-house Customs determination. In my view, however, the provision cannot constitutionally apply to put on the importer the onus of disproving obscenity. Otherwise entry of expressive materials could be denied by reason of the onus even where the standard of obscenity is not met, as for example, where an importer lacks the resources or the stamina to contest an initial determination. An importer has a *Charter* right to receive expressive material unless the state can justify its denial. It is not open to the state to put the onus on an individual to show why he or she should be allowed to exercise a *Charter* right. It is for the state to establish that a limitation on the *Charter* right is justified: *R. v. Oakes,* per Dickson, C.J. at pp. 136–7: "The onus of proving that a limit on a right or freedom guaranteed by the *Charter* is reasonable and demonstrably justified in a free and democratic society rests upon the party seeking to uphold the limitation."

As to the obscenity determination at the departmental level, I do not think s. 152(3) applies at all. The Crown does not contend that all expressive material entering Canada is presumptively obscene until shown to be otherwise. The earliest the reverse onus could apply with any logic is in the re-determination, but at that stage the importer is given neither sufficient notice nor a sufficient opportunity to be heard to discharge the onus. The reality is that once the front-line officer has made the initial determination that he or she considers the publication to be obscene, the question for the Deputy Minister or designate on the re-determination is whether the Department is ready, willing and able, if required, to establish in court that the detained material is obscene ...

As mentioned, s. 152(3) is not restricted to obscenity but has a broad application across the whole Customs process. It may be appropriate when dealing with imports of materials that ordinarily would not have much constitutional sensitivity (such as Minister Nowlan's "cabbages and cucumbers") to put the onus on the importer at the court level to show that the Customs official has made an erroneous tariff classification. What may work as a general rule in circumstances where Customs procedures are not limited by constitutional rights does not, however, work in relation to constitutionally protected expressive materials. In these circumstances, however, the proper order should be limited to the matters pertinent to the disposition of this appeal. I would therefore declare that s. 152(3) is not to be construed and applied so as to place on an importer the onus to establish that goods are not obscene within the meaning of s. 163(8) of the *Criminal Code*. The burden of proving obscenity rests on the Crown or other person who alleges it ...

Iacobucci, J.: – The *Customs Tariff*, s. 114, states that "[t]he importation into Canada of any goods enumerated or referred to in Schedule VII is prohibited." Schedule VII, Code 9956(a), prohibits importation of:

Books, printed paper, drawings, paintings, prints, photographs or representations of any kind that
(a) are deemed to be obscene under subsection 163(8) of the *Criminal Code*.

Several aspects of this regulatory scheme warrant comment. The first is that the initial classification decision, according to s. 58 of the *Customs*

Act, is to be made by "[a]n officer." Section 2 of the Act states that a customs officer includes any "person employed in the administration or enforcement" of the *Customs Act*, and any member of the Royal Canadian Mounted Police. In practice, these decisions are made by Customs Inspectors and Commodity Specialists, the front-line customs officers. The statute does not designate any specialized officers to make obscenity determinations. Instead, any one of the approximately 4,000 customs officers working at the border can prohibit a book from entering the country. The officers receive minimal training with regard to obscenity determinations and are not required to have any specialized knowledge of art or literature.

At high-volume border crossings, such as the Toronto region, certain Commodity Specialists are given special responsibilities over obscenity determinations. Goods suspected of being obscene are detained and forwarded to a Commodity Specialist for classification. However, John Shearer, the Director General of the Tariff Programs Division, testified that working on obscenity classifications is perceived to be more stressful and limiting career-wise. As a result, as Smith, J. recognized, "Customs employees generally consider this work to be undesirable, not all officers participate in it and those assigned to it are regularly moved from these duties into other areas, generally after three to six months" ((1996), 18 BCLR (3d) 241, at para. 44).

Section 58 is also notable for its failure to offer any guidance as to how the tariff classification is to be made. It does not provide for even the simplest of hearings. It does not allow the importer to present evidence, call witnesses, or submit written arguments. It does not require the officer to provide reasons for the decision to prohibit. It does not even require the officer to read or view the material in question ... Customs officers' review of imported materials is frequently superficial and context-insensitive. A typical example is provided by the testimony of Scenery Slater, a Customs Inspector at the Vancouver Mail Centre, describing how she would review a videotape:

[W]e would view it on fast forward. And if there was – there was a scene or scenes we deemed might be potentially prohibited, we rewind and slow it down to verify, and do this through the entirety of the tape.

When asked whether she would typically read a book in its entirety, she responded as follows:

That was rarely necessary. It's – what you – what you would initially do is you would try to determine the gist of the book ... If you started reading it and the general nature was sort of sensationalistic in a sexual manner, and you might flip through to make sure the entirety is like that, go to various sections throughout ... You would find – try to find at least two to three instances of having something prohibited and then once you hit three in the – it was deemed that the rest of the book was of the same nature you would prohibit it there without reading the rest of it.

Several Customs officers testified that they did not even attempt to judge the political, artistic, or literary merit of a particular work. Mr Shearer freely admitted that customs officers do not hold themselves out to be experts on artistic or literary merit. Moreover, Customs officers often do not understand the context in which a book was written. For example, Linda Murphy, the Director of the PID, admitted her lack of understanding of "the S and M practices engaged in by some people in our society." Another Customs officer admitted that she had not recognized Marguerite Duras as a major French novelist of the twentieth century, and that she generally did not have enough time to investigate the literary credentials of the authors whose books appear before her for review ... Incorrect determinations are the inevitable result of these factors ... Behind the statistics are countless anecdotes of incorrect seizures ... An importer or exporter with a history of dealing in pornography is also susceptible to increased scrutiny. During the time period relevant to this appeal, Customs officers in British Columbia inspected virtually every shipment of books and magazines headed to Little Sisters ... While Little Sisters and its suppliers are routinely targeted, mainstream bookstores receive more favourable treatment ... Similarly, books that were prohibited when destined for Little Sisters were widely available at other general interest bookstores in Vancouver, and even at the Vancouver Public Library ... A discussion of the facts as brief as this cannot capture adequately the complexities of the record compiled in this appeal. Nevertheless, I hope to have conveyed a basic portrayal of the Customs legislation and its enforcement.

III ANALYSIS ...

I agree with my colleague Binnie, J.'s defence of the harm-based approach to obscenity set out by this Court in *Butler, supra*. In particular,

I agree with his conclusions that the *Butler* test does not distinguish between materials based on the sexual orientation of the individuals involved or characters depicted. It seems to me that the *Butler* test applies equally to heterosexual, homosexual and bisexual materials ... We differ, however, over the crucial issue of whether the Customs legislation itself is responsible for the constitutional violations documented in this case, or whether it is only the legislation's application that was at fault ... Consequently, I disagree with my colleague Binnie, J.'s interpretation of this Court's decisions in *Hunter v. Southam Inc.*, [1984] 2 SCR 145, *R. v. Morgentaler*, [1988] 1 SCR 30, and *R. v. Bain*, [1992] 1 SCR 91. In my opinion, these cases illustrate the vigilance of this Court in protecting *Charter* rights when the legislative scheme in question is being applied in an unconstitutional fashion. Regardless of whether the legislation is under- or over-inclusive, if it lends itself to the repeated violations of *Charter* rights, as does the legislative scheme here, the legislation itself is partially responsible and must be remedied ... *Morgentaler* also rejected the argument that any problems were a product of maladministration, not the legislation itself ...

In this case, Binnie, J. argues that a failure at the implementation level can be addressed at that level. As will be discussed below, however, the government has provided little reason to believe that reforms at the implementation level will adequately protect the expressive rights involved or that any such reforms will not be dependent on exemplary conduct by Customs officials to avoid future violations of constitutional rights ... When the problems at the review stages are also taken into consideration, it is clear that the legislative scheme must take significant responsibility for the violations of expressive rights that have been documented in this case. This is not surprising when one considers that the Customs legislation was designed to deal with mechanical, objective determinations under a taxing regime and not nuanced judgments on literary and expressive values that are inherently subjective. I therefore conclude that it is the Customs legislation itself which is largely responsible for the infringement of s. 2(b) *Charter* rights in this case.

E   Is the Violation of Section 2(b) Justified Under Section 1?

...

The government's burden under s. 1 is to justify the *actual* infringement on rights occasioned by the impugned legislation, not simply that occasioned by some hypothetical ideal of the legislation. In my view, my colleague Binnie, J. incorrectly analyzes the s. 1 justification with regard only to the Customs legislation when properly administered. Examining such a hypothetical ideal runs the risk of allowing even egregious violations of *Charter* rights to go unaddressed. Obviously any substantive standard for obscenity will have difficulties in application, regardless of the institutional setting in which it is applied. As we recognized in *Butler* and *Keegstra*, this will not necessarily be cause for concern. Where, however, the challenge is to the procedures by which the law is enforced, the fact that far more materials are prohibited than intended is extremely relevant ...

What is challenged primarily in this appeal is not the exclusion of obscenity from this country; instead, it is the legislation which establishes the procedural mechanism for doing so, by which a great deal of non-obscene works are detained or prohibited. The narrow ambit of the government's legitimate purpose will be important to remember when determining whether the Customs legislation is a proportional response to the danger posed by the entry of obscene materials to Canada ...

In light of the Customs legislation's failure to acknowledge effectively the unique *Charter* concerns raised by expressive materials, I conclude that it is not minimally intrusive. As noted above, the only accommodation made for expressive materials is that their review under s. 67 is done by a superior court rather than by the Canadian International Trade Tribunal. In my view, this is insufficient to safeguard the fundamental *Charter* rights at stake. The sheer number of contested prohibitions, and the cost of challenging them through the various levels of administrative review, make it completely impracticable for the appellants to contest each one of them up to the s. 67 level. Thus the one accommodation provided is not even triggered for the vast majority of prohibitions ...

The common law has a long tradition disfavouring prior restraint ... As Thomas Emerson argued in "The Doctrine of Prior Restraint" ... the "worst evils of the system are likely to accumulate" where the system "entrusts the prevention of communication to an executive official." This is not to criticize the character of those charged with enforcing the Customs legislation. I have no doubt that they are generally honest, well-intentioned, hard-working civil servants. Emerson's point, to the contrary, is that the institutional dynamics of prior restraint commonly produce the kinds of "grave systemic problems" found in this case ... The flaws in the Customs regime are not the product of simple bad faith or maladministration, but rather flow from the very nature of prior restraint itself.

READING QUESTIONS ON *LITTLE SISTERS*

1 Do you agree with Iacobucci, J. that the fault lies with the legislation, not just with its administration? Are his arguments specific to prior restraint of free expression, or more general? How are they related to the views of Hobbes and Fuller, above?
2 Do you agree with Binnie, J. that a reverse onus is appropriate for "cabbages and cucumbers"? Or would that too violate values related to the rule of law?
3 In evaluating legislation, should judges assume it will be administered perfectly? Imperfectly? Sloppily? How might one justify the appropriate standard?
4 Both Iacobucci, J. and Binnie, J. say that *Butler* applies to homosexual as well as heterosexual materials. Is this claim convincing? How might one apply it, given the role that the court, following MacKinnon, gives to pornography in the subordination of women?
5 How do you suppose Cossman, above, would respond to the decision?

L.W. Sumner
The Hateful and the Obscene (2004)

Sumner argues that the Supreme Court of Canada has only paid lip service to Mill's harm principle in its treatment of pornography and hate speech. He criticizes the overly broad conception of social harm on which recent decisions rest, and then offers an alternative approach to freedom of expression that is more narrowly focused on actual harm caused.

Nearly forty years of judicial infatuation with community standards has not brought us measurably closer to an objective test of obscenity. In fact, it has not even resulted in a great deal of advance over the subjectivity and inconsistency of the old *Hicklin* test. The reference to community standards of tolerance, introduced into obscenity adjudication in 1962, has not prevented judges from relying on their personal levels of tolerance (or standards of taste) in determining whether the materials before them are obscene. Instead of deciding, on the basis of no evidence beyond the work itself, whether some erotic material has a "tendency to deprave and corrupt," judges are now required to determine when its depiction of sex is "degrading or dehumanizing." Their ritual genuflection toward community standards does little to disguise the essential arbitrariness of this exercise.

THE TYRANNY OF THE COMMUNITY

Although the foregoing problems are serious, there are also deeper, more philosophical, objections to the use of the community standards test in obscenity adjudication. In order to highlight these objections, we need to make the following (unrealistic) assumptions: (1) at any given time there is a strong consensus, at least among the majority of Canadians, concerning the kinds of erotic materials whose distribution they are prepared to tolerate; (2) empirical evidence is available concerning this consensus which could be presented by the crown in the course of obscenity prosecutions; (3) the consensus is sufficiently determinate and stable as to constitute "fair notice" whether particular materials exceed community standards of tolerance. Even under these ideal conditions for its practicability the community standards test would still be objectionable in principle.

To see why this is so, we need to return to J.S. Mill's Harm Principle, according to which the risk of harm to others is the only legitimate ground for legal restraint of an activity.[1] The Harm Principle excludes two competing justifications for restraints on liberty: paternalism (the protection of individuals against harm to which they willingly expose themselves) and moralism (the prohibition of activities with no potential for harm, to self or others, on the ground that they are immoral). The *Hicklin* test, with its reliance on the "tendency to deprave and corrupt," was openly moralistic; as long as the test was in force, pornographic materials were condemned on the ground either that they were themselves indecent or that they encouraged indecent acts.[2] In the *Hicklin* case itself, Chief Justice Cockburn found the objectionable portions of the pamphlet at issue to consist of "a series of paragraphs, one following upon another, each involving some impure practices, some of them of the most filthy and disgusting and unnatural description it is possible to imagine."[3] This language of impurity and contamination permeates the case law during the *Hicklin* era, right through to the 1950s.[4] The demise of the test was occasioned in no small part by a growing disquiet with legal moralism as a justification for restraints on liberty,[5] accompanied by the conviction that a firmer basis needed to be found for the legal regulation of pornography. Following the introduction of the statutory definition of obscenity, the courts sought this basis in contemporary community standards. However, as long as these were interpreted as standards of decency, the rationale for regulating erotic materials remained moralistic.[6] Even under the *Hicklin* test courts recognized that public opinion about decency would be subject to change over time.[7] Since judges could not be expected to ascertain an eternal Platonic truth (if there is one) about the boundary between decency and indecency, reliance on contemporary community standards was inevitable. The community standards test therefore could not move obscenity adjudication out of the shadow of moralism until the standards in question were reinterpreted as providing a measure not of decency but of tolerance.

At least in principle, there is a clear difference between a standard of tolerance and a standard of taste or morality, since people may regard certain activities as indecent, and therefore prefer not to engage in them, while being prepared to tolerate their practice by others. Recall Chief Justice Dickson's definitive statement of the distinction: "What matters is not what Canadians think is right for themselves to see. What matters is what Canadians would not abide other Canadians seeing ..."[8] This shift of focus from taste to tolerance is supposed to provide us with a more defensible justification for restricting liberties – to manufacture, distribute, and (by implication) consume erotic materials. The rationale can no longer be that these materials are indecent or scurrilous or otherwise immoral. Nor, since community intolerance is an unreliable indicator of genuine harm, can it be that they are harmful. So what is it? Stripped to its essentials, this is what the majority is saying to a minority with different tastes: "You will not be permitted to exercise your taste, not because its exercise would be harmful to society, nor even because it would be immoral, but simply because we are not prepared to tolerate it. It *will* not be tolerated because we think it *should* not be tolerated."

Reliance on the majority's limits of tolerance as a principle of restraint has been frequently, and justly, criticized either as objectionably conservative or as institutionalizing a (sexist or heterosexist) bias.[9] But these are mere symptoms of the fundamental problem. When Mill wrote the essay *On Liberty*, the danger against which he thought individual liberty principally needed protection was what he called the "tyranny of the majority," which included "the tyranny of the prevailing opinion and feeling ... [and] the tendency of society to impose ... its own ideas and practices as rules of conduct on those who dissent from them ... and compel all characters to fashion themselves upon the model of its own."[10] The Harm Principle was Mill's proposed line of defence against this tyranny: unless it is possible to demonstrate a significant risk of social harm, there is no case for a restraint of liberty. The Harm Principle of course forbids moralism as a ground of restraint, whether in the form of the *Hicklin* test or a community standard of decency. But in protecting individuals against the tyranny of the majority it also forbids restraint on the basis of a community standard of tolerance.

The rationale behind the Harm Principle is obvious: since harm is (by definition) an evil, no one has an unqualified liberty-right to inflict it on others. The fact that some activity is socially harmful is therefore easily recognizable as a reason (in principle) for its legal regulation. There is no similar rationale for the community standards test: the fact that the majority is not prepared to tolerate some activity is, taken by itself, no reason at all for restricting it. Indeed, it appears to confuse the existence of intolerance with the justification for it; whereas harm can count as a reason for refusing to tolerate an activity, the mere fact that it is not tolerated cannot. The task of the courts is to determine what forms of expression must be tolerated, since they are protected by section 2(b) of the *Charter*. This important question cannot be settled by ascertaining what forms of expression are in fact tolerated. The idea that important individual rights can be circumscribed by the tolerance level of the majority is misconceived from the outset, since one of the principal functions of rights (and of their constitutional entrenchment in the *Charter*) is to safeguard minorities against the majoritarian decision making represented by the legislature.

Another way of putting this is to say that, if community intolerance is a poor epistemic indicator of genuine harm, reliance on community standards to identify the realm of the obscene effectively recognizes moral distress as a kind of harm. In order to determine whether particular erotic materials will be legally tolerated, courts must try to determine whether most Canadians would morally tolerate them. But in that case the issue is decided by the level of moral distress experienced by some (the majority) at the very idea that others (the minority) are consuming these materials. This is not enough, by itself, to show that this result was reached through an application of the Harm Principle. But that step is easy to supply as well. According to the *Butler* court the rationale for regulating pornography in Canada has always been harm-based: it is the conception of the harm done by pornography which has shifted over time. Whereas this was once conceptualized as moral harm done to the male consumer, the locus of the harm has now been transferred to other groups considered to be vulnerable (especially women and children). What has all this to do with the appeal to community standards? It might be thought one thing to regulate pornography on a harm-based ground and quite another to do so by reference to the community's alleged standards of tolerance. The former fits unproblematically within the Harm Principle as traditionally conceived (that is, without expanding it by recognizing moral distress as a kind of harm) while the latter does not. But the court did not make this distinction; instead, it relied on community standards of tolerance as the measure of harm. In doing so, the court maintained an official allegiance to the Harm Principle, but only at the cost of treating communal moral distress – grounded in a shared standard of tolerance – as a harm. Violent pornography counts as harmful, not because it can be causally linked to sexual violence (the court recognized that the evidence on this question is inconclusive), but because most people think it is so linked and are therefore not willing to tolerate its consumption by anyone (else).

Just as the inadequacies of moralism gradually became apparent to an earlier generation of judges and scholars, so questions are now being raised about tolerance as a basis for restraint. These questions achieved some degree of judicial recognition in the Supreme Court's decision in *Towne Cinema*, where for the first time social harm was acknowledged as a relevant factor. Recall the disagreement in that decision between Chief Justice Dickson and Justice Wilson over whether harm was to be determined independently of the community standards test. Ultimately, in *Butler*, the court favoured Wilson's opinion (that community standards are the appropriate measure of social harm) over Dickson's (that the two factors could diverge, so that independent evidence of harm would be appropriate). Some commentators on the *Butler* decision have hailed it as the final step in the evolution from moralism to a harm test for obscenity.[11] It is certainly true that the *Butler* court devoted considerable attention to the harm question, at least so far as it concerned depictions of sex which are "degrading or dehumanizing."[12] However, it also subsumed that question under the community standards test.[13] The result is an unstable union of two quite different grounds for the legal regulation of pornography: harm and tolerance. While the former is the only legitimate ground, the *Butler* decision suggests that the harm test is to be applied by means of the community standards test, on the assumption that community standards of tolerance are based, at least in part, on the perception of harm. It is difficult to think of any other legal context in which the fact that some activity is harmful is taken to be established by people's belief that it is.[14] If, for instance, the state wishes to justify restrictions on smoking in public places, then it must provide evidence that exposure to secondhand smoke is a health hazard, not just that people think it is.[15] Only in the case of pornography is mere opinion considered to be sufficient to establish the fact of the matter.

Whether pornography has the potential for social harm (and, if so, what kind of harm) is a complex empirical question for whose resolution it is appropriate to consult the best available social-scientific evidence. It is not a question to be answered by a public opinion survey. If the evolution of judicial and academic thinking about obscenity has brought us now to the point of accepting the harm test as dispositive, then we should apply that test directly by requiring evidence of the harm caused by pornography. Doing so will render the community standards test redundant and obsolete. The test was devised in the first place to fill the legislative vacuum left by the vague and unhelpful "undue exploitation" definition of obscenity. Over the course of some forty years, it has gradually evolved from its roots in moralism to an unreliable surrogate for a harm test. It cannot now carry judicial thinking about obscenity any farther along the road to an open endorsement of the Harm Principle; indeed, it is an obstacle to further progress in that direction. The *Butler* court inherited the community standards test which had already been shown (in *Towne Cinema*) to have at best an uneasy relationship with the harm test. The court had the opportunity to steer the course of obscenity adjudication in a new direction by repudiating community standards altogether, and it did not have the courage to do so. Now it is time to decide, as a matter of political morality, what can justify restraints on the freedom to circulate erotic materials. If it is the majority's level of tolerance, then the community standards test still has a role to play. But if it is the risk of harm, then the test has outlived its usefulness.

CONCLUSION

The definition of obscenity in Canada is a judicial construct filling a legislative vacuum. Having been given nothing more specific to work with than the unhelpfully vague phrase "the undue exploitation of sex," the courts have attempted to operationalize it by adopting the community standards test as a reference point. Doing so has raised a number of legal problems: In a country as diverse as Canada, how can we speak of a national community? If there is such a community, how do we determine what its level of tolerance is for (some particular kind of) erotic materials? In the absence of a national consensus, is the community standard decided by the majority? If so, how are triers of fact to determine what the majority view is when they are given no empirical evidence on the question? How do we avoid having judges substitute their own personal tolerance level for that of the community? If this is what judges are doing, does the obscenity law not fail to provide potential offenders with "fair notice" of the legal status of their actions?

Although these practical difficulties attending the application of the obscenity law are serious enough, there is also a deeper and more philosophical issue raised by the community standards test. Criminalizing conduct solely on the ground that the majority are not prepared to tolerate it is inconsistent with Mill's Harm Principle and with the rejection in liberal societies of legal moralism. In its *Butler* decision and thereafter, the Supreme Court has insisted that restrictions on expressive freedom must be harm-based rather than morality-based. Since there is no good reason to think that the community's level of tolerance accurately tracks harmfulness, there remains a contradiction at the heart of Canadian obscenity adjudication.

...

AN IMMODEST PROPOSAL

I draw from the foregoing guidelines the conclusion that a defensible policy concerning the regulation of expression must (1) focus on harm to the exclusion of all extraneous considerations, (2) rest on reliable evidence of all alleged harms, (3) balance the harms of expression against those of restraint, (4) employ only measures of harm reduction which promise to be effective, and (5) among equally effective measures prefer those whose costs to expressive interests are lower. Our question now is what such a policy might look like.

My strategy in trying to answer this question will be to work from the "inside out," beginning with the limits to expressive freedom for which the most compelling justification is available and then applying the lessons learned to the more problematic and ambiguous cases. Our starting point will be the child pornography law (s. 163.1 of the *Criminal Code*), whose purpose is to prevent the sexual abuse or exploitation of children.[16] Because children are sexually abused in the making of most child pornography, and also because these materials can be used by pedophiles to recruit children for abuse, the linkage in this case between the expressive material and the harm it does is particularly direct and well verified. Besides its narrower focus and the more reliable evidence of the harm it aims to prevent, the child pornography law has the further advantage over the obscenity statute of working with a content-based definition of the material it is targeting which is free of reliance on community standards. On the other hand, the law intrudes more deeply into expressive freedom by virtue of criminalizing not just the production or distribution of child pornography but also its mere possession. As the Supreme Court recognized in the *Sharpe* case, the possession offence can be justified only if the definition of child pornography is no broader than it needs to be in order to prevent the harms in question. So let us begin by examining that definition more closely.

Because it is rather complicated, it will be useful to work with a simplified catalogue of prohibited materials. Roughly speaking, the child pornography law targets the following kinds of expression:[17]

1 Visual materials (photographs, films, videos, drawings, etc.) which
   (a) graphically depict children engaged in intimate sexual activity, or
   (b) graphically depict adults engaged in intimate sexual activity, wherethe adults are represented as children, or
   (c) depict nudity in children for a sexual purpose, or
   (d) advocate or counsel any sexual offence against children.
2 Written materials (stories, diaries, essays, etc.) which
   (a) depict any sexual offence against a child for a sexual purpose, or
   (b) advocate or counsel any sexual offence against children.

This list makes it clear that the sweep of the law is very wide indeed. The question is whether it is too wide to satisfy the *Oakes* test of minimal impairment. In that light, some of the categories seem particularly problematic. Two of them, 1(d) and 2(b), include purely argumentative materials, such as an essay advocating some form of sexual activity between adults and children. Whatever we might think of such advocacy, it is difficult both to conceptualize it as child pornography and to find a convincing rationale for its prohibition.[18] I am aware of no evidence implicating materials of this sort in actual harm to children, since they involve no children in their production and would be of little use in recruiting children for abuse. Furthermore, any prohibition of the circulation of an idea is a content restriction which makes particularly deep inroads into expressive freedom. If, on the other hand, these clauses are meant to capture (visual or verbal) depictions of child sexual activity which, by virtue of having the function of sexual stimulation, implicitly endorse this activity then they would seem to be redundant, since such depictions are captured elsewhere in the definition.

A broader, and more difficult, question arises from the fact that, even if we delete these two problematic clauses, the definition still includes not only visual materials whose production involves the actual sexual abuse of children but also materials (both visual and verbal) in whose production real children were not implicated, including stories (2(a)), drawings or computer-generated simulations (1(a)), and visual materials depicting adults as children (1(b)). In these latter cases no harms to participants are in question. The rationale for their inclusion must therefore rest entirely on the prevention of more indirect harms to third parties, especially the potential use of such materials to lure children into abusive situations. As far as I am aware, there is no evidence that erotic stories have any such potential, so it is difficult to make out a good case for including any written materials within the purview of the law.

Visual materials in which the depiction is simulated or virtual are a harder case. Category 1(b), for example, prohibits visual representations of sexual activity involving persons who are not actually underage but are depicted as such. This provision is obviously intended to prevent circumvention of the law by using adult models or performers who are dressed or otherwise made to look much younger. Much material of this sort exists; indeed, it is the standard fare on commercial websites claiming to offer explicit sexual images involving "young" models. However, it is of little interest to collectors of child pornography or to pedophiles hoping to recruit children for abuse. While it could in principle be used for this purpose, there is no reason to think that it would be more successful than other forms of adult pornography which are perfectly legal. In any case, the principal target for law enforcement agencies is material depicting very young (pubescent or pre-pubescent) children for whom there are no plausible adult surrogates.[19] The provision is also inherently difficult to enforce. While producers of sexually explicit materials can be required to document the age of all models or performers (and most are willing to comply, if only to stay on the safe side of the law), how are we to decide when someone over the age of eighteen is being depicted as underage (unless the scenario somehow makes that clear)? It is doubtful, therefore, whether this component of the definition of child pornography has any useful function.

What then of real-looking but computer-generated images of children in sexual scenarios? This question was recently adjudicated by the U.S. Supreme Court in *Ashcroft*. In the *Child Pornography Prevention Act* of 1996 Congress expanded the federal prohibition of child pornography so as to include sexually explicit images that appear to depict minors but were produced by means other than using real children (such as computer-imaging technology). In its decision the court struck down this expansion on the ground that "virtual child pornography" lacked the direct connection to the sexual abuse of children that was involved in "real" pornography. Moreover, the court concluded, the claim that virtual materials could still be used to groom or seduce children was too speculative to justify a content restriction on expression. The effect of the court's decision was to confine the definition of child pornography to materials whose production involved the use of real children.[20]

Given its decision in *Sharpe*, there is no reason to think that the Canadian court would draw a distinction between real and virtual child pornography. On this issue, therefore, we are offered two diametrically opposed positions: continuing to include visual depictions of child sexual abuse whether or not real children were involved in their production or restricting the definition of child pornography to visual records of actual abuse. The choice between these alternatives is not an easy one. However, especially in light of the possession offence, which trenches particularly deeply on individual freedom, it would be consonant with the evidence-based approach which I have advocated to expand the definition no farther than reliable evidence of harm. That evidence is incontrovertible in the case of materials produced by abusing children. Furthermore, the possession offence has a particularly compelling rationale in this case, since it can be argued that consumer demand for "real" pornography stimulates the market for more production and therefore more abuse. Where this rationale is absent, it is reasonable to demand reliable evidence of the use of virtual pornography to groom victims. Absent such evidence, the safer route is to limit the definition of child pornography to its narrowest confines.

If we consolidate our results to this point then we are left with categories 1(a) and 1(c), understood in each case to include only materials depicting real children. However, even category 1(a) is not without its defects. Unlike category 1(c), it lacks the condition that the depiction must be "for a sexual purpose," which the Supreme Court has glossed as meaning that it could be "reasonably perceived as intended to cause sexual stimulation."[21] In its present formulation, therefore, it could capture explicit depictions of child sexual activities which had an educational or scientific, rather than a sexual, purpose. In its 1993 version the child pornography law provided an exception for materials with an educational, scientific, or medical purpose.[22] However, the amendments tabled by the government in Bill C-20 would delete this paragraph in favour of a (much vaguer) "public good" defence.[23] In that case, it becomes imperative that educational or scientific materials, with no stimulative function, not be caught by the definition in the first place. The qualifier "for a sexual purpose" should therefore be read into the formulation of category 1(a). This has the effect of bringing the materials in this category within the accepted notion of pornography, which requires that their purpose be sexual arousal.

One further difficulty with the definition remains. For the purpose of section 163.1 a child is defined as someone under the age of eighteen. This age limit has the advantage both of being somewhat conservative and of being in line with similar provisions in many other jurisdictions, especially the United States. It is therefore widely recognized and observed by producers and distributors of mainstream pornography.[24] There is a case to be made for Canadian law harmonizing with international standards in this area. However, the use of eighteen as a cut-off point is curiously at odds with the other *Criminal Code* provisions concerning sexual offences against children (ss. 151–153). Simplifying considerably, those provisions absolutely prohibit sexual contact only with children under the age of fourteen (ss. 151 and 152). Between the age of fourteen and seventeen, such contact is prohibited only where a relationship of trust, authority, or dependency exists with the child – in other words, where there is reason to suspect exploitation of the child (s. 153). Now it could be argued that using a child in the production of pornography is tantamount to exploiting such a relationship, but it is difficult to see how this could be made out where the pedophile is a stranger or someone only casually connected to the child. The section as written seems aimed principally at those who have an established relationship with the child (parents, guardians, teachers, coaches, etc.). The amendments introduced by the government in Bill C-20 add an exploitative relationship to the prohibited list in section 153, where the following factors are to be taken into account in determining when a relationship is exploitative: age difference, the evolution of the relationship, and the degree of control or influence over the child. This provision arguably harmonizes better with the child pornography law, since most pedophiles may satisfy the conditions for an exploitative relationship with the children they recruit to appear in visual pornography. However, it is noteworthy that the government elected the foregoing change in the characterization of sexual offences against children instead of raising the age of consent (say, to sixteen). That decision might well have been a sound one, since a rigid age of consent risks criminalizing many forms of innocuous sexual contact with (and between) underage adolescents. However, it does leave the sexual offence provisions (whose age of consent is fourteen) out of step with the child pornography provision (whose age of consent is eighteen). It is difficult to understand why it would be unlawful to depict sexual activity (with a sixteen-year-old, for instance) which is itself perfectly lawful. A case could therefore be made for enforcing a single age of consent for both sexual activities and depictions of such activities, somewhere between fourteen at the lower end and eighteen at the upper.[25] However, a better alternative would be to incorporate sections 151 to 153 into section 163.1 by defining child pornography as any graphic visual depiction, for a sexual purpose, of child nudity or of intimate sexual activity involving children which would itself be a sexual offence.

While in its present form the child pornography law is overbroad, and therefore trenches too deeply on freedom of expression, it is clear that a version of the law which is more narrowly targeted in this way would easily surpass the threshold for criminal legislation. In light of both the similarities and the differences between the child pornography and obscenity laws, it is natural now to ask whether the same case can be made for criminal legislation regulating (at least some) adult pornography. One thing that is clear by now is that the harm done by pornography, whatever it might be, cannot be measured by any appeal to community standards. This implies, at a minimum, that the current obscenity law in Canada, with its obsolete reference to "undue exploitation of sex," must go.[26] It is the vagueness and unworkability of that definition that led the judiciary to rely on community standards to define the boundary between the obscene and the acceptable. If we are to have an obscenity law at all then, like the child pornography law, it must bite the bullet and provide an operational definition of obscenity in terms of both content and function. In the case of child pornography that project is feasible, since we can specify the objectionable content in terms of sexual images of children. No parallel content-based definition seems possible in the case of obscenity. During the 1980s the government of the day made two attempts to replace section 163 of the *Criminal Code* with legislation which defined obscenity in terms of a catalogue of prohibited depictions.[27] Both attempts failed, in part because any such catalogue was found to be too inflexible to accommodate evolving standards of sexual morality and tolerance. Whatever its other defects, at least the community standards criterion was capable of moving with the times. But the deeper problem was that "bad" pornography (for which legal regulation might be appropriate) cannot be distinguished from "good" pornography simply on the basis of the sexual activities it depicts or the body parts it displays. The same content – the sexual scenario itself – is capable of depiction in "good" or "bad," pornographic or non-pornographic, ways.

The *Butler* decision in 1992 went a considerable distance toward resolving the very considerable legal uncertainty throughout the 1980s as to which erotic depictions were to be regarded as obscene. Henceforth, the problematic representations were of sexual violence or degradation; depictions of sexual scenarios free of these features, however explicit they might be, were to fall outside the prohibited area. While this was doubtless a step forward, it did not solve the underlying definitional problem. For one thing, even a very explicit depiction of sexual violence or degradation can be produced for a number of different purposes, only one of which is sexual stimulation or arousal.[28] In order to capture the specifically pornographic the sexual *purpose* must be added to the sexual *content*. But even when that is done it is virtually impossible to contour the definition of "bad" pornography (the obscene) so as to map onto the harm whose prevention is the sole legitimate rationale of obscenity legislation. Consider, for example, visual depictions of the following two scenarios:

The gang-rape scenario. The repeated rape of a young woman is explicitly depicted in such a way as to be sexually arousing for a male audience. While she is initially shown to be resisting her attackers, she eventually comes to welcome and enjoy the violation.

The BDSM scenario. Two women are shown engaging in consensual sadomasochistic activities in which the "top" subjects the "bottom" to bondage and mild forms of torture. While the depiction is clearly meant to be sexually stimulating, the bottom is shown to be an active participant in the scenario and capable of calling an end to it whenever she chooses.

In both cases the activity depicted is violent and the depiction has the purpose of sexual arousal. Both therefore fall within the category of violent pornography. Yet while the first depiction clearly endorses violence against women by eroticizing it, it is far from clear that the second does so or that there is any identifiable kind of harm we might expect to flow from it. (Perhaps it would stimulate other couples – same-sex or otherwise – to experiment with consensual BDSM, but so what?) The difference between the two depictions is that only the first expresses an attitude of hatred or contempt toward women; in eroticizing forced sexual violence against them it degrades them to the status of objects or things. This further element – the endorsement of a degraded status for women – is not picked up by a content-based definition of obscenity, even when the content is violent and its depiction is for a sexual purpose. It is that element, however, which appears to constitute the potential harm of misogynist pornography and to provide the sole legitimate rationale for exercising legal control over it.

As we have seen, the strongest rationale for exercising such control over child pornography is to prevent the sexual abuse of children involved in its production. However, when we turn to participant harms in the case of adult pornography, imposing content restrictions on the product appears to be fundamentally misdirected. Unlike the case of children, exploitation or abuse of adult women, however frequently it occurs, is not an essential feature of the production process. Given the evident demand for pornography, criminalizing its production will succeed only in driving it underground, making the enforcement of fair employment practices impossible. The preferable route is to regard this as another problem of working conditions to be dealt with through enforcement of regulations in the workplace.[29] As the "adult" film industry goes increasingly mainstream, it should be required to adopt the normal protections for workers against harassment and duress: standardized contracts, minimum wages, supervision of shoots, the ability to organize effective associations or unions, and so on. With the constant risk of sexually transmitted diseases there are potentially serious health concerns to be dealt with as well, but they are best addressed as workplace health and safety issues.

The harms most frequently associated with pornography are its encouragement of sexual violence against women and its reinforcement of women's inferior social status. As we saw in the previous chapter, the supporting evidence for these effects is, for the most part, inconclusive at best. Given an initial presumption in favour of expressive liberty, inconclusive evidence is insufficient to surmount the threshold for criminal regulation. If the purpose of the obscenity law is to prevent these diffuse and systemic harms, then it must specifically target erotic materials which are misogynist in the attitudes they express toward women. Misogynist attitudes, however, can also be expressed in visual or verbal materials with no erotic content whatever (for instance, in novels or films portraying female characters as brainless). What this suggests is that the focus on the sexual, which is the hallmark of an obscenity law, is fundamentally misdirected. Pornography is problematic when it constitutes hate literature concerning women. But in that case the appropriate vehicle for its legal regulation is legislation targeting not the obscene but the hateful.

The logic of the obscenity law therefore takes us to the hate law. As I conceive it, this is the crux of the matter concerning defensible limits to expressive freedom and the hardest case to decide. Setting aside its details, section 319(2) of the *Criminal Code* prohibits any public communication intended to promote hatred against an "identifiable group." What is most obviously problematic about the statute, and the principal source of civil libertarian objections to it, is that it criminalizes the circulation of hateful opinions whether or not they have any discernible effect on the level of hostility toward their target groups. It is the nature of the views – whether they are hateful or not – that matters for the purpose of the law, not whether they actually succeed in influencing attitudes. As far as the law is concerned, it does not matter whether a hate message evokes nothing but ridicule or repudiation, as long as the intent of the message, as interpreted from its content and the context of its dissemination, was to promote hatred.

The most common argument in favour of regulating hate speech is that it contributes to a general climate of hostility or bigotry directed against target minorities which can in turn encourage or reinforce practices of discrimination or violence. The main problem with this argument, as with the parallel argument concerning pornography and women, is that we have very little hard evidence of this causal relationship. Because the attitudinal effects attributed to hate messages are diffuse and systemic, they are difficult both to measure and to trace to one particular cause. It is undeniable that members of racial and ethnic minorities in Canada have been victims of both discrimination and hate crimes (whether against persons or property). But it is far from clear just how much of this inequality and violence can be attributed to the circulation of hate messages. Because the groups most responsible for these messages operate clandestinely on the margins of Canadian society, they are likely to have little influence on mainstream public opinion. It might well be that the principal consequence of allowing them to voice their views openly and frankly, without codes and subtexts, would be to marginalize and discredit them even further.

The recent episode involving David Ahenakew provides a case in point. Ahenakew has been an influential aboriginal leader, with a long history of achievements in advancing Native rights and interests in Canada in general and Saskatchewan in particular. However, in December 2002, at a meeting of the Federation of Saskatchewan Indian Nations on the subject of health care, he made a number of strongly anti-Semitic remarks, including the suggestion that the Nazis were justified in initiating the Holocaust. Unlike the rantings of obscure white supremacists, these remarks received prominent media attention. They also elicited an overwhelming backlash of condemnation, not only from Jewish groups but also from Native leaders, politicians, the media, and so on. Ahenakew was stripped of every position he occupied as a Native leader and faces expulsion as well from the prestigious Order of Canada. There is no doubt that Ahenakew's remarks constituted hate propaganda, within the meaning of the statute. However, there is little likelihood that they succeeded in promoting any hatred against Jews or strengthening anti-Semitic attitudes in Canada. Six months after the event the Attorney General of Saskatchewan finally decided to proceed with charges against Ahenakew under section 319(2). However, it is difficult to see what the point of the prosecution might be. The overwhelming adverse reaction to his remarks would seem to serve by itself as an adequate deterrent, both to him and to others of like opinion.

The Ahenakew incident illustrates two important points. Recall the condition that criminal sanctions should be employed only "when the harm caused or threatened is serious, and when the other, less coercive or less intrusive means do not work or are inappropriate." Both discrimination and hate violence certainly qualify as serious harms. However, there appear to be less intrusive means available of neutralizing any contribution that hate speech might make to these practices. One of these means is precisely the kind of counterspeech elicited by Ahenakew's remarks. By the time the uproar over his comments had subsided and he had been denounced by every influential source of public opinion, the net effect was a forceful reminder of the evils of anti-Semitism. The antiracism cause was arguably better served by having Ahenakew speak his mind and arouse a firestorm of opposition than it would have been had he been intimidated into silence by the fear of prosecution. The other point has to do with an argument commonly used to support the criminalization of hate speech, namely that it serves as a vehicle for society to express its condemnation of racial hatred and bigotry. This purely symbolic function of law is, of course, rejected by a harm-based approach. But in any case the Ahenakew incident is a timely reminder that we don't need courts to voice our repugnance concerning racism when so many other authoritative social institutions can be relied on to do this.

There are further problems with the hate propaganda law in its present form. When it was first enacted in 1970 it may have made sense to restrict the scope of its protection to groups identified by "colour, race, religion or ethnic origin." However, subsequent developments in law and public policy have resulted in a longer list of social groups considered to be vulnerable to discrimination and/or violence. The *Canadian Human Rights Act*, adopted in 1977, currently prohibits discrimination based on "race, national or ethnic origin, colour, religion, age, sex, sexual orientation, marital status, family status, disability or conviction for an offence for which a pardon has been granted." Meanwhile, section 15 of the *Charter*, which came into effect in 1985, excludes discrimination based on "race, national or ethnic origin, colour, religion, sex, age or mental or physical disability" (sexual orientation has subsequently been "read in" to this list by the Supreme Court). Even more to the point, section 718.2 of the *Criminal Code* provides for penalty enhancement in the case of offences motivated by "bias, prejudice, or hate based on race, national or ethnic origin, language, colour, religion, sex, age, mental or physical disability, sexual orientation or any other similar factor." In light of all these precedents, the much shorter list of protected groups in section 319(2) seems arbitrary. If the aim of the statute is to prevent hostility toward religious, racial, or ethnic groups then why would this protection not be extended equally to other groups, such as women and gays and lesbians, who have also been, and continue to be, victims of both discrimination and hate-motivated violence?[30] If the statute is defensible at all, simple consistency requires that the scope of its protection be extended.

I have argued above that the sole defensible rationale for the obscenity law would be much better served by expanding the list of protected groups to include women. Others have made the same case on behalf of gays and lesbians,[31] a case that was recently acknowledged by the House of Commons when it passed a private member's bill adding "sexual orientation" to the definition of an "identifiable group."[32] While these expansions are required by the internal logic of section 319(2), they also have the effect of accentuating another problem with the law, namely the inevitable vagueness of the notion of hatred. In *Keegstra* (1990) the Supreme Court interpreted hatred of a group to include only the most intense feelings of antipathy or detestation toward members of the group.[33] While this gloss helps somewhat to focus the concept by excluding the milder forms of dislike or ill-will, it still leaves much room for interpretation. When does the expression of strong feelings of disapproval or condemnation, directed at a group as such, cross the line into promoting hatred toward the group?

Consider the question of sexual orientation. What are we to make of the opinion, frequently voiced in mainstream outlets such as newspapers and academic journals, that any sexual activity between same-sex partners is inherently immoral or evil? During recent public debates in Canada concerning the legal recognition of same-sex marriages, Alphonse de Valk, the editor of a prominent Catholic magazine, published an opinion piece in a major Toronto newspaper claiming that homosexual acts are narcissistic, unnatural, pathological, and "grave moral aberrations."[34] Likewise, in an earlier article published in the *Notre Dame Journal of Law, Ethics and Public Policy*, John Finnis, professor of law at Oxford University, argued that gay sex is immoral, evil, and worthless and likened it to prostitution, masturbation, bestiality, and sex between strangers.[35] In saying such things were de Valk and Finnis promoting hatred against gays and lesbians? It is arguable that they contributed to a climate in which members of this "identifiable group" would be regarded with aversion or contempt, and that this is the effect they intended (or at least should reasonably have foreseen). I am confident, however, that most people would dismiss as ridiculous any attempt to bring criminal sanctions to bear on opinions such as these, however hateful they might be, when they are expressed by respectable figures in a mainstream newspaper or an academic journal. How then could we justify applying the law to the expression of equally intense negative opinions (whether against gays or any other vulnerable minority) by less respectable sources (such as hate groups)? If the notion of promoting hatred is broad enough to apply, at least in principle, to the publication of opinions like those of de Valk and Finnis then it is overly broad.

The root problem with the hate propaganda law lies in the very idea of criminalizing speech on the ground that it might contribute to an atmosphere of hostility toward a particular social group. That problem merely becomes more visible if the roster of protected groups is expanded (as the rationale behind the law surely requires), but it also afflicts the law in its present form. What makes the law particularly difficult to defend is the fact that hate speech (whoever the target group might be) is political speech. Recall that in his defence of "liberty of discussion," Mill was particularly concerned to safeguard the expression of opinions concerning "morals, religion, politics, social relations and the business of life."[36] Criminal regulation of hate speech aims precisely at the expression of opinions in this vital territory – odious opinions, to be sure, but opinions none the less. Because the expressive interests at stake in political speech, broadly defined in this way, are so important, the regulation of such speech requires a particularly strong justification. The argument that hate speech should be criminalized because of its potential contribution to a climate of hostility fails to surpass this justificatory threshold.

This failure is all the more evident when doubts can be raised about the effectiveness of any such regulation. Since most hard-core hate propaganda (the kind generated by hate groups) is now disseminated via the Internet, it may lie beyond the effective reach of Canadian law. The Canadian Human Rights Tribunal proceeding against Ernst Zundel has shown that human rights law can be used against websites which are either situated in Canada or, while situated abroad, are controlled by Canadian residents. There is no reason to think that criminal proceedings could not succeed as well. But what does success accomplish? In Zundel's case the effect of the proceeding was to secure his relocation from Canada to the United States, from where his website remains as accessible to Canadians as it ever was. We might congratulate ourselves at ridding the country of a notorious anti-Semite (even if only temporarily), but how has that accomplishment diminished the electronic circulation of hate messages within our borders? How, indeed, could we ever diminish that circulation by means of law without unacceptable intrusion into the domain of individual liberty?[37] Individual endusers may, of course, choose to block access from their computers to hate sites (or, more frequently, pornography sites) by means of filtering software.

But the imposition of such filters by government at the level of, say, service providers would stand no chance of surviving constitutional scrutiny.[38] With the notable exception of child pornography, where the downloading or even mere viewing of images has been defined as an offence, existing Canadian law appears to be utterly ineffective at preventing the electronic circulation within the country of objectionable materials.

For all of the foregoing reasons, the principal argument in favour of the hate propaganda law – that it can play an important part in preventing discrimination or violence against vulnerable groups by reducing the general level of hostility toward them – appears to be insufficient. Because this is not the only argument in support of it, it would be premature to conclude that the law is indefensible. However, the case against regulating hate speech by means of human rights legislation appears to be conclusive. The sole purpose of such legislation is to prohibit discriminatory practices against stipulated social groups. Therefore the justification for including the communication of hate messages as itself a discriminatory practice must be that it will tend to promote and reinforce other such practices. If that justification is weak then there is no reason for human rights law to concern itself with the mere expression of hateful attitudes concerning the protected groups, as opposed to concrete discriminatory practices reflecting those attitudes.

Two other arguments for the criminalization of hate speech remain to be considered. One is that hate messages are hurtful to members of the target minorities when they are directed specifically at them, whether in the form of verbal abuse, telephone threats, graffiti spray-painted on sacred places, or whatever. In these cases the harm done by the communication is direct and verifiable. However, in virtually all of them the means chosen for delivering the message is itself an offence: criminal harassment, uttering a threat, mischief, and so on. Where there is evidence that these offences are hate-motivated, which will generally be provided by the content of the message, then they can be treated as hate crimes for the purpose of penalty enhancement.[39] In other cases, such as neo-Nazi rallies in Jewish neighbourhoods, context (time, manner, or circumstance) restrictions should suffice to ensure that the offending messages are not imposed on an unwilling target audience. In none of these instances does there seem to be a need to address the problem by imposing a general content restriction on hate speech.

To this point we have found a sharp contrast between hate propaganda and child pornography: in the latter case, but not the former, the material subject to legal regulation is implicated in a concrete and verifiable way in the causation of a specific kind of harm. However, we still need to consider the possibility that hate groups play a role in the causal nexus of hate violence analogous to the role of the pedophile in the sexual abuse of children. There is little doubt that the functions of hate messages disseminated by such groups include both recruitment of new members and motivation of adherents to commit hate crimes against members of target groups. This function makes for a much more direct causal relationship between the message and the violence, one which is not mediated by shifts in the overall climate of public opinion about minorities. However, it also opens up the possibility of treating the communication of hate messages, under certain circumstances, as incitement to this violence. The circumstances would be the ones cited by Mill in his discussion of the advocacy of tyrannicide, which would qualify as an instigation "only if an overt act has followed, and at least a probable connexion can be established between the act and the instigation."[40] In the previous chapter I cited some instances of hate crimes committed by members, or former members, of known hate groups and clearly inspired by the ideology of those groups. In those cases in which the motivation for the crime can be traced back in a reasonably direct way to hate messages communicated by the groups, there seems no reason not to regard the latter as having incited the violence and as being liable to prosecution on that basis.

As far as hate speech is concerned, the focus of our attention has been on section 319(2) of the *Criminal Code* – the hate propaganda law at stake in the *Keegstra* case. Less attention is usually devoted to section 319(1), which prohibits communications in any public place which incite hatred against an identifiable group "where such incitement is likely to lead to a breach of the peace." These two subsections of section 319, together with section 318, which prohibits the advocacy or promotion of genocide, constitute the *Criminal Code* provisions concerning hate speech. If, as I think, the principal concern about hate speech is its capacity for inciting violence on the part of those who are in its thrall, then a case can be made for deleting section 319(2) as unnecessarily intrusive of expressive interests and instead reworking section 319(1) so as to apply to cases in which the causation of hate crimes can be traced back to the influence of particular hate messages. Where this is the case, the incitement can itself be classified as a hate crime. This approach is compatible with, indeed requires, expansion of the list of protected groups in section 319(1) to include women, as well as gays and lesbians.

In that case the producers or distributors of misogynist pornography would be vulnerable to prosecution for incitement if it could be shown that their publications inspired specific acts of sexual violence against women. In this way both the hate propaganda law and the obscenity law could be subsumed in legislation prohibiting the incitement of hate violence.

My conclusion, therefore, is that no law imposing a content restriction on hate speech can be justified.[41] In reaching this conclusion I am acutely conscious that, as a straight white gentile male, I am not a member of any of the groups whose security and equality (an expanded version of) hate propaganda legislation is meant to protect; the view of the matter from within those groups might be very different. None the less, my claim is that legislation of this sort cannot survive an objective cost-benefit analysis: the equality benefits it promises are too tenuous and uncertain to balance the liberty costs which it imposes. Since my conclusion flows from this kind of consequentialist balancing, it has no more certainty than this methodology can bestow upon it. But the same uncertainty would afflict a case in favour of hate speech regulation. Calculations of consequences on a large social scale are always open to doubt, especially when they depend on the evidence available at a particular time. My conclusion is based on the best evidence I have been able to locate; should new evidence come to light, or should the level of racism, sexism, and homophobia in Canada undergo a significant increase then it may need to be rethought. Meanwhile, I advance it with as much confidence as the nature of consequentialist argumentation will permit.

The policy directions defended to this point will also dictate an abolitionist conclusion for the mechanisms of prior restraint: censorship by Customs officials or film review boards. Since they impose content restrictions by means of bureaucratic procedures which provide complainants with few of the protections and safeguards they would enjoy in a court of law, these regulatory regimes have a particularly high justificatory threshold to surmount. Nothing in their history suggests that they are capable of meeting this challenge. The long, sorry episode of the *Little Sisters* case revealed the arbitrariness of Customs censorship, its persistent homophobia, and its stubborn resistance to change for everyone to see. Even the Supreme Court majority that upheld the constitutionality of the enabling legislation went out of its way to chastise the Customs bureaucracy for its administration of its censorship procedures. It is difficult to share the majority's naïve confidence that

Customs could be trusted to do better; in its insistence that the fault lay in the legislation, rather than merely in its application, the dissenting minority had much the better of the argument. In any case, as more and more sexually explicit (and hateful) materials enter the country in electronic form, vigilance at the border will become less and less relevant. The time is overdue for Customs to get out of the business of intercepting expressive materials and focus its attention instead on tariffs and duties.

It can be argued that the provincial film review boards do a somewhat better job of applying the *Butler* criteria to pornographic films and videos, allowing the merely sexually explicit through and screening out the violent or degrading. However, deciding what actually constitutes sexual violence or degradation calls for sophisticated judgment, and the boards are still reliant for guidance on (what they perceive as) community standards of tolerance. The very idea that everyone within a board's jurisdiction will be prevented from seeing a film simply because the majority are thought to disapprove of its distribution should be deeply disturbing to anyone who cares about expressive freedom. Furthermore, the boards are still capable of reaching ludicrous decisions about mainstream films, as the Ontario board did in the *Fat Girl* episode. They can play an important educative role by classifying films and videos, thereby alerting potential viewers to their contents. But their power to prohibit distribution outright, or to demand cuts as a condition of distribution, should be removed from them.

The underlying problem with systems of prior restraint – one which applies with equal force to both Customs and the film boards – was articulated nearly a half-century ago by Thomas Emerson: "The function of the censor is to censor. He has a professional interest in finding things to suppress ... The long history of prior restraint reveals over and over again that the personal and institutional forces inherent in the system nearly always end in a stupid, unnecessary, and extreme suppression."[42] The alternative to prior restraint is not no restraint, since, where appropriate, expressive materials can be regulated through the procedures of criminal law. The concern is sometimes expressed that removal of the prior restraint mechanisms would overload the court system as cases come to be pursued instead by the police. However, even if the existing hate and obscenity laws were kept in place, the *Keegstra* and *Butler* decisions have gone a considerable way toward clarifying the criteria for the hateful and the obscene. Law enforcement officials could then limit their attention to expressive materials that were obviously pushing the boundaries of the acceptable. In any case, the pressure on the courts would be considerably reduced if those laws were abandoned in favour of a more targeted focus on the incitement of hate violence (sexual or otherwise). There would be far fewer cases in which the incitement charge could be made out, but they are the ones that matter.

CONCLUSION

The policy directions outlined in the preceding section can be summed up in four points: (1) *A slimmed down child pornography law*: the possession offence retained within the context of a narrower definition of child pornography; (2) *No (further) content restrictions*: no criminal or human rights legislation prohibiting expressive materials on the basis of obscene or hateful content; (3) *More use of context restrictions*: in particular, an expanded criminal prohibition of expressive materials inciting hate violence; (4) *No prior restraint*: no censorship of expressive materials by Customs officials, film boards, or other bureaucracies. This is the policy which, I contend, results from the consistent application of a principled normative framework – one which is both harm-centred and evidence-based. Because it defines a considerably more expansive right of free expression than the one the Canadian courts have been willing to protect, advocating a policy of this sort places me at odds with every major Supreme Court decision on free expression since 1990, with the exception of the *Zundel* decision in 1992 which struck down the "spreading false news" section of the *Criminal Code*. All of the remaining decisions – *Keegstra*, *Taylor*, *Butler*, *Little Sisters*, even *Sharpe* – I am committed to regarding as mistaken. They have all either upheld laws – criminal legislation governing hate propaganda and obscenity, human rights legislation governing hate propaganda, and Customs legislation authorizing censorship of hate and obscenity – which I believe ought to have been struck down, or have failed to deal adequately with a law – legislation governing child pornography – which, while acceptable in principle, remains overbroad in its current form.

The common defect in all of these decisions is the court's attenuation of the requirement that a restriction of expressive freedom be justified by means of credible evidence of the harm done by the form of expression in question. In place of this requirement the court has imposed a much lower justificatory threshold on Parliament by demanding no more than a "reasonable basis" for the restriction. What has been lost sight of in this process is the section 1 requirement that limits to *Charter* rights be "demonstrably justified in a free and democratic society." Where no reliable evidence has been presented that expressive materials can significantly impair important interests, such as security or equality, then the case for limiting freedom has not been demonstrated. In showing this degree of deference to the legislature, the court has doubtless been acting on what it regards as its proper function in a system of checks and balances, and a stricter level of scrutiny would certainly have elicited more complaints about "judicial activism." For better or worse, however, the court has been assigned the task of interpreting and applying the *Charter*, and there is nothing objectionably activist in taking seriously the section 1 condition for justifying limits to expressive freedom.

The aim of this book has been to articulate a framework for determining limits to the right of free expression and to apply it to the particular cases of hate propaganda and pornography. This process has eventuated in a blueprint for a society that strikes an appropriate balance between the potentially competing values of liberty and equality. Having sketched the outcome I favour, I will conclude with a note of pessimism about the prospects of ever achieving it. There are only two means available for expanding the range of expressive freedom: politics and law. But there is little likelihood that any political party will assign a high priority to legal reforms which will be seen as privileging the activities of hatemongers and pornographers, neither of whom form or could form a particularly effective lobby. Meanwhile, the Supreme Court has had its way with these issues and has shown no interest in revisiting them. Being neither a politician nor a lawyer, I have no way forward to propose. As a philosopher I must limit myself to mapping the promised land, leaving to others the task of getting us there.

NOTES

1 Harm to others is a necessary condition of justified restraint, not a sufficient one. Whether legal restrictions on socially harmful activities are justified is to be determined by a cost-benefit balance. However, restrictions on socially harmless activities are always unjustified.

2 Alternatively, the *Hicklin* test might be interpreted as aiming to prevent harm, either to the morals of the consumers of pornography themselves or to public morals. This interpretation, however, requires the legitimacy of the notion of "moral harm."

3 *Hicklin* (1868), 371.

4 Just two years before the adoption of the "undue exploitation" definition which would eventually supplant the *Hicklin* test, Justice Laidlaw could interpret the "tendency to deprave and corrupt" as the tendency to suggest impure thoughts or "to influence certain persons to do impure acts; or ... to imperil the prevailing standards of public morals" (*American News* (1957), 157).

5 The earliest influential public statement of this disquiet occurred in Sir John Wolfenden, *Report of the Committee on Homosexual Offences and Prostitution* (London, 1957): "We do not think that it is proper for the law to concern itself with what a man does in private unless it can be shown to be so contrary to the public good that the law ought to intervene in its function as the guardian of that public good" (21). The most sustained philosophical critique of legal moralism during this period was H.L.A. Hart, *Law, Liberty, and Morality* (New York, 1966).

6 Note Justice Judson's language in *Brodie* (1962), where he could interpret "undue exploitation" as "excessive emphasis on the theme [of sex] for a base purpose" and characterize materials guilty of such emphasis as "dirt for dirt's sake" (704). The same moralistic language persisted in subsequent cases; see, for example, *Duthie Books* (1966), 280; *Great West News* (1970), 309. As recently as 1988, material deemed to fail the community standards test could be dismissed as "depraved sludge" (*Pereira-Vasquez* (1988), 291). Even after the adoption of a standard of tolerance, courts continued to endorse moralism as a basis for restraint: "A free society depends for its vitality on a moral foundation. No such society can exist or continue to exist, absent the presence and preservation of a strong moral fibre. This in part is fostered by Parliamentary proscription. I have no doubt that you cannot legislate morality, but it is a legitimate exercise of responsible Government to deter corruption and create a climate in which healthy attitudes are nourished and encouraged within the community. Sexual morality in children and their attitudes in this regard form an important part of the total spectrum of moral integrity" (*Macmillan* (1976), 312).

7 See *Dominion News* (1963), 117.

8 *Towne Cinema* (1985), 508.

9 For the charge of conservatism, see Richard Moon, "R. v. Butler: The Limits of the Supreme Court's Feminist Re-Intrepretation of Section 163," (1993), 25 Ottawa Review at 368–9. The accusation of male bias is made in Kathleen E. Mahoney, "Canaries in a Coal Mine: Canadian Judges and the Reconstruction of Obscenity Law." In *Freedom of Expression and the Charter* (1991), 152–3, and of heterosexist bias in Paul Wollaston, "When

Will They Ever Get It Right? A Gay Analysis of *R. v. Butler*" (1992), Dalhousie Journal of Legal Studies at 257–8.

10 J.S. Mill, *On Liberty*, in *Essays on Politics and Society*, 220.

11 See, for example, Kathleen E. Mahoney, "The Canadian Constitutional Aproach to Freedom of Expression in Hate Propaganda and Pornography" (1992), 35 Law and Contemporary Problems at 103–5; Karen Busby, "LEAF and Pornography: Litigating on Equality and Sexual Representations" (1994), 9 Canadian Journal of Law and Society at 176. The Supreme Court itself now routinely refers to the *Butler* decision as having been "harm-based" (see, for example, *Little Sisters* (2000), 1154, 1155).

12 *Butler* (1992), 478–86.

13 This subsumption was reaffirmed by the court in *Little Sisters* (2000), 1162–3.

14 Jamie Cameron, "The Past, Present, and Future of Expressive Freedom under the Charter" (1997), 35 Osgoode Hall Law Journal at 65: "Simply believing that expression is harmful or has a bad influence is not sufficient to justify limits under section 1 of the *Charter*."

15 These evidentiary issues concerning harm were on prominent display in *RJR-MacDonald* (1995), where the court faced the question of the justifiability of restrictions on the advertising and promotion of tobacco products. While members of the court disagreed over the kind of evidence the government should be expected to provide of the harmfulness of these forms of expression, no one suggested that an opinion poll might suffice.

16 This purpose connects s. 163.1 closely with the provisions in the *Criminal Code* (ss. 151–3) dealing with sexual offences against children. These sections are grouped together in the *Code* under the general heading of "Sexual Offences," whereas s. 163.1 is grouped (along with s. 163, the obscenity statute) under the heading of "Offences Tending to Corrupt Morals." While the association of the child pornography and obscenity sections is understandable (since both deal with pornography), it is also misleading since the purpose of s. 163.1 is to prevent serious physical and psychological harm to children, not the corruption of anyone's morals.

17 I have incorporated into this catalogue both the glosses on the definition of child pornography offered by the Supreme Court in *Sharpe* and also the provisions in Bill C-20 (on the assumption that the latter will make their way into law).

18 This particular concern about overbreadth is not merely speculative. In 1997 an Ontario judge convicted Narcisse Kuneman under sec. 163.1 for possession, *inter alia*, of a copy of an advocacy piece entitled "Men Loving Boys Loving Men" originally published in 1977 in the gay maga-

zine *The Body Politic* ("1977 Sex Article Back in Court," *Globe and Mail*, 13 May 2003, A6). Bruce Ryder has argued that material advocating sexual offences against children should be removed from the definition of child pornography and instead treated as hate propaganda for the purpose of (an expanded version of) s. 319(2) ("The Harms of Child Pornography Law" (2003), 36 U.B.C. Law Review at 114). However, it is far from clear that the advocacy of sexual activities which are offences under ss. 151–3 necessarily constitutes the wilful promotion of hatred against children, and it seems to me a considerable stretch to treat "Men Loving Boys Loving Men" as a piece of hate literature. In any case, I consider, below, the case for expanding the range of protected groups in s. 319(2).

19 Robert Matthews of the Ontario Provincial Police has said that his unit does not bother with any material in which there is the slightest doubt whether the person depicted is under eighteen (Interview, 2002).

20 The same limitation for s. 163.1 is advocated in Ryder, "Harms of Child Pornography Law."

21 *Sharpe* (2001), 82.

22 S. 163.1(6).

23 This defence will also replace the existing artistic merit defence. Earlier we looked at the Supreme Court's interpretation of "artistic merit," which appears to have the implication that the defence can be invoked whenever the materials in question can be fitted into some recognizable category of artistic product. The proposed public good defence not only closes this potentially damaging loophole; it also applies both to the materials themselves and to their production, distribution, or possession. It will therefore potentially cover possession of prohibited materials for a legitimate purpose, such as education or research.

24 Many commercial websites contain explicit disclaimers to the effect that all models depicted are eighteen or over. Producers of hard-core videos also tend to be vigilant in enforcing the minimum age, if only to avoid needless legal complications.

25 In this connection it is interesting that the child pornography law was initially intended to define a child as someone under the age of sixteen; see Stan Persky and John Dixon, *On Kiddie Porn: Sexual Representation, Free Speech, and the Robin Sharpe Case* (2001), 58ff.

26 In any case, a thorough overhaul of the obscenity statute is long overdue, since it still prohibits the publication or distribution of crime comics, the public exhibition of disgusting objects, and the advertisement of abortifacients and drugs for restoring sexual virility or curing venereal diseases (s. 163(1)(b), (2)(b)(c)(d)).

27 Bill C-114 received first reading on 10 June 1986, while bill C-54 received first reading on 4 May 1987.

28 Some of the most graphic depictions of rape occur in mainstream films such as *The Accused* (1988), whose aim was not to glorify rape but to explore some of its legal ramifications, including the complicity of onlookers.

29 This approach is advocated in Drucilla Cornell, *The Imaginary Domain: A Discourse on Abortion, Pornography, and Sexual Harassment* (1995), 112ff, and James Weinstein, *Hate Speech, Pornography, and the Radical Attack on Free Speech Doctrine* (1999), 165–6.

30 I assume here that rape (where the victim is female) is a hate crime directed at women.

31 Jonathan Cohen, "More Censorship or Less Discrimination? Sexual Orientation Hate Propaganda in Multiple Perspectives" (2000) 46 McGill Law Journal at 46.

32 Bill C-250, sponsored by Svend Robinson, passed third reading on 19 September 2003.

33 *Keegstra* (1990), 777–8.

34 "Under False Pretences," *Toronto Star*, 31 August 2003, A17.

35 John M. Finnis, "Law, Morality and 'Sexual Orientation'" (1995) 9 Notre Dame Journal of Law, Ethics, and Public Policy.

36 Mill, *On Liberty*, 244–5.

37 "the current infrastructure of the internet renders the network so difficult to control that the objectives of restrictive state policies in the area of internet speech cannot be achieved without implementing measures inconsistent with the tenets of democracy" (Julien Mailland, "Freedom of Speech, the Internet, and the Costs of Control; The French Example" (2001), 33 New York University Journal of International Law and Politics at 1181–2).

38 Filtering software is notoriously inefficient at blocking access to objectionable Internet content, both because it can be circumvented and also because it inevitably blocks legitimate sites as well. From a constitutional point of view, its imposition would therefore fail both the rational connection and minimal impairment tests. For a critique of Internet filters, see Bennett Haselton, "A Critique of Filtering," in *Technical, Business, and Legal Dimensions of Protecting Children from Pornography on the Internet: Proceedings of a Workshop* (2002).

39 I take no stand here on the justifiability of penalty enhancement for hate crimes; for arguments on both sides of the issue see J.B. Jacobs and K. Potter, *Hate Crimes: Criminal Law and Identity Politics* (1998), and Frederick M. Lawrence, *Punishing Hate: Bias Crimes under American Law* (1999).

40 Mill, *On Liberty*, 228n.
41 On this question I am therefore changing my mind yet again; see Sumner, "Hate Propaganda and Charter Rights," *Free Expression: Essays in Law and Philosophy* (1994).
42 Thomas I. Emerson, "The Doctrine of Prior Restraint." (1955), 20 Law and Contemporary Problems at 659.

READING QUESTIONS ON SUMNER

1 Sumner argues that the community-standards test represents "the tyranny of the community" rather than a focus on genuine harm. What is his argument?
2 Sumner argues that content-based definitions of obscenity failed to differentiate between the material that is degrading to women and material that is not. How is this argument related to his general endorsement of the harm principle?
3 Sumner recommends dealing with problems of exploitation in the production of pornography through workplace health and safety regulation. Do you regard this as realistic?
4 In his discussion of hate speech, Sumner considers the example of David Ahenakew, and questions whether anything can be accomplished by punishment, given the adverse reaction to his remarks. Is this line of argument consistent with Sumner's more general recommendation of cost/benefit analysis as a model of justification? If a law is justified by its general results, is that a sufficient ground for applying it in a particular case?

APPENDIX 1

The Canada Act and the Canadian Charter of Rights and Freedoms

CANADA ACT 1982
U.K., 1982, c. 11
An Act to give effect to a request by the Senate and
House of Commons of Canada

Whereas Canada has requested and consented to the enactment of an Act of the Parliament of the United Kingdom to give effect to the provisions hereinafter set forth and the Senate and the House of Commons of Canada in Parliament assembled have submitted an address to Her Majesty requesting that Her Majesty may graciously be pleased to cause a Bill to be laid before the Parliament of the United Kingdom for that purpose.

Be it therefore enacted by the Queen's Most Excellent Majesty, by and with the advice and consent of the Lords Spiritual and Temporal, and Commons, in this present Parliament assembled, and by the authority of the same as follows:

1. *The Constitution Act, 1982* set out in Schedule B to this Act is hereby enacted for and enacted shall have the force of law in Canada and shall come into force as provided in that Act.

2. No Act of the Parliament of the United Kingdom passed after the *Constitution Act, 1982* comes into force shall extend to Canada as part of its law.

3. So far as it is not contained in Schedule B, the French version of this Act is set out in Schedule A to this Act and has the same authority in Canada as the English version thereof.

4. This Act may be cited as the *Canada Act 1982*.

CONSTITUTION ACT, 1982
Schedule B to Canada Act 1982 (U.K.)

PART I
CANADIAN CHARTER OF RIGHTS AND FREEDOMS

Whereas Canada is founded upon principles that recognize the supremacy of God and the rule of law:

Guarantee of Rights and Freedoms

1. *The Canadian Charter of Rights and Freedoms* guarantees the rights and freedoms set out in it subject only to such reasonable limits prescribed by law as can be demonstrably justified in a free and democratic society.

Fundamental Freedoms

2. Everyone has the following freedoms:
   (a) freedom of conscience and religion;
   (b) freedom of thought, belief, opinion and expression, including freedom of the press and other media of communication;
   (c) freedom of peaceful assembly; and
   (d) freedom of association.

Democratic Rights

3. Every citizen of Canada has the right to vote in an election of members of the House of Commons or of a legislative assembly and to be qualified for membership therein.

4. (1) No House of Commons and no legislative assembly shall continue for longer than five years from the date fixed for the return of the writs at a general election of its members.

(2) In time of real or apprehended war, invasion or insurrection, a House of Commons may be continued by Parliament and a legislative assembly may be continued by the legislature beyond five years if such continuation is not opposed by the votes of more than one-third of the members of the House of Commons or the legislative assembly, as the case may be.

5. There shall be a sitting of Parliament and of each legislature at least once every twelve months.

Mobility Rights

6. (1) Every citizen of Canada has the right to enter, remain in and leave Canada.

(2) Every citizen of Canada and every person who has the status of a permanent resident of Canada has the right

(a) to move and to take up residence in any province; and

(b) to pursue the gaining of a livelihood in any province.

(3) The rights specified in subsection (2) are subject to

(a) any laws or practices of general application in force in a province other than those that discriminate among persons primarily on the basis of province of present or previous residence; and

(b) any laws providing for reasonable residency requirements as a qualification for the receipt of publicly provided social services.

(4) Subsections (2) and (3) do not preclude any law, program or activity that has as its object the amelioration in a province of conditions of individuals in that province who are socially or economically disadvantaged if the rate of employment in that province is below the rate of employment in Canada.

Legal Rights

7. Everyone has the right to life, liberty and security of the person and the right not to be deprived thereof except in accordance with the principles of fundamental justice.

8. Everyone has the right to be secure against unreasonable search or seizure.

9. Everyone has the right not to be arbitrarily detained or imprisoned.

10. Everyone has the right on arrest or detention

(a) to be informed promptly of the reasons therefor;

(b) to retain and instruct counsel without delay and to be informed of that right; and

(c) to have the validity of the detention determined by way of *habeas corpus* and to be released if the detention is not lawful.

11. Any person charged with an offence has the right

(a) to be informed without unreasonable delay of the specific offence;

(b) to be tried within a reasonable time;

(c) not to be compelled to be a witness in proceedings against that person in respect of the offence;

(d) to be presumed innocent until proven guilty according to law in a fair and public hearing by an independent and impartial tribunal;

(e) not to be denied reasonable bail without just cause;

(f) except in the case of an offence under military law tried before a military tribunal, to the benefit of trial by jury where the maximum punishment for the offence is imprisonment for five years or a more severe punishment;

(g) not to be found guilty on account of any act or omission unless, at the time of the act or omission, it constituted an offence under Canadian or international law or was criminal according to the general principles of law recognized by the community of nations;

(h) if finally acquitted of the offence, not to be tried for it again and, if finally found guilty and punished for the offence, not to be tried or punished for it again; and

(i) if found guilty of the offence and if the punishment for the offence has been varied between the time of commission and the time of sentencing, to the benefit of the lesser punishment.

12. Everyone has the right not to be subjected to any cruel and unusual treatment or punishment.

13. A witness who testifies in any proceedings has the right not to have any incriminating evidence so given used to incriminate that witness in any other proceedings, except in a prosecution for perjury or for the giving of contradictory evidence.

14. A party or witness in any proceedings who does not understand or speak the language in which the proceedings are conducted or who is deaf has the right to the assistance of an interpreter.

Equality Rights

15. (1) Every individual is equal before and under the law and has the right to the equal protection and equal benefit of the law without discrimination and, in particular, without discrimination based on race, national or ethnic origin, colour, religion, sex, age or mental or physical disability.

(2) Subsection (1) does not preclude any law, program or activity that has as its object the amelioration of conditions of disadvantaged individuals or groups including those that are disadvantaged because of race, national or ethnic origin, colour, religion, sex, age or mental or physical disability.

Official Languages of Canada

16. (1) English and French are the official languages of Canada and have equality of status and equal rights and privileges as to their use in all institutions of the Parliament and government of Canada.

(2) English and French are the official languages of New Brunswick and have equality of status and equal rights and privileges as to their use in all institutions of the legislature and government of New Brunswick.

(3) Nothing in this Charter limits the authority of Parliament or a legislature to advance the equality of status or use of English and French.

17. (1) Everyone has the right to use English or French in any debates and other proceedings of Parliament.

(2) Everyone has the right to use English or French in any debates and other proceedings of the legislature of New Brunswick.

18. (1) The statutes, records and journals of Parliament shall be printed and published in English and French and both language versions are equally authoritative.

(2) The statutes, records and journals of the legislature of New Brunswick shall be printed and published in English and French and both language versions are equally authoritative.

19. (1) Either English or French may be used by any person in, or in any pleading in or process issuing from, any court established by Parliament.

(2) Either English or French may be used by any person in, or in any pleading in or process issuing from, any court of New Brunswick.

20. (1) Any member of the public in Canada has the right to communicate with, and to receive available services from, any head or central office of an institution of the Parliament or government of Canada in English or French, and has the same right with respect to any other office of any such institution where

(a) there is a significant demand for communications with and services from that office in such language; or

(b) due to the nature of the office, it is reasonable that communications with and services from that office be available in both English and French.

(2) Any member of the public in New Brunswick has the right to communicate with, and to receive available services from, any office of an institution of the legislature or government of New Brunswick in English or French.

21. Nothing in sections 16 to 20 abrogates or derogates from any right, privilege or obligation with respect to the English and French languages, or either of them, that exists or is continued by virtue of any other provision of the Constitution of Canada.

22. Nothing in sections 16 to 20 abrogates or derogates from any legal or customary right or privilege acquired or enjoyed either before or after the coming into force of this Charter with respect to any language that is not English or French.

Minority Language Educational Rights

23. (1) Citizens of Canada

(a) whose first language learned and still understood is that of the English or French linguistic minority population of the province in which they reside, or

(b) who have received their primary school instruction in Canada in English or French and reside in a province where the language in which they received that instruction is the language of the English or French linguistic minority population of the province,

have the right to have their children receive primary and secondary school instruction in that language in that province.

(2) Citizens of Canada of whom any child has received or is receiving primary or secondary school instruction in English or French in Canada, have the right to have all their children receive primary and secondary school instruction in the same language.

(3) The right of citizens of Canada under subsections (1) and (2) to have their children receive primary and secondary school instruction in the language of the English or French linguistic minority population of a province

(a) applies wherever in the province the number of children of citizens who have such a right is sufficient to warrant the provision to them out of public funds of minority language instruction; and

(b) includes, where the number of those children so warrants, the right to have them receive that instruction in minority language educational facilities provided out of public funds.

24. (1) Anyone whose rights or freedoms, as guaranteed by this Charter, have been infringed or denied may apply to a court of competent jurisdiction to obtain such remedy as the court considers appropriate and just in the circumstances.

(2) Where, in proceedings under subsection (1), a court concludes that evidence was obtained in a manner that infringed or denied any rights or freedoms guaranteed by this Charter, the evidence shall be excluded if it is established that, having regard to all the circumstances, the admission of it in the proceedings would bring the administration of justice into disrepute.

General

25. The guarantee in this Charter of certain rights and freedoms shall not be construed so as to abrogate or derogate from any aboriginal, treaty or other rights or freedoms that pertain to the aboriginal peoples of Canada including

(a) any rights or freedoms that have been recognized by the Royal Proclamation of October 7, 1763; and
(b) any rights or freedoms that now exist by way of land claims agreements or may be so acquired.[1]

26. The guarantee in this Charter of certain rights and freedoms shall not be construed as denying the existence of any other rights or freedoms that exist in Canada.

27. This Charter shall be interpreted in a manner consistent with the preservation and enhancement of the multicultural heritage of Canadians.

28. Notwithstanding anything in this Charter, the rights and freedoms referred to in it are guaranteed equally to male and female persons.

29. Nothing in this Charter abrogates or derogates from any rights or privileges guaranteed by or under the Constitution of Canada in respect of denominational, separate or dissentient schools.

30. A reference in this Charter to a province or to the legislative assembly or legislature of a province shall be deemed to include a reference to the Yukon Territory and the Northwest Territories, or to the appropriate legislative authority thereof, as the case may be.

31. Nothing in this Charter extends the legislative powers of any body or authority.

Application of Charter

32. (1) This Charter applies

(a) to the Parliament and government of Canada in respect of all matters within the authority of parliament including all matters relating to the Yukon Territory and Northwest Territories; and

(b) to the legislature and government of each province in respect of all matters within the authority of the legislature of each province.

(2) Notwithstanding subsection (1), section 15 shall not have effect until three years after this section comes into force.

33. (1) Parliament or the legislature of a province may expressly declare in an Act of Parliament or of the legislature, as the case may be, that the Act or a provision thereof shall operate notwithstanding a provision included in section 2 or sections 7 to 15 of this Charter.

(2) An Act or a provision of an Act in respect of which a declaration made under this section is in effect shall have such operation as it would have but for the provision of this Charter referred to in the declaration.

(3) A declaration made under subsection (1) shall cease to have effect five years after it comes into force or on such earlier date as may be specified in the declaration.

(4) Parliament or the legislature of a province may re-enact a declaration made under subsection (1).

(5) Subsection (3) applies in respect of a re-enactment made under subsection (4).

Citation

34. This Part may be cited as the *Canadian Charter of Rights and Freedoms*.

NOTE

1 Paragraph 25 (b) was amended by the *Constitution Amendment Proclamation, 1983*. It originally read "(b) any rights or freedoms that may be acquired by the aboriginal peoples of Canada by way of land claims settlement."

APPENDIX 2

An Overview of the Canadian Legal System: Division of Powers and Essentials of Procedure

While the focus of most of the readings in this book is the role of moral reasoning in the law, understanding of those issues is enhanced by an understanding of the ways in which particular issues arise and are resolved within a legal order. Not every dispute involves legal rights, and not every dispute involving legal rights makes it to trial. Canada's legal order shares important features with many of the world's legal systems, though it differs from other systems in various ways. This appendix is meant as a quick tour through the structure of legal order in general and in particular the structure of the Canadian legal order.

The Canadian legal system exhibits the classic liberal division of powers between three branches of government – the legislature, the executive, and the judiciary. According to the doctrine of the division of powers, the legislature – the democratically elected representatives of the people – make law, while the executive – a body of professional government employees – implement and enforce the law. The judiciary, who in Canada are unelected officials appointed by the government, interpret the law when a question arises about what it requires in a particular case.

The rationale for dividing power in this way is doing so secures the rule of law. Law is legitimate when it is made by the legislature for it then reflects the will of the people. Executive action to implement and enforce the law is legitimate as long as the officials stay within the limits set by the law. Thus, civil servants are charged with carrying out broadly defined government policies. Judicial interpretation of the law is legitimate as long as it is confined to seeing to it that the executive officials stay within the limits set by the law rather than whatever they would themselves consider appropriate.

In this scheme, judges are given the role of ultimately determining what the law is, but are subject to the duty to confine their determinations to what the law requires. If they confine their interpretative role in this way, society is governed by laws rather than by the personal whims of people holding power. Citizens can be secure in the knowledge that government officials may not act except when the law gives them the warrant to do so.

In Canada, the role of determining the law is the task of the superior courts of general jurisdiction of each province. These have different names according to the province, for example, Ontario Court (General Division), or in Alberta and other provinces, the Court of Queen's Bench. These courts have general jurisdiction in that they have the power to hear and decide any question of law. Appeals against their decisions are to the provincial courts of appeal. In addition, federal courts hear some cases in specialized areas of the law. Appeals against the decisions of both provincial and federal courts can be made to the Supreme Court of Canada. The Supreme Court agrees to hear only a small proportion of the cases appealed to it, and normally decides which cases to hear based on the legal significance of the issues they raise. Judges are appointed to all of these courts by the federal government, and enjoy lifetime tenure so as to protect their independence.

In order to bring a case before a court, the person bringing it must have *standing*. In private disputes, private citizens who claim to have been wronged by others have standing to sue. In general private citizens only have standing to challenge government action if they can claim that some right of theirs is jeopardized by it. However, in certain circumstances, parties before a court can argue on the basis of the constitutional rights of third parties. Also, courts have discretion to grant intervenor status to interested parties in appellate cases in which they have an indirect interest. Intervenors can raise broader constitutional issues that the parties to the dispute may not have raised themselves.

Public law governs the relationship between government and citizen as well as between the different branches of government. But judges also decide cases arising in private law, the law which regulates the interactions between individuals. The courts may have to decide whether an agreement between two people is a valid contract, or who is liable in the case of an unintended injury. They may have to determine who owns a piece of land, or whether someone can recover from someone else who was unjustly enriched at their expense. In Canada (unlike the United States) questions of private law are always tried by judges rather than juries. In answering questions in a private law case, judges often need to sort out difficult questions of fact – who did what, and when – as well as questions of law concerning the legal rights and duties of the parties. In considering facts in matters of private law, judges decide in favor of the party whose claim is supported by the balance of the evidence. Since one of the two parties will lose in a private dispute, fairness requires that the one with the stronger case should prevail. In order to limit frivolous litigation, the losing party in a private suit must pay the legal expenses of the winner. In private law cases, both parties enjoy the right of appeal. However, only issues of law can be raised on appeal. Facts must be taken to be as the trial court found them.

Canada has two distinctive systems of private law. In Quebec, private law is codified in the *Code Civile*. In the rest of Canada, private law is largely a matter of common law. The difference is important, because at the core of common-law reasoning is the appeal to precedent – the way cases have been decided before. Precedents can be drawn from other common-law jurisdictions, including foreign ones. By contrast, decisions in civil law systems are presented as the consequences of the explicit provisions of the civil code. As a result, decisions sometimes look as though they are the result of a straightforward deductive process. However, the generality with which such provisions must be framed still leaves space for judicial creativity, and judges are aware of prior judicial understandings of how the law should be interpreted.

In private law, judges are upholding the rule of law because individuals know that any private dispute which the law regulates will be settled by an impartial application of the law. Just as it is essential that citizens know that judges will keep government officials within the law, so it is essential that individuals know that their fellows will have to deal with them in the manner prescribed by law.

Criminal law falls into public rather than private law, because the state investigates and prosecutes criminal offences. Because of the grave consequences which attend criminal conviction, the standard of proof is higher in criminal law – facts must be proven beyond a reasonable doubt. For the same reasons, people accused of crimes are presumed innocent until proven guilty. Those accused of crimes with sentences of less than two years are subject to summary trial without a jury. Those accused of more serious crimes are entitled to trial by jury, though they may elect to be tried by a judge. In a jury trial, the jury's role is limited to determining facts. In Canada (unlike the United States) both the Crown and the accused are allowed to appeal a criminal decision, but only on the basis of questions of law. Often the grounds for appeal turn on the judge's instruction to the jury, or on the trial judge's decisions about the admissibility of evidence. The criminal law in Canada is codified in a single federal *Criminal Code*.

In common-law systems, it is sometimes difficult to determine what principle or principles a judicial decision stands for, since principles must be inferred from the judge's reasoning or argument justifying the decision. If several judges hear the matter, some might dissent from the majority on some issues but not others, while others concur with the result, but offer different reasons for it. Finally, even when all the judges support the judgment given by one judge, the opinion might include arguments which are in tension with each other. The common law is found in the judgments of the superior courts and changes over time at the hands of judges. When a judge decides an issue in a common-law legal order, that judgment becomes a precedent – it has authority for judges deciding similar issues. The weight of the authority it has will vary on a number of dimensions, the extent to which it has been followed, the place of the judge in the judicial hierarchy, and, indeed, the merits of the judgment. In some parts of the law, especially private law, the law in a common-law legal order might be made almost entirely by judges. In other parts, such as the criminal law, the common law will be a complex overlay of judicial interpretation of statutory codification. But it will also serve as an underlay, or a background for interpretation, since the principles that were codified were in the first instance principles developed by judges. The role of precedent in common-law systems means that the subsequent development of the law will often depend on the particular cases that make it to trial, which in turn depends in part on the resources available to the parties.

Public law includes the rules of public international law, the law which governs relations between states. Public international law also governs the interpretation of treaties. For example, if Canada and the United States have an extradition treaty, and some American states have the death penalty while Canada does not, does Canada need to send an American fugitive convicted of a capital crime in one of those states to certain death? (In private matters, the rules governing the choice of laws are no less complex, and govern such questions as which law applies to the property of a couple married in France, but residing in Canada at the time of their divorce.) Public law also includes constitutional law and administrative law. Some issues in constitutional law seem to have little to do with particular individuals, as in the questions relating to the division of political power in the Canadian federal system between the central federal government and the provincial governments. But the division of powers is important to the ability of various bodies to make law. If a lawmaking body overreaches its mandate, individuals may be illegally deprived of advantages to which they are entitled. Since the enactment of the *Charter* in 1982, Canada has had a written constitution. Even in jurisdictions without a written constitution (such as Britain), courts sometimes engage in constitutional review.

Issues of public law reveal the complexities of the division of powers. Governments often enact statutes which delegate broad powers to officials

to elaborate and implement policies, rather than attempting to anticipate details in advance. In order to protect their agencies from the intrusion of the superior courts into this kind of policy making, governments have often at the same time set up tribunals to decide the legal questions which arise in the course of elaborating and implementing the statute. For example, questions of labor law are decided by provincially appointed labor relations boards, and human rights codes by specially appointed tribunals. To what extent can the decisions of such bodies be immunized from the supervision by the superior courts? Courts have generally recognized the authority of tribunals to decide such issues, subject to their own "review power." Courts will intervene if the tribunal either overreaches what the court deems to be its statutory authority, or offends against any of the procedural values – the values of fair process which the courts deem it their constitutional duty to protect. Courts always retain a residual power of review because of their role as final arbiters of the boundaries between the branches of government.

Since the enactment of the *Charter of Rights and Freedoms* in 1982, a new range of constitutional issues has preoccupied the courts. These of course pertain to whether statutes or official action under statutes offend against *Charter*-protected rights and values. The Canadian *Charter* has an unusual structure in two respects. First, Section 1 requires a court to ask a further question after a finding that a *Charter*-protected right or value has been violated. This is the question whether that violation can itself be justified by the values of a "free and democratic society," and whether the violation is proportional to the problem it is supposed to address. Second, Section 33 permits a legislature or parliament to "override" a judicial determination of constitutionality subject to the conditions set out in the section. Thus, while judges have the final say over what the law is, legislatures retain the power to temporarily override those decisions.

The *Charter* may seem to undermine the division of powers. It clearly gives judges the power to decide on whether the laws made by democratically elected parliaments are valid in accordance with their interpretation of very broadly defined values, for example, the right to free speech. That is, judges may not merely be keeping officials within the limits of the law as it is, but deciding what the law ought to be. In this the *Charter* only makes more visible and dramatic a pervasive feature of legal orders. Virtually all legal systems include such concepts as "good faith," "reasonableness," and "fair play," all of which are open to moral interpretation. That judicial interpretation is partly creative and not merely deductive is explicitly recognized in the Canadian legal system.

Glossary of Legal and Philosophical Terms

Terms and Definitions

This section contains some technical terms that will be found in the readings. The definitions and discussions are intended to give a bare handle on the terms, and thus are an aid to the readings rather than a replacement for them.

Atomism. The view that the social world is made up of isolated individuals each making perfectly independent choices about how to live. The label "atomism" is more often offered as a criticism of others' view than as a view put forward by anyone.

Autonomy. The individual's right to decide for herself how to live her life.

Comity. The recognition by one legal system of another legal system's laws. Extradition treaties are one example of comity; the acceptance of marriages or divorces made abroad is another.

Common law. Systems of law descended from the British common-law system. (The common law was originally the law common to the King's courts, and thus contrasted with manorial and cannon law.) The distinctive feature of common-law systems is the way in which judges appeal to previously decided cases in deciding novel ones. The law is to be found in cases, rather than statutes. Most modern common-law systems include statutes as well, but these are standardly interpreted in light of settled cases.

Commensurability. Two things are said to be commensurable if there is some basis for comparing them. Things are said to be incommensurable if no such

basis exists. For example, love and money are usually thought to be incommensurable, because no amount of money can replace a lost love.

Communitarianism. The view that an individual is the product of a particular social and cultural environment. The meaningful choices as to how to live for an individual are the choices informed by this environment. Thus, communitarians suppose that choices to reject the ways of one's culture are often not worthy of protection.

Consequentialism. The moral position which evaluates actions based on the balance of good over bad consequences which they bring or might bring about. An argument in favor of something that claims its implementation would reduce violent crime is consequentialist. Consequentialist arguments always require factual support because they depend on claims about what would happen if various policies were adopted.

Constitutionalism. The view that the basic essentials of a political regime should lie outside the reach of ordinary processes of majority rule. Not all advocates of constitutional democracy suppose a written constitution is necessary. In Britain, for example, there is no written constitution, but the powers of government are limited.

Deontological. The moral position that supposes that acts should be evaluated on the basis of some intrinsic quality. For example, claims about rights, and appeals to fairness and desert are deontological. Both deontological and consequentialist arguments can be found on both sides of almost every political debate. Many complex positions will appeal to both kinds of arguments.

Egalitarianism. The view that the allocation of resources and opportunities has to be substantially equal.

Habeas corpus. The right against unlawful imprisonment. For example, prisoners who have not been promptly charged with any crime can be freed under *habeas corpus.*

Legal moralism. The position that the state can legitimately coerce people into ways that do not accord with their own views of the best way to live. *Pure* legal moralists suppose that there is a correct answer about how best to live; *impure* legal moralists suppose it is up to each society to answer questions about the appropriate moral content of law for itself. Opponents of

legal moralism often appeal to the "harm principle," which holds that the only legitimate basis for restrictions on liberty is the prevention of harm to others.

Legal positivism. The view that the law that exists on any matter exists as a matter of publicly ascertainable fact. That is, finding out what the law is does not require any sort of controversial moral argument.

Liberalism. The view that the fundamental role of the state is to enable people to freely decide how best to live their own lives. Different liberals have very different views about how best to protect individual liberty, as well as different views about which individual choices are most important. Some suppose that liberty requires an unregulated capitalist market; others that the state must make sure that individuals have a fair share of resources and opportunities in order to be able to freely decide what life is best for them. All liberals share an abstract commitment to rejecting paternalism, though they disagree about the implications of this commitment.

Libertarianism. The view that the only legitimate role of the state is in protecting negative liberty. Libertarians standardly reject economic redistribution as an illicit interference with property rights.

Majoritarianism. The view that the law should implement the preferences of the majority whatever these happen to be. Majoritarianism can be understood as a democratic position, but is at odds with the view that democracy requires certain constitutional safeguards.

Natural law. Defenders of natural law insist that whether or not anything counts as law will depend on its specific content. For the natural lawyer, wicked legal systems are not legal systems at all; they need to be understood as exercises of naked power. Natural lawyers disagree among themselves about just what moral content a legal system must have, but they agree that the proper role of positive law is to articulate and implement natural law.

Negative liberty. Defenders of negative liberty understand liberty as the absence of external impediments to individual preferences. One has this kind of liberty when the state limits its coercive interference in the lives of individuals to the minimum necessary to prevent individuals from harming each other.

Neutrality. The refusal by the state to take a stand on contested views about the good life. A neutral state will not treat opera any differently than it does football. A difficult question for theories of liberal neutrality is whether traditional practices that discriminate against women are best thought of as contested conceptions of the good which the state has no business correcting, or as injustices which are within the scope of its proper concern.

Normative claim. A claim about how things should be. Normative claims aim to guide action. Thus, they contrast with descriptions of how things are. There are a wide variety of types of normative claims. Moral claims are normative, as are aesthetic claims and claims of etiquette, though few suppose that any of these is simply a special case of the others. Legal claims are also action-guiding. One of the central questions of jurisprudence concerns the nature of legal normativity. The dispute between positivists and anti-positivists turns on whether the normative element in legal claims is a special case of the normativity of moral claims.

Paternalism. Actions by the state that are done to protect people from themselves. For example, a law outlawing bungee-jumping is paternalistic because it seeks to protect people from the consequences of their own choices. By contrast, drunk-driving laws are not paternalistic because one of their aims is to protect people from the choices of others.

Perfectionism. The position which requires the state to aid or even coerce people into living out their lives in accordance with some ideal of what makes life valuable. For example, state support of the arts is sometimes defended on perfectionist grounds.

Positive liberty. The view that individuals have to have certain things before the idea of negative liberty and autonomy makes any sense. Defenders of positive liberty differ in their views about what it requires. Some emphasize the role of various social conditions that are said to enable individual choice. Others stress the importance of such things as political participation or community to any life that is truly free.

Reasonable person. Anglo-American legal systems use the construct of a reasonable person to articulate standards of care and judgment. The reasonable person is neither the rational person who acts effectively to realize his or her ends, nor the typical or average person. Instead, the reasonable

person is the person who shows appropriate regard for the interests of others, and takes appropriate care in avoiding injury to them. Reasonableness standards reflect views both about what is important to the security of those who might be harmed, and about the importance of people being able to go about their own affairs. The reasonable person also appears in the law of self-defence, as the measure of the care one must take in assessing whether one's life is in peril. The reasonable person standard is sometimes called an *objective* standard because it abstracts away from the personal features of the person being judged.

Utilitarianism. The most prominent kind of consequentialist position. Utilitarians say that policies and institutions should be assessed on the basis of their ability to bring about the best overall balance of good over bad consequences. The most popular candidate for good consequences is the satisfaction of people's preferences – that is, the aggregate sum of what various people in fact want and desire.

Sources and Credits

Jean Hampton, "Democracy and the Rule of Law," in Ian Shapiro, ed., *The Rule of Law: Nomos* vol. 36 (1994) 13–44, reprinted by permission of New York University Press.

Charles Taylor, *Multiculturalism and the Politics of Recognition* (1992), 37–44, reprinted by permission of Princeton University Press.

Nitya Iyer, "Categorical Denials: Equality Rights and the Shaping of Social Identity" (1993–4) *Queen's Law Journal* 179–207, reprinted by permission of the author.

Wil Waluchow, "Constitutions as Living Trees: An Idiot Defends" (2005) 28 *Canadian Journal of Law and Jurisprudence* 207–47, reprinted by permission of the author.

Kent Roach, "Dialogic Judicial Review and Its Critics," in Grant Huscroft and Ian Brodie, eds., *Constitutionalism in the Charter Era* (2004) 49–104, reprinted by permission of the LexisNexis Canada Inc.

Mark Tushnet, "Weak-Form Judicial Review: Its Implications for Legislature," in Grant Huscroft and Ian Brodie, eds., *Constitutionalism in the Charter Era* (2004) 213–31, reprinted by permission of the Lexis Nexis Canada Inc.

David Cole, "Judging the Next Emergency: Judicial Review and Individual Rights in Times of Crisis" (2002) 101 *Michigan Law Review* 2565–95, reprinted by permission of the Michigan Law Review.

Joel Feinberg, "Pornography and the Criminal Law" (1979) 40 *University of Pittsburgh Law Review* 567–73, reprinted by permission of the author and of the editors of the *University of Pittsburgh Law Review*.

T.M. Scanlon, "A Theory of Freedom of Expression," *Philosophy and Public Affairs* vol. 1, no. 2 (winter 1972) 204–26 (some notes omitted; remaining notes renumbered), reprinted by permission of Princeton University Press.

Seana Valentine Shiffrin, "Speech, Death, and Double Effect" (2003)